The Great Father

FRANCIS PAUL PRUCHA

The Great Father

The United States Government

and the American Indians

Volumes I and II

Unabridged

UNIVERSITY OF NEBRASKA PRESS

LINCOLN AND LONDON

Acknowledgments for the use of
copyrighted material appear on pp. xxxi–xxxii.
Copyright 1984 by
the University of Nebraska Press
All rights reserved
Manufactured in the United States of America
The paper in this book meets the
minimum requirements of American
National Standard for Information Sciences—
Permanence of Paper for
Printed Library Materials,
ANSI Z39.48-1984

Library of Congress
Cataloging in Publication Data
Prucha, Francis Paul.
The great father.
Includes index.
1. Indians of North America –
Government relations.
I. Title.
E93.P9654   1984
323.1′197073   83-16837
ISBN 0-8032-3668-9 (alk. paper)
ISBN 0-8032-8734-8 (pbk)
First Bison Book (combined and unabridged
Volumes I and II) printing: 1995
Most recent printing indicated by
the last digit below:
10   9   8   7   6   5   4   3   2   1

For the Jesuits of Marquette University,
with whom I have lived and worked
for many years

When your GREAT FATHER and his chiefs see those things, they will
know that you have opened your ears to your GREAT FATHER's voice,
and have come to hear his good Councils.

Lewis and Clark, in presenting American flags
and medals to Oto chiefs, 1804

Friends and Brothers,—The business part of our Council is closed.
But we have seen who are your great men. We stand here to put medals
around their necks. . . . All these medals have on one side of them
your GREAT FATHER's face, and on the other side is his pipe, his
peace hatchet, and his hand.

Friends and Brothers,—You are never to forget that this is a great gift. It
comes from your GREAT FATHER himself, who sends it to you by our
hands. It is a new heart. Your GREAT FATHER has told us to come up here,
and put it in the breast of his great Chippeway children. No bad blood
belongs to this heart. It is an American heart, and is full of good blood;
and if you will open your ears and listen well, and never forget your
GREAT FATHER's message, it will make you all happy.

Thomas L. McKenney at treaty negotiations
with the Chippewa Indians, 1826

They [the Indians] look to our government for protection; rely upon
its kindness and its power; appeal to it for relief to
their wants; and address the president as their GREAT FATHER.

John Marshall in
Cherokee Nation v. *Georgia*, 1831

This is a great day for you and for us. A day of peace and friendship
between you and the whites for all time to come. You are about to be
paid for your lands, and the GREAT FATHER has sent me today to treaty
with you concerning the payment. . . . And the GREAT FATHER wishes you
to have homes, pastures for your horses and fishing places. He wishes you
to learn to farm and your children to go to a good school; and he now
wants me to make a bargain with you, in which you will sell your lands
and in return be provided with all these things.

Isaac I. Stevens at a council with Nisqually,
Puyallup, and Squaxon Indians, 1854

My friends: Your GREAT FATHER whose heart is right, and who
loves his red as well as his white children, has heard there is trouble
between the whites and Indians on the plains. He has heard that
there is war and that blood has been shed. He is opposed to war
and loves peace and his heart is sad. He has sent all these
big Chiefs to see you and to ascertain what is wrong. . . .
Now, if your GREAT FATHER did not love you, he would not send
all these big Chiefs so many hundred of miles to hunt you up
and converse with you. We are sent here to enquire of you
and find out what is the trouble between the white men and you.

Nathaniel G. Taylor, president of the Indian Peace
Commission, speaking to Sioux Indians, 1867

Nothing is more indispensable than the protecting and guiding
care of the Government during the dangerous period of transition from
savage to civilized life. . . . [The Indian] is overcome by a feeling
of helplessness, and he naturally looks to the "GREAT FATHER" to
take him by the hand and guide him on. That guiding hand must
necessarily be one of authority and power to command confidence
and respect. It can be only that of the government which the Indian is
accustomed to regard as a sort of omnipotence on earth. Everything
depends upon the wisdom and justice of that guidance.

Secretary of the Interior Carl Schurz in an
article in the *North American Review*, 1881

[The Indians] are the wards of the Nation. From time immemorial,
the Indians have been taught to call the President of this mighty
republic the "GREAT FATHER," and all communications from them to
the Indian Office are addressed in that way. In their speeches, they say
that they regard the President as a father, that they are his children,
and they look to him for protection, for justice, for succor, for advice.

Commissioner of Indian Affairs Thomas J. Morgan
in an address entitled "A Plea for the Papoose"

Contents

Andrew Jackson and Removal. Motivation for Removal.
Controversy and Debate. The Cherokee Cases.

VOLUME II

Maps

Illustrations

Tables

Preface

The relations of the federal government of the United States with the American Indians through two centuries form a major component of American political history. From the beginnings of the nation, when some Indian tribes were political and military entities of power and independence with whom the young nation had to come to terms, to the present, when newly energized tribal organizations once again emphasize a government-to-government relation with the United States, Indians as tribes or as individuals have been persistently in the consciousness of officials of all three branches of the federal government.

I have long recognized the need for a comprehensive history of the relations between the United States government and the Indians. Excellent one-volume surveys of the subject exist, and there are now a great many scholarly studies of selected periods or particular aspects of American Indian policy. But what I have attempted here is a survey of the full scope of American Indian policy from the time of the Revolutionary War to 1980. I have sought to provide a reasonably complete discussion of the course of Indian policy development and implementation, with its many vicissitudes, and to indicate in the footnotes the essential documents and secondary works in which this history is set forth.

Because federal policies have rested on past experience, no full understanding of any part of the story is possible without seeing what went before or without examining the working out of the programs. I have learned from this comprehensive study that there was much more fundamental unity and continuity in the government's policy than I had previously thought from looking only at selected partial aspects or at limited chronological periods.

The officials of the federal government in the executive branch and in Congress faced a serious problem as greatly diverse cultures came into contact and often conflict within the expanding territorial limits of the United States. The Indian cultures were amazingly rich and diverse; but the Indian groups quickly fell far behind the white society in numbers and technical skills, and they were in general no match for the economically and militarily powerful United States. When the Indian tribes, early in the nineteenth century, lost their powerful European allies in the New World—with whose assistance they might have hoped to hold off the onslaught of white American advance—it was clear to both Indians and whites that the United States dealt with the Indians from a position of dominance.

Cries for extermination of the Indians occasionally sounded by aggressive frontiersmen and exasperated frontier commanders were rejected by United States officials responsible for Indian affairs. These officials instead sought to treat the Indians honorably, even though they acted within a set of circumstances that rested on the premise that white society would prevail. The best term for this persistent attitude is *paternalism*, a determination to do what was best for the Indians according to white norms, which translated into protection, subsistence of the destitute, punishment of the unruly, and eventually taking the Indians by the hand and leading them along the path to white civilization and Christianity. The relationship was sometimes described, as it was by Chief Justice John Marshall in 1832, as resembling that of a ward and its guardian. The modern emphasis on the trust responsibility of the federal government toward the Indians has elements of the same attitude.

In the nineteenth century, it was common for Indians to refer to the president (head and symbol of the United States government) as the Great Father, and the term was adopted by government officials as well. It was an appropriate usage for the paternalistic attitude of the federal government toward the Indians as dependent children. The Great Father rhetoric largely disappeared after 1880, but paternalism continued and sometimes increased. Federal concern for the education, health, and economic development of its wards colored the history of Indian policy in the twentieth century. And when, in the decades of the 1960s and 1970s, the renewal of Indian self-determination came to the fore, it was protest against continuing governmental paternalism that gave form to the movement.

Paternalism was considered by its white practitioners as a humane Christian approach to the serious problems that faced the nation in its relations with the Indians, and it was accepted by many Indians as welcome and necessary support. But paternalism also had its oppressive aspects, and criticism of it has frequently arisen, sometimes in the form of a desire to get the government out of the Indian business and let the Indians fend for themselves within the larger white society and sometimes in the form of criticism of the weakening of the Indians' ability to direct their own destiny. Throughout the two centuries covered by this study, however, the controlling force in Indian-white relations has been the policy determined by the white government, not the wishes of the Indians.

This history is divided into two volumes at roughly 1880. The year is a neat chronological dividing point, for each volume thus covers a century, but it is more than that, too. Although nothing of startling historical importance happened in that precise year, the date can be used to note the end of an era marked by diplomatic dealings with the Indian tribes and marred by almost incessant military encounters with them in one region or another. The century after 1880, in contradistinction, was dominated by a new movement to destroy old tribal relations and traditional customs and to accomplish the ultimate acculturation and assimilation of individual Indians into white society.

As in my previous historical studies of Indian-white relations in the United States, large parts of which are incorporated in this book, I concentrate on the history of federal Indian policy and do not treat in detail the history of the Indian communities. I do this in part as a matter of expediency, because it is possible to survey the course of government policy in a single work, whereas it is not possible to treat the "Indian story" in such a unified way, given the great diversity of Indian groups and of individual responses within those groups. But my approach is justified also, I think, because the policies and programs of the United States have had a determining influence on the history of the Indian tribes. In the period of Indian-white contact that I cover, no history of a tribe can be understood without a detailed consideration of treaties, land cessions, the reservation system, and Indian educational programs, for example, which formed the substance of government policy and action.

I have boldly carried the story to 1980, for historical studies of Indian affairs have for too long emphasized events of the nineteenth century. Indian communities, like all human societies, have changed and developed through time, and their relations with the United States government have also changed. The policies and programs of the twentieth century are as important for understanding the status of Indians today in American society as are those of the nineteenth. There are difficulties, of course, in moving so close to the present in the writing of history, before the outcome of laws and decisions can be evaluated. Readers will appreciate that, in the case of many recent events, I have been unable to give the proportion of attention to them that later historians may find appropriate. But I have attempted to describe the multifarious developments that occurred and to indicate the arguments and purposes that lay behind them.

FRANCIS PAUL PRUCHA, S.J.
Marquette University

Acknowledgments

In a study of this size, reliance on the work of other scholars and the assistance of archivists and librarians is manifest. I cannot begin to thank adequately the staffs of the National Archives, Library of Congress, Milwaukee Public Library, Harvard University Library, State Historical Society of Wisconsin, Newberry Library, Huntington Library, Department of the Interior Library, and Marquette University Library, as well as many others, who have helped in one way or another. Historians and other scholars who have contributed to my knowledge and understanding are altogether too many to name, for I have spoken or corresponded with a great many persons interested in Indian-white relations in the United States, and I have read their books and articles. I owe special mention, however, to Robert F. Berkhofer, Ray Allen Billington, William T. Hagan, Reginald Horsman, Robert M. Kvasnicka, Frederick Merk, Robert Pennington, Martin Ridge, Robert M. Utley, Herman J. Viola, Wilcomb E. Washburn, and Mary E. Young. To my students, too, I owe much gratitude.

My research in Indian affairs has been materially aided by grants and fellowships from the Social Science Research Council, National Endowment for the Humanities, John Simon Guggenheim Foundation, Charles Warren Center for the Study of American History, and Huntington Library. De Rance, Incorporated, has generously provided research funds and has added a sizable subvention for the publication of these volumes. Marquette University, the Marquette Jesuit Community, and the Wisconsin Province of the Society of Jesus have supported my studies in many ways.

In writing this comprehensive history of the federal government's relations with the American Indians, I have drawn on several of my own previously published studies. For permission to use sections verbatim from the following works, I thank the editors and publishers:

American Indian Policy in the Formative Years: The Indian Trade and Intercourse Acts, 1790–1834. Harvard University Press. Copyright © 1962 by the President and Fellows of Harvard College.

The Sword of the Republic: The United States Army on the Frontier, 1783–1846. Macmillan Company. Copyright © by Francis Paul Prucha.

"Andrew Jackson's Indian Policy: A Reassessment." *Journal of American History* 56 (December 1969): 527–39.

Indian Peace Medals in American History. Copyright © 1971 by the State Historical Society of Wisconsin.

"The Image of the Indian in Pre-Civil War America," in *Indiana Historical Society Lectures, 1970–1971.* Copyright © 1971 Indiana Historical Society.

"American Indian Policy in the 1840s: Visions of Reform," in *The Frontier Challenge: Responses to the Trans-Mississippi West*, ed. John G. Clark. Copyright © 1971 by the University Press of Kansas.

American Indian Policy in Crisis: Christian Reformers and the Indian, 1865–1900. Copyright 1976 by the University of Oklahoma Press.

The Churches and the Indian Schools, 1888–1912. Copyright © 1979 by the University of Nebraska Press.

Introduction to *Cherokee Removal: The "William Penn" Essays and Other Writings*, by Jeremiah Evarts. Copyright © 1981 by the University of Tennessee Press.

Indian Policy in the United States: Historical Essays. Copyright © 1981 by the University of Nebraska Press.

The maps were prepared by the Cartographic Laboratory of the University of Nebraska–Lincoln. Picture and map credits are listed separately on pp. 607–8 and 1259–60.

The Great Father

Volume I

ABBREVIATIONS

ASP:IA   *American State Papers: Indian Affairs*, 2 vols. (Washington: Gales and Seaton, 1832–1834).

CIA Report   Annual Report of the Commissioner of Indian Affairs. For the period 1824–1920, the edition in the congressional serial set is used and the serial number is given.

GPO   United States Government Printing Office.

JCC   *Journals of the Continental Congress*, 34 vols. (Washington: U.S. Government Printing Office, 1904–1937).

Kappler   Charles J. Kappler, comp., *Indian Affairs: Laws and Treaties*, 5 vols. (Washington: U.S. Government Printing Office, 1904–1941). Unless otherwise indicated, references are to vol. 2.

OIA   Records of the Office [Bureau] of Indian Affairs, National Archives, Record Group 75.

OIA CCF   Records of the Office [Bureau] of Indian Affairs, Central Classified Files, National Archives, Record Group 75.

OIA Circulars   Records of the Office [Bureau] of Indian Affairs, Procedural Issuances: Orders and Circulars, National Archives, Record Group 75 (M1121).

OIA LR   Records of the Office [Bureau] of Indian Affairs, Letters Received, National Archives, Record Group 75 (M234).

OIA LS   Records of the Office [Bureau] of Indian Affairs, Letters Sent, National Archives, Record Group 75 (M21).

OSI   Records of the Office of the Secretary of the Interior, National Archives, Record Group 48.

OSI CCF   Records of the Office of the Secretary of the Interior, Central Classified Files, National Archives, Record Group 48.

SW IA LS   Records of the Office of the Secretary of War, Letters Sent, Indian Affairs, National Archives, Record Group 75 (M15).

WNRC   Washington National Records Center, Suitland, Md.

Note: For documents in the congressional serial set the number of the Congress and session are given in this abbreviated form: 92–1.

PROLOGUE

The Colonial
Experience

Images of the Indians. Christianization.

Invasion of the Indian Lands.

Trade Relations. British Imperial Policy.

The United States government in its relations with the American Indians built upon English colonial and imperial experience. The policy it developed was in many respects, of course, a response to specific conditions on the frontier, but little if anything was begun entirely de novo. Two centuries of English contact with the natives in the New World had provided a rich set of conceptions about the Indians and numerous examples of policies and programs concerning the interaction of the two cultures. There were colonial precedents for all the interfaces between white government and Indian groups—missionary contacts, military encounters, trade relations, and land transfers—upon which the new nation could draw. And after individual colonies seemed unable to regulate the settlers and maintain honorable and tranquil relations with the Indians, imperial programs of control furnished models of centralized management of Indian affairs that were clear in the minds of the Founding Fathers. To understand the foundation on which the United States erected its complex and evolving policy, one must look, however sketchily, at English and other European beginnings in America.[1]

1. There is an immense literature dealing with Indian affairs in the European colonial period. Douglas Edward Leach, *The Northern Colonial Frontier, 1607–1763* (New York: Holt, Rinehart and Winston, 1966), and W. Stitt Robinson, *The Southern Colonial Frontier, 1607–1763* (Albuquerque: University of New Mexico Press, 1979), offer general accounts that place Indian relations in a broad context. Recent general works of value are

IMAGES OF THE INDIANS

When Christopher Columbus struck the Western Hemisphere by chance in his attempt to sail west around the world to the riches of the Orient, he found not only land but peoples. Unable to comprehend that he was opening up a "new" world and confident that he had touched some outlying reaches of the Indies, he called the inhabitants *Indians*, a name that has lasted for five centuries despite its descriptive inaccuracy and the occasional attempts to substitute a more suitable name. These peoples were numerous and magnificently diverse, and it was immediately evident that they were different from the Europeans who came in contact with them. The Indians had to be accommodated into the intellectual patterns of the Western European mind, and practical conventions for dealing with them had to be developed.

The Europeans dealt with the Indians as they perceived them, and this perception came ultimately from detailed observation. Explorers, churchmen, traders, governors, scientists, and casual travelers all were fascinated by the strange land and its inhabitants and produced a voluminous literature about the Indians. No aspect of Indian life and customs was unexamined or unreported. The early Spanish reports were eagerly devoured by curious Europeans, who translated them into their own languages. And as the Portuguese, French, English, and Dutch followed the Spanish to America, they created their own reservoir of facts, surmises, and fanciful tales about the Indians.[2] The accumulated images of the Indians, however, were

---

Gary B. Nash, *Red, White, and Black: The Peoples of Early America* (Englewood Cliffs, New Jersey: Prentice-Hall, 1974), and Wilbur R. Jacobs, *Dispossessing the American Indian: Indians and Whites on the Colonial Frontier* (New York: Charles Scribner's Sons, 1972). Two works that present sharply conflicting views of the Puritans and the Indians are Alden T. Vaughan, *New England Frontier: Puritans and Indians, 1620–1675,* rev. ed. (New York: W. W. Norton and Company, 1979), and Francis Jennings, *The Invasion of America: Indians, Colonialism, and the Cant of Conquest* (Chapel Hill: University of North Carolina Press, 1975). An excellent study on the middle colonies is Allen W. Trelease, *Indian Affairs in Colonial New York: The Seventeenth Century* (Ithaca: Cornell University Press, 1960). Views of southern Indians are well treated in Richard Beale Davis, *Intellectual Life in the Colonial South, 1585–1763,* 3 vols. (Knoxville: University of Tennessee Press, 1978), 1: 103–256. A perceptive analysis of writings on colonial Indian matters is James Axtell, "The Ethnohistory of Early America: A Review Essay," *William and Mary Quarterly,* 3d series 35 (January 1978): 110–44. See also Axtell, *The European and the Indian: Essays in the Ethnohistory of Colonial North America* (New York: Oxford University Press, 1981).

2. A number of historians have recently examined the writings of Englishmen in the early period of colonization to extract views about Indians and their relations to Europeans. The fullest compendium of such views is H. C. Porter, *The Inconstant Savage: England and the North American Indian, 1500–1600* (London: Duckworth, 1979), but it offers few clear themes. Bernard W. Sheehan, *Savagism and Civility: Indians and English-*

not free of preconceptions. The Europeans already had established patterns into which to cast the inhabitants of the New World, who, since they lived in or close to the state of nature, were commonly called "savages."[3] Two basic images developed, contradictory in content.

The first was that of the "noble savage," natural man living without technology and elaborate societal structures. Naked without shame, unconcerned about private ownership and the accumulation of material wealth but sharing all things unselfishly, and free from the problems of government, the Indian represented an idyllic state from which the European had strayed or fallen. Dwelling in an earthly paradise, the Indians were a living example of a golden age, long past in European history but now suddenly thrust again upon the world's consciousness. John Donne in 1597 wrote, "The unripe side of the earth produces men like Adam before he ate the apple." And Marc Lescarbot, a Frenchman who visited the New World in 1606 and whose report was quickly published in an English translation, noted that the Indians lived in common, "the most perfect and most worthy life of man," a mark of the "ancient golden age." This good Indian welcomed the European invaders and treated them courteously and generously. He was handsome in appearance, dignified in manner, and brave in combat, and in all he exhibited a primitivism that had great appeal to many Europeans.[4]

The second pattern was that of the "ignoble savage," treacherous, cruel, perverse, and in many ways approaching the brute beasts with whom he shared the wilderness. In this view, incessant warfare and cruelty to captives marked the Indians. Ritual cannibalism and human sacrifice were the ultimate abominations; but countless descriptions of Indian life noted the squalor, the filth, the indolence, the lack of discipline, the thievery, and the hard lot accorded Indian women. Not a few Englishmen saw the

---

men in Colonial Virginia (Cambridge: Cambridge University Press, 1980), emphasizes the disparity that Englishmen saw between the savagism of the Indians and their own civility. Karen Ordahl Kupperman, *Settling with the Indians: The Meeting of English and Indian Cultures in America, 1580–1640* (Totowa, New Jersey: Rowman and Littlefield, 1980), in contrast, argues that the English writers recognized civility in the Indians and judged them basically as a "common sort" of person similar to the common sort of Englishmen. An excellent general account of white conceptions of the Indians is Robert F. Berkhofer, Jr., *The White Man's Indian: Images of the American Indian from Columbus to the Present* (New York: Alfred A. Knopf, 1978).

3. The term *savage* must be understood in its early meaning of a person who lived in the wilderness in a state of nature, without necessary connotations of cruelty and ruthlessness. There is an extended discussion of the terms *Indian* and *savage* in Berkhofer, *White Man's Indian*, pp. 3–31. See also Jennings, *Invasion of America*, pp. 73–81.

4. Donne and Lescarbot are quoted in Sheehan, *Savagism and Civility*, pp. 22, 31. Paradisiacal imagery, primitivism, and the noble savage concept are discussed in Sheehan, pp. 9–36, and in Berkhofer, *White Man's Indian*, pp. 28, 72–80.

Indians with their superstitions and inhuman practices as literally children of the Devil.[5]

The threads of these two conceptions intertwined in strange ways, and one or the other was drawn upon as suited the occasion. What persisted, however, were the notions of otherness, dependency, and inferiority. "Savagism" (whether noble or ignoble) was contrasted with "civility"; natural life in the wilds was opposed to disciplined life in civil society. There was little doubt in the minds of the Europeans (pace those who used the noble savage concept to condemn evils in their own society) that savagism was an inferior mode of existence and must give way to civility (civilization). The Indians were "younger brethren," dependents whom persons in superior positions claimed the right and obligation to shape into a new and civilized mold, by persuasion if possible and ultimately by force.[6]

The concept of savagism and inferiority did not imply racism, that is, a belief that the Indian was an inherently different kind of being incapable of rising out of an inferior condition. There was little question in the minds of Englishmen that the Indians were human beings like themselves, a belief firmly planted in the scriptural account of Adam as the single progenitor of all men. Nor was color an obstacle, for the brownness or tawny complexion of the Indians was considered to be the result of conditioning by the elements or by the use of cosmetics on persons born basically white. Not until the very end of the seventeenth century was there any reference to Indians as red, and then the term may have had symbolic meaning or arisen from the use of war paint.[7] The dichotomy between noble and ignoble savagism was never completely resolved, for the a priori images were fixed, and from time to time these simplistic positions resurfaced in theoretical discussions of the Indians.

As the English experience deepened, the theoretical concepts of noble and ignoble savagery (though long continued in imaginative literature) were replaced by more realistic and complex appraisals based on practical encounters. Remnants of Indian tribes remained in the developing colonies, often in a state of abject dependency, but the Indians who received the attention of the English colonial authorities in the century preceding the

5. Sheehan, *Savagism and Civility*, pp. 37–88.

6. Sheehan, *Savagism and Civility*, makes a strong case for the contrast between the two states, but he crystallizes the concepts unduly. Kupperman, *Settling with the Indians*, especially pp. 170–71, discusses the tutelary role of the English in regard to the natives. She argues that the exploitation of the Indians came not because of ideas of racial superiority on the part of the English but because of the ultimate powerlessness of the natives.

7. See Wesley Frank Craven, *White, Red, and Black: The Seventeenth-Century Virginian* (Charlottesville: University Press of Virginia, 1971), pp. 39–41; Vaughan, *New England Frontier*, rev. ed., p. xv.

independence of the United States were separate groups existing outside the areas of concentrated English settlement. More or less independent "nations" (like the Cherokees and other southern Indians and the Six Nations of the Iroquois in the north) entered into the diplomatic relations of the age along with a multiplicity of other political entities—French and Spanish as well as English colonies. These Indian groups were recognized and dealt with as distinct political entities, and forms of political structure familiar to Europeans were frequently attributed to them whether or not they accurately reflected the actual political organization of the tribes.[8] Yet the white goal continued to be the ultimate transformation of the Indians with whom they came into contact, a "civilizing" process that reached its apogee in the United States at the end of the nineteenth century.

CHRISTIANIZATION

The civility toward which the English hoped to bring the savages of the New World had as its companion Christianity. Although the two could be separated in theory, in practice they were nearly always combined. Thus an Englishman promoting colonization in 1583 could speak of doing "a most excellent worke, in respect of reducing the savage people to Christianity and civilitie." Or, as William Crashaw phrased it in 1610: "We give the Savages what they most need. 1. Civilitie for their bodies. 2. Christianitie for their soules." With sincere convictions, although without much actual success in the end, the English colonizers placed conversion of the Indians high among their objectives.[9]

Indeed, God's providence in permitting the discovery of the New World by the Christian nations of Europe was considered a mandate for Christianization. A writer reasoned in 1577 "that Christians have discovered these countries and people, which so long have byen unknowne, and they not us: which plainly may argue, that it is Gods good will and pleasure, that they should be instructed in his divine service and religion, whiche from the beginning, have been nouzeled and nourished in Atheisme, gross ignorance, and barbarous behavior." Despite repeated fears and assertions that the Indians were the children of Satan, Europeans generally believed

---

8. Edward H. Spicer, *A Short History of the Indians in the United States* (New York: Van Nostrand Reinhold Company, 1969), pp. 11–44, has a good discussion of the "many nations" interacting.

9. Christopher Carleill, "A Briefe and Summary Discourse upon the Intended Voyage to the Hithermost Parts of America," and "Crashaw's Sermon," quoted in Sheehan, *Savagism and Civility*, pp. 117, 124. See Sheehan's chapter on conversion, pp. 116–43, and Davis, *Colonial South*, 1: 176–96.

that conversion was possible and repeatedly asserted missionary motives for colonization. The first charter of the Virginia Company of 1606 included the declaration that propagation of the gospel was a principal purpose of the enterprise, and instructions to Governor Thomas Gates directed conversion of the natives "as the most pious and noble end of this plantation." Attempts were made to provide schools in which the Indian children could learn both religion and civil manners. Plans and collection of funds for a college at Henrico in Virginia were an early indication of the attempts in the southern colonies, and the idea never died. The results, to be sure, were minimal, for the Indians remained attached to their old ways, and missionary enthusiasm waned in the face of so little success. Frontier settlers had little interest in converting the natives, and what initiative there was came from the coastal areas or England.[10]

The Puritans of New England, of course, made conversion of the Indians a major justification of their undertaking. The Massachusetts charter charged the officers to "Wynn and incite the Natives . . . [to] the onlie true God and Saviour of Mankinde," and the oath of the governor directed him to "doe your best endeavor to draw on the natives of this country . . . to the true God." The seal of the Governor and Company of Massachusetts Bay, 1629, shows an Indian crying out, "Come over and help us."[11]

The goal of conversion remained throughout the period of settlement. Impressive work was done by the missionary Thomas Mayhew on Martha's Vineyard, and John Eliot, the "apostle to the Indians," won fame for his missionary zeal and effectiveness among the Indians as he established "praying towns" of natives. Parliament promoted the good work by chartering in 1649 the Society for Propagation of the Gospell in New-England. Education was at the heart of the endeavor, and the establishment of an Indian college at Harvard was an indication of the Puritans' determination. But even with the determination, zeal, and notable success of a few missionaries, the total number of converted Indians remained small, in part, no doubt, because of the total transformation required by the Puritans of their converts.[12]

10. Dionyse Settle, *A True Reporte of the Laste Voyage into West and Northwest Regions*, quoted in Sheehan, *Savagism and Civility*, p. 119; Davis, *Colonial South*, 1: 188–90.

11. Vaughan, *New England Frontier*, pp. 235–308; quotations p. 236. The seal is reproduced in Jennings, *Invasion of America*, p. 229.

12. A harsh view of Puritan missionary efforts, contrasting with that of Vaughan, is found in Jennings, *Invasion of America*, pp. 228–53. Jennings is especially critical of Eliot, whose fame as an Indian missionary he labels fraudulent. A similarly critical view is expressed in Neal E. Salisbury, "Red Puritans: The 'Praying Indians' of Massachusetts Bay and John Eliot," *William and Mary Quarterly*, 3d series 31 (January 1974): 27–54. Sympathetic portraits of Eliot are provided in Ola Elizabeth Winslow, *John Eliot: "Apostle*

Of particular note among Christians who preached to the Indians were the Quakers, members of the Society of Friends. Their founder, George Fox, instructed his American followers in 1667 to "go and discourse with some of the *Heathen Kings,* desiring them to gather their Council and People together, that you may declare *God's Everlasting Truth,* and his *Everlasting Way of Life and Salvation* to them, knowing that *Christ* is the promise of *God* to them, *a Covenant of Light to the Gentiles.*" The Friends followed that admonition and did missionary and educational work among the Indians with a gentleness and lack of arrogance that maintained mutual good feelings even though it did not result in any converts to Quakerism. The Quakers followed a policy of nonviolence toward the Indians and showed a willingness to accept Indian culture unknown among other groups of colonists; the common dichotomy between "savagery" and "civilization" had no place in their worldview. The Quaker colony established by William Penn had peaceful relations with the Indians, the result in part of Penn's insistence that lands be fairly purchased from the Indians; and the reputation of Penn and his followers for fair dealing was strong in the nineteenth century and has lasted to the present day.[13]

The great missionary upsurge in the United States after 1800 had a long history of colonial efforts as precedent, but in the English colonies, as later, mundane affairs overshadowed missionary work and at times seemed to obliterate it altogether.

INVASION OF THE INDIAN LANDS

The great distinguishing feature of English relations with the Indian groups was replacement of the Indians on the land by white settlers, not conversion and assimilation of the Indians into European colonial society. The

---

to the Indians" (Boston: Houghton Mifflin Company, 1968), and Samuel Eliot Morison, "John Eliot, Apostle to the Indians," in *Builders of the Bay Colony* (Boston: Houghton Mifflin Company, 1930), pp. 289–319. A strong emphasis on Puritan relations with the Indians as sacral rather than secular history is given in the documents and commentary in Charles M. Segal and David C. Stineback, *Puritans, Indians, and Manifest Destiny* (New York: G. P. Putnam's Sons, 1977). See also William Kellaway, *The New England Company, 1649–1776: Missionary Society to the American Indians* (New York: Barnes and Noble, 1961).

13. Frederick B. Tolles, "Nonviolent Contact: The Quakers and the Indians," *Proceedings of the American Philosophical Society* 107 (April 15, 1963): 93–101; Rayner Wickersham Kelsey, *Friends and the Indians, 1655–1917* (Philadelphia: Associated Executive Committee of Friends on Indian Affairs, 1917); Thomas E. Drake, "William Penn's Experiment in Race Relations," *Pennsylvania Magazine of History and Biography* 68 (October 1944): 372–87.

Spanish colonies to the south were marked by subjugation of a massive concentrated native population and its use as a primary labor force in exploiting the mineral and agricultural resources of the conquered lands. The Spaniards, in addition, carried on large-scale missionary efforts to Christianize the Indians, and the church was as significant as the state in the development of Spanish America. The preponderantly male Spanish colonists, moreover, took Indian women as wives and concubines, incorporating the Indians biologically as well as socially into Spanish society. None of these situations obtained in the English colonies to any large extent. The difference can be explained in part by the diverse attitudes toward other peoples of the southern and the northern Europeans, but it was the fundamental nature and place of English colonization that determined the case. The Indians did not present the same usefulness to the English that they did to the Spanish. There were no heavy Indian populations to be turned into a labor force and at the beginning no real need, for the English came to settle and cultivate the land. Nor was intermarriage or other liaison between the whites and Indians called for on a large scale among the family-oriented English colonists.[14]

An underlying condition of English settlement was the depopulation that had previously occurred among the Indian tribes with whom the first Englishmen had come in contact. European diseases, of which smallpox was only the most important among many, struck the Indians with devastating force, for the inhabitants of the New World had developed no immunity to Old World diseases. Large areas were stripped of once heavy populations, and the cleared fields of the former inhabitants were taken over by white settlers, who often saw the hand of Providence in their good fortune.[15]

The replacement of the Indians on the land became the basis for enduring conflict with the Indians who remained, and Indian wars marked the English experience as they did that of the United States. In the very beginning, the natives received the English colonists hospitably, greeted them

14. Nash, *Red, White, and Black*, pp. 65–67.

15. Indian demography has become a subject of great interest, and new estimates of aboriginal populations have greatly increased previous figures. A now classic article is Henry F. Dobyns, "Estimating Aboriginal American Population: An Appraisal of Techniques with a New Hemispheric Estimate," *Current Anthropology* 7 (October 1966): 395–416; see also Dobyns, *Native American Historical Demography: A Critical Bibliography* (Bloomington: Indiana University Press, 1976). There is a discussion of the effect of European diseases on the Indians in Alfred W. Crosby, Jr., *The Columbian Exchange: Biological and Cultural Consequences of 1492* (Westport, Connecticut: Greenwood Publishing Company, 1972), pp. 35–63. See also Wilbur R. Jacobs, "The Tip of an Iceberg: Pre-Columbian Indian Demography and Some Implications for Revisionism," *William and Mary Quarterly*, 3d series 31 (January 1974): 123–32.

with signs of friendship, and supplied them with food. But the image of savagism in the minds of the Europeans included a strong element of treachery on the part of the savages, and English behavior toward the Indians soon brought real enmity to the surface. It became evident to the Indians that the colonists were moving in to stay, and as the English expanded, encroaching upon Indian lands and in many cases treating the inhabitants despicably, the Indians resisted with force; sometimes young warriors acted without tribal approval, sometimes considered attacks were planned and executed by skilled tribal leaders. Indian rivalries, too, contributed to the conflicts, for by aiding one or another group that eagerly sought help against its enemies, the English became involved in intertribal wars. The Europeans for their part looked for Indian allies in their own conflicts. Sooner or later most tribes became attached in some fashion to French, Spanish, or British imperial systems. The pattern of hostility and open war thus began early and was a dominant part of Indian-white relations until almost the end of the nineteenth century.[16]

The first case was the massacre of 1622 in Virginia, in which the Indians under Opechancanough rose up against the white settlers who had invaded their lands and quickly killed a quarter to one-third of the population. English reaction was immediate and vengeful; the massacre was used as an excuse for a massive retaliation against the Indians, for it was looked upon as proof that Indians could not be trusted, even when professing friendship. Soon after, in New England, the Pequot War of 1637 began formal conflicts between the Indians and the English. The Pequots, moving into the Connecticut River Valley, met Puritans migrating into the same region and posed a threat to the peaceful expansion of the Massachusetts Bay Colony. Pequot harassment of the settlements brought war as the English attacked the hostile Indians in order to protect the nascent colony in Connecticut. Such conflicts set a pattern. A new surprise attack by Indians in Virginia in 1644, which killed five hundred whites, brought new reprisals, and Bacon's Rebellion of 1676 had strong anti-Indian origins. In 1675–1676 King Philip's War in New England furnished still another case of warfare instigated by the Indians in a desperate attempt to stop the advancing tide of English settlement.[17]

16. An excellent comprehensive study that covers colonial Indian wars is Douglas Edward Leach, *Arms for Empire: A Military History of the British Colonies in North America, 1607–1763* (New York: Macmillan Company, 1973); see especially pp. 42–79.

17. Alden T. Vaughan, "'Expulsion of the Savages': English Policy and the Virginia Massacre of 1622," *William and Mary Quarterly*, 3d series 35 (January 1978): 57–84; Vaughan, "Pequots and Puritans: The Causes of the War of 1637," ibid. 21 (April 1964): 256–69; Douglas Edward Leach, *Flintlock and Tomahawk: New England in King Philip's War* (New York: Macmillan Company, 1958). Most accounts of the English colonial experience deal with these conflicts.

These wars were brutal encounters—"savage" warfare on both sides—and confirmed the English in attitudes of fear and hatred toward the Indians. The terms of peace imposed on the defeated Indians were harsh and drawn up to ensure the future security of expanding white settlements. As in the aftermath of the Virginia massacre of 1622, the Indians were killed or forced out of the areas of white settlement. In some cases reserved lands with set boundaries were marked out for them, but white pressures against these reservations were incessant. Hopes for intermingling and coexistence of the whites and the Indians eventually collapsed.

Forced conquest, of course, was not the only means by which lands were transferred to white ownership. There was much theoretical discussion about the rights of savage, non-Christian peoples to the land they occupied, of whether the Indians and similar people could claim lands against Christian nations; and the idea that the lands in the New World were a *vacuum domicilium*, a wasteland, open for the taking, had wide acceptance. The God-fearing Puritans of Massachusetts Bay Colony found religious justification for dispossessing the Indians, and John Winthrop, the colony's first governor, declared: "The whole earth is the lords Garden & he hath given it to the sonnes of men, wth a general Condicion, Gen: 1.28. Increase & multiply, replenish the earth & subdue it. . . . And for the Natives of New England they enclose noe land neither have any settled habitation nor any tame cattle to improve the land by, & soe have noe other but a naturall right to those countries Soe as if we leave them sufficient for their use wee may lawfully take the rest, there being more than enough for them & us."[18] This argument echoed through the decades in the words of later religion-minded men.

The supremacy of the cultivator over the hunter was a classic weapon in the arsenal of the dispossessors. The argument was given legal expression in the writings of the eighteenth-century Swiss jurist Emmerich de Vattel, whose *Law of Nations* became a standard handbook. He wrote:

> There is another celebrated question, to which the discovery of the new world has principally given rise. It is asked if a nation may lawfully take possession of a part of a vast country, in which there are found none but erratic nations, incapable by the smallness of their numbers, to people the whole? We have already observed in establishing the obligation to cultivate the earth, that these nations can-

18. *Conclusions for the Plantation in New England*, quoted in Albert K. Weinberg, *Manifest Destiny: A Study of Nationalist Expansionism in American History* (Baltimore: Johns Hopkins Press, 1935), pp. 74–75; Wilcomb E. Washburn, "The Moral and Legal Justifications for Dispossessing the Indians," in James Morton Smith, ed., *Seventeenth-Century America: Essays in Colonial History* (Chapel Hill: University of North Carolina Press, 1959), pp. 15–32.

not exclusively appropriate to themselves more land than they have occasion for, and which they are unable to settle and cultivate. Their removing their habitations through these immense regions, cannot be taken for a true and legal possession; and the people of Europe, too closely pent up, finding land of which these nations are in no particular want, and of which they make no actual and constant use, may lawfully possess it, and establish colonies there. We have already said, that the earth belongs to the human race in general, and was designed to furnish it with subsistence; if each nation had resolved from the beginning, to appropriate to itself a vast country, that the people might live only by hunting, fishing, and wild fruits, our globe would not be sufficient to maintain a tenth part of its present inhabitants. People have not then deviated from the views of nature in confining the Indians within narrow limits.[19]

Aside from conquest in a "just war" and the aggressive encroachment of individual settlers, however, the English colonies generally did not simply dispossess the Indians as though they had no rights of any kind to the land. The vast claims in the New World made by European monarchs on the slightest pretence of "discovery" were claims against other European monarchs, not against the aboriginal inhabitants of those lands, and the handsome grants made to trading companies or individual proprietors in the form of colonial charters (with their extravagant language of lands extending from sea to sea) were of the same nature. The English settlers took steps to "quiet the Indian title" to the land before they took possession— "extinguishing the Indian title" was the terminology commonly used in later times by the United States.[20] But this did not solve all problems, for the Indian and the white systems of land tenure were quite different. The Indians had a notion of communal ownership of land, the English one of individual ownership in fee simple; neither fully understood the concept of the other.

Many years of actual contact between the groups were necessary before settled relations were agreed upon. But as European exploration and colonization increased, a theory in regard to the territory in America gained general acceptance, a theory developed by the European nations without consultation with the natives but one that did not totally disregard the In-

---

19. Emmerich de Vattel, *The Law of Nations; or, Principles of the Law of Nature, Applied to the Conduct and Affairs of Nations and Sovereigns* (Northhampton, Massachusetts: Simeon Butler, 1820), pp. 158–59 (bk. 1, chap. 18, para. 209).

20. There is a long discussion of colonial practices in regard to Indian lands in Cyrus Thomas, "Introduction," in Charles C. Royce, comp., *Indian Land Cessions in the United States*, Eighteenth Annual Report of the Bureau of American Ethnology, 1896–1897, part 2 (Washington: GPO, 1899), pp. 527–639.

dians' rights. According to this theory, the European discoverer acquired the right of preemption, the right to acquire title to the soil from the natives in the area—by purchase if the Indians were willing to sell or by conquest—and to succeed the natives in occupying the soil if they should voluntarily leave the country or become extinct. Discovery gave this right against later discoverers; it could hardly make claim against the original possessors of the soil, the native Indians. In practice, nevertheless, and eventually in theory, absolute dominion or sovereignty over the land rested in the European nations or their successors, leaving to the aborigines the possessory and usufructuary rights to the land they occupied and used.[21]

Although there were many cases in which individual colonists acquired land directly from Indians by purchase or some other sort of deed, abuses arose in these private arrangements. Colonial laws struck at the difficulty by declaring null and void all bargains made with the Indians that did not have governmental approval.[22] Not only did such laws seek to remove causes of resentment among the Indians by preventing unjust and fraudulent purchases, but they aimed as well at preserving the rights of the Crown or the proprietor to the land, which would be seriously impaired by extinguishment of Indian titles in favor of private persons. The preamble of the South Carolina act of December 18, 1739, called attention to this double motivation behind the restrictive legislation of the colonial governments, noting that "the practice of purchasing lands from the Indians may prove of very dangerous consequence to the peace and safety of this Province, such purchases being generally obtained from Indians by unfair representation, fraud and circumvention, or by making them gifts or presents of little value, by which practices, great resentments and animosities have been created amongst the Indians towards the inhabitants of this Province," and that "such practices tend to manifest prejudice of his Majesty's just right and title to the soil of this Province, vested in his Majesty by the surrender of the late Lords Proprietors."[23]

A common vehicle for dealing with the Indians for land, as also for more generalized relations of trade and of peace and war, was the treaty negotiation. Formal and stately ceremonials marked the interchanges, in which

21. Washburn, "Moral and Legal Justifications for Dispossessing the Indians," pp. 16–18, points out the "speculative" nature of the claims advanced by the European discoverers.

22. *The Colonial Laws of Massachusetts* (Boston, 1889), p. 161; *The Colonial Laws of New York from the Year 1664 to the Revolution*, 5 vols. (Albany: J. B. Lyon, 1894–1896), 1: 149; James T. Mitchell and Henry Flanders, eds. *The Statutes at Large of Pennsylvania from 1682 to 1801*, 16 vols. (Harrisburg, 1896–1911), 4: 154–56; Thomas Cooper, ed., *The Statutes at Large of South Carolina*, 10 vols. (Columbia: A. S. Johnston, 1836–1841), 3: 526.

23. *Statutes at Large of South Carolina*, 3: 525–26.

the English colonists adapted their proceedings to the deliberate and highly metaphorical patterns of the Indians. The eighteenth-century treaties with the Iroquois, for example, were dramatic documents indicating a shrewdness and eloquence on the part of the Indians that were often a match for the self-interest of the whites. It is in the treaties that one sees best the acceptance by Europeans of the nationhood of the Indian groups that became a fixed principle in the national policy of the United States, although the colonial treaties for the most part were in the form of reports of the speeches and negotiations as well as articles of agreement (all sealed with the presentation of strings and belts of wampum or other gifts), rather than in the cold legal contract form in which United States treaties were cast.[24]

The treaties did not solve the problem of the steady pressure of white settlers on the Indian hunting grounds, and it is difficult to explain the slowness with which the imperial government came to realize the danger of these white encroachments. Continuing to rely on presents in order to keep the Indians attached to the English cause, officials only gradually awakened to the realization that the way to keep the Indians happy would be to remove the causes of their resentment and discontent.

Conferences between the Indians and the Albany Congress in 1754 emphasized the point, for the Indians made known their resentment in unmistakable terms. "We told you a little while ago," said one speaker for the Mohawks, "that we had an uneasiness on our minds, and we shall now tell you what it is; it is concerning our land." Again and again in the course of the conferences, Indians complained of the steady encroachment of whites onto their lands through purchases that the Indians refused to acknowledge or without any semblance of title at all.[25] No matter how great the

24. There is an intelligent discussion of colonial treaty making in Davis, *Colonial South*, 1: 239–54; the process of treaties and gift giving in the north is treated in Wilbur R. Jacobs, *Diplomacy and Indian Gifts: Anglo-French Rivalry along the Ohio and Northwest Frontier, 1747–1763* (Stanford: Stanford University Press, 1950); Dorothy V. Jones, *License for Empire: Colonialism by Treaty in Early America* (Chicago: University of Chicago Press, 1982), discusses British treaty making after 1763. A useful list with synopses of printed Indian treaties is given in Henry F. DePuy, *A Bibliography of the English Colonial Treaties with the American Indians, Including a Synopsis of Each Treaty* (New York: Lenox Club, 1917), but it is necessary to read the full treaties to appreciate their nature. A handsomely printed compilation is Julian P. Boyd, ed., *Indian Treaties Printed by Benjamin Franklin, 1736–1762* (Philadelphia: Historical Society of Pennsylvania, 1938). An ongoing compilation is *Early American Indian Documents: Treaties and Laws, 1607–1789* (Washington: University Publications of America, 1979–). The dramatic quality of the treaties is analyzed in Lawrence C. Wroth, "The Indian Treaty as Literature," *Yale Review* 17 (July 1928): 749–66.

25. E. B. O'Callaghan, ed., *Documents Relative to the Colonial History of the State of New-York*, 15 vols. (Albany: Weed, Parsons and Company, 1853–1887), 6: 853–92.

presents made to the tribes, gifts could not cover over the fundamental reasons for Indian hostility to the English.

TRADE RELATIONS

Colonial bargaining with the Indians for land was but one aspect of the transactions between the two races. Trade in general was the great point of contact, and the exchange of goods became a complex mixture of economic, political, and military elements. Trade was of inestimable importance to the colonies economically, but political considerations came to overshadow all else. Peace and at times the very existence of the colonies depended on Indian attachment to the English. Presents to the Indians were long a favored method of ensuring the allegiance of the tribes, and constant efforts to prevent abuses in dealing with the Indians aimed to secure peace on the frontiers. But the fundamental policy in Indian affairs was to make the Indians dependent on the English in their trade. The colonists were instructed to encourage the Indians to trade with them "SO THAT they may apply themselves to the English trade and NATION rather than to any other OF EUROPE."[26] This was especially true in the case of the Iroquois, whom the English determined to attach to themselves at all costs in their conflict with the French. Because trade became the great means of cementing political alliance, the object was to get the trade; it was less important whether the furs and other goods were needed or not.[27] But the rivalry to capture the Indian trade was not limited to that between the European nations in the New World. It existed, too, among the English colonies.

Important as trade was to both the English and the Indians, it was also the source of almost endless trouble, and it became necessary for the colonial governments to protect the interests of the commonwealth against uncontrolled private gain. Fraud and illegal practices on the part of traders stirred up Indian indignation and anger and thus led to frequent retaliations against the white community. In an attempt to prevent abuses, multifarious legislation regulating the conditions of the trade was enacted. Different systems were tried, modified, abandoned, and tried again. Some-

26. Leonard W. Labaree, ed., *Royal Instructions to British Colonial Governors, 1670–1776*, 2 vols. (New York: D. Appleton-Century Company, 1935), 2: 464.

27. See the introduction in Peter Wraxall, *An Abridgment of the Indian Affairs Contained in Four Folio Volumes: Transacted in the Colony of New York, from the Year 1678 to the Year 1751*, ed. Charles H. McIlwain (Cambridge: Harvard University Press, 1915). My discussion on trade is taken largely from Francis Paul Prucha, *American Indian Policy in the Formative Years: The Indian Trade and Intercourse Acts, 1790–1834* (Cambridge: Harvard University Press, 1962), pp. 6–10.

times a strict public monopoly of the trade was set up; more often, the trade was in the hands of private traders, who were hedged about by strict and detailed regulations. Because the Indian trade had such close bearing on the public welfare, the colonial governments insisted on strict measures of control.

The universal means of regulation was a licensing system. This was the only way to keep trade open to all qualified persons and at the same time provide protection against traders of bad character. The need for such protection was manifest, for, as a South Carolina law of 1707 declared, "the greater number of those persons that trade among the Indians in amity with this Government, do generally lead loose, vicious lives, to the scandal of the Christian religion, and do likewise oppress the people among whom they live, by their unjust and illegal actions, which if not prevented may in time tend to the destruction of this Province."[28] Often bond was required of traders, and violators of the regulations were punished by revocation of license, forfeiture of bond and stores, or some specified fine. Frequently trade was restricted to designated localities, the better to enforce the licensing system. Commissioners and agents were appointed to manage trade, issue licenses, enforce laws, and adjudicate disputes arising from trade.[29]

Regulation of trade was critical in the case of two items—firearms and liquor—because of their explosive potentialities. Just as the colonists were forbidden to buy land from the Indians, so were they restricted in the sale of arms and rum. For obvious reasons it was necessary to prevent the supplying of hostile Indians with weapons, and laws were enacted for that purpose, especially in the early days of the colonies, when survival against the Indians was of primary concern.[30] Of far greater moment, however, were the restrictions placed on the sale of liquor to the natives. The Indian propensity toward strong drink and the disastrous results that inevitably followed were universal phenomena. Traders throughout the long history of

28. *Statutes at Large of South Carolina*, 2: 309–16.

29. An example of an orderly and comprehensive law was the South Carolina "Act for the better regulation of the Indian Trade, and for appointing a Commissioner for that purpose" of August 20, 1731. It came after years of controversy among various elements of the colony for control of the trade and bitter experience with Indian wars resulting from ill-managed affairs. Ibid., 3: 327–34. Verner W. Crane, *The Southern Frontier, 1670–1732* (Durham: Duke University Press, 1928), pp. 202–3, asserts that under this law the regulation of the Indian trade was "probably as well planned and as efficiently enforced as any such system could have been under colonial conditions, and in view of the vast extent of the Carolina Indian country." The law became an Indian trading code for the whole southern frontier, for Georgia modeled its regulations on it.

30. Francis X. Moloney, *The Fur Trade in New England, 1620–1676* (Cambridge: Harvard University Press, 1931), pp. 102–4; *Archives of Maryland*, 62 vols. (Baltimore: Maryland Historical Society, 1883–1945), 1: 346.

the fur trade relied upon rum and whiskey in their dealings with the Indians. The unscrupulous merchant did not hesitate to debauch the Indian with liquor in order to cheat him out of his furs. And the Indians' revenge more often than not was taken out indiscriminately upon the settlers close at hand. Governor George Thomas of Pennsylvania sensed the danger that was common to all the colonies. "I cannot but be apprehensive," he told the assembly in 1744, "that the Indian trade as it is now carried on will involve us in some fatal quarrel with the Indians. Our Traders in defiance of the Law carry Spirituous Liquors amongst them, and take Advantage of their inordinate Appetite for it to cheat them out of their skins and their wampum, which is their Money, and often to debauch their wives into the Bargain. Is it to be wondered at then, if when they Recover from the Drunken fit, they should take severe revenges?"[31]

In an attempt to meet the difficulty, the colonies enacted prohibitions against the sale of rum and other liquors to the Indians. Often the prohibition was absolute. Stiff fines were provided for violators, forfeiture of stores was common, and in some cases authorization was given to destroy the liquor. Such absolute prohibitions met with opposition even from the respectable traders, who could not then compete with the irregular traders or the Dutch and the French. Prohibitions were often relaxed and sometimes removed altogether.[32]

Unfortunately, the whole business of liquor restriction was largely futile, for the Indians' thirst would be quenched by foul means if fair means were denied. The moral fiber of the general run of traders was too frayed to permit a stand against liquor when the profits were so enticing, and even the colonial authorities at times found it necessary or expedient to give the Indians rum. The experience of the colonies showed the seemingly insatiable thirst of the Indians and the willingness of depraved traders to quench it.

Despite all the concern, regulation of the Indian trade by the individual colonies was a failure. The frontiers were too extensive and the inhabitants too widely scattered to permit adequate control of intercourse with the Indians. The Indians could not be induced or forced to bring their furs to central markets where the trade could be supervised and regulations enforced, so trade was left practically free and unrestricted. Anyone could engage in it by obtaining a license. The fur trade was thus in the hands of a great

31. Quoted in George Arthur Cribbs, "The Frontier Policy of Pennsylvania," *Western Pennsylvania Historical Magazine* 2 (January 1919): 25.

32. *Colonial Laws of Massachusetts*, p. 161; *Statutes at Large of South Carolina*, 2: 190; *Statutes at Large of Pennsylvania*, 2: 168–70; *Colonial Laws of New York*, 1: 657, 888. See Moloney, *Fur Trade in New England*, pp. 104–8, for discussion of liquor in the New England fur trade.

number of individuals, many of them lawless, unprincipled, and vicious. Even if one leaves out of the picture the offensive traders and focuses on the respectable merchants and colonial officials, there is little to praise, for Indian regulations could become hopelessly entangled in factional politics. There was no uniformity among the colonies, no two sets of like regulations. Abuses prohibited by one colony were tolerated by the next, and the conditions could hardly be amended while each colony was left to govern its own trade and to be guided in part by rivalry with its neighbors. The failure was apparent to all. The corruption, fraud, and mischievous dealings of the traders continually aroused the resentment of the Indians.

BRITISH IMPERIAL POLICY

The important precedents in Indian affairs for the patriot leaders who established the government of the United States were the recent actions and plans of the British government looking toward imperial control. For there was no question that colonial management had failed. Trade was not adequately controlled; the English settlers steadily moved into Indian lands; the Indians were resentful and showed their ill humor by incessant attacks upon the settlements. The hardest fact of all had to be faced: the Indians by and large adhered to the French in the imperial war that broke out between England and France in 1754.[33]

In 1755 the first step was taken to remove Indian affairs from the incompetent hands of the colonists and center political control in the hands of the imperial government. On April 15 William Johnson, longtime friend of the Iroquois, was appointed superintendent of Indian affairs for the northern department, and in the following year Edmond Atkin was named to a similar post in the south; he was replaced in 1762 by the more famous John Stuart. The superintendents had full charge of political relations between the British and the Indians. Their responsibilities were numerous: protecting the Indians as well as they could from traders and speculators, negotiating the boundary lines that were called for after 1763, distributing presents given to the Indians in the attempt to gain and maintain their goodwill, and enlisting Indians in wartime to fight on the British side. The superintendents, too, exercised what control they could over the fur trade, although management of the trade remained to a great extent in colonial hands.[34] The problems of the Indian trade caught the eye of the Board of

33. My discussion of imperial policy is taken from Prucha, *American Indian Policy in the Formative Years*, pp. 11–25.

34. A modern scholarly biography of Johnson is Milton W. Hamilton, *Sir William Johnson: Colonial American, 1715–1763* (Port Washington, New York: Kennikat Press,

Trade in London, but the intricate nature of the trade and the sensitiveness of the colonies to their longtime prerogatives caused the board to move slowly. Although indications of the movement toward imperialization of the trade can be seen in the declarations of the board, nothing substantial had been done by 1763.

The purchase of Indian lands also engaged the attention of the Board of Trade. Restrictions placed by individual colonies upon the purchase of Indian lands by private persons had not worked well, for single colonies could not grasp the overall pressure along the frontier, and the provincial governments themselves were causing alarm among the tribes by their own purchase of lands. Imperial control was imperative if peace and harmony with the Indians was to be maintained.

As early as 1753, in its instructions to the governor of New York, the board initiated a new policy in regard to the purchase of Indian lands. The governor was instructed to permit no more purchases of land by private individuals, "but when the Indians are disposed to sell any of their lands the purchase ought to be made in his Majesty's name and at the publick charge." A similar measure for improving the regulation of Indian affairs was proposed at the Albany Congress. Then on December 2, 1761, a general order was issued to the governors in the royal colonies that forbade them to issue grants to any Indian lands. All requests to purchase land from the Indians would have to be forwarded to the Board of Trade and would depend upon directions received from the board. The governors, furthermore, were to order all persons who "either wilfully or inadvertently" had settled on Indian lands to leave at once and were to prosecute all persons who had secured titles to such lands by fraud.[35]

1976); it is to be supplemented with a second volume that is to carry the life beyond 1763. Of older biographies, the best is Arthur Pound, *Johnson of the Mohawks: A Biography of Sir William Johnson, Irish Immigrant, Mohawk War Chief, American Soldier, Empire Builder* (New York: Macmillan Company, 1930). See also *The Papers of Sir William Johnson,* 14 vols. (Albany: University of the State of New York, 1921–1965). On Atkin, see Wilbur R. Jacobs, ed., *Indians of the Southern Colonial Frontier: The Edmond Atkin Report and Plan of 1755* (Columbia: University of South Carolina Press, 1954), and John C. Parish, "Edmond Atkin, British Superintendent of Indian Affairs," in *The Persistence of the Westward Movement and Other Essays* (Berkeley: University of California Press, 1943), pp. 147–60. John R. Alden, *John Stuart and the Southern Colonial Frontier: A Study of Indian Relations, War, Trade, and Land Problems in the Southern Wilderness, 1754–1775* (Ann Arbor: University of Michigan Press, 1944), treats fully Stuart's career; chapter 9 gives a good discussion of the office of superintendent.

35. Oliver M. Dickerson, *American Colonial Government, 1696–1765: A Study of the British Board of Trade in Its Relation to the American Colonies, Political, Industrial, Administrative* (Cleveland: Arthur H. Clark Company, 1912), p. 340; Labaree, *Royal Instructions,* 2: 467–68; O'Callaghan, *New York Colonial Documents,* 7: 478–79.

Little by little the idea grew of establishing an official and defined boundary line to separate Indian lands from lands of the whites. Pennsylvania, in fact, provided a precedent in the Treaty of Easton, October 24, 1758, by which the governor returned to the Indians all of the trans-Allegheny lands that had been purchased from the Six Nations in 1754 at Albany. A line was drawn between the whites and the Indians, and neither was to violate the territory of the other. The British ministry ratified this colonial agreement, accepting it under the stress of war, it is true, but binding itself by a solemn commitment that could not be ignored at the conclusion of the hostilities.[36]

Conciliation of the Indians was of prime importance to the British government at the end of the war with the French. British officials knew that justice in the treatment of the Indians was required and that justice demanded strong measures to restrain, if not prevent, encroachment on Indian lands. A document drawn up in May 1763 explicitly proposed an Indian boundary line along the western edge of the colonies, although the motive behind it seems to have been to forestall the formation of western colonies (which would not fit in well with a mercantilist scheme of empire) rather than to placate Indians. A similar document, drawn up by the secretary of the Board of Trade, while considering the wisdom of limiting the extent of the colonies, saw also the need to designate the land between the ridge of the Appalachians and the Mississippi "as lands belonging to the Indians." Both documents were incorporated into a report of the Board of Trade of June 8, 1763.[37] There were in fact two groups in the ministry: expansionists, who were eager for the spread of the colonists to the west, and anti-expansionists, who wished to restrict settlements to the seaboard. The boundary line was agreed to by both, the latter looking upon it as a permanent western wall for the colonies, the former as a temporary expedient needed at once to satisfy the Indians and to be the basis from which an ordered and regulated movement westward could be made.[38]

---

36. Lawrence H. Gipson, *The British Empire before the American Revolution*, vol. 9: *The Triumphant Empire: New Responsibilities within the Enlarged Empire, 1763–1766* (New York: Alfred A. Knopf, 1956), p. 51. A facsimile reproduction of Franklin's printing of "Minutes of Conferences, held at Easton, in October, 1758," is in Boyd, *Indian Treaties Printed by Franklin*, pp. 213–43.

37. The documents are cited in Prucha, *American Indian Policy in the Formative Years*, pp. 16–17.

38. See chapters 6–8 in Clarence W. Alvord, *The Mississippi Valley in British Politics: A Study of the Trade, Land Speculation, and Experiments in Imperialism Culminating in the American Revolution*, 2 vols. (Cleveland: Arthur H. Clark Company, 1917), 1: 157–228. A more recent study, which revises some of Alvord's conclusions, is Jack M. Sosin, *Whitehall and the Wilderness: The Middle West in British Colonial Policy, 1760–1775* (Lincoln: University of Nebraska Press, 1961).

The theoretical deliberations were interrupted by news from America, which, though it did not change the basic direction in which British policy was moving, demanded emergency action. Word arrived in August of Pontiac's Rebellion, with its threat of disaster to the whole back country. Sir William Johnson wrote to the Lords of Trade on July 1 reporting the blockade of Detroit, the defeat of a detachment on the way there from Niagara, the destruction of the fort at Sandusky with its garrison (and the apprehension that a similar fate had befallen the other outposts), the cutting off of communications with Fort Pitt, the destruction of several settlements, the murder of many traders, and in general "an universal pannic throughout the Frontiers."[39]

This was no time for debating where the line should be drawn, for running a carefully surveyed boundary, or for solving the disputed point about the wisdom of westward expansion for the colonies. Some action was needed at once to pacify the Indians. They must be convinced that the encroachment of the whites was at an end and that they could return with confidence to their peaceful ways, assured that they need no longer fear a steady and ruthless expulsion from their hunting grounds. The Indians must be convinced that the British government meant to honor the commitments made to them in both the north and the south. A boundary line needed to be drawn quickly, and the ridge of the Appalachians was accepted as the dividing line. On October 7, George III incorporated it into his famous Proclamation of 1763. The document proclaimed three things: it established the boundaries and the government for the new colonies of Florida and Nova Scotia acquired by the Peace of Paris; it offered specific encouragement to settlement in the new areas; and it established the boundary line as a new policy in Indian affairs.[40]

By this proclamation, the governors and commanders in chief of the new colonies were forbidden to issue any warrants for survey or patents for lands beyond the boundaries set for their colonies. The officials of the older colonies were forbidden "for the present, and until our further Pleasure be known," to permit surveys or to grant lands beyond the watershed of the Appalachians. Second, the proclamation formally reserved the Indian country for the Indian nations—"all the Lands and Territories lying to the Westward of the Sources of the Rivers which fall into the Sea from the West and North West." The king's subjects were prohibited from making purchases or settlements in the restricted territory, and any person who had already moved into the Indian country was ordered to leave at once.

The Appalachian boundary line proclaimed in 1763, occasioned by the

39. O'Callaghan, *New York Colonial Documents*, 7: 526.
40. The Proclamation of 1763 is printed in Adam Shortt and Arthur G. Doughty, eds., *Documents Relating to the Constitutional History of Canada, 1759–1791*, rev. ed. (Ottawa: J. de L. Taché, 1918), pp. 163–68.

war whoop of the Indians, was provisional. The Lords of Trade realized that the ordinary process of instructions to the governors was too slow for a time of crisis. They knew, too, that it was impossible during an Indian war (especially one as serious as the uprising of Pontiac) to proceed with the detailed surveying necessary for laying out the line itself. But the point-by-point negotiation with the Indians over the location of the line was only postponed, not abandoned. In 1764, in its outline of a plan for the management of Indian affairs, the Board of Trade emphasized the necessity of a carefully drawn line, to be worked out by the agents with the Indians.[41]

Almost immediately the laborious work began. In 1765 the line was marked out in South Carolina and continued into North Carolina in 1767. During 1768–1769 the line was drawn west of Virginia's settlements— with some reluctance on the part of Virginia, which did not want to appear to give up its claims to the western regions. In the north the responsibility lay with Sir William Johnson. At a conference with the Six Nations in the spring of 1765 he obtained the approval of the Indians, and in 1768, by the Treaty of Fort Stanwix, he settled the northern boundary line. By 1768 then, the boundary line, determined by solemn agreements with the Indians, extended from Canada to Florida. The concept of such a line by then had become ineradicable; but the line itself moved constantly westward as new treaties and new purchases drove the Indians back before the advancing whites.[42]

The Proclamation of 1763 was not a carefully worked out plan for management of the West and regulation of affairs with the Indians, and it did not remove the confusion in colonial Indian trade regulations. The Board of Trade recognized the necessity "of speedily falling upon some method of regulating Indian commerce & polity, upon some more general and better established system than has hitherto taken place." At the same time that it proposed the boundary line to the king it undertook to gather information on which to build an adequate set of regulations for the trade by writing to Sir William Johnson and to John Stuart for their opinions and proposals.[43] When the reports of the superintendents were in, the board set about to formulate a comprehensive imperial program for the fur trade.

41. O'Callaghan, *New York Colonial Documents*, 7: 641. The British government augmented the proclamation with special instructions to the colonial governors to enforce its restrictions. See instructions to the governors of East Florida, West Florida, and Quebec, 1763, and to the governors of Virginia and Pennsylvania, 1765, in Labaree, *Royal Instructions*, 2: 473–74, 479–80.

42. Max Farrand, "The Indian Boundary Line," *American Historical Review* 10 (July 1905): 782–91; John C. Parish, "John Stuart and the Cartography of the Indian Boundary Line," in *Persistence of the Westward Movement*, pp. 131–46; O'Callaghan, *New York Colonial Documents*, 7: 665; 8: 111–37.

43. Lords of Trade to Sir William Johnson, August 5, 1763, O'Callaghan, *New York Colonial Documents*, 7: 535–36.

On July 10, 1764, the board proposed a plan that had as its object "the regulation of Indian Affairs both commercial and political throughout all North America, upon one general system, under the direction of Officers appointed by the Crown, so as to sett aside all local interfering of particular Provinces, which has been one great cause of the distracted state of Indian affairs in general." The plan included an imperial department of Indian affairs independent both of the military commander in America (whose control had irked the Indian superintendents) and of the colonial governments. The board honestly faced the problems that existed in America and provided a competent set of rules for carrying on an orderly and peaceful trade.[44]

The fur trade was declared to be free and open to all British subjects, and to better regulate it two districts were designated, with lists of tribes to be considered in each district. For the southern district, all trade was to be carried on at the Indian towns; in the north, fixed posts for trade were to be designated. The trade would be taken completely out of the hands of the colonies, all colonial laws regulating Indian affairs repealed, and control placed with the agent or superintendent of each district, who was to be assisted by deputies, commissaries, interpreters, smiths, and missionaries. So that the superintendents could have a free hand, the plan expressly forbade interference in the conduct of Indian affairs by the commander in chief of His Majesty's forces in America and by the governors and military commanders of the separate colonies, although the cooperation of these officials was enjoined. It empowered agents or their deputies to visit the tribes yearly and to act as justices of the peace.

Persons wishing to trade would be required to obtain licenses from the governor or commander of their respective colonies and to give bonds for the observance of the regulations. The licenses would run for one year only, and each trader was required to specify in his license the town or post at which he intended to trade. Fines and imprisonment would hold for those trading without a license. Trade would be governed by tariffs of prices "established from time to time by the commissaries . . . in concert with the Traders and Indians." No trader could supply Indians with liquor or rifled guns or give them credit for goods beyond the sum of fifty shillings.

Affairs continued to drift, for unfortunately the Plan of 1764 was never formally adopted, and in 1768 it was officially abandoned. The sum of twenty thousand pounds a year, which the plan was estimated to cost, was too heavy for the British government to bear, and the Stamp Act troubles had shown the impossibility of raising the money in the colonies. Colonial

44. Lords of Trade to Sir William Johnson, July 10, 1764, ibid., pp. 634–36. The "Plan for the Future Management of Indian Affairs" is printed ibid., pp. 637–41. The Plan of 1764 was sent to Johnson and Stuart for their criticisms and "further lights" and to numerous other colonial officials as well.

opposition, too, contributed to the decision to put aside the imperial pro-gram and return affairs to the colonies.[45] But the superintendents used the plan as a guide in the conduct of Indian affairs, and it foreshadowed later legislation of the United States.

The return of regulation of the fur trade to the colonies was a strange reversal. The Board of Trade was aware that the colonies had failed, and that the misconduct of the ill-regulated traders had "contributed not a little to involve us in the enormous expences of an Indian war." Un-daunted, with eyes consciously or unconsciously blinded to reality, the board trusted that the ill effects of past neglect and inattention would induce colonial officials in the future to more caution and better management.

The results were what might have been expected. The ministry perhaps thought the Indian boundary line alone would forever remove the causes of friction between the Indians and the English, but the American settlers could not be restrained. Control of the fur trade was no more exact. The failure of the colonies to enact the necessary legislation caused great rest-lessness among the Indians. Superintendent Stuart described the condi-tions in his department as chaotic, for the old lawless traders were still at work, and settlements were constantly appearing across the boundary line. The failure of the colonies to agree upon any sort of general regulations resulted in intolerable conditions in the West. Some interposition of Par-liament for the regulation of the fur trade on an imperial basis was neces-sary, and one last attempt was made. By the Quebec Act of 1774 the west-ern areas were placed under the Quebec government. In this way the Board of Trade hoped to provide the necessary regulation.

The mind of the British ministry was revealed in the instructions sent to Governor Guy Carleton of Quebec at the beginning of January 1775. They enunciated again the freedom of the fur trade for all His Majesty's subjects and directed that regulations be drawn up, "giving every possible facility to that Trade, which the nature of it will admit, and as may consist with fair and just dealing towards the Savages." The need for fixed times and places for the trade, for tariffs of prices for goods and furs, and for pro-hibiting the sale of rum and other liquors was again indicated. Governor Carleton received a copy of the Plan of 1764, which was to serve as his guide when drawing up the rules for trade.[46] It was a return to the former plan for imperializing the West, but it came too late. The Revolutionary War and the establishment of the independent United States threw these problems into the hands of the new nation.

It was certainly not clear at the time that the United States would

45. Peter Marshall, "Colonial Protest and Imperial Retrenchment: Indian Policy, 1764–8," *Journal of American Studies* 5 (April 1971): 1–17.

46. Instructions to Carleton, January 3, 1775, Shortt and Doughty, *Canadian Consti-tutional Documents*, pp. 419–33.

quickly grow to a position of dominance and threaten not only the lands but the tribal existence of Indians living east of the Mississippi. The vast majority of the Indians, who lived west of the Appalachians, were neither subjected politically nor dominated culturally by the United States; they continued to maintain their independence and to seek a secure place in the international circumstances of the time by fighting or by negotiation. Their ability to obtain material and moral support from the British in the north and the Spanish in the south made them a force that the United States government could not ignore but had to respect and conciliate. When the nation entered on its independent existence, Indian relations were a very important item on its agenda.

PART ONE

Formative Years

The United States, on declaring its independence from the British Empire, inherited a responsibility that had not been well fulfilled by either the Crown or the individual colonies—a responsibility to maintain just and peaceful relations with the Indian tribes while at the same time allowing (if not indeed encouraging) the expansion of white society west from the Atlantic coast. Building on past experience and experimenting with new policies and procedures as problems arose, the nation little by little developed a set of principles to follow in its dealings with the Indians. The form of this federal program had been determined by 1834, when Congress codified previous legislation.

The program was carried out in an age when land was the most important element in the economic life of the nation. The population was largely rural, subsisting on the land. Accumulation of land was a means to wealth, power, and prestige, and land speculation was a big business. On a continent that seemed illimitable, "free land" was beckoning toward the west, and few could withstand the pull. "Land was the nation's most sought-after commodity in the first half-century of the republic," one historian of the public domain has written, "and the effort of men to acquire it was one of the dominant forces of the period."[1] It seemed only reasonable to the land-hungry

---

1. Malcolm J. Rohrbough, *The Land Office Business: The Settlement and Administration of American Public Lands, 1789–1837* (New York: Oxford University Press,

whites that the Indians, who made little use of their vast territories, should somehow give way to them.

American statesmen were part of this milieu, but they were determined that the advance of the frontier should be orderly and peaceful. Order was to be achieved, in the first place, by restrictions and regulations governing the intercourse between whites and Indians. These measures were intended as a tight web to hold back unruly frontiersmen, thus preserving the honor of the nation by enforcement of the agreements made between the United States and the Indians in formal treaties. The major restrictive elements were the following:

1. Protection of Indian rights to land by setting definite boundaries for the Indian country, prohibiting whites from entering the area except under certain controls, and removing illegal intruders.

2. Control of the disposition of Indian lands by denying the right of private individuals or local governments to acquire land from the Indians by purchase or any other means.

3. Regulation of Indian trade by determining the conditions under which individuals might engage in the trade, prohibition of certain classes of traders, and competition with private traders in the form of government trading houses.

4. Control of the liquor traffic by regulating the flow of intoxicating liquor into the Indian country and later prohibiting it altogether.

5. Provision for the punishment of crimes committed by members of one race against the other and compensation for damages suffered by one group at the hands of the other, in order to remove the occasions for private retaliation that led to frontier hostilities.[2]

Behind this legislative program stood the military force of the United States. The army was small and often not well disciplined (for heavy reliance was placed on militia), but power was there in fact or potentially to enforce the laws against obstreperous whites and to subjugate hostile Indians when attempts at peaceful relations failed.

The government policy had positive features as well as negative ones, however. It was the goal of the United States to civilize, Christianize, and

---

1968), p. xii. See also chapter 7, "The People and the Land," in Curtis P. Nettels, *The Emergence of a National Economy, 1775–1815* (New York: Holt, Rinehart and Winston, 1962), pp. 130–55, and Paul W. Gates, *The Farmer's Age: Agriculture, 1815–1860* (New York: Holt, Rinehart and Winston, 1960). There is stimulating discussion of the importance of land in Michael Paul Rogin, *Fathers and Children: Andrew Jackson and the Subjugation of the American Indian* (New York: Alfred A. Knopf, 1975), pp. 76–110.

2. These points are taken from Francis Paul Prucha, *American Indian Policy in the Formative Years: The Indian Trade and Intercourse Acts, 1790–1834* (Cambridge: Harvard University Press, 1962), p. 2.

educate the Indians so that they could ultimately be absorbed into the mainstream of American society. To this end, the government and Christian missionary societies cooperated to bring the "blessings of Christian civilization" to the Indians. Their programs and activities rested upon an intellectual or theoretical base that held that the Indian was inherently equal to the white man, but the belief in the potentiality of the Indians for civilization should not obscure the concomitant view that the existing condition of Indian society was far inferior to that of the whites. Innate equality of all men did not mean actual equality of diverse cultures. The Indians, it was clear to the whites, did not yet enjoy the advantages of civilization, and descriptions of their unflattering state abound, no doubt often exaggerated because seen through the ethnocentric eyes of the whites or played up to make the demand for educational civilizing programs more urgent. The result in white society was the growth of benevolence (an inclination to perform charitable acts toward the "untutored savages") and philanthropy (an effort to increase the well-being of the less fortunate Indians), which coalesced into an abiding paternalism (providing for the Indians' needs in a fatherly way without giving them responsibility).

It is true that the Indian tribes during and after the Revolutionary War were treated by the United States as independent sovereign nations. Treaties of peace were signed with them, and land cessions were acquired only through formal diplomatic mechanisms. Yet to emphasize such events is to mistake the true status of the United States in relation to the Indian tribes. The Indians, who had once been able to play off one European power against another for their own security and advantage, now faced a *single* power, the United States, a political state that soon greatly overshadowed them in population and resources. The United States knew it was superior to the Indians, not only in religious beliefs, literary accomplishments, and other cultural patterns, but also in population, in technological and agricultural achievements, and ultimately, therefore, in power. Even Thomas Jefferson had no illusion on this score and assumed that the Indians also had none. He urged humanity in dealing with the tribes, but he was willing to fall back upon fear if necessary. He wrote to a territorial governor in 1803: "We presume that our strength and their weakness is now so visible, that they must see we have only to shut our hand to crush them."[3]

As the century advanced, the disparity between the white and Indian societies became more pronounced. John C. Calhoun, as secretary of war, was outspoken. Although he promoted the education of the Indians and

---

3. Jefferson to William Henry Harrison, February 27, 1803, *The Writings of Thomas Jefferson*, ed. Andrew A. Lipscomb, 20 vols. (Washington: Thomas Jefferson Memorial Association, 1903–1904), 10: 370–71.

acknowledged "partial advances" in the attempts to civilize them, he saw the need for more radical measures. "They must be brought gradually under our authority and laws," he reported to Congress in 1820, "or they will insensibly waste away in vice and misery. It is impossible, with their customs, that they should exist as independent communities, in the midst of civilized society. They are not, in fact, an independent people, (I speak of those surrounded by our population,) nor ought they to be so considered. They should be taken under our guardianship; and our opinion, and not theirs, ought to prevail, in measures intended for their civilization and happiness. A system less vigorous may protract, but cannot arrest their fate." He asserted that "nominal independence" of the Indians was opposed to their happiness and civilization, for they had none of the advantages of real independence but suffered all the disadvantages of a state of complete subjugation.[4]

William Clark, too, from his vantage point as superintendent of Indian affairs in the west, pointed to changes that had occurred in relations between the United States and the Indians as a result of the military victories by American troops. Once a "formidable and terrible enemy," the Indians were no longer to be feared, he wrote; their "power had been broken, their warlike spirit subdued, and themselves sunk into objects of pity and commiseration." Clark outlined a paternal system of education for the Indians and urged their removal outside the states and territories to accomplish it.[5]

The view of the Indians that these men had—and many others shared it—did not call for extermination of the Indians but for humanity and benevolence. The policy makers, from George Washington and Henry Knox on, were imbued with a vision of the United States as the great republican model for the world, and they were continually conscious of the duties of justice toward a less favored people. Secretary of War Knox did not want the world to class the United States with Spain, which had destroyed the Indians of Mexico and Peru. Almost forty years later, John Quincy Adams's secretary of war, James Barbour, declared: "Next to the means of self-defence, and the blessings of free government, stands, in point of importance, the character of a nation. Its distinguishing characteristics should be, justice and moderation. To spare the weak is its brightest ornament."[6]

Added to this basically secular concern was the immense weight of Christian concern. The goal of the rising Protestant missionary endeavors was to evangelize the whole world, to bring Christ's message to all man-

4. Report of January 15, 1820, ASP:IA, 2: 200–201; Report of February 8, 1822, *House Report* no. 59, 17–1, serial 66, pp. 6–7.
5. Report of March 1, 1826, *House Report* no. 124, 19–1, serial 138.
6. Report of Knox, December 29, 1794, ASP:IA, 1: 543–44; Report of Barbour, February 3, 1826, *House Document* no. 102, 19–1, serial 135, p. 5.

kind. And the instrument for that great work was to be a United States committed to Christian principles. Deeply imbued with a sense of mission, of carrying out God's commands of justice and compassion, active Christians reinforced the national policy of paternalism to the Indians. It was not enough to lament past failings in regard to the Indians. A committee of the American Board of Commissioners for Foreign Missions in 1824 condemned failures to improve the civil, moral, and religious condition of the Indians, injustices in acquiring Indian lands and furs, and devastating wars against the natives. It viewed these acts as "national sins, aggravated by our knowledge and their ignorance, our strength and skill in war and their weakness; by our treacherous abuse of their unsuspicious simplicity, and especially by the light and privileges of Christianity, which we enjoy, and of which they are destitute." The only way to avert the just vengeance of God for these wrongs—and "to elevate our national character, and render it exemplary in the view of the world"—was to speed the work of civilizing and elevating the Indians.[7]

Thus the formative years brought into sharp focus the anomalies in relations between the United States and the Indian tribes that would persist through the decades. The federal government promoted the expansion of settlers westward, thus exerting great pressure on Indian lands, while it tried to ease the resulting conflict by regulating the whites and acculturating the Indians. The United States signed treaties with the Indian tribes, recognized an independent nationhood, and in many ways acted as though the Indian chiefs were in fact the rulers of sovereign political entities. Yet it hedged the tribes around with restrictions on their freedom of action, dictated treaty terms to chiefs unable or afraid to reject them, and set about to change the fundamental cultural patterns of the Indians in a self-righteous paternal manner.

7. Memorial of the American Board of Commissioners for Foreign Missions, March 3, 1824, ASP:IA, 2: 446.

CHAPTER I

Peace after the Revolution

The Policy of the Continental Congress.

Early Treaties and Ordinances. The Constitution

and Indian Policy. Treaty-Making Principles

and Practices. Indian Rights to the Land.

The colonies, engaged in a war with the mother country, were much concerned about the Indian nations at their backs. Unless the Indians could be neutralized or persuaded to join the patriots, the struggle for independence would be seriously jeopardized. And when the Revolutionary War had been won, Indian problems remained an important business in the establishment of the new nation.

THE POLICY OF THE CONTINENTAL CONGRESS

A coordinated Indian policy began to take shape during the Revolutionary War, even before independence was declared.[1] The individual colonies were well aware of Indian matters, and some of them sent commissioners to the tribes. But the Indian problem could not be handled adequately by disparate provincial practices, and on July 12, 1775, less than three months after Lexington and Concord, the Continental Congress inaugurated a federal Indian policy with a report from a committee on Indian affairs. Declaring that "securing and preserving the friendship of the Indian Nations, ap-

1. Much of the material in this chapter is taken from Francis Paul Prucha, *American Indian Policy in the Formative Years: The Indian Trade and Intercourse Acts, 1790–1834* (Cambridge: Harvard University Press, 1962), pp. 27–43. See also Walter H. Mohr, *Federal Indian Relations, 1774–1788* (Philadelphia: University of Pennsylvania Press, 1933).

pears to be a subject of the utmost moment to these colonies" and noting that there was reason to fear that the British would incite the Indians against the rebelling colonies, the committee recommended that steps be taken to maintain the friendship of the Indians. Congress thereupon established three departments: a northern department including the Six Nations and the Indians to the north of them; a southern department including the Cherokees and all others to the south of them; and a middle department containing the tribes living in between. It appointed commissioners for each department, who were to treat with the Indians "in the name, and on behalf of the united colonies"; they were to work to preserve peace and friendship with the Indians and, in the quaint understatement of the report, "to prevent their taking any part in the present commotions." Agents appointed by the commissioners would spy out the conduct of the British superintendents and their men and seize any British agents who were stirring up the Indians against the patriots.[2]

Congress on July 13 appointed the commissioners for the northern and middle departments, but it left the nomination of those for the southern department to the council of safety of South Carolina. That Benjamin Franklin, Patrick Henry, and James Wilson were chosen for the middle department is an indication of the importance attached to the matter.[3]

Indian matters were entwined with the still greater problem of the western lands, for administration of the lands and management of the Indians who were on the lands went hand in hand. Washington observed in 1783, "The Settlmt. of the Western Country and making a Peace with the Indians are so analogous that there can be no definition of the one without involving considerations of the other."[4] But the questions of managing the Indians and controlling trade with them did have a separate identity and were considered separately by the Continental Congress. The decisions made by that Congress and the principles incorporated into the Articles of Confederation gave a decisive turn to American Indian policy.

As with all the major questions involved in forming the new government, so with Indian policy the basic decision concerned the authority to

2. JCC, 2: 174–77. The great extent of Indian concerns can be seen in *Index, Journals of the Continental Congress*, comp. Kenneth E. Harris and Steven D. Tulley (Washington: National Archives and Records Service, 1976), and *Index: The Papers of the Continental Congress*, comp. John P. Butler, 5 vols. (Washington: National Archives and Records Service, 1978).

3. JCC, 2: 183, 192, 194.

4. Washington to James Duane, September 7, 1783, *The Writings of George Washington from the Original Manuscript Sources, 1745–1799*, ed. John C. Fitzpatrick, 39 vols. (Washington: GPO, 1931–1934), 27: 139–40. See Merrill Jensen, *The Articles of Confederation: An Interpretation of the Social-Constitutional History of the American Revolution* (Madison: University of Wisconsin Press, 1940), for details of the western land problem and how it was tied in with the Indian question.

be given to the federal government. The imperial experiment in unified management of the Indians had made its mark on the minds of the delegates to Congress, and a majority believed that Indian affairs belonged to the central government. Benjamin Franklin, the leading personality in the Congress, had offered a plan of union at Albany in 1754 that provided that the president-general, with the advice of the grand council, should control Indian affairs. Now he included the idea in a draft for a confederation that he proposed to Congress on July 21, 1775. He offered two articles. First, no colony could engage in offensive war against the Indians without the consent of Congress, which would be the judge of the justice and necessity of the war. Second, a perpetual alliance, both offensive and defensive, should be made with the Six Nations. For them, as well as for all other tribes, boundaries should be drawn, their land protected against encroachments, and no purchases of land made except by contract drawn between the great council of the Indians and the Congress. Agents residing among the tribes would prevent injustices in the trade and provide for the "personal Wants and Distresses" of the Indians by occasional presents. The purchase of land from the Indians was to be "by Congress for the General Advantage and Benefit of the United Colonies."[5]

The committee appointed to draft the Articles of Confederation put the task into the hands of the able writer John Dickinson, a Pennsylvanian like Franklin and an advocate of congressional control of the western lands. His draft, submitted on July 12, 1776, elaborated Franklin's plan; in the general enumeration of powers granted the central government, Dickinson included "Regulating the Trade, and managing all Affairs with the Indians."[6]

Congressional control of Indian affairs, however, was not accepted by all, and the debate on July 26 indicated a decided divergence of views. The opposition came chiefly from South Carolina, which wanted to handle Indian affairs as a colony. Georgia, on the other hand, was quite willing for Congress to assume the burden because the state could not afford the presents for the Indians that its position as a buffer against hostile tribes demanded. In the end, the overall necessities of controlling the Indians prevailed, for, as James Wilson pointed out, the Indians refused to recognize any superior authority, and only the United States in Congress assembled

5. The Albany proposal of June 28, 1754, "Short Hints toward a Scheme for a General Union of the British Colonies on the Continent," is in *The Papers of Benjamin Franklin*, ed. Leonard W. Labaree, 21 vols. to date (New Haven: Yale University Press, 1959–), 5: 361–64; it is based on an earlier sketch of a union drawn up by Franklin, June 8, 1754, ibid., pp. 335–38. The 1775 draft is in JCC, 2: 197–98. Jensen, *Articles of Confederation*, p. 152, points out that Franklin's draft reflected his views as a Pennsylvanian and a land speculator, siding with the landless states in insisting on control of the western lands by Congress.

6. Dickinson's draft is in JCC, 5: 546–54.

could have any hope of dealing with them adequately. Above all else, rivalries between colonies in treating with the Indians had to be avoided.[7]

On August 20 Congress accepted an amended draft. The Franklin-Dickinson articles about alliances with the Indians, about maintaining their boundaries, and about purchase of their lands—as well as Dickinson's strong statements about federal control of boundaries of colonies and of the western lands—were omitted. Only the following simple statement appeared: "The United States Assembled shall have the sole and exclusive right and power of . . . regulating the trade, and managing all affairs with the Indians, not members of any of the States."[8]

Even this did not satisfy the advocates of state control, who were jealous of individual state authority within their own territories, and corrective amendments were offered. Congress rejected two alternative amendments before agreeing to the provision that appeared in the ratified document. In its long enumeration of the powers of Congress, the Articles of Confederation declared: "The United States in Congress assembled shall also have the sole and exclusive right and power of . . . regulating the trade and managing all affairs with the Indians, not members of any of the States, provided that the legislative right of any State within its own limits be not infringed or violated."[9]

Thus the management of Indian affairs and the regulation of Indian trade fell to the federal government. The principle was enunciated, but it was not crystal clear, for the proviso cast a heavy blur over the article and the power that it actually gave to Congress and prohibited to the states. James Madison in Number 42 of *The Federalist* poked fun at the article, ridiculing it as "obscure and contradictory," as "absolutely incomprehensible," and as inconsiderately endeavoring to accomplish impossibilities. It must be admitted that Madison was moved to make the Articles of Confederation look black so that the new Constitution would look so much the brighter. But practical experience gave him and other critics of the Articles a sound foundation for their opposition. At critical moments in Indian affairs, some of the states refused to abdicate in favor of Congress.

The debates over the Articles of Confederation and the subsequent practice under this frame of government, nevertheless, clarified one element of Indian relations: the concept of the Indian country was strengthened. Not only was the Indian country the territory lying beyond the boundary lines, forbidden to settlers and to unlicensed traders, but it was also the area over which federal authority extended. Federal laws governing the Indians and

7. JCC, 6: 1077–79; Jensen, *Articles of Confederation*, p. 155; Mohr, *Federal Indian Relations*, pp. 182–84.

8. JCC, 5: 674–89.

9. Ibid., 9: 844–45.

the Indian trade took effect in the Indian country only; outside they did not hold.

The Articles of Confederation were approved by Congress in 1777, but they did not take effect until 1781, for Maryland refused to ratify until the landed states had ceded their western claims to the United States. Meanwhile, the course of the war was in the hands of the Continental Congress and its committees.[10]

The British had the more advantageous position in the war and in large measure retained the allegiance of the Indians. John Stuart and his deputies in the south and the successors of Sir William Johnson in the north made use of their authority and influence with the Indians to prevent them from following the colonists in opposition to the king. The British not only had better agents than the patriots could muster; they had powerful arguments, too, which they did not fail to exploit.[11] It was plain that the causes of complaint among the Indians—the abuses of traders and the encroachment of white settlers—all came from the colonists. The British imperial officials, on the other hand, had a good record of trying to deal justly with the Indians, of protecting their rights to their lands and their peltries, and of furnishing the goods needed for trade. The British agents did not hesitate to call these facts to the attention of the Indians. One deputy reminded the Cherokees, "But for the care of the Great King they could not have had a foot of land left them by the White." John Stuart, haranguing the Choctaws and Chickasaws at Mobile in May 1777, urged them to follow the Cherokees in taking up the hatchet against the Americans. He pointed out the difficulties that the royal superintendents had experienced in protecting Indian rights against the colonists, and he concluded that "as it is the declared intention of the Rebels to possess themselves of your Lands, it also becomes your duty and interest to unite yourselves with other nations for your mutual defense and protection and to attach yourselves firmly to the King's cause, to whose goodness and protection you have been and are so much indebted."[12]

The ineffectiveness of the revolutionary government in supplying the Indians with essential trade goods was a serious disadvantage in seeking Indian support. It was all well and good to urge the Indians to desert the British by remaining neutral or by actively joining the colonial forces, but these positions (certainly the latter) meant loss of trade ties with the Brit-

10. The Indians' part in the war is treated extensively in Barbara Graymont, *The Iroquois in the American Revolution* (Syracuse: Syracuse University Press, 1972), and James H. O'Donnell III, *Southern Indians in the American Revolution* (Knoxville: University of Tennessee Press, 1973).

11. Mohr, *Federal Indian Relations*, pp. 42–43.

12. The quotations are in Helen L. Shaw, *British Administration of the Southern Indians, 1756–1783* (Lancaster, Pennsylvania: Lancaster Press, 1931), pp. 96–97, 109–10.

ish, who alone could adequately supply the Indians' needs. The Americans could not honestly promise to replace the British as suppliers of goods, and this the Indians undoubtedly knew.

At first, the best the patriots could hope for was to keep the Indians neutral in the conflict. As delegates of the Continental Congress told the Iroquois in July 1775, "This is a family quarrel between us and Old England. You Indians are not concerned in it. We don't wish you to take up the hatchet against the king's troops. We desire you to remain at home, and not join on either side, but keep the hatchet buried deep."[13] That sentiment gradually changed, however, and the colonists, like the British, began to seek positive assistance from the Indians. In this they had little success. Some New England tribal remnants, it is true, aided Washington in the siege of Boston. But the only important groups to espouse the cause of the patriots were the Tuscaroras and Oneidas of the Six Nations, largely, it seems, because of the influence among them of the New England missionary Samuel Kirkland.

Although there was no consolidated uprising of Indians along the western frontier—which could have been a serious if not fatal blow to colonial aspirations—there were sporadic outbreaks, enough to keep settlers on edge and give consternation to the Congress that was directing the war. This phase of the Revolutionary War, perhaps, can best be considered a continuation of the tension between the two races that had already become a way of life in the West. But there is little doubt that the borderland warfare was aggravated by British encouragement of the Indians.[14]

There were only a few instances of formal entry into the war by Indians. The Cherokees in 1776, against the advice of John Stuart, mounted an attack on the back country of the Carolinas. It was a disastrous venture. In an unusual show of intercolonial cooperation, militia from Virginia, North Carolina, and South Carolina united to crush the Indians. The Cherokees signed treaties in which they ceded large sections of land. This was the end of organized Indian harassment in the south.[15]

In the north, the protagonists were members of the Iroquois confederacy who elected to side actively with the British. Ably directed by Guy John-

---

13. JCC, 2: 182.

14. The matter of who was to blame for the use of Indians is considered in Jack M. Sosin, "The Use of Indians in the War of the American Revolution: A Re-assessment of Responsibility," *Canadian Historical Review* 46 (June 1965): 101–21. He concludes: "To [General Thomas] Gage belongs the major blame for exaggerating the involvement on the patriot side and encouraging the wise-scale employment of the savages. Fortunately for the American Frontier, Carleton and John Stuart did not initially follow his orders and the settlers were thus given two years to prepare. At that point both sides, seeking to increase their manpower, actively tried to obtain warriors for offensive operations, but the British were more successful than the Americans in enlisting them."

15. O'Donnell, *Southern Indians*, pp. 34–53.

son, who had succeeded his uncle as superintendent in the north, and greatly influenced by the remarkable Mohawk chief Joseph Brant, the Mohawks and Senecas and their friends took an active part in the attempt in 1778 to cut off New England from the rest of the colonies. As General St. Leger drove east from Niagara along the Mohawk Valley to meet General Burgoyne coming from the north toward Albany, his army was heavily augmented by Indian allies. They played a significant role in the battle of Oriskany, as colonial troops sought to relieve the beleaguered garrison at Fort Stanwix.[16]

Burgoyne's defeat at Saratoga signaled the failure of the British plans, but the Iroquois power remained a distinct threat aimed at the heart of the colonies. It was to destroy this danger and to show the Indians that the colonial government could and would strike strongly against the tribes who had decided to fight with the British that Washington sent a well-planned expedition into Iroquois country in 1779 under General John Sullivan. Following a deliberate scorched earth policy, Sullivan's army moved north into the heart of the Iroquois confederacy. Swinging wide through western New York, the troops destroyed villages and crops, without, however, managing to destroy the Indians, who faded away ahead of the approaching army. The policy of destruction left blackened ruins and a bitterness that was not easily erased.[17] Retaliatory raids by the Indians heightened the hatred.

The British from their post at Detroit instigated Indian war parties against the settlements south of the Ohio. To cut off this danger, George Rogers Clark, sent out by Virginia, attacked the Illinois towns and then recaptured Vincennes from the British commander Henry Hamilton, greatly bolstering the morale of western patriots. It was less than a total victory, for the Indians continued to be dependent on trade with the whites; and it was the British, not the Americans, who could provide the needed trading system. Moreover, Clark did not receive the reinforcements he required to proceed against Detroit, and for the last two years of the war he was on the defensive against continual Indian attacks.[18]

Although the Indian campaigns in the war had little effect on the out-

16. These campaigns are treated in general histories of the Revolutionary War. See, for example, Christopher Ward, *The War of the Revolution*, 2 vols. (New York: Macmillan Company, 1952), 2: 477–91.

17. A brief account of the expedition is Donald R. McAdams, "The Sullivan Expedition: Success or Failure," *New-York Historical Society Quarterly* 54 (January 1970): 53–81. See also George S. Conover, comp., *Journals of the Military Expedition of Major General John Sullivan against the Six Nations of Indians in 1779* (Auburn, New York: Knapp, Peck and Thomson, 1887).

18. The war in the west is discussed in Don Higginbotham, *The War of American Independence: Military Attitudes, Policies, and Practice, 1763–1789* (New York: Macmillan Company, 1971), pp. 319–31, and Ward, *War of the Revolution*, 2: 850–65.

come, they did leave a lasting heritage. On the one side, Indian participation in the Revolutionary War had far-reaching effects upon the Indian communities themselves. The war, with the pull in opposite directions by the British and the colonists, fragmented the Iroquois confederacy and in general demoralized the eastern and southern tribes. Those who had agreed to aid Great Britain had succumbed to promises of support of land claims and generous provisions for trade. They discovered to their astonishment that at the end of the war these were disregarded. The British did not insist that Indian rights be protected in the Treaty of Paris that ended the war in 1783, and the Indians were left on their own to deal with the victorious colonists. Important, too, was the heritage of hostility between whites and Indians to which the war contributed so strongly. It is true that such fundamental causes of conflict as white desire for land existed independently of the war, but the atrocities on the frontiers, on the part of both Indians and whites, intensified antagonism and reinforced a pattern that might, in other circumstances, have been modified if not eliminated. It seemed only natural and proper to the founders of the nation that Indian affairs be placed under the War Department.

After the war had run its course and peace loomed on the horizon, the problem of the Indians and the western lands again came to the fore. The ascendency and unique authority of Congress in regard to Indian affairs had to be asserted again and again. The committee appointed to report on the land cessions of the states and on the petitions of various land companies declared on May 1, 1782, that a clearer definition of congressional jurisdiction over Indian affairs was imperative. The recommendations of the committee indicate that the authority given Congress in the Articles of Confederation was not well understood by the states and their citizens. Among a series of resolutions dealing with the creation of new states to the west, the committee felt obliged to include two that reasserted the principle that the sole right of "superintending, protecting, treating with, and making purchases of" the Indian nations living beyond the boundaries of the states belonged to Congress.[19]

When the Revolutionary War ended, the Treaty of Paris signed with Great Britain in 1783 recognized the independence of the United States and designated the Mississippi River and the Great Lakes as the western and northern boundaries of the new nation. But because the treaty made no provision for the Indian tribes, they were considered technically still at war. It behooved the new nation to come to terms with the tribes at once, for the great desideratum was peace. Prolonged hostilities on the frontier could well have collapsed the young nation in the first precarious years of its existence.

19. JCC, 22: 230–31.

The Congress under the Articles of Confederation, aware of the unrest and threatened dangers in the north, south, and west, acted quickly and responsibly to ensure peace. A committee report to Congress on April 21, 1783, made a series of recommendations: suspension of all offensive movements against the Indians as preparation for a final peace; appointment of four commissioners (eastern, northern, western, and southern) to inform the Indians of the decision; and purchase of presents to have on hand when the Indians assembled for a treaty of peace. Congress was also concerned about the steady encroachment onto Indian lands. A proclamation of September 22, 1783, forbade settling on lands inhabited or claimed by the Indians outside of state jurisdiction and purchasing or otherwise receiving such lands without the express authority and direction of Congress. It declared, moreover, that any such purchases or cessions were null and void.[20]

A new report submitted by a committee on Indian affairs on October 15, 1783, proposed a policy for dealing with the Indians of the northern and middle departments only, for the committee disclaimed competency in regard to the southern Indians because of insufficient data. The first problem to be faced was that of drawing the proper boundary lines to designate lands reserved to the Indians. The lines should be drawn "convenient to the respective tribes, and commensurate to the public wants"; that is, restricting the Indians enough so that the lands would be available to fulfill pledges made to soldiers during the war for land bounties. This land should be obtained from the Indians without any considerable expenditure, which the state of public finances would in no case allow. After all, the committee argued, the Indians had been on the losing side in the war. They could with justice be treated as conquered nations and their lands taken from them by right of conquest. And even if the right of conquest were waived, the destruction wrought by Indians and the outrages and atrocities they had committed required atonement and a reasonable compensation for the expenses incurred by the United States. The Indians could accomplish this act of justice only by agreeing to the boundaries proposed. The committee, however, was composed of realists, who recommended some compensation for Indian claims rather than risk another Indian war and the tremendous expense it would bring.[21]

The committee proposed further that a general conference be held with the tribes in order to receive them back into the favor and friendship of the United States. The conference should determine the boundary lines that would divide the white settlements from the villages and hunting grounds

20. Ibid., 24: 264; 25: 602.
21. Ibid., 25: 680–94. The committee that drew up this report relied heavily on the opinions and advice of George Washington, expressed in a letter to the committee head, James Duane, September 7, 1783, *Writings of George Washington*, 27: 133–40. Much of the wording of the report is identical with that in Washington's letter.

of the Indians and thus remove as far as possible the occasion for "future animosities, disquiet and contention." The government commissioners should demand hostages for the return of all prisoners but indicate at the same time the nation's preference for clemency instead of rigor in dealing with the defeated Indians. They should tell the Indians that the government was disposed to be kind to them, to supply their wants through trade, and to draw a veil over the past.

The committee drew up in detail the line to be proposed to the Indians. For the Oneida and Tuscarora tribes, who had adhered to the colonial cause during the war, it recommended special assurances of friendship and recognition of their property rights. And the importance of the Indian trade was not forgotten; to prevent violence, fraud, and injustice toward the Indians, the trade must be regulated and the traders required to give security that they would follow the regulations. To this end, the committee recommended that a group be appointed to draw up an ordinance for regulating the Indian trade.

The committee appointed to consider Indian affairs in the south returned an almost identical report on May 28, 1784.[22]

EARLY TREATIES AND ORDINANCES

Outlining a policy in the halls of Congress was easy enough; the test came in carrying out the actual negotiations with the Indians. In the north and west this was accomplished shortly by the treaties of Fort Stanwix, October 22, 1784, Fort McIntosh, January 21, 1785, and Fort Finney (at the mouth of the Great Miami), January 31, 1786. The first, drawn up with the Six Nations, limited the Indians to an area in western New York and distributed goods to them pursuant to "the humane and liberal views of the United States." The second was a treaty with Delawares, Wyandots, Chippewas, and Ottawas by which these western Indians were allotted an area of land and by which they ceded to the United States other lands formerly claimed by them. The last was a similar agreement with the Shawnees. In these negotiations the idea of a boundary line was taken for granted; the basic problems were exact determination of the line, the conflict of state and federal authority in dealing with the tribes, and the grounds for demanding cessions from the Indians.[23]

The sole and exclusive right of Congress to treat with the Indian tribes was challenged by New York commissioners, who had already come to an agreement with the Six Nations and who caused trouble at the Fort Stan-

22. JCC, 27: 453–64.
23. The treaties are printed in Kappler, pp. 5–8, 16–18.

wix negotiations, but the federal commissioners completed the treaty. No provisions were made for trade, however.[24]

The United States in these first treaties after the Revolutionary War thought it was dealing with conquered tribes or nations. Although Congress spoke of liberality toward the vanquished and realized that some moderation of claims might be necessary to avoid a renewal of fighting, its commissioners dictated the boundary lines and offered no compensation for the ceded lands. To this highhanded arrangement the Indians, abetted by the British, continued to object. They had never asked for peace, they insisted, but thought that the Americans desired it, and they had had no idea that they were to be treated as conquered peoples.[25]

Furthermore, although the lands west of the boundary lines were guaranteed to the Indians and the United States promised to restrict the encroachment of whites, white aggressions continued. George Washington, after a tour of the West in 1784, reported the extent of the menace:

> Such is the rage for speculating in, and forestalling of Lands on the No. West side of Ohio, that scarce a valuable spot within any tolerable distance of it, is left without a claimant. Men in these times, talk with as much facility of fifty, a hundred, and even 500,000 Acres as a Gentleman formerly would do of 1000 acres. In defiance of the proclamation of Congress, they roam over the Country on the Indian side of the Ohio, mark out lands, Survey, and even settle them. This gives great discontent to the Indians, and will unless measures are taken in time to prevent it, inevitably produce a war with the western Tribes.[26]

The government seemed powerless to hold back the onslaughts of the advancing whites, and by 1786 the northwest Indians, out of disgust with the whole policy of the United States, were ready to repudiate all the engagements made with them since the close of the war.

In the south, the difficulties were, if anything, even greater because of the tenacity with which the Indians held to their lands, the mounting pressure of white settlers on the lands, the history of hostility of the tribes

24. For a discussion of troubles with the New York commissioners, see Henry S. Manley, *The Treaty of Fort Stanwix, 1784* (Rome, New York: Rome Sentinel Company, 1932). Barbara Graymont, "New York State Indian Policy after the Revolution," *New York History* 57 (October 1976): 438–74, shows how New York continued to treat with the Indians within its borders, contrary to federal policy, and in the end largely stripped the Indians of their lands.

25. Mohr, *Federal Indian Relations*, pp. 93–138; Reginald Horsman, "American Indian Policy in the Old Northwest, 1783–1812," *William and Mary Quarterly* 18 (January 1961): 35–39.

26. Washington to Jacob Read, November 3, 1784, *Writings of George Washington*, 27: 486.

against the whites, and the serious interference by state officials in the federal government's handling of Indian affairs. A special committee again reported recommendations for dealing with these southern tribes similar to those proposed a year earlier. Emphasis was placed on the precise determination of a boundary line marking the Indian country, and the Indians were authorized to drive off unlawful intruders, who would forfeit the protection of the United States.[27] After troubles with North Carolina and Georgia, which objected to the composition of the board of commissioners, a series of treaties was negotiated with the Cherokees, Choctaws, and Chickasaws at Hopewell, South Carolina, at the end of 1785 and the beginning of 1786. These treaties fixed boundaries for the Indian country, withdrew United States protection from settlers on the Indian lands who did not leave within six months, made arrangements for the punishment of criminals, and declared in solemn tones that "the hatchet shall be forever buried." They stipulated further that "the United States in Congress assembled shall have the sole and exclusive right of regulating the trade with the Indians, and managing all their affairs in such manner as they think proper," and declared that "until the pleasure of Congress be known," any citizen of the United States could trade with the tribes.[28]

The new nation faced innumerable difficulties, and it was imperative that the Indians remain at peace. This happy end could be attained only by a policy of justice toward the Indians and protection of their rights and property against unscrupulous traders, avaricious settlers, and ubiquitous speculators. With this in mind, Congress on August 7, 1786, enacted an Ordinance for the Regulation of Indian Affairs. With an eye, no doubt, to North Carolina and Georgia, the exclusive right of Congress under the Articles of Confederation to deal with the Indians was once more reasserted. The ordinance established southern and northern Indian departments, divided by the Ohio River, and authorized a superintendent of Indian affairs for each. These men were to hold office for two years unless sooner removed, reside in or near their districts, and "attend to the execution of such regulations, as Congress shall, from time to time, establish respecting Indian Affairs." The plan placed the superintendents under the secretary of war and directed them to correspond regularly with him and to obey his instructions. The superintendents and their deputies had power to grant trading licenses. They could not engage in the trade themselves, however, and had to take an oath to fulfill their obligations and to post a

27. JCC, 28: 118–20.

28. Kappler, pp. 8–16. Details on the appointment of commissioners are in JCC, 27, and in Merritt B. Pound, *Benjamin Hawkins: Indian Agent* (Athens: University of Georgia Press, 1951). See also Mohr, *Federal Indian Relations*, pp. 139–72, and Kenneth Coleman, "Federal Indian Relations in the South, 1781–1789," *Chronicles of Oklahoma* 35 (Winter 1957–1958): 435–58.

bond for the faithful discharge of their duties. All traders needed a license, good for one year at a fee of fifty dollars, and had to give bond of three thousand dollars for strict observance of the laws and regulations. Only citizens of the United States could reside among the Indians or trade with them.[29]

The Ordinance of 1786 was backed up in February 1787 by a set of instructions sent to the superintendents. "The United States are fixed in their determination," the instructions read in part, "that justice and public faith shall be the basis of all their transactions with the Indians. They will reject every temporary advantage obtained at the expence of these important national principles." The directive told the superintendents to seek out the causes of Indian unrest and correct them as much as possible; to cultivate trade with the Indians as an object of special importance but to allow no traders to engage in the trade without the proper licenses; and to investigate the character and conduct of the traders. To aid in the enforcement of the ordinance, the commanding officers of frontier posts were ordered to render such assistance as was necessary and as the state of their commands would allow. These were general instructions; the fine points of treating with the Indians and managing the trade were left to the "prudence, fidelity and judgment" of the agents.[30]

The regulations and grand utterances of the general government were largely ignored, and affairs got out of hand. The frontier was too extensive, the enforcing agencies inadequate, and the concern with other matters more pressing. Georgia on November 3, 1786, less than three months after the ordinance had restated the sole and exclusive right of Congress to deal with the Indian tribes, signed the Treaty of Shoulderbone, in which a small body of Creeks pretending to speak for the nation signed and gave up the Indian claims to all lands in Georgia east of the Oconee River. The encroachments continued apace, and the trade regulations of the ordinance were not followed; there is no record of any licenses being issued in the south under its provisions.

Again, in the Northwest Ordinance of July 13, 1787, the federal government voiced its position: "The utmost good faith shall always be observed towards the Indians, their lands and property shall never be taken from them without their consent; and in their property, rights and liberty, they shall never be invaded or disturbed, unless in just and lawful wars authorised by Congress; but laws founded in justice and humanity shall from time to time be made, for preventing wrongs being done to them, and for preserving peace and friendship with them."[31]

The continual reassertion by Congress of its ideas of justice toward the Indians began to have a hollow sound. Part of the problem undoubtedly came from the haziness (at least professed in the minds of some) about the

---

29. JCC, 31: 490–93.   30. Ibid., 32: 66–69.   31. Ibid., pp. 340–41.

exact authority of Congress, and the intermeddling of the states in Indian affairs aggravated the difficulties of the general government.

Mincing no words, a congressional committee on southern Indian affairs in August 1787 went to the heart of the matter. It insisted on the authority of Congress over independent Indian tribes and condemned the acts of states (specifically Georgia and North Carolina) in dealing with Indian tribes. It demanded that Congress give serious attention to the repeated complaints of the Indians about encroachments upon their lands, "as well because they [the encroachments] may be unjustifiable as on account of their tendency to produce all the evils of a general Indian war on the frontiers." It urged an investigation of the causes of hostilities and a policy of strict justice to both sides. "An avaricious disposition in some of our people to acquire large tracts of land and often by unfair means," the committee noted, "appears to be the principal source of difficulties with the Indians," and it made note of the settlements that were appearing on the lands of the Cherokees and Creeks contrary to treaties made with those tribes.[32]

Admittedly it was difficult to determine accurately the titles to land, but more embarrassing was the misunderstanding about the extent of federal power in governing Indian matters. It was on this point that the committee made its strongest comments. It insisted upon the just claims of the Indians to their lands and asserted that the power needed to manage affairs with the Indians could not be divided between the states and the federal government.[33]

Still the encroachments continued. General Henry Knox, secretary of war under the Confederation, reported to Congress in July 1788 the unprovoked and direct outrages against Cherokee Indians by inhabitants on the frontier of North Carolina in open violation of the Treaty of Hopewell. The outrages were of such extent, Knox declared, "as to amount to an actual although informal war of the said white inhabitants against the said Cherokees." The action he blamed on the "avaricious desire of obtaining the fertile lands possessed by said indians of which and particularly of their ancient town of Chota they are exceedingly tenacious," and he urged Congress to take action to uphold the treaty provisions and thus the reputation and dignity of the Union. He recommended that Congress issue a proclamation warning the settlers to depart, and if they did not, to move in troops against them. "Your Secretary begs leave to observe," he concluded his report, "that he is utterly at a loss to devise any other mode of correct-

---

32. Ibid., 33: 455–62.
33. Ibid., pp. 458–59. The precise point at issue was the meaning of the proviso in the Articles of Confederation about not restricting the legislative right of any state within its own borders.

ing effectually the evils specified than the one herein proposed. That he conceives it of the highest importance to the peace of the frontiers that all the indian tribes should rely with security on the treaties they have made or shall make with the United States."[34]

Congress did not disappoint Knox. On September 1 it issued the recommended proclamation—that universal but generally useless prescription for such ills as the secretary of war described. The proclamation cited the provisions of the Treaty of Hopewell and the boundary lines drawn therein, and it ordered the intrusions and the outrages to cease, enjoining all who had settled on the Cherokee lands to leave at once. It directed the secretary of war to have troops in readiness to disperse the intruders.[35]

That Knox and Congress were not sure of their ground is shown by the deference they both paid to the state of North Carolina. Knox assumed that North Carolina would place no obstruction in the way of federal action, but he recommended nevertheless that the state be requested to concur. Congress sent copies of the proclamation to the executives of North Carolina and Virginia, asking their cooperation.

Congress did not retreat from the position that Indians were a uniquely federal concern. The hazy proviso in the ninth Article of Confederation and the highhanded action of New York and North Carolina caused difficulties, it is true, but the high councils of state, by constant reiteration of the principles, managed to make it stick. The centrifugal force of state sovereignty and state pride was never strong enough to destroy the centralization of Indian control.

The new federal government had to tread with great care, and it could not always act according to the theories it propounded. The practical problems of dealing with the Indians at the end of the war had to be met by practicable measures, not high-flown theory. The one basic requirement of the new government that never faded from the consciousness of its leaders was peace on the frontier. The government needed peace in which to get firmly established, and it had to tailor its practice to this great end.

Knox came to realize that agreements with the Indians based upon the right of conquest did not work and that adherence to such a policy would continually endanger the peace of the frontier. The British and colonial practice of purchasing the right of the soil from the Indians was the only method to which the Indians would peaceably agree, and Knox urged a return to that policy. To establish claims by the principle of conquest would mean continuous warfare. He recommended, therefore, that the land ceded by the northwest Indians be compensated for and that future cessions be acquired by purchase. By the treaties signed at Fort Harmar on January 9, 1789, with the Six Nations and some of the northwest Indians, the lands

34. JCC, 34: 342–44.   35. Ibid., pp. 476–79.

granted to the United States at Fort Stanwix and Fort McIntosh were paid for. Small as the payments were, they marked the abandonment of the policy that the lands from the Indians had been acquired by conquest.[36]

THE CONSTITUTION AND INDIAN POLICY

After the concern of the Continental Congress with Indian affairs and the discussion aroused when the Articles of Confederation were drawn up, it is surprising to find so little about Indian matters in the Constitutional Convention of 1787. It was almost as if the presence of Indians on the frontiers had slipped the minds of the Founding Fathers and provisions were made for carrying on relations with them only as an afterthought. The lack of debate on the question indicates, perhaps, the universal agreement that Indian affairs should be left in the hands of the federal government. It was not the purpose of the men who wrote the Constitution, of course, to provide explicit details for congressional or executive action. Grants of powers and responsibilities were made to the federal government, enabling Congress to work out the detailed laws that were necessary to achieve the end proposed, but the Constitution is meager indeed on the subject of Indians, and what does appear was not the product of long debate.

The statesmen who gathered in Philadelphia in the summer of 1787 had come together to correct weaknesses in the federal compact. It was natural, then, that disregard of federal authority in Indian matters by the states should find a place in the discussions. In James Madison's mind, at least, the problem was clear, and when the Committee of the Whole discussed the Paterson plan on June 19, he asked, "Will it prevent encroachments on the federal authority?" The Articles of Confederation had failed in this regard, and one of the examples adduced by Madison was that "by the federal articles, transactions with the Indians appertain to Congs. Yet in several instances, the States have entered into treaties & wars with them." When the Committee of Detail presented its draft of a constitution to the convention on August 6, however, no provision was made for dealing with the Indians. To remedy this omission, Madison proposed on August 18, among other additions to the powers of the federal legislature, that Congress have power "to regulate affairs with the Indians, as well within as without the limits of the United States." His proposal was referred to the Committee of Detail.[37]

36. Mohr, *Federal Indian Relations*, p. 132; Kappler, pp. 18–25.
37. Max Farrand, ed., *The Records of the Federal Convention of 1787*, 4 vols. (New Haven: Yale University Press, 1911–1937), 1: 316; 2: 321. Madison had Georgia specifically in mind. In his "Preface to Debates in the Convention of 1787" he wrote: "In certain cases the authy of the Confederacy was disregarded, as in violations not only of the

This broad grant of power, "to regulate affairs with the Indians," was considerably cut down by the committee, which merely added to the clause granting Congress the power "to regulate commerce with foreign nations, and among the several States" the words "and with the Indians, within the Limits of any State, not subject to the laws thereof." In the report of the Committee of Eleven, submitted on September 4, the Indian clause was reduced again, this time to the simple phrase "and with the Indian tribes." The convention agreed to this wording the same day without any opposition.[38]

These five words would seem to be scant foundation upon which to build the structure of federal legislation regulating trade and intercourse with the Indian tribes. Yet through them, plus treaty-making and other powers, Congress exercised what amounted to plenary power over the Indian tribes. John Marshall noted in *Worcester* v. *Georgia*: "[The Constitution] confers on Congress the powers of war and peace; of making treaties, and of regulating commerce with foreign nations, and among the several States, and with the Indian tribes. These powers comprehend all that is required for the regulation of our intercourse with the Indians. They are not limited by any restrictions on their free action. The shackles imposed on this power, in the confederation, are discarded." There have been questions about the precise derivation of congressional power over the Indians, of course. Some jurists emphasize the commerce clause; others find the bulk of congressional power in the treaty clause; some add authority from the general welfare, national defense, and national domain clauses of the Constitution. In 1886 the Supreme Court spoke of federal power that grew out of the peculiar nature of the relations between the two races, independent of grants of authority in the Constitution. But whatever the ultimate source of congressional power, the federal legislature established by the Constitution has never felt hampered for want of authority.[39]

Treaty of peace; but of Treaties with France & Holland, which were complained of to Congs. In other cases the Fedl authy was violated by Treaties & wars with Indians, as by Geo." Ibid., 3: 548.

38. Ibid., 2: 367, 493, 495, 499. There is little evidence that Indian matters entered into the debates over ratification of the Constitution. Georgia, however, seems to have quickly ratified because of a desire to gain stronger protection against hostile Indians. James Jackson, Georgia's representative in Congress, declared on August 11, 1789, as he was demanding federal aid against the Creeks, that the Georgians "must procure protection here or elsewhere. In full confidence that a good, complete, and efficient Government would succor and relieve them, they were led to an early and unanimous adoption of the Constitution." Quoted in Randolph C. Downes, "Creek-American Relations, 1782–1790," *Georgia Historical Quarterly* 21 (June 1937): 172–73.

39. *Worcester* v. *Georgia*, 6 Peters 559. An analysis of the scope of federal power over Indian affairs is in *Felix S. Cohen's Handbook of Federal Indian Law*, 1982 edition (Charlottesville, Virginia: Michie, Bobbs-Merrill, 1982), pp. 207–28.

TREATY-MAKING PRINCIPLES AND PRACTICES

The Constitution, with its division of powers among the three branches of government, necessitated a working out in practice of the grants of authority only briefly enumerated in the document itself. This was particularly true in regard to treaty making, which was stated in these terms: "[The President] shall have power, by and with the advice and consent of the Senate, to make treaties, provided two thirds of the senators present concur." Two questions arose: Were agreements with the Indian tribes to follow regular treaty procedures? How precisely did the Senate advise and consent in regard to treaties? Both questions were answered in 1789 and 1790 as President Washington dealt with the Senate concerning the treaties at Fort Harmar of January 1789 and the treaty with the Creeks at New York of August 1790.[40]

The Fort Harmar treaties, although negotiated before the government under the Constitution was set up, were submitted to the Senate on May 25, 1789, by Henry Knox, who went to the Senate in person as a representative of the president to explain the circumstances under which the treaties had been concluded. When the Senate postponed action on the treaties, President Washington sent a communication to that body on September 17, 1789, in which he expressed his opinion about the nature of Indian treaties and their ratification. He argued that it was the custom among nations to have the treaties negotiated by commissioners ratified by the government that had appointed them. "This practice has been adopted by the United States, respecting their treaties with European Nations," he noted, "and I am inclined to think it would be adviseable to observe it in the conduct of our treaties with the Indians: for tho' such treaties, being on their part, made by their Chiefs or Rulers, need not be ratified by them, yet being formed on our part by the agency of subordinate Officers, it seems to be both prudent and reasonable, that their acts should not be binding on the Nation until approved and ratified by the Government."[41]

A committee appointed to consider the president's message reported the following day that it did not consider formal ratification of Indian

40. Ralston Hayden, *The Senate and Treaties, 1789–1817: The Development of the Treaty-Making Functions of the United States Senate during Their Formative Period* (New York: Macmillan Company, 1920), pp. 11–39. The pertinent documents are carefully edited in *Documentary History of the First Federal Congress of the United States of America, March 4, 1789–March 3, 1791,* ed. Linda Grant De Pauw, vol. 2: *Senate Executive Journal and Related Documents* (Baltimore: Johns Hopkins University Press, 1974).

41. *Senate Executive Journal and Related Documents,* pp. 40–41.

treaties by the Senate necessary, for the signing of the treaties by both parties without further ratification by the governments had been the common practice. But the Senate rejected this opinion and proceeded on September 22 to "advise and consent that the President of the United States ratify" the Treaty of Fort Harmar with the northwest tribes.[42] Thus was the precedent established, in accordance with Washington's view, that Indian treaties—like those with foreign nations—be formally approved by the Senate before they took effect.

While the case of the Fort Harmar treaties was still pending, the Senate and the president began to work out the functioning of the treaty-making power. On August 6 a committee of the Senate was appointed "to wait on the President of the United States, and confer with him on the mode of communication proper to be pursued between him and the Senate, in the formation of Treaties, and making appointments to Offices." On August 8 and again on August 10, the committee conferred with the president. Although Washington believed that nominations to office could be made by written communications, he felt differently about treaties. "In all matters respecting Treaties," as the report of the conference expressed his sentiment, "oral communications seemed indispensably necessary; because in these a variety of matters are contained, all of which not only require consideration, but some of them may undergo much discussion; to do which by written communications would be tedious without being satisfactory." Although Washington did not want a hard and fast rule that would not permit accommodation to varying circumstances, in the matter of treaties he looked upon the Senate as a council with whom he would discuss in person any pending negotiations.[43] The procedure was put to the test in the case of a treaty with the Creek Indians.

On August 22 and August 24, 1789, President Washington and Secretary of War Knox met with the Senate in the Senate chamber and laid before the members a set of facts concerning relations with the southern tribes.

> To conciliate the powerful tribes of Indians in the southern District, amounting probably to fourteen thousand fighting Men, and to attach them firmly to the United States, may be regarded as highly worthy of the serious attention of government.
>
> The measure includes, not only peace and security to the whole southern frontier, but is calculated to form a barrier against the Colonies of an European power, which in the mutations of Policy, may one day become the enemy of the United States. The fate of the

42. Ibid., pp. 42–43.
43. Ibid., pp. 24, 29–30; notes on conference of August 8, 1789, *Writings of George Washington*, 30: 373–74; Washington to Madison, August 9, 1789, ibid., pp. 374–75.

southern States therefore, or the neighbouring Colonies, may principally depend on the present measures of the Union towards the
southern Indians.

The serious encroachment into Cherokee lands in violation of the Treaty
of Hopewell, Washington believed, could not be immediately resolved because North Carolina, whence the incursions came, had not yet ratified
the Constitution and joined the Union, and the Chickasaws and Choctaws
were far enough to the west to prevent immediate conflicts with white settlers. But the Creek problem needed immediate attention because of hostilities between the Creeks and the Georgians.[44]

The Creek situation illustrates well the complicated Indian affairs that
faced President Washington. The Creeks were the strongest and best organized of the southern Indians, although they maintained the nature of a
federation of somewhat independent towns organized as the Upper Towns
and the Lower Towns. They formed a buffer between the new states and
the Spanish, who had regained jurisdiction over Florida in 1783. The Creeks,
like other Indian tribes, were increasingly dependent upon trade goods procured from white centers, and they had established patterns of trade to the
south, largely though the firm of Panton, Leslie, and Company, with headquarters at Pensacola. Their relations with the state of Georgia were critical. Georgia, ignoring the established principle that only the federal government could negotiate with the Indian nations for cessions of land, had
concluded a series of treaties with a minority of Creek chiefs in which the
Indians had ceded land for white use. These treaties of Augusta (1783),
Galphinton (1785), and Shoulderbone (1786) were contested by a majority
of the Creeks, who denied their validity.[45] The spokesman for the Creeks
was the astute leader Alexander McGillivray, the son of a Scottish Loyalist
trader and a French-Indian mother. Although he got his support largely
from the Upper Towns, he represented himself successfully as chief of all
the Creeks. He refused to accept the Georgia treaties and bolstered his
position by strong ties with Panton and with Spanish officials, from whom
he customarily received a pension.[46]

Washington outlined for the Senate his proposed solution to this im-

44. *Senate Executive Journal and Related Documents*, pp. 31–37.

45. The treaties are printed ibid., pp. 165–69, 180–83. American relations with the
Creek Indians are covered in Downes, "Creek-American Relations, 1782–1790," pp.
142–84, and Randolph C. Downes, "Creek-American Relations, 1790–1795," *Journal of
Southern History* 8 (August 1942): 350–73. See also Clyde R. Ferguson, "Andrew Pickens
and U.S. Policy toward the Creek Indians, 1789–1793," *Kansas Quarterly* 3 (Fall 1971):
21–28.

46. On McGillivray, see John Walton Caughey, *McGillivray of the Creeks* (Norman:
University of Oklahoma Press, 1938); Arthur Preston Whitaker, "Alexander McGillivray,
1783–1789," *North Carolina Historical Review* 5 (April 1928): 181–203; Whitaker,

passe—to negotiate with the Creeks for conveyance of the lands actually occupied by the Georgians through a federal treaty, in case commissioners sent to investigate the claims of the two parties should decide against Georgia—and he posed seven questions about the pending negotiations, to which he asked for and received answers from the Senate.[47]

The conferences between the president and the Senate were marked by constraint and tension, and the procedure proved unsatisfactory to both parties. The Senate wanted to examine the documents of the case at leisure, and Washington was irked by such delay. When he left the chamber, the president declared that "he would be damned if he ever went there again." And in fact he never did, although he continued to keep the Senate informed about the progress of negotiations with the Creeks.[48]

It was the goal of the United States to come to an agreement with McGillivray and the Creeks in order to settle the peace on the southwest frontier, to vindicate federal authority against Georgia in dealing with the Indian nations, and to draw the Creeks away from the Spanish into American channels of trade. In the fall of 1789 the government sent commissioners to meet with the Creeks at Rock Landing, Georgia, but when it became apparent that the commissioners were going to stand behind Georgia's claims, the Indians withdrew and the conference broke up with nothing accomplished.[49] In 1790 another attempt was made. Through the good offices of Senator Benjamin Hawkins of North Carolina (who later gained fame as agent to the Creeks), Washington sent Colonel Marinus Willett to persuade McGillivray to come to the seat of government in New York. The chief agreed, and with great fanfare he and his party of chiefs and warriors arrived in New York to negotiate with Washington and Knox. Although he was carefully watched and to some extent importuned by Span-

---

"Alexander McGillivray, 1789–1793," ibid. (July 1928): 289–309; and J. Leitch Wright, Jr., "Creek-American Treaty of 1790: Alexander McGillivray and the Diplomacy of the Old Southwest," *Georgia Historical Quarterly* 51 (December 1967): 379–400. A sprightly, popular article is Gary L. Roberts, "The Chief of State and the Chief" (Washington and McGillivray), *American Heritage* 26 (October 1975): 28–33, 86–89.

47. *Senate Executive Journal and Related Documents*, pp. 33–36.

48. The story of Washington's encounter with the Senate is reported in *Memoirs of John Quincy Adams*, ed. Charles Francis Adams, 12 vols. (Philadelphia: J. B. Lippincott and Company, 1874–1877), 6: 427, and told in detail in William Maclay, *The Journal of William Maclay: United States Senator from Pennsylvania, 1789–1791* (New York: Albert and Charles Boni, 1927), pp. 125–29. Material on the Creek treaty matter appears in *Senate Executive Journal and Related Documents*, pp. 55, 86–87, 88–89, 90–91.

49. Instructions to the commissioners, August 29, 1789, and the long report of the commissioners, November 17, 1789 (which includes transcriptions of pertinent documents) are in *Senate Executive Journal and Related Documents*, pp. 202–41. See also Lucia Burk Kinnaird, "The Rock Landing Conference of 1789," *North Carolina Historical Review* 9 (October 1932): 349–65.

ish and British representatives, who followed the proceedings with considerable self-interest, McGillivray signed a treaty of peace and land cession on August 7, 1790.[50]

In the treaty the Creeks acknowledged themselves "to be under the protection of the United States of America and of no other sovereign whosoever" and agreed not to hold treaties with individual states or persons. For a small annuity, the Indians agreed to cede lands actually occupied by Georgia settlers, but they refused to accede to the rest of Georgia's claims based on her treaties with the Creeks. The United States solemnly guaranteed the Creek lands lying beyond the boundary line established by the Treaty of New York. It promised also to furnish "useful domestic animals and implements of husbandry," in order that the Creek nation might be led "to a greater degree of civilization and to become herdsmen and cultivators instead of remaining in a state of hunters." There is no doubt that the treaty was made possible by a number of secret articles. One of these authorized duty-free trade through United States ports if Creek trade channels through Spanish territories were cut off (which effectively guaranteed to McGillivray control over Creek trade through American ports, which he then held over trade through Spanish). Another made McGillivray an agent of the United States in the Creek nation with the rank of brigadier general and an annuity of twelve hundred dollars. Others presented medals, commissions, and one hundred dollars a year to lesser Creek chiefs and promised to educate and clothe Creek youths.[51]

When it came time to negotiate with the Cherokees, Washington again sought Senate advice before the negotiations were carried out. But this time all was done by written communication; neither Washington nor Knox met personally with the Senate. The questions proposed for advice and consent were very general and did not deal with alternatives that might arise in the negotiations. The Senate, too, replied briefly. But it was noted in ratification that the completed treaty conformed to the instructions given to the commissioners by the president and that those instructions were founded upon the prior advice and consent of the Senate.[52]

50. Wright, "Creek-American Treaty of 1790." This article analyzes the influence of the Nootka Sound controversy between England and Spain and the Yazoo land grants on McGillivray's decision to go to New York to treat with the United States, and it traces the activities of the Spanish and British in New York.

51. The Senate ratified the treaty on August 12, 1790, *Senate Executive Journal and Related Documents*, pp. 96–97. The original treaty and the secret articles are reprinted ibid., pp. 241–50. The treaty is in Kappler, pp. 25–28; the secret provisions are printed in Hunter Miller, ed., *Treaties and Other International Acts of the United States of America*, 8 vols. (Washington: GPO, 1931–1948), 2: 344.

52. Hayden, *The Senate and Treaties*, pp. 33–34; *Senate Executive Journal and Related Documents*, pp. 94–96; ASP:IA, 1: 123–29.

Later treaties during Washington's administration for the most part dispensed with prior consultation, and when the president's cabinet, in considering the Treaty of Greenville in 1795, was asked whether the executive should consult ahead of time with the Senate, the members unanimously said no.[53] It became the established procedure in treaties with the Indians, as in other treaties, for the executive to negotiate and sign the treaties and only then to submit them to the Senate for action.

The United States government thus treated with Indian tribes with the same legal procedures used for foreign nations, a practice that acknowledged some kind of autonomous nationhood of the Indian tribes. When Chief Justice John Marshall in 1831 and 1832 examined the history of American relations with the Cherokees and other tribes, he strongly emphasized that point. "They [the Cherokees] have been uniformly treated as a state from the settlement of our country," Marshall said in *Cherokee Nation* v. *Georgia*. "The numerous treaties made with them by the United States recognize them as a people capable of maintaining the relations of peace and war, of being responsible in their political character for any violation of their engagements, or for any aggression committed on the citizens of the United States by an individual of their community."[54] In *Worcester* v. *Georgia* Marshall was even more explicit.

> The Constitution, by declaring treaties already made, as well as those to be made, to be the supreme law of the land, has adopted and sanctioned the previous treaties with the Indian nations, and consequently admits their rank among those powers who are capable of making treaties. The words "treaty" and "nation" are words of our own language, selected in our diplomatic and legislative proceedings, by ourselves, having each a definite and well understood meaning. We have applied them to Indians, as we have applied them to the other nations of the earth. They are applied to all in the same sense.[55]

However the theory was expressed—and there were those like Andrew Jackson who early argued that it was a mistake to sign treaties with Indians—the practice became deeply ingrained. Many of the basic relations between the United States and the tribes were determined by treaties, and the obligations incurred endured after the treaty-making process itself ended.

53. Hayden, *The Senate and Treaties*, pp. 34–37.
54. *Cherokee Nation* v. *Georgia*, 5 Peters 16.
55. *Worcester* v. *Georgia*, 6 Peters 559. For a discussion of the scope and legal force of treaties, see *Cohen's Handbook of Federal Indian Law*, 1982 ed., pp. 62–70. For a discussion of the importance of treaty making, see Dorothy V. Jones, *License for Empire: Colonialism by Treaty in Early America* (Chicago: University of Chicago Press, 1982), pp. 157–86.

Although Indian treaties and those with foreign nations had a legal similarity, it would be a mistake to push the sameness too far. In fact, the Indian groups were not like foreign nations, and the negotiations with them often differed markedly from those with England or France. The Indian tribes, either willingly or because forced to do so, acknowledged in the very treaties themselves a degree of dependence upon the United States and a consequent diminution of sovereignty. In the treaties at Hopewell in 1785–1786, the Cherokees, Chickasaws, and Choctaws acknowledged themselves "to be under the protection of the United States of America, and of no other sovereign whosoever." Similar clauses appeared in the treaties of Fort McIntosh and Fort Harmar with the northwest Indians, in the Treaty of Fort Stanwix with the Six Nations, and in the Creek treaty of New York. And the Hopewell treaties proclaimed: "For the benefit and comfort of the Indians, and for the prevention of injuries or oppressions on the part of the citizens or Indians, the United States in Congress assembled shall have the sole and exclusive right of regulating the trade with the Indians, and managing all their affairs in such manner as they think proper." Other clauses specified provisions for trade and for the extradition of whites who committed crimes within the Indian nations.[56]

Although the treaties did not touch the autonomy of the tribes in internal affairs, they made it clear that in relations with whites, the Indian nations accepted significant restrictions. The tribes were not free to deal directly with European nations, with individual states, or with private individuals, a point enunciated by Marshall in his Cherokee decision in 1831 in unequivocal fashion. "They and their country are considered by foreign nations, as well as by ourselves," he said, "as being so completely under the sovereignty and dominion of the United States, that any attempt to acquire their lands, or to form a political connexion with them, would be considered by all as an invasion of our territory, and an act of hostility." It was such considerations that led the chief justice to denominate the Indian tribes, not independent foreign nations, but "domestic dependent nations."[57]

INDIAN RIGHTS TO THE LAND

One indication of the lack of full sovereignty among the Indian tribes was the insistence by the United States on the principle of preemption of In-

56. Kappler, pp. 9–16. Similar statements appeared in subsequent treaties. See, for example, the treaty with the Cherokees, 1791, ibid., pp. 29–32.

57. *Cherokee Nation* v. *Georgia*, 5 Peters 17–18. The Creeks in 1790 agreed that they would "not hold any treaty with an individual State, or with individuals of any State"; the Cherokees in 1791 agreed that they would "not hold any treaty with any foreign power, individual state, or with individuals of any state." Kappler, pp. 25, 29.

dian lands, inherited from the European nations who had developed it in the course of their New World settlement. Thomas Jefferson relied upon this accepted view when the British minister asked him in 1792 what he understood to be the American right in the Indian soil. The secretary of state replied: "1st. A right of pre-emption of their lands; that is to say, the sole and exclusive right of purchasing from them whenever they should be willing to sell. 2d. A right of regulating the commerce between them and the whites. . . . We consider it as established by the usage of different nations into a kind of *Jus gentium* for America, that a white nation settling down and declaring that such and such are their limits, makes an invasion of those limits by any other white nation an act of war, but gives no right of soil against the native possessors." The following year he was even more emphatic in replying to queries posed by Washington to his cabinet. "I considered our right of pre-emption of the Indian lands," Jefferson remarked, "not as amounting to any dominion, or jurisdiction, or paramountship whatever, but merely in the nature of a remainder after the extinguishment of a present right, which gave us no present right whatever, but of preventing other nations from taking possession, and so defeating our expectancy; that the Indians had the full, undivided and independent sovereignty as long as they choose to keep it, and that this might be forever."[58]

Henry Knox entertained the same views, although he based them less on theoretical reasoning about the law of nations than did Jefferson. For the secretary of war, the common principles of human decency and the honor and dignity of the nation were reason enough to protect the rights of the Indians. "It is presumable," he wrote to Washington on June 15, 1789, "that a nation solicitous of establishing its character on the broad basis of justice, would not only hesitate at, but reject every proposition to benefit itself, by the injury of any neighboring community, however contemptible and weak it might be, either with respect to its manners or power. . . . The

58. *The Writings of Thomas Jefferson*, ed. Andrew A. Lipscomb, 20 vols. (Washington: Thomas Jefferson Memorial Association, 1903), 1: 340–41; 17: 328–29. See also the strong statement in support of Indian rights in Jefferson to Henry Knox, August 10, 1791, ibid., 8: 226–27; and Jefferson to Knox, August 26, 1790, *The Papers of Thomas Jefferson*, ed. Julian P. Boyd, 19 vols. to date (Princeton: Princeton University Press, 1950–), 17: 430–31. Jefferson's proposed amendment to the Constitution to ratify the Louisiana Purchase contained a statement of respect for Indian rights: "The right of occupancy in the soil, and of self-government, are confirmed to the Indian inhabitants, as they now exist. Pre-emption only of the portions rightfully occupied by them, & a succession to the occupancy of such as they may abandon, with the full rights of possession as well as of property & sovereignty in whatever is not or shall not cease to be so rightfully occupied by them shall belong to the U.S." Quoted in Annie H. Abel, "The History of Events Resulting in Indian Consolidation West of the Mississippi," *Annual Report of the American Historical Association for the Year 1906* (Washington, 1908), 1: 241. Abel argues that in 1803 Jefferson looked upon the Indian possession as only temporary.

Indians being the prior occupants, possess the right of the soil. It cannot be taken from them unless by their free consent, or by the right of conquest in case of a just war." Knox adverted to the opinion that the Indians had indeed lost their rights by reason of defeat with the British in the Revolution, but he pointed out that Congress in 1788 and 1789 had waived the right of conquest and had conceded to the Indians rights to the lands they possessed. "That the Indians possess the natural rights of man, and that they ought not wantonly to be divested thereof, cannot be well denied," Knox declared, and he recommended that these rights be ascertained and declared by law. "Were it enacted that the Indians possess the right to all their territory which they have not fairly conveyed," he wrote, "and that they should not be divested thereof, but in consequence of open treaties, made under the authority of the United States, the foundation of peace and justice would be laid."[59]

The principle of preemption was vital in Washington's policy. General Rufus Putnam concluded a treaty of peace with the Wabash and Illinois Indians in 1793 that included the following article: "The United States solemnly guaranty to the Wabash, and the Illinois nations, or tribes of Indians, all the lands to which they have just claim; and no part shall ever be taken from them, but by a fair purchase, and to their satisfaction. That the lands originally belonged to the Indians; it is theirs, and theirs only. That they have a right to sell, and a right to refuse to sell. And that the United States will protect them in their said just right." In sending the treaty to the Senate for consideration, the president requested a change in this statement of absolute Indian ownership "to guard . . . the exclusive pre-emption of the United States to the land of the said Indians." The Senate, reluctant to amend the document without further negotiations with the Indians involved, in the end rejected the treaty, but not because of any disagreement with the principle of preemption.[60]

Such views of Indian rights to the land were the basis of the dealings of the United States with the Indians. However great the pressures for dispossession of the Indians, the legal principles were clear. Judicial decisions regarding Indian rights to the land stressed either the possessory right of the Indians or the limitations of that right—the "sacred" right of occupancy or the "mere" right of occupancy—but all agreed that the aboriginal title involved an exclusive right of occupancy but not the ultimate ownership.[61]

59. Knox to Washington, June 15, 1789, and January 4, 1790, ASP:IA, 1: 13, 61. See also Knox to Washington, July 7, 1789, ibid., pp. 52–54.

60. ASP:IA, 1: 338; Hayden, *The Senate and Treaties*, pp. 34–37.

61. Felix S. Cohen, *Handbook of Federal Indian Law* (Washington: GPO, 1942), p. 293.

CHAPTER 2

War and Defense

Subjugating the Indians Northwest of the Ohio River.

Unrest and Retaliation in the South.

Probing the New West. The War of 1812.

American Dominion—North, West, and South.

The goal of Washington and Knox was peace, a peace to be obtained and preserved by just and humane treatment of the Indians. Yet there was war on the frontiers, undeclared war between the frontiersmen and the Indians in raids and counterraids. The federal government soon came to realize that military might was an indispensable ingredient of the policy it pursued. When treaties, laws, proclamations, and trade provisions by themselves failed to ensure tranquility on the frontier, military force was needed to enforce the stipulations of the treaties and the legislation and to back up the decisions of the agents and the War Department. Moreover, from time to time it was employed to crush resisting hostile tribes and force them to submit to land cessions and other demands of white society.[1]

The United States, of course, absolutely rejected a war of extermination against the Indians. Henry Knox, in a long memoir relative to the Indians northwest of the Ohio that was sent to President Washington on June 15, 1789, weighed carefully the two alternatives: overwhelming the Indians by military force or treating them with justice in seeking cessions of land. He concluded that to crush the Indians would require men and money "far exceeding the ability of the United States to advance, consistently with a

1. This chapter relies heavily on Francis Paul Prucha, *The Sword of the Republic: The United States Army on the Frontier, 1783–1846* (New York: Macmillan Company, 1969)—especially chapters 2–8, pp. 17–137—and some sections are taken directly from the book. The book has more extensive documentation than is presented here.

due regard to other indispensable objects." To treat the Indians by a "conciliatory system" would not only cost far less but, more important, would absolve the nation from "blood and injustice which would stain the character of the nation . . . beyond all pecuniary calculation."[2]

Yet conditions on the frontiers again and again got out of hand, and the United States not only called up militia but, contrary to its republican pronouncements against a standing army, built a regular army to serve on the frontier. The purpose of this army was to enforce peaceful measures for regulating relations between whites and Indians and, when these failed, to provide a defense against hostile Indians and occasionally a striking force to subdue them.[3]

SUBJUGATING THE INDIANS NORTHWEST OF THE OHIO RIVER

A crisis approached in the Old Northwest as waves of white settlers appeared along the Ohio, floating down the river by the thousands in flatboats and barges. Major John Doughty at Fort Harmar wrote to Knox that between April 6 and May 16, 1788, "181 boats, 406 souls, 1,588 horses, 314 horned cattle, 223 sheep and 92 wagons" had passed his post. "It will give you some idea," he added, "of the amazing increase flowing into the western world from the old Atlantic states."[4]

The Indians refused to accept this invasion. They did not acknowledge the treaties of Fort McIntosh and Fort Finney, which had not been approved by the confederacy of the northwest Indians, and they refused to accept the idea that they had been defeated along with the British in the Revolutionary War. Supported by the British in Canada, they maintained that the Ohio River was the boundary that the Americans should not cross. But they were willing to treat again with the United States, provided that all land cessions were "by the united voice of the confederacy" and that partial treaties be considered null and void. Protesting a sincere desire for friendship and peace, the confederated Indians begged the United States "to prevent your surveyors and other people from coming upon our side [of] the Ohio river."[5]

2. ASP:IA, 1: 12–14.

3. An excellent study of the creation of the regular army is Richard H. Kohn, *Eagle and Sword: The Federalists and the Creation of the Military Establishment in America, 1783–1802* (New York: Free Press, 1975).

4. Quoted in North Callahan, *Henry Knox: General Washington's General* (New York: Rinehart and Company, 1958), p. 317.

5. "Speech of the United Nations, at their Confederate Council, held near the mouth of the Detroit river, the 28th November and 18th December, 1786," ASP:IA, 1: 8–9. The speech is also printed in *Documentary History of the First Federal Congress of the United States, March 4, 1789–March 3, 1791*, ed. Linda Grant De Pauw, vol. 2: *Senate*

The issue was joined. The Americans were intent on settling north of the Ohio, and the Indians were equally resolved that the Ohio was to be a permanent and irrevocable boundary between the white settlers and themselves. The Treaty of Fort Harmar, in which the United States benefited from rifts among the Indians, renewed the land cessions and paid for them, and Arthur St. Clair, governor of the Northwest Territory, ended the council on a pious note as he told the Indians: "I fervently pray to the Great God that the peace we have Established may be perpetual."[6] His words were soon echoing in mockery through the forests.

Although the War Department was not to be pushed precipitously into military action, pressure for war became too strong for Knox to resist as reports of Indian incursions and atrocities poured in from the west, and the military engagements with the northwest tribes began.[7] General Josiah Harmar, having been directed by the secretary of war to "extirpate, utterly, if possible," the banditti who were wreaking havoc on the frontier, on September 20, 1790, launched a punitive attack against the Miami towns. His expedition, formed mostly of militia from Kentucky and Pennsylvania, was routed by the Indians. Rufus Putnam at the Ohio Company settlement declared: "Our prospects are much changed. in stead of peace and friendship with our Indian neighbours a hored Savage war Stairs us in the face. the Indians in stead of being humbled by the Destruction of the Shawone Towns & brought to beg for peace, appear dutermined on a general War, in which our Settlements are already involved." The Indians, Putnam reported, "were much elated with there success & threatened there should not remain a Smoak on the ohio by the time the Leaves put out."[8]

Executive Journal and Related Documents (Baltimore. Johns Hopkins University Press, 1974), pp. 146–48. Knox's discussion of the document in the Senate on May 25, 1789, is given ibid., pp. 3–6.

6. Quoted in Randolph C. Downes, *Frontier Ohio, 1788–1803* (Columbus: Ohio State Archaeological and Historical Society, 1935), p. 16.

7. Reports on Indian disturbances are in ASP:IA, 1: 84–96. There are many histories dealing with the Indian wars in the Northwest. See James Ripley Jacobs, *The Beginning of the U.S. Army, 1783–1812* (Princeton: Princeton University Press, 1947), pp. 40–188; Randolph C. Downes, *Council Fires on the Upper Ohio: A Narrative of Indian Affairs in the Upper Ohio Valley until 1795* (Pittsburgh: University of Pittsburgh Press, 1940), pp. 310–38; Downes, *Frontier Ohio;* Kohn, *Eagle and Sword,* pp. 91–127; William H. Guthman, *March to Massacre: A History of the First Seven Years of the United States Army, 1784–1791* (New York: McGraw-Hill Book Company, 1975). See also the discussion of Indian policy in terms of the northwest campaign in Reginald Horsman, *Expansion and American Indian Policy, 1783–1812* (East Lansing: Michigan State University Press, 1967), pp. 84–103.

8. Quotations are in Knox to Harmar, June 7, 1790, ASP:IA, 1: 97–98, and *The Memoirs of Rufus Putnam and Certain Official Papers and Correspondence,* ed. Rowena Buell (Boston: Houghton, Mifflin and Company, 1903), pp. 113, 247. Special works on Harmar's campaign include Randolph G. Adams, "The Harmar Expedition of 1790,"

The next to try to chastise the Indians was Governor St. Clair, who was given command with a commission as major general. He was a man of parts, with a substantial if not distinguished military career in the Revolutionary War, and Congress gave him additional troops. His chances of success in a punitive expedition against the Indians were greater than those of the hapless Harmar, but delays in getting supplies and in establishing a chain of posts north of Fort Washington led to a late fall campaign, and the troops, still largely militia, fared no better than Harmar's. An attack by the Indians on November 4, 1791, destroyed St. Clair's army. The general was exonerated of blame for the failure of the campaign, which was laid in large part on the undisciplined troops. John Cleves Symmes, one of the three judges of the Northwest Territory, wrote to a friend in Philadelphia after the debacle: "Too great a proportion of the privates appeared to be totally debilitated and rendered incapable of this service, either from their youth (mere boys) or by their excessive intemperance and abandoned habits. These men who are to be purchased from the prisons, wheelbarrows and brothels of the nation at two dollars per month, will never answer our purpose for fighting of Indians."[9]

St. Clair's defeat was a national disaster, and it proved that a makeshift force was not enough to face the competent chiefs and warriors of the Indians. Knox called for an adequate military force of disciplined troops, and Congress responded on March 5, 1792, with an "Act for making farther and more effectual Provision for the Protection of the Frontiers of the United States" that authorized more regular infantry and militia cavalry. President Washington appointed another Revolutionary War general, Anthony Wayne, to lead a new campaign against the Indians.[10]

Ohio State Archaeological and Historical Quarterly 50 (January–March 1941): 60–62; Howard H. Peckham, "Josiah Harmar and His Indian Expedition," ibid. 55 (July–September 1946): 227–41; John P. Huber, "General Josiah Harmar's Command: Military Policy in the Old Northwest, 1784–1791" (Ph.D. dissertation, University of Michigan, 1968).

9. Symmes to Elias Boudinot, January 12, 1792, *Quarterly Publication of the Historical and Philosophical Society of Ohio* 5 (July–September 1910): 95–96. A study of St. Clair's campaign and reaction to it is William Patrick Walsh, "The Defeat of Major General Arthur St. Clair, November 4, 1791: A Study of the Nation's Response, 1791–1793" (Ph.D. dissertation, Loyola University of Chicago, 1977). Official documents of the campaign are in ASP:IA, 1: 136–202.

10. ASP:IA, 1: 197–202; 1 *United States Statutes* 241–43; *Annals of Congress*, 2d Congress, 1st session, pp. 337–55. General Wayne has received extensive treatment by historians; see Harry Emerson Wildes, *Anthony Wayne: Trouble Shooter of the American Revolution* (New York: Harcourt, Brace and Company, 1941); Thomas Boyd, *Mad Anthony Wayne* (New York: Charles Scribner's Sons, 1929); Dwight L. Smith, "Wayne's Peace with the Indians of the Old Northwest, 1795," *Ohio State Archaeological and Historical Quarterly* 59 (July 1950): 239–55. Extensive correspondence between Wayne and the secretaries of war is in Richard C. Knopf, ed., *Anthony Wayne, A Name in Arms: The*

As Wayne set about to organize and discipline his troops for war, a new peace offensive was begun. The chances for success were not auspicious, for the victory over St. Clair had greatly heightened the Indians' spirit and reunited the tribes in their determination to defend their lands and their civilization against the whites. "The Indians began to believe them Selves invisible, and they truly had great cause of triumph," as General Putnam observed.[11] In these views the Indians got full support from the British until they had developed an exaggerated opinion of the aid they could count on in their struggle with the Americans. The Indians adopted an adamant stand that rejected all compromise. The United States, for its part, was now willing to withdraw its insistence on the Fort Harmar Treaty line, and its commissioners were sent deep into the Indian country to treat with the Indians. In July 1793 the commissioners arrived at Detroit, but their meeting with the Indians did not ensure peace. The arrogant chiefs on August 16 insisted that the Americans withdraw from all the lands north of the Ohio. The ultimatum was unacceptable to the commissioners, and they returned empty-handed.[12] Wayne in the meantime had reorganized the troops into the Legion of the United States, assembled raw material for an army, and with extreme measures to ensure military discipline, worked diligently to whip the soldiers into shape for Indian fighting.

To Wayne's irritation, Knox kept hoping that peaceful measures would obviate the need for a new campaign to chastise the Indians. He tried to explain to Wayne at the beginning of 1793 that all avenues for peace must be explored before the signal for war could be sounded. "We shall always possess the power of rejecting all unreasonable propositions," he wrote. "But the sentiments of the great mass of the Citizens of the United States are adverse in the extreme to an Indian War and although these sentiments would not be considered as sufficient cause for the Government to conclude an infamous peace, yet they are of such a nature as to render it adviseable to embrace every expedient which may honorably terminate the conflict." Knox cited the president's hope that fair and humane motives exhibited by the United States would themselves pacify the tribes and his fear that with war "the extirpation and destruction of the Indian tribes" was inevitable. Nor could the young nation afford to ignore world opinion. "The favorable opinion and pity of the world is easily excited in favor of the oppressed," Knox noted. "The indians are considered in a great degree of this description—If our modes of population and War destroy the tribes

---

Wayne-Knox-Pickering-McHenry Correspondence (Pittsburgh: University of Pittsburgh Press, 1960); official documents are in ASP: IA, 1: 487–95, 524–29.

11. *Memoirs of Rufus Putnam*, p. 116.

12. An account of the peace negotiations, with extensive citation of sources, is given in Kohn, *Eagle and Sword*, pp. 148–54.

the disinterested part of mankind and posterity will be apt to class the effects of our Conduct and that of the Spaniards in Mexico and Peru together—." Nevertheless, if every measure for peace was found unavailing without a "sacrifice of national character," Knox "presumed" the citizens would unite to prosecute the war with vigor.[13]

What Knox called the "procrastinated and fruitless, but absolutely necessary negociations with the hostile Indians" consumed the summer of 1793.[14] But when it became clear in September that the peace overtures were a failure, Wayne prepared for an active campaign. He moved north of Fort Washington and spent the winter building a post he called Fort Greenville. From there in the spring and summer of 1794 he prepared his advance against the tribes, and on August 20 at the Battle of Fallen Timbers the Indians fled headlong in defeat. The British at nearby Fort Miami, not willing to risk open conflict with United States troops, closed their gates in the face of the retreating Indians and with this action ended the Indians' final hope of succor from those who had encouraged their defiance of the Americans.[15]

Wayne at once set about to consolidate his victory. He built Fort Wayne at the headwaters of the Wabash and by November was back at his headquarters at Greenville. He negotiated with the Indians, who were stunned by their defeat and the failure of the British to support them; he was determined to conclude a treaty even if he had to treat at a place chosen by the Indians. In the summer the chiefs began to assemble at Greenville. Their hope of maintaining the Ohio boundary was now gone, and on August 3, 1795, they agreed to Wayne's terms, giving up once and for all the two-thirds of Ohio and the sliver of Indiana marked by the Treaty of Greenville line.[16]

Peace with the Indians in the northwest was supported by diplomatic negotiations with the British, whose occupation of military posts on American soil after the Revolutionary War encouraged the Indians and exasperated the United States. Jay's Treaty, signed in 1794, although highly un-

13. Knox to Wayne, January 5, 1793, Knopf, *Anthony Wayne*, pp. 165–66.

14. Knox to Wayne, November 25, 1793, ibid., p. 285.

15. There is a detailed description of the battle, with references to primary sources, in Jacobs, *Beginning of the U.S. Army*, pp. 173–76. The part played by the British in encouraging the Indians to resist Wayne is shown in Reginald Horsman, "The British Indian Department and the Resistance to General Anthony Wayne, 1793–1795," *Mississippi Valley Historical Review* 49 (September 1962): 269–90. Relations between the British and the Indians, both north and south, is thoroughly treated, to a large extent from British sources, in J. Leitch Wright, Jr., *Britain and the American Frontier, 1783–1815* (Athens: University of Georgia Press, 1975).

16. Kappler, pp. 39–45. For a careful analysis of the terms of the treaty and their origin, see Dwight L. Smith, "Wayne and the Treaty of Green Ville," *Ohio State Archaeological and Historical Quarterly* 63 (January 1954): 1–7.

popular among some segments of the population because it failed to settle maritime grievances against Great Britain, was an effective instrument for peace in the West, for the British agreed to evacuate the troublesome posts and turn them over to the United States on June 1, 1796. The provision in the treaty that permitted Indian traders from Canada to operate unrestricted within American territory was a continuing threat to American sovereignty because of the inimical influence of the traders upon the Indians, yet the transfer of Fort Mackinac, Detroit, and the other posts was a significant recognition of American authority that was not lost upon the Indians.[17]

UNREST AND RETALIATION IN THE SOUTH

In the region south of the Ohio River, American sovereignty was maintained as precariously as in the Old Northwest. Much of the present state of Tennessee, most of Alabama and Mississippi, and large parts of Georgia were held by the Cherokees, Creeks, Chickasaws, and Choctaws. Spain, in possession of the Floridas and Louisiana and claiming jurisdiction as far north as the Tennessee River, sought to control the trade of the southern tribes and, by entering into alliances with them, to use the Indians as a barrier against the advancing American settlers. Baron de Carondelet, who became governor of Louisiana at the end of 1791, if he did not indeed encourage an American-Indian war would at least have welcomed such a conflict.[18]

Despite serious provocation and the clamor for military support from whites in the region, the federal government refused to declare war in the south. It had committed its meager regular army to resolving the question of effective American sovereignty in the Northwest Territory, and it had no resources to commit in another direction. Nor could the United States afford to antagonize or irritate Spain while delicate negotiations were under way over the southern boundary of the United States and navigation of the Mississippi. The Indian problem was merged with the boundary dispute, and one could not be negotiated or solved without the other.

17. On Jay's Treaty, see Samuel Flagg Bemis, *Jay's Treaty: A Study in Commerce and Diplomacy*, rev. ed. (New Haven: Yale University Press, 1962).

18. A survey of conditions in the Old Southwest is Thomas P. Abernethy, *The South in the New Nation, 1789–1819* (Baton Rouge: Louisiana State University Press, 1961). Specifically on Indian problems, see Jane M. Berry, "The Indian Policy of Spain in the Southwest, 1783–1795," *Mississippi Valley Historical Review* 3 (March 1917): 462–77; Randolph C. Downes, "Indian Affairs in the Southwest Territory, 1790–1796," *Tennessee Historical Magazine*, 2d series 3 (January 1937): 240–68; Arthur P. Whitaker, "Spain and the Cherokee Indians, 1783–1798," *North Carolina Historical Review* 4 (July 1927): 252–69; Horsman, *Expansion and American Indian Policy*, pp. 66–83.

With the northwestern tribes emboldened by their victories over Harmar and St. Clair, Knox hastened to conciliate the southern nations, lest they be drawn into the war against the United States. At least to keep them neutral was his aim, at best to induce them to join the American forces against the tribes of the northwest. To this end early in 1792 he sent Leonard Shaw, a young Princeton graduate, as a special emissary to the Cherokees, bearing medals for the chiefs and presents for the nation and a speech of friendship from President Washington. He entrusted to Shaw similar gifts and messages for delivery to the Choctaws and Chickasaws. The annuities due the Cherokees were quietly increased by 50 percent.[19]

Indian attacks and white retaliation continued. A group of Cherokees who had broken away from the parent nation, the Chickamaugas, were forced to seek new hunting lands along the Cumberland River and incessantly pressed upon the growing white settlement there. They were joined by Creeks, whose predilections of hostility against the Americans were aggravated by the activities of the Spanish and by English adventurers in their midst.[20]

In the face of impending war, William Blount, governor of the Territory South of the River Ohio (or Southwest Territory), called up the militia until in the fall of 1792 he had fourteen companies of infantry and a troop of cavalry in service. He fully expected an offensive move by the federal government against the hostile tribes. Instead he got a warning and then a stinging rebuke from the secretary of war. In August, before the worst of the storm, Knox had told him that war in the territory would be considered "by the general government as a very great, and by the mass of the citizens of the middle and eastern States as an insupportable evil," and Blount was urged to remove every just pretence of grievances on the part of the Indians. This was not very encouraging, and although Blount then described in detail the disturbances with which he was faced, Knox's reply was extremely critical. In the first place, the president did not feel authorized to direct offensive operations against the Indians. Declaring war was a power reserved to Congress, which hesitated to act because "the extension of the Northern Indian War to the Southern Tribes would be a measure into which the Country would enter with extreme reluctance." Second, Knox

19. ASP:IA, 1: 203–6, 247–48, 265–66; Kappler, pp. 32–33. The presentation of American medals to these Indians (among whom the Choctaws and Chickasaws, at least, were considered by Spain to be within its sphere of interest) greatly incensed Spanish officials, and Secretary of State Jefferson had some explaining to do to the Spanish agents in Philadelphia. Some of the certificates, signed by Governor William Blount, presented to the Choctaws with medals are now in the Archivo General de Indias in Madrid. The story is told in Francis Paul Prucha, *Indian Peace Medals in American History* (Madison: State Historical Society of Wisconsin, 1971), pp. 6–8.

20. See James P. Pate, "The Chickamaugas: A Forgotten Segment of Indian Resistance on the Southern Frontier" (Ph.D. dissertation, Mississippi State University, 1969).

strongly suggested that it was the whites, not the Indians, who were responsible for the frontier encounters. The United States, he told Blount, "never will enter into a War to justify any sort of encroachment of the Whites." He then criticized Blount for calling out more militia and keeping them in service for a longer time than was necessary.[21]

Blount continued to hope for offensive war against the Indians, but the failure of peace negotiations with the northern Indians in the summer of 1793 and the extreme measures taken by the whites destroyed the chances that the federal government would come in aggressively on the side of the frontiersmen. The governor and the Tennesseeans then moved ahead on their own with an invasion into the Cherokee and Creek country more extensive than any since the Revolutionary War. Mounted militia under General John Sevier penetrated the Indian country, defeated the Indian warriors, and laid waste their towns. The failure to get adequate federal support maddened the frontiersmen, and when news of victory at Fallen Timbers was received, an offensive force was sent to destroy the Chickamauga towns. Before Blount could stop these illegal movements, the deed was done by Major James Ore and the territorial militia.[22]

The chastisement of the Chickamaugas and the triumph of Anthony Wayne—which left the military forces of the United States free to deal with the southern Indians if need be—brought peace to the Cherokee frontier, for the body of the Cherokees had already been appeased by the increase in their annuities. The Creeks still remained a problem, but Blount's efforts to stir up the Cherokees and Chickasaws against them were quashed by the federal government. "It is plain that the United States are determined, if possible, to avoid a direct or indirect war with the Creeks," Knox's successor, Timothy Pickering, told Blount. "Congress alone are competent to decide upon an offensive war, and congress have not thought fit to authorize it."[23]

While the Southwest Territory and its governor were contending with the Cherokees and Creeks, another border contest was being fought in Georgia, where continuing conflict between state and national jurisdiction over Indian affairs further complicated matters. The Treaty of New York with the Creeks in 1790 had been ineffective, for Georgia had not been consulted about the treaty and refused to back down on her claims to In-

---

21. Correspondence between Blount and Knox, August 1792 to January 1793, printed in Clarence E. Carter, ed., *The Territorial Papers of the United States*, 26 vols. (Washington: GPO, 1934–1962), 4: 163–64, 175, 208–16, 220–34.

22. The failure of the peaceful federal Indian policy, which led to military action by the settlers in Tennessee, is discussed in Craig Symonds, "The Failure of America's Indian Policy on the Southwestern Frontier, 1785–1793." *Tennessee Historical Quarterly* 35 (Spring 1976): 29–45. For Ore's campaign, see Downes, "Indian Affairs in the Southwest Territory," pp. 260–61.

23. Pickering to Blount, March 23, 1795, Carter, *Territorial Papers*, 4: 386–93.

dian lands. Independent action by Georgia to overwhelm the Creeks was severely condemned by the federal government, and Georgia was reined in.[24] The United States agreed, however, to negotiate again with the Creeks in June 1796 at Colerain on the St. Mary's River, but to no avail. The Creeks refused to cede their lands, and this treaty did no more than ratify the Treaty of New York and reassert peace between the nation and the United States.[25]

When Henry Knox retired at the end of 1794, he left a forthright statement about defense of the western frontiers, both north and south.[26] He reasserted his policy of peace through justice, which meant calming Indian fears for their lands by control of the avaricious whites. Until the Indians could be quieted on this point and rely upon the United States government to protect their country, he argued, "no well grounded hope of tranquillity can be entertained." He sought to constrain the war in the northwest and prevent its spread to the south, where the Indians were stronger and where an open war could lead to serious diplomatic repercussions. In ending his public career he sounded the same high note of moral righteousness that had always marked his hope for peaceful relations with the Indians. "As we are more powerful, and more enlightened than they are," he wrote, "there is a responsibility of national character, that we should treat them with kindness, and even liberality." He noted the "melancholy reflection" that the United States in its dealings with the aborigines had been more destructive than the conquerors of Mexico and Peru, and he feared that future historians might mark the causes of this destruction in "sable colors."

In practical terms, Knox proposed a line of military posts garrisoned by regular army troops along the frontier within the Indian country. He wanted fifteen hundred men at posts on the southwestern frontier stretching from the St. Mary's River on the border of Georgia to the Ohio. North of the Ohio, in addition to the posts on American soil soon to be surrendered by the British, he advocated one at the Miami village on the Wabash and connecting posts south on the Wabash toward the Ohio and northeast on the Maumee toward Lake Erie, plus a post at Presque Isle. Knox outlined here a cordon of military posts strung along the border of contact between the Indians and the whites that became a staple of American defense policy. Regular army garrisons, at the crucial meeting points of the two cultures, were to restrain the whites and overawe the Indians and protect the two

24. See correspondence between Governor Edward Telfair of Georgia and Knox, April–September 1793; ASP:IA, 1: 264–65, 368–70. See also John K. Mahon, "Military Relations between Georgia and the United States, 1789–1794," *Georgia Historical Quarterly* 43 (June 1959): 138–55.

25. Kappler, pp. 46–49.

26. Knox to Washington, December 29, 1794, ASP:IA, 1: 543–44. The following quotations are from this document.

races from each other. "If to these vigorous measures," Knox concluded, "should be combined the arrangement for trade, recommended to Congress, and the establishment of agents to reside in the principal Indian towns, . . . it would seem that the Government would then have made the fairest experiments of a system of justice and humanity, which, it is presumed, could not possibly fail of being blessed with its proper effects—an honorable tranquillity of the frontiers."

Knox's wise plans called for adequate regular troops to man the posts, troops whose very presence on the frontier would uphold American authority without war. With the cessation of hostilities in the northwest, however, Congress turned to consider whether the military establishment that had been called into being to pacify the Indians should be continued. Secretary of War Pickering and his successor James McHenry submitted observations and recommendations to guide the lawmakers. Congress did not listen. The committee on the military establishment, viewing the end of hostilities against the Indians, decided that "the force to be provided for the defensive protection of the frontiers, need not be so great as what had been contemplated for carrying on the war against the different tribes of hostile Indians, and which is the basis of the present military establishment," and Congress on May 30, 1796, reduced the size of the army.[27]

In the Treaty of San Lorenzo (Pinckney Treaty), signed with Spain on October 27, 1795, the United States won recognition of the thirty-first parallel as its southern boundary and navigation rights on the Mississippi. Then the Louisiana Purchase in 1803 changed the whole complexion of Mississippi valley defense and Indian relations, for the withdrawal of the Spanish from New Orleans and the acquisition of the right bank of the Mississippi from its source to its mouth removed the obstacles to western commerce that had long irritated frontiersmen. Spain, however, was still present in the Floridas, which cut off the south from the Gulf of Mexico, and the southern Indians maintained their hold on vast stretches of territory. The Creeks, supported by British traders and the Spanish, remained a special problem, but there was relative quiet until the approach of the War of 1812.[28]

PROBING THE NEW WEST

The Louisiana Purchase nearly doubled the territorial size of the United States and provided a new empire of unmeasured extent and almost totally

27. Pickering to Committee on the Military Establishment, February 3, 1796, and McHenry to the committee, March 14, 1796, *American State Papers: Military Affairs*, 1: 112–14; committee report, ibid., p. 112; 1 *United States Statutes* 483–86.

28. On the treaty with Spain, see Samuel Flagg Bemis, *Pinckney's Treaty: A Study of America's Advantage from Europe's Distress, 1783–1800* (Baltimore: Johns Hopkins

unknown character. Occupying and establishing American sovereignty over the land and its people brought new problems and new opportunities in government relations with the Indians.

In the southern part of the Louisiana Purchase, with its concentrations of white population in New Orleans and outlying regions, the United States moved quickly to replace the Spanish and French and to institute civil government of its own. There were few Indians in the area. But north of the thirty-third parallel, a region first erected into the District of Louisiana (attached for administration to Indiana Territory) and then into the Territory of Louisiana, the land was largely wilderness and, aside from St. Louis and a few other small settlements along the Mississippi and its tributaries, the Indians were the lords of the land.

To serve as first governor of the new territory, President Jefferson appointed General James Wilkinson, who combined in his one person both civil and military authority over the region. The War Department, which directed his duties on military and Indian matters, charged Wilkinson in vague terms to "conciliate the friendship & esteem, of the Indian generally of that extensive Country, & to produce peace & harmony, as well among the several nations and tribes, as between them & the white inhabitants," but at the same time demanded of him strict adherence to "the most riged economy" and forbade him to establish any permanent military posts.[29]

Although Wilkinson's fame has been tarnished by his association with Aaron Burr and his machinations with Spanish officials in the western regions, he had a fundamental grasp of the problems facing the United States with its new empire, in regard to the British and the Spanish and the influence of these powers through their traders upon the Indians. His experience in campaigns in the Old Northwest had given his mind a distinctly anti-British set, and what he learned at his post in St. Louis did little to change it. Of immediate concern was the danger from British traders. Wilkinson knew that he could not suddenly cut off the British merchandise that furnished the regular supplies of the Indians, but he urged the

Press, 1926), pp. 280–355, and Arthur P. Whitaker, *The Mississippi Question, 1795–1803: A Study in Trade, Politics, and Diplomacy* (New York: D. Appleton-Century, 1934), pp. 51–78.

29. Secretary of war to Wilkinson, April 19, 1805, Carter, *Territorial Papers*, 12: 116–17. There are three biographies of Wilkinson, all critical of the man, as their titles show: Thomas Robson Hay and M. R. Werner, *The Admirable Trumpeter: A Biography of General James Wilkinson* (Garden City, New York: Doubleday, Doran, and Company, 1941); James Ripley Jacobs, *Tarnished Warrior: Major-General James Wilkinson* (New York: Macmillan Company, 1938); Royal Ornan Shreve, *The Finished Scoundrel* (Indianapolis: Bobbs-Merrill, 1933). A more favorable view of Wilkinson is presented in Francis S. Philbrick, *The Rise of the West, 1754–1830* (New York: Harper and Row, 1965).

secretary of state and the secretary of war to warn the British that the trade would be stopped and to make the warning public. To enforce the interdiction Wilkinson recommended the immediate establishment of a military post at the mouth of the Wisconsin River and another at the Mandan villages or at the falls of the Missouri, with customs officers to seize contraband goods. "These arrangements being once accomplished," he predicted, "in a very few years the trade of the Mississippi and Missouri, would take its ancient and natural course to New Orleans."[30]

Officials in Washington did not move as strongly as Wilkinson wanted to occupy the new regions, and the government did no more than build Fort Belle Fontaine near the confluence of the Missouri with the Mississippi. The general did not let up. He issued a proclamation prohibiting foreign citizens from trading along the Missouri River, and then he poured out his concern about Spanish dangers to the secretary of war, proposing an apt analogy from his experience on the Ohio frontier a decade earlier:

> The relative position of the Spaniards in New Mexico, of the United States on the Mississippi, & the intermediate hordes of Savages, may be compared to the former relations of the British Posts on the Lakes, our settlements on the Ohio, & the intervening tribes of savages, who so long Jeopardized our frontier & defied our Force; and the Policy is so obvious, we ought not to doubt, that the Spaniards (however blind) will exert themselves to Erect a strong Barrier of hostile Savages, to oppose us in time of War, & to harrass our frontier in time of Peace.—The Anology of circumstances fails indeed, in several important essentials unfavourable to us,—The Theatre before us is much more extensive—we are here feeble & far removed from substantial succour—The Savages are as ten to one—They are known to the Spaniards & unknown to us—and their Habits of Life, put it out of our Power to destress or destroy them.[31]

No doubt Wilkinson perceived political dangers that never would materialize, but he saw with a clear eye the importance of the Indians in the scheme of western empire.

While Wilkinson was worrying about the effect of British and Spanish influence on the western Indians, President Jefferson, fired by a dream of empire of his own, set about to gain accurate information about the land and its inhabitants. How could one *possess* the new land if he did not *know* it?

The most daring and dramatic of the expeditions was that of Meriwether

30. Wilkinson to the secretary of war and Wilkinson to the secretary of state, July 28, 1805, Carter, *Territorial Papers*, 12: 169, 173–74.

31. Proclamation and related documents, ibid., 13: 200–203; Wilkinson to the secretary of war, September 22 and December 30, 1805, ibid., pp. 230, 357–58.

Lewis and William Clark and their corps of discovery to the Pacific and back in 1804–1806. Along with the gathering of scientific data, trade with the Indians and peaceful relations with them were uppermost in Jefferson's mind as he sent the explorers out. Lewis emphasized to Clark "the importance to the U. States of an early friendly and intimate acquaintance with the tribes that inhabit that country, that they should be early impressed with a just idea of the rising importance of the U. States and of her friendly dispositions towards them, as also her desire to become usefull to them by furnishing them through her citizens with such articles by way of barter as may be desired by them or usefull to them."[32]

As they ascended the Missouri, Lewis and Clark carefully informed the Indians that the French and Spanish had withdrawn from the waters of the Missouri and the Mississippi and that the "great Chief of the Seventeen great nations of America" was now the one to whom they must turn: "He is the only friend to whom you can now look for protection, or from whom you can ask favours, or receive good council, and he will take care that you shall have no just cause to regret this change; he will serve you, & not deceive you." Lewis described the power and great number of the Americans, and he promised to arrange for trade. With considerable ceremony the chiefs were given silver medals with Jefferson's image on one side and symbols of peace and friendship on the other, along with American flags, chiefs' coats, and other presents, with the admonition from the president: "He has further commanded us to tell you that when you accept his flag and medal, you accept therewith his hand of friendship, which will never be withdrawn from your nation as long as you continue to follow the council which he may command his chiefs to give you, and shut your ears to the councils of Bad birds." The chiefs were told to turn in their French, Spanish, and British flags and medals, for it was no longer proper for them to keep these emblems of attachment to any great father except the American one.[33]

When Lewis returned, he discussed the problems of protecting the region and its fur trade. He pointed to the dangers of giving British traders a free hand on the upper Missouri, thus allowing the Indians to fall under the traders' influence and permitting them "to be formed into a rod of iron,

---

32. Lewis to Clark, June 19, 1803, Donald Jackson, ed., *Letters of the Lewis and Clark Expedition with Related Documents, 1783–1854*, 2d ed., 2 vols. (Urbana: University of Illinois Press, 1978), 1: 59. The literature on Lewis and Clark is voluminous. The most complete edition of their journals is Reuben Gold Thwaites, ed., *Original Journals of the Lewis and Clark Expedition, 1804–1806*, 8 vols. (New York: Dodd, Mead and Company, 1904–1905), but it needs to be supplemented with editions of more recently discovered documents. See the enlightening study by Paul Russell Cutright, *A History of the Lewis and Clark Journals* (Norman: University of Oklahoma Press, 1976).

33. Lewis and Clark to the Oto Indians, August 4, 1804, Jackson, *Letters of the Lewis and Clark Expedition*, 1: 203–8.

with which, for Great Britain, to scourge our frontier at pleasure." He proposed restricting British traders, opening the trade under fair competition to American merchants, and prohibiting Americans themselves from unrestricted hunting and trapping in the Indian country. It was his hope, he wrote, to combine "philanthropic views toward those wretched people of America," with means "to secure to the citizens of the United States, all those advantages, which ought of right exclusively to accrue to them, from the possession of Upper Louisiana." This would take a delicate balance, Lewis knew, and in his rough outline of points to be considered he included this shrewd observation: "The first principle of governing the Indians is to govern the whites—the impossibility of doing this without establishments, and some guards at those posts."[34]

While Lewis and Clark were still working their way across the Great Divide, General Wilkinson himself sent out two exploratory expeditions with similar goals. On July 30, 1805, he ordered a young lieutenant of the First Infantry, Zebulon Montgomery Pike, up the Mississippi River to seek its source. Pike was told to gather geographical and scientific knowledge, to locate proper points for military posts, and "to spare no pains to conciliate the Indians and to attach them to the United States." The written orders said nothing about counteracting the influence of British traders in the northwest, but it is clear from the attention given to the matter that Pike had strong directions from Wilkinson to this effect. Pike got as far as Leech Lake (somewhat short of the source of the Mississippi), where he found a British trader operating on American soil. He asserted American rights in no uncertain terms in a letter to the trader, and in council with the Chippewas he directed them to turn in their British medals and flags. But a single expedition to the upper Mississippi was not enough to undo the British traders' influence over the Indians. Pike's remonstrances meant little after he had disappeared downriver, and the power of the British traders over the Indians at the outbreak of the War of 1812 is proof that Pike's expedition alone was not enough.[35]

Pike in 1806 made a second trip, this time to probe the activities of the Spanish and their influence over the Indians in the southwest. He was instructed to make contact with the Comanches, to make peace between them and other tribes, and to induce some of their chiefs to visit Washing-

34. Thwaites, *Journals of the Lewis and Clark Expedition*, 7: 378, 387–88.

35. For journals and other documents of Pike's two expeditions, see Donald Jackson, ed., *The Journals of Zebulon Montgomery Pike with Letters and Related Documents*, 2 vols. (Norman: University of Oklahoma Press, 1966); also W. Eugene Hollon, *The Lost Pathfinder: Zebulon Montgomery Pike* (Norman: University of Oklahoma Press, 1949). Wilkinson's directive to Pike, July 30, 1805, is in Jackson, *Pike*, 1: 3–4; Pike's letter to trader Hugh McGillis, February 6, 1806, and his speech to the Chippewas, February 16, 1806, appear ibid., pp. 257–58, 263–64.

ton, where their friendship could be cultivated and they could be impressed with the power and authority of the United States.[36] Pike found clear evidence of Spanish influence over the Indians; and when he ventured too far west, he was arrested by Spanish troops, taken into Mexico, and not released for several weeks.

Acquaintance with the Indians in the vast Trans-Mississippi West was just beginning, but the importance of the tribes and their trade in the diplomatic relations of the continent was clearly seen. The War of 1812 soon emphasized the point.

THE WAR OF 1812

As the century advanced, there were new signs of Indian unrest on the frontiers, and the fragile peace achieved by a combination of negotiation and military force began to crumble. William Clark, who on his return from the expedition of discovery began a long career as Indian agent and superintendent at St. Louis, noted in late 1807 that the Indians on the upper Missouri "Shew Some hostile Simtoms," which he attributed to British action, and he feared that British traders had already made inroads on the upper Missouri.[37]

The War Department could not be entirely quiet in the face of continued remonstrances from responsible men of good judgment on the frontier, and it began to push trading houses and military garrisons into the Mississippi Valley. Factories and posts were established in 1808 among the Osages (Fort Osage) and near the mouth of the Des Moines River on the upper Mississippi (Fort Madison). "The principal object of the Government in these establishments," the superintendent of Indian trade wrote, was "to secure the Friendship of the Indians in our country in a way the most beneficial to them and the most effectual & economical to the United States."[38] The new posts did not prevent the drift toward open war, yet Congress refused to strengthen the military defense of that remote frontier, doing no more than to authorize six companies of rangers for the protection of settlers from Indian incursions. Meanwhile, farther east, advancing white settlement pushed against the Treaty of Greenville line and revived the temporarily quieted antagonisms of the Indians.

The celebrated Shawnee chief Tecumseh and his brother, the Prophet, soon appeared on the scene. Tecumseh by all accounts was a great man, noted for his humanity and uprightness of character. The Prophet preached resistance to the whites and a return to primitive ways, and Tecumseh be-

36. Wilkinson to Pike, June 24, 1806, Jackson, *Pike,* 1: 285–87.
37. Clark to the secretary of war, June 1, September 12, and December 3, 1807, Carter, *Territorial Papers,* 14: 126–27, 146–47, 153–54.
38. John Mason to John Johnson, May 20, 1808, ibid., pp. 185–87.

came a political leader, determined to stop the westward advance of the whites. Arguing that no sale of Indian land could be valid unless approved by all the tribes, he set about to form a confederacy that would unite the Indians in blocking white aggrandizement. For aid in this great project Tecumseh depended upon the British and from them drew arms and ammunition.[39] With the increased tension between Great Britain and the United States that grew out of the *Chesapeake* affair in 1807, the British in Canada were quite willing to renew the active allegiance of the Indians. The vision of Tecumseh thus reopened problems that the Americans thought had been resolved at Fallen Timbers and Greenville. American sovereignty north of the Ohio had not yet been secured in the face of rising Indian apprehensions, and from 1807 to the War of 1812 Indian relations in Indiana and Illinois territories steadily worsened.

Tecumseh and his brother won many supporters among the northwest Indians, and in 1808 the Prophet and his followers moved to the upper Wabash at the mouth of Tippecanoe Creek. This concentration of warriors on the Wabash alarmed William Henry Harrison, governor of Indiana Territory, who was convinced that serious trouble was brewing. Yet in the face of growing Indian intransigence, Harrison concluded a treaty at Fort Wayne on September 30, 1809, with the Miamis, Weas, and Delawares by which he purchased a large tract of land in Indiana. The treaty greatly agitated Tecumseh even though no Shawnee lands were involved, and in 1810 he visited Harrison at Vincennes, where he threatened the governor with hostile gestures and announced that he would never submit to the Fort Wayne treaty. A truce was arranged, but no ultimate compromise seemed possible. The following summer Tecumseh appeared again with a large retinue. He told Harrison he was on his way south to bring the southern nations into his confederacy.[40]

Harrison made use of the opportune absence of the Shawnee leader to advance against the Prophet's town. With regular troops, militia, and volunteers, he moved north from Vincennes in September 1811. In early November he sought a parley with the Indians, which failed to materialize. On November 7 the Indians attacked Harrison's army and were repulsed

39. On Tecumseh, see Glenn Tucker, *Tecumseh: Vision of Glory* (Indianapolis: Bobbs-Merrill, 1956). A brief popular account is Alvin M. Josephy, Jr., "'These Lands Are Ours . . . ,'" *American Heritage* 12 (August 1961): 14–25, 83–89. A scholarly study that emphasizes the importance of the Prophet is R. David Edmunds, *The Shawnee Prophet* (Lincoln, University of Nebraska Press, 1983).

40. The troubles between Harrison and Tecumseh and the Prophet are discussed in Dorothy Burne Goebel, *William Henry Harrison: A Political Biography* (Indianapolis: Historical Bureau of the Indiana Library and Historical Department, 1926), pp. 109–27, and Tucker, *Tecumseh*, pp. 134–231. See also *Messages and Letters of William Henry Harrison*, ed. Logan Esarey, 2 vols. (Indianapolis: Indiana Historical Commission, 1922); ASP:IA, 1: 776–80, 797–811.

only after severe fighting in which Harrison's losses were heavy. This Battle of Tippecanoe was described by Harrison as "a complete and decisive victory," but in the end it settled nothing. The Prophet's town was burned and his followers were scattered, but enmity against the whites only increased. Another step had been taken toward all-out war to see who would control the Old Northwest.[41]

The causes of the War of 1812 have been argued by historians at great length, but frontier disquiet cannot be discounted. Indian components of the war were a continuation of the prewar conflict, and they set the stage for the military history of the American frontier in the decades after 1815. The Indians, by and large, maintained or renewed their allegiance to the British, and the armies that the Americans met on the northwestern frontier were composed of more Indian troops than white. Tecumseh's dream of an Indian confederation, maintaining a united front against American territorial advance, seemed possible when the British were once again openly fighting the Americans.[42]

In the territory stretching west of Lake Michigan, the British and their Indian allies immediately reasserted control. Fort Mackinac fell on July 17, 1812, and Fort Dearborn (established in 1803 on the site of future Chicago) was evacuated on August 15 and most of its inhabitants massacred by the Indians as they marched out. More important was the disastrous surrender of Detroit on August 16 by General William Hull, who feared the massacre of the women and children by the Indian allies of the British if the city were taken by force.

The surrender of Hull's army left consternation and confusion on the frontier, and the Indians were emboldened by the American disaster. In Ohio, where settlement was heavy and concentrated, little was to be feared, but in thinly settled Indiana and Illinois fears of Indian raids were

---

41. Reports of Harrison to the secretary of war, November 8 and 18, 1811, *Messages and Letters of Harrison*, 1: 614–15, 618–30. Accounts of the drift toward war are in Jacobs, *Beginning of the U.S. Army*, pp. 356–63, and Louise Phelps Kellogg, *The British Regime in Wisconsin and the Northwest* (Madison: State Historical Society of Wisconsin, 1935). See also Christopher B. Coleman, "The Ohio Valley in the Preliminaries of the War of 1812," *Mississippi Valley Historical Review* 7 (June 1920): 39–50.

42. For British Indian policy before the war and the part played by the Indians in the war, see Reginald Horsman, "British Indian Policy in the Northwest, 1807–1812," *Mississippi Valley Historical Review* 45 (June 1958): 51–66; Horsman, "The Role of the Indian in the War," in Philip P. Mason, ed., *After Tippecanoe: Some Aspects of the War of 1812* (East Lansing: Michigan State University Press, 1963), pp. 60–77; and George F. G. Stanley, "The Indians in the War of 1812," *Canadian Historical Review* 31 (June 1950): 145–65. On the general course of the war, see Henry L. Coles, *The War of 1812* (Chicago: University of Chicago Press, 1965); Alec R. Gilpin, *The War of 1812 in the Old Northwest* (East Lansing: Michigan State University Press, 1958); Reginald Horsman, *The War of 1812* (New York: Alfred A. Knopf, 1969); and John K. Mahon, *The War of 1812* (Gainesville: University of Florida Press, 1972).

well-founded. The governors of the two territories ordered mounted militia to patrol the frontier, and a camp was established in southern Illinois for militia and the United States rangers. But clearly a new northwestern army would have to be organized to repair the damage done by Hull's defeat. The work fell to William Henry Harrison, who moved successfully against the British in upper Canada as soon as Admiral Oliver H. Perry had won control of the supply lines in the Great Lakes. At the Battle of the Thames on October 5, 1813, Harrison defeated Colonel Henry Proctor and his Indian allies. The Indians, ably led by Tecumseh, offered stiff resistance, but Tecumseh was soon killed and the Indians followed the British in flight. The Americans had made a great step toward redeeming the northwest, but attempts to regain Fort Mackinac and control of the upper Mississippi were rebuffed. The upper Mississippi remained in British hands, and the assertion of United States authority there had to await the postwar era.

Meanwhile a parallel story unfolded in the south. The hostile Creeks with their Spanish allies were the counterpart to Tecumseh's confederacy, and the Battle of Horseshoe Bend destroyed the Indians' hopes as did the Battle of the Thames and the death of Tecumseh. Whereas the Chickasaws and Choctaws took little part in the war and some of the Cherokees joined the United States forces, the Creeks developed a hostile faction that posed a serious threat. Certain of the young Creeks were influenced by Tecumseh, who visited the nation in 1811 and again in 1812 to solicit southern Indian support for his confederacy. Although older chiefs warned against Tecumseh, the great Shawnee came with a bagful of magic tricks and on his second visit brought encouraging news of American defeats. With promises that Spanish and British aid would support the Indians he won over the young warriors, or Red Sticks, among them William Weatherford (Red Eagle), a nephew of Alexander McGillivray. When a party of Red Sticks returning from a trip to Pensacola (where the Spanish governor had supplied them with ammunition) were attacked by white frontiersmen, the Indians retaliated by massacring the men, women, and children at Fort Mims, a stockade forty miles north of Mobile. The United States was electrified, and campaigns to crush the hostile Red Sticks were immediately mounted.[43]

The most important of these was led by Andrew Jackson, commander of the Tennessee militia. He quickly assembled volunteers, augmented them with regular infantry, and prepared to strike the Creeks in their stronghold in eastern Alabama. On March 27, 1814, aided by a contingent of Cherokees, Jackson crushed the hostile Creeks at Horseshoe Bend, a fortified position on the Tallapoosa River in the heart of the Creek country. Jackson

43. A recent detailed and well-documented account of Indian matters in the south during the War of 1812 is Robert V. Remini, *Andrew Jackson and the Course of American Empire, 1767–1821* (New York: Harper and Row, 1977), pp. 187–245.

did not intend to lose his advantage. He moved down the river and built Fort Jackson where the Coosa and Tallapoosa rivers join to form the Alabama. From this headquarters his troops scoured the country for hostile Indians. Not many were found, for most of the Red Sticks fled into Spanish Florida and some, including William Weatherford, turned themselves in at Fort Jackson. Jackson now forsook his militia status and accepted a commission as brigadier general in the regular army. He was almost immediately promoted to major general and given command of the Seventh Military District, which included Tennessee, Louisiana, and Mississippi Territory. In this position he concluded a treaty with the Creeks at Fort Jackson on August 9. It was the friendly Creeks who attended the council, for the hostiles had been killed or had fled, and the chiefs protested the terms of the treaty. Jackson insisted, nevertheless, on large land cessions west of the Coosa and along the Florida border, as buffers between the Creeks and Chickasaws and Choctaws on the west and the Spanish on the south.[44]

On August 27 Jackson was at Mobile, where he strengthened defenses constructed a year earlier and enabled the garrison to drive back an attack of the British. In early November, after receiving a new increment of mounted volunteers, he seized Pensacola, driving out the British who had been using it as a port and military depot. These southern escapades confirmed the action at Horseshoe Bend, for the Creeks might now well despair of active assistance from the British or the Spanish in the south. Jackson was ready to protect New Orleans if any British general should be so foolhardy as to make a direct attack by sea.

The treaty of peace signed at Ghent on December 27, 1814, provided for a return to the status quo before the war and left unmentioned the basic maritime problems that had done so much to bring on the war, and it is easy to assert that the war accomplished nothing. This was certainly not the case on the frontier in the northwest and the southwest. The crushing defeats of the Indians at the Thames and at Horseshoe Bend and the failure of the British (or the Spanish) to substantiate Indian claims against the Americans put a new complexion on the Indian problems in the West.

AMERICAN DOMINION—NORTH, WEST, AND SOUTH

The Indians, against whom so much of the American force in the War of 1812 had pressed, were not a party to the Treaty of Ghent. The ninth arti-

44. Kappler, pp. 107–10. A detailed history of the Creek War is Frank Lawrence Owsley, Jr., *Struggle for the Gulf Borderlands: The Creek War and the Battle of New Orleans, 1812–1815* (Gainesville: University Presses of Florida, 1981).

cle of the treaty, however, provided that the United States would undertake to put an end to all hostilities with Indian tribes with whom it might
still be at war at the time of ratification of the treaty and to restore to those
tribes "all the possessions, rights, and privileges" that they had enjoyed
previous to the war.[45] Accordingly, President Madison on March 11, 1815,
appointed three commissioners to treat with the Indians who had fought
against the United States, to notify all the tribes on the Mississippi and its
tributaries who were at war with the United States that peace had been
concluded with Great Britain, and to invite them to a council to sign a
treaty of peace and amity. Peace was to be the only purpose of the treaties;
other matters could be attended to at a later time. The commissioners
were to inform the Indians that the government intended to establish
strong military posts high up the Mississippi and between the Mississippi
and Lake Michigan and to open trading houses at these posts or at other
suitable places for their accommodation. Twenty thousand dollars' worth
of presents was placed at the disposal of the commissioners—"blankets,
strouds, cloths, calicoes, handkerchiefs, cotton stuffs, ribands, gartering,
frock coats, flags, silver ornaments, paints, wampum, looking-glasses,
knives, fire-steels, rifles, fusils, flints, powder, tobacco, pipes, needles,
&c.," according to the enumeration of the secretary of war, who specified
that the goods should equal in quality those that the Indians were accustomed to get from the British.[46]

On May 11 the commissioners met at St. Louis and prepared talks to be
sent out to the Indian chiefs. News of continuing hostility among the
tribes made it difficult to find messengers to carry the tidings into the Indian nations, but eventually thirty-seven talks were dispatched by means
of army officers, Indian agents, Frenchmen, or Indians themselves (who
promised to deliver the messages to more remote tribes with whom they
were in contact). The Indians gathered at Portage des Sioux, a convenient
spot on the west bank of the Mississippi above the mouth of the Missouri
and a few miles below the mouth of the Illinois. There, between July 18
and October 28, 1815, thirteen treaties were signed with the western Indians. These were peace pacts, providing that "every injury or act of hostility by one or either of the contracting parties against the other shall be
mutually forgiven and forgot," promising "perpetual peace and friendship"

45. There is a detailed account of the negotiations at Ghent, including Indian matters, in Bradford Perkins, *Castlereagh and Adams: England and the United States,
1812–1823* (Berkeley: University of California Press, 1964), pp. 81–127. See also A. L.
Burt, *The United States, Great Britain, and British North America: From the Revolution to the Establishment of Peace after the War of 1812* (New Haven: Yale University
Press, 1940), pp. 345–72.

46. Monroe to commissioners, March 11, 1815, ASP:IA, 2: 6; Monroe to John Mason,
March 27, 1815, ibid., p. 7.

between the Americans and the Indians, agreeing to the exchange of prisoners, and confirming previous treaties. In the next three years, other western tribes, absent from Portage des Sioux, signed similar treaties.[47]

Meanwhile, other negotiations were carried on with the Indians of Ohio, Indiana, and Michigan. These Indians had technically been at peace with the United States when the Treaty of Ghent had been ratified, and the provisions of that treaty did not apply; but "hostile excitement" among the Indians induced the secretary of war to appoint a commission to conciliate them and explain to them the provisions of the treaty. "The object of these explanations will be to counteract any suppositions that the treaty of peace has placed Great Britain in a new and more advantageous relation to the Northwest Indians," the acting secretary of war wrote to the commissioners on June 9, 1815; "to supersede the idea that the Indians have acquired by the treaty a more independent political character than they possessed before; and to beget a just confidence in the power as well as the resolution of our Government to maintain its rights against every opposition." The War Department considered the introduction of military posts and factories into the Indian country of increasing importance, and it directed the commissioners to inform the Indians that "in order to aid and protect them, and also to guard against encroachment upon the property and people of the United States" the president intended to establish a chain of posts from Chicago to St. Louis. A treaty was signed with the Indians on September 8 at Spring Wells near Detroit, in which peace was reaffirmed and the Indians who had continued hostilities after 1811 were pardoned.[48]

These treaties of friendship would be no more than paper documents unless the United States carried out its resolve to establish military posts on the Great Lakes and in the upper Mississippi Valley. Such action was imperative if the United States did not want to forfeit for a second time its control over the Indian tribes of the northwest. Americans in the West pleaded for military establishments that would check the Indians, weaken or destroy their adherence to the British, and protect and extend the American fur trade in the region. The point was well made by Governor Lewis Cass of Michigan Territory, who traced most of the difficulties he had with Indians to the problem of British traders among the northwestern tribes. He asserted that the British were about to renew their activities with increased energy, for large supplies of trade goods had arrived at Malden,

47. Kappler, pp. 126–33, 138–40, 156–59. For an excellent account of the treaty negotiations, see Robert L. Fisher, "The Treaties of Portage des Sioux," *Mississippi Valley Historical Review* 19 (March 1933): 495–508. Copies of the treaties and related documents about the negotiations are in ASP:IA, 2: 1–12.

48. Kappler, pp. 117–19. Documents dealing with these negotiations are in ASP:IA, 2: 12–25.

across from Detroit, and there had been an influx of agents and subordinate officers. As an effective check on their operations, Cass proposed blocking off with military posts the channels of communication by which the British traders and their goods infiltrated into the United States.[49]

The War Department quickly moved to establish new military posts and reestablish old ones at strategic spots. In 1816 the post at Chicago (Fort Dearborn) was reoccupied and Fort Howard at Green Bay was constructed. At the same time troops pushed up the Mississippi to build Fort Crawford at the mouth of the Wisconsin River. Indian agencies were established in the shadows of these posts.[50]

That was but a beginning. When John C. Calhoun accepted the post of secretary of war in October 1817, he brought to the office a pronounced spirit of nationalism and a dream of vindicating American authority over its largely nominal empire west of the Mississippi. With the disasters of the recent war etched deeply in his memory, he presented his arguments. The Indians in the West, composed of warlike and powerful tribes, were unacquainted with American power and at the same time were "open to the influence of a foreign Power"; with the expansion of American settlements, they were becoming close neighbors. A new thrust of American force into the region was thus necessary to overawe the tribes and to cut off once and for all the intercourse between the Indians and the British trading posts. "This intercourse," Calhoun said, "is the great source of danger to our peace; and until that is stopped our frontiers cannot be safe." The Treaty of Ghent had ended the British right to trade with the Indians, and Congress in 1816 had prohibited foreigners from trading with the Indians within the territory of the United States, but Calhoun admitted that "the act and instructions to Indian agents can have but little efficacy to remedy the evil." He would have preferred to persuade the British through diplomatic means to end the trade and the generous distribution of presents to the Indians, but until the British acted, new military posts would "put in our hand the power to correct the evil."[51]

Calhoun wanted military posts at Sault Ste. Marie, on the Mississippi at the mouth of the Minnesota (St. Peter's), and on the Missouri at the Mandan villages or even the mouth of the Yellowstone. He believed that re-

49. Cass to A. J. Dallas, July 20, 1815, Carter, *Territorial Papers*, 10: 573–75.

50. For general histories of the military expansion into the northwest after the War of 1812, see Henry P. Beers, *The Western Military Frontier, 1815–1846* (Philadelphia, 1935); Edgar B. Wesley, *Guarding the Frontier: A Study of Frontier Defense from 1815 to 1825* (Minneapolis: University of Minnesota Press, 1935); and Francis Paul Prucha, *Broadax and Bayonet: The Role of the United States Army in the Development of the Northwest, 1815–1860* (Madison: State Historical Society of Wisconsin, 1953).

51. Calhoun to Alexander Smyth, December 29, 1819, *American State Papers: Military Affairs*, 2: 33–34.

straining and overawing the Indians and destroying their contacts with the British traders and posts were primarily military matters. "Trade and presents, accompanied by talks calculated for the purpose," he noted, "are among the most powerful means to control the action of savages; and so long as they are wielded by a foreign hand our frontiers must ever be exposed to the calamity of Indian warfare." Of two great objects in view, he said, "the permanent security of our frontier is considered by far of the greatest importance." But the second object was also much in his mind: the enlargement and protection of the American fur trade. The military posts, by enforcing the prohibition on foreign traders, would permit unrestricted access to the trade by American traders. When the posts were all established and occupied, asserted Calhoun with a certain tone of exultation, "the most valuable fur trade in the world will be thrown into our hands."[52]

In 1818 Calhoun issued orders for the implementation of his plan. General Thomas A. Smith was to move up the Missouri to build a permanent post at the mouth of the Yellowstone, but the expedition faltered—hampered by congressional opposition to the cost—and the troops got no farther than Council Bluffs, above present-day Omaha, where they constructed Fort Atkinson. Calhoun's call for a strong post on the upper Mississippi was better answered. Troops moving from Detroit to Green Bay, then along the Fox-Wisconsin waterway and up the Mississippi, established in 1819 the impressive fort at the mouth of the Minnesota that eventually was named Fort Snelling.[53]

The failure to fulfill Calhoun's plan for advancing high up the Missouri emboldened the Indians of the region and lessened the chances of attaching them to the American government. The Indians were alert to what they considered American failures, and their arrogance seemed to grow whenever American force or resolution weakened. Attacks on St. Louis fur traders along the Missouri and its tributaries in 1823 by Arikaras and Blackfeet caused a special outcry. Benjamin O'Fallon, the United States Indian agent at Fort Atkinson, wrote in intemperate language to his superior in July, 1823: "I was in hopes that the British traders had some bounds to their rapacity—I was in hopes that during the late Indian war, in which they were so instrumental in the indiscriminate massacre of our people,

---

52. Calhoun to Henry Atkinson, March 27, 1819, *Correspondence of John C. Calhoun*, ed. J. Franklin Jameson, Annual Report of the American Historical Association for the Year 1899, vol. 2 (Washington, 1900), p. 159.

53. For this military advance, see Prucha, *Sword of the Republic*, pp. 140–51, and works cited there. See also Roger L. Nichols, "The Army and the Indians, 1800–1830: A Reappraisal, the Missouri Valley Example," *Pacific Historical Review* 41 (May 1972): 151–68, which challenges my view of the army's success.

they had become completely satiated with our blood, but it appears not to have been the case.—Like the greedy wolf, not yet gorged with the flesh, they guard over the bones—they ravage our fields, and are unwilling that we should glean them—although barred by the treaty of Ghent, from participating in our Indian trade, they presume [to do so] . . . becoming alarmed at the individual enterprise of our people, they are exciting the Indians against us."[54]

At the same time, General Edmund P. Gaines, commanding the Western Division, wrote to the secretary of war: "If we quietly give up this trade, we shall at once throw it, and with it the friendship and physical power of near 30,000 efficient warriors, into the arms of England, who has taught us in letters of blood (which we have had the magnanimity to forgive, but which it would be treason to forget) that this trade forms the rein and curb by which the turbulent and towering spirit of these lords of the forest can alone be governed." Gaines argued that to let the Arikaras and Blackfeet go unpunished would be to surrender the trade and the influence it exerted over the Indians to England.[55]

Colonel Henry Leavenworth and a company of 220 men from the Sixth Infantry, augmented by fur traders and Sioux, moved up the Missouri to the Arikara villages, where Leavenworth came to terms with the Indians. On his return to Fort Atkinson, he announced the successful outcome of the expedition: "The blood of our countrymen have been honorably avenged, the Ricarees humbled, and in such a manner as will teach them and other Indian tribes to respect the American name and character."[56]

Leavenworth's dealings with the Indians were not considered severe enough by the traders, who were more insistent than either the agents or the army officers in cries for strong government action. The trading interests had a powerful advocate in Senator Thomas Hart Benton, who broadcast their petitions in a national arena. In March 1824 Benton introduced a bill authorizing commissioners to negotiate treaties of friendship with the

54. Quoted in Donald McKay Frost, *Notes on General Ashley, the Overland Trail, and South Pass* (Worcester: American Antiquarian Society, 1945), pp. 83–84. Other information on the problems of the upper Missouri fur trade after the War of 1812 is in Dale L. Morgan, *The West of William H. Ashley: The International Struggle for the Fur Trade of the Missouri, the Rocky Mountains, and the Columbia, with Explorations beyond the Continental Divide, Recorded in the Diaries and Letters of William H. Ashley and His Contemporaries, 1822–1838* (Denver: Old West Publishing Company, 1964).

55. Gaines to John C. Calhoun, July 28, 1823, *American State Papers: Military Affairs*, 2: 579.

56. Leavenworth's final report and other documents are in Doane Robinson, ed., "Official Correspondence Pertaining to the Leavenworth Expedition of 1823 into South Dakota for the Conquest of the Ree Indians," *South Dakota Historical Collections* 1 (1902): 179–256.

Missouri River tribes and directing that a military post be built on the upper Missouri. It is interesting to note that Benton entitled his measure a bill "to enable the President to carry into effect the treaty made at Ghent, the 24th of December, 1814, excluding foreigners from trade and intercourse with Indian tribes within the United States, and to preserve the fur trade within the limits of the said United States." Not all of the Senate, however, was as convinced of the need as was Benton. His provision for building a fort was stricken out, and the title of the bill was changed. The most that he could get was authorization for a military escort to accompany the treaty commissioners.[57]

The expedition, led by Henry Atkinson and Benjamin O'Fallon, signed treaties of friendship in the summer of 1825 with the tribes they met along the way, but they discovered no British influence in the area they covered.[58] The dangers so loudly proclaimed by the American fur traders had evaporated as the British traders had shifted westward toward the rich beaver of the Rockies.

In the south, the federal government presumed that all Indian difficulties had ended with the Treaty of Fort Jackson with the Creeks. Besides the huge land cession, the Indians had promised to abandon all communication or intercourse with any British or Spanish posts and to permit the establishment of American forts and roads in the territory they still retained. It was a harsh peace, imposed, as the preamble to the treaty stated, because of the "unprovoked, inhuman, and sanguinary war" waged by the Creeks against the United States. But many Indians, unwilling to accept defeat, joined the Seminoles in Florida, where they continued to be a lively threat to white settlers moving onto the vacated lands. Here they were encouraged by British adventurers in their belief that the lands taken away from them at Fort Jackson would be returned now that the War of 1812 had ended. The American government, however, did not consider that the Treaty of Ghent in any way negated the treaty made with the Creeks at Fort Jackson.[59]

To maintain peace on this perilous frontier was the task of General

57. *Senate Journal*, 18–1, serial 88, pp. 239, 281, 432; *Annals of Congress*, 18th Congress, 1st session, pp. 432–45, 450–61.

58. For the Atkinson–O'Fallon expedition, see Roger L. Nichols, *General Henry Atkinson: A Western Military Career* (Norman: University of Oklahoma Press, 1965), pp. 90–108; Nichols, ed., "Report of the Yellowstone Expedition of 1825," *Nebraska History* 44 (June 1963): 65–82; ASP:IA, 2: 595–609. The journal of the expedition is in Russell Reid and Clell G. Gannon, eds., "Journal of the Atkinson–O'Fallon Expedition," *North Dakota Historical Quarterly* 4 (October 1929): 5–56; the treaties signed are in Kappler, pp. 225–46.

59. Kappler, pp. 107–9. For a scholarly account of the southern frontier from 1815 to 1821, see James W. Silver, *Edmund Pendleton Gaines, Frontier General* (Baton Rouge: Louisiana State University Press, 1949), pp. 54–88.

Gaines, who attempted to overawe the warlike Indians with a show of force. He built Fort Scott at the confluence of the Flint and Chattahoochee rivers, almost on the Florida border, and from there and from Fort Montgomery in Alabama (to which he moved in January 1817) Gaines carried on a running war with recalcitrant Indians along the border. He was soon joined by General Andrew Jackson, who, convinced that the Spanish were encouraging the Indians, boldly invaded Florida. There he seized two British traders, tried them by court-martial, and summarily executed them.[60]

Unmindful of the storm of controversy that would soon arise because of his execution of the two British subjects on Spanish soil, Jackson moved next against Pensacola. On May 25 he invested the Spanish post and three days later accepted its surrender. His proclamation of May 29 announced the appointment of one of his army officers as civil and military governor of Pensacola and the application of the revenue laws of the United States. His justification was explicit: "The Seminole Indians inhabiting the territories of Spain have for more than two years past, visited our Frontier settlements with all the horrors of savage massacre—helpless women have been butchered and the cradle stained with the blood of innocence. . . . The immutable laws of self defense, therefore compelled the American Government to take possession of such parts of the Floridas in which the Spanish authority could not be maintained."[61]

Jackson moved north to Fort Montgomery, where on June 2, 1818, he sent long letters to President Monroe and to Secretary of War Calhoun reporting what he had done and insisting upon the necessity of holding the posts in Florida he had taken. He told Calhoun: "The Seminole War may now be considered at a close. Tranquility [is] again restored to the Southern Frontier of the United States, and as long as a cordon of military posts is maintained along the gulf of Mexico America has nothing to apprehend from either foreign or Indian hostilities."[62]

Jackson returned to Nashville in triumph, leaving the diplomats to pick up the pieces. The Spanish minister, Don Luis de Onís, demanded the prompt restitution of St. Marks, Pensacola, and all other places wrested from Spain by Jackson's forces, as well as an indemnity for all losses and the punishment of the general. The posts were returned, but the general was not punished, and resolutions in Congress condemning his action were voted down.[63]

General Gaines meanwhile kept watch on the southern frontier, where

---

60. Jackson's role is treated in Remini, *Andrew Jackson*, pp. 341–424, and in other biographies of Jackson.

61. *Correspondence of Andrew Jackson*, ed. John Spencer Bassett, 6 vols. (Washington: Carnegie Institution of Washington, 1926–1933), 2: 374–75.

62. Jackson to Monroe and Jackson to Calhoun, June 2, 1818, ibid., pp. 377, 380.

63. See the references cited in Prucha, *Sword of the Republic*, p. 133 n; the political

the problems were not as completely solved as Jackson had asserted. The Indians had not been decisively beaten in combat, and until Florida finally passed into American possession in 1821, there was a continual threat of Spanish intrigue with the Indians. St. Augustine was a point of special concern, and Gaines was all for moving against it. His hands were tied against aggressive action, however, lest the delicate negotiations with Spain for the purchase of Florida become still more entangled.

---

repercussions of Jackson's highhanded operations in Florida are discussed in Remini, *Andrew Jackson*, pp. 366–77.

CHAPTER 3

Trade and Intercourse Laws

Legislation to Control the Frontier Whites.

Regulating the Trade in Furs. The Crusade against

Ardent Spirits. Crimes in the Indian Country.

Removal of Intruders on Indian Lands.

Military action against the Indians to push them back before the advancing whites was not a suitable basis for governing the relations between the United States and the Indians. Washington and Knox, both men of high integrity and experienced in Indian affairs, rejected an all-out war of subjugation against the tribes. The alternative was conciliation of the Indians by negotiation, a show of liberality, express guarantees of protection from encroachment beyond certain set boundaries, and a fostered and developed trade. But it was not enough to deal only with the Indians, for white settlers and speculators ignored the treaties and guarantees. Plainly, something more was needed than the treaties, which had been so largely disregarded.[1]

LEGISLATION TO CONTROL THE FRONTIER WHITES

In response to the insistent pleas of the executive, Congress supplied a series of laws for regulating trade and intercourse with the Indians. These laws, originally designed to implement the treaties and enforce them

1. This chapter is a condensation of material in Francis Paul Prucha, *American Indian Policy in the Formative Years: The Indian Trade and Intercourse Acts, 1790–1834* (Cambridge: Harvard University Press, 1962), pp. 43–50, 66–84, 93–212, and some parts are taken directly from that work.

against obstreperous whites, gradually came to embody the basic features of federal Indian policy. The first law was approved on July 22, 1790. Continuing the pattern set in the Ordinance of 1786 and earlier colonial legislation, it first of all provided for the licensing of traders and established penalties for trading without a license. Then it struck directly at the current frontier difficulties. To prevent the steady eating away of the Indian country by individuals who privately acquired lands from the Indians, it declared such purchases invalid unless made by a public treaty with the United States. To put a stop to the outrages committed against Indians by whites who invaded the Indian country, the act provided punishment for murder and other crimes committed by whites against the Indians in the Indian country.[2]

The bill as it was introduced called for the appointment of a military officer as superintendent, but strong opposition to this in the House of Representatives because it "blended the civil and military characters" forced its elimination. In the Senate an article to authorize the purchase of trade goods by the government for sale to the Indians through the superintendents and agents was likewise removed.[3] The law in its final form was to be in force "for the term of two years, and from thence to the end of the next session of Congress, and no longer." Congress was feeling its way and was not ready to commit the nation to a permanent measure.

Despite the legislation, frontier disturbances continued in both north and south, and military force had to be used to restrain the Indians and defend the whites. Washington, however, did not abandon his hope for a rule of law and justice. In his message to Congress in October 25, 1791, he laid down basic principles to govern the relations of the United States with the Indians. The president hoped to avoid all need of coercion, and to this end he sought "to advance the happiness of the Indians, and to attach them firmly to the United States." He offered a six-point program:

1. an "impartial dispensation of justice" toward the Indians;

2. a carefully defined and regulated method of purchasing lands from the Indians, in order to avoid imposition on them and controversy about the reality and extent of the purchases;

3. promotion of commerce with the Indians, "under regulations tending to secure an equitable deportment toward them";

4. "rational experiments" for imparting to the Indians the "blessings of civilization";

5. authority for the president to give presents to the Indians;

6. an "efficacious provision" for punishing those who infringed Indian rights, violated treaties, and thus endangered the peace of the new nation.

2. 1 *United States Statutes* 137–38.
3. *Annals of Congress*, 1st Congress, 2d session, p. 1575.

"A system corresponding with mild principles of religion and philanthropy toward an unenlightened race of men, whose happiness materially depends on the conduct of the United States," Washington concluded, "would be as honorable to the national character as conformable to the dictates of sound policy."[4] The president's message was referred to a special committee in the House, which in turn reported a bill, but the legislation died without debate or action.

Although the act of 1790 still continued in force, its life was about to expire, and Washington in his annual message of 1792 called this fact to the attention of Congress. His report was not optimistic, for troops were being raised and measures taken to put down the continuing hostilities, but he still hoped that legislation could be provided that would eliminate the causes of the conflict, and he again urged the matter upon Congress. It was necessary first of all, he told the lawmakers, to enforce the laws on the frontier and to check the outrages committed by the whites, which led to reprisals on the part of the Indians. The government should employ qualified agents, promote civilization among the friendly tribes, and develop some plan for carrying on trade with them "upon a scale equal to their wants."[5]

A new law, approved March 1, 1793, was a considerably stronger and more inclusive piece of legislation than its predecessor of 1790, for the seven sections of the earlier law were now expanded to fifteen. New sections authorized the president to give goods and money to the tribes "to promote civilization . . . and to secure the continuance of their friendship," and a long section was aimed at horse stealing, but the bulk of the new material was intended to stop criminal attacks of whites against the Indians and the irregular acquisition of their lands. This law, too, was temporary, with the same time limitations as the first one.[6]

A good part of Washington's program was written into these laws, which at least set up the machinery for the protection of Indian rights. Complaints of the Indians about encroachments could now be met by prosecutions for outrages committed by the whites. Peace, nevertheless, was not yet firmly won, and at the end of 1793 Washington urged still further congressional action. In addition to the immediate emergency, which certainly required attention, the president was looking ahead to measures

4. Fred L. Israel, ed., *The State of the Union Messages of the Presidents, 1790–1966*, 3 vols. (New York: Chelsea House, 1966), 1: 8–9. *House Journal*, 2d Congress, 1st session, pp. 445, 462.

5. Israel, *State of the Union Messages*, 1: 14. Citations to the *House Journal* for the first thirteen Congresses are from the reprint edition published by Gales and Seaton (Washington, 1826). A facsimile reprint of the original editions of the journals has been published by Michael Glazer, Inc. (Wilmington, Delaware, 1977).

6. 1 *United States Statutes at Large* 329–32.

that would "render tranquillity with the savages permanent, by creating ties of interest." He came back again to the second part of his two-pronged program. "Next to a rigorous execution of justice on the violators of peace," he said, "the establishment of commerce with the Indian nations, on behalf of the United States, is most likely to conciliate their attachment." Advocating a system of government trading houses that would replace the profit-seeking private traders, he hammered at the point again and again until he was finally heeded by Congress.[7]

The trade and intercourse laws were necessary to provide a framework for the trade and to establish a licensing system that would permit some control and regulation, but this was merely a restatement of old procedures. The vital sections of the laws were in answer to the crisis of the day on the frontier, and the provisions pertained to the tribes of Indians with whom the nation dealt as independent bodies. Neither President Washington nor the Congress was concerned with the remnants of tribes that had been absorbed by the states and had come under their direction and control. The laws sought to provide an answer to the charge that the treaties made with the tribes on the frontiers, which guaranteed their rights to the territory behind the boundary lines, were not respected by the United States. The laws were not primarily "Indian" laws, for they touched the Indians only indirectly. The legislation, rather, was directed against lawless whites and sought to restrain them from violating the sacred treaties. Even when severe crises were resolved by force, the restrictive elements of the intercourse laws were maintained, augmented, refined, and applied to later frontiers.

At first an attempt was made to combine the restrictive or protective features of Washington's program (that is, the regulation of traders, the prohibition of land purchases, the prevention and punishment of outrages against the Indians) with the positive features (the promotion of trade through government trading houses and the civilization of the Indians). But in the course of events the two elements of the president's plan for maintaining peaceful relations with the Indians became embodied in separate series of legislation. The laws "to regulate trade and intercourse with the Indian tribes, and to preserve peace on the frontier" became the main current that carried along the federal policy, which was in large measure one of controlling contact between the two races.

By the end of 1795 the hostile Indians north of the Ohio had been defeated by General Wayne, but the largely unrestrained invasion of the lands of the Creeks and Cherokees in Tennessee and Georgia caused a constant disruption of the peace, and Washington again asked Congress to act. He

7. Israel, *State of the Union Messages*, 1: 19–20. The trading factories are treated in detail in chap. 4 below.

repeated his plea for measures to protect the Indians from injuries inflicted by whites and to supply the necessities of the Indians on reasonable terms.[8] In response Congress passed the intercourse law of May 19, 1796. The new law specified in detail the boundary line between the whites and the Indians, the first designation of the Indian country in a statute law. The delineation was meant to indicate once again the government's intention to uphold the treaties, and though the line met with opposition in the House, efforts to remove it from the bill failed. Violent debate erupted over sections in the law aimed specifically at intruders on Cherokee lands, but again the supporters of the bill were able to maintain their ground. The measure was the only way, they argued, to satisfy the Indians and prevent invasion of their lands. As the bill finally emerged, unscathed by the attacks upon it, it was almost double the length of the law it replaced; but it, too, was only a temporary measure.[9]

Despite dissatisfaction with the law on the part of frontiersmen whose encroachments it curtailed, the law of 1796 did not wreak the havoc on the frontier that its opponents had feared, and it gave assurance to the Indians that the federal government was doing what it could to protect their rights. In 1799, two days before the law was due to expire, it was reenacted, passing both houses without amendment and with little debate.[10]

When Thomas Jefferson sent his first annual message to Congress in December 1801, he could remark that "a spirit of peace and friendship generally prevails" among the Indian tribes. The new president saw no need to depart from the Indian policies of his predecessors, and when the temporary laws for trading houses and for governing trade and intercourse expired, he asked Congress to renew them. The only modification he suggested was some restriction of the liquor traffic among the Indians, which he said the Indians themselves wanted. Accordingly, on March 30, 1802, a new trade and intercourse law was passed. It was for the most part merely a restatement of the laws of 1796 and 1799, but now the period of trial was over. The law of 1802 was no longer a temporary measure; it was to remain in force, with occasional additions, as the basic law governing Indian relations until it was replaced by a new codification of Indian policy in 1834.[11]

8. Israel, *State of the Union Messages*, 1: 30.

9. 1 *United States Statutes at Large* 469–74; *House Journal*, 4th Congress, 1st session, pp. 426, 433, 508, 510; *Senate Journal*, 4th Congress, 1st session, pp. 256–57; *Annals of Congress*, 4th Congress, 1st session, pp. 286–88, 893–905. Citations to the *Senate Journal* for the first thirteen Congresses are to the reprint edition published by Gales and Seaton (Washington, 1820–1821).

10. 1 *United States Statutes* 743–49.

11. Israel, *State of the Union Messages*, 1: 58; James D. Richardson, comp., *A Compilation of the Messages and Papers of the Presidents, 1789–1897*, 10 vols. (Washington: GPO, 1896–1899), 1: 334–35; 2 *United States Statutes* 139–46.

REGULATING THE TRADE IN FURS

The fur trade remained an important source of legitimate contact between the Indians and the whites, but after the removal of British and Spanish influence in the early years of the nineteenth century the political importance of the trade disappeared, for it was no longer necessary to win over the Indians from rival allegiances by drawing them into the American circuit of trade. Economically, too, the trade declined in importance, and by 1834 John Jacob Astor, the great fur mogul, had withdrawn from the business after complaining for years about its economic liabilities. Governmental interest in the trade then tended to become colored more and more by humanitarian interest, by the desire to protect the Indians from the injustices of wily traders and thus assure contentment and peace on the frontier. But under all the changing conditions trade regulation was an essential element in federal Indian policy, as the title "trade and intercourse" laws suggests.[12]

Congress did not have to look far for a method of regulation. It simply adopted the principles of the licensing system used for decades past, although it softened somewhat the requirements set forth in the Ordinance of 1786. The intercourse laws required licenses of all traders, bonds for the faithful observance of regulations governing the trade, and forfeiture of goods taken illegally into the Indian country. From time to time the legislation was strengthened by additional restrictions or increased fines, and the law of 1796 and subsequent laws authorized the use of military force to apprehend offenders.[13] These laws supplemented and strengthened the treaties signed with the tribes, which often dealt with trade and the federal government's right to regulate it.

The provisions of both the laws and the treaties seem unexceptionable. The licensing system was meant to furnish a check on the traders and make them abide by the rules of the trade. The bonds were high enough to eliminate the unstable, and the threat of confiscation of goods—with one-half to the informer—should have dampened any hopes for profitable trading outside the law. The facts, however, belied the surface impression. Year after year reports poured in about illegal trading and the inability of anyone to prevent it. Both north and south of the Ohio the territorial governors, serving ex officio as superintendents of Indian affairs, found it impossible

12. Useful information on the fur trade is found in Paul Chrisler Phillips, *The Fur Trade*, 2 vols. (Norman: University of Oklahoma Press, 1961). On John Jacob Astor and the American Fur Company, see Kenneth Wiggins Porter, *John Jacob Astor: Business Man*, 2 vols. (Cambridge: Harvard University Press, 1931), and David Lavender, *The Fist in the Wilderness* (Garden City, New York: Doubleday and Company, 1964).

13. 1 *United States Statutes* 137–38, 329–30, 473; 3 *United States Statutes* 682.

to cope with the illicit trade. With the addition of the Louisiana Purchase, the problems of regulating the trade spread over a vaster area and one where the legal lines were even less clearly drawn.

The problem of enforcing the intercourse laws can be understood and appreciated only in light of the character of the men with whom the enforcing agents had to contend. The traders were divided roughly into two classes. There were the licensed traders, often attached to some organized and responsible firm like the American Fur Company. They frequently were substantial men in the frontier communities, but their business tactics and the character of many of their employees were not above reproach, and they could interfere seriously with the process of the law by their political pressure and their astute discovery of legal technicalities. But there were also hordes of independent little traders, large numbers of whom were unlicensed—a breed of men irresponsible, lawless, in some cases depraved—who lived off clandestine intercouse with the Indians. The very nature of the fur trade called forth men to whom the restraints of civilized living meant little. They went off into the wilderness with their packs of goods and sought out the peltries of the Indians. Often they took Indian wives and adopted Indian ways, yet their loyalties were not transferred to the tribe, for they mercilessly exploited the Indians, debauched them with whiskey, and then robbed them of their furs. The fines and forfeitures of the laws meant little to them, for they had no property to lose. If they were temporarily driven off in one area, they quickly appeared again in another. There was trouble enough from both groups when it came to enforcing the intercourse laws— one lobbied to get favorable laws and interpretations and was intransigent in local courts against government officials who were too solicitous in the enforcement of the law, and the other totally disregarded legalities.

It seemed well-nigh impossible to stop the illegal trading by judicial process. The intercourse laws provided machinery, designating the action to be taken and the courts to be used, but the machinery was shaky and not very effective. Distances were too great, the time lag too long, and the difficulties of arranging for witnesses too serious for the laws to provide an effective deterrent or remedy for the illicit traffic. If some diligent and conscientious officer or agent did make the effort to bring a violator to trial, chances were that the judges would dismiss the case on a technicality or the jury side with the defendant. Too often the only reward for an officer who attempted to enforce the law was to be called into court himself to answer to charges of illegal trespass or arrest.[14]

14. Examples of the problems of enforcing officers are given in Prucha, *American Indian Policy in the Formative Years*, pp. 74–76.

The mischievous, unscrupulous, unlicensed trader caused untold troubles along the whole frontier, yet he was unorganized, and his total volume of trade was perhaps of little moment. It was his ubiquity and his furtive ways that made him such a nuisance, and it was his reliance on the illegal introduction of liquor to gain his ends that caused such consternation. More serious in many respects than his infractions, however, were the inroads on the trade made by foreign traders, chiefly the British along the Great Lakes and the upper reaches of the Mississippi and the Missouri.

British traders had deeply infiltrated the northwest area after the French were driven out in 1763. Operating under the direction of powerful companies, they exerted great influence over the Indians, who accepted their presents and depended upon them for goods. These traders were unmolested after the Revolutionary War, chiefly because the Americans were not prepared to replace them, and Jay's Treaty of 1794 specifically guaranteed their right to be there. Their posts at Michilimackinac and Prairie du Chien were important gathering points for Indians. There had always been irritation on account of these foreigners, and little by little they were pushed out of the trade south of the Great Lakes; but it was the War of 1812 that fully opened American eyes to the danger, for it was through the influence of traders that the Indians fought with the British against the United States in the war.

It is understandable that agitation should have arisen to eliminate the British traders altogether. By a law of April 29, 1816, licenses to trade with the Indians within the territorial limits of the United States were refused to noncitizens, although the president could permit such licenses if he thought the public interest demanded it. All goods taken into the Indian country by foreigners were subject to seizure and forfeiture if not yet traded to the Indians, and all peltries purchased from the Indians by foreigners were liable to seizure while still in the Indian country. The president was authorized to use military force to seize the goods or furs and to arrest violators of the act. Even foreigners who wished merely to pass through the Indian lands were required first to obtain a passport.[15]

The discretionary power of the president was invoked to allow some foreigners to continue in the trade. A sudden and absolute cutting off of noncitizens from the trade was impolitic, if not impossible, because there were not enough Americans to fill the vacuum that would have been created. The Indians had to be supplied with the goods on which they had become dependent, and for the time being it was necessary to rely on foreign traders. The president granted authority to Governor Lewis Cass of

15. 3 *United States Statutes* 332–33. There was little debate on the measure in Congress and apparently no opposition. *House Journal*, 14th Congress, 1st session, pp. 402, 647, 654; *Senate Journal*, 14th Congress, 1st session, p. 603.

Michigan Territory and to the Indian agents at Michilimackinac, Green Bay, and Chicago to issue licenses to foreigners, but only to reputable characters who were above suspicion.[16]

This presidential discretion in issuing licenses to foreigners was criticized in Congress, and on November 26, 1817, the president withdrew the power he had granted earlier to Cass and the agents. The law of 1816 was now to be carried fully into effect, and no licenses in the future were to be granted to anyone who was not an American citizen.[17] The exigencies of the trade, however, would not allow this drastic move. The traders themselves, no doubt, should be American citizens, but where could enough citizens be found to serve as boatmen and interpreters? It was necessary to rely on foreigners for these essential jobs—chiefly men of French extraction but of British citizenship, who congregated at such centers as Mackinac, Green Bay, and Prairie du Chien—and the president, after "farther information and reflection," permitted the use of such men under careful restrictions.[18] Yet, by the effects of the restrictive legislation and the steady growth of the power and influence of the American Fur Company, the British were generally forced out of the trade within the territory of the United States.

For some years after the War of 1812, the government sought to eliminate abuses in the fur trade by supplying the Indians through the government trading houses, or factories, but when Congress struck down the factory system in 1822, it was necessary to return to direct legislation. In fact, on the very day that the factories were abolished, Congress approved an amendment to the intercourse law of 1802 that raised the bonds required of licensed traders, demanded an annual report of licenses granted, and strengthened the restrictions on the whiskey trade. The law also protected Indians in suits over property with white citizens by placing the burden of proof upon the whites, and it authorized the appointment of a superintendent of Indian affairs at St. Louis.[19]

There was continued agitation to strengthen the hand of the government over the traders. One demand was for discretionary power on the part of the agents in issuing licenses, so that they could exclude unsavory characters, but such exclusion of citizens from the trade seemed to go against

16. William H. Crawford to Cass, May 10, 1816, *Wisconsin Historical Collections*, 19: 406–7; George Graham to Cass, October 29, 1816, Clarence E. Carter, ed., *The Territorial Papers of the United States*, 26 vols. (Washington, GPO, 1934–1962), 10: 667–68; Graham to Cass, May 4, 1817, SW IA LS, vol. D, p. 35 (M15, reel 4).

17. George Graham to Cass, November 26, 1817, SW IA LS, vol. D, p. 101 (M15, reel 4).

18. Calhoun to Cass, March 25, 1818, ibid., pp. 320–21; Cass to agents, April 23, 1818, *Wisconsin Historical Collections*, 20: 42–46.

19. 3 *United States Statutes* 682–83.

the American spirit of free enterprise. And any discretionary power over licenses greatly frightened the American Fur Company, which suspected there would be a severe limiting of the number of licenses granted; it fought through its political friends to quash such a "new-fangled obnoxious Indian system."[20] When Lewis Cass and William Clark, relying on their long experience as Indian superintendents, in 1829 repeated the recommendation of discretionary authority, the fur company did everything it could to block the proposal.

Another suggested panacea was to permit trading in the Indian country at designated sites only, where, with fewer places to keep an eye on, the agents could be more efficient in enforcing the law. In 1824 the proposal became law, and Secretary of War John C. Calhoun set up strict norms for the agents to follow: no more than one site for each tribe, no changes in designated sites without War Department approval, and forfeiture of bonds if trading was done at places not indicated on one's license.[21] There was an immediate outcry against the law from the American Fur Company, which found the designated sites neither convenient nor suitable, and some adjustments were made to accommodate the traders, but the law and the principle remained. Attempts to change the 1824 law failed, and the trade and intercourse law of 1834 continued to specify that no trade was to be carried on except at designated sites.

THE CRUSADE AGAINST ARDENT SPIRITS

The greatest source of difficulty in the Indian trade was whiskey. The "ardent spirits" smuggled into the Indian country made madmen of the Indians, yet the flow could not easily be stanched. It was an elemental problem, rooted in strong human drives—the Indians' fondness for drink and the heartless avarice of the whites. To protect the Indian from his own weakness the government needed to clamp down on the whiskey dealer.

The problem of the liquor traffic was as old as white settlement in America. Yet the first federal laws governing intercouse with the Indians made no mention of intoxicating liquors, just as there had been no discussion of the matter in the Continental Congress and no specific cnactments in regard to it. This may seem like a strange omission in view of the past troubles that had grown out of laxness in the matter, but it is likely that the legislators hoped that the licensing provisions of the laws would pro-

20. Ramsay Crooks to John Jacob Astor, May 30, 1820, American Fur Company Letter Books, 1: 305–6, photostatic copies at the State Historical Society of Wisconsin.
21. 4 *United States Statutes* 35–36; Calhoun to superintendents and agents, June 5, 1824, OIA LS, vol. 1, pp. 96–97 (M 21, reel 1).

vide the necessary restraints. They looked to the superintendents of Indian affairs and to the Indian agents to place the necessary brake upon the liquor trade. Nor was it clear at first that state or territorial ordinances could not take care of the problem. Officials on the frontier were in fact well aware of the whiskey menace, even though territorial governors and legislators took little action. That their steps were halting was due more to the dim twilight of authority between federal and local governments and to hesitation to act against the economic interests of the infant communities than to any malice toward the Indians or indifference to their plight.

The Territory North West of the River Ohio was still in its first stage of territorial government when the governor and judges proclaimed a comprehensive law governing Indian trade, not only forbidding under penalty of fine the distribution of intoxicating liquor to the Indians, but excluding foreigners from the trade and setting the high penalty of five hundred dollars for trading without a license. The law set a pattern for ineffectiveness. There was an uneasiness about the restrictions, and five years after enactment the law was quietly repealed with the notation that it was "partly supplied by an act of the United States." The governor of the territory found that his authority as superintendent of Indian affairs in large measure evaporated because it did not affect white settlements to which the Indians freely resorted for liquor.[22]

The inability or unwillingness of the territorial governments to cope with the whiskey problem brought numerous complaints to the federal officials as the nefarious traffic flourished. Even the Indians themselves, becoming aware of the evil effects of the liquor on their morals, health, and very existence, pleaded with President Jefferson for protection. When Jefferson in turn recommended to Congress that it restrict the trade, Congress inserted a special provision in the intercouse law of 1802 that authorized the president "to prevent or restrain the vending or distributing of spirituous liquors among all or any of the said Indian tribes." To implement the law, the secretary of war sent a circular of instructions to Indian officials, forbidding traders to vend ardent spirits. He addressed special letters as well to territorial governors, telling them not to allow traders to supply the Indians with spirituous liquors on any pretext whatever and to take licenses away from traders who disturbed the peace and harmony existing between the Indians and the whites.[23]

22. Theodore C. Pease, ed., *The Laws of the Northwest Territory, 1788–1800* (Springfield: Illinois State Historical Library, 1925), pp. 26–28, 256; letter of Winthrop Sargent, July 22, 1793, Carter, *Territorial Papers*, 3: 412; proclamation of Sargent, September 10, 1794, ibid., p. 423.

23. Jefferson to Congress, January 27, 1802, Richardson, *Messages and Papers*, 1: 334–35; 2 *United States Statutes* 146; Henry Dearborn to superintendents and agents,

The distinction between the Indian country and ceded territory was a major obstacle in the enforcement of the restrictions on whiskey, for it was accepted opinion that the federal regulations applied only to the lands still owned and occupied by Indians. Thus the territories and states had to take action themselves to extend prohibition against the liquor traffic to the ceded lands, but the legislatures were halfhearted in their measures. In 1808 President Jefferson pleaded with the governors to propose to the lawmakers the wisdom and humanity of restraining citizens from vending spirituous liquors to the Indians, and some action was taken in response to the request by most of the western territories.[24]

All the laws and regulations for regulating the trade were considered important in large measure because they would help to check the whiskey menace. The system of government trading houses, too, was strongly supported by humanitarians because it might squeeze out the petty traders, who were the primary distributors of liquor. When Congress struck down the factories, it made a new attempt to prevent the introduction of liquor into the Indian country. The 1822 amendment to the intercourse law of 1802 that accompanied the act abolishing the trading houses authorized the president to direct Indian agents, superintendents of Indian affairs, and military officers to search the goods of all traders in case of suspicion or information that ardent spirits were being carried into the Indian lands. If liquor was found, all the goods were to be forfeited, the trader's license was to be canceled, and his bond was to be put in suit.[25] But the new amendment availed little. There were still ambiguities and loopholes in the law, and the American Fur Company was able to overreach the government agents and army officers in executing it when they received permission from Governor Cass to import liquor in order to compete with British traders along the northern border.[26]

Then in February 1827 came a new tightening of the prohibition against liquor. "Upon this point," the head of the Indian Office wrote to Cass, "any discretion which may have been heretofore given not provided for by law, you will consider as withdrawn. The laws will govern." Cass objected to

September 14, 1802, SW IA LS, vol. A, p. 276 (M15, reel 1); Dearborn to William Henry Harrison, September 3, 1802, Carter, *Territorial Papers*, 7: 74; Dearborn to William C. C. Claiborne, September 11, 1802, Dunbar Rowland, ed., *The Mississippi Territorial Archives*, vol. 1 (Nashville: Brandon Printing Company, 1905), p. 552.

24. Jefferson to executives, December 31, 1808, *The Writings of Thomas Jefferson*, ed. Andrew A. Lipscomb, 20 vols. (Washington: Thomas Jefferson Memorial Association, 1903), 12: 223–24. For state and territorial response, see Prucha, *American Indian Policy in the Formative Years*, pp. 106–8.

25. 3 *United States Statutes* 682–83.

26. Prucha, *American Indian Policy in the Formative Years*, pp. 110–14.

the order because he had permitted whiskey only to prevent the utter ruin of American trade. Furthermore, Cass pointed out, his use of the discretionary power was not contrary to the laws, but was expressly allowed by the acts of 1802 and 1822. But he assumed that the president's intention now was to allow no more exceptions, so he discontinued such licenses.[27] The American Fur Company did not accept this rebuff. It soon made a new application for the privilege it had previously enjoyed, and on June 15, 1831, Secretary of War John H. Eaton restored to Cass the discretionary power that had been withdrawn in 1827. This was a temporary respite, for a new law of 1832 destroyed altogether the possibility of a discretionary grant.[28]

There were other ways to take liquor into the Indian country under the protection of authority. Permission was granted to carry in whiskey for use of the boatmen employed in trading, as the prohibition under the laws of 1802 and 1822 was only against introducing the article for use in trade with the Indians. This was a loophole through which large amounts of liquor poured into the Indian country, and any ruse to get by inspecting officers seemed to succeed. A second method was to demand liquor for the white settlements, such as Green Bay or Prairie du Chien, which were not, strictly speaking, Indian country.[29]

However diligent the agents and army officers were, the whiskey merchants were always one step ahead. The licensed traders used whatever schemes they could concoct to gain permission to take in liquor, and they slipped easily into illegal practices. The unlicensed traders operated altogether beyond the law. No section of the frontier was free of disturbance. From Florida, Alabama, Mississippi, Michigan, Arkansas, and Missouri reports flowed into the War Department from officers and agents lamenting the state of affairs, which all the current laws were quite inadequate to remedy. The legislation to date had concentrated on regulating the trade; because such measures were ineffective, the next step would be absolute prohibition of spirituous liquor in the Indian country.

This step was taken in 1832, when Congress bluntly declared: "No ardent spirits shall be hereafter introduced, under any pretence, into the Indian country." It was an all-inclusive prohibition that allowed for no exceptions and that applied to traders and nontraders alike.[30] For a short period

---

27. Thomas L. McKenney to Cass, February 20, 1827, OIA LS, vol. 3, p. 390 (M21, reel 3); Cass to McKenney, March 25, 1827, OIA LR, Michigan Superintendency (M234, reel 419); McKenney to Cass, April 19, 1827, OIA LS, vol. 4, p. 24 (M21, reel 4).

28. Eaton to Cass, June 15, 1831, Carter, *Territorial Papers*, 12: 294 and n.

29. Prucha, *American Indian Policy in the Formative Years*, pp. 115–20.

30. 4 *United States Statutes* 564. The law said that no liquor could be *introduced* into Indian country, and the agent of the American Fur Company on the upper Missouri

the strong prohibition seemed to have a good effect. The War Department sent strongly worded instructions to the Indian agents to carry out the provisions of the new law, and army officers were given new energy in searching out the forbidden goods, even though they still faced the possibility of legal action against them by the American Fur Company for their diligence.

Attempts were made to get permission to introduce limited amounts of whiskey as exceptions to the law, but the War Department was now adamant. Lewis Cass, who as governor of Michigan Territory had looked with favor upon such requests under the earlier laws, as secretary of war firmly refused permission even to his friends of the American Fur Company, although he continued to be bothered about details in the execution of the new law.

CRIMES IN THE INDIAN COUNTRY

When the white and red races met on the American frontier, there occurred innumerable violations of the personal and property rights of one group by members of the other. Murders and robberies were all too frequent between peoples who were nominally at peace, and some provision had to be made to preserve law and order or constant warfare would result. If private retaliation was not to be the rule, then crimes had to be defined and legal machinery established to mete out justice. These provisions for criminal court procedure formed an essential part of the Indian intercourse laws.

No matter how the sovereignty of the Indian nations might be defined, the establishment of an Indian country outside the jurisdiction of the states created special problems. Here was another indication of the anomaly of the Indian situation, for there were no formal precedents to go by. As in other elements of federal Indian policy, the legislation dealing with crimes in the Indian country grew bit by bit, until in the law of 1834 the main pieces were finally assembled into a whole.

The first measures taken to regularize criminal procedure in cases arising between Indians and white citizens were special articles included in the early treaties for the apprehension and punishment of criminals. Indians, or whites taking refuge among Indians, who had committed murder or other serious crimes against any citizen of the United States were to be delivered up to American authorities by the tribe and punished according to the laws of the United States. If, on the other hand, a white citizen committed the crime against an Indian, he was to be punished just as though

---

sought to evade it by distilling whiskey *within* the Indian country. The story is told in Prucha, *American Indian Policy in the Formative Years*, pp. 136–37.

the crime had been against another white citizen, and this punishment according to some of the treaties was to be exacted in the presence of the Indians. A special section added the injunction that private retaliation was not to be practiced on either side.[31]

The earlier intercourse laws, in an attempt to guarantee respect for the treaties on the part of whites, were concerned particularly with whites who committed crimes against Indians in the Indian country. The act of 1790 equated a crime against an Indian with the same deed committed against an inhabitant of one of the states or territories. The white offender was to be subject to the same punishment and the same procedure was to be followed as though the offense had been committed outside the Indian country against a white. Procedures for apprehending, imprisoning, and bailing in such crimes were to follow the Judiciary Act of 1789.[32]

These basic provisions of 1790 were expanded in succeeding acts because, as Washington pointed out in his annual message of 1792, "more adequate provision for giving energy to the laws throughout our interior frontier, and for restraining the commission of outrages upon the Indians" was necessary. The bill that was introduced in response to the message contained much that the president wished for, but strong opposition developed to the section of the bill that provided for punishment of crimes committed in the Indian country—the very heart of the measure if it were to bring an end to the outrages caused by the whites. The argument was advanced that the treaties or the laws of the states already provided for these cases and that it would be an absurdity to enact them again. The law, furthermore, would operate unfairly by striking whites without reaching out equally to Indians. But wiser counsels carried the day. "If the Government cannot make laws to restrain persons from going out of the limits of any of the States, and commit murders and depredations," one congressman asserted, "it would be in vain to expect any peace with the Indian tribes."[33]

In the intercourse law of 1793, "murder, robbery, larceny, trespass or other crimes" were named, and a new section specified the proper courts to be used. Yet this was not strong enough. Washington bluntly told Congress in December 1795: "The provisions heretofore made with a view to the protection of the Indians from the violences of the lawless part of our frontier inhabitants, are insufficient. It is demonstrated that these violences can now be perpetrated with impunity, and it can need no argument

31. See, for example, treaties with the Cherokees (1785), Choctaws (1786), Chickasaws (1786), Shawnees (1786), Wyandots (1789), and Creeks (1790), Kappler, pp. 8ff.

32. 1 *United States Statutes* 138.

33. Israel, *State of the Union Messages*, 1: 14; *Annals of Congress*, 2d Congress, 2d session, pp. 750–51.

to prove that unless the murdering of Indians can be restrained by bringing the murderers to condign punishment, all the exertions of the Government to prevent destructive retaliations by the Indians will prove fruitless and all our present agreeable prospects illusory."[34]

Acting on Washington's recommendation, Congress wrote into the intercourse law of 1796 detailed provisions for restraining outrages on both sides, including the death penalty for anyone convicted of going into Indian country and there murdering an Indian. Property taken or destroyed was to be paid for by the culprit or by the United States Treasury, and if Indians crossed over the line into white lands and committed crimes, satisfaction was to be demanded from the tribe. All of this was predicated on the condition that no private satisfaction be exacted. The provisions of the 1796 law were reenacted with little change in the temporary law of 1799 and in the permanent law of 1802. But it was not until 1817 that Congress ordained punishment for Indians who committed crimes against whites within the Indian country.[35]

The United States government was determined to provide an adequate judicial system for the Indian country and intended that Indians and whites be treated with equal justice. In practice, however, there were serious discrepancies, for the universal resort to legal procedures to gain satisfaction and justice envisaged by the laws simply did not obtain. Serious disturbances were solved by crushing defeats of the Indians and by their removal to lands farther away rather than by strict enforcement of the laws.

The laws, however, were by no means completely ineffective. Against Indian criminals they were invoked again and again. If an Indian committed a crime against a white—and murder was the offense foremost in mind—the criminal was demanded from the tribe for punishment by the United States. If the accused Indian was not delivered up, a military expedition was sent to apprehend him, or hostages were seized and held until the criminal appeared. The culprit was guarded by the federal troops and turned over by them to a civil court in a nearby territory or state for trial. In many cases this procedure worked satisfactorily. However reluctant the Indian tribes might have been to turn over their members to the United States for punishment, they had a remarkably good record in doing so. Whether this was due to their sense of justice or to the threat or use of military force cannot be determined, and it is impossible to tell what percentage of Indian murderers were actually brought to trial. Certainly many murders went unpunished. In 1824, Thomas L. McKenney, head of the Indian Office, wrote to both Lewis Cass and William Clark about the "alarm-

34. 1 *United States Statutes* 329–31; Israel, *State of the Union Messages*, 1: 30.
35. 1 *United States Statutes* 470–73, 744–48; 2 *United States Statutes* 39–40, 141–45; 3 *United States Statutes* 383.

ing extent to which murders are committed in the North and West," and he urged them to take special action to prevent recurrence.[36]

Even when court action was initiated, the simple frontier communities frequently became tied up in the legal proceedings. To find suitable counsel, to call adequate witnesses, to empanel a proper jury—all this was a complicated and time-consuming process. The local courts had insufficient means to confine prisoners while awaiting trial, it was not always easy to determine which court had proper jurisdiction, and collection of evidence was a difficult and thankless task. The whole process was expensive and, in the minds of army officers upon whom much of the responsibility fell, wrongly conceived. Some officers wanted to throw out the legal procedures of white civilization and punish Indian offenders on the spot. This sort of action the Indians would understand, and it would be effective in checking their depredations. But the government refused to modify the policy of treating Indians on a par with whites as far as legal forms were concerned. All along the frontier, army officers sought out criminals in the Indian country, confined them in the post guardhouses, and then sent them under military guard to civil authorities for trial.[37]

For crimes committed by whites against Indians the laws made specific provision, gradually becoming more explicit. If the offenses were committed within a territory or a state, the criminal code of that civil jurisdiction sufficed. Within the Indian country, offenses of whites against Indians were punishable in federal courts when the offenses were specified in the federal statutes, and the intercourse laws declared that crimes in any of the states or territories against a white citizen should also be considered crimes if committed in the Indian country against an Indian. But the crimes were so numerous and widespread that their control by judicial means proved impossible. The frequency of offenses committed against Indians by frontier whites, among which outright murder was commonplace, was shocking. It was often a question of who was more aggressive, more hostile, more savage—the Indian or the white man. The murders and other aggressions of whites against Indians provided one of the great sources of friction between the two races. Lack of enforcement made a mockery of the statutes. The typical frontier community could not be brought to convict a man who injured or murdered an Indian, and confusion as to the status of the federal courts in the territories delayed effective action.

Letters and directives and official proclamations, even when backed by

36. McKenney to Cass and Clark, November 1, 1824, OIA LS, vol. 1, p. 214 (M21, reel 1).

37. See Francis Paul Prucha, *Broadax and Bayonet: The Role of the United States Army in the Development of the Northwest, 1815–1860* (Madison: State Historical Society of Wisconsin, 1953), pp. 84–88.

all the goodwill in the world, were no match for the singular Indian-hating mentality of the frontiersmen, upon whom depended conviction in the local courts. In Indiana Territory, for example, the criminal law broke down, and Governor Harrison lamented the sad state of justice toward the Indians. In his message to the legislature in 1806 he unhesitatingly admitted that, although the laws provided the same punishment for offenses committed against Indians as against white men, "experience . . . shows that there is a wide difference in the execution of those laws. The Indian always suffers, and the white man never."[38]

The federal government made repeated efforts to bring white offenders to justice, and no doubt some Indians were influenced by the good intentions of the United States, even though white citizens were never kept in check. One measure taken to appease the Indians was to issue a proclamation in the name of the president, offering a handsome reward for the apprehension of the criminal. The ineffectiveness of such proclamations in actually bringing the criminals to justice in the frontier communities can be presumed, and the government more frequently resorted to compensating the families of murdered Indians by payment of a fixed sum of money or goods. The War Department directed the Indian agents to offer such pecuniary satisfaction in cases where the murderers could not be apprehended, in order to satisfy the families and show the willingness of the government to do justice. A sum of one to two hundred dollars for each Indian murdered by whites was suggested by the secretary of war in 1803, and this amount was regularly given.[39]

Theft was another cause of conflict, and the chief concern was horses. Aside from outright murders and massacres by the Indians, nothing was so likely to embroil the two races on the frontier as horse stealing, for horses were of elemental necessity for the frontiersman. The white's need and the Indian's cupidity and stealth made for an explosive combination that threatened to blow up one frontier after another. The petitions that reached the War Department regularly coupled horse stealing with murder as the scourge of living near the Indians.[40]

It was necessary to get at the evil indirectly, first of all by eliminating the market for the stolen stock. If the Indians could not dispose of the horses by ready sale, there would be no further incentive for large-scale

38. *Messages and Letters of William Henry Harrison*, ed. Logan Esarey, 2 vols. (Indianapolis: Indiana Historical Commission, 1922), 1: 199–200.

39. See proclamations dated February 27 and March 1, 1804, SW IA LS, vol. A, pp. 443, 447 (M15, reel 1). For use of compensation, see letters of Dearborn to various agents, ibid., pp. 352–53, 373, 417; Calhoun to Thomas Forsyth, March 15, 1819, ibid., vol. D, p. 269 (M15, reel 4); Calhoun to John McKee, July 21, 1819, Carter, *Territorial Papers*, 18: 657.

40. Carter, *Territorial Papers*, 4: 72, 129; 16: 188–89.

thefts. Such was the logic behind the provisions that were written into the intercourse laws, beginning with the law of 1793 and repeated in subsequent laws. To purchase a horse from any Indian or from any white person within the Indian country required a special license, and a report of all horses purchased was to be made to the agent who issued the license. For every horse purchased or brought out of the Indian country without a license, a fine was imposed. Furthermore, to plug another loophole, any person who purchased a horse that he knew had been brought out of the Indian country without a license was to forfeit the value of the horse.[41] But there were no convictions under these licensing and forfeiture provisions of the intercourse laws, and the laws soon became a dead letter.

The intercourse law of 1796, though it continued the restrictions on the purchase of horses in the Indian country, tried a new approach to the problem, one aimed less at justice than at preventing injustice from causing frontier disturbances. This was a guarantee of government compensation for theft of horses or other injuries if satisfaction could not be obtained from the guilty party, either by application to the tribe in the case of thefts by Indians or by recourse to the courts in the case of injuries perpetrated by whites. The War Department was eventually flooded with claims for stolen horses and occasionally for other property, and it did not know just what to do about the claims because often they were submitted on the least provocation without clear evidence that Indians were the real culprits and without going through the procedure prescribed by the laws. Yet faulty as the operation of the law was, it regularized this point of contact between the two races. By providing machinery for recovery of losses by peaceful means, it eliminated any justification for private retaliation and was largely successful in removing this friction, except on the rawest frontiers before they were amenable to juridical procedures. In numerous cases injured whites received compensation for their losses out of the annuities due the Indians, and in some cases—although apparently far fewer—the Indians were paid for injuries sustained from the whites. Frequently large numbers of claims on both sides were summarily provided for in treaties made with specific tribes.[42]

Because it was generally admitted that offenses among Indians within the tribe or nation were tribal matters that were to be handled by the tribe and were of no concern to the United States government, crimes committed by Indians against other Indians did not fall within the scope of the intercourse laws. The sovereignty of an Indian tribe, no matter how it might be circumscribed in other respects, was certainly considered to ex-

41. 1 *United States Statutes* 330.
42. Cases regarding horse stealing are discussed in Prucha, *American Indian Policy in the Formative Years,* pp. 205–11.

tend to the punishment of its own members. Up to the mid-nineteenth century, indeed, there were no laws or treaty provisions that limited the powers of self-government of the tribes with respect to internal affairs. Indian tribal sovereignty existed long before the coming of the whites and did not depend upon federal legislation. Yet the United States formally indicated its respect for this tribal authority by embodying in the law of 1817 that established federal jurisdiction over Indian offenses the declaration that the law did not extend "to any offense committed by one Indian against another, within any Indian boundary."[43] Intertribal wars, however, were of continuing interest to the United States, for they could endanger the lives and property of white citizens on the frontier. Indian agents were directed to use whatever advice, persuasion, or presents might be needed to prevent hostilities between tribes, but they were not to involve the United States on either side.[44]

REMOVAL OF INTRUDERS ON INDIAN LANDS

The conflict between the whites and Indians that marked American Indian relations was basically a conflict over land. Although the American government recognized Indian rights to the land and attempted by law, treaty, and special proclamation to ensure justice to the aborigines, the views of the frontiersmen were of a different nature altogether. Theorizing about rights of preemption played little part in the thinking of the settler or of the eastern speculator in western lands. Their doctrine was simpler and earthier, and they had their own ideas about *jus gentium*: they saw the rich lands of the Indians and they wanted them. Their philosophy was summed up by John Sevier, one of the most aggressive of the frontier leaders. "By the law of nations, it is agreed that no people shall be entitled to more land than they can cultivate," he said. "Of course no people will sit and starve for want of land to work, when a neighbouring nation has much more than they can make use of."[45]

In the conflict with the frontiersmen, the government did not back down in its principles; it in fact tightened its restrictions and strengthened the machinery of enforcement. But as the spearhead of settlement fluctu-

---

43. 3 *United States Statutes* 383.

44. John Smith to William Clark, September 8, 1810, SW IA LS, vol. C, pp. 49–50 (M15, reel 3); Calhoun to James Miller, June 29, 1820, ibid., vol. D, pp. 458–59 (M15, reel 4).

45. Sevier to James Ore, May 12, 1798, Robert H. White, ed., *Messages of the Governors of Tennessee*, 5 vols. (Nashville: Tennessee Historical Commission, 1952–1959), 1: 58,

ated back and forth across the West, driving ever deeper into territories once solely Indian, the pious principles of the legislators ran into the unprincipled practices of the settlers. The men actually on the land generally had the better of it, for they again and again deflected the enforcing army of government and in the end forced the Indians off the land. This is the story that has attracted so many writers and led to a widely held opinion that the Indians were ruthlessly dispossessed with nothing done to protect their rights. Quite the contrary, for the Indians were not completely deserted. Explicit treaties were made guaranteeing their rights, and stringent laws were enacted to ensure respect for the treaties. Various measures were undertaken to enforce the laws, which were not completely ineffective. It is true that in the end the Indians were pushed back by the onrush of whites, but what order and peace there was on the frontier came in large part from the enforcement of the intercourse laws against unlawful encroachment on Indian lands.

The prohibition of private purchase of lands from the Indians, which had been part of the colonial and imperial policy, continued as a fixed policy of the United States. The First Congress incorporated this principle into the intercourse law of 1790. The restriction entered as section 4 read: "no sale of lands made by any Indians, or any nation or tribe of Indians within the United States, shall be valid to any person or persons, or to any state, whether having the right of pre-emption to such lands or not, unless the same shall be made and duly executed at some public treaty, held under the authority of the United States." The same prohibition was included in the act of 1793, with an added clause setting a fine and imprisonment for any person treating directly or indirectly with the Indians for title to land. The law recognized, however, the right of agents of the states, with the approval of the United States commissioners, to be present at treaty making and to propose and adjust with the Indians the compensation for lands within the states whose Indian title would be extinguished by the treaty. This section was reenacted in the laws of 1796, 1799, and 1802.[46] The principle was clearly stated, and the practice had been uniform for decades. Federal commissioners were appointed to treat with the Indians for their lands, and Congress appropriated funds for compensating the Indians.

Treaties entered into with the Indians for cessions of land had the universal corollary that the unceded lands would be guaranteed against inva-

---

46. 1 *United States Statutes* 138, 330–31, 472, 746; 2 *United States Statutes* 143. Despite arguments in the 1970s that these provisions applied also to acquisition of lands from remnants of Indian tribes by such states as Massachusetts, the context in which the laws were passed indicates that the legislators did not have such cases in mind. See discussion below, "Land Claims and Conflicts," in chapter 46.

sion by whites. Thus all the treaties entered into by the Continental Congress guaranteed the remaining lands of the Indians, and the later ones expressly forbade whites to settle on Indian land under sanction of forfeiting the protection of the United States and becoming subject to punishment by the Indians. The same provisions were written into the first treaties made under the Constitution. Congress, therefore, in drawing up the intercourse law of 1790, considered it unnecessary to make specific prohibition of encroachment on the Indian country.

The open violations of the treaties, however, necessitated additional legislative measures against the illegal settlers, and the intercourse law of 1793 provided a maximum fine of one thousand dollars and imprisonment for twelve months for anyone who settled on Indian lands or surveyed or marked boundaries on such lands with a view to settlement. The president, furthermore, was authorized to remove all unlawful settlers by such measures as he might judge necessary. From that time on, the successive laws included sections aimed specifically at the aggressive frontiersmen. The act of 1796, which was copied in substance by the subsequent acts, forbade whites to cross over the Indian boundary line to hunt or to drive their livestock there to graze. Even to enter the Indian country south of the Ohio required a special passport issued by the governor of one of the states or by a commander of a frontier military post. Unauthorized settlers would lose any claim they might have to the lands they settled on or surveyed and suffer fine and imprisonment as well, and the president could use force to remove them.[47]

The federal government was determined to defend the integrity of the Indian country, but the United States itself was sometimes forced to seek concessions from the Indians. This occurred particularly in two cases: the acquisition of land within the Indian country for military posts, agencies, and trading houses, and acquisition for roads connecting important settlements or major segments of American territory. Getting land for the military posts and other government establishments caused little trouble because the troops of the United States were generally looked upon with respect by the Indians. Military forces within the Indian lands were more a protection than a threat and did not form a wedge for whites to intrude into the forbidden lands. The agencies and factories also worked for the benefit of the Indians.

The running of roads through the Indian country was a more controversial question, for the Indians frequently objected to such invasion of their lands. The War Department instructed its agents to proceed with great caution in persuading the Indians to grant permission for the roads and to offer

47. 1 *United States Statutes* 330, 470.

suitable inducements and compensation. With requests for the roads also went requests for sites of land on which "houses of entertainment" might be set up for the refreshment of the travelers, and one inducement used to win the agreement of the Indians was that the Indians themselves might profit from running such establishments. Though permission was sometimes delayed, the United States generally won its point, and treaties with the Indians contained specific articles authorizing the roads. Some of the intercourse laws mentioned roads when outlining the lands reserved to the Indians.[48]

Such small and authorized encroachments on Indian lands were insignificant in comparison with the illegal onrush of settlers, whose pressure was usually so great that the United States could not enforce the intercourse laws with any complete success. The Indians, who made valiant attempts to stave off the onslaught when it became apparent that the federal government was powerless to protect their rights, were little by little crushed, liquidated, or driven west. But the laws of Congress, the proclamations of the president, and the orders issued by the War Department did provide a brake on the westward rolling juggernaut.[49]

In the end, the force of the intruders was too great to be held back. Temporarily it could be halted, but the intruders were a mobile lot. They had moved in easily the first time, and if they were removed by military force, they could just as easily return. When the troops departed from the area, back streamed the settlers. Although the government repeatedly directed the Indian agents and the military commanders to carry out the law, little was accomplished. Then came the War of 1812 and the Creek War of 1813 – 1814, which turned attention to more serious troubles. The outcome of it all was what had already come to be expected—an expectation that no doubt took much of the edge off the zeal of officers responsible for removing the intruders. The more frequently the government acquiesced in the illegal settlements, the more difficult it became to take effective action. The settlers knew that they would be treated considerately. They had little fear that civil action would succeed against them, and there was an increasing number of examples of government action to cover such settlements through formal treaties that extinguished the Indian title.

A serious weakness in the protection of the Indian country was the shortage of troops to enforce the removal of intruders. The peacetime establishment of the regular army was altogether inadequate to the task. An

---

48. Secretary of war to William C. C. Claiborne, July 9, 1803, Carter, *Territorial Papers*, 5: 221–22; secretary of war to Benjamin Hawkins, February 11, 1804, ibid., pp. 306–7; Albert Gallatin to John Badollet, August 14, 1806, ibid., 7: 378–80; Kappler, pp. 30, 55, 56.
49. Prucha, *American Indian Policy in the Formative Years*, pp. 147–65.

attempt was made to use Indian troops, but because they were the beneficiaries of the action, the government balked at paying them for their
military service. In Georgia, the incessant intrusion onto Cherokee lands
led finally to the enrollment of volunteer troops at regular army pay to
drive out the violators. Joseph McMinn, as Cherokee agent, ordered the
mustering in of the volunteers and dispatched them to drive out the settlers. Armed with large butcher knives to cut down the corn of the intruders and with many mounted on horses they themselves had supplied, the
volunteers drove into the trouble spots, destroying the crops and burning
fences and houses. The intruders showed considerable hostility, and in the
engagement one of the settlers was killed by the troops, for which the
officers and two of the privates were haled into court.[50]

Even where regular troops were available, the officers often hesitated
to act, for they risked court action. "Every subaltern in the command
knows," reported one civilian traveler, "that if he interferes between an Indian and a white man, he will be sued instantly in the courts of the State.
When I was at Prairie du Chien, there were several of the officers who had
been cited to appear in court for having, pursuant to order, removed 'squatters' from the Indian lands over the Mississippi. The Indians then despise
the agent, because he is clothed with no military authority; and the pioneer despises the military, because their hands are tied by the local civil
power, whatever it be."[51]

Certain elemental conditions formed the basis of these difficulties.
Given the nature of American western settlement, there was an inherent
antagonism between the frontiersmen and any governmental force that
tried to inhibit their activities. The deep-seated desire for land found the
restrictions of the government an obstruction. Americans were expansion-
minded; it seemed part of their very nature. Too often the government was
helpless, even had it had the will, to hold in check the men who squatted
on land not yet officially open to them, whether it was public land or Indian country.[52]

On top of this foundation there was often built a superstructure of personal animosity. Martinets of army officers who expected the free-living

50. Ibid., pp. 165–66. Examples of problems in enforcing the laws are given ibid., pp.
166–85.

51. Charles F. Hoffman, *A Winter in the West*, 2 vols. (New York: Harper and Brothers, 1835), 2: 86–87.

52. On March 3, 1807, a law was approved that forbade settling on public lands on
which the Indian title had been extinguished but which were not yet surveyed and
opened to settlement. 2 *United States Statutes* 445–46. The federal government had no
more success in restraining such squatters than it had in preventing settlement on Indian
lands. See Paul W. Gates, *History of Public Land Law Development* (Washington: Public
Land Law Review Commission, 1968), pp. 219–21.

citizens on the frontier to jump with military precision at the sound of their voice—commandants little loved by soldier and civilian alike—did not supply the diplomacy necessary for the smooth running of the frontier communities. Indian agents, zealous beyond measure, perhaps, for the interests of their charges and overbearing in their self-importance, who could not get along with either the military or the traders and settlers, added their own measure of intolerance. Frontier entrepreneurs or budding lawyers, who dreamed of their community as the future pride of the West (with whose ascent they too would be propelled upward), developed fanatical hatred of the army officers who attempted to clamp down on their manifold operations.

The history of intrusions on Indian lands, of course, raises the difficult question of the sincerity of the government in its policy of protecting Indian rights to the land. Certainly the legal basis was firm enough, and the doctrines of preemption and of Indian sovereignty were endorsed by the Supreme Court in a series of famous decisions. In *Fletcher* v. *Peck*, in 1810, the court asserted that the "nature of the Indian title, which is certainly to be respected by all courts, until it be legitimately extinguished, is not such as to be absolutely repugnant to seizin in fee on the part of the State."[53] In 1823, in *Johnson and Graham's Lessee* v. *McIntosh*, the court expanded this doctrine when it considered the case of two claimants to the same piece of land, one of whom had received the title directly from the Indians, the other by a patent from the government. Chief Justice Marshall, in giving the decision of the court, furnished a long disquisition about the nature of the Indian title to land and expatiated on the traditional doctrine of preemption. With numerous citations of colonial precedents to back up his contention, he maintained that the United States, or the several states, had the exclusive power to extinguish the Indian right of occupancy. Although the "absolute ultimate title" rested with the European discoverers, the Indians kept the right of occupancy. This right, Marshall declared, "is no more incompatible with a seizin in fee, than a lease for years, and might as effectually bar an ejectment." He continued, "It has never been contended that the Indian title amounted to nothing. Their right of possession has never been questioned."[54]

The laws and proclamations were explicit, and there were many instances of vigorous action to drive off illegal settlers. Yet in the long run, the settlers nearly always won out. Why did the government not take more effective measures to prevent encroachment? The answer lies partly in the insufficiency of the forces available to carry out the legislative measures and executive decisions. Indian agents simply lacked the necessary means.

53. *Fletcher* v. *Peck*, 6 Cranch 87.
54. *Johnson and Graham's Lessee* v. *McIntosh*, 8 Wheaton 543.

The civil authorities could not be relied upon to prosecute or convict violators; and the army on the frontier was too small to police the whole area
successfully.

But behind these failures was a larger issue. The federal government
was sincerely interested in preventing settlement on Indian lands only up
to a point, and it readily acquiesced in illegal settlement that had gone so
far as to be irremediable. The policy of the United States was based on an
assumption that white settlement should advance and the Indians withdraw. The federal government was interested primarily in seeing that this
process was as free of disorder and injustice as possible. It meant to restrain and govern the advance of the whites, not to prevent it forever. It
supported Indian claims as far as it could out of justice and humanity to
the Indians and above all as far as it was necessary to keep a semblance of
peace and to maintain Indian goodwill so that land could continue to be
ceded by the tribes. In the early decades of the nineteenth century the federal government was convinced that once the Indians had been permanently settled on lands west of the Mississippi, the problems of encroachment and of removing intruders would be unhappy memories of the past.
And in the end it looked for the civilization of the Indians and their assimilation into white society.

The energy of the government in removing intruders was, in fact, proportionate, either directly or inversely, to a number of other circumstances: to
the length of time during which the Indian claims were expected to be
maintained; to the seriousness of Indian objections to the intruders, as removal was often the only way to prevent an Indian war; to the necessity of
convincing the Indians of the government's good faith in order to keep
them in a proper frame of mind for some impending treaty at which more
concessions of land were to be sought; to the pressures of white settlement, for full-scale drives into an area usually led to new treaties of cession
rather than to removal of the whites; to the boldness and aggressiveness of
the agents and military commanders in enforcing the laws; to the military
forces available in the area where encroachment was threatened; to the
strength of frontier opposition to military action against the intruders; and
to the color of title that the settlers on Indian lands could display, as well
as the character of the settlers themselves.

CHAPTER 4

Government Trading
Houses (Factories)

Beginnings of the Factory System.

Jeffersonian Expansion.

Attack and Support.

The End of the Factories.

If military subjugation in the manner of Anthony Wayne was one way to assure peace on the frontier—and peace remained the great desire of President Washington—establishing friendship on the basis of trade was a preferable alternative. In his recommendations for a just and humane Indian policy at the end of the Revolutionary War, Washington wrote: "I think, if the Indian Trade was carried on, on Government Acct., and with no greater advance than what would be necessary to defray the expence and risk, and bring in a small profit, that it would supply the Indians upon much better terms than they usually are; engross their Trade, and fix them strongly in our Interest." The subsequent course of events did not change his mind about the benefits of a trading policy that would be fair to the Indians and free of abuses. He insisted that the trade must be free of fraud and extortion, supply goods plentifully and without delay, and provide a market for Indian commodities at a stated and fair price. Private traders were motivated by hope of profit and took advantage of the Indians to gain their end, Washington argued; therefore the government, which was interested only in reimbursement of costs, should undertake the trade itself. He looked to Congress for appropriate authorization, and when no action was forthcoming, he repeated his recommendation.[1]

1. George Washington to James Duane, September 7, 1783, *Writings of George Washington,* ed. John C. Fitzpatrick, 39 vols. (Washington: GPO, 1931–1944), 27: 137–38; annual messages of October 25, 1791, December 3, 1793, and November 19, 1794, Fred L.

BEGINNINGS OF THE FACTORY SYSTEM

The system of government trading houses that Washington envisaged was soon begun. A committee of the House of Representatives reported favorably on the president's proposal on December 1, 1794, noting that "it would conduce to the honor and prosperity of the United States to cultivate peace with the Indian tribes" and that "the establishment of trading houses, under the direction of the President of the United States, would have a tendency to produce this laudable and benevolent effect." On February 28, 1795, Congress took the plan under consideration. Congress was sympathetic, for as Josiah Parker of Virginia noted, some legislation of the sort was necessary "to conciliate the affections of a distressed and unhappy people, and as it might prevent the expenses of a war with them." The Indians, it was argued, "had common sense enough not to quit allies who supplied them with articles which they wanted, till we also made some effectual establishments of that kind." The measure, too, was seen as a part of a total system for dealing with the Indians: military force to protect the frontier from Indian incursions, laws to prevent white frontiersmen from "predatory invasion into the Indian country," and trading houses to supply the Indians' wants and to detach "their habits of trade and their affections from a foreign nation." Without the third element in the system, the first two would be ineffective. "It was clear as a sunbeam," one representative remarked, "that the establishment of a trade must be the foundation of amity."[2]

Congress was cautious, but it was willing to let the president try the matter as an experiment. It appropriated $50,000 to purchase goods for the Indians in 1795 and directed that the goods be sold under the direction of the president.[3]

With such small funds, only a small and experimental beginning could

---

Israel, ed., *The State of the Union Messages of the Presidents, 1790–1966*, 3 vols. (New York: Chelsea House, 1966), 1: 9, 19–20, 26. The government trading houses that resulted from Washington's insistence have been thoroughly studied by historians. Two extensive studies are Ora Brooks Peake, *A History of the United States Indian Factory System, 1795–1822* (Denver: Sage Books, 1954), which has many data but is not well presented; and Aloysius Plaisance, "The United States Government Factory System, 1796–1822" (Ph.D. dissertation, Saint Louis University, 1954), a careful, detailed study. See also Herman J. Viola, *Thomas L. McKenney: Architect of America's Early Indian Policy, 1816–1830* (Chicago: Swallow Press, 1974), pp. 6–70. Articles on individual factories are cited below.

2. ASP:IA, 1: 524; *Annals of Congress*, 3d Congress, 2d session, pp. 1262–63, 1276.

3. 1 *United States Statutes* 443. The laws generally speak of "trading houses" and "agents" in charge of them, but the terms "factory" and "factor" were also in common use. I use the terms interchangeably.

be made. Passing over the Six Nations, which were closely surrounded by white settlements, and the tribes north of the Ohio River, still negotiating for peace after Wayne's victory, the War Department decided to apply the money among the southern Indians only.[4] For the Creeks a factory was set up at Colerain, on the St. Marys River in Georgia, a point of easy access for goods and sufficiently close, it was mistakenly judged, to the Creeks.[5] To supply the Cherokees, and to a lesser extent the Chickasaws, another trading house was begun at Tellico Blockhouse in eastern Tennessee, where there was already a military post to which the Indians were accustomed to resort. There was some difficulty in obtaining supplies because of the need to provide General Wayne with goods for his treaty negotiations and for annuity payments to the Chickasaws, but goods were sent off in the fall as soon as they could be procured. Two-thirds of the funds were used for the Creek factory because it could be more easily supplied.

The success of this initial outlay prompted Congress in the next session to formalize the program of trading houses. The arguments in favor were much the same as they had been earlier—that private traders of the young nation were unable to compete with the strong British traders and that development of commerce with the Indians, whatever it might cost, was less expensive than war. Suggestions that it was no business of the government to engage in trade and motions for delay were overcome, and the measure became law on April 18, 1796.[6]

The law of 1796 gave the president authority to establish such trading houses on the southern and western frontiers or in the Indian country as he judged best for carrying on a "liberal trade" with the Indians. Money was provided for agents and clerks, to be appointed by the president, who were prohibited from engaging in any trade on their own account. To the fund of the previous year Congress now added $150,000, and the law di-

---

4. An account of the establishment of the first two houses is given in a report of Secretary of War Timothy Pickering, December 12, 1795, ASP:IA, 1: 583–84.

5. Colerain proved quite unsatisfactory, and in 1797 the factory was moved to Fort Wilkinson on the Oconee River. In 1806 it was moved to the site of Fort Hawkins and in 1817 to Fort Mitchell in Alabama. An excellent article on the Creek factory (in its various locations) is Ray H. Mattison, "The Creek Trading House: From Colerain to Fort Hawkins," *Georgia Historical Quarterly* 30 (September 1946): 169–84. Another account of Colerain, based on the William Eaton Papers in the Huntington Library, San Marino, California, is Louis B. Wright and Julia Macleod, "William Eaton, Timothy Pickering, and Indian Policy," *Huntington Library Quarterly* 9 (August 1946): 387–400. The relation of the United States Indian agent and the first two southern factories is explored in George D. Harmon, "Benjamin Hawkins and the Federal Factory System," *North Carolina Historical Review* 9 (April 1932): 138–52.

6. Debate on the bill is recorded in *Annals of Congress*, 4th Congress, 1st session, pp. 229–32, 240–43, 282–85.

rected that prices were to be set at such a level that this capital stock not be diminished. Lest the trade in any way hinder the ultimate goal of civilizing the Indians in the white man's pattern, the law forbade agents to accept in trade guns, clothing, cooking utensils, or "any instrument of husbandry" obtained by the Indians in their intercourse with whites. The act was to run for two years and to the end of the next session of Congress thereafter.[7]

For some unexplained reason, the new legislation did not result in an expansion of the system, perhaps because President John Adams, a New Englander, did not push it aggressively.[8] Colerain (moved to Fort Wilkinson in 1797 in order better to supply the Creeks) and Tellico continued to be the only trading houses in operation, and when the legislation lapsed on March 3, 1799, no one seemed to notice. The end of the legislation did not liquidate the capital fund or remove the factors from their positions, and the system continued, law or no law.

JEFFERSONIAN EXPANSION

Thomas Jefferson stirred up the whole matter anew when he became president, for unlike his predecessor he had a deep and abiding interest in Indian affairs. His secretary of war, Henry Dearborn, reporting on the operation of the factories up to the end of 1801, found that not only had the capital not diminished, but it had increased 3 or 4 percent. He judged that the system had had a "very salutary effect on the minds of the Indians," and that such commerce had "a powerful tendency toward strengthening and confirming the friendship of the Indians to the people and Government of the United States, and toward detaching them more and more from the influence of neighboring Governments." He urged extension of

7. 1 *United States Statutes* 452–53.

8. Adams appeared to have little interest in Indian problems while he was president, although he later prided himself on observing peace. "I was engaged in the most earnest, sedulous, and, I must own, expensive exertions to preserve peace with the Indians, and prepare them for agriculture and civilization, through the whole of my administration," he wrote. "I had the inexpressible satisfaction of complete success. Not a hatchet was lifted in my time; and the single battle of Tippecanoe has since cost the United States a hundred times more money than it cost me to maintain universal and perpetual peace. . . . My labors were indefatigable to compose all difficulties and settle all controversies with all nations, civilized and savage." Adams to James Lloyd, March 31, 1815, *The Works of John Adams*, ed. Charles Francis Adams, 10 vols. (Boston: Little, Brown and Company, 1850–1856), 10: 153. For a discussion of Adams's views and activities, see Frederick M. Binder, *The Color Problem in Early National America as Viewed by John Adams, Jefferson and Jackson* (The Hague: Mouton, 1968), pp. 32–47.

the system. Noting the lapse of authorization for the factories, Jefferson asked Congress to revive the system and to extend it.[9]

On April 30, 1802, Congress obliged by renewing the act of 1796 and extending it until March 4, 1803.[10] A new flurry of activity resulted. Trading houses were established in 1802 at Fort St. Stephens among the Choctaws on the Tombigbee River in Alabama, at Chickasaw Bluffs among the Chickasaws in western Tennessee, at Fort Wayne in Indiana, and at Detroit.[11]

There was no letup. Jefferson sent a special message to Congress at the beginning of 1803 in which he urged continuation of the trading houses, for they were an integral part of what he considered an essential Indian policy. The pressure on Indian lands had been so great that many Indians were resisting further diminution of their land. "It hazards their friendship and excites dangerous jealousies and perturbations in their minds," Jefferson said, "to make any overture for the purchase of the smallest portions of their land." Two measures, he believed, were called for. One was to encourage the Indians to abandon hunting and to adopt the agriculture and husbandry of the whites, proving to them that less land would maintain them better under such operations than their traditional mode of living. The second was to multiply trading houses among them and thus put within their reach means of domestic comfort. Jefferson hoped thus to arrange a mutually advantageous exchange—the Indians would give up unnecessary lands and receive the means to carry on the white man's agricultural existence. He pointed out to Congress that the system was succeeding with its liberal trade policies. Private traders, both foreign and domestic, were undersold and driven from the field, and the nation was ridding itself of a class of men who constantly endeavored to excite the

9. Report of Henry Dearborn, December 8, 1801, ASP:IA, 1: 654–55; Jefferson to Congress, January 28, 1802, ibid., p. 653.

10. 2 *United States Statutes* 173.

11. The Choctaw factory at Fort St. Stephens was moved to Fort Confederation, farther up the Tombigbee, in 1817; the factory at Chickasaw Bluffs was moved to Spadra Bluffs on the Arkansas River in 1818. A detailed history of the operation of the Choctaw factory is given in Aloysius Plaisance, "The Choctaw Trading House, 1803–1822," *Alabama Historical Quarterly* 16 (Fall–Winter 1954): 393–423. For the history of the Chickasaw Bluffs factory, see Plaisance, "The Chickasaw Bluffs Factory and Its Removal to the Arkansas River, 1818–1822," *Tennessee Historical Quarterly* 11 (March 1952): 41–57. Information on one of the factors at Spadra Bluffs is given in George L. Montagno, "Matthew Lyon's Last Frontier," *Arkansas Historical Quarterly* 16 (Spring 1957): 46–53. Invoices, inventories, and memorials from the factory at Fort Wayne, 1802–1811, are printed in Bert J. Griswold, ed., *Fort Wayne, Gateway of the West, 1802–1813* (Indianapolis: Historical Bureau of the Indiana Library and Historical Department, 1927), pp. 401–663. They furnish an exhaustive listing of the trade goods sent to the factory and of the furs received.

Indian mind with suspicions, fears, and irritations toward the Americans.[12]

In a private letter to William Henry Harrison, governor of Indiana Territory, the president spoke eloquently and candidly about his views. "Our system," he told Harrison, "is to live in perpetual peace with the Indians, to cultivate an affectionate attachment for them, by everything just and liberal which we can do for them within the bounds of reason, and by giving them effectual protection against wrongs from our own people." But fundamentally, he hoped "to draw them to agriculture, to spinning and weaving." Then, as they came to need less land they would willingly sell to the whites. "To promote this disposition to exchange lands, which they have to spare and we want, for necessaries, which we have to spare and they want," he said, "we shall push our trading houses, and be glad to see the good and influential individuals among them run in debt, because we observe that when these debts get beyond what the individuals can pay, they become willing to lop them off by a cession of lands." With the trading houses underselling private traders, the country would "get clear of this pest without giving offence or umbrage to the Indians."[13]

Congress kept the system afloat by renewing the 1796 act again in 1803, and in 1805 it appropriated $100,000 for additional trading houses. New factories appeared in 1805 at Chicago, at Belle Fontaine on the Missouri River just north of St. Louis, at Natchitoches on the Red River in Louisiana, and at Arkansas Post on the Arkansas River. A year later another was opened at Sandusky, Ohio.[14]

With such far-flung and increasing activity, it was necessary to do more than revive from time to time the original law of 1796, and in 1806 Congress supplied more comprehensive legislation for the system. In addition to repeating the main provisions of the earlier legislation, it set the sum for trading goods, including previous appropriations, at $260,000 and authorized a superintendent of Indian trade to take charge of the whole business

12. Message of January 18, 1803, James D. Richardson, comp., *A Compilation of the Messages and Papers of the Presidents*, 10 vols. (Washington: GPO, 1896–1899), 1: 340–41.

13. Jefferson to Harrison, February 27, 1803, *The Writings of Thomas Jefferson*, ed. Andrew A. Lipscomb, 20 vols. (Washington: Thomas Jefferson Memorial Association, 1903–1904), 10: 369–71. In a similar letter to Secretary of War Dearborn, August 12, 1802, Jefferson spoke of the trading houses as "the cheapest & most effectual instrument we can use for preserving the friendship of the Indians." Clarence E. Carter, ed., *The Territorial Papers of the United States*, 26 vols. (Washington: GPO, 1934–1962), 7: 67–69.

14. 2 *United States Statutes* 207, 338. There is an account of the Chicago factory in Milo Milton Quaife, *Chicago and the Old Northwest, 1673–1835* (Chicago: University of Chicago Press, 1913), pp. 296–309. For the history of the factory at Arkansas Post, see Aloysius Plaisance, "The Arkansas Factory, 1805–1810," *Arkansas Historical Quarterly* 11 (Autumn 1952): 184–200, and Wayne Morris, "Traders and Factories on the Arkansas Frontier, 1805–1822," ibid., 28 (Spring 1969): 32–40.

under the direction of the president. But Congress still could not see the trading houses as any more than a temporary expedient and provided that the act was to run for three years only.[15]

The creation of the Office of Indian Trade was a milestone in developing the federal machinery for dealing with Indian problems. Before 1806 there had been no official in the government whose full duties concerned the Indians; the secretary of war, under the president, looked after what business there was. The goods for the factories were purchased by a succession of purchasing agents operating in Philadelphia. Now, with the superintendent of Indian trade, there was someone who could attend to the important trading functions and who gradually became the focus for nonmilitary Indian matters.

The first superintendent was John Shee of Philadelphia, appointed on July 8, 1806. He was a shadowy figure who made no appreciable mark on the office, and he was replaced in October 1807 by John Mason, president of the Bank of Columbia in the District of Columbia. Mason was an able officer, and the factory system expanded in his early years, with additional houses established in 1808 at Fort Osage on the Missouri River, at Mackinac Island, and at Fort Madison on the west bank of the Mississippi at the mouth of the Des Moines River. These new posts reflected the advance of the American frontier; as the Indians were pushed westward by white settlement, old factories were closed, and new ones, more convenient for the changing circumstances of the trade, were substituted. In 1809, while extending the life of the system for another three years, Congress appropriated an additional $40,000 for the trade and authorized an additional clerk in the office of the superintendent.[16]

Much of the formalizing of the activities and duties of the factors was the work of Mason, who sent full instructions to these agents. He dictated the percentage of markup on the goods sold, where to ship their furs and peltries, restrictions on their trading activities, and the kind of accounts they were to keep. The factors were to sell to Indians only, except in "very particular and pressing cases" and then with an additional charge of 10 percent. Credit was allowed "with caution, to principal chiefs of good character." The sale of liquor was strictly prohibited.[17]

It was an active and relatively thriving business. At the beginning of 1812, Mason, reporting on the preceding four years, showed $290,000 employed out of the $300,000 of capital stock authorized and a profit for the period of $14,171.30. The southern factories were doing poorly, however,

---

15. 2 *United States Statutes* 402–4.

16. 2 *United States Statutes* 544–45.

17. Circular of Mason to agents, December 12, 1807, ASP: IA, 2: 520–21; Mason to Matthew Irwin, September 9, 1808, *Wisconsin Historical Collections*, 19: 326–30.

for they depended largely on deerskins, for which the home market was deficient, whereas the northern factories, dealing chiefly in hatters' furs, for which the home demand was greater than the supply, generally showed sizable profits. The northern posts also received other goods from the Indians—buffalo tallow and candles at Fort Osage, maple sugar at Mackinac, and lead at Fort Madison.[18] Mason and his successor carried on their activities from headquarters in Georgetown, whither the office had been moved from Philadelphia in 1807. Using the former Bank of Columbia building, a three-story brick building still standing on M Street in Georgetown, the Office of Indian Trade with its small staff and long hours conducted its manifold business.[19]

Apparently satisfied with the operation of the factories in these years, Congress continued the system in 1811 with a new basic law. Repeating most of the 1806 act and its supplements, the new law specifically authorized the factors and in a very general way described their duties. The capital stock of $300,000 was continued, and the president was authorized to open additional houses. An indication of the growing responsibility of the superintendent of Indian trade was the directive that in future he was to purchase and distribute, in addition to the goods for the trading houses, all the goods needed for annuities and presents to the Indians and for treaty purposes.[20]

Mason seems to have handled these duties effectively, but he and his successor operated within a bureaucratic snarl that must have been disconcerting at best. No clear administrative responsibility was given to the superintendent, although he seems to have operated vaguely within the War Department, which had general charge of Indian affairs. The secretary of war approved the dates for auctioning off the furs collected, and accounts relating to annuities and presents were reviewed by the War Department. The Indian trade accounts, on the other hand, had to be sent to the Treasury. Because the War Department and the Treasury Department were eventually serviced by different auditors and comptrollers, the separation of the paper work was troublesome. The appointment of factors and the opening and closing of factories, of course, had to be done under the eye of the president.[21]

18. Report of Mason, January 13, 1812, with attached documents, ASP:IA, 1: 782–94. A previous, less detailed report of April 12, 1810, showed a diminution of the capital amounting to roughly $44,500. Ibid., pp. 768–75.

19. An excellent description of the routine is given in Viola, *McKenney*, pp. 10–20. Extensive details on the operations of the Office of Indian Trade also appear in Peake, *Indian Factory System*, and Plaisance, "United States Government Factory System."

20. 2 *United States Statutes* 652–55.

21. Viola, *McKenney*, pp. 8–9, 306–7. Although the act of 1806 did not specify subordination of the superintendent of Indian trade to the secretary of war (his work was to be done under the direction of the president, with accounts sent to the Treasury Depart-

MAP 1: United States Factory System, 1795–1822

Fort Mackinac
St. Peters
Green Bay
Prairie du Chien
Detroit
Chicago
Fort Armstrong
Fort Wayne
Sandusky
Fort Madison
Fort Edwards
Fort Osage
Belle Fontaine
Marais des Cygnes
Spadra Bluffs
Chickasaw Bluffs
Hiwassee
Tellico
Arkansas Post
Sulphur Fork
Fort Confederation
Fort Wilkinson
Fort Hawkins
Natchitoches
Fort Mitchell
Fort St. Stephens
Colerain

Minnesota R.
Mississippi R.
Wisconsin R.
Des Moines R.
Missouri R.
Wabash R.
Ohio R.
Arkansas R.
Red R.
Mississippi R.
Tennessee R.
Alabama R.
Tombigbee R.
Oconee R.
Ocmulgee R.

(modern state lines shown)

The connection of the factory system with the War Department was important on the frontier, for the association of the factories and the military posts was very close. The success of the government trading operations was due in part to the protection and assistance given to the factories by

ment), it is interesting to note that Thomas L. McKenney's appointment as superintendent was signed by the secretary of war as well as by the president and bore the seal of the War Department. Commission, in Huntington Library, HM 1926.

TABLE 1: Government Trading Houses (Factories), 1795–1822

1. COLERAIN (Georgia)
   Established 1795; moved to Fort
   Wilkinson 1797

2. TELLICO (Tennessee)
   Established 1795; moved to
   Hiwassee 1807

3. FORT WILKINSON (Georgia)
   Established 1797; moved to
   Ocmulgee Old Fields 1806;
   designated Fort Hawkins 1808

4. FORT ST. STEPHENS (Alabama)
   Established 1802; moved to Fort
   Confederation 1817

5. CHICKASAW BLUFFS (Tennessee)
   Established 1802; moved to
   Spadra Bluffs 1818

6. FORT WAYNE (Indiana)
   Established 1802; closed 1812

7. DETROIT (Michigan)
   Established 1802; closed 1805

8. CHICAGO (Illinois)
   Established 1805; destroyed 1812;
   reopened 1815; closed 1821

9. BELLE FONTAINE (Missouri)
   Established 1805; closed 1808

10. NATCHITOCHES (Louisiana)
    Established 1805; moved to
    Sulphur Fork 1818

11. ARKANSAS POST (Arkansas)
    Established 1805; closed 1810

12. SANDUSKY (Ohio)
    Established 1806; destroyed 1812

13. OCMULGEE OLD FIELDS (Georgia)
    Established 1806; designated
    Fort Hawkins 1808

14. HIWASSEE (Tennessee)
    Established 1807; closed 1811

15. FORT OSAGE [Fort Clark] (Missouri)
    Established 1808; reopened at Arrow
    Rock 1813; reestablished 1815;
    closed 1822

16. FORT MACKINAC (Michigan)
    Established 1808; captured by
    British 1812

17. FORT MADISON (Iowa)
    Established 1808; closed 1812

18. FORT HAWKINS (Georgia)
    Designated 1808; moved to Fort
    Mitchell 1817

19. GREEN BAY (Wisconsin)
    Established 1815; closed 1821

20. PRAIRIE DU CHIEN (Wisconsin)
    Established 1815; closed 1822

21. FORT CONFEDERATION (Alabama)
    Established 1817; closed 1822

22. FORT MITCHELL (Alabama)
    Subagency of Fort Hawkins 1816;
    principal factory 1817; closed 1819

23. FORT JOHNSON [Le Moin] (Illinois)
    Branch of Prairie du Chien 1817;
    moved to Fort Edwards 1819

24. SPADRA BLUFFS (Arkansas)
    Established 1818; closed 1822

25. SULPHUR FORK (Arkansas)
    Established 1818; closed 1822

26. FORT EDWARDS (Illinois)
    Established 1819; moved to Fort
    Armstrong 1821

27. MARAIS DES CYGNES (Missouri)
    Branch of Fort Osage 1820; inde-
    pendent factory 1821; closed 1822

28. FORT ARMSTRONG (Illinois)
    Established 1821; closed 1822

29. ST. PETERS (Minnesota)
    Authorized 1821 as consolidation
    of Green Bay and Chicago; never
    opened

Note: Dates are approximate, for dates of authorization and actual opening, and dates
for termination and actual closing, were not always the same.

the regular army garrisons. All but four of the trading houses were in the shadow of an existing military post or were themselves the occasion for the building of a fort. The forts protected the factories, the presence of the soldiers enhanced the factors' prestige in the eyes of the Indians, and the troops were sometimes the only labor force on hand to build the factories, transport their goods, and aid in the beating and packing of furs.[22]

ATTACK AND SUPPORT

The promising state of the factories was devastated by the War of 1812. The British and the Indians seized the trading houses at Mackinac, Chicago, Sandusky, and Fort Wayne, and the army officer at Fort Madison ordered the destruction of the store there to prevent the goods from falling into the hands of the enemy. The estimated loss was $43,369.61.[23]

This serious economic blow was quickly overcome, however. When Mason reported on the operation of the system from 1811 through 1815, he was able to indicate a net gain of nearly $12,500, even accounting for the destruction during the war. In 1815 the post at Chicago was reopened, and two new ones—at Green Bay and at Prairie du Chien—were established. Congress in the same year continued its game of renewing the enabling legislation, this time until March 4, 1817.[24]

More dangerous than the physical losses of the war were the changed conditions of the American fur trade after the Treaty of Ghent. The spirit of enterprise blossomed forth with the rise of American nationalism that came at the end of the war. When foreign traders were prohibited from the fur trade in 1816, the American Fur Company of John Jacob Astor began to push steadily for control of the fur trade in the area of the Great Lakes and the upper Mississippi. The years between the War of 1812 and the abolition of the factories in 1822 were years of dramatic conflict between the increasingly powerful private fur trading interests—powerful both economically and politically—and the embattled but defiant supporters of the government trading houses. The attacks and counterattacks filled official reports and the public press and provide a detailed picture of the American fur trade in the years after the war.

Some of the criticism of the factories came from western officials, who,

22. Francis Paul Prucha, *The Sword of the Republic: The United States Army on the Frontier, 1783–1846* (New York: Macmillan Company, 1969), pp. 99–101, 207.

23. Mason to William H. Crawford, February 9, 1816, ASP:IA, 2: 67–68, also Table Fm, p. 59. These and numerous other reports on the factory system are attached to the report sent to the Senate by Secretary of War Crawford, March 13, 1816, ibid., pp. 26–88.

24. Report of Mason, February 9, 1816, ASP:IA, 2: 67–68; 3 *United States Statutes* 239.

although friendly with private fur traders, might have been expected to know enough about conditions on the frontier to offer objective and valuable advice. One such person was Ninian Edwards, governor of Illinois Territory since 1809, who flatly told the secretary of war: "For my part, I have never been able to discover, and I defy any man to specify, a solitary public advantage that has resulted from it [the factory system] in this country." The system, he said, was "neither calculated to conciliate and accommodate the Indians, nor for successful competition with British traders." It was not extensive enough to provide for all the Indian tribes, and defects in its functioning—such as restrictions on credit and the requirement that the Indians bring in their furs to the factories—made it "good policy to abandon it."[25]

Another critic was the governor of Michigan Territory, Lewis Cass. As early as 1814 Cass had noted that the trading factories and "our economy in presents" had led the Indians to scorn the United States. "The Government," he told the secretary of war, "should never Come in contact with them, but in cases where its Dignity, its strength or its liberality will inspire them with respect or fear." After the War of 1812 he argued that there was sufficient private American capital to carry on the fur trade effectively and that there was no need then for the government to engage in the business; that, in fact, such mercantile enterprise made the government "obnoxious and contemptible" to the Indians. Since the Indians, if sober, were shrewd bargainers, the private traders could not take undue advantage of them. All that was necessary on the part of the government was to exclude liquor from the Indian country. "Believing as I do," Cass asserted, "that the system itself is radically incorrect I cannot but recommend its abolition."[26]

The Reverend Jedidiah Morse, reporting to the secretary of war in 1821 on conditions in the Indian country, returned a similar verdict. He found that the general consensus was against the system, and he advocated its abolition.[27]

The government officials responsible for the program were not so ready

25. Edwards to William H. Crawford, November 1815, ASP:IA, 2: 62–67.

26. Cass to John Armstrong, September 3, 1814, Carter, *Territorial Papers*, 10. 4/6; Cass to John C. Calhoun, September 14, 1818, *Wisconsin Historical Collections*, 20: 82–86. Cass had no sooner written to the secretary of war than he had second thoughts about his absolute rejection of the factory system, admitting that his opinion was "more speculative than practical." Consequences of abolition, he admitted, might be equally injurious. Cass to Calhoun, October 1, 1818, Records of the Office of Indian Affairs, Field Office Records, Michigan Superintendency, Letters Sent by the Superintendent, National Archives, Record Group 75 (M1, reel 4).

27. Jedidiah Morse, *A Report to the Secretary of War of the United States: On Indian Affairs* (New Haven: S. Converse, 1822), pp. 60–61. For an extensive survey of the criticism, see Peake, *Indian Factory System*, pp. 184–203.

to give up. Secretary of War William Crawford in 1816 advocated not only its continuation but its extension, with capital stock increased to $500,000. He wanted to use some of the extra money to establish a supply depot at St. Louis under an assistant superintendent, who would furnish goods not only to the government trading houses, but to respectable private traders under strict regulations. The financial problems of the factories did not overly concern Crawford, however, for profits were not the inducement for continuing them. "That inducement, if it exists at all," he observed, "must be found in the influence which it gives the Government over the Indian tribes within our limits, by administering to their wants, increasing their comforts, and promoting their happiness. The most obvious effect of that influence is the preservation of peace with them, and among themselves." He hoped by trade to develop in the Indians a concern for private property, and he showed unmistakably the growing humanitarian concerns of the advocates of the factories. His views, he concluded, were "substantially founded upon the conviction that it is the true policy and earnest desire of the Government to draw its savage neighbors within the pale of civilization." If, on the contrary, the goal was to gain all their lands as quickly as possible, then the trade ought to be abandoned to private interests. "The result," Crawford asserted, "would be continued warfare, attended by the extermination or expulsion of the aboriginal inhabitants of the country to more distant and less hospitable regions." But not for a moment would he accept such a policy, an idea "opposed to every act of the Government, from the declaration of independence to the present day." He wanted a "humane and benevolent policy" that would ultimately incorporate the Indians into "the great American family of freemen."[28]

Crawford had the strong support of John Mason, whose views he was no doubt echoing. But Mason resigned on April 1, 1816, pleading the necessity of attending to his private business because of his large family.[29]

Mason was replaced by Thomas Loraine McKenney, one of the key figures in the development of American Indian policy, a sentimental and romantic man who could not always keep his accounts straight, who lived beyond his means, and who was continually trying to advance his importance in the political circles of the day, but withal a sincere humanitarian committed to the welfare and betterment of the Indians. McKenney, born in Maryland in 1785, was a merchant in Georgetown when the War of 1812 broke out. After military duty in the war, he sought a federal office suited to his talents. At last he obtained the superintendency of Indian trade. Taking office on Good Friday, April 12, 1816, the pious McKenney prayed: "Al-

28. Report of Crawford to the Senate, March 13, 1816, ASP:IA, 2: 26–28.
29. Mason to Crawford, March 6, 1816, ASP:IA, 2: 70; Records of the Office of Indian Trade, Letters Sent, vol. C, p. 495, National Archives, Record Group 75 (M16, reel 3).

mighty God! This day I have sworn faithfully and honestly, to discharge
the duties of Superintendent of Indian Trade—but as man in his best estate
is weak and helpless, always liable to err; and continually subject to the
casualties which often involve his good name, and his dearest interests,—I
do most humbly beseech Thee to grant me in all my labors the assistance
of thy Holy Spirit, through Jesus Christ our Lord. Amen."[30] McKenney
needed spiritual succor, for he bore the brunt of the growing attacks made
by the American Fur Company, some of which were aimed at him personally, not merely at the factory system.

McKenney used his office to further two intense and abiding views. One
was an abhorrence of private traders, whom he saw as the source of immeasurable evil in the Indian country. "In the course of my Superintendence of the trade established with the several Indian Tribes," he wrote to
the chairman of the House Committee on Indian Affairs in 1818, "it has
become part of my duty to take cognizance of such checks as are known to
operate against it. Among these, and foremost in this train, is the conduct
of the private traders, than which it is impossible to conceive of any thing
more obnoxious, if viewed in relation to the morals of the Indians; or more
destructive of that pacific result which the U.S. factories are or may be calculated to produce."[31]

An example of McKenney's concern were the reports he received from
Arkansas, where the traders were "almost literally drown[ing] that country
with whiskey" and stirring up the Indians against the government posts.
McKenney told the secretary of war:

> Indeed I am of opinion that this influence destroyed, a power
> would exist in the Factory . . . in withholding from them their looked
> for supplies, or granting them, as their bad or good conduct should
> dictate. But the Traders not only make them independent of the Gov^t
> supplies, (which however is done at the cost of exactions and the
> most unexampled debauchery) but stimulate them to become hos-
> tile, with a view to their entire monopoly of their trade, which the
> prostration of the Factory would enable them to realize upon terms
> even more enriching than those which their inebriating policy al-
> ready ensures to them.

McKenney's views were strongly supported by Major Thomas Biddle and
by Colonel Henry Atkinson from their experiences on the military expedition up the Missouri River. Biddle saw the "impossibility of civilizing the

30. Prayer by McKenney, April 12, 1816, written on the back of his commission from
President Madison, dated April 2, 1816, Huntington Library, HM 1926.
31. McKenney to Henry Southard, January 6, 1818, *Wisconsin Historical Collections*, 20: 12–16.

Early Indian Policy

1. Jefferson Indian Peace Medal

Thomas Jefferson was a key figure in the formulation of early Indian policy. His view of the unity of mankind and thus the innate equality of Indians and whites became the basis of humanitarian concern for the Indians and of the drive to educate them in the white man's civilization. This large medal bearing the president's likeness was the beginning of a series of round silver medals presented to Indian chiefs as a symbol of their allegiance to the United States.

2. Hopethle-Mico, a Creek Chief

The famous American artist John Trumbull made this pencil sketch of Hopethle-Mico when a Creek delegation came to New York in 1790 to negotiate a treaty with the United States. The artist wrote: "I had been desirous of obtaining portraits of some of these principal men, who possessed a dignity of manner, form, countenance and expression, worthy of Roman senators."

When a delegation of Osages and other Indians from the West came east in 1804 to confer with officials of the United States, some of them were drawn in crayon by the French artist Charles B. Saint Mémin. Payouska, an Osage chief, wears a large medal, an arm band, and a military uniform—all gifts highly prized by the Indians.

Although Secretary of War Henry Knox hoped to maintain peace with the Indians by dealing fairly with them, warfare broke out in the area north of the Ohio River when whites invaded the Indian lands. Fort Washington was established in 1789 at the site of present-day Cincinnati to serve as a base for military expeditions against the hostile Indians. After the Indians defeated the troops led by Josiah Harmar and Arthur St. Clair, General Anthony Wayne crushed Indian resistance at the Battle of Fallen Timbers in 1794.

3. Payouska, an Osage Chief

4. Henry Knox

5. Anthony Wayne

6. Fort Washington

7. William Clark

8. Meriwether Lewis

9. Zebulon M. Pike

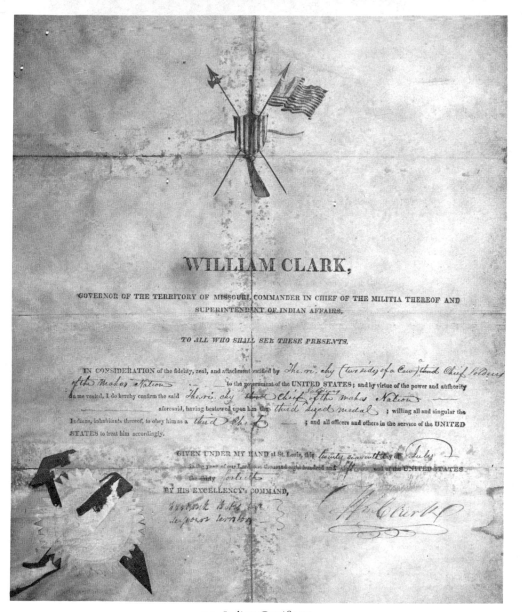

WILLIAM CLARK,

GOVERNOR OF THE TERRITORY OF MISSOURI, COMMANDER IN CHIEF OF THE MILITIA THEREOF AND
SUPERINTENDENT OF INDIAN AFFAIRS.

TO ALL WHO SHALL SEE THESE PRESENTS.

IN CONSIDERATION of the fidelity, zeal, and attachment testified by *The.ri. chy (twen idy of a Caw) thud Chief Soldier* *of the Mahas Nation* to the government of the UNITED STATES; and by virtue of the power and authority in me vested, I do hereby confirm the said *The.ri. chy thud Chief of the Mahas Nation* aforesaid, having bestowed upon him the *thud Sized medal*; willing all and singular the Indians, inhabitants thereof, to obey him as a *thud Chief*; and all officers and others in the service of the UNITED STATES to treat him accordingly.

GIVEN UNDER MY HAND at St. Louis, this *twenty seaventh* day of *July* in the year of our Lord one thousand eight hundred and *fifteen* and of the UNITED STATES the thirty *fortieth.*

BY HIS EXCELLENCY'S COMMAND,

10. Indian Certificate

Exploratory expeditions sought to convince the Indians in the West of the goodwill of the United States government. The Lewis and Clark expedition of 1804–1806 was the most dramatic, and after its return Clark became a key official in dealing with the Indians. Pike's two expeditions— one to the upper Mississippi and another across the central plains—were means of extending the influence of the United States against the British and Spanish.

The portraits of these three men were painted in his Philadelphia studio by Charles Willson Peale.

As governor of Missouri Territory, William Clark presented medals and certificates to Indian chiefs who came to Portage des Sioux in the summer of 1815 to make peace after the War of 1812. This certificate with a small medal was given to a minor Omaha chief.

11. Pawnee Council

12. Fort Snelling

Samuel Seymour, official artist with Stephen H. Long's exploring expedition, painted a picture of the council with the Pawnee Indians held in October 1819. The painting served as the basis for this engraving from Edwin James's *Account of an Expedition from Pittsburgh to the Rocky Mountains*.

Fort Snelling, established in 1819, was a key post in the West. This painting by Captain Seth Eastman, who commanded Fort Snelling in the 1840s, was one of a series of pictures of military forts done by Eastman when he was called upon in the 1870s to decorate the room of the House Committee on Military Affairs in the United States Capitol.

McKenney (painted by Charles Loring Elliott) and Calhoun (painted by John Wesley Jarvis) were significant leaders in the formulation of American Indian policy. The former served as superintendent of Indian trade (1816–1822) and as first head of the Indian Office within the War Department (1824–1830) and the latter was secretary of war (1817–1825). The two men worked closely together to develop a policy that would lead the Indians toward the ways of white society.

13. Thomas Loraine McKenney

14. John C. Calhoun

15. Wisconsin Territorial Seal

16. Astor Indian Medal

17. Lewis Cass

The seal designed by William Wagner for the Territory of Wisconsin in 1838 showed by its Latin motto, *Civilitas successit barbarum*, the pervasive belief of the age in stages of society progressing from savagery to barbarism to civilization.

John Jacob Astor's American Fur Company, in its competition with the trading houses of the United States, produced silver medals for the Indians in imitation of the official medals distributed by the federal government.

Cass, as governor of Michigan Territory (1813–1831) and as secretary of war (1831–1836) was a dominant force in American Indian affairs. This daguerreotype of about 1850–1855 shows the firm character of the man that impressed the Indians and won their respect.

Indians, when exposed to the temptations and delusions of interested traders," and both he and Atkinson recommended that all private trading be prohibited and that the government take over the entire business.[32]

The second major interest of McKenney, in which he built upon the work of his predecessor but went far beyond it, was the use of the factories as positive agencies for promoting the education and civilization of the Indians. He expected the factors to be more than tradesmen; they were to be key men in spreading the gospel of agriculture and domestic arts, to supply necessary tools and information, and to be models of what could be done in taming the wilderness.[33] But in addition to his instructions to the men at the trading houses, McKenney hoped to inaugurate a federal policy of education and civilization, and in this he broadly expanded his position as superintendent of Indian trade.

When President Madison asked Congress to resume "the work of civilization" with the Indians and the House Committee on Indian Affairs requested information of McKenney, the superintendent not only urged expansion of the factory system ($200,000 for eight new factories and a supply depot at St. Louis), but he proposed a network of schools to be run by the missionary societies and supervised by the superintendent of Indian trade.[34]

McKenney and his friends worked hard to push the school system, but their maneuvering was conducted in an atmosphere of near desperation, for the defenders of the factories were being forced to the wall by their attackers. McKenney may, in fact, have hoped that turning the system into a great civilizing and Christianizing agency would increase the prospects of its staying alive and, if this were the case, that his salary would also be increased as the system expanded.[35]

Undoubtedly there were problems in the factory system after the War of 1812. Although the trading houses made a reasonable recovery from the devastation of the war, the panic of 1819, which struck a severe blow at the whole economy, brought losses to the factories and a call upon Congress to cut federal spending. Returns from the sale of furs declined, and charges of mismanagement were easy to make. McKenney made excuses for the factories: the short term authorizations for the system gave it no permanence

---

32. McKenney to John C. Calhoun, July 16, 1819, Carter, *Territorial Papers*, 19: 86; Thomas Biddle to Henry Atkinson, October 29, 1819, ASP:IA, 2: 201–3; Atkinson to Calhoun, November 26, 1819, ibid., p. 204.

33. See, for example, McKenney to George C. Sibley, October 21, 1816, in Office of Indian Trade, Letters Sent, vol. D, pp. 152–53 (M16, reel 4).

34. Viola, *McKenney*, pp. 33–35; see McKenney to Isaac Thomas, December 14 and 23, 1816, January 3, 1817, Office of Indian Trade, Letters Sent, vol. D, pp. 200–209, 209–15, 217–25 (M16, reel 4).

35. For the outcome of the education drive, see below, pp. 148–54.

and did not allow for major improvements; the restrictions on giving credit and presents to the Indians weakened its competitive stance against private traders; the prohibition against liquor turned many Indians toward more freehanded traders; and the machinations of the private traders harassed the factors in the field.[36]

McKenney continued to insist that an expanded factory system, with tightened control of private traders if they could not be excluded entirely from the trade, was the proper policy of the government. His emphasis was on the humanitarian effects of the government system, which were simply impossible under private traders motivated only by gain. He declared in 1818 that an end to the government factory system would cause the whole system of Indian reform to "tumble into ruins, and blast, at once, the happiness of thousands of Indians who now enjoy its benefits." He concluded:

> The existing Government system has its foundation in *benevolence*, and *reform*. Those are the two pillars, on which it rests. The Factors employed by the United States do not go to supply the more helpless parts of our Family with articles necessary for their support and security against the elements, and upon terms that embrace no more than a preservation of the capital employed, only, but also with implements of husbandry; with suitable instructions how to use them; and with invitations to seek their support from the Earth, and exchange, for her certain compensation, the uncertain products of the chase. The instructions [to] the Factors also, direct them to cultivate among the Indians a regard for, and attachment to our Government and Country.[37]

THE END OF THE FACTORIES

In the long run, McKenney's vision of benevolence and reform was overcome by John Jacob Astor and his political friends, who were alarmed by McKenney's efforts to maintain and expand the government system at the expense of private traders. Ramsay Crooks and Robert Stuart, Astor's lieutenants in the American Fur Company, wrote to Astor at the beginning of 1818 lamenting the competition of the factories, which had "become so

36. See the discussion of McKenney's defense of the factory system in Viola, *McKenney*, pp. 47–70.

37. McKenney to Calhoun, August 19, 1818, *Wisconsin Historical Collections*, 20: 69. Other statements of value are McKenney to Henry Southard, March 19, 1818, ibid., pp. 37–41; McKenney to Southard, November 30, December 30, 1820, March 17, 1821, Office of Indian Trade, Letters Sent, vol. F, pp. 99–104, 104–7, 151–53 (M16, reel 6); McKenney to Henry Johnson, December 27, 1821, ASP:IA, 2: 260–65.

numerous, and are of late provided with such extensive means, as threatens in a very few years more, to annihilate private competition, and throw the whole trade into the hands of Government." Astor was quick to pass on the complaint to Calhoun. "We have been great sufferers," he wrote, "so much so, that it would indeed be ruinous to continue the Trade under such circumstances."[38] And he sent Crooks to Washington to explain the "difficulties" in person. Crooks became a steady lobbyist against the factories, and a general harassment of the system started to come from Congress, beginning with a resolution asking the secretary of war to report "a system for providing for the abolition of the existing Indian trading establishment."[39]

That the concept of government trading houses had at best an uncertain hold on the mind of Congress is evident from the congressional refusal to extend the system more than a short period at a time. In March 1817 the factories were authorized until May 1, 1818; then their life was extended until March 1, 1819; in 1819 they were granted a reprieve for one more year, then for another one, and finally in 1821 for still another single year.[40] At each renewal the contest grew more bitter between the supporters of the factories and their opponents; after 1820 there was an all-out attempt on the part of the American Fur Company to have Congress do away with the system altogether. Crooks expressed his determination in a candid letter to Astor, who was then in Europe.

> I shall follow your advice in again visiting Washington, and will use every fair means to obtain a decision on the Public Trading House system. Last session a respectable majority voted against their continuance, but Congress had to rise on the 3d March without having time to act finally on the subject, in consequence of the Government Officers having resorted to every means in their power to delay its consideration. It will be brought forward early this session, and I have reason to think will be warmly supported, for enough is now known of the subject to excite enquiry, and if a thorough investigation is had, the abolition of these useless establishments is in my opinion sure. Great efforts will be made by Mr McKenney, & his

38. Crooks and Stuart to Astor, January 24, 1818, *Wisconsin Historical Collections,* 20: 26; Astor to Calhoun, March 4, 1818, *Papers of John C. Calhoun,* ed. Robert L. Meriwether, W. Edwin Hemphill, and Clyde N. Wilson, 14 vols. to date (Columbia: University of South Carolina Press, 1959–), 2: 191–92. There is an account of the American Fur Company's opposition to the factory system in Kenneth Wiggins Porter, *John Jacob Astor, Business Man,* 2 vols. (Cambridge: Harvard University Press, 1931), 2: 709–14.

39. *House Journal,* 15–1, serial 4, p. 420. Calhoun's reply of December 5, 1818, is in ASP: IA, 2: 181–85; it follows closely McKenney to Calhoun, August 14, 1818, *Wisconsin Historical Collections,* 20: 66–79.

40. 3 *United States Statutes* 363, 428, 514, 544, 641.

friends to save the Factories. His official reports to the Indian Committee will villify the Traders, and whine over the unfortunate &
helpless conditions of the poor Indians, who will be left to the mercy
of these unprincipled private traders; but all this will avail him little,
for his canting is too well known, and his only resource will be falsehood, to which he has more than once resorted. Exposition will become necessary, and may involve us in a paper war, but the consequences must be encountered; for I cannot, and will not tamely
submit to his scurilous abuse.[41]

The American Fur Company and the St. Louis fur traders enlisted the
aid of Senator Thomas Hart Benton, who entered the Senate in 1821 and
who became a great supporter of western interests. With vigorous rhetoric
and biting sarcasm, he railed against the factories in 1822. He asserted that
great abuses had been committed in the purchase of goods by the superintendent, who had bought some goods ill suited to the Indian trade and others of bad quality and had purchased goods at high prices in eastern markets when they would have cost less in western ones. He accused the
superintendent of mismanagement in the disposition of goods to the Indians and in the sale of the furs and peltries taken in trade. Benton was at
his best in ridiculing allegedly useless goods purchased for the factories. In
the list of items sent out in 1820, he hit upon eight gross of jew's harps. He
had fun regaling the Senate with examples of music that would sooth savage breasts. The jew's harps, he said, were

> precisely adapted to the purposes of the superintendent, in reclaim-
> ing the savage from the hunter state. The first state after that, in the
> road to refined life, is the pastoral, and without music the tawney-
> colored Corydons and the red-skinned Amaryllises, *"recubans sub
> tegmine fagi,"* upon the banks of the Missouri and the Mississippi,
> could make no progress in the delightful business of love and senti-
> ment. Even if the factories should be abolished, these harps might
> not be lost. They might be "hung upon the willows," and Æolus, as
> he passes by, might discourse upon them melancholy music, "soft
> and sad," adapted to the vicissitudes of human affairs, the death of
> the factories, and the loss of that innocent age they were intended to
> introduce.[42]

This was unfair, of course, for jew's harps were a standard article in the
Indian trade, and Benton's friends of the American Fur Company sent large

---

41. Crooks to Astor, November 30, 1821, American Fur Company Letter Books, 2:
177–78, photostatic copies at the State Historical Society of Wisconsin.

42. *Annals of Congress*, 17th Congress, 1st session, pp. 319–20.

numbers of them to the frontier. But Benton offered more than amusing ridicule. He produced reports from Indian agents John Biddle and Benjamin O'Fallon, from John R. Bell, an army officer who had accompanied the expedition of Stephen H. Long in 1820, and from Ramsay Crooks himself, all denouncing the iniquities of the factory system. O'Fallon, in addition, condemned the misdeeds of McKenney and his agents, who were alleged to be growing rich in the service.[43]

Benton did his work well. He succeeded in amending a bill introduced for the abolition of the factories by providing that the business of liquidating the factories be taken out of the hands of McKenney and the factors and assigned to special agents. So amended, the bill to terminate the factory system became law on May 6, 1822.[44] Ramsay Crooks congratulated Senator Benton on the victory: "The result is the best possible proof of the value to the country of talents, intelligence, & perseverance; and you deserve the unqualified thanks of the community for destroying the pious monster, since to your unwearied exertions, and sound practical knowledge of the whole subject, the country is indebted for its deliverance from so gross and [un]holy an imposition."[45] The two had sufficient reason for rejoicing. The trade now became the unimpeded domain of the private traders and the powerful fur company.

Although the law specified that the factories be closed on June 3, 1822, in fact the process dragged out for a number of years. Benton's insistence that the closing be done by others than McKenney and his agents indicated his hope that evidence of fraud and mismanagement would be uncovered. McKenney tried in vain to get permission for the present employees to close out the business. Instead, George Graham, who at one time had served as acting secretary of war, was put in charge of the liquidation. He was familiar with the operations of the factory system, but the other special agents knew little about the business. Considerable losses were incurred as Graham and his men sought to sell or otherwise dispose of the property. An investigation by the House of Representatives exonerated McKenney in 1823 of any misdeeds in his handling of the factory business, but it was not until 1833 that all his accounts were straightened out.[46]

In the heyday of the factories during Jefferson's administration, the

43. The reports of these critics are printed in ASP:IA, 2: 326–32. A long rebuttal by McKenney with supporting documents appears ibid., pp. 354–64. The same material is printed in *Senate Document* no. 60, 17–1, serial 59.

44. 3 *United States Statutes* 679–80.

45. Crooks to Benton, April 1, 1822, American Fur Company Letter Books, 2: 241.

46. The story of the liquidation of the factories and of the charges brought against McKenney for mismanagement is told in Viola, *McKenney*, pp. 71–84. For documents on the closing of the factories, see *House Report* no. 104, 17–2, serial 87; *House Report* no. 129, 18–1, serial 106; and *House Document* no. 61, 18–2, serial 116.

United States had written into treaties with the Sacs and Foxes and with the Osages a promise to establish and permanently maintain trading houses near them. With the abolition of the factories, these obligations were quietly abrogated by new treaties, in which the tribes agreed to release the government from its promise in return for payment in goods—$1,000 worth for the Sacs and Foxes and $2,329.40 for the Osages—taken from the closing factories.[47]

It cannot be said that the conduct of the Indian trade by the federal government was a failure, for the system was never really given a full chance. Unable to concede that circumstances might demand a government monopoly of the trade in order to end abuses and to supply the Indians fairly with the goods they needed, the government admitted a dual system, allowing private traders to engage in the trade (under a less than rigorous licensing system) while at the same time engaging in the trade itself on a nonprofit basis. Once the private traders came into their own after the War of 1812, they squeezed out the factory system, which had never had more than halfhearted support from Congress, despite the strong rational arguments made in its behalf by McKenney, Calhoun, and other ardent supporters. The ineffectiveness of the factories, which their critics charged, was belied by the opposition itself, for the violence of the attacks is indication enough that the factories were offering serious competition. It may be that the proponents put too much burden on the system. Instead of working to correct recognized economic weaknesses, they intended to use the trading houses as a measure for benevolence and reform, humanitarian notions that could not stand up against the hardheaded, if not ruthless, economic policies of John Jacob Astor.[48] But the hope of some fair means by which the Indians could be supplied recurred again and again, and the dream of civilizing them came to depend on other means than the factory system, on which Thomas L. McKenney had pinned such high hopes.

47. Kappler, pp. 76, 95, 201–2.
48. The two final chapters in Peake, *Indian Factory System*, summarize the various reasons proposed for the system's failure.

Civilization
and Education

Much of the legislative program that established Indian policy aimed to avoid conflicts between white citizens and the Indians. It was thus largely negative and restrictive, as it sought to regulate trade and intercourse between the two races. Even the government trading houses, although they contained certain positive features in supplying the Indians with useful goods at fair prices and with good example, had as their primary objective the elimination of abuses in the fur trade.

Parallel to these restraining activities was a positive constructive attempt to change the Indians and their cultural patterns. Operating under the principles of the Enlightenment and of Christian philanthropy, government officials proposed to bring civilization to the Indians. It is here that the benevolent and paternalistic aspects of Indian policy appear most clearly. Although the first attempts were feeble and sporadic, they foreshadowed increasingly powerful efforts through the nineteenth century to Americanize the Indians.

CIVILIZATION

The proposals made to better the condition of the Indians all gave evidence of a deepseated and common conviction of what *civilization* meant, even though most of the officials concerned never bothered to think philosophically about the concept. They relied on the accepted wisdom of the day, which reflected ideas that were part of their Western European heritage.[1] *To civilize* meant to bring to a state of civility out of a state of rudeness and barbarism, to enlighten and refine. It meant as a minimum to lead persons who lived a natural life in the wilderness, relying upon hunting and gathering, to a state of society dependent upon agriculture and domestic arts (spinning and weaving); to this was added instruction in reading, writing, arithmetic, and the truths of the Christian religion.

The place of American Indians in the scheme of civilization depended on the way Americans viewed the Indians. Opinions varied from the extreme disdain of the aggressive frontiersman, who equated the Indians with wild beasts of the forest fit to be hunted down at will, to the romantic ideas of novelists like James Fenimore Cooper and poets like Henry Wadsworth Longfellow, who exalted the superhuman qualities of the "noble savage." But in between, among the responsible and respected public figures in the first decades of United States development, there was a reasonable consensus that was the underpinning of official policy toward the Indians.[2]

Among the first generation of American statesmen, Thomas Jefferson was surely the most important theorizer about the aborigines. He was a man of tremendous speculative interests, a scientist (according to the definition of his age) as well as a political philosopher, and one who so influenced his generation that we correctly speak of his age in American history as "Jeffersonian." Jefferson, setting a pattern that was not to be successfully challenged, considered the Indian to be by nature equal to the white man. Although he strongly suspected that the black was an inferior creature, he never for a moment relegated the Indian to such status. Thus he wrote un-

1. An excellent analysis of the history and meaning of the term *civilization* is in Charles A. Beard and Mary R. Beard, *The American Spirit: A Study of the Idea of Civilization in the United States* (New York: Macmillan Company, 1942), especially chapters 3–5, pp. 62–276. .

2. Several works deal with images of the Indian and theoretical speculatons about race. The most comprehensive is Robert F. Berkhofer, Jr., *The White Man's Indian: Images of the American Indian from Columbus to the Present* (New York: Alfred A. Knopf, 1978). See also Roy Harvey Pearce, *The Savages of America: A Study of the Indian and the Idea of Civilization* (Baltimore: Johns Hopkins Press, 1953), and a critique of the book by David Bidney, "The Idea of the Savage in North American Ethnohistory," *Journal of the History of Ideas* 15 (April 1954): 322–27. There are valuable insights in Winthrop D. Jordan, *White over Black: American Attitudes toward the Negro, 1550–1812* (Chapel Hill: University of North Carolina Press, 1968), although the book touches on Indians only incidentally. I also rely in this section on Francis Paul Prucha, "The Image of the Indian in Pre-Civil War America," *Indiana Historical Society Lectures, 1970–1971* (Indianapolis: Indiana Historical Society, 1971), pp. 2–19, from which some parts are taken directly.

equivocally in 1785: "I believe the Indian then to be in body and mind equal to the whiteman."[3]

His arguments rested on two principles. In the first place, he believed in an essential, fixed human nature, unchangeable by time or place, and he applied his principle of unity of mankind to the Indians. In the second place, as an ardent American, Jefferson could not accept a position that would have made the American natives a basically ignoble breed. In fact, his most detailed and most eloquent defense of the qualities of the Indians came in his *Notes on the State of Virginia*, in which he refuted the criticism of things American that appeared in the celebrated work of the French naturalist Georges Louis Leclerc de Buffon, who described the Indian as deficient in stature, strength, energy, mental ability, and family attachments. These aspersions Jefferson answered fully, and he entered a point-by-point refutation of the slanders. He insisted that the Indian's "vivacity and activity" of mind was equal to that of the white in similar situations. And he quoted from the famous speech of Chief Logan, declaring that the whole orations of Demosthenes and Cicero could not produce a single passage superior to the chief's oratory. Physically, too, the Indians were a match for the whites. They were brave, active, and affectionate.[4]

Unable to ignore weaknesses in Indian life and customs as they existed before his eyes, Jefferson (like most of his contemporaries) explained the difference by environment. If the circumstances of their lives were appropriately changed, the Indians would be transformed. In that happy event, Jefferson asserted, "we shall probably find that they are formed in mind as well as in body, on the same module with the 'Homo sapiens Europeaus.'"[5]

So convinced was he of the racial equality or uniformity that he urged physical as well as cultural amalgamation of the Indians with the whites. "In truth," he wrote to the Indian agent Benjamin Hawkins, "the ultimate point of rest & happiness for them is to let our settlements and theirs meet and blend together, to intermix, and become one people." In his disappointment that during the War of 1812 the British had again stirred up Indian animosity toward the Americans, Jefferson lamented: "They would

3. Jefferson to François-Jean Chastellux, June 7, 1785, *The Papers of Thomas Jefferson*, ed. Julian Boyd, 19 vols. to date (Princeton: Princeton University Press, 1950–), 8: 186. The views of Jefferson and the Jeffersonians about the Indians are examined in Bernard W. Sheehan, *Seeds of Extinction: Jeffersonian Philanthropy and the American Indian* (Chapel Hill: University of North Carolina Press, 1973), part 1; Daniel J. Boorstin, *The Lost World of Thomas Jefferson* (New York: Henry Holt Company, 1948), pp. 81–88; Frederick M. Binder, *The Color Problem in Early National America as Viewed by John Adams, Jefferson, and Jackson* (The Hague: Mouton, 1968), pp. 82–119.

4. For Jefferson's refutation of Buffon, see his *Notes on the State of Virginia* (Richmond: J. W. Randolph, 1853), pp. 62–69, 215–18.

5. Ibid., p. 67.

have mixed their blood with ours, and been amalgamated and identified with us within no distant period of time. . . . but the interested and unprincipled policy of England has defeated all our labors for the salvation of these unfortunate people."[6]

Since the Indian by nature possessed the capacity for civilization, Jefferson admitted the responsibility of the whites to aid the natives in attaining that great goal. He knew, of course, that the Indians could not be transformed at a single stroke; but the movement toward civilization he held to be inexorable, and unless the Indians moved with the tide, they would surely be destroyed. That they would indeed move and eagerly accept white aid was judged to be a corollary of their rational nature. If there was a sense of urgency in Jefferson's hope for Indian melioration, it came from his conviction that haste was necessary because of the extraordinary pressures of white civilization.

Jefferson had a linear view of civilization; he saw an inevitable movement from the savagery of the Indians toward the European culture of his own coastal region. This he expressed in a striking comparison of geographical states with temporal ones. He wrote:

> Let a philosophic observer commence a journey from the savages of the Rocky Mountains, eastwardly towards our seacoast. These [the savages] he would observe in the earliest stage of association living under no law but that of nature, subsisting and covering themselves with the flesh and skins of wild beasts. He would next find those on our frontiers in the pastoral state, raising domestic animals to supply the defect of hunting. Then succeed our own semi-barbarous citizens, the pioneers of the advance of civilization, and so in his progress he would meet the gradual shades of improving man until he would reach his, as yet, most improved state in our seaport towns. This, in fact, is equivalent to a survey, in time, of the progress of man from the infancy of creation to the present day.[7]

Jefferson here expressed succinctly the "stages of society" theory that dominated the minds of the nineteenth century, the idea that the set stages of savagery, barbarism, and civilization followed one another inevitably, as the history of all human societies had shown. If the whites had gone through that process over the centuries, there was no reason to doubt that the Indians would follow the same route.[8]

6. Jefferson to Hawkins, February 18, 1803, *The Works of Thomas Jefferson*, ed. Paul Leicester Ford, 12 vols. (New York: G. P. Putnam's Sons, 1904–1905), 9: 447; and Jefferson to Baron von Humboldt, December 6, 1813, ibid., 11: 353.

7. Jefferson to William Ludlow, September 6, 1824, *The Writings of Thomas Jefferson*, ed. Andrew A. Lipscomb, 20 vols. (Washington: Thomas Jefferson Memorial Association, 1903–1904), 16: 74–75.

8. The long history of the theory of stages of society based on different modes of sub-

Jefferson and his contemporaries did not think that the Indians would take as long to reach civilization as had their own European ancestors. The process could be speeded up by radical changes in the conditions of Indian society, and the Jeffersonians and their heirs set about to make those changes. Jefferson strongly urged the Indians to accept the white man's ways. And for this he had a single formula. The hunter state must be exchanged for an agricultural state; the haphazard life dependent upon the chase must give way to a secure and comfortable existence marked by industry and thrift; private property must replace communal ownership. By example and by education these changes could be wrought. The central point was conversion to farming, which was proper enough in light of Jefferson's agrarian propensities.

In Jefferson's mind there was no contradiction or equivocation in working for the Indians' advancement and at the same time gradually reducing the land they held. It was not an opposition of policies, one working for the education and civilization of the Indians, the other seeking to relieve them of their land for the benefit of the whites. These were two sides of the one coin. At the same time that the whites called for more land, the Indians, by conversion to an agricultural existence, would need less land, and they would exchange their excess land for the trade goods produced by the whites. Nor was Jefferson unmindful of benevolence toward the Indians. "In leading them thus to agriculture, to manufactures, and civilization," he told Congress on January 18, 1803; "in bringing together their and our sentiments, and in preparing them ultimately to participate in the benefits of our Government, I trust and believe we are acting for their greatest good."[9]

Although Jefferson was the chief theorist, his view was common. In the early days of the Continental Congress the doctrine received formal approval in a resolution of 1776, which declared that "a friendly commerce between the people of the United Colonies and the Indians, and the propagation of the gospel, and the cultivation of the civil arts among the latter,

---

sistence is traced in Ronald L. Meek, *Social Science and the Ignoble Savage* (Cambridge: Cambridge University Press, 1976). A classic account of the theory came near the end of the nineteenth century in Lewis Henry Morgan, *Ancient Society; or, Researches in the Lines of Human Progress from Savagery through Barbarism to Civilization* (New York: Henry Holt and Company, 1877). An interesting example of the pervasiveness of the theory can be seen in the Territory of Wisconsin, which in 1838 adopted an official seal picturing an Indian surrounded by a farmer, a steamboat, a pile of lead ingots, a lighthouse, a schoolhouse, and a representation of the territorial capitol, with the Latin motto *Civilitas Successit Barbarum*. See John O. Holzheuter, "Wisconsin's Flag," *Wisconsin Magazine of History* 63 (Winter 1979–1980): 91–121.

9. Jefferson to Benjamin Hawkins, February 18, 1803, *Works*, ed. Ford, 9: 447; James D. Richardson, comp., *A Compilation of the Messages and Papers of the Presidents, 1789–1897*, 10 vols. (Washington: GPO, 1896–1899), 1: 352.

may produce many and inestimable advantages to both," and Congress directed the commissioners for Indian affairs to investigate places among the Indians for the residence of ministers and teachers. Secretary of War Knox, in his first report on Indian affairs under the Constitution, admitted that the civilization of the Indians would be "an operation of complicated difficulty," which would require deep knowledge of human nature and patient perseverance in wise policies, but he did not doubt its possibility. Missionaries, he thought, should be appointed to reside among the Indians and supplied with the necessary implements and stock for farming. In instructions to General Rufus Putnam, whom he sent in 1792 to treat with the Indians near Lake Erie, Knox directed Putnam to make clear to the Indians the desire of the United States to impart to them "the blessings of civilization, as the only mean[s] of perpetuating them on the earth" and to inform them that the government was willing to bear the expense of teaching them to read and write and to practice the agricultural arts of the whites.[10]

President Washington was moved by similar considerations when he outlined an Indian policy for the United States. He had asked Congress in 1791 to undertake experiments for bringing civilization to the Indians and in the following year repeated his plea. Thereupon Congress in the intercourse law of 1793 provided that "in order to promote civilization among the friendly Indian tribes, and to secure the continuance of their friendship," the president might furnish them with domestic animals and the tools of husbandry, as well as other goods and money. Temporary agents sent to the tribes would have the same purposes, and twenty thousand dollars a year was allowed for the gifts and for payment of the agents. Washington in 1795 noted with pleasure that the results of the law seemed promising, and the law of 1796 retained the civilization provision, although the appropriation was cut to fifteen thousand. This measure was repeated in the laws of 1799 and 1802.[11]

Even Lewis Cass, whose eighteen years as governor of Michigan Territory (1813–1831) had given him close contacts with the Indians and led him often to judge harshly the present conditions of the Indians, basically agreed with Jefferson. While leaving untouched as much as possible the peculiar aboriginal institutions and customs, he wanted to encourage the Indians to adopt individual ownership of property, assist them in opening farms and procuring domestic animals and agricultural implements, and employ honest and zealous men to instruct them as far and as fast as their

10. JCC, 4: 111; Knox to Washington, July 7, 1789, ASP:IA, 1: 53–54; Knox to Putnam, May 22, 1792, ibid., p. 235.

11. Washington's messages of October 25, 1791, November 6, 1792, and December 8, 1795, Fred L. Israel, ed., *The State of the Union Messages of the Presidents, 1790–1966,* 3 vols. (New York: Chelsea House, 1966), 1: 9, 14, 30.

capabilities permitted. Education was essential. Cass openly despaired of doing very much to change the habits or opinions of adult Indians. "Our hopes," he asserted, "must rest upon the rising generation. And, certainly, many of our missionary schools exhibit striking examples of the docility and capacity of their Indian pupils, and offer cheering prospects for the philanthropist." His aid to the missionary teacher Isaac McCoy indicated a willingness to promote in practice what he preached in principle. William Clark, Cass's counterpart on the Mississippi and Missouri rivers, has been characterized as a "Jeffersonian man on the frontier," who believed that Indian assimilation could be attained by altering the Indians' environment.[12]

Emphasis on the Enlightenment thought of the Jeffersonians in the formation of American policy, however, overlooks an even more important and enduring influence: the dominance of evangelical (that is, biblical) Christianity in American society. The views about the nature of the Indians and the possibility of their transformation held by the rationalists and the churchmen were much the same if not identical. But the basis was different. One built on the philosophy of the Enlightenment, on the laws of nature discovered in God's creation by rational man. The other was a product of a surge of evangelical religion that came with the Second Great Awakening at the turn of the century, a new missionary spirit, a revivalism that was to be a dominant mark of Protestant Christian America for a full century and more. The unity of mankind, firmly anchored in the story of man's creation in Genesis, became and remained a fundamental tenet in the nation's Indian policy.

Thomas L. McKenney, as superintendent of Indian trade and then head of the Office of Indian Affairs, whose influence on federal Indian affairs was unmatched between the War of 1812 and the removal of the Indians to west of the Mississippi after 1830, was a good example of the strong Christian influence among the policy makers. McKenney, of Quaker background, can hardly be considered a man of the Enlightenment. He was a *Christian* humanitarian, for whom the civilization and Christianization of the Indians was of great moment. He was unequivocal in his stand on the equality of the races and the reasons for his opinion. In a letter of 1818 asking for a copy of a manuscript by Lewis Cass on Indian relations, McKenney said: "I will be gratified, I am sure, with a perusal of Gov. Gass's view of our Indian relations. I hope he has considered them as Human Beings,—because, if he has not, I shall believe the good book is profane to him, which says, 'of *one blood*,' God made all the nations to dwell upon

12. Report of the secretary of war, November 31, 1831, *House Executive Document* no. 2, 22–1, serial 216, pp. 27–34; Cass, "Indians of North America," *North American Review* 22 (January 1826): 115, 118–19; Jerome O. Steffen, *William Clark: Jeffersonian Man on the Frontier* (Norman: University of Oklahoma Press, 1977).

the face of the earth.'"[13] As a tireless instigator of missionary efforts for the Indians, McKenney cooperated with the missionary societies that sprang up or were revitalized at the beginning of the century.

AGRICULTURE AND DOMESTIC INDUSTRY

The work of civilization got well under way first among the Cherokees, for the secretaries of war told the agents to that nation that it would be a principal object of their work to introduce among the women the art of spinning and weaving and among the men "a taste for raising of stock and Agriculture." They enjoined the agents to operate a school to teach the women and promised them spinning wheels and other apparatus necessary for producing linen and cotton cloth and the agricultural implements and livestock essential for the farms. A specified sum of money was authorized for these projects.[14]

The civilization of the Indians by instructing them in agricultural and household arts, of course, received vigorous support from Thomas Jefferson. In his first annual message to Congress, Jefferson enthusiastically reported success in the program under the intercourse laws; that the Indians had already come to realize the superiority of these means of obtaining clothing and subsistence over the precarious resources of hunting and fishing; and that instead of decreasing in numbers they were beginning to show an increase. The president expressed his views freely in his talks to the Indians. He told the Miamis, Potawatomis, and Weas, for example, on January 7, 1802: "We shall with great pleasure see your people become disposed to cultivate the earth, to raise herds of useful animals and to spin and weave, for their food and clothing. These resources are certain, they will never disappoint you, while those of hunting may fail, and expose your women and children to the miseries of hunger and cold. We will with pleasure furnish you with implements for the most necessary arts, and with persons who may instruct how to make and use them."[15]

---

13. McKenney to Christopher Vandeventer, June 21, 1818, Christopher Vandeventer Collection, Clements Library, University of Michigan (note supplied by Herman J. Viola). McKenney's humanitarianism is fully discussed in Herman J. Viola, *Thomas L. McKenney: Architect of America's Early Indian Policy, 1816–1830* (Chicago: Swallow Press, 1974).

14. James McHenry to Thomas Lewis, March 30, 1799, and Henry Dearborn to Return J. Meigs, May 15, 1801, SW IA LS, vol. A, pp. 29–35, 43–49 (M15, reel 1). The importance of these civilizing measures can be seen from the prominent position they are given in the long instructions to the agents.

15. Message of December 8, 1801, Israel, *State of the Union Messages*, 1: 58; SW IA LS, vol. A, p. 143 (M15, reel 1).

Jefferson's views were ardently promoted by Secretary of War Henry Dearborn, who kept up a constant battery of instructions to the agents on the use of implements made available under the intercourse laws. He wrote in the name of the president to the territorial governors of the Northwest Territory, Mississippi Territory, and Indiana Territory to encourage them to promote energetically the government's plan for civilizing the Indians, and he authorized the employment of blacksmiths and carpenters, necessary to keep the plows and other implements in working order.[16] Dearborn expressed his optimism to the Creek agent in 1803:

> The progress made in the introduction of the arts of civilization among the Creeks must be highly pleasing to every benevolent mind, and in my opinion is conclusive evidence of the practicability of such improvements upon the state of society among the several Indian Nations as may ultimately destroy all distinctions between what are called Savages and civilized people. The contemplation of such a period however distant it may be is highly pleasing, and richly compensates for all our trouble and expense; and to those Gentlemen who have and shall be the individual agents in effecting such an honorable and benevolent system it must not only afford the most pleasant self approbation, but command the warmest plaudits of every good man.[17]

When word reached the War Department that one of the Indian agents was obstructing the work of civilization being carried on within his agency by a missionary establishment, he was warned that if he did not cease his opposition to the views of the government in this matter, he would be removed from his position.[18]

Jefferson, as he neared the end of his administration, saw in the state of Indian affairs a vindication of the policy of civilization. Those tribes who were "most advanced in the pursuits of industry" were the ones who were most friendly to the United States. The southern tribes, especially, were far ahead of the others in agriculture and the household arts and in proportion to this advancement identified their views with those of the United States.[19]

It is impossible to know the full operation of the annual fifteen thou-

---

16. Dearborn to William Lyman, July 14, 1801, and to Charles Jouett, September 6, 1802, SW IA LS, vol. A, pp. 92–93 (M15, reel 1); Dearborn to William C. C. Claiborne, William H. Harrison, and Arthur St. Clair, February 23, 1802, ibid., p. 166. See also Dearborn to Silas Dinsmoor, May 8, 1802, in which the intentions of the government in its Indian policy are again clearly stated. Ibid., pp. 207–8.

17. Dearborn to Benjamin Hawkins, May 24, 1803, ibid., pp. 349–50.

18. John Smith to William Wells, July 9, 1807, ibid., vol. B, p. 324 (M15, reel 2). For a full account of the case, see Joseph R. Parsons, Jr., "Civilizing the Indians of the Old Northwest, 1800–1810," *Indiana Magazine of History* 56 (September 1960): 208–13.

19. Message of October 27, 1807, Israel, *State of the Union Messages*, 1: 91–92.

sand dollars authorized by the intercourse laws, for the Treasury Department kept no special account under that heading, and when the Senate in 1822 asked for information on the annual disposition of the fund, little was forthcoming from either the War Department or the Treasury. Secretary of War Calhoun, however, reported that he thought the principal expenditure had been made through the Cherokee, Creek, Chickasaw, and Choctaw agents for spinning wheels, looms, agricultural implements, and domestic animals.[20]

The annual fund provided by the intercourse laws for promotion of civilization among the Indians was not the only source from which the government could draw in providing plows and looms, blacksmiths and carpenters; for many of the treaties signed with the tribes also provided for such aid. The Treaty of New York with the Creeks and the Treaty of Holston with the Cherokees were early examples. The Delawares in 1804 were promised a yearly sum "to be exclusively appropriated to the purpose of ameliorating their condition and promoting their civilization," plus the employment of a person to teach them how to build fences, cultivate the earth, and practice the domestic arts. In addition, the United States agreed to deliver draft horses, cattle, hogs, and agricultural implements. Similar arrangements were made with other tribes, and sometimes the tribes were allowed to choose between annuities in the form of goods or money and special aids for developing agriculture. Furthermore, treaties often stipulated blacksmiths or other artificers and teachers in agricultural or domestic arts.[21]

Abortive attempts were made in 1821 and 1822 to make the licensed traders responsible for promoting the agricultural advance of the tribes they served. A bill introduced in January 1821, aiming primarily at the abolition of the factories and the tighter control of independent Indian traders, also included special features to promote the civilization of the Indians. The bill directed traders to live in fixed abodes on the land leased from the Indians, to set up blacksmith shops there for the Indians, to cultivate grain and fruit and raise domestic animals, to sell seed and stock to the Indians, and to induce them to become cultivators and livestock breeders. For his license, each trader would pay an annual fee that was to be used to buy seed and stock for the Indians and to build mills for them. Congress, however, did not act on the bill, and when the measure was reintroduced in January 1822, it again made no progress through the House.[22]

20. Calhoun to James Monroe, February 21, 1822, and report of William Lee, February 19, 1822, ASP:IA, 2: 326.

21. Kappler, pp. 28, 31, 36, 42, 70–71, 75, 93, 95, 186, 200.

22. *Annals of Congress*, 16th Congress, 2d session, pp. 958–59; *House Journal*, 17–1, serial 62, pp. 157, 543; original bill (H.R. 41), 17th Congress, 1st session.

CHRISTIANIZATION

The United States government accepted as allies in its work of civilization the Christian churches of the land, whose missionary energies were directed in part toward the Indians. These were in the main Protestant efforts; the early Catholic missionary work within the boundaries of the United States was sparse, and not until the end of the nineteenth century did Catholic missionaries come into prominence. But even Protestant missionaries at the beginning of the new nation were not much in evidence. Only a dozen missionaries survived at the end of the Revolutionary War to Christianize the Indians. But the Second Great Awakening that began at the end of the century stimulated new endeavors, and soon there was a group of eager missionary societies whose purpose it was to evangelize the heathen, including the Indians in their own nation. The most important of these groups was the American Board of Commissioners for Foreign Missions, founded in Boston in 1810 by Presbyterians and Congregationalists. Their goal, in good Protestant fashion, was to bring the gospel to the unenlightened.[23]

The churches engaged in a long and inconclusive debate over the precedence to be given to civilizing and to Christianizing. Did an Indian need to be civilized first, so that Christianity could "take"? "The Gospel, plain and simple as it is, and fitted by its nature for what it was designed to effect," one missionary wrote, "requires an intellect above that of a savage to comprehend. Nor is it at all to the dishonor of our holy faith that such men must be taught a previous lesson, and first of all be instructed in the emollient arts of life." Others held as firmly that the gospel itself was the greatest civilizing power. "Instead of waiting till Civilization fit our Indian neighbors for the gospel," one advocate said, "let us try whether the gospel will not be the most successful means of civilizing them."[24] But it was largely a theoretical squabble, for the two processes, civilizing and Christianizing, were inextricably mixed. When missionaries went among the Indians, they went to educate and to convert, and it would be difficult to tell where one activity ended and the other began. Nor did it matter to the government, which came to depend upon the church societies for civilizing work among the Indians without intending to promote any particular religion.

23. The best study of Protestant missionary efforts among the Indians before the Civil War is Robert F. Berkhofer, Jr., *Salvation and the Savage: An Analysis of Protestant Missions and American Indian Response, 1787–1862* (Lexington: University of Kentucky Press, 1965; reprinted with a new preface, New York: Atheneum, 1972).

24. Thaddeus M. Harris, *A Discourse, Preached November 6, 1823* (Boston, 1823), p. 8, and John M. Mason, *Hope for the Heathen: A Sermon Preached . . . before the New*

It was quietly understood, by government officials as well as by church leaders, that the American civilization offered to the Indians was *Christian* civilization, that Christianity was a component of civilization and could not and should not be separated from it. By the end of the nineteenth century, concepts of religion and civilization became entwined in the Americanism of the Protestants, but the seeds of such a union were well sprouted at the beginning of the nation's life. The missionary's goal, seen in this light, differed little from the goal of Washington, Jefferson, and other public statesmen. Take, for example, this statement of the United Foreign Missionary Society in 1823:

> Let then, missionary Institutions, established to convey to them the benefits of civilization and the blessings of Christianity, be efficiently supported; and, with cheering hope, you may look forward to the period when the savage shall be converted into the citizen; when the hunter shall be transformed into the mechanic; when the farm, the work shop, the School-House, and the Church shall adorn every Indian village; when the fruits of Industry, good order, and sound morals, shall bless every Indian dwelling; and when throughout the vast range of country from the Mississippi to the Pacific, the red man and the white man shall everywhere be found, mingling in the same benevolent and friendly feelings, fellow citizens of the same civil and religious community, and fellow-heirs to a glorious inheritance in the kingdom of Immanuel.[25]

To achieve such ideals, the mission stations among the Indians were primarily educational institutions, instructing the Indian children not only in piety, but in traditional learning and in industrious work habits.[26] As such, they were actively encouraged and supported by the United States government. Thus when the Presbyterian missionary Gideon Blackburn approached Jefferson and Dearborn in 1803 about aid for a school among the Cherokees, he was warmly received and permitted to open his school. Although he was told that he could expect no compensation from the government for his services, the secretary of war nevertheless instructed the Cherokee agent to erect a schoolhouse and to give necessary aid to start

---

York Missionary Society . . . , November 7, 1797 (New York, 1797), p. 43, both quoted in Berkhofer, *Salvation and the Savage*, pp. 4–5. See the discussion in Berkhofer, pp. 4–15.

25. Records of the UFMS Board of Managers, May 5, 1823, quoted in Berkhofer, *Salvation and the Savage*, pp. 10–11.

26. Berkhofer, *Salvation and the Savage*, devotes a separate chapter to each of these areas of instruction and furnishes a detailed picture of the schools and other mission work of the church societies.

the project, "which should not require more than two or three hundred dollars for the first six months of its application."[27]

The first mission of the American Board of Commissioners for Foreign Missions was founded at Brainerd, Tennessee, in 1816 and received similar assistance from the government. Cyrus Kingsbury, founder of the school, applied to the War Department for support on the grounds that extending to the Indians the blessings that whites enjoyed was "not only a dictate of humanity, and a duty enjoined by the Gospel, but an act of justice." Secretary of War William H. Crawford greeted the request favorably; he told Kingsbury:

> the agent will be directed to erect a comfortable school-house, and another for the teacher and such as may board with him. . . . He will also be directed to furnish two ploughs, six hoes, and as many axes, for the purpose of introducing the art of cultivation among the pupils. Whenever he is informed that female children are received and taught in the school, and that a female teacher has been engaged, capable of teaching them to spin, weave, and sew, a loom and half a dozen spinning-wheels, and as many pair of cards, will be furnished. He will be directed, from time to time, to cause other school-houses to be erected, as they shall become necessary, and as the expectation of ultimate success shall justify the expenditure.

If the mission succeeded, Crawford assured the missionary, Congress would notice the good work and that "the means of forwarding your beneficent views will be more directly and liberally bestowed by that enlightened body."[28]

Kingsbury had explicit goals, which could easily be seconded by the War Department and the Indian agents. "I considered it to be the grand object of the present undertaking," he wrote to the American Board on November 26, 1816, "to impart to them that knowledge which is calculated to make them useful citizens, and pious Christians. In order to do this, it appeared necessary to instruct them in the various branches of common English

27. Dearborn to Meigs, July 1, 1803, SW IA LS, vol. A, pp. 354–55 (M15, reel 1); Dearborn to Blackburn, July 1, 1803, ibid., pp. 355–56; Dearborn to Blackburn, January 12, 1804, ibid., pp. 422–23. Blackburn continued his school until 1810, when ill health and financial difficulties forced him to withdraw.

28. Kingsbury to Crawford, May 2, 1816, and Crawford to Kingsbury, May 14, 1816, ASP:IA, 2: 477–78. Information on the Brainerd school is given in Viola, *McKenney*, pp. 32–33, and in Robert Sparks Walker, *Torchlights to the Cherokees: The Brainerd Mission* (New York: Macmillan Company, 1931). The Indian missionary work of Kingsbury is treated in Arthur H. DeRosier, Jr., "Cyrus Kingsbury: Missionary to the Choctaws," *Journal of Presbyterian History* 50 (Winter 1972): 267–87.

education, to form them to habits of industry, and to give them a competent knowledge of the economy of civilized life."[29]

THE ROLE OF THOMAS L. MCKENNEY

The close union of minds between government and the churches was exhibited in the attempt to make the factory system into a primary civilizing agency. Such was the dream, if not the obsession, of Thomas L. McKenney while he was superintendent of Indian trade from 1816 to 1822.[30] McKenney used his office to further his paramount interest, the civilization and Christianization of the Indians, and he sounded at times more like a missionary than a public official. "It is enough to know that Indians are Men," he wrote to a missionary of the American Board early in his tenure, "that like ourselves they are susceptible of pleasure, and of pain—that they have souls, the term of whose duration is co-extensive with our own—that like us they must live forever; and that we have the power not only to enhance their happiness in this world, but in the next also; and by our councils, and guidance, save souls that otherwise must perish!" He declared that the government was founded on pillars of mercy, that it was run by men who "would joyfully administer to them [the Indians] the cup of consolation, nor withhold it because of the color which an Indian Sun has burned upon their brothers."[31] As superintendent of Indian trade McKenney worked in close concert with missionaries to the Indians, prodding, encouraging, and supporting their efforts and interceding for them with the secretary of war.

McKenney's first goal was to turn the Indians toward agriculture, which would promote an interest in private property, stimulate hard work, and provide the stability and settled existence that the missionaries needed to build Christian communities. Despite a considerable lack of enthusiasm on the part of the Indians, he sent agricultural equipment and seeds to the factories and wanted the factors to encourage the Indians to trade for such goods by setting up model gardens and farms. "This is the way you will most effectually promote the *great object of the Govt.* towards these unenlightened people," he wrote. "Invite their attention to agriculture and the arts, and help them, for they are helpless. Our object is not to keep these Indians hunters eternally. We want to make citizens out of them, and

29. Quoted in Walker, *Torchlights*, p. 22.
30. There is ample discussion of McKenney's interest in civilizing the Indians through the factory system in Viola, *McKenney*, chap. 3, "The Factories and Indian Reform," pp. 21–46.
31. McKenney to Elias Cornelius, July 26, 1817, Records of the Office of Indian Trade, Letters Sent, vol. D, pp. 374–75, National Archives, Record Group 75 (M16, reel 4).

they must be first anchored to the soil, else they will be flaying about whilst there is any room for them in the wilderness or an animal to be trapped."[32]

McKenney also helped the missionaries directly. He sent letters and packages for them under his franking privilege, urged factors to support missionaries visiting their regions, and persuaded Secretary of War Calhoun to endorse missionary activities.[33]

Cyrus Kingsbury's work at Brainerd so impressed McKenney that he soon was actively promoting a network of similar schools in the Indian country. As he urged an expansion of the factory system to "serve the great object of humanity" by fostering cultural improvement among the Indians, he added to the proposal a system of schools to be run by the missionary societies under his supervision. He worked closely with the Kentucky Baptist Society for Propagating the Gospel among the Heathen and the American Board of Commissioners for Foreign Missions, who hoped to get government support for the Indian educational work they planned.[34]

McKenney was much encouraged by President James Monroe, who in his first annual message to Congress in December 1817 noted the rapid extinguishment of Indian titles in both north and south, and said:

> In this progress, which the rights of nature demand and nothing can prevent, marking a growth rapid and gigantic, it is our duty to make new efforts for the preservation, improvement, and civilization of the native inhabitants. The hunter state can exist only in the vast uncultivated desert. It yields to the more dense and compact form and greater force of civilized population; and of right it ought to yield, for the earth was given to mankind to support the greatest number of which it is capable, and no tribe or people have a right to withhold from the wants of others more than is necessary for their own support and comfort. It is gratifying to know that the reservations of land made by the treaties with the tribes on Lake Erie were made with a view to individual ownership among them and to the cultivation of the soil by all, and that an annual stipend has been pledged to supply their other wants. It will merit the consideration of Congress whether other provision not stipulated by treaty ought to be made for these tribes and for the advancement of the liberal and humane policy of the United States toward all the tribes within our limits, and more particularly for their improvement in the arts of civilized life.[35]

32. McKenney to Matthew Lyon, May 18, 1821, ibid., vol. F, p. 197 (M16, reel 6).

33. See the case of the Osage mission of the United Foreign Missionary Society, discussed in Viola, *McKenney*, pp. 27–32.

34. Ibid., pp. 33–37.

35. Israel, *State of the Union Messages*, 1: 152–53.

Working with Henry Southard, chairman of the House Committee on Indian Affairs, and other sympathetic congressmen, McKenney fought hard for a national school system for the Indians, to be supported by profits from an expanded factory system. "I certainly think," he told Southard, "Congress has it completely in its power to erect out of the materials of Indian reform a monument more durable and towering than those of ordinary dimensions, a monument as indestructible as justice, interesting as humanity—and lasting in time."[36] He and his missionary friends lobbied earnestly for the measure, and the House committee reported a bill on January 22, 1818, to extend the factory system with the addition of eight new factories and to provide schools for the Indians. The committee's arguments were typical of those advanced by the humanitarians: "In the present state of our country, one of two things seems to be necessary: either that those sons of the forest should be moralized or exterminated. Humanity would rejoice at the former, but shrink with horror from the latter. Put into the hands of their children the primer and the hoe, and they will naturally, in time, take hold of the plough; and, as their minds become enlightened and expand, the Bible will be their book, and they will grow up in habits of morality and industry, leave the chase to those whose minds are less cultivated, and become useful members of society." The committee noted the success of missionary societies in Africa and Asia and pointed out that the obstacles to be overcome among the Indians were considerably less.[37]

The bill submitted by the committee proposed to use profits from the factory system to support education of the Indians by directly endowing schools and by helping missionary societies to support their schools. The second provision was removed by amendment and a limit was set on the first of $10,000 annually, but the bill still did not pass. Perhaps it departed too much from the basic principle of the factory system, which specified that no profits were to be made out of the government trade with the Indians in order to undersell and gradually force out the petty traders.[38]

This was but a temporary delay, for McKenney did not waver in his resolve, and he stimulated a flood of petitions to Congress from religious groups in behalf of a measure (now left unspecified) for "the *security, preservation,* and *improvement* of the Indians." President Monroe reasserted the need to civilize the Indians, and the House committee reporting on the president's message in January 1819 praised the successful work being done by missionary societies among the Indians, asserting that "a more en-

36. McKenney to Southard, January 15, 1818, Office of Indian Trade, Letters Sent, vol. E, pp. 99–100 (M16, reel 5).

37. Report of January 22, 1818, ASP:IA, 2: 150–51.

38. *House Journal,* 15–1, serial 4, p. 169; original bill (H.R. 50), 15th Congress, 1st session.

ergetic and extensive system is necessary, to improve the various Indian tribes, in agriculture, education, and civilization." At the same time, it reported a bill authorizing the president to select such tribes as he thought best prepared for the change and to use whatever means seemed proper to civilize them.[39] When Senator Jeremiah Morrow of Ohio, chairman of the Senate Committee on Indian Affairs, asked McKenney how much money should be appropriated yearly for the civilization of the Indians, McKenney was quick to reply: "One hundred thousand dollars, annually. It is little enough since we got the Indians' land for an average of 2¾ cents the acre." The prudent senator cut the sum to ten thousand dollars and introduced a bill to that effect, which replaced the House bill.[40] What was won, however, was not an elaborate school system tied to the factories, but an annual appropriation for a civilization fund independent of the factories, which continued after the factories themselves were destroyed.

THE CIVILIZATION FUND AND INDIAN SCHOOLS

The "act making provision for the civilization of the Indian tribes adjoining the frontier settlements" became law on March 3, 1819. It appropriated ten thousand dollars annually for use at the president's discretion to further the civilization of the tribes wherever practicable by employing "capable persons of good moral character, to instruct them in the mode of agriculture suited to their situation; and for teaching their children in reading, writing, and arithmetic." The president and the secretary of war decided not to use the fund directly, but rather to spend it through the "benevolent societies" that had already established schools for the education of Indian children or would do so in future (under the encouragement of the fund). Secretary of War Calhoun issued a special circular that invited interested individuals or groups to apply for a share of the fund and called for information about their resources, the kind of education they proposed to impart, and the number of students to be instructed.[41]

The civilization fund was not without its critics. Congress repeatedly asked for reports on the functioning of the program and passed resolutions inquiring into the expediency of repealing the law. On May 4, 1822, Repre-

39. Message of Monroe, November 16, 1818, Israel, *State of the Union Messages*, 1: 163–64; report of Henry Southard, January 15, 1819, ASP:IA, 2: 185–86.

40. Congressional action can be followed in *House Document* no. 91, 15–2, serial 22; *Senate Journal*, 15–2, serial 13, pp. 288, 289, 323; and *House Journal*, 15–2, serial 16, pp. 188, 331, 333, 339. Morrow's interchange with McKenney is reported in Viola, *McKenney*, pp. 41–43.

41. 3 *United States Statutes* 516–17; report of Calhoun, January 15, 1820, ASP:IA, 2: 200–201; circular of September 3, 1819, ibid., p. 201.

sentative Thomas Metcalfe of Kentucky sought to eliminate the measure altogether by amendments to the supplementary intercourse act of 1822. He inveighed against the civilization fund on the grounds of inutility and cited numerous historical examples to show that all such attempts to civilize the Indians had ended in failure. Despite such attacks the annual appropriation continued, and the House Committee on Indian Affairs in 1824 reported enthusiastically on the program. The committee noted the twenty-one schools then in existence, all but three of which had been established after the act of 1819, and the more than eight hundred pupils "whose progress in the acquisition of an English education exceeds the most sanguine expectations that had been formed." It believed that the large contributions made toward the schools by the missionary societies had been stimulated by the annual appropriation of the government.[42]

When McKenney was appointed to head the Office of Indian Affairs in 1824, he continued to fight aggressively for the program. One of his early acts was to send a blistering circular to the Indian superintendents and agents reminding them of the solicitude of the government for the improvement of the Indians by means of the school system and the ten thousand dollars' annual appropriation for its support. It was the duty of the superintendents, McKenney declared, to "*sanction*, and *second*, this plan of renovating the morals and enlightening and improving these unfortunate people." Those who opposed the plan were opposing the government itself, paralyzing its program, and bringing the program into contempt in the eyes of the Indians, whom it was designed to benefit. McKenney continued to be enthusiastic about the program and its salutary effects. In November 1824 he reported 32 schools in operation, with 916 children, and he accepted the optimistic reports of the school directors as proof that nothing insuperable stood in the way of complete reformation of the Indians' lives. A year later he had lost none of his enthusiasm, and in 1826 he recommended that the annual allotment be increased, so great were the benefits being derived from the schools. Annual reports showed a steady increase in the number of schools, the enrollment of Indian pupils, and the religious groups taking part. These groups, encouraged by the government aid, devoted more and more from their private funds to the enterprise.[43]

Indian schools were materially aided also by special treaty provisions.

42. *Annals of Congress*, 17th Congress, 1st session, pp. 1792–1801; *House Report* no. 92, 18–1, serial 106.

43. Circular of August 7, 1824, OIA LS, vol. 1, p. 170 (M21, reel 1); McKenney to James Barbour, December 13, 1825, ibid., vol. 2, pp. 298–306 (M21, reel 2); McKenney to Calhoun, November 24, 1824, ASP:IA, 2: 522–24; McKenney to Barbour, November 20, 1826, ibid., pp. 671–72. A complete account of disbursements of the civilization fund, showing amounts, to whom payments were made, and purposes of grants, 1820–1844, is given in *House Document* no. 247, 28–1, serial 443.

Treaties with the Chippewas and the Potawatomis in 1826, for example, authorized an annual grant for schools, to be continued as long as Congress thought proper. Similarly, treaties with Winnebagos, Menominees, Kickapoos, Creeks, Cherokees, and others stipulated money for education. As the policy continued, sizable funds were provided. In the year 1834, thirty-five thousand dollars was due for schools under treaty provisions.[44]

Of special note among the attempts to provide white education for Indian youths was the Choctaw Academy, established in 1825 under the sponsorship of Richard M. Johnson, representative and senator from Kentucky and later vice president of the United States. Under the Choctaw Treaty of Doak's Stand in 1820, funds for education were provided from the sale of ceded lands, and in 1825 a new treaty added a six-thousand-dollar annuity for twenty years to support Choctaw schools. The chiefs desired to use part of the funds for a school outside the Choctaw Nation, where the influence of white civilization would be stronger. When the federal government approved the request, Johnson quickly seized upon the occasion to have the school established on his property near Great Crossings, in Scott County, Kentucky. The Baptist General Convention undertook the venture, and the Reverend Thomas Henderson was engaged to superintend the school. What developed was a boarding school for Indian boys that taught the standard elements of an English education and supplied training in mechanic arts. The students were primarily Choctaws, sent from the Indian Territory, but the school was open to other Indians and to local white boys as well. Johnson was a good promoter, no doubt in part because he profited from the venture, and Henderson an able director, and the school flourished for fifteen years. It reached its top enrollment of 188 in 1835.[45]

The goal of the Choctaw Academy was well expressed in 1831 by Elbert Herring, head of the Office of Indian Affairs:

Many Indian youths . . . have already returned to their respective tribes, carrying with them the rudiments of learning, the elements of

44. Kappler, pp. 36, 193, 220, 274, 282, 287, 304, 307; George Dewey Harmon, *Sixty Years of Indian Affairs: Political, Economic, and Diplomatic, 1789–1850* (Chapel Hill: University of North Carolina Press, 1941), p. 380.

45. Kappler, pp. 193, 212. The history of the Choctaw Academy can be traced in the documents printed in *House Document* no. 109, 26–2, serial 384; expenses are tabulated in *House Document* no. 231, 27–2, serial 404. An excellent series of letters from Johnson to Henderson is in Thomas Henderson Papers (photostats), State Historical Society, Madison, Wisconsin. See also Mrs. Shelley D. Rouse, "Colonel Dick Johnson's Choctaw Academy: A Forgotten Educational Experiment," *Ohio Archaeological and Historical Publications* 25 (1916): 88–117; Carolyn Thomas Foreman, "The Choctaw Academy," *Chronicles of Oklahoma* 6 (December 1928): 543–80; Foreman, "The Choctaw Academy," ibid. 9 (December, 1931): 382–411; 10 (March 1932): 77–114.

morals, and the precepts of religion; all apparently calculated to subdue the habits, and soften the feelings of their kindred, and to prepare
the way for the gradual introduction of civilization and Christianity.
That such will be the result of the intellectual and moral cultivation
of a portion of the young of their respective tribes, on the life and
character of the Indians in their confederacies, cannot be predicted
with certainty. It is, however, an experiment creditable to our national council, and meriting its further patronage. It is an experiment
consecrated by our best feelings, delightful to the view of the patriot,
and dear to the heart of philanthropy; but time alone can disclose its
efficacy.[46]

The efficacy of the Indian schools was in fact not always evident. In the
formative years the system was inadequate, and even enthusiastic promoters like Thomas McKenney came to realize that. Because of the small
number of schools provided, only a few children in each tribe could be educated, and they were not enough to influence the character of the whole
tribe. Even those who enrolled in school often did not profit because at the
completion of their studies they had no means and little incentive to pursue a new life. So the student's only alternative was, as McKenney noted,
"to turn Indian again; and too often by his improved intelligence he becomes the oppressor of his less cultivated brothers." McKenney wanted to
furnish the educated Indians with land, a house, and agricultural implements, but no funds for the purpose were available.[47]

As the 1820s advanced, the initial expansion of Indian education occasioned by the civilization fund began to slacken. By 1830, there were fifty-
two schools with 1,512 students, but that was not a large proportion of the
total number of Indian children, even of the tribes where schools had been
established.[48] It had been McKenney's hope that once the system had
proved itself, Congress would increase the annual fund, but Congress refused to do so. When McKenney left office in 1830, he saw how far short of
his optimistic goals the reality was, and he came to support voluntary removal of the tribes as necessary for their preservation and improvement.
The deepseated conviction that the destiny of the Indians was acculturation and assimilation into white society had not changed; if it could not be
accomplished east of the Mississippi, then it would have to be pursued in
the West.

46. CIA Report, 1831, serial 216, p. 172.
47. Viola, *McKenney*, p. 194.
48. CIA Report, 1830, serial 206, pp. 166–68.

JEDIDIAH MORSE'S REPORT

The congruence of missionary and government endeavors on behalf of the Indians is well illustrated in the inspection of Indian tribes made in 1820 by the Reverend Jedidiah Morse, noted Congregational clergyman, editor, and geographer. Then in his sixtieth year, Morse had accepted commissions from two missionary societies to visit the Indians in order to acquire knowledge about them that would aid in devising plans for advancing their civilization and welfare. He proposed as well to serve as an agent of the federal government in his tour. President Monroe approved the plan, and Secretary of War Calhoun sent Morse an official commission, with an allowance of five hundred dollars and the promise of more if his expenses should exceed that amount. Calhoun expressed a desire for a prompt report so that the government could "avail itself of it in the future application of the fund for the civilization of the Indians."[49]

Morse received detailed instructions about what he was to look for: "the actual condition of the various tribes . . . in a religious, moral, and political point of view." Calhoun wanted information on the number of the Indians, the extent of their territory, their mode of life, and the character and disposition of their chiefs. He further directed Morse:

> You will also particularly report on the number of schools, their position, the number and character of the teachers, the number of scholars of each sex, the plan of education, with the degree of success which appears to attend the respective schools, and the disposition which appears to exist in the tribes, and with their chief men, to promote among them education and civilization. You will also report your opinion as to the improvements which may be made, and the new establishments, to promote the object of the government in civilizing the Indians, which can be advantageously formed.

Calhoun asked as well for a report on the character of the Indian trade and on any other points that might be useful to the government.[50]

Morse reported to Congress and the president on various parts of his charge from time to time and then in 1822 published a full report with extensive appendixes. It was an illuminating view by an intelligent and sympathetic observer, and no doubt it was well received by the federal officials.[51]

49. Calhoun to Morse, February 7, 1820, Jedidiah Morse, *A Report to the Secretary of War of the United States on Indian Affairs* (New Haven: S. Converse, 1822), p. 11. Calhoun included a copy of this letter in a report to the House of Representatives on the civilization of the Indians, January 19, 1822, ASP:IA, 2: 273–74.

50. Calhoun to Morse, February 7, 1820, Morse, *Report*, p. 12.

51. Calhoun in his report of February 8, 1822, on civilization of the Indians referred

Morse had a high view of the Indians, "an intelligent and noble part of our race, and capable of high moral and intellectual improvement," and he firmly declared: "They are a race who on every correct principle ought to be saved from extinction, if it be possible to save them." He did not hesitate to offer plans to the government for this great end. He proposed an Indian college, liberally endowed by the government and run by a missionary society, in which Indian youth could be trained as teachers and leaders of their own peoples. His main plan, however, was for the establishment of "education families" composed of missionaries, teachers, and mechanics, who would serve among the Indians to instruct them and lead them into the paths of civilization by example as well as by precept. The government agents, too, would be members of these families and if possible might be nominated by the missionary groups. Morse saw in the regulations sent by Calhoun to the agents on February 29, 1820, the inchoate form of what he was proposing, for Calhoun had directed: "It is considered to be the duty of all persons who may be employed or attached to any institution, not only to set a good example of sobriety, industry, and honesty, but, as far as practicable, to impress on the minds of the Indians the friendly and benevolent views of the Government towards them, and the advantage to them in yielding to the policy of Government, and co-operating with it in such measures as it may deem necessary for their civilization and happiness."[52]

Morse knew that there were persons who argued that the Indians were not capable of civilization, but he gave them little countenance. "It is too late to say that Indians cannot be civilized," he asserted. "The facts referred to [in his appendix], beyond all question, prove the contrary. The evidence of actual experiment in every case, is paramount to all objections founded on mere *theory* or . . . in naked and unsupported *assertions*."[53]

Nor would there be any lack of funds, if only the government would devote to the purpose a reasonable proportion of the money it gained from selling the Indian lands ceded by treaty to the United States. Morse admitted that "the work of educating and changing the manners and habits of nearly half a million Indians, as they are now situated, is acknowledged to be great, and arduous, and appalling." But he had great faith in God—and in the United States. His outlook in 1822 was not untypical of the new missionaries and of men like McKenney and Calhoun, who directed the Indian affairs of the nation. But their optimism and benevolence were cooled by the failure of Congress to respond fully and by the mundane economic desires of so many of their countrymen.

---

to Morse's *Report* for more detailed information. *House Document* no. 59, 17–1, serial 66.

52. Morse, *Report*, pp. 23, 65–96, 292. Calhoun's directive is also in ASP:IA, 2: 273.
53. Morse, *Report*, p. 81.

In order to aid the government in pursuing the good work, Morse dreamed up an elaborate American Society for Promoting the Civilization and General Improvement of the Indian Tribes within the United States, to be composed of members from each state and territory and from all religious denominations, under the patronage of the chief officers of the government. It was to be a scientific organization that would gather accurate information, identify past failures and their causes, and propose remedies, and it would look to Congress for the funds to carry on its work. The society would be "an eye to the Government, and act the part of pioneers and surveyors to them in pursuing an important object in an unexplored wilderness."[54]

Morse moved boldly ahead with his scheme. In February 1822 he sent a prospectus to important individuals, with a copy of the constitution of the society and an invitation to join and to subscribe funds. The list of goals to be pursued was formidable—gathering information about the character of the Indians and their country, conducting agricultural experiments to ascertain the best crops and domestic animals for Indian advancement, determining the most suitable locations for "education families"—in short, doing all "which such a Society can do, to accomplish its grand object THE CIVILIZATION OF THE INDIANS." The prospectus and the constitution set forth an amazing array of ex officio officers and members, including the past presidents of the United States, the vice president, members of Congress, cabinet officers, justices of the Supreme Court, governors of states and territories, Indian superintendents and agents, commanding officers of military posts, professors of colleges and seminaries, and on and on. Morse himself was shown as corresponding secretary and signed an attached circular that urged cooperation in the "arduous work."[55]

Morse made a strong argument for voluntary associations. "In extensive, complicated, and arduous works of benevolence, requiring large means, and powerful influence to carry them forward with success," he wrote, "individuals, associations, and whole communities, have each their appropriate duties. Individuals begin these works; they devise and suggest. Associations combine their wisdom, and ripen suggestions into plan and system; and thus the way is prepared for the nation to examine and approve; and then to lend the means and patronage necessary for their accomplishment."[56]

The argument had little effect. There was one meeting of the society in Washington in 1824. But none of the distinguished gentlemen listed in Morse's prospectus had been approached beforehand; and the important

54. Ibid., pp. 75–76.
55. *A New Society for the Benefit of Indians: Organized at the City of Washington, February, 1822* (n.p., n.d.). The constitution is also printed in Morse, *Report*, pp. 284–90.
56. *First Annual Report of the American Society for Promoting the Civilization and General Improvement of the Indian Tribes in the United States* (New Haven: S. Converse, 1824), p. 13.

men needed to make the organization a success begged to be excused. John Adams declined—although he hoped everything possible could be done for the happiness of the Indians—because he believed the responsibility and powers to effect those ends lay with the officials of government, not with a voluntary organization. Thomas Jefferson refused to participate for much the same reasons, denying the need of a "collateral power" to achieve functions already being handled by government officials under law and fearing that "this *wheel within a wheel* is more likely to produce collision than aid." He also feared the magnitude of the organization with all its ex officio members and the fact that clergymen would make up nineteen-twentieths of the whole. "Can this formidable array be reviewed without dismay?" he asked. All the Supreme Court justices also refused. Secretary of War Calhoun accepted, as did James Madison. But the society collected no funds with which to carry on its activities. Yet it had done some good, Morse believed, in awakening the community to look at the condition of the Indians and preparing it to act for their relief.[57]

Morse, of course, had strong allies among his fellow churchmen. At the same time that he was promoting his society to aid the Indians, he joined with others of the American Board of Commissioners for Foreign Missions to memoralize Congress "to extend the blessings of civilization and Christianity, in all their variety, to the Indian tribes within the limits of the United States." Asserting that "the object of the Government and of the board is one, and, indeed, is common to the whole community," the memorial expressed forcefully Christian humanitarian views. It noted past neglect of the Indians, which would bring down God's vengeance upon the nation if reform was not undertaken. It offered "indubitable evidence of the practicability of educating Indians" for full civilization. And it repeated Morse's plan for a college to educate Indian teachers.[58]

Morse died in 1826, and no more was heard of his society. It was but one in a long line of voluntary associations organized and supported by Christian philanthropy specifically for the improvement and welfare of the Indians. The American Board of Commissioners for Foreign Missions, a well-organized and well-supported missionary organization, in many ways fulfilled the purposes that Morse had in mind for his abortive society.

Whether the initiative came from government officials like Thomas L. McKenney and John C. Calhoun or from zealous citizens like Jedidiah Morse and the missionaries of the American Board, the goal of civilizing and Christianizing the Indians remained an important element in government policy well into the twentieth century and helped to give that policy its strongly paternalistic bent.

57. Ibid., pp. 20–24 and passim.
58. The memorial, presented in the House on March 3, 1824, is in *House Document* no. 102, 18–1, serial 97, and in ASP:IA, 2: 446–48.

CHAPTER 6

The Indian
Department

Superintendents and Agents. Headquarters

Organization. Assistance from Military

Commanders. Presents and Annuities.

Peace Medals and Delegations.

Implementation of United States Indian policy depended upon special personnel within the War Department appointed to deal with the Indians. The aggregate of these persons was given the general designation "Indian department," a term covering the officials and clerks in the office of the secretary of war who were assigned to Indian matters and the superintendents, agents, subagents, interpreters, clerks, and mechanics who carried on the work in the field. The term did not necessarily indicate a fixed organization, and it seems to have been used in the first place as a category for accounting for funds. The word *department* was initially applied also to geographical units, such as the northern and southern districts or departments designated in the Ordinance of 1786, but the geographical divisions of Indian administration soon came to be known as superintendencies, agencies, and subagencies, corresponding to the title of the persons in charge. As the laws governing intercourse with the Indians expanded in scope and were expressed with greater precision, so the official standing and duties of the men in the Indian department also became more clearly defined, until in 1834 a definitive organization was established by law.[1]

1. This chapter is based in large part on Francis Paul Prucha, *American Indian Policy in the Formative Years: The Indian Trade and Intercourse Acts, 1790–1834* (Cambridge: Harvard University Press, 1962), pp. 51–65, 250–74, and sections are taken directly from that work. General accounts of the development of the Indian department can be found in Laurence F. Schmeckebier, *The Office of Indian Affairs: Its History, Activities and*

SUPERINTENDENTS AND AGENTS

Antecedents of the Indian department are found in the colonial agents sent among the Indians, the British superintendents, the special commissioners sent out by the Continental Congress, and the Indian superintendents authorized by the Ordinance of 1786. Most directly concerned were the superintendents, for their office was quietly carried over when the Constitution replaced the Articles of Confederation. On September 11, 1789, Congress provided two thousand dollars for the governor of the Northwest Territory, both as his annual salary and "for discharging the duties of superintendent of Indian affairs in the northern department," thus beginning the practice of making territorial governors ex officio superintendents of Indian affairs. In 1790 the law establishing the Territory South of the River Ohio declared that "the powers, duties and emoluments of a superintendent of Indian affairs for the southern department, shall be united with those of the governor." This office of southern superintendent lapsed in 1796 when Tennessee became a state, but in the same year Benjamin Hawkins was appointed "principal temporary agent for Indian affairs south of the Ohio River"; Hawkins exercised wide supervision over the southern Indians, although he was especially responsible for the Creeks. When Mississippi Territory was set up in 1798, the office of southern superintendent was joined to the office of governor of the new territory. The law of May 7, 1800, which established Indiana Territory by dividing the original Northwest Territory, declared that "the duties and emoluments of superintendent of Indian affairs shall be united with those of governor"; subsequent laws setting up new territories included a similar clause.[2]

The first trade and intercourse law (1790) authorized the superintendents to issue licenses for trade and to enforce the licensing provisions, and it referred to "such other persons as the President of the United States shall appoint" to issue and recall licenses. But no specific provision was made for appointing agents or establishing agencies. To care for particular Indian problems, however, special agents were appointed in 1792. These men—three sent to the southern Indians and one to the Six Nations—had no connection with the intercourse law. They were charged instead with special diplomatic missions. The primary object of the agent sent to the

---

Organization (Baltimore: Johns Hopkins Press, 1927), pp. 1–42, and Felix S. Cohen, *Handbook of Federal Indian Law* (Washington: GPO, 1942), pp. 9–12. An extensive historical account of legislation dealing with Indian agencies is in *House Report* no. 474, 23–1, serial 263. *House Document* no. 60, 23–1, serial 255, gives data on persons employed in the Indian department.

2. 1 *United States Statutes* 50, 54, 68, 123, 550; 2 *United States Statutes* 59, 309, 331, 515.

Cherokees was to keep the southern Indians from joining the warring tribes north of the Ohio and attach the Indians more firmly to the interests of the United States. The agent sent to the Creeks sought to quiet disturbances among them, to see that the Treaty of New York was complied with, and finally to obtain three hundred Creek warriors to join the federal troops against the northern Indians. The duties of the agents sent to the Chickasaws and the New York Indians were of a similar nature.[3]

A new turn in the development of Indian agencies came with the second intercourse law (1793). A section dealing with measures to civilize the Indians authorized the president "to appoint such persons, from time to time, as temporary agents, to reside among the Indians, as he shall think proper." The commissions and instructions sent to these agents emphasized their responsibility to civilize the Indians by means of agriculture and domestic arts and referred to them officially as "temporary agents." The duties assigned them ran the wide range of Indian relations set forth in the intercourse laws, and eventually the word *temporary* was dropped from their title.[4] Under this authorization appeared the permanent Indian agents, assigned to particular tribes or areas, who became indispensable in the management of Indian affairs.

The work of the agents paralleled the development of the intercourse laws. At first their duties were set down in very general terms: to maintain the confidence of the Indians, to keep them attached to the United States, and to impress upon them the government's desire for peace and justice. As the intercourse laws made more specific the means by which peace was to be preserved and justice maintained, the agents' duties were also specified, in order to see that the laws were carried out.

The government also appointed subagents, but there seems to have been no special authorization for them as distinct from the agents. They were appointed at first as assistants to the agents; eventually they were assigned to separate locations with duties similar to those of the agents. All these men came under the general superintendence of the territorial gover-

3. Instructions to Leonard Shaw, February 17, 1792, ASP:IA, 1: 247–48; Henry Knox to James Seagrove, February 20, 1792, ibid., pp. 249–50; Knox to William Blount, April 22, 1792, ibid., p. 253; instructions to Israel Chapin, April 28, 1792, ibid., pp. 231–32.

4. 1 *United States Statutes* 331. Benjamin Hawkins in 1796 was appointed "Principal Temporary Agent for Indian Affairs South of the Ohio River." Thomas Lewis in 1799 was appointed "Temporary Indian Agent in the Cherokee Nation," William Lyman in 1801 was appointed "Temporary Agent for Indian Affairs in the Northwestern and Indiana Territories," and Silas Dinsmoor in 1802 was appointed "Temporary Agent for the Choctaw Nation." But the commissions issued to Charles Jouett and Richard Graham in 1815 called them simply "Agent of Indian Affairs." Appointments of these men are in SW IA LS, vol. A, pp. 29–35, 44–49 (M15, reel 1); and Clarence E. Carter, ed., *The Territorial Papers of the United States*, 26 vols. (Washington: GPO, 1934–1962), 5: 146–50; 7: 26–29; 17: 190–91, 196–200.

nors and reported through them to the War Department. They were directed to keep records of the happenings at their agencies and to note the condition of the Indians, the natural history of the area, and the progress of the Indians in civilization.[5]

In 1818 there were fifteen agents and ten subagents among the Indians, and on April 16 of that year Congress regularized the appointment of these men; they were to be nominated by the president and appointed by and with the consent of the Senate, but the law did not actually establish the offices that the appointees were to fill. Nor did the law of April 20, 1818, which set the pay of agents and subagents, formally establish the agencies. These laws and the succeeding appropriation bills that provided "for pay of the several Indian agents as allowed by law" merely took the agencies for granted.[6]

The 1822 amendment to the intercourse law of 1802 repeatedly mentioned agents, their authority in restricting the whiskey traffic, their duties in issuing licenses, and the reports required of them by the War Department. The act, furthermore, authorized the appointment of a superintendent of Indian affairs at St. Louis with power over the Indians who frequented that place (a necessary arrangement after the admission of Missouri as a state), and a special agent for the tribes in Florida.[7]

However indefinite and insecure their legislative foundation was before 1834, the agents were accepted as a regular part of the Indian service; the War Department came to rely on them more and more heavily in the enforcement of Indian policy, a reliance explicitly indicated in the instructions and regulations given to them. Of these instructions, the most important were the detailed ones drawn up for the early agents, which—with some necessary changes in geographical names and territorial officers—continued to be sent to Indian agents until 1815. After a preamble which enjoined upon the agent zealous endeavors to introduce the civilized arts of agriculture and spinning and weaving (an injunction worked into the body of the instructions in the 1815 version), the document directed the agent point by point in his enforcement of the laws and in the records and

5. Dearborn to Governors William C. C. Claiborne, William H. Harrison, and Arthur St. Clair, February 23, 1802, SW IA LS, vol. A, pp. 166–68 (M15, reel 1); Dearborn to Agents William Lyman, Samuel Mitchell, John McKee, and William Wells, February 27, 1802, ibid., pp. 172–73.

6. 3 *United States Statutes* 428, 461.

7. 3 *United States Statutes* 682–83. In the interval between the end of Missouri Territory with its governor as ex officio superintendent of Indian affairs and the commission to William Clark, who became superintendent under the act of 1822, the Indian agents were charged to correspond directly with the War Department. This was a general practice, but in some cases agents within states were made subordinate to a nearby territorial governor.

reports required.[8] The War Department augmented these initial instructions with specific directives, either to promulgate some change in policy or to answer questions of policy and procedure posed by the agents themselves. From time to time, too, the secretary of war issued additional general instructions to the superintendents of Indian affairs for their own guidance and for transmittal to the agents under their charge.

An agent's duties were in large part reportorial. He was to keep an eye out for violations of the intercourse laws and to report them to the superintendents, to the military commanders of the frontier posts, or to the War Department. Action and further directions to the agent in most cases came from his superior officers. But the critical work of dealing with the Indians and the frontier whites devolved upon the agent, and the success of the work depended upon the character of the man, the respect he won from the tribes among whom he lived, and the authority of his position in the eyes of the whites. Fortunately, the United States had a number of capable and distinguished men of a character and integrity that gave stature to the office of Indian agent and that enabled the agents by their personal influence alone to ease the conflicts between whites and Indians without reliance on either civil court procedures or military force.[9]

HEADQUARTERS ORGANIZATION

The work of directing the superintendents and agents rested upon the secretary of war and the clerks of the War Department whom he chose to as-

8. The instructions of James McHenry to Thomas Lewis, March 30, 1799, SW IA LS, vol. A, pp. 29–35 (M15, reel 1), is the oldest extant copy. It is possible that McHenry merely transcribed instructions that had been issued earlier to other agents. Other instructions are cited in n. 4 above.

9. The work of the agents is discussed in Edgar B. Wesley, *Guarding the Frontier: A Study of Frontier Defense from 1815 to 1825* (Minneapolis: University of Minnesota Press, 1935), pp. 16–30; Ruth A. Gallaher, "The Indian Agent in the United States before 1850," *Iowa Journal of History and Politics* 14 (January 1916): 3–55. For the work and character of two important agents for the early period, see Merritt B. Pound, *Benjamin Hawkins: Indian Agent* (Athens: University of Georgia Press, 1951); Frank L. Owsley, Jr., "Benjamin Hawkins, the First Modern Indian Agent," *Alabama Historical Quarterly* 30 (Summer 1968): 7–13; Lawrence Taliaferro, "Auto-biography of Major Lawrence Taliaferro: Written in 1864," *Minnesota Historical Collections* 6 (1887–1894): 189–225. For the two most important superintedents, see John L. Loos, "William Clark, Indian Agent," *Kansas Quarterly* 3 (Fall 1971): 29–38; Jerome O. Steffen, *William Clark: Jeffersonian Man on the Frontier* (Norman: University of Oklahoma Press, 1977); Francis Paul Prucha, *Lewis Cass and American Indian Policy* (Detroit: Wayne State University Press, 1967); Ronald Gregory Miriani, "Lewis Cass and Indian Administration in the Old Northwest, 1815–1836" (Ph.D. dissertation, University of Michigan, 1975).

sign to the task, for in the first decades of the new nation there was no formally established office charged specifically with Indian affairs. Dealings with the Indians were considered a special category of the War Department's activities, however, and separate letterbooks were maintained for correspondence concerned with Indian matters.

When the office of superintendent of Indian trade was established in 1806, it became an unofficial focus for Indian affairs, supplying information and advice to the secretary of war and corresponding with citizens who were interested in the Indians. But the abolition of the factories in 1822 removed even this semblance of an Indian center in the War Department.[10]

Then on March 11, 1824, Secretary of War Calhoun, by his own order and without special authorization from Congress, created in the War Department what he called the Bureau of Indian Affairs. Calhoun appointed his friend Thomas L. McKenney to head the office and assigned him two clerks as assistants. The duties of the new position were set forth in the letter of appointment: to take charge of the appropriations for annuities and current expenses, to examine and approve all vouchers for expenditures, to administer the fund for the civilization of the Indians, to decide on claims arising between Indians and whites under the intercourse laws, and to handle the ordinary Indian correspondence of the War Department.[11]

Despite Calhoun's designation, the new section was not commonly called the Bureau of Indian Affairs. McKenney for the first few months headed his letters Indian Office and then uniformly used Office of Indian Affairs. Indian matters from the superintendents and agents passed through his hands, as well as business with persons outside the government. The correspondence was voluminous, and McKenney was generally also called upon to prepare the reports on Indian affairs requested by Congress of the secretary of war. He and his clerks formed a sort of Indian secretariat within the War Department, but it did not take him long to become dissatisfied with this setup. The work of handling disbursements, immense correspondence with the agents, preparation and execution of treaties, care for Indian schools, and regulation of Indian trade all rested with McKenney, but the authority and responsibility still resided in the secretary of war. "It was the weight of these concerns, added to their importance, which led to the creation, *by the Executive*, of this office. But, with its constitution, no power was conveyed," McKenney complained. "The business, though it be arranged, has yet, at every step, to be carried up to the head of the Department, without regard to its importance, otherwise the most unimportant

10. The manifold work of the Office of Indian Trade under Thomas L. McKenney is well treated in Herman J. Viola, *Thomas L. McKenney: Architect of America's Early Indian Policy, 1816–1830* (Chicago: Swallow Press, 1974).

11. *House Document* no. 146, 19–1, serial 138, p. 6.

correspondence upon matters of mere detail, is not authorized, *except by the general confidence of the head of the Department in the Officer in charge of the Indian business.*" What McKenney wanted was for Congress to create an office of Indian affairs, with a responsible head, to whom would be referred all matters arising out of Indian relations.[12]

McKenney drew up a bill embodying his suggestions that was introduced in the House of Representatives on March 31, 1826. It called for the appointment of a general superintendent of Indian affairs who would have the responsibility for keeping the records on Indian affairs, conducting all correspondence arising out of Indian relations, handling and adjusting financial accounts before transmitting them to the Treasury, and, in general, for doing all things in relation to Indian affairs that had hitherto rested with the secretary of war directly. The bill was committed to the Committee of the Whole, but there was no further action in that Congress, and subsequent attempts to get the bill passed also failed.[13]

McKenney's proposal for congressional action was picked up by Lewis Cass and William Clark and included in their plan for reorganizing Indian affairs, which they prepared at the behest of the secretary of war in 1829. In the Twenty-second Congress the measure was introduced again, this time by the Senate Committee on Indian Affairs, and it passed both houses without difficulty. The bill, which became law on July 9, 1832, authorized the president to appoint a commissioner of Indian affairs, under the secretary of war, who was to have "the direction and management of all Indian affairs, and of all matters arising out of Indian relations." The secretary of war was to assign clerks to the new office, without, however, increasing the total number of clerks in the War Department, and an annual salary of three thousand dollars was specified for the commissioner. Ironically, the new position was established only after McKenney had been removed from office.[14]

ASSISTANCE FROM MILITARY COMMANDERS

The army on the frontier was sent there for military defense and to uphold American authority in remote regions of the nation, but the military men who commanded the frontier forts had an important role as the power be-

12. McKenney to James Barbour, November 15, 1825, ibid., pp. 6–9.

13. *House Journal*, 19–1, serial 130, p. 394; original bill (H.R. 195), 19th Congress, 1st session, March 31, 1826; *House Journal*, 20–1, serial 168, pp. 72–73, 105; original bill (H.R. 29), 20th Congress, 1st session, January 2, 1828.

14. 4 *United States Statutes* 564. The first commissioner of Indian affairs was Elbert Herring; authoritative biographical sketches of Herring and the succeeding commissioners appear in Robert M. Kvasnicka and Herman J. Viola, eds., *The Commissioners of Indian Affairs, 1824–1977* (Lincoln: University of Nebraska Press, 1979).

hind the decisions and policies of the Indian agents and as the last resort of the territorial governors in dealing with hostile Indians or recalcitrant whites. It was no accident that Indian agencies and government trading houses were usually in the shadow of a military post.

The instructions sent to the Indian agents directed them to apply to the military commanders for aid in carrying out their duties, and the army officers received explicit directives time after time from the War Department to assist the agents in the enforcement of the laws and treaties. The legal justification for this assistance was written into the intercourse laws beginning with the law of 1796, which provided that the president of the United States could employ such military force as he judged necessary to remove illegal settlers on lands belonging to the Indians or secured to them by treaty and to apprehend any person found in the Indian country in violation of the laws. Furthermore, the law directed the military force of the United States, when called upon by civil magistrates, to assist in arresting offenders against the law and committing them to safe custody for trial according to law.[15]

The army officers' hands, however, were pretty well tied, for any hint of militarism was deeply feared. Recommendations made by Knox and others for use of courts-martial to try frontier offenders were never accepted by Congress, and the intercourse laws carefully provided that, in apprehending persons who were in the Indian country illegally, military troops should convey them immediately by the nearest convenient and safe route to the civil authority of the United States in an adjoining state or territory for trial. The law of 1796 directed that persons apprehended by the military could be detained no more than ten days between arrest and removal to the civil authorities. In 1799 the period of detention was reduced to five days, and as a further precaution against tyrannical action (which American frontiersmen always suspected on the part of the military) the law directed that the officers and soldiers having custody of a prisoner should treat him "with all the humanity which the circumstances will possibly permit; and every officer and soldier who shall be guilty of maltreating any such person, while in custody, shall suffer such punishment as a court-martial shall direct." Military officers, if requested to do so by the persons in custody, were required to conduct those persons to the nearest judge of the supreme court of any state, who, if the offense were bailable, might take proper bail if offered. By a special supplement to the intercourse laws in 1800, this provision was extended to justices of inferior or county courts, unless the defendant had been charged with murder or some other capital offense.[16]

Close cooperation was required of the agents and the military command-

---

15. 1 *United States Statutes* 470, 473–74.
16. 1 *United States Statutes* 748; 2 *United States Statutes* 40.

ers, not only by the intercourse laws themselves, but also by the repeated directives coming from the secretary of war, the general in chief, and the head of the Office of Indian Affairs. Unfortunately, the official directives could not smooth out all the rough edges in human relations between the army officers and the civilian Indian agents. Both groups were under the direction and surveillance of the secretary of war, but frequent conflicts of authority arose, to the detriment of efficient enforcement of the intercourse laws. Legally, and according to accepted practice, routine peacetime Indian relations were to be in the hands of the civilian superintendents and agents. Troops were to be called upon by them only when physical force or the threat of its use was necessary. Alexander Hamilton, then major general in the "provisional army" authorized to meet a threat of war from France, expressed the policy in a letter to a frontier commander in 1799:

> You are aware that the Governors of the North Western Territory and of the Mississippi Territory are severally *ex officio* Superintendants of Indian Affairs. The management of those affairs under the direction of the Secretary of War appertains to them. The military in this respect are only to be auxiliary to their plans and measures. In saying this, it must not be understood that they are to direct military dispositions and operations; But they are to be the organs of all negociations and communications between the Indians and the Government; they are to determine when and where supplies are to be furnished to those people and what other accommodations they are to have. The military in regard to all such matters are only to aid as far as their Cooperation may be required by the superintendants; avoiding interferences without previous concert with them, or otherwise than in conformity with their views. This will exempt the military from a responsibility which had better rest elsewhere: And it will promote a regular and uniform system of Conduct towards the Indians, which Cannot exist if every Commandant of a Post is to intermeddle separately and independently in the management of the concerns which relate to them.[17]

Yet many army officers were unwilling to take orders directly from civilian officers of the government, even from the superintendents and agents who were, like them, under the War Department. Specific orders coming explicitly from the secretary of war or down through the chain of command to the post commandant were considered necessary before military officers would heed the requests of agents for help. Such orders were a normal procedure, however, and the agents were supported by the War Department in their call for military assistance, although the post comman-

17. Hamilton to J. F. Hamtramck, May 23, 1799, Carter, *Territorial Papers*, 3: 24–25.

ders could be slow to respond and quick to find excuses for taking no action.[18]

Difficulties sometimes arose because of interference in Indian affairs on the part of army officers, who did not always wait to get a cue from the agents and whose garrisons were at times a point of infection in the Indian country, to which the Indians flocked for free food and even liquor. One Indian agent recommended to Governor Lewis Cass in 1815 that the relative powers of the agents and the commanding officers be more clearly pointed out. "For want of this definition of powers," he asserted, "the officers of the two departments are very apt to fall out, and the publick interest receive much injury." Lawrence Taliaferro, the able Indian agent at St. Peter's, for example, had been directed when he assumed his post to consult with the post commander at Fort Snelling and keep him informed of all his proceedings as agent. "It is of the first importance," Secretary of War Calhoun had written him, "that, in such remote posts, there should be a perfect understanding between the officers, civil and military, stationed there, to give energy and effect to their operations." Nevertheless, in his long tenure in the office of agent, Taliaferro was often at odds with the commander of Fort Snelling.[19]

The disputes and controversies between agents and officers were more than balanced by the energy and zeal with which most of the frontier commanders undertook to carry out the federal government's Indian policy. In removing intruders, confiscating liquor, restraining Indian hostilities, and conducting treaties and conferences, the army officers were able and devoted supporters of the government and of the intercourse laws.

PRESENTS AND ANNUITIES

Whatever the legal formality of treaties between sovereign nations, the relations between the United States government and the Indian tribes called forth procedures and practices that indicated special relationships that hardly existed even analogously between the United States and the nations of Europe. One was the widespread use of presents to Indian leaders. It had been European practice during the colonial era and continued to be British

18. The travail of the military commanders in dealing with Indian affairs is described in Francis Paul Prucha, *Broadax and Bayonet: The Role of the United States Army in the Development of the Northwest, 1815–1860* (Madison: State Historical Society of Wisconsin, 1953), pp. 53–103, and in Prucha, *The Sword of the Republic: The United States Army on the Frontier, 1783–1846* (New York: Macmillan Company, 1969), pp. 193–209.

19. Benjamin F. Stickney to Cass, September 27, 1815, Carter, *Territorial Papers*, 10: 597; Calhoun to Taliaferro, December 27, 1819, SW IA LS, vol. D, p. 350 (M15, reel 4).

practice among the Indians in Canada and along the border to provide gifts to Indian tribes and their chiefs. As the Indians came to depend more and more upon European goods, such gifts formed an indispensable diplomatic tool in gaining the good will and allegiance of Indian tribes. Great amounts of money were expended to "brighten the chain of friendship," and as the outlay of free goods continued, many Indians became almost completely dependent upon them.[20]

The young United States could not eliminate the practice. If it wanted to win the adherence of crucial Indian nations, it would have to continue gift giving—and it did. The Continental Congress beginning in 1776 provided for the purchase of goods to be distributed to the Indians as presents in order to cultivate their goodwill and friendship. And early treaties negotiated under the Articles of Confederation provided "in pursuance of the humane and liberal views of Congress" for the distribution of goods to the tribes for their use and comfort.[21]

President Washington was alert to the need for presents, and in the six-point program for advancing the happiness of the Indians and attaching them to the United States proposed in 1791, he asked that the president "be enabled to employ the means to which the Indians have been long accustomed for uniting their immediate interests with the preservation of peace." The presents were to be employed also as a means of bringing the Indians around to the civilization of the whites. Secretary of War Knox, in his first long report on Indian affairs, recommended gifts of sheep and other domestic animals for chiefs and their wives in an attempt to instill in the Indians a "love for exclusive property." And the intercourse laws provided that "in order to promote civilization among the friendly Indian tribes, and to secure the continuance of their friendship," the president could furnish them with domestic animals and the implements of husbandry.[22]

Competition with the British offered a strong incentive for distributing presents to Indians. Lewis Cass, as governor of Michigan Territory, gave the matter great emphasis, and in a memorandum of 1816 concerning In-

---

20. An excellent study of the use of presents in colonial times is Wilbur R. Jacobs, *Diplomacy and Indian Gifts: Anglo-French Rivalry along the Ohio and Northwest Frontier, 1748–1763* (Stanford: Stanford University Press, 1950). Jacobs provides great detail not only on the use and significance of the presents but on the kinds of goods provided. The use of presents among the southern tribes is indicated in Wilbur R. Jacobs, ed., *Indians of the Southern Colonial Frontier: The Edmond Atkin Report and Plan of 1755* (Columbia: University of South Carolina Press, 1954).

21. JCC, 4: 378, 410; 7: 127; 8: 542, 550; 24: 225; 25: 688–89; Kappler, pp. 6, 8.

22. Fred L. Israel, ed., *The State of the Union Messages of the Presidents, 1790–1966*, 3 vols. (New York: Chelsea House, 1966), 1: 9; Knox to Washington, July 7, 1789, ASP:IA, 1: 53–54; 1 *United States Statutes* 331, 472, 746–47; 2 *United States Statutes* 143; 4 *United States Statutes* 738.

dian affairs he provided a detailed rationale for giving presents. In the first place, he saw a moral obligation to provide for the Indians who had given up "the fairest portion of their Country" to the whites and who now found it difficult to subsist by means of hunting. Without the "annual gratuities" they had come to expect from the government, Cass found it "difficult to conceive how they could support and clothe themselves." Cass, charged with maintaining peace on his remote frontier, looked upon the distribution of presents as essential for that end. "Whatever has a tendency to conciliate the minds of the Indians and to render less unpleasant those obnoxious circumstances in our intercourse with them, which cannot be removed," he wrote, "will have a powerful effect in continuing our existing relations with them. The importance of presents in this point of view is too striking to require any particular illustration." This was especially true in competition with the British, and Cass pointed to the experience of the War of 1812, in which the British had used presents to great advantage. Moreover, presents were required to secure the attachment of influential chiefs and to prevent Indians from committing depredations on the property of white citizens. Finally, the distribution of presents by agents of the United States was necessary "to give dignity, influence and importance to the Agent, and attention to his representations." Governor Cass added a detailed proposal for procedures in distributing presents to get the most good out of them and suggested $20,000 a year in presents for the Indians of his region.[23]

Cass's proposal was not fully implemented, and as annuities under treaties and trade goods from the factory system provided alternatives, the use of presents as a wholesale means of supplying the needs of the Indians declined. But the influence of presents upon chiefs, to get them to agree to American proposals, continued unabated. The appropriate distribution of gifts where they would do the most good, in a thinly veiled form of bribery, became an accepted part of treaty making.

A special form of gift giving was rations, distributed gratuitously from time to time to the Indians. These were generally provided at treaty negotiations for the large groups of participating Indians, and the reorganization of the Indian department in 1834 authorized the president to grant such rations as could be spared from army provisions to Indians visiting military posts or Indian agencies on the frontier.[24]

As more and more land was ceded by the Indians in treaties with the

23. Francis Paul Prucha and Donald F. Carmony, eds., "A Memorandum of Lewis Cass: Concerning a System for the Regulation of Indian Affairs," *Wisconsin Magazine of History* 52 (Autumn 1968): 40–41, 45–50.

24. 2 *United States Statutes* 85. The provision, with the addition of the words "or agencies," was repeated in the law of 1834. 4 *United States Statutes* 738.

United States, the payments for these lands in the form of annuities proportionately increased. The annuities, together with rations and other gratuities that continued through the decades, became an essential means of support for many tribes. The distribution of the annuities—either in cash or in goods—became one of the primary activities of the Indian department and one of its biggest headaches.

The annuities, as the name suggests, were annual payments either for a specified period of years or in perpetuity. At first the payments were small, mere token payments, such as the $1,500 a year to the Creeks in the Treaty of New York in 1790 and the $1,000 a year to the Cherokees in the Treaty of Holston in 1791, although both those treaties also provided for "certain valuable goods" to be delivered immediately to the nation.[25] But year by year, as the treaties of cession multiplied, considerable sums were appropriated annually to meet the treaty obligations. When Cass and Clark in 1829 recommended consolidation of annuity appropriations into a single bill, the list of funds due under various treaties totaled $214,590.[26]

In some cases the treaties specified a money payment to the tribe; in many other cases the annuity was to be in the form of goods or services. Thus in the treaty of 1794 with the Six Nations, in addition to $10,000 worth of goods delivered at once, the United States agreed to expend "yearly forever" a sum of $4,500 "in purchasing clothing, domestic animals, implements of husbandry, and other utensils suited to their circumstances, and in compensating useful artificers, who shall reside with or near them, and be employed for their benefit." Stipulations that annuity payments be used for education were also common in the treaties.

To procure the goods needed for annuity payments was no small task. The work was entrusted by a law of 1792 to an agent of the Treasury Department who supervised the purchases of supplies for the military, naval, and Indian services. In 1795 Congress created the office of purveyor of public supplies for the procurement of government goods.[27] In 1811, after the office of superintendent of Indian trade had been established, the superintendent was charged with the purchase and distribution of annuity goods as well as of goods needed for the trading houses. The great variety of items

25. Kappler, pp. 26, 30.
26. *Senate Document* no. 72, 20–2, serial 181, pp. 52–57.
27. 1 *United States Statutes* 280, 419. A letterbook of the commissioner of the revenue, 1794–1796, is in Records of the Revenue Office Relating to the Treasury of the War Department, National Archives, Record Group 75. The work of the purveyor is discussed in the biography of the man who held the job from 1803 to 1812: Jacob E. Cooke, *Tench Coxe and the Early Republic* (Chapel Hill: University of North Carolina Press, 1978), pp. 413–21. For details on annuity goods, see Journal of Superintendent of Military Stores, Annuity Goods, 1794–1811, Records of the Indian Tribal Claims Branch, WNRC, Suitland, Maryland.

required and the frequent difficulties in locating appropriate stocks created an immense amount of work and worry for his office. After the dissolution of the factory system and the institution of the Office of Indian Affairs in the War Department, the head of that office carried on the work. The fact that Thomas L. McKenney, the last superintendent of Indian trade, became the first head of the Indian Office made possible some continuity in the enterprise.[28]

No matter who was responsible for distributing goods or money to the Indians, accounting for both was a major task. When the annuities and presents were added to funds appropriated for the salaries of agents and their supporting personnel, for transportation, for buildings, and for contingent expenses, the sums involved were large, and it seemed impossible (granted the problems of communication and the incompetence of some of the men who handled accounts) to keep the records straight. McKenney had great trouble clearing his accounts for annuities and presents, as well as for trade goods, when the factories were closed. When he became head of the Indian Office, he had even more money to account for; in some years he was responsible for the disbursement of up to a million dollars.[29]

Regulations and laws dealing with accounting for funds were extensive and became increasingly detailed. When Lewis Cass printed a two-page broadside in Detroit, dated September 15, 1814, called "Regulations for the Indian Department," he prescribed in detail the procedures for distributing presents and keeping accounts on them, details that took up most of the broadside. The law of 1822 tightening the regulation of trade had a special section on accounting for Indian department funds, and judging from the correspondence it called forth, that part of the law most interested the secretary of war.[30]

Accounting procedures remained a special problem and seemed to give officials of the Indian department more trouble than did the actual dealings with the Indians. Henry R. Schoolcraft, the longtime Indian agent at Sault Ste. Marie, expressed a general view when he wrote graphically in 1828, "The derangements in the fiscal affairs of the Indian department are in the extreme. One would think that appropriations had been handled with a pitchfork. . . . And these derangements are only with regard to the

28. An account of McKenney's work in procuring Indian supplies is in Viola, McKenney, pp. 12–16.

29. Ibid., pp. 80–84, 105, 175–76. Indian office disbursements in 1824 amounted to $424,978.50 and in 1825 to $671,470.59; McKenney estimated that they would be $1,082,474.68 in 1826. McKenney to James Barbour, April 21, 1826, OIA LS, vol. 3, pp. 44–45 (M21, reel 3). In attached statements, McKenney gives a breakdown for each year.

30. Calhoun to Clark, May 28, 1822, SW IA LS, vol. E, pp. 258–61 (M15, reel 5); Calhoun to William P. DuVal, June 11, 1822, Carter, Territorial Papers, 22: 452–55; Calhoun to the territorial governors, March 18, 1823, ibid., 19: 502.

north. How the south and west stand, it is impossible to say. But there is a screw loose in the public machinery somewhere." Such criticisms McKenney was willing to accept; he knew well enough, he said, "how slip-shod almost every thing is," but he insisted that only Congress could remedy the situation.[31] In 1834 the president was authorized "to prescribe such rules and regulations as he may think fit . . . for the settlement of the accounts of the Indian department." The distribution of annuities usually took place at the Indian agencies, to which the Indians were summoned for the occasion. There the agent, with the support of the military post commander, gave the money or goods to the chiefs, who in turn distributed them to the Indians. In some cases the annuities went directly to individuals, but in 1834 Congress stipulated that annuities were to be paid to the chiefs or to such other persons as the tribe designated. At the request of the tribe, according to the same legislation, money annuities could be commuted to goods.[32]

Cash annuities, although easier to provide than goods, came under frequent attack, for the money quickly passed from the Indians' hands into the pockets of traders. McKenney called the payment of money a "radical defect." It was a practice, he said, that "furnishes a lure to the avaricious— and gives the means of indulgence to these untutored people, in all their propensities to drunkenness & idleness; & is known, to have produced from the beginning, *no other fruits.*"[33] Annuities continued to be of great concern to the government officials responsible for Indian affairs.

PEACE MEDALS AND DELEGATIONS

One practice in dealing with the Indian chiefs that the United States took over from the British and other European nations was the presentation of silver medals to chiefs and warriors as tokens of friendship and as signs of allegiance and loyalty on the part of those who accepted them. These peace medals came to play a prominent part in American Indian policy.[34] Medals were given to Indian chiefs on such important occasions as the

31. Henry R. Schoolcraft, *Personal Memoirs of a Residence of Thirty Years with the Indian Tribes on the American Frontier* (Philadelphia: Lippincott, Grambo and Company, 1851), p. 319; McKenney to P. S. Duponceau, October 1, 1828, OIA LS, vol. 5, pp. 140–42 (M21, reel 5).

32. 4 *United States Statutes* 737–38.

33. McKenney to William P. DuVal, December 26, 1825, OIA LS, vol. 2, p. 330 (M21, reel 2); McKenney to Eli Baldwin, October 8, 1829, ibid., vol. 6, p. 105 (M21, reel 6).

34. A complete history of the peace medals, their production, and their use is Francis Paul Prucha, *Indian Peace Medals in American History* (Madison: State Historical Society of Wisconsin, 1971). Sections of that book are used here.

signing of a treaty, a visit of Indians to the national capital, or a tour of Indian country by some federal official. They were distributed, too, by Indian agents on the frontier at their own discretion but according to established norms. The proposed regulations for the Indian department drawn up in 1829 by Cass and Clark set forth a simple outline of rules to govern the use of medals:

> In the distribution of medals and flags, the following rules will be observed:
>   1. They will be given to influential persons only.
>   2. The largest medals will be given to the principal village chiefs, those of the second size will be given to the principal war chiefs, and those of the third size to the less distinguished chiefs and warriors.
>   3. They will be presented with proper formalities, and with an appropriate speech, so as to produce a proper impression upon the Indians.
>   4. It is not intended that chiefs should be appointed by any officer of the department, but that they should confer these badges of authority upon such as are selected or recognized by the tribe, and as are worthy of them, in the manner heretofore practised.
>   5. Whenever a foreign medal is worn, it will be replaced by an American medal, if the Agent should consider the person entitled to a medal.[35]

Although these regulations were never formally adopted, they represented the generally accepted practice on the frontier.

The practice became so firmly established, indeed, that it was impossible to conduct satisfactory relations with the Indians without medals. Thomas L. McKenney made this clear to the secretary of war at the end of 1829. "So important is its continuance esteemed to be," he wrote, "that without medals, any plan of operations among the Indians, be it what it may, is essentially enfeebled. This comes of the high value which the Indians set upon these tokens of Friendship. They are, besides this indication of the Government Friendship, badges of power to them, and trophies of renown. They will not consent to part from this ancient *right*, as they esteem it; and according to the value they set upon medals is the importance to the Government in having them to bestow."[36]

When the United States was in competition with the British for the friendship of the tribes, the medals were of supreme importance, for the chiefs signified their switch from adherence to the British to loyalty to

35. *Senate Document* no. 72, 20–2, serial 181, pp. 77–78.
36. McKenney to John H. Eaton, December 21, 1829, OIA LS, vol. 6, p. 199 (M21, reel 6).

the United States by formally turning in their British medals and accepting in their place those bearing the likeness of the American president. The medals, perhaps even more than the flags that also were presented to chiefs, carried the full weight of national allegiance. They were personal marks, worn with pride upon the breasts of the chiefs, and unlike flags were nearly indestructible. Within the tribes, too, possession of a medal gave rank and distinction; and despite protestations of government officials to the contrary, by awarding medals the United States commissioners sometimes designated or "made" the chiefs with whom they dealt.

President Washington presented large oval silver medals to Alexander McGillivray and his Creek associates by the secret clauses of the Treaty of New York in 1790 and sent similar medals to the Cherokees, Choctaws, and Chickasaws in subsequent years and to the Seneca chief Red Jacket in 1792. General Wayne distributed Washington medals at Greenville. When Lewis and Clark ascended the Missouri in 1804, they took along a large supply of medals, mostly Jefferson medals (in three sizes) with the bust of the president on the obverse and clasped hands with the words PEACE AND FRIENDSHIP on the reverse. The explorers confiscated Spanish and British medals and replaced them with American ones. As the years passed, these medals flooded the frontier, especially after the War of 1812, when they played a significant part in the campaign to gain the loyalty of the Indians in the Great Lakes region and on the upper Mississippi and Missouri.[37] The urgency appears in a letter of William Clark to the secretary of war in 1831:

> I beg leave to S[t]ate to you the necessity of my being Supplied with *Medals* for Indian Chiefs, within the Superintendency of St. Louis. At the Treaties which have been latterly negotiated, with various Tribes of the Indians of the Missouri and Mississippi rivers, application was made in council by their chiefs "for *Medals* with the face of the President (their great father) to place near their heart, which would give them power and Strength to follow his Councils, and enforce the provisions of their Treaties"—as I had no medals, and the commissioners being in favour of their application, a promise was made to those Chiefs, that I would ask the President (their great father) to grant their request, and that we had no doubt of his bestowing Medals, on Such Chiefs as were worthy of receiving that mark of distinction.[38]

Clark reported that British medals had been delivered up to the commissioners who had treated with the tribes on the upper Missouri in 1825

37. Prucha, *Indian Peace Medals*, pp. 3–53.
38. Clark to John H. Eaton, January 22, 1831, OIA LR, St. Louis Superintendency (M234, reel 749).

and that the chiefs were still waiting for the United States medals promised them. "I must beg leave to observe," he said, "that all western Tribes of Indians consider *Medals* of the bust of the President, one of the greatest marks of distinction which they can receive from the government and which is worn suspended from their neck as authority in important council with the white people, their negotiations with other tribes, and in making themselves known to Strangers. Medals & Flags are the greatest *boast* of a chief among those distant Tribes, who considers himself supported by the Gov^t bestowing on him those marks of distinction, in ad[d]ition to the influence he has with his own tribe and is so considered by other tribes.

The distribution of medals to the chiefs of the northwestern and western tribes, Clark believed, had had a salutary effect in gaining security for American traders and in easing tensions among the tribes themselves. "To effect in part these objects," he concluded, "a proper distribution of *Medals*, Flags & Chief Coats will give an influence which no other means within my knowledge can be applied with as little expense."[39]

Federal officials took great pains to procure medals of respectable artistic merit, for as McKenney noted in connection with the John Quincy Adams medals, "they are intended, not for the Indians, only, but for posterity." Notable artists and diesinkers were hired to design and produce the medals, and the United States Mint in Philadelphia handled the striking of them.[40]

Another device for attaching Indians to the United States government was to invite delegations of important tribal leaders to the seat of government to confer with the president, the secretary of war, and the commissioner of Indian affairs. These Indian delegates sometimes came to negotiate treaties and sometimes to present grievances, but the occasions were used also to impress them with the size and power of the United States and its people. The Indians visited the sights of the capital, met dignitaries at the White House, inspected navy yards and fortifications, and often stopped to see Philadelphia and New York before they returned home. The trials of entertaining the Indians in Washington were many, but the practice continued—often at the insistence of the Indians.[41]

39. Ibid.
40. McKenney to Samuel Moore, October 13, 1825, OIA LS, vol. 2, p. 188 (M21, reel 2). For details on production of the medals, see Prucha, *Indian Peace Medals*, pp. 73–138.
41. There is considerable literature on delegations. The best account is Herman J. Viola, *Diplomats in Buckskins: A History of Indian Delegations in Washington City* (Washington: Smithsonian Institution Press, 1981). See also Katharine C. Turner, *Red Men Calling on the Great White Father* (Norman: University of Oklahoma Press, 1951), and John C. Ewers, "'Chiefs from the Missouri and Mississippi,' and Peale's Silhouettes of 1806," *Smithsonian Journal of History* 1 (Spring 1966): 1–26.

The Indian Office, which entertained the delegations and performed the steadily increasing duties that federal relations with the Indians entailed, was a modest bureau in the early years of the nineteenth century. Its organization and much of its work began informally, but as the years passed its role became ever more critical, and like other bureaucracies it grew and grew. The Indian Office assumed the paternalistic mantle that theoretically belonged to the Great Father, the president.

PART TWO

Indian Removal

American Indian policy is sometimes thought of as a movement between two extremes. On one hand was the idea of assimilating the Indians into white American society through the acculturative processes of private property, an agricultural (as opposed to a hunter) economy, formal education in English letters, and Christianization. On the other was the idea of segregation or separateness; the Indians could maintain their limited political autonomy, their special languages, and their customs and religions but only outside the limits of white society, either in protected enclaves or, preferably, beyond the western frontier of white settlement. In the nineteenth century at least, there was no concept of a truly pluralistic society.

The removal of the eastern Indians that dominated the second quarter of the century, if the dichotomy above is accepted, falls of course on the side of separateness. It was an admission that the speedy acculturation and absorption of the Indians into white society (and even the biological intermingling of the races) that was the goal of the Jeffersonians had not been attained and was perhaps unattainable. Yet this was not a simple matter of either assimilation or segregation. Removal was the policy adopted to solve the problem of alien groups claiming independence within established states and territories of the United States, the problem of groups of human beings with communal cultures still only partially dependent upon agriculture owning large areas of land that were coveted for the dynamic white agricultural systems of both the north and the south, and the problem of friction that occurred along the lines of contact between the two societies and the deleterious effect that contact almost universally had upon Indian individuals and Indian society.

These problems were real problems for both the United States government and its people and for the Indian tribes. They could not be easily waved aside simply by appeals to public morality and justice. They resulted in a great complexity of practical situations that confounded sincere Christian statesmen as well as zealous missionaries and for which even aggressive and ruthless white expansionists found no easy answers. Indian leaders, too, saw the complexity, and they arrived at a variety of adaptive responses as they sought to maintain some degree of self-determination in the face of the obvious power and advantages of the United States. Nor was removal complete segregation, a cutting off of the Indian groups from white contact and connections by banishment beyond the Mississippi. In some respects the policy and the process brought increased rather than lessened interference in domestic Indian affairs on the part of the Great Father. And when the emigrant Indians were settled in their western homes, the drive for educating, civilizing, and Christianizing them took on new vigor. Acculturation and to a large extent assimilation was still the ultimate goal, slowed down and delayed as it seemed to have been in the East.

Indian removal has been popularly associated with the Five Civilized Tribes of the southeastern United States and dramatized in the Cherokees' Trail of Tears, but it was a phenomenon that affected Indians north of the Ohio River as well. The total picture must encompass both groups, and it must include in addition the developments in the Indian department and its administration that were occasioned by the massive relocation of the tribes.

The debates over removal policy touched fundamental questions. In 1828 Secretary of War Peter B. Porter had complained that there was no clear definition of the nature of the relations between the United States and the Indians. On one side he saw advocates of "primitive and imprescriptible rights in their broadest extent" contending that the tribes were independent nations with sole and exclusive right to the property and government of the territories they occupied. On the other side he recognized extremists who considered the Indians "mere tenants at will, subject, like the buffalo of the prairies, to be hunted from their country whenever it may suit our interests or convenience to take possession of it."[1]

The controversy over removal in the 1830s might have been expected to widen the split between the opposing forces, for each side presented an extreme position. Yet when the dust stirred up by the debates began to settle, the definition that Porter had asked for began to appear. It is true that the

---

1. Report of Peter B. Porter, November 24, 1828, *American State Papers: Military Affairs*, 4: 3.

supporters of the removal bill won their point in Congress and that the
Indians were ejected from the eastern states. Hostile attitudes toward
the Indians were often victorious in practice on much of the frontier, too,
but official United States Indian policy had a firmer and more balanced
foundation than the selfish interests of frontiersmen. That policy came to
rest on treaties (including the removal treaties), which uniformly guaranteed Indian rights, as well as on the intercourse laws and War Department
regulations, which implemented the treaties and restricted the contacts
between whites and Indians in order to protect both parties, and on the
decisions of the Supreme Court, such as those of 1831 and 1832 dealing
with the Cherokees, which vindicated Indian rights. The tremendous
weight of the arguments put forth in the 1830s by those who opposed
forced and ruthless removal stirred the conscience of much of the nation
and to a large extent reinforced the concern for Indian welfare and improvement that had been part of official attitudes from the beginning.

Ultimate evaluation of Indian removal is difficult. Removal brought
neither the utter collapse of Indian society and culture direly predicted by
the critics of Jackson's program nor the utopia in the West that advocates
envisaged. Like so many human affairs, it had elements of good and evil, of
humanitarian and philanthropic concern for the Indians and fraud and corruption practiced by unscrupulous men. How it might finally have turned
out cannot be determined, for the development of the emigrant Indians in
the West was cut short by new forces of expansion in the 1840s and 1850s
and then by the cataclysm of the Civil War.

CHAPTER 7

The Policy of
Indian Removal

Formulation of the Policy. Andrew Jackson and

Removal. Motivation for Removal. Controversy

and Debate. The Cherokee Cases.

Although it has been common to ascribe the removal of the Indians in the 1830s to Andrew Jackson, his aggressive removal policy was in fact the culmination of a movement that had been gradually gaining momentum in government circles for nearly three decades. Whites had steadily encroached upon Indian lands, and new treaties of cession had been negotiated from time to time to validate the incursions. But this was a piecemeal process, and there were dreams that the problems could be eliminated once and for all by inducing the eastern Indians to exchange their lands for territory west of the Mississippi, leaving the area between the Appalachians and the Father of Waters free of encumbrance for white exploitation.[1]

FORMULATION OF THE POLICY

The idea of exchange of lands originated with Thomas Jefferson in 1803, when the addition of the vast Louisiana Purchase created conditions that would make removal feasible. Before the end of Jefferson's administration

1. The development of the removal policy has received extended treatment from historians. I follow here my earlier discussion in Francis Paul Prucha, *American Indian Policy in the Formative Years: The Indian Trade and Intercourse Acts, 1790–1834* (Cambridge: Harvard University Press, 1962), pp. 224–49. See also the old but still useful treatise by Annie H. Abel, "The History of Events Resulting in Indian Consolidation

gentle pressure was being placed on the Cherokees, to introduce to them the notion of exchanging their present country for lands in the West. The secretary of war directed the Indian agent to sound out the chiefs and let the subject be discussed in the nation so that prevailing opinion could be ascertained. Those who chose to live by hunting were to be especially encouraged to emigrate, but care was to be taken that the removal was the result of their own inclinations and not of force.[2]

Some Cherokees did go west, at first to hunt and then to settle, but the problems of the War of 1812 crowded out any serious thought of orderly emigration of the tribes. Not until Monroe's administration was the proposal discussed again in earnest. In January 1817 the Senate Committee on the Public Lands reported on the expediency of exchanging lands with the Indians and proposed that an appropriation be made to enable the president to enter into treaties with the Indians for that purpose. The aim of the measure was to obviate the "irregular form of the frontier, deeply indented by tracts of Indian territory," to consolidate the settlement of the whites, and to remove the Indians from intimate intercourse with the whites, a contact "by which the civilized man cannot be improved, and by which there is ground to believe the savage is depraved."[3]

President Monroe and Secretary of War John C. Calhoun worked earnestly for a change in the enduring situation of the Indians. The anomaly of large groups of savage or semicivilized tribes surrounded by civilized whites struck them with special force. The solution was either removal to the open western regions or a change from the hunter state. In a letter to Andrew Jackson in October 1817, Monroe asserted that "the hunter or savage state requires a greater extent of territory to sustain it, than is compatible with the progress and just claims of civilized life, and must yield to it." He returned to the same views in his annual message to Congress in December, adding that it was right that the hunter should yield to the farmer. The prickly question of land tenure would disappear if only the Indians could be removed beyond the Mississippi, and the War Department authorized its commissioners to make liberal offers to the eastern tribes in an attempt to induce them to accept willingly an exchange of lands. Monroe

---

West of the Mississippi," *Annual Report of the American Historical Association for the Year 1906*, 1: 233–450; also the more recent, heavily documented study, Ronald N. Satz, *American Indian Policy in the Jacksonian Era* (Lincoln: University of Nebraska Press, 1975), pp. 1–63. An example of popular treatments that are almost universally very sympathetic to the Indian cause is Dale Van Every, *Disinherited: The Lost Birthright of the American Indian* (New York: William Morrow, 1966).

2. Secretary of war to Return J. Meigs, March 25 and May 5, 1808, SW IA LS, vol. B, pp. 364, 377 (M15, reel 2).

3. *Senate Journal*, 14th Congress, 2d session, p. 95; report of Senate Committee on Public Lands, January 9, 1817, ASP:IA, 2: 123–24.

and Calhoun, as well as Jackson, were convinced that the good of the Indians demanded an end to their independent status within the white settlements and urged some action on Congress.[4]

The removal question was then given a new and dangerous twist by special circumstances surrounding the Cherokees in Georgia (and to a lesser extent the Creeks, Chickasaws, and Choctaws in Alabama and Mississippi). The Cherokees were settled within the boundaries of Georgia on lands which they had always held. These Indians were not nomads; they had an abiding attachment to their lands and were determined to hold them at all costs, no matter what the United States might offer them as an inducement to move. One of the ironies of the situation was that the very progress in civilization of the Cherokees made them less willing to depart. The United States, through government officials directly and through the encouragement given to missionary societies, had urged the Indians to adopt white ways by tilling the soil and developing the domestic arts of spinning and weaving. Formal education in English language schools, also, had led to a cadre of leaders—mostly mixed-bloods—who could deal effectively with white society. The remarkable invention of a Cherokee syllabary by Sequoyah made it possible for great numbers of Cherokees to learn to read in their native tongue. Assisted by the missionaries of the American Board, the Cherokees at the end of the decade of the 1820s began to publish their own newspaper, the *Cherokee Phoenix*, which printed material in English and in the Cherokee language and which became an important vehicle for disseminating views of the Cherokees, both within their own nation and to the white world. Some of the Indian leaders, too, had adopted the whites' system of black slavery and had established extensive plantations, rivaling their white counterparts. Contemporaries differed in their opinions about the actual extent of progress in white cultural patterns. Was it evident only in the small group of mixed-bloods, who sought to manipulate the destinies of the Indian nations for their own interests, or was the general mass of the population also affected? Whatever the case, the "civilized tribes" of the southeastern United States did not correspond to the Indian tribes pictured as hunters who needed to transform themselves into agriculturalists that was a common part of the rhetoric justifying removal.[5]

4. Monroe to Jackson, October 5, 1817, *Correspondence of Andrew Jackson*, ed. John Spencer Bassett, 6 vols. (Washington: Carnegie Institution, 1926–1933), 2: 331–32; message of December 2, 1817, Fred L. Israel, ed., *The State of the Union Messages of the Presidents, 1790–1966*, 3 vols. (New York: Chelsea House, 1966), 1: 152–53; C. Vandeventer to Lewis Cass, June 29, SW IA LS, vol. D, pp. 176–79 (M15, reel 4); Calhoun to Joseph McMinn, July 29, 1818, ibid., pp. 191–94. See also Monroe's message of November 16, 1818, Israel, *State of the Union Messages*, 1: 163–64; Calhoun's report of January 15, 1820, ASP:IA, 2: 200–201.

5. Most accounts of the Cherokees and other southern tribes note their cultural

Georgia and the United States had signed a compact on April 24, 1802, by which Georgia ceded to the United States its western land claims. In return, the United States agreed to extinguish the Indian title to lands within the state and turn them over to Georgia as soon as this could be done peaceably and on reasonable terms. As the land greed of the Georgians increased through the years, the federal government was accused of failing in its part of the bargain, for the government had not extinguished the Indian title to the Georgia lands. Complaints reached Washington both from the Cherokees—who looked with apprehension on the threats of Georgia and on the federal government's renewed appropriations for a treaty to extinguish the Indian claims—and from the Georgians. The governor of Georgia censured the federal government for its tardiness and weakness, asserting that the Indians were mere tenants at will who had only a temporary right to use the lands for hunting; he insisted that Georgia was determined to gain the Cherokee lands.[6]

To these criticisms President Monroe replied in a special message to Congress on March 30, 1824, defending the course of the government, asserting that the Indian title was in no way affected by the compact with Georgia, and denying any obligation on the part of the United States to force the Indians to move against their will. He reiterated his strong opinion that removal would be in the best interests of the Indians, but he refused to be pushed by Georgia beyond the strict import of the compact. The president's message did nothing to soothe the irritation of the Geor-

---

transformation, but the description is frequently based on enthusiastic accounts of the missionaries and other whites. See, for example, Grace Steele Woodward, *The Cherokees* (Norman: University of Oklahoma Press, 1963), pp. 139–56. For insight into white acculturated Indians, see Ralph Henry Gabriel, *Elias Boudinot, Cherokee, and His America* (Norman: University of Oklahoma Press, 1941). Much information about the state of Cherokee acculturation is given in William G. McLoughlin and Walter H. Conser, Jr., "The Cherokees in Transition: A Statistical Analysis of the Federal Cherokee Census of 1835," *Journal of American History* 64 (December 1977): 678–703. Studies of Indian slave-holders are Theda Perdue, *Slavery and the Evolution of Cherokee Society, 1540–1866* (Knoxville: University of Tennessee Press, 1979); Perdue, "Cherokee Planters: The Development of Plantation Slavery before Removal," in *The Cherokee Indian Nation: A Troubled History,* ed. Duane H. King (Knoxville: University of Tennessee Press, 1979), pp. 110–28; R. Halliburton, Jr., *Red over Black: Black Slavery among the Cherokee Indians* (Westport, Connecticut: Greenwood Press, 1977); Daniel F. Littlefield, Jr., *Africans and Creeks: From the Colonial Period to the Civil War* (Westport, Connecticut: Greenwood Press, 1979).

6. Charles C. Royce, "The Cherokee Nation of Indians: A Narrative of Their Official Relations with the Colonial and Federal Governments," *Annual Report of the Bureau of Ethnology, 1883–1884* (Washington: GPO, 1887), pp. 233–38. The compact of 1802 is printed in Clarence E. Carter, ed., *The Territorial Papers of the United States,* 26 vols. (Washington: GPO, 1934–1962), 5: 142–46.

gians, whose governor in another communication to the president commented with much severity upon the bad faith that for twenty years had characterized the conduct of the executive officers of the United States.[7]

As Monroe neared the end of his term, he increased his insistence that steps be taken to preserve the rapidly degenerating tribes, now increasingly threatened by Georgia. He told Congress on December 7, 1824, of the Indians' deplorable conditions and the danger of their extinction. To civilize them was essential to their survival, but this was a slow process and could not be fully attained in the territory where the Indians then resided. Monroe had no thought of forceful ejection; even if it aimed at the security and happiness of the Indians, he said, it would be "revolting to humanity, and utterly unjustifiable." There was only one solution: the Indians must be invited and induced to take up their home in the West. The plan would be expensive, Monroe admitted, but he saw no other solution.[8]

Before Congress had time to act, Monroe sent it a special message on removal based upon a report of Calhoun dated January 24, 1825. The president urged a liberal policy that would satisfy both the Cherokees and the Georgians. He asked for "a well-digested plan" for governing and civilizing the Indians, which would not only "shield them from impending ruin, but promote their welfare and happiness." He was convinced that such a plan was practicable and that it could be made so attractive to the Indians that all, even those most opposed to emigration, would be induced to accede to it in the near future. The essence of his proposal was the institution of a government for the Indians in the West, one that would preserve order, prevent the intrusion of the whites, and stimulate civilization. "It is not doubted," Monroe told Congress, "that this arrangement will present considerations of sufficient force to surmount all their prejudices in favor of the soil of their nativity, however strong they may be." To convince the Indians of the sincere interest of the government in their welfare, he asked Congress to pledge the solemn faith of the United States to fulfill the arrangements he had suggested, and he recommended sending commissioners to the various tribes to explain to them the objects of the government.[9]

Congress acted at once to implement the president's message. On the day following the message, Senator Thomas Hart Benton wrote to Calhoun that the Committee on Indian Affairs in the Senate had unanimously adopted the system recommended by Monroe, and Calhoun sent Benton a

7. Monroe's message and numerous documents relating to the compact of 1802 are printed in *Senate Document* no. 63, 18–1, serial 91. See also Royce, "Cherokee Nation of Indians," pp. 238–40.

8. Israel, *State of the Union Messages*, 1: 228.

9. Report of Calhoun, January 24, 1825, ASP:IA, 2: 542–44; message of Monroe, January 27, 1825, James D. Richardson, comp., *A Compilation of the Messages and Papers of the Presidents, 1789–1897*, 10 vols. (Washington: GPO, 1896–1899), 2: 280–83.

draft of a bill. The measure, introduced by Benton on February 1, followed precisely the recommendations Monroe had made, authorizing the president to acquire land from the western Indians and to treat with the eastern tribes for removal. It directed the president, furthermore, "to pledge the faith of the nation" that the emigrating tribes would be guaranteed permanent peace, protection from intrusion, and aid in improving their condition and in forming a suitable government, and to appoint commissioners to visit the tribes to induce them to move. A sum of $125,000 was to be appropriated to carry out the provisions of the bill. It was a promising beginning, but although the bill passed the Senate, it failed in the House.[10]

The matter was by no means dead, however. In December 1825 a House resolution charged the Committee on Indian Affairs to inquire into the expediency and practicability of establishing a territorial government for the Indians west of the Mississippi, and on February 21, 1826, a new bill was introduced.[11] This bill represented the current view of the administration, for John Cocke, chairman of the House committee, had sent a copy of the earlier bill to Secretary of War James Barbour, asking for his opinion. "The Committee are desirous," Cocke said, "to cooperate with the views of the President in relation to the Indians within the limits of the U. States." Barbour in reply argued for removal of the Indians as the only means to preserve them. He suggested the following outline for a bill:

1. The country west of the Mississippi to be set aside for the exclusive use of the Indians.

2. Removal of the Indians as individuals, instead of as tribes.

3. Establishment of a territorial government for the Indians, to be maintained by the United States.

4. When circumstances permitted, extinction of tribes and distribution of property among individuals.

5. The condition of those Indians who remained in the East to be left unchanged.[12]

Barbour's letter was read and discussed in a cabinet meeting on February 7. Although President Adams noted that Barbour's paper was "full of benevolence and humanity," he wrote: "I fear there is no practicable plan by which they can be organized into one civilized, or half-civilized, Government. Mr. Rush, Mr. Southard, and Mr. Wirt all expressed their doubts

10. Benton to Calhoun, January 28, 1825, OIA LR, Miscellaneous (M234, reel 429); Calhoun to Benton, January 31, 1825, OIA LS, vol. 1, pp. 334–35 (M21, reel 1). The course of the bill (S. 45) can be followed in the Senate and House *Journals*, in serials 107 and 112.

11. *House Journal*, 19–1, serial 130, pp. 97, 276 (H.R. 113).

12. Cocke to Barbour, January 11, 1826, OIA LR, Miscellaneous (M234, reel 429); Barbour to Cocke, February 3, 1826, ASP:IA, 2: 646–49.

of the practicability of Governor Barbour's plan; but they had nothing more effective to propose, and I approved it from the same motive."[13]

The bill failed to pass, however, and at the beginning of the following session of Congress, the House called upon the secretary of war for detailed information on the condition of the Indians, their willingness to migrate, and the probable expense of removal. McKenney answered the request for Barbour in a serious and reasonable document in which he honestly admitted lack of information on much of what the House wanted to know and recognized the difficulties involved in carrying out removal. Yet he insisted strongly that the program was possible and that the Indians could be brought to accept it if they were approached in the right way.[14]

On July 26, 1827, the Cherokee Nation adopted a written constitution patterned after that of the United States in which the Indians asserted that they were one of the sovereign and independent nations of the earth with complete jurisdiction over their own territory. This move on their part caused great alarm. The secretary of war wrote to the Cherokee agent, warning that the constitution could not be understood as changing the relations that then existed between the Indians and the government of the United States. In the House of Representatives the Committee on the Judiciary and then the Committee on Indian Affairs were directed to inquire into the matter, and a special report was requested from the president. Georgia, of course, was indignant and angered by the "presumptuous document."[15]

Because Congress provided no legislation to relieve the situation, Georgia finally began to move against the Cherokees, contending that it could not abide an *imperium in imperio* within the state. Georgia's line of action was to extend the authority of the state and its laws over the Cherokee lands. This would in effect withdraw the Cherokee territory from the status of Indian country, bring control of the lands into Georgia's hands, and by overt as well as subtle pressure force the Indians out. The resolutions of a committee of the Georgia legislature that were approved on December 27, 1827, gave an indication of the direction of the wind. After condemning the bad faith of the federal government for not having extinguished the

---

13. *Memoirs of John Quincy Adams, Comprising Portions of His Diary from 1795 to 1848*, ed. Charles Francis Adams, 12 vols. (Philadelphia: J. B. Lippincott and Company, 1874–1877), 7: 113. William Clark in his long comments on Barbour's letter showed general agreement. Clark to Barbour, March 1, 1826, ASP:IA, 2: 653–54.

14. McKenney to Barbour, December 27, 1826, OIA LS, vol. 3, pp. 273–85 (M21, reel 3).

15. The Cherokee Constitution is printed in *House Document* no. 91, 23–2, serial 273, pp. 10–19. For congressional action, see *House Journal*, 20–1, serial 168. The president's report with accompanying documents is in *House Executive Document* no. 211, 20–1, serial 173.

Cherokee title, the committee put forth Georgia's position, that the lands within the limits of the state belonged to it absolutely and that because the Indians were merely tenants at will, the state could end that tenancy at any time. The committee insisted that Georgia had the right to extend its authority and laws over the whole territory and to exact obedience to them from all. Another resolution was a thinly veiled threat of the use of force, if necessary, to accomplish Georgia's aims.[16]

The situation grew steadily more serious. How could the claims of the state of Georgia be reconciled with justice to the Indians? John Quincy Adams in his final message to Congress reviewed the problem:

> As independent powers, we negotiated with them [the Indians] by treaties; as proprietors, we purchased of them all the lands which we could prevail upon them to sell; as brethren of the human race, rude and ignorant, we endeavored to bring them to the knowledge of religion and of letters. The ultimate design was to incorporate in our own institutions that portion of them which could be converted to the state of civilization. In the practice of European States, before our Revolution, they had been considered *as children* to be governed; as tenants at discretion, to be dispossessed as occasion might require; as hunters to be indemnified by trifling concessions for removal from the grounds from which their game was extirpated. In changing the system it would seem as if a full contemplation of the consequences of the change had not been taken. We have been far more successful in the acquisition of their lands than in imparting to them the principles or inspiring them with the spirit of civilization. But in appropriating to ourselves their hunting grounds we have brought upon ourselves the obligation of providing them with subsistence; and when we have had the rare good fortune of teaching them the arts of civilization and the doctrines of Christianity we have unexpectedly found them forming in the midst of ourselves communities claiming to be independent of ours and rivals of sovereignty within the territories of the members of our Union. This state of things requires that a remedy should be provided—a remedy which, while it shall do justice to those unfortunate children of nature, may secure to the members of our confederation their rights of sovereignty and of soil.[17]

The House Committee on Indian Affairs, which considered the proposals of President Adams and Secretary of War Peter B. Porter, agreed that

16. *Acts of the General Assembly of the State of Georgia, 1827* (Milledgeville, 1827), pp. 249–50.

17. Message of December 2, 1828, Israel, *State of the Union Messages*, 1: 287. For a study of Adams's changing views about the Indians, see Lynn Hudson Parsons, "'A Per-

removal was necessary because of the crisis growing out of the controversy with the states. The elementary question to be answered was, How are the Indians to be preserved? The committee found only one way: to remove the Indians from the states and establish them on lands beyond the limits of any state or territory. "The policy of urging them to leave their country for another would be deplored," the committee asserted, "if it were not believed to be the only effectual measure to secure the prosperity and happiness of themselves and their posterity." The committee reported a bill to appropriate fifty thousand dollars to enable the president to aid the Indians in their migration westward, but the measure was not passed.[18]

ANDREW JACKSON AND REMOVAL

Then Andrew Jackson—a man of forthright views who did not hesitate to speak his mind and a man who had ample Indian experience to give weight to his utterances—became president of the United States. Jackson had early decided that it was farcical to treat with the Indian tribes as though they were sovereign and independent nations, and he could point to considerable evidence to show that treaties had never been a success.[19]

Jackson himself had been a United States commissioner in drawing up treaties with the southern Indians. As his experience with the Indians

---

petual Harrow upon My Feelings': John Quincy Adams and the American Indian," *New England Quarterly* 46 (September 1973): 339 79.

18. *House Report* no. 87, 20–2, serial 190, pp. 1–3.

19. Jackson's relations with the Indians and his role in their removal from east of the Mississippi have been variously commented upon. Many historians have viewed his opinions and his actions harshly, heaping on him most of the opprobrium for the removal policy. For an extreme example, see Edward Pessen, *Jacksonian America: Society, Personality, and Politics*, rev. ed. (Homewood, Illinois: Dorsey Press, 1978), p. 296, which describes Jackson's position as "a blending of hypocrisy, cant, and rapaciousness, seemingly shot through with contradictions. Inconsistencies however are present only if the language of the presidential state papers is taken seriously. . . . When the lofty rhetoric is discounted and viewed for what is was—sheer rationale for policy based on much more mundane considerations—then an almost frightening consistency becomes apparent." A more seious and balanced appraisal of Jackson's policy, is Satz, *American Indian Policy in the Jacksonian Era*. The events get a special twist in the psychohistory by Michael Paul Rogin, *Fathers and Children: Andrew Jackson and the Subjugation of the American Indian* (New York: Alfred A. Knopf, 1975). Rogin suggests that Jackson was a victim of separation anxiety because of his parents' early death and that he proved his manhood by destroying Indians. Although the book has much good material, its argument is not convincing. A favorable view that attempts to understand the complex situation facing Jackson is Francis Paul Prucha, "Andrew Jackson's Indian Policy: A Reassessment," *Journal of American History* 56 (December 1969): 527–39.

grew, he began to question openly the wisdom of the traditional procedure. In March 1817, while military commander in the South, he had complained to President Monroe about the absurdity of making treaties with the Indians, whom he considered subjects of the United States with no sovereignty of their own. Congress, Jackson maintained, had as much right to legislate for the Indians as for the people of the territories, and he strongly urged—for the good of the Indians, he insisted, as well as for the good of the nation—that Congress make use of this right to prescribe the Indian bounds and to occupy and possess parts of their lands when the safety, interest, or defense of the country should render it necessary. Due compensation was to be given, of course, just as in any exercise of the right of eminent domain. The Indians, he said, "have only a possessory right to the soil, for the purpose of hunting and not the right of domain, hence I conclude that Congress has full power, by law, to regulate all the concerns of the Indians."[20]

Monroe had found Jackson's view "new but very deserving of attention," and, encouraged no doubt by the favorable reception of his views in high circles, Jackson had stuck to his position. In 1820 he wrote to Secretary of War Calhoun on the subject of Indian affairs. The message was the same. It was absurd to treat with the Indians rather than legislate for them. It was "high time to do away with the farce of treating with the Indian tribes." Again his views were approved, but Calhoun was unable to get Congress to modify the treaty system.[21] During the seven and one-half years that Calhoun held the position of secretary of war, with the conduct of Indian affairs under his department, forty treaties were signed with the Indian nations. The picture had not changed. The solemnities were still observed; the documents spoke formally of grants and guarantees as though the great powers of the world were negotiating.

Jackson brought his early views with him when he entered the White House. He was convinced that the Indians could no longer exist as independent enclaves within the state. They must either move west or become subject to the laws of the states.

Assured of presidential sympathy, Georgia took new action against the Cherokees. At the end of 1828 the Georgia legislature added Cherokee lands to certain northwestern counties of Georgia. A year later, it extended the laws of the state over these lands, effective June 1, 1830. Thereafter the Cherokee laws and customs were to be null and void.[22] The Cherokees

20. *Correspondence of Andrew Jackson*, 2: 279–81.

21. Monroe to Jackson, October 5, 1817, ibid., pp. 331–32; Jackson to Calhoun, September 2, 1820, and January 18, 1821, ibid., 3: 32, 36–38; Calhoun to Jackson, November 16, 1821, ibid., p. 132.

22. William C. Dawson, comp., *A Compilation of the Laws of the State of Georgia* (Milledgeville: Grantland and Orme, 1831), pp. 198–99.

immediately protested and made representations to the president and to Congress.

Jackson, whatever his shortcomings in dealing with the Indians, was not one to hide his realistic intentions behind pleasant phrases, for, as he had written to an Indian commissioner a few years earlier, "with all Indians, the best plan will be to come out with candor."[23] Through the instrumentality of Secretary of War John H. Eaton, Jackson answered the Cherokees. Bluntly he told them that they had no hope of succor from the federal government. The letter of Eaton to the delegation of the Cherokees on April 18, 1829, was an unequivocal statement of the Jackson policy.[24]

Eaton informed the Indians that by the Declaration of Independence and the treaty of 1783 all the sovereignty which pertained to Great Britain had been conferred upon the states of the Union. "If, as is the case," he told the Indians, "you have been permitted to abide on your lands from that period to the present, enjoying the right of the soil, and privilege to hunt, it is not thence to be inferred, that this was any thing more than a permission, growing out of compacts with your nation; nor is it a circumstance whence, now to deny to those states, the exercise of their original sovereignty." The treaties with the Indians, which for the supporters of Indian rights were a great arsenal of arguments, were turned to his own uses by the secretary of war. The "emphatic language" of the Treaty of Hopewell, he told the Cherokees, could not be mistaken. The United States *gave peace* to the Indians and took them again into favor and under her protection. The treaty *allotted* and *defined* the hunting grounds. It secured to the Indians the privilege of pursuing game and protection from encroachment. "No right, however, save a mere possessory one, is by the provisions of the treaty of Hopewell conceded to your nation. The soil, and the use of it, were suffered to remain with you, while the Sovereignty abided precisely where it did before, in those states within whose limits you were situated." Later treaties, after renewed hostilities, were similar to the Treaty of Hopewell, guaranteeing occupancy and possession of the Indian country. "But the United States, always mindful of the authority of the States, even when treating for what was so much desired, peace with her red brothers, forbore to offer a guarantee adverse to the Sovereignty of Georgia. They could not do so; they had not the power." The compact of 1802, Eaton added, had nothing to say about sovereignty. Both parties to the compact knew well where it lay: with the state. There was nothing to be offered to the Cherokees but the urgent recommendation that they move west of the Mississippi.

23. Jackson to John D. Terrill, July 29, 1826, *Correspondence of Andrew Jackson*, 3: 308–9.

24. Eaton to Cherokee delegation, April 18, 1829, OIA LS, vol. 5, pp. 408–12 (M21, reel 5). This document was seen at the time—by both friends and foes of Jackson—as epitomizing Jackson's position.

The same doctrine was set forth by Jackson's attorney general, the Georgian John M. Berrien, who insisted that the United States had granted peace to the Cherokees in 1785 as a "mere grace of the conqueror."[25] The argument might have sounded plausible in 1830, but in 1783 and the years following, Congress did not look much like a conqueror imposing terms on the conquered Indians. With nervous anxiety, the United States then sought to keep the Indians at peace at all costs rather than risk any more hostilities, which a new nation in its weakness could ill afford.

Jackson moved ahead boldly. In his first message to Congress, on December 8, 1829, he addressed himself to the problems of the "condition and ulterior destiny of the Indian tribes within the limits of some of our States." He called attention to the fact that some of the southern Indians had "lately attempted to erect an independent government within the limits of Georgia and Alabama," that the states had countered this infringement on their sovereignty by extending their laws over the Indians, and that the Indians in turn had appealed to the federal government. Did the federal government have a right to sustain the Indian pretensions, he asked. His answer was forthright. The Constitution forbade the erection of a new state within the territory of an existing state without that state's permission. Still less, then, could it allow a "foreign and independent government" to establish itself there. On these grounds, he told Congress, he had informed the Indians that their attempt to establish an independent government would not be countenanced by the executive of the United States, and he had advised them either to emigrate beyond the Mississippi or to submit to the laws of the states. He came back to the old argument: if the Indians remained in contact with the whites they would be degraded and destroyed. "Humanity and national honor demand that every effort should be made to avert so great a calamity." The solution was to set apart an ample district west of the Mississippi, to be guaranteed to the Indian tribes as long as they occupied it. There they could be taught the arts of civilization.[26]

Jackson denied any intention to use force. "This emigration should be voluntary, for it would be as cruel as unjust to compel the aborigines to abandon the graves of their fathers and seek a home in a distant land." The protestation had a hollow ring, for the Indians were to be informed that if they remained they would be subject to the state laws and would lose much of their beloved land. With a touch of sarcasm, the president pronounced it visionary for the Indians to hope to retain hunting lands on

25. "Opinion of the Attorney General as to the Right Acquired to the Soil under Existing Treaties with the Cherokees," March 10, 1830, *House Executive Document* no. 89, 21–1, serial 197, pp. 45–46.
26. Israel, *State of the Union Messages*, 1: 308–10.

which they had neither dwelt nor made improvements, "merely because they had seen them from the mountain or passed them in the chase."[27]

Following the suggestion of the president, the House and the Senate each introduced an Indian removal bill. The bills were similar in nature, and the House version was dropped in favor of the Senate bill. The measure, like the president's message, made no mention of coercion to remove the Indians, and on the surface it seemed harmless and humane enough, with its provisions for a permanent guarantee of possession of the new lands, compensation for the improvement left behind, and aid and assistance to the emigrants. But those who knew the policy and practice of Jackson and the Georgians and the adamant stand of the Indians against removal understood that force would be inevitable.

MOTIVATION FOR REMOVAL

The strongest pressure for removal of the Indians from Georgia and the other southeastern states came from the land hunger of the whites. When the cotton plantation system began its dynamic drive west across the gulf plains after the War of 1812, a movement stimulated by the invention of the cotton gin and the seemingly endless demand for cotton to feed the new mills in England and the Northeast, the lands held by the Indians seemed an enormous obstacle. All of the Five Civilized Tribes—Cherokee, Creek, Choctaw, Chickasaw, and Seminole—had sloughed off rims of territory by treaties of cession in the period 1815–1830, a paring down that opened much good land to white exploitation. But all the tribes insisted on retaining their heartlands, sizable blocks of territory that seemed to Georgia and the new states of Mississippi and Alabama (admitted to the Union in 1817 and 1819, respectively) to be alien enclaves in their midst. It was possible for some years to postpone the conflict, as free land was taken up and as Georgia continued to expect action from the federal government in regard to Cherokee lands under the compact of 1802. But in the 1820s the push for new lands intensified, and the vehemence of the demands of the southern states increased. An added element was the discovery of gold within the Cherokee Nation in 1829. As would be the case with strikes in the Far West later in the century, the word of gold fired the Georgians with new enthusiasm for Cherokee lands, and many rushed into the region in violation of the Indians' territorial rights.

There was no effective check upon the covetousness for land. Land was the most important commodity in early nineteenth-century America, and

27. Ibid., p. 310.

the sale of the public domain was a major source of funding for the national government before the Civil War. White society, both northern and southern, had a fundamental belief that the land was there to be exploited and that the Indians were not making full use of its possibilities. Governor George C. Gilmer of Georgia declared in 1830 that "treaties were expedients by which ignorant, intractable, and savage people were induced without bloodshed to yield up what civilized peoples had a right to possess by virtue of that command of the Creator delivered to man upon his formation—be fruitful, multiply, and replenish the earth, and subdue it." To the House Committee on Indian Affairs, which reported the removal bill in 1830, the practice of extinguishing Indian titles by money payments was "but the substitute which humanity and expediency have imposed, in place of the sword, in arriving at the actual enjoyment of property claimed by the right of discovery, and sanctioned by the natural superiority allowed to the claims of civilized communities over those of savage tribes." Semi-literate frontiersmen justified their encroachment on Chickasaw lands by challenging the government to remove them from "fine fertile countrys lying uncultivated."[28]

There were strong arguments made for the rights of the Indians to their lands, but they ultimately foundered on the deepseated conviction that the white man had a superior right to the land. The Jacksonian and Georgian contention that the Indians had only a possessory right to the soil—a "mere right of occupancy"—was not a spur-of-the-moment argument to cover white cupidity for Indian lands. There had long been an overriding reluctance to admit any title in fee for Indians. Despite the Jeffersonian principle that the salvation of the Indians lay in private ownership of land, treaties negotiated with them generally had fallen short of providing fee simple ownership either to individual Indians or to tribes.[29]

The Jacksonian drive to relocate the Indians west of the Mississippi, however, failed to appreciate their attachment to their ancestral homes. The ancestors of the whites who now sought Indian lands had themselves emigrated from their homelands, and thousands of white citizens each year were pulling up their roots and moving west. If whites, seeking a better condition, could adjust to the pains of removal, why not the Indians. Jackson told a Choctaw leader in 1830:

> The attachment you feel for the soil which encompasses the bones of
> your ancestors is well known. Our forefathers had the same feeling

28. Gilmer statement quoted in Albert K. Weinberg, *Manifest Destiny: A Study of Nationalistic Expansionism in American History* (Baltimore: Johns Hopkins Press, 1935), p. 83; *House Report* no. 227, 21–1, serial 200, pp. 6–7; petition of intruders on Chickasaw lands, September 5, 1810, in Carter, *Territorial Papers*, 6: 107.

29. Robert W. McCluggage, "The Senate and Indian Land Titles, 1800–1825," *Western Historical Quarterly* 1 (October 1970): 415–25.

when a long time ago, to obtain happiness, they left their lands beyond the great waters, and sought a new and quiet home in those distant and unexplored regions. If they had not done so, where would have been their children? And where the prosperity they now enjoy? The old world would scarcely have afforded support for a people who, by the change their fathers made, have become prosperous and happy. In future time, so will it be with your children.[30]

By liberal terms and inducements, the promoters of removal hoped to persuade the Indian tribes that it would be to their benefit to move away from the stresses and pressures that came from existence within the state and that the advantages would overcome the attachment to their ancestral lands. Such a voluntary move was made by considerable numbers of Indians, but the great majority preferred to stay where they were, and they insisted on their right to do so.

Desire for Indian lands was not the only motivation for removal. The concern about states' rights and the fear of a bitter federal-state jurisdictional contest that might even lead to military conflict was not simply a rationalization for base economic motives but a very real issue in the pre-Civil War period. The demands made for federal protection of the Indians in their own culture on their ancestral lands within the states in the East ran up against the hard fact that the United States government could not risk an all-out confrontation with Georgia. The federal government did not have a standing army of sufficient strength to protect the enclaves of Indian territory from the encroachments of the whites. Jackson could not withstand Georgia's demands for the end of the *imperium in imperio* represented by the Cherokee Nation and its new constitution, not because of some inherent immorality on his part but because the political situation of America would not permit it.

The jurisdictional dispute cannot be simply dismissed. Were the tribes independent nations? The question received its legal answer from the Supreme Court when John Marshall defined the Indian tribes as "domestic dependent nations." But aside from the judicial decision, were the Indians, in fact, independent, and could they have maintained their independence without the support—political and military—of the federal government? The answer, clearly, was no, as writers at the time pointed out. The federal government could have stood firm in defense of the Indian nation against Georgia, but this would have brought it into head-on collision with a state that insisted its sovereignty was being impinged upon by the Cherokees. This was not a conflict that anyone in the federal government wanted.

30. Jackson to Greenwood LeFlore, August 23, 1830, quoted in Arthur H. DeRosier, Jr., *The Removal of the Choctaw Indians* (Knoxville: University of Tennessee Press, 1970), p. 119.

President Monroe had been slow to give in to the demands of the Georgians. He had refused to be panicked into hasty action before he had considered all the possibilities. But eventually he became convinced that stubborn resistance to the southern states would solve nothing, and from that point on he and his successors, Adams and Jackson, sought to solve the problem by removing the cause. They wanted the Indians to be placed in some area where the problem of federal versus state jurisdiction would not arise, where the Indians could be granted land in fee simple by the federal government and not have to worry about what some state thought were its rights and prerogatives.

There was also, it must be admitted, genuine humanitarian concern for the Indians, in which their voluntary removal out of contact with whites appeared to be a viable, indeed perhaps the only, answer. Despite the optimism of supporters of the programs for civilizing the Indians, an uncomfortable conclusion had become increasingly clear: the contact of Indians with white civilization had deleterious effects upon the Indians. The efforts at improvement were vitiated or overbalanced by the steady pressure of white vices, to which the Indians succumbed. Instead of prospering under white tutelage, Indians in many areas were degenerating and disappearing. That men as knowledgeable in Indian ways as Thomas L. McKenney, William Clark, and the Baptist missionary Isaac McCoy were longtime and ardent promoters of Indian removal should give us pause in seeing only insatiable land hunger or Jacksonian villainy behind the policy.[31] The promoters of the program argued that only if the Indians were removed beyond contact with whites could the slow process of education, civilization, and Christianization take place. Insofar as removal was necessary to safeguard the Indian, to that extent the intercourse laws had failed.

A shift of attitude can be seen in Thomas L. McKenney. His enthusiastic reports on the progress of the Indian schools and Indian civilization in general were replaced by more dismal reporting. Although he had for some time been favorable to the voluntary removal of groups of Indians, he asserted that his tour through the Indian country in 1827 had opened his eyes to the degradation of the eastern tribes. When asked to report in 1830 on the previous eight years of the program for civilizing the Indians, he no longer considered salvation possible in the present location of the tribes. The condition of the Florida Indians he described as "in all respects truly deplorable. It is not known that they have advanced a single step in any

---

31. Recent scholarly studies of these three men make clear their humanitarian concern for the Indians. See Herman J. Viola, *Thomas L. McKenney: Architect of America's Early Indian Policy, 1816–1830* (Chicago: Swallow Press, 1974); Jerome O. Steffen, *William Clark: Jeffersonian Man on the Frontier* (Norman: University of Oklahoma Press, 1977); George A. Schultz, *An Indian Canaan: Isaac McCoy and the Vision of an Indian State* (Norman: University of Oklahoma Press, 1972).

sort of improvement; and as to the means of education, when offered to them, they were refused." The Indians in the Northwest, he reported, "pretend to nothing more than to maintain all the characteristic traits of their race. They catch fish, and plant patches of corn; dance, paint, hunt, get drunk, when they can get liquor, fight, and often starve." Their condition, however, was far better than that of the Creeks and better than most of the Choctaws. McKenney agreed that those Choctaws who had benefited by instruction were better off than they had been before. "But these were, to my eye," he said, "like green spots in the desert. The rest was cheerless and hopeless enough. Before this personal observation, I was sanguine in the hope of seeing those people relieved, and saved, where they are. But a sight of their condition, and the prospect of the collisions which have since taken place, and which have grown out of the anomalous relations which they bear to the States, produced a sudden change in my opinion and my hopes."[32]

The paternalism of this position, of course, is inescapable. In a typically benevolent frame of mind McKenney wrote in 1829: "Seeing as I do the condition of these people, and that they are bordering on destruction, I would, were I empowered, take them *firmly* but *kindly* by the hand, and tell them they must go; and I would do this, on the same principle that I would take my own children by the hand, firmly, but kindly and lead them from a district of Country in which the plague was raging." President Jackson expressed a similar view in private correspondence in 1829. He said: "You may rest assured that I shall adhere to the just and humane policy towards the Indians which I have commenced. In this spirit I have recommended them to quit their possessions on this side of the Mississippi, and go to a country to the west where there is every probability that they will always be free from the mercenary influence of White men, and undisturbed by the local authority of the states: Under such circumstances the General Government can exercise a parental control over their interests and possibly perpetuate their race."[33]

The idea of parental or paternal care was pervasive. Once removal was accomplished, Jackson told Congress in 1832, "there would be no question of jurisdiction to prevent the Government from exercising such a general control over their affairs as may be essential to their interest and safety."[34]

An example of humanitarian support of removal (although interwoven

32. Report of McKenney, March 22, 1830, *Senate Document* no. 110, 21–1, serial 193, pp. 2–3. For a critical, but unconvincing, appraisal of McKenney, see Richard Drinnon, *Facing West: The Metaphysics of Indian-Hating and Empire-Building* (Minneapolis: University of Minnesota Press, 1980), pp. 165–90.

33. McKenney to Eli Baldwin, October 28, 1829, OIA LS, vol. 6, p. 140 (M21, reel 6); Jackson to James Gadsden, October 12, 1829, *Correspondence of Andrew Jackson*, 4: 81.

34. Richardson, *Messages and Papers of the Presidents*, 2: 565–66.

with political interests) was the organization set up in New York City to promote Jackson's removal policy. When prominent church groups spoke out against that policy, McKenney gathered a group of clergymen and lay-men (mostly Dutch Reformed) to counteract the cry that the government was embarked upon an un-Christian enterprise. On July 22, 1829, the Board for the Emigration, Preservation, and Improvement of the Aborig-ines of America was established. McKenney, in addressing the board on August 12, argued removal in humanitarian and religious terms; his con-cern was to preserve the Indians from complete degradation and to enable them to improve and civilize themselves outside of contact with whites. The board, however, was short-lived. It sent a memorial to Congress and issued a pamphlet containing addresses and other documents; but when McKenney was removed from office by Jackson in August 1830, the organi-zation collapsed.[35]

CONTROVERSY AND DEBATE

The Cherokee Indians strongly protested Georgia's action and carried their arguments to the federal government. The politically astute leaders, gener-ally mixed-bloods who were wise in the ways of whites, kept delegations in Washington to watch developments and to present the Cherokee posi-tion to federal officials. On February 17, 1829, the Cherokee delegation ad-dressed a letter to the secretary of war, pointing to the tribes' national and territorial rights and to Georgia's violations of these rights in extending jurisdiction over the Indian lands. Ten days later the Cherokees presented a memorial to Congress in which they made the same points, appealing to the federal government to protect them in their legal rights and to uphold the treaty obligations that the United States had entered into with the tribe.[36]

The Indian action was ineffective in reversing the position of the Jack-son administration. The removal bill introduced in February 1830 was re-

35. Francis Paul Prucha, "Thomas L. McKenney and the New York Indian Board," *Mississippi Valley Historical Review* 48 (March 1962): 635–55. McKenney's address and other pertinent documents are printed in *Documents and Proceedings Relating to the Formation and Progress of a Board in the City of New York, for the Emigration, Preserva-tion, and Improvement, of the Aborigines of America* (New York, 1829). Some of the material is also printed in Thomas L. McKenney, *Memoirs, Official and Personal* (New York: Paine and Burgess, 1846).

36. The letter of February 17 could not be located, but its contents can be determined by the specific reply it occasioned, Eaton's letter of April 18, 1829. The Cherokee memo-rial of February 27, 1829, is printed in *House Document* no. 145, 20–2, serial 187. See also Cherokee memorials of November 5, 1829, and December 18, 1829, in *House Report* no. 311, 21–1, serial 201, pp. 2–9; and Creek memorial of February 3, 1830, against the actions of Alabama, in *House Report* no. 169, 21–1, serial 199.

ported favorably by the Committee of Indian Affairs in both the House and the Senate. The Senate committee urged removal of the Indians to the west, "where they can be secured against the intrusion of any other people; where, under the protection of the United States, and with their *aid*, they can pursue their plan of civilization, and, ere long, be in the peaceable enjoyment of a civil government of their own choice, and where Christian and philanthropist can have ample scope for their labors of love and benevolence." The House committee, in a long exposition of the administration's views, spoke in the same benevolent terms.[37]

This position was countered by a campaign in support of the Cherokees' rights that sought, even before the congressional committees had made their formal reports, to arouse the public conscience against the removal scheme and to convince Congress to support the Indian nations against Georgia and the other states. The campaign, although on the surface a great outpouring of Christian sentiment and a spontaneous upsurge of public opinion, was in fact largely the inspiration and the work of one man, the secretary of the American Board of Commissioners for Foreign Missions, Jeremiah Evarts.

Evarts, born in Vermont in 1781 and a graduate of Yale University, was a lawyer, but he devoted most of his short life to the cause of religion and especially Christian missions. He became associated with the American Board shortly after its founding in 1810 and in 1821 became its secretary. Evarts had close acquaintance with the Cherokees and other southern tribes because of the American Board's missions among them. He had traveled through the Indian country, counted numerous Indian leaders among his personal friends, and had studied their history and legal claims. If any man ever held an absolutely sure position, it was Jeremiah Evarts in regard to the rights of the Cherokee Indians to stay where they were in Georgia and the obligation of the United States to protect those rights without delay or equivocation. But Evarts was more than an expert on the legal rights of the Cherokees. He was a man with a vision of a world fully evangelized, of universal conversion to Christ, and he saw the new American nation as the vehicle of this great work. The movement of Christian benevolence, reaching its height as the Indian question came to the fore, became for Protestant Americans of Evarts's persuasion a great national mission. Evarts insisted upon Christian influence on civil society and upon the obligation of committed Christians to call to task civil rulers if they departed from the path of justice and morality. It was no self-righteous, carping attitude that motivated such criticism but a profound patriotic view that God had called this nation to a special mission—to be a special beacon of good-

37. *Senate Document* no. 61, 21–1, serial 193; *House Report* no. 227, 21–1, serial 200.

ness in a corrupt world—and that God in his vengeance would rain disaster and destruction on America if it, as a nation, sinned against that covenant.[38]

Evarts was convinced that the federal government's refusal to protect the Cherokees against the clamors of Georgia would be a moral wrong, a sin of great magnitude. The only way to prevent it would be through an outcry by the Christians of the nation, protesting against the threatened action with such a loud and persistent voice that the national leaders would turn aside from their sinful plans. Evarts set about to stir up the conscience of the nation and to direct its indignation and sense of outrage into effective channels in the national councils.

The first and most significant work of Evarts in support of the Cherokees was a series of twenty-four articles that appeared in the *National Intelligencer* between August 5 and December 19, 1829, under the pseudonym William Penn. The articles began with a statement of the moral crisis facing the nation in the removal question, the national sin that would bring God's sure punishment if the obligations to the Indians were cast aside, and then moved to a detailed analysis of the Cherokee treaties and their recognition of the Cherokees as a nation. The Penn essays were the fullest and best statement of the Cherokee case and the obligations of the United States to support it. They were reprinted in numerous newspapers and periodicals and widely circulated in pamphlet form. Churchmen and congressmen alike drew their arguments from Evarts's writings, and they looked to him to instruct them as they moved against the Jackson policy and Georgia's actions.[39]

Evarts initiated a widespread campaign of submitting memorials to Congress in favor of the Cherokees and against the removal bill. His strategy was to enlist individuals or groups to organize in major cities public meetings that would endorse a memorial written by Evarts. The first such memorial came from New York City at the end of December 1829. It presented information on the rights of the Indians and their treaties, drawn

38. I follow here the introduction by Francis Paul Prucha to Jeremiah Evarts, *Cherokee Removal: The "William Penn" Essays and Other Writings* (Knoxville: University of Tennessee Press, 1981). Biographical material on Evarts is found in E. C. Tracy, *Memoir of the Life of Jeremiah Evarts, Esq.* (Boston: Crocker and Brewster, 1845); J. Orin Oliphant, ed., *Through the South and West with Jeremiah Evarts in 1826* (Lewisburg, Pennsylvania: Bucknell University Press, 1956); "Biography: Sketch of the Life and Character of Jeremiah Evarts, Esq.," *Missionary Herald* 27 (October 1831): 305–13; (November 1831): 337–46; *Dictionary of American Biography*, s.v. Evarts, Jeremiah, by H. W. Howard Knott. There is an excellent discussion of Evarts' world view in Oliphant, *Jeremiah Evarts*, pp. 8–19.

39. Jeremiah Evarts, *Essays on the Present Crisis in the Condition of the American Indians: First Published in the National Intelligencer, under the Signature of William Penn* (Boston: Perkins and Marvin, 1829).

largely from the Penn essays, and ended with an earnest plea that Congress intervene on the behalf of the Indians in order to "save the nation, by prompt and decisive measures, from the calamity that hangs over it." The memorial did not get a friendly reception in Congress, where Georgia senators and congressmen lashed out against it for impeaching the character and conduct of the southern states. Representative Richard H. Wilde was especially vehement, ridiculing the attempt of the memorialists to meddle in other people's business, and he voiced his disgust over "these everlasting political homilies—this mawkish mixture of sentiment and selfishness—this rage for instructing all the world in their appropriate duties."[40]

Evarts and his friends were chastened, and they moderated their condemnatory language in future memorials, but they were undaunted and stepped up their petition campaign. Another long memorial prepared in Boston was submitted on February 8; then short petitions in the same vein were distributed to friends around the country, to be signed by concerned Christians and forwarded to Congress. Evarts made use of the network of parishes already in touch with the American Board offices and enlisted the aid of special zealots like George B. Cheevers, later to be a well-known abolitionist, who as a student at Andover Seminary pushed with great vigor the campaign to save the Cherokees and thus the sacred honor of the nation.[41]

The final argument of Evarts and other opponents of Indian removal shifted away from the question of legal rights to the inexpediency of emigration. While the supporters of the policy spoke of exchanging eastern lands for lands of equal or better quality in the West, the critics described in the most dismal terms those districts set aside to receive the emigrants. Thus Evarts in the final number of the Penn essays spoke of the misery that removal would bring to thousands of innocent persons, and a memorial he prepared in early 1831 described how the despondent Indians would sink into anarchy and how the temptations of the open land to the west would counteract the forces that had led them to adopt agriculture in the East. Vagrant white men and savage Indians would press upon them, and

40. "Memorial unanimously adopted by a meeting of citizens of the City of New York, convened by a public notice," December 28, 1829, in Records of the U.S. Senate, Memorials and Petitions, Committee on Indian Affairs, 21A–G8, National Archives, Record Group 46; *Register of Debates in Congress*, 6: 7–8.

41. The Boston memorial is in *House Report* no. 245, 21–1, serial 200. Cheever's work can be followed in the Cheever Family Papers, American Antiquarian Society, Worcester, Massachusetts; see also Robert M. York, *George B. Cheever: Religious and Social Reformer, 1807–1890*, University of Maine Studies, 2d ser. no. 69 (Orono, Maine: University Press, 1955). The petitions are in Records of the U.S. Senate, Memorials and Petitions, Committee on Indian Affairs (RG 46), and Records of the U.S. House of Representatives, Memorials and Petitions, Committee on Indian Affairs (RG 233). A good many are published in the serial set of congressional documents.

the very nature of the land assigned them was unknown. That little was in fact known about the lands in the West did not stop fanciful descriptions to suit the purpose of Jackson's opponents.[42]

While Evarts was masterminding the petition campaign, he was simultaneously engaged in another publicity endeavor on behalf of his particular views on the Indian question. This was caused by the appearance in the *North American Review* for January 1830 of a long article by Lewis Cass, governor of Michigan Territory. In the article, which was nominally a review of the pamphlet published by the New York Board for the Emigration, Preservation, and Improvement of the Aborigines of America, Cass came out strongly in favor of Jackson's program of removal, even though he had in the past been critical of the policy. Evarts called the article "the most important thing that has transpired of late, on this subject," and he declared that the piece was "distinguished for servility and sycophancy." He told a friend, "This man wishes to trim his sails, in such a manner as to catch the breeze of government favor and patronage." Evarts succeeded in evoking articles and pamphlets that refuted Cass's position, and Congress and the public were thus made more fully aware of the Boston missionaries' position.[43]

Through all this agitation, Evarts kept in close touch with what was going on in Congress. His chief point of contact in Washington was Theodore Frelinghuysen, Whig senator from New Jersey, a man of similar Christian outlook whose active promotion of such Christian programs as the Sunday School Union and temperance brought him the title of the "Christian statesman." Frelinghuysen corresponded frequently with Evarts about the Indian question and about another of Evarts's campaigns, prohibition of the Sunday mails. Evarts corresponded also with other sympathetic members of Congress, some of whom regularly solicited his advice.[44] As the debate on removal intensified in Congress, Evarts went to

42. A good many historians have accepted the arguments of Jackson's opponents without careful examination, and some have gone so far as to assert that the United States government turned to removal when Major Stephen H. Long submitted his report in 1820 on the desert conditions west of the Mississippi. See the refutation of this position in Francis Paul Prucha, "Indian Removal and the Great American Desert," *Indiana Magazine of History* 59 (December 1963): 299–322.

43. Lewis Cass, "Removal of the Indians," *North American Review* 30 (January 1830): 62–121; Evarts to Eleazar Lord, January 8, 1830, Evarts Family Papers, Yale University Library. An example of the anti-Cass pamphlets was George B. Cheever, *Removal of the Indians: An Article from the American Monthly Magazine; An Examination of an Article in the North American Review; and an Exhibition of the Advancement of the Southern Tribes, in Civilization and Christianity* (Boston: Peirce and Williams, 1830).

44. Frelinghuysen to Evarts, January 11 and February 22 and 24, 1830, Evarts Family Papers; Frelinghuysen to Evarts, February 1, 1830, Letters to Jeremiah Evarts, Library of Congress. See also correspondence with Isaac C. Bates, Edward Everett, and Ambrose

Washington to follow the course of events from close at hand and to offer advice and assistance to the Indians and their defenders. The debates, most of which he listened to from the gallery, increased his concern and confirmed the harsh judgments he had already made—both about the callousness of the Jackson party and about the apathy of the well-meaning Christians of the nation. He applauded the speeches of Senator Frelinghuysen, who spoke for six hours against the administration measure, and of Senator Peleg Sprague of Maine, as well as the similar speeches in the House of Henry R. Storrs of New York, William E. Ellsworth of Connecticut, and Edward Everett and Isaac C. Bates of Massachusetts; and he condemned the arguments of those who spoke in favor of removal.[45]

Jeremiah Evarts and his friends tried to make the removal question simply a moral issue. Would the United States government honor its treaty obligations to the Cherokees, recognize their nationhood, and protect them against the illegal pretensions of Georgia? Or would Jackson and the Georgians drive ahead in their evil ways and make the nation liable to God's punishment? "Nothing can save us," George Cheever wrote, "unless the public mind be universally aroused from its lethargy, and an appeal made, so loud, simultaneous, and decisive, as shall astonish the world at the power of moral feeling in the heart of the country, and cause the most inveterate and bold supporters of national iniquity to tremble."[46]

Yet beneath the surface of this bombast was a strong party feeling; each side accused the other of operating not on moral principles but on political ones. Evarts was particularly pointed in charging the supporters of removal with acting in "the spirit of party." It is clear, nevertheless, that Evarts got all his support from Whigs and other anti-Jackson men and that the fight against removal was used as one means to embarrass the Jackson administration. The administration's supporters, indeed, insisted that the op-

---

Spencer in Evarts Family Papers. Evarts's concern to prohibit the distribution of mail on Sunday was almost as deep as his concern for the Indians—and for the same reason: he feared that the nation, by desecrating the Sabbath, would incure divine wrath. His campaign of petitions against the Sunday mails was comparable to that against Cherokee removal and no more successful.

45. The anti-removal speeches are printed in Jeremiah Evarts, ed., *Speeches on the Passage of the Bill for the Removal of the Indians, Delivered in the Congress of the United States, April and May, 1830* (Boston: Perkins and Marvin, 1830); they are reported in *Register of Debates in Congress*, 6: 305ff and 580ff. Evarts wrote an account of the debate that appeared in seven issues of the *New-York Observer* in the summer and fall of 1830 under the title "History of the Indian Bill." Evarts's stay in Washington is fully reported, in large part through quotations from letters and reports of Evarts, in Tracy, *Jeremiah Evarts*, pp. 353–82. See also Satz, *American Indian Policy in the Jacksonian Era*, pp. 20–31.

46. Cheever, *Removal of the Indians*, p. 10.

position to the removal bill was a matter of party politics and that the sudden feeling for the Indians was a ruse to defeat the president on an important measure. Wilson Lumpkin of Georgia declared that every one of the supporters of the Cherokees was an opponent of Jackson on political grounds, and Jackson himself claimed that the opposition to the bill was part of the "secrete workings of Duff Green, Calhoun and Co."[47]

The Senate passed the removal bill 28 to 19 on April 24 and the House by the narrower margin of 102 to 97 on May 26, and Jackson signed it on May 28, 1830. On its face it was a "liberal" measure that Jackson hoped would win over the Indians. It authorized the president to mark off lands west of the Mississippi "not included in any state or organized territory, and to which the Indian title has been extinguished," and to exchange such districts for lands held by the eastern Indians. The president was "solemnly to assure the tribe or nation with which the exchange is made, that the United States will forever secure and guaranty to them, and their heirs or successors, the country so exchanged with them." The act provided payment for improvements made on present lands, for aid and assistance in emigrating and for the first year after removal, and for protection of the Indians in their new home and the "same superintendence and care" over the tribes that was authorized in their present places of residence. The act specifically noted that it did not authorize or direct the violation of any existing treaties. For carrying out these provisions, Congress appropriated five hundred thousand dollars.[48] The symbol that the act had become was perhaps more important than its specific provisions. Its passage meant congressional authorization of the removal policy that Jackson's administration had announced, and steps were quickly taken to begin treaty negotiations for removal.

The opponents of removal did not admit defeat, however. They noted the slim margin of victory in the House and that Jackson's Maysville Road bill veto on May 27 lost him some of his supporters. Evarts declared that "there is great reason to hope for an expression of public opinion, that will compel the government to be cautious, and will ultimately vindicate the rights of the Indians." Congress adjourned on May 31, three days after Jackson signed the Removal Act, and Evarts pinned his hopes on repeal of the law in the next session of Congress, or at least on the prevention of any further appropriations.[49]

47. Wilson Lumpkin, *The Removal of the Cherokee Indians from Georgia*, 2 vols. (Wormsloe, Georgia, 1907; New York: Dodd, Mead and Company, 1907), 1: 74; Jackson to John Coffee, April 24, 1831, *Correspondence of Andrew Jackson*, 4: 269. The political maneuvering is well described in Satz, *American Indian Policy in the Jacksonian Era*, chapters 1 and 2, pp. 9–63.

48. 4 *United States Statutes* 411–12.

49. Tracy, *Jeremiah Evarts*, pp. 374–81.

While in Washington, Evarts, who conferred frequently with the Cherokee delegates, wrote an address to be signed by the Cherokees on their departure from the capital, a statement that was ultimately issued instead by the Cherokee National Council and published in the *Cherokee Phoenix* of July 24, 1830. It was addressed to the people of the United States as a plea for support against removal, and it offered a succinct and compelling statement of the Cherokee position in opposition to the arguments of Georgia and President Jackson.[50]

Passage of the removal bill did not resolve the controversy. If anything, agitation against the administration measure grew stronger as Jackson began to get the movement under way. During 1830 Evarts redoubled his efforts. He edited and published a collection of the chief speeches in Congress against the Indian bill, and he continued his writing against removal.[51] When the second session of the Twenty-first Congress approached (it opened on December 6), Evarts began a new campaign of petitioning in favor of the Indians, the most significant result of which was a memorial in late January 1831 from the Prudential Committee of the American Board. It was Evarts's last effort, for he was seriously ill. After a futile attempt to regain his health in Cuba, he died on May 10, three months after his fiftieth birthday.[52]

For all practical purposes, the Christian crusade against the removal of the Indians died with Evarts. There were, to be sure, a large number of petitions sent to Congress in early 1831, a sizable proportion of them undoubtedly the result of his agitation. Many of these memorials simply repeated the arguments and pleas of the previous year. Others called for the outright repeal of the Removal Act and for refusal to ratify treaties made under it. Still others emphasized the enforcement of the Indian intercourse law of 1802, which prohibited encroachment on Indian lands. Although many were referred to the committees on Indian affairs, others were merely tabled. They had little or no effect on Congress or the administration. Jackson was further goaded by the Senate, which demanded an accounting of his enforcement of the intercourse law in Georgia. The president replied with a strong vindication of his course of action in withdrawing federal

---

50. "Address of the 'Committee and Council of the Cherokee nation in General Council convened' to the people of the United States," *Cherokee Phoenix and Indians' Advocate*, July 24, 1830; Tracy, *Jeremiah Evarts*, p. 432. The address is printed in Tracy, pp. 442–48. Tracy notes that the last two paragraphs were added by the Cherokee council.

51. Included among these writings were "Removal of the Indians," *North American Review* 31 (October 1830): 396–442, and two new "William Penn" articles, *National Intelligencer*, November 24 and 27, 1830.

52. "Memorial of the Prudential Committee of the American Board of Commissioners for Foreign Missions," January 26, 1831, *Senate Document* no. 50, 21–2, serial 204. Evarts's illness and death is treated in Tracy, *Jeremiah Evarts*, pp. 410–17.

troops from the Cherokee lands as soon as Georgia had extended her laws over the area.[53] Soon the petitions and the pamphlets and the press agitation died away almost entirely. Opposition to the removal policy by then had moved to the courts.

THE CHEROKEE CASES

Having failed in their appeals to the president and to Congress, the Cherokees took their case to the Supreme Court.[54] At the urging of Senators Daniel Webster and Frelinghuysen and Representative Ambrose Spencer of New York, the Indians engaged William Wirt as their legal adviser. Wirt, who as attorney general in the Monroe and Adams administrations had approved the removal policy, had changed his mind and was convinced that a court decision in favor of the Cherokees would embarrass Jackson. With the aid and advice of such important Whig lawyers as Webster and James Kent, with funds provided by the Cherokee Nation, and with an encouraging statement of sympathy for the Indians' cause from Chief Justice John Marshall, Wirt (aided by John Sergeant) prepared a case. The Cherokee Nation filed suit in the Supreme Court against the state of Georgia; it sought an injunction against Georgia's encroachment on the Indian territory in violation of the tribe's treaty rights. Wirt contended that the Cherokees were a sovereign nation, not subject to Georgia's territorial jurisdiction, and that the laws of Georgia were null and void because they were repugnant to treaties between the United States and the Cherokees, to the intercourse law of 1802, and to the Constitution by impairing contracts arising from the treaties and by assuming powers in Indian affairs that belonged exclusively to the federal government.[55]

---

53. Jackson's message to the Senate, February 22, 1831, and accompanying documents, *Senate Document* no. 65, 21–2, serial 204.

54. I follow here in large measure the article by Joseph C. Burke, "The Cherokee Cases: A Study in Law, Politics, and Morality," *Stanford Law Review* 21 (February 1969): 500–531. See also Satz, *American Indian Policy in the Jacksonian Era*, pp. 44–50, and William F. Swindler, "Politics as Law: The Cherokee Cases," *American Indian Law Review* 3, no. 1 (1975): 7–20. All these accounts stress the political implications of the Cherokee cases. The crisis for the Supreme Court that these cases occasioned is the theme of Charles Warren, *The Supreme Court in United States History*, rev. ed., 2 vols. (Boston: Little, Brown and Company, 1937), 1: 729–79.

55. Wirt's views were expressed in *Opinion on the Right of the State of Georgia to Extend Her Laws over the Cherokee Nation* (Baltimore: F. Lucas, Jr., 1830). The arguments of Sergeant and Wirt before the Supreme Court were printed in Richard Peters, *The Case of the Cherokee Nation against the State of Georgia* (Philadelphia: John Grigg, 1831). Wirt's interest in the case and his unusual request for a show of opinion from John Marshall before undertaking the case are reported in John P. Kennedy, *Memoirs of the*

Marshall's decision in *Cherokee Nation* v. *Georgia*, March 18, 1831, began with a statement of concern for the Cherokees. "If Courts were permitted to indulge their sympathies," he said, "a case better calculated to excite them can scarcely be imagined." But rather than look at the merits of the case, he moved instead to "a preliminary inquiry." Did the Supreme Court have jurisdiction? Was the Cherokee Nation a foreign state and thus, under the Constitution, able to sue as a plaintiff in the Supreme Court? Marshall admitted that the Cherokees formed "a distinct political society, separated from others, capable of managing its own affairs and governing itself." He noted the treaties by which the United States recognized the tribe as capable of maintaining the relations of peace and war and of being responsible for violations of their political engagements. But were the Indians, in fact, a *foreign* state? Marshall's answer was no, that the relation of the Cherokees and the United States was something different, "perhaps unlike that of any other two people in existence." He noted that the commerce clause of the Constitution listed foreign nations, the several states, and Indian tribes and concluded that the three categories were distinct. He wrote:

> The Indian territory is admitted to compose a part of the United States. In all our maps, geographical treatises, histories, and laws, it is so considered. In all our intercourse with foreign nations, in our commercial regulations, in any attempt at intercourse between Indians and foreign nations, they are considered as within the jurisdictional limits of the United States, subject to many of those restraints which are imposed upon our own citizens. They acknowledge themselves in their treaties to be under the protection of the United States; they admit that the United States shall have the sole and exclusive right of regulating the trade with them, and managing all their affairs as they think proper. . . .
>
> Though the Indians are acknowledged to have an unquestionable, and, heretofore, unquestioned right to the lands they occupy, until that right shall be extinguished by a voluntary cession to our government; yet it may well be doubted whether those tribes which reside within the United States, can, with strict accuracy, be denominated foreign nations. They may, more correctly, perhaps, be denominated domestic dependent nations. They occupy a territory to which we assert a title independent of their will, which must take effect in point

---

Life of William Wirt: Attorney-General of the United States, rev. ed., 2 vols. in 1 (Philadelphia: J. B. Lippincott and Company, 1860), 2: 253–58. See also Marvin R. Cain, "William Wirt against Andrew Jackson: Reflection on an Era," *Mid-America* 47 (April 1965): 113–38.

of possession when their right of possession ceases. Meanwhile they are in a state of pupilage. Their relation to the United States resembles that of a ward to his guardian.

They look to our government for protection; rely upon its kindness and its power; appeal to it for relief to their wants; and address the president as their great father. They and their country are considered by foreign nations, as well as by ourselves, as being so completely under the sovereignty and dominion of the United States, that any attempt to acquire their lands, or to form a political connexion with them, would be considered by all as an invasion of our territory, and an act of hostility.[56]

Associate Justices John McLean, Henry Baldwin, and William Johnson concurred with the decision that the court lacked jurisdiction. Baldwin and Johnson did not agree, however, with Marshall's analysis of the status of the Indian tribes, for they denied that the Cherokees had any political or property rights in Georgia.[57] Thus the court for the present sidestepped a critical confrontation with Jackson and Georgia, and the Jacksonites looked upon the decision as a vindication of their position.

Two justices, Smith Thompson and Joseph Story, dissented, for they believed that the Cherokees were a foreign state, but they did not deliver formal opinions. To counteract the publicity given the decisions of Baldwin and Johnson, Marshall urged Thompson and Story to make public their views; Thompson wrote out his opinion, which Story also accepted.[58] The Thompson opinion renewed hope for the Indian cause, for it indicated the possibility that the court might favor the Cherokees if another case were brought before it. The documents of *Cherokee Nation* v. *Georgia* were publicly aired in a publication for private sale by the court reporter, Richard Peters. In addition to the opinions of the justices, the book included the briefs of the Cherokees' counsel, the treaties with the Cherokees, the opinion of James Kent on the Cherokee claims, and the trade and intercourse law of 1802.[59] Anti-Jackson agitation took on new life, and Jackson was painted as a "nullifier" who refused to enforce the intercourse law. At the meeting of the National Republicans in Baltimore in December 1831, called in order to name candidates for the 1832 election, much was made of Jackson's villainy regarding the Cherokee issue.

The legal cause of the Indians, meanwhile, entered a new stage. Georgia, under a law that took effect on March 1, 1831, forbade whites to reside in

56. 5 Peters 15–20.
57. The concurring opinions of Baldwin and Johnson are printed ibid., pp. 20–50.
58. Thompson's dissent, although not written until the court had rendered its decision, is printed ibid., pp. 50–80.
59. Peters, *Case of the Cherokee Nation*.

the Cherokee country without a license, for the state hoped to remove the missionaries who encouraged and advised the Indians in their adamant stand against removal. When the missionaries did not leave, they were arrested and imprisoned. Two of them, Samuel A. Worcester and Elizur Butler, refused to accept pardons or licenses. The American Board of Commissioners for Foreign Missions, with which these men were affiliated, hired William Wirt and John Sergeant again to bring the Cherokee cause against Georgia to the Supreme Court. Here was a case to test the Georgia-Cherokee controversy that was clearly within the jurisdiction of the court. It was also a case with important political implications, for both Sergeant and Wirt accepted nomination for public office before the Supreme Court took up the case, the former as vice presidential candidate for the National Republican Party and the latter as presidential candidate for the Anti-Masonic Party. They had much at stake in a decision that would reflect adversely upon Jackson as he sought a second term.

Marshall's decision in the case of *Worcester* v. *Georgia*, delivered on March 3, 1832, was a forthright vindication of the Cherokee position, for he declared unconstitutional the extension of state law over Cherokee lands. In his long opinion, the chief justice again examined the status of the Indian tribes and now came to a conclusion that emphasized the political independence of the Cherokees considerably more than had his decision of the previous year.

> The Indian nations had always been considered as distinct, independent political communities, retaining their original natural rights, as the undisputed possessors of the soil, from time immemorial with the single exception of that imposed by irresistible power, which excluded them from intercourse with any other European potentate than the first discoverer of the coast of the particular region claimed; and this was a restriction which those European potentates imposed on themselves, as well as on the Indians. The very term "nation," so generally applied to them, means "a people distinct from others." The Constitution, by declaring treaties already made, as well as those to be made, to be the supreme law of the land, has adopted and sanctioned the previous treaties with the Indian nations, and consequently admits their rank among those powers who are capable of making treaties. The words "treaty" and "nation" are words of our own language, selected in our diplomatic and legislative proceedings, by ourselves, having each a definite and well understood meaning. We have applied them to Indians, as we have applied them to the other nations of the earth. They are applied to all in the same sense.

Marshall argued that the nationhood of the Indians was not destroyed by treaties acknowledging the protection of the United States, for "the settled doctrine of the law of nations is, that a weaker power does not surrender its independence—its right to self-government, by associating with a stronger, and taking its protection." The Cherokee Nation, therefore, was "a distinct community, occupying its own territory, with boundaries accurately described, in which the laws of Georgia can have no force, and which the citizens of Georgia have no right to enter, but with the assent of the Cherokees themselves, or in conformity with treaties, and with the acts of Congress." All intercourse with the Indian nations was vested, not in the state, but in the federal government.[60]

The Supreme Court issued a special mandate ordering the Georgia court to reverse its conviction of Worcester and release him, but there were loopholes in federal laws that made the court's action ineffective. United States marshals could not be sent to free the prisoners until the state judge had refused formally to comply with the order. But Georgia completely ignored the court's proceedings, and no written refusal was forthcoming. Anyway, the Supreme Court adjourned before it could report Georgia's failure to conform. Nor was there any other procedure that Jackson could adopt, even if he had wanted to. He himself declared that "the decision of the supreme court has fell still born, and they find that they cannot coerce Georgia to yield to its mandate."[61]

William Wirt and other opponents of Jackson made use of the *Worcester* decision to charge the president with failure to enforce federal laws, even though they knew that he was powerless to act in the case, and anti-Jacksonites made much of the continual imprisonment of the missionaries. In typical campaign rhetoric, the *Boston Daily Advertiser* asked: "Will the Christian people of the United States give their sanction, by placing him again in office, to the conduct of a President who treats the ministers of the Christian religion with open outrage, loads them with chains, drags them from their peaceful homes to prison, commits them to defiance of law like common criminals to the penitentiary, and violently keeps them there, against the decision of the highest law authority affirming their innocence?"[62]

For his part, Jackson hoped that the impossibility of enforcing the Supreme Court's decision might help to convince the Indians that voluntary removal would be the only practicable solution. He urged Governor Wil-

60. 6 Peters 559–63.

61. Jackson to John Coffee, April 7, 1832, *Correspondence of Andrew Jackson*, 4: 430. Historians still like to quote an alleged Jackson aphorism—"Well, John Marshall has made his decision; now let him enforce it!"—even though it is extremely unlikely that he made such a statement and it is clear that he had no legal grounds for acting. The matter is laid to rest effectively in Warren, *Supreme Court*, 1: 755–68; see also Burke, "Cherokee Cases," pp. 524–28.

62. Quoted in Burke, "Cherokee Cases," p. 528.

son Lumpkin of Georgia not to act in any way that would exacerbate the conflict, and Lumpkin agreed to act in concert with the federal government. The president asked Georgia to pardon the missionaries, and the American Board persuaded them to accept the release.[63]

The rapprochement was due in large part to the nullification threat from Georgia's neighboring state South Carolina, which came in the critical months after *Worcester* v. *Georgia*. Jackson moved cautiously lest he drive Georgia into the nullification camp; but more important, Jackson's opponents saw the danger to the Union that arose from South Carolina's action, and they tempered their criticism of Jackson as he stood firm against nullification. In the end, unionist sentiment proved greater than sympathies for the Cherokees, and the Indians' devoted friends on the American Board urged them to sign a removal treaty. Even Senator Frelinghuysen in April 1832 came to the conclusion that the Indians should move if offered a liberal treaty.[64]

Undoubtedly the Cherokee controversy lost votes for the Democratic Party in the election of 1832, but it was not an issue of sufficient weight to defeat the popular president. When Jackson was handily reelected in November 1832, hope for preserving the Cherokees in their old homes practically vanished.

63. Ibid., p. 530.
64. Edwin A. Miles, "After John Marshall's Decision: *Worcester* v. *Georgia* and the Nullification Crisis," *Journal of Southern History* 39 (November 1973): 519–44.

CHAPTER 8

The Emigration of
the Southern Tribes

Choctaws. Creeks. Chickasaws.

Investigating the Lands in the West.

Seminoles and the Florida War.

Cherokees and the Trail of Tears.

The test of the removal policy was not the passage of the Removal Act or the legal decisions in the Cherokee cases of the Supreme Court. It came in the implementation of the policy during the administrations of Jackson and Martin Van Buren. The decade of the 1830s was matched by no other in American history as a dramatic period in relations between the United States government and the Indians. Removal treaties with the Five Civilized Tribes were negotiated—under various levels of duress—between 1830 and 1835, and by 1840 the bulk of the southeastern Indians, some sixty thousand tribesmen, were settled in the Indian Territory, now the state of Oklahoma, to continue their national existence. This uprooting of Indian nations from their ancestral homes was a traumatic experience and has become for many the most powerful symbol of white inhumanity toward the Indians. It was, however, a complex and confusing event, and the government was ill prepared for the tremendous physical task of moving so many thousands of men, women, and children and establishing them in the undeveloped regions west of the Mississippi.[1]

1. A long-accepted descriptive work on the removal process of the southern tribes is Grant Foreman, *Indian Removal: The Emigration of the Five Civilized Tribes of Indians* (Norman: University of Oklahoma Press, 1932); it is not a well-balanced account, however, for it overemphasizes the hardships and miseries.

CHOCTAWS

The first of the southern Indians to emigrate were the Choctaws, who moved from their homes in Mississippi to the region assigned them in what is now southeastern Oklahoma. Their removal was a sort of test case that exhibited the governmental pressures, tribal factionalism, hardships on the march, and troubles in establishing the nation in the West that marked the whole removal process.[2]

The Choctaws had long experienced white pressures upon their nation. In 1801, 1803, 1805, and 1816 they had reluctantly signed treaties of cession with the United States by which large areas passed into the hands of the whites.[3] Although the Indians had retained most of central Mississippi, the creation of the state in 1817 brought increased demands for the Indian lands. After some unsuccessful attempts at negotiations, the United States (with Andrew Jackson as principal commissioner) signed the Treaty of Doak's Stand with the Choctaws on October 18, 1820. The preamble noted that it was "an important object with the President of the United States, to promote the civilization of the Choctaw Indians, by the establishment of schools amongst them; and to perpetuate them as a nation, by exchanging, for a small part of their land here, a country beyond the Mississippi River, where all, who live by hunting and will not work, may be collected and settled together." The Choctaws, in exchange for five million acres in west central Mississippi, received some thirteen million acres between the Arkansas and Canadian rivers and the Red River, partly in Arkansas Territory and partly to the west. The residents of Arkansas were hostile to the treaty, which would bring more Indians into the territory, and the Choctaws for their part were reluctant to leave Mississippi. In 1825, by a treaty signed in Washington, a new boundary line was drawn along the western border of Arkansas and additional annuities were provided for the Choctaws.[4]

Under the Removal Act of 1830, Jackson sought to eliminate the re-

2. The fullest work on Choctaw removal is Arthur H. DeRosier, Jr., *The Removal of the Choctaw Indians* (Knoxville: University of Tennessee Press, 1970), but it gives too much weight to differences between the removal policies of Calhoun and Jackson. A good brief account is Muriel H. Wright, "The Removal of the Choctaws to the Indian Territory, 1830–1833," *Chronicles of Oklahoma* 6 (June 1928): 103–28. Ronald N. Satz, *American Indian Policy in the Jacksonian Era* (Lincoln: University of Nebraska Press, 1975), pp. 64–96, treats Choctaw removal as a "test case." See also Foreman, *Indian Removal*, pp. 19–104.

3. Kappler, pp. 56–58, 69–70, 87–88, 137. These treaties are discussed in DeRosier, *Removal of the Choctaw Indians*, pp. 28–37.

4. Kappler, pp. 191–95, 211–14; DeRosier, *Removal of the Choctaw Indians*, pp. 53–99.

maining Choctaws from Mississippi by the cession of all the lands they still owned in the state, and some of the Choctaws were receptive to the idea. Greenwood LeFlore, a mixed-blood Choctaw courted by the government and encouraged by the Methodist missionary Alexander Talley, drafted a removal treaty very favorable to the Indians and sent it to the president for acceptance. Although Jackson took the unprecedented step of submitting the "treaty" to the Senate for its advice, nothing came of the move, for the Senate refused to consider the document. Jackson then sent Secretary of War John Eaton and his old friend John Coffee to treat with the Choctaws in Mississippi, where they met with a huge gathering of five to six thousand Indians at Dancing Rabbit Creek in September 1830. Having sent the missionaries away from the treaty grounds lest they influence the Indians, Eaton and Coffee warned the Indians that if they did not move they would have to submit to state laws and thus lose their tribal existence. By providing generous land allotments and other benefits to tribal leaders, the commissioners were able to sign a treaty with the Choctaws on September 27.[5] The Choctaws agreed to relinquish all their lands east of the Mississippi and in return received "in fee simple to them and their descendants, to inure to them while they shall exist as a nation and live on it" the territory that had already been marked out in the treaty of 1825. The national existence of the Indians in the West was strongly guaranteed by the United States in the fourth article:

> The Government and people of the United States are hereby obliged to secure to the said Choctaw Nation of Red People the jurisdiction and government of all the persons and property that may be within their limits west, so that no Territory or State shall ever have a right to pass laws for the government of the Choctaw Nation of Red People and their descendants; and that no part of the land granted them shall ever be embraced in any Territory or State; but the U.S. shall forever secure said Choctaw Nation from, and against, all laws except such as from time to time may be enacted in their own National Councils, not inconsistent with the Constitution, Treaties, and Laws of the United States; and except such as may, and which have been enacted by Congress, to the extent that Congress under the Constitution are required to exercise a legislation over Indian Affairs. But the Choctaws, should this treaty be ratified, express a wish that Congress may grant to the Choctaws the right of punishing by their own laws, any

---

5. Kappler, pp. 310–19; DeRosier, *Removal of the Choctaw Indians*, pp. 116–28. Older accounts of the treaty are Henry S. Halbert, "The Story of the Treaty of Dancing Rabbit," *Publications of the Mississippi Historical Society* 6 (1902): 373–402; George Strother Gaines, "Dancing Rabbit Creek Treaty," *Historical and Patriotic Series of Alabama State Department of Archives and History*, 10 (1928): 1–31.

white man who shall come into their nation, and infringe any of their national regulations.

The United States, moreover, agreed to protect the Choctaws from domestic strife and from foreign enemies "on the same principle that the citizens of the United States are protected." Annuities from older treaties would continue, and the treaty authorized an additional twenty thousand dollars for twenty years. In addition, the United States was to provide houses for chiefs, schools, mechanics, and miscellaneous goods, and to educate forty Choctaw youth for a period of twenty years.

The treaty showed the ambivalence of the removal policy: whereas it made every effort to clear Mississippi of tribal Indians and included all sorts of inducements to encourage emigration, it at the same time allotted lands to Indians within the ceded territory east of the Mississippi. There were three categories of such allotments. First, 80 to 320 acres went to heads of families, according to the amount of land they had under cultivation. They were expected to sell these lands in order to pay for their improvements and to have money to pay debts or to aid in beginning a new life in the West. If no private sale was made, the United States would buy the allotments for fifty cents an acre. A second type of reservation went to persons who had some claim upon the government. These "special reservations" ranged from 320 to 2,560 acres, and some were floating claims that could be located anywhere within the cession; many of these grants were made in supplementary articles to the treaty signed on September 28. Most of these allottees sold their lands to speculators. The third type of grant was intended for those who desired to stay in the state—640 acres to heads of families and lesser amounts to others—to be granted in fee simple after five years of residence. The agent, William Ward, did not register all such claims as the treaty directed, however, seriously upsetting the intended operation of the system. All in all, the disposition of these lands and the settlement of claims arising from their sale led to nearly interminable conflicts between the Indians, bona fide settlers, and land speculators that delayed removal and unsettled land titles for years following the treaty.[6]

The Choctaw treaty was the sort of treaty, recognizing Indian political and property rights, that the Jackson administration hoped would make removal easy to swallow. There was considerable grumbling about its provisions among some of the Choctaws and a flaring up of intratribal animosities, however, and the government moved to counteract opposition.

6. The best discussion of these problems is Mary E. Young, *Redskins, Ruffleshirts, and Rednecks: Indian Allotments in Alabama and Mississippi, 1830–1860* (Norman: University of Oklahoma Press, 1961), pp. 47–72. Documents concerning Choctaw reservations are in *Senate Document* no. 266, 23–1, serial 240.

It promised to give the position of removal agent east of the Mississippi to George S. Gaines, a longtime trader among the Choctaws who was highly respected by them. Gaines led an exploration party west to investigate the nature of the lands designated for the tribe, and the party bought back a favorable report. The attitude of the tribe toward the treaty was ultimately neither enthusiasm nor opposition, but resignation. Chief David Folsom wrote: "We are exceedingly tired. We have just heard of the ratification of the Choctaw Treaty. Our doom is sealed. There is no other course for us but to turn our faces to our new homes toward the setting sun."[7]

The treaty specified emigration in three groups, the first in the fall of 1831 and the others in 1832 and 1833. The federal government would remove the Indians "under the care of discreet and careful persons, who will be kind and brotherly to them" and furnish them with ample corn and beef or pork for twelve months in their new homes. Some of the Indians, estimated at about one thousand, moved on their own before the official emigrant groups were organized, but most awaited the government's assistance. The operation, directed by the army's commissary general of subsistence, George Gibson, was carefully planned, with supplies accumulated along the route of travel and civilian agents and army officers appointed to oversee the actual movement. But confusion soon appeared, as the agents and army officers bickered among themselves and as maldistribution of rations caused delays. Late departures exposed the emigrants to unusually severe winter storms, and the Indians experienced great misery en route, even though the army officers who met them in the West exerted extraordinary efforts to meet the needs of the desperate travelers. Alexis de Tocqueville, who observed the Choctaws crossing the Mississippi at Memphis in 1831, wrote:

> It was then in the depths of winter, and that year the cold was exceptionally severe; the snow was hard on the ground, and huge masses of ice drifted on the river. The Indians brought their families with them; there were among them the wounded, the sick, newborn babies, and old men on the point of death. They had neither tents nor wagons, but only some provisions and weapons. I saw them embark to cross the great river, and the sight will never fade from my memory. Neither sob nor complaint rose from that silent assembly. Their afflictions were of long standing, and they felt them to be irremediable.[8]

In an attempt to better organize the removal process, Secretary of War Cass in April 1832 relieved all civilian agents and put the entire removal

7. Quoted in DeRosier, *Removal of the Choctaw Indians*, p. 128.
8. Alexis de Tocqueville, *Democracy in America*, ed. J. P. Mayer and Max Lerner, trans. George Lawrence (New York: Harper and Row, 1966), pp. 298–99. See also the

operation in military hands under General Gibson, and on May 15 he issued a set of regulations to govern the later removals.[9] The removals of
1832 and 1833 went more smoothly, but jurisdictional disputes disrupted
the emigration, and in 1832 the appearance of cholera in the Mississippi
Valley caused still further alarm and hardship. Altogether about 12,500
Choctaws settled in the Indian Territory; some 600 more remained in Mississippi, on allotments provided by the treaty or simply as vagrants. Little
by little, many of them drifted west to join their brethren, but Choctaws
still remain in the state today. The total expenditure for the Choctaw removal, including the treaty negotiations, was more than $5 million, a
larger sum than the Jackson administration had estimated for the removal
of all the eastern tribes. From the sale of the Choctaw cession, however,
the federal government received more than $8 million, and after long nego-
tiations about that sum and about other Choctaw claims, the United
States paid the Choctaws about $3 million.[10]

The Choctaw emigration was not the model removal project that Jackson had intended—administrative mixups, high costs, bad weather, and
tribal factionalism saw to that—but neither was it so disastrous as to form
a hindrance to other removals.

CREEKS

The situation of the Creeks in Alabama and Georgia was much like that of
the Choctaws. The Creek Nation had had long dealings with the federal
government and with the southern states and in 1790 under the leadership
of Alexander McGillivray had come to terms with the United States and
placed itself under federal protection. But the Creeks were deeply divided,
and when the Red Sticks became openly hostile during the War of 1812,
their resounding defeat by Andrew Jackson at the Battle of Horseshoe Bend
led to the massive cession of territory in Georgia and Alabama at the

account quoted in George Wilson Pierson, *Tocqueville in America* (Garden City, New
York: Doubleday and Company, 1959), pp. 379–81.

9. *Senate Document* no. 512, 23–1, serial 244, pp. 343–49. The five volumes of *Senate Document* no. 512, serials 244–248, contain correspondence and other documents
assembled by the commissary general of subsistence in response to Senate resolutions
and cover the period between November 30, 1831, and December 27, 1833. These volumes are a very rich resource for the removal operations in 1832 and 1833. A description
of the contents is provided in George Gibson to Cass, October 31, 1834, in serial
244, p. 3.

10. DeRosier, *Removal of the Choctaw Indians*, p. 163. For an account of the Choctaw claims controversy, see W. David Baird, *Peter Pitchlynn: Chief of the Choctaws*
(Norman: University of Oklahoma Press, 1972).

MAP 2: Land Cessions of the Five Civilized Tribes

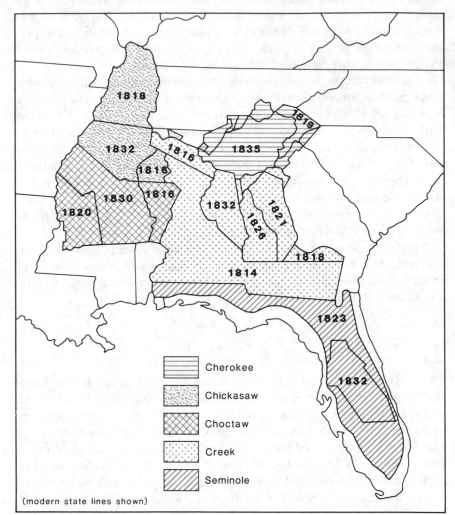

Cherokee

Chickasaw

Choctaw

Creek

Seminole

(modern state lines shown)

Treaty of Fort Jackson in 1814. In 1818 and 1821 other parcels of land were ceded in Georgia.[11]

In 1825 another large cession was made at the Treaty of Indian Springs, which included a provision for a grant of land in the Indian Territory in exchange for the ceded lands. This treaty had been negotiated by a small pro-removal faction led by William McIntosh against the clear stipulation of Creek law providing for the execution of any chief who subscribed to an unauthorized land cession, and McIntosh and some of his associates were

11. Kappler, pp. 107–10, 155–56, 195–98.

killed by order of the Creek council. When President John Quincy Adams learned of the fraudulent nature of the treaty, he determined to make a new treaty, which he did in Washington in 1826. This treaty validated the cession of land in Georgia, sought to adjust amicably the dissension between the Creek factions, and provided for removal to lands to be selected in the West. Prosperous mixed-blood members of the McIntosh faction migrated to the Indian Territory and laid out plantations in the Arkansas and Verdigris valleys.[12]

The Creeks who remained in Alabama were soon subjected to pressures from the state, which added the Creek territory to organized counties and extended the jurisdiction of local courts over the Indians, and from white intruders on their lands. Federal officials used such actions to support their arguments that the only salvation for the Creeks lay in removal from the state. Finally, on March 24, 1832, Chief Opotheyahola and other Creek leaders signed a treaty in Washington with Lewis Cass.[13]

The treaty was not specifically a removal treaty. Although the Creeks ceded to the United States all their lands east of the Mississippi, they were to receive allotments within the cession (a full section to each of ninety principal chiefs and a half-section to all other heads of families). The Indians were authorized to sell these allotments "to any other persons for a fair consideration," or to remain on the lands themselves and after five years receive a fee simple title. The United States was "desirous that the Creeks should remove to the country west of the Mississippi and join their countrymen there" and agreed to pay for the emigration and one year's subsistence in the West, but the treaty specifically stated that it was "not to be construed so as to compel any Creek Indian to emigrate but they shall be free to go or stay, as they please." The Creek territory west of the Mississippi was solemnly guaranteed to the Indians, and their right to govern themselves free from interference by any state or territory was recognized "so far as may be compatible with the general jurisdiction which Congress may think proper to exercise over them."

The treaty stipulated that intruders on the Creek lands in Alabama would be removed until the lands were surveyed and allotments selected (except for whites who had made improvements without expelling Creeks

---

12. Ibid., pp. 214–17, 264–68. A subsequent treaty of November 15, 1827, provided for the cession of Creek lands in Georgia that had not been included in the 1826 treaty. Ibid., pp. 284–86. For discussion of the treaty, see Annie H. Abel, "The History of Events Resulting in Indian Consolidation West of the Mississippi," *Annual Report of the American Historical Association for the Year 1906*, 1: 344–57; and Angie Debo, *The Road to Disappearance* (Norman: University of Oklahoma Press, 1941), pp. 88–95.

13. Kappler, pp. 341–43. Creek memorials prior to the treaty that complained of the acts of Alabama and demanded protection are printed in *Senate Document* no. 53, 21–1, serial 193, and *House Document* no. 102, 22–1, serial 218.

from theirs, who could remain to gather their crops). When all the reservations had been made, they would amount to a little more than two million acres out of the approximately five million in the cession. The surplus land would be open to white entry.

The treaty, on its face, seemed like a reasonable document, for it supported Creeks who chose to emigrate and provided for those who preferred to stay; but its actual operation was disastrous for the Creeks. Despite its promises to evict intruders, the federal government in fact was unwilling or unable to do so, and the Creek lands were quickly overrun. Moreover, the Indians, unused to handling financial matters, were victimized by speculators, who moved in to gain title to the allotments and force the Indians off the land. The frauds were spectacular and widespread, making a mockery of the treaty intentions, and the government seemed impotent to stem the speculators' chicanery. The commissioner of Indian affairs, on receiving the report of a commission sent to investigate, declared in exasperation in 1838: "It is shocking to reflect on the disclosures elicited. They embrace men of every degree. Persons, heretofore deemed respectable, are implicated in the most disgraceful attempts to defraud those who are incapacitated from protecting their own interests; whose presence, as far from being any interruption to the plundering of themselves, was sometimes sought, as their instrumentality was used to effect their own ruin. This conduct, derogatory to civilized men, was not inaptly termed 'land stealing.'"[14]

Whites intimidated the Indians, who looked in vain for their promised protection. The whole Creek Nation was in a state of turmoil and bitterness resulting from the premature and illegal action of the whites, and a government attempt to get the Creeks to sign a new treaty that would provide for immediate removal came to nothing. Only a small number migrated in 1834, but the Indians, hoping that everything would be adjusted satisfactorily, continued their preparations for removal. Prospects looked good until the Indians discovered that the contract for their removal had been let to a company of men who had been active in defrauding them of their lands. The tension on both sides mounted, and destitute Indians sought refuge wherever they could find it, some moving into Cherokee country in Alabama and Georgia. The smoldering situation broke into open fire in the spring of 1836. Georgia militia attacked Creeks who had encamped on Georgia soil, and roving bands of Creeks began to attack and kill whites and destroy their property.[15]

14. T. Hartley Crawford to Joel R. Poinsett, May 11, 1838, *House Document* no. 452, 25–2, serial 331, p. 15. A detailed history of the Creek frauds is given in Young, *Redskins, Ruffleshirts, and Rednecks*, pp. 73–113. See also Foreman, *Indian Removal*, pp. 129–39.

15. I follow here the discussion of the Creek troubles in Francis Paul Prucha, *The*

As the alarming reports reached Washington, Secretary of War Cass issued orders to remove the Creeks as a military measure. He ordered General Thomas S. Jesup to inaugurate a military operation against the Indians, subdue them, and force their removal to the West. In the "Creek War" of 1836 several thousand troops were ordered into the Creek country. General Winfield Scott, leaving behind his Seminole difficulties in Florida, arrived at Savannah on May 22 and assumed general command of the war. He sent Jesup to Alabama to direct the operations of the Alabama militia toward the Creeks on the Chattahoochee River, and he himself planned to advance toward the same objective from the east. Between them, the two forces would find and defeat the Indians. Before Scott could perfect his preparations, however, Jesup acted on his own against the hostiles. Fearing that he could no longer restrain the militia, who were eager for action as reports of new Indian ravages came in, he moved directly into the heart of the Indian country. In a few days he had located the principal Creek camp and had captured the leader, Eneah Micco, and three or four hundred of the warriors. The whites' success quieted the Indians, and Jesup wrote to Scott that he had brought tranquility once more to the frontier.[16]

The subdued Creeks were now removed to the West. Dejected warriors, handcuffed, chained, and guarded by soldiers, left Fort Mitchell on July 2, followed by wagons and ponies carrying the children and old women and the sick. On July 14 almost 2,500 Indians, including 800 warriors, were embarked at Montgomery and conveyed down the Alabama River to Mobile, thence to New Orleans and up the rivers to the western lands of the Creeks. The remainder of the hostiles left Montgomery on August 2. The friendly Creeks soon followed their brothers west. In all, 14,608 Creeks were removed in 1836, including 2,495 enrolled as hostile. A number of Creek warriors who had enlisted for service in Florida against the Seminoles were released too late to emigrate in 1836 and followed the next year.[17]

CHICKASAWS

The Chickasaw Nation in northern Mississippi and northwestern Alabama suffered the same disabilities in relations with its white neighbors as

---

Sword of the Republic: The United States Army on the Frontier, 1783–1846 (New York: Macmillan Company, 1969), pp. 258–61.

16. The military strategy and campaign are treated in Charles W. Elliott, *Winfield Scott: The Soldier and the Man* (New York: Macmillan Company, 1937), pp. 310–21. Letters and reports dealing with the operations are in *House Document* no. 154, 24–2, serial 304, and *American State Papers: Military Affairs*, 7: 168–365.

17. Foreman, *Indian Removal*, pp. 152–90; "Statements of the Probable Number of

did the other southern tribes. Because they blocked white expansion into rich lands, the Chickasaws were ultimately forced to give in to the pressures put upon them by the states and the federal government, to cede all their lands east of the Mississippi, and to move west. Their removal, however, was more tranquil and the return they got for their lands more equitable than was the case with the other tribes.[18]

In 1816 and 1818, in treaties for which Andrew Jackson was one of the United States commissioners, the Chickasaws had ceded lands in Alabama, Tennessee, and Kentucky north of the Mississippi boundary in return for annuities and reservations of land for certain chiefs.[19] But they were firm in their refusal to part with the heart of their domain in northern Mississippi, and attempts of the government to win their agreement to removal in 1826 came to naught. The nation was politically and economically in the control of mixed-bloods, of whom the Colbert family was dominant. These leaders, although identifying themselves with tribal interests and thus gaining support of the full-bloods, managed to run the nation for their own benefit as well as that of the tribe, and they dealt skillfully with federal officials.

Immediately after the passage of the Removal Act, President Jackson himself met the Chickasaw leaders at Franklin, Tennessee, where the Indians signed a provisionary treaty on August 31, 1830, with Secretary of War John Eaton and John Coffee, the United States commissioners. By it the Indians ceded their lands east of the Mississippi in return for sizable individual allotments within the ceded territory, but the cession was contingent upon the location of a suitable territory in the West as the ultimate home of the Chickasaws. Because the Indians' investigating party failed to agree upon such a district, the treaty was null and void, and Jackson did not submit it to the Senate for ratification.[20]

The will of the Chickasaws not to move from Mississippi had been broken by encroachments of whites on their lands and by the action of the state in extending jurisdiction over the nation, erasing the tribal government and destroying the power of the chiefs. The Indians' appeal to Jackson against these evils met the same response given to the Cherokees, Choctaws, and Creeks: "To these laws, where you are, you must submit;— there is no preventive—no other alternative. Your great father cannot, nor can congress, prevent it. . . . [Your great father's] earnest desire is, that you

---

Creek Warriors Engaged in Hostilities against the United States during the Years 1836 and 1837," *American State Papers: Military Affairs*, 7: 951–52.

18. Chickasaw removal is treated in Arrell M. Gibson, *The Chickasaws* (Norman: University of Oklahoma Press, 1971), pp. 122–83, and Foreman, *Indian Removal*, pp. 193–226.

19. Kappler, pp. 135–37, 174–77.

20. This unratified treaty is printed ibid., pp. 1035–40.

may be perpetuated and preserved as a nation; and this he believes can only be done and secured in your consent to remove to a country beyond the Mississippi."[21]

With the failure of the Franklin treaty, the United States moved quickly to new negotiations carried on by John Coffee, and on October 20, 1832, at the Chickasaw council house at Pontotoc Creek, a new treaty was signed. "The Chickasaw Nation," the preamble read, "find themselves oppressed in their present situation; by being made subject to the laws of the States in which they reside. Being ignorant of the language and laws of the white man, they cannot understand or obey them. Rather than submit to this great evil, they prefer to seek a home in the west, where they may live and be governed by their own laws."[22]

The new treaty was similar to the Franklin treaty. Chickasaw lands were ceded to the government; they would be surveyed immediately and placed on sale, to be sold for what the market would bring. Meanwhile, each adult Indian received a temporary homestead (ranging from one section to four sections, depending on the size of the family). The money from the sale of these temporary reservations and of the surplus lands would be placed in a general fund of the Chickasaw Nation, and from it would come the costs of survey and of removal. In 1834 amendments were made to the Pontotoc treaty for the benefit of the Chickasaws; the size of the temporary homesteads was increased and provision was made for land for orphans. Moreover, the temporary lands were granted in fee simple, and the proceeds from their sale would now go to the individuals holding the land. The treaty provided for a tribal commission to supervise the sales and to judge the competence of individuals to assume direct control over the sale money.[23]

As the survey and sale of the lands in Mississippi proceeded, Chickasaw commissioners sought a satisfactory territory in the West. It had always been the intention of the United States that the Chickasaws would share the western lands assigned to the Choctaws, but the two tribes had been unable to come to an agreement. Finally, on January 17, 1837, at Doaksville in the Choctaw Nation, a treaty was signed; it provided for the purchase by the Chickasaws of the central and western sections of the Choctaw lands for $530,000, and it granted the Chickasaws certain privileges within the Choctaw Nation.[24] The Chickasaws then began their emigra-

21. *Niles' Register*, September 18, 1830, quoted in Gibson, *Chickasaws*, p. 154.

22. Kappler, pp. 356–62.

23. Ibid., pp. 418–25.

24. Ibid., pp. 486–88. The Chickasaw district was more specifically defined in treaties of November 5, 1854, and June 22, 1855, and the region west of the ninety-eighth meridian was leased to the United States as a home for other Indians. Ibid., pp. 652–53, 706–14.

tion; a roll of the tribe prepared for the removal showed 4,914 Chickasaws and 1,156 slaves.

The Chickasaws left Mississippi in relatively prosperous financial condition. A minimum price of $1.25 an acre had been set for the sale of their individual homesteads, and some of the land brought more, for an upturn in the business cycle made abundant capital available for investment in the Indian lands. The unallotted lands—over 4,000,000 acres out of the entire cession of 6,422,400 acres—were sold at public auction under a graduation principle and brought about $3.3 million to the Chickasaw general fund. The movement was placed in charge of A. M. M. Upshaw, from Tennessee, who enrolled tribesmen from four districts of the nation, and the movement proceeded in orderly fashion. But there were delays in the migration and the inevitable problems of cheating and exploitation in the contracting for supplies, and the Chickasaws did not escape misery and suffering in the emigrant camps, on the way, and in the establishment of their new homes. Ethan Allen Hitchcock, sent to Indian Territory to investigate charges of fraud, reported defective supplies at exorbitant prices and found bribery, perjury, and forgery in the transactions.[25]

INVESTIGATING THE LANDS IN THE WEST

As the removal process moved into full gear with the treaties made with the Choctaws, Creeks, and Chickasaws, the United States government took steps to ease the process by turning its attention to the lands to which the emigrating Indians were directed. In order to make sure that the Indians located on suitable lands and that no conflicts arose among the different tribes, Congress in July 1832 authorized the appointment of three commissioners to investigate the western lands, to select tracts for the incoming Indians, and to adjudicate conflicting claims. The commission, composed of Montfort Stokes, former governor of North Carolina, the Dutch Reformed minister John F. Schermerhorn, and a Connecticut businessman, Henry I. Ellsworth, received from Secretary of War Cass a detailed set of instructions, in which Cass urged them to satisfy the Indians

---

25. Young, *Redskins, Ruffleshirts, and Rednecks,* pp. 114–54; Gibson, *Chickasaws,* pp. 163–83. Hitchcock's investigations covered Creeks, Choctaws, and Cherokees as well as Chickasaws, and his report was a severe indictment of the contract system of supplying the emigrating Indians. See Hitchcock to Secretary of War J. C. Spencer, April 28, 1842, *House Report* no. 271, 27–3, serial 428, pp. 28–43; his observations are reported also in *Fifty Years in Camp and Field: Diary of Major-General Ethan Allen Hitchcock,* ed. W. A. Croffut (New York: G. P. Putnam's Sons, 1909), and *A Traveler in Indian Territory: The Journal of Ethan Allen Hitchcock, Late Major-General in the United States Army,* ed. Grant Foreman (Cedar Rapids, Iowa: Torch Press, 1930).

and thus preserve peace in the area. He told them particularly to welcome the Indian delegations sent to look at the land to see that they were pleased. "You will perceive," Cass said, "that the general object is to locate them all in as favorable positions as possible, in districts sufficiently fertile, salubrious & extensive, & with boundaries, either natural or artificial, so clearly defined, as to preclude the possibility of dispute. There is country enough for all, & more than all. And the President is anxious, that full justice should be done to each, & every measure adopted be as much to their satisfaction, as is compatible with the nature of such an arrangement."[26]

The Stokes Commission, in its report of 1834, judged the land favorably. It declared that the country acquired from the western Indians for the purpose of providing land for the Indians coming from the East was "very extensive," running from the Red River to 43° 30′ north latitude, and from the western boundary of Missouri and Arkansas to the hundredth meridian. The climate did not "materially vary from the climate, in the corresponding degrees of latitude, in the Atlantic States, some distance in the interior from the seaboard," and the soil was of great diversity, such "as generally is found in the States bordering on the Mississippi." The commissioners reported considerable game but predicted that it would soon be destroyed as the eastern Indians moved in. They wrote:

> The question then arises, "is the country able to furnish them a support in any other way; and particularly is it calculated for the purposes of agriculture?" And this question the commissioners answer unhesitatingly in the affirmative. They are of opinion that there is a sufficiency of good first rate soil, now belonging to those tribes who already have lands assigned to them, and in sufficient quantity still undisposed of, to assign to such tribes as may hereafter choose to remove there, to support them, if they will settle down like our white citizens and become agriculturists.[27]

The Stokes Commission was perhaps bound to support the government's contention that lands west of the Mississippi were suitable for the emigrant Indians, but its report fitted into a pattern of favorable comments on the land from other men who knew the region firsthand. As early as 1826, when removal was recommended by Secretary of War Barbour, William Clark at St. Louis commented on the proposal as follows: "The country west of Missouri and Arkansas, and west of the Mississippi river, north

26. *House Executive Document* no. 2, 22–2, serial 233, pp. 32–37. The question of the quality of the land assigned to the emigrant Indians is discussed in Francis Paul Prucha, "Indian Removal and the Great American Desert," *Indiana Magazine of History* 59 (December 1963): 299–322.

27. Report of the commissioners, February 10, 1834, *House Report* no. 474, 23–1, serial 263, pp. 82–84.

of Missouri, is the one destined to receive them. From all accounts, this country will be well adapted to their residence; it is well watered with numerous small streams and some large rivers; abounds with grass, which will make it easy to raise stock; has many salt springs, from which a supply of the necessary article of salt can be obtained; contains much prairie land, which will make the opening of farms easy; and affords a temporary supply of game."[28]

In May 1828 Congress appropriated fifteen thousand dollars for an exploration of the country west of the Mississippi and authorized commissioners to accompany the Indians. The commissioners in their reports described the territory as far as they had examined it and set forth both advantages and disadvantages. In general, however, the reports were favorable. One of the commissioners—Isaac McCoy, a longtime advocate of colonizing the Indians in the West—declared that "the country under consideration is adequate to the purpose of a permanent and comfortable home for the Indians; and whatever may be the obstacles which at present oppose, they may nevertheless be located there without recourse to any measure not in accordance with the most rigid principles of justice and humanity." George B. Kennerly, who led the expedition composed of deputations of the Choctaws, Chickasaws, and Creeks, reported, "There is a sufficient quantity of well timbered and watered land on the Arkansas and its tributaries for the whole of the southern Indians, if a proper distribution be made."[29]

Other reports on inspection of the lands proposed for the eastern Indians were of like tenor. A treaty with the Delaware Indians for removal west of Missouri provided that the land be inspected and agreed upon before the treaty would take effect. The agent appointed to accompany the Indians in their tour was again Isaac McCoy. His report to the secretary of war in April 1831 described in some detail the lands extending about two hundred miles west of the Missouri and Arkansas lines. "I beg leave, sir, to state distinctly," he reported, "that I am confirmed in an opinion often expressed, that the country under consideration may safely be considered favorable for settlement: [in] the distance, on an average of two hundred miles from the State of Missouri and Territory of Arkansas, water, wood, soil, and stone, are such as to warrant this conclusion." McCoy noted that the Delawares were so anxious to move to the new tract that they did not wait for the United States aid promised in the treaty. This, he asserted, furnished *"the best comment on the suitableness of that country for the permanent residence of the Indians."*[30]

28. ASP:IA, 2: 653.

29. 4 *United States Statutes* 315; *House Report* no. 87, 20–2, serial 190, pp. 24–25.

30. Kappler, pp. 204–5; *Senate Document* no. 512, 23–1, serial 245, pp. 435–36. Another report of McCoy, February 1, 1832, is printed in *House Document* no. 172, 22–1,

Such positive reports, which in fact accurately described the lands that were designated to receive the emigrant Indians, substantially refuted the cries of alarm made by such men as Jeremiah Evarts and George B. Cheever. The negative reports brought back by some Indian groups who went west to look at the lands are understandable, for the Indians found undeveloped wilderness in contrast with the improved lands in their old homes. But the Indians after relocation did not find the agricultural potential of the region insufficient for their economic well-being and development. The injustice came, not from having to settle on poor lands, but from the ultimate lack of secure and permanent enjoyment of the lands they did receive.

SEMINOLES AND THE FLORIDA WAR

The Seminoles, an amalgam of Creeks who had gradually drifted into Florida and native tribes there with whom they mixed, numbered no more than five thousand, but they showed a resistance to removal that kept the United States army occupied for seven years and that was never completely overcome. The United States government had made a decision that the Seminoles were to be removed; then it tried with main force to carry out the decision, even though it soon became apparent that the land thus to be freed of the Indians was not of significant value to the whites and that if the Seminoles had been left alone the expense and grief of the conflict might have been avoided.[31]

---

serial 219; journals of McCoy's exploring expeditions are printed in *Kansas Historical Quarterly* 5 (August 1936): 227–77; 5 (November 1936): 339–77; 13 (August 1945): 400–462. McCoy's exploring work is discussed in George A. Schultz, *An Indian Canaan: Isaac McCoy and the Vision of an Indian State* (Norman: University of Oklahoma Press, 1972), pp. 101–22. See also J. Orin Oliphant, ed., "Report of the Wyandot Exploring Delegation, 1831," *Kansas Historical Quarterly* 15 (August 1947): 248–62.

31. I follow here the discussion in Prucha, *Sword of the Republic*, pp. 269–306. The Seminole removal and the war it caused have had extended historical treatment. A full scholarly account is John K. Mahon, *History of the Second Seminole War, 1835–1842* (Gainesville: University of Florida Press, 1967). An older history by a participant that contains a good many documents is John T. Sprague, *The Origin, Progress, and Conclusion of the Florida War* (New York: D. Appleton and Company, 1848). A recent careful study of relations of the United States and the Seminoles is Virginia Bergman Peters, *The Florida Wars* (Hamden, Connecticut: Archon Books, 1979). See also Mark F. Boyd, "The Seminole War: Its Background and Onset," *Florida Historical Quarterly* 30 (July 1951): 3–115. The printed government documents dealing with the war are voluminous, for as the war dragged on and the promised terminations did not materialize, Congress repeatedly called for explanations from the president and the secretary of war. The reports, often with extensive reprinting of correspondence, orders, and other documents, make it possible to reconstruct the war in great detail. See annual reports of the War Department; *American State Papers: Military Affairs*, volumes 5–7; serial set of congressional docu-

The removal of the Seminoles had complications that were not present in the removal of the other tribes. It was not simply a matter of exchanging the lands that the Indians claimed in Florida for lands beyond the Mississippi—although, indeed, this might have been matter enough for dispute. The Seminole problem was also a problem of black slaves. For many years slaves from the southern states had fled as fugitives to the Indian settlements in Florida, where they often became slaves of the Seminoles. The Indians may have augmented the number of slaves by the purchase of others in the white manner; but whatever their origin, the blacks enjoyed a less restrictive existence among the Seminoles than with white masters in Georgia or Alabama. They lived in a kind of semi-bondage, more like allies than slaves of the Indians. Many lived in their own villages as vassals of the chief whose protection they enjoyed, contributing shares of the produce from their own fields rather than labor on the lands of the owner.

The demands of the white masters of the fugitives became increasingly insistent. Claims were presented which the Seminoles, who kept no legal records of their slaves, could not easily refute in court. More and more frequently raiding parties from the north invaded the Seminole lands and attempted to carry off by force the blacks who were claimed as slaves. The Seminole War was perhaps as much a movement on the part of the slave owners to recover the property they claimed as it was a war to acquire Indian land for white use. And the blacks clearly sensed that fact. Although about a tenth of the Seminoles sided with the United States in the conflict over removal, acting as guides and interpreters against their blood brothers, the blacks all fought bitterly against the whites until assurance was given that enrollment for removal to the West did not mean placing oneself within the clutches of some white slave owner who stood by waiting to enforce his claims.[32]

The removal issue proper can be traced in three treaties between the Seminoles and the United States. The first of these was the Treaty of

---

ments; and Clarence E. Carter, ed., *The Territorial Papers of the United States*, 26 vols. (Washington: GPO, 1934–1962), vols. 25 and 26.

32. All the serious accounts of the war call attention to the importance of the blacks. The best consideration of the problem is in a series of articles by Kenneth W. Porter of which the following are the most general: "Florida Slaves and Free Negroes in the Seminole War, 1835–1842," *Journal of Negro History* 28 (October 1943): 390–421; "Osceola and the Negroes," *Florida Historical Quarterly* 33 (January–April 1955): 235–39; and "Negroes and the Seminole War, 1835–1842," *Journal of Southern History* 30 (November 1964): 427–50. The abolitionist Joshua R. Giddings claimed that the war was instigated by slave-holders; see his *The Exiles of Florida; or, The Crimes Committed by Our Government against the Maroons, Who Fled from South Carolina and Other Slave States, Seeking Protection under Spanish Laws* (Columbus, Ohio: Follett, Foster and Company, 1858), pp. 270–71.

Camp Moultrie, signed on September 18, 1823, in which the Florida Indians were induced to give up all their claims to Florida and in return were granted a reservation of land in central Florida, which by executive proclamation was slightly increased in 1824 and 1826 to include more tillable land. By the treaty the Indians agreed to prevent runaway slaves from entering their country and to aid in the return of slaves who had escaped. They were granted $6,000 worth of livestock and an annuity of $5,000 for twenty years.[33]

Much of the land thus reserved for the Indians was not well suited for cultivation, and the Indians did not abide by the reservation lines. The Seminoles were irritated by whites who were allowed to invade the reservation in search of slaves, and they retaliated by raids upon white settlements outside the reservation boundaries. Many of the Indians remained in their old homes when whites came into the area to settle, and there was increasing agitation for the removal of the Indians altogether from Florida. When the Removal Act of 1830 made provision for removal treaties, the Seminoles were also pressured into moving. A treaty was signed with the Indians on May 9, 1832, at Payne's Landing. The Indians were near destitution, and the promise of food and clothing in the treaty eased the negotiations. But the Seminoles would not agree to removal until they had had an opportunity to inspect the land and determine its suitability. The treaty, accordingly, provided that the government would send a party of the Indians to the West, where they could themselves judge the land that would be set aside for them. The members of the Seminole delegation arrived at Fort Gibson in November 1832, and they were shown the territory that was to be theirs in the Creek country. They were persuaded to sign an agreement stating that they approved the land. This Treaty of Fort Gibson, March 28, 1833, although it was not accepted by the Seminoles as a whole, was considered by the United States as fulfilling the provisions of the Payne's Landing treaty, and the government demanded that the Indians carry out the treaty and move out of Florida.[34]

The Seminoles did not think that the Fort Gibson agreement expressed the approval of their whole nation, and they did not want to be an integral part of the Creek Nation as the United States desired. The usual impasse had arrived. The government pointed to the treaty and insisted that it be

33. Kappler, pp. 203–7. For a detailed, reasonable account of the treaty and its background that is less condemnatory than most accounts, see John K. Mahon, "The Treaty of Moultrie Creek, 1823," *Florida Historical Quarterly* 40 (April 1962): 350–72.

34. Kappler, pp. 344–45, 394–95. John K. Mahon, "Two Seminole Treaties: Payne's Landing, 1832, and Ft. Gibson, 1833," *Florida Historical Quarterly* 41 (July 1962): 1–21, is a careful analysis of the treaties and the charges of fraud. Because the evidence is "fragmentary and often contradictory," Mahon arrives at no apodictic judgments. But he concedes that the Seminoles did not regard the treaties as just and that their refusal to abide by them led to war.

fulfilled. The Indians denied that they had made the agreements specified and refused to move. As the tension increased, the stage was set for war.

Indian Agent Wiley Thompson made plans for concentrating the Indians in preparation for emigration, and the Indians were told that if they did not come voluntarily, military force would be used. As the army closed in to force removal, the Indians struck. Thompson was murdered on December 28, 1835, outside Fort King, and on the same day Major Francis L. Dade and a company of troops were ambushed and killed. The uprising electrified the Florida frontier, and the War Department hastened to act, but the Indians could not easily be routed from their fastnesses in the Everglades. One commander after another tried his best to bring the embarrassing affair to a successful conclusion, yet the war dragged on and on, despite optimistic announcements from the commanding generals and the War Department that the war had finally been brought to an end. It was a sad and distressing affair, and it included episodes—such as the capture and imprisonment of the Seminole leader Osceola when he came in to parley under a white flag and the hiring of bloodhounds from Cuba to track down the elusive Indians—that roused strong public criticism of the war. Even a delegation of Cherokees who offered their good services in an attempt to bring the war to a conclusion was ineffective.[35]

In 1838 General Thomas S. Jesup, then directing the war, concluded that the removal of the Seminoles was not practicable and that to insist upon it would prolong a useless war without any hope of a satisfactory outcome. "In regard to the Seminoles," he told Secretary of War Joel R. Poinsett in February 1838, "we have committed the error of attempting to remove them when their lands were not required for agricultural purposes; when they were not in the way of the white inhabitants; and when the greater portion of their country was an unexplored wilderness, of the interior of which we were as ignorant of as of the interior of China. We exhibit, in our present contest, the first instance, perhaps, since the commencement of authentic history, of a nation employing an army to explore a country (for we can do little more than explore it), or attempting to remove a band of savages from one unexplored wilderness to another." But the secretary of war would not relent in carrying out the removal policy as em-

35. For the course of the war, see the accounts in Prucha, *Sword of the Republic*, pp. 273–300; Mahon, *Second Seminole War*; and Peters, *Florida Wars*, pp. 105–263. Osceola, the most famous of the Seminole leaders, has been given considerable attention; see the articles (including those on his capture) in *Florida Historical Quarterly* 33 (January–April 1955). A general account of the use of bloodhounds is James W. Covington, "Cuban Bloodhounds and the Seminoles," ibid. 33 (October 1954): 11–19. An extended discussion of the Cherokee mission is in Edwin C. McReynolds, *The Seminoles* (Norman: University of Oklahoma Press, 1957), pp. 197–206. See also "Report of Cherokee Deputation into Florida," *Chronicles of Oklahoma* 9 (December 1931): 423–38; and *House Document* no. 285, 25–2, serial 328.

bodied in the Treaty of Payne's Landing. "The treaty has been ratified," he told Jesup, "and is the law of the land; and the constitutional duty of the president requires that he should cause it to be executed. I cannot, therefore, authorize any arrangement with the Seminoles, by which they will be permitted to remain, or assign them any portion of the Territory of Florida as their future residence."[36]

So the war continued. Little by little some bands of Indians gave up and were moved from Florida, but others continued their desperate raids in the hope of driving off the white invaders. In the end, under Colonel William Jenkins Worth, the army harried most of the Indians into removal. In February 1842 Worth wrote to the commanding general of the army suggesting that a halt be called to the hostilities. "I believe there has been no instance," he began, "in which, in the removal of Indians, some, more or less, have not been left." And he declared the "utter impracticability" of securing by force the few Seminoles still left in Florida.[37] His observations were heeded, after some hesitation lest the honor of the country and the gallantry of the army be compromised, and the president on May 10 announced the decision in a special message to Congress. He noted the presence in Florida of only about 240 remaining Indians, of whom 80 were judged to be warriors, and asserted that "further pursuit of these miserable beings by a large military force seems to be as injudicious as it is unavailing." He continued that he therefore had authorized the commanding officer in Florida to declare that hostilities against the Indians had ceased. In accordance with these directives, Colonel Worth on August 14, 1842, declared the war at an end.[38] An estimated 2,833 Seminole Indians had been located in new lands in the Indian Territory.

So ended the bitterest episode in the annals of Indian removal. All but the irremovable remnant tallied by Worth had been killed or removed. In addition, more than 1,500 white soldiers had lost their lives and the costs of the war reached the staggering total of $20 million.

CHEROKEES AND THE TRAIL OF TEARS

Just as the Cherokee Nation was the chief focus of the controversy over the removal policy, so it furnished the most controversial episode in the

36. Jesup to Poinsett, February 11, 1838, quoted in Sprague, *Florida War*, pp. 200–201; Poinsett to Jesup, March 1, 1838, ibid., pp. 201–2. For a similar statement of the secretary of war, see Poinsett to Jesup, July 25, 1837, *House Document* no. 78, 25–2, serial 323, pp. 32–33.

37. Worth to Scott, February 14, 1842, quoted in Sprague, *Florida War*, pp. 441–44. Worth's correspondence on the Florida campaign is in *House Document* no. 262, 27–2, serial 405.

38. Message of President Tyler, May 10, 1842, James D. Richardson, comp., *A Com-*

actual emigration to the West.[39] The agitation of the 1830s, however, obscures the fact that many Cherokees had already emigrated and established themselves in the Indian Territory. Some had migrated west with the permission of the government during the administrations of Jefferson and Madison, and by 1816 the agent estimated that at least two thousand Cherokees were in Arkansas.[40] Their status there was precarious, for they were challenged by Osage Indians in the region and by incoming white settlers as well. To regularize the situation, the Cherokees, by treaties of July 8, 1817, and February 27, 1819, ceded large sections of their holdings in the East in return for a guaranteed tract in Arkansas between the Arkansas and White rivers. The treaties provided that all white citizens were to be removed from the western districts, but there were the usual difficulties as the whites looked with covetous eyes upon the rich Indian lands.[41] Then in 1828 the western Cherokees exchanged their lands in what is now Arkansas for seven million acres in the northeastern corner of the present state of Oklahoma, and they were granted as well the so-called Cherokee Outlet, extending west to the limits of United States jurisdiction at the hundredth meridian. This was in intent a removal treaty; its purpose was

> to secure to the Cherokee nation of Indians, as well those now living within the limits of the Territory of Arkansas, as those of their friends and brothers who reside in States East of the Mississippi, and who may wish to join their brothers of the West, *a permanent* home, and which shall, under the most solemn guarantee of the United States, be, and remain, theirs forever—a home that shall never, in all future time, be embarrassed by having extended around it the lines, or placed over it the jurisdiction of a Territory or State, or pressed upon by the extension, in any way, of any of the limits of any existing Territory or State.[42]

---

pilation of the Messages and Papers of the Presidents, 10 vols. (Washington: GPO, 1896–1899), 4: 154; Order no. 28, Headquarters Ninth Military Department, August 14, 1842, quoted in Sprague, *Florida War*, p. 486. The emigration of the Seminoles is recounted in Foreman, *Indian Removal*, pp. 364–86.

39. A recent retelling of the Cherokee story is Samuel Carter III, *Cherokee Sunset, a Nation Betrayed: A Narrative of Travail and Triumph, Persecution and Exile* (Garden City, New York: Doubleday and Company, 1976).

40. Return J. Meigs to William H. Crawford, February 17, 1816, enclosed in John Mason to Crawford, March 2, 1816, Carter, *Territorial Papers*, 15: 121–23.

41. Kappler, pp. 140–44, 177–79. For a discussion of Cherokee problems in Arkansas, see Francis Paul Prucha, *American Indian Policy in the Formative Years: The Indian Trade and Intercourse Acts, 1790–1834* (Cambridge: Harvard University Press, 1962), pp. 173–78.

42. Kappler, pp. 288–92.

The Indians west of Arkansas were known as the Old Settlers or Cherokees West, and they developed their own government and a prosperous agricultural economy along the rivers of the area. Here they were joined from time to time by small parties of eastern Cherokees who enrolled for emigration before a total removal treaty had been negotiated. By 1836 more than six thousand Cherokees had moved west.[43]

Despite the success of the Cherokees in the West, the great bulk of the nation adamantly refused to consider removal. Encouraged by the favorable decision of the Worcester case and influenced by political leaders who controlled the national councils, they repeatedly importuned the federal government—both the executive and Congress—to protect them where they were.[44]

Jackson's administration was embarrassed by the Cherokees' failure to accept the inducements to emigrate. Secretary of War Cass met again and again with the Cherokee delegations and explained the president's desire to aid them, but he insisted that if they chose to remain in the East, they must accept both the privileges and disabilities of other citizens. The unwillingness of the Cherokees to emigrate exasperated the secretary of war. "It was hoped that the favorable terms offered by the Government would have been accepted," he wrote to Wilson Lumpkin, then governor of Georgia. "But some strange infatuation seems to prevail among these Indians. That they cannot remain where they are and prosper is attested as well by their actual condition as by the whole history of our aboriginal tribes. Still they refuse to adopt the only course which promises a cure or even an alleviation for the evils of their present condition." Little by little Cass grew less patient in his dealings with the Cherokees, telling them curtly in 1834 that there was little use in reviving discussion with them, since the government's position had not changed. Jackson himself in March 1835 spoke bluntly to the Cherokees: "I have no motive, my friends, to deceive you. I am sincerely desirous to promote your welfare. Listen to me therefore while I tell you that you cannot remain where you now are. Circumstances that cannot be controlled and which are beyond the reach of human laws render it impossible that you can flourish in the midst of a civilized community. You have but one remedy within your reach. And that is to remove to the west and join your countrymen who are already

43. CIA Report, 1836, serial 301, p. 402. Emigration 1829–1835 totaled 2,698. *Senate Document* no. 403, 24–1, serial 283, pp. 1–2. There is a brief account of the Old Settlers in Morris L. Wardell, *A Political History of the Cherokee Nation, 1838–1907* (Norman: University of Oklahoma Press, 1938), pp. 4–7.

44. Memorial of January 5, 1832, *House Document* no. 45, 22–1, serial 217. Other memorials are the following: May 3, 1830, *House Report* no. 397, 21–1, serial 201; January 15, 1831, *House Document* no. 57, 21–1, serial 208; May 17, 1834, *Senate Document* no. 386, 23–1, serial 242.

established there. And the sooner you do this the sooner will commence your career of improvement and prosperity."[45]

Andrew Jackson and his supporters seemed convinced that there were two groups of Cherokees, the "real" Indians making up the majority of the Cherokee Nation, whose deplorable conditions made them willing and eager to migrate, and the mixed-blood chiefs, who selfishly opposed removal and threatened their subjects with reprisals if any agreed to removal. Thomas L. McKenney advanced the argument in 1829 as part of his program for the New York board that supported Jackson's removal policy. When the *Cherokee Phoenix* flatly denied his assertion and declared that "the great body of the tribe are *not anxious to remove*," McKenney took pains to gather together a number of documents from persons in the Indian country that substantiated his claims of the Indians' desire to emigrate and the use of threats to stop those who wanted to go and had them published in the New York *Evening Post*. As late as 1835, Commissioner of Indian Affairs Elbert Herring reported, "There can be little doubt that bad advisement, and the intolerant control of chiefs adverse to the measure, have conduced to the disinclination of a large portion of the nation to emigrate, and avail themselves of the obvious benefit of the contemplated change."[46]

Whatever the truth of this analysis, only a few Indians enrolled for emigration; the main body of the nation would not budge. The condition of the Cherokees in the East steadily worsened, as white encroachments continued to destroy their property and threaten their lives, and the federal government showed no signs of weakening its stand. A part of the Cherokees, thereupon, decided that the inevitable had to be faced and prepared to negotiate for removal. This group, known as the "treaty party," was led by Major Ridge, who had fought with Andrew Jackson against the Creeks at Horseshoe Bend; his educated and politically active son John Ridge; and his two nephews, the brothers Elias Boudinot and Stand Watie. Its appearance, beginning in 1832–1833, split the Cherokee Nation into factions of bitter opposition that persisted for decades. The "anti-treaty party," representing the bulk of the nation, was led by the elected principal chief, John Ross, a mixed-blood who was one-eighth Cherokee.[47]

45. Cass to John Martin, John Ridge, and William S. Coodey, January 10, 1832, OIA LS, vol. 8, p. 407 (M21, reel 8); Cass to Lumpkin, December 24, 1832, ibid., vol. 9, pp. 486–89 (M21, reel 9); Cass to John Ross and others, February 2, 1833, and March 13, 1834, ibid., vol. 10, pp. 18–21, and vol. 12, pp. 187–88 (M21, reels 10 and 12); Jackson to the Cherokees, March 16, 1835, ibid., vol. 15, p. 169 (M21, reel 15).

46. Francis Paul Prucha, "Thomas L. McKenney and the New York Indian Board," *Mississippi Valley Historical Review* 48 (March 1962): 649; CIA Report, 1835, serial 286, p. 262. See also CIA Report, 1832, serial 233, p. 161. The question is discussed in Mary E. Young, "Indian Removal and Land Allotment: The Civilized Tribes and Jacksonian Justice," *American Historical Review* 64 (October 1958): 33–35.

47. A history of the Ridge party that presents a reasonable and sympathetic account

This factionalism was used by the Reverend John F. Schermerhorn, appointed United States commissioner to treat with the Cherokees. When the Ross party rejected his overtures, he signed a removal treaty with the Ridge faction at New Echota on December 29, 1835. In an unusual preamble to the treaty, the government sought to justify its dealing with what was only a small portion of the whole tribe. The commissioners, the statement said, had called a meeting of the general council for December 21 at New Echota, at which they would be prepared to make a treaty with the Cherokees who assembled there. Those who did not come would be considered to have given their assent and sanction to whatever was transacted at the council. Ross and his supporters boycotted the meeting, so the Ridge party alone attended and signed the treaty. On this shaky foundation the United States procured its removal treaty with the Cherokees. A vehement protest came from the Cherokee national council, which passed a resolution condemning the work of the unauthorized New Echota meeting; and in a memorial to the Senate, Ross elaborated his position, protesting that "the instrument entered into at New Echota, purporting to be a treaty, is deceptive to the world, and a fraud upon the Cherokee people." There was a public outcry as well and a vigorous debate in the Senate; but on May 18, 1836, the Senate approved the treaty by a single vote.[48]

By the treaty, the Cherokees ceded all their lands east of the Mississippi and for $5 million released their claims upon the United States. The seven million acres of land granted the Cherokees in the treaty of 1828 plus the outlet to the west were confirmed, and additional lands were granted. Articles excluding the western lands from state or territorial jurisdiction and granting protection against unauthorized intruders and against domestic and foreign enemies, similar to those in the other removal treaties, were included. Provision was made also for the emigration, for one year's subsistence, and for allotments for Indians who desired to stay in the East. The treaty specified that the removal was to be accomplished within two years after ratification of the treaty.

The treaty party emigrated with little trouble; the state officials treated them considerately, and they were, in general, economically well-off. They

---

of their arguments and decisions is Thurman Wilkins, *Cherokee Tragedy: The Story of the Ridge Family and the Decimation of a People* (New York: Macmillan Company, 1970). A memorial of November 28, 1834, is a good statement of the Ridge party's argument that removal was inevitable for preservation of the nation; *House Document* no. 91, 23–2, serial 273, pp. 1–7. The best work on Ross is Gary E. Moulton, *John Ross, Cherokee Chief* (Athens: University of Georgia Press, 1978).

48. Kappler, pp. 439–49; "Memorial and Protest of the Cherokee Nation," March 8, 1836, and other documents in *House Document* no. 286, 24–1, serial 292; memorial of December 15, 1837, *House Document* no. 99, 25–2, serial 325. See also the discussion of Ross's activities in Moulton, *John Ross*, pp. 73–79.

established their farms and plantations among the western Cherokees. The remainder, having rejected the treaty as a valid instrument, refused to move, and Ross used every opportunity in his attempts to reverse the treaty's provisions. He encouraged his followers to stand firm, and few enrolled for emigration. Numerous petitions poured into Congress from religious and philanthropic supporters of the Cherokees, protesting the execution of the 1835 treaty.[49]

A strenuous denial of the validity of the treaty was submitted to Congress in early April 1838. It bore the signatures of 15,665 Cherokees and appealed to Congress once more for protection against the throngs of Georgians invading their lands as the deadline for removal approached. It closed with this plea: "We never can assent to that compact; nor can we believe that the United States are bound, in honor or in justice, to execute on us its degrading and ruinous provisions. It is true, we are a feeble people; and, as regards physical power, we are in the hands of the United States; but we have not forfeited our rights, and if we fail to transmit to our sons the freedom we have derived from our fathers, it must not only be by an act of suicide, it must not be with our own consent."[50]

Ross also carried on a pamphlet campaign to stir up public support for his cause and to condemn and weaken the opposing treaty party.[51] Such actions brought a vigorous response from Elias Boudinot as spokesman for the Ridge faction, in memorials to Congress and appeals to the nation. In a statement "To the Public," January 1838, and in long open letters to John Ross, Boudinot set forth the position held by the treaty party:

> Without replying to these charges [of Ross] in this place, we will state what *we* suppose to be the great cause of our present difficulties—our present dissensions. *A want of proper information among the people.* We charge Mr. Ross with having deluded them with expectations incompatible with, and injurious to, their interest. He has prevented the discussion of this interesting matter, by systematic measures, at a time when discussion was of the most vital importance. By that reason the people have been kept ignorant of their true condition. They have been taught to feel and expect what *could not* be realized, and what Mr. Ross himself must have known *would not*

---

49. For memorials against the New Echota Treaty, see *House Documents* nos. 374, 384, 385, and 404, 25–2, serial 330; *Senate Documents* nos. 388, 389, 390, 402, 416, and 417, 25–2, serial 318.

50. Memorial of February 22, 1838, *House Document* no. 316, 25–2, serial 329.

51. John Ross, *Letter from John Ross, Principal Chief of the Cherokee Nation of Indians, in Answer to Inquiries from a Friend Regarding the Cherokee Affairs with the United States* (Philadelphia, 1836); Ross, *Letter from John Ross, the Principal Chief of the Cherokee Nation: To a Gentleman of Philadelphia* (Philadelphia, 1837).

be realized. This great delusion has lasted to this day. Now, in view of such a state of things, we cannot conceive of the acts of a *minority* to be so reprehensible or unjust as are represented by Mr. Ross. If one hundred persons are ignorant of their true situation, and are so completely blinded as not to see the destruction that awaits them, we can see strong reasons to justify the action of a minority of fifty persons to do what the majority *would do* if they understood their condition —to save a nation from political thraldom and moral degradation.[52]

As the crisis continued, Ross sought finally to replace the New Echota Treaty with one of his own design, but his proposals were unacceptable, and the government would not depart from the provisions of the 1835 treaty.[53]

The general air of dissension within the Cherokee country and the fear that the New Echota treaty would not be carried out by the mass of the Cherokees had caused Secretary of War Cass to assign Brigadier General John E. Wool to the Cherokee country on June 20, 1836. Wool was ordered to ascertain the designs of the Cherokees and to take command of Tennessee volunteers raised by the governor of Tennessee. Cass directed him to reduce the Cherokees to submission if they should begin any hostilities and if necessary to call for more troops from the governors of Tennessee, Georgia, and North Carolina.[54]

Wool, whose sympathies lay with the Indians, did not find his task an appealing one. "The whole scene since I have been in this country has been nothing but a heart-rending one, and such a one as I would be glad to get rid of as soon as circumstances will permit," he wrote on September 10, 1836.[55] He anxiously hoped for a force of regular troops to be sent to him that fall, but he received only a curt note from the War Department that "there is no portion of the regular army that can be placed at your disposal." He was told to make use of the volunteers. When Wool attempted

52. Statement of Boudinot, *Senate Document* no. 121, 25–2, serial 315; see also the other material printed in this document. Boudinot also resorted to pamphlets: *Documents in Relation to the Validity of the Cherokee Treaty of 1835: Letters and Other Papers Relating to Cherokee Affairs, Being in Reply to Sundry Publications Authorized by John Ross* (Washington: Blair and Rives, 1838); *Letters and Other Papers Relating to Cherokee Affairs: Being in Reply to Sundry Publications Authorized by John Ross* (Athens, Georgia: Southern Banner, 1837).

53. Poinsett to John Ross and others, May 18, 1838, *House Document* no. 376, 25–2, serial 330; report of Senate Committee on Indian Affairs, June 5, 1838, *Senate Document* no. 466, 25–2, serial 318.

54. My account of military action against the Cherokees relies on Prucha, *Sword of the Republic*, pp. 262–68.

55. Quoted in James Mooney, *Myths of the Cherokee*, Nineteenth Annual Report of the Bureau of American Ethnology, 1897–1898, part 1 (Washington: GPO, 1900), p. 127.

to protect the Indians in the Cherokee country in Alabama, where their oppression was particularly notorious, he was charged by the governor and legislature of the state with having usurped the powers of the civil tribunals, disturbed the peace of the community, and trampled upon the rights of the citizens. The president referred the charges to a military court of inquiry, whch met in Knoxville in September 1837. The court completely vindicated Wool, but such maneuverings to protect the reputation of the general did nothing to ease the tense situation in the Cherokee country.[56]

When the deadline for removal, May 23, 1838, approached and the Indians were still on their old lands, the government ordered General Winfield Scott to the Cherokee country "with a view to the fulfillment of the treaty." Scott, on May 10, issued an address to the Cherokee chiefs. "The President of the United States," he told them bluntly, "has sent me, with a powerful army, to cause you, in obedience to the Treaty of 1835, to join that part of your people who are already established in prosperity on the other side of the Mississippi." He stressed his determination to carry out his orders and pointed to the troops already occupying the Indian country and the "thousands and thousands . . . approaching from every quarter." He urged them to move with haste, thus to spare him "the horror of witnessing the destruction of the Cherokees." The general directed his troops to treat the Indians with kindness and humanity as they were rounded up and gathered in concentration points for the movement west, but contemporary reports included lurid stories of harshness and inhumanity.[57]

The emigrating Indians were organized into detachments, but only about three hundred had departed when Scott called a halt to the exodus for the rest of the hot summer season. The Cherokee leaders then made an agreement with Scott whereby they themselves would take charge of the emigration when it began again in the fall, and the operation became a project of the Rosses. Officers were appointed by the Cherokee council, and a quasi-military order was maintained on the march. When the drought that had further delayed the departure was broken in October, the caravans began their march overland to Nashville and Memphis. The emigrants numbered about thirteen thousand, including black slaves; they carried along whatever of their belongings they had managed to save. The Indian leaders themselves were responsible for the good behavior of the nation, and no

56. The proceedings of the court of inquiry are in *House Document* no. 46, 25–1, serial 311.

57. Documents on Scott's operations are in *House Document* no. 453, 25–2, serial 331; Scott's part in the removal is treated in Elliott, *Winfield Scott,* pp. 345–55. Examples of reports of harsh treatment of the Cherokees appear in *Niles' National Register* 54 (August 18, 1838): 385, and in Mooney, *Myths of the Cherokee,* p. 130.

military escort was deemed necessary. The journey, with its late start, occurred during the hardest months of the year, and this Trail of Tears reaped a heavy harvest of misery and death.[58]

The difficulties in implementing the removal policy in regard to the Cherokees and the other southern tribes—the fraudulent nature of some of the treaties, the dishonesty and chicanery involved in the disposition of the Indians' lands, the bitter military conflict in Florida, and the hardships and misery of the movement—did not weaken the resolve of federal officers, from the president down, who favored the policy. Having committed themselves absolutely to eliminating the Indian nations east of the Mississippi, Jackson and his associates and their successors in office continued to expound the advantages of the program for both the Indians and the whites. Jackson himself, the great father, gave his final benediction to the removal

---

58. Descriptions of the emigration are given in Foreman, *Indian Removal*, pp. 279–312. Moulton, *John Ross*, pp. 95–106, discusses the removal under Ross and the subsequent controversy over removal expenses.

The number of Cherokees who perished on the Trail of Tears is a historiographical problem. Because of the injustice involved in the removal and the hardships endured, it is easy to accept uncritically greatly exaggerated figures. The crusading secretary of the Indian Rights Association declared in 1890: "The march through the wilderness caused the death of at least half the tribe." Herbert Welsh, *The Indian Question: Past and Present* (Philadelphia, 1890), p. 7. The historian Ralph Henry Gabriel wrote in 1929, "A third of the people perished in the autumn and winter of 1838 when the Cherokee followed what they called the 'trail of tears.'" Gabriel, *The Lure of the Frontier: A Story of Race Conflict* (New Haven: Yale University Press, 1929), p. 128. A commonly accepted figure, however, is four thousand, or one-fourth of the sixteen thousand total presumed to have emigrated. Thus Annie Abel's influential and usually well-documented monograph makes the undocumented assertion, "More than one-fourth are said to have perished on the way." Abel, "Indian Consolidation," p. 404. And Grant Foreman's widely accepted history says in a footnote, "All told, about 4,000 died during the course of capture and detention in temporary stockades, and the removal itself." *Indian Removal*, p. 312 n. The "more than one-quarter died" statistic is accepted by Mary Young, who depends on the testimony in 1839 of Dr. Elizur Butler, whom she regards as "a reliable witness, and perhaps the best qualified of his contemporaries to make a general estimate," but then she admits that "the proportion of deaths which can be positively confirmed runs between five and six per cent of the emigrants." Mary Young, "Indian Removal and the Attack on Tribal Autonomy: The Cherokee Case," in *Indians of the Lower South: Past and Present*, ed. John K. Mahon (Pensacola: Gulf Coast History and Humanities Conference, 1975), pp. 135–37. Figures given for the twelve emigrating parties in T. Hartley Crawford to Joel R. Poinsett, August 8, 1840, *House Report* no. 1098, 27–2, serial 411, pp. 9–10, show that fewer than 10 percent died on the journey. This is a demographic problem and has been treated as such in the study of Donald R. Englund, "A Demographic Study of the Cherokee Nation" (Ph.D. dissertation, University of Oklahoma, 1973). By comparing different censuses and rates of natural increase before and after removal, Englund concludes that about two thousand of the sixteen thousand died in the removal.

policy in his "Farewell Address" of March 4, 1837. "The States which had so long been retarded in their improvement by the Indian tribes residing in the midst of them are at length relieved from the evil," he said, "and this unhappy race—the original dwellers in our land—are now placed in a situation where we may well hope that they will share in the blessings of civilization and be saved from that degradation and destruction to which they were rapidly hastening while they remained in the States; and while the safety and comfort of our own citizens have been greatly promoted by their removal, the philanthropist will rejoice that the remnant of that ill-fated race has been at length placed beyond the reach of injury or oppression, and that the paternal care of the General Government will hereafter watch over them and protect them.[59]

President Van Buren, upon whom rested the responsibility for removing the Cherokees and for the conduct of the Seminole War, asserted in 1837 that "the most sanguine expectations" of the friends and promoters of removal had been realized, and he contrasted the "certain destruction" that awaited the tribes within the states and territories with the near utopia that could be developed in the West. He spoke the following year of the "misrepresentation" and "unjust imputations" made about removal and declared that the wisdom and necessity of the policy had never been doubted by "any calm, judicious, disinterested friend of the Indian race accustomed to reflection and enlightened by experience."[60]

Whatever the views, whether the extreme praise of the Jacksonites, who seemed blinded to the evils that accompanied the policy, or the severe condemnation of the anti-removal critics, who ignored the real problems facing the United States in adjusting the rights and interests of the two races, the southern Indian nations in fact had been removed, and only scattered remnants remained east of the Mississippi. The relations of the United States government with them thereafter were based upon that fundamental condition.

59. Richardson, *Messages and Papers of the Presidents*, 2: 541.
60. Message of December 5, 1837, Fred L. Israel, ed., *The State of the Union Messages of the Presidents, 1790–1966*, 3 vols. (New York: Chelsea House, 1966), 1: 490–91; message of December 3, 1838, ibid., p. 509.

CHAPTER 9

Removal of the
Northern Indians

Clearing the Old Northwest. Potawatomi

Dispersal. Sacs and Foxes and the

Black Hawk War. Other Tribes.

New York Indians. The Role of the Traders.

Public attention focused on the removal of the Five Civilized Tribes from the southeastern states. It was the Cherokees' conflict with Georgia that held the attention of the federal government and of the public in the development of the removal policy and in the Removal Act of 1830. But this removal policy was also intended to apply to the Indians north of the Ohio River, who remained on lands sought by the expanding agricultural society of the North. They, like their southern brothers—with the notable exceptions of groups that migrated to Canada and others that remained on reservations within their old territories—were removed to the Indian country west of the Mississippi River.[1]

CLEARING THE OLD NORTHWEST

Whereas the southern Indians were organized into five sizable Indian nations, with relatively well-defined land holdings that stretched back to time immemorial, the northern tribes were numerous, sometimes frac-

1. Grant Foreman, *The Last Trek of the Indians* (Chicago: University of Chicago Press, 1946), pp. 17–158, deals with the removal of the northern tribes, but the book is principally concerned with the actual emigrations. Ronald N. Satz, "Indian Policy in the Jacksonian Era: The Old Northwest as a Test Case," *Michigan History* 60 (Spring 1976): 71–93, is an indictment of the removal policy that suffers from trying to prove a case.

tionalized into scattered bands, and often with land claims overlapping or ill-defined as the result of frequent migrations. In the removal period a great variety of Indian communities in the Old Northwest (Kaskaskias, Peorias, Shawnees, Ottawas, Wyandots, Miamis, Potawatomis, Menominees, Delawares, Sacs and Foxes, Piankashaws, Weas, Kickapoos, Chippewas, Sioux, and New York Indians) negotiated treaties with the United States, and in the same period treaties were signed with Indians holding lands in Iowa, Missouri, and Minnesota in order to clear those regions, or parts of them, of Indian inhabitants. It was a continuous and complicated process.

Most of the Indians involved had a long history of shifting locales. The Delawares, for example, at the beginning of the historic period were located in what is now New Jersey and Delaware, and in the course of time they established themselves along the Susquehanna River in eastern Pennsylvania, in the Allegheny valley in western Pennsylvania, and in eastern Ohio, central Indiana, southern Missouri, and eastern Kansas. At the end of three centuries of movement there are now surviving groups of Delawares in Oklahoma, Kansas, Wisconsin, and Ontario.[2] The Shawnees had a similar history, perhaps even more diverse, for they appeared in the southeast and in Pennsylvania as well as in the Old Northwest; there are "Shawneetowns" scattered across the eastern United States. Migration had been a way of life for the Shawnees until they were moved west of Missouri in 1832.[3] Although these may be extreme cases, none of the Indians north of Ohio occupied precisely the same lands in 1830 that their ancestors had held when French traders first came in contact with them in the seventeenth century. The emigration of these tribes in the Jacksonian era was part of their migration history, which continued even after their first settlements west of the Mississippi.

Nor was the relation of the United States government with these groups in the 1830s, after the passage of the Removal Act, a new departure. Rather, it was a continuation of policies and actions that had been going on for more than three decades (although without doubt new impetus was given by the 1830 legislation). Removal, in the sense of an exchange of lands within the states and territories east of the Mississippi for lands in the West, was only one part of the story. Many of the treaties provided for ces-

---

Useful articles on the individual tribes appear in *Handbook of North American Indians*, vol. 15: *Northeast*, ed. Bruce G. Trigger (Washington: Smithsonian Institution, 1978).

2. See C. A. Weslager, *The Delaware Indians: A History* (New Brunswick: Rutgers University Press, 1972). The endpaper maps graphically depict the Delaware migrations.

3. Jerry E. Clark, *The Shawnee* (Lexington: University Press of Kentucky, 1977), p. 3. An elaborate map of Shawnee locations and movements is in Charles Callender, "Shawnee," in Trigger, *Northeast*, p. 623.

sion of Indian lands to the United States and the concentration of the displaced Indians on remaining lands, with the privilege of hunting on the
ceded lands until they were surveyed and sold—a process that had been
taking place for many years.[4] Indeed, by 1830 most of Ohio, Indiana, and
Illinois had already been freed of Indian title in a succession of treaties between Indian groups and the United States government. What remained in
these states were enclaves of natives, subsisting on agriculture and government annuities, surrounded by whites. Pressures for the release of these
final Indian holdings became irresistible. The attitude of the whites is
sharply reflected in the repeated memorials sent to Congress by the legislature of Indiana. One of January 1829 was an epitome of frontier sentiment:

> The continuance of these few savages within our limits, who
> claim so large a space of the best soil, not only circumscribes, in its
> practical effects, the usefulness of the privileges we enjoy as a free
> and independent State, but tends materially to impede a system of
> internal improvements essential to the prosperity of our citizens, and
> in a degree jeopardizes the peace and tranquillity of our frontier,
> which it is our right and duty to secure. It is evident, that, although
> the Indians within our boundaries have been supported by large an-
> nuities, although the game has greatly decreased, yet agricultural
> pursuits are almost entirely neglected; and thus the large extent of
> country they yet claim is not only unprofitable to them, but, by its
> contiguity to the [Wabash] canal, is calculated to retard the settle-
> ment, the revenue, and the prosperity of the State.[5]

In the northern territories, Michigan and Wisconsin, on the other hand,
white settlement, even after the opening of the Erie Canal in 1825, was
confined to the southern and central tiers of counties. The rest of the region retained much of its Indian population and in addition became a
refuge for Indians displaced from other areas. Secretary of War Calhoun's
1825 proposal on Indian removal, in fact, included the suggestion that the
Indians living in the northern parts of Indiana and Illinois and in Michigan,

---

4. James A. Clifton classifies the treaties with the Indians in the Old Northwest,
1830–1839, as follows: seventeen provided for reduction of land base without removal;
three provided for permissive removal; eight provided for obligatory removal. His low
total of twenty-eight results from omitting treaties that confirmed or supplemented earlier ones and from combining a number of treaties made with separate bands of Potawatomis, which were in fact a single action of ceding reservations made earlier. Clifton,
"Escape, Evasion, and Eviction: Adaptive Responses of the Indians of the Old Northwest
to the Jacksonian Removal Policy in the 1830s," an unpublished paper furnished me by
Clifton.

5. Memorial of the General Assembly of the State of Indiana, January 22, 1829, *Senate Document* no. 22, 21–2, serial 203, p. 3. See similar memorials in *House Document*
no. 68, 21–2, serial 208, and *House Document* no. 129, 23–2, serial 273.

Ohio, and New York be moved to the region west of Lake Michigan and north of Illinois.[6]

The situation in the Old Northwest also differed from that in the South because of the proximity of British Canada. Many of the tribes in the region had had close economic and political ties with the British. They had sided with the British in the War of 1812 and after the war continued to frequent the British posts (notably at Malden across from Detroit). This friendly association of the Indians with the British north of the border would perhaps have given the United States pause had it planned the ruthless dispossession of the Indians pictured by some writers. But more important than the possibility of succor in time of trouble was the open haven that Canada offered for Indians in the United States. It would be wrong to think of removal from the Old Northwest only as a migration to the future states of Iowa, Kansas, or Oklahoma, for large numbers of Potawatomis, Ottawas, and Chippewas, as well as smaller numbers of other tribes, moved into Canada.[7]

In treaties with the Indians of the Old Northwest, provision was frequently made for reserves of land within the cession for individuals or small bands. The practice began with the treaties of 1817, and thereafter it was difficult not to follow that precedent, for such reservations were a means for the Indians to escape (at least for the time being) the nearly inexorable pressure for emigration to lands west of the Mississippi. The guaranteed reserves, however, were an awkward intrusion into the removal policy. At first they were patented in fee to the individuals, but the Senate, in ratifying treaties, came to look askance at this procedure, and later treaties specified either that these lands were to be held "in the same manner as Indian reservations had been heretofore held," with preemption rights in the United States government, or that individual grants could not be disposed of without the approval of the president. But in practice there was no objection to the sale of these lands, and permission was easy to obtain. Once the practice of reserves had been established, it was almost impossible to obtain a treaty of cession from the northwest Indians without them. The reserves were not only a hedge against removal; they were

6. Calhoun report, January 24, 1825, ASP:IA, 2: 542–44.

7. On the Potawatomis, see James A. Clifton, *The Prairie People: Continuity and Change in Potawatomi Indian Culture, 1665–1965* (Lawrence: Regents Press of Kansas, 1977), pp. 301–9; Clifton, *A Place of Refuge for All Time: Migration of the American Potawatomi into Upper Canada, 1830 to 1850* (Ottawa: National Museums of Canada, 1975). For Ottawa movement to Canada, see Robert F. Bauman, "Kansas, Canada, or Starvation," *Michigan History* 36 (September 1952): 287–99. There is discussion of Indians moving to Canada in the reports of T. Hartley Crawford of Janaury 15, 1839, *House Document* no. 107, 25–3, serial 346, and April 7, 1840, *House Document* no. 178, 26–1, serial 366.

also a means of individual profit, for the Indians could dispose of them for a reasonable price and sometimes more. Traders and other land speculators hoped to get the lands from the Indians by sale or in payment of debts.[8]

To the federal government, desirous of clearing the states of Indians altogether, the reservations became an irritant and an obstacle, yet so insistent were the Indians that there was great temptation to allow the individual grants in order to obtain new cessions. In 1833 Secretary of War Cass instructed the commissioners dealing with the Potawatomis at Chicago:

> Decline, in the first instances, to grant any reservations either to the Indians or others, and endeavor to prevail upon them all to remove. Should you find this impracticable, and that granting some reservations will be unavoidable, that course may be taken in the usual manner, and upon the usual conditions. But I am very anxious that individual reservations should be circumscribed within the narrowest possible limits. The whites and half-breeds press upon the Indians, and induce them to ask for these gratuities, to which they have no just pretensions; and for which neither the United States nor the Indians receive any real consideration. The practice, though it has long prevailed, is a bad one, and should be avoided as far as possible.

In the Chicago case, cash payments were provided "to satisfy sundry individuals, in behalf of whom reservations were asked, which the Commissioners refused to grant." In 1843 the Senate resolved that no more individual reservations should be allowed in treaties.[9]

The passage of the Removal Act, of course, stimulated increased action in regard to the northern tribes. President Jackson in February 1831 appointed James B. Gardiner of Ohio to treat with the Ohio Senecas, and upon Gardiner's success the president commissioned him as a special agent to confer with other Indians in Ohio and explain to them the necessity of moving beyond the Mississippi. In July and August 1831 Gardiner negotiated removal treaties with the Shawnees and the Ottawas in which they ceded all their lands in Ohio and accepted designated districts in the western Indian country beyond the state of Missouri. With the Wyandots Gardiner had less success. Although pressed upon by white settlements, these Indians first demanded an investigation of the land proposed for their

8. Paul W. Gates, "Indian Allotments Preceding the Dawes Act," in John G. Clark, ed., *The Frontier Challenge: Responses to the Trans-Mississippi West* (Lawrence: University Press of Kansas, 1971), pp. 147–58. For a discussion of the type of tenure the Indians had in the reserves, see Robert W. McCluggage, "The Senate and Indian Land Titles, 1800–1825," *Western Historical Quarterly* 1 (October 1970): 415–25.

9. Cass to commissioners, April 8, 1833, *Senate Document* no. 512, 23–1, serial 246, p. 652; Kappler, p. 402 (see Schedule A for individuals so rewarded, pp. 404–6); *Journal of the Executive Proceedings of the Senate*, 6: 170, 184.

residence in the West. When an unfavorable report was returned, the Wyandots refused to emigrate. The treaty that Gardiner signed with them on January 19, 1832, authorized the cession of sixteen thousand acres for which the Indians would be paid $1.25 an acre as the land was sold. The treaty provided that the band "may, as they think proper, remove to Canada, or to the river Huron in Michigan, where they own a reservation of land, or to any place they may obtain a right or privilege from other Indians to go."[10]

Congress in 1832 authorized treaties to extinguish the title of the Kickapoos, Shawnees, and Delawares at Cape Girardeau in Missouri and of the Piankashaws, Weas, Peorias, and Kaskaskias in Illinois, as well as for dealing with the Shawnees and Menominees. In October the Indians concerned assembled at Castor Hill, the home of Superintendent William Clark near St. Louis, where treaties were signed between October 24 and 29 by which the lands in Missouri and Illinois were given up and new lands west of the Missouri accepted.[11] The northern part of the Indian country in the West was gradually taking shape as the home of the northern Indians.

POTAWATOMI DISPERSAL

The Potawatomi Indians were an example of drawn out, piecemeal removal of Indians from the Old Northwest.[12] Altogether, between 1789 and 1837, members of this tribe signed thirty-nine treaties with the United States. By 1828 the Potawatomis had given up most of their lands except for parcels in Indiana, Michigan, Illinois, and Wisconsin. In that year Lewis Cass and Pierre Menard met with the Winnebagos and united bands of Potawatomis, Chippewas, and Ottawas at Green Bay for a preliminary agreement on cession of the lead-mining regions on the east side of the Mississippi; and the next year at Prairie du Chien the united bands ceded their claims to a tract along the Mississippi south of Prairie du Chien in Wisconsin and Illinois, as well as a large parcel of land south of the Fox

10. Foreman, *Last Trek of the Indians*, pp. 65–85; Carl G. Klopfenstein, "The Removal of the Wyandots from Ohio," *Ohio Historical Quarterly* 66 (April 1957): 119–36. Pertinent documents from *Senate Document* no. 512 are cited in Foreman; the treaties are in Kappler, pp. 325–40.

11. 4 *United States Statutes* 564, 594; Kappler, pp. 365–67, 370–72, 376–77, 382–83. There is discussion of the treaties in Foreman, *Last Trek of the Indians*, pp. 60–65.

12. I have depended upon the general accounts of Potawatomi removal that appear in Clifton, *Prairie People*, pp. 179–245, 279–346; R. David Edmunds, *The Potawatomis: Keepers of the Fire* (Norman: University of Oklahoma Press, 1978), pp. 240–72; and Foreman, *Last Trek of the Indians*, pp. 100–125.

River and west of Chicago, in return for annuities, special grants for chiefs, and payment of debts to traders.[13]

Another broad grouping of Potawatomis, those in Indiana and Michigan, who had been extensively missionized and in many ways acculturated to the white man's ways, negotiated with Cass and Menard in 1828 at Carey Mission on the St. Joseph River in southwestern Michigan. There the Indians ceded their holdings in the region; annuities and other benefits were provided, traders' debts were covered, and grants of land (one-half to two sections in size) were stipulated for certain individuals.[14]

After the Black Hawk War of 1832, Potawatomi bands met United States commissioners again on the Tippecanoe River in Indiana. These Indians were split into bitter factions, each looking out for its own interests, and the commissioners solved the problem by signing three separate treaties between October 20 and 27, 1832, with different groupings of Indians. The Potawatomis of "the Prairie and Kankakee" band relinquished title to lands in eastern Illinois along the Kankakee River. Those from Indiana villages gave up their claims in that state, and the third faction, chiefly from the St. Joseph River region, ceded all claims to lands in Illinois, Indiana, and Michigan. In order to expedite the negotiations, the United States agreed to small reservations of land within the ceded districts for individuals and for village bands. Some 120 such reserves were stipulated in the three treaties; they satisfied the desire of the Indians to remain (even on reduced land holdings), but they seriously interfered with the government's intention of removing the Indians from the states. The Indians made use of the importunity of the government to drive a harder bargain than in previous negotiations, and large sums of money and goods were involved. The influence of traders, too, was evident, for the treaties provided generously for the payment of debts, and the purchase of large quantities of goods for the Indians further enriched the merchants.[15]

By these various treaties the Potawatomis ceded most of their land base, and the tribesmen were concentrated in small reservations of bands scattered through Michigan, Indiana, and Illinois. They now owned in common only a single large tract in northeastern Illinois and southeastern Wisconsin. The conditions of the Potawatomis were deteriorating, and it

13. Kappler, pp. 292–94, 297–300. Beginning with a treaty at Chicago in 1821, the United States dealt with the Illinois-Wisconsin Potawatomis in conjunction with small groups of Chippewas and Ottawas associated with them. For all practical purposes these "united bands" were Potawatomis; the treaties applied only to them and to the limited numbers of others in close association with them. The treaties confused this fact by sometimes listing the Ottawas or the Chippewas first.

14. Kappler, pp. 294–97.

15. Ibid., pp. 353–56, 367–70, 372–75. These treaties are discussed in the books by Clifton and Edmunds.

MAP 3: Potawatomi Land Cessions—An Example of
the Piecemeal Removal of the Northern Tribes

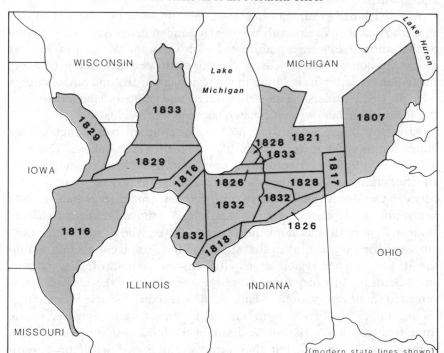

appeared inevitable that they would soon be pressured to remove altogether
from the states and territories that had been their home. Some migrated
voluntarily, joining Kickapoos who moved to Texas, settling in the Kickapoo reservation in Kansas, or establishing themselves on Manitoulin Island. For the rest, plans were soon under way for a treaty at Chicago in the
fall of 1833.

The Chicago negotiation was a spectacular affair.[16] Large numbers of Indians appeared, and whites of all persuasions seeking personal fortunes
were quickly on hand to gain whatever they could. The British traveler
Charles Joseph Latrobe, passing through the village of Chicago, described
the scene:

16. A general account of the treaty is Anselm J. Gerwing, "The Chicago Treaty of
1833," *Journal of the Illinois State Historical Society* 57 (Summer 1964): 117–42. An
excellent portrayal of the many interests at work in the negotiations is in James A.
Clifton, "Chicago, September 14, 1833: The Last Great Indian Treaty in the Old Northwest," *Chicago History* 9 (Summer 1980): 86–97. Documents pertaining to the treaty are
printed in Milo M. Quaife, ed., "The Chicago Treaty of 1833," *Wisconsin Magazine of
History* 1 (March 1918): 287–303.

You will find horse-dealers, and horse-stealers,—rogues of every description, white, black, brown, and red—half-breed, quarter-breeds,
and men of no breed at all;—dealers in pigs, poultry, and potatoes;—
men pursuing Indian claims, some for tracts of land, others, like our
friend Snipe, for pigs which the wolves had eaten;—creditors of the
tribes or of particular Indians, who know they have no chance of getting their money, if they do not get it from the Government agents;—
sharpers of every degree; pedlars, grog-sellers; Indian agents and Indian traders of every description, and Contractors to supply the Pot-
tawattomies with food. The little village was in an uproar from
morning to night, and from night to morning; for, during the hours of
darkness, when the housed portion of the population of Chicago
strove to obtain repose in the crowded plank edifices of the village,
the Indians howled, sang, wept, yelled, and whooped in their various
encampments. With all this, the whites seemed to me to be more
pagan than the red men.[17]

The forceful demands of the American commissioners, led by George B.
Porter, governor of Michigan Territory, were met by the skillful tactics of
the Indian negotiators, the mixed-bloods Billy Caldwell and Alexander
Robinson. The Wisconsin and Illinois Potawatomis signed first on September 26. Those from Michigan needed more persuading to part with their
small tracts and did so only with the proviso that they would not have to
migrate to the West; they affixed their signatures the next day. The treaty
stipulated the exchange of lands, some five million acres in the West, including a triangle between the original western boundary of the state of
Missouri and the Missouri River known as the Platte Purchase, for an
equal amount of land given up. Debts to traders were covered, payments
were made to specified Indians, and a twenty-year annuity was included.
The Indians agreed to emigrate as soon as possible, the cost to be borne by
the United States.[18]

The Senate was slow to ratify the treaty (which it finally did on February 21, 1835), for some of the traders' debts rightly looked suspicious. The
state of Missouri, moreover, desired the Platte Purchase for itself and at
the time of the Chicago treaty was already making plans to acquire it. The
Missouri senators succeeded in having the Senate amend the treaty to substitute land in Iowa for the Platte Purchase. It took some pains to get the
Potawatomis to agree to the amendment, and in the end a special commit-

17. Charles Joseph Latrobe, *The Rambler in North America, MDCCCXXXII–
MDCCCXXXIII*, 2 vols. (London: R. B. Seeley and W. Burnside, 1835), 2: 206–7.

18. Kappler, pp. 402–15. A biography of Billy Caldwell is James A. Clifton, "Merchant, Soldier, Broker, Chief: A Corrected Obituary of Captain Billy Caldwell," *Journal
of the Illinois State Historical Society* 71 (August 1978): 185–210.

tee of only seven men signed the revision in the name of the tribe. Even then the Indians insisted on occupying the Platte Purchase temporarily, and it was only after much irritation on both sides and the threat of military force that the emigrants moved into Iowa, where a subagency was established for them at Council Bluffs.[19]

While the united bands were struggling for some sort of stability west of the Mississippi, the United States began negotiations to eliminate the pockets of Potawatomis that remained in the states on the reserves stipulated in the 1832 treaties. Most of the lands allotted to individual Indians soon passed into white hands. Then, in a series of treaties in 1834 and 1836, the enclaves held by bands were ceded to the United States for considerations of goods, money, payment of debts, and annuities, and their inhabitants agreed to move off the land. A number of the treaties specified removal "to a country provided for them by the United States, west of the Mississippi river." Through the years many of the Indians affected by these treaties migrated into Kansas, settling on a reserve along the Osage River. In the removal of one band in 1838, that led by Chief Menominee, military force was used against the resisting Indians, and the hardships endured in the emigration were long remembered.[20] Other individuals and groups drifted northward in Michigan and Wisconsin and never left the eastern states at all, and about twenty-five hundred (nearly a third of the total Potawatomi population) moved into Canada.[21]

In 1846 a treaty was signed by both large groups of Potawatomis (those in Iowa and those on the Osage River reservation) in an attempt on the part of the United States to pull together into one unit the disparate strands of the Potawatomi people with whom it had been dealing—"to abolish all minor distinctions of bands by which they have heretofore been divided, and . . . to be known only as the Pottowautomie Nation, thereby reinstating the national character." The Indian signatories agreed to cede to the

19. The Platte Purchase issue is discussed in R. David Edmunds, "Potawatomis in the Platte Country: An Indian Removal Incomplete," *Missouri Historical Review* 68 (July 1974): 375–92. See also documents in *Senate Document* no. 206, 24–1, serial 281, and *Senate Document* no. 348, 24–1, serial 283.

20. Kappler, pp. 428–31, 457–61, 462–63, 470–72. There is a brief account of the removal of Menominee's band in Edmunds, *Potawatomis*, pp. 266–68. See also Irving McKee, ed., *The Trail of Death: Letters of Benjamin Marie Petit* (Indianapolis: Indiana Historical Society, 1941).

21. The Potawatomis were not simply shoved around by the paternal government of the United States, but they investigated and took advantage of options open to them in their adaptive response to white pressures. "A fair number of Potawatomis were shopping around in those days," Clifton notes, "inspecting, testing, and comparing the alternative possibilities of Iowa, Kansas, northern Wisconsin, or Canada before finally settling in somewhere. Their freedom of movement in this period was far greater than has generally been appreciated." *Prairie People*, p. 285.

United States their reservations in Iowa and eastern Kansas for $850,000. In return the United States sold them (for $87,000) a new reservation along the Kaw River, land recently ceded by the Kansa Indians.[22] The single national existence never materialized, however, for the united bands from Iowa (designated finally as the Prairie Potawatomi) did not coalesce with the more acculturated tribesmen who had moved to the Kaw from the Osage River (designated ultimately as the Mission or the Citizen Band).[23]

SACS AND FOXES AND THE BLACK HAWK WAR

The dispossession of the Sacs and Foxes, a confederation of once powerful tribes in the Great Lakes and upper Mississippi regions, was notable because it involved the Black Hawk War, a military conflict that in its small way was as embarrassing to the Jackson administration as the Florida War. The war was neither a planned aggression on either side nor a last-ditch stand of noble natives against Indian-hating frontiersmen. A disgruntled war chief, who sought ascendency over a rival chief of saner mind and who naively relied on the counsel of unreliable lieutenants, was opposed by reluctant and hesitant regular army commanders and undisciplined volunteers. A wiser decision here, a tighter rein there, would have obviated the dangers and provided a peaceful settlement.[24]

Black Hawk, the chief protagonist, was a Sac warrior with a long history of anti-American views and actions. In the War of 1812 he had joined actively with the British, and after the war he made regular trips to the British at Malden, which reinforced the hostilities toward the Americans of his followers, who became known as the British band. Black Hawk rejected the treaty made by William Henry Harrison with Sacs and Foxes at

22. Kappler, pp. 557–60.

23. Clifton, *Prairie People*, pp. 347–402. The history of the Citizen Band is given in Joseph Francis Murphy, "Potawatomi Indians of the West: Origins of the Citizen Band" (Ph.D. dissertation, University of Oklahoma, 1961).

24. I follow here the account in Francis Paul Prucha, *The Sword of the Republic: The United States Army on the Frontier, 1783–1846* (New York: Macmillan Company, 1969), pp. 211–31. The most complete history of the Black Hawk War is Frank E. Stevens, *The Black Hawk War, Including a Review of Black Hawk's Life* (Chicago: Frank E. Stevens, 1903); an excellent brief narrative and appraisal of the war is Reuben Gold Thwaites, "The Story of the Black Hawk War," *Wisconsin Historical Collections* 12 (1892): 217–65; a more recent retelling of the story is William T. Hagan, *The Sac and Fox Indians* (Norman: University of Oklahoma Press, 1958), pp. 92–204. For a recent popular account, see Cecil Eby, *"That Disgraceful Affair": The Black Hawk War* (New York: W. W. Norton Company, 1973). An exhaustive, carefully edited collection of documents is Ellen M. Whitney, ed., *The Black Hawk War, 1831–1832*, 2 vols. in 4 parts (Springfield: Illinois State Historical Library, 1970–1978).

St. Louis in 1804 by which the chiefs on hand ceded their extensive holdings east of the Mississippi, in western Illinois and southwestern Wisconsin. Although later treaties confirmed the cession and Black Hawk himself signed at least one of them, he refused to depart from his village of Saukenuk and the lands in Illinois near the mouth of the Rock River.[25]

The treaty of 1804 had permitted the Indians to remain on the ceded lands until they were surveyed and sold, and there was no crisis until Illinois settlers moved into the region in large numbers and at the end of the 1820s threatened the village of Saukenuk itself. Then removal of the Indians from Illinois became a political issue. Governor Ninian Edwards repeatedly called upon the federal government to move the Indians out altogether, and his political existence seemed to depend upon the success of his endeavors.[26]

Many of the Sacs and Foxes considered removal west of the Mississippi inevitable and, following the leadership of Keokuk, began to establish new villages along the Iowa River. Keokuk continually preached acquiescence in the demands of the United States, and he persuaded many to follow his counsel. Not so Black Hawk. The older leader set himself squarely against Keokuk. He refused to leave Saukenuk and rallied around himself the dissenters of like mind.[27]

A preliminary encounter occurred in 1831 as Black Hawk and his followers returned to Illinois after their winter hunt and began to plant corn. General Edmund P. Gaines moved up the Mississippi to Rock Island with new troops and called a council, attended by both Black Hawk and Keokuk. Keokuk pleaded with Black Hawk's followers to desert their leader for more peaceful policies, and he succeeded in winning over some of the band, but Black Hawk himself remained defiant. Only when militia called out by Governor John Reynolds (who had succeeded Edwards in 1830) appeared to drive out the Indians did Black Hawk retreat quietly across the Mississippi. In a new council called by Gaines, which Black Hawk reluctantly attended, the Sacs and Foxes signed Articles of Agreement and Ca-

25. Kappler, pp. 74–77, 120–22, 126–28, 250–55. The best source on Black Hawk is Donald Jackson, ed., *Black Hawk (Ma-Ka-Tai-Me-She-Kia-Kiak): An Autobiography* (Urbana: University of Illinois Press, 1955).

26. Correspondence on the matter can be found in *The Edwards Papers: Being a Portion of the Collection of the Letters, Papers, and Manuscripts of Ninian Edwards*, ed. E. B. Washburne (Chicago: Fergus Printing Company, 1884). See also the letters of Edwards and Reynolds in Evarts B. Greene and Clarence W. Alvord, eds., *The Governors' Letter-Books, 1818–1834* (Springfield: Illinois State Historical Library, 1909).

27. A masterful analysis of the background of the war is Anthony F. C. Wallace, *Prelude to Disaster: The Course of Indian-White Relations Which Led to the Black Hawk War of 1832* (Springfield: Illinois State Historical Library, 1970). This appeared as the introduction to Whitney, *Black Hawk War*.

pitulation in which they agreed to stay west of the Mississippi and abandon all communication with the British. "I touched the goosequill to this
treaty," Black Hawk admitted, "and was determined to live in peace."[28]

The quiet was short-lived. On July 31 a body of Sac and Fox warriors
surprised an unarmed camp of Menominees near Fort Crawford and slew
twenty-eight of the camp in vengeance for the massacre of Fox chiefs by
Sioux and Menominees the year before. The outrage convinced many
whites that they would be the next victims, and the government quickly
demanded the murderers, ordering General Henry Atkinson with military
reinforcements to Rock Island to restrain the Sioux and Menominees from
an attack on the Sacs and Foxes. The intertribal conflict also reenergized
Black Hawk. He championed those who refused to surrender the guilty
braves and thus drew new elements into his depleted band and strengthened his position against his rival Keokuk, under whose domination he
chafed. Advised by supporters that aid would be forthcoming from the
British and from other Indian tribes, he and his band on April 6, 1832,
recrossed the Mississippi into Illinois. There were about five hundred
mounted warriors, together with the old men and the women and children
of his band, who swelled the total number to an estimated two thousand.

Fearful of handling the explosive situation with his small regular force,
Atkinson called upon Governor Reynolds for mounted militia. When
Black Hawk refused to depart peacefully, the army began operations against
the recalcitrant Indians, pursuing the Black Hawk band up the Rock River.
The mounted Illinois militia moved faster than Atkinson's foot soldiers.
Unfortunately, they were an undisciplined group, whose camp one regular
officer described as a "multitude of citizen volunteers, who were as active
as a swarming hive; catching horses, electioneering, drawing rations, asking questions, shooting at marks, electing officers, mustering in, issuing
orders, disobeying orders, galloping about, 'cussing and discussing' the
war, and the rumors thereof."[29] When they overtook the Indians near the
Wisconsin border, Black Hawk, who realized now that he had been duped
by his advisers and that no British or other aid was coming, sought to surrender. But the party he sent under a white flag was set upon by the excited
volunteers. Believing that his peace overtures had been rejected, Black
Hawk attacked and routed the militia camp. The war had now become a
bloody affair, and there was no drawing back on either side.

28. Jackson, *Black Hawk: An Autobiography*, p. 129. Governor Reynolds tells the
story of the Black Hawk War and his part in it in *My Own Times: Embracing Also, the
History of My Life* (Belleville, Illinois, 1855), pp. 320–421. Documents are in *House Executive Document* no. 2, 22–1, serial 216, pp. 180–97.

29. Philip St. George Cooke, *Scenes and Adventures in the Army; or, Romance of
Military Life* (Philadelphia: Lindsay and Blakiston, 1857), p. 158.

New volunteers were called up, and Atkinson began a slow pursuit of the Indians into Wisconsin. The delay was embarrassing to Jackson, who was seeking reelection. Going over the head of General Gaines, in whose department the conflict was raging, he ordered Major General Winfield Scott to assume general conduct of the war and ordered that all the troops that could be spared from the seacoast, the lakes, and the lower Mississippi be concentrated in the theater of war. Scott and his troops from the East never got into action, for they were caught by an epidemic of the dread Asiatic cholera as they traversed the Great Lakes and were quarantined in Chicago. Atkinson was left to push his campaign against the fleeing Indians, who soon realized that all was lost and sought only to find refuge across the Mississippi. Suffering desperately from want, they were finally overtaken just as they reached the Mississippi and were cut down at the mouth of the Bad Axe River. Some of the band made it across the Mississippi, but before they could reach safety with Keokuk, they were massacred by their old enemies the Sioux.[30]

Black Hawk, who had escaped the final carnage, was captured by a party of Winnebagos and turned in to the Indian agent at Prairie du Chien. He and his sons and two associates were sent in irons to Jefferson Barracks. In 1833 he and other prisoners were taken east, where they were briefly imprisoned at Fortress Monroe. They also saw President Jackson and enjoyed a triumphal tour of eastern cities in the process. On their release, Black Hawk was given into the custody of Keokuk and lived out his life in peaceful retirement.

The Black Hawk War need never have occurred, had there been honorable dealings with the Indians and a firm policy toward both the Indians and the whites. Squatters had been allowed to violate treaty obligations by invading the Sacs in their ancient lands before the area had been sold by the government. An earlier concentration of regular troops on the upper Mississippi might have kept the Indians better in check, and a less cautious commander than Atkinson might have successfully stopped the movement of Black Hawk's band up the Rock River before hostile acts had occurred. The shameful violation of the flag of truce by the volunteers precipitated open warfare just as Black Hawk had decided to surrender. Again at the Wisconsin River and at the Bad Axe River attempts of the Indians to surrender were misunderstood or rejected by the whites.

The war was a turning point in the history of the Sacs and Foxes. Once a

---

30. An excellent account of Scott's troop movement to Chicago with the difficulties encountered is in Charles W. Elliott, *Winfield Scott: The Soldier and the Man* (New York: Macmillan Company, 1937), pp. 259–73. The war from Atkinson's standpoint can be traced in Roger L. Nichols, *General Henry Atkinson: A Western Military Career* (Norman: University of Oklahoma Press, 1965), pp. 152–75.

powerful confederation that the United States was forced to respect, the Indians now succumbed to liquor and other white vices, declined precipitously in population, and were rent by internal factions. At the conclusion of the war in 1832 General Scott and Governor Reynolds, as United States commissioners, negotiated a treaty of cession with the Indians at Fort Armstrong. The preamble spoke fancifully of the Black Hawk War as "an unprovoked war upon unsuspecting and defenceless citizens of the United States, sparing neither age nor sex," carried on by "certain lawless and desperate leaders, a formidable band, constituting a large portion of the Sac and Fox nation." Accordingly, the United States demanded of the Indians a considerable cession of land: a wide strip along the Mississippi running almost the length of the future state of Iowa, "partly as indemnity for the expense incurred, and partly to secure the future safety and tranquillity of the invaded frontier." The Indians agreed to move from the cession, known as the Black Hawk Purchase, by July 1, 1833; and "to prevent any future misunderstanding," no one would be allowed to hunt, fish, or plant crops in the cession after that date. The government allowed a reserve of four hundred square miles along the Iowa River, including Keokuk's village, and provided an annuity of $20,000 for thirty years.[31]

This was the beginning of the complete liquidation of the estate of the Sacs and Foxes in Iowa. In 1836 they sold the reserve along the Iowa River, and in the following year, at a conference in Washington called to ease the conflicts between the Sacs and Foxes, the Sioux, and the Winnebagos, Keokuk sold another 1.25 million acres lying directly west of the Black Hawk Purchase. The United States commissioners repeatedly urged the Indians to move entirely from Iowa, where they suffered increasingly from the pressure of incoming white settlers. In 1841 unsuccessful negotiations attempted to persuade the Sacs and Foxes to accept a reserve in southwestern Minnesota. Then in October 1842, in negotiations with Governor John Chambers of Iowa Territory, the Indians gave in. They parted with their remaining lands in Iowa in return for the assignment of a "tract of land suitable and convenient for Indian purposes, to the Sacs and Foxes for a permanent and perpetual residence for them and their descendants" at some unspecified place on the Missouri River or its tributaries. They received also an annual payment of 5 percent of a sum of $800,000 and blacksmiths and gunsmiths. They refused to agree to payment in the form of funds set aside for agricultural and educational purposes, for the Sacs and Foxes consistently rejected the white man's schools and his religion. They were allowed three years to move from the western half of the cession, and they eventually gathered at the headwaters of the Osage River in Kansas.[32]

31. Kappler, pp. 349–51.
32. Ibid., pp. 474–78, 495–96, 546–49; Hagan, *Sac and Fox Indians*, pp. 205–24;

OTHER TRIBES

Each of the many tribes involved in removal from the Old Northwest had its own history, but many fitted a general pattern: a succession of treaties of cession following the War of 1812, increasing pressure on the remaining lands by white settlers supported by the state and federal governments, new cessions with reserved lands for chiefs and other individuals or bands that refused to migrate beyond the Mississippi, degradation and deterioration of the tribes because of drunkenness and indolence (often a result of the annuities on which many of the Indians depended for existence), and finally, as conditions worsened and pressures increased, acquiescence in treaties that demanded removal from the states to reservations laid out in the Indian country to the west.

Such was the case of the Miamis. In 1818 at the Treaty of St. Mary's, in Ohio, they relinquished the major part of their lands in central Indiana, accepting reservations of important tribal sites as well as reserves for individuals and a perpetual annuity of $15,000. Eight years later, under demands from citizens of Indiana who wanted Miami lands for canals and other transportation routes judged essential for the development of the state, the Miamis gave up claims to lands north and west of the 1818 cession (land also ceded by the Potawatomis) for increased annuities, some reserved land, payment of debts, and other considerations. But the treaty gave only temporary quiet to the Indians. The stimulus of the Removal Act, the canal-building fever that hit the state after the great success of the Erie Canal, and anti-Indian sentiment created by the Black Hawk War all contributed to new demands for Miami removal. Government attempts to get cessions in 1833 failed, but the Indians' resistance was weakened, and in October 1834 a new treaty was signed at the Forks of the Wabash. For considerable remuneration in cash, annuities, and payment of traders' debts, the Miamis ceded some of the reserves delineated in previous treaties. Jackson refused to approve the treaty because it did not provide for the removal of the Indians, but the Indians held firm, and the treaty was finally ratified on December 22, 1837. The inhabitants of Indiana strongly criticized the treaty for failing to rid the state of Indians, and it was clear that new negotiations would soon be undertaken. A tentative success for the United States came in November 1838. The Miamis ceded more land and the government promised to guarantee to the tribe "a country west of the

---

Donald J. Berthrong, "John Beach and the Removal of the Sauk and Fox from Iowa," *Iowa Journal of History* 54 (October 1956): 313–34. In 1851–1852 a group of Foxes, dissatisfied with the Kansas lands and tiring of confederation with the Sacs, returned to Iowa and located among the white settlers; their number was augmented from time to time, and they were finally recognized by the federal government.

Mississippi river, to remove to and settle on, *when the said tribe may be disposed to emigrate from their present country.*" Although they did not then agree to leave Indiana, the Miamis did agree to explore the region in the West.[33]

Finally, in 1840, the chiefs (who had long adamantly resisted removal) agreed to accept emigration. A new treaty required the movement of about half the Miamis only because many of the tribe were exempted. But partial removal was accepted by the citizens of Indiana, for nearly all the tribal lands were made available for white exploitation. Although the treaty specified that removal was to take place within five years, that time was in the end extended; finally, in 1846–1847, the Miamis made the trek to a reservation in Kansas. The tribe by then was decimated; the agent at the reservation certified the arrival of only 323 persons.[34]

The fate of the Winnebago Indians, who were moved from place to place unconscionably, was particularly sad. Once having claimed a large area in what is now southwestern and south central Wisconsin, they, like the other tribes, were dispossessed to make room for white miners and farmers. The Winnebagos participated in the Treaty of Prairie du Chien of 1825, which set boundaries to their claims: roughly, the Rock River, the Black River, and the Wisconsin River. But the peace was interrupted in 1827 when Red Bird, taking vengeance for white assaults upon the Winnebagos, murdered members of a white family near Prairie du Chien. The government moved quickly with a show of military force to quell any widespread disturbance, and Red Bird and his accomplices surrendered to the United States commissioners.[35] Then, in quick succession, the Winnebagos signed treaties in 1829 and 1832 that extinguished their title to lands south of the Wisconsin River. By the 1832 treaty, the United States, realizing that the Wisconsin lands remaining to the Winnebagos would not support the tribe, granted to them the so-called Neutral Ground, a tract across the Mississippi lying between the lands of the Sacs and Foxes on the south and the Sioux on the north. Some Winnebagos moved to the new reservation, but they were insecure in the war zone between the hostile western tribes.[36]

The United States government wanted the Winnebagos to move en-

33. Kappler, pp. 278–81, 425–28, 519–24. The removal of the Miamis is thoroughly covered in Bert Anson, *The Miami Indians* (Norman: University of Oklahoma Press, 1970), pp. 177–233.

34. Kappler, pp. 531–34. An analysis of Miami population is given in Anson, *Miami Indians*, p. 226.

35. An elaborate description of Red Bird and his surrender is given in Thomas L. McKenney, "The Winnebago War of 1827," *Wisconsin Historical Collections* 5 (1868): 179–87.

36. Kappler, pp. 300–303, 345–48; Louise Phelps Kellogg, "The Removal of the Winnebago," *Transactions of the Wisconsin Academy of Sciences, Arts and Letters* 21 (1924): 23–29.

MAP 4: Indian Land Cessions in the North

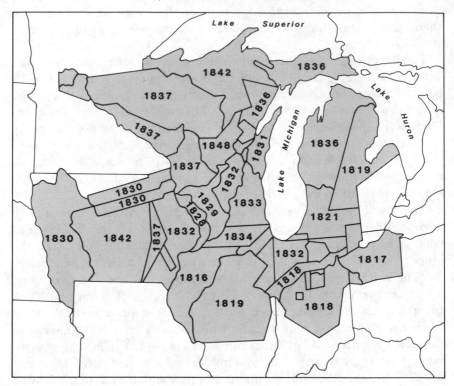

tirely beyond the Mississippi, which the tribe refused to do. In 1837, however, a delegation of Winnebagos was induced to travel to Washington.
There, in a clearly illegal treaty (for the delegation had no authority to sell),
they were pressured into signing away the rest of their Wisconsin land.
They were told, through the deception of the interpreter, that they would
have eight years to move, whereas in fact the treaty specified only eight
months. The treaty, pushed for execution by the United States, created a
permanent division in the tribe. One group decided it would be best to
abide by the treaty and in a series of subsequent treaties with the federal
government moved from one location to another—in 1846 from the Neutral Ground in Iowa to a reservation along the Mississippi at the Crow
Wing River in central Minnesota, in 1855 to a better spot farther south in
Minnesota at Blue Earth (half of which they ceded in 1859), and in 1862, as
a result of the agitation arising from the Sioux uprising of that year, from
Blue Earth to a barren spot along the Missouri River in Dakota, from which
they ultimately moved to Nebraska, where a reservation was provided for
them. The treaty-abiding faction, with whom these later negotiations were

conducted, amounted to about half the Winnebagos. The defiant remainder hid out in central Wisconsin, from which they were periodically rounded up and moved to join their fellow tribesmen, only to drift back to scattered enclaves in Wisconsin.[37]

The Chippewa (or Ojibway) Indians in Michigan, Wisconsin, and Minnesota did not take part in the general emigration of the northern tribes to the western Indian country. They also felt the pressures of white advance —farmers, lumbermen, and miners—and ceded most of their once large estate to the United States, but they managed to preserve reservations within their old territories, where they remain today.

The Chippewas of the Lake Superior region were inveterate foes of the Sioux, whom they at one time had driven out of lands east of the Mississippi. The incessant warfare of the two tribes was an unsettling condition on the frontier, and one of the purposes of the 1825 Treaty of Prairie du Chien was to adjudicate the rivalry and establish a line of demarcation between the hostile groups. That treaty, however, was but a prelude to further negotiations with the Chippewas, who faced aggressive whites coming into the region, as well as the Sioux. In 1837 at Fort Snelling, Henry Dodge, governor of Wisconsin Territory, signed a treaty with them in which they parted with a large tract of timberland in eastern Minnesota and north central Wisconsin in return for annuities, settlement of traders' claims, and cash to influential mixed-bloods. The Chippewas also retained the right to hunt, fish, and gather rice on the ceded lands until the president directed their removal. Meanwhile miners invaded the copper lands of the Indians along the southern shore of Lake Superior, and in 1842 by a treaty signed at La Pointe the Chippewas sold their hunting grounds as far east as Marquette, Michigan, for similar considerations. Not until 1850 did the president order the Indians to prepare for removal from the ceded lands, but even then the Indians refused to consider moving entirely from their homelands. The outcome was a new treaty in 1854 in which the Indians accepted a group of small permanent reservations scattered across northeastern Minnesota, northern Wisconsin, and the Upper Peninsula.[38]

37. Nancy Oestreich Lurie, "Winnebago," in Trigger, *Northeast*, pp. 697–700. See also the report of the Committee on Indian Affairs, March 17, 1836, *Senate Document* no. 252, 24–1, serial 281, which urges removal of the Winnebagos to south and west of the Missouri River; *House Document* no. 229, 25–3, serial 349, and *Senate Document* no. 297, 26–1, serial 359, which deal with Winnebago removal and the claims arising therefrom.

38. Negotiations with the western Chippewas are treated in Edmund Jefferson Danziger, Jr., *The Chippewas of Lake Superior* (Norman: University of Oklahoma Press, 1978), pp. 68–90; and Danziger, "They Would Not Be Moved: The Chippewa Treaty of 1854," *Minnesota History* 43 (Spring 1973): 175–85. The treaties are in Kappler, pp. 491–93, 542–45, 648–52.

The eastern bands of Chippewa met a similar fate in the state of Michigan. In 1819 they ceded a huge wedge of land extending from Lake Huron into central Michigan and in 1836 (with the Ottawas) gave up the northwest quarter of the Lower Peninsula. But no wholesale removal was involved, for reserves were provided, and the Indians retained the right to use the land until it was settled by whites.[39]

The Sioux Indians, too, succumbed to the forces demanding removal from the Old Northwest. They took part in the Treaty of Prairie du Chien in 1825, in which lines were drawn between them and the Sacs and Foxes to the south and their Chippewa enemies to the north, although the northern line was of little consequence in ending the hostilities between the two tribes. In 1830 they were again at Prairie du Chien, in negotiations aimed at ending conflicts between them and the Sacs and Foxes, and each tribe ceded a twenty-mile-wide strip of territory along the dividing line to create the Neutral Ground later given to the Winnebagos. The buffer strip was ineffective. Then at Washington in 1837 the Sioux were induced to cede their holdings east of the Mississippi (in what is now Wisconsin) in return for $300,000 to be invested at 5 percent, cash payments to relatives and friends of the tribe, $90,000 to pay debts due traders, and annuities in goods and provision for agricultural development. How much the Indians profited is questionable, for the annuities became a crutch for their subsistence and delayed the day when they could support themselves, and dependence upon the annuities created troubles if payment was late. For the government the treaty was one more advance in clearing the region east of the Mississippi of Indian titles. Not until the treaties of Traverse des Sioux and Mendota in 1851 were the Sioux forced to part with sizable tracts west of the river.[40]

The Menominee Indians resisted removal from their Wisconsin homes, but like others they were forced to relinquish vast territories of farmland and timberland to white pioneers, and they gave up valuable land as well to New York Indians migrating to Wisconsin. As participants in the Prairie du Chien Treaty of 1825, they had their claims defined, but the boundary between the Menominees and the Chippewas was not set. In 1827 at the Treaty of Butte des Morts, therefore, Lewis Cass and Thomas L. McKenney dealt anew with the tribe. The negotiations furnished a remarkable example of federal commissioners directing internal tribal matters, for Cass and McKenney in effect appointed a head chief with whom they could

39. Kappler, pp. 185–87, 540–56; Elizabeth Neumeyer, "Michigan Indians Battle against Removal," *Michigan History* 55 (Winter 1971): 275–88.

40. Kappler, pp. 305–10, 493–94; Roy W. Meyer, *History of the Santee Sioux: United States Indian Policy on Trial* (Lincoln: University of Nebraska Press, 1967), pp. 39–61. For a discussion of the 1851 treaties, see below, pp. 438–39.

deal. Cass told the assembled Indians that without a chief they appeared "like a flock of geese without a leader. Some fly one way & some another. Tomorrow at the opening of the Council, we will proceed to appoint a principal chief for the Menomonies." McKenney made the same point the following day in forceful rhetoric:

> Your great Father, who lives in the Great Village towards the rising sun, has heard confused sounds from the lands where his Menomonie children hunt. He thinks it is because there are too many mouths here & that all speak at once. He wants one mouth, that he may hear more distinctly, & one pair of ears to hear through, & a pair of eyes to see for him. He said to your father & me—*Go*, select from my Menomonie children the best man & make him Chief. Give him good things. Put a Medal around his neck, & a robe over his shoulders, & give him a flag. . . . Tell him his great Father takes him fast by the hand today—that this medal unites them.[41]

Oshkosh was named head chief and Caron second chief, and these men were the first to affix their marks to the treaty.[42] The treaty defined the boundaries between the Chippewas and the Menominees, but much of the discussion concerned the question of lands for Indians from New York who had migrated to Wisconsin. That question was deferred to the decision of the president. When the Senate in ratifying the treaty modified it to protect the interests of the New York Indians, the Menominees refused to accept the amended document. The issue was not settled until 1831, when the Menominees ceded specific lands along the Fox River to the New York Indians and specified tracts along the east shore of Lake Winnebago for the Stockbridge and Brotherton Indians. The Menominees also gave up their claims to the lands lying east of Green Bay, the Fox River, and Lake Winnebago. When the Indians objected to the 1831 treaty, a new agreement was drawn up in 1832 that somewhat modified the provisions. This was

41. Treaty journal, Documents Relating to the Negotiation of Ratified and Unratified Treaties with Various Indian Tribes, National Archives, Record Group 75 (T494, reel 2).

42. The designation of chiefs by the commissioners did not escape criticism. McKenney felt obliged to justify his action to the secretary of war: "I have already stated, that the persons employed to hold treaties with the Indian tribes in the Territory of Michigan, during the year 1827, did not undertake to 'constitute and appoint an Indian Chief,'" he wrote. "But in conformity to immemorial usage, as well of the British and French, as of our Government, the ceremony of recognizing those as chiefs who were reported by their bands as their acknowledged leaders, was observed by 'those persons' in putting medals around their necks. Further than this, and the giving of what was considered good advice, at the time, for their own and their people's government, nothing was done. All such signed the treaty, and after they received the medals." McKenney to James Barbour, March 24, 1828, OIA LS, vol. 4, pp. 362–63 (M21, reel 4).

but the beginning in the decline of the Menominee estate, for in 1836 the tribe ceded its land along the western shore of Green Bay and west of Lake Winnebago, as well as a strip of pinelands along the Wisconsin River.[43]

When Wisconsin became a state in 1848, new attacks were made on the Menominee holdings. In October, Indian Commissioner William Medill forced upon the now weakened tribe a removal treaty. The Indians gave up their remaining lands in Wisconsin and were assigned a tract on the Crow Wing River in central Minnesota. But ultimately they refused to move west. Exploring parties reported unfavorably on the Crow Wing land, and President Millard Fillmore extended the right of the Menominees to remain on their lands. With the support of white citizens, the Indians moved to new lands along the Wolf River in 1852. In 1854 the United States confirmed this reservation in place of the Minnesota tract. The adamant refusal of the Menominees to move across the Mississippi had succeeded, although the new Menominee Reservation amounted to but a fraction of the aboriginal holdings.[44]

NEW YORK INDIANS

The disposition of lands in Wisconsin was complicated by the emigration to that region of Indians from New York State at the very time the United States government was trying to extinguish the titles of the resident tribes. Federal officials like Secretary of War Calhoun, however, had spoken of the region west of Lake Michigan as a refuge for Indians from the East, and Lewis Cass wrote of the Iroquois in 1830: "It is very desirable to place them in that Country. Their habits and the strong pecuniary ties, which bind them to the United States would ensure their fidelity, and they would act as a check upon the Winnebagos, the worst affected of any Indians upon our borders."[45] Jedidiah Morse, too, in his report to Calhoun on his investigation of the West in 1820, praised the fertility of the Green Bay region. He told Calhoun: "Should it be thought expedient, and be found practicable, to collect the remnants of tribes now scattered, and languishing and wasting away among our white population, and to colonize them for the purpose of preserving them from utter extinction, and of educating them to the best advantage, and with the greatest economy, some portions

43. Kappler, pp. 281–83, 319–25, 377–82, 463–66; Patricia K. Ourada, *The Menominee Indians: A History* (Norman: University of Oklahoma Press, 1979), pp. 71–98.

44. Kappler, pp. 572–74, 626–27; Ourada, *Menominee Indians*, pp. 99–126.

45. Cass to Calhoun, November 11, 1820, quoted in Joseph Schafer, *The Winnebago-Horicon Basin: A Type Study in Western History* (Madison: State Historical Society of Wisconsin, 1937), p. 42. See also Albert G. Ellis, "Advent of the New York Indians into Wisconsin," *Wisconsin Historical Collections* 2 (1855): 415–49.

of these Territories will, I think, unquestionably be found better suited to these objects, than any other in our country, and as such I deliberately recommend them to the attention of the government."[46]

There was pressure, too, from the Ogden Land Company in New York, which held preemption rights to the Indian lands and which was eager to free the lands of Indian title. An additional and potent force was a mixed-blood named Eleazar Williams, a remarkable self-promoter (who among other things claimed to be the lost dauphin of France), who became the self-proclaimed leader of the emigration. Williams was able to interest only a group of Oneidas, however, for most of the Indians of the Six Nations refused to leave New York. To them he joined the Stockbridge Indians (Mohicans originally located in Massachusetts, and highly acculturated to white ways, who had migrated to New York in the 1780s and who now had a small admixture of Munsees). In addition, the Brotherton Indians, remnants of New England tribes that had settled in New York near the Stockbridges, joined the migration. In 1821 Williams led a mixed group of these Indians west to investigate possibilities, and arrangements were made with the local Indians (Menominees and Winnebagos) for grants of land along the Fox River. In 1822 the emigration began, and it continued through the decade.

The status of these intruding Indians was not well established, and their presence was resented by the local tribes. Because the negotiations at Butte des Morts in 1827 merely passed the problem to the president for resolution, it was not until the treaties of 1831–1832 with the Menominees (after a special commission had reported to the president on the issue) that the Oneidas, Stockbridges, and Brothertons were provided for. The Oneidas received a sizable tract west of the Fox River (which was severely reduced in 1836), and the Brothertons and Stockbridges were allotted lands along the eastern shore of Lake Winnebago.[47]

The Stockbridges, though a small group, furnish an excellent example of a sharp division of an Indian tribe into one faction seeking acculturation and citizenship (the Citizens Party) and another wishing to maintain traditional Indian community organization (the Indian Party) and the complications caused by the division in relations with the United States government. Each side attempted to win the government to its position with a steady stream of petitions and delegations sent to Washington. In a treaty

46. Jedidiah Morse, *A Report to the Secretary of War of the United States on Indian Affairs* (New Haven: S. Converse, 1822), appendix, p. 15. Schafer, *Winnebago-Horicon Basin*, pp. 35–57, gives a general account of the New York Indian immigration.

47. Kappler, pp. 319–25, 377–82; John H. Eaton to commissioners, June 9, 1830, in "McCall's Journal of a Visit to Wisconsin in 1830," *Wisconsin Historical Collections* 12 (1892): 172–77; report of the commissioners, September 20, 1830, in "Documents Illustrating McCall's Journal," ibid., pp. 207–14.

of 1839 half the Stockbridge reserve was sold and provisions were made for those who desired to maintain tribal cohesion to migrate west of the Mississippi, but few actually left Wisconsin. Then in 1843 Congress passed a law that granted citizenship to the Stockbridges and Brothertons and provided for the "subdivision and allotment in severalty" of the remaining lands. The Brothertons accepted the legislation and ended their federal status, but the Indian party of the Stockbridges strongly objected and refused citizenship. They were successful in 1846 in persuading Congress to repeal the 1843 law. This action, in turn, upset the members of the Citizens Party, who did not want to give up their citizenship, and the affairs of the tribe were in turmoil as each party sought to gain the federal money due the tribe. Finally in 1848 the tribe ceded all its lands in Wisconsin, and the Citizens Party patented tracts of land within the cession. The Indian Party was to move to Minnesota but in the end did not move across the Mississippi, and in 1856 they were provided land in the southwest corner of the Menominee Reservation. The configuration of Indian reservations in Wisconsin was thus set.[48]

THE ROLE OF THE TRADERS

It is easy to think of the treaties by which the Indian title to land was extinguished as compacts between two parties, the Indian tribe and the United States government—and such, legally, they were. But in fact there was sometimes an influential and occasionally dominating third party: traders. When the fur trade flourished, traders supplied the Indians with goods in return for furs, but as the hunting lands were circumscribed and the fur-bearing animals disappeared, the Indians paid the traders from their annuities, or the government bought large quantities of goods for the Indians directly from the traders. As cessions multiplied and annuities and other payments grew, the traders became more and more involved in the treaty process. Indians were indebted to the traders for goods received on credit; the debts could be recovered only by provisions in the treaties for cash annuities, by which the Indians could pay the debts, or by direct allotment of funds in the treaties to cover specified debts.[49]

48. Kappler, pp. 529–30, 574–82, 742–56; 5 *United States Statutes* 645–47; 9 *United States Statutes* 55–56. A detailed study of the Stockbridges is Marion Johnson Mochon, "Stockbridge-Munsee Cultural Adaptations: 'Assimilated Indians,'" *Proceedings of the American Philosophical Society* 112 (June 21, 1968): 182–219. The complicated relations with the United States can be followed in John Porter Bloom, ed., *The Territorial Papers of the United States*, vols. 27–28: *The Territory of Wisconsin* (Washington: National Archives and Records Service, 1969–1975), and in OIA LR, Green Bay Agency (M234, reels 315–36). See also Schafer, *Winnebago-Horicon Basin*, pp. 58–76.

49. The best general account of the role of the trader is James L. Clayton, "The Im-

The allowance of traders' claims in the treaties began with the Osage treaty of 1825, in which the Indians, as a mark of friendship toward favorite traders, agreed to payment of certain debts by the United States. The practice became almost universal in the treaties signed in subsequent years with the Indians in the Old Northwest. And as the pressures for removal increased and removal treaties seemed necessary at any price, the rewards for the Indians and for the traders were considerable. The Potawatomi treaties of 1832, for example, together provided well over $100,000 for paying traders' claims, and the Winnebago treaty of 1837 authorized nearly twice that much.[50]

In addition, because the treaty negotiations were usually eased by generous handouts to the attending Indians, and because the treaties often specified large payments in goods as well as in cash, the traders profited by furnishing these supplies, often at inflated prices. The traders, moreover, had a deep interest in the lands allotted individual Indians in the treaties, for such lands often quickly fell into their hands. So much influence did traders have over the Indians that in many cases the government would have been unable to procure the treaties of cession it wanted without providing adequately for the traders' interests.

The exorbitance of many traders' claims called for government investigation and adjudication lest unscrupulous merchants grow inordinately rich at the expense of the Indians and the United States Treasury. The Senate from time to time refused to ratify treaties until the claims against the Indians were checked, and the War Department established regulations for the payment of claims. Special commissions were sometimes established to decide on claims and adjust the payments among diverse claimants, and they were given detailed instructions. Those investigating the claims under the Winnebago treaty of 1837 were told:

> You will require the respective creditors to deposit with you transcripts of their claims, exhibiting names, dates, articles, prices, and the original consideration in each claim. . . . If original books or en-

pact of Traders' Claims on the American Fur Trade," in David M. Ellis, ed., *The Frontier in American Development: Essays in Honor of Paul Wallace Gates* (Ithaca: Cornell University Press, 1969), pp. 299–322. Other studies, which deal with more restricted areas or tribes, are Paul Wallace Gates, "Introduction," in *The John Tipton Papers*, comp. Glen A. Blackburn and ed. Nellie Armstrong Robertson and Dorothy Riker, 3 vols. (Indianapolis: Indiana Historical Bureau, 1942), 1: 3–53; and Robert A. Trennert, "A Trader's Role in the Potawatomi Removal from Indiana: The Case of George W. Ewing," *Old Northwest* 4 (March 1978): 3–24. Trennert has expanded his account of the traders in *Indian Traders on the Middle Border: The House of Ewing, 1827–54* (Lincoln: University of Nebraska Press, 1981).

50. See table 15, "Fur Traders' Debt Claims Provided For by Treaty Funds, 1825–1842," in Clayton, "Traders' Claims," p. 303.

tries cannot be produced, their loss or destruction must be proved. The sale of spirituous liquors to Indians being prohibited by the laws of the United States, no item of charge on that account will, under any circumstances, be allowed. . . . If [the claim] be against an individual Indian, he should be called before you, and each item in the account be explained to him and his assent or dissent to it required.

The Indian Office recognized the forces pulling in two directions and instructed the commissioners further: "The moral duty of paying every just claim should be pressed upon the Indians; and, in receiving their statements, you will bear in mind the danger arising on the one hand from the disposition to evade an obligation; and on the other, from the exercise of improper influence by any of the claimants."[51] The commissioners found it impossible to carry out their duties with the exactitude wanted by the commissioner of Indian affairs, but they went about their business carefully and made judgments on the validity of the claims presented. In some cases claims were scaled down or disallowed altogether.

The attitude of the traders toward removal was often ambivalent. These men shared the sentiments of other white settlers that the Indians should be moved to the west to clear the land for white exploitation, and often they had a direct interest in the ceded lands. Yet it was not easy to part with the large profits they made in supplying the Indians where they were. Even though most traders realized that removal was inevitable, they worked to delay the emigration as much as possible. Each new treaty could be another bonanza. In 1838 the commissioner of Indian affairs asserted that disturbances arising in the removal of the Indians were caused "by the large indebtedness of the Indians to their traders, and to the undue influence of the latter over them." He said he was confident "that their influence is not only prejudicial to the Indians, but has been frequently exercised to defeat negotiations with them, and to prevent the accomplishment of objects sanctioned by treaties, and others devised and calculated to promote their welfare and permanent improvement."[52]

It was the government's unwavering objective to rid the East of Indians, and since it was necessary to get the traders' acquiescence if not active support, measures were taken to circumvent any obstructionism. Thus in the Potawatomi removal the government threatened to pay no more claims until the Indians had emigrated. Then on March 3, 1843, the Senate

51. C. A. Harris to commissioners, July 26, 1838, *House Document* no. 229, 25–3, serial 349, pp. 5–6; the undated report of the commissioners appears ibid., pp. 14–21. For other accounts of investigation of claims, see Trennert, "Trader's Role," and Clayton, "Traders' Claims."

52. C. A. Harris to J. R. Poinsett, February 12, 1838, *Senate Document* no. 198, 25–2, serial 316, p. 2.

resolved that in future negotiations of treaties with the Indians "no reservations of land should be made in favor of any person, nor the payment of any debt provided for."[53] But many old debts were still outstanding, and claims dragged on and on, much to the irritation of the overburdened Indian Office. In later treaties the claims of the traders against the Indians had to be recognized if the desired cessions were to be obtained. Even though the government did not pay the traders directly, large sums were provided to enable the Indians "to settle their affairs and comply with their present just engagements."[54]

53. *Journal of the Executive Proceedings of the Senate*, 6: 170, 184.

54. Sioux treaties of 1851, Kappler, pp. 589, 591; and Lucile M. Kane, "The Sioux Treaties and the Traders," *Minnesota History* 32 (June 1951): 65–80.

CHAPTER 10

The Emigrant Indians
in the West

Transplanted Indian Nations.

Military Defense of the Frontier.

Benevolence and Reform.

Advocates of removal justified the policy on the grounds that emigration
to the West would benefit the Indians. Out of the reach of established
states and territories, the Indian tribes could continue their national existence unmolested by encroaching whites and jurisdictional controversies.
West of the Mississippi the federal government could provide for the protection and improvement of the Indians.

Because of the dramatic nature of the removal, especially of the southern tribes, it is easy to ignore the sequel of the removal itself and to assume
that once the Indians had been shipped out of the way of the whites, the
government breathed a sigh of relief and washed its hands of the whole
affair. That was far from the case, for in the decade following removal the
United States diligently—though not always effectively—worked to fulfill
the vision Jackson had enunciated in his first annual message to Congress:
"There [in the West] they may be secured in the enjoyment of governments
of their own choice, subject to no other control from the United States
than such as may be necessary to preserve peace on the frontier and between the several tribes. There the benevolent may endeavor to teach
them, to raise up an interesting commonwealth, destined to perpetuate the
race and to attest the humanity and justice of this Government."[1]

1. Fred L. Israel, ed., *The State of the Union Messages of the Presidents, 1790–1966,*
3 vols. (New York: Chelsea House, 1966), 1: 310.

Secretary of War Lewis Cass, in his first annual report on November 21, 1831, declared: "A crisis in our Indian affairs has evidently arrived, which calls for the establishment of a system of policy adapted to the existing state of things, and calculated to fix upon a permanent basis the future destiny of the Indians." Cass hoped by careful planning for the future to repair the errors and unpleasantness of the past. He was convinced that removal was the only means by which the Indians could be preserved and improved. But, granted the migration to the West, what steps should be taken to protect and encourage the Indians there? He suggested a seven-point program, a list of principles to govern relations with the Indians in their new circumstances.

1. A solemn declaration that the country assigned to the Indians would be theirs forever and a determination that white settlement should never encroach upon it.

2. A determination, accompanied by proper surveillance and proper police, to exclude all liquor from the Indians' new territory.

3. The employment of adequate military force in the vicinity of the Indians in order to prevent hostility between the tribes.

4. Encouragement to the Indians to adopt severalty of property.

5. Assistance to all who needed it for opening farms and procuring domestic animals and agricultural implements.

6. Restraint as much as possible from involvement with the peculiar institutions and customs of the Indians.

7. Employment of persons to instruct the Indians, moving as far and as fast as they were capable.

This, it was apparent, was not a detailed blueprint for Indian laws or regulations, but it offered a general policy background that the lawmakers would find useful.[2]

TRANSPLANTED INDIAN NATIONS

The Indian nations were not destroyed by removal, for the utter degradation and collapse predicted by the opponents of Jackson's removal program did not occur. Although most of the northern tribes that emigrated to the West were small in population and economically and politically weak, the Indian nations from the southeast moved to the Indian Territory in strength and with treaty guarantees that protected their land holdings and their political autonomy. The turmoil of removal brought great hardships to those who were forced to depart their traditional homes against their will, and

2. Report of the secretary of war, November 21, 1831, *House Executive Document* no. 2, 22–1, serial 216, pp. 27–34.

tribal divisions occasioned or aggravated by removal disrupted the tranquility of the communities. Yet the southern nations showed tremendous resilience in reestablishing an orderly and productive existence beyond the Mississippi. Organized governments continued, agricultural development (including large plantations run in part by slave labor) quickened, school systems were established, and missionary endeavors were renewed and encouraged.

The report of Ethan Allen Hitchcock, who was sent west by the War Department in 1841 to investigate charges of fraud and corruption in the business of removal, furnished a picture of established communities, which he compared favorably with those of white frontier Americans. "There was nothing to distinguish appearances from those of many of our border people," he wrote of a visit to a Cherokee home, "except the complexion (Cherokee) and superior neatness." Hitchcock described the homes, plantations, government, schools, Christian churches, and general society of the Indian groups, and he reported prosperity rather than depression or desperation among those with whom he came in contact. He noted, however, that the political and economic leadership was largely in the hands of mixed-bloods.[3]

Similar positive notes came from the government agents in contact with the tribes. The superintendent of the Western Territory wrote glowing reports of the progress and condition of the Choctaws, Chickasaws, Creeks, Seminoles, and Cherokees living under his jurisdiction. "Civilization is spreading through the Indian country," he noted as early as 1840, "and where but a few years past the forest was untouched, in many places good farms are to be seen; the whole face of the country evidently indicating a thrifty and prosperous people, possessing within themselves the means of raising fine stocks of horses, cattle, and hogs, and a country producing all the substantials of life with but a moderate portion of labor." The superintendent of Indian affairs at St. Louis in 1846 reported rapid improvement among many of the tribes in agriculture and the general comforts of life. He listed the Shawnees, Wyandots, Delawares, Kickapoos, Munsees, Stockbridges, Ottawas, and Potawatomis as the tribes among whom improvements were most visible, and he attributed this success to the influence of the missionaries and their schools.[4]

3. *A Traveler in Indian Territory: The Journal of Ethan Allen Hitchcock, Late Major-General in the United States Army*, ed. Grant Foreman (Cedar Rapids, Iowa: Torch Press, 1930); quotation is from p. 23. Excellent summary descriptions are given in a series of letters by Hitchcock to the secretary of war in 1841 and 1842, printed in appendix, pp. 233–62.

4. Report of William Armstrong, October 1, 1840, CIA Report, 1840, serial 375, p. 310; report of Thomas H. Harvey, September 5, 1846, CIA Report, 1846, serial 493, p. 282.

The Cherokees were the most important of the Indian nations in the West, and they best exemplified the rapid establishment of a viable society in the new lands. Yet they were sharply divided politically. The Old Settlers, Cherokees who had voluntarily emigrated to Arkansas and then into the Indian Territory before the agitation for removal in the 1830s, were economically well established in their western homes and had a loosely organized but effective government that dealt with the federal government as a distinct entity. In 1834 they numbered fifty-eight hundred. A second division was the treaty party of the Ridges, Elias Boudinot, and Stand Watie. Having promoted the Treaty of New Echota of 1835, they emigrated peacefully under its provisions and settled in the West with the Old Settlers. Because they had cooperated with the United States in the removal policy, they were generally favored by United States officials who became entangled in Cherokee intratribal conflicts. Finally, there was the Ross party, the group that had opposed removal and emigrated only when forced to do so in 1838. This was the most populous faction, with perhaps fourteen thousand adherents. John Ross considered himself the principal chief of *all* the Cherokees, thus irritating the treaty party and the Old Settlers, who feared his domination. The arrival of this anti-treaty group in the West brought dissension and conflict.[5]

The conflict was severely exacerbated by the vengeance taken by the Ross party against treaty party leaders for having ceded the eastern lands. On June 22, 1839, Major Ridge, John Ridge, and Elias Boudinot were brutally murdered; Stand Watie, also marked for death, escaped. Although it was clear that this was a planned political assassination, John Ross denied any complicity or approval of the deed; but he could not completely shake the accusations made against his party. The federal government remained critical of him and continually called for punishment of the murderers. Under the rubric of maintaining domestic peace within the Cherokee Nation, Matthew Arbuckle, commander at Fort Gibson in the Cherokee

---

5. Useful accounts of the Cherokees in the Indian Territory after removal are Morris L. Wardell, *A Political History of the Cherokee Nation, 1838–1907* (Norman: University of Oklahoma Press, 1938), pp. 3–117, and Grant Foreman, *The Five Civilized Tribes* (Norman: University of Oklahoma Press, 1934), pp. 281–426. The events from John Ross's viewpoint are told in Gary E. Moulton, *John Ross, Cherokee Chief* (Athens: University of Georgia Press, 1978), pp. 107–65; from that of Stand Watie of the treaty party in Kenny A. Franks, *Stand Watie and the Agony of the Cherokee Nation* (Memphis: Memphis State University Press, 1979), pp. 54–113. A brief treatment is Gerard Reed, "Postremoval Factionalism in the Cherokee Nation," in Duane H. King, ed., *The Cherokee Indian Nation: A Troubled History* (Knoxville: University of Tennessee Press, 1979), pp. 148–63. Documents dealing with the divisions among the Cherokees appear in *Senate Document* no. 347, 26–1, serial 359; *Senate Document* no. 140, 28–2, serial 457; *House Document* no. 185, 29–1, serial 485.

country, took an active part in Cherokee political affairs and openly represented the interests of the Old Settlers.⁶

Although members of the Cherokee factions agreed to an Act of Union in 1839 and 1840, the groups were still at odds among themselves and with United States military commanders, and the following years were filled with turmoil at times approaching civil war. All three parties sent delegations to Washington to plead their causes and to seek a settlement by the federal government, but the form that a solution might take was not easily agreed upon. Should the Cherokees be divided into two tribes (the Ross party in one and his opponents, the treaty party and the Old Settlers, in the other), or was a unified Cherokee Nation still possible? On April 13, 1846, President James K. Polk sent a special message to Congress on the matter. He noted the unprovoked murders and other disturbances in the Cherokee Nation that had gone unpunished, and he spoke approvingly of the army's attempts to suppress those outrages under the provision of the treaty of 1835, by which the United States had agreed "to protect the Cherokee Nation from domestic strife and foreign enemies." But in the end he concluded: "I am satisfied that there is no probability that the different bands or parties into which it [the Cherokee Nation] is divided can ever again live together in peace and harmony, and that the well-being of the whole requires that they should be separated and live under separate governments as distinct tribes." The House Committee on Indian Affairs reported a bill including all that Polk had asked for. It noted the obligations owed by the United States to the minority anti-Ross party, which had cooperated in the removal policy, and it justified the intervention of the United States against the Ross majority because of the wardship status of the Indians. It unanimously recommended division into two tribes. "The people must be separated," the report read; "the continuance of the present social compact, unchecked and unrestrained as it exists at present, will inevitably end in the fatal destruction of the minority parties."⁷

Such action led John Ross, who above all wanted a unified nation, to persuade Polk to approve a treaty that would keep the Cherokees intact. The president thereupon appointed commissioners to negotiate with

6. A balanced account of Arbuckle's action is given in Brad Agnew, *Fort Gibson: Terminal on the Trail of Tears* (Norman: University of Oklahoma Press, 1980), pp. 185–211; this book is a valuable study of Fort Gibson and Indian removal. An account unduly hostile toward Arbuckle is Foreman, *Five Civilized Tribes.*

7. James K. Polk to Congress, April 13, 1846, *House Document* no. 185, 29–1, serial 485, pp. 1–2; this document also contains a long report of the commissioner of Indian affairs on the Cherokee conflict, memorials from the three factions, and several other pertinent documents submitted to Congress by the president in support of his message. Further documents are in *Senate Document* no. 301, 29–1, serial 474. The report of the House Committee on Indian Affairs, June 2, 1846, is in *House Report* no. 683, 29–1, serial 490.

MAP 5: Location of Indians in the Indian Territory, after Removal

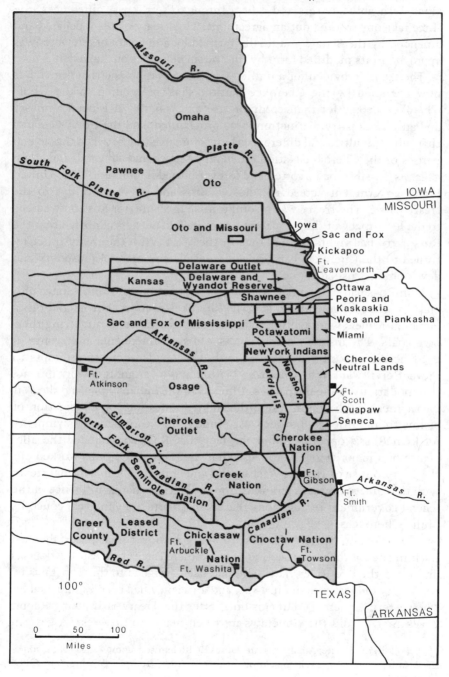

the three Cherokee delegations in Washington in order to heal all dissension. With able advisers and a firm intent to settle past differences, the three factions worked out an agreement. This treaty of 1846, debated and amended by the Senate and finally ratified by a majority of one vote, was approved in its modified form by the Indian delegates on August 14.[8]

The treaty provided for a unified Cherokee Nation and that "the lands now occupied by the Cherokee Nation shall be secured to the whole Cherokee people for their common use and benefit." A general amnesty and an end to party distinctions was proclaimed, and the treaty declared that "all difficulties and differences heretofore existing between the several parties of the Cherokee Nation are hereby settled and adjusted, and shall, as far as possible, be forgotten and forever buried in oblivion." The United States government agreed to adjust claims and pay indemnities to the treaty party.[9] The treaty was a compromise measure, for Ross now agreed to the legitimacy of the 1835 treaty, and the Old Settlers admitted that the Ross party had rights to the lands in the West. With the treaty, quiet returned to the Cherokee Nation, and a decade and more of prosperity and development ensued.

John Ross had frequently protested against actions of United States officials in what he considered strictly Cherokee matters, but he and other factional leaders were willing to use federal assistance in furthering their own goals. The military commanders and superintendents and agents in the Cherokee country were faced with difficult decisions in attempts to prevent civil war in the Cherokee Nation and to promote a workable accommodation among the parties. Officials of the Indian Office and the War Department, with whom rested the ticklish questions of adjudication of claims to annuities and other treaty funds, were torn between sympathy for John Ross's opponents and the fact that Ross commanded the allegiance of a majority of Cherokees. That the three delegations worked out the compromise of 1846 in Washington and embodied it in a formal treaty with the United States is an indication of the tremendous influence of the federal government in questions that were, in principle, internal concerns of the Cherokees.

The Choctaw Nation, the first to sign a removal treaty, reestablished itself in the southeastern section of the Indian Territory, west of Arkansas and along the Red River. This land had been assigned to the Choctaws by the Treaty of Doak's Stand in 1820, and an agency had been established for the western Choctaws, but not until after the Treaty of Dancing Rabbit Creek in 1830 did the Choctaws move en masse to the West. A govern-

8. Polk to the Senate, August 7, 1846, James D. Richardson, comp., *A Compilation of the Messages and Papers of the Presidents, 1789–1897*, 10 vols. (Washington: GPO, 1896–1899), 4: 458–59.

9. Kappler, pp. 561–65.

ment based on the three districts of the Choctaw Nation was set up, and agricultural development was promoted. Using funds specified in their treaties, the Choctaws built anew a flourishing school system, and Protestant missionaries zealously provided schools and churches.[10] The Choctaw leader Peter Pitchlynn drew a pleasant picture of the advances of his nation in 1849:

> Our constitution is purely republican, the gospel ministry is well sustained, and our schools are of a high order. Our people are increasing in numbers. Peace dwells within our limits, and plenteousness within our borders.
>
> Schools, civilization upon Christian principles, agriculture, temperance and morality are the only politics we have among us; and adhering to these few primary and fundamental principles of human happiness, we have flourished and prospered: hence we want none other. We wish simply to be let alone, and permitted to pursue the even tenor of our way.[11]

The Choctaws were joined by Chickasaws from northern Mississippi, who settled on the western section of the Choctaw lands (which they purchased from the Choctaws), with certain privileges in the Choctaw Nation. This condition dissatisfied the Chickasaws, for they wished to live under a strictly independent government, and in 1848 they adopted a formal constitution, in part as a means to prevent the diversion of their large tribal funds to the Choctaws. By 1854 contention between the two tribes had reached such a point that commissioners were appointed to seek agreement on separate jurisdictions and a set boundary line. A treaty signed that year at Doaksville in the Choctaw Nation defined the boundary; in 1855 a treaty concluded in Washington more carefully established relations between the two tribes.[12]

Chickasaw development in the West proceeded slowly, for with the death of Levi Colbert in 1834 there was no effective unified leadership, and the scattering of the settlements further fragmented the tribe. More serious was the general debilitation brought on, ironically, by the good terms received by the Chickasaws in their removal treaty. Hitchcock, who visited them in 1842, reported: "All accounts seem to agree that the Chickasaws are perhaps in a worse condition than either of the other emigrant

10. Angie Debo, *The Rise and Fall of the Choctaw Republic* (Norman: University of Oklahoma Press, 1934), pp. 58–79; Foreman, *Five Civilized Tribes*, pp. 17–94. Useful statistics on population and maps are provided in Jesse O. McKee and Jon A. Schlenker, *The Choctaws: Cultural Evolution of a Native American Tribe* (Jackson: University Press of Mississippi, 1980).

11. Remonstrance of Peter Pitchlynn, January 20, 1849, *House Miscellaneous Document* no. 35, 30–2, serial 544, p. 3.

12. Kappler, pp. 652–63, 706–14.

tribes resulting in part from their dependence upon what seemed in fact a more favorable treaty than that made by any other tribe." The Chickasaws seemed to lapse into a kind of apathy, depending on treaty annuities for their subsistence.[13]

Because of their exposed position, the Chickasaws suffered more than other tribes from raids by the warlike Kiowas, Comanches, and Kickapoos. "We are placed entirely on the frontier and surrounded by various bands of hostile Indians," Chickasaw leaders wrote to the president, "and we wish to know of our Great Father if he will not have some of his men placed at some suitable situation in our District to protect our lives and property, both of which are at the mercy of these roving bands."[14] In response to such pleas, the secretary of war in 1841 directed the construction of a new military post in the Chickasaw District to check the raiding tribes. Fort Washita was built near the mouth of the Washita River in 1842, and in 1851 another post, Fort Arbuckle, was established northwest of Fort Washita. Yet the Chickasaws were slow to move into their own district; a census of the tribe in 1844 showed a population of 4,111, three-fourths of whom still lived among the Choctaws. In 1853, however, a new count showed 4,709, with only one-tenth living outside the Chickasaw District.[15] By the mid-1850s the tribe appeared regenerated, with new leadership and social and economic development.

The Creek Indians moved to lands in the Indian Territory between the Cherokees and the Choctaws, although at first they clustered near Fort Gibson because they feared the wild tribes of the prairies. Like other tribes, they were divided, the Lower Creeks settling along the Arkansas River and the Upper Creeks along the Canadian. In 1840 the two groups united in a general council, but only later were the animosities between them quieted. Their factionalism, together with heavy population losses occasioned by the removal, delayed Creek development in the West.[16]

A further complication was the emigration of the Seminoles who had been forced out of Florida by the Seminole War. They were assigned a district within the Creek lands, between the Canadian River and its North Fork. But they objected to a union with the Creeks, and many stayed encamped near Fort Gibson. A principal bone of contention was the status of black slaves among the Seminoles, for these slaves enjoyed a good deal

13. Hitchcock, *Traveler in Indian Territory*, p. 176; Arrell M. Gibson, *The Chickasaws* (Norman: University of Oklahoma Press, 1971), pp. 184–226; Foreman, *Five Civilized Tribes*, pp. 97–144.

14. Quoted in Gibson, *Chickasaws*, p. 189.

15. Ibid., pp. 191–93.

16. Angie Debo, *The Road to Disappearance* (Norman: University of Oklahoma Press, 1941), pp. 108–41; Foreman, *Five Civilized Tribes*, pp. 147–219.

more freedom than the slaves of the Creeks, and they seemed to the Creeks to pose a threat to their own slave society. In a treaty signed at the Creek Agency on January 4, 1845, the difficulties were at least partially resolved, although the slavery problem continued and the Seminoles were irked by their incomplete independence from the Creeks. Finally, in 1856, following the pattern of separating the Choctaws and Chickasaws, a treaty was concluded in Washington by which the Seminoles received a new tract of land west of the Creek settlements. Once they had moved to these lands they were no longer subject to Creek laws.[17]

In spite of internal dissensions, the growth of these nations in the Indian Territory presaged an era of peace and prosperity that was taken as a sign of the wisdom of removal and the potentialities of the Indians to adapt to white ways. Such hopes were cut short by the Civil War, which reopened old animosities within the tribes and brought new economic and social disruptions.

MILITARY DEFENSE OF THE FRONTIER

Development of the Indian communities in the West depended upon a peaceful existence, free of attacks by outside enemies whether white or Indian. Critics of the removal policy had voiced a fear that the emigrant Indians would be insecure in their new homes, facing wild Indians of the plains who would resist the intrusion of tens of thousands of eastern Indians, most of them unprepared to fend off attacks. The emigrant Indians, moreover, would need protection against the encroachments of whites, protection that the Jackson administration had asserted was impossible in the East because of state jurisdictional problems but which the government could and would provide in the Trans-Mississippi West, where its authority was unchallenged. The federal government was mindful, also, of white citizens on the western frontier who, rightly or wrongly, feared the new heavy concentration of Indians on their borders. As removal proceeded, therefore, the United States developed elaborate plans for western defense to meet these needs.[18]

17. Kappler, pp. 550–52, 756–63. The problem of the slaves is thoroughly treated in Daniel F. Littlefield, Jr., *Africans and Seminoles: From Removal to Emancipation* (Westport, Connecticut: Greenwood Press, 1977), pp. 36–179; much of the same material is used in Littlefield, *Africans and Creeks: From the Colonial Period to the Civil War* (Westport, Connecticut: Greenwood Press, 1979), pp. 110–232.

18. I use here material from Francis Paul Prucha, *The Sword of the Republic: The United States Army on the Frontier, 1783–1846* (New York: Macmillan Company, 1969), pp. 339–60.

The removal of the eastern Indians, which poured thousands of tribesmen into the region west of Missouri and Arkansas, upset the haphazard system of establishing one fort at a time for frontier protection as local conditions required. What was needed now was a comprehensive, coordinated plan for the whole western frontier that would both maintain peace and fulfill the obligations the federal government had assumed to protect the transplanted Indians. The first full-scale plan came from Secretary of War Cass shortly before he left that office to become minister to France. On February 19, 1836, Cass presented a detailed proposal to House and Senate committees on military affairs. He estimated that when the removal of the eastern Indians was complete, about 93,500 emigrants would have been added to the indigenous tribes of the plains for a total of 244,870 between the Mississippi and the Rocky Mountains. These numbers were bound to increase the difficulties among the tribes and between the Indians and the whites. A sufficient military force along the frontier was needed to overawe the Indians, to intercept any bands that might attempt raids on white settlements, and to provide the means of concentrating troops wherever they might be needed.[19]

To accomplish these ends, Cass proposed the building of a military road along the frontier, running from the Red River near Fort Towson in the south to the Mississippi near Fort Snelling in the north. Along this line he wanted to construct stockaded posts. Forts east of the line would be abandoned as quickly as possible and their troops transferred to the western line. The plan met immediate approval, and on July 2, 1836, Congress passed "an act to provide for the better protection of the western frontier" that embodied his proposals and appropriated the hundred thousand dollars he had requested to carry them out. The president was authorized to survey and open a military road from the Mississippi to the Red River and to have military posts constructed along the road wherever they would be judged most proper for the protection of the frontier. Two weeks later Cass sent instructions to the commission of army officers selected to lay out the road and determine the posts.[20] But then the whole project bogged down, for new councils in the War Department rejected the plan as an answer to western defense problems.

Benjamin F. Butler, who replaced Cass as secretary of war, expressed only reserved approval of the line of posts, noting that "though it will be sufficient, if well garrisoned, to protect our own frontier, [it] will not be all

19. Report of Cass, February 19, 1836, and accompanying papers, *American State Papers: Military Affairs*, 6: 149–55; the documents also appear in *House Report* no. 401, 24–1, serial 294.

20. 5 *United States Statutes* 67; Cass to commissioners, July 16, 1836, *House Document* no. 278, 25–2, serial 328, pp. 9–12.

that caution and good faith will require." Butler had in mind the solemn pledges given to the emigrating Indians that they would be protected in their new homes, and he wrote an eloquent appeal for the fulfillment of those promises. To preserve peace among the different tribes of emigrant Indians and to protect them from their savage neighbors would require posts inside the Indian country as well as on the exterior line. But Butler's greatest concern was to protect the Indians from the encroachments of whites. The pledges given by the government to prevent whites from intruding on Indian lands had been given in the utmost sincerity, he said, and they could not be fulfilled without a strong military force—"a force adequate to repress the encroachments of the civilized and more powerful race."[21]

Butler served only an interim term and was not in office long enough to carry on a successful fight for his highly honorable proposals. He was succeeded by Joel R. Poinsett, whose primary concern was to protect whites from hostile Indians and who shortly drew up a plan for western defense based on principles that he considered diametrically opposed to the underpinnings of Cass's proposal. Basing his plan on a report of Acting Quartermaster General Trueman Cross, Poinsett rejected Cass's idea of a road running north and south along the frontier and insisted that proper defense demanded lines of communication running *perpendicular* to the line of settlement, from the populated interior of the country to the exposed frontier. With a view both to protecting the border settlements from incursions of savage tribes and to fulfilling obligations toward the emigrant Indians, Cross had asked for 7,000 men to protect the border settlements, including large disposable forces at Fort Leavenworth, Fort Gibson, and Fort Towson, and a reserve of 1,500 men at Jefferson Barracks. Poinsett supported this request; he called for 5,000 troops to man the exterior and interior lines of posts, plus reserves at Jefferson Barracks and at Baton Rouge, which he thought would "both insure the safety of the western frontier, and enable the government to fulfill all its treaty stipulations, and preserve its faith with the Indians." He added a proposal, however, for an auxiliary force of volunteer troops, to be instructed a certain number of days each year by regular army officers at regular army posts, in order to have on hand a trained reserve force.[22]

21. Report of Butler, December 3, 1836, *American State Papers: Military Affairs*, 6: 815.

22. Poinsett's plan of December 30, 1837, and accompanying documents, *American State Papers: Military Affairs*, 7: 777–86, and *House Document* no. 59, 25–2, serial 322. Another plan was submitted by General Edmund P. Gaines, which is in *House Document* no. 311, 25–2, serial 329; it is discussed at length in James W. Silver, *Edmund Pendleton Gaines, Frontier General* (Baton Rouge: Louisiana State University Press, 1949), pp. 216–57.

All the proposals suggested a series of military posts as a military cordon in the West, and a line of forts was maintained that corresponded roughly with the master plans, even though specific locations often were determined by local circumstances. By 1844 the pre-Mexican War defense arrangements were set. In that year Fort Wilkins was established on Keweenaw Peninsula in Lake Superior to meet defense needs arising from the influx of miners into that copper region. To the secretary of war for whom the post was named, the new fort formed "one point in a new cordon, which the general extension of our settlements and the enlargement of our territories by Indian treaties" made necessary.[23] With Fort Wilkins the top link in the chain, the exterior line of posts in that year comprised Fort Snelling, Fort Leavenworth, Fort Scott, Fort Gibson, Fort Towson, and Fort Washita. The interior posts were Fort Mackinac and Fort Brady on the Great Lakes, Fort Winnebago at the portage between the Fox and Wisconsin rivers, Fort Crawford at Prairie du Chien, Forts Atkinson and Des Moines in Iowa, and Jefferson Barracks. In the south Fort Smith and Fort Jesup also served the Indian frontier.

The officers and men of these posts gave a sense of security to the whites in the West, and they furnished an available military force that was called upon to restrict white encroachments on Indian lands and lessen (although they could not control) the machinations of whiskey vendors. In this they carried out the stipulations of Indian treaties, fulfilling many promises made by the United States to the tribes. Although there were clashes between the plains Indians and the emigrants, there were no serious intertribal wars, and the maps of the Census Bureau that show frontier lines testify to the success of the line of forts in restraining white advance, for there is a sharp line between white settlement and regions reserved for the emigrated and indigenous tribes.

Although the emigrated Indians were much on the minds of government officials as they established the defense line in the West, the army did not neglect the plains Indians, with whom new contacts were continually being made. With the organization of a dragoon regiment in 1832 —the first regular mounted troops on the frontier—the army began a series of summer expeditions into the prairies and plains west of the emigrated tribes in order to overawe and keep at peace the western tribes. From Fort Gibson, Fort Leavenworth, and Fort Des Moines, the dragoons between 1834 and 1845 crisscrossed the Indian country and invaded the lands of the Comanches, Kiowas, Pawnees, Sioux, Cheyennes, and other western Indians, bringing a show of power into their lands and on occasion meeting with the tribes in council. In all this, the army served as an agent

23. Report of William Wilkins, November 30, 1844, *Senate Document* no. 1, 28–2, serial 449, p. 114.

of the federal government in regulating the advance of the white frontier and easing the intercultural conflicts that inevitably resulted.[24]

Army commanders on the frontier played a significant role in the management of Indian affairs, both between the Indians and the federal government and within the tribes themselves. Imbued with the same paternalistic spirit that marked the civilian officials of the government, the army officers felt called upon to impress and control Indians as they would unruly children. But they were also a significant buffer between the frequently helpless Indians and unscrupulous frontier whites or warlike Indians to the west, and they could be a source of support and influence that was cultivated by tribal factions for their own purposes.

BENEVOLENCE AND REFORM

When Indian removal was over—or nearly so—the federal government returned to a concentrated effort at civilization and Christianization.[25] By 1840 the bulk of the eastern Indians had emigrated, and as they settled into their new lives, new humanitarian efforts were made to move them rapidly into the white man's ways. With relative tranquility on the frontier and the traumas of the removal process over, the wounds began to heal as the tribes adjusted to their new conditions. Under such circumstances, it is understandable that concerns for Indian advancement should have assumed something of their old prominence.

The 1840s were a decade of intense reforming spirit in America, a decade that saw the "first great upsurge of social reform in United States history," a high point in reform movements that began about 1815 and continued to the Civil War.[26] Betterment for all mankind seemed within easy

24. Prucha, *Sword of the Republic*, pp. 365–94.

25. Much of the material in this section is taken from Francis Paul Prucha, "American Indian Policy in the 1840s: Visions of Reform," in John G. Clark, ed., *The Frontier Challenge: Responses to the Trans-Mississippi West* (Lawrence: University Press of Kansas, 1971), pp. 81–110.

26. The quotation is from Arthur M. Schlesinger, *The American as Reformer* (Cambridge: Harvard University Press, 1950), p. 3. The reform movements in antebellum America have received much attention. For surveys, see Alice Felt Tyler, *Freedom's Ferment: Phases of American Social History to 1860* (Minneapolis: University of Minnesota Press, 1944); Ronald G. Walters, *American Reformers, 1815–1860* (New York: Hill and Wang, 1978); and Clifford S. Griffin, *Their Brothers' Keepers: Moral Stewardship in the United States, 1800–1865* (New Brunswick: Rutgers University Press, 1960). A useful collection of contemporary essays is Walter Hugins, ed., *The Reform Impulse, 1825–1850* (Columbia: University of South Carolina Press, 1972); modern essays are reprinted with an excellent introduction in David Brion Davis, ed., *Ante-Bellum Reform* (New York: Harper and Row, 1967). The intellectual setting in which movements for

reach, and concern for society's unfortunates (the delinquent, the insane, the indigent poor, the deaf, and the blind) appeared everywhere. Crusades for peace, women's rights, temperance, education, and the abolition of slavery marched with reforming zeal and a strange naiveté through the land. Words like *benevolence, philanthropy,* and *perfectability* slipped easily from men's tongues. The plans for civilizing and Christianizing those Indians who had been moved from the main arena of American life partook of this evangelizing spirit. It was part of the continuing revivalist atmosphere that so marked America in the nineteenth century and made Americans into a reforming people.

Indian welfare in the 1840s was not the object of a formal "reform movement," with voluntary organizations and national attention—as were temperance, women's rights, or abolition, and as Indian reform became in the last decades of the century. But the men who directed Indian affairs reflected their times. They spoke the same evangelical Protestant perfectionist rhetoric that distinguished the other reformers. They shared in the vital optimism of the age and hoped for no less for the Indians than the professional reformers did for other unfortunate groups within the nation. The policies of the 1840s must be understood in this context.

Removal itself continued to be seen as part of the total drive to civilize the Indians. The men in charge of Indian affairs in the 1840s were convinced of the wisdom of the removal policy and eager to make it work for the Indians. "It will be the end of all," T. Hartley Crawford, the commissioner of Indian affairs appointed by President Van Buren, wrote after his first year in office, "unless the experiment of the Government in the Indian territory shall be blessed with success." He admitted that the outcome was uncertain, but he was not disheartened, and he urged perseverance.[27]

As Crawford warmed to his job, he became bolder in his praise of removal as essential for Indian betterment. He considered other alternatives that might have been pursued—assimilation of Indians into the mass of white society and life as farmers on their lands in the East—and rejected them as infeasible. Removal to the West, he judged, was "the only expedient—the wisest, the best, the most practicable and practical of all." His view of the advantages to the Indians was idyllic, his goals utopian. The Indians, he prophesied, would find "a home and a country free from the apprehension of disturbance and annoyance, from the means of indulging a most degrading appetite [for liquor], and far removed from the temptations of bad and sordid men; a region hemmed in by the laws of the United

---

bettering the conditions of the Indians must be placed is treated in Perry Miller, *The Life of the Mind in America from the Revolution to the Civil War* (New York: Harcourt, Brace and World, 1965); see especially the section on benevolence, pp. 78–84.

27. CIA Report, 1839, serial 363, p. 346.

States and guarded by virtuous agents, where abstinence from vice, and the practice of good morals, should find fit abodes in comfortable dwellings and cleared farms, and be nourished and fostered by all the associations of the hearthstone. In no other than this settled condition can schools flourish, which are the keys that open the gate to heaven and God." Imbued with this attitude, he could not but urge the speedy removal of those Indians who had not yet migrated.[28]

The great means to bring about the transformation in the Indians that the reformers wanted—as it had been since early in the century—was education. There continued to be no doubt in the minds of responsible officials of the federal government that the Indians were ultimately educable. These men admitted that the present state of many of the Indians was one of semi-barbarism, but they did not believe in a racial inferiority that was not amenable to betterment. "It is proved, I think, conclusively," Crawford remarked of the Indian race, "that it is in no respect inferior to our own race, except in being less fortunately circumstanced. As great an aptitude for learning the letters, the pursuits, and arts of civilized life, is evident; if their progress is slow, so has it been with us and with masses of men in all nations and ages." Circumstances and education alone made the difference between them and the whites; and Indian agents, missionaries, and traders contributed evidence that the Indians were susceptible of improvement. There would be no racial obstacle to their eventual assimilation into the political life of the nation.[29]

So schools for the Indians were advocated with even greater enthusiasm than Thomas L. McKenney and his pioneering missionary friends had displayed, as befitted an age in which education was considered the "universal utopia."[30] The promotion of schools as the agency to swing the Indians from a state considered to be barbarous, immoral, and pagan to one that was civilized, moral, and Christian took on new exuberance when the Indians were safely ensconced in the West, where the "experiment" could be carried out unhindered. Indian schools, Commissioner Crawford asserted in 1839, formed "one of the most important objects, if it be not the greatest, connected with our Indian relations. Upon it depends more or less even partial success in all endeavors to make the Indian better than he is."

---

28. CIA Report, 1840, serial 375, pp. 232–34. Crawford's vision was shared by the secretaries of war. See report of Joel R. Poinsett, December 5, 1840, *Senate Document* no. 1, 26–2, serial 375, p. 28; report of John C. Spencer, November 26, 1842, *Senate Document* no. 1, 27–3, serial 413, p. 190.

29. CIA Report, 1844, serial 449, p. 315; report of Thomas H. Harvey, October 8, 1844, ibid., p. 435; report of William Wilkins, November 30, 1844, *Senate Document* no. 1, 28–2, serial 449, p. 127.

30. The phrase is from a chapter heading in Arthur A. Ekirch, Jr., *The Idea of Progress in America, 1815–1860* (New York: Columbia University Press, 1944), p. 195.

The commissioner hammered tirelessly at this theme. "The greatest good we can bestow upon them," he said in 1842, "is education in its broadest sense—education in letters, education in labor and the mechanic arts, education in morals, and education in Christianity."[31]

The initial problem was how to intrigue the Indians, both the youths to be educated and their parents, into accepting the schooling. It was all too evident that simply duplicating white schools in the Indian country or sending Indians to the East for formal education was not the answer. Learning in letters alone was not appreciated by the Indians and did not give any practical advancement to young Indians, who became misfits within their own communities. The answer, rather, lay in manual labor schools, whose full importance was made explicit by Crawford:

> The education of the Indian is a great work. It includes more than the term imports in its application to civilized communities. Letters and personal accomplishments are what we generally intend to speak of by using the word; though sometimes, even with us, it has a more comprehensive meaning. Applied to wild men, its scope should take in much more extensive range, or you give them the shadow for the substance. They must at the least be taught to read and write, and have some acquaintance with figures; but if they do not learn to build and live in houses, to sleep on beds; to eat at regular intervals; to plough, and sow, and reap; to rear and use domestic animals; to understand and practise the mechanic arts; and to enjoy, to their gratification and improvement, all the means of profit and rational pleasure that are so profusely spread around civilized life, their mere knowledge of what is learned in the school room proper will be comparatively valueless. At a future day, more or less remote, when those who are now savage shall have happily become civilized, this important branch of Indian interest may be modified according to circumstances; but at present, when every thing is to be learned at the school, and nothing, as with us, by the child as it grows up, unconsciously and without knowing how or when, the manual labor school system is not only deserving of favor, but it seems to me indispensable to the civilization of the Indians; and their civilization, with a rare exception here and there, is as indispensable to real and true Christianity in them.[32]

This apotheosis of white cultural traits and insistence upon them, willy-nilly, for the Indians is an overpowering indication of the ethnocentric, paternalistic viewpoint of the white reformers. Once the Indians

---

31. CIA Report, 1839, serial 363, p. 343; CIA Report, 1842, serial 413, p. 386.
32. CIA Report, 1844, serial 449, p. 313.

accepted the new way of life, they would see the advantages of education in arts and letters, and the desire to attain it would motivate the Indians to attend and promote traditional schools. As civilization advanced, Christianity could be promoted, and moral improvement would follow. The desire for material well-being would stimulate industry, which would in turn accelerate the whole process. It was a wonderful white man's carousel.

The practical model for the Indian Office was the manual labor school established at the Methodist Shawnee mission in eastern Kansas in 1839, which seemed to embody all the characteristics needed to reach the goal. The school, built with church funds aided by substantial grants from the Indian civilization fund of the government, drew students from several tribes—Shawnee, Delaware, Kansas, Peoria, Potawatomi, Wyandot, Ottawa, and a scattering of others—and provided training for both boys and girls in useful agricultural and domestic skills, as well as in the English language.[33] Crawford considered the school "the strongest evidence I have yet seen of the probability of success, after all our failures, in the efforts made by benevolent and religious societies, and by the Government, to work a change in Indian habits and modes of life; while it is conclusive proof that these sons of the forest are our equals in capacity."[34] For its good work, and even more as a harbinger of greater things to come within the Indian country, the school won praise from the highest sources. Manual labor schools for the Indians became the goal of the War Department and the Indian Office.[35]

Two other principles in connection with manual labor education were adopted by the Indian Office. One was that Indian schools should teach girls as well as boys, if civilization were to be forwarded. When Crawford, early in his term of office, noted that more boys than girls were being educated, he asked, "Upon what principle of human action is this inequality founded?" And he set forth his argument in strong terms:

> Unless the Indian female character is raised, and her relative position changed, such an education as you can give the males will be a rope

33. Valuable details on the founding and operation of the Shawnee mission school are given in Martha B. Caldwell, comp., *Annals of Shawnee Methodist Mission and Indian Manual Labor School* (Topeka: Kansas State Historical Society, 1939), and J. J. Lutz, "The Methodist Missions among the Indian Tribes in Kansas," *Transactions of the Kansas State Historical Society* 9 (1905–1906): 170–93. A good theoretical analysis of early missionary manual labor schools is Robert F. Berkhofer, Jr., "Model Zions for the American Indian," *American Quarterly* 15 (Summer 1963): 176–90.

34. CIA Report, 1840, serial 375, p. 243. Crawford got his information from a report of John B. Luce, November 11, 1840, ibid., pp. 387–88. See also the reports of the beginning of the school in CIA Report, 1839, serial 363, pp. 433–34.

35. Report of W. L. Marcy, December 5, 1846, *Senate Document* no. 1, 29–2, serial 493, p. 60; CIA Report, 1846, serial 493, p. 227.

of sand, which, separating at every turn, will bind them to no ame-
lioration. Necessity may force the culture of a little ground, or the
keeping of a few cattle, but the savage nature will break out at every
temptation. If the women are made good and industrious house-
wives, and taught what befits their condition, their husbands and
sons will find comfortable homes and social enjoyments, which, in
any state of society, are essential to morality and thrift. I would therefore advise that the larger proportion of pupils should be female.[36]

"The conviction is settled," he reiterated in 1841, "that the civilization of
these unfortunate wards of the Government will be effected through the
instrumentality of their educated women, much more than by their taught
men."[37] Although the commissioner's goals were never met, promotion of
female education continued.

A second principle, gradually developed during the decade, was that
Indian youths should be taught in the Indian country where they lived
and not sent off to eastern schools. This reversed the tradition of sending
select Indian boys to schools in the East, where it was supposed that they
could more quickly absorb the white man's civilization and take it back
to their tribes. Thus the Cherokees John Ridge and Elias Boudinot had
been educated at Cornwall, Connecticut, and many Indians had attended
Richard M. Johnson's Choctaw Academy in Kentucky.

Crawford advised from the first against sending Indians away from
home to distant schools, and in 1844 Secretary of War Wilkins argued that
education should be diffused as equally as possible through the whole tribe
by establishing common schools within the Indian country. The education
of a few individuals in a school away from their tribe did not promote the
designs of the government, Wilkins said, for he was afraid that men more
highly educated than the mass of the tribes might employ their talents for
selfish acquisition and oppression of their uneducated brothers. By 1846
the Indian Office had clearly decided to adhere to the new policy.[38] "The
practice so long pursued of selecting a few boys from the different tribes,
and placing them at our colleges and high schools," Commissioner William Medill repeated in 1847, "has failed to produce the beneficial results
anticipated; while the great mass of the tribe at home were suffered to remain in ignorance." He intended to discontinue the plan as soon as existing arrangements could be changed and apply the resources of the Indian

36. CIA Report, 1839, serial 363, p. 344.
37. CIA Report, 1841, serial 401, p. 241.
38. CIA Report, 1839, serial 363, p. 344; report of Wilkins, November 30, 1844, *Senate Document* no. 1, 28–2, serial 449, p. 127; report of Marcy, December 5, 1846, *Senate
Document* no. 1, 29–2, serial 493, p. 60.

Office solely to schools within the Indian country, where education could be extended to both sexes and generally spread throughout the tribe.[39]

To carry out the educational reform considerable money was expended in the Indian country. The civilization fund of $10,000 a year was apportioned among the various missionary societies in small amounts.[40] The effect of these allowances in stimulating contributions by missionary groups is hard to evaluate, for other federal funds also were poured into the mission schools. Chief among these were funds specified for education in treaties made with the Indians or designated from annuity money by the tribes themselves for educational purposes. Thus the Choctaw treaty of 1830 stipulated that the government would pay $2,000 annually for twenty years for the support of three school teachers, and the tribe voted in 1842 to apply $18,000 a year from its annuities to education.[41] A treaty with the Ottawas and Chippewas in 1836 specified that, in addition to an annuity in specie of $30,000 for twenty years, $5,000 each year would be granted for teachers, schoolhouses, and books in their own languages, and $3,000 more for missions. These payments were to run for twenty years and as long thereafter as Congress would continue the appropriation. In 1845, $68,195 was provided by treaties for Indian education, to which was added $12,367.50 from the civilization fund. Subsequent treaties added to the school funds available. A treaty with the Kansas Indians in 1846, for example, called for the investment of the sum paid for ceded lands, and $1,000 a year from the interest was directed to schools. The treaty of 1846 with the Winnebagos stated that $10,000 of the cession payment would be applied to the creation and maintenance of one or more manual labor schools.[42] To these government funds were added the money supplied by the missionary societies. The government also built schools and churches and supplied agricultural implements and domestic equipment that could be used in the sort of education advocated by white leaders of the 1840s.

Although the number of students in the Indian schools was small, the optimism of the Indian Office and the missionaries was not without foundation. The Choctaws, who were more interested in education than many of the tribes, offered an example of what was possible. They began to build

39. CIA Report, 1847, serial 503, p. 749. See also report of Marcy, December 2, 1847, *Senate Executive Document* no. 1, 30–1, serial 503, p. 70.

40. A year-by-year listing of expenditures from the fund for the period 1820–1842 appears in *House Document* no. 203, 27–3, serial 423. See also George D. Harmon, *Sixty Years of Indian Affairs: Political, Economic, and Diplomatic, 1789–1850* (Chapel Hill: University of North Carolina Press, 1941), appendix, table V, pp. 378–79.

41. Kappler, p. 315; P. P. Pitchlynn to William Armstrong, December 12, 1842, in CIA Report, 1843, serial 431, pp. 367–68.

42. Kappler, pp. 451–52, 553, 566; Harmon, *Sixty Years of Indian Affairs*, appendix, table VII, p. 381.

schools as soon as they arrived in the West. The missionaries of the American Board reported eleven schools with 228 Choctaw students in 1836, in addition to which there were five schools supported by the Choctaw Nation and the three district schools provided by the 1830 treaty. In 1842 a comprehensive system of schools was begun. Spencer Academy and Fort Coffee Academy were opened in 1844, Armstrong and New Hope academies two years later. The national council also supported four schools established earlier by the American Board. By 1848 the Choctaws had nine boarding schools supported by tribal funds, and neighborhood schools had been opened in many communities.[43] The commissioner of Indian affairs reported progress as well among the other tribes. The Cherokees especially made remarkable advances and had a better common school system than that of either Arkansas or Missouri.[44]

Comparative numbers give some indication of the progress, although reports were often incomplete. In 1842 forty-five schools (out of a total of fifty-two) reported 2,132 students enrolled. In 1848 there were sixteen manual labor schools with 809 students and eighty-seven boarding and other schools with 2,873 students; in 1849, although some reports were missing, a further increase in students was noted.[45]

These schools could not have existed without the devoted work of Christian missionaries, and Indian education was a beneficiary of the missionary impulse of the Protestant churches that was an important element in the reform ferment of the age. The Indian Office felt this influence strongly, for its goals and those of the missionary societies were identical: practical, moral, and religious education of the Indians that would bring both Christianity and civilization to the aborigines. Reliance on the missionaries, indeed, was uppermost in the minds of federal officials. Commissioner Crawford noted in his report of 1839: "No direction of these institutions [Indian schools] appears to me so judicious as that of religious and benevolent societies, and it is gratifying to observe the zeal with which all the leading sects lend themselves to this good work; discouragements do not seem to cool their ardor, nor small success to dissuade them from persevering efforts." So successful was the Methodist school in Kansas that the War Department was eager to support similar establishments directed by other religious groups, "equally zealous, no doubt, in spreading the light

43. Debo, *Choctaw Republic*, pp. 60–61; documents 69–72 in CIA Report, 1843, serial 431, pp. 367–72. Spencer Academy is a good example of the cooperation of several agencies in the Indian schools. It was started with $2,000 from the government's civilization fund and $6,000 from Choctaw annuities, and it was directed and run by Presbyterian missionaries. See W. David Baird, "Spencer Academy, Choctaw Nation, 1842–1900," *Chronicles of Oklahoma* 45 (Spring 1967): 25–43.

44. CIA Report, 1847, serial 503, p. 750; Foreman, *Five Civilized Tribes*, p. 410.

45. Document 83 in CIA Report, 1842, serial 413, pp. 520–22; CIA Report, 1849, serial 570, p. 956.

of the Gospel among the Indians, and equally disposed to advance their moral culture."[46]

Agents in the field who were close to the missionaries and their work strongly praised the efforts of the churches, and officials in Washington uncritically accepted the highly favorable reports sent in by the missionaries themselves. The eagerness to see success in these ventures, unwarranted as it might have been at times, reflects the utopian, reform-minded views of the age.[47]

The general reports of progress were highly optimistic. Government officials held firm to their views of the perfectibility of the Indians, of their ability to attain the civilization of the whites. They eagerly seized upon whatever evidence pointed in that direction, convinced as they were that the advances in education among some of the tribes proved conclusively that all Indians were amenable to such attainments, immediately or in the near future. They were sure their efforts had contributed to the good result, and they spoke in justification of the faith they had had. Only a few voices were raised in opposition, not to deny the possibilities or even some of the accomplishments, but to point to the slowness of the progress.

By the end of the decade success seemed assured and was in fact proclaimed from on high. Secretary of War W. L. Marcy in December 1848 reported: "No subject connected with our Indian affairs has so deeply interested the department and received so much of its anxious solicitude and attention, as that of education, and I am happy to be able to say that its efforts to advance this cause have been crowned with success. Among most of the tribes which have removed to and become settled in the Indian country, the blessings of education are beginning to be appreciated, and they generally manifest a willingness to co-operate with the government in diffusing these blessings." The schools, he concluded, afforded evidence that nearly all of the emigrated tribes were rapidly advancing in civilization and moral strength, and he gave full credit to the Indian Office for the improved condition of the numerous tribes. In the same year, William Medill, then commissioner of Indian affairs, acknowledged the earlier decline of the Indians and the disappearance of some aboriginal groups. "Cannot this sad and depressing tendency of things be checked, and the past be at least measurably repaired by better results in the future?" he asked. His

46. CIA Report, 1839, serial 363, p. 343; report of Joel R. Poinsett, December 5, 1840, *Senate Document* no. 1, 26–2, serial 375, p. 28.

47. See Epilogue, "The Harvest Unreaped," in Robert F. Berkhofer, Jr., *Salvation and the Savage: An Analysis of Protestant Missions and American Indian Response, 1787– 1862* (Lexington: University of Kentucky Press, 1965), pp. 152–60, for a critical appraisal of the missionaries' success up to 1860. Reports of the missionaries appear in such sources as the *Annual Report* of the American Board of Commissioners for Foreign Missions and in the board's journal, *The Missionary Herald*, as well as in reports attached to the annual reports of the commissioner of Indian affairs.

answer was cautious but reassuring: "It is believed they can, and, indeed, it has to some extent been done already, by the wise and beneficent system of policy put in operation some years since, and which, if steadily carried out, will soon give to our whole Indian system a very different and much more favorable aspect."[48]

The optimism of the next commissioner of Indian affairs, Orlando Brown, knew no bounds, but his report of 1849 differed only in degree and not in kind from the enthusiastic appraisals of his predecessors. "The dark clouds of ignorance and superstition in which these people have so long been enveloped seem at length in the case of many of them to be breaking away, and the light of Christianity and general knowledge to be dawning upon their moral and intellectual darkness," he wrote. Brown gave credit for the change to the government's policy of moving the Indians toward an agricultural existence, to the introduction of the manual labor schools, and to instruction by the missionaries in "the best of all knowledge, religious truth—their duty towards God and their fellow beings." The result was "a great moral and social revolution" among some of the tribes that he predicted would be spread to others by adoption of the same measures. Within a few years he believed that "in intelligence and resources, they would compare favorably with many portions of our white population, and instead of drooping and declining, as heretofore, they would be fully able to maintain themselves in prosperity and happiness under any circumstance of contact or connexion with our people." In the end he expected a large measure of success to "crown the philanthropic efforts of the government and of individuals to civilize and to christianize the Indian tribes." He no longer doubted that the Indians were capable of self-government. "They have proved their capacity for social happiness," he concluded, "by adopting written constitutions upon the model of our own, by establishing and sustaining schools, by successfully devoting themselves to agricultural pursuits, by respectable attainments in the learned professions and mechanic arts, and by adopting the manners and customs of our people, so far as they are applicable to their own condition."[49]

This was a bit too much, for the Indians did not reach utopia. But it was quite in tune with the age, when zealous reformers saw no limit to the possibilities for ameliorating and perfecting the human condition, when the insane were to be cured, the slaves freed, the prisons cleansed, and women's rights recognized, and when Sunday schools would flourish. Government officials and their missionary allies hoped for no less for the American Indians.

48. Report of Marcy, December 1, 1848, *House Executive Document* no. 1, 30–2, serial 537, p. 84; CIA Report, 1848, serial 537, pp. 385–86.
49. CIA Report, 1849, serial 570, pp. 956–57.

CHAPTER 11

New Structures
and Programs

Development of the Indian Department.

Proposals for an Indian State.

Annuities and Liquor Regulation.

The removal of the eastern Indians not only meant the relocation of tens of thousands of Indians in the Trans-Mississippi West, radically changing the distribution of the tribes with whom the United States government dealt, but it also necessitated a modification and codification of the laws and regulations governing Indian relations. The Indian bureaucracy (which had grown piecemeal during the previous decades) was regularized, an up-to-date trade and intercourse law was enacted, and plans were proposed for Indian government in the West. In addition, special problems growing out of annuity payments and the liquor traffic were once again directly countered with legislative remedies.

DEVELOPMENT OF THE INDIAN DEPARTMENT

The first step was congressional authorization in 1832 of a commissioner of Indian affairs to replace the head of the Indian Office appointed by the secretary of war on his own authority (Thomas L. McKenney and his two successors, Samuel S. Hamilton and Elbert Herring). Congress specified that the new official, who would be under the direction of the secretary of war, would manage all Indian affairs.[1] This formalization had been a dream

1. 4 *United States Statutes* 564.

of McKenney's, which he had promoted unsuccessfully for many years before he was removed from office in 1830.

The first to serve in the long line of commissioners extending up to the
1970s was Elbert Herring, who carried over from the older office and who
served until 1836. Herring was a politician with no experience in Indian
affairs, but he was an enthusiastic supporter of the removal policy and programs determined by Andrew Jackson and Lewis Cass. He fitted well into
the paternalistic, benevolent Christian reform pattern of the time and
urged the transformation of Indian society from a system of communal to
one of private property, concluding that the "absence of the *meum* and
tuum in the general community of possessions, which is the grand conservative principle of the social state, is a perpetual operating cause of the *vis
inertiae* of savage life." He recommended a new political system for the
tribes, the education of Indian youth, and the introduction of Christianity,
"all centering on one grand object—the substitution of the social for the
savage state."[2] Herring's successor, Carey A. Harris, was likewise a firm
supporter of the removal policy. A Tennessee newspaperman and lawyer
who had become chief clerk in the War Department and a close associate
of Cass and Jackson, Harris served as commissioner for only two years,
when he was forced to resign because of a scandal arising out of speculation in Indian allotments.[3]

In 1834 Congress went far beyond the establishment of the commissionership by undertaking a wholesale revamping of the Indian department and its activities. First, it put a firm legislative foundation under the
Indian service, made explicit provisions for Indian agents, whose status
had been somewhat irregular, and established systematic accounting procedures in order to eliminate the confusion and embarrassment that had
frequently arisen in financial matters. Second, it restated and codified Indian policy as it had been embodied in trade and intercourse laws during
the preceding four and a half decades of United States history, bringing to
culmination earlier legislation, ripened now. Third, it intended to fulfill
the pledges made to the Indians upon removal that adequate provision
would be made for their protection and for their government.[4]

The first and second of these measures were not revolutionary. Their

2. CIA Report, 1832, serial 233, p. 163; see also CIA Report, 1834, serial 266, pp.
238–39, 241. A brief biographical sketch of Herring is provided in Ronald N. Satz,
"Elbert Herring, 1831–36," in Robert M. Kvasnicka and Herman J. Viola, eds., *The Commissioners of Indian Affairs, 1824–1977* (Lincoln: University of Nebraska Press, 1979),
pp. 13–16.

3. Ronald N. Satz, "Carey Allen Harris, 1836–38," in Kvasnicka and Viola, *Commissioners of Indian Affairs*, pp. 17–22.

4. I use material here from Francis Paul Prucha, *American Indian Policy in the Formative Years: The Indian Trade and Intercourse Acts, 1790–1834* (Cambridge: Harvard
University Press, 1962), pp. 250–69.

ultimate source was earlier legislation based on past experience, as well as numerous recommendations made through the years to perfect United States policy toward the Indians. There were, moreover, important proximate sources through which the past was brought to focus on the present. Such were the detailed recommendations submitted to the secretary of war in February 1829 by Lewis Cass and William Clark, the report of the Stokes Commission sent out by the secretary of war in 1832 to investigate the new home allotted to the emigrating Indians, and finally, the report of the House Committee on Indian Affairs, which presented the draft of the new Indian bills to Congress in 1834.

The trade and intercourse laws from 1790 to 1802, with occasional later amendments, had grown little by little, and they needed to be augmented and pulled together in a single piece of legislation. This need, plus the frustrating difficulties arising from the lack of well-founded administrative procedures in the War Department for handling Indian affairs, struck Peter B. Porter with special force when he became secretary of war in the spring of 1828. "In the few weeks that have elapsed since I had the honor to be called to this Department," Porter wrote to Governor Cass in July 1828, "I have found no portion of its extensive and complicated duties so perplexing, and the performance of which has been less welcome, than those which appertain to the Bureau of Indian Affairs." This was not due to deficiencies in the character of the men charged with the duties, he asserted, but came rather from "the want of a well digested system of principles and rules for the administration of our Indian concerns." His purpose in writing Cass and in sending a similar letter to William Clark at St. Louis was to invite the two men to Washington to draw up a code of regulations for Indian affairs that could be presented to Congress for its action. "The long and intimate acquaintance which you have both had with the Indian character," he told them, "—your knowledge of their interests, their habits, wants, wishes and capabilities would render your aid and advice in the formation of such a system, peculiarly useful and desirable."[5]

Both Cass and Clark responded enthusiastically to Porter's proposal. Clark thought that the existing laws were "not sufficiently explicit & consistent" to punish offences against the laws and regulations, and Cass wanted "some established principles to regulate the discretion which now exists." Working together in Washington, they produced a long report, which Porter sent to the Senate on February 9, 1829.[6]

5. Porter to Cass, July 28, 1828, OIA LS, vol. 5, pp. 56–57 (M21, reel 5). See also report of the secretary of war, November 24, 1828, *Senate Document* no. 1, 20–2, serial 181, pp. 20–21.

6. Clark to Porter, August 27, 1828, OIA LR, St. Louis Superintendency (M234, reel 748); Cass to Porter, September 8, 1828, ibid., Michigan Superintendency (M234, reel 420). The report of Cass and Clark is in *Senate Document* no. 72, 20–2, serial 181.

In answer to Porter's demand for a bill that would "embrace the whole policy of the government, and comprise all its legislation on Indian intercourse, and every other subject connected therewith, in one statute," the two men submitted the draft of a bill with fifty-six sections. It was made up in large part of transcriptions—more or less literal—from previous laws, incorporating most of the intercourse act of 1802, a law of 1800 providing for visits of Indians to the seat of government, provisions of the law of 1816 excluding foreigners from the Indian trade, the law of 1817 providing for crimes committed in the Indian country, the law of 1818 concerning the manner of appointing Indian agents, the law of 1819 establishing an annual $10,000 civilization fund, the supplementary intercourse law of 1822, the provisions of 1824 designating sites for the trade, and sections of other laws that touched upon Indian trade, Indian agents, or the accounting for public funds. There was also much that was new: additions and modifications of earlier legislation embodying the views of Cass and Clark for ameliorating the existing state of affairs. These pertained to regularizing and specifying the appointment and duties of Indian department personnel and to improving methods for handling financial accounts. Discretionary power for agents in granting licenses was recommended, along with tighter restriction in general of access to the Indian country.

The proposed bill was accompanied by a set of "Regulations for the Government of the Indian Department." These in many places repeated the provisions in the bill but also added details of procedure for carrying the law into effect. There were sections governing the civil and fiscal administration of the Indian department, and others that prescribed the limits of agencies, listed the designated trading posts, and provided rules for treating with the Indians, paying annuities, issuing licenses, processing claims for indemnification for losses suffered by either race, using the civilization fund, prohibiting liquor, and accounting for funds.[7]

A third item was a bill to consolidate into one statute all the provisions for payment of annuities due from the United States to the Indians. This was a sensible proposal, intended to eliminate the unnecessary complications of accounting for funds under diverse headings.[8]

The work of Cass and Clark bore witness to their competence in Indian affairs. The proposed bills, it is true, included a few items that were no longer of current importance, but they provided adequately for a workable department and new legislation and regulations to correct evils not taken care of by the earlier laws. The men skillfully worked into one bill and one set of regulations diverse matters that had been scattered through the statutes and War Department directives. They attempted in their regulations

7. The regulations are printed ibid., pp. 75–82.
8. Ibid., pp. 52–57.

to codify existing practice where it was satisfactory and introduce new procedures where greater clarity or strength was needed. The proposed bill was accompanied by an extensive section-by-section commentary that made clear the thinking behind the proposals and gave insight into Indian affairs at the time.

The proposals were submitted to the Senate by Porter with the earnest recommendation that they receive early consideration. McKenney, too, praised them; the report was, he declared, "able and judicious," and the accompanying bill "ample and apposite," although he objected to the mode of accounting that Cass and Clark had proposed and offered alternative suggestions. McKenney picked out for special emphasis the provisions in the bill and regulations that would grant discretion to the agents in issuing licenses to traders. That this discretionary power was a crucial point in the regulation of Indian intercourse can be seen from the violent opposition it stirred up in the American Fur Company.[9] Congress took no action on the Cass-Clark report as it stood, but the recommendations were not ineffectual, for they served as a ready reference for those who advocated some updating of the laws governing relations with the Indians, and much of the report was incorporated into the bills that became law in 1834.

Removal invigorated the concern to update the legislative basis of Indian affairs. The Stokes Commission of 1832, besides investigating the land in the West, was charged to gather information that would be essential in developing a sound policy for governing future relations with the Indians. "In the great change we are now urging them [the Indians] to make," Secretary of War Cass warned the commissioners, "it is desirable that all their political relations, as well among themselves as with us, should be established upon a permanent basis, beyond the necessity for any future alteration. Your report upon this branch of the subject will be laid before Congress, and will probably become the foundation of a system of legislation for these Indians."[10]

The commissioners submitted a long and useful report, full of details on the condition of the western tribes and the character of the territory to be allotted to the emigrating Indians. They emphasized the necessity for governmental action to suppress hostilities among Indian groups and recommended in detail the military posts in the West that they considered essential. They noted the high prices charged the Indians for goods by white traders and urged that the government care for Indian wants by supplying annuities in goods at reasonable cost. The commissioners stressed the im-

9. CIA Report, 1829, serial 192, pp. 167–68; McKenney to John H. Eaton, January 21, 1830, OIA LS, vol. 6, pp. 237–38 (M21, reel 6).

10. Instructions of Cass, July 14, 1832, *House Executive Document* no. 2, 22–2, serial 233, pp. 32–37.

portance of freeing the Indian country of white citizens and preventing whites from grazing their livestock or trapping on Indian lands. They strongly suggested the organization of the Indian territory and an annual grand council of Indians. So anxious were they to avoid contacts between the whites and the Indians that they recommended a neutral strip of land five miles wide between the lands of the two races on which all settlement was to be prohibited.[11]

President Jackson in his annual message of December 1833 called attention to the need for a reorganization of Indian affairs to meet new conditions. In response, the House Committee on Indian Affairs presented a full-scale report on May 20, 1834. The report relied heavily on the Cass-Clark proposals of five years earlier and on the report of the Stokes Commission, which had been submitted on February 10. Accompanying the report was a trio of bills—for organizing the Indian department, for a new trade and intercourse law, and for establishing a government for the Indians in the West.[12]

Because the authorization for a commissioner of Indian affairs in 1832 met the demand that had been made for a centralized office to handle Indian matters, the committee turned immediately to the problem of Indian superintendencies and agencies. They discovered legislative and administrative confusion. They found four superintendents, eighteen agents, twenty-seven subagents, and thirty-four interpreters on duty with the Indian department, drawing a total annual compensation of $57,222. They were dismayed at the lack of legal foundation for the offices that these men filled and insisted that the creation of the offices and the fixing of the salaries "should not be left to Executive discretion or to legislative implication." For help in drawing up a suitable bill, the committee turned to the secretary of war, asking him "to furnish them with a general bill, reorganising the Indian Department & in fact defining as far as possible the Indian service." Cass replied with alacrity and made arrangements to meet personally with the committee.[13]

The bill reported by the committee on May 20 withdrew the superintendence of Indian affairs from the governors of Florida and Arkansas territories, and from the governor of Michigan Territory as soon as a new

11. Report of commissioners, February 10, 1834, *House Report* no. 474, 23–1, serial 263, pp. 78–103.

12. Message of December 3, 1833, Fred L. Israel, ed., *The State of the Union Messages of the Presidents, 1790–1966,* 3 vols. (New York: Chelsea House, 1966), 1: 386–87; *House Report* no. 474, 23–1, serial 263.

13. House committee to Cass, February 25, 1834, OIA LR, Miscellaneous (M234, reel 435); Cass to committee, February 26, 1834, Office of the Secretary of War, Reports to Congress, vol. 3, National Archives, Record Group 107. No copy of a written report to the committee including a detailed bill could be found.

territory should be organized west of Lake Michigan. It continued the superintendency at St. Louis for all Indians west of the Mississippi who were not within the bounds of any state or territory. The superintendents were given general direction over agents and subagents, including the power to suspend them for misconduct. Authorized agencies were listed in the bill, a terminal date for others was set, and the rest were declared abolished. The establishment of subagencies, however, and the appointment of subagents was left in the hands of the president. The powers and responsibilities of the agents and subagents, especially in regard to issuing licenses, were extended. To care for miscellaneous needs, the president was empowered to require military officers to perform the duties of Indian agent. The limits of the agencies were to be determined by the secretary of war according to tribes or by geographical boundaries. The bill made provision, too, for hiring and paying interpreters, blacksmiths, and other mechanics.

A second concern of the committee in the Indian department bill was the payment of annuities; the bill provided that no payments be made on an individual basis, but that the whole annuity be paid to the chiefs or to other persons delegated by the tribes. If the Indians requested, the annuity could be paid in goods, and all goods for the Indians were to be purchased by an agent of the government and under sealed bids if time permitted—in an attempt to prevent the exorbitant markup on goods that the western commissioners had reported.

The bill contained additional items collected from previous legislation: the prohibition that no person employed in the Indian department could engage in trade with the Indians; authorization for the president to furnish domestic animals and implements of husbandry to the Indians in the West; and a grant of rations to Indians who visited military posts or agencies on the frontier. The bill also authorized the president to prescribe the necessary rules and regulations for carrying out the act. The committee pushed this bill as an economy measure, as well as a clarification of former uncertainties, and it submitted data to show that the bill would effect an annual saving of over $80,000. The bill became law on June 30 exactly as it had been submitted by the committee.[14]

The new legislation established a well-organized Indian department with a considerable reduction of personnel, effecting its economy in part by placing additional burdens upon the military officers on the frontier. The post commanders were often called upon to assume the duties of Indian agent, and the quartermaster officers were frequently responsible for the funds disbursed to the Indians in annuity payments. To govern the officers in these tasks the adjutant general sent them copies of the 1834

14. 4 *United States Statutes* 735–38.

TABLE 2: Field Organization of the Indian Department, 1837

ACTING SUPERINTENDENCY OF MICHIGAN	Upper Missouri Agency
Michilimackinac Agency	Upper Missouri Subagency
Saginaw Subagency	Council Bluffs Subagency
Sault Ste. Marie Subagency	Great Nemahaw Subagency
	Osage River Subagency
SUPERINTENDENCY OF WISCONSIN	
TERRITORY	ACTING SUPERINTENDENCY
Sac and Fox Agency	OF THE WESTERN TERRITORY
St. Peter's Agency	Choctaw Agency
Prairie du Chien Subagency	Creek Agency
Green Bay Subagency	Cherokee Agency
Lapointe Subagency	Osage Subagency
Crow Wing River Subagency	Neosho Subagency
SUPERINTENDENCY OF ST. LOUIS	MISCELLANEOUS
Fort Leavenworth Agency	Chickasaw Agency
Council Bluffs Agency	Ohio Subagency
	New York Subagency

Source: "Regulations Concerning Superintendencies, Agencies, and Subagencies, April 13, 1837," in *Office Copy of the Laws, Regulations, Etc., of the Indian Bureau, 1850* (Washington: Gideon and Company, 1850).

laws and special sets of regulations, and he directed them to follow instructions given them by the commissioner of Indian affairs, by order of the secretary of war.[15]

The second bill of the committee, which on June 30 became the intercourse law of 1834, was a good example of continuity in American Indian policy.[16] It offered no sharp break with the past but embodied, occasionally in modified form, the principles that had developed through the previous decades. One who has seen the provisions of the earlier laws feels much at home here. What changes did occur were generally the culmination of longterm agitation for correction of abuses. The committee in drawing up this bill relied heavily on the proposals made by Cass and Clark in 1829.

The act began with a definition of the Indian country. The principle of the earlier intercourse laws, in which "the boundary of the Indian country was a line of metes and bounds, variable from time to time by treaties," was rejected by the committee because the multiplication of treaties made it difficult to ascertain just what was Indian country at any given moment. Instead, the new law declared: "All that part of the United States west of the Mississippi, and not within the states of Missouri and Louisiana, or the

15. Circular to post commanders, July 12, 1834, Adjutant General's Office, Letters Sent, vol. 11, pp. 42–43, National Archives, Record Group 94.

16. 4 *United States Statutes* 729–35.

Territory of Arkansas, and also, that part of the United States east of the Mississippi river, and not within a state to which the Indian title has not been extinguished, for the purposes of this act, be taken and deemed to be the Indian country." The law accepted the removal of the Indians as an accomplished fact. The Indians in the southern states were no longer considered to be in Indian country, and in territories east of the Mississippi, as Indian titles were extinguished, the lands would cease automatically to be Indian country. West of the Mississippi the designation of Indian country could be changed only by legislative enactment.

The licensing system for trading with the Indians was continued, but it was strengthened by the grant of discretionary authority to the agents in issuing licenses and by the requirement that all trading be done at designated sites. The use of presidential authority to withhold goods from certain tribes and to revoke licenses to trade with them, which Cass and Clark had proposed as a means of bringing pressure to bear on the Indians when the public interest demanded it, became part of the new law. To protect the integrity of the Indian country, restrictions were made more explicit and fines were often increased. Other sections of previous laws were included—provisions for indemnification of thefts and damages, for bringing criminals to justice, for restricting the whiskey traffic, for use of military forces, and so on. The law in its final form differed little from the bill introduced by the committee.

In one respect the 1834 law marked a new direction in the relations of the United States with the tribes. The War Department in the past had been careful not to interfere in purely Indian squabbles. Although it deprecated the hostilities that frequently broke out between tribes, it had adopted a hands-off policy. In the law of 1834 the government committed itself to the opposite policy, as it had already done to some extent in particular treaties with the Indians. Hostilities had been stimulated by the closer contacts between tribes that resulted from the emigration of eastern Indians to the West, and these hostilities were an increasing cause of concern to frontiersmen and fur traders. Cass and Clark had argued in 1829 that "no well founded objection can be foreseen" to the president's use of military force to prevent or terminate hostilities between tribes. They based their proposal on the principle that "the relation of the government of the United States to the Indian tribes, is, in many respects, a paternal one, founded upon the strength and intelligence of the one party, and the weakness and ignorance of the other." They charged the Indians with wars "as ceaseless as they are causeless, originating they know not why, and terminating they care not when," arising often out of the desire of young men of a tribe to prove their valor. The government had a direct interest in suppressing such wars, both to protect American citizens who fell in the way of war parties and to preserve the Indians themselves. The law of 1834 gave the War Department statutory authorization, under the direction of the president, to use military force to end or prevent Indian wars.

A milestone in American Indian policy had been reached in 1834, and the United States looked to the future with an Indian policy that was considered reasonable and adequate. The two laws passed in 1834 summed up the experience of the past; they offered the well-grounded legal basis for the Indian service that had been so long in coming and embodied the principles for regulating contacts between whites and Indians that had proved necessary through the preceding decades. The continually changing boundaries of the Indian country that had kept Indian relations in a state of flux were now stabilized, it was hopefully assumed, by the removal of the Indians to the West. With a tempered enthusiasm the president and the secretary of war commended the nation for what had been accomplished and looked forward to less troubled times—although in 1834 the worst of the tribulations for the emigrating Indians were yet to come.[17]

PROPOSALS FOR AN INDIAN STATE

The third bill reported by the House Committee on Indian Affairs in 1834 was one for organizing a western territory to provide a political system for the emigrant Indians. It was one episode in continuing agitation on the part of well-meaning officials and reformers for a unified or confederated government for all the Indians in the West, an "Indian state" that might eventually become a regular part of the Union. The proposals reflected paternalistic white thinking, not Indian views, for many of the tribes rejected them.[18]

It is impossible to pinpoint an originator of the concept of the Indian state, for it had appeared in a variety of forms even before Indian removal became a national issue. An early proponent was the Reverend Jedidiah Morse, whose report in 1822 to Secretary of War Calhoun was full of innovative ideas. Morse thought in terms of a colony for the Indians in what is now Wisconsin and the Upper Peninsula of Michigan. "Let this territory be reserved exclusively for Indians," he wrote, "in which to make the pro-

17. The great influx of Indians into the West after the passage of the laws in 1834 soon indicated the need for changing some of the administrative arrangements, but change came slowly. See the recommendations made by T. Hartley Crawford to Joel R. Poinsett, December 30, 1839, *House Document* no. 103, 26–1, serial 365. The various changes are well described in Edward E. Hill, *The Office of Indian Affairs, 1824–1880: Historical Sketches* (New York: Clearwater Publishing Company, 1974).

18. A careful, heavily documented study of a century of such proposals is Annie Heloise Abel, "Proposals for an Indian State, 1778–1878," *Annual Report of the American Historical Association for the Year 1907*, 1: 87–104.

posed experiment of gathering into one body as many of the scattered and other Indians as choose to settle here, to be educated, become citizens, and in due time to be admitted to all the privileges common to other territories and States in the Union."[19] Official attention was turned in that direction by President Monroe. In his annual message of December 7, 1824, he spoke of the need to move the Indians to western lands, which would be divided into districts with "civil governments . . . . established in each," and in his special removal message of January 27, 1825, he called for "a well-digested plan for their government and civilization" and for providing in the Indians' western territory "a system of internal government which shall protect their property from invasion, and, by the regular program of improvement and civilization, prevent that degeneracy which has generally marked the transition from the one to the other state." He then spoke at greater length about the government:

> The digest of such a government, with the consent of the Indians, which should be endowed with sufficient power to meet all the objects contemplated—to connect the several tribes together in a bond of amity and preserve order in each; to prevent intrusions on their property; to teach them by regular instruction the arts of civilized life and make them a civilized people—is an object of very high importance. It is the powerful consideration which we have to offer to these tribes as an inducement to relinquish the lands on which they now reside and to remove to those which are designated. It is not doubted that this arrangement will present considerations of sufficient force to surmount all their prejudices in favor of the soil of their nativity, however strong they may be.[20]

Monroe did not specify the nature of the government, but Calhoun's report, on which he based his special message, seemed to look in the direction of ultimate statehood, for it spoke of a system "by which the Government, without destroying their independence, would gradually unite the several tribes under a simple but enlightened system of government, and laws formed on the principles of our own." Congress showed interest in these proposals to constitute a regular territory for the Indians in the West, and Senator Thomas Hart Benton introduced a bill, drafted by Calhoun, that passed the Senate but failed in the House of Representatives.[21]

The matter came up again in the John Quincy Adams administration,

19. Jedidiah Morse, *A Report to the Secretary of War of the United States on Indian Affairs* (New Haven: S. Converse, 1822), appendix, p. 314.

20. James D. Richardson, comp., *A Compilation of the Messages and Papers of the Presidents, 1789–1897*, 10 vols. (Washington: GPO, 1896–1899), 2: 261, 281–82.

21. Calhoun report of January 24, 1825, ASP:IA, 2: 544. The congressional action is traced in Abel, "Proposals for an Indian State," p. 92.

and Secretary of War James Barbour prepared a bill which recommended among other things the establishment of a territorial government for the Indians, to be placed in the hands of the president, subject to the control of Congress. He suggested "a legislative body, composed of Indians, (to be selected in the early stages by the President, and eventually to be elected by themselves,) as well for the purpose of enacting such laws as would be agreeable to themselves, as for the purpose of exciting their ambition."[22] Although Adams and his cabinet concurred, no legislation was forthcoming. But the idea was by no means dead.

It was kept alive, to a large extent, through the efforts of the Baptist missionary Isaac McCoy. Many whites were concerned simply with the removal of the Indians from the East, but McCoy was interested in what would happen to them in the West. He early developed an obsession for Indian "colonization," urging the formation of an Indian colony where the tribes could be protected from the onslaughts of whites and led to a new civilized and Christianized existence. This vision of an Indian Canaan included plans for some sort of unified territorial government, supplied at first in the form of a few simple laws and regulations by the United States. McCoy had an idea of a single national Indian identity that would somehow absorb the separate tribes, and he envisaged his colony developing into a state of the Union.[23]

Thomas L. McKenney from his post in the War Department's Indian Office encouraged the missionary. He wrote to the secretary of war early in 1829: "It is my decided opinion, which I respectfully submit, that nothing can preserve our Indians, but a plan well matured and suitably sustained, in which they shall be placed under a Government, of which they shall form part, and in a colonial relation to the United States. . . . In a colony, of course, the existing divisions among the Tribes would be superseded by a general Government over the whole; and by a parcelling out of the lands among the families. . . . It does appear to me that as a first step in this business of Colonization, a general arrangement should be made in regard to the lands and the limits—a Government simple in its form, but effective, ought to be extended over those who have already emigrated."[24] The Stokes Commission of 1832, moreover, in its detailed report on conditions facing

22. ASP:IA, 2: 648.

23. George A. Schultz, *An Indian Canaan: Isaac McCoy and the Vision of an Indian State* (Norman: University of Oklahoma Press, 1972), pp. 78–100; William Miles, "'Enamoured with Colonization': Isaac McCoy's Plea of Indian Reform," *Kansas Historical Quarterly* 38 (Autumn 1972): 268–86. The crystallization of McCoy's plan came in his *Remarks on the Practicability of Indian Reform, Embracing Their Colonization* (Boston, 1827; 2d ed., New York, 1829).

24. McKenney to Peter B. Porter, January 31, 1829, OIA LS, vol. 5, pp. 289–90 (M21, reel 5).

the Indians in the West, suggested the organization of the Indian territory "for the sole purpose of enforcing the laws of the United States, as far as they are applicable to the Indian country," with a governor, secretary, marshal, prosecuting attorney, and judiciary to be set up at Fort Leavenworth. In addition, the commissioners called for an annual grand council of the Indians.

> Here distant tribes may meet to settle difficulties, make peace, renew their friendship, and propose salutary regulations for their respective tribes. Here, too, improvements in the arts could be exhibited, and the savage tribes permitted to see and taste the fruits of civilization; here, also, the Government could communicate instruction and advice to her red children. It is not improbable that the tribes may, ere long, adopt some general articles of confederation for their own republic not inconsistent with the wishes of Government.[25]

The extensive reorganization of Indian affairs that came in 1834 included a fundamental concern for an Indian state. The House committee intended its third bill to meet "the obligations of the United States to the emigrant tribes"; it was "to provide for the establishment of the Western Territory and for the security and protection of the emigrant and other Indian tribes therein." The three bills were considered "parts of a system," and the committee urged that they all be passed together.[26]

The third bill established boundaries for an Indian territory west of Arkansas and Missouri that would be reserved forever for the Indian tribes. It pledged the faith of the United States to guarantee the land to the Indians and their descendants. Each of the tribes was to organize a government for its own internal affairs, and a general council would be established as a governing body for the voluntary confederation of the tribes envisaged by the bill. The president would appoint a governor, who would have a veto over acts of the council, power to reprieve offenders sentenced to capital punishment (with pardoning power reserved to the president), and considerable authority in settling difficulties between tribes, executing the laws, and employing the military forces of the United States. The confederation would send a delegate to Congress, and the committee expressed a hope of eventual admission of the territory as a state into the Union.

The three bills of the committee, although introduced in the House on May 20, 1834, were not debated until June 24, close to the adjournment of

25. Report of commission, February 10, 1834, *House Report* no. 474, 23–1, serial 263, pp. 100–101.

26. The bill for the western territory is in *House Report* no. 474, 23–1, serial 263, pp. 34–37; discussion of the bill in the committee report is on pp. 14–22.

Congress on June 30. The lateness of the session may well have enabled the first two bills to be pushed through without much change, but strong opposition arose to the bill on the western territory, the most radical of the three, which had no real precedents. After considerable and violent debate, it foundered in the House and was postponed to the next session and to ultimate failure.[27]

The bill was severely criticized. John Quincy Adams immediately assailed it on the basis of unconstitutionality. "What consitutional right had the United States to form a constitution and form of government for the Indians?" he demanded. "To erect a Territory to be inhabited exclusively by the Indians?" Samuel F. Vinton of Ohio spoke with much severity against almost every part of the bill, charging that it would establish an absolute military despotism in the West that would be in the hands of the president ruling through the appointed governor. Critics like Adams and Vinton were not to be hurried into accepting the bill and demanded that it be postponed until it could be given full consideration. Adams admitted that he had read neither the committee's report nor the bills before that very day and had not suspected that any such bill as this was included among them. The admission of an exclusively Indian state to the Union was a seminal idea, he said, and might set a dangerous precedent. Was the House prepared upon a half-hour's notice, he asked, "totally to change the relations of the Indian tribes to this country?" He objected, too, to the power given to the president by the bill—power that rightly belonged to Congress. William S. Archer of Virginia argued that the bill did not provide an Indian government but would "establish and enforce the Government of the United States within the sacred territory set apart as the exclusive abode" of the Indians. Millard Fillmore of New York doubted the propriety of the bill as a piece of legislation. To him it seemed more nearly an act of treaty making. Horace Everett of Vermont calmly and ably defended the report of the committee and the western territory bill, answering point by point the arguments of the critics, denying in large part that the criticisms had any validity when applied to the circumstances of the Indians and their present state of civilization. Everett was seconded by other members of the committee, but the demand to postpone consideration of the bill was too strong to withstand.[28] The bill was taken up again at the beginning of the second session of the Twenty-third Congress in December 1834, but once again Congress adjourned before action was taken.[29]

There were repeated attempts to resurrect the idea of a western Indian state. Isaac McCoy had not given up his dream, and he enlisted Senator

27. *House Journal*, 23–1, serial 253, pp. 645, 833, 834.

28. *Register of Debates in Congress*, 23d Congress, 1st session, pp. 4763–79 (June 25, 1834).

29. *House Journal*, 23–2, serial 270, pp. 65, 425, 430–33.

John Tipton of Ohio in his cause. The Senate considered a bill introduced by Tipton in 1836 that proposed "to unite the tribes as one people, and to allow them to meet annually by delegates to enact laws for the government of the whole, without infringing the rights of the tribes severally to manage their own internal affairs"—all subject to the approval of the president. The confederation would send a delegate to Congress. The argument of Tipton's Committee on Indian Affairs was couched in terms of the necessity of a system of government if the Indians were to improve their condition from a state of savagery to one of civilization.[30] In 1837 and again in 1839 the Senate passed bills to promote territorial organization of the Indians. But the House refused to approve the legislation, despite a strong push for the measure on the part of Everett and Caleb Cushing of Massachusetts.[31]

The executive branch of the government had endorsed the measure. President Jackson himself thought in terms of a confederacy of the southern Indians in the West, developing their own territorial government, which should be on a par with the territories of the whites and eventually take its place in the Union. He backed the suggestions of the commissioner of Indian affairs and the secretary of war for developing a confederated Indian government.[32]

In the end all the suggestions and recommendations and partial successes in Congress came to nothing. The arguments made against the bill in 1834 remained strong, and the House was unwilling to approve such an innovative measure as an Indian state in the Union. But even if the paternal plans for a regulated confederated government in the western territory

30. *Senate Report* no. 246, 24–1, serial 281. The whole report is an excellent statement of the McCoy proposal for removal and organization of the Indians west of Arkansas and Missouri.

31. Abel, "Proposals for an Indian State," pp. 97–98; Schultz, *Indian Canaan*, pp. 177–81, 188–95. To promote his vision of the territorial organization and development of Indians in the West, McCoy published four issues of *The Annual Register of Indian Affairs within the Indian (or Western) Territory,* 1835–1838. See the 1837 issue, pp. 52–56, for one set of arguments for territorial government. McCoy declared: "Most of the tribes within the Territory have expressed a desire to become united in one civil compact, and to be governed by laws similar to those of the United States." In 1844 the American Indian Mission Association, of which McCoy was secretary, submitted memorials to Congress again urging the establishment of a territory for Indians. *Senate Document* no. 272, 28–1, serial 434; *Senate Document* no. 76, 28–2, serial 451.

32. See Jackson to John Coffee, February 19, 1832, *Correspondence of Andrew Jackson,* ed. John Spencer Bassett, 6 vols. (Washington: Carnegie Institution of Washington, 1926–1935), 4: 406; message of Jackson, December 5, 1836, Israel, *State of the Union Messages,* 1: 465–66. Lengthy discussion of the matter of an Indian state is in CIA report, 1836, serial 297, pp. 385–95; see also CIA Report, 1837, serial 321, p. 566, and "Report of Mr. McCoy Relative to a Government for the Western Territory," ibid., pp. 618–24.

had passed congressional barriers, it is not likely that such an organization could have been set up effectively, for strong Indian groups were also vehemently opposed. If to many whites a unified Indian state seemed wise and feasible, to the Indians it violated tribal nationalism. The Five Civilized Tribes, the most politically sophisticated of the emigrated Indians, upon whom any successful confederated government would have had to depend, refused to consider such a move. Though they met in occasional intertribal councils, they held fast to their own tribal identities and independent governments, and their removal treaties gave a legal foundation to their position. The tribes were to have (as the Choctaw treaty, for example, provided) "the jurisdiction and government of all the persons and property that may be within their limits west, so that no Territory or State shall ever have a right to pass laws for the government of the Choctaw Nation of Red People and their descendants."[33] These nations established viable governments of their own, which they steadfastly protected against federal encroachment.

When a Cherokee delegation in 1838 expressed fears that a form of government might be imposed upon the Cherokees in the West that they were not prepared for and did not want, Secretary of War Poinsett assured them that "no form of government will be imposed upon the Cherokees without the consent of the whole nation, given in council, nor shall their country be erected into a territory without such previous concurrence." As the Choctaw delegate Peter Pitchlynn insisted in 1849, when the territorial idea surfaced again, the scheme was "fruitful of evil, and only evil, to all the Indian tribes." It was, he said, "beautiful in theory, but in practice, would be destructive to all the long cherished hopes of the friends of the red men, as it would introduce discord, dissensions, and strife among them," and he pointed to differences in land tenure, levels of civilization, language, and laws and customs.[34]

The very treaties on which the Indians depended for their independence, of course, provided opening wedges for the interposition of United States government action or influence. Laws passed by the Choctaw national council, for example, were to be "not inconsistent with the Constitution, Treaties, and Laws of the United States," and the prohibition on outside legislation excepted such laws "as may, and which have been en-

---

33. Kappler, p. 311; see also similar provision in Creek treaty of 1832, ibid., p. 343, and Cherokee treaty of 1835, ibid., p. 442.

34. Poinsett to John Ross and others, May 18, 1838, *House Document* no. 376, 25–2, serial 330, p. 3; "Remonstrance of Col. Peter Pitchlynn, Choctaw Delegate, against the passage of the bill to unite under one government the several Indian tribes west of the Mississippi river," January 20, 1849, *House Miscellaneous Document* no. 35, 30–2, serial 544. See also the memorial of Creek and Choctaw delegations, April 26, 1838, *Senate Document* no. 407, 25–2, serial 318.

acted by Congress, to the extent that Congress under the Constitution are required to exercise a legislation over Indian Affairs." The treaty, furthermore, obligated the United States "to protect the Choctaws from domestic strife and from foreign enemies."[35] But, in fact, no Indian territorial government or Indian state was set up.

ANNUITIES AND LIQUOR REGULATION

The settlement of the Indians in the Indian country west of the Mississippi and the new legislation organizing the Indian department did not eliminate all problems in Indian-white relations. The Indians, unfortunately, were not sequestered from contact with evil men. Traders under license were permitted in the Indian country, and they came to the emigrant Indians principally to provide goods in return for annuity money. Concern for the Indians in the 1840s included a critical attack upon the existing system of annuity payments and strenuous efforts to change the system.[36]

Commissioner of Indian Affairs T. Hartley Crawford, a state legislator and representative from Pennsylvania who took office in October 1838, complained in 1841: "The recipients of money are rarely more than conduit pipes to convey it into the pockets of their traders."[37] The annuities aggravated the very conditions that the Indian Office was trying to correct. So long as the Indians were assured of receiving their annual stipend, they did not exert themselves to earn a living, thus defeating the efforts of re formers to turn them into hard-working farmers. Much of the annuity money was spent for worthless goods or trivial objects, so that the bounty of the government was misappropriated. The annuity problem, furthermore, was closely tied to the problem of intemperance among the Indians, for the money was easily drained off into the pockets of whiskey vendors.[38]

The attack on the problem was made on several fronts, all aimed at directing the annuities toward the benefit of the Indians. A change was demanded, first, in the method of payment. The act of 1834 that reorganized the Indian department provided for payment to the chiefs, and the funds often did not reach the commonalty but were siphoned off by the chiefs and their friends for purposes that did not necessarily benefit the tribe as a whole. To correct this deficiency, Congress on March 3, 1847, granted dis-

35. Kappler, p. 311.

36. This section is based on Francis Paul Prucha, "American Indian Policy in the 1840s: Visions of Reform," in John G. Clark, ed., *The Frontier Challenge: Responses to the Trans-Mississippi West* (Lawrence: University Press of Kansas, 1971), pp. 93–101.

37. CIA Report, 1841, serial 401, pp. 238–39.

38. See, for example, the report of James Clarke, Iowa Superintendency, October 2, 1846, CIA Report, 1846, serial 493, p. 243.

cretion to the president or the secretary of war to direct that the annuities, instead of being paid to the chiefs, be divided and paid to the heads of families and other individuals entitled to participate, or, with the consent of the tribe, that they be applied to other means of promoting the happiness and prosperity of the Indians. The new law, in addition, struck boldly at the liquor problem. No annuities could be paid to Indians while they were under the influence of intoxicating liquor or while there was reason for the paying officers to believe that liquor was within convenient reach. The chiefs, too, were to pledge themselves to use all their influence to prevent the introduction and sale of liquor in their country. Finally, to protect the Indians from signing away their annuities ahead of time, the law provided that contracts made by Indians for the payment of money or goods would be null and void.[39]

The War Department immediately took advantage of the discretionary authority and sent instructions to superintendents and agents to pay the annuities in all cases to the heads of families and other individuals entitled to them.[40] Although there were complaints from parties adversely affected by the new policy, the Indian Office was well pleased. William Medill, Crawford's successor, declared in 1848, "in the whole course of our Indian policy, there has never been a measure productive of better moral effects."[41] Medill also aimed to cut down the Indian profligacy with annuity payments by dividing the annuities and paying them semi-annually and by encouraging the Indians to use them for worthwhile purposes that would lead to their civilization. The goal was always the same: "The less an Indian's expectations and resources from the chase, and from the government in the shape of money annuities," Medill said, "the more readily can he be induced to give up his idle, dissolute, and savage habits, and to resort to labor for a maintenance; and thus commence the transition from a state of barbarism and moral depression, to one of civilization and moral elevation."[42]

The influence of the traders upon the Indians and their catering to the

39. 9 *United States Statutes* 203–4.
40. William Medill to Thomas H. Harvey, August 30, 1847, CIA Report, 1847, serial 503, p. 756.
41. CIA Report, 1848, serial 537, p. 400. For the reaction of Thomas H. Harvey to the new legislation, see his report of October 29, 1847, CIA Report, 1847, serial 503, pp. 832–41. Commissioner Luke Lea in 1850, although he conceded "the general wisdom and justice of the policy," argued that it tended to reduce the position of the chiefs, through whom the government dealt with the tribes. CIA Report, 1850, serial 587, pp. 44–45.
42. CIA Report, 1847, serial 503, p. 746; CIA Report, 1848, serial 537, pp. 393–94, 400. See, however, the remarks of D. D. Mitchell, superintendent of Indian affairs at St. Louis, October 13, 1849, in which he criticized the semi-annual payment for small tribes. CIA Report, 1849, serial 570, p. 1068.

Indians' tastes for liquor and useless goods led to a proposal for a new "factory system." Commissioner Crawford broached the subject in his report of 1840. Emphatically asserting that he did not propose a return to the old factory system, which had been "rightly abolished," Crawford nevertheless called its principle valuable. Because of the increased annual disbursements to the Indian tribes, the improved facilities for transportation, the greater need of the Indians for protection as they became surrounded by white population, and the growing dependency of the Indians upon payments, he urged an alternative to the existing system that would be more beneficial to the Indians. He outlined his plan in some detail:

> I would make a small establishment of goods, suitable to Indian wants, according to their location, at each agency. I would not allow these goods to be sold to any one except Indians entitled to a participation in the cash annuities, and I would limit the purchases to their proportion of the annuity; so that the Government would, instead of paying money to be laid out in whiskey and beads, or applied to the payment of goods at two prices bought from others, meet the Indians to settle their accounts, and satisfy them that they received, in articles of comfort or necessity, the annuity due them for the year, at *cost*, including transportation. The Indians would be immensely benefited; and the expense would not be greater than that of the money-payments now almost uselessly made them.

Under such a system Crawford believed that the government Indian agents would gain the position of importance with the Indians that they ought to have. The Indians would look to the government as its best friend, for from it would come the goods they needed.[43]

In subsequent years Crawford repeated and strengthened his original recommendation. The House Committee on Indian Affairs took up the proposal in 1844 and reported a bill to authorize the furnishing of goods and provisions by the War Department, but the action died in the House. Crawford did not give up. His plan, he asserted, would increase the comfort of the Indians; the comfort in turn would be a "leading string . . . to conduct them into the walks of civilization," and general improvement of the Indians would soon be seen everywhere.[44] But when Crawford left office, his scheme died. It was too much to ask in an age of private enterprise that the government go back into the Indian trade. Control of the evils of the trade reverted to the old attempt to enforce the licensing system that had been part of the traditional setup.

43. CIA Report, 1840, serial 375, pp. 240–41.
44. CIA Report, 1842, serial 413, pp. 382–83; CIA Report, 1843, serial 431, p. 266; CIA Report, 1844, serial 449, pp. 312–13; *House Journal*, 28–1, serial 438, p. 1112.

A strong movement in that direction came in 1847, under the direction of Medill and Secretary of War W. L. Marcy. Although existing previous laws and regulations called for a careful surveillance of the traders and the elimination of those deemed unfit for dealing with the Indians, Medill found that lax enforcement had allowed licenses to be given to many persons who should never have been permitted to go into the Indian country. He insisted that licenses should be granted to "none but persons of proper character, who will deal fairly, and cooperate with the government in its measures for meliorating the condition of the Indians." He therefore drew up new and tighter regulations, which were promulgated by the War Department. The secretary of war reported in 1848 that the new regulations and the rigid supervision over the conduct of traders had put an end to many evils and abuses.[45]

All problems or obstacles in improving the Indians' condition seemed to stem from or to be aggravated by intemperance. The cupidity of white men, who were eager to sell vile concoctions to Indians at exorbitant prices, could not be struck at directly, and restrictions on the sale of liquor to Indians were impossible to enforce. A primary justification for removing the Indians to the West had been to place them in a home free from temptations. In an age of reform, when many considered excessive drinking an important factor in the problems of delinquency and dependency among the general public, temperance was to be one of the means that would open up "the fountains of hope" for Indians in the new lands.[46]

But removal alone did not prevent intemperance among the Indians. The whiskey vendors were if anything more virulent on the western frontier than in the settled regions of the East, and the means of stopping their nefarious commerce were less effective. In 1843 Crawford reported on the strenuous and unremitting exertions of the Indian department to prevent the use of ardent spirits by the Indians, describing attempts by the territories of Iowa and Wisconsin to prevent the trade. But his outlook was pessimistic that any final solution would come from legal enactments. His hope lay with the efforts of the tribes themselves, and he noted with pleasure that temperance societies had been organized in several of the tribes and that some tribes had passed laws of their own to put down the sale and use of whiskey.[47]

45. CIA Report, 1847, serial 503, pp. 750–51. The "Regulations Concerning the Granting of Licenses to Trade with the Indians," November 9, 1847, and the forms of licenses and bonds to be used are printed ibid., pp. 760–64. See also report of W. L. Marcy, December 1, 1848, *House Executive Document* no. 1, 30–2, serial 537, pp. 83–84.

46. CIA Report, 1840, serial 375, pp. 233–34. The temperance crusade is discussed in Alice Felt Tyler, *Freedom's Ferment: Phases of American Social History to 1860* (Minneapolis: University of Minnesota Press, 1944), pp. 308–50.

47. CIA Report, 1843, serial 431, pp. 270–71.

Crawford professed to see some signs of success. He and others worked diligently to promote temperance through education, but they did not neglect the frontal attack on the liquor trade that had long been a staple of American Indian policy. The law of 1832 creating the commissioner of Indian affairs had absolutely prohibited the introduction of liquor into the Indian country, and the trade and intercourse law of 1834 contained detailed provisions for prosecuting violators. But this legislation had not been completely successful, and the secretaries of war in 1843 and 1845 called for more.[48]

Finally, on March 3, 1847, Congress acted. In addition to the fines set by the act of 1834, the new law provided up to two years' imprisonment for anyone who sold or disposed of liquor to an Indian in the Indian country, and up to one year's imprisonment for anyone who introduced liquor, excepting such supplies as might be required for the officers and troops of the army. In all cases arising under the law, Indians were to be competent witnesses. The commissioner of Indian affairs and the secretary of war were not satisfied to let the law serve by itself, however. New regulations, dated April 13, 1847, were promulgated by the War Department, which called attention to the provisions of the new law and the pertinent sections of the law of 1834, then spelled out in detail just what duties were imposed by these laws upon the military officers and the Indian agents—who were enjoined to be vigilant in executing their duties and were threatened with removal from office if they did not succeed.[49]

Federal laws and regulations to control the liquor traffic had effect only within the Indian country and not in the adjoining states. In an attempt to prevent the Indians from crossing the line to obtain liquor, Secretary of War Marcy wrote a strong letter on July 14, 1847, to the governors of Missouri, Arkansas, and Iowa, invoking their aid. The stringent laws of Congress, he pointed out, failed to reach the most prolific source of the ills, which lay within the limits of the nearby states. He described the ills resulting from the trade and noted that the insecurity of frontier whites was often due to Indian retaliation for such injuries.[50]

The efforts to prevent whiskey from reaching the Indians met with limited success. But all the laws of Congress and the strenuous efforts of the

48. Report of J. M. Porter, November 30, 1843, *Senate Document* no. 1, 28–1, serial 431, p. 59; report of W. L. Marcy, November 29, 1845, *Senate Document* no. 1, 29–1, serial 470, p. 205. A thorough discussion of the evils of the liquor traffic among the Indians is Otto F. Frederikson, *The Liquor Question among the Indian Tribes in Kansas, 1804–1881* (Lawrence, Kansas, 1932).

49. 9 *United States Statutes* 203; regulations of April 13, 1847, CIA Report, 1847, serial 503, pp. 764–66.

50. Marcy to governors of Missouri, Arkansas, and Iowa, July 14, 1847, CIA Report, 1847, serial 503, pp. 767–69.

Indian agents and military officers on the frontier to enforce them did not end drunkenness. The frontier was too extensive and the profits to whiskey dealers too large to make complete prohibition possible. More reliance was urged upon a system of rewards and punishments operating directly on the Indians themselves, but even these were largely ineffective.[51] Abuse of liquor remained an abiding plague in Indian affairs.

51. CIA Report, 1848, serial 537, p. 402; CIA Report, 1849, serial 570, p. 939; report of W. L. Marcy, December 1, 1848, *House Executive Document* no. 1, 30–2, serial 537, pp. 83–84. See also Frederikson, *Liquor Question*, pp. 55–64, regarding the act of 1847 and its effect.

PART THREE

American Expansion
and the
Reservation System

The removal of the Indians from east of the Mississippi and their settlement beyond Arkansas and Missouri was accomplished by mid-century. The Five Civilized Tribes maintained their national identity in the Indian Territory and at varying rates overcame the trauma of their uprooting and emigration. The smaller tribes along the Missouri border were encouraged by government officials and Christian missionaries to strive for the good life, cultivating farms, learning mechanical arts, and educating their children in white schools. The Indians and the whites were generally at peace.

Just when the education and civilization of the border tribes seemed to be bearing such good fruit, however, dramatic events in the 1840s overturned the premises upon which American Indian policy had been based. The formal removal program had followed the earlier policy, more or less unplanned, of simply moving the Indians west out of the way of advancing white settlement. The definite line separating the Indian country from white lands, which had been defined in the intercourse law of 1796, had been gradually pushed westward, as the Indian tribes ceded land in exchange for annuities and for newly designated and newly guaranteed lands to the west. Some thought that the removals of the 1830s had culminated this process, and that in the "Western Territory" beyond Arkansas, Missouri, and Iowa the removed Indians would be finally secure behind a permanent line running from the Red River north and northeast to Lake Superior. Then, suddenly, before the end of the 1840s the concept of such a line was shattered, and it was not long before the barrier itself was physically destroyed. The expansion of the United States that in three short years added Texas (1845), the Oregon country (1846), and California and the rest of the Mexican Cession (1848), radically changed the relationship between the United States and the Indians.

The government now came face to face with new groups of Indians. There were the nomadic buffalo Indians of the northern and southern plains—Sioux, Cheyennes, Arapahos, Crows, Kiowas, Comanches, and Pawnees—warlike and untamed and uninterested in transforming themselves into English-speaking farmers. There were Indians like the Utes, Shoshonis, and Paiutes, subsisting at minimal levels in the mountains and in the wastelands of the Great Basin. There were the oasis Indians of the Southwest with their age-old patterns of life in the pueblos, warlike Apaches and Navajos raiding their peaceful Indian neighbors and the Mexican settlements, and numerous bands of California Indians, some affected by the Spanish mission experience but others living still undisturbed in the mountains. To the north were the Indians of the Pacific Northwest, fishing along the coast and hunting in the intermountain basins. These tribes were not totally unknown, of course, for early explorers had encountered and observed them; traders had met them on the Pacific coast, in the Rocky Mountains, and along the Santa Fe Trail; and some military reconnaissance expeditions had come upon Indian warriors.[1]

In Texas the white population that had created the Republic of Texas in 1836 had already challenged Indian occupation of the region. With the acquisition of the Oregon country and the Mexican Cession, American population in those areas swelled greatly, and the aboriginal inhabitants were increasingly pressed upon by aggressive pioneers who had scant concern for Indian rights of person or property. And to get to the riches of the Pacific coastal regions, emigrants cut across the hunting grounds of the plains Indians. The Indian country was invaded, crossed and crisscrossed, and it was no longer possible to solve the question of the Indians' destiny by the convenient scheme of repeated removal. The commissioner of Indian affairs in 1856 looked into the future with considerable perception. He saw railroads moving into the great plains as far as good lands extended and at the same time other railroads moving east from the Pacific coast settlements, followed in both cases by an active white population that would open farms and build cities.

> When that time arrives, and it is at our very doors, ten years, if our
> country is favored with peace and prosperity, will witness the most of

---

1. These military encounters are described in Francis Paul Prucha, *The Sword of the Republic: The United States Army on the Frontier, 1783–1846* (New York: Macmillan Company, 1969); see especially chaps. 12 and 18.

it; where will be the habitation and what the condition of the rapidly wasting Indian tribes of the plains, the prairies, and of our new States and Territories?

As sure as these great physical changes are impending, so sure will these poor denizens of the forest be blotted out of existence, and their dust be trampled under the foot of rapidly advancing civilization, unless our great nation shall generously determine that the necessary provision shall at once be made, and appropriate steps be taken to designate suitable tracts or reservations of land, in proper localities, for permanent homes for, and provide the means to colonize, them thereon.[2]

So reservations—in most cases small parcels of land "reserved" out of the original holdings of the tribes or bands—developed as an alternative to the extinction of the Indians.[3] The reservations, however, were thought of as a temporary expedient, for whites dealing officially with the Indians in the 1850s all accepted the idea that the nation within its new continental limits would become the abode of enterprising and prosperous American citizens. They had no notion of a pluralistic society or a divided land occupied in part by European immigrants and their descendants and in part by American Indians adhering to their own customs. The goal was to ease the immediate conflicts between the two cultures and to prevent, as far as it was in their power to do so, the utter destruction of the weaker party. It was for this end that segregation on reservations and application of the intercourse laws were considered so essential for Texas, Utah, New Mexico, California, and the Pacific Northwest and that revision of the intercourse laws was incessantly called for to make them more applicable to the new conditions. But beyond protection and preservation there was the ultimate goal of transformation: to induce the Indians all to become cultivators of the soil, to adopt the white man's language, customs, and religion, and, finally, to be self-supporting citizens of the commonwealth, a goal that all but a few believed was entirely practicable if only the proper means were applied. Agriculture, domestic and mechanical arts, English education, Christianity, and individual property (land allotted in severalty) were the elements of the civilization program that was to be the future of the Indians.

The policy makers were firm in their views of what constituted humanitarian concern and benevolence for their Indian charges. Having judged the civilization programs among the Five Civilized Tribes and the border Indians as marked with signs of ultimate success, they saw no reason why the same

2. CIA Report, 1856, serial 875, p. 574.

3. Robert A. Trennert, Jr., *Alternative to Extinction: Federal Indian Policy and the Beginnings of the Reservation System, 1846–51* (Philadelphia: Temple University Press, 1975), covers only a half-dozen years and the region east of the Rockies, but the main title of the book can be applied much more broadly.

causes would not produce the same effects among the new tribes that had fallen under United States jurisdiction.

The United States government had only one pattern for dealing with Indians. It held that Indians retained title to the lands they occupied (although there was considerable question whether this principle applied to the Indians and land that came to the United States from Mexico) and that these titles could be extinguished only by treaties, which would specify the lands ceded and the payment to be made for them. Yet the treaties with most of the tribes with whom the government now came into contact, following a precedent already well established in the East, were not the result of negotiations between two sovereign and independent powers. They were instead a convenient and accepted vehicle for accomplishing what United States officials wanted to do under circumstances that were frequently difficult. By treaty the government could provide Indian segregation on small reservations, throwing open the rest of the territory to white settlement and exploitation. On the reservations the restrictions and protection of the intercourse laws could be applied to restrain if not prevent deleterious contacts between the two races and to protect the remaining rights of the Indians. By treaty, too, the United States sought to provide the means for transforming the life of the Indians, for the negotiations were used to gain the acquiescence, at least nominal, of the Indians to an agricultural existence and "moral improvement and education."

The system was applied with indifferent success. In many cases the treaty procedure came too late, after the destruction of the Indians was already far advanced, and the federal government was inexcusably slow in looking after Indian affairs in the remote regions of the Far West. The single pattern was applied with little appreciation of the varying Indian cultures it was supposed to replace, and on occasion the treaties signed in the field were not ratified by the Senate, leaving the status of the Indians and their lands in a sort of limbo. Often, application of the treaty provisions was possible only after resisting Indians had been overwhelmed and crushed by military force.

The men in the Indian service whose lot it was to seek solutions for the new Indian problems facing the nation after the territorial acquisitions of the 1840s took faltering steps, and Congress was no more sure-footed. But out of it all developed a reservation system that became a staple of United States Indian policy for the future.

CHAPTER 12

The Indian Office:
Men and Policies

Department of the Interior. Commissioners

of the 1850s. An Expanded Indian Department.

Perennial Problems: Annuities and Liquor.

The Challenge of Scientific Racism.

The changed relations with the Indians that came with American expansion to the Pacific were accompanied by changes in the administration of Indian policy, for new conditions called for corresponding responses. Yet there were constants. Problems that had plagued the conduct of Indian affairs in the East, then in mid-America, reappeared in relations with the far western tribes. And the paternalistic concern for the transformation of the Indians continued, now applied to the newly contacted Indian groups.

DEPARTMENT OF THE INTERIOR

In 1849 Indian affairs were transferred from the War Department, which had been responsible for them since the beginning of the nation, to a newly created executive department called the Department of the Interior. Congress, in organizing the government after the Constitution had been adopted, had put Indian relations into the charge of the War Department with hardly a second thought, for the Revolutionary War had placed the Indians for the most part on the side of the British, and contact with them had been as adversaries. Henry Knox, who had been in charge of the War Department under the Articles of Confederation, continued in that position in Washington's cabinet, so there was a welcome continuity in dealing with the Indians. The seemingly interminable border conflicts between encroaching frontiersmen and resisting Indians, and the serious outbreaks of war in the Old Northwest in the 1790s and both north and south during the War of 1812 made it reasonable to keep Indian affairs under the secretary of war—even though the administration of them (through superintendents, agents, and factors) was a civilian operation. The officials of the Indian department were civilian employees of the War Department, not military men, except in rare temporary cases.

As circumstances changed and the Indians were no longer looked upon primarily as military foes, the logical reasons for having the secretary of war direct Indian affairs disappeared. What held the management of the Indians within the War Department was bureaucratic inertia and strong congressional disinclination to increase the size of the executive branch of the government by creating a new department and a new cabinet officer.

Agitation for an "interior" department began long before mid-century. Even when the national government was established there were proposals for a secretary of domestic affairs to balance a secretary of foreign affairs, but the decision at the time was for a Department of State, responsible for both domestic and foreign matters. The secretary of state, for example, was charged with management of the territories. Land business, because sale of the public domain was an essential element in the financial well-being of the nation, was appropriately placed under the secretary of the treasury. The rapid growth of the nation, however, soon put considerable stress on the national administrative organization, and by 1815 serious weaknesses appeared. Repeated moves were made to relieve the burdens of the existing departments by shifting offices that did not strictly pertain to them into some sort of "home department." All of the plans called for including Indian affairs within the new department.[1]

In light of the strong arguments for a new department, coming from successive presidents and from Congress itself, it is difficult to explain the delay and postponement over a period of more than a quarter-century. Some argued that the nation had gotten along without an interior department and opposed tampering with the structure. More important, perhaps, was the republican fear of gradual and imperceptible aggrandizement of federal power over domestic matters. It continued to be obvious, nevertheless, that it was incongruous to have the Patent Office in the State Department, the management of public lands under the Treasury, and—in an era when serious Indian wars were considered a thing of the past—Indian affairs in the War Department.

The eventual success in gaining a new department came largely as a result of America's expansion in the 1840s, the acquisition of the Oregon

1. For the history of agitation for an interior or home department, see Henry Barrett Learned, "The Establishment of the Secretaryship of the Interior," *American Historical Review* 16 (July 1911): 751–73.

Removal and Concentration

18. Andrew Jackson as the Great Father

The removal policy that forced the emigration of eastern Indians to regions west of the Mississippi is closely associated with President Andrew Jackson, for he vigorously pursued the policy. Jackson, who was severely criticized by opponents of removal, thought he was acting in a paternal fashion for the Indians' best interests. This contemporary cartoon shows the president and his "children."

19. John Ross

As principal chief of the Cherokee Nation, John Ross firmly opposed all removal measures of the federal government. Although only one-eighth Cherokee by blood, Ross won the support of a majority of the nation because of his staunch defense of Cherokee rights. This portrait of 1848 is by John Neagle.

20. Major Ridge

A group of Cherokees led by Major Ridge, his son John Ridge, and his nephew Elias Boudinot decided to accept removal as the only means to preserve the Cherokee Nation. In December 1835 the Ridge party signed the Treaty of New Echota, which provided for the removal of the whole nation.

The removal of the Indians caused a great public debate, and religious leaders were found on both sides. Jeremiah Evarts, secretary of the American Board of Commissioners for Foreign Missions, led the attack on the removal policy, charging that to carry it out against the rights and wishes of the Indians would be a great national sin. Isaac McCoy, a Baptist missionary, on the other hand, spent much of his life promoting the movement and colonization of the eastern Indians in the West.

21. Jeremiah Evarts

22. Isaac McCoy

23. Black Hawk, Sac Chief

The removal of Indians from the region north of the Ohio River proceeded without serious resistance. The one exception was the Black Hawk War of 1832. Black Hawk refused to give up his ancestral lands in Illinois east of the Mississippi, and when troops were sent to evict him, the war began. This painting by George Catlin catches the nobility and defiant spirit of the chief.

24. Osceola, Seminole

The Second Seminole War, 1835–1842, was a long-drawn conflict with few heroes. Osceola, presented in this portrait by George Catlin, was a leader in the Seminole resistance to removal. He was captured when he came in to parley in 1837 and died the next year while imprisoned at Fort Marion.

The "permanent Indian frontier" west of Missouri and Iowa was broken by emigrants moving across the plains to the Pacific coast. One of the strongest advocates of legally opening the plains to white settlement was Senator Stephen A. Douglas of Illinois, who wanted to tie the nation together by transcontinental railroads.

The invasion of California by Americans after the discovery of gold in 1848 was a disaster for the California Indians, who were no match for the aggressive whites. One man who tried to protect the Indians was Edward Fitzgerald Beale, who as special agent (1852–1854) sought to establish reservations for them in a form reminiscent of the old Spanish missions.

25. Stephen A. Douglas

26. Edward Fitzgerald Beale

Treaties with Indians in the Pacific
Northwest in order to concentrate them
on reduced reservations were the work
largely of Isaac I. Stevens, governor of
Washington Territory. The treaty council of Stevens with the Flathead Indians
in July 1855 was sketched by Gusta-
vus Sohon.

27. Isaac I. Stevens

28. Flathead Treaty Council

Country and the Mexican Cession, which at a stroke greatly increased the "interior" concerns of the United States. The final move came from Robert J. Walker, Polk's secretary of the treasury, who for four years had experienced firsthand the overburdening of the existing departments. Walker proposed a new officer "to be called the Secretary of the Interior, inasmuch as his duties would be connected with those branches of the public service . . . associated with our domestic affairs." In the new establishment would repose the General Land Office taken from the Treasury Department, the Patent Office taken from the State Department, and the Pension Office and the Indian Office taken from the War Department. Walker argued most strongly in regard to the General Land Office, which with the increased public domain in California, Oregon, and New Mexico greatly increased the duties of the secretary of the treasury, and in regard to Indian matters. Of the latter he wrote:

> The duties now performed by the Commissioner of Indian Affairs are most numerous and important and must be vastly increased with the great number of tribes scattered over Texas, Oregon, New Mexico, and California, and with the interesting progress of so many of the tribes in Christianity, knowledge, and civilization. These duties do not necessarily appertain to war, but to peace, and to our domestic relations with those tribes. . . .
>
> This most important bureau, then, should be detached from the War Department, with which it has no necessary connexion.[2]

Walker prepared a bill, introduced on February 12, 1849, by Representative Samuel F. Vinton for the House Committee on Ways and Means. After small debate the measure passed the House by a considerable margin; the only substantial change was the substitution of Home Department for Department of the Interior in the title of the bill. The debate in the Senate was more pointed, for James M. Mason of Virginia and John C. Calhoun of South Carolina expressed the fear that the bill would tend to increase the powers of the federal government not specifically delegated to it by the Constitution. Other senators pointed out that the bill was adding no new duties but was merely giving better organization to those that already existed, and the bill passed the Senate by a vote of thirty-one to twenty-five. President Polk signed it on March 3, 1849, just as the Thirtieth Congress was ending and his Democratic administration was giving way to President Zachary Taylor and the Whigs.[3]

2. Report of R. J. Walker, December 9, 1848, *House Executive Document* no. 7, 30–2, serial 538, pp. 36–37.

3. *Congressional Globe*, 30th Congress, 2d session, pp. 514–18, 543–44, 669–80. Most of the debate concerned the duties of the secretary of the treasury and the need to divide them. The law is in 9 *United States Statutes* 395–97.

The law came to be because of the administrative burdens upon existing departments, especially the Treasury Department, and the new department was put together out of four parts that were sloughed off by others and did not fit together logically except that they all dealt with domestic matters. It was thus by chance, not by some sinister design, that the General Land Office, concerned with the disposal of the public domain in the interest of white settlers, and the Indian Office, responsible for protecting Indian rights to their land, came to be conflicting responsibilities of the same executive officer. The relation of the two responsibilities, however, was not lost on the sponsors of the bill, for Vinton saw a "peculiar fitness" in the arrangement, since "the business of the one was intimately interwoven with that of the other." Senator Jefferson Davis of Mississippi, who argued strongly for the bill, spoke of the incongruity of keeping the Indian bureau in the War Department. "When our intercourse with the Indian tribes was held under the protection of troops," he said, "and wars and rumors of wars came annually with the coming of grass, it was proper to place Indian relations under the War Department. Happily for them, honorably for us, the case has greatly changed, and is, I hope, before a distant day, to assume a character consonant with the relations of guardian and ward, which have been claimed by us as those existing between our Government and the Indian tribes. . . . War being the exception, peace the ordinary condition, the policy should be for the latter, not the former condition."[4]

There was no objection from the War Department about giving up its control of Indian affairs; no doubt the secretary was happy to be rid of the onerous duty. For the Indian Office, the new law of itself did not create any great problems. The work had been a civilian operation reporting to the secretary of war; it continued as it was, but reported now to the secretary of the interior. The lack of concern evidenced is remarkable in light of the excessive agitation that arose in the 1860s and 1870s about transfer of the Indian Office back to the War Department. The end of the 1840s was one of those times of rare tranquility on the frontier, when it was easy to believe that Indian wars were a thing of the past and that Indians were no longer a military matter. There seems to have been no sense of vested interests that sometimes hinder administrative changes.

When Indian disturbances broke out again in the 1850s, responsible people began to question whether military control of the whole Indian service might not be wise. In 1860, both Secretary of War John B. Floyd and Secretary of the Interior Jacob Thompson responded affirmatively to a Senate resolution asking about the expediency of moving Indian affairs back to

4. *Congressional Globe*, 30th Congress, 2d session, pp. 514, 678.

the War Department. As Thompson observed, the War Department had superior facilities for controlling and managing "the wild, roving, and turbulent tribes of the interior, who constitute the great majority of the Indians." The secretary, no doubt, would have welcomed handing on Indian problems to someone else, but a transfer bill introduced in May 1860 quickly died.[5]

COMMISSIONERS OF THE 1850S

If one counts Orlando Brown, the appointee of the Whig administration and the first commissioner of Indian affairs under the Department of the Interior, there were six commissioners in the dozen years during which the reservation system was developed in response to the problems created by American expansion. There was a rapid turnover of the high officers charged with managing Indian affairs as politicians of various stripes—generally without any special experience with Indians—stepped into the office amid the challenges from the expanded West. Yet a strong and consistent reservation policy developed to which the commissioners, whatever their background, adhered.

Brown's tenure was short. A leading Whig in Kentucky, a protégé of John Crittenden, and a man of literary and political talents, Brown had a disappointing career as commissioner. He had hoped for a cabinet post when Taylor became president and accepted the next highest opening, the Indian Office, only to find that Secretary of the Interior Thomas Ewing dominated the scene, both in handling Indian affairs and in handing out the patronage that the new department made available for hungry Whig office seekers. His humanitarian views about the progress of the emigrated Indians and his vision of a great social and moral revolution among them led him to believe that a like application of methods to the Indians in the newly acquired territories would produce like results. He accepted the framework for such a program from his predecessors—to concentrate the Indians in smaller areas in order to move them out of the way of the whites and to foster among them agriculture and the arts of civilized life. But Brown's unhappiness in his job led him to resign effective July 1, 1850.[6]

President Taylor appointed as Brown's successor a Mississippi lawyer and politician, Luke Lea, a man with no Indian experience who sought a federal job after failing in his bid for the governorship of Mississippi. Tay-

5. Floyd to Jefferson Davis, March 26, 1860, and Thompson to Davis, March 13, 1860, *Senate Report* no. 223, 36–1, serial 1040; *Senate Journal*, 36–1, serial 1022, p. 441.

6. CIA Report, 1849, serial 550, pp. 937–58; Robert A. Trennert, "Orlando Brown, 1849–50," in Robert M. Kvasnicka and Herman J. Viola, eds. *The Commissioners of Indian Affairs, 1824–1977* (Lincoln: University of Nebraska Press, 1979), pp. 41–47.

lor's sudden death on July 9, 1850, led to a shakeup in the cabinet. Ewing resigned as secretary of the interior, and his replacement, the Virginia Whig Alexander H. H. Stuart, left Indian matters largely in the hands of the Indian Office. Lea, like others before him, relied on the proposals of his predecessors in formulating his Indian policies. In the circumstances of the times, to be sure, he was sensitive to the demands of whites in the new territories, and he assumed without question the superiority of his own culture. "When civilization and barbarism are brought in such relation that they cannot coexist together," he wrote, "it is right that the superiority of the former should be asserted and the latter compelled to give way. It is, therefore, no matter of regret or reproach that so large a portion of our territory has been wrested from the aboriginal inhabitants and made the happy abodes of an enlightened and Christian people." Much of the conflict that had arisen, he declared, had been due to "the Indian's own perverse and vicious nature."[7]

Yet Lea adopted the unequivocal stand that the civilization of the Indians was a necessary and practicable goal of the federal government. Although he admitted the difficulties of the task and his own insufficiency in carrying it out, he declared that civilizing the Indians was "a cherished object of the government." He noted the critics who ridiculed any chance of success, but he was not to be turned aside. "It should be remembered . . . ," he said, "that to change a savage people from their barbarous habits to those of civilized life, is, in its nature, a work of time, and the results already attained, as evinced in the improved condition of several of our tribes, are sufficient to silence the most skeptical, and warrant the assurance that perseverance in the cause will achieve success." Any plan, he thought, would have to provide for the Indians' "ultimate incorporation into the great body of our citizen population."[8]

The immediate means to Lea's humanitarian end would be a national system of reservations, and in his first annual report he had worked out a clear statement of that policy in regard to "our wilder tribes."

> It is indispensably necessary that they be placed in positions where they can be controlled and finally compelled by sheer necessity to resort to agricultural labor or starve. Considering, as the untutored Indian does, that labor is a degradation, and that there is nothing worthy of his ambitions but prowess in war, success in the chase, and eloquence in council, it is only under such circumstances that his haughty pride can be subdued, and his wild energies trained to the more ennobling pursuits of civilized life. There should be assigned to

7. CIA Report, 1852, serial 658, p. 293; Robert A. Trennert, "Luke Lea, 1850–53," in Kvasnicka and Viola, *Commissioners of Indian Affairs*, pp. 49–55.
8. CIA Report, 1851, serial 613, pp. 273–74.

each tribe, for a permanent home, a country adapted to agriculture, of limited extent and well-defined boundaries; within which all, with occasional exception, should be compelled constantly to remain until such time as their general improvement and good conduct may supersede the necessity of such restrictions. In the mean time, the government should cause them to be supplied with stock, agricultural implements, and useful materials for clothing; encourage and assist them in the erection of comfortable dwellings, and secure to them the means and facilities of education, intellectual, moral, and religious.[9]

The beginning of Lea's term coincided with the appointment of Charles E. Mix as chief clerk in the Indian Office, a position second only to the commissioner and one of considerable influence, given its continuity in the midst of rapidly changing commissioners and the frequent absence of the incumbents from Washington. Mix was experienced, having entered the Indian Office as a clerk after the failure of his mercantile business in the Panic of 1837, and he had a reputation for integrity and efficiency. For eighteen years after his appointment in 1850 he was a force to be reckoned with, and he left the stamp of his views on Indian policy of the period. It is often difficult to determine how much of the work of the commissioners, including the writing of annual reports, was in fact the work of Mix.[10]

There can be no doubt, however, that much of the consistency of policy during the 1850s was due to this man. Mix in fact held the office of commissioner for a five-month period in 1858, and his report for that year marked him as strongly in favor of the reservation policy. His remarks formed a sort of paradigm of what was proposed during the decade. He noted "three serious, and, to the Indians, fatal errors" that had characterized past policy toward the Indians: "their removal from place to place as our population advanced; the assignment to them of too great an extent of country, to be held in common; and the allowance of large sums of money, as annuities, for the lands ceded by them." It was, he asserted, these mistakes in policy rather than any lack of capacity on the part of the Indians that had been responsible for the failure to "domesticate and civilize" them. By frequent changes in location and the holding of large bodies of land in common, the Indians were kept unsettled and failed to acquire experience in private property, and their large annuities fostered habits of indolence and profligacy and made them victims of unscrupulous traders

---

9. CIA Report, 1850, serial 587, pp. 35–36; see also CIA Report, 1852, serial 658, p. 300.

10. Harry Kelsey, "Charles E. Mix, 1858," in Kvasnicka and Viola, *Commissioners of Indian Affairs*, pp. 77–79. I have also profited from "Mr. Lincoln's Indian Bureau," an unpublished manuscript by Harry Kelsey, a copy of which was kindly supplied me by the author.

and speculators. The policy Mix advocated and helped to establish reversed, to some degree, all three of these "errors."[11]

Luke Lea served through President Millard Fillmore's term; he was replaced on March 24, 1853, by George W. Manypenny, an Ohio businessman and newspaper publisher who thus began a longterm interest in the welfare of the American Indians. Manypenny was a man of energy, intelligence, and honesty who won the enmity of western politicians for his courageous resistance to fraudulent claims against Indian annuities. He followed the tradition of his predecessors, and he no doubt felt the influence of Charles Mix.[12]

For the border tribes, who were blocking white expansion into Kansas and Nebraska, Manypenny wanted the Indians assigned to reduced reservations with provision for allotment of land in severalty. His commitment to a reservation system as a means of promoting the civilization of the Indians in the Far West was strong. Of the Indians in New Mexico and Utah, he wrote at the end of 1854: "Conventional arrangements are necessary . . . for the purpose of fixing them in proper locations, and giving to the department such influence and control over them as will enable it, as far as possible, to confine them thereon, and to induce them to resort to agriculture and kindred pursuits, instead of relying, as they now do, for support upon the uncertain and precarious supplies of the chase; and when that fails, upon the more hazardous and injurious practice of theft and plunder." Manypenny knew that no military force that might be sent to the territories could prevent depredations, unless by exterminating the Indians. The alternative was for the Indians to be "colonized in suitable locations, and, to some extent at least, be subsisted by the government, until they can be trained to such habits of industry and thrift as will enable them to sustain themselves."[13]

It was clear to Manypenny (as it was to Mix) that it was no longer possible to solve the question of the Indians' destiny by the convenient expedient of repeated removal. He hoped at first in dealing with the emigrated tribes along the border in Kansas and Nebraska to move them into the "colonies" established north and south, but he noted the Indians' resistance and ultimately promoted instead the assignment of permanent reservations, reduced in size to be sure, where the Indians already were.[14] The reservation policy that was developing in the 1850s, therefore, included as an essential component the establishment of fixed and permanent homes for the Indians.

11. CIA Report, 1858, serial 974, p. 354.

12. Robert M. Kvasnicka, "George W. Manypenny, 1853–57," in Kvasnicka and Viola, *Commissioners of Indian Affairs*, pp. 57–67.

13. CIA Report, 1854, serial 746, p. 222.

14. CIA Report, 1856, serial 875, p. 575.

Allotment of land in severalty was a necessary corollary of the reduced permanent reservations, and it was recommended strongly by Manypenny and his successors. The doctrine of private property was, of course, an essential part of the American way that the Indians had long been expected to accept. But it took on a special urgency as the reservation system got under way, for it lay "at the very foundation of all civilization."[15]

Manypenny faced the question of Indian civilization and Christianization more realistically than some of the workers in the field, who sent in accounts of rapid advancement in civilization among the tribes they served. The commissioner noted that after years of such flattering reports the Indians who had been under government supervision for all that time should have reached a high state of civilization. Yet that was far from the case. Nevertheless, he was mildly optimistic, following the long tradition of humanitarian concern for Indian betterment. He noted that "many have made an encouraging degree of progress, in acquiring the elements of a rude civilization," and that although much remained yet to be done "to secure and accomplish the full and complete regeneration of the Indians," the object was a noble one and fully deserving the attention and energies of the government and of "a great Christian people." His commitment to Christianity was firm, and his policy was suffused with his belief. He ended his annual report of 1854 with this statement: "As a Christian government and people, our obligations and duties are of the highest and holiest character, and we are accountable to the Maker of all men for the manner in which we discharge them. Having faithfully employed all the means placed within our reach to improve the Indian race, and preserve it from extinction, we can, with a good conscience and strong faith, leave the issue in the hands of our common Father."[16]

Manypenny served the full four-year term of Franklin Pierce's administration, something of a record for the 1850s. He was followed by James W. Denver, a representative from California, who served from April to December 1857 and again from November 1858 to March 1859, with Charles Mix serving in the interval. Denver's term was too short to influence Indian policy in any significant way, and Mix's management of affairs was no doubt pronounced.[17] Next came Alfred B. Greenwood, a Georgian by birth who had made his career in the frontier state of Arkansas. He, too, relied heavily on the chief clerk and worked diligently with him for an updating of Indian legislation. He accepted the policy of concentrating the Indians and recalled the belief of his predecessors that "the Indian possessed all the elements essential to his elevation to all the powers and sympathies which

15. The quoted phrase is from James W. Denver, CIA Report, 1857, serial 919, p. 292.
16. CIA Report, 1853, serial 690, p. 264; CIA Report, 1854, serial 746, pp. 230–31.
17. Donald Chaput, "James W. Denver, 1857, 1858–59," in Kvasnicka and Viola, *Commissioners of Indian Affairs*, pp. 69–75.

appertain to his white brother, and which only need proper development to enable him to tread with equal step and dignity the walks of civilized life." He asserted the wisdom of placing the Indians on reservations and introducing them to agriculture, then gradually restricting their possessions and finally dividing their reservations in severalty; and against critics who distrusted the system he expressed his confidence in its ultimate success.[18] But in the end Greenwood became entangled in the sectional crisis. Although he served out his term, he left Washington when Lincoln took office in April 1861 and actively served the South as a recruiter of Cherokee and Choctaw Indians for the Confederacy and as a member of the Confederate Congress.[19]

AN EXPANDED INDIAN DEPARTMENT

While the commissioners were developing and promoting a reservation policy for the Indians in the West, they were also concerned about the insufficiency of the administrative machinery they had to work with. Orlando Brown in 1849 noted "the present defective and inefficient organization" of his bureau. "However well adapted to the condition of things in 1834, when it was prescribed," he declared, "it is incompatible with the present state of affairs, and altogether inadequate to enable the Department to discharge, in a proper manner, the enlarged and more complicated trusts and duties now devolving upon it." He noted the movement of the eastern tribes to regions across the Mississippi, the increased transactions with the Indians under treaty stipulations, and the vast numbers of Indians added by the acquisition of Texas, Oregon, California, and New Mexico. One serious defect was the lack of a sufficient number of superintendents to handle Indian affairs in regions remote from the seat of government, regions where discretionary authority frequently needed to be exercised, and where superintendents could give "immediate and rigid supervision" to agents and subagents. Brown did not like to see the duties of agent and superintendent combined, nor did he like the ex officio arrangement by which territorial governors performed the duties of Indian superintendents. He boldly asked for "seven full and independent superintendencies"—four east of the Rockies, including Texas, and one each for Oregon, California, and New Mexico. Brown also pointed to the inadequate arrangement of agents and subagents. Only eleven agents were authorized by law, but subagents could be appointed at the discretion of the president,

18. CIA Report, 1860, serial 1078, pp. 249–50.
19. Gary L. Roberts, "Alfred Burton Greenwood, 1859–61," in Kvasnicka and Viola, *Commissioners of Indian Affairs*, pp. 81–87.

with the result that subagents often filled positions with duties and responsibilities that called for a full agent. He thought that if the salaries of the agents were increased, more competent men could be found for the agencies and many subagencies could be eliminated.[20]

Commissioner Brown, strongly supported by Secretary of the Interior Ewing, proposed to Congress the additional superintendents and agents that were needed. Separate bills were drawn up, one each for Oregon, California, New Mexico, and Texas. But the sectional controversy meant postponement of action on all but the Oregon bill, approved on June 5, 1850, which established an independent superintendency for Oregon and provided for three agents and the extension of the trade and intercourse laws over the territory.[21] Brown's successor, Lea, pushed for fulfillment of the Indian Office's proposals. Representative Robert W. Johnson, chairman of the Committee on Indian Affairs, offered amendments to the Indian appropriation bill that embodied the request. "The object of the series of amendments," he said, ". . . is to effect that reorganization of the Indian Department which the changed relations of our Government, her very considerable acquisition of territory, the increased number of tribes, and the amount of responsibility require." The amendments were included in the act, approved on February 27, 1851. At last, an expanded Indian department matched the expanded nation.[22]

The law repealed all previous authorization for Indian superintendents east of the Rockies and north of Texas and New Mexico and provided instead three superintendents for the Indians in those areas, to be appointed by the president with the advice and consent of the Senate. The president or the secretary of the interior was empowered to assign the superintendents to appropriate tribes. (The governor of Minnesota Territory, however, was to continue as ex officio superintendent until the president should direct otherwise.) In place of the twenty-three agents and subagents employed in the same region, the law authorized eleven Indian agents at a salary of fifteen hundred dollars a year and six other agents at a thousand dollars a year. The same law provided four agents for New Mexico and one for Utah and extended the intercourse laws over the tribes in those terri-

20. CIA Report, 1849, serial 550, pp. 952–56. Brown relied heavily on a report of W. Medill of December 30, 1846, written in response to a House request for information about possible changes in the public service for greater economy and efficiency, printed in *House Document* no. 70, 29–2, serial 500, pp. 10–14. See also the discussion of reorganization of the Indian department in Robert A. Trennert, Jr., *Alternative to Extinction: Federal Indian Policy and the Beginnings of the Reservation System, 1846–51* (Philadelphia: Temple University Press, 1975), pp. 45–60.

21. 9 *United States Statutes* 437.

22. *Congressional Globe,* 31st Congress, 2d session, pp. 616–19; 9 *United States Statutes* 586–87. See also Trennert, *Alternative to Extinction,* pp. 57–58.

tories. The Central Superintendency was established in place of the old St. Louis Superintendency, with responsibility for agents and Indians in present-day Kansas and Nebraska as well as the upper reaches of the Missouri, Platte, and Arkansas rivers. The Northern Superintendency assumed responsibility for the Indians in Wisconsin and Michigan and, after 1856, those in Minnesota. The Southern Superintendency replaced the old Western Superintendency and had charge of the Indians in the Indian Territory and the Osage Indians in southern Kansas.[23]

The separation of the territorial governors from ex officio duty as Indian superintendents, which was part of Orlando Brown's proposal, did not come at once. The problems that arose from this overburdening of frontier administrators, to say nothing of the frequent conflicts of interest, did not slacken; and with repeated recommendations from the Indian Office, Congress acted piece by piece. In 1850 a separate superintendency for Oregon was created. In 1856 the Minnesota Superintendency, in which the governor served as superintendent, was discontinued and its agencies added to the Northern Superintendency. And in 1857 the two offices were separated in the territories of Utah and New Mexico.[24]

If renovation was necessary in the field organization, the operation of the Indian service also loudly called for an overhaul. Some order, it is true, was achieved without legislative change when Charles Mix became chief clerk in 1850. Relying on an authorization of funds provided by Congress, Mix drew up a compilation of rules and regulations for the superintendents and agents in their multifarious business with the Indian Office. The 85-page pamphlet, entitled *Office Copy of the Laws, Regulations, Etc., of the Indian Bureau, 1850,* was a mélange of previous rules and directives. It included the intercourse law of June 30, 1834, in full, as well as the law of the same date organizing the Indian department. To these were added a series of so-called "revised regulations," issued from time to time by the secretary of war for carrying into effect the laws of 1834. These were intended to specify the boundaries and sites of existing superintendencies, agencies, and subagencies and to describe in detail the duties of the various officials and the procedures for carrying out trade regulations, for handling depredation claims, for managing the emigration of Indian groups, and for paying annuities. Similarly, detailed instructions about the revision of the inter-

23. A concise history of these superintendencies and the agencies attached to them is given in Edward E. Hill, *The Office of Indian Affairs, 1824–1880: Historical Sketches* (New York: Clearwater Publishing Company, 1974), pp. 28–31, 118–20, 174–75.

24. 9 *United States Statutes* 437; 11 *United States Statutes* 185. On territorial governors as ex officio Indian superintendents, see William M. Neil, "The Territorial Governor as Indian Superintendent in the Trans-Mississippi West," *Mississippi Valley Historical Review* 43 (September 1956): 213–37.

course laws in 1847 were included. The manual included copies of the numerous forms on which the various reports were to be submitted.[25]

The manual by itself might have been a dead letter had it not been for the zeal with which Mix managed the office. He called to task agents who did not follow the letter of the regulations, and in his long term in the Indian Office he was able to develop a uniformity of practice that had been badly needed amid the rapid turnover of personnel. The manual in its original form was rudimentary, without table of contents or index, but it remained as it was until 1869, when a few slight revisions were made.[26]

There was some gain in having the existing legislation and explanatory regulations set forth in a single place and a chief clerk on duty to see that the proper forms were used and that reports went through the proper channels. But clearly more was needed. It was the constant refrain of the commissioners of Indian affairs that new legislation was necessary. Thus Manypenny wrote in a typical statement in 1854: "Experience has proven the law approved June 30, 1834, 'to regulate trade and intercourse with the Indian tribes, and to preserve peace on the frontier,' to be inadequate to meet and dispose of all the varied questions and difficulties which frequently arise under, and grow out of, the existing state of our Indian relations."[27]

What bothered Manypenny, in addition to the general inapplicability of old laws to new circumstances, was the inadequacy of the law of 1834 to protect the persons and property of the Indians. He saw what was happening to the Indians as they succumbed to the pressures of the invading whites, and he remarked, "The rage for speculation and the wonderful desire to obtain choice lands, which seems to possess so many of those who go into our new territories, causes them to lose sight of and entirely overlook the rights of the aboriginal inhabitants." He concluded: "Humanity, Christianity, national honor, unite in demanding the enactment of such laws as will not only protect the Indians, but as shall effectually put it out of the power of any public officer to allow these poor creatures to be despoiled of their lands and annuities by a swarm of hungry and audacious speculators, attorneys, and others, their instruments and coadjutors."[28]

The same plea was made by Manypenny's successors.[29] Finally, in Feb-

25. *Office Copy of the Laws, Regulations, Etc., of the Indian Bureau, 1850* (Washington: Gideon and Company, 1850). The congressional authorization is in 9 *United States Statutes* 558.

26. The manual is discussed briefly in Kelsey, "Mr. Lincoln's Indian Bureau," pp. 25–27.

27. CIA Report, 1854, serial 746, p. 225. See also CIA Report, 1855, serial 810, p. 335.

28. CIA Report, 1856, serial 875, pp. 572–75.

29. CIA Report, 1857, serial 919, p. 300; CIA Report, 1858, serial 974, p. 364; CIA Report, 1859, serial 1023, pp. 389–90. See the long and detailed discussion about inequities and inadequacies in the existing laws in the report of Elias Rector, superintendent

ruary 1859, Congress directed the commissioner of Indian affairs "to prepare rules and regulations for the government of the Indian service, and for trade and intercourse with the Indian tribes and the regulation of their affairs," which would have effect only when enacted by Congress. Commissioner Greenwood worked to comply with the request, but nothing came of the effort.[30]

There was some growth in the office staff in Washington, but it was not at all proportionate to the increased work that devolved upon the commissioners. Manypenny complained in 1856 that the work "had swelled to an extent almost incredible." The tasks of the office had doubled since 1852, yet the office staff remained the same size.[31]

PERENNIAL PROBLEMS: ANNUITIES AND LIQUOR

The question of the proper manner of paying annuities to the Indians was reopened in the 1850s, as the pendulum of arguments swung back again to an earlier position. The legislation of 1847, which provided for per capita payment of the annuities rather than payment to the chiefs as the law of 1834 had directed, in its turn was now a cause of complaint. The praise that had been showered on the 1847 law by Commissioner Medill, in the minds of his successors in the 1850s, was sadly misplaced. Luke Lea, in his first year in office, found "material objections" to the practice. Although the law had allowed the tribes to set apart some of their annuity payments for national and charitable purposes, in fact they had not done so. Nor did he like the slighting of the chiefs that came with a per capita payment, for it was through the chiefs that the government carried on business with the tribes, and he thought they deserved a larger share than the "common Indians." Moreover, if the chiefs were passed by, their authority within the tribes was weakened and disorder resulted. Congress took no action on Lea's recommendations, however, and in 1857 James Denver raised the same questions in a forceful way. He declared that the "great body of the Indians can be managed only through the chiefs" and predicted that the per capita payments would break down the domestic government of the Indians and thus foster lawlessness.[32]

The policy makers were caught between two contradictory positions

of the Southern Superintendency, September 24, 1857, CIA Report, 1857, serial 919, pp. 479–93.

30. 11 _United States Statutes_ 401; CIA Report, 1859, serial 1023, pp. 389–90.
31. CIA Report, 1856, serial 875, pp. 571–72.
32. CIA Report, 1850, serial 587, pp. 44–45; CIA Report, 1857, serial 919, pp. 295–96.

and could not easily extricate themselves. They held, on one hand, that the tribes were independent governments (as far as domestic matters were concerned), for which the chiefs were essential figures who needed to be treated with special respect. On the other hand, they saw the abuses that crept in with the large payments to the chiefs, who could succumb to the pressures of outside manipulators interested in pocketing the annuity payments themselves. Thus Manypenny in 1853 condemned the conversion of the private debts of a few Indians into "national debts" to be paid out of the annuities.[33]

It was clear to the officials of the 1850s, however, as it would be to their successors through the decades, that annuities in *money*, whether paid directly to individuals or distributed through the chiefs, were an unmitigated evil. Instead of advancing the Indians toward civilization and self-support, the money was looked upon as a substitute for work, and the Indians became increasingly dependent on what amounted to a dole. Commissioner Manypenny declared that the money-annuity system had done "as much, if not more, to cripple and thwart the efforts of the government to domesticate and civilize our Indian tribes, than any other of the many serious obstacles with which we have had to contend." He wanted payments to the Indians to be in the form of goods, agricultural implements, and stock animals or in the form of "means of mental, moral, and industrial education and training."[34] As he set about to negotiate treaties with the Indians, he saw to it that payments were not permanent, but that they would gradually be reduced over a set period of years. Moreover, the payments were placed under the control of the president, who could use the funds as he saw fit to contribute to the civilization and improvement of the tribes. A set provision was inserted in most of the treaties in this or similar form:

> All which several sums of money shall be paid to the said . . . tribes, or expended for their use and benefit under the direction of the President of the United States, who may, from time to time, determine, at his discretion, what proportion of the annual payments, in this article provided for, if any, shall be applied to and expended, for their moral improvement and education; for such beneficial objects as in his judgment will be calculated to advance them in civilization; for buildings, opening farms, fencing, breaking land, providing stock, agricultural implements, seeds, &c., for clothing, provisions, and merchandise; for iron, steel, arms and ammunition; for mechanics, and tools; and for medical purposes.[35]

33. CIA Report, 1853, serial 690, p. 261.
34. Ibid., pp. 260–61.
35. Treaty with the Oto and Missouri Indians, 1854, Kappler, p. 609.

Because, as Manypenny reported at the end of 1856, since March 4, 1853, fifty-two treaties had been entered into with various tribes (thirty-two already ratified and twenty still under consideration), his policy had significant effect. Moreover, the policy inaugurated in the previous decade of paying annuities semi-annually was revived. It appeared to have a good effect in countering the tendency of many Indians to spend their funds wastefully and then sink back into a long period of misery until the next annual payment arrived.[36]

An old problem, not unconnected with the receipt of annuity payments, was the liquor traffic to the Indians. Even the new and tighter strictures of the law of 1847 were not enough. "The appetite of the Indian for the use of ardent spirits," Manypenny lamented in 1855, "seems to be entirely uncontrollable, and at all periods of our intercourse with him the evil effects and injurious consequences arising from the indulgence of the habit are unmistakably seen. It has been the greatest barrier to his improvement in the past, and will continue to be in the future, if some means cannot be adopted to inhibit its use." The federal system was in large part to blame, for the federal government had done almost all it could to end the sale or use of liquor in the Indian country, but it could not legislate for the states and territories that were adjacent to or surrounded the tribal lands. All it could do was to urge proper legislation, but nothing truly effective was provided.[37]

THE CHALLENGE OF SCIENTIFIC RACISM

The men in the Indian Office held firm to the principles of Indian civilization that had carried over from earlier decades. They accepted without serious question the prevailing doctrine that Indians were fully human beings like their white neighbors, that they were emerging (in varying degrees) from a state of savagery or barbarism, and that it was the responsibility of a Christian nation and its government to take them in hand like a good father, punishing them when necessary but supplying them with the patterns and means of a civilized existence based on agriculture (ultimately with private property holdings) and providing teachers and missionaries for their moral, intellectual, and industrial advancement. They saw no philosophical conflict in their acceptance and promotion of an expanding white society that was moving into the vast regions acquired in the previous decade and their benevolent concern for the Indians who were threatened with being crushed by the American advance. They believed in the superiority of their way of life and hoped to convince—or compel—the

36. CIA Report, 1856, serial 875, p. 571; CIA Report, 1855, serial 810, pp. 336–37.
37. CIA Report, 1855, serial 810, p. 340; see also CIA Report, 1850, serial 587, p. 45.

Indians to accept it as the only alternative to extermination. The fact that partial extermination resulted from the contacts of the two races, notably in California, was not the result of plan but of the insufficiency of the reservations and other means offered and the slowness of the Indians to accept the salvation offered them so insistently. There is no indication that the policy makers departed from the norms and principles of the evangelical Christian society in which they lived, even though we know nothing about their personal involvement in the rising Christian revivalism that marked the decade of the 1850s in the North.[38]

They lived at a time, however, when the optimism of humanitarians in regard to the Indians' progress was challenged by the rise of the so-called American School of Ethnology, the first serious attempt to develop a scientific racism. This group of investigators and writers denied the unity of mankind and preached a multiplicity of races, some innately inferior to others. Caught between the biblical chronology of man's existence on earth (the Protestant divine James Ussher had set the creation of the world at 4004 B.C.) and clear evidence that distinct races had existed for thousands of years, these men rejected the monogenesis of traditional Judeo-Christian belief and opted for polygenesis, that is, separate creation of the white, black, red, brown, and yellow races. Much of their evidence was furnished by Samuel G. Morton, who collected and measured human skulls. In his *Crania Americana*, published in Philadelphia in 1839, he concluded that the Indians were a distinct race, whose characteristics were physical and not based merely on environment, and he wrote disparagingly about Indian capabilities.[39]

Whereas Morton was circumspect and careful not to appear to challenge biblical beliefs headon, his most famous follower, Dr. Josiah C. Nott of Mobile, was a polemicist and propagandist who delighted in stinging the clergy and other religious traditionalists. As early as 1844 he began to write

---

38. Only Manypenny came from the region where revivalism was strong, and he sounds most like the revivalists. Three commissioners—Brown, Lea, and Greenwood—were southerners, and southern tradition was a heavily biblical one, with unspeculative reliance upon religious fundamentals.

39. Samuel George Morton, *Crania Americana; or, A Comparative View of the Skulls of the Various Aboriginal Nations of North and South America, to Which Is Prefixed an Essay on the Varieties of the Human Species* (Philadelphia: J. Dobson, 1839), pp. 81–82. Morton repeated the same views in a talk before the Boston Society of Natural History in 1842, printed as *An Inquiry into the Distinctive Characteristics of the Aboriginal Race of America*, 2d ed. (Philadelphia: John Pennington, 1844). A good account of Morton and the American School is given in William R. Stanton, *The Leopard's Spots: Scientific Attitudes toward Race in America, 1815–1859* (Chicago: University of Chicago Press, 1960). I have also relied on Reginald Horsman, "Scientific Racism and the American Indian in the Mid-Nineteenth Century," *American Quarterly* 37 (May 1975): 152–68, although I disagree with his conclusions.

about the inferiority of non-Caucasian races, and in 1854, together with the Egyptologist George R. Gliddon, he published *Types of Mankind*, which gathered evidence that the races came from separate creations and were different in their capacities. "In America," the two wrote, "the aboriginal barbarous tribes cannot be forced to change their habits, or even persuaded to successful emigration: they are melting away from year to year. . . . It is as clear as the sun at noon-day, that in a few generations more the last of these Red men will be numbered with the dead." They saw the Indians of America as "one great family, that presents a prevailing type," and offered this description: "Small and peculiarly shaped crania, a cinnamon complexion, small feet and hands, black straight hair, wild, savage nature, characterize the Indian everywhere."[40]

It should be noted that Nott and others of his stripe were more concerned with blacks than with Indians, and their arguments in favor of the existence of inferior races offered a scientific argument for slavery. That may help explain why Nott received favorable notice in some segments of the Democratic and southern press. The *Democratic Review* flirted with the new ideas, and the *Southern Quarterly Review* and *DeBow's Review* (published in New Orleans) openly accepted inherent differences in the races, heeding the animadversions of the ethnologists about Indians.[41]

The American School, however, made no perceptible headway against the views of the Indian policy makers, imbued as they were with the pervasive evangelical religious atmosphere of the day. Even in regard to the blacks, neither the North nor the South accepted the scientists' conclusions about the inferiority of blacks as a basis for action. The North could not accept a doctrine that lent comfort to slavery, and the South, with its deep commitment to religion, relied on the Bible for support of slavery, not on a science that would force rejection of the Bible.[42] In regard to the In-

40. J. C. Nott and George R. Gliddon, *Types of Mankind; or, Ethnological Researches, Based upon the Ancient Monuments, Paintings, Sculptures, and Crania of Races, and upon Their Natural, Geographical, Philological, and Biblical History* (Philadelphia: Lippincott, Grambo and Company, 1854), pp. 69–70.

41. There is an extended discussion of the articles on the diversity of races and the inferiority of the Indian that appeared in these journals in Horsman, "Scientific Racism," pp. 160–64.

42. John S. Haller, Jr., *Outcasts from Evolution: Scientific Attitudes of Racial Inferiority, 1859–1900* (Urbana: University of Illinois Press, 1971), p. 78. See also Stanton, *Leopard's Spots*, pp. 193–95. Historians who assert that the makers of Indian policy were influenced by the American School are Reginald Horsman in "Scientific Racism," Thomas F. Gossett, in *Race: The History of an Idea in America* (Dallas: Southern Methodist University Press, 1963), and Russel B. Nye, in *Society and Culture in America, 1830–1860* (New York: Harper and Row, 1974). These authors do not offer convincing evidence that these views were the dominant ones and none at all to show that they formed the basis for government policy. See "Scientific Racism and Indian Policy," in

dians, the efforts to educate and Christianize them in the 1840s and after make it clear that the government policy makers and their missionary partners maintained a uniform—and in some cases a very strong—adherence to the traditional positions. There were few indications that they were aware of the new scientific theories, and if scientific racism was adverted to at all, it was rejected.

In 1851, the year Samuel Morton died, Commissioner Luke Lea made a typical assertion: "The history of the Indian furnishes abundant proof that he possesses all the elements essential to his elevation; all the powers, instincts, and sympathies which appertain to his white brother; and which only need the proper development and direction to enable him to tread with equal step and dignity the walks of civilized life. . . . That his inferiority is a necessity of his nature is neither taught by philosophy, nor attested by experience." George W. Manypenny noted the slowness of the Indians' progress, but he did not think ultimate success was impossible. "I believe," he said in 1855, "that the Indian may be domesticated, improved, and elevated; that he may be completely and thoroughly civilized, and made a useful element of our population." Both Lea and Manypenny, however, were aware of what the latter called "erroneous opinions and prejudices in relation to the disposition, characteristics, capacity, and intellectual powers of the race" and considered them obstacles and drawbacks in the rapid improvement of the Indians.[43] These men and their predecessors in the 1840s clearly did not accept the view of the Indian proposed by Morton, Gliddon, and Nott. They did not subscribe to the racist positions of *DeBow's Review.* Their viewpoints and their actions (especially in regard to education for the Indians) continued to follow the pattern of evangelical Christianity of the first decades of the century.

Thomas L. McKenney, appearing on the lecture circuit in the 1840s with lectures on the "origin, history, character, and the wrongs and rights of the Indians," held firm to monogenesis. He wrote:

> I am aware that opinions are entertained by some, embracing the theory of multiform creations; by such, the doctrine that the whole family of man sprang from one original and common stock, is denied. There is, however, but one source whence information can be derived on this subject—and that is the Bible; and, until those who base their

---

Francis Paul Prucha, *Indian Policy in the United States: Historical Essays* (Lincoln: University of Nebraska Press, 1981), pp. 180–97, which I draw on here.

43. CIA Report, 1851, serial 613, p. 274; CIA Report, 1855, serial 810, pp. 338, 340. For the views of Henry R. Schoolcraft, see Stanton, *Leopard's Spots*, p. 192; for those of Lewis Henry Morgan, see Carl Rezek, *Lewis Henry Morgan: American Scholar* (Chicago: University of Chicago Press, 1960).

convictions on Bible testimony, consent to throw aside that great land-mark of truth, they must continue in the belief that "the Lord God formed *man* of the dust of the ground, and breathed into his nostrils the breath of life, when he became a living soul." Being thus formed, and thus endowed, he was put by his Creator in *the* garden, which was eastward in Eden, whence flowed the river which parted, and became the four heads; and that from his fruitfulness his species were propagated.

The propagation of the entire human race from "an original pair," McKenney asserted, "is a truth so universally admitted, as to render any elaborate argument in its support superfluous." Because the Eden of Adam and Eve was not in America, the Indians could not have been indigenous to America. McKenney believed they were of Asiatic origin and had migrated to the New World by way of Bering Strait. He argued in his lectures against those who said that the Indian was irreclaimable.[44]

The American School of Ethnology is of interest primarily to historians of science. The polygenesis doctrine, on which the diversity of human species and the inferiority of the nonwhite races rested, was replaced by the evolutionary theories of Charles Darwin, whose *Origin of Species* was published in 1859.[45] Morton and Nott and their friends turned out to be scientific oddities, their cranial measurements relegated to the attic like the phrenology with which they flirted. The dominance of evangelical Protestant views in Indian policy after the Civil War was, if anything, stronger than it had been before.

44. Thomas L. McKenney, *Memoirs, Official and Personal: With Sketches of Travels among the Northern and Southern Indians* (New York: Paine and Burgess, 1846), 2: 14–15.

45. There was a strange recurrence in the 1970s of the notion of separate creation of the Indians among some Indians, who asserted that the Indians were always in the New World and did not migrate here. This appeared to be part of the movement to reassert the importance of Indianness.

CHAPTER 13

A Pathway to
the Pacific

Colonization of the Western Tribes.

Kansas-Nebraska and the Indians.

Military Action on the Plains.

The territorial acquisitions of the 1840s were both the result of and a stimulus to population movements to the Pacific slope. Although large numbers moved by sail around Cape Horn and others risked the shorter distance through the Isthmus of Panama, great hordes of emigrants chose the course across the continent. In 1843 the first mass movement to Oregon took place, jumping off from Independence, Missouri, and moving along the overland route to the Willamette Valley in Oregon. The spectacle was repeated in 1844 and 1845, and by 1848 more than fourteen thousand emigrants had impressed the Oregon Trail indelibly on the landscape and on the American consciousness. Some turned south from Fort Hall and sought California instead of Oregon; the trickle of immigrants became a torrent when news of the discovery of gold in California in 1848 reached the East.[1] Meanwhile, there was heavy traffic as well on the Santa Fe Trail, which had been laid out in 1822 and which became a major passageway to the Southwest and California.

---

1. There are plentiful statistics on the emigrants in John D. Unruh, Jr., *The Plains Across: The Overland Emigrants and the Trans-Mississippi West, 1840–60* (Urbana: University of Illinois Press, 1979). See chapter 5, "Emigrant-Indian Interaction," pp. 156–200.

COLONIZATION OF THE WESTERN TRIBES

These great movements of population had two effects on Indian affairs. In the first place, they cut directly through the lands of the Indians, making a wide swath that upset the ecological patterns by destroying large numbers of game (chiefly buffalo) and forcing the Indians to seek new hunting grounds; this in turn led to increased intertribal irritations. Although direct conflicts between the Indians and the Oregon and California emigrants were few, and in many cases the Indians offered vital assistance to the intruders, the ultimate result shook apart the existing economic and political structures on the plains into an irreparable shambles—which it became the responsibility of the federal government to deal with. In the second place, the increasing population of the West (the population of California in the census of 1850 was ninety-three thousand, that of Oregon Territory thirteen thousand, and that of Utah Territory eleven thousand) meant that the Indians were surrounded. No longer was it possible to keep moving the tribesmen vaguely "to the west." Whites and their lines of communication moved upon the Indians with seemingly inexorable force from both directions, east and west, and the process speeded up still more after the Civil War.

To meet the crisis, the officials of the federal government, whether Democrats of Whigs, had one solution. This was to free the great middle section of the plains of its Indian inhabitants by moving them to two great "colonies," one already well established in the south as the Indian Territory and a comparable one to be laid out north of the lines of travel.[2] The idea had been slowly developing. Commissioner of Indian Affairs T. Hartley Crawford in 1841 spoke of "an Indian territory in the northern part of Iowa" as a "counterpoise to the southwestern Indian territory," with a "dense white population . . . interposed between the two settlements." And his successor, William Medill, in 1848 noted that the government had "commenced the establishment of two colonies for the Indian tribes that we have been compelled to remove; one north, on the head waters of the Mississippi, and the other south, on the western borders of Missouri and Arkansas." These officials were thinking primarily of locations for the Indians transferred from east of the Mississippi, but no great mental gymnastics were required to expand the notion to the tribes of the plains. Medill in fact urged removing the Omahas and the Otos and Missouris, keeping the Pawnees north of the Platte, and restraining the Sioux to their northern

2. An old but still very useful treatment of this whole matter is James C. Malin, *Indian Policy and Westward Expansion* (Lawrence, Kansas, 1921). See also Robert A. Trennert, Jr., *Alternative to Extinction: Federal Indian Policy and the Beginnings of the Reservation System, 1846–51* (Philadelphia: Temple University Press, 1975).

regions. He looked forward to the day when "an ample outlet of about six geographical degrees will be opened for our population that may incline to pass or expand in that direction; and thus prevent our colonized tribes from being injuriously pressed upon, if not swept away."[3]

There were attempts as early as the mid-1840s to provide territorial organization for the central plains, looking toward the joining of the west coast with the east, the protection of the emigrants, and the populating of the region by whites. Secretary of War William Wilkins in 1844 recommended that the areas on both sides of the Platte be organized as a territory. Senator David Atchison of Missouri and Senator Stephen A. Douglas of Illinois introduced bills in 1844–1845 for organizing the region, and Douglas took pride in the fact that from that time forward he tirelessly advocated the measure. The Indian barrier set up with the removal of the Indians from east of the Mississippi was anathema to him. "It was obvious to the plainest understanding," he wrote later, "that if this policy should be carried out and the treaty stipulations observed in good faith it was worse than folly to wrangle with Great Britain about our right to the whole or any part of Oregon—much less cherish the vain hope of ever making this an Ocean-bound Republic. This Indian Barrier was to have been a colossal monument to the God terminus saying to christianity, civilization and Democracy 'thus far mayest thou go, and *no* farther.'"[4]

Orlando Brown enthusiastically adopted the earlier proposals, and Luke Lea said he concurred in the policy of his predecessors—"by a partial change in their [the Indians'] relative positions, to throw open a wide extent of country for the spread of our population westward, so as to save them from being swept away by the mighty and advancing current of civilization, which has already engulfed a large portion of this hapless race." There was an ample outlet south of the colonized tribes, he said, but another was needed farther north, "leading more directly towards our remote western possession."[5]

But the humanitarian concerns of the previous decade were not suddenly dropped in the face of the new circumstances and the imperious demands for some easing of the tensions caused by the migrating and expanding white population. All the proposals for colonization had a second

3. CIA Report, 1841, serial 401, p. 231; CIA Report, 1848, serial 537, pp. 388, 390.

4. Douglas to J. H. Crane, D. M. Johnson, and L. J. Eastin, December 17, 1853, *The Letters of Stephen A. Douglas*, ed. Robert W. Johannsen (Urbana: University of Illinois Press, 1961), pp. 269–70. The report of Wilkins is in *House Executive Document* no. 2, 28–2, serial 463, p. 124. There is a discussion of the attempts of Senators Atchison and Douglas to get Congress to organize Nebraska Territory in Malin, *Indian Policy and Westward Expansion*, pp. 38–40.

5. CIA Report, 1849, serial 570, p. 946; CIA Report, 1850, serial 587, p. 39. Lea repeated his statement of policy the next year in CIA Report, 1851, serial 613, p. 268.

component or argument: it was necessary to consolidate the Indians in order to preserve them and to civilize them. The interest in settling the Indians in circumstances where they could be "improved" by education and manual labor, which had been an essential part of the civilization plans from the beginning of the century, continued to be viewed as a kind of panacea for the Indian problem. Medill explicitly urged application of the old policy to the new situation. He wrote in 1848:

> The policy already begun and relied on to accomplish objects so momentous and so desirable to every Christian philanthropist, is, as rapidly as it can safely and judiciously be done, to colonize our Indian tribes beyond the reach, for some years, of our white population; confining each within a small district of country, so that, as the game decreases and becomes scarce, the adults will gradually be compelled to resort to agriculture and other kinds of labor to obtain a subsistence, in which aid may be afforded and facilities furnished them out of the means obtained by the sale of their former possessions. To establish, at the same time, a judicious and well devised system of manual labor schools for the education of the youth of both sexes in letters—the males in practical agriculture and the various necessary and useful mechanic arts, and the females in the different branches of housewifery, including spinning and weaving; and these schools, like those already in successful operation, to be in charge of the excellent and active missionary societies of the different Christian denominations of the country, and to be conducted and the children taught by efficient, exemplary, and devoted men and women, selected with the approbation of the Department by those societies; so that a physical, intellectual, moral, and religious education will all be imparted together.[6]

He recalled the case of other tribes, "not long since colonized," who a few years before had been nomads and hunters, opposed to labor, and distrustful of schools and missionaries, but who now desired to educate their children. He declared that they were "becoming prosperous and happy from having learned how to provide certain and comfortable support for themselves and their families by the cultivation of the soil and other modes of labor." But the biggest change he saw was in the condition of Indian women, who had been drudges and slaves but now were beginning to assume their true position as equals.[7]

Medill's successors sang the same song. Orlando Brown waxed eloquent about the effects of civilization and education among the tribes moved

6. CIA Report, 1848, serial 537, p. 386.
7. Ibid.

from the East and expected the same results if the same methods were applied to the more western Indians.[8] Luke Lea asserted: "If timely measures are taken for the proper location and management of these tribes, they may, at no distant period, become an intelligent and Christian people, understanding the principles of our government, and participating in all its advantages."[9]

The federal government took steps to carry out these designs—to open up the passage to the Far West and to promote the civilization of the Indians—by a series of Indian treaties in the early 1850s. The first of these was the Treaty of Fort Laramie, signed September 17, 1851, with the Sioux, Cheyennes, Arapahos, Crows, Assiniboins, Gros Ventres, Mandans, and Arikaras. The treaty was negotiated by David D. Mitchell, a onetime fur trader who was superintendent of Indian affairs at St. Louis and an active advocate of clearing a central passageway to the Pacific. He was aided by Thomas Fitzpatrick, Indian agent for the Upper Platte Agency. The Indians agreed to cease hostilities among themselves and "to make an effective and lasting peace." They recognized the right of the United States to establish roads and military posts in their territory, and they agreed to make restitution for wrongs committed on whites lawfully passing through their lands. The treaty spelled out in detail the boundaries for each of the tribes in an attempt, generally unsuccessful, to keep them apart. In return the United States promised to protect the Indians from white depredations and to pay annuities of fifty thousand dollars a year for fifty years (reduced to ten years, with a possible five-year extension, by an amendment proposed by the Senate and later ratified by the tribes). The annuities were to be paid in "provisions, merchandize, domestic animals, and agricultural implements, in such proportions as may be deemed best adapted to their condition by the President of the United States."[10]

Mitchell reported optimistically on the results of the treaty. He said that the presents distributed at the council satisfied the Indians for all past destruction of buffalo, grass, and timber caused by the emigrating whites. And he justified the large annuity because it was needed to save the Indians. He wrote: "Humanity calls loudly for some interposition on the part of the American government to save, if possible, some portion of these ill-fated tribes; and this, it is thought, can only be done by furnishing them the means, and gradually turning their attention to agriculture." The veteran Jesuit missionary Pierre-Jean DeSmet, who attended the council, spoke highly of the peaceful behavior of the Indians and approved the

8. CIA Report, 1849, serial 570, pp. 956–57.
9. CIA Report, 1851, serial 613, p. 268. See also CIA Report, 1850, serial 587, pp. 35–36.
10. Kappler, pp. 594–95.

treaty, which he said would be "the commencement of a new era for the Indians—an era of peace."[11]

The treaty was considered highly successful by the Americans, but the powerful Sioux with their Cheyenne and Arapaho allies, in a sense, dominated the conference. The treaty was a recognition of Sioux power and did little effectively to curb it, for the Sioux continued to expand their domination of the hunting grounds, and wars between them and the United States were not long in coming.[12]

In 1853 Thomas Fitzpatrick by himself negotiated a treaty with the southern plains tribes—Comanches, Kiowas, and Apaches—at Fort Atkinson on the Santa Fe Trail in southwestern Kansas. The provisions were similar to those of Fort Laramie: agreements of peace among the Indians and with the whites, right of passage through the territories for the whites, and permission for military and other posts on Indian lands. The annuities were set at eighteen thousand dollars a year for ten years, with a possible five-year extension; a special article provided that if the United States decided it would be wise to establish farms among the Indians for their benefit, the annuities could be changed into a fund for that purpose.[13]

Fitzpatrick had no trouble with the Indians about the rights of way through their country, which had long been conceded, although he heard strenuous objections to the military posts, which "destroy timber, drive off the game, interrupt their ranges, excite hostile feelings, and but too frequently afford a rendezvous for worthless and trifling characters." The Indians similarly objected to reservations of land for depots and roads, but Fitzpatrick saw no alternative and felt that the concessions finally made by the Indians were "extremely fortunate." He wrote in his report of 1853:

> In view of the fact that at no distant day the whole country over which those Indians now roam must be peopled by another and more enterprising race, and also of the consideration that the channels of

11. CIA Report, 1851, serial 613, pp. 288–90; Hiram Martin Chittenden and Alfred Talbot Richardson, *Life, Letters, and Travels of Father Pierre-Jean DeSmet, S.J., 1801–1873,* 4 vols. (New York: Francis P. Harper, 1905), 2: 675–84. For a detailed analysis of the ratification of the amendment reducing the annuities, see Harry Anderson, "The Controversial Sioux Amendment to the Fort Laramie Treaty of 1851," *Nebraska History* 37 (September 1956): 201–20.

12. Richard White, "The Winning of the West: The Expansion of the Western Sioux in the Eighteenth and Nineteenth Centuries," *Journal of American History* 65 (September 1978): 319–43, traces the powerful advance of the Sioux. The 1851 treaty council is used perceptively by Raymond J. DeMallie as a case study of treaty making in his "Touching the Pen: Plains Indian Treaty Councils in Ethnohistorical Perspective," in Frederick C. Luebke, ed., *Ethnicity on the Great Plains* (Lincoln: University of Nebraska Press, 1980), pp. 41–46.

13. Kappler, pp. 600–602.

commerce between the east and west will eventually, in part at least, pass through their country, it was regarded as incumbent to provide, as far as practicable, for any action the government might see proper to take upon the subject. Already the idea of a great central route to the Pacific by railway has become deeply impressed upon the public mind; and while many courses are contemplated two of them at least are designed to pass through this section of the country. Should the results of explorations now in progress determine it thus, the acknowledgment contained in this clause of the treaty may be found of inestimable value. It will afford all the concession necessary for locations, pre-emptions, reservations, and settlements, and avoid, besides, the enhanced costs of secondary treaties with these tribes. Moreover, it will open a rich vein of wealth in what is now a wilderness, and that, too, without additional public burden.[14]

KANSAS-NEBRASKA AND THE INDIANS

The agitation for a railroad to the Pacific, to which Fitzpatrick alluded in his report, was an important force in clearing the central region of its Indian inhabitants. Some sort of transcontinental road linking the Mississippi Valley with the Pacific, and thus with the riches of the Orient, had been urged by Asa Whitney in the mid-1840s; by 1853 the need was so universally agreed upon that Congress authorized surveys to determine the most appropriate route. The War Department sent out four scientific parties to investigate the possibilities in the north, in the south, and through the central regions. The search for a railroad route also had deep political implications, for each section had strong advocates of a railroad. A southern route would pass through Louisiana, Texas, and the Territory of New Mexico to California—politically organized areas that would offer protection and encouragement to settlement along the road. It was therefore incumbent upon the proponents of a central route to see that the lands through which it would pass were politically organized. And in addition to the need for a railroad, there was continued pressure for settlement of the lands west of the Indian frontier line from restless farmers who felt unjustly obstructed from the "normal" development of the West by the Indian barrier. Congress moved steadily toward creation of a Nebraska territory, which became the goal—one might almost say the obsession—of Senator Douglas.[15]

14. CIA Report, 1853, serial 690, pp. 362–63.
15. Douglas's role is well analyzed in Robert W. Johannsen, *Stephen A. Douglas* (New York: Oxford University Press, 1973), pp. 390–434. The complex issues involved in

In a letter dated December 17, 1853, to a convention for promoting Nebraska to be held in St. Joseph, Missouri, Douglas voiced his own aspirations and those of many in the nation.

How are we to develope, cherish and protect our immense interests and possessions on the Pacific, with a vast wilderness fifteen hundred miles in breadth, filled with hostile savages, and cutting off all direct communication. The Indian barrier must be removed. The tide of emigration and civilization must be permitted to roll onward until it rushes through the passes of the mountains, and spreads over the plains, and mingles with the waters of the Pacific. Continuous lines of settlement with civil, political and religious institutions all under the protection of law, are imperiously demanded by the highest national considerations. These are essential, but they are not sufficient. No man can keep up with the spirit of this age who travels on anything slower than the locomotive, and fails to receive intelligence by lightning. We must therefore have Rail Roads and Telegraphs from the Atlantic to the Pacific, through our own territory. Not one line only, but many lines, for the valley of the Mississippi will require as many Rail Roads to the Pacific as to the Atlantic, and will not venture to limit the number. The removal of the Indian barrier and the extension of the laws of the United States in the form of Territorial governments are the first steps toward the accomplishment of each and all of those objects.[16]

Congress, hoping at last to satisfy both the North and the South in regard to the thorny question of slavery in the central area, passed the Kansas-Nebraska Act in May 1854, which, while repealing the Missouri Compromise prohibition on slavery, provided for two territories whose inhabitants themselves under "popular sovereignty" would decide for or

---

the Nebraska question are treated in Roy F. Nichols, "The Kansas-Nebraska Act: A Century of Historiography," *Mississippi Valley Historical Review* 43 (September 1956): 187–212, and James C. Malin, *The Nebraska Question, 1852–1854* (Lawrence, Kansas, 1953). The Indian aspects of the Nebraska territorial agitation get special attention in Roy Gittinger, "The Separation of Nebraska and Kansas from the Indian Territory," *Mississippi Valley Historical Review* 3 (March 1917): 442–61, and Malin, *Indian Policy and Westward Expansion.* See also Robert R. Russel, *Improvement of Communication with the Pacific Coast as an Issue in American Politics, 1783–1864* (Cedar Rapids, Iowa: Torch Press, 1948), pp. 150–67.

16. Douglas to J. H. Crane, D. M. Johnson, and L. J. Eastin, December 17, 1853, in Douglas, *Letters*, pp. 270–71. The letter was originally printed, with a long introduction, in James C. Malin, "The Motives of Stephen A. Douglas in the Organization of Nebraska Territory: A Letter Dated December 17, 1853," *Kansas Historical Quarterly* 19 (November 1951): 321–53.

against slavery. Whatever the ultimate motivations of the men who voted for the bill, the long agitation for territorial organization that culminated in the act provided a tremendous impetus to the new direction in Indian policy. While the territorial debate was engaging Congress in 1853–1854, in fact, the Indian Office was taking steps to free the region of Indian title and thus open it for settlement.

That difficult task was the responsibility largely of George W. Manypenny, a man whose humanitarian sentiments toward the Indians were frequently enunciated. Manypenny believed that for the Indians' sake the western territories should be organized and that the Indians should be placed as much as possible out of the paths of emigrants to the Pacific. "Objections have been urged to the organization of a civil government in the Indian country," he wrote in 1853; "but those that cannot be overcome are not to be compared to the advantages which will flow to the Indians from such a measure, with treaties to conform to the new order of things, and suitable laws for their protection."[17]

Under an authorization of Congress of March 3, 1853, Manypenny energetically moved ahead to fit the Indians into "the new order of things."[18] He visited most of the border tribes, held councils with them, and did his best to get agreement from them for the cession of their lands. The Indians were ill-disposed to such a measure, having been excited and irritated by exploring parties of whites already invading their territory. At first they were opposed to any sale at all, but eventually they agreed on condition that they could keep small reserves in the areas where they were then situated—a policy that the commissioner objected to, for he wished them to move out entirely.[19] In Washington between March 15 and June 5, 1854, he negotiated nine treaties with the Indians who lived along the eastern border of the new territories: Otos and Missouris, Omahas, Delawares, Shawnees, Iowas, Sacs and Foxes of the Missouri, Kickapoos, Kaskaskias, Peorias, Piankashaws, Weas, and Miamis.[20]

The treaties were pretty much of a piece; the Oto and Missouri treaty of March 5 can be taken as an example. It provided for the cession of the tribes' holdings west of the Missouri River and designated a reduced area

17. CIA Report, 1853, serial 690, p. 251. On Manypenny see Henry E. Fritz, "George W. Manypenny and *Our Indian Wards,*" *Kansas Quarterly* 3 (Fall 1971): 100–104; and Robert M. Kvasnicka, "George W. Manypenny, 1853–57," in Robert M. Kvasnicka and Herman J. Viola, eds., *The Commissioners of Indian Affairs, 1824–1977* (Lincoln: University of Nebraska Press, 1979), pp. 57–67.

18. 10 *United States Statutes* 238–39.

19. CIA Report, 1853, serial 690, pp. 249–50.

20. Kappler, pp. 608–46. These tribes held about 15 million acres, all of which were ceded except for about 1,342,000 acres retained by the tribes in reduced reservations. CIA Report, 1854, serial 746, pp. 213–14.

within the old reservation to which the Indians agreed to remove within a year. A significant characteristic of this treaty, as of all these treaties, was the provision for allotting lands in the newly designated reserve in farm-sized plots to individual Indians. The president was given the discretionary authority to survey the land, set it off in lots, and assign the lots in speci-fied amounts (a quarter-section to a family, 80 acres to single adults, and so on) to all Indians who were "willing to avail of the privilege" and would locate on the lots as a permanent home. There were to be regulations for bequeathing the land and restrictions on its lease or sale. If the Indians left the land to "rove from place to place," their patents would be revoked and their annuities withheld until they returned and "resumed the pursuits of industry." Any residue of land after all the Indians had received an allot-ment was to be sold for the benefit of the Indians.

In return, the United States agreed to pay the Otos and Missouris an-nuities on a sliding scale from twenty thousand to five thousand dollars over the next thirty-eight years. The president would decide what propor-tion, if any, was to be paid in money and what proportion expended for education and other means to civilization. Another twenty thousand dol-lars was granted to help the Indians to move, subsist for a year, and estab-lish themselves on their farms. Moreover, the government would build a grist and saw mill and a blacksmith shop and for ten years would employ a miller, a blacksmith, and a farmer. Punishment in the form of withholding annuities was prescribed for anyone who would drink liquor or bring it into the Indians' lands. Thus were these Indians, who had been subjected to the civilizing policies of the government for a number of decades, to be finally incorporated into white society. The continued Indian residence in Kansas and Nebraska, however, was not intended to impede the westward movement of the whites, for the Indians agreed in the treaties to allow "all the necessary roads and highways, and railroads, which may be constructed as the country improves" to run through their lands, with just compensa-tion to be paid in money.[21]

Good as the intentions of the federal officials were in attempting to pro-vide permanent homes for the Indians in eastern Kansas and Nebraska (as much as possible on individual homesteads), they did not reckon fully with the special problems facing Kansas in the mid-1850s and with what Manypenny called "the wonderful desire to obtain choice lands" on the part of individuals, land companies, and railroads that "causes them to lose sight of and entirely overlook the rights of the aboriginal inhabitants." The conflict between the pro-slavery and anti-slavery forces that turned the

---

21. Clauses in the various treaties pertained to the special conditions of each tribe; the treaties with the Delawares and the Shawnees were the most complex. Most of the treaties made land grants to missionary societies who maintained schools for the Indians.

southern territory into Bleeding Kansas caught the hapless Indians in a devastating situation. As Manypenny neared the end of his tenure as commissioner, he described the pathetic conditions, which were beyond his power to control. The general disorder and the influx of lawless men and speculators slowed down the surveys and the selection of homes for the Indians. He lamented the hindrances to effective use of the means of civilization provided in the treaties.

> The schools have not been as fully attended, nor the school buildings, agency houses, and other improvements, as rapidly constructed as they might otherwise have been. Trespasses and depredations of every conceivable kind have been committed on the Indians. They have been personally maltreated, their property stolen, their timber destroyed, their possession encroached upon, and divers other wrongs and injuries done them. . . . In the din and strife between the anti-slavery and pro-slavery parties with reference to the condition of the African race there, and in which the rights and interests of the red man have been completely overlooked and disregarded, the good conduct and patient submission of the latter contrasts favorably with the disorderly and lawless conduct of many of their white brethren, who, while they have quarrelled about the African, have united upon the soil of Kansas in wrong doing toward the Indian![22]

Manypenny hoped that with the return of peace and order to the territory the good citizens would hasten to repair the wrong and injury done to the Indians by lawless men. But he was much too sanguine in his expectations. The Indian reserves were extraordinarily attractive to designing speculators; leaders of Indian factions made use of the uncertain times for their own benefit; and the federal government was powerless—or lacked the will to exert power—to fulfill its promises to protect the Indians, who had declared in the treaties of 1854 that they would abide by the laws of the United States in conflicts with citizens and expected to be protected and to have their own rights vindicated in turn by the United States.[23]

A special case was that of the Wyandot Indians, who had moved from Ohio in 1843 to a reserve at the mouth of the Kansas River. The Wyandots were highly acculturated to white ways, and some of their leaders played an important part in the agitation for a Nebraska territory. In January 1855

22. CIA Report, 1856, serial 875, p. 572.
23. A detailed and critical account of the conflicts over Indian lands in Kansas after 1854 is in Paul Wallace Gates, *Fifty Million Acres: Conflicts over Kansas Land Policy, 1854–1890* (Ithaca: Cornell University Press, 1954). What happened to the Indian reserves in Kansas is described in H. Craig Miner and William E. Unrau, *The End of Indian Kansas: A Study of Cultural Revolution, 1854–1871* (Lawrence: Regents Press of Kansas, 1977).

they negotiated a treaty with Manypenny in which they declared that, "having become sufficiently advanced in civilization, and being desirous of becoming citizens, it is hereby agreed and stipulated, that their organization, and their relations with the United States as an Indian tribe shall be dissolved and terminated." The Wyandots were declared to be citizens of the United States, and their land was divided among the members of the tribe. Despite the advances of the tribe, however, many Wyandots were not able to prosper under the new conditions, and in February 1867 this portion—including some who, "although taking lands in severalty, have sold said lands, and are still poor," and others who were "unfitted for the responsibilities of citizenship"—decided "to begin anew a tribal existence" and remove to the Indian Territory on land ceded by the Senecas.[24]

MILITARY ACTION ON THE PLAINS

The plans of federal officials for opening a wide passageway west through the plains were interrupted by Indian hostility, brought on by the inexorable pressure of white population sometimes compounded by the imprudent and foolish actions of a few men. Indian hostility became so general by the end of the 1850s that one could speak of a plains Indian barrier of Sioux, Cheyennes, Arapahos, Kiowas, and Comanches extending from the Mexican to the Canadian border. This barrier did not crumble until a decade or more after the Civil War. The United States army, maintaining small forts along the trails and in trouble spots in the West, at first followed a defensive strategy, acting the role of policeman. Then, as Indian raids multiplied, it modified its policy to consider the whole tribe or band responsible for the raids of its members, and it mounted offensive campaigns against them.[25]

The first encounter arose out of the chance Indian killing of a cow belonging to an emigrant Mormon on the trail near Fort Laramie. A rash young lieutenant, John L. Grattan, marched out of the fort on August 19, 1854, to arrest the Indian accused of the cow's death. When the Brulé chief Conquering Bear, at whose camp the culprit was sought, failed to deliver

24. Kappler, pp. 677–81, 960–63. The complicated story of the indefinite land grants to certain members of the tribe made when the Indians moved from Ohio and confirmed in the 1855 treaty—called Wyandot "floats"—is told in Homer E. Socolofsky, "Wyandot Floats," *Kansas Historical Quarterly* 36 (Autumn 1970): 241–304. See also Raymond E. Merwin, "The Wyandot Indians," *Transactions of the Kansas State Historical Society* 9 (1905–1906): 73–88.

25. The best discussion of this subject is Robert M. Utley, *Frontiersmen in Blue: The United States Army and the Indian, 1848–1865* (New York: Macmillan Company, 1967), pp. 108–41.

him, Grattan opened fire, killing the chief. The Sioux fought back and quickly destroyed Grattan and his whole detachment. Emboldened, other Indians attacked the trail along the Platte. The Indian Office criticized the army's action, for under the intercourse law there should have been recourse to the Indian agent for compensation for the butchered animal. But the army decided to teach the Sioux a lesson.[26]

Secretary of War Jefferson Davis placed Colonel William S. Harney in command, and in the summer of 1855 Harney and the troops he had assembled at Fort Kearny moved against the Brulés. Early in September they destroyed the Indians' village near Ash Hollow on the North Platte in western Nebraska. Harney reported heavy casualties for the Sioux: eighty-six killed, five wounded, and about seventy women and children captured. "Never for years," wrote one of the officers in his journal after the battle, "has there been such an utter rout and disorganization of a band of Indians." Then the troops marched through the heart of the Sioux lands from Fort Laramie to Fort Pierre on the Missouri. At Fort Pierre in March 1856 Harney held a council with the Sioux chiefs and cowed them into agreeing to refrain from hostilities.[27] But the harsh action did little to encourage genuinely peaceful sentiments among the Indians. Harney's expedition was simply the first major challenge to the powerful Sioux advance on the northern plains, a movement that paralleled the advance of white Americans into the same region.[28]

Cheyenne Indians, continuing their raids of the Pawnees despite the treaty at Fort Laramie in 1851, disturbed the central plains, and they soon became the target of army action. The Cheyennes struck at emigrants on the trail along the Platte, and the army planned an offensive for the spring of 1857. During May and June a column of troops under Colonel Edwin

26. Lloyd E. McCann, "The Grattan Massacre," *Nebraska History* 37 (March 1956): 1–25; CIA Report, 1854, serial 746, pp. 224, 304–6.

27. Report of Harney, September 5, 1855, *Senate Executive Document* no. 1, 34–1, serial 811, pp. 49–51; Ray H. Mattison, ed., "The Harney Expedition against the Sioux: The Journal of Capt. John B. S. Todd," *Nebraska History* 43 (June 1962): 89–130 (quotation from p. 114); "Council with the Sioux Indians at Fort Pierre," *House Executive Document* no. 130, 34–1, serial 859. The treaty signed by Harney with the Indians at Fort Pierre, an action not in accordance with Indian Office procedures, was rejected by the Senate.

28. White, "Winning of the West," pp. 341–42. White writes: "The warfare between the northern plains tribes and the United States that followed the Fort Laramie Treaty of 1851 was not the armed resistance of a people driven to the wall by American expansion. In reality these wars arose from the clash of two expanding powers—the United States, and the Sioux and their allies. If, from a distance, it appears that the vast preponderance of strength rested with the whites, it should be remembered that the ability of the United States to bring this power to bear was limited. The series of defeats the Sioux inflicted on American troops during these years reveals how real the power of the Tetons was."

Vose Sumner moved up the Platte while a parallel operation under Major John Sedgewick followed the Arkansas. The Indians disappeared before the troops advancing west, but then the columns joined and turned back east to invade the Cheyenne homelands. Along the Solomon River in western Kansas hostile Cheyennes were driven back, and in the followup operation a principal Cheyenne village was destroyed. At that point Sumner's command was called for duty in Utah, and he was forced to suspend his operations. But he had done enough to subdue the Indians. When the Indian agent for the Upper Arkansas met with the tribes to distribute presents in the summer of 1858, he noted that Sumner had worked "a wondrous change in their dispositions toward the whites." The Cheyennes especially were anxious for a new treaty. "They said they had learned a lesson last summer in their fight with Colonel Sumner," the agent reported; "that it was useless to contend against the white man, who would soon with his villages occupy the whole prairie. They had eyes and were not blind. They no longer listened to their young men who continually clamored for war."[29]

The Cheyennes' chastisement kept them quiet even during the Pike's Peak gold rush of 1858–1859, when hordes of gold seekers cut across the central plains from the Missouri to the Rockies. But the increased emigration and its effect upon the Indians gave the Indian Office one more argument for its reservation policy. Commissioner Alfred B. Greenwood noted at the end of 1859 the exasperation that the oncoming whites caused the Indians by dispersing or killing off the game. Only assurances that the government would not let them suffer, he thought, had kept the Indians peaceful. He continued:

> They have also been brought to realize that a stern necessity is impending over them; that they cannot pursue their former mode of life, but must entirely change their habits, and, in fixed localities, look to the cultivation of the soil and the raising of stock for their future support. There is no alternative to providing for them in this manner but to exterminate them, which the dictates of justice and humanity alike forbid. They cannot remain as they are; for, if nothing is done for them, they must be subjected to starvation, or compelled to commence robbing and plundering for a subsistence. This will lead to hostilities and a costly Indian war, involving the loss of many lives, and the expenditure of a much larger amount of money than

29. Report of Agent Robert C. Miller, August 17, 1858, CIA Report, 1858, serial 974, p. 450; S. L. Seabrook, "Expedition of Col. E. V. Sumner against the Cheyenne Indians, 1857," *Collections of the Kansas State Historical Society* 16 (1923–1925): 306–15. Pertinent documents are printed in LeRoy R. Hafen and Ann W. Hafen, eds., *Relations with the Indians of the Plains, 1857–1861* (Glendale, California: Arthur H. Clark Company, 1959), pp. 15–153.

would be required to colonize them on reservations, and to furnish them with the necessary facilities and assistance to enable them to change their mode of life.

Greenwood urged Congress to appropriate funds for the negotiation of new treaties with the tribes.[30]

While a precarious peace settled on the northern plains, the Kiowas and Comanches continued their raids on the Texas frontier. Although they suffered numerous casualties inflicted by United States cavalry and the Texas Rangers, the Indians kept up their hostility throughout the decade. Even an extensive summer campaign of regular troops in 1860 through southern Kansas and western Indian Territory failed to quench the fires.[31]

In the antebellum years neither the army with its offensive operations on the plains and its network of military posts nor the Indian Office with its treaties of peace and civilization and its commitment to a reservation system had completely opened the way for unharassed travel or settlement on the Great Plains.

30. CIA Report, 1859, serial 1023, p. 385.

31. These operations are described in detail in Utley, *Frontiersmen in Blue,* pp. 125–40. See also Brad Agnew, "The 1858 War against the Comanches," *Chronicles of Oklahoma* 49 (Summer 1971): 211–29, and the documents in Hafen and Hafen, *Relations with the Indians of the Plains,* pp. 191–299.

CHAPTER 14

Texas, New Mexico,
and Utah

The Indian Situation in Texas.

Reservations for Texas Indians.

Indian Affairs in New Mexico.

Indians, Mormons, and Gentiles.

The developing reservation policy of the United States met severe tests in Texas and in the regions acquired from Mexico as a result of the Mexican War. There was no lack of resolve on the part of federal officials in Washington or the superintendents and agents they sent into the field. These men held fast to the notion that the Indians must be forced to end their nomadic habits and their raids against the settlements and accept a new existence by living within specified boundaries and depending for subsistence on cultivation of the soil and stock raising. Only thus would there be order in the land and the Indians be protected against extermination. But wherever the federal government turned there were special problems that were only slowly appreciated and that came close to shattering the humanitarian dreams of the policy makers. In Texas state autonomy and self-interest was the special obstacle, in New Mexico the long tradition of raiding the Mexican settlements, and in Utah the overriding presence of the Mormons.

THE INDIAN SITUATION IN TEXAS

The government's reservation policy in Texas failed utterly, for it could not be built securely on the foundation inherited from the Republic of Texas.[1]

1. For useful accounts of the history of federal Indian policy in Texas, see Lena Clara

After Texas gained its independence from Mexico in 1836, its Indian policy vacillated between two extremes. President Sam Houston, who served 1836–1838 and again 1841–1844, and the last president of the Republic, Anson Jones (1844–1846), followed a policy of friendship and conciliation, even in the face of continuing Indian raids upon the settlements. President Mirabeau Buonaparte Lamar, who served between Houston's two terms, on the other hand, was determined to remove or exterminate the Indians, and he organized volunteer troops and rangers to subjugate the hostile tribes. Cherokee Indians, who had peacefully moved into east Texas from Arkansas about 1820, were driven out of Texas by military force in 1839, and other immigrant Indians were threatened with a like fate.[2] Although agents and commissioners were appointed from time to time to deal with the Indians, the Republic of Texas acknowledged no Indian rights to the land, and the Indians roamed over the central and western regions of Texas, following their nomadic hunting life. They passed freely between Texas and lands still under Mexican jurisdiction, moreover, complicating the relations of Texas with Mexico.[3] When Texas was annexed in 1845, the United States inherited an unsolved Indian problem of serious dimensions.

The federal government worked under special handicaps. In the first place, the annexation provisions left control of the public lands in Texas in

---

Koch, "The Federal Indian Policy in Texas, 1845–1860," *Southwestern Historical Quarterly* 28 (January 1925): 223–34; 28 (April 1925): 259–86; 29 (July 1925): 19–35; 29 (October 1925): 98–127; George Dewey Harmon, "The United States Indian Policy in Texas, 1845–1860," *Mississippi Valley Historical Review* 17 (December 1930). 377–403; Alban W. Hoopes, *Indian Affairs and Their Administration: With Special Reference to the Far West, 1849–1860* (Philadelphia: University of Pennsylvania Press, 1932), pp. 178–99; and Robert A. Trennert, Jr., *Alternative to Extinction: Federal Indian Policy and the Beginnings of the Reservation System, 1846–51* (Philadelphia: Temple University Press, 1975), pp. 61–93. Valuable collections of documents are *Texas Indian Papers*, ed. Dorman H. Winfrey and James M. Day, 4 vols. (Austin: Texas State Library, 1959–1961); and *The Indian Papers of Texas and the Southwest, 1825–1916*, ed. Dorman H. Winfrey and James M. Day (Austin: Pemberton Press, 1966).

2. For the history of Indian affairs under the republic, see Anna Muckleroy, "The Indian Policy of the Republic of Texas," *Southwestern Historical Quarterly* 25 (April 1922): 229–60; 26 (July 1922): 1–29; 26 (October 1922): 128–48; 26 (January 1923): 184–206; and A. K. Christian, "Mirabeau Bounaparte Lamar," *Southwestern Historical Quarterly* 24 (July 1920): 39–80. On the Texas Cherokees, see Ernest William Winkler, "The Cherokee Indians in Texas," *Quarterly of the Texas State Historical Association* 7 (October 1903): 95–165; Albert Woldert, "The Last of the Cherokees in Texas, and the Life and Death of Chief Bowles," *Chronicles of Oklahoma* 1 (June 1923): 179–226; Dorman H. Winfrey, "Chief Bowles of the Texas Cherokee," *Chronicles of Oklahoma* 32 (Spring 1954): 29–41; Mary Whatley Clarke, *Chief Bowles and the Texas Cherokees* (Norman: University of Oklahoma Press, 1971).

3. Ralph A. Smith, "Indians in American-Mexican Relations before the War of 1846," *Hispanic American Historical Review* 43 (February 1963): 34–64.

the hands of the state, not the federal government as was the case with the other states and territories. That meant that the United States assumed responsibility for Indian affairs in the new state without ownership and jurisdiction over lands that could be granted and guaranteed to Indian tribes as reservations, and it was unable, without the consent of Texas, to extend the federal trade and intercourse laws (which applied to federally controlled Indian country) for the protection of the Texas Indians from white crimes, encroachment, and trade abuses.[4]

Second, by article 11 of the Treaty of Guadalupe Hidalgo at the end of the Mexican War in 1848, the United States accepted serious obligations. It agreed to restrain the Indians from incursions into Mexico and to exact satisfaction for incursions that could not be prevented. The treaty made it unlawful for inhabitants of the United States to purchase captives or property seized by the Indians in Mexico, and the United States government agreed to rescue Mexican captives brought into the country and return them to Mexico. In addition, the treaty declared: "The sacredness of this obligation shall never be lost sight of by the said Government, when providing for the removal of the Indians from any portion of the said territories, or for it's being settled by citizens of the United States; but on the contrary special care shall then be taken not to place it's Indian occupants under the necessity of seeking new homes, by committing those invasions which the United States have solemnly obliged themselves to restrain." A clause in the original treaty obliged the United States not to furnish firearms or ammunition to the Indians, but this was struck out by the Senate. The amendment, Secretary of State James Buchanan informed Mexico, was "adopted on a principle of humanity": if the Indians could not live by the chase, they were all the more likely to raid Mexican and American settlements for sustenance. Given the lack of federal control over the affairs of Texas and New Mexico, these stipulations were never effectively carried out, and the United States, with a sigh of relief, extricated itself from the responsibilities in the Gadsden Treaty of 1853. A large part of the payment under that treaty was considered an indemnity for Indian incursions.[5]

---

4. One of the conditions of annexation was that Texas "shall also retain all the vacant and unappropriated lands lying within its limits, to be applied to the payment of the debts and liabilities of said Republic of Texas, and the residue of said lands, after discharging said debts and liabilities, to be disposed of as said State may direct." 5 *United States Statutes* 798; 9 *United States Statutes* 108.

5. Treaty of Guadalupe Hidalgo, February 2, 1848, in Hunter Miller, ed., *Treaties and Other International Acts of the United States*, 8 vols. (Washington, GPO, 1931–1948), 5: 219–22, 251, 256; Gadsden Treaty, December 30, 1853, ibid., 6: 296–97. A full discussion is given in J. Fred Rippy, "The Indians of the Southwest in the Diplomacy of the United States and Mexico, 1848–1853," *Hispanic American Historical Review* 2 (August 1919): 363–96. See also Paul Neff Garber, *The Gadsden Treaty* (Philadelphia: University of Pennsylvania Press, 1923), pp. 25–40.

Finally, the military forces available to the federal government, by which it might have enforced by military might what persuasion and diplomacy failed to accomplish, were never numerous enough to patrol the long frontier lines and the even longer international boundary with anything more than minimal effect. In 1849 the army completed a string of posts along the Mexican boundary and at the same time established a cordon of forts along the line of Texas settlement from Fort Worth on the Trinity River to Fort Martin Scott west of Austin, with the purpose of keeping marauding Indians out of the settled areas. The frontier posts, manned largely by infantry, were unable to restrain the mounted Indians, nor were they effective in holding back the tide of white settlers. By 1851 the Texans had moved across the defense line and were demanding a new chain of posts. To satisfy them, Fort Belknap was established on the Brazos River west of Fort Worth, and a new series of posts appeared on a line running southwest to Fort Clark near the Rio Grande. Some of the earlier forts were closed and their men and supplies moved to the new establishments. With these forts and others built throughout the 1850s to protect communication lines, the troops tried valiantly but unsuccessfully to maintain peace.[6]

Despite the peculiarities of the situation, the federal government proceeded pretty much according to the main outlines of its developing policy for dealing with the new Indians it encountered as the result of western territorial acquisitions. In September 1845 it began by dispatching a peace commission to conciliate the Indians. The two commissioners, Pierce M. Butler and M. G. Lewis, called a council of the tribes in Texas for January 1846, but it was not until May that the Indians—Comanches, Anadarkos, Caddos, Lipans, and others—assembled on the Brazos River at a place called Council Springs. By that time the war with Mexico had commenced, and the need to keep the restive Indians peaceful was of great importance.[7] On May 15 the tribes signed a treaty with the traditional provisions: the Indians acknowledged themselves to be under the exclusive protection of

6. A brief summary of the military defense is given in Robert M. Utley, *Frontiersmen in Blue: The United States Army and the Indian, 1848–1865* (New York: Macmillan Company, 1967), pp. 71–75. A more detailed account appears in W. C. Holden, "Frontier Defense, 1846–1860," *West Texas Historical Association Year Book* 6 (1930): 35–64. See also Rupert Norval Richardson, *The Frontier of Northwest Texas, 1846 to 1876: Advance and Defense by the Pioneer Settlers of the Cross Timbers and Prairies* (Glendale, California: Arthur H. Clark Company, 1963); Averam B. Bender, *The March of Empire: Frontier Defense in the Southwest, 1848–1860* (Lawrence: University of Kansas Press, 1952).

7. Details of the negotiations are given in Butler and Lewis to William Medill, August 8, 1846, *Senate Report* no. 171, 30–1, serial 512, pp. 29–37. The report is printed also in *House Document* no. 76, 29–2, serial 500. For the record kept by a Cherokee Indian who accompanied Butler and Lewis, see Grant Foreman, ed., "The Journal of Elijah Hicks," *Chronicles of Oklahoma* 13 (March 1935): 68–99.

the United States and agreed to keep peace with the Americans and with other Indians; the United States assumed sole right to regulate trade and intercourse with them; the Indians agreed to give up all captives; punishment for crimes between Indians and whites was provided for (there was a separate article on horse stealing); the United States promised to erect trading houses and agencies on the borders of the tribes; special provision was made to prohibit the liquor traffic; and there was, finally, the usual provision, at the discretion of the president, for blacksmiths, schoolteachers, and "preachers of the gospel." Other articles, attempting to define the jurisdiction of the United States and the state of Texas in Indian affairs, were stricken out on the insistence of the Texas delegation in Congress, so that the treaty could at length be ratified and proclaimed on March 8, 1847.[8]

Even before ratification, initial steps were taken to provide for the Texas Indians. On March 3, 1847, Congress authorized $20,000 for presents, $3,650 for a special agent and two interpreters for a year, and $10,000 "to carry into effect the treaty with the Comanches and other tribes of Indians."[9]

The agent appointed, Robert S. Neighbors, was an especially happy choice. Neighbors, who had moved to Texas in 1836 when he was twenty, had served with distinction in the Texas Revolution and under the Republic of Texas (as army officer and Indian agent). He understood the Indians' situation, was sympathetic to their plight, and stood irrevocably committed to protecting their interests; he acted as an effective and persuasive diplomat under conditions that gave him little to work with.[10] Neighbors was a realist in appraising the situation. He wrote to the commissioner of Indian affairs soon after he took office:

> For the last few months our settlements have extended very rapidly, and, unless checked, will continue to do so; also, frequently large parties of surveyors penetrate many miles into the country now occupied by the Indians. These movements keep the Camanches and many other tribes in continual excitement; and unless some measures can be adopted by the department to check the surveyors, it will finally lead to serious difficulties. From these causes the Camanches are in a doubtful state of quietness, and there is no telling how soon there will be a general outbreak among them. The present

8. Kappler, pp. 554–56; Grant Foreman, "The Texas Comanche Treaty of 1846," *Southwestern Historical Quarterly* 51 (April 1948): 313–32.

9. 9 *United States Statutes* 204.

10. Kenneth F. Neighbours, "Robert S. Neighbors in Texas, 1836–1859: A Quarter Century of Frontier Problems" (Ph.D. dissertation, University of Texas, 1955); Neighbours, "Robert S. Neighbors and the Founding of Texas Indian Reservations," *West Texas Historical Association Year Book* 31 (1955): 65–74.

laws of Texas do not acknowledge that the Indians have any right of soil; and those persons holding land claims contend that they have the privilege of locating wherever they choose.[11]

Neighbors, nevertheless, believed that peace was possible. He called a great council of the tribes at the end of September 1847 in order to explain the treaty of 1846 and to allay their fears, and he persuaded Governor J. Pinckney Henderson of Texas to reinstate the laws of the Republic of Texas regarding intercourse with the Indians and to designate a temporary line above the settlements separating Indians from whites.[12] But with the withdrawal of heavy troop concentrations in Texas at the end of the Mexican War and the continued advance of the surveyors and settlers came new raids and hostility along the frontier.

RESERVATIONS FOR TEXAS INDIANS

There seemed to be only one practicable solution. Texas must grant lands for reservations on which the Indians could be settled and turned into farmers and where the federal government could protect them from lawless whites. All the responsible federal officials were of one mind on this. Neighbors in March 1849 outlined his own specifications for a workable plan: (1) a boundary line established by treaty, which would extinguish Indian claims to all the land needed by Texas; (2) acquisition from Texas by the United States of sufficient territory to establish a permanent location for the Indians; (3) extension of the federal trade and intercourse laws over the Indians of Texas; (4) a general agency, with at least three subagents; and (5) necessary military posts in the Indian country. John H. Rollins, the Whig who succeeded Neighbors when his term of office expired in 1849, came to the same conclusion: "Nothing short of a country for the Indians, over which the laws of the United States regulating our Indian intercourse and relations were extended, together with a temporary support for the Indians," he wrote, "could be safely adopted as a permanent policy." Like many others, he argued, too, on the basis of economy, asserting that "it would be incalculably less expensive to purchase a country for the Indians, remove them to it, and support them until they had made some advance in agriculture, than to deprive them by force of a country which they very

11. Neighbors to William Medill, June 2, 1847, CIA Report, 1847, serial 503, pp. 893–94. The full report, pp. 892–96, gives an excellent picture of the conditions and how Neighbors met them.

12. Neighbors to Medill, October 12, 1847, CIA Report, 1847, serial 503, pp. 903–6; Neighbors to Medill, November 18, 1847, *Senate Report* no. 171, 30–1, serial 512, pp. 9–10.

properly thought their own, to say nothing of the duty of humanity, or the sudden and violent interruption which a prolonged and uncertain war would cause to the prosperity and progress of this and other frontier States." George T. Howard, who became agent when Rollins died in September 1851, spoke of "the absolute necessity for some provision being made for the settlement of these Indians, and for supplying them with the necessary means to commence the cultivation of the soil." He believed so strongly in the need that he recommended buying or leasing land from private individuals if Texas did not grant some reservation lands. "Until a territory is procured for them," he wrote, "all attempts to control and civilize them will prove abortive." When Neighbors was reappointed special agent for Texas Indians in May 1853, he began to work with unabated energy for the realization of a reservation system.[13]

The agents on the spot, judging the conditions as they experienced them firsthand, were seconded by the commissioners of Indian affairs and the secretaries of the interior. These men in Washington no doubt were influenced by what the highly respected agents were proposing, but it cannot be overlooked that the plans for Texas reservations accorded precisely with the philosophy of the general government for handling Indian relations. The Indians were to be persuaded to stop their hunting over a vast area, claiming lands that were increasingly sought by white settlers; to settle as agriculturalists on limited reserves out of the way of the whites, where they would soon become self-sufficient again in the new economic pattern; and to adopt the cultural attributes of white civilization through education and Christianization. The statements of Medill, Brown, and Lea and their successors were not pious abstractions; these men advocated what they considered a practical solution, one that as Christian officials they had judged successful in dealing with tribes that had moved to the new frontier west of the Mississippi. They saw no reason to doubt its efficacy in dealing with the wild tribes of Texas.[14]

In 1850 Congress authorized two more agents to serve in Texas and thirty thousand dollars for procuring information, for collecting statistics, and for making treaties with and giving presents to the Indian tribes on the borders of Mexico. The instructions to the three-man commission appointed for these purposes—Charles S. Todd, Robert B. Campbell, and

13. Neighbors to William J. Worth, March 7, 1849, CIA Report, 1849, serial 550, p. 964; Rollins to C. S. Todd, March 25, 1851, CIA Report, 1851, serial 613, p. 518; Howard to Luke Lea, June 1, 1852, quoted in Hoopes, *Indian Affairs and Their Administration*, p. 187; Howard to Lea, August 15, 1852, CIA Report, 1852, serial 658, p. 430.

14. There is an especially pointed statement of this policy in CIA Report, 1848, serial 537, p. 386. For remarks on Texas Indian policy, see CIA Report, 1847, serial 513, pp. 751–52; CIA Report, 1848, serial 537, p. 408; CIA Report, 1849, serial 550, pp. 941–42; CIA Report, 1850, serial 587, p. 44.

Oliver Temple—said little about treaties but emphasized the necessity of gathering information about the attitude of the Indians toward the United States, about where to locate agencies, and about what kind of presents were necessary, information that would be useful guidance to the Indian Office in determining how to deal with the Indians of Texas. The commissioners were told to inquire into "everything relating to the character of the several tribes: their manners, habits, customs, mode of living—whether by agriculture, the chase, or otherwise; the extent of their civilization, their religion or religious ceremonies—whether Christian or Pagan; what their religious rites; whether marriages are held sacred among them, and whether a plurality of wives is tolerated." In addition, they were to report on the topography and resources of the country and the nature of Indian claims and tenure. Unfortunately, little came from the commission, for Congress refused to appropriate additional funds for it and abrogated its authority to negotiate treaties. Its report was brief and of limited value, but the commissioners did urge settling the Indians within definite boundaries, a "salutary and philanthropic policy [that] may tend to their civilization, by leading them to cultivate the soil, to acquire individual property, and domesticate themselves, so far at least as to become herdsmen, instead of living like wandering Arabs."[15]

Although Congress in 1850 extended the trade and intercourse laws over New Mexico and Utah territories, it did not do so for the state of Texas, and Lea felt obliged to instruct the agents in Texas: "You will . . . have no right to resort to force in the execution of your official duties; and an attempt to do so would not only be without the sanction of law, but might be regarded as derogatory to the rights and dignity of a sovereign State. Hence the means you will employ in carrying out the views and policy of the Government must be altogether of a mild and persuasive character." Lea pleaded for action in setting aside lands for the Indians. The amount of reserved territory, he asserted, would be small. Without it the Indians were forced either to starve or to steal, nor should Texas complain about depredations that the state itself was largely responsible for. The Indians, he said in 1851, "certainly have the right to live somewhere; and nowhere, more certainly, than on the lands which they and their fathers have occupied for countless generations." He insisted that reservations were "indispensable to a proper adjustment of Indian affairs" in Texas.[16]

15. 9 *United States Statutes* 555, 556; A. S. Loughery, acting commissioner of Indian affairs, to Todd, Campbell, and Temple, October 15, 1850, CIA Report, 1850, serial 587, pp. 153–55; Luke Lea to Todd, Campbell, and Temple, April 3, 1851, CIA Report, 1851, serial 613, pp. 301–2; Todd, Campbell, and Temple to Lea, August 23, 1851, ibid., pp. 302–6.

16. CIA Report, 1851, serial 613, p. 272; Lea to John H. Rollins, John A. Rogers, and Jesse Stem, November 25, 1850, ibid., p. 515; CIA Report, 1852, serial 658, p. 299.

As conditions worsened in Texas, the state finally saw the necessity of what federal officials had been requesting for almost a decade. After giving up hope that all Indians could be removed from the state, it moved slowly toward the reservation system. In 1851, a joint committee on Indian affairs of the Texas legislature proposed such a plan. The report, heavily influenced by the committee chairman (none other than Robert Neighbors, who had been elected to the house after his removal as Indian agent), offered the following proposal:

> The State could adopt no better or more humane plan to relieve our border citizens from the petty thefts and depredations committed by those Indians residing in our State in detached bands, and under the control of no direct agency by setting apart small tracts or parcels of land near the United States military posts selected on our frontier, to be occupied by these Indians, subject to the pleasure of the State. By adopting the plan proposed, they will at once settle down, cultivate the soil, turn attention to stockraising, etc., instead of depending on the chase, which, at least, affords an uncertain and scanty subsistence, and often drives them to acts of theft upon the stock of our citizens, to supply the deficiency required for the support of their old men and families.[17]

Little by little the idea matured, for the existing state of affairs could not continue much longer.

Finally, on February 6, 1854, the Texas legislature offered reservations for the Indians. The law provided that up to twelve leagues of land be set aside for use of the Indians within the state. The land, to be selected and surveyed by the United States, was to be laid out so far as possible in square tracts, numbering three or fewer, and these were to be located no more than twenty miles east or south of the northernmost line of United States military posts. Jurisdiction over the territory selected for the Indians was ceded to the United States government "so far as to enable it to extend any act of Congress now existing, or hereafter to be passed, regulating trade and intercourse with the Indian tribes," but the state retained its jurisdiction over non-Indians. The federal government was authorized to settle the Indians on the reserve, "exercise entire control and jurisdiction" over them, and establish necessary agencies and military posts. The lands would revert to the state should the Indians abandon them.[18]

17. *Senate Journals of the State of Texas*, 1851–1852, quoted in Harmon, "Indian Policy in Texas," p. 389. Harmon discusses the moves toward reservation grants on pp. 387–94.

18. Williamson S. Oldham and George W. White, *A Digest of the General Statute Laws of the State of Texas* (Austin: John Marshall and Company, 1859), pp. 238–39. By a

With these provisions, Neighbors and his superiors in Washington moved to establish their long-desired colonies. In the summer of 1854 the agent, in company with Captain R. B. Marcy of the United States army, selected two reserves. One, of 37,152 acres, was located at the main fork of the Brazos River about ten miles south of Fort Belknap. Another, of 18,576 acres, was located on the Clear Fork of the Brazos at Camp Cooper.[19] It took some time to gather the Indians, but in March 1855 the semi-agricultural tribes —Caddos, Wacos, Tawakonis, Anadarkos, Tonkawas, Keechies, and a few Delawares—began to colonize the Brazos reserve. In September Neighbors counted 794 Indians located there, and he spoke enthusiastically of their agricultural progress. "There can be no doubt of the success of the policy," he wrote, "and I would earnestly commend it to the fostering care of the general government as the most humane and economical that could possibly be followed, and one, that, in a very short time, will relieve our frontier forever from the scenes of murder and theft that have retarded the extension of civilization for so many years." The Brazos reservation appeared to fulfill all the agent's hopes, as year by year he reported more Indians settled, more fields under cultivation, and more crops harvested. The hopes were not only for tranquility on the frontier, but for the Indians' advancement as well, and Neighbors was not disappointed. "There has been great improvement for the last year in the moral and physical condition of the Indians now settled," he wrote in 1856. "They are gradually falling into the customs and dress of the white man; and by being well clothed, having houses to live in, and [being] relieved from the continued anxieties attending a roving life, their health has greatly improved, and they now, for the first time for several years, begin to raise healthy children." A school for the Indian children was successfully begun, too. The glowing reports, however, referred largely to the Brazos reserve; the Comanche reserve, with In-

---

law of February 4, 1856, Texas provided another five leagues of land west of the Pecos River as a reservation for the Indians in that area. Ibid., pp. 239–40. This third reservation was never established because the difficulties with the first two precluded extension of the reservation system in Texas, and Congress prohibited the use of appropriations for the new reservation. 11 *United States Statutes* 400; CIA Report, 1859, serial 1023, p. 383. By a law of July 28, 1856, Texas extended the intercourse laws of the United States insofar as they prohibited the introduction of liquor into the Indian country for a distance of ten miles from the boundary lines of the reservations. Oldham and White, *Laws of the State of Texas*, p. 240.

19. Kenneth F. Neighbours, "The Marcy-Neighbors Exploration of the Headwaters of the Brazos and Wichita Rivers in 1854," *Panhandle-Plains Historical Review* 27 (1954): 26–46; W. Eugene Hollon, *Beyond the Cross Timbers: The Travels of Randolph B. Marcy, 1812–1887* (Norman: University of Oklahoma Press, 1955), pp. 169–86; R. B. Marcy, *Thirty Years of Army Life on the Border* (New York: Harper and Brothers, 1866), pp. 170–214.

dians less ready to settle down, made much less progress, both in numbers and in agricultural production.[20]

The letters of Neighbors and the other agents convinced the officials in Washington for a time of the program's success. But the legal problems of protecting the Indians on the reservations were never solved. Although the Texas legislature had done what it could to provide federal jurisdiction over the reservations, Congress, for its part, never officially extended the trade and intercourse laws to Texas, so that federal officials had no weapon against the whites who were introducing liquor and in other ways abusing the Indians.[21]

The location of hundreds of Indians on the two reserves did not solve the Indian problem in Texas. Nonreservation Indians, many if not most of whom came into the state from Mexico, New Mexico, or Indian territory, continued their depredations. In the minds of the enraged Texans it was difficult to draw a sharp distinction between those Indians and Indians on the reservations. Indeed, many Texans believed that reservation Comanches were guilty of raids and other outrages. Tension increased as the border warfare heightened, for neither state nor federal officials were able to end the attacks. What hopes for peace there might have been were destroyed on December 27, 1858, when a group of whites attacked a party of peaceful Indians on a hunting expedition and murdered seven men and women in their sleep. Neighbors reported it as "the most cold-blooded murder of women and children that has ever transpired since the revolution made Texas a republic, and exceeds all the brutality attributed to the wild Comanches." He saw the act as part of an "organized conspiracy against the Indian policy of the general government, for the purpose of breaking up the reserves in Texas." The whites feared retaliation from the Indians, and some sought openly to attack the Indians on the reserves, who dared not leave their limits and clustered around the agency in fear.[22]

20. Neighbors to Charles E. Mix, September 10, 1855, CIA Report, 1855, serial 810, pp. 497–502; Neighbors to George W. Manypenny, September 18, 1856, CIA Report, 1856, serial 875, pp. 724–27; Neighbors to Mix, September 16, 1858, CIA Report, 1858, serial 974, pp. 524–27. Descriptions of the reservations are given in Kenneth F. Neighbours, "Chapters from the History of Texas Indian Reservations," *West Texas Historical Association Year Book* 33 (1957): 3–16. There is an account of the Comanche reservation in Rupert N. Richardson, "The Comanche Reservation in Texas," *West Texas Historical Association Year Book* 5 (1929): 43–65, and in his *The Comanche Barrier to South Plains Settlement: A Century and a Half of Savage Resistance to the Advancing White Frontier* (Glendale, California: Arthur H. Clark Company, 1933), pp. 211–66. For an account of the Indian-white contact focused on the Comanches, see T. R. Fehrenbach, *Comanches: The Destruction of a People* (New York: Alfred A. Knopf, 1974).

21. The agents and commissioners of Indian affairs continued to call for congressional action; see, for example, CIA Report, 1858, serial 974, pp. 359–60, 529–36.

22. Neighbors to J. W. Denver, January 30, 1859, CIA Report, 1859, serial 1023,

The futility of the government's reservation policy was soon apparent. In February 1859 Neighbors urged the immediate removal of the reservation Indians outside the borders of Texas to land recently obtained from the Choctaws and Chickasaws. Even if the United States poured in military forces to protect the reserves, the Indians under the circumstances could hardly progress in the arts of civilization. At the end of March the Indian Office directed the agents to make the move so that the Indians could be "protected from lawless violence, and effective measures adopted for their domestication and improvement," and accordingly instructions were sent in mid-June.[23] After a survey of the proposed lands with some of the chiefs and the superintendent of the Southern Superintendency, Elias Rector, who would assume responsibility for the Indians in their new home, the move was made. In August, protected by United States cavalry on the march, 1,050 Indians from the Brazos reserve and 380 Comanches migrated to Indian Territory—out of the "heathen land of Texas," "out of the land of the Philistines," as Neighbors described it to his wife.[24] Having seen his charges to the new reservation, Neighbors returned to Fort Belknap. He had long been under attack by certain Texans for his defense of Indian rights, and on September 14, 1859, as he went about his business in town, he was murdered by a stranger.[25]

The reservation as a panacea was thus strikingly ineffective in Texas. The federal government, unwilling to tangle with the Texans, who emphasized states' rights, was delayed in establishing reservations for the Indians because of state control of public lands. When, through a grant by the state, land was set aside for the Indians, the government proved unable to protect the settled Indians from lawless and aggressive Texas frontiersmen. Even if it had forced a showdown, the agitation and resulting tension would have weakened if not destroyed the conditions under which an agricultural civilization program, one of the primary goals of reservation life, would have

p. 595; numerous documents that tell the story of white aggression against the Indians are printed ibid., pp. 588–632.

23. Neighbors to Denver, February 14, 1859, CIA Report, 1859, serial 1023, p. 605; Mix to Neighbors, March 30, 1859, ibid., pp. 631–32; A. B. Greenwood to Neighbors, June 11, 1859, ibid., pp. 650–51.

24. Neighbors to Greenwood, July 24, 1859, ibid., p. 687; Neighbors to Lizzie A. Neighbors, August 8, 1859, quoted in Koch, "Indian Policy in Texas," p. 122; Kenneth F. Neighbours, "Indian Exodus out of Texas in 1859," *West Texas Historical Association Year Book* 36 (1960): 80–97. Texas in 1875 finally declared the reserves abandoned and provided for squatters and other homesteaders on the lands. John Sayles and Henry Sayles, *Early Laws of Texas*, 3 vols. (St. Louis: Gilbert Book Company, 1888), 3: 301–3.

25. Statement of M. Leeper, September 15, 1859, CIA Report, 1859, serial 1023, pp. 701–2; Kenneth F. Neighbours, "The Assassination of Robert S. Neighbors," *West Texas Historical Association Year Book* 34 (1958): 38–49.

been possible. The federal government chose to retreat instead, holding its policy intact.

The removal, of course, brought no peace to Texas. Marauding Indians devastated the settlements, and defense of the Texas frontier remained a serious problem until the ultimate subjugation of the southern plains tribes in the 1870s.

INDIAN AFFAIRS IN NEW MEXICO

The United States began its formal relations with the Indians of New Mexico during the Mexican War, and its relations in the first instance were primarily military.[26] The advance of General Stephen Watts Kearny into the region in 1846 as part of the American strategy in the Mexican War set the pattern for government action. Kearny's column came as a conquering army, promising to bring peace and order to a land torn by depredations and fear. The Pueblo Indians in their settled towns along the Rio Grande were beset by their hostile Navajo neighbors and threatened periodically by the warlike Apaches and Comanches raiding from the southern plains, and they hastened to greet the American soldiers with gestures of friendship. The Americans looked upon the Pueblos, who had been considered citizens by the Mexican government, as "civilized Indians," living in organized communities and dependent upon agriculture for subsistence.

Quite different were the "wild," more nomadic Apaches and Navajos, tending their sheep and horses but living in large part by raids on the Mexicans. It was these Indians who created such an uproar in the region and who were the basic problem for the United States government. Kearny came with a strong feeling of American superiority, which he expected the Indians to recognize, and he hoped to gain support for his occupation from the Mexicans by his offers of protection against the hostile Indians. He told the people of Las Vegas, the first major settlement he encountered, on August 15, 1846: "From the Mexican government you have never received protection. The Apaches and the Navajhoes come down from the mountains and carry off your sheep, and even your women, whenever they

26. The best studies of early Indian affairs in New Mexico are Trennert, *Alternative to Extinction*, pp. 94–130, and Hoopes, *Indian Affairs and Their Administration*, pp. 161–78. The place of Indian affairs in the whole political picture can be seen in Howard R. Lamar, *The Far Southwest, 1846: A Territorial History* (New Haven: Yale University Press, 1966), pp. 56–108. Military activities against the Indians are studied in Utley, *Frontiersmen in Blue*, pp. 142–74, and Bender, *March of Empire*, pp. 149–70. See also Averam B. Bender, "Frontier Defense in the Territory of New Mexico, 1846–1853," *New Mexico Historical Review* 9 (July 1934): 249–72, and "Frontier Defense in the Territory of New Mexico, 1853–1861," ibid. (October 1934): 345–73.

please. My government will correct all this. It will keep off the Indians, protect you in your persons and property." As he moved victorious to Santa Fe, he repeated his assurances, proclaiming that he would protect the peaceful inhabitants against the Indians.[27]

There was no trouble with the Pueblos, whose delegates met peacefully with Kearny and convinced him of their friendship. The other tribes were less easily handled. Colonel Alexander W. Doniphan moved into Navajo country and negotiated with the chiefs. An agreement was signed on March 22, for the Navajos were initially impressed by the American power and agreed to stop their raids against the Mexicans and to return captives and stolen property.[28] Peace seemed to be at hand as Kearny proceeded on to California and Doniphan into Mexico, leaving Charles Bent on the spot in charge of a provisional territorial government set up by Kearny. Bent made recommendations to the Indian Office for the appointment of agents and subagents and urged that a delegation of Indians be sent to Washington to impress them with the power of the United States. But the territory was not yet a part of the United States, and the Indian Office could not act. Continued military control was the only alternative.[29]

It did not take long for Indian unrest to reappear. Mexicans, unhappy with the American occupation, plotted to overthrow the government and enlisted Pueblo support. An uprising at Taos on January 19, 1847, killed Governor Bent and other officials and ended the idea of peaceful occupation, although the revolt was quickly put down by military force. Soon the wild Indians renewed their depredations, and Indian affairs in New Mexico deteriorated, as the success of Navajo and Apache raids emboldened other tribes to attack the Americans, especially along the Santa Fe Trail. American military force in New Mexico was not enough to guarantee the peace that Kearny had so sanguinely promised.[30]

The end of the Mexican War and the ratification of the Treaty of Guadalupe Hidalgo in 1848 did not greatly change the military picture in New Mexico, although the provision by which the United States agreed to stop Indian raids into Mexico added considerably to the responsibilities of the

27. W. H. Emory, "Notes of a Military Reconnaissance from Fort Leavenworth, in Missouri, to San Diego, in California," *Senate Executive Document* no. 7, 30–1, serial 505, p. 27; "Proclamation to the Inhabitants of New Mexico by Brigadier General S. W. Kearny," August 22, 1846, *House Executive Document* no. 19, 29–2, serial 499, pp. 20–21.

28. An account of Doniphan's expedition is in John Taylor Hughes, *Doniphan's Expedition: Containing an Account of the Expedition against New Mexico* (Cincinnati: U. P. James, 1847), reprinted in William Elsey Connelley, *Doniphan's Expedition and the Conquest of New Mexico and California* (Topeka, 1907), pp. 115–524. The text of the agreement appears on p. 307.

29. Trennert, *Alternative to Extinction*, p. 103.

30. Ibid., pp. 104–12.

army commanders. Lieutenant Colonel John M. Washington, the new military governor, intended to pacify the hostile tribes and then make them accept American control, in line with the conventional Indian policy of the day. "The period has arrived," he wrote to the War Department in February 1849, "when they [the Indians] must restrain themselves within prescribed limits and cultivate the earth for an honest livelyhood, or, be destroyed. . . . The particular location and extent of these limits and the inducements held out for a change from their present roving habits to the pursuit of agriculture, from the savage state to that of civilization, are well worthy of attention."[31]

The pacifying was no easy task. In all sections of the region Indian raids continued, and the citizens were enraged. "We are now," wrote one of them to the secretary of war in July 1849, "in actual war with four of the most powerful and numerous tribes on the continent, all living in close proximity to the territory and all making daily incursions into our settlements."[32] Prodded by such criticism, Governor Washington began a military operation against the Navajos in August, penetrating into their country. A first meeting with three chiefs broke up in a fight in which one Navajo was killed, but after a display of military force in Canyon de Chelly, Washington negotiated a treaty with other chiefs, who agreed to recognize American jurisdiction and to submit to the trade and intercourse laws, to return captives and stolen property and remain at peace, and to allow the federal government to determine their boundaries.[33] No sooner had the expedition returned to Santa Fe, however, than the Indians renewed their raids.

When the new Whig president Zachary Taylor entered office in 1849, the government provided for civilian administration of Indian affairs in New Mexico by transferring a midwestern agency to Santa Fe and appointing a South Carolina politician, James S. Calhoun, to be Indian agent.[34] Calhoun proved to be a man of marked ability who exhibited deep concern for the Indians and intelligently promoted an Indian policy that would end

31. Washington to Roger Jones, February 3, 1849, quoted ibid., p. 113.

32. Remarks of William S. Messervy, quoted ibid., p. 114.

33. Documents regarding Washington's Navajo expedition are in *House Executive Document* no. 5, 31–1, serial 569, pp. 104–15. The treaty is printed ibid., pp. 113–14. Continuing relations with the Navajos are studied in Frank D. Reeve, "The Government and the Navaho, 1846–1858," *New Mexico Historical Review* 14 (January 1939): 82–114. See also L. R. Bailey, *The Long Walk: A History of the Navajo Wars, 1846–68* (Los Angeles: Westernlore Press, 1964), pp. 14–20.

34. Calhoun's letter of appointment, April 7, 1849, is in *House Executive Document* no. 17, 31–1, serial 573, pp. 194–96. His early reports to the secretary of the interior and the commissioner of Indian affairs appear ibid., pp. 198–229. The standard work on Calhoun is Annie Heloise Abel, ed., *The Official Correspondence of James S. Calhoun While Indian Agent at Santa Fe and Superintendent of Indian Affairs in New Mexico* (Washington: GPO, 1915).

the troubles in the Southwest. He arrived in Santa Fe just as Governor Washington was preparing to launch his expedition into Navajo country, and he accompanied the troops in order to support the commander's attempt to impress the Indians with the authority of the United States. Before the year was out Calhoun had succeeded in negotiating with the Utes a treaty similar to that signed with the Navajos; it included promises by the Indians "to build up pueblos, or to settle in such other manner as will enable them most successfully to cultivate the soil, and pursue such other industrial pursuits as will best promote their happiness and prosperity," to cease their "roving and rambling habits," and to support themselves "by their own industry, aided and directed as it may be by the wisdom, justice, and humanity of the American people."[35]

Calhoun's proposal for adjusting Indian affairs in New Mexico was a display of military force that would end Indian depredations, then settlement of the Indians on reservations modeled after the Pueblo towns. The agent worked out a specific plan. Separated tracts of land, at least a hundred miles apart, would be assigned to the Navajos, Apaches, Utes, and Comanches. The Indians would be supplied with subsistence until they had learned to become self-sufficient. It would cost money, Calhoun admitted, but as he told the Indian Office, "to establish order in this territory, you must either submit to these heavy expenditures, or exterminate the mass of these Indians."[36]

Calhoun's plan depended on military force to keep the Indians on their reservations, and he called for the establishment of military posts in the Indian country. But he also demanded civilian agents for the tribes, to aid him in the civilizing aspects of his proposal. "The presence of Agents in various places in the Indian country," he told the commissioner of Indian affairs, "is indispensably necessary—their presence is demanded by every principle of humanity—by every generous obligation of kindness—of protection, and good government throughout this vast territory." He was especially insistent that agents be supplied to the Pueblos, not only to aid them in their agriculture, but to protect them from encroaching whites; and he urged the extension of the trade and intercourse laws to New Mexico so that the agents would have authority for their protective action.[37]

The hands of the commissioner of Indian affairs were tied, however, as long as New Mexico did not have a civil government and remained under military control, and the conflict between civilian and military officers over Indian affairs complicated an already difficult situation. The Indians

35. Kappler, pp. 585–87.
36. Calhoun to Orlando Brown, February 3, 1850, Abel, *Correspondence of Calhoun,* p. 141; Calhoun to Brown, March 30, 1850, ibid., p. 179.
37. Calhoun to Medill, October 15, 1849, ibid., pp. 56–57; Calhoun to Brown, November 16, 1849, ibid., pp. 78–81.

boldly kept up their attacks, and the army, forced to rely on infantry when cavalry were desperately needed against the mounted Indians, could do little but lament its own ineffectiveness. In addition, the strong movement of the New Mexicans for immediate statehood disturbed the Pueblos, who feared that the formation of a state before federal protection had been extended to them would result in loss of the civil and property rights they had enjoyed under Mexican rule and under American military government.[38]

Congress, caught up in the sectional controversy that emerged with the Mexican War, denied the New Mexican demands for statehood. Instead, on September 9, 1850, the Territory of New Mexico was established as part of the Compromise of 1850. The Senate, on January 7, 1851, confirmed the appointment of James S. Calhoun as first territorial governor and ex officio superintendent of Indian affairs, and at the end of February Congress authorized four Indian agents for New Mexico and extended the trade and intercourse laws over the territory.[39]

The military component of Indian affairs in New Mexico, nevertheless, continued to be of great moment. In November 1849 Secretary of War George W. Crawford detailed Colonel George A. McCall of the Third Infantry to investigate conditions in New Mexico. McCall's report of July 15, 1850, gave a detailed account of the geographical characteristics and agricultural capabilities of the land, of the Indians and their way of life, and of the possibilities of changing the ways of the various tribes. The Navajos he thought "might in a short time by judicious management be induced to give up their roving habits and settle themselves in permanent towns in the vicinity of their fields." At the other extreme, he wrote of the Jicarilla Apaches: "This band is considered as incorrigible, and it is believed they will continue to rob and murder our citizens until they are exterminated. I know of no means that could be employed to reclaim them." He noted how ignorant all the Indians were of the power of the United States and urged that groups of them be invited to Washington to see the "means and resources of the country to carry on a war."[40]

McCall's report called for military posts in the Indian country, and the War Department adopted his proposals. Colonel Edwin V. Sumner, who assumed military command in New Mexico, was directed to chastise the hostile Indians and move his troops out of the towns of the territory into the Indian country. Calhoun heartily agreed, for once the posts were estab-

38. The statehood movement is discussed in Trennert, *Alternative to Extinction*, pp. 122–23, and in more detail in Lamar, *Far Southwest*, pp. 73–82.

39. Abel, *Correspondence of Calhoun*, p. 296; 9 *United States Statutes* 447, 587.

40. On McCall, his work, and his reports, see George Archibald McCall, *New Mexico in 1850: A Military View*, ed. Robert W. Frazer (Norman: University of Oklahoma Press, 1968). The quotations are from pp. 100, 105, 108.

lished among the Indians, he could assign the agents to the tribes to begin the program of civilization. Sumner proceeded with the program. In 1851 he established Fort Union east of Santa Fe, as a depot for army supplies coming into the territory and as a base for troops sent out to protect the Santa Fe Trail, and Fort Defiance in the Navajo country. New posts near El Paso (Fort Fillmore) and at Valverde south of Albuquerque (Fort Conrad) placed more troops among the Indians.[41]

While the military policy was being implemented, Calhoun began placing his agents. Early in 1852 a Navajo agency was established at Fort Defiance and one was opened near Ojo Caliente for the southern Apaches. Here the agents began to distribute the seeds and farming implements that were to start the Indians on the way to becoming farmers.[42] At the time of Calhoun's untimely death in June 1852, the application of the new policy in New Mexico was well begun.

On July 1, 1852, a treaty was negotiated with the Mescalero Apaches including the typical provisions. The Indians declared "that they are lawfully and exclusively under the laws, jurisdiction, and government of the United States of America, and to its power and authority they do submit" and agreed to "perpetual peace and amity" with the government and people of the United States. The Indians bound themselves to treat Americans honestly and humanely, to allow free passage through their lands, and "to conform in all things to the laws, rules, and regulations" of the United States in regard to Indian tribes. Moreover, the treaty authorized the United States to "designate, settle, and adjust their territorial boundaries, and pass and execute in their territory such laws as may be deemed conducive to the prosperity and happiness" of the Indians. In return, the United States would grant to the Indians "donations, presents, and implements, and adopt such other liberal and humane measures as said government may deem meet and proper." Against the protestations of the Apache chiefs, the treaty included a provision that Indian raids into Mexico were to stop.[43]

However inappropriate such an idealistic treaty may have been in the circumstances, peace was maintained in New Mexico for two years; but Calhoun's successors were soon plagued with the old troubles. Although the Gadsden Purchase treaty eliminated the responsibility of the United

---

41. Sumner's operations and Calhoun's reaction are treated in Trennert, *Alternative to Extinction*, pp. 127–30. See also Robert M. Utley, "Fort Union and the Santa Fe Trail," *New Mexico Historical Review* 36 (January 1961): 36–48, and Bailey, *Long Walk*, pp. 25–39.

42. Data on the establishment of the agencies in the New Mexico Superintendency are given in Edward E. Hill, *The Office of Indian Affairs, 1824–1880: Historical Sketches* (New York: Clearwater Publishing Company, 1974), pp. 110–16.

43. Kappler, pp. 598–600.

States to prevent raids into Mexico, the new territory included more western Apaches within the boundaries of the United States—Indians who were not very amenable to the government's Indian policy.[44] In 1854 a war with the Jicarilla Apaches broke the peace, and other tribes were restless. The Utes attacked settlers on the upper Arkansas and Rio Grande, and military forces were sent out in early 1855 to subdue them. At the same time trouble with the Mescalero Apaches broke out, and army troops invaded their country. New military posts were built along the Rio Grande and in other trouble spots.[45]

The next move came from Congress, which in the summer of 1854 appropriated $30,000 for the negotiation of treaties with the Apaches, Navajos, and Utes in New Mexico. The money provided the opportunity to apply the policy that was maturing in the mind of the commissioner of Indian affairs, George W. Manypenny, who believed that the only solution was to extend to New Mexico (and to its sister territory, Utah) the system of reservations that was being developed elsewhere.[46]

David Meriwether, who had become governor in 1853, negotiated a series of treaties with the tribes in the summer of 1855, which embodied Manypenny's principles. All the treaties were quite similar, and the treaty with the Capote Utes on August 8 can be taken as an example. The Utes agreed to peaceful relations, a cession of all their land claims, and the acceptance of a specified reserve of about two thousand square miles at the headwaters of the San Juan River; but the more crucial articles imposed a regimen of civilization upon the Indians, who agreed to settle on the reservation within a year after ratification of the treaty and to "cultivate the soil, and raise flocks and herds for a subsistence." Furthermore, the president of the United States, at his discretion, could survey the reservation and allot parcels of land to individual Indian families. In return for the cession and the promises of the Indians, the United States would pay annuities: $5,000 annually for the first three years, $3,000 for the next three, and $2,000 for the following twenty years. The payments were to be made at the direction of the president, who could determine what proportion, if any, would be paid in money and what proportion might be expended for moral improvement and civilization. Additional articles prohibited the

---

44. See Ralph Hedrick Ogle, *Federal Control of the Western Apaches, 1848–1886*, with an introduction by Oakah L. Jones, Jr. (Albuquerque: University of New Mexico Press, 1970), pp. 31–45. This study was first published in *New Mexico Historical Review*, 1939–1940.

45. Utley, *Frontiersmen in Blue*, pp. 142–74, describes the military action in New Mexico, 1854–1861. The location of the posts is given in Francis Paul Prucha, *A Guide to the Military Posts of the United States, 1789–1895* (Madison: State Historical Society of Wisconsin, 1964).

46. CIA Report, 1854, serial 746, p. 222. The authorization for the treaties is in 10 *United States Statutes* 330.

making, selling, or using of spirituous liquors on the reservation and provided that the trade and intercourse laws would continue in force over the Indian lands.[47]

Here was a clear indication of the theoretical policy of the government to turn the Indians of the newly acquired territories into settled agriculturalists, no matter what the Indians' traditions and inclinations might be or what the capabilities of the land for farming. Meriwether reported that the Utes "very reluctantly consented to commence the cultivation of the soil for a subsistence"; but he had strong hopes that success with this relatively amicable band would have "a powerful effect upon all the other bands of this savage tribe."[48] Meriwether's chief concern in the treaties can be seen in his exultant report to Manypenny when he forwarded them: "Each treaty contains a stipulation requiring the Indians to *cultivate* the land assigned to them." The governor urged speedy action by the president and the Senate, but the Senate failed to approve the treaties. Yet the negotiations appear to have had some effect, for Manypenny reported at the end of 1856 that depredations in New Mexico had been less serious than in any of the previous years.[49]

On March 3, 1857, the position of superintendent of Indian affairs was separated from the territorial governor's office, and James L. Collins was appointed superintendent. In 1856 and again in 1857 Congress appropriated $47,500 for the Indian service in the Territory of New Mexico and "for making to the Indians in said Territory presents of goods, agricultural implements, and other useful articles, and in assisting them to locate in permanent abodes, and sustain themselves by the pursuits of civilized life." So even without ratification of the treaties Collins moved ahead with plans to concentrate the Utes on the San Juan and the Apaches along the Gila. The goal was to remove the Indians from the vicinity of the white settlements and to supervise them from nearby military posts. In 1859 Congress acted in regard to the Apaches, authorizing a reservation of one hundred square miles on or near the Gila River, and a small area was selected by the Indian Office and established by executive order.[50]

While plans for peaceful settlement of the Utes and the Apaches proceeded, the Navajos were engaged in war—predatory raids by the Indians and retaliation by federal troops. Only after a vigorous campaign in the winter of 1860–1861 were the Indians subdued and a peace negotiated. By

47. Kappler, vol. 5, p. 687.

48. Meriwether to Manypenny, August 14, 1855, ibid., p. 689. Kappler prints only two of the unratified treaties.

49. CIA Report, 1855, serial 810, p. 507; CIA Report, 1856, serial 875, p. 566. The action of the Senate on the treaties is in *Journal of the Executive Proceedings of the Senate*, 10: 31, 254–55.

50. 11 *United States Statutes* 79, 184, 185, 401.

then the Civil War had brought new circumstances, as both the military and civilian officials were forced to neglect Indian affairs for more pressing concerns.[51]

INDIANS, MORMONS, AND GENTILES

Indian affairs in Utah Territory, stretching from the Rocky Mountains to the Sierra Nevada north of the thirty-seventh parallel, were complicated by relations between the Mormons and the federal government. The Mormons were deeply interested in the Indians from a theological standpoint, for the Book of Mormon described them as Lamanites, descendants of Israelites who had migrated to the New World and who had fallen from grace. They were to be redeemed in the new age, and the Mormons actively sought Indian children for upbringing in their own families as a means of conversion.[52] The Mormons, moreover, had practical interests in Indian relations in the Great Basin, where the Utes, Shoshonis, and Paiutes occupied the lands into which Mormon immigrants poured in the 1840s and 1850s. The security and well-being of the Mormon settlements depended upon peaceful accommodation with the Indians, and Brigham Young repeatedly directed his followers to treat the Indians well. There was genuine concern for the civilization of the Indians that differed little from that exhibited by Christian humanitarians in the East, and Young appreciated the futility of war with the natives. "We have proved," he told the territorial legislature after two decades in Utah, "that the pacific, conciliatory policy is in every sense the better course for us to pursue. Experience has taught us that it is cheaper to feed the Indians than to fight them—a statement that has been so often repeated that it has become a recognized axiom among us." The peaceful policy, of course, did not always work, and Mormon frontiersmen experienced Indian wars and depredations as they encroached seriously upon the Indians.[53]

51. Utley, *Frontiersmen in Blue*, pp. 168–74. See also Frank McNitt, *Navajo Wars: Military Campaigns, Slave Raids, and Reprisals* (Albuquerque: University of New Mexico Press, 1972); and Bailey, *Long Walk*, pp. 83–142.

52. Mormon relations with the Indians are discussed in Juanita Brooks, "Indian Relations on the Mormon Frontier," *Utah Historical Quarterly* 12 (January–April 1944): 1–48; and Gustive O. Larson, "Brigham Young and the Indians," in Robert G. Ferris, ed., *The American West: An Appraisal* (Santa Fe: Museum of New Mexico Press, 1963), pp. 176–87. The setting of Indian affairs within the broader context of Mormon frontier development can be seen in Nels Anderson, *Desert Saints: The Mormon Frontier in Utah* (Chicago: University of Chicago Press, 1942). See also Leonard J. Arrington and Davis Bitton, *The Mormon Experience: A History of the Latter-Day Saints* (New York: Alfred A. Knopf, 1979), pp. 145–60.

53. Governor's message, January 22, 1866, in J. Cecil Alter, ed., "The Mormons and the Indians: News Items and Editorials from the Mormon Press," *Utah Historical Quar-*

Added to the problems of Indian-white relations common to all American frontiers was the question of Mormon domination of life in Utah, a serious irritant to the agents of the federal government who were responsible for Indian affairs there. The federal government, as the decade of the 1850s advanced, became greatly concerned that its authority in the territory was not respected by Brigham Young and the Mormons. Under these unfavorable circumstances, the United States attempted to provide an Indian policy in Utah.[54]

When the Mexican Cession was acquired by the Treaty of Guadalupe Hidalgo, the government transferred an older agency to Salt Lake just as it had moved an agency to Santa Fe. On April 7, 1849, John Wilson of Missouri was appointed to the Salt Lake post. His letter of appointment indicated how little the Indian Office knew about the Indians he was sent to serve, for he was issued no specific instructions and was asked instead to gather information about the tribes and their customs, their territory, their attitude toward whites, and whether the trade and intercourse laws could properly be applied.[55]

Little came of this early beginning; Wilson conferred with the Mormons in Utah in September, then he moved into California and soon resigned. A successor was appointed, but the Salt Lake Agency was abolished before he reached it. Some stability came with the establishment of the Territory of Utah in September 1850 and the appointment of Brigham Young as territorial governor and ex officio superintendent of Indian affairs.[56]

In February 1851 Congress extended the intercourse laws over Utah and provided an agent for the Utah Superintendency, who with two subagents reached Salt Lake City in the summer.[57] These men almost at once became embroiled in the controversies between Mormons and Gentiles (as the

---

terly 12 (January–April 1944): 65. For a brief account of the Walker War and the Gunnison massacre of 1853, for example, see Hoopes, *Indian Affairs and Their Administration*, pp. 141–46.

54. The best studies of Indian affairs in Utah before the Civil War are Dale L. Morgan, "The Administration of Indian Affairs in Utah, 1851–1858," *Pacific Historical Review* 17 (November 1948): 383–409, and Hoopes, *Indian Affairs and Their Administration*, chapter 5, "Indian Affairs in Utah, 1849–1860," pp. 131–59. Most of the pertinent documents are printed in "The Utah Expedition," *House Executive Document* no. 71, 35–1, serial 956, pp. 124–215.

55. William Medill to John Wilson, April 7, 1849, *House Executive Document* no. 17, 31–1, serial 573, pp. 182–84. Letters from Wilson dated Fort Bridger, August 22, 1849, and Great Salt Lake Valley, September 4, 1849, are printed ibid., pp. 104–12, 184–87.

56. Morgan, "Indian Affairs in Utah," pp. 383–84; Hoopes, *Indian Affairs and Their Administration*, pp. 131–34.

57. 9 *United States Statutes* 587; Jacob H. Holeman to Luke Lea, September 21, 1851, CIA Report, 1851, serial 613, pp. 444–46.

Mormons called all non-Mormons). The agent, Jacob H. Holeman, was especially critical of the Mormons. In November 1851 he wrote to the Indian Office from Salt Lake City to warn against the encroachments of the Mormons upon the Indians:

> I alluded in my report to the necessity of adopting such measures by the general government as would protect the Indians of this Territory; they are becoming very much excited by the encroachment of the Mormons, as they are making settlements throughout the Territory on all the most valuable lands, extending these settlements for near three hundred miles from this city. In the first settlements of this city and the adjoining country by the Mormons they at first conciliated the Indians by kind treatment; but when they once got a foothold, they began to *force their way*; the consequence was a war with the Indians, and in many instances, a most brutal butchery. This they fear will be the result wherever the Mormons may make a settlement. The Indians have been driven from their lands, and their hunting grounds destroyed, without any compensation therefor. They are in many instances reduced to a state of suffering bordering on starvation.

He felt that the Mormons were too self-interested to be allowed to have anything at all to do with the Indians officially.[58]

Holeman's correspondence continued to exhibit a strong prejudice against the Mormons, and the agent was in continual conflict with Young. His bias was not supported at first in Washington, however, and in 1853 he was replaced.[59] His successor died within a year, and the new agent, Dr. Garland Hurt, soon renewed Holeman's critical reports about the Mormons. Hurt was especially disturbed by the expansion of Mormon missions among the Indians and what he saw as a concerted drive to alienate the Indians from non-Mormons.[60]

Hurt took constructive steps to aid the Indians, and through his initiative the federal government began a program for Indians in Utah that paralleled its developing reservation system in other parts of the West. A great problem, however, was the lack of any treaty with the Indians by which some recognition of their lands and other rights against the whites might have been officially established. John Wilson had proposed that the Indian title to lands near the Great Salt Lake be extinguished "by treaty," and Agent Holeman had asserted that a treaty with the various tribes in Utah

58. Holeman to Lea, November 28, 1851, "Utah Expedition," pp. 128–29.
59. Conflict between the agent and the superintendent is treated in Morgan, "Indian Affairs in Utah," pp. 386–92.
60. Hurt to George W. Manypenny, May 2, 1855, "Utah Expedition," pp. 176–77.

would produce much good: "it would have the effect of preventing depre-dations on their lands, quieting their excitement against the whites, and ultimately save the Government from much trouble and expense."[61] Brigham Young was of the same mind. He wanted the government to promote schools and other measures to civilize the Indians, and he declared: "If previous to any such arrangements being made for their benefit it becomes necessary to enter into Treaty stipulations with them, then we should not delay that operation any longer, but go about it as speedily as possible."[62]

The Mormons were of course eager to have a valid title to their lands, which could come only with the extinguishment of Indian title by treaty, and they kept up pressure on Washington to arrange such a negotiation with the Indians. Commissioner Manypenny wanted to locate the Indians within specified boundaries and begin the process of civilization, and the Indian appropriation bill of July 31, 1854, spoke of distributing money appropriated for the Utah Indians "under treaty stipulations" or in some other way.[63]

But the movement for a treaty in Utah was abortive. Young provided estimates of goods needed for treating with the Indians, but in the end they were merely filed away because similar arrangements suggested for the Indians in New Mexico had been turned down by the Senate. Not until 1863 were any treaties signed with Indians in Utah Territory, and not until 1865 was a treaty negotiated (but never ratified) with the Utes.[64]

In the meantime, Hurt moved ahead with an alternative to formal reservations by establishing a farming system for the Indians' benefit. Building on some early moves by Brigham Young to provide farmers to instruct the Indians, Hurt undertook to teach them to farm in order to ease their destitution, an action cautiously approved by Commissioner Manypenny, who suggested hiring farmers on a temporary basis only. In late 1855 Hurt laid out a number of "reservations" where Indians were collected to farm. Although the agent forcefully justified his action, he was reined in, for he had spent money from contingent funds without official authorization. He thought such liberal action necessary to counteract Mormon missionary activity and to win over the Indians to a favorable view of the federal government.[65]

61. Wilson to Thomas Ewing, September 4, 1849, *House Executive Document* no. 17, 31–1, serial 573, p. 105; Holeman to Lea, September 21, 1851, CIA Report, 1851, serial 613, p. 446.

62. Young to Lea, November 30, 1851, OIA LR, Utah Superintendency (U/1–1852) (M234, reel 897, frame 217).

63. CIA Report, 1854, serial 746, p. 222; 10 *United States Statutes* 332.

64. Morgan, "Indian Affairs in Utah," p. 396; 10 *United States Statutes* 332; Kappler, pp. 848–53, 859–60.

65. Morgan, "Indian Affairs in Utah," pp. 397–401. Reports of Hurt's work are in CIA

In 1856 Congress appropriated $45,000 for the Utah Superintendency, and the financial strain on the farming program was eased, but the agent still had to maneuver around Brigham Young for the money. Hurt was convinced of the value of the farms. He attributed the tranquility on the frontier to his efforts to establish reservations for the Indians and to the introduction of a system of agriculture. "Though these reservations have been visited during this season by large bands of the wild Indians who live east of the Wasatch Mountains," he wrote to the commissioner of Indian affairs, "the influences which these farms exerted upon them through the home tribes, has enabled us to conduct our intercourse with them in a very tranquil manner."[66]

In addition to his repeated spats with the Gentile agents, Brigham Young did not get along well with the Indian Office in Washington. The governor complained of bureaucratic red tape that obstructed his handling of Indian affairs (believable even without any Mormon-Gentile antagonism), and Commissioner Manypenny suggested as early as 1854 that the ex officio superintendency be separated from the governor's office. He argued that Young's duties as head of the Mormon Church took much of his time and that the duties of Indian superintendent, which often had to be performed far from the seat of government, should properly be given to a different person.[67]

In 1857 relations between the United States and the Mormons in Utah approached a breaking point. Brigham Young's plan for a Mormon-dominated state, with economic and political as well as religious control, was in many ways a fact. Non-Mormons in Utah were antagonized, and their hostility spread across the nation. The announcement in 1852 that polygamy was a basic doctrine and practice of the Mormon Church added an emotional fervor to the cries of lawlessness and rebellion against the Mormons. President James Buchanan, over-hastily heeding complaints from a few federal officials in Utah and the public outcry, replaced Young as governor of Utah Territory with Alfred Cumming and sent a military expedition west to put down the alleged rebellion and to make sure that the new governor was accepted and respected. Congress on March 3, 1857, had already provided for independent superintendents of Indian affairs in

Report, 1855, serial 810, pp. 517–21; Hurt to Manypenny, August 30, 1856, "Utah Expedition," pp. 179–81.

66. 11 *United States Statutes* 79; Hurt to Denver, June 30, 1857, OIA LR, Utah Superintendency (H/685–1857) (M234, reel 898, frame 333).

67. Manypenny to Secretary of the Interior Robert McClelland, April 10, 1854, "Utah Expedition," pp. 165–66; CIA Report, 1854, serial 746, p. 225. Young's complaints about the attention—or lack of it—that he received from the Indian Office are strongly stated in Young to Manypenny, June 26, 1855, "Utah Expedition," pp. 170–75.

the western territories, and Jacob Forney was appointed to the new office for Utah Territory.[68]

As the Utah Expedition, commanded by Albert Sidney Johnston, moved toward Utah, the Mormons geared for war. Buchanan had neglected to inform Young of his replacement and of the military expedition, and the Mormon governor and his followers, when they received news of the advance of the troops, believed that the army was coming to destroy them. They prudently sought to engage the Indians on their side against the federal troops and the Gentile oppressors. Thus Young instructed one of the Mormon missionaries to the Indians in August 1857: "Continue the conciliatory policy towards the Indians, which I have ever recommended, and seek by works of righteousness to obtain their love and confidence, for they must learn that they have either to help us, or the United States will kill us both."[69]

In such an atmosphere of fear and hatred the Mountain Meadows massacre, one of the most brutal episodes in the long history of Indian-white conflicts in the West, occurred in September 1857. A company of emigrants from Arkansas and Missouri, passing through southern Utah to California, irritated both the Indians and the Mormons by their behavior. Encamped at a place called Mountain Meadows, they were besieged by hostile Indians. The Indians were aided by a number of Mormon men who, caught in the frenzy of the day, hoped to preserve the goodwill of the Indians and prevent the emigrants from carrying news to California that might stimulate an attack on the Mormons from that direction. Decoyed out of their encampment after giving up their arms in promise of safe conduct, the 120 emigrants were murdered by the Indians and the Mormons. Only 17 children were spared. Although Brigham Young by no means instigated or condoned the act, he tried to keep the Mormon participation in the affair quiet. The news of the massacre further fueled antagonism toward the Mormons.[70]

The "Mormon War" was in the end bloodless. The troops, arriving in the West too late in the year to move directly into Utah, wintered near Fort Bridger with some discomfort, for the Mormons had applied a scorched-earth policy to the vicinity. Conciliatory measures were begun, and Brigham Young, who had ordered the evacuation of Salt Lake City with direc-

68. There is a good account of the Utah Expedition and Mormon reaction to it in Leonard J. Arrington, *Great Basin Kingdom: An Economic History of the Latter-Day Saints, 1830–1900* (Cambridge: Harvard University Press, 1958), pp. 161–94.

69. Young to Jacob Hamblin, August 4, 1857, quoted in Brooks, "Indian Relations," p. 20.

70. A detailed critical study of the massacre is Juanita Brooks, *The Mountain Meadows Massacre* (Norman: University of Oklahoma Press, 1962; originally published in 1950). The author declares that Brigham Young was accessory after the fact.

tions to burn the city if the hostile troops moved in, agreed to accept peace. In the spring the troops passed peacefully through the nearly deserted city and established a military post (Camp Floyd) forty miles to the west, where they stayed until called back by the Civil War. Governor Cumming was amicably accepted by the Mormons, and Forney took over the duties of Indian superintendent.

Brigham Young continued to use his considerable influence with the Indians to further peaceful relations with them and to work for their civilization. When treaty negotiations with the Utes were undertaken in 1865, the agent did not hesitate to call upon Young for support.[71] Yet peaceful relations were not enough, for the white encroachment on Indian lands came faster than the government's plans for civilization and self-support could be carried out, and at the end of the decade many of the Indians were hungry, naked, and in desperate straits.

71. O. H. Irish to William P. Dole, June 29, 1865, CIA Report, 1865, serial 1248, pp. 317–20.

CHAPTER 15

California, Oregon, and Washington

A Reservation Policy for California.

Indian Affairs in the Oregon Country.

The Indians of Washington Territory.

The movement of American citizens to the Pacific coast and the incorporation of California and the Pacific Northwest into the American nation illustrate the deleterious effect upon the Indians of a policy applied from a great distance without a sound appreciation of local conditions and without adequate concern to protect Indian rights against the onslaught of American invaders on their aboriginal lands. Yet the government in the end applied to the Indians of the Pacific slope and the inland empire the same paternalistic patterns that marked the development of the reservation system in other parts of the nation.

A RESERVATION POLICY FOR CALIFORNIA

The relations of the United States with the Indians of California were particularly disastrous for the Indians, for the attempt of the federal government to protect them through treaty machinery was abortive, and the Indians were no match for the aggressive and often lawless gold seekers who flooded the region in 1849 and after.[1]

1. Indian policy in California has been well documented in William H. Ellison, "The Federal Indian Policy in California, 1846–1860," *Mississippi Valley Historical Review* 9 (June 1922): 37–67, and Alban W. Hoopes, *Indian Affairs and Their Administration:*

The United States, to begin with, was almost entirely ignorant of the Indians in the new acquisition. It knew neither the population, the number and organization of the bands and tribes, nor the status of the Indians under Mexico—a status that presumably was to be continued under the provisions of the Treaty of Guadalupe Hildalgo. The Americans, logically enough, grouped the Indians roughly into two categories. One was the mission Indians, who had come under the influence of Franciscan friars in the mission establishments that dotted the coast from San Diego to San Francisco Bay. These Indians had been drawn to live at the missions in order to be trained in agriculture, stock raising, and simple crafts, as well as to be instructed in Christianity. The missions enjoyed considerable prosperity and success. Stock was raised in large numbers there, and substantial yields of grain were harvested. The Indians, under the training and discipline of the priests, did the building, weaving, tanning, soap making, and other work needed to maintain the nearly self-sufficient communities. But by the time the Americans arrived the missions had been secularized by the Mexican government and the Indians by and large dispersed.[2] The rest of the native inhabitants were "wild Indians," who had little or no contact with whites and who subsisted by hunting, fishing, and gathering acorns. Estimates of the number of these two groups vary; a total of one hundred thousand at the time of American occupation may be a reasonable figure, representing a considerable decline from the estimated aboriginal population of more than three hundred thousand.[3]

With Special Reference to the Far West, 1849–1860 (Philadelphia: University of Pennsylvania Press, 1932), pp. 35–68. Some idea of Indian reaction to the policy in southern California can be gained from George Harwood Phillips, *Chiefs and Challengers: Indian Resistance and Cooperation in Southern California* (Berkeley: University of California Press, 1975). Accounts of the destruction of the Indians and their cultures are in Robert F. Heizer, ed., *The Destruction of the California Indians* (Santa Barbara: Peregrine Smith, 1974); Heizer, ed., *They Were Only Diggers: A Collection of Articles from California Newspapers, 1851–1866, on Indian and White Relations* (Ramona, California: Ballena Press, 1974); and Heizer and Alan J. Almquist, *The Other Californians: Prejudice and Discrimination under Spain, Mexico, and the United States* (Berkeley: University of California Press, 1971), pp. 23–91.

2. There has been a great deal of study of the missions and considerable controversy about whether their effect on the Indians was good or bad. An old but classic study is Herbert E. Bolton, "The Mission as a Frontier Institution in the Spanish-American Colonies," *American Historical Review* 23 (October 1917): 42–61. A survey of the historiography is John Francis Bannon, "The Mission as a Frontier Institution: Sixty Years of Interest and Research," *Western Historical Quarterly* 10 (July 1979): 303–22. For details on the California missions and missionaries, see the works of Maynard Geiger.

3. Ellison in "Federal Indian Policy in California," p. 40 and n., suggests "at least 100,000 or perhaps 125,000," basing his figure on contemporary reports and the estimates of ethnographers. A similar conclusion of "about 100,000," is given in Robert F. Heizer, "Treaties," in *Handbook of North American Indians*, vol. 8: *California*, ed.

After California was seized by United States troops under Stephen Watts Kearny in 1847, it was the military who first sought to establish some sort of official relations with the Indians and to prevent as much as possible the raids and counterraids between Indians and whites that threatened the peace of the country. Kearny, as military governor, hoped to conciliate the Indians by means of presents (which he urged the War Department to send), and in 1847 he appointed three subagents: John Sutter for Indians on the Sacramento River; Mariano G. Vallejo for those on the north side of San Francisco Bay; and J. D. Hunter for those at San Luis Rey.[4]

The federal government proceeded slowly in providing civil government for California, and it sought to determine as precisely as possible the actual state of affairs. In the spring of 1849 the president appointed Thomas Butler King to study conditions in California. The instructions to King from Secretary of State John M. Clayton included directions to secure information about "the number of the various Indian tribes which form a portion of the population of the Territories; their power, character and modes of life." King's report, dated March 22, 1850, offered scant help to the policy makers. He reported the impossibility of forming an accurate estimate of the number of Indians in the territory, but he noted that "the whole race seems to be rapidly disappearing." He greatly disparaged the Indians, who seemed to him "to be almost the lowest grade of human beings" without the slightest inclination to cultivate the land. "They have never pretended to hold any interest in the soil," he asserted, "nor have they been treated by the Spanish or American immigrants as possessing any." He did not think that the Mexican government had ever purchased any land from the Indians or otherwise extinguished their claims. But he suggested that it might be possible to collect the Indians and teach them the "arts and habits of civilization," although he did not hold out much hope for their preservation.[5]

Another official observer of Indian affairs was William Carey Jones, dis-

---

Robert F. Heizer (Washington: Smithsonian Institution, 1978), p. 701. The great work on the population of the California Indians has been done by Sherburne F. Cook; see his *The Conflict between the California Indians and White Civilization: Ibero-Americana*, nos. 21–24 (Berkeley: University of California Press, 1943); and *The Population of the California Indians, 1769–1970* (Berkeley: University of California Press, 1976).

4. Ellison, "Federal Indian Policy in California," p. 42; Hoopes, *Indian Affairs and Their Administration*, pp. 36–37. Documents on the appointment of, instructions to, and reports from the subagents can be found in two similar (though not identical) printings of government documents on the occupation of California: *Senate Executive Document* no. 18, 31–1, serial 557, and *House Executive Document* no. 17, 31–1, serial 573.

5. Clayton to King, April 3, 1849, *House Executive Document* no. 17, 31–1, serial 573, p. 11; Thomas Butler King, *California: Report of Hon. T. Butler King* (Washington: Gideon and Company, 1850), pp. 3–4. The report is also printed in *House Executive Document* no. 59, 31–1, serial 577.

patched to California to investigate the question of land titles. At the end of his instructions from the commissioner of the General Land Office, Jones was told explicitly what to look for: "You will make an inquiry into the nature of the *Indian rights* as existing under the Spanish and Mexican governments, and as subsisting when the United States obtained the sovereignty, indicating from authentic data the difference between the privileges enjoyed by the wandering tribes and those who have made actual settlements and established rancherias, and will report their general form, extent, and localities; their probable number, and the manner and form in which such rights have been regarded by the Spanish and Mexican governments."[6]

Jones's report was succinct. He declared that it was a constant principle of the Spanish colonial laws that the Indians "shall have a *right* to as much land as they need for their habitation, for tillage, and for pasturage." He noted that the mission Indians were to have rights to the land they used and that other grants were subject to these Indian rights. Nor did he believe a continuation of these principles would cause much inconvenience because of the small number of Indians involved. "A proper regard for long recognized rights, and a proper sympathy for an unfortunate and unhappy race," he said, "would seem to forbid that it should be abrogated, unless for a better." As for the "wild or wandering tribes," the Spanish recognized no title whatever to the soil.[7]

Influenced no doubt by these reports and intending to follow in California established principles of reservation policy, the government moved ahead, albeit somewhat clumsily, to provide enclaves of land for the Indians, as well as agents to look after their interests and conduct their relations with the United States.

In April 1849 a subagent, Adam Johnston, was appointed for the Sacramento and San Joaquin valleys. He appears to have managed his affairs competently and supplied officials in Washington with detailed reports about the state of affairs, but he soon faded into the background somewhat as Congress provided for commissioners and agents.[8] On September 28, 1850, Congress authorized the appointment of three agents for Indian tribes in California "to perform the duties now prescribed by law to Indian agents." Two days later it appropriated $25,000 to enable the president to

6. J. Butterfield to Jones, July 5, 1849, *House Executive Document* no. 17, 31–1, serial 573, p. 115.

7. William Carey Jones, *Report on the Subject of Land Titles in California: Made in Pursuance of Instructions from the Secretary of State and the Secretary of the Interior* (Washington: Gideon and Company, 1850), pp. 36–37.

8. Johnston's commission is given in *House Executive Document* no. 17, 31–1, serial 573, pp. 187–88. His reports are in *Senate Executive Document* no. 4, 33–special session, serial 688.

hold treaties with the California tribes; this sum was subsequently increased to $50,000.[9]

At this point there was considerable confusion. The act appointing the agents provided no appropriation for their salaries; the act authorizing treaties made no provision for treaty commissioners. The strange situation was resolved pragmatically: the men appointed as agents were charged with negotiating the treaties and paid from the treaty money. To this dual position of agent-commissioner, the president appointed Redick McKee of Virginia, George W. Barbour of Kentucky, and O. M. Wozencraft of Louisiana. These men arrived in California at the end of December and the beginning of January and set about energetically to negotiate treaties with the Indians. Their vague instructions stated that the goal of the government was to gain information about the Indians and their customs and "to make such treaties and compacts with them as may seem just and proper."[10] Operating as a group, the three men signed a treaty on March 19, 1851, with men whom they took to be the leaders of six tribes in the San Joaquin Valley, and on April 29 another treaty was made with sixteen tribes. Later, in order to speed the work, the commissioners split up, each moving to a designated region to continue the treaty making. By January 7, 1852, eighteen treaties had been negotiated and signed.[11]

The treaties were much alike. The Indians recognized the United States as sole sovereign over the land ceded to the United States by Mexico in 1848, and they placed themselves under the protection of the United States and agreed to keep peace. By each treaty a definite reservation was set aside for the tribes, and subsistence in the form of beef cattle was provided for them while they were moving and settling on the reservations. Annuities in the form of clothing, agricultural implements, and livestock were authorized, and farmers, blacksmiths, and schoolteachers were pro-

9. 9 *United States Statutes* 519, 558, 572.

10. CIA Report, 1850, serial 587, p. 42. The appointment letter is printed in *Senate Executive Document* no. 4, 33–special session, serial 688, p. 7; their instructions are in A. S. Loughery to McKee, Barbour, and Wozencraft, October 15, 1850, ibid., pp. 8–9. The reports of the three commissioners and journals of their activity appear in the same Senate document. See also Alban W. Hoopes, ed., "The Journal of George W. Barbour, May 1 to October 4, 1851," *Southwestern Historical Quarterly* 40 (October 1936): 145–53, and 40 (January 1937): 247–61; and Chad L. Hoopes, "Redick McKee and the Humboldt Bay Region, 1851–1852," *California Historical Society Quarterly* 49 (September 1970): 195–219.

11. The treaties are printed in Kappler, vol. 4, pp. 1081–1128. Official secrecy on the treaties was lifted by the Senate on January 18, 1905. A copy of the 1905 Senate printing of the treaties is in Records of the Office of Indian Affairs, Documents Relating to the Negotiation of Ratified and Unratified Treaties with Various Indian Tribes (T494, reel 8, frames 410–25), National Archives, Record Group 75. The idea that the secrecy was conspiratorial is considered and rejected in Harry Kelsey, "The California Indian Treaty Myth," *Southern California Quarterly* 55 (Fall 1973): 225–35.

vided for a period of years. The eighteen treaties set aside 11,700 square miles (7,488,000 acres) of land, about 7.5 percent of the state.[12]

The three commissioners did their work rapidly. Indeed, haste was necessary if conflicts between the onrushing whites and the Indians were to be prevented and the Indians protected in their rights. But they acted without the detailed knowledge of the Indians that modern anthropologists can provide. Although 139 tribes or bands were represented in the eighteen treaties, an enumeration in 1926 indicated that more than 175 tribes were not included in the treaties. Thirty years later, a study conducted under Indian Claims Commission litigation reported that of the 139 signatory groups, 67 were identifiable as tribelets, 45 were merely village names, 14 were duplicates spelled differently without the commissioners having been aware of the fact, and 13 were either unidentifiable or personal names.[13]

The irregularities, although indicative of the lack of precise information with which the whole process was carried out, in the end did not matter, for the Senate refused to ratify the treaties. There is some question whether, even at the beginning, a majority of the Senate intended to authorize treaties of cession rather than mere treaties of peace and friendship. A clearly worded measure introduced by John C. Frémont, one of California's first senators, "to treat with the Indian tribes of California having territorial claims in the State of California and to extinguish their land claims," with an appropriation of $100,000 for the negotiations, was substantially changed by the Committee on Indian Affairs. The new version made no mention of land claims, and the appropriation was excluded altogether from the authorization bill. There was considerable feeling in Congress that the California Indians had no land titles and therefore that no treaties were needed to extinguish them.[14]

12. These are calculations of Ellison, "Federal Indian Policy in California," p. 57, and they have been generally accepted by historians. The map of California in Charles C. Royce, *Indian Land Cessions in the United States,* Eighteenth Annual Report of the Bureau of American Ethnology, 1896–1897, part 2 (Washington: GPO, 1899), pl. 7, purports to show the lands ceded (all of California west of the Sierra Nevadas) and the reservations established, but the map is based on faulty information and assumptions. Heizer says: "There seems to be no basis whatsoever for this map beyond the vague impression of the U.S. Senate in 1852 that the California Indian tribes were agreeable to ceding to the United States the lands of California. Royce's map is, therefore, his own artifact deriving from the same assumption that the Senate made in 1852. But since it was already known in 1852 that many groups had not been treated with, either because they had not been encountered in the course of the wanderings of the three commissioners or because through lack of interpreters no communication was possible between the Americans and numbers of groups of native Californians, it must have been obvious that the 1851–1852 treaties did not, as was implied, cover the quieting of territorial claims ('title') of the Indians then living in the state." Heizer, "Treaties," pp. 703–4.

13. Heizer, "Treaties," p. 703.

14. Kelsey, "California Indian Treaty Myth," pp. 228–29.

But whatever the status of Indian titles, other aspects of the treaties drawn up by the three commissioners militated against their ratification. There was stong opposition from Californians, who saw large regions to be snatched from their grasp and reserved for the Indians, whom they despised. Furthermore, the costs of the treaties had grown to nearly a million dollars, far beyond the total of $50,000 that had been appropriated. The commissioners, working on the spot, had felt it necessary to contract for large numbers of cattle to feed the Indians, and they also provided for further subsistence and annuities in the treaties. Although Commissioner Luke Lea and the newly appointed superintendent of Indian affairs for California were solidly for ratification, the Senate voted with the opposition.[15]

The rejection of the treaties left Indian affairs in California in an uncertain state. For one thing, many of the claims made under the contracts let by the treaty commissioners were later declared fraudulent and never paid. More serious was the worsening condition of relations between the Indians and the miners and other settlers. This became the responsibility of Edward F. Beale, a highly competent and benevolent man with navy and army experience who was appointed the first Indian superintendent in California under congressional authorization of March 3, 1852.[16] Beale, arriving in San Francisco on September 16, immediately saw the urgency of the situation and quickly set about to give new shape to American policy. "The necessity of a speedy and permanent arrangement for this unhappy race is more apparent every day," he wrote at the end of October, "as our people are fast filling every habitable foot of ground in the entire state, to the exclusion of the original occupants." What he proposed was a considerable change from the traditional land cession and reservation policy embraced by the rejected treaties. He set forth his plan in brief tentative form as follows:

> In the first place, I propose a system of "military posts" to be established on reservations, for the convenience and protection of the

15. Ellison, "Federal Indian Policy in California," pp. 57–58. A strong statement about California opposition to the treaties is William H. Ellison, "Rejection of California Indian Treaties: A Study in Local Influence on National Policy," *Grizzly Bear* 37 (May 1925): 4–5, 86; 37 (June 1925): 4–5, supplement 7; 37 (July 1925): 6–7. Kelsey, "California Indian Treaty Myth," argues for the preeminence of the question of Indian land titles in the rejection of the treaties. A set of reprinted items is in George E. Anderson, W. H. Ellison, and Robert F. Heizer, *Treaty Making and Treaty Rejection by the Federal Government in California, 1850–1852* (Socorro, New Mexico: Ballena Press, 1978). The action of the Senate can be followed in the *Journal of the Executive Proceedings of the Senate*, vol. 8.

16. 10 *United States Statutes* 2–3. On Beale and his work, see Gerald Thompson, *Edward F. Beale and the American West* (Albuquerque: University of New Mexico Press, 1983), pp. 45–79; Richard E. Crouter and Andrew F. Rolle, "Edward Fitzgerald Beale and the Indian Peace Commissioners in California, 1851–1854," *Historical Society of South-*

Indians; these reservations to be regarded as military reservations or government reservations. The Indians to be invited to assemble within these reserves.

A system of discipline and instruction to be adopted by the agent who is to live at the post.

Each reservation to contain a military establishment, the number of troops being in proportion to the population of the tribes there assembled.

The expenses of the troops to be borne by the surplus produce of Indian labor.

The reservation to be made with a view to a change in location, when increase of white population may make it necessary.

A change of present Indian laws to be made, so as to suit the condition of this State and the proposed policy.[17]

Beale had in mind a reestablishment of the mission system on a secular basis, for he thought the missions had been an ideal means for channeling Indian labor into useful projects. "Every useful mechanic art, all necessary knowledge of agricultural pursuits, was here [at the mission] taught under a system of discipline at once mild, firm, and paternal," he wrote to Luke Lea. "It is this system, modified and adapted to the present time, which I propose for your consideration; nor can I conceive of any other which would preserve this unfortunate people from total extinction, and our government from everlasting disgrace."[18]

Beale began to implement his plan on a piece of land on the San Joaquin River, land passed over by the settlers as unworthy of their labor. Here he wanted to establish an Indian settlement. This should not be done by treaty, he insisted, and the land should be a *government* reservation to

---

ern *California Quarterly* 42 (June 1960): 107–32. An older biography of Beale is Stephen Bonsal, *Edward Fitzgerald Beale: A Pioneer in the Path of Empire, 1822–1903* (New York: G. P. Putnam's Sons, 1912).

17. Beale to Luke Lea, October 29, 1852, *Senate Executive Document* no. 4, 33–special session, serial 688, p. 374. Lea's own proposal was similar to what was being worked out in the central plains; he suggested forming the California Indians into "two grand colonies, to be suitably located: one in the northern and the other in the southern portion of the State." CIA Report, 1852, serial 658, p. 300.

18. Beale to Lea, November 22, 1852, *Senate Executive Document* no. 4, 33–special session, serial 688, p. 380. Phillips, in *Chiefs and Challengers*, pp. 128, 173, asserts that "the foundation of the reservation system that he [Beale] proposed to his superiors" was a report drawn up by a subagent appointed by Beale, Benjamin D. Wilson. The report is printed with an introduction and annotations in John Walton Caughey, ed., *The Indians of Southern California in 1852: The B. D. Wilson Report and a Selection of Contemporary Comment* (San Marino: Huntington Library, 1952).

which the Indians would have no title and from which they could be moved as occasion demanded.[19] He asked $500,000 to carry out his policy. His plea was that of a Christian humanitarian as he described the condition of the Indians:

> Driven from their fishing and hunting grounds, hunted themselves like wild beasts, *lassoed*, and torn from homes made miserable by want, and forced into slavery, the wretched remnant which escapes starvation on the one hand, and the relentless whites on the other, only do so to rot and die of a loathsome disease, the penalty of Indian association with frontier civilization. This is no idle declamation—I have seen it; and seeing all this, I cannot help them. I know that they starve; I know that they perish by hundreds; I know that they are fading away with a startling and shocking rapidity, but I cannot help them. Humanity must yield to necessity. They are not dangerous; therefore they must be neglected. I earnestly call the early attention of the government to this condition of affairs, and to a plan I have proposed in a previous letter for its relief. It is a crying sin that our government so wealthy and so powerful, should shut its eyes to the miserable fate of these rightful owners of the soil. What is the expense of half a million for the permanent relief of these poor people to a government so rich?[20]

Congress responded by authorizing the creation of five military reservations from the public domain that were not to exceed twenty-five thousand acres each. A quarter of a million dollars was appropriated to sustain the Indians and move them to the reservations.[21]

Beale enthusiastically pursued his plan, developing a promising reservation at Tejon Pass, but his work was checked by political opposition and by his own carelessness in his accounts.[22] Just as appropriations were being considered for California Indian affairs in May 1854, Beale was reported to be nearly $250,000 in arrears in his accounts. Although subsequent investigation exonerated him, the damage had been done. Congress cut the number of authorized reservations from five to three, which were to run between five and ten thousand acres each. Out of a total appropriation of $200,000 for continuing the removal and subsistence of the Indians, not more than $25,000 was to be used to extinguish competing white land

---

19. Beale to Lea, December 14, 1852, *Senate Executive Document* no. 4, 33–special session, serial 688, pp. 391–92.

20. Beale to Lea, November 22, 1852, ibid., p. 378.

21. 10 *United States Statutes* 238.

22. For the Tejon reservation, see Helen S. Giffin and Arthur Woodward, *The Story of El Tejon* (Los Angeles: Dawson's Book Shop, 1942), pp. 19–43.

titles to the reserved lands. While Congress was taking this action, Beale was removed from office.[23]

The plan that Beale had outlined, however, was continued by his successor, Thomas J. Henley, who was optimistic about the possibilities of the reservation system. He established Nome Lacke Reservation for Indians in the northern part of the state and then petitioned the government to restore the provision for five reserves. Congress agreed; it again authorized five reservations and appropriated $150,000 to move the Indians to the two additional reservations, which could be as large as 25,000 acres each. By September 1856 there were four permanent reservations: Tejon, Nome Lacke, Klamath (on the Klamath River), and Cape Mendocino (on the Pacific). In addition, three temporary farms had been established. Henley sent in glowing reports, the commissioner of Indian affairs looked optimistically at the developments, and Congress continued to provide large appropriations for the military reservation system.[24]

Doubts arose about the success of the California experiment, however. In 1858 a special agent, Godard Bailey, was dispatched to visit the reservations. His observations led him to conclude that Beale's plan of collecting the Indians on the reserves where they would be supported by their own labor was "a lamentable failure." He reported: "At present the reservations are simply government alms-houses, where an inconsiderable number of Indians are insufficiently fed and scantily clothed, at an expense wholly disporportioned to the benefit conferred. There is nothing in the system, as now practiced, looking to the permanent improvement of the Indian, or tending in any way to his moral, intellectual, or social elevation; the only attempts at anything of the sort that fell under my observation seeming to be rather the result of individual effort than to spring from the system itself."[25]

Congress in 1858 cut the appropriations for the removal and subsistence of the California Indians to $50,000—not enough to restore the reservations from their dilapidated condition. In these circumstances, Commissioner Charles E. Mix seriously challenged the favorable appraisal of his predecessors and asserted that "serious errors" had been committed. He

23. Ellison, "Federal Indian Policy in California," p. 63; 10 *United States Statutes* 332; *Congressional Globe*, 33d Congress, 1st session, pp. 1027–30, 1841–51, 1895, 1945, 1983.

24. Ellison, "Federal Indian Policy in California," pp. 64–65; 10 *United States Statutes* 698, 699; 11 *United States Statutes* 183, 330; Henley to George W. Manypenny, September 4, 1856, CIA Report, 1856, serial 875, pp. 787–97; Henley to J. W. Denver, September 4, 1857, CIA Report, 1857, serial 919, pp. 675–78. See also the annual reports of Manypenny in 1854, 1855, and 1856, and the report of J. W. Denver in 1857.

25. Bailey to Charles E. Mix, November 4, 1858, CIA Report, 1858, serial 974, pp. 649–57; quotation from p. 650.

thought that too much money had been expended and too much done for the Indians, with negligible results. He urged a system that would make the Indians self-sufficient without cost to the government. He wanted them put on good land and then forced to provide for themselves. All unauthorized whites were to be kept out, manual labor schools provided, and after a year the lands divided in severalty among the Indians. Mix's successor, A. B. Greenwood, closely followed this lead. Accepting Bailey's conclusions, as Mix had done, he asserted that "almost any change would be better than the present system as administered," and he recommended the abandonment of Beale's system and the repeal of the laws authorizing the superintendent and the agents in California, and their replacement by a system of two districts with precisely limited agents and other personnel. On June 19, 1860, a new law took effect that largely followed Greenwood's recommendations. It authorized the secretary of the interior to divide California into northern and southern districts. Two superintending agents were provided for, who could appoint a supervisor for each reservation "to instruct the Indians in husbandry," and no more than four laborers to aid each supervisor. The Indians were to be placed on small reservations, to which they would move by simple agreements, not by formal treaties.[26]

The new arrangement seemed little better than the old. President Lincoln's commissioner of Indian affairs, William P. Dole, a man with genuine concern for Indian rights whatever his other failings, found much to condemn when he took office in 1861. He saw the need for breaking up some of the reservations, for establishing others with more ample resources, and for correction of the "outrageous wrongs perpetrated, under color of law, against not only the property but also the persons and liberty of the Indians." None of the reserves in the southern district were free of white claims and none were adequate in extent to serve the Indians' needs, and in the northern district conditions were little better. The result was utter defeat of the purposes for which the reservations had been set up. Dole's analysis is an apt statement of the goals of the government's policy and a harsh, but justified, condemnation of conditions (seemingly beyond the will or power of the federal government to correct) that frustrated the goals.

Instead of being a retreat from the encroachments of the whites upon which they may concentrate and gradually become accustomed

---

26. CIA Report, 1858, serial 974, pp. 357–58; CIA Report, 1859, serial 1023, pp. 386–88; CIA Report, 1860, serial 1078, pp. 244–45; 12 *United States Statutes* 57. Instructions to the new superintending agents are printed in CIA Report, 1860, serial 1078, pp. 454–56.

to a settled mode of life, while *learning* the arts and advantages of civilization, and which at a proper time is to be subdivided and allotted to them in severalty, and thus a home furnished to each of them, around which shall cluster all those fond associations and endearments so highly prized by all civilized people, and they in a condition to appreciate the same, the reservation is a place where a scanty subsistence is doled out to them from year to year; they become accustomed to rely upon charity rather than their own exertions; are hemmed in by people by whom they are detested, and whose arts and customs they have neither the power nor inclination to acquire, and thus they become vagrants and vagabonds, accomplishing for themselves no desirable end, and are a nuisance to their white neighbors.[27]

The California Indians continued to live in a kind of limbo. Many of them settled on the reservations and developed a rancheria existence— little spots of poor land within the rich state to which they had no clear title and on which they were under constant threats of encroachment from white Americans. Their numbers declined by 1856, according to some estimates, to as few as twenty-five or thirty thousand.[28] These so-called "mission Indians" and their rights became a special subject of attention of the post-Civil War humanitarian Indian reformers.

The designation of the reservations in California under the rejected treaties, under Beale's and Henley's activities, and under the district superintending agents contributed to the development of the federal Indian reservation system, but the California experience was outside the main course of reservation history. The Indians were allowed no clear title to the land, and the small and scattered reserves of land presented quite a different situation from that on the Sioux reserve in Dakota, for example, or the Kiowa-Comanche reservation in Oklahoma set up by the treaties made by the peace commission in 1868, which fitted into the pattern of the northern and southern colonies advocated since the late 1840s.[29]

INDIAN AFFAIRS IN THE OREGON COUNTRY

The United States was slow to vindicate its claim to the Oregon Country, the vast area lying north of California and west of the Rocky Mountains,

27. CIA Report, 1861, serial 1117, pp. 639–40.
28. Cook, *Population of the California Indians*, p. xv.
29. Ellison, "Federal Indian Policy in California," argues that the California reservations were the origin of the United States reservation system and set the pattern for later reservation policy; Hoopes, *Indian Affairs and Their Administration*, follows his lead. These authors overlook the long history of setting aside lands with set boundaries for

and thus to assume responsibility for Indian relations in the area.[30] Although Yankee traders along the coast and occasional overland expeditions like those of Lewis and Clark and the Astorians gave the United States a claim to the region, the nation did not at first take much interest in such a remote spot. In 1818 the United States made an agreement of joint occupation for ten years with Great Britain, and in 1827 the agreement was extended. In the twenties and thirties, however, there was public agitation for the acquisition of Oregon. Representative John Floyd of Virginia tried to develop enthusiasm in Congress for Oregon and in December 1820 persuaded the House to appoint a committee to "inquire into the situation of the settlements upon the Pacific Ocean, and the expediency of occupying the Columbia River." The committee (with Floyd as chairman) submitted a report urging annexation that produced no tangible movement in regard to acquiring Oregon but did stir up public attention. In 1822 Floyd proposed another measure, and he continued to agitate for occupation of the Columbia River region. But the arguments in favor of the rich province were overcome by counterarguments that the Pacific region was too distant to be joined in one nation with the existing states.[31]

The agitation for Oregon did not cease. It was promoted by a Massachusetts school teacher, Hall Jackson Kelley, who carried on an extensive propaganda campaign that urged government support for a colony in Oregon to combat the growing influence of the British. His efforts to transplant a New England town to the Oregon wilderness came to nothing. A fellow New Englander, Nathaniel J. Wyeth, was little more successful, although he led a small party across the continent to the Willamette Valley in 1832 and left a journal of the expedition that is a valuable document on the westward crossing.[32]

---

specific tribes and the intention of leading the Indians to white civilization there. Note that Robert A. Trennert, Jr., *Alternative to Extinction: Federal Indian Policy and the Beginnings of the Reservation System, 1846–51* (Philadelphia: Temple University Press, 1975), does not mention California at all.

30. An authoritative general history of the region including an account of Indian affairs is Dorothy O. Johansen, *Empire of the Columbia: A History of the Pacific Northwest*, 2d ed. (New York: Harper and Row, 1967). Indian policy developments in Oregon and Washington are treated thoroughly in Hoopes, *Indian Affairs and Their Administration*, pp. 69–130.

31. *Annals of Congress*, 16th Congress, 2d session, p. 679. The report of Floyd's committee, in favor of occupying the Oregon Country, January 25, 1821, with a proposed bill is printed ibid., pp. 945–59. A detailed account of Floyd's activity is given in Charles H. Ambler, "The Oregon Country, 1810–1830: A Chapter in Territorial Expansion," *Mississippi Valley Historical Review* 30 (June 1943): 3–24.

32. On Kelley see Fred Wilbur Powell, *Hall Jackson Kelley: Prophet of Oregon* (Portland, Oregon: Ivy Press, 1917), and Powell, ed., *Hall J. Kelley on Oregon* (Princeton:

Of more significance for the settlement of Oregon and relations with the Indians was the work of Christian missionaries. In October 1831 four Indians of the Northwest appeared in St. Louis in the company of a group of traders. The story arose that they had come to seek missionaries to show them the road to heaven, and the publication of this story—in large part a fabrication—in the Methodist *Christian Advocate and Journal* in March 1833 pricked the Christian conscience.[33] Soon substantial missionary efforts aimed at Christianizing the Indians of Oregon and the establishment of permanent settlements there as a base of operation were under way. The first of these was a Methodist mission led by Jason Lee, who moved across the continent in 1834. Lee and his party established the first American agricultural community in the Willamette Valley. Supported by the Methodist Board of Missions and promoted by aggressive propagandizing in the East, the Methodist mission grew in size and by 1840 was a significant advertisement of the economic wonders of Oregon.[34]

The Methodists were followed by missionaries of the American Board of Commissioners for Foreign Missions. In 1835 Dr. Marcus Whitman and the Reverend Samuel Parker moved up the Missouri with a party of the American Fur Company and met with Indians in the Green River Valley. Encouraged by the reception the Indians gave them, Whitman returned east for helpers while Parker continued to the coast to seek out locations for missions. Whitman was authorized by the American Board to establish a mission among the Flatheads, and he and the Reverend Henry H. Spalding and their wives returned to the West in 1836. The Whitmans opened a mission among the Cayuse Indians at Waiilatpu, near Fort Walla Walla; the Spaldings set up one at Lapwai, in present-day Idaho, among the Nez Per-

---

Princeton University Press, 1932), which prints a number of Kelley's writings. For Wyeth's work, see "The Correspondence and Journals of Captain Nathaniel J. Wyeth, 1831–6," ed. F. G. Young, *Sources of the History of Oregon*, vol. 1, parts 3–6.

33. Two recent scholarly accounts of the story are in Clifford M. Drury, *Marcus and Narcissa Whitman and the Opening of Old Oregon*, 2 vols. (Glendale, California: Arthur H. Clark Company, 1973), 1: 28–50, and Alvin M. Josephy, Jr., *The Nez Perce Indians and the Opening of the Northwest* (New Haven: Yale University Press, 1965), pp. 93–103. Three older articles, presenting different views, are John Rothensteiner, "The Flat-Head and Nez Perce Delegation to St. Louis, 1831–1839," *St. Louis Catholic Historical Review* 2 (October 1920): 183–97; Francis Haines, "The Nez Perce Delegation to St. Louis in 1831," *Pacific Historical Review* 6 (March 1937): 71–78; and J. Orin Oliphant, "Francis Haines and William Walker: A Critique," ibid. 14 (June 1945): 211–16.

34. A careful study of Lee's mission is Robert J. Loewenberg, *Equality on the Oregon Frontier: Jason Lee and the Methodist Mission, 1834–43* (Seattle: University of Washington Press, 1976). See also Cornelius J. Brosnan, *Jason Lee: Prophet of the New Oregon* (New York: Macmillan Company, 1932). A brief, popular, and well-illustrated article is Michael Ames, "Missionaries' Toil for Soul and Survival: Introducing Christianity to the Pacific Northwest," *American West* 10 (January 1973): 28–33, 63.

ces. Another American Board mission was established at Fort Colville among the Spokanes.[35] Catholic missionaries, too, moved into the Oregon Country. Some came from Canada in response to appeals from French Canadians living in the Willamette Valley. Others, of whom the Jesuit Pierre-Jean DeSmet was the most famous, moved up the Missouri River. Father DeSmet opened a mission in the Bitterroot Valley in present-day Montana in 1841. These Catholic missions expanded in the interior regions of the Oregon Country, and the missionaries gained great influence with the Indians.[36]

The Protestant missions were less successful than the Catholic, in large part because of dissension among the missionaries. The discouraging reports led the American Board in 1842 to direct the closing of the Waiilatpu and Lapwai missions, keeping only the one among the Spokanes; but Whitman on a trip to the East in support of the missions won a reprieve.[37] Yet the missions did not prosper, and the Indians' lack of concern turned into hostility.

The missionary endeavors, especially the agricultural success of the Methodists in the Willamette Valley, building on the earlier agitation for the settlement of Oregon, helped to touch off a massive movement of Americans into Oregon. A migration of about a thousand emigrants left Independence, Missouri, in 1843 (guided by Marcus Whitman on his return from the East), and in the following years even larger companies swelled the American population in the Willamette Valley. By 1845 the population in Oregon was about six thousand, and the increase in American presence soon led to renewed pressure for sole American jurisdiction. The British, finding the fur trade declining and fearing the turbulent frontiersmen, moved from Fort Vancouver on the Columbia to Vancouver Island; and despite some braggadocio about "54° 40' or fight," the United States and Great Britain came to a peaceful agreement on June 15, 1846, by which the forty-ninth parallel boundary line was extended to the Pacific. The Oregon Country south of that line was now the undisputed posses-

35. The fullest and best account of the Whitmans is Drury, *Marcus and Narcissa Whitman.* See also Clifford M. Drury, *Henry Harmon Spalding, Pioneer of Old Oregon* (Caldwell, Idaho: Caxton Printers, 1936), and Clifford M. Drury, *Elkanah and Mary Walker: Pioneers among the Spokanes* (Caldwell, Idaho: Caxton Printers, 1940).

36. A thorough introduction to Catholic involvement with the Indians in the Pacific Northwest that is broader in scope than its title indicates is Robert Ignatius Burns, *The Jesuits and the Indian Wars of the Northwest* (New Haven: Yale University Press, 1966). On DeSmet, see H. M. Chittenden and A. T. Richardson, eds., *Life, Letters, and Travels of Father Pierre-Jean DeSmet, S.J., 1801–1873,* 4 vols. (New York: Francis P. Harper, 1905).

37. There is extended literature about the legend that Whitman "saved" Oregon by his trip to the East. An excellent analysis of the legend is in Drury, *Marcus and Narcissa Whitman,* 2: 375–86.

sion of the United States and its Indian affairs the concern of the federal government.

The United States government, however, was slow to accept its new responsibilities, and it made no immediate move to establish a territorial government or any administrative machinery to attend to Indian affairs. It is true that in 1842, while Oregon was still under joint occupation, Elijah White had been appointed Indian subagent for Oregon. He had successfully eased tensions between the whites and the Cayuse and Nez Perce Indians, but he made political enemies, and in 1845 he was removed from his position and not replaced.[38] The settlers, meanwhile, in good American fashion, in 1843 and 1845 had set up their own "provisional government," but they expected a formal territorial government to be set up. It was the Indian troubles in Oregon that finally produced some action in Congress.

When an epidimic of measles struck the Whitman mission, in which the whites under Dr. Whitman's care recovered while the Cayuse Indians ministered to by him died, the Indians were convinced that they had been poisoned as part of a missionary plot. On November 29, 1847, the Indians rose up against the mission and murdered Whitman, his wife, and a dozen others, taking captive the remaining women and children.[39] The outrage stirred up the people of Oregon, and in May the provisional legislature petitioned Congress for immediate territorial organization. The legislature noted, among other reasons for extending laws of the United States over the territory, that it had "no *power or right to treat with the Indian tribes,* nor means to pay them should we make a treaty," and that a general Indian war was likely. On August 14, 1848, President Polk signed the bill that created the Territory of Oregon, which made the governor ex officio superintendent of Indian affairs. The law specifically protected the rights of the Indians in the new territory "so long as such rights shall remain unextinguished by treaty between the United States and such Indians," and it vindicated the right of the United States to make laws and regulations regarding the Indians. As a stopgap measure, it provided funds for such presents to the Indians as might be required for the "peace and quietude of the country." Polk appointed as governor Joseph Lane, an able Kentucky politician, who was a hero of the Mexican War and later vice presidential candidate with Breckinridge in 1860. In the following March, Lane arrived in Oregon and declared the new government to be in operation. Lane's instruction of August 31, 1848, from the commissioner of Indian affairs di-

38. Hoopes, *Indian Affairs and Their Administration,* p. 70.

39. Drury, *Marcus and Narcissa Whitman,* 2: 205–65. For a history of the Cayuses, see Robert H. Ruby and John A. Brown, *The Cayuse Indians: Imperial Tribesmen of Old Oregon* (Norman: University of Oklahoma Press, 1972), and *The Spokane Indians: Children of the Sun* (Norman: University of Oklahoma Press, 1970).

rected him to collect information about the Indians in Oregon, the best arrangements for agencies, and the funds needed to manage Indian affairs in his territory.[40]

Lane observed the Indian situation by traveling through the territory, and he maintained a precarious peace. His views reflected the dominant white attitude toward Oregon's riches and the Indians who stood in the way of their exploitation. In his message to the Oregon legislature on July 17, 1849, he called attention to the wonders of the region and noted "how lavishly nature has bestowed her blessings on this favored land." Regarding the Indians, he told the legislators: "Surrounded as many of the tribes and bands now are, by the whites, whose arts of civilization, by destroying the resources of the Indians, doom them to poverty, want, and crime, the extinguishment of their title by purchase, and the locating them in a district removed from the settlements, is a measure of the most vital importance to them. Indeed, the cause of humanity calls loudly for their removal from causes and influences so fatal to their existence." Lane urged a memorial to Congress on the subject, and the Oregon legislature quickly responded with a long memorial dated July 20, 1849, that prayed for the purchase of the Indian lands and the removal of the Indians to some district "where their wretched and unhappy condition may be ameliorated."[41]

Lane's brief administration ended with the surrender by the Cayuses of the Whitman murderers, who were tried and executed in the summer of 1850. With the advent of Taylor's Whig administration, Democrat Lane was replaced as governor by John P. Gaines, who arrived in Oregon in August 1850. But by then Congress, following the urging of the territorial delegate from Oregon, Samuel R. Thurston, had made special provision for Indian affairs. Thurston's purposes were to extinguish all Indian title to lands west of the Cascade Mountains and to remove the Indians from that region to some location east of the mountains, and he urged that appropriate officials be appointed to handle Indian matters. Congress was sympathetic. On February 1, 1850, the House adopted Thurston's resolution, and on June 5 a law was approved that supported his desires. It called for the appointment of commissioners to negotiate treaties with the Oregon Indians to carry out his plans. Moreover, it removed the responsibility for

40. "Petition of Citizens of Oregon, praying that the laws of the United States may be extended over that Territory, &c.," *Senate Miscellaneous Document* no. 136, 30–1, serial 511, p. 4; 9 *United States Statutes* 323–31; William Medill to Lane, August 31, 1848, OIA LS, vol. 41, pp. 207–10 (M21, reel 41).

41. Lane to the secretary of war or commissioner of Indian affairs, October 22, 1849, *Senate Executive Document* no. 52, 31–1, serial 561, pp. 167–80; governor's message, July 17, 1849, ibid., p. 8; "Memorial of the Legislature of Oregon Praying for the Extinguishment of the Indian Title and the Removal of the Indians from Certain Portions of That Territory," July 20, 1849, *Senate Miscellaneous Document* no. 5, 31–2, serial 592.

Indian affairs from the territorial governor and authorized the appointment of a separate superintendent of Indian affairs, and it extended the intercourse law of 1834 over the Indians of Oregon Territory. One to three Indian agents were to be appointed by the president for Oregon.[42]

Anson Dart of Wisconsin was appointed superintendent, and three agents were named. Luke Lea instructed Dart to urge the Indians to live in peace and harmony among themselves, to induce them to engage in agricultural pursuits (encouraging them by prizes offered for the best crops), and to cooperate with the Christian missionaries working among the Indians without getting involved in sectarian disputes. The Indian, Lea said, has "but one alternative—early civilization or gradual extinction. The efforts of the government will be earnestly directed to his civilization and preservation, and we confidently rely upon their Christian teachers, that, in connection with their spiritual mission, they will aid in carrying out this policy." The adopted policy of the government toward the Indians of the West was repeatedly proclaimed. If the objectives of the civilization program for the Indians could be attained—"if they can be taught to subsist, not by the chase merely, a resource which must soon be exhausted, but by the rearing of flocks and herds, and by field cultivation, we may hope that the little remnant of this ill-fated race will not utterly perish from the earth, but have a permanent resting-place and home on some part of our broad domain, once the land of their fathers." Lea seemed to have no awareness that the Indians with whom Dart had to deal subsisted largely by fishing and that a change to an agricultural existence was neither wise nor easily accomplished.[43]

On October 25, 1850, three commissioners, including Governor Gaines, were appointed "to negotiate treaties with the several Indian tribes in the Territory of Oregon for the extinguishment of their claims to lands lying west of the Cascade Mountains." The goal of the government, they were told, was to free the land west of the Cascades entirely of Indian title and to move all the Indians to some spot to the east. Their instructions made it clear that the payments stipulated for the ceded lands were to be in objects beneficial to the Indians and that no part should be paid in money. The instructions specified agricultural assistance, hiring of blacksmiths and mechanics, employment of farmers to teach cultivation, physicians, and "ample provision for the purposes of education."[44]

The wishes of the Oregon settlers to clear the western part of Oregon of Indians, backed by the instructions of the federal government, ran up

---

42. *Congressional Globe*, 31st Congress, 1st session, p. 272; 9 *United States Statutes* 437.

43. Lea to Dart, July 20, 1850, CIA Report, 1850, serial 587, pp. 148–51.

44. A. S. Loughery, acting commissioner of Indian affairs, to J. P. Gaines, Alonzo H. Skinner, and Beverly S. Allen, October 25, 1850, CIA Report, 1850, serial 587, pp. 145–47.

against the Indians' adamant refusal to depart. The alternative was outlined by the commissioners:

> It will be impossible to remove the Indians of Willamette and lower Columbia valleys, without a resort to force, nor do we think it very desirable to do so. As before stated they are friendly and well disposed, they live almost entirely by fishing, and the wages they receive from the whites for their labor. They possess little or no skill as hunters or warriors. And to remove them from their fisheries and means of procuring labor from the whites would in our opinion insure their annihilation in a short time either from want or by the hands of their more warlike neighbors. General satisfaction we believe would be felt by the Indians and the citizens to allow them small reservations of a few sections and a portion of their fishing grounds.[45]

And this is what they provided in the six treaties they signed with the Indians in April and May 1851. Then the work of the commissioners was ended by an act of Congress of February 27, 1851, directing that all treaty making be carried on by regular officers of the Indian department, not by special commissioners. Superintendent Dart carried on the negotiations by himself. During the summer and fall of 1851 he signed thirteen treaties with Indian bands that freed more than six million acres of land of Indian title.[46]

For reasons that are difficult to pin down precisely, none of the treaties signed by the commissioners and by Dart were ever ratified. The failure to eliminate the Indians completely from west of the Cascades by providing residual reservations there for the tribes probably played an important part, for in this sense the treaties failed to accomplish what the congressional directive had stipulated. Some of the treaties, too, were negotiated with mere remnants of once more populous tribes. The Wheelappa band of Chinooks, with whom Dart signed a treaty on August 9, 1851, for example, had only two male survivors and a few women and children. And the cost of the annuities may have been another point of objection.[47]

45. Commissioners to Luke Lea, February 8, 1851, quoted in Hoopes, *Indian Affairs and Their Administration*, pp. 78–79. The commissioners made the same point when they submitted to the commissioner of Indian affairs the treaties containing provisions for reserved lands, contrary to the directions they had received. See commissioners to Lea, April 19 and May 14, 1851, CIA Report, 1851, serial 613, pp. 467–72.

46. The treaty making is discussed in detail in C. F. Coan, "The First Stage of the Federal Indian Policy in the Pacific Northwest, 1849–1852," *Oregon Historical Society Quarterly* 22 (March 1921): 46–65. In an appendix, pp. 65–89, Coan reprints the report of Dart to Lea, November 7, 1851, transmitting the treaties; also reprinted there are the few treaties that are extant. See also Hoopes, *Indian Affairs and Their Administration*, pp. 79–86.

47. Coan, "First Stage," pp. 59, 65.

The first round of treaties, then, did not bring a firm settlement of Indian problems facing the federal government in Oregon, and critical conditions remained. Whites moved into the territory in ever-increasing numbers, eager to lay their hands on the rich lands. Congress on September 27,
1850, by the so-called Donation Land Law, without concern for Indian
titles, had provided grants of 320 acres to American citizens or prospective
citizens who had resided in Oregon and cultivated the land for four years,
and settlers felt entitled to take land wherever they chose.[48]

In the summer of 1853 Anson Dart resigned, and Joel Palmer, an Oregon
pioneer, was appointed superintendent in his stead. Palmer, who served
until August 1856, directed Indian affairs in Oregon in a critical period. As
he took office troubles began with the Rogue River Indians, and a minor
war raged through the summer and early fall of 1853. The Indians were
subdued by army regulars and Oregon volunteers, and Palmer signed a
treaty of cession with the Indians at Table Rock on September 10, 1853. By
this treaty the Indians gave up their claims to land in Oregon and accepted
a small section of their lands as a temporary reserve until a permanent reservation could be established. Annuities in the form of specified goods
were provided, but article 7, added by the Senate, stipulated that the
annuities at the discretion of the president could be used instead to establish farms for the benefit of the Indians. The treaty was ratified on April
12, 1854.[49]

With this success behind him, Palmer proceeded to negotiate a series of
treaties with other tribes along the coast and with tribes in central Oregon
that eliminated Indian title over much of the area between the Cascades
and the coast, as well as a sizable section of the interior. Palmer had decided views about what the negotiations should include. In June 1853 he
painted a bleak picture of the Indians' condition as they were pressed upon
by the whites and as they succumbed to white vices and diseases, and then
he set forth his proposal:

> If the benevolent designs of the government to preserve and elevate
> these remnants of the aborigines are to be carried forward to a suc-

---

48. 9 *United States Statutes* 496–500; James M. Bergquist, "The Oregon Donation
Act and the National Land Policy," *Oregon Historical Quarterly* 58 (March 1957): 17–47.
A contemporary reaction to the Donation Land Law was provided by the superintendent
of Indian affairs in Washington Territory: "The inapplicability of the intercourse law, and
its being in conflict with the act of Congress donating lands to settlers, &c., of September 27, 1850, renders it almost impossible to do anything without extinguishing their
titles, and placing them in reservations where they can be cared for and attended to."
Isaac I. Stevens to George W. Manypenny, December 26, 1853, *Senate Executive Document* no. 34, 33–1, serial 698, p. 6.

49. Kappler, pp. 603–5.

cessful issue, there appears but one path open. A home remote from the settlements must be selected for them. There they must be guarded from the pestiferous influence of degraded white men, and restrained by proper laws from violence and wrong among themselves. Let comfortable houses be erected for them, seeds and proper implements furnished, and instruction and encouragement given them in the cultivation of the soil. Let school-houses be erected, and teachers employed to instruct their children; and let the missionaries of the gospel of peace be encouraged to dwell among them. Let completeness of plan, energy, patience and perseverance characterize the effort; and, if still it fail, the government will have at least the satisfaction of knowing that an honest and determined endeavor was made to save and elevate a fallen race.[50]

The Palmer treaties were pretty much of a piece and fitted well into the pattern established throughout the West in the 1850s.[51] There was little indication in them that two sovereign equals were negotiating. For lack of other acceptable and established procedures, the treaties were the vehicle chosen to accomplish what the United States government wanted as it reacted to cries from western settlers and to the philosophical principles dominant in government circles. The Indians were to be moved out of the way of the whites—not, as in the case of the removal of the eastern tribes, to open spaces in the West, but to limited reserves within their old, more extensive territorial claims or to other specified locations within the territory. Most of the treaties were made with "confederated tribes and bands," an often more or less arbitrary grouping for convenience. In all of them the chiefs and headmen of these bands acknowledged "their dependence on the Government of the United States" and promised to stay on friendly terms with the citizens, sometimes consenting "to submit to, and observe all laws, rules, and regulations which may be prescribed by the United States for the government of said Indians." They agreed, moreover, to grant rights of way through their lands for roads and railroads. All claims of the Indians to lands were given up in return for small reservations within their old limits, but most of the Palmer treaties included a blanket agreement to move from these reserves to other locations selected by the government

---

50. Palmer to Manypenny, June 23, 1853, CIA Report, 1853, serial 690, p. 449. Palmer's annual report of October 8, 1853, is printed in *Oregon Historical Society Quarterly* 23 (March 1922): 28–38.

51. The treaties negotiated by Palmer and the Oregon Indians are printed in Kappler, pp. 606–7, 655–60, 665–69, 714–19, 740–42. C. F. Coan, "The Adoption of the Reservation Policy in the Pacific Northwest, 1853–1855," *Oregon Historical Society Quarterly* 23 (March 1922): 3–27, deals with the treaty making in Oregon and Washington territories.

"should the President at any time believe it demanded by the public good and promotive of the best interests of said Indians."

All the treaties spoke specifically of "civilization." Annuity payments for ceded lands, set for a limited term of years, were not to be in money, but in goods conducive to the agricultural development of the Indians and for their moral improvement and education. The United States, moreover, agreed to erect blacksmith shops, hospitals, and schoolhouses and to furnish for a period of years the necessary mechanics, physicians, and teachers. The treaties authorized the president to survey the reservations and assign lots in severalty to Indians "willing to avail themselves of the privilege, and who will locate thereon as a permanent home." An attack was made on the liquor menace by providing that annuities be withheld from Indians guilty of intemperance; and no annuities could be taken to pay the debts of individuals. Although government officials no doubt rejoiced in the framework of existence for the Indians envisaged in the treaties, the negotiations were in fact a nearly complete capitulation of the tribesmen to superior power.

The treaties signed by Palmer with the Indians in 1853 and 1854 were ratified and proclaimed in good time. When war broke out again in 1855, the Senate delayed ratification of the later treaties until the spring of 1859, causing incalculable problems in dealing with the Indians, who did not understand why the benefits promised them in the treaties were not forthcoming.

THE INDIANS OF WASHINGTON TERRITORY

On March 2, 1853, Washington Territory (initially bounded by the forty-ninth parallel to the north, the Rocky Mountains to the east, and the Columbia River and the forty-sixth parallel to the south) was broken off from Oregon Territory. Isaac Ingalls Stevens was appointed territorial governor and ex officio superintendent of Indian affairs. Stevens, from Massachusetts, was a West Point graduate with service in the Mexican War, who resigned his commission in March 1853 to accept the new position in the West; he was thirty-five years old. At his request the War Department placed him in charge of the party surveying the northern route for a Pacific railroad, and he met with Indian groups as he moved west from St. Paul to Olympia, the territorial capital.[52]

52. A scholarly biography of Stevens that pays close attention to his handling of Indian affairs is Kent D. Richards, *Isaac I. Stevens: Young Man in a Hurry* (Provo: Brigham Young University Press, 1979). Hazard Stevens, *The Life of Isaac Ingalls Stevens*, 2 vols. (Boston: Houghton, Mifflin and Company, 1900), is by his son and must be used with

Soon after Stevens's arrival he wrote to the commissioner of Indian affairs of the "urgent necessity" that treaties be made at once with the Indians west of the Cascades, for settlers were moving in rapidly and the Indians would be driven from their homes. He realized, however, that the complete removal of the Indians from west of the Cascades was unrealistic. He noted the attachment of the Indians to their hereditary residences and that their customary means of subsistence by fishing would be seriously disrupted by removal into the interior. The solution was to provide small reserves for them in their present locations. Stevens urged as well treaties with the tribes in eastern Washington. "There is much valuable land, and an inexhaustible supply of timber, east of the Cascades," he wrote; "and I consider its speedy settlement so desirable that all impediments should be removed." Commissioner Manypenny strongly supported the need for treaties; and Stevens, on a visit to Washington, D.C., in the spring of 1854, added his own personal promotion of the idea. Congress appropriated $45,000 for negotiating treaties with the Indians in Washington Territory and another $80,000 for holding a council with "the Blackfeet, Gros Ventres, and other wild tribes of Indians, immediately within or adjacent to the eastern boundary of Washington Territory."[53]

Governor Stevens was an energetic and highly organized man, and his career as superintendent of Indian affairs was marked by a series of dramatic councils with the Indians at which treaties of peace, cession, and civilization were signed. In preparation for treating with the Indians, Stevens organized a commission, which met on December 7, 1854. The application of a pattern common to the whole nation is seen in the report of the meeting, for the commission read and discussed the recent treaties made by Commissioner Manypenny with the Otos and Missouris and with the Omahas. After considerable discussion of reservations, fishing stations, schools, and farms, George Gibbs, a talented Harvard graduate and ethnolo-

---

caution because of its favorable bias, but it contains detailed accounts of the Indian councils. An account of the Indian tribes met on the way west is given in Stevens's report of September 16, 1854, in CIA Report, 1854, serial 746, pp. 392–457; a final report appears in *Reports of Explorations and Surveys, to Ascertain the Most Practicable and Economical Route for a Railroad from the Mississippi River to the Pacific Ocean*, vol. 12, book 1 (*House Executive Document* no. 56, 36–1, serial 1054). A useful description of the Washington Superintendency is James R. Masterson, "The Records of the Washington Superintendency of Indian Affairs, 1853–1874," *Pacific Northwest Quarterly* 37 (January 1946): 31–57.

53. Stevens to Manypenny, December 26, 1853, *Senate Executive Document* no. 34, 33–1, serial 698, pp. 6–7; Stevens to Manypenny, December 29, 1853, ibid., pp. 13–14; Manypenny to Robert McClelland, February 6, 1854, ibid., pp. 1–2; 10 *United States Statutes* 330.

gist who was a member of the group, was delegated to prepare "a pro-
gramme of a Treaty" in accordance with the views of the commission.[54]

When the commission met again three days later, a draft of a treaty was
ready. Thus armed, the governor and his commissioners met on Christmas
Day with a number of tribes at Medicine Creek at the mouth of the Nisqually River. This was not to be a "negotiation" between two political
powers, of course, but an imposition upon the Indians of the treaty provisions Stevens brought with him, for he held a highly paternalistic view of
his relations with the tribes. As his wife remarked in a letter to her mother
that undoubtedly reflected her husband's opinions, the Indians "think so
much of the whites that a child can govern them." "Mr. Stevens," she said,
"has them right under his thumb—they are afraid as death of him and do
just as he tells them." On December 26 the governor spoke to the assembled Indians in a flowery and patronizing manner that expressed his
view of relations between the government and the tribesmen:

> This is a great day for you and for us. A day of Peace and Friendship
> between you and the Whites for all time to come. You are about to be
> paid for your lands, and the Great Father has sent me to-day to treat
> with you concerning the payment. The Great Father lives far off. He
> has many children: some of them came here when he knew but little
> of them or the Indians, and he has sent me to inquire into these
> things. We went through this Country last year, learned your num-
> bers and saw your wants. We felt much for you and went to the Great
> Father to tell him what we had seen. The Great Father felt for his
> children—he pitied them, and he has sent me here to-day to express
> those feelings, and to make a Treaty for your benefit.[55]

The prepared treaty was explained point by point to the Indians, who
signed it on December 26 without objection. The terms were very similar
to those in the treaties signed by Joel Palmer and the Oregon Indians, but
in addition to those terms, specific provision was made to protect the fishing rights of the Indians. The United States agreed to maintain for twenty
years an agricultural and industrial school for the children of the signatory
bands and for those of other tribes and bands, at a general agency to be set
up for the Puget Sound region. This treaty was promptly ratified.[56]

In quick succession, Stevens and his assistants signed similar treaties

54. "Records of the Proceedings of the Commission to hold Treaties with the Indian
Tribes in Washington Territory and the Blackfoot Country," Records of the Office of Indian Affairs, Documents Relating to the Negotiation of Ratified and Unratified Treaties
with Various Indian Tribes (T494, reel 5, frames 205–6).

55. Ibid. (frames 206–9). Margaret Stevens's letters of February 17 and 18, 1855, are
quoted in Richards, *Isaac I. Stevens*, p. 195.

56. Kappler, pp. 661–64.

with other groups of coastal Indians at Point Elliott (January 22, 1855), Point No Point (January 26), and Neah Bay (January 31). With that of Medicine Creek, these treaties cleared a wide area of land around Puget Sound, but they were not ratified until 1859.[57]

The summer and fall of 1855 were taken up by three great councils with the Indians in which Stevens, with his usual drive and energy, expected to impose on the Indians of the interior his vision of their future. The first was the Walla Walla Council in late May and early June, attended by Joel Palmer as well as Stevens and made up of delegations of Walla Walla, Cayuse, Umatilla, Yakima, and Nez Perce Indians. The Indians, aside from the generally friendly Nez Perces, were hostile, and concessions, including special cash annuities for the chiefs, had to be made to get signatures on the treaties. Two treaties were signed on June 9, one with the Walla Wallas, Cayuses, and Umatillas and a second with the Yakimas. Another on June 11 was signed with the Nez Perces. They contained the usual provisions for cessions, reservations, annuity payments, employment of mechanics, articles for agricultural development, and means for moral improvement and education. But the treaties were not the successes that Stevens assumed, for the chiefs were offended by the terms that the whites proposed and could see their crushing effect. The Jesuit missionary Joseph Joset commented: "The chiefs agreed to a mock treaty in order to gain time and prepare for war."[58]

In mid-July Stevens moved on to Hell Gate on the Clark Fork just beyond the northern end of the Bitterroot Valley for a council with Flathead, Kutenai, and Pend d'Oreille Indians. The treaty, similar to those at Walla Walla, was signed on July 16, 1855.[59] At Hell Gate, too, there was much agitation among the Indians as they argued about a proper location for the reduced reservation they were expected to accept. The deep Indian attachment for traditional homelands was not sufficiently appreciated by the whites, who looked chiefly at the economic potentialities of a reservation for sustaining the Indians in a peaceful agricultural existence, and the treaty was signed by the Indians with the understanding that the president would survey the region and designate an acceptable spot.[60]

57. Ibid., pp. 669–77, 682–85. Extracts from the proceedings at Point No Point are printed in Charles M. Gates, ed., "The Indian Treaty of Point No Point," *Pacific Northwest Quarterly* 46 (April 1955): 52–58.

58. Quoted in Burns, *Jesuits and the Indian Wars*, p. 79. There is an excellent account of the council and its background in Josephy, *Nez Perce Indians*, pp. 285–332; a shortened version is in Josephy, "A Most Satisfactory Council," *American Heritage* 16 (October 1965): 26–31, 70–76. The treaties are printed in Kappler, pp. 694–706.

59. Kappler, pp. 722–25.

60. The most thorough critical account of the council is in Burns, *Jesuits and the Indian Wars*, pp. 96–114. An incomplete version of the official minutes is in Albert J.

The final grand council was held in October with the Blackfeet, Flat-heads, and Nez Perces at the mouth of the Judith River in present-day Montana. It fulfilled a need, observed by Stevens when he crossed the con-tinent with the railroad survey expedition in 1853, for a treaty of peace be-tween the often warring tribes of the northern Rockies; and the $80,000 appropriated by Congress in 1854 had been for this purpose. Joel Palmer and Alfred Cumming, superintendent of the Central Superintendency, were named with Stevens as commissioners for the treaty. Manypenny told them that the principal objects were the establishment of well-defined and permanent relations of amity between the Indians and the United States and between the tribes themselves. "A cordial, firm, and perpetual peace should be established," the commissioner of Indian affairs directed; "a well understood recognition by the Indians of their allegiance to the United States, and their obligation to obey its laws, should be obtained, and a high regard on their part for its justice, magnanimity and power, should be fostered or inculcated."[61]

After some false starts occasioned by a delay in the arrival of goods to be distributed as presents, the council was opened on October 16 by Stevens and Cumming with thirty-five hundred Indians in attendance; Joel Palmer did not come. The treaty, signed on October 17, began with formal state-ments of perpetual peace between the United States and the Indians and between the signatory tribes themselves and with other tribes. Boundaries were specified for common hunting grounds for the Indians for a period of ninety-nine years, and the lands belonging exclusively to the Blackfeet were described. The United States agreed to provide the Blackfeet with cer-tain annuities and to instruct them in agricultural and mechanical pur-suits, to educate their children, and in other aspects to promote their "civi-lization and Christianization." This treaty was ratified by the Senate on April 15, 1856.[62] But those signed at the Walla Walla and Flathead councils had to wait for ratification until March 1859, together with those signed with the western Washington tribes and Palmer's Oregon Indian treaties.

Stevens used the Indian councils to promote his interests in the north-

---

Partoll, ed., "The Flathead Indian Treaty Council of 1855," *Pacific Northwest Quarterly* 29 (July 1938): 283–314. See also Burns, "A Jesuit at the Hell Gate Treaty of 1855," *Mid-America* 34 (April 1952): 87–114.

61. Manypenny to Cumming, Stevens, and Palmer, May 3, 1855, CIA Report, 1855, serial 810, pp. 530–31.

62. Kappler, pp. 736–40. For accounts of the council, see Burns, *Jesuits and the In-dian Wars*, pp. 117–23; John C. Ewers, *The Blackfeet: Raiders on the Northwestern Plains* (Norman: University of Oklahoma Press, 1958), pp. 214–22; and Alfred J. Partoll, ed., "The Blackfoot Indian Peace Council," *Frontier and Midland: A Magazine of the West* 17 (Spring 1937): 199–207.

ern railroad route. As he and his party traveled to the council sites, he continued to explore the land in terms of railroad possibilities. Even the military operations against the Indians were used for the same purpose, for, as he wrote in his final report on the survey, the military expeditions were always accompanied by one or two staff officers experienced in exploration, whose observations contributed materially to the knowledge of the country. Stevens was ever aware of the three tasks he was simultaneously engaged in: promoting a northern route for the transcontinental railroad, diligently working to build up a populous, enterprising white settlement in Washington Territory, and settling Indian affairs, by treaty and if need be by war. It is easy, in looking back to the 1850s, to see a serious conflict of interest in the governor-superintendent's position, but Stevens himself did not see it that way, for in his mind all were coordinated to produce a peaceful and prosperous region, of which he was an ardent advocate.

The delay in treaty ratification, which so seriously complicated Indian relations, was due primarily to the wars that broke out in 1855. Increasing penetration of their country by whites stirred up both the Rogue River Indians in Oregon and the Yakimas and their allies in central Washington. The simultaneous operations that resulted, the Rogue River War and the Yakima War, can be considered a single military endeavor. The troubles began while Stevens was still engaged in his council with the Blackfeet far to the east. Hostile acts by the Yakimas and the Oregon Indians, including the murder of Yakima Indian agent A. J. Bolen, called out volunteers to augment the military strength of the small regular army garrisons, and military operations continued in the two territories into the summer of 1856. The Rogue River and Umatilla hostiles in Oregon surrendered in June and were concentrated on the Coast Reservation. In Washington the interior Indians, joined by those around Puget Sound, carried on a longer struggle under the Yakima chief Kamiakin. Quarrels between Stevens and the military commander John Wool and recriminations over action of the volunteers did little to bring the war to a close, and military action brought only temporary pacification of the hostile Indians. Not until 1858, when defeat of a column under Lieutenant Colonel Edward J. Steptoe called forth strong punitive action by troops under Colonel George Wright, did peace return to the Northwest. After victories in the battles of Four Lakes and Spokane Plains, Wright traversed the Indian country, executing culprits accused of inciting attacks and, with the mediation of the Jesuit missionary Joset, gaining the submission of the defeated chiefs.[63]

63. The action in these wars can be followed in Robert M. Utley, *Frontiersmen in Blue: The United States Army and the Indian, 1848–1865* (New York: Macmillan Company, 1967), pp. 175–210; Burns, *Jesuits and the Indian Wars*, pp. 158–355. See also Robert Ignatius Burns, ed., "Pere Joset's Account of the Indian War of 1858," *Pacific North-*

The military action was decisive in Oregon and Washington. The Indians, unlike those in many parts of the nation, had moved beyond their guerilla warfare and, with well-defined war aims, met their enemy in open battlefield encounters, in which they were decisively defeated. The ending of the war opened the way for ratification of the treaties by the Senate on March 8, 1859. The movement to the reservations and the advance toward the white man's ways of life that those treaties specified became the lot of the Indians in the Pacific Northwest. "Reservation life proved fully as unhappy as they had expected," Robert Utley has written, "but the memory of Colonel Wright hung over them, and never again did they try to deflect their destiny by force of arms."[64]

The reservation policy that had determined Indian affairs in the Northwest was strongly supported by the successors of Palmer and Stevens. Absolom F. Hedges, who replaced Palmer in August 1856, envisaged self-supporting reservations and manual labor schools to civilize the Indians, although he was in office too short a time to accomplish much. On March 3, 1857, the separate superintendencies for Oregon and Washington were abolished and a joint superintendency provided, with James W. Nesmith as superintendent. Nesmith considered the ultimate civilization and Christianization of the Indians "utopian and impracticable." But he saw what happened when the whites and Indians were in contact and pleaded for ratification of the treaties so that the Indians could be placed on reservations where the intercourse laws could be enforced and peace and quiet maintained in the region.[65] The Presbyterian missionary Edward R. Geary, who replaced Nesmith in April 1859, had a more sanguine view of Indian advancement, holding firmly to the evangelical Christian view of Indian potentialities. "Amidst many failures," he wrote, "enough has been achieved to establish the improvability, intellectually, morally and socially, of the Indian race, and that the impediments to their elevation are not innate and peculiar, but such as would be found in any other portion of the human family, in the same conditions, and affected by the same influences." Geary noted the improvement that came with the final ratification of the treaties, but, because of Indian opposition, he could report little

---

west Quarterly 38 (October 1947): 285–307. Stevens's quarrels with the military are discussed in Kent Richards, "Isaac I. Stevens and Federal Military Power in Washington Territory," *Pacific Northwest Quarterly* 63 (July 1972): 81–86. Official documents on the wars are printed in *House Executive Document* no. 93, 34–1, serial 858, and in *House Executive Document* no. 76, 34–3, serial 906.

64. Utley, *Frontiersmen in Blue*, p. 209.

65. Hoopes, *Indian Affairs and Their Administration*, pp. 126–27; report of Nesmith, September 1, 1857, CIA Report, 1857, serial 919, pp. 605–6; report of Nesmith, August 20, 1858, CIA Report, 1858, serial 974, pp. 566–74.

progress in the education that he deemed so essential. Establishment of industrial schools, under the direction of religious men—"those who from a sentiment of humanity, guided and energized by the strong convictions of moral obligations, have devoted their lives to the efforts of Christian beneficence"—was his principal recommendation.[66]

66. Report of Geary, September 1, 1859, CIA Report, 1859, serial 1023, p. 753; report of Geary, October 1, 1860, CIA Report, 1860, serial 1078, pp. 408–9. The joint superintendency ended in early 1861.

PART FOUR

The
Civil War
Years

Indian affairs during the years of the Civil War were marked by two distinct situations. In the first place, the Civil War had a direct bearing on Indian relations in the Indian Territory and the neighboring state of Kansas. The defection of the slave-holding Indian nations from their treaty obligations to the Union and their signing of treaties of allegiance and alliance with the Confederate States of America brought them into the Civil War as formal participants, while loyal factions that fled to Kansas created additional problems for the federal government.

In the second place, this period in the West was one of continuing development and settlement, with throngs of whites moving into new areas in search of precious metals or agricultural riches. It was almost as though westerners were unaware of the great battle raging between the North and the South. The Pike's Peak gold rush of 1859 and the concurrent discoveries in Nevada were soon followed by the establishment of Colorado and Nevada territories in 1861; and Nevada achieved statehood in 1864. Then the mining frontiers moved rapidly both north and south, with political organization of new territories coming quickly in the wake of the first major strikes. Arizona Territory was created in 1863, and in the same year Idaho Territory was set up to satisfy the whites who had rushed into the Snake River region. New discoveries of precious metals in what is now western Montana led to thriving centers of population at Virginia City and Helena. In May 1864 Congress created Montana Territory. These advances cut deep into Indian lands, and the increased traffic they occasioned between the mining settlements and the more established sections of the country further exasperated the Indians. Meanwhile, growing white population on the central plains brought new pressure upon the Indian tribes there. Kansas grew in population from 107,206 in 1860 to 364,399 in 1870 and Nebraska (which became a state in 1867) from 28,841 to 122,993.

The Civil War years were filled with Indian-white conflicts growing out of white invasion of Indian lands. These serious encounters were aggravated by the weakening of federal authority in the West as regular troops were withdrawn and replaced by volunteers, who were often few in number, inexperienced in Indian control, and too frequently imbued with frontier hostility toward Indians. Yet the federal government, despite the fact that its energies were fully engaged in the great sectional struggle, could not totally ignore the Indians, and both the Indian service (working under the weight of a patronage system that placed political appointees in sensitive positions) and the army had to worry about the "second front."

The Lincoln government met the challenges by continuing the fundamental policies of the preceding decades: an absolute commitment to transformation of the Indians into the white man's civilization and the development of restricted reservations as the principal "first step" in that process. The principle was well expressed by the commissioner of Indian affairs in 1863 when he wrote to two special agents in Kansas in response to questions they had sent about allotment of Potawatomi lands: "The Government recognizes Indians who still continue their tribal organization as its wards, requiring and entitled to its protection and guardianship. It is the Policy of the Government to reclaim and civilize the Indians, and to induce them to abandon their tribal organizations and adopt the customs and arts of civilized society. That solution of all questions which relate to the disposition of the lands or other property which will most conduce to the desired result should be adopted."[1]

The special problems arising out of relations with the Five Civilized Tribes in the Indian Territory, the outbreak of Sioux Indians in Minnesota, and the subjugation of the Apaches and Navajos in New Mexico necessitated military action and in some cases military control, but in the end civilian management of the tribes by the Indian Office was vindicated.

Abraham Lincoln himself devoted little personal attention to Indian affairs. His own experience with Indians, like that of his predecessors, had been minimal. He had had little contact with Indians in Indiana and Illinois; and even his brief tour as a militia captain in the Black Hawk War

---

1. William P. Dole to Special Commissioners Wolcott and Ross, April 28, 1863, OIA LS, vol. 70, p. 494 (M21, reel 70).

had not furnished any real experience in dealing with Indians and their problems. In the Lincoln-Douglas debates of 1858, Douglas at Ottawa tried to make capital of Lincoln's desire to provide citizenship for "negroes, Indians and other inferior races." When Lincoln ignored the challenge about Indians, Douglas at Alton tried again, declaring that when the signers of the Declaration of Independence had said that all men were created equal, they "did not mean the negro, nor the savage Indians, nor the Fejee Islanders, nor any other barbarous race." Lincoln answered forthrightly, quoting from an earlier speech at Springfield: "I think the authors of that notable instrument intended to include *all* men. . . . They meant to set up a standard maxim for free society . . . [applicable] to all people, of all colors, every where."[2]

That Lincoln's humane principles applied to Indians there can be little doubt, but he held common white views about their destiny. In an address to a delegation of plains Indians at the White House in March 1863, he spoke of peace and the observation of treaties, but his advice to his "red brethren" was typical of his age: "The pale-faced people are numerous and prosperous because they cultivate the earth, produce bread, and depend upon the products of the earth rather than wild game for subsistence. . . . I can only say that I can see no way in which your race is to become as numerous and prosperous as the white race except by living as they do, by the cultivation of the earth."[3]

Lincoln could not give Indian problems high priority amid the other crises that filled his presidency; only when forced to look at them because of spectacular events such as the Sioux outbreak in Minnesota or the southern refugee Indian flight into Kansas or because of the prodding of reformers did he act personally in regard to the Indians. Mostly he left Indian matters in the hands of the secretary of the interior and, even more, the commissioner of Indian affairs.

2. *The Lincoln-Douglas Debates of 1858*, ed. Robert W. Johannsen (New York: Oxford University Press, 1965), pp. 45–46, 299, 304.
3. Report of the meeting in *Daily Morning Chronicle* (Washington), March 27, 1863, printed in *Collected Works of Abraham Lincoln*, ed. Roy P. Basler, 9 vols. (New Brunswick: Rutgers University Press, 1953–1955), 6: 151–52. A brief treatment of Lincoln and the Indians is Harry Kelsey, "Abraham Lincoln and American Indian Policy," *Lincoln Herald* 77 (Fall 1975): 139–48; a fuller treatment that is very critical of Lincoln is David A. Nichols, *Lincoln and the Indians: Civil War Policy and Politics* (Columbia: University of Missouri Press, 1978).

CHAPTER 16

The Southern Indians and the Confederate States

Tribes in the Indian Territory. Indian

Treaties with the Confederacy. War in

the Indian Territory. Peace Council at

Fort Smith. Reconstruction Treaties.

When secession and the Civil War occurred, Indian affairs took on a new dimension, for the Indian country in the West was of strategic importance in the war. Of vital concern to both the North and the South was the attitude of the southern Indians—especially the Cherokees, Creeks, Choctaws, Chickasaws, and Seminoles—now living in the area to which they had been removed, north of Texas and west of Arkansas.[1]

TRIBES IN THE INDIAN TERRITORY

The Five Civilized Tribes, or at least significant portions of them, were southern in sympathy as well as location. They were dominated by mixed-bloods, many of whom were slave-owners, and cultural affinity to the

1. The most complete and thoroughly documented study of these Indians in the war is the series of three volumes by Annie Heloise Abel under the general title *The Slaveholding Indians* (Cleveland: Arthur H. Clark Company), vol. 1 (1915): *The American Indian as Slaveholder and Secessionist: An Omitted Chapter in the Diplomatic History of the Southern Confederacy*; vol. 2 (1919): *The American Indian as Participant in the Civil War*; and vol. 3 (1929): *The American Indian under Reconstruction*. I have relied upon these volumes as a guide to printed sources, and the volumes themselves contain copies of a great many documents. A shorter general article is Annie Heloise Abel, "The Indians in the Civil War," *American Historical Review* 15 (January 1910):

southern states as well as practical political interests tilted them toward the seceding states. Even so, it is difficult to understand how Indian groups so recently uprooted from their traditional lands by Georgia, Alabama, Mississippi, and Tennessee—action vigorously opposed and condemned by northern states—could now forswear their allegiance and treaty obligations to the Union and ally themselves with the South. Despite large Unionist factions, especially among the Creeks and the Cherokees, all of the Five Civilized Tribes signed formal treaties with the Confederate States of America, and some of the smaller Indian groups in the Indian Territory joined them in this switch of allegiance.

Geographical location had a significant influence. The Choctaws and Chickasaws were located along the Red River adjacent to Texas, and the Choctaws were bordered on the east by Arkansas. Thus caught in a vise between two ardent members of the Confederacy, there was little likelihood that they could maintain a neutral or Unionist position even if they had been inclined to do so. The Creeks and Seminoles and even more the Cherokees, located farther north, could for a while think of neutrality and at least hope for effective support and succor from the North. The Cherokees held out the longest, and only under extreme pressure did the Union faction, led by John Ross, succumb.

The Indian department officials in the Indian Territory at the outbreak of the Civil War were largely southern sympathizers, for the federal patronage system had long emphasized local men. The agents, the agency employees, and the traders were southerners, in many cases from Arkansas and Texas. Douglas H. Cooper, a Mississippian appointed Choctaw and Chickasaw agent by President Buchanan, became a key military officer of the Confederacy in the West, and even among the agents appointed by Lincoln when he took office there were southern men who worked for secession. Elias Rector, superintendent of the Southern Superintendency, which was responsible for the Indians south of Kansas, was a cousin and close associate of Henry Rector, secessionist governor of Arkansas, and worked closely with him in drawing the Indians into the Confederate fold.[2]

There were, moreover, financial considerations. The trust funds of the Indians, invested by the federal government for the benefit of the tribes,

---

281–96. See also Sammy D. Buice, "The Civil War and the Five Civilized Tribes: A Study in Federal-Indian Relations" (Ph.D. dissertation, University of Oklahoma, 1970); and Ohland Morton, "Confederate Government Relations with the Five Civilized Tribes," *Chronicles of Oklahoma* 31 (Summer 1953): 189–204; 31 (Autumn 1953): 299–322.

2. Abel, *Indian as Slaveholder*, pp. 59–60. William H. Garrett, Creek agent, was from Alabama; Robert J. Cowart, Cherokee agent, was from Georgia; Matthew Leeper, agent for the Indians in the Leased District, was from Texas; and Andrew J. Dorn, Neosho River agent, was from Arkansas. Ibid., p. 82 n.

were almost entirely in southern stocks and bonds. There was a fear, played upon heavily by the secessionists, that these funds would be forfeited if the tribes maintained their attachment to the North.[3]

The southern Indians questioned the genuineness of the support of their interests by Lincoln's Republican administration. They recalled the remark of William H. Seward in a Chicago speech during the presidential campaign of 1860—"The Indian territory, also, south of Kansas, must be vacated by the Indians"—and it was easy to build up this chance remark in a political speech into a policy of once again contracting their territories. They were aware, too, of the defenseless nature of their situation as far as northern military support was concerned. In the late 1850s the War Department, despite vigorous protests by the secretary of the interior, had persisted in a general withdrawal of troops from the Indian Territory. When the war broke out, the remaining Union forces were withdrawn, and the military posts were occupied by Confederate forces. The Indians were left at the mercy of the Confederacy, and southern officials were quick to capitalize on all the points in their favor.[4]

The election of Lincoln and the secession of the Deep South could not be ignored by the Indian nations. The first to react formally, and apparently on their own initiative, were the Chickasaws. At a special meeting of their national legislature, the tribe on January 5, 1861, issued a call to the Choctaw, Creek, Cherokee, and Seminole nations to send commissioners to an intertribal conference "for the purpose of entering into some compact, not inconsistent with the Laws and Treaties of the United States, for the future security and protection of the rights and Citizens of said nations, in the event of a change in the United States."[5] The conference met at the Creek Agency on February 17, with scanty attendance by the Creeks, Seminoles, and Cherokees and no Chickasaws or Choctaws. The tone of the meeting was one of caution, set by John Ross in his instructions to the Cherokee delegates, which warned against premature action and pointed to the obligations of their treaties with the United States.[6]

3. Ibid., p. 61; George Dewey Harmon, "The Indian Trust Funds, 1797–1865," *Mississippi Valley Historical Review* 21 (June 1934): 23–30. The use of the trust funds in Confederate arguments to the Indians can be seen in David Hubbard to John Ross and Ben McCulloch, June 12, 1861, *The War of the Rebellion: A Compilation of the Official Records of the Union and Confederate Armies*, 70 vols. (Washington: GPO, 1880–1901), series 1, 13: 497; henceforth cited as *Official Records*.

4. Abel, *Indian as Slaveholder*, pp. 52–59. Seward's speech is in *The Works of William H. Seward*, ed. George E. Baker, 5 vols. (Boston: Houghton, Mifflin and Company, 1853–1884), 4: 363.

5. Quoted in Abel, *Indian as Slaveholder*, pp. 68–69 n.

6. Instructions of John Ross to Cherokee delegation, February 12, 1861, quoted ibid., p. 71 n.

Meanwhile, the Choctaws were striking out on their own. In a meeting on February 7, 1861, they passed a series of resolutions expressing the sentiments of their General Council in regard to the political disagreement between the North and the South. The Choctaws deprecated the unhappy state of affairs and hoped that the differences between the sections could be honorably adjusted, but they took an unequivocal stand in the case that did not occur:

> *Resolved further*: That in the event a permanent dissolution of the American Union takes place, our many relations with the General Government must cease, and we shall be left to follow the natural affections, education, institutions, and interests of our people, which indissolubly bind us in every way to the destiny of our neighbors and brethren of the Southern States, upon whom we are confident we can rely for the preservation of our rights of life, liberty, and property, and the continuance of many acts of friendship, general counsel, and material support.

The Choctaws made a special bow of amity toward Arkansas and Texas and directed that a copy of the resolutions be sent to the governors of the southern states.[7] Although one small party, of which Peter Pitchlynn was a member, hoped to maintain neutrality, the bulk of the nation was strongly for the Confederacy, and it convinced or intimidated the opposition.[8]

The Chickasaws did not act until after the Civil War had broken out. On May 25, 1861, their legislature, with the approval of Governor Cyrus Harris, threw in their lot with the South. They saw the secession and war as the dissolution of the United States under the Constitution, thus freeing them from their treaty obligations, and noted the failure of the Lincoln government, "pretending to represent said Union," to protect them. They predicted a bloody war that they could not escape. "Our geographical position, our social and domestic institutions, our feelings and sympathies," their resolution read, "all attach us to our Southern friends." Their rights, they believed, would be recognized and protected by the Confederate States, and "as a Southern people we consider their cause our own." The Chickasaws made a strong point of the fact that "the current of the events of the last few months has left the Chickasaw Nation *independent*," free to form such alliances as seemed best to it. They appealed to the neighboring tribes

7. *Official Records*, series 1, 1: 682, quoted in full in Abel, *Indian as Slaveholder*, pp. 73–74.

8. Angie Debo, *The Rise and Fall of the Choctaw Republic* (Norman: University of Oklahoma Press, 1934), pp. 80–109. Pitchlynn's part is discussed in W. David Baird, *Peter Pitchlynn: Chief of the Choctaws* (Norman: University of Oklahoma Press, 1972), pp. 126–28.

to join them in defending their territory from "the Lincoln hordes and Kansas robbers, who have plundered and oppressed our red brethren among them, and who doubtless would extend towards us the protection which the wolf gives to the lamb should they succeed in overrunning our country."[9]

In the face of such a sympathetic movement of the Indians toward the Confederacy, the federal Indian Office offered little to reassure the Indians. Perhaps unaware of the secessionist action taken by the Choctaws and the Chickasaws (for communications with the Indian Territory were almost nonexistent after the departure of Unionist agents and federal troops), Indian Commissioner William P. Dole on May 11, 1861, addressed a circular letter to the chiefs of the Five Civilized Tribes, telling them that neither Lincoln nor any government agents had any intention of interfering with their domestic institutions and that an appeal had been made to the War Department to furnish them the protection called for in their treaties with the United States. It was an ineffectual statement, carried to the Indians by the new southern superintendent, William G. Coffin, who was delayed in getting to his post, and it showed the ineffectiveness of the Indian Office's attempt to get action from the War Department, which by that date more than had its hands full elsewhere.[10]

INDIAN TREATIES WITH THE CONFEDERACY

The Confederacy was much more energetic in its concern for Indian affairs. It saw at once the strategic necessity of drawing the Indian Territory into its camp and the need to act expeditiously before the withdrawn federal troops could be replaced by volunteers, who might shore up any sagging Union sentiment among the Indians.

The provisional government of the Confederate States on February 21, 1861, resolved to open negotiations with the Indian tribes in the West, and four days later it proposed appointing agents to those tribes. On March 15, a Bureau of Indian Affairs was created in the War Department, and the next day David Hubbard was nominated by President Jefferson Davis to head the bureau.[11] While this administrative machinery was being set up, the Department of State under Robert Toombs was promoting the appoint-

9. The resolution is in *Official Records*, series 1, 3: 585–87. The Chickasaw part in the Civil War and Reconstruction is told in Arrell M. Gibson, *The Chickasaws* (Norman: University of Oklahoma Press, 1971), pp. 227–46.

10. Dole to Indian chiefs, May 11, 1861, CIA Report, 1861, serial 1117, pp. 650–51; Dole to Caleb B. Smith, May 30, 1861, ibid., pp. 651–52. See also Abel, *Indian as Slaveholder*, pp. 80–82.

11. Abel, *Indian as Slaveholder*, pp. 127–28.

ment of a special diplomatic agent to deal with the Indian tribes west of
Arkansas. In May the provisional Congress passed an act for the protection
of the Indian tribes, under which Albert Pike was appointed special agent
for negotiating treaties with the Indians. A native of New England, Pike
had become a prominent lawyer in Arkansas; he had also gained military
experience in the Mexican War, and he was even a poet of some renown.
He was an excellent choice for dealing with the Indians, for he respected
their rights and was generous in the guarantees he wrote into the treaties
he signed with them.[12]

Pike failed in his first attempt to persuade John Ross to align the Cherokee Nation with the Confederacy, but he passed on to quick success with
the other tribes. The Creeks signed a treaty on July 10, 1861, the Choctaws
on July 12, and the Seminoles on August 1.[13] All these treaties began with a
preamble that indicated the Confederacy's offer "to assume and accept the
protectorate of the several nations and tribes of Indians occupying the
country west of Arkansas and Missouri, and to recognize them as their
wards, subject to all the rights, privileges and immunities, titles and guar-
anties, with each of said nations and tribes under treaties made with them
by the United States of America" and the Indians' agreement thereto. It
was a formal transfer of allegiance and loyalty from the Union to the Confederacy. The tribes, moreover, agreed to offensive and defensive alliances
with the South.

The treaties recognized the existing territorial limits of the tribes, and
they guaranteed fee simple ownership of the lands within the boundaries.
The lands were never to be included in any state or territory, nor would a
tribe, without its consent, be organized as a territory or state. In many respects the treaties were the same as the earlier treaties with the United
States; but the new treaties were more generous to the tribes, and the tone
was one of conciliation rather than dictation, for Pike promised the Indians many things that they had been contending for with the United
States. The Indians were allowed more control of their trade, property
rights in slaves were guaranteed, and financial benefits were promised. It
was necessary for the rights of the Indians to be clearly recognized when
Indian alliances were so desperately sought by the Confederacy.

The treaties, as Pike negotiated them, contained a provision for Indian
delegates in the Confederate Congress, and the Choctaw-Chickasaw treaty
provided for ultimate statehood (to which the Creeks, Seminoles, and

12. Ibid., pp. 129–41. For a biography of Pike, see Walter L. Brown, "Albert Pike,
1809–1891" (Ph.D. dissertation, University of Texas, 1955).
13. The treaties are printed in *Official Records*, series 4, 1: 426–43, 445–66, 513–27.
They are exhaustively analyzed in Abel, *Indian as Slaveholder*, pp. 157–80. See also
Kenny A. Franks, "An Analysis of the Confederate Treaties with the Five Civilized
Tribes," *Chronicles of Oklahoma* 50 (Winter 1972–1973): 458–73.

Cherokees could be joined). President Davis objected to both these provisions as impolitic and unconstitutional, and the treaties were amended to leave the decision on delegates and admission of states to the House of Representatives and to Congress.[14]

Pike moved on from his success with these major tribes, which he treated with great solicitude, to negotiate with the lesser tribes in the Indian Territory. He went first to the Wichita and Comanche tribes in the Leased District, a region west of the ninety-eighth meridian that the United States in 1855 had rented from the Choctaws and Chickasaws for the settlement of Wichita Indians and other tribes and that passed under jurisdiction of the Confederate States by the Choctaw-Chickasaw treaty of July 12. These tribes were less important to the cause of the South than the Five Civilized Tribes and received few concessions. The two treaties, signed on August 12, were primarily treaties of peace and of promoting civilization, in large part to satisfy the citizens of Texas, who were ravaged by Indian raids. They contained little if anything to distinguish them from treaties made by the United States with the western tribes except, of course, that the Indians placed themselves "under the laws and protection of the Confederate States of America." They were full of the rhetoric of paternalism—promising the Indians their reserves "as long as grass shall grow and water run," providing for livestock and agricultural assistance, and asking of the tribes only "that they will settle upon their reserves, become industrious, and prepare to support themselves, and live in peace and quietness."[15]

The Cherokees were still outside the southern fold, but as Pike was negotiating in the west, John Ross abandoned his neutral stance and threw in his lot with the Confederacy. This was a surprising move, for Ross had formally declared his neutrality and his intention of holding firm to his treaty relationship with the United States. He had answered the pressures from Governor Rector of Arkansas firmly but politely, and to a Texas commission that visited him he reiterated his neutral stand. On May 17, 1861, in fact, Ross issued a formal proclamation of neutrality, reminding the Cherokees of their obligations to the United States and urging them to abstain from partisan discussions and actions.[16] When the Confederate Indian

14. Davis message of December 12, 1861, James D. Richardson, comp., *Compilation of the Messages and Papers of the Confederacy: Including the Diplomatic Correspondence, 1861–1865*, 2 vols. (Nashville: United States Publishing Company, 1905), 1: 149–51. The ratification action of the Confederate Congress is printed with each treaty in *Official Records*.

15. *Official Records*, series 4, 1: 542–54. See also Arrell M. Gibson, "Confederates on the Plains: The Pike Mission to Wichita Agency," *Great Plains Journal* 4 (Fall 1964): 7–16.

16. "Proclamation to the Cherokee People," May 17, 1861, *Official Records*, series 1, 13: 489–90.

commissioner, David Hubbard, tried to win Ross over in June by suggesting that the southern states had treated Indians far better than the northern and that the only hope for preserving the money, property, and slaves of the Cherokees lay in joining the Confederacy, the chief replied: "A comparison of Northern and Southern philanthropy, as illustrated in their dealings toward the Indians within their respective limits, would not affect the merits of the question now under consideration, which is simply one of duty under existing circumstances. I therefore pass over it, merely remarking that the 'settled policy' of former years was a favorite policy with both sections when extended to the acquisition of Indian lands, and that but few Indians now press their feet upon the banks of either the Ohio or the Tennessee."[17]

But there were strong forces undermining Ross's position of neutrality. The factionalism of the Cherokees was revived. The old treaty party, now led by Stand Watie and his nephew Elias C. Boudinot and supported by many half-bloods, among whom most of the slave-owners were found, were sympathetic to the southern cause. Ross's great dream of unity in the Cherokee Nation might be shattered if a North-South split grew, and he could lose his position of leadership if the Confederacy chose to deal with Watie, as indeed Pike hinted in June that it might do. Ross's position, moreover, was seriously weakened when federal troops withdrew from the Indian Territory in April 1861 and Confederate forces controlled the surrounding areas. Unionist Indian agents and northern missionaries had departed, and the treaties Pike had made with the other tribes still further undercut Ross. The attractive offers made by Pike no doubt also played a part, for the Confederate agent was promising things that Ross had sought for years to obtain from the federal government without success. And then, the decisive Confederate victory at Wilson's Creek near Springfield, Missouri, on August 10, 1861, made Confederate success in its bid for separation from the North seem possible.[18]

On August 21, at a national conference of the Cherokee Nation attended by nearly four thousand men, Ross announced his decision "to

17. David Hubbard to John Ross and Ben McCulloch, June 12, 1861, *Official Records*, series 1, 13: 497–98; John Ross to David Hubbard, June 17, 1861, ibid., pp. 498–99.

18. Analyses of Ross's change of mind are in Gary E. Moulton, *John Ross: Cherokee Chief* (Athens: University of Georgia Press, 1978), pp. 171–73, and Morris L. Wardell, *A Political History of the Cherokee Nation, 1838–1907* (Norman: University of Oklahoma Press, 1938), pp. 133–38. There has been much speculation about the genuineness of Ross's adherence to the Confederacy; he himself protested after the war that he had always at heart been loyal to the United States and was forced by circumstances to ally with the South. A refutation of that position was made by Albert Pike in a letter to the commissioner of Indian affairs, February 17, 1866, quoted in Abel, *Indian as Slaveholder*, pp. 134–40 n. The letter is a good statement of Pike's activities in 1861.

adopt preliminary steps for an alliance with the Confederate States." The council quickly passed resolutions supporting the chief. Pike was notified of the change of heart and asked to return to work out a formal treaty.[19]

At the same time, in accord with Pike's request, Ross invited the leaders of the Osages, Shawnees, Senecas, and Quapaws to Park Hill, his estate in the Cherokee Nation, and these tribes on October 2 and 4 signed treaties with the South. They placed themselves under the protection of the Confederate States forever and were guaranteed their property and other rights; in return they agreed to "make themselves parties to the existing war between the Confederate States and the United States of America, as the allies and wards of the former" and to furnish warriors for the war.[20] These small tribes, located in the northeastern section of the Indian Territory, were to block a Union invasion from the north.

The treaty with the Cherokees came finally on October 7. It was similar to those with the other Five Civilized Tribes and included the promises made by Pike: Cherokee Nation control over its lands, the right to incorporate other tribes into the nation, rights of self-government, control over the appointment of agents, a Cherokee court, a delegate in the House of Representatives, and provision for sale of the Neutral Lands, which the Cherokees owned in Kansas. As a kind of anti-climax, the Cherokee Council on October 31 adopted a declaration of independence, written by Pike, that stated the reasons for joining the Confederacy and declared the Cherokees a "free people, independent of the Northern States of America and at war with them by their own act."[21]

WAR IN THE INDIAN TERRITORY

The deep concern of the Confederacy to sign treaties with the tribes in the Indian Territory, of course, was not abstract concern for Indian rights and welfare but rested in part on the need for military alliance and aid in order to prosecute the war. This was uppermost in Pike's mind, for even before the provisional congress had adopted its bill for protection of the Indian country Pike had pointed out the absolute necessity of securing the territory militarily. He probably expected in fact to be appointed military com-

19. Ross's address and the council's resolutions are included in Joseph Vann to William P. Ross, August 21, 1861, *Official Records*, series 1, 3: 673–76. See also Abel, *Indian as Slaveholder*, pp. 217–27.

20. *Official Records*, series 4, 1: 636–66.

21. Ibid., pp. 669–87. A summary of the treaty is in Wardell, *Cherokee Nation*, pp. 139–41. The "Declaration of the people of the Cherokee Nation of the causes which have impelled them to unite their fortunes with those of the Confederate States of America," October 28, 1861, is in *Official Records*, series 1, 13: 503–5.

mander rather than diplomatic agent, and it was not long before he got such an appointment.[22]

Meanwhile, on May 13, 1861, the Confederacy assigned Brigadier General Ben McCulloch as military commander in the Indian Territory, with orders to prevent a federal invasion from Kansas or elsewhere and to engage the services of Indian troops to augment his white regiments. Although McCulloch could not persuade Ross to desert his neutrality at that time, he was successful with the other major tribes, and Pike's treaties with them provided for Indian troops to fight with the Confederacy. Even before the treaties were signed, many Choctaws and Chickasaws were recruited by Douglas Cooper, and after the treaties the recruiting of Indian troops went forward rapidly. Stand Watie had organized troops before the Cherokee treaty, and by the end of July 1861 a large Confederate Indian force was in the field. After the Cherokee treaty, a regiment of Cherokee "home guards" under Colonel John Drew was accepted by McCulloch. Then on November 22, 1861, the Indian Territory was established as a separate military department, with Albert Pike commanding as a brigadier general.[23]

The successful recruiting and organization of military commands among the Indians could not hide the division within some of the tribes between northern and southern factions. The Choctaws and Chickasaws were strong supporters of the South, but the Cherokees and the Creeks were seriously rent by the tenacity of Union factions. The full-blood Cherokees of the Ross party had joined the South without enthusiasm under the press of circumstances, and latent Union sentiment came to the surface whenever conditions seemed promising. Among the Creeks large numbers led by Opothleyohola resisted attempts to force them into the southern camp and fled as refugees into Kansas, where similar discontented refugees from other tribes joined them.[24]

It appeared to the loyal Indians that they had been abandoned by Lincoln and the North, and the president gave grounds for such a judgment by his vacillation and delay.[25] When Lincoln at length in January 1862 decided to retake the Indian Territory, he faced grave problems. Chief among these

22. Abel, *Indian as Slaveholder*, pp. 131–32.

23. Ibid., pp. 143–44, 207–15, 252 n.

24. The divisions of the tribes and the secret organizations—Pins or Keetoowah Society among the Cherokees, for example, supporting the Union and circles of the Knights of the Golden Circle among the tribes supporting the Confederacy—are discussed in Wardell, *Cherokee Nation*, pp. 121–23, and Abel, *Indian as Slaveholder*, pp. 86 n, 135 n, 216.

25. A detailed study that is very critical of Lincoln's actions in regard to the Indians is David A. Nichols, *Lincoln and the Indians: Civil War Policy and Politics* (Columbia: University of Missouri Press, 1978).

were the thousands of Indian refugees in Kansas. They crowded across the border in a state of destitution, for which there seemed to be no remedy. An army surgeon in February 1862 described them in this fashion:

> It is impossible for me to depict the wretchedness of their condition. Their only protection from the snow upon which they lie is prairie grass, and from the wind scraps and rags stretched upon switches; some of them had some personal clothing; most had but shreds and rags, which did not conceal their nakedness; and I saw seven, ranging in age from three to fifteen years, without one thread upon their bodies. . . . Why the officers of the Indian department are not doing something for them I cannot understand; common humanity demands that more should be done, and done at once, to save them from total destruction.[26]

The southern superintendent, William G. Coffin, who was with the refugees at their camp on the Verdigris River, reported, "The destitution, misery, and suffering amongst them is beyond the power of any pen to portray; it must be seen to be realized."[27]

At length the Indian Office moved to provide aid. Commissioner William P. Dole went to Kansas in late January. He found that Major General David M. Hunter was doing the best he could to assist the refugees with army provisions, but in mid-February Hunter ran out of supplies and turned over the problem to the Indian department. Dole wired the secretary of the interior: "Six thousand Indians driven out of Indian territory, naked and starving. General Hunter will only feed them until 15th. Shall I take care of them on the faith of an appropriation?" When Secretary of the Interior Caleb B. Smith told him to go ahead, Dole began to purchase supplies on credit for the Indians.[28] Congress sustained that action and on July 5 provided that the annuities of the hostile Indians in the Indian Territory should be applied for the relief of the refugees.[29] The solution of the refugee problem, however, was not relief, but return of the Indians to their homes in the Indian Territory and protection of them there.

26. A. B. Campbell to James K. Barnes, February 5, 1862, CIA Report, 1862, serial 1157, pp. 295–96.

27. W. G. Coffin to Dole, February 13, 1862, ibid., p. 289. A comprehensive study of the refugee problem is Edmund J. Danziger, Jr., "The Office of Indian Affairs and the Problem of Civil War Indian Refugees in Kansas," *Kansas Historical Quarterly* 35 (Autumn 1969): 257–75. See also Dean Banks, "Civil War Refugees from Indian Territory in the North, 1861–1864," *Chronicles of Oklahoma* 41 (Autumn 1963): 286–98.

28. The action is described in a report of Dole to Smith, June 5, 1862, CIA Report, 1862, serial 1157, pp. 291–93, to which other pertinent documents are attached.

29. *Congressional Globe*, 37th Congress, 2d session, p. 815; 12 *United States Statutes* 528.

Lincoln's ultimate decision to invade the Indian Territory was entangled in the serious political and military squabbles that engulfed Kansas. At the center of these was James H. Lane, an adventurous politician from Indiana who moved to Kansas in 1855. He had built up a strong political following but managed to quarrel with everyone who might hinder his ascent to power. As senator from the new state of Kansas, he persistently nagged Lincoln in order to get what he wanted. He was appointed brigadier general of volunteers (without resigning his Senate seat) and promoted an expedition into the Indian Territory manned by Indian troops and led by him. The Indian expedition was obstructed and delayed by disagreements between Lane and Hunter, who commanded the Kansas Department and who hoped to lead the expedition himself, and not until June 1862 was it ready to move. By then Hunter had been replaced by Brigadier General James G. Blunt, a friend of Lane's. The expedition was less grandiose than Lane had originally proposed, and its object was limited "to open the way for friendly Indians who are now refugees in Southern Kansas to return to their homes and to protect them there."[30]

As the expedition moved south under Colonel William Weer, the Confederate Indian forces were in sad disarray. The serious Confederate defeat at the Battle of Pea Ridge in Arkansas in April, in which General McCulloch was killed, had a dispiriting effect, and quarrels between Pike and General T. C. Hindman (who had taken over McCulloch's troops) further hindered effective operations. The advancing expedition moved easily into Tahlequah, the Cherokee capital. John Ross, arrested by the invading army, went north to Kansas with his family and other Cherokee refugees and then on to Washington and Philadelphia, where he waited out the war. During the late summer and fall the Union forces generally routed the Confederates they met, and large numbers of Indians deserted to the Union side. Only Stand Watie's soldiers seemed to hold together.[31]

The refugee problem was not solved by the invasion from Kansas; in fact, the returning army brought with it additional Indians fleeing the destruction in their homeland. John Ross made use of his exile to importune the president to do something for the refugees, although his efforts were impeded by lingering doubts about his loyalty to the Union. No immediate action was forthcoming. General Blunt wanted immediate removal, for the problem of caring for the refugees was staggering, but the officials of the Indian Office did not want the refugees to be sent back until they could be protected adequately from raids and from further suffering, and white sol-

30. L. Thomas to H. W. Halleck, March 19, 1862, *Official Records*, series 1, 8: 624. A full discussion of Lane and the Kansas problems is provided in Albert Castel, *A Frontier State at War: Kansas, 1861–1865* (Ithaca: Cornell University Press, 1958). The organization of the expedition is discussed in Abel, *Indian as Participant*, pp. 91–123.

31. Ibid., pp. 125–201.

diers hesitated to act vigorously in the Indian cause. The situation was further complicated by traders and contractors in Kansas who prospered by supplying provisions to the refugees. Finally in May 1864—under pressure from Senator Lane, who strongly advocated the Indians' return, and aware of the expense of maintaining the Indians in Kansas—Congress appropriated funds to move the Indians back into the Indian Territory and to aid destitute Indians. Under Superintendent Coffin's care, five thousand Indians were removed in June 1864, and Lincoln authorized funds to help them until they were able to fend for themselves.[32]

The last years of the war were disastrous for the Indian Territory. Guerilla warfare caused widespread destruction, and political disorganization resulted in corruption and exploitation.[33] The ground gained by the Five Civilized Tribes, as they had developed economically and socially in the Indian country between removal and the Civil War, was lost. The physical destruction was enormous, and the factionalism and political upheaval were equally demoralizing. The Indians were considered by many northerners to have lost all rights by their adherence to the Confederacy. But the Confederacy, which had made such grand promises of protection and financial benefits, had been unable to live up to those promises. When the war ended, mammoth problems of reconstruction faced the Indian Territory.

PEACE COUNCIL AT FORT SMITH

The United States government intended to deal strongly with the tribes that had joined the Confederacy. The Indians had thrown over their treaty obligations and concluded formal alliances with the South, and many of them had fought tenaciously for the Confederate cause. Stand Watie was the last Confederate general to surrender.

The government's sentiment toward these wayward tribes was expressed in a bill for the consolidation of the Indian tribes and the establishment of a civil government in the Indian Territory, passed by the Senate on March 2, 1865. The bill, sponsored by Senator James Harlan of Iowa, was on its

32. Nichols, *Lincoln and the Indians*, pp. 54–64: 13 *United States Statutes* 62. Ross's dealings with the Lincoln administration are treated in Gary E. Moulton, "John Ross and W. P. Dole: A Case Study of Lincoln's Indian Policy," *Journal of the West* 12 (July 1973): 414–23.

33. For the military history of the war see Abel, *Indian as Participant*, pp. 243–335, and Lary C. Rampp and Donald L. Rampp, *The Civil War in the Indian Territory* (Austin: Presidial Press, 1975). The failure of the Confederacy to live up to its treaties with the Indians and furnish adequate protection is analyzed in Kenny A. Franks, "The Implementation of the Confederate Treaties with the Five Civilized Tribes," *Chronicles of Oklahoma* 51 (Spring 1973): 21–33, and "The Confederate States and the Five Civilized Tribes: A Breakdown of Relations," *Journal of the West* 12 (July 1973): 439–54.

surface a proposal for territorial organization of the Indian Territory to bring it within the regular political framework of the United States. But behind such purpose lay the desire to open the rich lands to white exploitation. By territorial organization the unique proprietorship of all the lands that the removal treaties of the 1830s had placed forever in the hands of the Five Civilized Tribes would be shattered and the riches of the territory opened to all. The avarice for Indian lands that appeared in the 1850s fulfilled the prophecy of Jeremiah Evarts, who in opposing removal of the Indians in 1829, had written: "Twenty five years hence, there will be 4,000,000 of our population west of the Mississippi, and fifty years hence not less than 15,000,000. By that time, the pressures upon the Indians will be much greater from the boundless prairies, which must ultimately be subdued and inhabited, than it would ever have been from the borders of the present Cherokee country."[34]

Typical of the expansionist views were those of Robert J. Walker, territorial governor of Kansas, who had noted in his inaugural address of May 27, 1857, that the Indian Territory was "one of the most salubrious and fertile portions of this continent," admirably suited for growing cotton, and that it "ought speedily to become a State of the American Union." The treaties with the Indians were no obstacle, he thought, for like those of Kansas they could be replaced, and by selling their lands to whites the Indians could become "a most wealthy and prosperous people." Perhaps the western parts could be set aside for the Indians, and the eastern sections could be a white state. Of great importance to Walker was the need to cross the Indian Territory with railroads, to join Kansas with the Gulf of Mexico, and to join the Mississippi Valley to the Pacific coast.[35] President Buchanan in his first annual message to Congress had remarked on the rapid advance of the Five Civilized Tribes "in all the arts of civilization and self-government" and looked forward to the day, not far distant, when they would be "incorporated into the Union as one of the sovereign States."[36] This was not merely a Democratic dream, of course, for Seward's call for vacating the Indian Territory of Indians came from a prominent Republican who became secretary of state in Lincoln's cabinet.

---

34. Jeremiah Evarts, *Essays on the Present Crisis in the Condition of the American Indians: First Published in the National Intelligencer, under the Signature of William Penn* (Boston: Perkins and Marvin, 1829), p. 100. Evarts's predictions on population were close; the census of 1860 showed 4,536,475 persons west of the Mississippi; that of 1880 showed 11,259,360.

35. Quotations from John Ross, "Message of the Principal Chief of the Cherokee Nation to the National Committee and Council in General Council Convened," October 5, 1857, CIA Report, 1857, serial 919, pp. 509–10.

36. Message of December 8, 1857, in Fred L. Israel, ed., *The State of the Union Messages of the Presidents, 1790–1966*, 3 vols. (New York: Chelsea House, 1966), 1: 966.

Although the Confederate States made much of such expansionist statements in their campaign to woo the southern Indian tribes by pointing out the dangers that lay in store for them under the Union, the South was driven by the same greed (disguised as it might have been while the Confederate States needed the Indian alliances). Even Albert Pike, whose concern for the Indians has been noted, could voice less benevolent intentions; in his report to President Jefferson Davis on the negotiation of the treaties with the Indian tribes, he concluded:

If it should seem to any one that too much is conceded to any of these Indians, let him but learn the great extent and the varied resources of the Indian country, with its fine streams, its splendid scenery, its soil unexcelled in the world for fertility, its vast undulating prairies, on which all the herds of the world could feed, its capabilities to produce grain of every kind, hemp, tobacco, cotton, fruit, wine and wool; its immense basins of coal, its limestones, marbles, granite, iron, lead and salt, which will make it some day the very finest State of the Confederacy, and he will begin to comprehend that the concessions made the Indians are really far more for *our* benefit than for *theirs*; and that it is *we*, a thousand times more than they, who are interested to have this country, the finest, in my opinion, on the continent, opened to settlement and formed into a State.[37]

And the treaty with the Choctaws and Chickasaws, as Pike negotiated it, provided for their admission as one of the Confederate States, to which the other tribes could be joined.

Indian Commissioner Dole, to his credit, fought strenuously to prevent a territorial organization that would destroy the treaty guarantees made by the federal government. He saw no advantage in the innovation for governing the Indians, and he noted that the action would be "at variance with our long established Indian policy." Although he admitted that there was some question about the force of treaty obligations toward Indians who had joined the Confederacy, Dole insisted that the obligations were intact toward Indians who had remained loyal and that to violate them would "constitute a gross breach of national faith." Dole, however, was unable to stop the growing movement in Congress to organize the Indian Territory and the parallel proposal to remove the Indians from Kansas and concentrate them in part of the territory. Through Senator Lane's efforts, in fact, Congress in March 1863 attached to the Indian appropriation bill a provision for removal.[38]

37. Pike, "Report of the Commissioner of the Confederate States to the Indian Nations West of Arkansas," quoted in Gibson, "Confederates on the Plains," pp. 15–16.
38. Abel treats these movements in *Indian under Reconstruction*, pp. 235–41 and

On February 4, 1865, Lane offered a resolution directing an inquiry into the expediency of organizing a territorial government for the country lying between Kansas and Texas. On February 20, Senator James Harlan, who with Lane was a member of the Indian Committee, reported a bill. It was never debated in the House, but its sponsors were able to push it through the Senate before adjournment, and the "Harlan Bill" became an important expression of opinion from the Senate, which might later have to ratify treaties of peace with the Indian tribes of the Confederacy. The bill directed the establishment of a regular territory with set boundaries and a government similar to that in other territories. Executive officers were to be appointed by the president of the United States. A council elected by the tribes would share legislative power with the governor. A delegate would represent the territory in the United States Congress. According to an amendment offered by Senator James Doolittle, the arrangement would go into effect by means of treaties with the tribes.[39]

The United States called the tribal leaders to a conference at Fort Smith, Arkansas, in September 1865. There the Indians met with a special commission headed by Dennis N. Cooley, whom Andrew Johnson had appointed commissioner of Indian affairs in place of Dole in July. Cooley, who was from Dubuque, Iowa, was a friend and associate of Harlan, now secretary of the interior. Associated with Cooley on the commission were Elijah Sells, head of the Southern Superintendency, who had replaced Coffin in May; Thomas Wister, a well-known Quaker from Pennsylvania; General W. S. Harney; and Colonel Ely S. Parker, a Seneca Indian and aide-de-camp to General Ulysses S. Grant, who later became commissioner of Indian affairs. The secretary of the commission was Charles E. Mix of the Indian Office.[40]

---

nn. Dole's statements are from Dole to Caleb Smith, March 17, 1862, quoted ibid., pp. 235–36 n. The authorization of removal is in 12 *United States Statutes* 793.

39. *Congressional Globe*, 38th Congress, 2d session, pp. 589, 915, 1021–24, 1058, 1303–6, 1308–10. The provisions of the bill are printed ibid., pp. 1021–22. Abel, *Indian under Reconstruction*, pp. 244–66, quotes extensively from the Senate debates of February 23, 24, and March 2, 1865, and discusses the matter fully on pp. 218–67. Senator Lafayette S. Foster of Connecticut spoke strongly against the bill, arguing in terms reminiscent of the debate against removal in 1830 that the measure would be a violation of trust and a breach of faith.

40. The "Report of D. N. Cooley, as President of the Southern Treaty Commission," October 30, 1865, and the "Official Report of the Proceedings of the Council with the Indians of the West and Southwest, Held at Fort Smith, Arkansas, in September, 1865," are printed in CIA Report, 1865, serial 1248, pp. 480–96 and 496–537. A brief sketch of Cooley is Gary L. Roberts, "Dennis Nelson Cooley, 1865–66," in Robert M. Kvasnicka and Herman J. Viola, eds., *The Commissioners of Indian Affairs, 1824–1977* (Lincoln: University of Nebraska Press, 1979), pp. 99–108.

The goal of the commission was well summarized in a telegraph from Harlan to Cooley en route to Fort Smith: "The President is willing to grant them peace; but wants land for other Indians, and a civil government for the whole Territory." Cooley also carried to Fort Smith a copy of the Harlan Bill and a long letter of instructions from Secretary Harlan.[41]

When the conference opened on September 8, only the loyal factions of the tribes were on hand, for the secessionists were meeting at Armstrong Academy in the Choctaw Nation. But Cooley proceeded anyway to address the gathering as though he were talking to Confederate Indians, telling them they had forfeited their annuities and rights to land in the Indian Territory but that the president was willing to make new treaties with them. The delegates were startled by what they heard, for none of them had come with authority from their tribes to make treaties, but the next day Cooley continued in his course. He outlined for the Indians in seven points the stipulations that were to be included in the treaties.

1. Each tribe must enter into a treaty for the permanent peace and amity with themselves, each nation and tribe, and with the United States.

2. Those settled in the Indian territory must bind themselves, when called upon by the government, to aid in compelling the Indians of the plains to maintain peaceful relations with each other, with the Indians in the territory, and with the United States.

3. The institution of slavery, which has existed among several of the tribes, must be forthwith abolished, and measures taken for the unconditional emancipation of all persons held in bondage, and for their incorporation into the tribes on an equal footing with the original members, or suitably provided for.

4. A stipulation in the treaties that slavery, or involuntary servitude, shall never exist in the tribe or nation, except in punishment of crime.

5. A portion of the lands hitherto owned and occupied by you must be set apart for the friendly tribes in Kansas and elsewhere, on such terms as may be agreed upon by the parties and approved by government, or such as may be fixed by the government.

6. It is the policy of the government, unless other arrangement be made, that all the nations and tribes in the Indian territory be formed into one consolidated government after the plan proposed by the Senate of the United States, in a bill for organizing the Indian territory.

41. Harlan to Cooley, August 24, 1865, quoted in Roberts, "Cooley," p. 103; Harlan to commissioners, August 16, 1865, quoted in full in Abel, *Indian under Reconstruction,* pp. 219–26.

7. No white person, except officers, agents, and employés of the government, or of any internal improvement authorized by the government, will be permitted to reside in the territory, unless formally incorporated with some tribes, according to the usages of the band.[42]

The loyal Indians present argued that they had not willingly overturned their allegiance to the United States but had done so only under pressure. The Cherokees could point to their National Council's action in February 1863 revoking the treaty with the Confederate States and abolishing slavery. But Cooley was not easily turned aside from his position. He was especially harsh toward John Ross, whom he refused to acknowledge as principal chief of the Cherokee Nation. The conference underscored again the divisions within the tribes.

The Indian delegates, aside from their insistence that they were not authorized to negotiate new treaties with the United States, were strongly opposed to some of the points Cooley proposed. They were hesitant about incorporating the blacks into their nations, and they were especially hostile to the scheme of a territorial government that had been the heart of the Harlan Bill. Only Elias C. Boudinot, representing the southern Cherokees, was willing to accept territorial organization, a goal he continued to work for. The best that Cooley's commission could accomplish at Fort Smith was an agreement of amity between the tribes and the United States. In it the Indians acknowledged once more that they were under the exclusive jurisdiction of the United States, and they canceled and repudiated the treaties they had made with the Confederacy. In its turn the United States promised peace and friendship and renewed protection of the tribes.[43] The formal treaties would have to come later.

Secretary Harlan's concern about reconstruction of the tribes in the Indian Territory that had participated in the Civil War should not obscure the general continuity of his Indian policy with that of earlier officials. His long instructions to Cooley's commission included sections dealing with the western tribes that were part and parcel of the reservation system developed in the previous decade. Harlan was convinced that the nomadic Indians would have to be narrowly concentrated on reservations to be out of the way of a growing white population, and he instructed the commissioners in case they had occasion to deal with tribes to the west:

> You will impress upon them, in the most forcible terms, that the advancing tide of immigration is rapidly spreading over the country, and that the government has not the power or inclination to check it.

42. CIA Report, 1865, serial 1248, pp. 482–83.
43. The agreement is printed in the minutes of the council, CIA Report, 1865, serial 1248, pp. 514–15. Kappler prints it among unratified treaties, pp. 1050–52.

Our hills and valleys are filling up with an adventurous and rapidly increasing people, that will encroach upon and occupy the ancient abodes of the red man. Such seems to be an inevitable law of population and settlement on this continent. It leads to collisions, always followed by lamentable results, and sometimes by bloody and devastating wars. It is for the interest of both races, and chiefly for the welfare of the Indian, that he should abandon his wandering life and settle upon lands reserved to his exclusive use, where he will be protected in his rights and surrounded with every kindly and elevating influence by a paternal government.[44]

The western Indians were to be assigned tracts of land as remote as possible from the routes of whites to the West. Although Harlan admitted that "a sudden transition from a savage and nomadic life to the more quiet and confining pursuits of civilization is not to be expected," the lands were to be suitable for the ultimate adoption of pastoral and agricultural life. He insisted that the government would have to furnish the assistance necessary for a transition to a new way of life and improvement of the Indians' moral and intellectual condition. "The nation cannot adopt the policy of exterminating them," he said. "Our self-respect, our Christian faith, and a common dependence on an all-wise Creator and benefactor forbid it. Other nations will judge our character by our treatment of the feeble tribes to whom we sustain the relation of guardian. Morally and legally there is no distinction between destroying them and rendering it impossible for them to escape annihilation by withholding from them adequate means of support." Harlan was an active Methodist, as was Cooley, and this concern for Indian salvation and transformation cannot be dismissed as mere cant and hypocrisy. It was understood by Harlan and by the commissioners to whom he addressed it as in conformity with the worldview they had inherited—an acceptance of the inevitable (that is, Providential) advance of the white population and its culture, with efforts to protect and sustain the Indians until they should be able to cope with the onrush and be subsumed by it.[45]

Cooley's commission did not negotiate treaties with the western tribes. That work was accomplished in October, the month following the Fort Smith council, by a special United States commission. The treaties signed

44. Harlan to commissioners, August 16, 1865, in Abel, *Indian under Reconstruction*, p. 224.

45. Ibid., p. 225. Abel says the object of the Harlan bill was "nothing more and nothing less than capitalistic exploitation of southern Indian preserves," and she speaks freely of "cant and hypocrisy" in Cooley's invocation of a beneficent Great Spirit in his address to the assembled delegates at Fort Smith (pp. 183, 227). But this is to misunderstand the evangelical Protestant heritage in which Harlan, Cooley, and their associates, as well as the leaders of the Five Civilized Tribes, worked.

on the Little Arkansas with the Cheyennes, Arapahos, Comanches, Kiowas, and Kiowa-Apaches included the provisions Harlan had outlined in his instructions.[46]

RECONSTRUCTION TREATIES

The Fort Smith council adjourned on September 21, to meet again at the call of the secretary of the interior. In Washington in the spring and early summer of 1866 the representatives of the Five Civilized Tribes met with Cooley, Sells, and Parker and signed new treaties with the United States. The treaties had common provisions and built upon the points laid out by Cooley at Fort Smith, but considerable modifications were made to meet the protestations of the Indians. The tribes gave up sections of their land to make homes for Indians to be removed from Kansas and elsewhere; slaves were emancipated and slavery forever prohibited, and provisions were made for the freedmen; stipulations were included for a general council of all the tribes in the Indian Territory (looking toward territorial government, but for the present stopping short of it); and rights of way for railroads were provided for. The Seminoles gave up their entire territory and accepted a new region to the east. The Choctaws and Chickasaws sold their interests in the Leased District to the United States. The Creek land was cut in two. But the Cherokees, although they sold the Neutral Lands and the Cherokee Strip and gave the United States an option on the Cherokee Outlet, lost none of their lands; they agreed to admit other Indians to their territories west of the ninety-eighth meridian, however. The Choctaw-Chickasaw treaty and that of the Cherokees included provisions for survey of their lands and allotment of them in severalty whenever approved by the tribal councils.[47]

The treaties were signed with reunited tribes, although the divisions were by no means all healed. Among the Choctaws and Chickasaws there was little trouble, for there had been no fundamental split into loyal and secessionist parties. The Creeks and Seminoles patched up their divisions and sent national delegations to Washington to negotiate with the govern-

---

46. Kappler, pp. 887–95.
47. The treaties are printed in Kappler as follows: Seminole, March 21, 1866, pp. 910–15; Choctaw and Chickasaw, April 28, 1866, pp. 918–31; Creek, June 14, 1866, pp. 931–36; Cherokee, July 19, 1866, pp. 942–50. There is detailed coverage in Abel, *Indian under Reconstruction*, pp. 301–63. See also the following articles on the separate treaties: Harry Henslick, "The Seminole Treaty of 1866," *Chronicles of Oklahoma* 48 (Autumn 1970): 280–94; Gail Balman, "The Creek Treaty of 1866," ibid., pp. 184–96; Marion Ray McCullar, "The Choctaw-Chickasaw Reconstruction Treaty of 1866," *Journal of the West* 12 (July 1973): 462–70; Paul F. Lambert, "The Cherokee Reconstruction Treaty of 1866," ibid., pp. 471–89.

MAP 6: The Indian Territory, 1866–1888

ment. But among the Cherokees hostile factions persisted, and both groups were on hand in Washington. On March 3, 1865, the northern Cherokees, acting through the National Council, sent a delegation led by Ross, who was in ill health and close to the end of his life. A southern delegation, led by Elias C. Boudinot and William P. Adair, sought its own ends. Cooley dealt with both delegations, but he was favorably inclined toward the southern group, for it was sympathetic with his proposals for a territorial government and his encouragement of railroad development in the Indian Territory. He was not averse to considering a division of the Cherokee Nation into northern and southern parts, however. Cooley sent a treaty made with the southern delegates to the president in May, justifying his action at great length in an anti-Ross pamphlet he published at the same time entitled *The Cherokee Question*. But President Johnson refused to forward the treaty to the Senate. The commissioner of Indian affairs was then forced to come to terms with the northern delegation, with whom he finally signed the treaty that was ratified by the Senate. The treaty represented compromises on both sides. The southern faction was offered a degree of autonomy in the Canadian District, lying between the Arkansas and Canadian rivers, but the unity of the nation was preserved. John Ross died on August 1, 1866, and new leadership was found for the distracted nation.[48]

The Civil War was a crucial experience in the history of the southern Indians. Even though they could argue that their attachment to the Confederacy was the result of abandonment by the Union and duress from the Confederate government, it placed them in the position of conquered foes at the end of the war. Politicians in the North like Lane and Harlan were ready to use the occasion to bring about a fundamental change in the relations of the Cherokees and other nations with the United States. In this they were largely frustrated for the time being by the Indians, who managed to keep intact most of their national autonomy for another three decades. But northern sentiment in the post-Civil War years, even among notable friends of the Indians, never quite shook off the conviction that the treaty rights of the Indians had been destroyed by the tribes' defection, and the movement for territorial organization gathered momentum as the century progressed.[49]

48. There is an extended account of the treaty negotiations and the relations of the factions in Wardell, *Cherokee Nation*, pp. 194–207, and in Abel, *Indian under Reconstruction*, pp. 345–63. Cooley's pamphlet is *The Cherokee Question: Report of the Commissioner of Indian Affairs to the President of the United States, June 15, 1866, Being Supplementary to the Report of the Commissioners Appointed by the President to Treat with the Indians South of Kansas, and Which Assembled at Fort Smith, Ark., in September, 1865* (Washington: GPO, 1866). The pamphlet is reprinted, with introduction and notes to refute its anti-Ross position, in Joseph B. Thoburn, ed., "The Cherokee Question," *Chronicles of Oklahoma* 2 (June 1924): 141–242. The heated nature of the conflict between the two Cherokee parties can be seen in the small "pamphlet war" they conducted in the summer of 1866; the pamphlets are conveniently listed in Lester Hargrett, *The Gilcrease-Hargrett Catalogue of Imprints* (Norman: University of Oklahoma Press, 1972), pp. 55–56. Ross's last days are treated in Moulton, *John Ross*, pp. 184–96.

49. Some useful information on post-treaty reconstruction in the separate Indian nations is in M. Thomas Bailey, *Reconstruction in Indian Territory: A Story of Avarice, Discrimination, and Opportunism* (Port Washington, New York: Kennikat Press, 1972); Ohland Morton, "Reconstruction in the Creek Nation," *Chronicles of Oklahoma* 9 (June 1931): 171–79; and Hanna R. Warren, "Reconstruction in the Cherokee Nation," ibid. 45 (Summer 1967): 180–89.

CHAPTER 17

Indian Conflicts: A Series of Other Wars

Sioux Uprising in Minnesota.

War in the Southwest.

Bosque Redondo—The Great Experiment.

Sand Creek.

The Civil War was accompanied by a series of other wars that the United States government was forced to fight concurrently—wars with the Sioux in Minnesota and Dakota, with the Apaches and Navajos in Arizona and New Mexico, and with the Cheyennes, Arapahos, Kiowas, and Comanches in Kansas and eastern Colorado. Unlike the action of the southern tribes in the Indian Territory, which was an inextricable part of the Civil War, the Indian wars in the north and west were only indirectly related to the main event. They nevertheless put an additional strain on the resources of the Lincoln administration and were significant events in the history of the government's relations with the Indian tribes.

SIOUX UPRISING IN MINNESOTA

On August 18, 1862, without warning, the Sioux Indians of Minnesota rose up in fury against the white settlers. This was an outbreak of peculiar violence, and it tested severely the Indian policy of the federal government.[1]

1. The standard and best account of the Sioux uprising is William Watts Folwell, *A History of Minnesota*, 4 vols. (St. Paul: Minnesota Historical Society, 1921–1930), 2: 109–301. An excellent narrative that skillfully weighs the evidence and includes many illustrations is Kenneth Carley, *The Sioux Uprising of 1862* (St. Paul: Minnesota Historical Society, 1961). Briefer accounts of value are Roy W. Meyer, *History of the Santee*

Minnesota was the homeland of important Indians: in the north bands of Chippewas (Ojibwas) and in the south the Santee Sioux (Mdewakanton, Sisseton, Wahpeton, and Wahpekute bands). As white population moved into the Midwest in the 1830s and 1840s, these Indians were still relatively isolated and not immediately within the plans of the advancing whites, for they were beyond the Mississippi River, that chimerical boundary that was supposed to mark the western limits of American settlement. In 1837, it is true, the Chippewas ceded their Minnesota lands east of the Mississippi below the mouth of the Crow Wing River and the Sioux a thin triangle south of the Chippewa cession.[2] But for a dozen years or more, the rich agricultural lands of the Sioux in what is now the southern half of Minnesota were left undisturbed. With the admission of Wisconsin into the Union (1848), however, and the subsequent establishment of Minnesota Territory (1849), pressures began to mount for freeing more lands in Minnesota for settlement. The cry for the "Sulands" could not long be ignored.

On July 23, 1851, at Traverse des Sioux, the chiefs of the Wahpeton and Sisseton bands of the Upper Sioux ceded their lands in southern and western Minnesota for $1,665,000 in cash and annuity goods. Two weeks later, at Mendota across from Fort Snelling, the Lower Sioux (Mdewakanton and Wahpekute) signed away the southeastern quarter of Minnesota for $1,441,000. In return for some twenty-four million acres of rich land, the Sioux, in addition to the promised annuities, were provided with two reservations twenty miles wide stretching along both sides of the upper Minnesota River. The treaties, negotiated by Luke Lea, commissioner of Indian affairs, and Alexander Ramsey, governor and ex officio superintendent of Indian affairs in Minnesota Territory, were in large part designed by fur traders, of whom Henry Hastings Sibley, longtime trader with the Sioux at Mendota and later first governor of the state of Minnesota, was the most prominent. The traders, to whom the Indians were heavily in debt, wanted treaties that would provide funds for canceling those debts, and most of the cash payments stipulated by the government went into the traders' pockets, not into the hands of the Indians.[3]

Sioux: United States Indian Policy on Trial (Lincoln: University of Nebraska Press, 1967), pp. 109–54; Edmund Jefferson Danziger, Jr., *Indians and Bureaucrats: Administering the Reservation Policy during the Civil War* (Urbana: University of Illinois Press, 1974), pp. 95–130; and Theodore C. Blegen, *Minnesota: A History of the State* (Minneapolis: University of Minnesota Press, 1963), pp. 259–84. A popular account that emphasizes stories of settlers caught in the war is C. M. Oehler, *The Great Sioux Uprising* (New York: Oxford University Press, 1959). Military aspects of the war are treated in Louis H. Roddis, *The Indian Wars of Minnesota* (Cedar Rapids, Iowa: Torch Press, 1956).

2. Chippewa Treaty of St. Peters, July 29, 1837, and Sioux Treaty of Washington, September 29, 1837, Kappler, pp. 491–94.

3. Kappler, pp. 588–93. For the role of traders and politicians in the treaties, see

The treaties were also "civilizing" treaties, for the small reservations were intended to be the site of increased agricultural development for the Indians. The treaties had the usual agricultural, educational, and general civilization provisions. As the Indians moved to the reservations in 1853 and 1854, agency buildings were erected at both the Upper Sioux Agency and the Lower Sioux Agency, and the agent divided his time between them. Here the successive agents, aided by Christian missionaries, worked to change the Indians into white farmers. Joseph R. Brown, who became agent in September 1857, was especially active. He had had long experience as a fur trader and was married to a woman of Sioux blood, and he proceeded energetically to lead the Indians down the road of civilization envisaged in the 1851 treaties. "Sufficient progress has been made," he reported in 1858, "to dispel all doubt of the capacity of the Sioux for a thorough transformation from a state of heathen barbarism to that of civilized and useful members of community"—although he realized that the transformation would be a slow and painful process. Convinced that only individual ownership of land would make true civilization possible, Brown proposed to allot eighty-acre plots to individual families as a step toward private property and ultimate citizenship. Then in 1858 new treaties further restricted the reservations, as the lands lying north of the Minnesota River were ceded to the United States. These treaties endorsed Brown's program and provided for the allotment of eighty acres to heads of families and single individuals over twenty-one. The secretary of the interior, moreover, was given discretionary power over expenditure of the annuities, to use them in a way "best calculated to promote their interests, welfare, and advance in civilization."[4] The theory behind the system was well stated by Brown's successor: "The theory, in substance, was to break up the community system among the Sioux; weaken and destroy their tribal relations; individualize them by giving each a separate home and having them subsist by industry—the sweat of their brows; till the soil; make labor honorable and idleness dishonorable; or, as it was expressed in short, '*make white men of them*,' and have them adopt the habits and customs of white men."[5]

Although there were encouraging reports of success in the civilization program, there was in fact a deep division among the Sioux and growing hostility between the "farmer" Indians and the "blanket" Indians, who intended to keep their old ways. Persecution of the agriculturalists by the

---

Lucile M. Kane, "The Sioux Treaties and the Traders," *Minnesota History* 32 (June 1951): 65–80, and Meyer, *Santee Sioux*, pp. 72–87.

4. Report of Joseph R. Brown, September 30, 1858, CIA Report, 1858, serial 974, pp. 401–9; Kappler, pp. 781–89.

5. Thomas J. Galbraith to Clark W. Thompson, January 27, 1863, CIA Report, 1863, serial 1182, p. 398.

traditional party made it difficult for them to adhere to the programs of the agents and the missionaries. The superintendent of the Northern Superintendency wrote in the summer of 1860: "There is no doubt that at the present time a great struggle for ascendancy is taking place among the Sioux between the civilized or improvement Indians who have adopted our habits and customs and those who still retain the savage mode of life."[6] Conditions were becoming ripe for an explosion.

The Indians had specific grievances. The Great Father's promises in the treaty negotiations had never fully materialized, for the sums listed were drained away to pay traders' debts, and the Indians were further irritated by the attempts to substitute goods for money payments. In 1861, under the spoils system, the superintendent of the Northern Superintendency, the Sioux agent, and many of the agency employees were swept out of office to make room for Republicans who had aided the party effort in the 1860 election. Joseph Brown was replaced as agent by Thomas J. Galbraith, a man of no Indian experience who was characterized by an arrogance and inflexibility that boded ill for the handling of a delicate and dangerous situation. The Sioux, moreover, had been emboldened by the Spirit Lake Massacre in 1857, in which a renegade band of Wahpekutes under Inkpaduta raided and murdered settlers in northern Iowa and southern Minnesota. The perpetrators had not been punished, and the Indian Office had backed down from its initial purpose of strict punishment for the crimes.[7]

The Civil War, of course, had a decided effect. Withdrawal of regular troops was not unnoticed by the Indians. Although the men were replaced in part by Minnesota volunteers, the number of companies was cut in half and the new soldiers were inexperienced. The Sioux were restless, and there were rumors that the war would put an end altogether to the money coming from the federal government. Many men at the time also suspected machinations of Confederate agents among the Indians. Galbraith hinted darkly that rebel sympathizers had created disaffection among the Indians at his agency; Secretary of the Interior Caleb Smith feared a general Indian uprising in the West, and he suspected that British traders from Canada, in sympathy with the South, were at work. "I am satisfied," he wrote in November 1862 in a discussion of the causes of the Minnesota outbreak, "that the chief cause is to be found in the insurrection of the southern States." Ultimately these fears were admitted to have been groundless, but it is easy to see how they could have arisen in the excitement of the times.[8]

6. William J. Cullen to Alfred B. Greenwood, July 16, 1860, quoted in Meyer, *Santee Sioux*, pp. 107–8.

7. Folwell, *Minnesota*, 2: 223–25, 400–415; Meyer, *Santee Sioux*, pp. 97–101.

8. Galbraith to Thompson, January 27, 1863, CIA Report, 1863, serial 1182, p. 401; report of Smith, November 29, 1862, *House Executive Document* no. 1, 37–3, serial 1157, pp. 7–10.

All these proximate causes were built upon the fundamental opposition of large numbers of the Sioux to the civilization program. Agent Galbraith declared: "The radical moving cause of the outbreak is, I am satisfied, the ingrained and fixed hostility of the savage barbarian to reform, change, and civilization." He condemned the Sioux culture out of hand and saw behind it the working of the Devil. Nevertheless, his analysis of the cause of the war was not far different from that of Chief Big Eagle, an active participant in the conflict, who commented later on the causes of the uprising:

> The whites were always trying to make the Indians give up their life and live like white men—go to farming, work hard and do as they did—and the Indians did not know how to do that, and did not want to anyway. It seemed too sudden to make such a change. If the Indians had tried to make the whites live like them, the whites would have resisted, and it was the same with many Indians. The Indians wanted to live as they did before the treaty of Traverse des Sioux—go where they pleased and when they pleased; hunt game wherever they could find it, sell their furs to the traders, and live as they could.[9]

In 1862 there was unreasonable delay in the annuity payments. This would have remained only an irritation, no doubt, had not the Indians come to depend so heavily on the annuities. Because of bad crops they were in a state of near starvation. The agent and the missionaries made some moves to provide subsistence for the tribes, but at the time of the outbreak many of the Indians were desperate. In early August at the Upper Agency serious violence was prevented only by a show of military force from Fort Ridgely and a reluctant agreement by Galbraith to issue supplies (although he wanted to wait until the money annuities had arrived so that supplies and cash could be distributed together). On August 15 at the Lower Agency hungry and angry Indians were turned away because neither the agent nor the traders were willing to supply them. Trader Andrew Myrick said, "So far as I am concerned, if they are hungry let them eat grass."

The outbreak began with a simple enough event. On August 17, for inconsequential reasons and without premeditation, four Indians killed five white settlers in Acton Township. The Indians knew that the rash action would bring retaliation by the whites, and the chiefs debated about what course to pursue. In the end they decided for war. Led by Little Crow on

---

9. Galbraith to Thompson, January 27, 1863, CIA Report, 1863, serial 1182, p. 397; "Chief Big Eagle's Story," in Kenneth Carley, ed., "As Red Men Viewed It: Three Indian Accounts of the Uprising," *Minnesota History* 38 (September 1962): 129. Big Eagle also noted the abuses of the traders, the replacement of the agent and the superintendent, the rumors that the Union was losing the Civil War and that it would be a good time for the Indians to regain their lands, and intratribal politics.

August 18 the Indians stormed the Lower Agency in a surprise attack. Among those killed was Andrew Myrick, whose body was found with grass stuffed in his mouth. The outbreak spread rapidly, as the Indians decimated the outlying settlements and attacked Fort Ridgely and the town of New Ulm.

Panic seized the frontier in Minnesota and the neighboring states and territories, and official Washington picked up the exaggerated reports.[10] Commissioner Dole called the action "the most atrocious and horrible outbreak to be found in the annals of Indian history." He noted the Acton murders and reported:

> And now followed a series of cruel murders, characterized by every species of savage atrocity and barbarity known to Indian warfare. Neither age, sex, nor condition was spared. It is estimated that from eight hundred to one thousand quiet, inoffensive, and unarmed settlers fell victims to savage fury ere the bloody work of death was stayed. The thriving town of New Ulm, containing from 1,500 to 2,000 inhabitants, was almost destroyed. Fort Ridgely was attacked and closely besieged for several days, and was only saved by the most heroic and unfaltering bravery on the part of its little band of defenders until it was relieved by troops raised, armed, and sent forward to their relief. Meantime the utmost consternation and alarm prevailed throughout the entire community. Thousands of happy homes were abandoned, the whole frontier was given up to be plundered and burned by the remorseless savages, and every avenue leading to the more densely populated portions of the State was crowded with the now homeless and impoverished fugitives.[11]

The state of Minnesota and the United States reacted quickly to the outbreak. On August 19 Governor Ramsey placed Henry Sibley in command of a relief expedition; Sibley, with hastily gathered militia and volunteers, moved against the Indians. Ramsey pleaded with Washington for federal aid, but President Lincoln could not easily release men from the conduct of the Civil War. The serious problems of defense against the Indians—both real and imagined—did not disappear in the Northwest, how-

---

10. The absurdity of the panic can be seen in Milo M. Quaife, "The Panic of 1862 in Wisconsin," *Wisconsin Magazine of History* 4 (December 1920): 166–95.

11. CIA Report, 1862, serial 1159, pp. 170–71. Dole's estimates of casualties were high. No exact figures are available, but about 500 seems reasonable for massacred civilians and soldier deaths. Folwell analyzes the various estimates in an appendix in *Minnesota*, 2: 391–93; he notes that in the New York draft riots of July 1863 "more than twice as many murders were committed and much more property was destroyed by white savages than by Indians during the outbreak of 1862." Ibid., p. 213.

ever, and after the Second Battle of Bull Run, Lincoln, who for political as well as military reasons wanted to get rid of General John Pope, created a Department of the Northwest and sent Pope to command it.[12] The general arrived in St. Paul on September 16 and immediately took a hard line toward the Indians. "It is my purpose utterly to exterminate the Sioux if I have the power to do so," he wrote to Sibley, "and even if it requires a campaign lasting the whole of next year. Destroy everything belonging to them and force them out to the plains, unless, as I suggest, you can capture them. They are to be treated as maniacs or wild beasts, and by no means as people with whom treaties or compromises can be made."[13]

The Indians, although they had the initial advantage of surprise, were in the end no match for the forces of Sibley and Pope. A decisive victory by Sibley at Wood Lake on September 23 was the end of organized fighting by the Sioux in Minnesota. Indians who remained hostile fled west, and friendly chiefs arranged for the release of white captives. Large numbers of Sioux were captured or surrendered, and day by day more Indians, many of them on the point of starvation, gave themselves up.

Cries of vengeance filled the air, and a five-man military commission was quickly appointed to try the captive Indians. The commission worked with great haste; in ten days it tried 392 prisoners, condemning 303 to death. Pope and Sibley wanted the condemned men executed at once, and they telegraphed the names to Lincoln for confirmation of the sentences. Lincoln would not move so precipitously; he directed that the full records of the trials be sent to him for review.

The president was pressured greatly from both sides. Pope was adamant for a speedy execution. "The example of hanging many of the perpetrators of the late outrages," he declared, "is necessary and will have a crushing effect." Governor Ramsey hinted that private vengeance would take over if official action was denied, and private citizens and the newspapers of Minnesota warned the president of dire consequences if he failed to carry out the executions. Senator Morton Wilkinson and Minnesota Representatives Cyrus Aldrich and William Windom worked desperately to prevent a presidential pardon. In the Senate, Wilkinson regaled the members with lurid

12. The story of the Department of the Northwest is told in detail in Robert Huhn Jones, *The Civil War in the Northwest: Nebraska, Wisconsin, Iowa, Minnesota, and the Dakotas* (Norman: University of Oklahoma Press, 1960). See also Richard N. Ellis, *General Pope and U.S. Indian Policy* (Albuquerque: University of New Mexico Press, 1970), pp. 1–51.

13. Pope to Sibley, September 28, 1862, *The War of the Rebellion: A Compilation of the Official Records of the Union and Confederate Armies*, 70 vols. (Washington: GPO, 1880–1901), series 1, 13: 686 (hereafter cited as *Official Records*). See also Pope to Sibley, September 17, 1862, ibid., pp. 648–49.

stories of murdered men and violated women and got approval of a resolution requesting information from the president regarding evidence on the condemned prisoners.[14]

In a formal protest to Lincoln against a pardon of the convicted Sioux, the Minnesota legislators expressed the sentiments of their constituents:

> We *protest against the pardon* of these Indians, because, if it is done, the Indians will become more insolent and cruel than they ever were before, believing, as they certainly will believe, that their great father at Washington either justified their acts or is afraid to punish them for their crimes.
>
> We *protest against it* because, if the President does not permit these executions to take place under the forms of law, the outraged people of Minnesota will dispose of these wretches without law. These two peoples cannot live together. We do not wish to see mob law inaugurated in Minnesota, as it certainly will be, if you force the people to do it. . . .
>
> You can give us peace, or you can give us lawless violence. We pray you, sir, in view of all that we have suffered, and of the danger which still awaits us, *let the law be executed; let justice be done* our people.[15]

But calmer, more reasonable voices also were heard. The lawyers whom Lincoln assigned to study the trial transcripts were shocked by what they found—short trials, reliance on hearsay evidence, denial of due process and of counsel—and rejected many of the findings of the military commission. Henry B. Whipple, Espicopal Bishop of Minnesota, despite the unpopularity of his views in Minnesota, stood up strongly for careful justice, and he appealed to Lincoln through Senator Henry Rice: "We cannot hang men by the hundreds. Upon our own premises we have no right to do so. We claim that they are an independent nation & as such they are prisoners of war. The leaders must be punished but we cannot afford by an wanton cruelty to purchase a long Indian war—nor by injustice in other matters purchase the anger of God."[16]

14. John Pope to H. W. Halleck, October 10, 1862, ibid., series 1, 13: 724; *Congressional Globe*, 37th Congress, 3d session, p. 13. Lincoln's part is treated in David A. Nichols, *Lincoln and the Indians: Civil War Policy and Politics* (Columbia: University of Missouri Press, 1978), pp. 76–128. Nichols is harsh in his judgment of Lincoln, although he admits the humaneness of Lincoln's action in regard to the execution of the Sioux.

15. *Senate Executive Document* no. 7, 37–3, serial 1149, p. 4. The statement is full of lurid details about Indian atrocities.

16. Whipple to Rice, November 12, 1862, Whipple Papers, Minnesota Historical Society, quoted in Nichols, *Lincoln and the Indians*, p. 104. Whipple describes his opinions and actions in his autobiography, *Lights and Shadows of a Long Episcopate* (New York: Macmillan Company, 1899), pp. 105–32.

The strongest voice was that of Commissioner Dole, who understood the hysteria on the frontier and did not criticize Sibley and Pope but called for reasonable action. "I cannot reconcile it to my sense of duty to remain silent," he wrote to the secretary of the interior. Dole admitted that the Indians had committed "horrible and atrocious crimes" at which the country was justly incensed; but "an indiscriminate punishment of men who have laid down their arms and surrendered themselves as prisoners," he said, "partakes more of the character of revenge than the infliction of deserved punishment; that it is contrary to the spirit of the age and our character as a great, magnanimous, and Christian people." Dole had no exalted views of the Indians, but he believed that only the leaders should be punished, not the rank and file who followed them in blind obedience, and he urged a middle course upon the administration. He pleaded with Smith to "prevent the consummation of an act which I cannot believe would be otherwise than a stain upon our national character, and a source of future regret." Secretary Smith sent the plan to Lincoln with his endorsement of the "humane views" of the commissioner.[17]

It was not an easy question for Lincoln. He decided finally to uphold the sentence of death for only thirty-nine of the convicted men, and on December 6 he sent Sibley their names. He laid out the basis for his decision to the Senate. "Anxious to not act with so much clemency as to encourage another outbreak, on the one hand, nor with so much severity as to be real cruelty, on the other," Lincoln said, "I caused a careful examination of the records of the trials to be made, in view of first ordering the execution of such as had been proved guilty of violating females. Contrary to my expectations, only two of this class were found. I then directed a further examination, and a classification of all who were proven to have participated in *massacres*, as distinguished from participation in *battles*."[18] One of the thirty-nine men was reprieved at the last minute; the thirty-eight were hanged at Mankato in a spectacle attended by a large crowd on December 26, 1862.

Mass execution was not the only thing Minnesotans wanted. They demanded the total removal of the Sioux from the state. Citizens of St. Paul, in a memorial to the president, offered typical arguments: "The Indian's nature can no more be trusted than the wolf's. Tame him, cultivate him, strive to Christianize him as you will, and the sight of blood will in an

17. Dole to Caleb B. Smith, November 10, 1862, CIA Report, 1862, serial 1157, pp. 213–14; Smith to Lincoln, November 11, 1862, Lincoln Papers, Library of Congress (microfilm reel 43, no. 19500).

18. Lincoln to the Senate, December 11, 1862, *Senate Executive Document* no. 7, 37–3, serial 1149, pp. 1–2; Lincoln to Sibley, December 6, 1862, *Collected Works of Abraham Lincoln*, ed. Roy P. Basler, 9 vols. (New Brunswick: Rutgers University Press, 1953–1955), 5: 542–43.

instant call out the savage, wolfish, devilish instincts of the race." Only if
the Indians were removed from the state could Minnesotans feel secure. It
was a question "simply whether the Indian or the white man shall possess
Minnesota."[19]

The Lincoln administration acquiesced. On March 3, 1863, Congress
authorized the removal of the Sioux from the state, requiring that they be
located outside the limits of any existing state. Dole and Secretary of the
Interior John P. Usher (who had replaced Smith in January 1863) picked a
spot near Fort Randall on the upper Missouri. In May and June 1863 the
Sioux who had been encamped at Fort Snelling in the wake of the uprising
were loaded on steamboats for the long journey down the Mississippi and
up the Missouri to their new reservation at Crow Creek. It was a miserable, barren spot, and after three years the Sioux were moved to a new and
better reservation at the mouth of the Niobrara River in Nebraska. Meanwhile, the convicted Indians not executed at Mankato were moved to a
prison in Davenport, Iowa; only later were they allowed to join their families in Nebraska.[20]

The hapless Winnebago Indians were caught in the removal uproar.
Having already been moved from their Wisconsin homes—to Iowa in
1840, to the Crow Wing River in Minnesota in 1849, and then to Blue
Earth County, Minnesota, in 1855—they were now forced to relocate again
in order to satisfy the cries of Minnesotans against Indians in their midst
on lands coveted for their own use. By a law of February 21, 1863, Congress
authorized their removal, and they quickly followed on the heels of the
departing Santees, locating next to the Sioux reservation at Crow Creek.
The Winnebagos were unhappy in the new spot, and they moved en masse
to the Omaha reservation in Nebraska in 1864. The Indian Office recognized the fait accompli and purchased part of the Omaha reserve as a permanent home for the wandering Indians.[21]

The Sioux who fled Minnesota during the outbreak of 1862 were not
quickly pacified. They roamed the Dakota prairies and found some support
among the Yankton and Yanktonai Indians. General Pope feared a new attack by these Indians on the Minnesota frontier, and he mounted a punitive expedition into Dakota Territory against them. In 1863 General Sibley
moved west from Minnesota, while General Alfred Sully proceeded up the
Missouri. They scattered the Indians they met, but the expeditions settled

---

19. Memorial, *Senate Executive Document* no. 7, 37–3, serial 1149, p. 5.
20. 12 *United States Statutes* 819–20; *House Report* no. 13, 37–3, serial 1173. Details on the removal are given in William E. Lass, "The Removal from Minnesota of the
Sioux and Winnebago Indians," *Minnesota History* 38 (December 1963): 353–64, and
Danziger, *Indians and Bureaucrats*, pp. 11–30.
21. 12 *United States Statutes* 658–60; Kappler, pp. 872–73.

nothing. In 1864 Sully led another expedition into Dakota, where he was joined by Minnesota forces. In the Battle of Killdeer Mountain on July 28, 1864, the Sioux were defeated. Military posts were established along the Missouri, and the Indian raids gradually ceased.[22]

On February 19, 1867, the Sisseton and Wahpeton Sioux in Dakota signed a treaty in Washington according to which two reservations were established for them. One was a triangle of land in what is now the north-eastern corner of South Dakota (Sisseton Reservation), and the other extended south from Devils Lake in North Dakota. The treaty, designed to promote civilization among the Indians, called for the allotment of the reservations in quarter-section tracts. It further specified that Congress would take steps from time to time to enable the Indians to return to an agricultural life, "including, if thought advisable, the establishment and support of local and manual-labor schools; the employment of agricultural, mechanical, and other teachers; the opening and improvement of individual farms; and generally such objects as Congress in its wisdom shall deem necessary to promote the agricultural improvement and civilization of said bands."[23]

WAR IN THE SOUTHWEST

The drive in the 1850s against the warlike Indians in New Mexico and Arizona that promised success in pacifying them was ended by the outbreak of the Civil War. Many regular army troops were withdrawn from the scattered garrisons, leaving the Indians free to renew their raids against the inhabitants of the region. And the Confederate attempts to control the area by military expeditions and the organization of territory government created new confusion, for all Union forces had to be mobilized to meet the challenge of the southern attack.[24]

The Confederate invasion began with a move up the Rio Grande from El Paso by troops under John R. Baylor of the Texas Mounted Rifles, and the Union forces gave way. Forts Buchanan and Breckinridge near Tucson were abandoned, and then Fort Fillmore on the Rio Grande was evacuated and its troops attempted to march to Fort Stanton. On the way they surren-

22. A brief, well-documented account of these expeditions is in Robert M. Utley, *Frontiersmen in Blue: The United States Army and the Indians, 1848–1865* (New York: Macmillan Company, 1967), pp. 270–80. See also Folwell, *Minnesota*, 2: 265–301.

23. Kappler, pp. 957–59. The history of the Sioux on these reservations is told in detail in Meyer, *Santee Sioux*.

24. Confederate operations in the Southwest are discussed in Ray C. Colton, *The Civil War in the Western Territories: Arizona, Colorado, New Mexico, and Utah* (Norman: University of Oklahoma Press, 1959), pp. 3–99, which thoroughly exploits the documents printed in *Official Records*.

dered to Baylor, and Fort Stanton, unreinforced, was also abandoned. Baylor, in the flush of victory, set up a Confederate Territory of Arizona (composed of all of New Mexico south of the thirty-fourth parallel) and proclaimed himself governor. At the end of the year, a major Confederate military advance into the region was begun under the command of General Henry Hopkins Sibley, a former United States officer who had fought in New Mexico against the Indians in the 1850s.[25]

To meet this attack Brigadier General Edward R. S. Canby had to rely on New Mexico volunteers and a handful of remaining regulars. They were no match for Sibley, who advanced up the Rio Grande. On February 21, 1862, the Union forces were defeated at the Battle of Valverde, north of Fort Craig, and the Confederates, largely unimpeded, moved on to Albuquerque, which they took on March 2, and then to Santa Fe on March 10. The only remaining obstacle to control of all New Mexico was the great depot of supplies at Fort Union. But the invading army did not make it. Union forces, augmented by feisty Colorado volunteers under Major John M. Chivington, routed the Confederate army at Glorieta Pass on March 28, and the southerners retreated down the Rio Grande, never to return.[26]

A new phase in the history of New Mexico began in August 1862 with the arrival on the Rio Grande of a column of California volunteers under Brigadier General James H. Carleton, who on September 18 replaced Canby in command of the Department of New Mexico. For the rest of the war Carleton was the dominant figure in New Mexico. A man of ability and zeal, he was also arrogant and arbitrary, and he stubbornly pushed for the fulfillment of his vision of what New Mexico needed. With the Confederate threat removed, the new commander turned his attention to subduing the Indians. Joining with an old associate, Colonel Christopher (Kit) Carson of the New Mexico cavalry, Carleton set out to accomplish his objective: to end once and for all the depredations of the Apaches and the Navajos. To do this Carleton intended to adopt the guerilla tactics of the Indians themselves. "The troops must be kept after the Indians," he wrote in 1863, "not in big bodies, with military noises and smokes, and the gleam of arms by day, and fires, and talk, and comfortable sleeps by night; but in small parties moving stealthily to their haunts and lying patiently in wait for

25. Baylor's work, especially his harsh policy of extermination against the Indians, is treated in Martin Hardwick Hall, "Planter vs. Frontiersman: Conflict in Confederate Indian Policy," in *Essays on the American Civil War*, ed. William F. Holmes and Harold M. Hollingsworth (Austin: University of Texas Press, 1968), pp. 45–72. For a detailed narrative of Sibley's campaign, see Hall, *Sibley's New Mexico Campaign* (Austin: University of Texas Press, 1960).

26. In addition to Colton's and Hall's books, see Max L. Heyman, Jr., *Prudent Soldier: A Biography of Major General E. R. S. Canby, 1817–1873* (Glendale, California: Arthur H. Clark Company, 1959), pp. 137–87.

them; or by following their tracks day after day with a fixedness of purpose that never gives up." He intended to make no treaties short of total surrender, and when subjugation was achieved to move the Indians to an isolated reservation away from all contact with the white inhabitants of the territory, where they could be supported by the government until they could be transformed into agriculturalists and enlightened by teachers and Christian missionaries.[27]

Carleton turned first to the Mescalero Apaches of south central New Mexico. These Indians had been subdued in the mid-1850s, and Fort Stanton had been erected on the Rio Bonita in May 1855. But when the post was abandoned in the face of Confederate attack in 1861, the Apaches began to prey upon the white settlers. "This condition of the tribes is truly disheartening to the citizens," Indian Agent Lorenzo Labadi wrote in September 1862. "There is no security for life or property, and unless the government takes immediate steps to stop these depredations the country will be stripped of every species of property it now contains. The only permanent remedy for these evils is in the colonization of these Indians. Reservations should be at once located and the Indians forced to reside upon them."[28]

The general moved vigorously. He ordered Carson to reactivate Fort Stanton and directed the officers to kill the Indian men and capture the women and children, and to hold no council of peace with them. If the chiefs wanted peace, they would have to go to Santa Fe to submit. "The whole duty can be summed up in a few words," he told Carson: "The Indians are to be soundly whipped, without parleys or councils."[29] The troops kept up incessant pressure on the Apaches, and in November the chiefs appeared with the agent at Santa Fe to make peace. There Carleton revealed what he had in store for them. He had established a new military post (Fort Sum-

27. An extensive collection of documents concerning Carleton's operations in New Mexico, 1862–1865, that he furnished to the Doolittle Committee, is printed in the committee's report, *Condition of the Indian Tribes: Report of the Joint Special Committee, Appointed under Joint Resolution of March 3, 1865* (Washington: GPO, 1867; also printed as *Senate Report* no. 156, 39–2, serial 1279), pp. 98–322. The quotation is from Carleton to Edwin A. Rigg, August 6, 1863, ibid., p. 124. A biography of Carleton that treats him favorably is Aurora Hunt, *Major General James Henry Carleton, 1814–1873: Western Frontier Dragoon* (Glendale, California: Arthur H. Clark Company, 1958). An excellent brief account of Carleton's New Mexico career is Utley, *Frontiersmen in Blue*, pp. 231–60. Kit Carson's role can be followed in Edwin L. Sabin, *Kit Carson Days, 1809–1869*, rev. ed., 2 vols. (New York: Press of the Pioneers, 1935), 2: 694–724 and reprinted documents in appendix, pp. 846–91; and Clifford E. Trafzer, *The Kit Carson Campaign: The Last Great Navajo War* (Norman: University of Oklahoma Press, 1982).

28. Labadi to J. L. Collins, September 25, 1862, CIA Report, 1862, serial 1157, pp. 391–92. Labadi was speaking of the Navajos as well as of the Apaches.

29. Carleton to Joseph R. West, October 11, 1862, and Carleton to Carson, October 12, 1862, *Condition of the Indian Tribes*, pp. 99–101.

ner) on the Pecos River in eastern New Mexico at a spot called Bosque Redondo, after the round grove of cottonwoods there. The Indians who wanted peace were to move to the Bosque Redondo and take up a life of agriculture; the government would provide their subsistence and protect them until they could raise crops for themselves. By the end of March 1863 more than four hundred Apaches—the great bulk of the tribe—were at Fort Sumner. "My purpose," Carleton wrote to the adjutant general, "is to have them fed and kept there under *surveillance:* to have them plant a crop this year; to have them, in short, become what is called in this country a *pueblo.*" There missionaries could teach them the Gospel and open a school for the children, and the agent could instruct them in farming.[30]

Carleton next gave his attention to the Navajos, a far more numerous tribe with an estimated ten thousand people, compared with the four or five hundred Mescaleros. His plan for them, however, was the same as for the Apaches: to subdue the hostile elements of the tribes and move all to some distant reservation. The goal was similar to that preached by his predecessor, Canby, who had declared at the end of 1861 that there was "no choice between their absolute extermination or their removal and colonization at points so remote from the settlements as to isolate them entirely from the inhabitants of the Territory."[31] But whereas Canby probably had in mind some section of the traditional Navajo lands, Carleton soon decided that the Navajos as well as the Apaches were to settle at the Bosque Redondo.

While Colonel Carson was rounding up the Mescaleros, the offensive against the Navajos began with the establishment of Fort Wingate in western New Mexico in October 1862. Navajo chiefs responded by appearing in Santa Fe in December to seek peace, but Carleton let them know that he had no faith in their promises and sent them home. In April 1863 he informed two leading peace chiefs, Delgadito and Barboncito, that the peaceful Indians would have to be clearly separated from the warring tribesmen—in short, that they would have to move to the Bosque Redondo. When the chiefs rejected the proposal to move so far from home, Carleton issued an ultimatum, directing the commander at Fort Wingate to tell

30. Carleton to Carson, November 25, 1862, and Carleton to Lorenzo Thomas, March 19, 1863, ibid., pp. 101–2, 106. Carleton wrote to Bishop John B. Lamay of Santa Fe asking for a priest "of energy, and of all those qualities of patience, good temper, assiduity and interest in the subject so necessary in one who is wanted to teach the Indian children now at Fort Sumner, not only the rudiments of an education, but the principles and truths of Christianity." Carleton to Lamay, June 12, 1863, ibid., p. 112. An account of the Apaches is given in C. L. Sonnichsen, *The Mescalero Apaches* (Norman: University of Oklahoma Press, 1958), pp. 89–119.

31. Canby to assistant adjutant general, Western Department, December 1, 1861, *Official Records*, series 1, 4: 77–78. Canby's Indian campaigns are described in Heyman, *Prudent Soldier*, pp. 113–36, 157–60.

them that they would have until July 20 to come in. "We have no desire to make war on them and other good Navajoes," Carleton said, "but the troops cannot tell the good from the bad; and we neither can nor will tolerate their staying as a peace party among those against whom we intend to make war." After the deadline, "*every Navajo that is seen will be* considered hostile and treated accordingly."[32]

Carleton meant just what he said, and he began to lay plans for an invasion of the Navajo country. On June 15, 1863, he ordered Kit Carson to move into the area and "to prosecute a vigorous war upon the men of this tribe until it is considered at these Head Quarters that they have been effectually punished for their long continued atrocities." The army was to have only one message for the Indians: "Go to Bosque Redondo, or we will pursue and destroy you. We will not make peace with you on any other terms."[33]

As winter set in, Carleton planned an attack into the Canyon de Chelly, the final citadel of the Navajos. The Indians could not withstand the insistent attacks and the destruction of their crops, orchards, and livestock. After the invasion, they surrendered in large numbers, for they faced starvation and had lost all hope of turning back the determined white soldiers. By mid-March six thousand had come in. They were transported across New Mexico to the reservation on the Pecos in a Long Walk that recalled the Cherokees' Trail of Tears more than a quarter-century before. By the end of 1864, three-fourths of the total tribe—some eight thousand people—were at the Bosque Redondo. The remainder, refusing to surrender, fled westward to the deserts, out of contact with the settlements.[34]

Carleton was now ready to begin the massive experiment in Indian transformation that he had outlined for his superiors in September 1863:

> The purpose now is never to relax the application of force with a people that can no more be trusted than you can trust the wolves that run through their mountains; to gather them together, little by little,

32. Carleton to J. Francisco Chavez, June 23, 1863, *Condition of the Indian Tribes*, p. 116. An extensive collection of documents on the campaign against the Navajos with accompanying scholarly commentary is Lawrence C. Kelly, *Navajo Roundup: Selected Correspondence of Kit Carson's Expedition against the Navajo, 1863–1865* (Boulder, Colorado: Pruett Publishing Company, 1970).

33. General Orders no. 15, Headquarters, Department of New Mexico, June 15, 1863, and Carleton to Carson, September 19, 1863, in Kelly, *Navajo Roundup*, pp. 21–22, 52.

34. The campaign in the Canyon de Chelly and the surrender of the Navajos is described ibid., pp. 80–158. See also L. R. Bailey, *The Long Walk: A History of the Navajo Wars, 1846–68* (Los Angeles: Westernlore Press, 1964), pp. 145–71. A collection of stories of the Long Walk handed down among the Navajos is presented in Ruth Roessel, ed., *Navajo Stories of the Long Walk Period* (Tsaile, Arizona: Navajo Community College Press, 1973). A census of Indians at the Bosque Redondo, December 31, 1864, is given in *Condition of the Indian Tribes*, pp. 264–65.

on to a reservation, away from the haunts, and hills, and hiding-places of their country, and then to be kind to them; there teach their children how to read and write; teach them the arts of peace; teach them the truths of Christianity. Soon they will acquire new habits, new ideas, new modes of life; the old Indians will die off, and carry with them all latent longings for murdering and robbing; the young ones will take their places without these longings; and thus, little by little, they will become a happy and contented people, and Navajo wars will be remembered only as something that belongs entirely to the past. Even until they can raise enough to be self-sustaining, you can feed them cheaper than you can fight them.[35]

BOSQUE REDONDO—THE GREAT EXPERIMENT

There was much in favor of Carleton's dream to turn the Bosque Redondo into a model reservation. The site was distant enough from the concentrations of white settlement to prevent contact between the two races, and the open plains in which it was located made it difficult for Indians to flee unnoticed. The land along the Pecos was suitable for irrigated farming, and Carleton estimated that enough food could be grown to feed the large number of Indians. In fact, a good beginning was made. The Apaches were put to work to build irrigation ditches, prepare fields, and plant crops, and when the Navajos arrived, they too worked hard to make the reservation livable. Carleton was sanguine about the possibilities, and he looked ahead ten years to see the Navajos as the "happiest and most delightfully located pueblo of Indians in New Mexico—perhaps in the United States."[36]

Carleton's actions, of course, were not motivated solely by concern for Indian welfare, genuine as that may have been. Like others of his time, he was not unmindful of the rich possibilities of the land vacated by the Indians when they gathered on restricted reservations. As he turned over his immense file of correspondence in October 1865 to the congressional committee headed by Senator James Doolittle that was sent west to investigate Indian troubles, he called attention to documents that spoke of the mineral wealth of the Indian lands and remarked that unless the Indians, who

35. Carleton to Lorenzo Thomas, September 6, 1863, *Condition of the Indian Tribes*, p. 134.

36. Carleton to Lorenzo Thomas, March 6, 1864, ibid., p. 163. The development of the Bosque Redondo reservation and the difficulties encountered there are told in detail in Gerald Thompson, *The Army and the Navajo: The Bosque Redondo Reservation Experiment, 1863–1868* (Tucson: University of Arizona Press, 1976), and Lynn R. Bailey, *Bosque Redondo: An American Concentration Camp* (Pasadena: Socio-Technical Books, 1970).

did not mine the metals, were removed to reservations, the riches could not be safely exploited by the whites. The question, he said, was "shall the miners be protected and the country be developed, or shall the Indians be suffered to kill them and the nation be deprived of its immense wealth?" And as the Navajos came in for transfer to Fort Sumner in March 1864, he wrote to the adjutant general: "By the subjugation and colonization of the Navajo tribe, we gain for civilization their whole country, which is much larger in extent than the State of Ohio, and, besides being by far the best pastoral region between the two oceans, is said to abound in the precious as well as in the useful metals." But he pressed this argument in part at least in order to persuade the federal government to appropriate sufficient funds to make possible the transformation in living that he envisaged for the Navajos at the Bosque Redondo. "When it is considered what a magnificent pastoral and mineral country they have surrendered to us—a country whose value can hardly be estimated," he wrote, "the mere pittance, in comparison, which must at once be given to support them, sinks into insignificance as a price for their natural heritage."[37]

Carleton had a number of strong supporters. James L. Collins, former superintendent of Indian affairs for New Mexico, continued to promote the project, and Henry Connelly, the governor of New Mexico Territory, no doubt relieved that the Navajo problem was being solved, accepted Carleton's evaluation of the scheme. Kit Carson, of course, had only praise for the reservation. "A new era dawned upon New Mexico," he wrote about Carleton's policy at the end of his campaign, "and the dying hopes of the people were again revived." He urged a gentle but firm hand in leading the Indians "into the habits or customs of civilized life" and predicted that the Navajos at the Bosque Redondo in a few years would "equal if not excell our industrious Pueblos, and become a source of wealth to the Territory instead of being as heretofore its dread and impoverishers."[38]

It was not to be. Almost from the start weaknesses in the scheme began to appear, and outspoken critics condemned the operation. The chief of the critics was Michael Steck, former Mescalero Apache agent who had replaced Collins as superintendent in March 1863. Although Steck favored the settlement of the Apaches at Fort Sumner and thought they could prosper there, he came to oppose strongly the movement of thousands of Navajos to the same reservation. Carleton had noted that the Apaches and Navajos were related and spoke the same language, but Steck asserted that the two tribes had been "inveterate enemies, and it is folly to suppose

37. Carleton to James R. Doolittle, October 22, 1865, and Carleton to Lorenzo Thomas, March 6 and 12, 1864, *Condition of the Indian Tribes*, pp. 98, 163, 166–68.
38. Carson to assistant adjutant general, Department of New Mexico, May 20, 1864, in Kelly, *Navajo Roundup*, pp. 157–58; Utley, *Frontiersmen in Blue*, pp. 245–46.

MAP 7: The Long Walk of the Navajo Indians

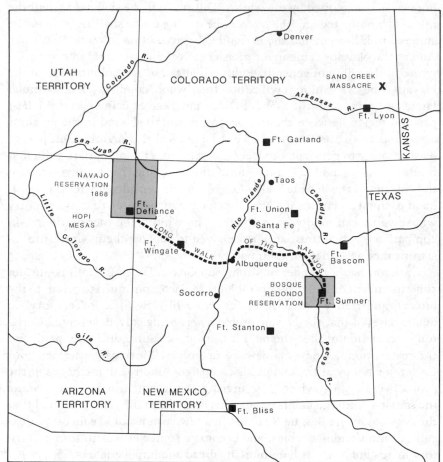

that they can agree upon the same reservation after having been so long at war." More important, the Bosque Redondo reservation, to his mind, was unequal to the demands of its large population, and millions of dollars would be required from the Treasury of the United States to give them subsistence. Steck wanted a reservation for the Navajos to be established on the Little Colorado River near their own country, where they would be contented and could to a large extent provide for themselves. The continuing controversy between the general and the superintendent obstructed any smooth operation of the reservation.[39]

39. Steck to William P. Dole, December 10, 1863, and October 10, 1864, CIA Report, 1864, serial 1220, pp. 324–31, 351–52. See also Edmund J. Danziger, Jr., "The Steck-

Even without the squabbling, there were problems on the reservation. The Navajos, used to a largely pastoral existence, objected to being cooped up on farms, with no provisions for extensive flocks and herds. They objected to Carleton's plans to have them live in concentrated villages, when they were used to smaller and more mobile units of habitation. But it was the forces of a harsh nature that ultimately destroyed the Bosque Redondo experiment. It is possible that with good crops and thus adequate food supplies the discontent of the Indians could have been overcome. But year after year the crops failed, destroyed by insects or drought. Goods supplied by the government were never adequate, and reduced rations were frequently the lot of the Indians. The Navajos were destitute, demoralized, and weakened by disease—far from the happy farmers that Carleton had predicted. Nor was the general able to develop his plans for education.[40] The reservation life, moreover, did not bring an end to Indian raiding in New Mexico, for dissident Apaches and Navajos still struck the settlements, and as conditions worsened at the Bosque Redondo, members of both tribes slipped away to join in the depredations.

To add to Carleton's troubles there were political murmurings against him in New Mexico Territory. The huge demand for supplies at Fort Sumner raised prices in the territory, and Carleton had to bear the brunt of the criticism. The Santa Fe *New Mexican*, a Republican newspaper fighting the Democrats who supported Carleton, ran numerous articles criticizing the general, and the legislature petitioned the federal government for his removal.[41] Early in January 1865, Carleton struck back in the propaganda war with a pamphlet entitled *To the People of New Mexico*, in which he presented his reasons for establishing the reservation. He noted the failure of all past attempts to subjugate and pacify the Navajos and declared that his plan was logically the best—as plain "as that two and two make four." Then he answered point by point the criticisms that had been directed at

---

Carleton Controversy in Civil War New Mexico," *Southwestern Historical Quarterly* 74 (October 1970): 189–203.

40. In pleading for funds for schools, Carleton wrote to the secretary of the interior: "The education of these children is the fundamental idea on which must rest all our hopes of making the Navajoes a civilized and Christian people. . . . You can figure to your own mind, 3,000 intelligent boys and girls with no one to teach them to read or write. Here is a field for those who are philanthropic which is ample enough to engage their attention and be the object of their charities for many years." Carleton to the secretary of the interior, March 30, 1865, *Condition of the Indian Tribes*, p. 224.

41. Long extracts from the *New Mexican* are printed with commentary in William A Keleher, *Turmoil in New Mexico, 1846–1868* (Santa Fe: Rydal Press, 1952) pp. 440–58. Extracts from the memorial of the legislature, January 21, 1866, are printed ibid., pp. 455–56. Keleher's book also contains a great many documents dealing with the whole New Mexico Indian problem; see pp. 275–512.

him. In the end he urged the New Mexicans to "wait patiently and hopefully until this great experiment has been thoroughly tested."[42]

The "great experiment" failed. New crop disasters precluded cutting the
tremendous costs of maintaining the reservation Indians, and the dissatisfaction of the Navajos increased. On December 21, 1866, General Ulysses
S. Grant instructed the commander of the Department of the Missouri to
turn over the Navajos, "now held as prisoners" at the Bosque Redondo, to
the Indian Office, but it was ten months before the actual transfer was accomplished on October 21, 1867. By that time General Carleton had given
up his command in New Mexico for service in the Department of Texas.
The Indian Office, unfortunately, was even less prepared financially than
the War Department to continue the operation, and it announced at the
end of 1867 that it was prepared to take care of the Indians at the Bosque
Redondo for only three months and then additional appropriations would
be necessary.[43] The New Mexico superintendent, A. B. Norton, who had
been appointed in February 1866, described the dismal failure of the
reservation:

> The soil is cold, and the alkali in the water destroys it. The corn crop
> this year is a total failure. Last year 3,000 bushels only was raised in
> 3,000 acres, and year before last six thousand bushels; continually
> growing worse instead of better. The self-sustaining properties of the
> soil are all gone. The Indians now dig up the muskite [mesquite] root
> for wood, and carry it upon their galled and lacerated backs for 12
> miles. . . . What a beautiful selection is this for a reservation. It has
> cost the government millions of dollars, and the sooner it is aban-
> doned and the Indians removed the better.

Norton insisted that the Indians stayed there only by force. "Free them
from military control and fear," he said, "and they would leap therefrom as
the bird from its open cage." His strong recommendation was to send them
back to their homeland.[44]

Congress authorized a Peace Commission in 1867, which, though mainly
concerned with the hostile tribes on the southern and northern plains, also

---

42. Gerald E. Thompson, ed., "'To the People of New Mexico': Gen. Carleton De-
fends the Bosque Redondo," *Arizona and the West* 14 (Winter 1972): 347–66.

43. Thompson, *Army and the Navajo*, pp. 123–50. See CIA Report, 1867, serial 1326,
part 2, p. 12.

44. Norton to N. G. Taylor, August 24, 1867, CIA Report, 1867, serial 1326, part 2,
p. 190. The problems of supplying subsistence at the Bosque Redondo were the concern
of the commissary general of subsistence, who wrote on January 16, 1868, that reports
from his subordinates "clearly indicate that the selection of that location as a place for
the attempt to civilize these Indians was unfortunate, and that it ought not to be further
continued, but that some more suitable location should be selected and the Indians
transferred to it." *House Executive Document* no. 248, 40–2, serial 1341, p. 8.

turned its attention to the Navajos. General William T. Sherman and Samuel Tappan, members of the commission who were sent to the Bosque Redondo, met with the Indians in late May 1868 and heard from them about the terrible conditions on the reservation and their earnest desires to return home. They could see for themselves the tragedy of the enforced stay at Fort Sumner, and on June 1 they signed a treaty with the Navajo chiefs providing for the Indians' return west. Boundaries were set for a reservation there; $150,000 was provided for removal and for the purchase of livestock; and all the customary stipulations for advancing the Indians in civilization were included.[45]

There was little problem in the return trip of the Navajos to their old lands, for they were eager to go, and they rejoiced as they saw the familiar landmarks. But it was not a simple return to the past, for the years at the Bosque Redondo left an indelible mark on the tribe. The Indians' clothing and housing had been influenced by the close contact with whites on the reservation, and a new sense of tribal unity had been fostered. More fundamentally, the Navajos put behind them their longtime raiding and depredations and settled on the reservation to work out their future. There was never again a Navajo war.[46]

SAND CREEK

When the Indians in Minnesota rose up against the white settlers in 1862, there was great consternation, for whites feared a widespread conspiracy among the Indians to attack all along the frontier while the nation was

45. John L. Kessell, "General Sherman and the Navajo Treaty of 1868: A Basic and Expedient Misunderstanding," *Western Historical Quarterly* 12 (July 1981): 251–72; Thompson, *Army and the Navajo*, pp. 151–57; Kappler, pp. 1015–20. The pervasiveness of the civilization policy of the government is seen here. Although the situation of the Navajos in New Mexico was quite different from that of the northern plains tribes who signed the Treaty of Fort Laramie in 1868, the provisions for selecting homesteads, for school attendance, and the like were almost identical.

46. Thompson, *Army and the Navajo*, pp. 158–65, analyzes the effects of the Bosque Redondo experience. An authoritative study of the Navajos, in a much-quoted statement, asserted in 1946: "Fort Sumner was a major calamity to The People; its full effects upon their imagination can hardly be conveyed to white readers. Even today it seems impossible for any Navaho of the older generation to talk for more than a few minutes on any subject without speaking of Fort Sumner. Those who were not there themselves heard so many poignant tales from their parents that they speak as if they themselves had experienced all the horror of the 'Long Walk,' the illness, the hunger, the homesickness, the final return to their desolated land. One can no more understand Navaho attitudes—particularly toward white people—without knowing of Fort Sumner than he can comprehend Southern attitudes without knowing of the Civil War." Clyde Kluckhohn and Dorothea Leighton, *The Navaho* (Cambridge: Harvard University Press, 1946), pp. 9–10.

engaged in the great struggle of the Civil War. There were, in fact, scattered raids along the emigrant and mail routes crossing the plains, and the general restlessness among the Sioux, Cheyennes, and Arapahos worried the Indian Office and the War Department and unnerved the territorial officials in the West, even though there was no general uprising.[47]

In 1861, at Fort Wise on the upper Arkansas, peaceful chiefs, including Black Kettle and White Antelope of the Cheyennes and Little Raven of the Arapahos, had agreed to give up the lands assigned them in the Treaty of Fort Laramie of 1851 and accept a reservation along the Arkansas. The land of the reservation was to be allotted in severalty to individual members of the tribes in order to promote "settled habits of industry and enterprise." The treaty provided annuities for fifteen years, totalling $450,000, to be spent at the discretion of the secretary of the interior for agricultural development among the tribes, and land for the support of schools. The Indians who signed the treaty agreed to induce the portions of the tribes not represented to join them in this great step toward civilization.[48]

The chiefs who agreed to the Fort Wise Treaty had no success in drawing others to such a radical change in their way of life, and most of the Indians continued to rely on hunting the buffalo that still roamed between the Platte and the Arkansas. Governor John Evans of Colorado Territory hoped to draw all the Indians to a great council in September 1863, where they would agree to settle on the upper Arkansas reservation, but no one appeared, for the traditional chiefs rejected the concept of the treaty. With the failure of the council, Evans expected and planned for war.[49] In this aggressive policy he was eagerly joined by the military commander of the District of Colorado, Colonel John M. Chivington, the hero of Glorieta

---

Henry F. Dobyns and Robert C. Euler, in *The Navajo People* (Phoenix: Indian Tribal Series, 1972), pp. 35–36, assert: "'The Long Walk' became a central fact of Navajo psychology for the next century, the foundation stone of Navajo-White relationships, and a fundamental conceptual watershed between the remote and increasingly meaningless past, and the actuality of United States domination. The United States forcefully pacified the Navajos and their 'Long Walk' drove that fact home to them."

47. The military action on the plains is described in Utley, *Frontiersmen in Blue*, pp. 281–99, and in Donald J. Berthrong, *The Southern Cheyennes* (Norman: University of Oklahoma Press, 1963), pp. 174–244. The Indian Office's concern is treated in Danziger, *Indians and Bureaucrats*, pp. 21–47. An excellent firsthand account of the guarding of the telegraph lines and the emigrant trail west of Fort Laramie is provided in William E. Unrau, ed., *Tending the Talking Wire: A Buck Soldier's View of Indian Country, 1863–1866* (Salt Lake City: University of Utah Press, 1979).

48. Kappler, pp. 807–11. This treaty is a splendid example of the government's sincere but unreasonable expectations of inducing the nomadic plains Indians to settle down on individual lots as agriculturalists.

49. A scholarly biography of Evans that is favorable to the governor is Harry E. Kelsey, Jr., *Frontier Capitalist: The Life of John Evans* (Denver: State Historical Society of Colorado and Pruett Publishing, 1969); see pp. 115–53.

Pass. Chivington, a Methodist minister turned soldier and politician, enjoyed unusual autonomy while his superiors were occupied with the Civil War.

The Civil War did not seriously interrupt the great migration of people to the West. The explosion of the mining frontier that followed the strikes in Colorado in 1858 continued unabated and largely unconcerned with the dramatic events taking place in the East. Stage and freight lines moved west across Kansas, and the burgeoning traffic of men and materials continued to cut sharply into the hunting grounds of the Indians, who reacted with sporadic raids on stations and settlements. Although the raids were often isolated and of limited destruction, the depredations over a wide area made it difficult to separate hostile Indians from peaceful ones. It was enough to alarm the Colorado settlements to the point of panic, and Evans and Chivington urged military action to crush the offending Indians and restore security to the territory.

One group of Cheyennes under Black Kettle and White Antelope, joined by a small number of Arapahos, wanted peace with the whites. These Indians met with Governor Evans and Colonel Chivington at Camp Weld near Denver on September 28, 1864. The whites sought only to determine the attitude of the Indians and made no formal peace arrangements, but their remarks were interpreted by the chiefs to mean peace, and the Indians turned in their arms at Fort Lyon (the former Fort Wise) and moved north to a camp along Sand Creek. There on the morning of November 29 they were attacked without warning by Colonel Chivington with troops of the First Colorado Cavalry and one-hundred-day enlistees of the Third Colorado Cavalry. Black Kettle raised an American flag and a white flag before his tent to indicate the peaceful nature of the camp, and White Antelope stood with his arms folded in a peaceful gesture as the whites advanced, but to no avail. The soldiers slaughtered the defenseless Indians in a most brutal manner, killing men, women, and children indiscriminately and mutilating in revolting fashion the bodies of those who fell. Black Kettle and others escaped, but about one hundred and fifty Indians, including White Antelope, were killed in this Sand Creek Massacre.[50]

50. The literature on Sand Creek is extensive, for the complexity of the event and of its origins has puzzled and intrigued historians and popular writers. Useful accounts are Stan Hoig, *The Sand Creek Massacre* (Norman: University of Oklahoma Press, 1961); Raymond G. Carey, "The Puzzle of Sand Creek," *Colorado Magazine* 41 (Fall 1964): 279–98; Janet Lecompte, "Sand Creek," ibid., pp. 315–35; and Lonnie J. White, "From Bloodless to Bloody: The Third Colorado Cavalry and the Sand Creek Massacre," *Journal of the West* 6 (October 1976): 535–81. For a discussion of the historical controversies about Sand Creek, see Michael A. Sievers, "Sands of Sand Creek Historiography," *Colorado Magazine* 49 (Spring 1972): 116–42; background information is supplied in William E. Unrau, "A Prelude to War," ibid., 41 (Fall 1964): 299–313, and Harry Kelsey, "Background to Sand Creek," ibid. 45 (Fall 1968): 279–300.

The atrocities at Sand Creek were celebrated with jubilation in Denver, where the returning volunteers were cheered in the streets and in the theaters as they displayed the grisly trophies of the campaign. But the savage treatment of the peaceful Indians brought nothing but revulsion and outcry in the East. There was no dearth of information, for three formal investigations of the event collected extensive testimony and spread it before the public in official reports. Here was a barbaric affair that sickened those who had hoped for Christian treatment of the Indians.

First on the scene was the Joint Committee on the Conduct of the War, which was directed by the House of Representatives on January 10, 1865, to investigate Sand Creek. In March the committee heard testimony in Washington, gathered affidavits, correspondence, and official reports, and added testimony from Chivington in Denver. The report, signed by Senator Benjamin F. Wade, was a devastating condemnation. Its description of the massacre was lurid and its criticism harsh. The soldiers, it said, "indulged in acts of barbarity of the most revolting character; such, it is to be hoped, as never before disgraced the acts of men claiming to be civilized." It spoke of the "fiendish malignity and cruelty of the officers who had so sedulously and carefully plotted the massacre" and accused Chivington of deliberately planning and executing "a foul and dastardly massacre which would have disgraced the veriest savage among those who were the victims of his cruelty."[51] Then a military fact-finding commission led by Samuel F. Tappan met in Denver to investigate the conduct of Colonel Chivington.[52]

At the same time the Joint Special Committee of Congress, headed by Senator Doolittle, undertook its study of the condition of the western Indians. One part of the committee, assigned to study Kansas, the Indian Territory, and the territories of Colorado, New Mexico, and Utah, made a special investigation of Sand Creek. It, too, took testimony in Washington in March and then traveled west to Fort Riley, Fort Lyon, and Denver, where interviews were held with participants and other interested parties.[53]

The voluminous hearings furnished tremendous ammunition for those who were aghast at the government's handling of Indian affairs and wanted immediate reform. No matter that the testimony on Sand Creek was often contradictory, that evidence was admitted without any critical norms, and that the investigators made no claim to objectivity.[54] No matter that the

51. "Massacre of Cheyenne Indians," in Report of the Joint Committee on the Conduct of the War, *Senate Report* no. 142, 38–2, serial 1214, pp. iii–v. Appended to the report are more than one hundred pages of testimony.

52. "Proceedings of a Military Commission Convened by Special Orders No. 23, Headquarters District of Colorado, Denver, Colorado Territory, Dated February 1, 1865, in the Case of Colonel J. M. Chivington, First Colorado Cavalry," *Senate Executive Document* no. 26, 39–2, serial 1277, pp. 2–228.

53. "The Chivington Massacre," *Condition of the Indian Tribes*, pp. 26–98.

54. Carey, "Puzzle of Sand Creek," pp. 297–98, points out the weaknesses in the

attack was undertaken by local troops and was not the result of official United States policy or plans. The Sand Creek Massacre became a cause célèbre, a never-to-be-forgotten symbol of what was wrong with United States treatment of the Indians, which reformers would never let fade away and which critics today still hold up to view.[55]

Sand Creek intensified Indian hostilities on the plains if it did not, indeed, set off new Indian warfare. Black Kettle and others who escaped were aided by the Northern Cheyennes and Arapahos and by the Comanches and Kiowas, and the Indians fought off the troops sent out to quiet them. The army planned an extensive campaign, but humanitarian outcries over Sand Creek and the desire of the Indians themselves for peace led to negotiations. A United States commission met with chiefs of the Cheyennes and Arapahos, Comanches, Kiowas, and Kiowa-Apaches on the Little Arkansas River. On October 14, 1865, the Cheyennes and Arapahos present signed a treaty in which they agreed to give up their lands in Colorado and accept a reservation which lay partly in Kansas and partly in the Indian Territory. Although they were permitted to range over their old lands, they agreed not to disturb roads, military posts, and towns of the whites. The government agreed to pay annuities for forty years. Three days later a similar agreement was concluded with the Kiowa-Apaches, and on the following day one with the Comanches and Kiowas, who were to get a reservation in the Indian Territory and in the panhandle of Texas. The treaties, although they brought a temporary peace, did not solve the problem because the reservations to be established never materialized. The control of Texas over its lands nullified the agreement with the Comanches and Kiowas, and Kansas refused to allow a reservation within its boundaries.[56]

At the end of the Civil War, when full attention could once more be directed to Indian problems, the nation was ready for a major overhaul of Indian policy.

---

techniques of the groups that investigated Sand Creek. He concludes: "Not one of the examining bodies can be credited with having done a reputable job of distinguishing between the valid testimony of eye-witnesses and the second-hand accounts of special pleaders, or of cutting through the jungle of half-truths, exaggerations, and untruths to determine, beyond reasonable doubt, what actually happened before, at, and after Sand Creek."

55. The Sand Creek Massacre gets emphatic treatment, for example, in Helen Hunt Jackson, *A Century of Dishonor* (New York: Harper and Brothers, 1881), pp. 343–58, and Dee Brown, *Bury My Heart at Wounded Knee* (New York: Holt, Rinehart and Winston, 1970), pp. 67–102. For a novelized treatment, see Michael Straight, *A Very Small Remnant* (New York: Alfred A. Knopf, 1963).

56. Kappler, pp. 887–95; Berthrong, *Southern Cheyennes*, pp. 224–44; William H. Leckie, *The Military Conquest of the Southern Plains* (Norman: University of Oklahoma Press, 1963), pp. 23–26.

CHAPTER 18

The Indian System
and Its Critics

Commissioner Dole and the Reservation System.

Protests against the Indian System.

Proposals for Military Control.

Lincoln's Republican administration, replacing the long rule of the Democrats (broken only by the Whig interlude of Zachary Taylor and Millard Fillmore) was much concerned about political patronage, and the Department of the Interior was full of rich plums. Caleb B. Smith, picked by Lincoln to be secretary of the interior, was an Indiana lawyer and politician who led his state's delegation to the Republican National Convention in Chicago in 1860, gave a seconding speech for Lincoln's nomination, and worked hard to deliver Indiana to Lincoln in the election. He had no real interest in the job or in the Washington bureaucracy, knew nothing about Indian affairs, and resigned as soon as an opportunity presented itself. Smith left much of the work of the Interior Department in the hands of John Palmer Usher, also from Indiana, who had been appointed assistant secretary of the interior in November 1861 and who succeeded him as secretary in January 1863. Usher was more interested in railroad affairs than in Indian matters, and though he appeared to hope sincerely for the welfare of the Indians, he did little or nothing to counteract the political and economic pressures that impinged upon Indian interests.[1]

1. On Smith, see Louis J. Bailey, "Caleb Blood Smith," *Indiana Magazine of History* 29 (September 1933): 213–39, and Richard J. Thomas, "Caleb Blood Smith: Whig Orator and Politician—Lincoln's Secretary of Interior" (Ph.D. dissertation, Indiana University, 1969). A generally favorable biography of Usher is Elmo R. Richardson and Alan W.

COMMISSIONER DOLE AND THE RESERVATION SYSTEM

The focus of federal Indian affairs during the Civil War era was William P. Dole, who served as commissioner of Indian affairs during the whole of Lincoln's administration—a longer term than any commissioner until William A. Jones (1897–1904). Dole, like Smith and Usher, had been a longtime resident of Indiana, although he had moved to Illinois in 1854, and he, like them, got his appointment as a reward for active campaigning for Lincoln. He was a personal friend of the president, and no doubt Lincoln agreed with his major Indian policies and actions. Although he knew nothing about Indians when he entered office, he took his responsibilities seriously and was considerably more than a political hack, despite his eager appointment of relatives and political friends to offices within his patronage. It was he who faced the crucial issues of the Confederate Indians, the refugees from the Indian Territory, the Minnesota Sioux outbreak, and long-continuing problems inherited from earlier administrations.[2]

The basic concern of Dole's administration was the extension and reform of the reservation system. In this he was no doubt influenced considerably by Charles Mix, who continued to hold his job as chief clerk in the Indian Office amid the political vicissitudes of the times. But Dole also had his own ideas. He wanted to isolate the Indian from contact with white settlements, and he wrote in his first annual report: "There seems to be no means by which he can be secured from falling an easy victim to those vices and temptations which are perhaps the worst feature of our civilization, and to which he seems to have an almost irresistible inclination." He noted that the multiplication of small reservations, notably in California and in Kansas, meant that the Indians would soon be entirely surrounded by whites. His recommendation was to concentrate the In-

---

Farley, *John Palmer Usher, Lincoln's Secretary of the Interior* (Lawrence: University of Kansas Press, 1960). The authors conclude, p. 63: "In dealing with the Indian tribes, he could not free himself from the traditional bonds of politics and patronage or resist the pressure of local attitudes." A harsh picture of Usher is presented in David A. Nichols, *Lincoln and the Indians: Civil War Policy and Politics* (Columbia: University of Missouri Press, 1978).

2. Because Dole managed Indian affairs, studies of government relations with the Indians during the Civil War concentrate on him. The most useful ones are those of Harry Kelsey: "William P. Dole and Mr. Lincoln's Indian Policy," *Journal of the West* 10 (July 1971): 484–92; "William P. Dole, 1861–65," in Robert M. Kvasnicka and Herman J. Viola, eds., *The Commissioners of Indian Affairs, 1824–1977* (Lincoln: University of Nebraska Press, 1979), pp. 89–98; and the manuscript, "Mr. Lincoln's Indian Bureau," a copy of which was kindly furnished me by the author. See also Donovan L. Hofsommer, "William Palmer Dole: Commissioner of Indian Affairs," *Lincoln Herald* 75 (Fall 1973): 97–114.

dians, moving those on the scattered reservations into larger reservations and then excluding all whites except "such soldiers and officers as may be actually required in order to preserve peace among the Indians, enforce the necessary police regulations, instruct the young, and render the necessary aid to adults while acquiring a knowledge of the arts of civilized life."[3] Dole hoped to apply his principle to the Indians in Kansas and went personally to Kansas to treat with them.

The concentrated reservation plan also entered into Dole's consideration of the problems arising from conflicts between the plains Indians and the advancing whites. "The white and the red man cannot occupy territory in common," he asserted in 1864, and he proposed to set aside three to five large blocks of the public domain for Indian use, "selected with especial reference to their adaptation to the peculiar wants and requirements of the Indians, and protected by the most stringent legislation against encroachments by the whites." The Indian Territory looked like the best place to Dole, and he assumed that the Indians who joined the Confederacy would have to make room after the war for other Indians who might be moved there. The congressional action in 1862 that authorized the president to abrogate treaties with the Indians "in a state of actual hostility to the government" opened the possibility of using lands in the Indian Territory for such a concentration.[4] Although Dole himself actually accomplished little, either with the settled Indians in eastern Kansas or with the plains Indians still active in the western part of the state, the policy of concentrating these Indians in the Indian Territory was in the end carried out.

Despite his inexperience, Dole immediately saw that an improvement could be made in the reservation system by recognizing "cattle husbandry as a means of subsistence for the Indians, equal in importance with the tillage of the soil." He realized that the arid conditions west of the hundredth meridian made agriculture a risky business, and he hoped to furnish the Indian, "who is naturally more of a herdsman than a cultivator," with a source of subsistence when crops failed. Treaties with the western tribes like the Shoshonis and Utes made during Dole's administration called specifically for provision of stock for herding or in general for goods judged by the president to be "suitable for their wants and condition either as hunters or herdsmen."[5]

Dole continued his predecessors' drive for allotment of Indian lands. "It seems perfectly manifest to me," he wrote in 1863, "that a policy designed

---

3. CIA Report, 1861, serial 1117, pp. 646–47; CIA Report, 1862, serial 1157, pp. 169–70; CIA Report, 1863, serial 1182, pp. 129–30; CIA Report, 1864, serial 1220, p. 149.

4. CIA Report, 1864, serial 1220, p. 149; 12 *United States Statutes* 528. Dole's views are also expressed in CIA Report, 1862, serial 1157, pp. 179–80.

5. CIA Report, 1861, serial 1117, p. 638; Kappler, pp. 849, 852, 858, 860.

to civilize and reclaim the Indians within our borders, and induce them to adopt the customs of civilization, must of necessity embrace, as one of its most prominent features, the ideas of self-reliance and individual effort, and, as an encouragement to those ideas, the acquisition and ownership of property in severalty." He saw a chance to improve the system, however, by insisting that allotments not be granted indiscriminately but only to an Indian who had demonstrated interest and ability—as "a special mark of the favor and approbation of his 'Great Father,' on account of his good conduct, his industry, and his disposition to abandon the ancient customs of his tribe, and engage in the more rational pursuits of civilization." The treaties negotiated during his administration all had some provision for individual ownership of Indian land.[6]

Dole acted out the role of the Great Father, and part of the role was that of teacher. The education and thereby the civilization of the Indians was not forgotten amid the pressure of other duties, and the place of religion in the process was still a prime consideration. Dole paid attention to the schools in his reports, accepting and promoting the manual labor boarding school as the ideal. He wrote to a friend in 1862:

> The best schools are the labor schools and *the more labor the better*. Book learning is useless to an Indian if he has not habits of industry with it. If he does not work for his living after he leaves school but returns to the chase or depends upon annuities and his wife's labor he is the *worse* for all we have expended on him, generally and very generally, at that. What I want then is a farm with a farmer whose heart is in it to teach the boys to work only mixing enough of books with it for a change and to make it of interest caring very little except that they should be taught to be self-sustaining. I have thought deeply about this . . . and have come to the conclusion that an honest, upright, true-hearted missionary, I care not of what church, who will with his family settle down with or near some of these people and by example and kindness teach them the arts of husbandry &c. &c. will do more good than all the traveling agents in the Union.[7]

Dole made his most significant mark on Indian policy by his insistence on the use of treaties to protect Indian rights. Whatever might be thought about the inappropriateness of dealing with nomadic Indian bands as sovereign nations, Dole was concerned about the question of Indian rights to

---

6. CIA Report, 1863, serial 1182, p. 130; see also CIA Report, 1861, serial 1117, p. 647.

7. Dole to Elijah White, June 9, 1862, Letterbook, Dole Papers, Huntington Library. Dole's reliance on missionaries in educational work is noted in CIA Report, 1861, serial 1117, p. 645.

land, especially in the huge area of the Southwest acquired from Mexico. The commissioner could see little sense in arguing about the Indian title to land in the Mexican Cession, for he believed that the Indians had moral if not legal rights to the land. He met squarely the argument that the Spanish and Mexicans had not recognized title for the nomadic tribes and therefore that the United States should not. "If this position is correct," he said in his report of 1861, "it would seem to follow that the policy so long pursued by our government in negotiating treaties with the Indians, and thus extinguishing their titles to land within our borders, has been radically wrong; for as the Indians occupied the territory of both nations prior to the advent of the European races upon this continent, it seems clear that they held lands in the territory of Mexico and the United States by precisely the same tenure." He believed that the transfer of the lands in the Southwest to the United States placed the Indians "within the protection of the general policy established by the United States for the government of other tribes" and that it would be an anomaly to treat the Indians in the Mexican Cession any differently from other Indians.[8]

The Indians of California, especially, needed attention, and Dole pressed for a just land settlement for them against the opposition of local citizens who did not want to see Indian rights to land secured. He painted a dismal picture of the Indians' condition in California, beset by encroaching whites and with no place of refuge or security. "The great error in our relations with the California Indians," he wrote in 1862, "consists . . . in our refusal to recognize their usufructuary right in the soil, and treat with them for its extinguishment; thereby providing for them means of subsistence until such time as they shall be educated to conform to the widely altered circumstances by which they are surrounded." Dole conceded that it was perhaps too late to make treaties, but he wanted the government to "do voluntarily that justice which we have refused to acknowledge in the form of treaty obligations." But Congress refused to cooperate, and nothing was done for California except a reorganization in 1864 by which the dual superintendencies established in 1860 were replaced by a single superintendent, who was to have charge of no more than four reservations, each with its own agent.[9]

Dole recognized an obligation on the part of the government to provide for destitute Indians—whether there were treaty arrangements calling for

---

8. CIA Report, 1861, serial 1117, p. 637.

9. CIA Report, 1862, serial 1157, p. 191; 12 *United States Statutes* 530; 13 *United States Statutes* 39. For an account of Indian-white conflicts in California during the Civil War, see Leo P. Kibby, "California, the Civil War, and the Indian Problem: An Account of California's Participation in the Great Conflict," part 2, *Journal of the West* 4 (July 1965): 384–403.

support or not. Senator John Sherman of Ohio did not agree, pointing out that no relief was proposed for whites driven out of the South, and asked, "Why, then, should we extend relief to Indians, when no one would call for that relief to loyal white people?" But Dole's concerns were more humane. Where he saw need, as among the refugee Indians in Kansas, Dole spent the money from other Indian accounts and then insisted that Congress pay it back.[10]

Dole busied himself also with questions of Indian trust funds, moneys appropriated in payment of land cessions that were invested, largely in state bonds, by the United States government for the benefit of the Indians. In the previous administration $871,000 of these securities had been stolen (Dole said "abstracted"), and the commissioner wanted them to be replaced. He argued, sensibly enough, that the loss should not be borne by the Indians, who were "dependent pupils and wards of this government," but by the government that had undertaken to invest the funds as guardian and custodian, and he urged that Congress appropriate at least the interest due the Indians on such bonds as a measure of manifest justice and wise policy. He advocated, moreover, the investment of all Indian trust funds in United States bonds rather than in those of the individual states. Congress on July 12, 1862, authorized the secretary of the treasury to credit each of the Indian tribes to which the stolen bonds pertained the sum of those funds, and it appropriated money to pay 5-percent interest on them. But this provision did not apply to the Cherokees and Potawatomis, and at the end of the year Dole recommended similar provisions for them and measures to prevent further "abstraction" of Indian funds. He continued to urge prudent investment and reinvestment of the Indians' money.[11]

PROTESTS AGAINST THE INDIAN SYSTEM

The politicization of the Indian service, which reached some sort of a zenith in Lincoln's administration precisely when the Civil War turned public and official attention away from Indian affairs, and the rampant corruption that accompanied it intensified the abuses that the Indians had long suffered. Although there was no concentrated movement for Indian

10. Kelsey, "Mr. Lincoln's Indian Bureau," pp. 78–82; *Congressional Globe*, 37th Congress, 2d session, p. 2149.

11. CIA Report, 1861, serial 1117, pp. 644, 817; CIA Report, 1862, serial 1157, pp. 194–95; CIA Report, 1863, serial 1182, pp. 156–57; CIA Report, 1864, serial 1220, p. 190; 12 *United States Statutes* 539–40. There is a long report on the stolen bonds in *House Report* no. 78, 36–2, serial 1105. See also George Dewey Harmon, "The Indian Trust Funds, 1797–1865," *Mississippi Valley Historical Review* 21 (June 1934): 29–30.

reform during the war years, private individuals kept the issue alive. Two men were especially insistent: John Beeson, an Oregonian who already had to his credit a long history of agitation on behalf of the Indians, and Protestant Episcopal Bishop of Minnesota Henry Benjamin Whipple.

Beeson was an Englishman who came to America in 1830 and settled in Illinois in 1834. Two decades later he was struck by the "Oregon fever" and moved in 1853. When the Rogue River War broke out between the Indians and the white settlers, Beeson's deep religious convictions led him to defend the Indians and to charge that the war was the result of white aggression. Such nonconformity with frontier attitudes made Beeson's life in Oregon impossible, and he returned to the East, where he devoted much of his time to promotion of Indian causes. He published in New York in 1857 A Plea for the Indians, in which he gave a history of the Oregon war and condemned the white savages for destroying the Indians, and in 1859 he spoke at Fanueil Hall in Boston, where he shared the platform with Edward Everett, Wendell Phillips, and other reformers in an appeal for Indian rights. In the following year he began publication of The Calumet, meant to be a vehicle for promoting reform in Indian affairs. Only one issue of the journal came from the presses, however, for the secession crisis turned attention away from Indian matters.[12]

The Civil War did not curb all of Beeson's activities. Firmly convinced that the war was not caused by slavery but was "an extension of the unneighborly, unChristian, and destructive practice which for generations had been operating against the Aborigines," he insisted that redress of Indian wrongs was "the first step in the order of national reform and self preservation." The reformer was received sympathetically by Lincoln, and in a meeting in 1864 the president told him: "My aged Friend. I have heard your arguments time and again. I have said little but thought much, and you may rest assured that as soon as the pressing matter of this war is settled the Indians shall have my first care and I will not rest untill Justice is done to their and your Sattisfaction."[13] Beeson interviewed other national

12. John Beeson, A Plea for the Indians, with Facts and Features of the Late War in Oregon (New York, 1857; rev. ed., 1859); Beeson, Are We Not Men and Brethren? An Address to the People of the United States (New York: National Indian Aid Office, 1859). For my discussion of Beeson and Whipple, I draw on Francis Paul Prucha, American Indian Policy in Crisis: Christian Reformers and the Indian, 1865–1900 (Norman: University of Oklahoma Press, 1976), pp. 4–10. An autobiographical sketch by Beeson is in Calumet 1 (February 1860): 4–9. A useful sketch of Beeson appears in Robert Winston Mardock, The Reformers and the American Indian (Columbia: University of Missouri Press, 1971), pp. 10–14.

13. Beeson to Lincoln, November 18, 1862, Department of the Interior, Indian Division, Letters Received, Miscellaneous, National Archives, Record Group 48. Lincoln's statement is quoted in Beeson to E. P. Smith, June 25, 1873, OIA LR, Miscellaneous P–520 (M234, reel 466, frame 302).

leaders, memorialized Congress, and organized public meetings in the eastern cities. When his funds ran out, he returned to Oregon in 1865, but his interest in Indian reform flared up periodically as he joined his voice to others who took up the cause of the Indians.[14]

Paralleling Beeson's activities was the more influential agitation of Bishop Whipple, whose stature as an Indian friend eventually made him a correspondent and confidant of important national leaders and whose powerful voice condemning wrongs could not be ignored as could the more fanatical utterances of Beeson. Whipple, after serving in a parish in Rome, New York, and for two years among the poor on the south side of Chicago, was elected the first Protestant Episcopal Bishop of Minnesota in 1859. In 1860 he took up residence at Faribault, which was his home for the rest of his life. Having thus been thrust into contact with both the Chippewas and the Sioux on that still primitive frontier, the new bishop investigated the condition of the Indians and became painfully aware of the injustices in the government's Indian system. He began an active crusade to right the wrongs suffered by the Indians, bombarding government officials all the way up to the president himself with letters and memorials.[15]

Whipple began his campaign while Buchanan was still in office. In a letter to the president he insisted that civilization and Christianization were the only hope for the Indians. He castigated the present condition of the Indian service, with the illegal sale of liquor and corruption prevalent among the traders. He predicted a Sioux uprising unless reforms were forthcoming. "Again and again I had declared publicly," he wrote, "that as certain as any fact in human history, a nation which sowed robbery would reap a harvest of blood."[16]

Whipple renewed his crusade with the Lincoln administration, attempting first to influence Caleb Smith, the new secretary of the interior, and

14. Beeson wrote many letters to government officials, in some of which he sought government employment as a special commissioner to the Indians. Examples are cited in Prucha, *American Indian Policy in Crisis*, p. 6 n. Beeson suggested using phrenology to pick out suitable agents, "such as have the requisite amount of benevolence, conscientiousness and intellect." *Plea for the Indians*, p. 126. In 1875 Beeson again proposed that Indian agents be "tested by the science of phrenology" so that appointments could be based on "native qualities and approved character." Address to the People of the United States, September 23, 1875, copy inclosed in Beeson to President Hayes, October 15, 1877, OIA LR, Miscellaneous (M234, reel 475). In 1862 Beeson suggested that the Indian Office organize a band of Indian singers to travel around the country giving concerts; this would do more to civilize the Indians, he said, "than all the Armies and Missionaries put together." Kelsey, "Mr. Lincoln's Indian Bureau," p. 101.

15. Whipple's career as an Indian reformer can be followed in his autobiography, *Lights and Shadows of a Long Espicopate* (New York: Macmillan Company, 1899), and in the Henry B. Whipple Papers, Minnesota Historical Society.

16. Whipple, *Lights and Shadows*, p. 105; Whipple to Buchanan, April 9, 1860, ibid., pp. 50–53.

Superintendent Clark Thompson and Agent Thomas Galbraith, the new
political appointees in charge of Minnesota Indians.[17] Then he appealed to
President Lincoln himself in a letter of March 6, 1862, writing "freely with
all the frankness with which a Christian bishop has the right to write to
the Chief Ruler of a great Christian Nation." He pointed to the rapid deterioration that had taken place among the tribes since they had signed away
much of their lands in treaties with the United States, and he especially
excoriated the Indian agents, who were selected to uphold the honor and
faith of the government without any attention to their fitness. "The Congressional delegation desires to reward John Doe for party work," the
bishop charged, "and John Doe desires the place because there is a tradition
on the border that an Indian Agent with fifteen hundred dollars a year can
retire upon an ample fortune in four years." He asked for simple honesty,
for agency employees who were men "of purity, temperance, industry, and
unquestioned integrity" rather than "so many drudges fed at the public
crib." He wanted the Indian to be treated as a ward of the government, with
aid in building a house and opening a farm and with adequate schools for
his children. And he insisted that law be provided for the Indians as it was
for the whites. Whipple was not ready to submit a detailed plan for a new
Indian system, but he urged instead that a commission of three men be
appointed to investigate Indian affairs and propose a new plan to remedy
the evils, a commission of men who would be "so high in character that
they are above the reach of political demagogues."[18]

Lincoln graciously acknowledged the communication and passed the
matter to the secretary of the interior, who indicated his agreement with
Whipple. "No one who has any knowledge of the manner in which their
[the Indians'] business is managed," Smith wrote, "can ignore the fact that
they are made victims of the avarice of those who are brought in communication with them, and that the Agents, selected by the United States, to
protect their interests, in many instances become the willing instruments
of designing men, who enrich themselves by obtaining the money which
the government intended should be expended for the benefit of the Indians." But he noted that the agents were usually local men who were not
well known to the president, and he excused himself from further consideration of the matter by sending Whipple's letter to the committees of Indian affairs in the House and Senate, with a recommendation that action
be taken to remedy the situation.[19]

Whipple's main concern was to end the evils caused by political ap-

17. Nichols, *Lincoln and the Indians*, pp. 132–33.
18. Whipple to Lincoln, March 6, 1862, *Lights and Shadows*, pp. 510–14.
19. Lincoln to Whipple, March 27, 1862, and Smith to Whipple, March 31, 1862,
Whipple Papers.

pointment of incompetent and corrupt men in the Indian service, which he believed could be done by the appointment of a commission "of some pure, large hearted & clear headed men to carry into effect the provisions of Congress." But he saw also, as he told Lincoln, "the absolute necessity of providing a government for your Indian wards," so that the good would feel its protection and the bad fear its punishment.[20]

Whipple worked hard with the two senators from Minnesota, Morton S. Wilkinson and Henry M. Rice, and with Representative Cyrus Aldrich, who chaired the House Committee on Indian Affairs. Rice alone seemed sympathetic, and he admitted that the problems would exist "so long as Agents and Superintendents, even Commissioners are appointed as rewards for *political service*." He was not sanguine, however, about correcting the system, and he confessed to Whipple that he feared "the demagogue, the politician, & those *pecuniarally interested*." From Wilkinson and Aldrich the bishop did not get even sympathy, for they openly expressed doubts that the Indians would profit much from any attention. Wilkinson saw no sense in trying to educate or convert the Indians until they had learned habits of industry: "Labor is the great civilizer." Aldrich bluntly told the bishop, "I do no[t] entirely agree with your views with regard to the capacities of the Indian race. . . . It is very questionable to my mind whether under the most favorable circumstances the native Aborigine 'to the manor born' is capable of attaining a high or even mediocre state of civilization." Whipple nevertheless held adamantly to his position. "If the world were against me," he had written to Rice, "I know I am right & I will never yield." He intended to appeal to the people if he could make no headway with Congress or the executive.[21]

The Sioux uprising tragically fulfilled Whipple's premonitions of serious trouble if the Indian system were not reformed. His zeal for the rights and welfare of the Indians was not cooled by the war. He went immediately to the scene of the disaster, taking care of the wounded and comforting the bereaved. He then took a courageous stand in support of the Indians by publishing in the St. Paul newspapers a plea to his fellow citizens not to wreak vengeance on the Indians, whose uprising had been the result of intolerable evils worked upon them by the Indian system. He went personally to Washington to plead with Lincoln for clemency for the Indians condemned to death by the military commission.

Working through Senator Rice, Whipple continued to urge the president

20. Whipple to Smith, April 10, 1862, and Whipple to Lincoln, April 16, 1862, ibid.
21. Separate letters of Whipple to Wilkinson, Rice, and Aldrich, April 30, 1861; Rice to Whipple, April 22 and 26, 1862; Wilkinson to Whipple, May 8, 1862; Aldrich to Whipple, June 12, 1862; Whipple to Rice, April 30, 1862, ibid. Aldrich presented a somewhat more sympathetic attitude toward reform in a letter to Whipple, June 26, 1862, ibid.

to bring about a wholesale reform in Indian affairs. Lincoln heard the appeal and in his state of the union address of December 1, 1862, told Congress: "I submit for your especial consideration whether our Indian system shall not be remodeled. Many wise and good men have impressed me with the belief that this can be profitably done."[22] This favorable reaction encouraged Whipple, who wrote to Lincoln, "With all my heart I thank you for your recommendation to have our whole Indian system reformed. It is a stupendous piece of wickedness and as we fear God ought to be changed." He kept hammering on the idea that a commission should be appointed to set up the reforms. To his cousin, General Henry W. Halleck, he wrote shortly after Lincoln's message: "This Indian system is a sink of iniquity. The President has recommended reform. You have his ear. Do, for the sake of these poor victims of a nation's wrong, ask him to put on it [the commission] something better than politicians."[23]

Lincoln continued to recommend reform in his annual messages, and Commissioner Dole was not unsympathetic. But Congress, too busy with the war and much concerned about vested interests in the current Indian system, took no action.[24] Senator Rice reported ruefully in February 1863: "I have no hope of anything being done to improve the condition of the Indians by this Administration." And Senator Wilkinson justified postponement of action on the basis that he was "greatly perplexed as to the details of the system to be adopted" and that any new system would take long and careful thought. The new representative from Minnesota, Ignatius Donnelly, took up Whipple's cause, but he expected nothing but hostility from those whose frauds he uncovered, and he urged the bishop to keep up his fight to arouse public opinion.[25]

Whipple returned to the charge in October 1864 with a blistering attack on the Indian system in the *North American Review*. It was a long recitation of fraud and corruption on the part of politically appointed men who entered upon their duties "with only one thought, and that is plunder." "The school is a miserable sham," the bishop declared, "the agricultural funds are wasted by improvidence, the annuity goods are lessened by fraud in the purchase or by theft after they are received, and the implements of

22. Fred L. Israel, ed., *The State of the Union Messages of the Presidents, 1790–1966*, 3 vols. (New York: Chelsea House, 1966), 2: 1074. Rice wrote to Whipple after his meeting with Lincoln: "I will do my best—Alas! the poor Indian is kept in a savage state by a great government—and his condition renders him, not an object of pity, but of plunder." Rice to Whipple, November 27, 1862, Whipple Papers.

23. Whipple to Lincoln, December 4, 1862, and Whipple to Halleck, December 4, 1862, Whipple Papers.

24. Messages of December 8, 1863, and December 6, 1864, Israel, *State of the Union Messages*, 2: 1092–93, 1104.

25. Rice to Whipple, February 3, 1863; Wilkinson to Whipple, March 1, 1863; Donnelly to Whipple, June 12, 1864, Whipple Papers.

husbandry are worthless." Whipple continued to insist, moreover, that a system of law should be provided for the Indians. "The Indians have been placed under conditions where their rude patriarchal government is destroyed or cannot be exercised," he charged. "We have recognized them as an independent nation, and then left them without a vestige of government or law. . . . The only human being in the United States who has none of the restraints or protection of law is the treaty Indian."[26]

It would be hard to show that the corruption and fraud in the Indian service was notably worse in the Civil War era than it had been in the 1850s. The insistent demands of Manypenny and others for revision of the intercourse laws for the protection of the Indians from sharpers who cheated them was indication enough of unsavory conditions. But cries for reform were largely unheeded until public opinion on some broad scale picked up the outcries. Bishop Whipple reported that on one of his trips to Washington to plead the Indians' cause before the president and the cabinet, Secretary of War Stanton had said to General Halleck, "What does Bishop Whipple want? If he has come here to tell us of the corruption of our Indian system and the dishonesty of Indian agents, tell him that we know it. But the Government never reforms an evil until the people demand it. Tell him that when he reaches the heart of the American people, the Indians will be saved."[27]

What reached the heart of the American people were spectacular events like the Sioux uprising of 1862 with its massacre of unsuspecting whites— and even more, Sand Creek with its massacre of unsuspecting Indians. The reports of official investigative bodies into the causes of continuous warfare on the plains, coming after the Civil War had ended, energized a reform movement of much broader scope than was possible for the single voice of a John Beeson or a Henry Whipple, though both men, especially Whipple, continued to be heard.

PROPOSALS FOR MILITARY CONTROL

The renewal and continuation of Indian hostilities through the Civil War period made it almost inevitable that the question of military control of Indian affairs should be a vital issue, and transfer of the Indians from the civilian Indian Office to the army was advanced as a practical "reform." Dole fought against any such move. In some cases, of course, he had to

26. Henry B. Whipple, "The Indian System," *North American Review* 99 (October 1864): 452–54.
27. Whipple, *Lights and Shadows*, p. 144. Whipple used this story in his preface to Helen Hunt Jackson's *A Century of Dishonor: A Sketch of the United States Government's Dealings with Some of the Indian Tribes* (New York: Harper and Brothers, 1881).

acquiesce in military management of the Indians. General Carleton's grand scheme for solving the Indian problems in New Mexico by concentrating the Apaches and the Navajos at the Bosque Redondo rested upon army responsibility during most of the experiment. Dole's hands were tied, for the Indian Office had no means at its disposal to give the large numbers of Indians subsistence.

Another challenge, more in theory this time than in practice, came from General Pope, whose encounter with the Indians in Minnesota had made him an instant Indian specialist. While engaged with hostile Indians, Pope's military commanders dealt with the Indians (including prisoners and captives) without much concern for the Indian Office, but Pope also wanted a general overhaul of federal Indian policy. In a letter to General Halleck on September 23, 1863, Pope strongly criticized existing policy and called for agreements with the hostile Indians that would be treaties of peace only, with no purchase of lands and no annuities of any kind. "Such conditions," he said, "only exhibit (in the eyes of the Indians) weakness on the part of the Government, and lead necessarily to the very hostilities they are intended to prevent. They stimulate the cupidity of unscrupulous men, both traders and others, and finally lead to that system of swindling and wrong to the Indians in which have originated nearly all of our Indian difficulties."[28]

Pope's most ambitious statement was the plan he drew up and forwarded to Secretary of War Stanton in February 1864.[29] The general was on strong ground as he painted in black colors the existing conditions of Indian affairs: the evils attendant on avaricious whites surrounding Indian reservations or having contact with more remote Indians who came in each year for annuity payments, the excesses of the liquor trade, and the accumulation of payments made to Indians in the pockets of traders and whiskey dealers. To these abuses he attributed the Indian outbreaks. He asserted that "our Indian policy has totally failed of any humanizing influence over the Indian, has worked him a cruel wrong, and has entailed a very great and useless expense upon the government," and he urged "a radical change in our whole Indian policy." He objected to "the principle of remunerating the Indian for land taken from him."

Pope's plan was twofold. For the "reserve and annuity Indians" along the frontier, he proposed to move them "with or without their consent" to some reservation within the settled portions of the country, take away

---

28. Pope to Halleck, September 23, 1863, *The War of the Rebellion: A Compilation of the Official Records of the Union and Confederate Armies*, 70 vols. (Washington: GPO, 1880–1901), series 1, 22: part 2, pp. 569–70 (hereafter cited as *Official Records*).

29. Pope to Stanton, February 6, 1864, *Official Records*, series 1, 34: part 2, pp. 259–63; the document is also printed in CIA Report, 1864, serial 1220, pp. 568–73.

their arms, stop the payment of their annuities, and spend any money due or appropriated for them in building villages and supplying them with food and clothing. The Indian here "would be placed under the most favorable circumstances to apply to him the influences of civilization, education, and Christianity with hopes of successful results, and without the surroundings which have hitherto made such instruction impossible." Pope hoped that by the second generation the Indians would be humanized and, if not made into good citizens, at least turned into harmless members of the community. "So long as Indians retain their tribal organization, and are treated in their corporate and not their individual capacity, the change of habit and of ideas necessary to effect this result or to humanize the Indians cannot be accomplished, nor can these results ever be obtained under any circumstances until the Indian is no longer an object of cupidity to the whites."

For the "wild Indians" of the West with whom treaties had not yet been made, Pope proposed military control. All these Indians should be gathered at some point beyond the "western limits of the great fertile region between the Mississippi river and the Rocky mountains," where the army would be left to deal with them without treaties and "without the interposition of Indian agents." Pope saw no reason to treat the Indians as sovereign nations with territorial rights. Treat them completely as wards of the government, he insisted, with the western tribes under complete military control and the partially civilized ones cared for far away from the disruptive forces they were encountering on the frontiers.

In addition to these general proposals there were specific proposals for the reform of trade regulations. Pope recognized the obvious fact, repeatedly enunciated by the commissioners of Indian affairs, that the existing trade and intercourse laws were ineffective and unenforcible in much of the Indian country. His solution, again, was tight military control of the traders.[30]

Although many of Pope's ideas—such as the need to educate and assimilate the Indians and the need for revision of the trade laws—had long been espoused by the Indian Office and although Dole was ready to admit that evils existed in the present system, the Indian Office refused to consider the general's plan. Dole at first simply ignored it, but when General Halleck arranged for its publication in the *Army and Navy Journal* and sent his cousin Bishop Whipple to promote the plan with the commissioner and with the president, Dole felt obliged to reply.[31] This he did in his annual report of 1864, in which he printed Pope's plan and his own refutation

30. Pope to Assistant Secretary of War C. A. Dana, September 9, 1864, enclosing Pope to Halleck, May 11, 1864, *Official Records*, series 1, 41: part 3, pp. 124–26.
31. See Halleck to Pope, April 14, 1864, *Official Records*, series 1, 34: part 3, p. 159.

of it. He admitted that serious mistakes had occurred in the management of Indian affairs, that the Indians had suffered great wrongs, and that Indian wars had resulted, but he charged that it would be difficult to demonstrate that any other policy would have had better results. He challenged Pope's assumption that there were lands in the West forever out of the way of white expansion and pointed not only to the immense expense that would be incurred by placing the Indians in areas where there were no means of subsistence but also to the dangers of bringing together mutually hostile tribes. He ridiculed the idea of easily removing Indians from their homelands without their consent, calling attention to the military operations in Florida, Oregon, California, and New Mexico occasioned by such attempts. Nor was Dole convinced that abuses and unwholesome contacts would be obviated by military control. "I have yet to learn," he said, "that the greed of military contractors is any less than is that of contractors drawn from the ranks of civilians; or that camp-followers and the 'hangers-on' around the military posts are more virtuous than are the classes of whites who assemble around our Indian reserves under the present policy."[32]

Dole insisted that it was best to stick with the policy then in effect, which, he declared, had been "gradually improving by experience." The plan of concentrating the Indians on reservations was relatively new and may not have brought all the results intended, but it was "a step in the right direction." He noted that under its operation many of the smaller tribes had been united, and that this was a beginning toward eventual consolidation of the various tribes into a single political organization; but he admitted that it would be a slow process and require patient and persevering effort. He concluded: "I freely confess that the subject is to my mind beset with difficulties, but at the same time am convinced that the object which all profess to seek, viz: ultimate reclamation and civilization of the Indian, is best to be attained by steadily persevering in our present policy, amending it from time to time as experience may suggest, and, as rapidly as may be found practicable, concentrating the Indians upon portions of the public domain suited to their wants and capacities."[33]

Dole's eloquent plea for continuing the treaty system was an outright rejection of Pope's contention that the military should be given arbitrary control of the Indians, to do what was considered necessary with or without their consent. Dole's position was that there should be a mutual understanding between the Indians and whites about the boundaries of the Indian territory, the laws that were to be applied to Indians, and "the reciprocal duties and obligations resting upon each race, whether regarded as

32. Dole to J. P. Usher, April 6, 1864, CIA Report, 1864, serial 1220, pp. 573–75.
33. Ibid., p. 575.

individuals or distinct communities." And he compared two methods by which that mutual understanding could be arrived at:

> First, by availing ourselves of our overwhelming numerical, physical, and intellectual superiority, we may set apart a country for the use of the Indians, prescribe the laws by which they shall be governed, and the rules to be observed in the intercourse of the two races, and compel a conformity on the part of the Indians; or, secondly, we may, as has been the almost universal practice of the government, after resorting to military force only so far as may be necessary in order to induce the Indians to consent to negotiate, bring about this understanding through the instrumentality of treaties to which they are parties, and as such have yielded their assent.[34]

Dole recognized that the overwhelming power of the United States enabled the government to adopt either of these methods, and the use of that power in imposing treaty agreements upon tribes who were not really free to give or withhold assent may have blurred any substantial difference between Dole's two methods. Yet the distinction that Dole saw was based on significant theoretical principles. The military plan advanced by Pope, he argued, entirely ignored the independence of the Indians and reduced them to absolute subjection, whereas the treaty system did not altogether deprive them of "their sense of nationality and independence as a people." Moreover, arbitrary military control would lead the Indians to regard the whites as "merciless despots and tyrants, who have deprived them of their homes and liberties," whereas treaties, although they rested on a recognition that the Indians as belligerents could not cope with the United States, might lead the Indians toward friendship and a gradual appreciation of the advantages and blessings of civilization. Dole asserted that the military plan was put forward for economic rather than humanitarian reasons, and he disputed even the economic benefits of it. He concluded that the advantages of the second method "seem so apparent that I can hardly realize that the former is seriously advocated." He remained firmly convinced that no better system could be found "for the management of the Indians" than the system then followed: "the fixing of the rights, duties, and obligations of each race towards the other through the instrumentality of treaties."[35]

In thus taking an adamant stand against turning the Indians over to the War Department, Dole maintained an essential principle of federal Indian policy at a time when it might have been easy to gain substantial public as well as official support for a transfer. It was an initial victory against a

34. CIA Report, 1864, serial 1220, p. 150.
35. Ibid.

campaign for turning Indian affairs over to military men that was to continue into the post–Civil War decades. More significantly, Dole refused to
consider Pope's recommendation to end the treaty system, cancel annuity
payments, and manage the Indians without in any way seeking their consent or legally establishing Indian rights and government responsibilities.[36]

There were not, then, any radical reforms in Indian affairs in the Civil
War era. The federal government continued and advanced the reservation
system that had been accepted during previous decades as the best solution to the intense problems facing the nation in its relations with the Indian tribes, and Dole and Lincoln met the special crises that arose with
what they believed to be fair-mindedness and humanity. But the public
furor that erupted over Sand Creek as the Civil War ended did not allow for
careful distinctions in placing blame. Commissioner Dole bore much of
the criticism aimed against the evils in Indian affairs, to which the Colorado
massacre called attention, and a few weeks after Lincoln's assassination, he
was forced out of office. Secretary of the Interior Usher also resigned. Andrew Johnson's appointees, James Harlan and Dennis N. Cooley, whose
work we have already seen, filled the offices of secretary of the interior and
commissioner of Indian affairs.

36. Pope's plan and Dole's rejection of it are discussed in Richard N. Ellis, *General
Pope and U.S. Indian Policy* (Albuquerque: University of New Mexico Press, 1970),
pp. 31–51. I do not agree with Ellis's strong charge that Dole "completely distorted
Pope's proposals."

The
Peace Policy

The Civil War was an economic conflict between competing agrarian and industrial societies and a great nationalistic drive on the part of the North to crush rising southern nationalism and thus preserve the Union. But it was also a great Christian crusade, a moral mandate fulfilled, a wiping away of the hideous blot of sinful slavery from the conscience of the nation. The emotional intensity of the northern endeavor was heightened still more by the religious dimensions of the struggle. It was God's work: "Mine eyes have seen the glory of the coming of the Lord. He is trampling out the vintage where the grapes of wrath are stored." The evil of chattel slavery, holding in bondage black brothers made in God's image, fired the abolitionists. Rejected at first by more prudent and traditional men, abolitionism spread in subtle and diverse ways. No matter how much politicians might protest that they urged no moves against slavery where it was protected by the Constitution, and that it was only the extension of slavery they abhorred, the question of the ultimate morality of slavery could not be quieted. Even before the Emancipation Proclamation it was clear that the Civil War was indeed a war to end slavery and to recover for the Christian nation the uprightness—in its own eyes and in the eyes of the world—it had lost by clinging to the monstrous practice of human bondage. In a Senate speech in January 1864, Senator James R. Doolittle of Wisconsin asserted his belief that "we shall come out of this struggle with slavery utterly done away with; that we shall be redeemed and regenerated as a people; that we shall stand hereafter, as we have stood heretofore, in the vanguard of the civilized nations—the power of all other powers on earth."[1] The Civil War, despite the carnage and destruction, was, in the minds of many, America's finest hour. The war reinforced the evangelical aspiration and sentiments of the nation, touching many with a new revivalist ardor that could not be suddenly cooled by Appomattox.

The end of the Civil War freed new energies, and America embarked upon expansion and development of a scope that few in antebellum days would have thought possible. Northern industry, stimulated by the war and encouraged by sympathetic and benevolent legislators, absorbed the energies and talents of many men, and the exuberance that came when the crushing burden of war was removed covered over the traumas of that past event. Exploitation of land and mineral resources moved at new speeds, and transcontinental railroads, rapidly becoming a reality, tied the nation together in new unity.

Evangelical reformism thrived in this new and ebullient atmosphere. The evils of slavery had been crushed, and radical reconstruction, with new amendments to the Constitution and military occupation of the defeated South, sought to guarantee a secure place in the nation for the freedmen—who also engaged the interests of the benevolent (Generals O. O. Howard, Samuel C. Armstrong, and Clinton B. Fisk come to mind) who were working to ease the transition from the life of a slave to that of a free citizen of the republic.

Yet evils still abounded that reforming spirits could not ignore. One of the most obvious and pressing at war's end was the condition of the Indians, now made manifest as never before. Even before the war had run its course, the trail of post–Civil War Indian reform had begun, for the massacre at Sand Creek in November 1864 became a popular symbol of what was wrong in the Indian service, and a great humanitarian outcry was the result.

The concern was fed by official reports of injustice toward the Indians, and the nation witnessed an upsurge of Christian sentiment demanding Christian justice for the Indians that would be proper to a Christian nation. This was a restatement of the paternal concern for Indian welfare that had existed for decades, and the program demanded little that was new. What was new was the totality of the agitation against perceived wrongs and the intensity with which evangelical Christians moved into Indian affairs. The Indian Office, officially charged with managing Indian affairs, seemed incapable of the task in the period of chaos and crisis. Congressional committees undertook to investigate Indian wrongs, and a carefully picked

1. William Frederick Doolittle, comp., *The Doolittle Family in America* (Cleveland: Sayers and Waite Printing Company, 1901–1908), p. 673.

special commission of civilians and military officers was established to propose and implement remedies.

The formal answer to the demands for reform came in the administration of Ulysses S. Grant. It has been called "Grant's peace policy," but the principles it embodied antedated 1869 and continued to the end of the century and beyond. The peace policy was almost as many-faceted as the Indian problem it hoped to solve. Basically it was a state of mind, a determination that since the old ways of dealing with the Indians had not succeeded, a new emphasis on kindness and justice was in order. Because states of mind do not begin and end abruptly with the passage of a law, the establishment of a commission, or a military disaster, but change more subtly and grow until they dominate an era, the peace policy cannot be precisely dated, nor can it be rigidly defined.[2]

An official description of the policy in its early days appeared in a statement in 1873 by Grant's secretary of the interior, Columbus Delano, that listed the aims and purposes of the administration's policy. In the first place, Delano noted, the policy aimed to place the Indians on reservations. There they could be kept from contact with frontier settlements and could be taught the arts of agriculture and other pursuits of civilization through the aid of Christian organizations cooperating with the federal government, and there "humanity and kindness may take the place of barbarity and cruelty." Second, the policy sought to combine with such humane treatment "all needed severity, to punish them for their outrages according to their merits, thereby teaching them that it is better to follow the advice of the Government, live upon reservations and become civilized, than to continue their native habits and practices." Third, it meant a determination to see that the supplies furnished to the Indians were of high quality and reasonably priced so that funds appropriated for the Indians would not

2. I use here material from Francis Paul Prucha, *American Indian Policy in Crisis: Christian Reformers and the Indian, 1865–1900* (Norman: University of Oklahoma Press, 1976), pp. 30–33. A number of other historians have studied the peace policy or particular aspects of it, and each has his own definition of what the policy included. The following are important works: Robert H. Keller, Jr., *American Protestantism and United States Indian Policy, 1869–82* (Lincoln: University of Nebraska Press, 1983); Peter J. Rahill, *The Catholic Indian Missions and Grant's Peace Policy, 1870–1884* (Washington: Catholic University of America Press, 1953); Robert Lee Whitner, "The Methodist Episcopal Church and Grant's Peace Policy: A Study of the Methodist Agencies, 1870–1882" (Ph.D. dissertation, University of Minnesota, 1959). The peace policy is discussed thoroughly as well in these books: Henry E. Fritz, *The Movement for Indian Assimilation, 1860–1890* (Philadelphia: University of Pennsylvania Press, 1963); Robert Winston Mardock, *The Reformers and the American Indian* (Columbia: University of Missouri Press, 1971); and Loring Benson Priest, *Uncle Sam's Stepchildren: The Reformation of United States Indian Policy, 1865–1887* (New Brunswick: Rutgers University Press, 1942).

be squandered. Fourth, through the aid of religious organizations, it aimed to procure "competent, upright, faithful, moral, and religious" agents to distribute the goods and to aid in uplifting the Indians' culture. Finally, "through the instrumentality of the Christian organizations, acting in harmony with the Government," it intended to provide churches and schools that would lead the Indians to understand and appreciate "the comforts and benefits of a Christian civilization and thus be prepared ultimately to assume the duties and privileges of citizenship." Forty years later, a formal description of the peace policy spoke broadly of "such legislation and administration in Indian affairs as by peaceful methods should put an end to Indian discontent, make impossible Indian wars, and fit the great body of Indians to be received into the ranks of American citizens."[3]

Underlying this new departure in Indian policy was the conscious intent of the government to turn to religious groups and religion-minded men for the formulation and administration of Indian policy. The peace policy might just as properly have been labeled the religious policy. Building on the long history of close relations between the federal government and missionary groups in Indian matters, the nation now went far beyond simple cooperation of church and state in educational and religious activities. It welcomed official church societies and church-related individuals into fuller partnership; and to a large extent these groups came to dominate official government policy and administration of Indian affairs, at first by direct participation, then by stirring up and channeling public opinion. In turning to religious organizations, the federal government abdicated much of its responsibility. Specific governmental functions were handed over to the churches, a development that indicated not only the failure of the governmental processes in regard to the "Indian question" but also the pervasive moral and religious influences on the national outlook.

Paradoxically, the period in which the peace policy was inaugurated was a time of Indian wars, and military force was employed to crush the resisting tribes. The need for troops in active service against Indians led to a vociferous demand that all Indian affairs be turned over to the army, which might be able to better control and manage the Indians than the civilian champions of the peace policy could and which might end the fraud that continued to mark the provision of goods to the Indians. The drive to transfer the Indian Office from the Interior Department to the War Department nearly succeeded. That the movement was halted is an indication of the depth of the nation's Christian humanitarianism.

3. Report of the Secretary of the Interior, 1873, *House Executive Document* no. 1, part 5, 43–1, serial 1601, pp. iii–iv; Merrill E. Gates, "Peace Policy," in Frederick Webb Hodge, ed., *Handbook of American Indians North of Mexico*, 2 vols. (Washington: GPO, 1907–1910), 2: 218–19.

The administrative structures of the peace policy introduced under Grant, it is true, largely failed, but the spirit of the policy did not die with them. The secretary of the interior in 1882 denied that the peace policy was connected with or dependent upon formal church participation in managing Indian affairs. "I do not know what you mean by the peace policy," he told the secretary of the Methodist board of missions. ". . . If however, you mean that peace is better than war and that civilization and labor are better for the Indian than his past and present condition, I agree with you."[4] In the decade and a half from 1865 to 1880 the principles of peace and civilization were refined and reformulated into a consistent and generally agreed upon program that in the following two decades would be enacted into law.

4. Henry M. Teller to J. M. Reid, August 5, 1882, *Report of the Board of Indian Commissioners*, 1882, p. 53.

CHAPTER 19

Stirrings
of Reform

Doolittle Committee.

Indian Peace Commission.

Civilization for the Indians.

Reform Impulses.

As demands for Indian reform burst out with new energy, a full-scale reform movement developed that substantially influenced relations between the federal government and the Indian tribes. Congress prepared the way with formal investigations of evil conditions in the West.[1]

DOOLITTLE COMMITTEE

On March 3, 1865, Congress created the Joint Special Committee "to inquire into the present condition of the Indian tribes, and especially into the manner in which they are treated by the civil and military authorities of the United States."[2] The committee, composed of three senators and four representatives, was chaired by Senator James R. Doolittle and is commonly called the Doolittle Committee. The chairman, a longtime active Baptist described by his family biographer as "the ideal type of cultured, Christian gentleman," was a good choice to head such a reform committee. He was a deeply religious man who saw in the American republic the

1. This chapter uses material from Francis Paul Prucha, *American Indian Policy in Crisis: Christian Reformers and the Indian, 1865–1900* (Norman: University of Oklahoma Press, 1976), pp. 14–29.
2. 13 *United States Statutes* 572–73.

special guidance of Divine Providence and who boldly proclaimed that the Declaration of Independence was "the new gospel of man's redemption" and the Fourth of July "the birthday of God's Republic, second only in history to the birth of Christ."[3]

Doolittle's committee split into three groups and toured the West to investigate conditions among the Indians. In addition, the committee sent a detailed questionnaire to military commanders, Indian agents, and others acquainted with the West asking about causes of the deterioration of the Indians, the best forms of land tenure, the effects of schools and missions, the use of annuities, and whether the Indian Office should be transferred to the War Department. The voluminous answers were attached to the committee's report, which, after long delay, was submitted on January 26, 1867. The committee noted that, except for the tribes in the Indian Territory, the Indian population was rapidly declining as the result of disease, intemperance, war, and the pressure of white settlement. The wars, it asserted, came in large part because of "the aggression of lawless whites." Viewing the loss of Indian hunting grounds as an important cause of decay, it spoke of the powerful effect of the railroads on the destruction of the buffalo. Although the committee decided that the Indian service should stay in the Interior Department, it recommended a system of five inspection districts, each to be served by a three-man inspection committee composed of an assistant commissioner of Indian affairs, an army officer, and a person chosen by the president on the recommendations of church groups or missionary boards.[4]

The importance of the Doolittle Committee lay, not in immediate legislation, but in the effect its report had upon the Christian conscience of reform-minded humanitarians in the East. Its bulky appendix was full of charges of fraud and corruption indicating the need for a new policy. The statements were inconsistent, the charges often unsubstantiated, and the facts many times in error. The large volume hardly presented an accurate

3. William Frederick Doolittle, comp., *The Doolittle Family in America* (Cleveland: Sayers and Waite Printing Company, 1901–1908), p. 692. The other members were Lafayette S. Foster of Connecticut and James W. Nesmith of Oregon from the Senate and Asahel W. Hubbard of Iowa, William Higby of California, Lewis W. Ross of Illinois, and William Windom of Minnesota from the House.

4. *Condition of the Indian Tribes: Report of the Joint Special Committee, Appointed under Joint Resolution of March 3, 1865* (Washington: GPO, 1867; also printed as *Senate Report* no. 156, 39–2, serial 1279), pp. 3–10. There is a summary and analysis of the responses to the questionnaire in Donald Chaput, "Generals, Indian Agents, Politicians: The Doolittle Survey of 1865," *Western Historical Quarterly* 3 (July 1972): 269–82. In March 1866 Doolittle had introduced a bill to establish just such a system of inspection as the committee recommended. The bill passed the Senate, but the House did not act on it. See Doolittle's support of the measure and debate on it in *Congressional Globe*, 39th Congress, 1st session, pp. 1449–50, 1485–92.

picture of the "condition of the Indian tribes," but no matter, for it furnished ammunition for those seeking a change.[5]

Even while the Doolittle Committee was formulating its report, renewed warfare in the West drove home the need for some better Indian policy. War broke out along the Bozeman Trail, which had been built through the Powder River hunting grounds of the Sioux to link the new mining regions of Montana with the Oregon Trail near Fort Laramie. The state of siege in which the Indians held the military posts established in 1865 and 1866 to protect the miners' wagon trains caused apprehension, but few saw it as a prelude to white defeat. Then on December 21, 1866, a rash lieutenant, William Fetterman, ignoring the admonitions of his superiors not to go beyond the protective range of Fort Phil Kearny, was ambushed by the Indians. He and his command of eighty men were wiped out, and the Fetterman Massacre made clear in the East the seriousness of the Indian situation in the West.[6] A special committee appointed to investigate the disaster reinforced the conclusions of the Doolittle Committee.[7]

The central plains, too, were on fire, and the news of the Fetterman ambush and of raiding parties into Texas brought near panic. To prevent what he believed would be a major outbreak in the spring of 1867, General Winfield Scott Hancock moved to overawe the Indians by striking at a Cheyenne village. The action only stirred up the Indians more, and the peace of the spring turned into war as the hostile Indians terrorized the regions on both sides of the Platte.[8]

Responsible officials agreed that a crisis had arrived in Indian policy, that the past ways of dealing with the Indians had not worked and were especially unsuited for post-Civil War conditions. They saw the inexorable movement of waves of white population, against which the Indians were defenseless. "Unless they fall in with the current of destiny as it rolls and surges around them," wrote General Grant's aide-de-camp, Ely S. Parker, who later became commissioner of Indian affairs, "they must succumb and be annihilated by its overwhelming force." Commissioner of Indian Affairs

5. A very critical analysis of the Doolittle report that points to the political motivation of many of the statements contained in it and charges that it was "incomplete and largely misleading" is Harry Kelsey, "The Doolittle Report of 1867: Its Preparation and Shortcomings," *Arizona and the West* 17 (Summer 1975): 107–20.

6. There is a useful analysis of the military situation in Robert A. Murray, *Military Posts in the Powder River Country of Wyoming, 1865–1894* (Lincoln: University of Nebraska Press, 1968), pp. 3–12, 73–101. Red Cloud's part in the Indians' fight against the road is discussed in James C. Olson, *Red Cloud and the Sioux Problem* (Lincoln: University of Nebraska Press, 1965), pp. 27–57.

7. CIA Report, 1867, serial 1326, pp. 2–3. Reports of the members of the commission are in *Senate Executive Document* no. 13, 40–1, serial 1308.

8. See reports in *Senate Executive Document* no. 13, 40–1, serial 1308; *House Executive Document* no. 240, 41–2, serial 1425.

Nathaniel G. Taylor declared in similar vein that the millions of whites advancing upon the Indians would "soon crush them out from the face of the earth, unless the humanity and Christian philanthropy of our enlightened statesmen shall interfere and rescue them." Both Parker and Taylor agreed, despite cries to the contrary in the press and in the utterances of some public figures, that "the sentiment of our people will not for a moment tolerate the idea of extermination."[9]

A recommendation with two closely related elements crystallized in the reports and statement of 1867. First was a reservation scheme by which the Indians of the plains would be moved out of the way of the whites who seemed about to crush them. Although this was by no means a novel idea, officials now asserted the urgency and absolute necessity of such an arrangement in order to save the Indians. The Indians should be made to move to the reservations, where they would be given livestock, agricultural implements, and spinning and weaving equipment to enable them to move toward self-support; schooling in letters and industry; and missionary instruction in Christianity; and where they could be isolated from all whites except government employees and others permitted on the reservations. The second element in the recommendation was for a special commission made up of respected citizens of integrity (Parker wanted to add also some of the "most reputable educated Indians, selected from the different tribes") to select and designate suitable ample reservations and then work to persuade the Indians to move to them.[10]

INDIAN PEACE COMMISSION

Out of these threads came the United States Indian Peace Commission, a congressional creation intended to take the business of negotiating with the Indians out of the hands of the executive and give it instead to a special group of civilian and military leaders with interest and competence in Indian affairs. The act of Congress of June 20, 1867, that established the commission, designating the civilian members of the commission and leaving to the president the responsibility of naming the military component, set its tasks in unmistakable language. The body had authority to call together the chiefs of the warring tribes, find the causes of hostility, and negotiate treaties that would "remove all just causes of complaint on their part, and at the same time establish security for person and property along the lines of railroad now being constructed to the Pacific and other thoroughfares of

9. Taylor to W. T. Otto, July 12, 1867, and Parker to Grant, January 24, 1867, *Senate Executive Document* no. 13, 40−1, serial 1308, pp. 5−6, 42−49.

10. Ibid.; see also Lewis V. Bogy to O. H. Browning, February 4, 1867, ibid., pp. 7−11.

travel to the western Territories, and such as will most likely insure civilization for the Indians and peace and safety for the whites." For Indians who did not then occupy reservations under treaty agreements, the commissioners were to select reservations that would become their permanent homes. But there was an iron hand in this velvet glove: if the commissioners failed to get the Indians to settle on reservations and thus secure peace, the secretary of war was authorized to call for volunteers for "the suppression of Indian hostilities."[11]

The men chosen by Congress were a humanitarian lot. The chairman of the commission was Nathaniel G. Taylor, who had been appointed commissioner of Indian affairs by President Johnson on March 26, 1867. Born in Happy Valley, Tennessee, Taylor had graduated from Princeton in 1840, practiced law, and served in the House of Representatives both before and after the Civil War. He made a name for himself as a Union man and won praise for his efforts to succor East Tennessee refugees during the Civil War. When Taylor, a man of deep religious sentiment who served for a time as a Methodist minister, retired from the Indian Office, he devoted himself to farming and preaching the gospel. Taylor had strong views about Indian policy, which dominated his annual reports and the initial report of the Peace Commission; there was not the slightest doubt in his mind about either the obligation or the possibility of civilizing the Indians in a Christian pattern.[12] Seconding him was a Bostonian who had moved to Colorado, Samuel F. Tappan, a noted supporter of Indian rights with a tinge of fanaticism in his makeup, who had chaired the military commission investigating Colonel Chivington and Sand Creek. Aligned with them was Senator John B. Henderson of Missouri, chairman of the Senate Committee on Indian Affairs and sponsor of the legislation that had created the commission. A fourth was John B. Sanborn, a native of Minnesota, who had risen to the rank of major general in the army and who in 1867 was out of the service and practicing law in Washington. He had served on the commission that investigated the Fetterman Massacre. These four men had been named explicitly in the law that established the commission.[13]

11. 15 *United States Statutes* 17. See the discussion in *Congressional Globe*, 40th Congress, 1st session, pp. 756–57.

12. "Nathaniel G. Taylor," in Oliver P. Temple, *Notable Men of Tennessee from 1833 to 1875: Their Times and Their Contemporaries* (New York: Cosmopolitan Press, 1912), p. 199; *Biographical Directory of the American Congress*, s.v. Taylor, Nathaniel G. See also William E. Unrau, "Nathaniel Green Taylor, 1867–69," in Robert M. Kvasnicka and Herman J. Viola, eds., *The Commissioners of Indian Affairs, 1824–1977* (Lincoln: University of Nebraska Press, 1979), pp. 115–22.

13. Representative William Windom of Minnesota had been named as a member of the commission, but he begged off because of other duties and suggested Tappan in his place. *Congressional Globe*, 40th Congress, 1st session, p. 756.

In addition to these the president appointed three army officers, well-qualified men with considerable experience in the West and, though firm believers in military control of the Indians, not averse to attempts at peace maneuvers. General William T. Sherman was in command of the Division of the Missouri and had overall responsibility for peace on the frontier. With him was Major General Alfred H. Terry, commander of the Department of Dakota, a scholarly young man of forty who had an excellent military record. The third general was William S. Harney, then retired in St. Louis, who had served on the Indian frontier and had many personal friends among the Indians. An extra member was Major General Christopher C. Augur, commander of the Department of the Platte, who at first substituted for Sherman but then became a regular member of the commission. A reasonable mixture of military firmness and humanitarian leniency, the commission boded well for a successful move toward peace.[14]

The Peace Commission went right to work. After an organizational meeting in St. Louis in August it moved up the Missouri, determined to council with the Indians and arrive at some peaceful understanding with them. A meeting with delegations of Sioux and Northern Cheyennes at North Platte, however, settled nothing, for Red Cloud and the Indians from the Powder River region did not attend. After announcing a new meeting at Fort Laramie for November, the commission returned to St. Louis and turned its attention to the southern plains. At Medicine Lodge Creek in southern Kansas in October 1867 it signed treaties with the Cheyennes, Arapahos, Kiowas, Comanches, and Kiowa-Apaches that assigned the Indians to two reservations in the western part of the Indian Territory, where the United States would furnish rations and other goods needed to turn them into happy farmers.[15] There was less success in the north, for Red Cloud refused to come in to Fort Laramie, declaring that he would not consider peace until the military forts along the Bozeman Trail were removed. The commission decided on a new council in the spring and adjourned.

On January 7, 1868, the commission submitted its first report, which was clearly from Taylor's hand although it was signed by all the members.[16] The report was a jeremiad, a denunciatory tirade against the evils in

14. For a view of the Peace Commission and its work through military eyes, see Robert G. Athearn, *William Tecumseh Sherman and the Settlement of the West* (Norman: University of Oklahoma Press, 1956), pp. 171–85, 196–211, 227–28; and John W. Bailey, *Pacifying the Plains: General Alfred Terry and the Decline of the Sioux* (Westport, Connecticut: Greenwood Press, 1979).

15. Kappler, pp. 977–89. A detailed story of the negotiations of the treaties from the reports of newspapermen who covered the event is Douglas C. Jones, *The Treaty of Medicine Lodge: The Story of the Great Treaty Council as Told by Eyewitnesses* (Norman: University of Oklahoma Press, 1966).

16. "Report to the President by the Indian Peace Commission," January 7, 1868, CIA

the Indian system. It found that an Indian sought to gain all his ends by war, the only means he knew. "If he fails to see the olive-branch or flag of truce in the hands of the peace commissioner, and in savage ferocity adds one more to his victims, we should remember that for two and a half centuries he has been driven back from civilization, where his passions might have been subjected to the influences of education and softened by the lessons of Christian charity." In councils with the Indians the commission inaugurated "the hitherto untried policy in connection with Indians, of endeavoring to conquer by kindness."[17]

The commissioners sought to understand Indian behavior in terms of white behavior under similar circumstances. They saw no inherent warlikeness in the Indians—only a reaction to evils that would be expected of whites themselves. "If the lands of the white man are taken," the report said, "civilization justifies him in resisting the invader. Civilization does more than this: it brands him as a coward and a slave if he submits to the wrong. Here civilization made its contract and guaranteed the rights of the weaker party. It did not stand by the guarantee. The treaty was broken, but not by the savage. If the savage resists, civilization, with the ten commandments in one hand and the sword in the other, demands his immediate extermination."[18]

The commission accepted the charge to remove the causes of complaint on the part of the Indians, but they found it "no easy task." "We have done the best we could under the circumstances," it reported, "but it is now rather late in the day to think of obliterating from the minds of the present generation the remembrance of wrong." The indictment of past policy was almost complete. "Among civilized men war usually springs from a sense of injustice. The best possible way then to avoid war is to do no act of injustice. When we learn that the same rule holds good with Indians, the chief difficulty is removed. But it is said our wars with them have been almost constant. Have we been uniformly unjust? We answer unhesitatingly, yes."[19]

The evangelical sentiment that suffused the report is seen best in the goal for the Indians that it proposed. There was no hint that the Indians should be protected to live forever as Indians; that would seem to fly in the face of God's plan for the progress of the republic. "We do not contest the

---

Report, 1868, serial 1366, pp. 486–510. The report is also printed in *House Executive Document* no. 97, 40–2, serial 1337. There is a good discussion of the Peace Commission and its work in Henry George Waltmann, "The Interior Department, War Department, and Indian Policy, 1865–1887" (Ph.D. dissertation, University of Nebraska, 1962), pp. 134–55.

17. CIA Report, 1868, serial 1366, pp. 487, 489.
18. Ibid., p. 492.
19. Ibid., p. 502.

every-ready argument that civilization must not be arrested in its progress by a handful of savages," the commission noted. "We earnestly desire the speedy settlement of all our territories. None are more anxious than we to see their agricultural and mineral wealth developed by an industrious, thrifty, and enlightened population. And we fully recognize the fact that the Indian must not stand in the way of this result. We would only be understood as doubting the purity and genuineness of that civilization which reaches its ends by falsehood and violence, and dispenses blessings that spring from violated rights."[20]

The solution was simple enough. The Indians must accept the civilization of the whites. "The white and Indian must mingle together and jointly occupy the country, or one of them must abandon it. If they could have lived together, the Indian by this contact would soon have become civilized and war would have been impossible. All admit this would have been beneficial to the Indian." To transform the Indians, to break down the antipathy of race, the commission set forth its recommendations: districts in the West set aside for the Indians, organized as territories, where agriculture and domestic manufactures should be introduced as rapidly as possible; schools to teach the children English; courts and other institutions of government; farmers and mechanics sent to instruct the Indians; and missionary and benevolent societies invited to "this field of philanthropy nearer home." The report declared: "The object of greatest solicitude should be to break down the prejudices of tribe among the Indians; to blot out the boundary lines which divide them into distinct nations, and fuse them into one homogeneous mass. Uniformity of language will do this—nothing else will. As this work advances each head of a family should be encouraged to select and improve a homestead. Let the women be taught to weave, to sew, and to knit. Let polygamy be punished. Encourage the building of dwellings and the gathering there of those comforts which endear the home."[21]

As practical suggestions, the commissioners recommended that money annuities be abolished forever and that domestic animals and agricultural and mechanical implements be substituted, that the intercourse laws be thoroughly revised, and that all agents and superintendents be relieved of office and only the competent and faithful reappointed. They declared that since peace, not war, with the Indians was the object, Indian affairs should be under civilian and not military control, and they recommended the formation of an independent Indian department.[22] It was the old program rejuvenated by a crusading zeal.

20. Ibid., p. 492.
21. Ibid., pp. 503–4.
22. Ibid., pp. 507–9. The generals as well as the civilians signed the full report, including the statement that Indian affairs belong under civilian control. But General Sher-

CIVILIZATION FOR THE INDIANS

Settlement with the northern tribes came at Fort Laramie in 1868. The way had been prepared by the government's willingness to withdraw its posts from the Powder River country, for as the Union Pacific moved westward, it would soon be possible to supply a new route to Montana west of the Big Horn Mountains. Little by little the tribes came in. A treaty was signed with the Brulé Sioux on April 29, with the Crows on May 7, and with the Northern Cheyennes and Northern Arapahos on May 10. But the other bands of Sioux appeared only slowly to affix their signatures to the treaty. The offending forts were dismantled and burned during the summer, and Red Cloud finally signed the treaty in November. The treaty set aside the Great Sioux Reserve west of the Missouri River in Dakota, and the chiefs agreed to settle at the agencies and accept reservation life. Meanwhile, the commissioners had gone about their business of negotiating with other western tribes at Fort Sumner, New Mexico, and Fort Bridger, Utah. All the treaties followed a common pattern supplied by the commission, with certain local or tribal variations. They were political documents of significance, for they declared that war between the tribes and the United States would "forever cease" and that peace between the parties would "forever continue," made arrangements for the punishment of wrongdoers, and established reservations with well-defined boundaries on which the Indians agreed to reside.[23]

The modern concern of Indians to protect a community land base has led to an emphasis on the land arrangements of these treaties (especially the 1868 treaty with the Sioux at Fort Laramie) that distorts their meaning in the context of the circumstances under which they were signed. These treaties were reformist documents aimed at attaining the humanitarian civilizing goals of the Peace Commission, even though the reforming tendencies were probably not well understood by the Indians and have been overlooked by historians because they were not effective. The treaties were intended to turn the nomadic warriors into peaceful farmers, and if the established reservations did not contain 160 acres of tillable land for each person (provided "a very considerable number of such persons shall be disposed to commence cultivating the soil as farmers"), the government agreed to set apart additional arable land adjacent to the reservations.

---

man later asserted that the report did not accurately reflect the officers' views. "We did not favor the conclusion arrived at," Sherman explained, "but being out-voted, we had to sign the report." Sherman to E. G. Ross, January 7, 1869, quoted in Waltmann, "The Interior Department, War Department, and Indian Policy," p. 149.

23. Kappler, pp. 998–1024.

Heads of families who wished to farm were authorized to select 320 acres, to be recorded in a "land book." Such land would no longer be held in common but "in the exclusive possession of the person selecting it, and of his family so long as he or they may continue to cultivate it." Single adults could similarly claim 80 acres. Indians who convinced the agent that they intended in good faith to cultivate the soil for a living were to receive seeds and agricultural implements for three or four years and instructions from the farmer, provided by the treaty. If more than one hundred Indians began to farm, an additional blacksmith was to be provided. To stimulate enterprise, the sum of five hundred dollars annually for three years was authorized as awards for the ten persons each year who were judged by the agent to have grown the most valuable crops.

"In order to insure the civilization of the tribes," these treaties declared, ". . . the necessity of education is admitted." The Indians pledged themselves to compel their children between the ages of six and sixteen, both boys and girls, to attend school, and the agent was charged to see that this stipulation was strictly complied with. For each thirty students who could "be induced or compelled to attend school," the government would provide a teacher "competent to teach the elementary branches of an English education." The provision was to continue for not less than twenty years, by which time, presumably, a large part of the tribes would be civilized and self-sufficient. To further encourage self-reliance, preference was to be given to Indians in the hiring of farmers, blacksmiths, millers, and other employees authorized by the treaties.

These treaties were a triumph of theory and faith over hard reality. Aside from the fact that cultivation of the soil in quarter- or half-section plots was infeasible in most of the area covered by the treaties and that successful enterprise tended to be in grazing rather than in agriculture, the Indians concerned were not prepared to conform suddenly to the philanthropists' views of the good life of English education and neat farms.

Taylor's faith and philosophy again showed clearly in his annual report of 1868, in which he devoted a long section to the questions "Shall our Indians be civilized? And how?" He began with the assumption that the Indians had rights; to deny that would "deny the fundamental principles of Christianity." The crucial question was how best to protect those rights and at the same time harmonize them with white interests. It was a question, he admitted, that had "long trembled in the hearts of philanthropists and perplexed the brains of statesmen," but he did not hesitate to propose an answer. He wrote: "History and experience have laid the key to its solution in our hands, at the proper moment, and all we need to do is to use it, and we at once reach the desired answer. It so happens that under the silent and seemingly slow operations of efficient causes, certain tribes of our

Indians have already emerged from a state of pagan barbarism, and are to-day clothed in the garments of civilization, and sitting under the vine and fig tree of an intelligent, scriptural Christianity."[24]

The historical examples were the Cherokees, Choctaws, Chickasaws, Creeks, and Seminoles, who had once, as savages, terrorized the colonial frontiers but who now lived as Christian and enlightened nations. "Thus the fact stands out clear, well-defined, and indisputable," Taylor concluded, "that Indians, not only as individuals, but as tribes, are capable of civilization and of christianization. Now if like causes under similar circumstances always produce like effects—which no sensible person will deny—it is clear that the application of the same causes, that have resulted in civilizing these tribes, to other tribes under similar circumstances, must produce their civilization." And what were these means? Reduction of territory, causing the Indians to resort to agricultural and pastoral pursuits; settlement in fixed locations; introduction of private property; and the work of Christian missionaries among the Indians.[25] Uniting Christian philanthropy with philosophy, Taylor had found a solution to the Indian problem. In this he was fully supported by Secretary of the Interior Orville H. Browning, whose views corresponded with those of the commissioner.[26]

The peace party could at first claim success, and for a time there were no serious disturbances. Then in August 1868 a group of Cheyennes with a few Arapahos and Sioux shattered the agreements made at Medicine Lodge Creek by an outbreak on the Salina and Solomon rivers in Kansas. Roving war parties killed and burned and raped on the frontiers of Kansas and Colorado. General Sherman increased military control in the West. He had been named by Congress to disburse the funds appropriated for carrying out the treaties, and although the secretary of the interior had stated that relations between his department and the Indians were to remain unchanged, Sherman had acted otherwise. In August he created two military districts, one for the Sioux under General Harney and one for the Cheyennes, Arapahos, Kiowas, and Comanches under General W. B. Hazen. The army officers were to act as "agents" for the Indians not on reservations.[27]

When the Peace Commission met again in Chicago in October, there was no longer agreement. Senator Henderson was detained in Washington

24. CIA Report, 1868, serial 1366, p. 476.

25. Ibid., pp. 477–78.

26. Maurice G. Baxter, *Orville H. Browning: Lincoln's Friend and Critic* (Bloomington: Indiana University Press, 1957), pp. 202–5.

27. William H. Leckie, *The Military Conquest of the Southern Plains* (Norman: University of Oklahoma Press, 1963), pp. 63–87; Olson, *Red Cloud and the Sioux Problem*, p. 78.

over the business of President Johnson's impeachment, and only Taylor and Tappan were left to defend a conciliatory position. The others had been convinced by the summer's warfare that military force was needed to coerce the hostile Indians, and the resolutions they passed reversed much of the previous report. The commissioners now urged provisions at once to feed, clothe, and protect the tribes "who now have located or may hereafter locate permanently on their respective agricultural reservations," and they urged that treaties with these tribes be considered to be in force whether ratified or not. The depredations committed by the Indians, the resolutions declared, justified the government in abrogating clauses of the Medicine Lodge treaties that gave the Indians the right to hunt outside their reservations. Military force should be used to compel Indians to move to the reservations. The tribes, insofar as existing treaties permitted, should no longer be considered "domestic dependent nations," and the Indians should be individually subject to the laws of the United States. Finally, in a sharp reversal of its previous stand, the commission recommended transferring the Bureau of Indian Affairs to the War Department. Commissioner Taylor, as chairman, signed the resolutions, but it was obvious from his annual report that he vigorously disagreed with them.[28]

Generals Sherman and Sheridan decided on a winter campaign to drive the tribes to their reservations, and they determined to harry and kill those who refused to settle down, with none too great care in separating those who were actually hostile from those who hoped to remain at peace. Lieutenant Colonel George A. Custer attacked the sleeping village of Black Kettle's Cheyennes on the Washita River on November 27, killing more than a hundred, including Black Kettle, and taking women and children prisoners. And Sheridan ordered a sweep against other Cheyenne villages downriver toward Fort Cobb, where Kiowas and Comanches had turned themselves in and promised peace. Hostile Cheyennes and Arapahos were pursued south until most of them were defeated and returned to the reservation. But the reservations for many of these southern plains Indians were merely places to recoup their strength between raids.[29]

REFORM IMPULSES

The report of the Peace Commission and the continuing warfare on the plains both gave new impetus to reformers interested in the Indians—the

---

28. Resolutions dated October 9, 1868, CIA Report, 1868, serial 1366, pp. 831–32.

29. Leckie, *Military Conquest of the Southern Plains*, pp. 88–132. A sympathetic history of Sheridan and his aggressive action against the Indians is Carl Coke Rister, *Border Command: General Phil Sheridan in the West* (Norman: University of Oklahoma Press, 1944).

warfare because it reemphasized the urgency to do something radical to end conditions that caused war, the report because it gave hope that the government would listen to men and women who promoted peace and justice. A deep impression was made on a number of reformers who had not been notably interested in Indian affairs before. Some were abolitionists, whose reforming zeal for the cause of the slaves made them fit subjects for appeals in behalf of another oppressed minority. One of these was Lydia Maria Child, who wrote when she read the Peace Commission's report: "I welcomed this Report almost with tears of joy. 'Thank God!' I exclaimed, 'we have, at last, an Official Document, which manifests something like a right spirit toward the poor Indians! Really, this encourages a hope that the Anglo-Saxon race are capable of civilization." Child countered at considerable length the argument that the Indians could not be civilized, for she was convinced of the unity of mankind.[30] "Nothing can ever change my belief that human nature is essentially the same in all races and classes of men," she wrote two years later, "and that its modifications for good or evil are to be attributed to the education of circumstances. My faith never wavers that men can be made just by being treated justly, honest by being dealt with honestly, and kindly by becoming objects of kindly sympathy."[31]

Other abolitionists—notably Wendell Phillips—took up the cause of Indian reform, adding the abused Indians to a long list of reform causes promoted in the *National Standard*, Phillips's personal sounding board.[32] Yet the direct effect of abolitionist leaders on post–Civil War Indian reform was slight, even though Child, Phillips, and other antislavery crusaders spoke out occasionally on Indian affairs. Partly because they had already expended a large part of their reservoir of reforming energies, partly because they did not center their whole attention on Indian reform but kept active in a variety of movements, and partly because they did not create effective or enduring organizations through which to channel their work, they did

30. Lydia Maria Child, *An Appeal for the Indians* (New York: William P. Thomlinson, n.d.), p 3; the essay first appeared in the *National Anti-Slavery Standard*, April 11, 1868.

31. Child to Aaron Powell, *National Standard*, August 27, 1870, p. 4, quoted in Robert Winston Mardock, *The Reformers and the American Indian* (Columbia: University of Missouri Press, 1971), p. 16. Child criticized some aspects of the Peace Commission's report, however: she objected to forcing English upon the Indians and to the punishment of polygamy. "We have so long indulged in feelings of pride and contempt toward those we are pleased to call 'subject races' that we have actually become incapable of judging them with any tolerable degree of candor and common sense." *Appeal for the Indians*, p. 8.

32. The Reform League, which Phillips helped to found in 1870, and its journal, the *National Standard* (which replaced the *National Anti-Slavery Standard*), supported blacks, Chinese immigration, women's rights, temperance, and prison reform, as well as Indian rights. Irving H. Bartlett, *Wendell Phillips, Brahmin Radical* (Boston: Beacon Press, 1961), pp. 370–71.

not shape the course of Indian policy. But this is not to deny their importance in helping to stir up public interest, in attracting other reformers to
the cause, and in contributing substantial weight to the whole movement.[33]

The Indians and the Indian wars also drew the attention of Alfred Love
and his Universal Peace Union, which added humanitarian treatment of
the Indians to its other peace-orientated reforms. The organization at its
convention in Washington in January 1868 sent a petition to Congress on
Indian matters, adding its voice to the growing concern, although Indian
activities were only a small part of the Union's work.[34]

The stirring reports of the serious state of Indian affairs brought still
other responses. The condemnation of evil and proposals for good struck
sympathetic chords among many persons of humanitarian and philanthropic bent, who turned to Indian reform once they had been awakened to
the needs. One such response was the formation in 1868 of the United
States Indian Commission in New York City under the instigation of Peter
Cooper. The purpose of this collection of Protestant ministers and other
benevolent gentlemen was "to array on the side of justice and humanity
the influence and support of an enlightened public opinion, in order to secure for the Indians that treatment which, in their position, we should demand for ourselves." These men condemned the failure of the government
to fulfill its treaty obligations, the outrages upon Indians by white citizens
and soldiers (especially Sand Creek), the degradation and deterioration of
the Indians by venereal disease brought in with military troops in Indian
country, and the lack of honest and faithful Indian agents. Once the nation
was informed about Indian wrongs, they thought, "their united voice will
demand that the honor and the interests of the nation shall no longer be
sacrificed to the insatiable lust and avarice of unscrupulous men."[35] Cooper,
an industrialist turned philanthropist, had a long history of humanitarian
concern, including antislavery agitation, and his Cooper's Union in New
York City not only offered industrial classes but provided a forum for

33. Mardock, in *Reformers and the American Indian* and in "The Anti-Slavery Humanitarians and Indian Policy Reform," *Western Humanities Review* 12 (Spring 1958):
131–45, argues that most of the men and women who took up the Indian cause after the
Civil War had previously been involved with the antislavery movement, but the evidence
in his own writings tends to disprove this. It is certainly not true that the *leaders* in the
post-Civil War Indian reform movement had been *leaders* in the antislavery movement.
The abolitionists cited by Mardock (Lydia Maria Child, Wendell Phillips, and Henry
Ward Beecher) had no sustained effect on Indian reform after the war.

34. See Robert Winston Mardock, "Alfred Love, Indian Peace Policy, and the Universal Peace Union," *Kansas Quarterly* 3 (Fall 1971): 64–71.

35. Memorial to Congress, July 14, 1869, *House Miscellaneous Document* no. 165,
40–2, serial 1350. The formation of the commission is described in Mardock, *Reformers
and the American Indian*, p. 33.

reform speakers of many persuasions. Vincent Colyer, an officer of the New York YMCA, served as secretary of the Indian Commission, and the Reverend Henry Ward Beecher was a prominent member. John Beeson supported the commission and urged that it be allowed to nominate commissioners and other persons employed in Indian affairs, and Bishop Whipple at a meeting on October 19 read a report on the condition of the tribes.[36] When General Hazen requested a visitor to study the conditions of the Kiowa and Comanche Indians at Fort Cobb, the commission sent Colyer to investigate.[37]

Of all the groups concerned about a Christian approach to Indian policy, none was more symbolic (if not actually influential) than the Society of Friends. The Quakers from colonial days on showed an interest in just and humane treatment of the Indians, and the story of William Penn's peaceful dealings with the Indians was repeated so widely that it became embedded in the general American consciousness in mythic form. There were few Americans, moreover, who were not acquainted with Benjamin West's painting of Penn's legendary treaty with the Indians in one of its manifold reproductions.[38] Although the Quakers' active Indian work in antebellum days was largely with the tribes in New York State, and although their concern for the blacks and the antislavery movement far overshadowed their interest in the Indians, the Quakers easily shifted to a new concern for Indians when the conditions after the Civil War demanded it. They offered a statement of principles in 1866 that, although it was probably not widely circulated, could have served as a platform for the new Christian peace policy: "From the earliest period at which the Religious Society of Friends had intercourse with the Indians, it has been their endeavor to treat them with kindness and justice, to guard them against the imposition and fraud to which their ignorance exposed them; to meliorate and improve their condition; and to commend the benign and heavenly principles of the Christian religion to their approval and acceptance by an upright example consistent therewith." The statement contrasted "the history of much of the public and more private dealings with the Indians," which it found "stained by fraud and bloodshed," with such pacific and religious behavior. Coercion and violence had failed to civilize and Christianize the Indians and thus to secure peace and harmony, and the Quakers asked whether it would not be well "for government and its officers to try the effect of just

36. Mardock, *Reformers and the American Indian*, pp. 33–34.
37. Leaflet of the commission, February 3, 1869.
38. Ellen Starr Brinton, "Benjamin West's Painting of Penn's Treaty with the Indians," *Bulletin of Friends' Historical Association* 30 (Autumn 1941): 99–189; Clyde A. Milner II, *With Good Intentions: Quaker Work among the Pawnees, Otos, and Omahas in the 1870s* (Lincoln: University of Nebraska Press, 1982), pp. 6–7.

and pacific measures; to substitute for the sword the benign and winning persuasion which flows from the spirit of the Gospel, and teaches us to do to others as we would that they should do to us."[39]

When disturbances on the frontier in the late 1860s attracted the attention of the nation, the Quakers did not fail to react. The conference of the Yearly Meetings of the Liberal Quakers (Hicksite) at Baltimore in 1868 sent a memorial to Congress praying "that the effusion of blood may cease, and that such just and humane measures may be pursued as will secure a lasting peace, and tend to the preservation and enlightenment of those afflicted people, whom we regard as the wards of the nation." The assembly urged "benevolent efforts to improve and enlighten the Indians" and that only persons "of high character and strict morality" be sent among them as agents. The next year, shortly after the release of the Peace Commission's report, these Quakers renewed their appeal to Congress for the Indians. "Let the effort be made in good faith," they said, "to promote their education—their industry—their morality. Invite the assistance of the philanthropic and Christian effort, which has been so valuable an aid in the elevation of the Freedmen, and render it possible for justice and good example to restore that confidence which has been lost by injustice and cruelty." The memorial strongly opposed turning over the Indian Office to the military and expressed a common worry among religious men about the venereal dangers that lurked at military posts. "May you be enabled, as representatives of a Christian nation," the Quakers ended their address to Congress, "to legislate respecting the Indians in the fear of the Almighty, and be guided by His wisdom."[40] A similar memorial was sent by the Orthodox Friends.

By 1869 the Indians were in the forefront of reformers' minds. The drive to protect them from avarice and corruption and to draw them ultimately into the Christian civilization of the humanitarians gathered momentum as one group after another turned with new interest toward them. The administration of Ulysses S. Grant, remembered for the opprobrious corruption called Grantism, paradoxically brought to fruition a policy dominated by evangelical Protestant men and principles.

39. *A Brief Sketch of the Efforts of Philadelphia Yearly Meeting of the Religious Society of Friends, to Promote the Civilization and Improvement of the Indians* (Philadelphia: Friends' Book Store, 1866), pp. 1, 55–56.

40. *Memorial of the Religious Society of Friends . . . Now Assembled in Conference in the City of Baltimore, of the Six Yearly Meetings or General Assemblies of Our People* [1868]; Memorial of Religious Society of Friends, January 21, 1869, *House Miscellaneous Document* no. 29, 40–3, serial 1385.

CHAPTER 20

Structures of the Peace Policy

The Board of Indian Commissioners.

Churches and the Agencies.

Failure of the Structures.

The End of Treaty Making.

The demand of religiously motivated men and women for reform in Indian affairs could not be disregarded. The evangelical outcry led not only to national consciousness of the flagrant evils in the Indian service and the wars in the West but to most unusual administrative developments. The governmental structures that marked the peace policy were a remarkable manifestation of reliance of the "Christian nation" on professedly Christian men and principles in an attempt to establish the just and humane administration that was so ardently called for in the 1860s.[1]

THE BOARD OF INDIAN COMMISSIONERS

The first sign of the change came from President Grant himself, who in his inaugural address on March 4, 1869, declared: "The proper treatment of the original occupants of this land—the Indians—is one deserving of careful study. I will favor any course toward them which tends to their civilization and ultimate citizenship."[2] Encouraged by this clear sign of willing-

1. In this chapter I draw on Francis Paul Prucha, *American Indian Policy in Crisis: Christian Reformers and the Indian, 1865–1900* (Norman: University of Oklahoma Press, 1976), pp. 33–71.
2. *Inaugural Addresses of the Presidents of the United States from George Washington 1789 to Richard Milhous Nixon 1969* (Washington: GPO, 1969), p. 121.

ness to listen to Christian advocates, a group of Philadelphia philanthropists determined to press for an independent commission to watch over Indian affairs, an idea that had frequently been recommended as a means of rectifying the corruption and attendant evils in the Indian service.[3] The leader in this effort was William Welsh, who exemplified the Christian humanitarians upon whom the new policy depended. An Episcopalian layman, who with his brothers had amassed a sizable mercantile fortune, Welsh devoted much of his apparently boundless energy to public service. "Into how many of the secular interests of the community Mr. Welsh threw the weight of his influence, and the vigor of his active powers, I do not know," the Reverend M. A. DeWolfe Howe said in a memorial sermon for Welsh in 1878. "He spent no effort in winning popular favor. I think he would have refused any office in the exercise of which he could not hope to accomplish some positive religious good. He did not feel that he had time for any occupation in which he could not advance the cause and kingdom of Christ."[4]

Welsh, in 1868, called a meeting of like-minded men, and a committee representing different religious bodies was appointed to call upon the president and the secretary of the interior. The committee told Grant that although the government could do something by itself to aid the Indians, "without the co-operation of Christian philanthropists the waste of money would be great, and the result unsatisfactory." If philanthropists could be associated with the secretary of the interior, "the lost confidence of Congress could be regained, the Indians made more hopeful, and the whole Christian community aroused to co-operate with the Government in 'civilizing, Christianizing, and ultimately making citizens of the Indians.'"[5] Prominent among the group speaking thus candidly to the president was a friend of Grant's, George Hay Stuart, a wealthy Philadelphia merchant

3. See, for example, Henry B. Whipple, "What Shall We Do with the Indians" (1862), in *Lights and Shadows of a Long Episcopate* (New York: Macmillan Company, 1899), p. 518. A treaty with the Chippewas in 1863 had authorized the president to appoint a board of visitors from Christian denominations to attend annuity payments and to report regularly on the qualifications and behavior of persons living on the reservation. Kappler, p. 854. Instructions from the commissioner of Indian affairs to the committee are in CIA Report, 1863, serial 1182, pp. 458–59. The Joint Special Committee under Senator Doolittle had recommended inspection boards, and in 1868 the New York reform group called the United States Indian Commission had memorialized Congress to appoint unpaid, politically independent men to work in Indian affairs. *House Miscellaneous Document* no. 165, 40–2, serial 1350.

4. M. A. DeWolfe Howe, *Memorial of William Welsh* (Reading, Pennsylvania, 1878), p. 21.

5. The report of the committee is printed in *Taopi and His Friends; or, the Indians' Wrongs and Rights* (Philadelphia: Claxton, Remsen and Haffelfinger, 1868), pp. 73–84. The quotations are from pages 76 and 78.

who had been active in Presbyterian church work, temperance and anti-slavery movements, Sunday school work, and the Young Men's Christian Association. Stuart was, as the editor of his autobiography asserted, "a Christian merchant who is at once zealously Christian and diligently a man of business," whose joy it was "to testify everywhere and to all men of his love of the Saviour."[6]

On March 24, 1869, Grant and Secretary of the Interior Jacob D. Cox cordially received the delegation and accepted their ideas. Stimulated by Welsh's continuing efforts, Congress on April 10, 1869, authorized the president to "organize a board of Commissioners, to consist of not more than ten persons, to be selected by him from men eminent for their intelligence and philanthropy, to serve without pecuniary compensation," who under the president's direction should "exercise joint control with the Secretary of the Interior" over the disbursement of Indian appropriations.[7]

The establishment of this Board of Indian Commissioners, through a series of fortuitous concatenations, set post–Civil War Indian policy ever more firmly in the pattern of American evangelical revivalism. The chain of religious reformers from Charles G. Finney, the great revivalist preacher, to the board was remarkable but very clear. That it was so is indisputable testimony to the grip that religious thought had upon the public councils of the day.

Revivalism, so often associated with its rural manifestations in the Second Great Awakening of the decades after 1800, came to the fore again in the 1850s as an urban phenomenon. The years 1857–1858 were its high point, as widely publicized interdenominational revival meetings took place in the major cities of the United States that were attended by throngs of businessmen and others. These revivalist stirrings exhibited what later became major themes of American Protestantism—lay leadership, a drive toward interdenominational cooperation, and emphasis, not on theological argument, but on ethical behavior, which supported an intense concern for social reform.[8]

The outstanding manifestation and agent of the new awakening was the Young Men's Christian Association. Founded in England in 1844, the YMCA movement spread quickly in America after associations were organized in Montreal and Boston in 1851. The YMCA was the product of the successive waves of revivals that swept the nation in the nineteenth century. It reflected Finney's pragmatic concern for ethical action *now*, and it

6. Introduction by Robert Ellis Thompson to *The Life of George H. Stuart: Written by Himself* (Philadelphia: J. M. Stoddart and Company, 1890), pp. 20–21.

7. 16 *United States Statutes* 40.

8. The fullest account of this revival is Timothy L. Smith, *Revivalism and Social Reform in Mid-Nineteenth-Century America* (Nashville: Abingdon Press, 1957).

was a laymen's organization of unabashed interdenominational scope. "In all this," says the modern historian of the movement, "the Y.M.C.A. mirrored American Protestantism. Its faith rested upon a naive belief in the Bible as the unique, supernatural repository of all truth, knowledge, and morality. Its God was that of the Book, especially concerned for sinners whose day-to-day conduct failed to measure up to current Protestant usage. The Association was, for the most part, a move by the 'better' people in behalf of those for whom they felt a real compassion and responsibility."[9]

The revivals of 1857–1858 had a far-reaching effect upon the YMCA, for it had been the most important promotional agency for those nationwide revivals. Out of such circumstances came the YMCA's great work during the Civil War, the United States Christian Commission.[10]

When the war began, the YMCA directed its attention to the Union soldiers. Immediately after the Battle of Bull Run on July 21, 1861, the New York association sent two of its leaders, one of them Vincent Colyer, "to minister to the temporal and spiritual necessities of the wounded and dying men who crowded the hospitals in and near the capital."[11] The association organized a continuing mission to the soldiers, but Colyer soon became convinced that a national organization was needed to care for the religious needs of the troops. He and his New York supporters issued a call to associations across the country to appoint "army committees" and for these committees to meet in New York. In mid-November 1861 a convention of delegates from fifteen associations met in New York. On November 16 the convention established the twelve-member Christian Commission, which was to take charge of the army work of the YMCA and to act as a clearing house for religious work with the troops. Most of those appointed to the commission were YMCA leaders. The chairman was George H.

---

9. C. Howard Hopkins, *History of the Y.M.C.A. in North America* (New York: Association Press, 1951), pp. 45–46. Hopkins's volume is a thorough scholarly treatment of the YMCA; see also L. L. Doggett, *History of the Young Men's Christian Association* (New York: International Committee of Young Men's Christian Associations, 1896), and Sherwood Eddy, *A Century with Youth: A History of the Y.M.C.A. from 1844 to 1944* (New York: Association Press, 1944). The YMCA, with some internal controversy, limited its membership to members of "evangelical churches." Although in 1869 it defined what it meant by evangelical—maintaining the Holy Scriptures as "the only infallible rule of faith and practice," belief in the divinity of Christ, and belief in Christ as "the only name under heaven given among men whereby we must be saved from everlasting punishment"—it refused to name the churches that were evangelical. But clearly it excluded Unitarians and Universalists on one hand and Roman Catholics on the other, to say nothing of Jews and nonbelievers. There is a good discussion of the matter in Hopkins, *Y.M.C.A.*, pp. 362–69.

10. Hopkins, *Y.M.C.A.*, pp. 81–84.

11. Cephas Brainerd, *The Work of the Army Committee of the New York Young Men's Christian Association, Which Led to the Organization of the United States Christian Commission* (New York, 1866), quoted in Hopkins, *Y.M.C.A.*, p. 88.

Stuart, then president of the Philadelphia YMCA and chairman of the YMCA Central Committee.

The commission directed an army of volunteer workers who collected funds and materials, and it sent delegates into the hospitals and army camps to distribute stores, circulate good reading material among the men, aid chaplains in encouraging prayer meetings and discouraging vice, and assist surgeons on the battlefield. It was motivated by a sincere and open love of Christ and represented "the forces of Christianity developed and exemplified amid the carnage of battle and the more perilous tests of hospital and camp."[12]

The Christian Commission worked closely with the government. It sought and received the approbation and commendation of the president, the secretaries of war and navy, and the army generals. It set a useful pattern of a committee of distinguished men, without government positions and without pay, who took over duties and activities that might well have been considered the responsibility of government officials and who worked closely (though not always without friction) with both civilian and military officers.

The idea of the Christian Commission and the work it had done was much in the air when the Board of Indian Commissioners was conceived and organized. And when it came time to appoint the board, Grant called upon his old friend Stuart, who went to Washington to advise the president. "Stuart," Grant told him, "you and Welsh have got me into some difficulty by the passage of this bill which requires me to appoint a Board of Commissioners, and I have sent for you to help me." When Stuart asked how he could be of use, Grant replied, "I want you to name some likely men from the different sections of the country, and representing various religious bodies, who will be willing to serve the cause of the Indians without compensation." The industrialist obliged, suggesting men from Boston, New York, Philadelphia, Pittsburgh, Chicago, and St. Louis. Grant added a name of his own and insisted that Stuart himself be on the board.[13]

Secretary Cox, in inviting men to serve on the board, noted that the pur-

12. Edward P. Smith, *Incidents of the United States Christian Commission* (Philadelphia: J. B. Lippincott and Company, 1869), p. 5. The work of the commission can be traced also in Lemuel Moss, *Annals of the United States Christian Commission* (Philadelphia: J. B. Lippincott and Company, 1868), and in the commission's *Annual Report*, issued 1863–1866. A useful secondary account is M. Hamlin Cannon, "The United States Christian Commission," *Mississippi Valley Historical Review* 38 (June 1951): 61–80.

13. Stuart, *Life of George H. Stuart*, pp. 239–41. On the back of a telegram from Secretary of the Interior Cox to Stuart, April 13, 1869, seeking his consultation on the formation of the board, Stuart wrote: "Asked & went to Washington on receipt & helped to form the Indian Board of Commissioners *nearly all* of whom were named by me." George Hay Stuart Papers, Library of Congress.

pose was "that something like a Christian Commission should be estab-
lished having the civilization of the Indians in view & laboring to stimu-
late public interest in this work."[14] In fact, the continuity between the old
Christian Commission of the Civil War, which had ended its labors on
January 1, 1866, and the new Board of Indian Commissioners was striking.
Stuart's work as national chairman of the Christian Commission made
him think largely of his coworkers in the commission when he supplied
Grant with a list of names for the board. William E. Dodge, appointed from
New York, was a businessmen whose life had paralleled Stuart's. An active
Presbyterian, with antislavery, temperance, Sunday school, foreign mis-
sion, Bible Society, and YMCA interests and engagements, Dodge had orga-
nized the New York Branch of the Christian Commission in 1862 and presided at its fund-raising meetings. He was a deeply religious man, firmly
impressed with the fundamental articles of the Calvinist creed.[15] Another
New Yorker on the original Board of Indian Commissioners was Nathan
Bishop, who had served as chairman of the executive committee of the
New York Branch of the Christian Commission. He was a Baptist educator
and philanthropist, active in a variety of church societies and organizations. From Chicago came John V. Farwell, a leading dry goods merchant
and a supporter of the revivalist Dwight L. Moody, who had been chairman
of that city's branch of the Christian Commission; and from Boston, Edward S. Tobey, a Congregational shipping magnate, who had been chairman of the Christian Commission there.[16]

The Board of Indian Commissioners thus comprised a good number of
wealthy Christian gentlemen with recent firsthand experience, and generally applauded success, in a public philanthropic enterprise of notable extent, an enterprise that had sought and received aid for a good cause from
people of goodwill across the nation and in which the cooperation between
lay figures and the government had been very close. These old associates of
Stuart were joined by William Welsh, who fittingly was chosen first chairman of the board, and by the Pittsburgh industrialist Felix R. Brunot.
Brunot, who replaced Welsh as chairman on November 17, 1869, had a
background in YMCA service, support of temperance and Sunday obser-

14. Cox to William Welsh, April 15, 1869, printed in *Taopi and His Friends*, pp.
82–83. A similar letter to William E. Dodge is in D. Stuart Dodge, *Memorials of William E. Dodge* (New York: Anson D. F. Randolph and Company, 1887), p. 168.

15. See Dodge, *Memorials of William E. Dodge*; Richard Lowitt, *A Merchant Prince
of the Nineteenth Century: William E. Dodge* (New York: Columbia University Press,
1954); and Carlos Martyn, *William E. Dodge: The Christian Merchant* (New York: Funk
and Wagnalls, 1890).

16. *Dictionary of American Biography*, s.v. Bishop, Nathan, by Thomas Woody, and
Tobey, Edward Silas, by Sidney Gunn; John V. Farwell, Jr., *Some Recollections of John V.
Farwell* (Chicago: R. R. Donnelley and Sons, 1911).

vance, and other good works that was similar to Stuart's. Other members of the first board were Robert Campbell, a St. Louis merchant and banker suggested by Stuart, and Henry S. Lane of Indiana, chosen by Grant to fulfill political obligations. The Quaker John D. Lang was appointed in 1870.[17]

The relation of the board to the churches was not defined in the law, but it was obviously very close. Although the original members were not official representatives of their particular denominations, they all reflected the dominant Protestant character of American Christianity. And when new members were appointed after 1875, they asserted that they had been nominated by and therefore represented their particular churches.[18] There were no Roman Catholics on the board, even though Catholics were heavily involved in Indian missionary work, and it seems reasonable to suppose that none would have been welcome.[19]

The work to which the Board of Indian Commissioners was to devote its attention was spelled out in considerable detail in a letter sent to the members on May 26, 1869, by Ely S. Parker, commissioner of Indian affairs. Acknowledging their desire for the "humanization, civilization, and Christianization of the Indians," Parker posed a series of questions for

17. Clinton B. Fisk, who became chairman of the Board of Indian Commissioners in 1874, had been a member of the Christian Commission. The Reverend Edward P. Smith, commissioner of Indian affairs 1873–1875, had served as field secretary of the commission. Hiram Price, named commissioner of Indian affairs in 1881, had served on the commission's Iowa committee.

18. Clinton B. Fisk said at his first meeting of the board in January 1875: "Most of us who are here today, I believe, are here by the nomination of the religious bodies which we represent." *Report of the Board of Indian Commissioners*, 1874, p. 123. In 1878, A. C. Barstow, then board chairman, testified: "He [President Grant] asked each of the religious bodies to recommend to him an able man to act upon the Board of Indian Commissioners. I represented upon the board the American Board of Commissioners for Foreign Missions." And E. M. Kingsley declared: "I have been a member of the Board of Indian Commissioners by the nomination of the Presbyterian Board of Foreign Missions, since, I think, February, 1875." *Senate Miscellaneous Document* no. 53, 45–3, serial 1835.

19. Some weak attempts to involve Catholics centered on the Reverend George Deshon, a Paulist priest who had been a classmate of Grant's at West Point. When asked about the matter in 1896, Deshon replied: "Prest Grant never offered to put a Catholic in the Board of Indian Comrs. . . . F. D. Dent, Grant's brother in law, and who was a long time in the White House, asked me if I would be willing to be one of the Commissioners, and I declined. He said Grant would appoint me if I would consent. I did not see that I could do the least good in that crowd of bigots who would ignore me and bolster themselves by serving with a Catholic man on the board and therefore I declined." Joseph A. Stephan to George Deshon, January 15, 1896, and Deshon to Stephan, January 18, 1896, Papers of the Bureau of Catholic Indian Missions, 1896, District of Columbia, Marquette University Library. See also references to Father Deshon and the peace policy in Peter J. Rahill, *The Catholic Indian Missions and Grant's Peace Policy, 1870–1884* (Washington: Catholic University of America Press, 1953). Not until 1902 were Catholics allotted positions on the board.

their consideration. It was an awesome list, which must have frightened the members; and it indicated the kinds of problems the Grant administration was interested in. What should be the legal status of the Indians and what were their rights and obligations under existing laws and treaties? Should treaties continue to be made with the tribes, and if not, what sort of legislation would be required? Should Indians be placed on reservations, and how could this be accomplished? Should a distinction be made in dealing with the localized, civilized Indians and the roving tribes of the plains and mountains? What line should be drawn between civil and military rule of the Indians? Were changes required in the trade and intercourse laws because of changed conditions in the country? And what changes should be made in the procedures for purchasing goods for the Indians and in methods of paying annuities? In order to carry out effectively its duties, the board was given authority to inspect the agencies and the records of the Indian Office, to be present at annuity payments and at councils with the Indians, to supervise the purchase of goods and to inspect the purchases, and to offer advice in general on plans for civilizing the Indians and on the conduct of Indian affairs.[20]

The powers were not clear and strong enough to satisfy William Welsh, who wanted the full joint control with the secretary of the interior that he thought had been directed by Congress. He feared that the board had been relegated to "a mere council of advice," and being unwilling "to assume responsibilities without any power of control," he resigned from the board only a month after its organization.[21]

The rest of the board entered upon its duties with energy and goodwill. The board appointed a purchasing committee (Stuart, Dodge, Farwell, and Campbell, all businessmen of competence and integrity) to cooperate with the government in purchasing supplies for the Indian department, and three of the members (Brunot, Bishop, and Dodge) made an extensive trip to the Indian country during the summer. At the end of the year, despite

---

20. Parker to board members, May 26, 1869, *Report of the Board of Indian Commissioners*, 1869, pp. 3–4. Grant in an order of June 3, 1869, promulgated regulations for the board. Ibid., pp. 4–5. The members of the board were all called to Washington for a meeting at which the questions were posed and arrangements made. The minutes of the early meetings of the board, from May 26, 1869, to February 3, 1870, are printed in *Minutes of the Board of Indian Commissioners* (Washington: H. Polkinhorn and Company, 1870). They give an excellent picture of how the board got under way, of meetings with government officials, of the appointment of Colyer as paid secretary, and so on. The complete minutes of the board, correspondence, and other records are in Records of the Office of Indian Affairs, Records of the Board of Indian Commissioners, National Archives, Record Group 75.

21. William Welsh, *Indian Office: Wrongs Doing and Reforms Needed* (Philadelphia, 1874), pp. 1–2.

problems of organization arising from Welsh's resignation, the ill health of some of the members, and the pressure of other duties, the board submitted a long and outspoken report, largely the work of Brunot. The report was a powerful denunciation of past Indian relations and, although it admitted that recommendations should not be the "result of theorizing," a remarkably complete prospectus of policies and programs to come.

The righteous indignation of these Christian philanthropists pervaded the report:

> While it cannot be denied that the government of the United States, in the general terms and temper of its legislation has evinced a desire to deal generously with the Indians, it must be admitted that the actual treatment they have received has been unjust and iniquitous beyond the power of words to express.
>
> Taught by the government that they had rights entitled to respect; when those rights have been assailed by the rapacity of the white man, the arm which should have been raised to protect them has been ever ready to sustain the aggressor.
>
> The history of the government connections with the Indians is a shameful record of broken treaties and unfulfilled promises.
>
> The history of the border white man's connection with the Indians is a sickening record of murder, outrage, robbery, and wrongs committed by the former as a rule, and occasional savage outbreaks and unspeakably barbarous deeds of retaliation by the latter as the exception.

The cause was clear: "Paradoxical as it may seem, the white man has been the chief obstacle in the way of Indian civilization. The benevolent measures attempted by the government for their advancement have been almost uniformly thwarted by the agencies employed to carry them out." The board saw no inherent problem in the Indians themselves, who had been made suspicious, revengeful, and cruel by the treatment they had received from the whites. They denied that the Indians would not work and pointed to the example of the Five Civilized Tribes and the Yankton Sioux. "The reports of the Indian Bureau," they asserted with the optimism of true reformers, "will be found to abound in facts going to prove that the Indian, as a race, can be induced to work, is susceptible of civilization, and presents a most inviting field for the introduction of Christianity."[22]

For men with little experience in Indian affairs, the members of the board confidently set forth preliminary recommendations for future dealings with the tribesmen. They urged that Indians be collected on small

22. *Report of the Board of Indian Commissioners,* 1869, pp. 7–9.

contiguous reservations making up a large unit that would eventually become a state of the Union. On the reservations the Indians should be given land in severalty, and tribal relations should be discouraged. They recommended the abandonment of the treaty system and the abrogation of existing treaties "as soon as any just method can be devised to accomplish it." Money annuities should cease, for they promoted idleness and vice. The board urged the establishment of schools to teach the children English and wanted teachers nominated by religious bodies. Christian missions should be encouraged and their schools fostered. "The religion of our blessed Saviour," they said, "is believed to be the most effective agent for the civilization of any people." They insisted upon an honest observation of treaty obligations, appointment of agents "with a view to their moral as well as business qualifications, and aside from any political consideration," and fair judicial proceedings for Indian criminals. "The legal status of the uncivilized Indians," they decided, "should be that of wards of the government; the duty of the latter being to protect them, to educate them in industry, the arts of civilization, and the principles of Christianity; elevate them to the rights of citizenship, and to sustain and clothe them until they can support themselves."[23]

It was just the sort of platform one would expect from the Christian merchant princes who made up the Board of Indian Commissioners. Whether they were conscious of it or not, they intended to apply to the "uncivilized" Indians of the plains and mountains the same prescriptions made for more eastern Indians in antebellum days.

The tours of board members of the West enabled them to gather firsthand information on which to base their continuing recommendations. If they carried with them their own prejudices and saw Indian matters from their own perspective, they nevertheless furnished an element of articulate concern for the Indians that could be ridiculed and often pushed aside but never completely ignored. Especially hard working was Felix Brunot. "Mr. Brunot saw that the task before him was tremendous," his sympathetic biographer recorded. "There was a race to civilise, there were agents to humanise, and there was a great nation to educate in the principles of Christian love toward an oppressed and heathen race." For five years Brunot spent his life on the work of the board—traveling to New York and Washington for meetings and consultations, writing articles and letters to stir up concern for the Indians, drawing up the reports of the board, and visiting the Indian tribes in the West during the summer months.[24] The secretary of the board, Vincent Colyer, in the first year alone submitted reports on the condition of the Indians he visited in Kansas, the Indian Ter-

23. Ibid., p. 10.
24. Charles Lewis Slattery, *Felix Reville Brunot* (New York: Longmans, Green and Company, 1901), pp. 147–48.

ritory, Texas, New Mexico, Arizona, and Colorado, as well as a long report on the Indians of Alaska. In 1871 he submitted another long report on the Apaches of New Mexico and Arizona.[25]

Of more practical significance than the investigative reports of members was the board's work in supervising the purchase of supplies for the Indians in an attempt to end the fraud and corruption in the Indian service. Poor goods were contracted for at high prices, and merchants and their friends grew rich by cheating the government and the Indians. In July 1870 Congress directed the board to inspect all goods purchased for the Indians, and the experienced businessmen who made up the special purchasing committee worked year after year to correct abuses. The committee was optimistic—it was convinced, it reported in 1871, "that all 'Indian rings' can be broken up, and that the wards of the nation, who have been so long the victims of greedy and designing men, ought and must be treated in a manner worthy of the highest moral obligations of a Christian government." Even with the loopholes that provided opportunity for continuing fraud, substantial savings and a rise in the quality of goods resulted from the committee's supervision.[26]

Meanwhile, the executive committee of the board examined the accounts and vouchers presented to the Indian Office for payment, a duty given to the board by Congress in 1871. The task was onerous and had not been solicited by the board, but it was an essential part of sharing responsibility with the secretary of the interior in the disbursement of funds. Millions of dollars' worth of bills and vouchers were examined each year, and the committee rejected those that were improper or unreasonable. Although the secretary of the interior frequently overruled the committee's decisions, the vigilance of these philanthropists saved the government large sums of money.[27]

25. *Report of the Board of Indian Commissioners, 1869*, pp. 30–55, 81–164; ibid., 1871, pp. 32–86. The 1871 report was printed separately as *Peace with the Apaches of New Mexico and Arizona: Report of Vincent Colyer, Member of the Board of Indian Commissioners, 1871* (Washington: GPO, 1872).

26. 16 *United States Statutes* 360; *Report of the Board of Indian Commissioners, 1870*, pp. 21–23; ibid., 1871, p. 161. See the reports of the purchasing committee in the annual reports of the board. The report for 1875, pp. 19–24, is a long recital of specific cases that revealed "the tricks, subterfuges, evasions, and combinations" that the purchasing committee experienced, and its attempts to defeat them. George H. Stuart, who served as chairman of the committee, tells of its work in *Life of George H. Stuart*, pp. 242–45.

27. 16 *United States Statutes* 568. In 1871, for example, the executive committee examined 1,136 vouchers, representing a cash disbursement of $5,240,729.60, of which it rejected or suspended $153,166.20. In 1873 it examined 1,656 vouchers, representing disbursement of $6,032,877.65, of which 39 vouchers representing $426,909.96 were turned down as fraudulent or questionable. *Report of the Board of Indian Commissioners, 1871*, p. 11–12; ibid., 1873, p. 9.

Still another function of the board was its liaison with the missionary societies engaged in Indian work. At a meeting in Washington each winter the board met with representatives of the missionary groups to discuss Indian matters. These conferences, which were usually attended by the commissioner of Indian affairs, were a valuable forum for promoting Indian reform, and they served to confirm and strengthen the religious reform sentiment of the day. They brought the evangelical churches into semi-official association with the men who formulated Indian policy and furnished a useful platform from which to preach the reforms devised.[28]

CHURCHES AND THE AGENCIES

The second structural component of Grant's peace policy was the apportionment of the Indian agencies among church groups, with the understanding that the missionary boards would nominate the agents and other employees at the agencies. By such an arrangement, it was hoped, the evils resulting from dishonest and incompetent agents would be obviated. This extreme measure, an admission by the government that it was unable to carry out its obligations by ordinary procedures, was a striking example of the conviction in public as well as private circles that only by emphasis on moral and religious means would the Indians be led along the path to civilization.

The roots of the program were diverse. It was perhaps an obvious conclusion that if evils were caused because bad men were appointed agents, then the evils could be corrected by appointing good men. If religious men had provided such a positive influence for good among the Indians as missionaries and teachers, certainly the good effects could be increased by broadening the scope of their activities. Bishop Whipple had recommended such a move, and army officers noted that missionaries had often succeeded with the Indians where military and civilian officers had failed.[29]

The postwar allotment of agencies to religious bodies began with the Quakers. The memorial from the Baltimore assembly of the seven Yearly Meetings of Friends in January 1869 indicated a renewed concern for In-

28. Reports of the winter missionary conferences are included in the *Report of the Board of Indian Commissioners*, except that of 1872, which was published separately as *Journal of the Second Annual Conference of the Board of Indian Commissioners with the Representatives of the Religious Societies Cooperating with the Government, and Reports of Their Work among the Indians* (Washington: GPO, 1873). Catholic missionaries, except in a few isolated instances at the beginning, did not attend the conferences.

29. Robert H. Keller, Jr., *American Protestantism and United States Indian Policy, 1869–82* (Lincoln: University of Nebraska Press, 1983), pp. 20–21. Keller's work is the best general study of this aspect of the peace policy.

Peace Policy and Indian Wars

29. Henry B. Whipple

The Protestant Episcopal Bishop of Minnesota, Henry B. Whipple, was a longtime reformer in Indian affairs. Whipple pleaded with President Lincoln to change the conditions of fraud and corruption in the Indian service, and he took the side of the Indians after the outbreak in Minnesota of 1862. His interest in Indian affairs continued through the rest of the century.

The Peace Commission authorized by Congress in 1867 negotiated treaties with the Indians on both the southern and northern plains in an attempt to bring peace to the West by locating the tribes on reservations. The members of the commission were, left to right, Alfred H. Terry, William S. Harney, William T. Sherman, Nathaniel G. Taylor, Samuel F. Tappan, and Christopher C. Augur. In the center is a Sioux woman.

The Peace Commission met with Cheyenne, Arapaho, Kiowa, Comanche, and Kiowa-Apache Indians at Medicine Lodge Creek in southern Kansas in October 1867. The treaties signed there provided for reservations for the Indians in the western part of the Indian Territory. This drawing is by Hermann Stieffel.

The peace policy after the Civil War is associated with the presidency of Ulysses S. Grant. This peace medal was produced at that time for presentation to the Indians; it is full of messages and symbols of peace and an agricultural life.

30. Medicine Lodge Creek Treaty Council

31. United States Indian Peace Commission

32. Grant Indian Peace Medal

33. Felix R. Brunot

34. William T. Sherman

35. Ely S. Parker

Brunot, Sherman, and Parker played key roles in the peace policy. The first, as head of the Board of Indian Commissioners, directed the work of that reforming group. The second represented the military point of view that the Indians needed to be handled with force and not by ineffective good wishes. The third, a Seneca Indian, was Grant's first commissioner of Indian Affairs, who helped to inaugurate the peace policy.

The Modoc War of 1873 was a severe test of the peace policy. When a peace commission led by General Canby met with the Modocs on Good Friday 1873, the Modoc leader Captain Jack killed Canby by shooting him at short range, and other members of the commission were killed or wounded. Captain Jack was later executed for the murder, and the Modoc tribe was exiled to the Indian Territory.

36. Edward R. S. Canby

37. Captain Jack, Modoc

38. Carl Schurz

Schurz, a political refugee from Germany, was a notable political reformer. As secretary of the interior in President Hayes's administration (1877–1881), he took an active part in Indian affairs. He hoped by education and the individualization of Indian land holdings to enable the Indians to make their way in American society.

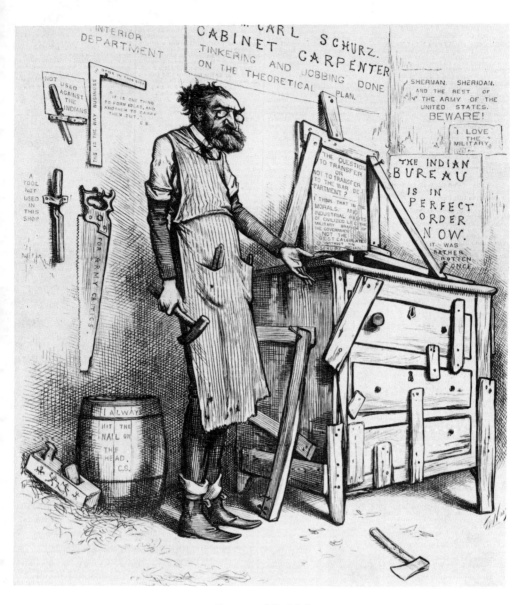

39. Cartoon of Carl Schurz

By reform of the Indian Bureau, Secretary Schurz hoped to diffuse military attacks upon civilian control of Indian affairs. Thomas Nast, in *Harper's Weekly* for January 25, 1879, pokes fun of Schurz's endeavors, which in the end were more successful than the cartoon suggests.

41. Chief Joseph, Nez Perce   40. George Armstrong Custer

Custer, the "boy general" of the Civil War, was flamboyant and impetuous. The annihilation of his troops of the Seventh Infantry at the Battle of the Little Bighorn in June 1876 stunned the nation. The subsequent military campaigns to chastise the Indians destroyed the power of the Indians on the northern plains and forced them to reservations.

Chief Joseph received national attention when he led the flight of the Nez Perce Indians from the military forces of the United States in 1877. After his surrender to General Nelson A. Miles, he was taken to the Indian Territory, where he insistently demanded return to his homeland in the Pacific Northwest, a plea sympathetically supported by many reformers.

dians, and on January 25 a delegation of Quakers met with president-elect Grant to urge an Indian policy based on peace and Christianity and the selection of religious employees for the agencies as far as practicable. To this group Grant is said to have replied: "Gentlemen, your advice is good. I accept it. Now give me the names of some Friends for Indian agents and I will appoint them. Let us have peace." A similar committee of Philadelphia Friends also visited Grant. The committees were impressed with his cordial attitude and his apparently earnest desire to begin a more peaceful and humane policy toward the Indians.[30]

Grant moved quickly to implement the Quakers' proposal. On February 15, 1869, Ely S. Parker, then Grant's aide-de-camp, wrote to Benjamin Hallowell, secretary of the Quaker conference, asking for a list of Quakers whom the Society of Friends would endorse as suitable persons to be Indian agents. He added that Grant also wished to assure him "that any attempt which may or can be made by your Society, for the improvement, education, and Christianization of the Indians, under such Agencies, will receive . . . all the encouragement and protection which the laws of the United States will warrant him in giving."[31] The Quakers, after some hesitation about accepting posts on the distant and exposed frontier, responded favorably, and by mid-June both the Orthodox and Hicksite Friends had appointed superintendents and agents and organized special comittees to deal with Indian matters. The Hicksite Friends were given the Northern Superintendency, comprising six agencies in Nebraska; the Orthodox Friends received the Central Superintendency, comprising the Indians in Kansas and the Kiowas, Comanches, and a number of other tribes in the Indian Territory. Secretary of the Interior Cox noted: "The Friends were appointed not because they were believed to have any monopoly of honesty or of good will toward the Indians, but because their selection would of itself be understood by the country to indicate the policy adopted, namely, the sincere cultivation of peaceful relations with the tribes and the choice of agents who did not, for personal profit, seek the service, but were sought for it because they were at least deemed fit for its duties."[32]

30. T. C. Battey in introduction to Lawrie Tatum, *Our Red Brothers and the Peace Policy of President Ulysses S. Grant* (Philadelphia: John C. Winston and Company, 1899), pp. 17–18; *Report of the Joint Delegation Appointed by the Committees on the Indian Concern of the Yearly Meetings of Baltimore, Philadelphia and New York* (Baltimore: J. Jones, 1869). The Quakers' concern in Indian matters is well treated in Rayner W. Kelsey, *Friends and the Indians, 1655–1917* (Philadelphia: Associated Executive Committee of Friends on Indian Affairs, 1917); see especially pp. 162–99.

31. The letter is printed in Kelsey, *Friends and the Indians*, p. 168, and appears in many of the Quaker reports; it was considered the basic authorization for their participation.

32. Report of the Secretary of the Interior, 1869, *House Executive Document* no. 1,

For the other agencies Grant appointed army officers, a move that was not surprising in light of the reduction of the army that had come in 1868. He did this for reasons of economy, since the officers otherwise would be on pay but not on duty; and they were thought to be a "corps of public servants whose integrity and faithfulness could be relied upon, and in whom the public were prepared to have confidence." But this solution to the problems of political patronage was soon upset, for Congress on July 15, 1870, forbade army officers to accept civil appointments. Although such action can be explained by the desire of spoilsmen to regain a foothold in the Indian service by means of political appointments, there had been strong opposition to the army officers on the part of reform elements as well. The massacre of Piegan Indians by troops under Colonel E. M. Baker on January 23, 1870, an action approved by General Sheridan, caused a great humanitarian outcry. Such was the effect of army attempts to civilize the Indians, the critics declared. In the House of Representatives, during debate on the Indian appropriation bill, Daniel Voorhees of Indiana pointed to the "curious spectacle" of the president of the United States "upon the one hand welcoming his Indian agents in their peaceful garments and broadbrims coming to tell him what they had done as missionaries of a gospel of peace and of a beneficent Government, and upon the other hand welcoming this man, General Sheridan, stained with the blood of innocent women and children!"[33]

Vincent Colyer, secretary of the Board of Indian Commissioners, was convinced that missionaries and soldiers as agents formed an inconsistent combination. Fearing, however, that if the army officers were removed the evils of political appointments would return, he began a campaign to enlist other denominations besides the Quakers in the Indian service. With the approval of Cox and Grant, Colyer sought help from the various missionary boards, and he slowly gained their support. His goal was clearly a humanitarian one. He contended against army control because that would mean only policing the Indians, not reclaiming or civilizing them, and by extended church control the efforts of the politicians to regain their sway would be thwarted.[34]

41–2, serial 1414, p. x. Quaker participation is treated in Clyde A. Milner II, *With Good Intentions: Quaker Work among the Pawnees, Otos, and Omahas in the 1870s* (Lincoln: University of Nebraska Press, 1982).

33. Report of the Secretary of the Interior, 1869, p. x; 16 *United States Statutes* 319; *Congressional Globe*, 41st Congress, 2d session, p. 1581. See the discussion of the Piegan incident in Robert W. Mardock, *The Reformers and the American Indian* (Columbia: University of Missouri Press, 1971), pp. 67–73.

34. Colyer's view and his successful efforts to enlist other denominations to nominate agents are seen in his correspondence with officials of the various churches, printed

President Grant's motives are more difficult to isolate. Some observers credited his experience as a young army officer in the Pacific Northwest for his concern to right the wrongs suffered by the Indians. His own religious views and religious experience were hardly strong enough to have been a dominant element in his policy making, yet it seems reasonable that his desire to end the warfare that had so long marked Indian-white relations led him to accept the Quakers and other sincerely religious men as instruments to that end. At any rate, Grant justified his initial action in his first annual message to Congress. "The Society of Friends is well known as having succeeded in living in peace with the Indians in the early settlement of Pennsylvania, while their white neighbors of other sects in other sections were constantly embroiled," he said. "They are also known for their opposition to all strife, violence, and war, and are generally noted for their strict integrity and fair dealings. These considerations induced me to give the management of a few reservations of Indians to them and to throw the burden of the selection of agents upon the society itself. The result has proven most satisfactory." When the army agents were removed, it was a logical step to expand the system, to offer the agencies to other religious groups, who could be expected "to Christianize and civilize the Indian, and to train him in the arts of peace."[35]

Commissioner of Indian Affairs Parker strongly endorsed the scheme. "The plan is obviously a wise and humane one," he remarked. "Under a political management for a long series of years, and the expenditure of large sums of money annually, the Indians made but little progress toward that healthy Christian civilization in which are embraced the elements of material wealth and intellectual and moral development. . . . Not, therefore, as a denier resort to save a dying race, but from the highest moral conviction of Christian humanity, the President wisely determined to invoke the coöperation of the entire religious element of the country, to help, by their labors and counsels, to bring about and produce the greatest amount

---

in *Report of the Board of Indian Commissioners*, 1870, pp. 93–100. The sense of urgency and the pressure put on the missionary boards can be seen in the correspondence of Colyer, Cox, and Delano with the Reverend John C. Lowrie, secretary of the Presbyterian mission board, August–December 1870, in American Indian Correspondence, MS In 25 B–1–C, Presbyterian Historical Society, Philadelphia.

35. Fred L. Israel, ed., *The State of the Union Messages of the Presidents, 1790–1966*, 3 vols. (New York: Chelsea House, 1966), 2: 1199, 1216–17. Henry G. Waltman, in "Circumstantial Reformer: President Grant and the Indian Problem," *Arizona and the West* 13 (Winter 1971); 323–42, attempts to evaluate Grant's personal contribution to the reform of Indian policy. He concludes that "Grant was a well-intentioned, but shortsighted and inconsistent would-be Indian reformer whose identification with the Peace Policy was, in some respects, more symbolic than substantial."

of good from the expenditure of the munificent annual appropriations of money by Congress, for the civilization and Christianization of the Indian race."[36] These high-sounding sentiments were not mere rhetoric. Grant and Parker were convinced that a peace policy must work. The assignment of the agencies to the churches appeared to be a wonderful solution, in tune with the idealistic, humanitarian sentiments of the day.

Vincent Colyer, so much involved in the formulation and promotion of the scheme, was soon at work allotting the agencies to the various denominations. The only enunciated principle appeared at the end of 1870 in Grant's annual message to Congress, in which he declared his determination "to give all the agencies to such religious denominations as had heretofore established missionaries among the Indians, and perhaps to some other denominations who would undertake the work on the same terms, i.e., as a missionary work." But this was much too vague to be satisfactory, and Colyer was forced to make an initial division on the basis of his own scanty information about the agencies and the missionary work being performed at them. Colyer's original plans, which he admitted were "simply suggestions," were modified when the agencies were actually assigned, and changes in apportioning the agencies occurred throughout the existence of the policy.[37]

The distribution caused immediate dissatisfaction, and one religious group after another complained about being slighted or overlooked. The vagueness of criteria for appointment was partly to blame. Different principles were proposed, as they fitted the purposes of the churches concerned. One argument was that an agency belonged to whichever group had started the first mission there, whether or not it had been a success. Catholics insisted that agencies, according to Grant's statement, should be assigned to churches that had missionaries at them in 1870 and, if more than one group was represented, to the one that had been there first. At other times Catholics argued that the Indians themselves should choose which denomination they wanted. A Baptist member of the Board of Indian Commissioners proposed distribution according to denominational size, for the Baptists felt cheated in getting fewer agencies than the Episcopalians and Presbyterians, who had fewer adherents. The board argued that no church

36. CIA Report, 1870, serial 1449, p. 474.
37. Israel, *State of the Union Messages*, 2:1216; Colyer to Cox, August 11, 1870, *Report of the Board of Indian Commissioners*, 1870, p. 98. There is a listing of the assigned agencies and the number of Indians at each in CIA Report, 1872, serial 1560, pp. 461–62, and a slightly different listing in *Report of the Board of Indian Commissioners*, 1872, pp. 29–46. For a tabular listing of apportionments for 1870, 1872, and 1875, with a complete list of agencies assigned to each group and a statement of previous missionary efforts at each agency, see Keller, *American Protestantism and Indian Policy*, appendix 1, pp. 219–22.

TABLE 3: Distribution of Indian Agencies to Church Groups, 1872

Church	Agency	State or Territory	Number of Indians
AMERICAN BOARD OF COMMISSIONERS FOR FOREIGN MISSIONS	Sisseton	Dakota Territory	1,496
BAPTIST	Cherokee	Indian Territory	18,000
	Creek	Indian Territory	12,300
	Walker River	Nevada	6,000
	Paiute	Nevada	2,500
	Special	Utah Territory	3,000
			41,800
CATHOLIC	Tulalip	Washington Territory	3,600
	Colville	Washington Territory	3,349
	Grande Ronde	Oregon	870
	Umatilla	Oregon	837
	Flathead	Montana Territory	1,780
	Grande River	Dakota Territory	6,700
	Devils Lake	Dakota Territory	720
			17,856
CHRISTIAN	Pueblo	New Mexico Territory	7,683
	Neah Bay	Washington Territory	604
			8,287
CONGREGATIONAL	Green Bay	Wisconsin	2,871
	Chippewas of Lake Superior	Wisconsin	5,150
	Chippewas of the Mississippi	Minnesota	6,455
			14,476
FRIENDS (HICKSITE) Northern Superintendency	Great Nemaha	Nebraska	313
	Omaha	Nebraska	969
	Winnebago	Nebraska	1,440
	Pawnee	Nebraska	2,447
	Oto	Nebraska	464
	Santee Sioux	Nebraska	965
			6,598
FRIENDS (ORTHODOX) Central Superintendency	Potawatomi	Kansas	400
	Kaw	Kansas	290
	Kickapoo	Kansas	598
	Quapaw	Indian Territory	1,070
	Osage	Indian Territory	4,000
	Sac and Fox	Indian Territory	463
	Shawnee	Indian Territory	663
	Wichita	Indian Territory	1,250
	Kiowa	Indian Territory	5,490
	Upper Arkansas	Indian Territory	3,500
			17,724

TABLE 3, *continued*

Church	Agency	State or Territory	Number of Indians
LUTHERAN	Sac and Fox	Iowa	273
METHODIST	Hoopa Valley	California	725
	Round Valley	California	1,700
	Tule River	California	374
	Yakima	Washington Territory	3,000
	Skokomish	Washington Territory	919
	Quinaielt	Washington Territory	520
	Warm Springs	Oregon	626
	Siletz	Oregon	2,500
	Klamath	Oregon	4,000
	Blackfeet	Montana Territory	7,500
	Crow	Montana Territory	2,700
	Milk River	Montana Territory	19,755
	Fort Hall	Idaho Territory	1,037
	Michigan	Michigan	9,117
			54,473
PRESBYTERIAN	Choctaw	Indian Territory	16,000
	Seminole	Indian Territory	2,398
	Abiquiu	New Mexico Territory	1,920
	Navajo	New Mexico Territory	9,114
	Mescalero Apache	New Mexico Territory	830
	Tularosa or Southern Apache	New Mexico Territory	1,200
	Moquis Pueblo (Hopi)	Arizona Territory	3,000
	Nez Perce	Idaho Territory	2,807
	Uintah Valley	Utah Territory	800
			38,069
PROTESTANT EPISCOPAL	Whetstone	Dakota Territory	5,000
	Ponca	Dakota Territory	735
	Upper Missouri	Dakota Territory	2,547
	Fort Berthold	Dakota Territory	2,700
	Cheyenne River	Dakota Territory	6,000
	Yankton	Dakota Territory	1,947
	Red Cloud	Dakota Territory	7,000
	Shoshone	Wyoming Territory	1,000
			26,929
REFORMED DUTCH	Colorado River	Arizona Territory	828
	Pima and Maricopa	Arizona Territory	4,342
	Camp Grant	Arizona Territory	900
	Camp Verde	Arizona Territory	748
	White Mountain or Camp Apache	Arizona Territory	1,300
			8,300

TABLE 3, *continued*

Church	Agency	State or Territory	Number of Indians
UNITARIAN	Los Pinos	Colorado Territory	3,000
	White River	Colorado Territory	800
			3,800
		Total	239,899

Source: CIA Report, 1872, serial 1560, pp. 461–62.

had a *right* to any agency, and that the quality of work done by the churches or the simple resolution of competing claims might call for a change. The welfare of the Indians, it insisted, was paramount to the benefit to be received by any church. Sometimes the rival groups were left to work out exchanges and other agreements among themselves.[38]

What the government wanted from the churches was a total transformation of the agencies from political sinecures to missionary outposts. The religious societies were expected not only to nominate strong men as agents but to supply to a large extent the subordinate agency personnel. Teachers especially were desired, men and women with a religious dedication to the work that would make up for the low pay and often frightening conditions. The churches, too, it was assumed, would pursue more energetically and more effectively the strictly missionary activities already begun now that conflicts between government agents and missionaries would no longer be an obstacle. The commissioner of Indian affairs, in fact, asserted in 1872 that "the importance of securing harmony of feeling and concert of action between the agents of the Government and the missionaries at the several agencies, in the matter of the moral and religious advancement of the Indians, was the single reason formally given for placing the nominations to Indian agencies in the hands of the denominational societies."[39] Agency physicians, interpreters, and mechanics, if they were of solid moral worth, could all contribute to the goal of civilizing and Christianizing the Indians.

Utopia seemed to be within grasp. The reports of the secretaries of the interior, the commissioners of Indian affairs, the Board of Indian Commissioners, and Grant himself rang loud with praise for the new policy.

38. Keller, *American Protestantism and Indian Policy*, pp. 34–35.
39. CIA Report, 1872, serial 1560, p. 461.

Both the Board of Indian Commissioners and the church-run agencies, despite the early praise, were soon in trouble. The romantic ideal of depoliticizing the Indian Office and the administration of the agencies by the appointment of high-minded, religiously motivated individuals ran up against the hard rock of practical operations within an old political system. The Board of Indian Commissioners felt the pressures first. As the board members began their work, all seemed to go smoothly, and the secretaries of the interior lauded their efforts and "the healthful effect of their influence and advice."[40] But the board soon found that its attempts to do good were blocked by powerful forces and its advice and recommendations ignored or contradicted. Goodwill and integrity on the part of the board's members met greed in the "Indian ring" and corruption among public officials. The board underwent a crisis in 1874 from which it only slowly recovered.

The problem was one of authority. Could there in fact be "joint authority" between the Department of the Interior and the quasi-private group of unpaid, philanthropic businessmen? Brunot, conscientiously trying to find out precisely what power the board had in supervising expenditures, submitted the documents relating to the board to the attorney general for a ruling. Although the ruling upheld the board's authority, in practice its recommendations were often set aside. Many disbursements, moreover, were not cleared through the board at all, and contracts were awarded without competitive bids.[41]

One element in the conflict was an attack on Commissioner of Indian Affairs Parker for alleged questionable dealings in procuring Indian supplies. The attack, led by William Welsh, who had lost none of his interest in Indian affairs by his resignation from the board, resulted in a congressional investigation of the Office of Indian Affairs. The investigating committee found "irregularities, neglect, and incompetency," but it exonerated Parker of fraud or corruption. Nevertheless, Parker resigned in July 1871, charging the whole affair to the enmity of those "who waxed rich and fat from the plundering of the poor Indians"; he declared it was "no longer a pleasure to discharge patriotic duties."[42] Although the *Nation* exulted that

40. Report of the Secretary of the Interior, 1870, *House Executive Document* no. 1, 41–3, serial 1449, p. ix; ibid., 1871, *House Executive Document* no. 1, part 5, 42–2, serial 1505, p. 3.

41. *Report of the Board of Indian Commissioners*, 1873, pp. 6–9. Congress in 1872 provided that the board's approval was not a prerequisite for payment of vouchers. 17 *United States Statutes* 186.

42. Welsh, *Indian Office*; William Welsh, *Summing Up Evidence before a Commit-

a revolution had taken place by "the complete overthrow of a most gigantic system of wrong, robbery, hypocrisy, greed, and cruelty, and in the triumph of right, of official integrity, of administrative economy, and of the principles of a Christian civilization," the oppressive pressures on the board did not end.[43] Parker's forced resignation was countered by the forcing from office of Vincent Colyer, the board's secretary, whose investigation and reports on Indian affairs in the Southwest had won him the enmity of Secretary of the Interior Columbus Delano.[44]

By 1874 matters had come to an impasse, and all the original members of the Board of Indian Commissioners resigned. "It was obvious, towards the close of 1873," Brunot's biographer wrote, "that the original members of the Board of Indian Commissioners could not serve much longer. They freely gave of their busy lives for the sake of the Indians, but when they found repeatedly during the last year that their recommendations were ignored, that bills, laboriously examined by them and rejected by them, were paid, that gross breaking of the law in giving contracts was winked at, and that many important matters were not submitted to them at all, then they decided that their task was as useless as it was irritating."[45]

The passing of the original members marked the end of one phase of the board's existence; the new members appointed in 1874, although they dif-

---

tee of the House of Representatives, Charged with the Investigation of Misconduct in the Indian Office (Washington: H. Polkinhorn and Company, 1871); House Report no. 39, 41 3, serial 1464, pp. ii; Norton P. Chipman, Investigation into Indian Affairs, before the Committee on Appropriations of the House of Representatives: Argument of N. P. Chipman, on Behalf of Hon. E. S. Parker, Commissioner of Indian Affairs (Washington: Powell, Ginck and Company, 1871); "Writings of General Parker," Publications of the Buffalo Historical Society 8 (1905): 526–27. Arthur C. Parker, The Life of General Ely S. Parker (Buffalo: Buffalo Historical Society, 1919), pp. 150–61, has nothing but praise for Parker's career as commissioner of Indian affairs. A detailed and balanced account of the investigation of Parker and of his conflict with Welsh and the Board of Indian Commissioners appears in William H. Armstrong, Warrior in Two Camps: Ely S. Parker, Union General and Seneca Chief (Syracuse: Syracuse University Press, 1978), pp. 152–61.

43. Nation 13 (August 17, 1871): 100–101.

44. In October 1871 Brunot had refused an offer of the position of commissioner of Indian affairs, perhaps suspecting even then that conditions were hostile to the reforms he envisaged. Delano to Brunot, October 17, 1871, Records of the Board of Indian Commissioners, Minutes of Board Meetings, vol. 1, p. 61; Brunot to Delano, October 19, 1871, ibid., p. 62. Grant wrote to Stuart about the matter: "I will be careful that no one is apt'd Ind. Com. who is not fully in sympathy with a humane policy towards the indians. I will see too that he has the full confidence of the Peace [Board of Indian] Commissioners." Grant to Stuart, July 22, 1871, George Hay Stuart Papers, Library of Congress.

45. Slattery, Brunot, p. 217. See also Dodge, Memorials of William E. Dodge, pp. 177–78.

fered little from the old in background and religious outlook, were less inclined to set themselves up in opposition to the official government departments.[46] The old board members had attempted what was perhaps
impossible: to assume direct responsibility for Indian finances and for Indian policy in general. But the seeds they planted would germinate and
blossom later. The new board, weak though it was, continued the idea that
the moral and religious sentiments of the nation should be represented in
the formulation and administration of Indian policy. Brunot and his colleagues were the first example of highly motivated men in a corporate,
united attempt to change the course of government action from outside
the administrative structure. The idea would not die; it lived on in the reform sentiment that came to dominate the 1880s and 1890s.

The assignment of agencies to churches that had looked so promising in
principle did not work well in practice. Fundamentally, the missionary societies were not prepared to handle the tremendous responsibility suddenly cast upon them. It was not as simple as many sanguine persons had
thought to supply competent Christian men to run the agencies. Such men
were not available in large numbers, and the missionary boards were none
too astute in selecting agents. Amid the words of praise for the new system
in the official reports were clear indications that men of inadequate character and competence had been appointed. In 1873 the Board of Indian Commissioners noted that "a vastly better class of men" had been given to the
Indian service and that "at the present time a large majority of the agents
are, it is believed, honest men." But the basic criticism remained: some of
the agents were men with no real sympathy for the missionary effort. Of
the eight hundred agency employees under control of the churches, many
did not display Christian character, and some of them were from the worst
social classes in the country. Until such difficulties were overcome, the
work of Christianization would yield little fruit.[47]

Nor were the auxiliary services of education and missionary work effectively pursued, for most of the missionary boards found that providing for
the Indian service was a distasteful responsibility. Among many of the
churches, the Indians had to compete with foreign infidels, who captured
the imagination of the communicants and most of the missionary funds.

---

46. Congressional debates on the board and its continued existence and on internal
dissension within the board are discussed in Loring Benson Priest, *Uncle Sam's Stepchildren: The Reformation of United States Indian Policy, 1865–1887* (New Brunswick:
Rutgers University Press, 1942), pp. 47–52. Priest takes too limited a view of the board's
work and its successes, however.

47. Report of the Secretary of the Interior, 1872, *House Executive Document* no. 1,
part 5, 42–3, serial 1560, p. 9: *Report of the Board of Indian Commissioners, 1871*, p. 11;
ibid., 1873, pp. 24–25. For a heavily documented account of troubles in the peace policy
agencies, see Keller, *American Protestantism and Indian Policy*, pp. 107–25.

In truth, the internal effectiveness of the whole policy was open to serious doubt, although the demands of the agencies were met differently by the different churches. The Quakers and the Episcopalians, who helped to originate the peace policy, met the challenge most effectively. The Roman Catholics, although they felt they were persecuted, also performed well. The Methodists, who had been most favored in the distribution of the agencies, did the least.[48]

Equally serious as the lack of sustained interest on the part of the churches was the interdenominational rivalry. Maintaining a position against a conflicting group was, unfortunately, often a more powerful motivation than concern for the welfare of the Indians. Examples of these fights abounded; they were all disedifying if not scandalous. If many could be explained by pettiness and denominational bias, the conflict between the Protestant mission groups and the Roman Catholics was nothing less than flagrant bigotry. The peace policy of Grant came at a time when Protestant missionary interest in the Indians was waning and Catholic activity in Indian missions and the Indian schools had begun a remarkable upsurge. This changing relation in the strength of the rival mission groups in itself explains much of the friction, for the Protestants, whose long dominance had not been seriously challenged before, now faced a threat from growing "Romanism."[49]

In its origins, the peace policy, both in the Board of Indian Commissioners and in the plan for allotting the agencies to the churches, was a Protestant affair. When the allotments were made, the Catholics were shocked to receive only seven agencies; on the basis of their previous missionary work they had expected thirty-eight. Their leaders protested, but to respond to Catholic complaints once the assignments had been made would have meant taking agencies away from groups to which they had been given. In order to protect their own interests against what appeared to them as a unified bloc of Protestants, therefore, the Catholics in 1874 organized a central agency, the Bureau of Catholic Indian Missions, to direct the work of the missions in the field and to lobby in Washington for

48. Keller, *American Protestantism and Indian Policy*, pp. 47–66, gives a denomination-by-denomination evaluation of the Protestant performance. For an evaluation of the Quaker agents of the Northern Superintendency, see Milner, *With Good Intentions*. For the work of the Methodists, see Robert Lee Whitner, "The Methodist Episcopal Church and Grant's Peace Policy: A Study of the Methodist Agencies, 1870–1882" (Ph.D. dissertation, University of Minnesota, 1959). Whitner concludes, p. 281: "The record of the Missionary Society of the Methodist Episcopal church as a participant in the peace policy was largely a failure. It did little to improve the service or the condition of the Indians. It did much to perpetuate sectarianism and intolerance and bigotry in America."

49. There are extended discussions of denominational conflict in Keller's book and Whitner's dissertation. See also the account in Priest, *Uncle Sam's Stepchildren*, pp. 31–36.

mission needs. The conflicts were numerous on the reservations, where Catholic and Protestant agents and missionaries carried on quite un-Christian feuds.[50]

Much was made of the question of religious liberty. Did assignment of an agency to a particular religious group exclude other denominations from the reservation? The Catholics, particularly, cut off by apportionment from a number of reservations where they had traditionally done missionary work, insisted on the right to preach and to teach the Indians on reservations officially assigned to Protestants. The controversy grew to considerable proportions, and no solution seemed in sight until a Protestant group in turn was excluded from carrying on its ministrations to Indians at a Catholic agency. Then the whole matter took on a new light, and ultimately a regulation from Secretary of the Interior Carl Schurz in 1881 declared that Indian reservations would be open to all religious denominations, except where "the presence of rival organizations would manifestly be perilous to peace and order" or where treaty stipulations would be violated.[51]

But religious liberty was not very broadly conceived in nineteenth-century America. The Mormons, who had done a good deal of missionary work among the Indians, did not participate in the peace policy. Nor were the southern branches of the great Protestant denominations allotted agencies, even though the Southern Methodists, for example, had been active Indian missionaries. What was more serious was the complete disregard for the religious views and the religious rights of the Indians themselves. Quakers, Methodists, Episcopalians, and all the other Protestants, fighting for the religious liberty of their own groups on the reservations, made no move to grant so much as a hearing to the Indian religions. The record of the Catholics was no better. They criticized Protestant bigotry and called for freedom of conscience, but that freedom did not extend to native religions, which were universally condemned. The missionaries were not in-

---

50. Strong Catholic attacks on Grant's policy appeared in *Address of the Catholic Clergy of the Province of Oregon, to the Catholics of the United States, on President Grant's Indian Policy, in Its Bearings upon Catholic Interests at Large* (Portland, Oregon: Catholic Sentinel Publication Company, 1874); and *Catholic Grievances in Relation to the Administration of Indian Affairs: Being a Report Presented to the Catholic Young Men's National Union, at Its Annual Convention, Held in Boston, Massachusetts, May 10th and 11th, 1882* (Richmond, Virginia, 1882). A thorough study of the Bureau of Catholic Indian Missions and of the work of the Catholics under the peace policy in the Sioux agencies in Rahill, *Catholic Indian Missions and Grant's Peace Policy*.

51. Rahill, *Catholic Indian Missions and Grant's Peace Policy*, pp. 273–307; R. Pierce Beaver, *Church, State, and the American Indians: Two and a Half Centuries of Partnership in Missions Between Protestant Churches and Government* (St. Louis: Concordia Publishing House, 1966), pp. 157–61; Keller, *American Protestantism and Indian Policy*, pp. 177–84. Schurz's statement is quoted in Rahill, p. 306.

terested in the Indians' right to maintain and defend their own religion. By religious freedom they meant liberty of action on the reservations for their own missionary activities.

It quickly became clear that the assignment of agencies to the churches did not solve the "Indian problem." Good intentions of Christian men were not enough to correct evils of a complex nature or overcome a long history of mismanagement. Failure to study or appreciate the Indian side of the question, to adopt or build upon the societal forms that persisted in the Indian communities, weakened all the missionary efforts. And although most of the church groups professed a sincere regard for the well-being and advancement of the Indians, all this was thought of completely in terms of transforming them into acceptable Christian citizens. Catholics and Protestants alike saw little worth preserving in the Indian groups they sought to convert and civilize.

Internal weaknesses and dissensions in the various missionary groups together with the interdenominational bickering and open conflict alone would have doomed the policy. But external forces, too, were at work. The policy of church agencies would have brought difficulties in times of the highest moral rectitude in government circles; in fact, it was attempted in a decade noted in American history as a low point in public morals. "Grantism" became a term for fraud and corruption in high federal office, and the Indian service was one of the more lucrative areas in which politicians and spoilsmen could grow rich. It is understandable that rapacious individuals would not stand idly by when the source of rich spoils was cut off by the missionary policy. Almost from the very start of the program, pressures of political patronage were at work, undermining the system. Secretary of the Interior Cox, a man of integrity and one of the architects of the peace policy, resigned in October 1870. Under his successor, Columbus Delano, the Interior Department provided one scandal after another, and Delano was forced to resign in 1875. During his term he made it clear to the churches that he had the final say in the appointment of agents, and he frequently presented agents to the missionary boards for their rubber-stamp approval. Being a "good Christian brother," he told the Board of Indian Commissioners, was "not enough to make a man a satisfactory agent."[52]

The White House, too, manipulated agency appointments for political friends, and even the Board of Indian Commissioners on occasion interfered for special appointments. More subtle but even more significant were the pressures exerted by Congress, many of whose members and their constituents did not understand or could not abide a church-dominated Indian service. If the agents themselves were church-appointed, at least room among the subordinate officials on the reservations could be made for a

---

52. *Report of the Board of Indian Commissioners*, 1870, p. 112.

friend in need of a job. Missionary boards did not know just how to counteract senatorial pressure for or against confirmation of particular individuals and often gave in rather than fight the issue. Senators frequently insisted that agents be appointed from men who lived in the state concerned,
thus severely limiting the churches' freedom of choice. But politicians
were not the only group with unclean hands. Church leaders, too, were not
above some conniving to satisfy friends of the church.[53]

Public denunciation of the peace policy was rare in the East, where the
press was favorable to the humane attempt to deal with the Indians. If
Grant was attacked, little or nothing was said about Indian policy. Western
opinion, though not unanimous, was hostile. In areas where Indians were
close at hand and often warlike, "peace" policies did not win much support. Extermination of the Indians was openly advocated; but a Montana
paper declared sarcastically that the government would never allow any
more punitive expeditions against the Indians because "some poor red-
skinned pet of the Government, with its Quaker policy would get hurt,
and tender-hearted philanthropists in the east would be thrown into con-
vulsions of grief."[54] How much the rabid utterances of the western press
affected the course of the policy is difficult to determine. Extreme ranting
most likely only confirmed the eastern humanitarians in their resolve.
Voter influence on representatives in Congress was not uniform, for western delegations did not vote as a bloc in opposition to the Grant policies.[55]

When Rutherford B. Hayes succeeded Grant in 1877, the policy of
church-appointed agents was clearly on a downhill course. Carl Schurz,
the reform-minded Liberal Republican whom Hayes appointed secretary of
the interior, developed quite a different tone from that of the previous administration, and the religious character of the men in office did not seem
any longer to be of prime importance. The board of inquiry that Schurz
appointed soon after taking office to investigate irregularities in the Indian
service criticized the appointment of agents "because of a sentiment"
rather than on the basis of business qualifications, and it said that to en-
trust the church-appointed agents with such great power and responsibility was to "undertake through pigmies the solution of a problem that has
engaged the best efforts of statesmen and philanthropists ever since the
days of the republic." Although admitting that it was possible for business

---

53. Keller, *American Protestantism and Indian Policy*, pp. 93–97.

54. *Montanian* (Virginia City), August 24, 1871, quoted ibid., p. 99. For other western
views see the discussion in Keller, pp. 98–101, and Henry E. Fritz, *The Movement for
Indian Assimilation, 1860–1890* (Philadelphia: University of Pennsylvania Press, 1963),
pp. 109–19.

55. Keller, *American Protestantism and Indian Policy*, pp. 103–5, discusses early
congressional debate on the peace policy.

acumen and religious convictions to coexist, the board asserted that religious convictions alone were not enough to stem the corruption in the Indian service or to prevent the avarice of contractors and frontiersmen.[56]

The churches became less and less involved in appointing the agents, and the denominations that had been in the forefront in instigating the policy became disillusioned and withdrew. The Friends, finding cooperation with the Indian Office impossible and suffering from a general weariness, resigned from the duty of supplying agents.[57] The Episcopalians, too, lost interest, and their nominations were ignored. In 1882, when the secretary of the Methodist board, J. M. Reid, wrote to Secretary of the Interior Henry M. Teller to inquire why the nominations for the Michigan and Yakima agencies had not been honored, the secretary replied that he would no longer consult religious bodies in the appointment of Indian agents. "I do not believe," he said, "that the government has discharged its duty when it shall have made its appropriations and then turned the matter over to the churches of the land to deal with as their different interests may dictate."[58] So the Methodists, like all the rest, were, as the chairman of the Board of Indian Commissioners remarked, "mustered out of the service."

THE END OF TREATY MAKING

A concomitant movement for fundamental change in American Indian policy that culminated early in Grant's administration was an attack on the treaty system. From President Grant down, reformers called for abandonment of the system that had been an essential element in the relation between the United States government and the Indian tribes from the inception of the nation. Those who had some historical sense realized that the treaties at first had been a good deal more than "a mere form to amuse the quiet savages, a half-compassionate, half-contemptuous humoring of

56. *Report of Board of Inquiry Convened by Authority of Letter of the Secretary of the Interior of June 7, 1877, to Investigate Certain Charges against S. A. Galpin, Chief Clerk of the Indian Bureau, and Concerning Irregularities in Said Bureau* (Washington, GPO, 1878), p. 63.

57. Tatum, *Our Red Brothers*, pp. 285–86; Kelsey, *Friends and the Indians*, pp. 184–85, 196. An account of the Friends' difficulties under Hayes is in *Extracts from the Minutes of a Convention of Delegates from the Seven Yearly Meetings of Friends Having Charge of the Indians in the Northern Superintendency* (Philadelphia, 1878).

58. J. M. Reid to H. M. Teller, July 31, 1882, and Teller to Reid, August 5, 1882, printed in *Report of the Board of Indian Commissioners*, 1882, pp. 52–54. The discussion at the meeting of the Board of Indian Commissioners and the church groups at which these letters were read indicated that the policy had come to an end with all the groups.

unruly children," as Commissioner Francis A. Walker observed in 1873. The Indians at one time had had enough power to make a favorable cession of lands a diplomatic triumph for the United States. "The United States were clearly the stronger party in every such case," Walker noted; "but the Indians were, in the great body of instances, still so formidable, that to wrest their lands from them by pure, brutal violence would have required an exertion of strength which the government was ill prepared to make."[59]

Early in the nineteenth century perceptive men had seen the incongruity of treating the Indian tribes as equals, but the decisions of Chief Justice John Marshall in the Cherokee cases strengthened the position of the Indian tribes. Then, as demands for reform in Indian affairs grew during and immediately after the Civil War, the treaty system came under increasing scrutiny. The attack was part of the movement to end Indian tribal organization and make Indians wards of the government and then ultimately individualized citizens. The disparities between the United States and the tribes were noted along many lines. A statement drawn up by Bishop Whipple and sent to the president in 1862 by the General Conference of the Episcopal Church declared that it was "impolitic for our Government to treat a heathen community living within our borders as an independent nation, instead of regarding them as wards." Whipple's statement two years later in the *North American Review* was even stronger. "Our first dealing with these savages is one of those blunders which is worse than a crime," he wrote. "We recognize a wandering tribe as an independent and sovereign nation. We send ambassadors to make a treaty as with our equals, knowing that every provision of that treaty will be our own, that those with whom we make it cannot compel us to observe it, that they are to live within our territory, yet not subject to our laws, that they have no government of their own, and are to receive none from us; in a word, we treat as an independent nation a people whom we will not permit to exercise one single element of that sovereign power which is necessary to a nation's existence." Ostensibly the United States government and the Indians were the parties to the treaties, Whipple said, but in actuality the "*real* parties" were the Indian agents, the traders, and the politicians, and the real design was to pay worthless debts due to traders and to create places where political favorites could be rewarded.[60]

Reformers, moreover, blamed the treaty system for the conflicts and wars that arose between the Indians and whites over land. In stinging words, Felix Brunot indicted the whole system:

59. Francis A. Walker, *The Indian Question* (Boston: James R. Osgood and Company, 1874), pp. 8–9.
60. Whipple, *Lights and Shadows*, p. 139; Henry B. Whipple, "The Indian System," *North American Review* 99 (October 1864): 450–51.

The United States first creates the fiction that a few thousand savages stand in the position of equality in capacity, power, and right of negotiation with a civilised nation. They next proceed to impress upon the savages, with all the form of treaty and the solemnity of parchment, signatures and seals, the preposterous idea that they are the owners in fee of the fabulous tracts of country over which their nomadic habits have led them or their ancestors to roam. The title being thus settled, they purchase and promise payment for a portion of the territory, and further bind themselves in the most solemn manner to protect and defend the Indians in the possession of some immense remainder defined by boundary in the treaty, thus becoming, as it were, *particeps criminis* with the savages in resisting the "encroachments" of civilisation and the progressive movement of the age. Having entered into his last-named impracticable obligation, the fact of its non-performance becomes the occasion of disgraceful and expensive war to subdue their victims to the point of submission to another treaty. And so the tragedy of war and the farce of treaty have been enacted again and again, each time with increasing shame to the nation.[61]

Brunot's colleagues on the Board of Indian Commissioners echoed his sentiments. The board in its first report recommended unequivocally: "The treaty system should be abolished." And it went a step further in proposing that when a "just method" could be devised, existing treaties should be abrogated. Individual members of the board, in their inspection reports, repeated the same principle.[62] The highest government officials agreed with the reformers. Commissioner Parker, who had a long career of upholding the rights of the Seneca tribe to which he belonged, declared flatly in 1869 that the treaty system should no longer be continued. He considered the Indians to be wards of the government, whose title to the land was a "mere possessory one," and he condemned the treaty procedures for falsely impressing upon the tribes a notion of national independence. "It is time," he said, "that this idea should be dispelled, and the government cease the cruel farce of thus dealing with its helpless and ignorant wards." President Grant told the Board of Indian Commissioners that he believed the treaty system had been a mistake and ought to be abandoned.[63]

Before the reformers could organize effectively enough to bring an end to treaty making, however, the system was destroyed by Congress for rea-

61. Slattery, *Brunot*, p. 156.
62. *Report of the Board of Indian Commissioners*, 1869, p. 10; see also John V. Farwell to Brunot, November 4, 1869, ibid., pp. 28–29.
63. CIA Report, 1869, serial 1414, p. 448; minutes of May 27, 1869, Minutes of the Board of Indian Commissioners, vol. 1, pp. 6–7.

sons that had little to do with humanitarian reform. The end came as the result of a conflict of authority between the House of Representatives and the Senate. The fundamental problem was that making treaties was a function of the president and the Senate, and if dealings with the Indians were confined to treaties the House of Representatives was left out completely except to appropriate funds for arrangements it had no hand in making.

One crucial point at issue was the disposition of Indian lands. The Indian Office, by negotiating treaties with the Indians, could manipulate Indian land cessions in the interests of railroads or land companies. The territory freed of Indian title would not revert to the public domain and thus not become subject to the land laws that frontier settlers had fought to gain in their own interests. By means of the treaty process, one-fourth of the lands of Kansas passed from Indian ownership to individuals, land speculating companies, and railroads without ever becoming part of the public domain or coming under congressional control. Such disposal denied settlers the benefits of the Homestead Act of 1862 and gave no voice to the popularly elected House of Representatives, where land reform sentiment was strongest.[64] The most celebrated case was a treaty signed with the Osages in 1868 by which eight million acres of land was to be sold to railroad interests at about twenty cents an acre. News of the treaty precipitated strong opposition in the House, and the treaty was defeated. This was a striking example of what could happen to the public land system, and congressional opponents of the treaty-making power made full use of it in their attacks upon the defenders of the system.[65]

Another problem arose in 1869 in connection with the treaties negotiated in 1867 by the Peace Commission. The Senate inserted into the Indian appropriation bill for fiscal year 1870 certain funds necessary for implementing the treaties, but the House refused to concur. The Fortieth Congress ended on March 4, 1869, without providing any funds for the Indian Office for the year beginning July 1. When the new Congress met, the impasse continued until a compromise was reached whereby Congress voted a lump sum of two million dollars over and above the usual funds

64. Paul Wallace Gates, *Fifty Million Acres: Conflicts over Kansas Land Policy, 1854–1890* (Ithaca: Cornell University Press, 1954), pp. 6–8.

65. The debate in the House over the Osage treaty appears in *Congressional Globe*, 40th Congress, 2d session, pp. 3256–66. Gates discusses the matter fully in *Fifty Million Acres*, pp. 194–211. But he does not notice the other groups in opposition to the treaty-making power, and he attributes the end of treaty making too exclusively to the Osage land question. Furthermore, he writes from the standpoint of the settlers, as though their interests were always to be considered paramount. The Indian Office (aside from the temptations to fraud) could very well have negotiated for the sale of Indian lands, with the sale money to be used for the benefit of the Indians, rather than turning all the lands over to the public domain to be homesteaded without cost by white settlers.

"to enable the President to maintain the peace among and with the various tribes, bands, and parties of Indians, and to promote civilization among said Indians, bring them, where practicable, upon reservations, relieve their necessities, and encourage their efforts at self-support." The House, refusing to give up its principle of demanding equal voice with the Senate on Indian matters, added a provision that the legislation should not be construed to ratify or approve any treaty made since July 20, 1867. This was a meaningless action legally because the treaties had already been ratified by constitutional procedures, but it assuaged the pique of the House over its inferior position. A similar statement was included in the Indian appropriation bill for 1871, with the added provision that nothing should "affirm or disaffirm any of the powers of the Executive and Senate over the subject." Inadvertently, this disclaimer was omitted from the final engrossed bill, but it was formally passed with the appropriation act for the next fiscal year.[66]

The House realized that it was making little headway, for it was ultimately forced to approve the appropriations needed to carry out treaties ratified by the Senate, and the provisos tacked on to the bills had little if any legal effect. For the House to get an equal voice in Indian affairs the treaty system would have to be abolished altogether. Although some members of the House argued that such a move would be unconstitutional, their position was weakened by a decision of the Supreme Court that acts of Congress could supersede or abrogate treaties. The Senate was willing to end treaty making if treaties already ratified were held inviolate, so the way was cleared for the necessary legislation, which came finally in an obscure clause in the Indian appropriation act of March 3, 1871. Added to a sentence providing funds for the Yankton Indians was the statement: "*Provided,* That hereafter no Indian nation or tribe within the territory of the United States shall be acknowledged or recognized as an independent nation, tribe, or power with whom the United States may contract by treaty; *Provided,* further, That nothing herein contained shall be construed to invalidate or impair the obligation of any treaty heretofore lawfully made and ratified with any such Indian nation or tribe."[67]

The end of treaty making created a paradox. The question of what constitutional basis the federal government had for dealing with the Indians (aside from trade) had been answered largely by pointing to the treaty-

66. 16 *United States Statutes,* 40, 570. Debate on the matters is in *Congressional Globe,* 40th Congress, 3d session, pp. 1698–1708, 1813, 1891; 41st Congress, 1st session, pp. 170–73, 417–18, 557–73; 41st Congress, 2d session, pp. 1575–81, 4971–73, 5606–8.

67. 16 *United States Statutes* 566. See Laurence F. Schmeckebier, *The Office of Indian Affairs: Its History, Activities, and Organization* (Baltimore: Johns Hopkins Press, 1927), pp. 58–66; Priest, *Uncle Sam's Stepchildren,* pp. 95–99.

making power. Now Congress struck down this chief constitutional basis. As a matter of fact, however, the old processes could not be completely abandoned. Whether or not a group of Indians was recognized as "an independent nation, tribe, or power," dealings between it and the United States called for formal agreements by which Indian consent was obtained. This was especially true in land cessions. Such agreements differed from the treaties chiefly in that they were ratified not by the Senate alone but by both houses of Congress. Even legislative terminology showed that the old ways and attitudes had not been erased by the law of 1871. An act of May 1, 1876, for example, provided payment for a commission "to treat with the Sioux Indians for the relinquishment of the Black Hills country in Dakota Territory."[68] Congress did not simply legislate for the Indians as for other inhabitants of the United States, in the way Andrew Jackson and others following him had wanted.

The abolition of treaty making, only to be replaced by agreement making, did not satisfy reformers who objected to the perpetuation of tribal existence that such agreements acknowledged. Objectionable, too, was the continuation of treaty arrangements that had been concluded prior to 1871, for these still rested upon a basis of tribal sovereignty. The humanitarians concerned with the Indians' rights insisted that treaty rights of the past be respected at all costs—but to consider the Indians simultaneously both sovereign peoples and wards of the government, as Commissioner Edward P. Smith pointed out in 1873, involved "increasing difficulties and absurdities." "So far, and as rapidly as possible," Smith declared, "all recognition of Indians in any other relation than strictly as subjects of the Government should cease." He admitted, however, that this would require "radical legislation."[69] By 1876 problems arising in the Indian Territory, where the Five Civilized Tribes had maintained a strong national existence, led the secretary of the interior to assert that the sooner the idea of treating with the various tribes in the Indian Territory as though they possessed a sort of independent power and nationality were done away with, the earlier would some practical solution for their government be reached. And Commissioner J. Q. Smith was even more pointed in his remarks: "There is a very general and growing opinion that observance of the strict letter of treaties with Indians is in many cases at variance both with their best interests and with sound public policy."[70]

68. 19 *United States Statutes 45.*
69. *CIA Report, 1873, serial 1601, p. 371.*
70. *Report of the Secretary of the Interior, 1876, House Executive Document* no. 1, part 5, 44–2, serial 1749, p. viii; CIA Report, 1876, serial 1749, p. 389. A strong, detailed criticism of the treaty system appeared in Elwell S. Otis, *The Indian Question* (New York: Sheldon and Company, 1878), pp. 117–97.

Old ways did not change as easily as the legal forms. Even outside the Indian Territory, tribal leaders in some cases continued to exercise more authority on the reservations than the Indian agents, who were supposed to be directing the destinies of the nation's wards. Criticism of tribal authority and objections to consulting with the chiefs about government policy grew rather than diminished after the abolition of the treaty system.[71]

71. George E. Hyde, *A Sioux Chronicle* (Norman: University of Oklahoma Press, 1956), gives numerous examples of the conflict and tension between the agents and the Sioux tribal leaders. See also Priest, *Uncle Sam's Stepchildren*, pp. 102–4.

CHAPTER 21

Military Challenge

Indian Wars.

The Army and the Indian.

The Transfer Issue.

The End of the Military Phase.

The period of the post-Civil War peace policy was marked, paradoxically, by continual Indian wars. Neither the philanthropists on the Board of Indian Commissioners nor the agents appointed by the churches were able to reverse conditions that led to Indian resistance, and the civilian men who dominated the Indian Office did not succeed in eliminating the need for military action. The promoters of the peace policy, in fact, developed a modus vivendi with the army, a fragile balance between the Indian Office and the War Department. Indian Commissioner Ely S. Parker in the early days of the peace policy spoke of "a perfect understanding" between the officers of the two departments. He summarized the policy of the government in the following terms: "that they [the Indians] should be secured their legal rights; located, where practicable, upon reservations; assisted in agricultural pursuits and the arts of civilized life; and that Indians who should fail or refuse to come in and locate in permanent abodes provided for them, would be subject wholly to the control and supervision of military authorities, to be treated as friendly or hostile as circumstances might justify."[1]

1. CIA Report, 1869, serial 1414, p. 447. There is a tremendous literature on the post-Civil War Indian wars. The best scholarly survey is Robert M. Utley, *Frontier Regulars: The United States Army and the Indian, 1866–1891* (New York: Macmillan Company, 1973), on which I have confidently relied. The wars with the plains Indians are popularly

Francis A. Walker, Parker's successor, likewise saw no inconsistency in making use of soldiers when Indians needed chastisement, while at the same time pursuing the peace policy on the reservations. Walker had little patience with recalcitrant Indians and little sympathy for their situation, and he had no qualms about using military men to restrain refractory tribesmen. He insisted that such action was neither an abandonment of the peace policy nor disparagement of it. The reservation policy from the beginning, he said, demanded "that the Indians should be made as comfortable on, and as uncomfortable off, their reservations as it was in the power of the Government to make them," and he saw the use of military force not as war but as discipline.[2]

The limited use of military police power that Walker envisaged in 1872, however, gave way to all-out war. The military encounters of the 1860s with the Apaches and Navajos in the Southwest, with the Cheyennes and Arapahos in the central plains, and with the Sioux in the Powder River Valley along the Bozeman Trail turned out to be, not the final examples of Indian wars cut short by the peace policy, but the beginning of a decade or more of desperate fighting in the West. This resurgence of violence brought into question the very foundation on which the policy of peaceful relations was based and created a strong movement for military management of the Indians in place of civilian control—a movement that came close to swamping the peace policy altogether.

INDIAN WARS

On the southern plains the Kiowas and Comanches, for whom raiding had become a way of life, would not stay confined to the reservation assigned to them by the Treaty of Medicine Lodge Creek. Led by aggressive leaders like Satanta and Satank, these Indians left the reservation time and again to raid across the Red River into Texas. Lawrie Tatum, the Iowa Quaker farmer who had been sent to the Kiowas as agent in 1869 under the peace

---

treated in Ralph K. Andrist, *The Long Death: The Last Days of the Plains Indian* (New York: Macmillan Company, 1964). Some of the material in this chapter is taken from Francis Paul Prucha, *American Indian Policy in Crisis: Christian Reformers and the Indian, 1865–1900* (Norman: University of Oklahoma Press, 1976), pp. 72–102, 123–25, 234–36.

2. Walker discussed his views on Indian policy at great length in CIA Report, 1872, serial 1560, pp. 391–493; the quotation is from p. 394. See also Francis A. Walker, *The Indian Question* (Boston: James R. Osgood and Company, 1874), which reprints part of his 1872 report and two articles dealing with the Indian question in general and with Indian citizenship.

policy, tried desperately to make a nonviolent policy work. He seemed for a while to make some headway; but he resorted to withholding rations to force the chiefs to return white captives taken on the raids, and ultimately, when such coercion proved insufficient to restrain the Indians, he called for military assistance. Having thus violated the basic tenets of the peaceful Quakers, he got into trouble with his superiors, and at the end of March 1873 he resigned. Periodic promises of peace on the part of the Indians, interspersed with murderous raids off the reservation, kept the Red River frontier in a state of turmoil. The Cheyennes, too, joined in the depredations, and in June 1874 an attack by Kiowas, Comanches, and Cheyennes on a trading establishment at Adobe Walls in the Texas panhandle signaled the beginning of a full-scale war. Strong columns of troops were sent into the western part of the Indian Territory and into the Staked Plains of northwestern Texas to corral and subdue the Indians and force them to the reservations. But not until June 1875 were the last of the hostiles rounded up, the Red River War brought to a close, and the Indian prisoners of war sent to Fort Marion, Florida. With the defeat of the three tribes peace finally came to the southern plains.[3]

The peace policy was severely tried also by the Modoc War, a flaring up of hostilities along the Oregon-California border in 1872–1873 that grew out of Indian resistance to white pressures on their homelands.[4] The Modocs lived around Tule Lake, which stretched across the border, and they included in their lands along the southern edge of the lake a forbid-

3. Utley, *Frontier Regulars*, pp. 207–33; William H. Leckie, *The Military Conquest of the Southern Plains* (Norman: University of Oklahoma Press, 1963), pp. 133–235. There are many details on the conflict in W. S. Nye, *Carbine and Lance: The Story of Old Fort Sill* (Norman: University of Oklahoma Press, 1937). The Quaker agent's own story is in Lawrie Tatum, *Our Red Brothers and the Peace Policy of President Ulysses S. Grant* (Philadelphia: John C. Winston and Company, 1899). See also Lee Cutler, "Lowrie Tatum and the Kiowa Agency, 1869–1873," *Arizona and the West* 13 (Autumn 1971): 221–44.

4. The best histories of this war are Keith A. Murray, *The Modocs and Their War* (Norman: University of Oklahoma Press, 1959), and Erwin N. Thompson, *Modoc War: Its Military History and Topography* (Sacramento: Argus Books, 1971); Thompson's book is a detailed analysis of the military action prepared originally for the National Park Service. A more popular account is Richard H. Dillon, *Burnt-Out Fires: California's Modoc Indian War* (Englewood Cliffs, New Jersey: Prentice-Hall, 1973). Jeff C. Riddle, *The Indian History of the Modoc War and the Causes That Led to It* (San Francisco, 1914), is an account written, with the help of D. L. Moses, by the son of Frank and Tobey Riddle, interpreters in the negotiations between the whites and the Modocs. Official documents dealing with the war and the trial of the murderers from both War Department and Interior Department files are printed in "Modoc War," *House Executive Document* no. 122, 43–1, serial 1607. See also "Report of A. B. Meacham, Special Commissioner to the Modocs, upon the Late Modoc War," *CIA Report*, 1873, serial 1601, pp. 442–50.

ding region of lava beds, a remarkable stronghold against attacking forces. The Modocs were little affected by the mining frontier, for no gold was found in their vicinity, but their grasslands attracted ranchers, who soon clamored to have the Indians out of the way. In 1864, in response to these white cries, the United States government negotiated a treaty with the Indians by which they were moved to a reservation twenty-five miles to the north.[5] They had to share the reservation with the Klamath tribe; and the Modocs, on alien ground and outnumbered by the Klamaths, were restless and unhappy. One of the Modoc leaders, called Captain Jack by the whites, soon led his followers back to their old homes along Lost River, which ran into Tule Lake from the north. But white ranchers had moved there in the Indians' absence, and the return of Captain Jack and his band caused consternation and panic. Early negotiations with Captain Jack, endeavoring to get him to return to the reservation, came to nothing.

When Grant became president in 1869, he appointed as superintendent of Indian affairs for Oregon a faithful Republican named Alfred B. Meacham, an ardent temperance man moved by deep reforming instincts. Born in Indiana in 1826, Meacham had migrated to California during the gold rush and had then moved on to Oregon. As Indian superintendent he was a staunch supporter of Grant's peace policy and undertook to carry out its reform principles. He talked Captain Jack into returning to the reservation, but pressures from the Klamath Indians and the Indian agent drove Captain Jack again to Lost River in April 1870. The use of army troops in an attempt to force the Modocs back to the reserve led in 1872 to armed conflict, and the Modoc War was under way. The Indians holed up in the lava beds, from which the army without enthusiasm and without success sought to dislodge them, even though General Edward R. S. Canby, commanding the Department of the Columbia, himself assumed direction of the campaign.

To overcome this expensive and embarrassing impasse, a peace commission, headed by Meacham, was appointed on January 29, 1873. But negotiations made little progress. The Modocs themselves were divided, and the army tightened the pressure on the area held by the Indians. Captain Jack, his hand forced by more desperate members of his band, at length agreed to the treacherous murder of General Canby and the peace commissioners when they came unarmed to the next council. On Good Friday, April 11, 1873, the deed was done. At a signal from Captain Jack the Indians rose up armed, and Jack himself, drawing a pistol he had concealed under his coat, shot General Canby at pointblank range. The Reverend Eleasar Thomas, a member of the peace commission, was quickly killed,

5. Kappler, pp. 865–68.

too, by an Indian named Boston Charley. Meacham, who started to flee when the trouble broke out, was grazed by bullets and fell unconscious. He was partially scalped when a cry that soldiers were coming drove off his assailant, and he was found still alive when the rescuers arrived and eventually recovered. The other member of the commission escaped unharmed.

The disaster shocked the nation. Much of the sympathy that had supported the Modocs, who had been far outnumbered by the soldiers in the conflict, was destroyed, and cries for vengeance against the murderers resounded. The army intensified its drive until at last, giving up before hopeless odds, the Indians surrendered. Some of the criminals were granted amnesty for aiding in the capture of Captain Jack, but six of the Modocs were sentenced to death by a military commission at Fort Klamath.[6] On October 3, Captain Jack and three of his companions were executed at Fort Klamath; two lesser participants had their sentences commuted by President Grant to life imprisonment at Alcatraz.

The Modoc murders touched off a nationwide attack on Grant's peace policy. Western opposition was intense, and even supporters of the policy were stunned by the murder of the commissioners and agreed that stiff punishment was in order. It did not take long, however, for the peace advocates to renew their insistent urging that the peace policy be continued, and they spoke strongly against recurring white attacks upon the Indians —which, they charged, deserved as strict an accounting as that meted out to the Modocs. Meacham himself held no grudge against the Indians and devoted the rest of his life to Indian reform. He toured the lecture circuit with talks of his Modoc adventure, founded a journal devoted to Indian matters, *The Council Fire*, and served the government on special commissions.[7]

After the sentences of the military tribunal had been executed, the remaining 153 Modocs were exiled from their homeland. They were taken by the army to Fort McPherson, Nebraska, and there turned over to agents of the Interior Department, who moved them to the Indian Territory and placed them in charge of the Quapaw Agency. "The Indian is greatly attached to his tribal organization," Secretary Delano asserted, "and it is be-

---

6. "Proceedings of a Military Commission Convened at Fort Klamath, Oregon, for the Trial of Modoc Prisoners," *House Executive Document* no. 122, 43–1, serial 1607, pp. 131–83.

7. Biographical details are found in Meacham's own writings: *Wigwam and Warpath: or the Royal Chief in Chains* (Boston: John P. Dale and Company, 1875); *Wi-ne-ma (The Woman-Chief) and Her People* (Hartford: American Publishing Company, 1876); and "The Tragedy of the Lava-Beds," in T. A. Bland, *Life of Alfred B. Meacham* (Washington: T. A. and M. C. Bland, 1883). The fullest account of Meacham's life and works is Edward Sterl Phinney, "Alfred B. Meacham, Promoter of Indian Reform" (Ph.D. dissertation, University of Oregon, 1963).

lieved that this example of extinguishing their so-called national existence and merging their members into other tribes, while in reality a humane punishment, will be esteemed by them as the severest penalty that could have been inflicted, and tend by its example to deter hostile Indians in future from serious and flagrant insurrection."[8] The Modocs lived quietly and productively as farmers in the Indian Territory until in 1909 those who were left were allowed to return to the Klamath reservation in Oregon.

In Arizona and New Mexico the Apaches carried on a continual guerilla war with the troops sent to subdue them. Attempts to isolate friendly groups from those who continued depredations led to strong criticisms from local whites, who feared that the "feeding stations" were merely refugees for marauding Indians. On April 30, 1871, a force of Tucson citizens attacked the unsuspecting Apaches at Camp Grant, murdered and mutilated them, and carried off children into slavery. The Camp Grant Massacre speeded up attempts to apply the peace policy in Arizona, and in July 1871 Vincent Colyer was dispatched there to make peace with the Apaches and establish them on reservations. The outraged Arizonans ridiculed Colyer's attempts, but a good many Apaches gathered at temporary reservations set up at military posts, and General O. O. Howard, following in Colyer's path, made peace with the Chiricahua chief Cochise and induced more Indians to come into the agencies. A system of reservations was established, and a sizable number of Apaches gathered at them. Still the raiding continued, and in 1872–1873 General George Crook mounted a successful offensive against the bands. More Apaches settled on the reservations, and for several years peace was maintained in Arizona. Despite conflict between John Clum, the young civilian agent who assumed control of the San Carlos Agency in 1874, and the army officers, the Apaches were concentrated at San Carlos. The peace, however, did not end the raids into Mexico, carried on from both Arizona and New Mexico. Under Victorio, a Warm Springs Apache, the frontier was again terrorized until the chief was killed in 1880. And then new leaders, of whom Geronimo became the best known, continued the guerilla warfare until they too were tracked down. Geronimo finally surrendered in 1886.[9]

8. Report of the Secretary of the Interior, 1873, *House Executive Document* no. 1, part 5, 43–1, serial 1601, pp. ix–x.

9. Utley, *Frontier Regulars*, pp. 170–74, 192–98, 369–93. Colyer's report on the Apaches was printed in pamphlet form as *Peace with the Apaches of New Mexico and Arizona: Report of Vincent Colyer, Member of the Board of Indian Commissioners, 1871* (Washington: GPO, 1872). Specialized writings on the Apache wars are numerous. A comprehensive work is Dan L. Thrapp, *The Conquest of Apacheria* (Norman: University of Oklahoma Press, 1967). A recent scholarly biography of Geronimo is Angie Debo, *Geronimo: The Man, His Time, His Place* (Norman: University of Oklahoma Press, 1976).

Another challenge to civilian control of the Indians came in the conflicts with the Sioux. The Treaty of Fort Laramie in 1868 had left unceded lands in the Powder River country as hunting lands of the Sioux, but it had also set aside the Great Sioux Reserve west of the Missouri River in Dakota, and the chiefs had agreed to settle at the agencies and accept reservation life. Many of the Indians, lured by the government's rations, went to the agencies, but some, like Sitting Bull, remained on the unceded lands and refused to settle down. The nonreservation Indians were considered "hostile," for they occasionally raided Montana settlements and fought the advancing railroad surveyors who entered their lands. The Sioux were irritated, too, by the invasion of the Black Hills by a military expedition under George A. Custer in 1874 that confirmed the rumors that gold was there and stimulated the miners to invade the forbidden hills.

As long as the Indians were able to subsist by hunting in the Powder River Valley, it was impossible to control them fully. Only on the reservations would they be completely dependent upon the United States, and in December 1875 runners were sent to the Sioux to announce that all who were not at the agencies by January 31, 1876, would be hunted down by the army and brought in by military force. The midwinter deadline made compliance impossible, but in any event the Indians did not intend to obey. On February 1, 1876, the secretary of the interior declared that all Indians not on the reservations were to be considered hostile and asked the secretary of war to take appropriate action. General Sheridan, now in command of the Division of the Missouri, wanted a winter campaign, but delays prevented a full-scale attack until April and May, when three columns moved in toward the Sioux and their Cheyenne allies. One column headed eastward from Fort Ellis in Montana, a second moved north along the old Bozeman Trail from Fort Fetterman, and a third, including part of the Seventh Cavalry under Custer, traveled west from Fort Abraham Lincoln on the Missouri. Seriously underestimating the size of the opposing Indian force, Custer launched a premature attack on the Indian camp on the Little Bighorn on June 25, and he and his entire force were annihilated.[10]

News of the disaster on the Little Bighorn arrived in the East just as the centennial of the signing of the Declaration of Independence was being celebrated. The report stunned the nation, and heavy army reinforcements

10. Perhaps more has been written about Custer's battle than about any other Indian-related event in United States history. A well-documented survey of the whole conflict with the Sioux is Utley, *Frontier Regulars*, pp. 236–95. Utley also provides an excellent brief survey of the Little Bighorn battle that illuminates the strategy and tactics used in *Custer Battlefield National Monument, Montana* (Washington: National Park Service, 1969). A reasonable, detailed account is Edgar I. Stewart, *Custer's Luck* (Norman: University of Oklahoma Press, 1955). A recent reinterpretation is John S. Gray, *Centennial Campaign: The Sioux War of 1876* (Fort Collins, Colorado: Old Army Press, 1976).

were sent into Montana to hunt down the bands of Sioux and Cheyenne who had scattered after the fight. Such pressure was more than the Indians could withstand, and little by little during the fall and winter the bands surrendered at the agencies. Even the most recalcitrant at length came in. Crazy Horse with a band of more than a thousand surrendered at Camp Robinson, Nebraska, on May 6, 1877. Sitting Bull with his adherents fled into Canada determined never to submit to reservation life, but finally he, too, came back and gave up in July 1881. The Sioux war had accomplished what the peace policy had been unable to; it had forced the Indians to abandon their hunting grounds and accept government control on the reservations.

The defeat of the Sioux did not end all military action in the north, however. The traditionally peaceful Nez Perces in 1877 startled the nation with a new military conflict. When the Nez Perce Reservation had been reduced in 1863, some of the Indians, mostly those who had resisted the attempts to convert them to Christianity, refused to accept the treaty. Chief Joseph was among these "nontreaty" Indians, and he and his band continued to live in their beloved Wallowa Valley in eastern Oregon. Increasing white encroachments there laid the groundwork for trouble, and the United States was eager to persuade these tribesmen to join their relatives on the Lapwai Reservation in Idaho. It seemd a hopeless endeavor. Two special commissions sent to investigate the matter in 1873 reached contrary conclusions about the appropriateness of forcing the band to move, and in 1876 a new group made another attempt to reach a solution. This commission recommended that, as long as it remained peaceful, Joseph's band be allowed to remain in the Wallowa Valley, with troops sent in to ensure order. If the band did not quietly settle down there, it should be forced to move to the reservation. General Howard was given responsibility for the peace, and in a series of meetings with Chief Joseph he finally won the Indian's consent to go to Lapwai.[11]

Before the movement could be accomplished, hostilities broke out. In June 1877 young men of the band, avenging the murder of an Indian by whites, killed a party of settlers. General Howard's troops were ordered in and war began. The Indians' choice was flight. By skillful maneuvers, Joseph and the military leaders of the band moved east through the Lolo Pass into the Bitterroot Valley of Montana, down into Yellowstone Park, and then north, seeking to reach asylum in Canada. Pursued by Howard's soldiers and with occasional military encounters, the fleeing Indians executed one of the great military movements in history. They had almost

11. CIA Report, 1877, serial 1800, pp. 405–8; "Report of Civil and Military Commission to Nez Perce Indians, Washington Territory and the Northwest," December 1, 1876, ibid., pp. 607–13.

reached their objective when they were cut off by troops from Fort Keogh under General Nelson A. Miles. With many warriors dead and the rest exhausted and the women and children cold and starving, Chief Joseph surrendered at the Bear Paw Mountains on October 5.[12]

In 1878 and 1879, Bannocks, Shoshonis, and Paiutes in Idaho, Nevada, and eastern Oregon, upset by increasing white pressures on their lands, rose up in minor wars against the whites. Military expeditions directed by General Howard tracked down the hostiles through the rugged country of the Rockies and Great Basin and forced them back to their reservations.[13]

In neighboring Colorado, the Utes faced similar encroachment. By a treaty of 1868 they had been guaranteed a reservation in the western quarter of Colorado. Two agencies were to be maintained, one on the White River for bands in the north and the other on the Los Pinos River for three bands in the south, and provisions were made for education, for individual homesteads, and for stock, seeds, and implements to start the Utes on the road toward civilization.[14] The expanding mining frontier in Colorado soon encroached upon the reserved lands, however, and a United States commission, headed by Felix Brunot of the Board of Indian Commissioners, succeeded in gaining from the Indians in 1873 a large cession of land in the southern part of the reservation. The Utes remained at peace and under Chief Ouray exhibited loyalty and friendship to the United States. But white pressures upon their lands did not let up; and after Colorado had become a state in 1876 they became incessant as the state's inhabitants, its government, and the press shouted in ever louder chorus, "The Utes must go!" The tension between the two races was aggravated by government failures to provide promptly the goods and services promised in the treaties.

A violent outbreak might have been avoided but for a change in agents at the White River Agency in 1878. In that year, Agent H. E. Danforth, a nominee of the Unitarians under the peace policy, was replaced by Nathan C. Meeker. Meeker, born near Cleveland, Ohio, in 1817, had had

12. Utley, *Frontier Regulars*, pp. 296–321. The Nez Perces and the war have received much attention from historians. Histories of the tribe that include accounts of the conflict and its aftermath are Francis Haines, *The Nez Perces: Tribesmen of the Columbia Plateau* (Norman: University of Oklahoma Press, 1955), and Alvin M. Josephy, Jr., *The Nez Perce Indians and the Opening of the Northwest* (New Haven: Yale University Press, 1965). Histories specifically of the war are Merrill D. Beal, *"I Will Fight No More Forever": Chief Joseph and the Nez Perce War* (Seattle: University of Washington Press, 1963), and Mark H. Brown, *The Flight of the Nez Perce* (New York: G. P. Putnam's Sons, 1967). See also Mark H. Brown, "The Joseph Myth," *Montana: The Magazine of Western History* 22 (Winter 1972): 2–17.

13. Utley, *Frontier Regulars*, pp. 322–32.

14. Kappler, pp. 990–93. A comparison of this Ute treaty of 1868 with the one made in 1863 (ibid., pp. 856–59) indicates the new emphasis on means to promote civilization.

an intriguing career. Something of a visionary, he became converted to the agrarian socialism of Fourier and lived for several years in a phalanx in Ohio. For a while he served as agricultural editor of the *New York Tribune*, but he had not lost his utopian dreams. On a trip to the West in 1869 Meeker determined to set up an ideal agricultural community, and with Horace Greeley's enthusiastic support he founded Union Colony in eastern Colorado. The community, soon named Greeley, prospered, but Meeker himself seemed always to be in debt. When he was offered the Indian agency at White River, therefore, he saw it as a way to a sure income. But he also looked upon it as an opportunity to try his agricultural principles as a solution to the Indian problem—to build a Union Colony among the Utes. Meeker moved the agency downriver to a spot more suitable for his agricultural plans and began to plow, fence, and irrigate the meadows favored by the Indians as grazing grounds for their ponies. He met adamant opposition from some members of the tribe, who had no interest in farming and who objected to Meeker's plowing up their lands. When the agent realized their growing antagonism, he called for military support, and troops under Major Thomas T. Thornburgh were dispatched to strengthen his position. Thornburgh's troops were attacked as they entered the reservation, and the major and eleven of his soldiers were killed. At the same time, the agency was assaulted; Meeker and eight others were killed, and Meeker's wife and daughters were taken captive. It was a tragic ending for a good man whose obstinacy and lack of understanding of the Indians brought his death. Even Clinton B. Fisk, chairman of the Board of Indian Commissioners, who might have been expected to sympathize with the aggressive civilizing program Meeker had attempted, declared the agent "destitute of that particular tact and knowledge of the Indian character which is required of an agent; a man of too many years to begin with, unhappily constituted in his mental organization for any such place." Fisk viewed Meeker's whole administration as a failure.[15]

Although the uprising, the work of a small group of Indians, was quickly quieted through the good offices of Ouray and the concentration of additional troops in the area, the effect upon the Coloradans was electrifying. It was just the occasion they sought to demand a war of extermination

15. The Ute problems and the conflict they led to at White River are discussed in CIA Report, 1879, serial 1910, pp. 82–98. Two studies that treat the episode in detail are Robert Emmitt, *The Last War Trail: The Utes and the Settlement of Colorado* (Norman: University of Oklahoma Press, 1954), and Marshall Sprague, *Massacre: The Tragedy of White River* (Boston: Little, Brown and Company, 1957). See also the documents in *Senate Executive Document* no. 31, 46–2, serial 1882; *House Executive Document* no. 83, 46–2, serial 1925; *House Miscellaneous Document* no. 38, 46–2, serial 1931. Fisk's statement appears ibid., p. 45.

against the Utes. Secretary of the Interior Schurz moved at once to prevent an expensive and destructive war, which he was sure would come if the situation of the Utes in Colorado could not be radically changed. He sent a special agent to get back the captives and then to obtain the surrender of the guilty Indians. Schurz was chiefly interested in a plan for long-range settlement of the difficulties, a plan he expressed in succinct terms: "settlement of the Utes in severalty, so as to promote the civilization of the Indians, and to open the main part of the Ute reservation to development by white citizens, thus removing a source of constant irritation between the latter and the Utes." An agreement was signed in Washington on March 6, 1880, by representatives of the Ute tribe that provided for removal of the White River Utes to the Uintah Reservation in Utah and for the band of Uncompahgre and Southern Utes to settle on lands on the Grand and the La Plata rivers.[16]

THE ARMY AND THE INDIAN

The Indian wars made the army an agent of the United States government in the control and management of Indians that was on a par, or at least almost so, with the Indian Office. And the ultimate goal of the two services was the same: to locate the Indians on reservations with set boundaries, where they could be educated and trained for American citizenship. It was in methods and the nature of their tasks that the Interior Department and the War Department differed.[17]

The post-Civil War army, composed of officers and men who stayed with the army as a career at the end of the sectional struggle, entered a period of rapid professionalization. The commanding officers had their eyes set on European models of what an up-to-date army preparing for conventional warfare should be. The schools and the manuals and theorists like Emory Upton sought to change the American military forces into a thoroughly modern and professional organization.

But the actual work of the postwar army was Indian fighting, a highly unorthodox warfare, which the army somehow considered not its primary mission but only a passing phase. So the military men were not well geared to meet the enemy they actually confronted, an enemy with quite uncon-

16. Report of the Secretary of the Interior, 1879, *House Executive Document* no. 1, part 5, 46–2, serial 1910, pp. 16–19. The quotation is from "Agreement with Ute Indians of Colorado," *House Report* no. 1401, 46–2, serial 1937, p. 2. The agreement is in *Senate Executive Document* no. 114, 46–2, serial 1885; it is also printed as part of the law in 21 *United States Statutes* 200–202.

17. For discussion of the army's role I have relied chiefly on Utley, *Frontier Regulars*, pp. 44–58.

ventional characteristics. To begin with, the Indians could not readily be classified as hostile or friendly, so the enemy was seldom clearly identified. Who was friend and who was foe was never absolutely resolved, for the lines of division shifted rapidly, and the Indians wore no sharply distinguishing uniforms and did not draw up in organized array.

Moreover, the army did not develop a sharp ideological stand of hostility toward its Indian foes. Although the soldiers and their officers saw the horrors of savage warfare, they could also view the Indians through eyes that recognized the fraud, corruption, and injustice heaped upon the tribes. "Ambivalence, therefore," Robert Utley has noted, "marked military attitudes toward the Indians—fear, distrust, loathing, contempt, and condescension, on the one hand; curiosity, admiration, sympathy, and even friendship, on the other."[18] Humanitarians in the East, harping on Sand Creek (which was not a work of the regular army) or the Piegan Massacre and picking up exasperated statements of General Sherman and General Sheridan about refractory bands of Indians, charged that the army's policy was one of extermination. Such accusations were wide of the mark, for the impulse to civilize the Indians was as strong in the army as it was among humanitarian reformers and government officials.[19]

Some military men, in fact, were noted for their sincere concern for the Indians and their welfare and have been labeled "humanitarian soldiers."[20] Outstanding, perhaps, was General George Crook, a man who served in the West for a third of a century and who had a well-deserved reputation as an aggressive Indian fighter. But he also developed a philosophy of Indian relations based on honesty, justice, and concern for Indian civilization. He supported the Ponca Indians in their flight from the Indian Territory, spoke out in support of the Cheyenne chief Dull Knife and of the Bannock Indians in their conflicts with the United States, and during his second tour of Arizona, 1882–1886, worked out a positive program for the economic welfare of the Apaches that sought to convert them into capitalistic farm-

18. Ibid., p. 45.

19. See, for example, General Sherman's views in a letter "to a friend in Washington," April 17, 1873, in *Army and Navy Journal* 10 (April 26, 1873): 586–87. Sherman's policies and actions are well described in Robert G. Athearn, *William Tecumseh Sherman and the Settlement of the West* (Norman: University of Oklahoma Press, 1956). On Sheridan, see Carl Coke Rister, *Border Command: General Phil Sheridan in the West* (Norman: University of Oklahoma Press, 1944). A highly complimentary view of the army generals by a reformer is the statement of William Welsh in *Journal of the Second Annual Conference of the Board of Indian Commissioners with the Representatives of the Religious Societies Cooperating with the Government, and Reports of Their Work among the Indians* (Washington: GPO, 1973), pp. 47–48.

20. This theme has been developed in two articles by Richard N. Ellis, "The Humanitarian Soldiers," *Journal of Arizona History* 10 (Summer 1969): 53–66, and "The Humanitarian Generals," *Western Historical Quarterly* 3 (April 1972): 169–78.

ers.[21] In his later years, Crook's views toward Indian policy were almost indistinguishable from those of the civilian reformers with whom he came to have close contact. Crook believed firmly in the Indians' competence to survive and advance if given a chance. "I wish to say most emphatically," he wrote, "that the American Indian is the intellectual peer of most, if not all, the various nationalities we have assimilated to our laws, customs, and language. He is fully able to protect himself, if the ballot be given and the courts of law not closed against him." When the general died in 1890, he was eulogized as "a tower of strength to all who labored for Indian civilization."[22]

Another western commander of moderate views was General John Pope, who changed the exterminationist views he had expressed at the time of the Sioux outbreak in Minnesota in 1862. His long subsequent career in the West—he commanded the Department of the Missouri from 1870 to 1883—taught him much about the Indians and about the short-comings of existing Indian policy. Although he directed campaigns against the warring Indians, he voiced concern for their future, relieved their suffering at the end of the wars, and sought to protect them from rapacious whites. His goal, like that of the reformers, was the eventual assimilation of the Indians into white society. General Oliver Otis Howard, too, was more than an Indian fighter. Known as the "Christian general" and renowned for his work as head of the Freedmen's Bureau, Howard approached the Indians with deep religious sentiments. His piety irritated some of his associates, but he sincerely hoped for peaceful means of dealing with the Indians. Like so many others, he concluded that there would be no lasting end to Indian troubles until the Indians got land in severalty and protection of the law and were assimilated into American culture. He pushed for Indian education and for an end to the reservation system.[23] Other officers—like Benjamin Grierson, who cooperated closely with the

21. James T. King, "George Crook: Indian Fighter and Humanitarian," *Arizona and the West* 9 (Winter 1967): 333–48. King asserts that Crook "conceived and put into practice one of the most enlightened Indian policies in the history of the American frontier" and that his career provides "insight into the element of humanitarianism which lies neglected among the more martial characteristics of the military frontier." See also King, "'A Better Way': General George Crook and the Ponca Indians," *Nebraska History* 50 (Fall 1969): 239–56. Crook's own story has been edited by Martin F. Schmitt, *General George Crook: His Autobiography* (Norman: University of Oklahoma Press, 1946).

22. Crook to Herbert Welsh, January 3, 1885, printed in *Letter from General Crook on Giving the Ballot to Indians* (Philadelphia, 1885), a leaflet distributed by the Indian Rights Association; *Report of the Indian Rights Association*, 1890, pp. 52–53.

23. Ellis, "Humanitarian Generals," pp. 169–70, 174–76; Richard N. Ellis, *General Pope and U.S. Indian Policy* (Albuquerque: University of New Mexico Press, 1970), pp. 230–42: John A. Carpenter, *Sword and Olive Branch: Oliver Otis Howard* (Pittsburgh: University of Pittsburgh Press, 1964), pp. 267–68.

MAP 8: The United States Army and the Indians—
The Plains and Mountains, 1865–1880

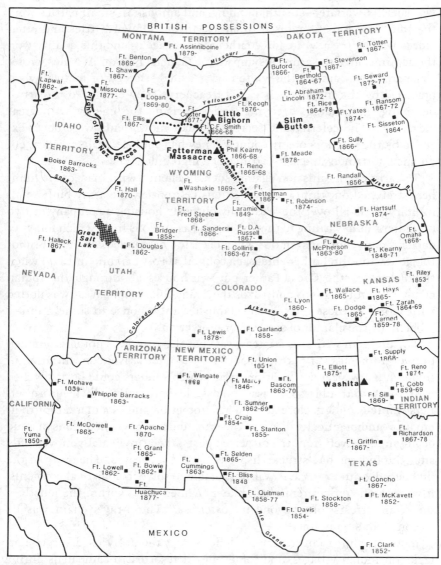

Quaker agent among the Kiowas and Comanches, Ranald Mackenzie, who fed the defeated and starving Indians, and Richard Henry Pratt, whose assignment to care for the prisoners of the Red River War started him on a lifelong career in Indian education and assimilation—add further testimony.

The work of troops in the West was more that of a police force than of a conventional army, as Commissioner Francis A. Walker had discerned: not war, but discipline. The basic unconventionality was that Indian warfare was guerilla warfare—stealth, cunning, and ambush in small parties were the rule. The Indians refused to engage in long-drawn battles and often faded away before a white force rather than engage it, and this quality won the admiration of the army. A sympathetic General Nelson A. Miles wrote: "The art of war among the white race is called strategy, or tactics; when practised by the Indians it is called treachery. They employed the art of deceiving, misleading, decoying, and surprising the enemy with great cleverness. The celerity and secrecy of their movements were never excelled by the warriors of any country. They had courage, skill, sagacity, endurance, fortitude, and self-sacrifice of a high order."[24]

To carry out its mission against such an enemy, with inadequate numbers stretched out thinly over an extensive frontier, the army built small military posts all over the West, tiny outposts housing a company or two of soldiers, as a warning to the Indians and as stations from which forays of detachments could march out when occasion demanded. As Felix Brunot told Red Cloud and other chiefs at a council at Fort Laramie in 1871, when trouble arose "the Great Father put war-houses all through the Indian country."[25] In the 1860s and 1870s the Trans-Mississippi West was dotted with scores of these forts, each established in response to some military problem or the clamor of settlers for protection.

The problem with this strategy was that the army was not large enough to man a fort at every critical spot. Yet the alternative, concentration of troops at a few strategic locations from which soldiers could be dispatched in strength to trouble spots, was impossible, both politically (because settlers wanted soldiers close at hand for protection and as a market for their produce) and practically (because the army did not have the means of rapid deployment). Even from the dispersed posts, the army usually moved only after the Indians had struck, dispersed, and disappeared. The army in the first decades after the Civil War was unable to solve its logistical problems. It was, as one officer remarked, like a chained dog, "within the length of the chain irresistible, beyond it powerless." The army's chain was its wagon train supply line.[26]

In an attempt to overcome its deficiencies, the army used surprise attacks on Indian villages, and sometimes it resorted to campaigns during

24. Nelson A. Miles, *Serving the Republic: Memoirs of the Civil and Military Life of Nelson A. Miles* (New York: Harper and Brothers, 1911), pp. 117–18.

25. CIA Report, 1871, serial 1505, p. 440. The locations of the regular army posts are indicated in Francis Paul Prucha, *A Guide to the Military Posts of the United States, 1789–1895* (Madison: State Historical Society of Wisconsin, 1964).

26. G. W. Baird, "General Miles's Indian Campaigns," *Century Magazine* 42 (July 1891): 351, quoted in Utley, *Frontier Regulars*, p. 48.

the winter, when the Indians were accustomed to curtail their operations and were often ill-prepared to beat back an attacker. Such tactics were "total war," for the women and children were nearly always intermingled with the fighting men and often took part in the fighting. The inability to distinguish between combatants and noncombatants raised questions that greatly disturbed the humanitarians and many military leaders as well. Another tactic was to employ Indians against other Indians, a common occurrence in all the Indian wars. Tribal rivalries and enmity made it possible to use Crows and Pawnees, for example, against the Sioux. General Crook in Arizona used scouts from the same tribe he was fighting.

Military leaders, unable to set aside planning and organization of the army for future possible wars with conventional enemies, stumbled along in their campaigns against their unconventional Indian foes, whom they were trying more to control than to destroy. The punishment they meted out often fell on the innocent as well as on the guilty, for the two were difficult to distinguish, and this destruction blackened the record of the army. Yet neither in theory nor in fact was the result extermination or genocide. It is impossible to establish an accurate record of Indian deaths in the post-Civil War Indian wars, but the casualties on both sides from armed conflict were in total small.[27] The tragedy was in the destruction of the Indians' traditional way of life, which was the conscious goal of both military and civilian officials.

THE TRANSFER ISSUE

Military actions against hostile Indians led to renewed agitation for transferring the Indian Office to the War Department.[28] This was a serious challenge to civilian control of Indian affairs, for the proposals did not envisage

27. Don Russell, "How Many Indians Were Killed?" *American West* 10 (July 1973): 42–47, 61–63. Russell concludes: "Weighing all factors, it seems improbable that more than 3,000 Indians were killed in all the U.S. Army's fights. Even if all the wildest claims be taken at face value, the total would not exceed 6,000. That is by no means the 'policy of exterminating Indians, tribe by tribe' alleged by those entirely ignorant of Indian warfare. Remember, too, that these small figures are to be compared, not with the number of Indians existing at any one time, whether 700,000 in 1492 or 250,000 in 1890, but rather with the total number of Indians who lived during the entire century" (p. 47).

28. Loring B. Priest, *Uncle Sam's Stepchildren: The Reformation of United States Indian Policy, 1865–1887* (New Brunswick: Rutgers University Press, 1942), pp. 15–27, treats the transfer issue with special emphasis on congressional action and public opinion. A brief survey article is Donald J. D'Elia, "The Argument over Civilian or Military Indian Control, 1865–1880," *Historian* 24 (February 1962): 207–25. A discussion of the issue in the early postwar years, with special emphasis on Kansas, is in Marvin H. Garfield, "The Indian Question in Congress and in Kansas," *Kansas Historical Quarterly* 2 (February 1933): 29–44.

a simple return to conditions that existed before the creation of the Department of the Interior in 1849. The earlier period had hardly been a period of *military* control; the Indian Office had been a civilian enterprise under the direction of a civilian commissioner of Indian affairs, with civilian superintendents (often ex officio the governors of the territories) and civilian agents and other agency personnel. Only on relatively rare occasions had army officers filled the posts of Indian agents, and conflicts between the two services, although both were under the single jurisdiction of the secretary of war, had frequently occurred.[29] Persons in the 1860s and 1870s who knew the history of the Indian service did not advocate a simple transfer of the bureau from one department to another with little change in outlook, activities, or character of personnel. They proposed putting the Indians into the hands of army men on active military duty. A complete transfer was urged, and General Sherman provided a description of the plan:

> Each military post has its quartermaster and commissary, who can, without additional cost, make the issues directly to the Indians, and account for them; and the commanding officer can exercise all the supervision now required of the civil agent, in a better manner, because he has soldiers to support his authority, and can easily anticipate and prevent the minor causes which have so often resulted in Indian wars. In like manner, our country is divided into military departments and divisions, commanded by experienced general officers named by the President, who can fulfill all the functions now committed to Indian superintendents; and these, too, have near them inspectors who can promptly investigate and prevent the incipient steps that are so apt to result in conflict and war.[30]

General Grant himself had casually recommended such a change in 1866, and when he became president, he had followed his convictions by appointing army officers to most of the Indian agencies. This seemed so reasonable to him that he did little theorizing about the matter. As humanitarian activity increased, however, the arguments for military control had to be expounded more explicitly. The military men and their supporters asserted that the proposals of the Indian reformers could not be carried

29. Francis Paul Prucha, *Broadax and Bayonet: The Role of the United States Army in the Development of the Northwest, 1815–1860* (Madison: State Historical Society of Wisconsin, 1953), pp. 93–95.

30. Sherman to W. A. J. Sparks, January 19, 1876, *House Report* no. 354, 44–1, serial 1709, p. 9. It should be noted that in the face of criticism against military control, Sherman later suggested that the War Department could employ civilian agents for the peaceful tribes and use military ones only for warlike tribes. Sherman to Alvin Saunders, November 27, 1878, *Senate Miscellaneous Document* no. 53, 45–3, serial 1835, p. 220.

out by mere moral suasion. Sherman, reviewing the work of the Peace Commission in assigning the Indians to reservations, wrote: "To labor with their own hands, or even to remain in one place, militates with all the hereditary pride of the Indian, and *force* must be used to accomplish the result." The War Department, he argued, was the only branch of the government that could act with the promptness and vigor necessary to carry out the plans and purpose of the commission. Nor could he abide a divided command. He wrote his brother John in the summer of 1868 that he would have to spend the rest of his days on the Indian frontier "unless the Indians are wholly taken charge of by the War or Interior Dept."[31]

Secretary of War J. M. Schofield similarly argued that it was inefficient and uneconomical to split the responsibility for Indian affairs between two departments. If the Interior Department could manage the Indians by itself, all right; but if the army was needed to protect the railroads and settlements, why not let the army officers act as Indian agents and save the expense of employing civilians. The army officers, moreover, with their military reputation and commissions at stake, could be depended upon for an honest administration of Indian affairs.[32]

As the peace policy progressed and the Indian agencies were handed over to representatives of the religious denominations, the opponents of civilian control found a rich field for criticism. Each failure of the peace policy, each act of Indian hostility, could be used to show that the humanitarians from the East, who had little contact with the wild Indians of the West, were unfit to formulate and carry out a practical Indian policy. Instances of failure by peaceful methods were taken to be automatic proof that Indian affairs belonged in the hands of the military.

Strong support of the army came from the West, where frontier governors, legislators, and newspaper editors called for aggressive military action against the Indians.[33] Nor did transfer lack support in the East. After the Fetterman disaster the *Nation* recommended transfer as the "primal remedy for our evils." Lamenting the *divisum imperium* that marked Indian management, it supported Sherman's stand of sole military control.

---

31. Report of Sherman, November 1, 1868, *House Executive Document* no. 1, 40–3, serial 1367, pp. 5–6; Sherman to John Sherman, July 30, 1868, William T. Sherman Papers, Library of Congress.

32. Report of Schofield, November 20, 1868, *House Executive Document* no. 1, 40–3, serial 1367, pp. xvii–xviii.

33. Garfield, "The Indian Question," pp. 29–37, 44. Memorials to Congress from the Kansas legislature in 1869 and 1874 urging transfer are in *Senate Miscellaneous Document* no. 29, 40–3, serial 1361, and *Senate Miscellaneous Document* no. 75, 43–1, serial 1584. Similar memorials from the California legislature in 1876 and 1878 are in *House Miscellaneous Document* no. 92, 44–1, serial 1701, and *House Miscellaneous Document* no. 19, 45–2, serial 1815.

What could the troops do if they had sole responsibility, the editor asked. "The answer is," he declared, "the troops could *corral* the Indians; they could keep them away from the emigrant routes; could establish a healthful state of non-intercourse; could remove the temptations to plunder by forcing the Indians away from certain prescribed regions. In this way they would effectually police the 'short route' to Montana and the Pacific."[34]

The Protestant churches were strongly committed to the Interior Department and its civilian peace program and universally opposed transfer, but the Catholic position was mixed. Catholic missionaries, squeezed out of some reservations by the allotment of agencies under Grant's peace policy, hoped that army control might give them a free hand to operate where they chose. Felix Brunot asserted that all denominations opposed transfer "except the Roman Catholics," and Indian Commissioner E. A. Hayt, in a personal letter to the secretary of the Baptist Home Missionary Society in 1878, remarked, "If the transfer to the Army takes place, which seems extremely probable, the Catholics boast that they will then be allowed to go to every agency in the United States, and I think their boast is not an empty one." The Bureau of Catholic Indian Missions, it is true, aligned itself with the Indian Office in opposing transfer, but strong Catholic voices called for a return of the Indian service to the War Department.[35]

There was continuing support for transfer in the House of Representatives, and Congress considered the issue for more than a decade. Debate first arose at the end of January 1867, when a bill for transfer passed the House by a narrow margin. Although western senators urged the need of force to manage Indian affairs, the Senate defeated the bill. The report of the Peace Commission against transfer, signed as it was by Generals Sherman, Augur, and Terry, dampened the agitation for the measure, but when the commission reversed its decision the way was cleared for a new attempt, and on December 8, 1868, a new transfer bill, introduced by Representative James Garfield, passed the House by a substantial margin. The Senate again refused to conform, despite attempts made in February 1869 to add an amendment to the Indian appropriation bill that would provide for transfer. Then, the inauguration of Grant's peace policy made any strong movement toward military control out of the question for the time being. Military actions like that of Major Baker against the Piegans in

---

34. *Nation* 4 (January 17, 1867): 52. But note that the journal had modified its position by 1879; see ibid. 28 (January 2, 1869): 7–8.

35. Charles Lewis Slattery, *Felix Reville Brunot, 1820–1898* (New York: Longmans Green, 1901), pp. 229–30; Hayt to S. S. Cutting, June 3, 1878, Records of the Office of the Commissioner of Indian Affairs, vol. 1878, p. 113, National Archives, Record Group 75; Peter James Rahill, *The Catholic Indian Missions and Grant's Peace Policy, 1870–1884* (Washington: Catholic University of America Press, 1953), pp. 120–21, 160, 204–5. See also *Council Fire* 1 (July 1878): 98.

January 1870 were made the most of by critics of the army's handling of Indian affairs and no doubt had an important effect upon the outcome of the issue. The increased incidence of Indian hostilities in the 1870s, however, kept the issue alive, and political considerations in the election year of 1876 again made the transfer measure an important one, even before the Custer massacre added new fuel. On April 21, 1876, the House passed a new measure, but the bill failed once again in the Senate, which continued to side with the civilian reformers.[36]

The failure of Congress to pass a transfer measure, despite incessant agitation on the part of military supporters, was due to the desperate struggle to maintain civilian control—and with it the peace policy—that came from the humanitarian Christian reformers. The peace policy had been launched in fear of military control of Indian affairs and developed in an atmosphere of constant threat that army dominance would be reasserted. Such insecurity kept the reformers alert to the least wind blowing in the direction of army control; their outbursts against the army made the arguments of the advocates of transfer seem moderate and mild-mannered by comparison.

At first everything seemed promising. The Joint Special Committee on the Condition of the Indian Tribes in its report of 1867, after weighing carefully the arguments for and against the transfer of the Indian Office, concluded unanimously that Indian affairs should remain in the Department of the Interior. The Peace Commission, likewise, after a careful analysis of conditions in the West, decided against transfer in its initial report of January 7, 1868. "If we intend to have war with them [the Indians] the bureau should go to the Secretary of war," it declared. "If we intend to have peace it should be in the civil department." The commission felt that the chief tasks of the Indian Office were to educate and instruct the Indians in peaceful acts. "The military arm of the government," it flatly asserted, "is not the most admirably adapted to the discharge of duties of this character." Not one army man in a thousand, the commissioners thought, would like to teach Indian children to read and write or Indian men to farm.[37] But renewal of war in the West that summer led to reversal of the commission's stand in its meeting at Chicago in October.

36. *Congressional Globe*, 39th Congress, 2d session, pp. 891–98, 1712–20; ibid., 40th Congress, 3d session, pp. 17–21, 39–43, 880–83, 1376–78; *Congressional Record*, 4: 2657–74, 2682–86, 3962–65; *House Report* no. 240, 44–1, serial 1708; *House Report* no. 354, 44–1, serial 1709. There is extensive and valuable testimony from both sides about the army and the Indians and specifically the transfer issue in *House Report* no. 384, 43–1, serial 1624.

37. *Condition of the Indian Tribes: Report of the Special Joint Committee* (Washington: GPO, 1867), pp. 6–7; "Report of the Indian Peace Commissioners," January 7, 1868, *House Executive Document* no. 97, 40–2, serial 1337, pp. 20–21.

To counteract this change of mind on the part of such a distinguished group, which would threaten the hopeful goals of the reformers, Commissioner of Indian Affairs Taylor, who as president of the Peace Commission had refused to vote for transfer when the commission as a whole reversed its position, issued a powerful report. His eleven-point indictment of military control of Indian matters, issued as part of his annual report on November 23, 1868, exhausted the arguments of the civilian reformers. This comprehensive and forceful statement was a manifesto to which later militants could add little. Like many other reformers, however, Taylor was abler in pointing out the evils he considered inherent in military control than in offering convincing proof that civilian control could furnish the answer to the Indian problem. In a strange mixture of reformers' rhetoric, evangelical preaching against evil, and innuendoes about the motives of the military men, he set forth his arguments. That the intemperance of his language and the absurdity of some of his charges might weaken his position seems not to have crossed his mind.

Taylor argued that transfer would mean the maintenance of a large standing army in peacetime, an expensive undertaking and one contrary to the republican principles of the nation. Previous military management of the Indians, he charged, had been a failure and must "in the very nature of things, always prove a failure," for soldiers were trained for war and were not competent to teach the arts of civilization. "Will you send professional soldiers, sword in one hand, musket in the other, and tactics on the brain," he asked, "to teach the wards of the nation agriculture, the mechanic arts, theology and peace? You would civilize the Indian! Will you send him the sword? You would inspire him with the peaceful principles of Christianity! Is the bayonet their symbol? You would invite him to the sanctuary! Will you herald his approach with the clangor of arms and the thunder of artillery?" Taylor, like most of the reformers, had an obsessive fear of the demoralizing influences and diseases that came to Indians who associated with the soldiers at military posts. "If you wish to exterminate the race," he wrote in one flight of rhetoric, "pursue them with ball and blade; if you please, massacre them wholesale, as we sometimes have done; or, to make it cheap, call them to a peaceful feast, and feed them on beef salted with wolf bane; but for humanity's sake, save them from the lingering syphilitic poisons, so sure to be contracted about military posts." As for the reversal of opinion in the Peace Commission, Taylor charged that to the military men's desire for more power.[38]

Grant's acceptance of the peace policy presented to him by the religion-minded reformers for a time quieted the fears of military dominance, and the early agreements about dividing authority over the reservation and the

38. CIA Report, 1868, serial 1366, pp. 467–75.

hostile nonreservation Indians brought a temporary truce. But the rise in hostilities in the West and the consequent attacks on the peace policy brought renewed defense from the anti-military party. In order to gain information from the reservations in support of its own position, the Board of Indian Commissioners on August 1, 1875, sent a circular letter to each agent, asking whether military forces were stationed at or near the agency, what the troops were used for, and how the Indians reacted to the military presence. The agent was to report his own judgment on the influence of the troops "in respect to morality, good order, and progress in civilization" and to furnish other information "bearing upon the wisdom of increasing or diminishing the use of the Army in the management of Indian affairs." In a related question, the agents were asked about the use of Indian police and whether they might replace military forces. The replies substantiated the anti-military leanings of the board. Nearly all the agents who had had experience with troops near the reservations reported that the Indians viewed the troops with dislike and apprehension and that the effect of the common soldiers upon the moral condition of the Indian was universally bad.[39]

The board could thus report its views with confidence. The work now, it insisted, was to educate and civilize the Indians, not to subdue them, and this was eminently civilian, not military work. Charging that the men who enlisted in the army during times of peace were "among the most vicious of our population," the board asserted that when a military post and an agency were close together bad results were certain to follow. Moreover, the army acted arbitrarily and with the use of force, which in itself led to more Indian hostilities. So, the members righteously concluded: "We cannot see any benefit whatever that is likely, or even possible, to result from relegating the care of the Indians to the Army. The Army is admirable in its place, but its function is not that of civil government in a republic like ours."[40]

Commissioner of Indian Affairs Edward P. Smith backed the board. In a long discussion of the whole transfer issue, he argued that the Peace Commission had voted against transfer in 1868 and that conditions in 1875 called for it even less. He noted that at five-sixths of the agencies no soldiers were needed, and at half of the remainder troops were required only to assist the agent in arresting turbulent men. "So far, then, as eleven-twelfths of the Indian agencies are concerned," he concluded, "the question of putting them under the control of the War Department has no more pertinency than that of putting the almshouse and city schools under the metropolitan police." Rather, the very process of civilization was hindered

39. *Report of the Board of Indian Commissioners*, 1875, pp. 64–103.
40. Ibid., pp. 14–15.

by the presence of the soldiers. "The first lesson to be given the Indian is that of self-support by labor with his own hands—the last lesson which a man in uniform teaches," he said. And he added the usual little piece on "the inevitable demoralization of intemperance and lewdness" which the soldiers brought to Indian reservations. But Smith was more than willing that the onerous task of supplying the Indian agencies be taken over by the army.[41]

A few reformers faltered. William Welsh, who had taken such an active part in initiating the peace policy, finally despaired of ridding the Indian service of graft and came out for army control, but he was almost alone, and his defection brought other men back into the fray. Felix Brunot, then no longer on the Board of Indian Commissioners, published an open letter, dated May 22, 1876, to his former colleague on the board, William E. Dodge, that was a new testimonial to the anti-military policy. He pointed once more to the good effects of the peace policy and counted up the acres plowed, the cattle raised, and the Indian children in school. And he ridiculed the idea that military control would mean economy, one of the chief arguments of the army men. Most of the agencies were not even near a military post; and he asked whether it was intended to move the Indians to the forts or the forts to the reservations. "If it is merely proposed to detach army officers from the posts to perform the duties of agents," he added, "I reply that any one acquainted with the nature of those duties must be aware that the agent can have time for nothing else, and if there are enough superfluous officers of a proper rank who can be spared from the posts to perform them, the army needs to be reduced." Bishop Whipple wrote to thank Brunot for his stand: "I think your manly letter at the time Mr. Welsh was disposed to turn our Indians over to the army prevented it."[42]

The crisis that came with Custer's defeat brought the reformers back into the fight. The Board of Indian Commissioners made a great stir about the question of economy in its report of 1877, providing comparative figures to show that costs had been greater under the War Department than under the Interior Department. But it did not want such practical issues to crowd out the main issue. "In all our dealings with the Indians, in all our legislation for them," it declared, "their civilization and ultimate citizenship should be the one purpose steadily pursued. That is the only aim worthy of us as a great Christian nation. And the attainment of this end will hardly be possible by military means." In the following year, the board repeated once again all the old arguments, emphasizing now, however, that the Indians themselves were opposed to transfer to military control. The Five Civilized Tribes publicly denounced the proposed transfer. The dele-

41. CIA Report, 1875, serial 1680, pp. 520–23.
42. Slattery, *Brunot*, pp. 233, 236–37.

gates of these nations in the capital met on February 12, 1878, to oppose a new transfer bill and addressed a long memorial to Congress in which they praised the peace policy inaugurated under Grant and echoed the reformers' pleas for keeping the Indians out of the hands of the military. "Do you desire to save from further destruction your Indian population?" they asked Congress. "Is it your purpose to civilize and christianize them, so as to prepare them eventually for citizenship? Then in the name of civilization, christianity, and humanity, we earnestly ask you to make no change in the present general management unless it be to create an independent Indian department."[43]

In this campaign the opponents of transfer had the support of the *Council Fire*. Alfred B. Meacham was particularly aggressive, and he wrote in May 1878:

> What means the clamor for a transfer of the Indian to the War Department?
>
> It means to make business for the War Department. No well-informed man will assert that it is for *the good of the Indian*. Everybody knows better. Those who clamor for change give as a reason that by so doing we will get rid of the Indian rings. This is all bosh. The Indian rings are no worse than the army rings. . . . If West Point is the only institution which graduates honest men then our Christian civilization is a lie. It is an insult to our peace-loving people to intimate that military men are superior to civilians in business integrity.

For the defeat of transfer "that unwise and barbarous measure"—the journal took much of the credit. Former Commissioner of Indian Affairs George W. Manypenny also entered the lists, although a bit late to affect the outcome of the contest, with a detailed recital of military inhumanity to the Indians in a book called *Our Indian Wards*.[44]

The opposing sides were careful to seek supporting evidence from their friends. The Board of Indian Commissioners sent its questionnaire of 1875 to the civilian agents who were part of the Interior Department structure

43. *Report of the Board of Indian Commissioners*, 1877, pp. 5–6; ibid., 1878, pp. 9–16; *The Indians Opposed to the Transfer Bill: United Action of the Delegations of the Cherokee, Creek, Seminole, Chickasaw, and Choctaw Nations in Opposition to the Measure: They Protest against It, and Give Their Reasons for So Doing* (Washington: Gibson Brothers, 1878), p. 10.

44. *Council Fire* 1 (May 1878): 66; 6 (March 1883): 38–39; 6 (October 1883): 139–40. Manypenny wrote: "It is submitted that the facts given ought to silence, now and hereafter, the clamor in which military officers have indulged against the civil administration of Indian affairs, and forever dispose of the question of the restoration of the Indian bureau to the war department—a theme on which these officers (with but few exceptions) have indulged, with an assurance amounting to audacity." *Our Indian Wards* (Cincinnati: Robert Clarke and Company, 1880), p. xxv; see also pp. 373–94.

and who would have been eliminated under the army's proposals. No wonder the respondents were almost unanimous in asserting that what was needed was civilian effort to educate and civilize the Indians. The House Committee on Military Affairs in 1876, on the other hand, seeking advice on the expediency of transferring the Indian service to military control, sent its questionnaire to sixty high-ranking army officers, all but two of whom recommended the transfer as a measure of "expediency, wisdom, and economy." Not until 1878 was there an attempt by an investigating group to get both sides of the story, and then the report was a four-to-four split.[45]

When the campaign for transfer was renewed in Congress in 1878, the Senate succeeded once more in stopping a transfer amendment added to the Indian appropriation bill. A joint committee appointed to investigate the subject, after exhaustive testimony that repeated endlessly all the old arguments on both sides, could not overcome its partisan differences and submitted two reports—the Democrats urging transfer and the Republicans opposing it. By that time the issue had lost much of its urgency, and later congressional action was half-hearted and indecisive.[46]

Much of the credit for the victory against transfer belongs to Carl Schurz, whose reform of the Indian Office weakened one of the main lines of attack by military men against Interior Department control. Schurz publicly stood up to the generals who criticized civilian administrators. On the other side, in 1876, just at a crucial point when military advocates seemed to be winning, the impeachment of Secretary of War William Belknap for malfeasance in office and his subsequent resignation gave the opponents of War Department control a new argument. Did the nation, they asked, want Indian affairs turned over to such a corrupt office? One representative spoke of the spectacle of the "House marching to the Senate for the impeachment of the head of that Department, a Department all bad and worse with every revelation, and at the same time giving it new privileges and powers and fresh responsibilities."[47]

In all events, the humanitarians had won. The Board of Indian Commissioners rejoiced in 1879 that the "general sentiment of the country sustained our views and Congress refused to endorse a measure so fraught with evil and so subversive of the good results of the last ten years of hu-

45. *Report of the Board of Indian Commissioners*, 1875, p. 64; *House Report* no. 354, 44–1, serial 1709, pp. 4–5; *Senate Report* no. 693, 45–3, serial 1837.

46. *Congressional Record*, 7: 3876–77, 4192–4200, 4234–39, 4685–86; *House Report* no. 241, 45–2, serial 1822; *Senate Miscellaneous Document* no. 53, 45–3, serial 1835.

47. *Congressional Record*, 4: 2658. See the discussion of Schurz's role in Claude Moore Fuess, *Carl Schurz: Reformer* (New York: Dodd, Mead and Company, 1932), pp. 255–57, and Hans L. Trefousse, *Carl Schurz: A Biography* (Knoxville: University of Tennessee Press, 1982), pp. 242–47.

mane policy adopted by the government." Schurz, in his final report as secretary of the interior in 1880, renewed once more the arguments for civilian handling of the Indian service, but he noted how little military significance there was then in Indian affairs, and his tone indicated that he knew the fight was over.[48]

While the transfer issue was being debated, an alternative to the either-or proposition of Interior Department or War Department management of Indian affairs was also considered. A recommended solution to the disturbing conflict was that the Indian Office be elevated into an independent department on a par with Interior and War, although this was less satisfactory to military proponents than to civilian reformers. Commissioner Taylor, after his long condemnation of the threatened transfer in 1868, admitted that Indian affairs had not been much more satisfactory under the Interior Department than they had under the War Department prior to 1849. "There is too much cargo for the capacity of the vessel," he wrote, "and too much vessel and freight for the power of the machinery. We have crammed into a bureau, which under the supervisory and appellate power is a mere clerkship, all the large, complex, difficult and delicate affairs that ought to employ every function of a first-class department." The remedy was simple: launch a new Department of Indian Affairs. It was an intelligent and reasonable suggestion—one indicated by the Peace Commission in January 1868 as its own ultimate preference.[49]

The idea frequently recurred, but it made little headway. An independent department as the solution to fraud and graft in the Indian service was pushed by Felix Brunot and the original Board of Indian Commissioners in 1874, and the administration's failure to give the proposal a hearing was used as an excuse by the board for resigning en masse. The report of the joint committee in 1879 noted the proposal and recommended it because the committee viewed the Indian Office as important enough that its chief should communicate directly with the president. The committee, however, did not urge immediate legislation on the subject. Carl Schurz alluded to the idea in his final report; he was favorably inclined but not sure that it would be wise to enlarge the size of the cabinet.[50] The proposal never got the aggressive support needed to make it a reality.

The transfer issue was the greatest challenge that the peace program of

48. *Report of the Board of Indian Commissioners,* 1879, p. 8; Report of the Secretary of the Interior, 1880, *House Executive Document* no. 1, part 5, 46–3, serial 1959, pp. 16–19.

49. CIA Report, 1868, serial 1366, p. 474; "Report of the Indian Peace Commissioners," January 7, 1868, *House Executive Document* no. 97, 40–2, serial 1337, p. 21. See also S. F. Tappan to William T. Sherman, February 8, 1868, William T. Sherman Papers, Library of Congress.

50. *Senate Report* no. 693, 45–3, serial 1837, p. xix; Report of the Secretary of the Interior, 1880, *House Executive Document* no. 1, part 5, 46–3, serial 1959, p. 19.

the Christian Indian reformers had to meet. The persistent advocacy of military management of Indian affairs was an explicit denial that civilian methods, on which the peace policy depended, could succeed. The contest kept the air filled with charges and countercharges, forced the reformers to defend their policy both in theory and by practical accomplishments, and kept the public agitated over the Indian question. Scraping by with the narrowest of victories in Congress, the reformers stuck to their position until the succession of crises passed and they were able to begin anew with an aggressive humanitarian program for turning the Indians into standardized Americans.

THE END OF THE MILITARY PHASE

The military phase of Indian relations had practically ended by the early 1880s, at the same time that the church-appointed agency program of the peace policy collapsed. General Sherman, in his final report as general of the army, October 27, 1883, noted the changed situation:

> I now regard the Indians as substantially eliminated from the problem of the Army. There may be spasmodic and temporary alarms, but such Indian wars as have hitherto disturbed the public peace and tranquillity are not probable. The Army has been a large factor in producing this result, but it is not the only one. Immigration and the occupation by industrious farmers and miners of land vacated by the aborigines have been largely instrumental to that end, but the *railroad* which used to follow in the rear now goes forward with the picket-line in the great battle of civilization with barbarism, and has become the *greater* cause.[51]

Four great transcontinental lines cut across the West, and branch lines and lesser railroads crisscrossed the country that had once been the sole domain of the Indians. The logistical problems that had hampered the United States army's supply in the Trans-Mississippi West and made the mobile Indians more than an even match were solved by the railroads. The rapid extension of the lines made it possible to transport troops and supplies quickly to areas where they were needed. The increase in western settlement, moreover, made it advisable to abandon many of the small outposts. Secretary of War Robert T. Lincoln noted at the end of 1884 that "the Army has enjoyed almost complete rest from active field operations," and he remarked about the "unprecedented quiet among the Indians."[52]

51. *House Executive Document* no. 1, 48–1, serial 2182, pp. 45–46.
52. Report of the Secretary of War, 1884, *House Executive Document* no. 1, part 2, 48–2, serial 2277, p. 5.

The railroads, so emphasized by Sherman, had another effect. They speeded the destruction of the buffalo on the plains and thereby destroyed the Indians' independence and ability to wage war. At the end of the Civil War, great herds of buffalo blackened the landscape. By the mid-1870s the buffalo were largely gone in Kansas, and after 1883, the year of the last large kill, nearly all the herds vanished. New tanning methods and cheap transportation increased the market for buffalo hides, and hunters with their high-powered rifles covered the plains, slaughtering the huge beasts by the thousands and often leaving the flesh to rot and the bones to whiten on the plains.[53] The slaughter was applauded by both the civilian and the military officers of the government concerned with the Indians, for the disappearance of the Indians' means of subsistence would force them into the dependent condition that was to be the first step toward their transformation into hard-working, self-supporting farmers. Secretary of the Interior Delano wrote as early as 1874: "The buffalo are disappearing rapidly, but not faster than I desire. I regard the destruction of such game . . . as facilitating the policy of the Government, of destroying their hunting habits, coercing them on reservations, and compelling them to begin to adopt the habits of civilization." In the same year General Sheridan suggested that the Texas legislature award medals to the buffalo hunters in gratitude. "These men have done more in the last two years, and will do more in the next year, to settle the vexed Indian question," he said, "than the entire regular army has done in the last thirty years. They are destroying the Indian's commissary."[54] The end of the buffalo meant the end of the life that the plains Indians had known and was a fundamental condition for establishing the reservation system for the once nomadic Indians.

53. The buffalo have been thoroughly treated in general studies that all include material on their destruction and the effect it had on the Indians. See, for example, Francis Haines, *The Buffalo* (New York: Thomas Y. Crowell Company, 1970); Thom McHugh, *The Time of the Buffalo* (New York: Alfred A. Knopf, 1972); David A. Dary, *The Buffalo Book: The Full Saga of the American Animal* (Chicago: Swallow Press, 1974). The slaughter of the buffalo is treated specifically in E. Douglas Branch, *The Hunting of the Buffalo* (New York: D. Appleton-Century Company, 1929; reprint with introduction by J. Frank Dobie, Lincoln, University of Nebraska Press, 1962), and Wayne Gard, *The Great Buffalo Hunt* (New York: Alfred A. Knopf, 1959).

54. *House Report* no. 384, 43–1, serial 1624, p. 99; Mari Sandoz, *The Buffalo Hunters: The Story of the Hide Men* (New York: Hastings House, 1954), p. 173, quoted in Utley, *Frontier Regulars*, p. 413.

CHAPTER 22

Reservation Policy

Consolidation of Reservations.

Indian Resistance to Removal.

Revision of Reservation Policy.

The post-Civil War Indian Office and the Indian reformers inherited a reservation policy that had developed gradually during the previous decades, and the concentration of Indians on reservations was the underpinning of Grant's peace policy.[1] Commissioner Ely S. Parker's question to the new Board of Indian Commissioners asking whether the Indians should be placed on reservations received a unanimous affirmative answer. The board declared in its first report:

> The policy of collecting the Indian tribes upon small reservations contiguous to each other, and within the limits of a large reservation, eventually to become a State of the Union, and of which the small reservations will probably be the counties, seems to be the best that can be devised. Many tribes may thus be collected in the present Indian territory. The larger the number that can be thus concentrated the better for the success of the plan; care being taken to separate hereditary enemies from each other. When upon the reservation they should be taught as soon as possible the advantage of individual ownership of property; and should be given land in severalty as soon

1. This chapter is taken largely from Francis Paul Prucha, *American Indian Policy in Crisis: Christian Reformers and the Indian, 1865–1900* (Norman: University of Oklahoma Press, 1976), pp. 107–31.

as it is desired by any of them, and the tribal relation should be discouraged.[2]

CONSOLIDATION OF RESERVATIONS

The views of the Board of Indian Commissioners accorded well with those of responsible men in Grant's administration. Secretary of the Interior Jacob D. Cox looked not to a new reservation policy but to "an enlarged and more enlightened application of the general principles of the old one." He saw two objects in the policy: "First, the location of the Indians upon fixed reservations, so that the pioneers and settlers may be freed from the terrors of wandering hostile tribes; and second, an earnest effort at their civilization, so that they may themselves be elevated in the scale of humanity, and our obligation to them as fellowmen be discharged." Cox, in agreement with the Board of Indian Commissioners, saw that larger concentration would obviate many of the evils that arose when small reservations were surrounded by the unscrupulous frontier whites, and he hoped that moving less advanced tribes into contact with more civilized ones would have a beneficial result. He was sanguine about the prospects of concentrating the tribes in the Indian Territory and the organization of a territorial government over them. In the north and west of the Rockies he wanted the same sort of development, although he realized that there it would take more time.[3]

With Columbus Delano, Cox's successor, consolidation of tribes in the Indian Territory became almost an obsession, and he began to play a numbers game, trying to fit all the Indians into one large reservation. He counted 172,000 Indians outside the Indian Territory, occupying 96,155,785 acres—558 acres per capita. Inside the Indian Territory he found only one person to every 630 acres. "Could the entire Indian population of the country, excluding Alaska and those scattered among the States . . . be located in the Indian Territory," he decided, "there would be 180 acres of land, *per capita*, for the entire number, showing that there is ample area of land to afford them all comfortable homes." At the same time he candidly admitted that the acres given up by the assembling tribes could be thrown open to white settlement and cultivation. He wanted the Indians to realize that if they did not cooperate in this scheme to preserve them in the consoli-

2. *Report of the Board of Indian Commissioners*, 1869, pp. 3, 9; minutes of May 26, 1869, Minutes of the Board of Indian Commissioners, vol. 1, p. 4, National Archives, Record Group 75.

3. Report of the Secretary of the Interior, 1869, *House Executive Document* no. 1, 41–2, serial 1414, pp. viii–ix.

dated reservation, they would inevitably be inundated or crushed by the rapidly growing tide of white emigration.[4]

In this work of reducing the Indians' reservations, Felix Brunot of the Board of Indian Commissioners played a large part. Negotiations with the Crows, carried on in 1873 by Brunot, which were intended to move the Indians from their reservation on the Yellowstone River in southern Montana to one in the Judith Basin and reduce their lands by four million acres, delighted the people of Montana. The territorial governor thanked Brunot for his work and attributed the success of the negotiations to "the ability and patience by which the negotiations were conducted, aided by the friendly feeling that has been brought about by the humane policy of the President towards the Indian tribes." To the disappointment of the whites, Congress failed to ratify the agreement, and the Crows stayed for the time being on their lands along the Yellowstone. But the case shows both the sincere desire of humanitarians like Brunot to reduce the Indians' land holdings and how the "friendly feeling" that was a conscious part of the peace policy worked toward the ultimate dispossession of the Indians.[5]

An even more personal involvement of Brunot in reducing the reservations came in his dealings with the Utes. Ouray, chief of the Utes, was steadfast at first in his refusal to sell any lands. When Brunot met Ouray at a council in 1872, the chief told him of the capture of his young son fifteen years before by a party of Cheyennes and Arapahos. Brunot and the secretary of the Board of Indian Commissioners, Thomas Cree, undertook to recover the long-lost son, who was found in Texas and united with his father in the office of the board in Washington. The young Indian, unfortunately, died on his way home. "But the gratitude which he [Ouray] felt toward Mr. Brunot and Mr. Cree," Brunot's biographer wrote, "did what a special commission could not do, and when Mr. Brunot told him he thought it right for him to sell a portion of his reservation, Ouray threw all his strong influence in favour of the sale, though a year before he intended opposition to the bitter end." Brunot did "what neither commissioners nor armies could accomplish"; after six days of patient negotiation on his part the Utes ceded five million acres, the southern half of their reservation in southwestern Colorado.[6]

Secretary Delano remarked in 1873 that the efforts of the Indian Office

4. Ibid., 1871, *House Executive Document* no. 1, part 5, 42–2, serial 1505, pp. 6–7; ibid., 1872, *House Executive Document* no. 1, part 5, 42–3, serial 1560, pp. 5–7.

5. Charles Lewis Slattery, *Felix Reville Brunot, 1820–1898* (New York: Longmans, Green and Company, 1901), pp. 207–13. The agreement is in Kappler, vol. 4, pp. 1142–47.

6. Slattery, *Brunot*, pp. 191–92, 214–15. The agreement of September 13, 1873, is in Kappler, vol. 1, pp. 151–52. The story of Ouray's lost son is told in Ann W. Hafen, "Efforts to Recover the Stolen Son of Chief Ouray," *Colorado Magazine* 16 (January 1939): 53–62.

had been "unremitting," and he continued to urge the Indians to exchange reservations lying within the range of advancing settlements and railroad construction for other locations. Even the Sioux in Dakota and Montana did not escape his solicitous attention. He noted the unproductive soil and the severity of the winters in those northern regions, conditions that hindered all attempts to improve the Indians' condition through agriculture and grazing. Rejecting the older idea of a northern as well as a southern reserve, he wanted to move these northern Indians en masse to the Indian Territory, where "both climate and soil are so favorable for the production of everything necessary to sustain and make them comfortable." Delano lamented the obstinacy of the Sioux, who refused to move, but he thought that time would ultimately overcome their objections.[7]

Delano's plans did not die when he was forced out of office in 1875. His successor, Zachariah Chandler, continued to urge them, although he was willing to use a reservation in Minnesota and another in the southern part of Washington Territory in addition to the Indian Territory as the new permanent homes for the scattered Indians. He also seemed less enthusiastic about what all this would do for the Indians and more concerned about saving money and trouble for the government. His report of 1876 neatly summed up the arguments:

> Briefly, the arguments are all in favor of the consolidation; expensive agencies would be abolished, the Indians themselves can be more easily watched over and controlled, evil-designing men be the better kept away from them, and illicit trade and barter in arms, ammunition, and whiskey prevented; goods could be supplied at a great saving; the military service relieved; the Indians better taught, and friendly rivalry established among them, those most civilized hastening the progress of those below them, and most of the land now occupied as reserves, reverting to the General Government, would be open to entry and sale.[8]

It might be suspected that men like Delano, whose record was none too clean, were more interested in freeing Indian lands for white exploitation than in Indian welfare, but they no doubt honestly believed that the Indians had to be moved from their present situations if they were to survive

7. Report of the Secretary of the Interior, 1873, *House Executive Document* no. 1, part 5, 43–1, serial 1601, pp. vii–viii; ibid., 1874, *House Executive Document* no. 1, part 5, 44–2, serial 1639, p. xii.

8. Ibid., 1876, *House Executive Document* no. 1, part 5, 44–2, serial 1749, p. vi. Chandler was merely repeating the arguments and proposals put forth by Commissioner of Indian Affairs John Q. Smith in his annual report, CIA Report, 1876, serial 1749, pp. 385–87. Two years later Commissioner E. A. Hayt drew up a bill to consolidate the tribes further. CIA Report, 1878, serial 1850, p. 440.

and advance. It was the almost universal opinion of the age and a doctrine that went back clearly as far as Thomas Jefferson. Views like Delano's on Indian consolidation were accepted as part of the humanitarians' package of Indian reform. "Since the inauguration of the present Indian policy," the Board of Indian Commissioners declared in 1876, "this board has not ceased to recommend the consolidation of agencies where it can be effected without infringing existing treaties. The time has now arrived when the Government must, if it would see an impulse given to the work of Indian civilization, take decided ground and prompt action upon this important subject." The board was convinced that "the public sentiment in and out of Congress will see the great advantage of this important advance movement in Indian civilization." Tribes that occupied small reservations and had made little progress, if moved to large reservations, would profit from the encouragement of their more advanced brethren and would learn by daily observation "that thrift, enterprise, and energy do always produce their legitimate fruits of civilization and self-dependence." Moreover, a system of law could be more easily introduced, early allotment of land could be provided, and tribal relations could be broken up. Such action, the board concluded, would "go far toward the successful solution of the Indian problem, which has so long perplexed our nation, puzzled our statesmen, and disturbed our philanthropists."[9]

INDIAN RESISTANCE TO REMOVAL

The theorists who elaborated schemes for consolidating all the Indians in one big reservation reckoned too little with the Indians, whom they were so willing to move around like pieces on a chessboard. The Indians were deeply attached to their homelands, and the topographical and climatic conditions were psychologically if not physically of tremendous importance to their well-being. Sioux, long acclimated to the northern plains, foresaw only misery and disaster if they had to move to the actually better lands in the Indian Territory. In the 1870s, while government officials and humanitarians were concocting fine schemes to remove the Indians to a few large reservations in order to save money and at the same time speed

---

9. *Report of the Board of Indian Commissioners,* 1876, pp. 4–6. The board repeated its recommendations in subsequent years. In 1878, a resolution submitted to the Senate asserted that there were 300,000 Indians on 300,000,000 acres of public land in the United States, or about 1,000 acres for each Indian, whereas whites were restricted to a 160-acre homestead for a family. The creation of four Indian reservations or territories was proposed, two west of the Rockies and two east, with the provision that Indians who cut loose from the tribe could take out homesteads where they were. *Senate Miscellaneous Document* no. 16, 45–2, serial 1785.

the civilization process, three disastrous removals propelled the issue into the public consciousness.

The most famous removal was that of the Ponca Indians from their reservation along the Missouri River to the Indian Territory. It was, in fact, the spark that ignited a new flame of concern for the rights of the Indians. The cause was just, the propaganda arising from it was spectacular, and the interest of eastern philanthropists in the Indians burned with new intensity.[10]

The Poncas, a small peaceful Siouan tribe, in 1865 had been guaranteed a reservation of 96,000 acres along the Missouri north of the Niobrara River. Three years later, however, the United States in the Fort Laramie treaty with the Sioux—without consulting the Poncas—ceded the entire Ponca reservation to the Sioux, the Poncas' traditional enemies.[11] Although the United States admitted that the transfer to the Sioux had been a mistake, the government's resolution of the problem was not to restore the lands, which might have irritated the Sioux, but to remove the Poncas to the Indian Territory. Over their objections, the Indians in 1877 were escorted south by federal troops and settled on the Quapaw reserve.

The hardships of the journey and the change in climate brought great misery and many deaths to the Poncas, and even after they had found a new and more favorable location within the Indian Territory, they remained restless and unhappy and longed to return to their old home in the north. "I am sorry to be compelled to say," Commissioner of Indian Affairs Ezra Hayt lamented, "the Poncas were wronged, and restitution should be made as far as it is in the power of the government to do so." Secretary of the Interior Schurz echoed these sentiments, but Congress paid no heed to the reports, and the Indians' condition remained precarious.[12]

One of the chiefs, Standing Bear, could endure the situation no longer. Taking along the body of his dead son, who had succumbed to malaria, and followed by a small portion of the tribe, he started out in January 1879 to return north. Reaching Nebraska early in the spring, the group settled

10. The story of Ponca removal is traced in Earl W. Hayter, "The Ponca Removal," *North Dakota Historical Quarterly* 6 (July 1932): 262–75; and Stanley Clark, "Ponca Publicity," *Mississippi Valley Historical Review* 29 (March 1943): 495–516. An account by one of the men who fought for the Poncas' rights, with reprints of important documents, is Zylyff [Thomas Henry Tibbles], *The Ponca Chiefs: An Attempt to Appeal from the Tomahawk to the Courts* (Boston, 1880; reprinted with an introduction by Kay Graber, Lincoln: University of Nebraska Press, 1972). An excellent account of the Ponca affair and the reaction of the reformers is in Robert Winston Mardock, *The Reformers and the American Indian* (Columbia: University of Missouri Press, 1971), pp. 168–91.

11. Kappler, pp. 875–76, 998.

12. Report of the Secretary of the Interior, 1877, *House Executive Document* no. 1, part 5, 45–2, serial 1800, pp. vii–viii; CIA Report, 1877, serial 1800, pp. 417–19. The quotation from Hayt is in CIA Report, 1878, serial 1850, p. 467.

down for the time being with the Omaha Indians, their longtime friends. The plight of Standing Bear and his followers had by this time become a public issue, and a group of citizens of Omaha, encouraged by General Crook, took up their case. When federal troops arrived to arrest the runaways and return them to the Indian Territory, prominent lawyers of the city drew up a writ of habeas corpus to prevent the chief's return, and on April 30 the matter was brought before Judge Elmer S. Dundy of the United States District Court. In the celebrated case of *Standing Bear* v. *Crook*, Judge Dundy ruled that "an Indian is a 'person' within the meaning of the laws of the United States, and has, therefore, the right to sue out a writ of habeas corpus in a federal court." Since he could find no authority for forcing the Poncas back to the Indian Territory, Dundy ordered their release.[13]

The Ponca affair had important repercussions on Indian reform, for a man much involved in the origins of the Standing Bear case in Omaha soon mounted a campaign in the East to stir up public support for the Poncas. He was Thomas Henry Tibbles, one of the strangest characters in the history of Indian reform. Tibbles had been a member of John Brown's band in Kansas, a guide and scout on the plains, an itinerant preacher, a Pullman car conductor, and a newspaper reporter. When the Poncas returned north, he was an assistant editor of the Omaha *Herald*. According to his own testimony, he was the prime mover in the Standing Bear case, and after the chief's release he resorted to the lecture platform to keep the Ponca issue alive. Accompanied by Standing Bear and Susette La Flesche, an Omaha Indian girl known as Bright Eyes, he appeared in Chicago and in several eastern cities to relate the wrongs of the Poncas, condemn the government for its actions, and appeal for support of the Indians' cause.[14]

The greatest success of Tibbles was in Boston, where a group of prominent men (including John D. Long, governor of Massachusetts, and Frederick O. Prince, mayor of Boston) organized the Boston Indian Citizenship Committee to fight for the rights of the Poncas and other Indians. The principal thrust of the group's program was to demand respect for the Indians' rights, including the return to their original reservation, and to denounce the federal government for its part in the Ponca removal. Tibbles fitted well into the program and spoke to enthusiastic audiences in Boston. Bright Eyes and Standing Bear, appearing on stage in Indian dress, added a strong personal touch to the proceedings.

The bête noire of Tibbles and the Boston reformers was Secretary of the Interior Carl Schurz, who had assumed his duties just as the actual move-

13. 25 *Federal Cases* 695–701. The quotation is at 700–701.

14. *Dictionary of American Biography*, s.v. Tibbles, Thomas Henry, by W. J. Ghent; publisher's preface in Thomas Henry Tibbles, *Buckskin and Blanket Days; Memoirs of a Friend of the Indians* (Garden City, New York: Doubleday, 1957). Autobiographical material appears in *Buckskin and Blanket Days* and in Zylyff, *Ponca Chiefs*.

ment of the Poncas to the Indian Territory got under way. In public speeches and published letters, the Boston committee and its supporters on one side and Secretary Schurz on the other engaged in acrimonious debate in which neither side adhered strictly to the facts. The atrocity stories of Tibbles and Bright Eyes were countered by Schurz's descriptions of the favorable condition of the Poncas in the Indian Territory. At a public meeting in Boston on December 3, 1880, presided over by Governor Long, Tibbles delivered an enthusiastically received diatribe against Schurz and his handling of the Ponca case, and other speeches were made by Long, Prince, Bright Eyes, and Wendell Phillips. Schurz replied to the talks in an open letter to Governor Long dated December 9, 1880, in which he urged that justice be accorded the government officials as well as the Indians; he argued that to move the Poncas back to Dakota, as the Boston group demanded, would cause new misery to the Indians and open the door to white invasions of the Indian Territory. This brought a long and denunciatory reply from Boston renewing the charges against the secretary.[15]

Schurz was also engaged in a public exchange with Helen Hunt Jackson, who had heard Tibbles and Bright Eyes in Boston in November 1879 and became a zealous convert to the cause of Indian reform. Schurz quashed an attempt to carry the Standing Bear case to the Supreme Court, and he urged Jackson and her friends, who were collecting funds for further legal action on Indian rights, to use the money for Indian education rather than pour it into the pockets of attorneys in futile cases.[16]

Still another of Schurz's opponents was Senator Henry L. Dawes of Massachusetts, with whom he tangled over the accidental killing of Standing Bear's brother, Big Snake, at the Ponca agency on October 31, 1879.[17] In a Senate inquiry into the killing, Dawes insinuated that the government had plotted the shooting of the Ponca chief; he then alluded to Schurz's German background: "It has been a relief to me, however, in examining

15. T. H. Tibbles, *Western Men Defended: Speech of Mr. T. H. Tibbles in Tremont Temple, Boston, Mass., December, 1880* (Boston: Lockwood, Brooks and Company, 1880); Schurz to Long, December 9, 1880, *Speeches, Correspondence and Political Papers of Carl Schurz*, ed. Frederic Bancroft, 6 vols. (New York: G. P. Putnam's Sons, 1913), 4: 50–78; Schurz to Edward Atkinson, November 28, 1879, ibid., 3: 481–89; *Secretary Schurz: Reply of the Boston Committee, Governor John D. Long, Chairman: Misrepresentations Corrected and Important Facts Presented* (Boston: Frank Wood, 1881).

16. The exchange of letters is printed in Helen Hunt Jackson, *A Century of Dishonor: A Sketch of the United States Government's Dealings with Some of the Indian Tribes* (New York: Harper and Brothers, 1881), pp. 359–66. Another expression of Schurz's views appears in his brief statement "The Removal of the Poncas," *Independent* 32 (January 1, 1880): 1.

17. Reports on the killing of Big Snake are printed in *Senate Executive Document* no. 14, 46–3, serial 1941. See also the testimony in *Senate Report* no. 670, 46–2, serial 1898, pp. 245–51. A useful article is J. Stanley Clark, "The Killing of Big Snake," *Chronicles of Oklahoma* 49 (Autumn 1971): 302–14.

our treatment of these weak and defenseless people, to find that these methods are not American in their origin, but bear too striking a resemblance to the modes of an imperial government carried on by espionage and arbitrary power. They are methods which I believe to be unique, and which I trust will never be naturalized."[18] In reply Schurz addressed an open letter to Dawes and gave every senator a copy on his desk as his only means of replying to Dawes's privileged congressional remarks. The letter was a devastating refutation of the senator's charges. The agitation in the Big Snake affair was, said Schurz, a new illustration of the fact that it was "difficult to exaggerate the malignant unscrupulousness of the speculator in philanthropy hunting for a sensation."[19]

The verbal combat between the reformers and the secretary of the interior did not prevent the working out of a solution to the Ponca problem, although nearly every move of the administration was subject to critical attack. A special Senate committee investigating the Ponca removal strongly condemned the government's action but split over a remedy. The majority report advocated returning the Poncas to their old home, whereas a minority report sided with Schurz in recommending that the Indians be indemnified but kept in the Indian Territory.[20] At the end of 1880 President Hayes appointed a special commission to confer with the Poncas, both those in the Indian Territory and those in Nebraska, and to recommend action. The commission, headed by General George Crook and made up of General Nelson A. Miles, William Stickney of the Board of Indian Commissioners, and William Allen of Boston, recommended that the Poncas in the Indian Territory remain there and that provision be made for those who wanted to stay in the north with Standing Bear. The decision of the commission was in accord with a declaration of wishes presented to the president by a delegation of Poncas from the Indian Territory on December 27, 1880, that indicated their desire to remain on the lands they then occupied and to relinquish all interest in their former reservation on the Missouri.[21]

18. *Congressional Record*, 11: 1958.

19. Carl Schurz, *An Open Letter in Answer to a Speech of Hon. H. L. Dawes, United States Senate, on the Case of Big Snake* (Washington, 1881). The letter, dated February 7, 1881, is printed also in *Speeches of Schurz*, 4: 91–113. The quotation is from p. 102. An account of the controversy, based in large part on the Dawes Papers in the Library of Congress, is in Loring Benson Priest, *Uncle Sam's Stepchildren: The Reformation of United States Indian Policy, 1865–1887* (New Brunswick: Rutgers University Press, 1942), pp. 78–79. Schurz's biographer, Claude Moore Fuess, in *Carl Schurz: Reformer* (New York: Dodd, Mead and Company, 1932), pp. 252–77, believes that Schurz was completely vindicated in his conflicts with the humanitarian reformers.

20. *Senate Report* no. 670, 46–2, serial 1898.

21. The commission's report and a copy of its proceedings are in *Senate Executive Document* no. 30, 46–3, serial 1941. Included is a minority report submitted by Allen,

Hayes recommended that immediate action be taken in line with the Crook commission report and the Ponca request. At last Congress acted; on March 3 it appropriated $165,000 to enable the secretary of the interior "to indemnify the Ponca tribe of Indians for losses sustained by them in consequence of their removal to the Indian Territory, to secure to them land in severalty on either the old or new reservation, in accordance with their wishes, and to settle all matters of difference with these Indians." All that remained was to gain Sioux approval for the Poncas of Standing Bear's party to remain in the north, and this was accomplished by a special agreement drawn up with a Sioux delegation in Washington in August 1881.[22]

The controversy over the Poncas between Schurz and the reformers, although it kept the country much alive to Indian problems, was unfortunate, for it obscured the fundamental agreement of both sides in their desire to promote justice for the Indians. In large part, no doubt, the attacks on Schurz by the evangelical reformers reflected the fundamental differences of the two parties. Schurz was a severely practical and unsentimental man. His program was one of "policy," not of religious motivation. A man more different in background and outlook from the general run of Indian reformers can hardly be imagined, yet Schurz's Indian policy—attack upon corruption and inefficiency in the Indian Office, support of civilian as opposed to military control of Indian affairs, allotment of land in severalty and sale of "surplus" lands, and an aggressive educational program for Indians—were all in line with what the friends of the Indian came to espouse so ardently later in the 1880s.

Senator Dawes, for his part, learned the danger of opposing the administration. After Schurz left office, Dawes wrote concerning the new secretary of the interior, Samuel J. Kirkwood, who had defended Schurz's position on the Poncas: "Of course we widely differ from him but an open conflict with this new administration, as with the last, on the Indian policy, must be avoided if possible, or we shall be very much disabled. . . . Let us, Boston and all, try to pull with Washington, but to be sure and pull the hardest!"[23] The reform groups learned, too, to base their arguments on sound information and not to be carried away, as they had been in the first flush of their reform enthusiasm, by such exaggerated tales as those told by Tibbles and Bright Eyes.[24]

---

who was unwilling to believe that the Indians had genuinely decided to stay in the Indian Territory.

22. Hayes letter of February 1, 1881, *Senate Executive Document* no. 30, 46–3, serial 1941, pp. 1–4; 21 *United States Statutes* 422; agreement with Sioux, *House Executive Document* no. 1, 47–1, serial 2018, pp. 39–40.

23. Dawes to Allen, August 11, 1881, Dawes Papers, quoted in Priest, *Uncle Sam's Stepchildren,* p. 79.

24. Tibbles, whose first wife died in 1879, married Bright Eyes in 1881.

Another celebrated case that illustrated the weakness of the consolidation policy was the flight of a band of Northern Cheyennes from the Indian Territory in 1878.[25] Following military action on the northern plains after Custer's defeat, a party of these Indians had been placed on the reservation of the Southern Cheyennes and Arapahos near Fort Reno. The Indians suffered greatly in their new home, and the subsistence supplied by the government was inadequate. On September 9, 1878, about three hundred of them led by chiefs Dull Knife and Little Wolf fled the reservation and headed north to join their friends the Sioux. When troops of the United States army were sent to stop the Indians and return them to the Indian Territory, the flight became a running fight, and the Cheyennes killed a number of settlers in their passage through Kansas.

When the Indians reached the Platte, they separated into two groups. One of them under Dull Knife moved westward toward Fort Robinson; the party surrendered on October 23 and was imprisoned at the fort. The post commandant received orders to transport the Indians back to the Indian Territory, but they steadfastly refused to go, and the officer attempted to freeze and starve them into submission. Able to endure the torture no longer and frightened by the seizure of one of their leaders, the Indians broke out of their quarters on the night of January 9. Weakened by the ordeal of their imprisonment, they were easy prey for the soldiers who pursued them, and fifty or sixty men, women, and children were killed in flight. Some were captured and returned to the south, while Dull Knife and others escaped to the Sioux. The other group, led by Little Wolf, had continued north, hoping to reach Montana. They were induced to surrender on March 25, 1879, and were taken to Fort Keogh, where they were allowed to remain.

Commissioner Hayt blamed the affair upon unwarranted dissatisfaction on the part of the Indians and asserted that Dull Knife's band contained "the vilest and most dangerous element of their tribe." With elaborate statistics he attempted to prove that the Indians had not been maltreated or underfed in the Indian Territory.[26] But other evidence soon became available. A select committee of the Senate appointed to investigate the case

---

25. A full account of the event is given in George Bird Grinnell, *The Fighting Cheyennes* (New York: Charles Scribner's Sons, 1915), chapters 19–20. Mari Sandoz, *Cheyenne Autumn* (New York: McGraw-Hill Book Company, 1953), tells the story of the Indians in dramatic style. See also Verne Dusenberry, "The Northern Cheyenne," *Montana Magazine of History* 5 (Winter 1955): 23–40.

26. CIA Report, 1878, serial 1850, pp. 455–57. Hayt's views were supported by Secretary Schurz in Report of the Secretary of the Interior, *House Executive Document* no. 1, part 5, 45–3, serial 1850, pp. vii–ix. See also CIA Report, 1879, serial 1910, pp. 80–82, and a letter of T. J. Morgan, April 23, 1890, *Senate Executive Document* no. 121, 51–1, serial 2686, pp. 2–9.

returned a critical report in June 1880 based on abundant testimony taken at Fort Reno and on interviews with Indians imprisoned in Kansas. Its findings sharply contradicted Hayt's report and described the government's lack of compliance with treaty agreements and the disastrous conditions that resulted from the shortage of supplies. "It is impossible to say," the committee reported, "that these were or were not the causes that led three hundred Indians in a body to escape from the Territory and to return to Dakota. They were doubtless provoking causes to that hegira, but the Indians were also strongly impelled by a longing desire to return to their native country, and by a feeling of disgust towards their new location." The committee noted, too, that the band had left the reservation not as a marauding party but simply with the intention of escaping to their former homes, and that they had begun to fight only when attacked by the army. The handling of Dull Knife's band at Fort Robinson was severely condemned.[27]

The committee's conclusion was decisive: there was no hope of civilizing Indians and making them self-supporting in a location where they were discontented. Unless they were living in a place they could look upon as home, it was unlikely that they would ever gain the independence of feeling that would lead them to work for their own living. "If they are compelled to accept a prison as a home," the report said, "they will naturally prefer to compel the keepers to feed and clothe them. They will remain pensioners upon our humanity, having lost all pride of character and all care of anything except to live." Moreover, the concentration of Indians in large numbers in one place was out of line with the changing relations between the government and the Indians. "They are already surrounded and separated into limited districts by the intervening white settlements," the senators noted, "and the time is near at hand when they must become members of the same communities with the white people."[28]

Ironically, at the very time Dull Knife and Little Wolf were fleeing north, another band of Northern Cheyennes led by Little Chief was moving south into the Indian Territory from western Nebraska. This group, too, was severely dissatisfied with its new surroundings and in the summer of 1879 sent a delegation to Washington to beg permission to join their tribesmen at Fort Keogh. Although Commissioner Hayt reported that the delegation was induced to return cheerfully to the Indian Territory, the case was by no means closed. In 1881, after continued petitioning, Little Chief's band was transferred to the Sioux reservation at Pine Ridge, and in

27. *Senate Report* no. 708, 46–2, serial 1899, pp. xvi–xviii. The failure of the attempt to force the Cheyennes into white agricultural patterns is studied in Ramon Powers, "Why the Northern Cheyenne Left Indian Territory in 1878: A Cultural Analysis," *Kansas Quarterly* 3 (Fall 1971): 72–81.

28. *Senate Report* no. 708, 46–2, serial 1899, p. xxi.

1883, under congressional authorization, the Northern Cheyennes still in the Indian Territory were allowed to follow.[29]

The Sioux reservation in Dakota did not completely satisfy the Cheyennes, however, and little by little they drifted west into Montana to join their brethren, for whom a reservation, eventually extended to the Tongue River, had been established by executive order on November 26, 1884. No attempts were made to restrain this voluntary migration of the Indians. Captain J. M. Bell, acting agent at Pine Ridge, urged in 1886 that the departing Cheyennes be brought back by force or imprisoned when they arrived at Fort Keogh. "Until measures of this kind are adopted," he reasoned, "they will continue roaming from place to place, and will accomplish nothing in the way of civilization." But Commissioner of Indian Affairs Hiram Price demurred, and Secretary of the Interior L. Q. C. Lamar declared: "These straying Indians, a restless element at their old agencies, appear to be satisfied in their new location, and it is not deemed advisable to force them to return to the Sioux Reservation."[30] This was a clear admission of the failure of the concentration policy.

Still another example of the impossibility of forcing northern Indians into the Indian Territory was the case of Chief Joseph's band of Nez Perces. When these Indians surrendered to General Miles in northern Montana in October 1877, Miles had promised that they could return to Idaho in the spring to settle down peacefully on the reservation. General Sherman overruled this humane decision. Declaring that the Indians were prisoners of war and that they "should never again be allowed to return to Oregon or to Lapwai," Sherman directed that the Nez Perces be imprisoned at Fort Leavenworth until they could be turned over to the Indian Office for disposition.[31] Transported down the Yellowstone and the Missouri to Fort Leavenworth, the miserable Indians were encamped in unhealthy lowlands along the river, where, ill provided for and pining for the clear mountain streams of their homeland, they succumbed to sickness, and many died.

---

29. The story of Little Chief and of the transfer of the Cheyennes to Dakota can be traced in CIA Report, 1880, serial 1959, p. 109; CIA Report, 1881, serial 2018, pp. 41–42; CIA Report, 1882, serial 2100, p. 50; CIA Report, 1883, serial 2191, p. 39.

30. Executive order in *House Document* no. 153, 55–3, serial 3807, p. 145; letters of J. M. Bell, J. D. C. Atkins, and L. Q. C. Lamar, in *Senate Executive Document* no. 212, 49–1, serial 2341. The movement of the Cheyennes on their own accord from Pine Ridge to Tongue River upset the supply of subsistence, and the Indian Office repeatedly asked Congress for aid in relieving the Indians' misery. See *Senate Executive Document* no. 208, 48–1, serial 2168; *House Executive Document* no. 17, 49–1, serial 2387; *Senate Executive Document* no. 212, 49–1, serial 2341; and *Senate Executive Document* no. 121, 51–1, serial 2686.

31. Report of Sherman, November 7, 1877, *House Executive Document* no. 1, 45–2, serial 1794, p. 15.

Commissioner Hayt had noted in his report for 1877 that "humanity prompts us to send them back and place them on the Nez Perce reservation." Yet he saw an "insuperable difficulty in the way." The murder of whites by members of Chief Joseph's band at the beginning of the outbreak meant that the Indians would find neither peace nor safety in their old haunts. Indictments had in fact been issued in Idaho for certain Nez Perces, and the memory of the murders would continue to be an obstacle to the return of the band. "But for these foul crimes," Hayt asserted, "these Indians would be sent back to the reservation in Idaho. Now, however, they will have to be sent to the Indian Territory; and this will be no hardship to them, as the difference in the temperature between that latitude and their old homes is inconsiderable." The Nez Perces at Fort Leavenworth were turned over by the army to agents of the Indian Office, and on July 21, 1878, they headed south to be settled on a section of the Quapaw Reservation. It was hoped that there, under the guidance of the Quaker agent, the desolate Indians would soon become self-supporting, as the Modocs had done in the same location.[32]

The Indians did not recover, and more of the band sickened and died. Two members of the Board of Indian Commissioners who visited them in August 1878 found Joseph absolutely averse to remaining in the Indian Territory. "Seldom have we been in councils where the Indians more eloquently or earnestly advocated their side of the question," they reported. "Joseph's arraignment of the Army for alleged bad faith to him after the surrender of himself and people to General Miles was almost unanswerable."[33] The commissioners ordered medical supplies for the Indians and made arrangements for a better tract of land on the Quapaw reserve for the Nez Perces, but these actions hardly struck at the heart of the matter.

When Hayt visited Joseph the following October, he was informed in unmistakable terms of the chief's dissatisfaction. The Indian insisted that he had been promised by Miles and Howard that he would be allowed to return to Idaho and that he had surrendered under that condition, and he complained about the quality of the region selected for his people in the Indian Territory. Hayt, like all who came in contact with the Nez Perce leader, was impressed with his intelligence, character, and integrity, and he tried to convince the chief that his people were prevented from returning to Idaho for their own protection and welfare. He attempted a limited accommodation, moreover, by taking Joseph west on a trip of exploration to

---

32. CIA Report, 1877, serial 1800, p. 409. Two thoroughly documented studies of the Nez Perces in the Indian Territory are J. Stanley Clark, "The Nez Perces in Exile," *Pacific Northwest Quarterly* 36 (July 1945): 213–32, and Berlin B. Chapman, "Nez Perces in Indian Territory: An Archival Study," *Oregon Historical Quarterly* 50 (June 1949): 98–121.

33. *Report of the Board of Indian Commissioners*, 1878, pp. 47–48.

seek a better spot for his band. A place on Salt Creek in the Cherokee Outlet near the Poncas seemed to please the chief, and Hayt believed that he
would agree to settle there. Hayt had been accompanied by E. M. Kingsley,
a member of the Board of Indian Commissioners, who was favorably impressed with Joseph's argument about Miles's promise and about bad conditions in the Indian Territory. "This statement is believed to be true in the
main," Kingsley noted, "and, if so, Joseph stands before the American people a victim of duplicity; his confidence wantonly betrayed; his substance
pillaged; an involuntary exile from home and kindred; his 'cause' lost; his
people rapidly wasting by pestilence; an object not of haughty contempt or
vulgar ridicule, but of generous, humane treatment and consideration."[34]

The wheels of justice moved very slowly and none too surely. Still reluctant to send the Indians back among hostile frontiersmen, the government in June settled the Nez Perces on the new tract in the Cherokee Outlet. Joseph was not reconciled. He told the reformer Alfred B. Meacham in
July: "You come to see me as you would a man upon his deathbed. The
Great Spirit Chief above has left me and my people to our fate. The white
men forget us, and death comes almost every day for some of my people.
He will come for all of us. A few months more and we will be in the
ground. We are a doomed people."[35] Such dire predictions were not fulfilled, and the tribe's condition improved as the Indians engaged in agriculture and stock raising; but the basic dissatisfaction remained.

Finally in 1883 arrangements were made for the return of thirty-three
women and children to Idaho. Philanthropists, encouraged no doubt by
this break in the government's position, carried on a campaign to return
the rest of the Nez Perces to the Pacific Northwest, and numerous memorials were sent to Congress for that purpose.[36] Congress now acted. A law
of July 4, 1884, authorized the secretary of the interior to remove the Nez
Perces from the Indian Territory if he judged proper. In May 1885, 118 of
the band settled on the Lapwai Reservation in Idaho, where they were
warmly received by friends and relatives. The remaining 150, because of
continuing threats from Idaho citizens against some of them, were sent on
to the Colville Reservation in Washington, where adjustment was slow.[37]
Chief Joseph's eternal hope that he might eventually return to the Wallowa
Valley was never fulfilled.

34. CIA Report, 1878, serial 1850, pp. 464–65; *Report of the Board of Indian Commissioners*, 1878, p. 51.
35. *Council Fire* 2 (October 1879): 145.
36. The memorials can be traced through the indexes to the House and Senate *Journals*, 48th Congress, 1st session. Some of the memorials came from citizens of Kansas,
who may have been moved as much by a desire to free the Cherokee Outlet as by philanthropic motives.
37. 23 *United States Statutes* 90, 378; CIA Report, 1885, serial 2379, p. 57.

REVISION OF RESERVATION POLICY

The cases of the Poncas, northern Cheyennes, and Nez Perces uncovered evils in forced removals that no one could hide and that policy makers could not ignore, whatever theoretical advantages there might have been in moving small tribes to large reservations and consolidating the agencies. Men who had held firmly to a removal policy were forced by the course of events to change their ground. Carl Schurz noted in 1880 that when he had taken charge of the Department of the Interior three and a half years earlier, the prevailing opinion seemed to be that it was best for the Indians to be gathered together where they could be kept out of contact with the whites and where their peaceful conduct could be ensured by a few strong military posts. He had accepted that view himself, but as he learned more from experience he realized that it was a "mistaken policy." In his new wisdom, he argued that it was more in accordance with justice as well as experience to respect the home attachments of the Indians and to introduce them to agricultural and pastoral pursuits in the lands they occupied, provided the lands were capable of sustaining the tribe. Moreover, he began to see that large reservations would become impracticable as the pressure of white settlement increased. "The policy of changing, shifting, and consolidating reservations," he declared, ". . . was therefore abandoned."[38]

In 1881, however, Schurz's successor Kirkwood tried to return to a policy of consolidation. He counted 102 reservations west of the Mississippi, occupied by about 224,000 Indians. Attached to these reservations were sixty-eight agencies, and nearby, for the protection of the whites and the Indians, were thirty-seven military posts. The expenses of this multiplication of agencies and forts disturbed Kirkwood. He believed that, if all the Indians could be gathered together into four or five reservations, the savings would be great and the benefit to the Indians proportionate. He urged Congress to appoint a commission to make recommendations about consolidation.[39]

Kirkwood could not reverse the new trend of thought. The humanitarian reformers resolved in 1884 that "careful observation has conclusively proved that the removal of Indians from reservations which they have long occupied, to other reservations far distant from the former and possessing different soil and climate, is attended by great suffering and loss of life." The reformers were moving rapidly away from support of any kind

38. Report of the Secretary of the Interior, 1880, *House Executive Document* no. 1, part 5, 46–3, serial 1959, pp. 3–4.

39. Report of the Secretary of the Interior, 1881, *House Executive Document* no. 1, part 5, vol. 1, serial 2017, pp. v–vi.

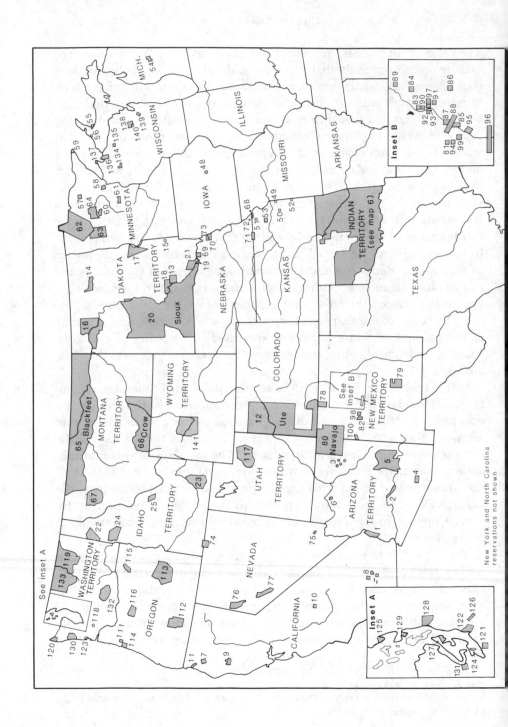

New York and North Carolina
reservations not shown

ARIZONA TERRITORY
1. Colorado River
2. Gila River
3. Moqui Pueblo
4. Papago
5. White Mountain
6. Suppai

CALIFORNIA
7. Hoopa Valley
8. Mission
9. Round Valley
10. Tule River
11. Klamath River

COLORADO
12. Ute

DAKOTA TERRITORY
13. Crow Creek
14. Devils Lake
15. Flandreau
16. Ft. Berthold
17. Lake Traverse
18. Old Winnebago
19. Ponca
20. Sioux
21. Yankton

IDAHO TERRITORY
22. Coeur d'Alene
23. Ft. Hall
24. Lapwai
25. Lemhi

INDIAN TERRITORY
26. Arapaho and Cheyenne
27. Cherokee
28. Chickasaw
29. Choctaw
30. Creek
31. Kansas
32. Kiowa and Comanche
33. Modoc
34. Nez Perce
35. Osage
36. Ottawa
37. Pawnee
38. Peoria
39. Ponca
40. Potawatomi
41. Quapaw
42. Sac and Fox
43. Seminole
44. Seneca
45. Shawnee
46. Wichita
47. Wyandot

IOWA
48. Sac and Fox

KANSAS
49. Black Bob
50. Chippewa and Munsee
51. Kickapoo
52. Miami
53. Potawatomi

MICHIGAN
54. Isabella
55. L'Anse
56. Ontonagon

MINNESOTA
57. Bois Forte
58. Fond du Lac
59. Grand Portage
60. Leech Lake
61. Mille Lac
62. Red Lake
63. White Earth
64. Winnebagoshish

MONTANA TERRITORY
65. Blackfeet
66. Crow
67. Jocko

NEBRASKA
68. Iowa
69. Niobrara
70. Omaha
71. Oto
72. Sac and Fox
73. Winnebago

NEVADA
74. Duck Valley
75. Moapa Valley
76. Pyramid Lake
77. Walker River

NEW MEXICO TERRITORY
78. Jicarilla Apache
79. Mescalero Apache
80. Navajo

Pueblos
81. Jemez
82. Acoma
83. San Juan
84. Picuris
85. San Felipe
86. Pecos
87. Cochiti
88. Santo Domingo
89. Taos
90. Santa Clara
91. Tesuque
92. San Ildefonso
93. Pojoaque
94. Zia
95. Sandia
96. Isleta
97. Nambe
98. Laguna
99. Santa Ana
100. Zuni

NEW YORK
101. Allegany
102. Cattaraugus
103. Oil Spring
104. Oneida
105. Onandaga
106. St. Regis
107. Tonawanda
108. Tuscarora

NORTH CAROLINA
109. Cheoah Boundary
110. Qualla Boundary

OREGON
111. Grande Ronde
112. Klamath
113. Malheur
114. Siletz
115. Umatilla
116. Warm Springs

UTAH TERRITORY
117. Uinta Valley

WASHINGTON TERRITORY
118. Chehalis
119. Colville
120. Makah
121. Nisqually
122. Puyallup
123. Shoalwater
124. Squaxin Island
125. Lummi
126. Muckleshoot
127. Port Madison
128. Snohomish or Tulalip
129. Swinomish
130. Quinaielt
131. Skokomish
132. Yakima
133. Columbia

WISCONSIN
134. Lac Court Oreilles
135. Lac du Flambeau
136. La Point (Bad River)
137. Red Cliff
138. Menominee
139. Oneida
140. Stockbridge

WYOMING TERRITORY
141. Wind River

Source: Annual Report of the Commissioner of Indian Affairs, 1880.

of reservation system, whether scattered or consolidated, and urged now that the Indians be given the right to take homesteads on the lands they had traditionally occupied. Consolidation of the Indians in the Indian Territory met strong objections also from the white population in Missouri, Kansas, Texas, and Arkansas, who fought the concentration of more Indians in their vicinity. Although in fact they had nothing to fear from the Indians, the fuss they raised convinced Secretary of the Interior Lamar in 1885 that the scheme was impracticable. "The policy of change and unsettlement," he said, "should give way to that of fixed homes with security of title and possession, and hereafter the civilizing influences and forces already at work among the Indians should be pushed forward upon the lands which they now occupy."[40]

Yet the idea of Indian removals and concentration within the Indian Territory could not be completely scotched. Commissioner of Indian Affairs J. D. C. Atkins in the late 1880s, in the hope of easing white pressure upon vacant lands within the territory, advocated anew filling up the area by moving in various Indian groups. He met violent opposition from the reformers. "We ought by this time to have learned something from the experience in regard to such removals," one wrote. "Nearly all of our wars have originated in irritations growing out of them; our pauperizing policy of feeding and clothing Indians grew out of them, as this was an inducement offered, and it would be difficult to find a tribe whose removal has not proved to be a long step backward in their progress. The Commissioner should make a study of the past before he urges to its adoption this policy which has been fruitful of evil, and evil alone, hitherto."[41]

But if consolidation of reservations was given up as a realizable ideal, reduction of the existing reservations continued to be strongly pushed. Secretary Kirkwood, although he preferred consolidation, at least wanted to cut the size of those reservations that were "entirely out of proportion to the number of Indians thereon." Henry M. Teller, a former senator from Colorado, who followed Kirkwood as secretary of the interior, strongly advocated such reduction. He admitted the necessity of the reservations but did not think their size should be disproportionate to the needs of the Indians. "Very many of these reservations," he noted, "contain large areas of valuable land that cannot be cultivated by the Indians, even though they were as energetic and laborious as the best class of white agriculturists. All such reservations ought to be reduced in size and the surplus not needed

40. *Lake Mohonk Conference Proceedings*, 1884, pp. 15–16; Report of the Secretary of the Interior, 1885, *House Executive Document* no. 1, part 5, vol. 1, 49–1, serial 2378, pp. 27–28. Lamar largely repeats CIA Report, 1885, serial 2379, pp. 8–12.

41. CIA Report, 1886, serial 2467, pp. 88–90; Charles C. Painter, *The Proposed Removal of Indians to Oklahoma* (Philadelphia: Indian Rights Association, 1888), p. 6.

ought to be bought by the government and opened to the operation of the homestead law, and it would then soon be settled by industrious whites, who, as neighbors, would become valuable auxiliaries in the work of civilizing the Indians residing on the remainder of the reservation." The reduced lands should be vested in the tribe in fee simple. Teller urged that his plan be adopted for the Crow reservation in Montana Territory. Of the 4,713,000 acres in that reserve, Teller estimated that at least three million could be disposed of, leaving the Indians about 600 acres apiece, enough for them to become self-sufficient in agriculture or stock raising. Proceeds from the sale of the surplus lands, if properly used to buy herds for the Crows, could make the Indians self-supporting in a few years.[42]

The reformers continued to see great advantages in such a program. The pressure of the whites on Indian lands would be lessened if not entirely removed, the land left in Indian hands could be given a sure title, proceeds from the sale of the excess lands could replace direct appropriations for Indian subsistence and welfare, and the Indians would be driven closer to an agricultural pattern.

42. Report of the Secretary of the Interior, 1881, *House Executive Document* no. 1, part 5, vol. 1, 47–1, serial 2017, pp. v–vi; ibid., 1882, *House Executive Document* no. 1, part 5, vol. 1, 47–2, serial 2099, p. viii; ibid., 1884, *House Executive Document* no. 1, part 5, vol. 1, 48–2, serial 2286, pp. xiii–xiv. The Crow reservation, however, was not reduced until 1891.

CHAPTER 23

The Indian Service: Policies and Administration

An Array of Commissioners. Fraud and

the "Indian Rings." Inspectors and

Special Agents. Policies and

Programs. Law and Order.

The Indian service, upon which rested much of the responsibility for solving the "Indian problem" of the post-Civil War decades, was itself a large part of the problem. The fraud and abuses that Bishop Whipple had railed against in the early 1860s became a much-publicized national concern in the years that followed, and the Indian service was a primary example of the corruption that tainted Grant's administration. To protect and aid the Indians without at the same time curtailing the expansion of white population in the West created a problem of major dimensions for the Indian Office. Commissioner Dennis Cooley saw it clearly as he neared the end of his term. He wrote in 1866:

> It does not seem a great task to attend to the business of directing the management of about three hundred thousand Indians; but when it is considered that those Indians are scattered over a continent, and divided into more than two hundred tribes, in [the] charge of fourteen superintendents and some seventy agents, whose frequent reports and quarterly accounts are to be examined and adjusted; that no general rules can be adopted for the guidance of those officers, for the reason that the people under their charge are so different in habits, customs, manners, and organization, varying from the civilized and educated Cherokee and Choctaw to the miserable lizard-eaters of Arizona; and that this office is called upon to protect the Indians,

whether under treaty stipulations or roaming at will over his wild hunting-grounds, from abuse by unscrupulous whites, while at the same time it must concede every reasonable privilege to the spirit of enterprise and adventure which is pouring its hardy population into the western country; when these things are considered, the task assigned to this bureau will not seem so light as it is sometimes thought.[1]

The tensions would have taxed the abilities of wise and competent men. Yet, somehow, in spite of all the experiments with philanthropic advisers and church-related agents, the men who ran the Indian service, although they promoted the civilization programs that had become a standard element of Indian policy, left much to be desired.

AN ARRAY OF COMMISSIONERS

In the first decade and a half after the Civil War, the period in which the Indian peace policy took form, ten men held the office of commissioner of Indian affairs, if one counts the short period in which William P. Dole carried over into Andrew Johnson's administration. This was an average tenure of about a year and a half, a very short time given the reform ferment and the frontier turmoil of the time. Commissioner Cooley, who directed the crucial work of dealing with the Indian nations in the Indian Territory after the war, was appalled by the waste and corruption of the Indian service, but Congress was too busy with other matters to pay attention to the call for reform. Cooley's successor, Lewis Vital Bogy, a flexible Missouri politician, failed to win confirmation from the Senate, which accused him of fraudulent contracts for Indian goods. More significant in directing Indian affairs was Nathaniel G. Taylor, the Methodist minister and Tennessee politician whose humanitarian sentiments put a strong stamp of Christian philanthropy on Indian Office documents and activities, but whose convictions on Indian perfectability often got in the way of his grasp of the present situation. Ely S. Parker, the Seneca, who formally began the peace policy of Grant, resigned under a cloud in 1871, just as the program was getting under way.[2]

The peace policy was then directed by a group of commissioners with

1. CIA Report, 1866, serial 1284, pp. 1–2.
2. For Bogy, see William E. Unrau, "Lewis Vital Bogy, 1866–67," in Robert M. Kvasnicka and Herman J. Viola, eds., *The Commissioners of Indian Affairs, 1824–1977* (Lincoln: University of Nebraska Press, 1979), pp. 109–14, and William E. Unrau, "Politics, Bureaucracy, and the Bogus Administration of Indian Commissioner Lewis Vital Bogy, 1866–1867," *American Indian Law Review* 5 (Summer 1977): 185–94.

strong views about Indian policy and the civilization of their charges. The first of these, Francis A. Walker, was an anomaly. A brilliant economist and statistician who had directed the Ninth Census, Walker was appointed to the Indian Office to keep him on the government payroll when census salary appropriations were cut. Although he had no previous Indian experience, he quickly grasped the situation and the needs of the office. In spite of the fact that he held office only temporarily—from late 1871 to early 1873—he wrote a long and forceful annual report in 1872 (later incorporated with two other essays into a book called *The Indian Question*) in which he advanced his philosophy of firmness in settling Indians on definite reservations and a strong commitment to protecting their rights once they arrived there. A practical man with little trace of the sentimentality that marked Christian reformers like Nathaniel Taylor, Walker nevertheless had strong humanitarian instincts and deep concern for fair treatment of the Indians. At the end of his term he wrote:

> In good faith and good feeling we must take up this work of Indian civilization, and, at whatever cost, do our whole duty by this un-happy people. Better that we should entail a debt upon our posterity on Indian account, were that necessary, than that we should leave them an inheritance of shame. We may have no fear that the dying curse of the red man, outcast and homeless by our fault, will bring barrenness upon the soil that once was his, or dry the streams of the beautiful land that, through so much of evil and of good, has become our patrimony; but surely we shall be clearer in our lives and freer to meet the glances of our sons and grandsons, if in our generation we do justice and show mercy to a race which has been impoverished that we might be made rich.[3]

Edward P. Smith, who succeeded Walker, was the epitome of a peace policy commissioner. He was the son of a clergyman who, after obtaining a degree from Yale, entered the seminary and in 1856 was ordained a Congregational minister. His baptism in public good works came when he was with the United States Christian Commission during the Civil War as the commission's general field agent with the Army of the Cumberland; later he was field secretary for the central office of the commission. After 1866 he worked with the American Missionary Association in New York City and was nominated by that body to be an Indian agent under the peace policy, and in February 1871 he became agent of the Chippewas in Minnesota.

3. Francis A. Walker, "The Indian Question," *North American Review* 116 (April 1873): 388. See also Francis A. Walker, *The Indian Question* (Boston: James R. Osgood and Company, 1874); CIA Report, 1872, serial 1560, pp. 391–493; H. Craig Miner, "Francis A. Walker, 1871–73," in Kvasnicka and Viola, *Commissioners of Indian Affairs*, pp. 135–40.

He was strongly recommended for the position of commissioner of Indian affairs by Secretary Delano and by the Board of Indian Commissioners and was appointed to that office on March 20, 1873, bringing with him a commitment to the reforms urged by the Christian humanitarians. He held no brief with Indians as sovereign tribes and promoted incessantly the movement toward individual allotment of land, American law for the Indians, and progress toward self-support; and in true missionary fashion he continually reported in optimistic terms the advancement he saw among the Indians. Ironically, Smith fell victim himself to the demand for reform, for his actions as Chippewa agent in regard to timber sales led to a formal investigation. Although he was cleared of any wrongdoing in the Chippewa affair, he was attacked again during an investigation of charges of fraud against the Red Cloud agent in 1875, and in December of that year he resigned.[4]

John Q. Smith, who followed, continued the reform principles of his predecessors, but he left no strong mark on the office or on Indian affairs. His term, from December 1875 to September 1877, was a high point for charges of fraud against the Indian service, and although he himself escaped any charges of personal corruption, he was removed from office soon after Carl Schurz became secretary of the interior.[5]

Smith's successor was Ezra A. Hayt, a businessman from New Jersey with close ties to the Board of Foreign Missions of the Reformed Church, which had secured his appointment on the Board of Indian Commissioners in 1874. He was an effective member of the board and during most of his time on it was chairman of the purchasing committee. In that capacity he came into conflict with the Indian Office. Following an investigation of flour purchased for Indians in the Indian Territory, over which Hayt and Commissioner J. Q. Smith strongly disagreed, President Grant demanded that Hayt resign from the board, which he did on January 20, 1877. Schurz, seeking a man of high integrity to replace Smith as commissioner of Indian affairs, appointed Hayt to the position. Hayt carried out his duties with energy and aggressive promotion of a civilization program for the Indians. When he suffered the usual attacks from persons critical of all Indian Office actions and was blamed for disturbances (the Northern Cheyenne and the Ute troubles, for example) that had their roots in earlier administrations, he was strongly backed by Schurz. But when evidence of irregularities at the San Carlos Agency were uncovered that incriminated him, Hayt became a liability in Schurz's campaign of reform, and the secretary removed him from office at the end of January 1880.[6]

4. Richard C. Crawford, "Edward Parmelee Smith, 1873–75," in Kvasnicka and Viola, *Commissioners of Indian Affairs*, pp. 141–47.

5. Edward E. Hill, "John Q. Smith, 1875–77," ibid., pp. 149–53.

6. Roy E. Meyer, "Ezra A. Hayt, 1877–80," ibid., pp. 155–66.

Under such circumstances, the Hayes administration sought a man of unassailable integrity. It found him in a Michigan representative, Roland E. Trowbridge, whose background showed no interest in Indians but whose college classmate and close friend was Rutherford B. Hayes. Honesty was Trowbridge's hallmark, and he suffered no charges of corruption. But he made no innovations in the service, and illness forced long absences from his duties. After less than a year in office and without even signing the annual report (which was submitted by the acting commissioner, H. R. Clum), Trowbridge resigned in March 1881.[7]

FRAUD AND THE "INDIAN RINGS"

These commissioners, including two ordained Protestant ministers and other upright Christian gentlemen of close church affiliation, were unable to stem the abuses that plagued the Indian service, for they faced conditions that stimulated fraud and corruption in official Indian-white relations. As land cessions multiplied and the money and other goods due the Indians increased, the chances for unscrupulous whites to cash in on the payments grew almost without bounds. Disposition of such resources as timber from Indian reservations offered still other opportunities for robbing the Indians through fraudulent contracts. Not only was this a matter of plain injustice to the nation's wards, but cheating the Indians of their rightful due frequently led to reprisals. Supplying goods to the Indians—a multimillion dollar business by the 1870s—was the chief arena for illegal and unjust economic gain at the expense of the government and the Indians. There seemed to be endless ways of cheating by the supply of inferior or insufficient goods for full or inflated prices, and the huge transportation costs of moving masses of goods from eastern markets to the far distant and often isolated agencies offered still other prizes. Although it was never possible to put one's finger on them precisely, "Indian rings"— some sort of conspiratorial aggregation of suppliers and Indian service personnel and sometimes corrupt Indian leaders—seemed to be everywhere.[8]

The creation of the Board of Indian Commissioners was one attempt to correct the evils by having an independent, disinterested group of high-minded businessmen supervise the purchase of Indian goods. The purchasing committee of the board performed valuable and to some extent effec-

7. Michael A. Goldman, "Roland E. Trowbridge, 1880–81," ibid., pp. 167–72.

8. Although charges against *the* "Indian ring" or against "Indian rings" were widespread, there was no agreement about who precisely was involved. For one study of their operations, see George H. Phillips, "The Indian Ring in Dakota Territory, 1870–1890," *South Dakota History* 2 (Fall 1972): 345–76.

tive service by checking the bids and inspecting the goods supplied, and the board was optimistic. It reported in 1871 "that all 'Indian rings' can be broken up, and that the wards of this nation, who have been so long the victims of greedy and designing men, ought and must be treated in a manner worthy of the highest moral obligations of a Christian government." But it soon enough discovered the "tricks, subterfuges, evasions, and combinations" of the men who became rich from the Indian business.[9]

One of these subtle schemes was described by George Stuart, who chaired the first purchasing committee of the board:

I . . . soon discovered how it was that the "Indian Ring" was enabled to make such immense profits out of the annual supplies furnished to the government for its Indian wards. The advertisements for such goods specified certain classes, number one, number two, etc., each class containing several articles, so that the bidders had to bid for the whole of a class of goods, and the lowest *total* bid obtained the award. At the foot of the advertisement specifying the several classes, it was stated that "the government reserves the right to diminish or increase the quantity taken of any of the articles of any class." On further examination, I found [that] a bidder who was said to have made a large fortune out of the government had bid about half-price for a large quantity of goods called for by one article in one of the classes, and nearly double its market value for an article in the same class of which a very small quantity was called for. On this class his bid was, very naturally, the lowest. Finally, I found that he ultimately supplied a very small quantity of the article for which he had bid half-price, and a very large quantity of the article for which he had bid nearly double its market value.[10]

No matter how much the board's supervising functions may have helped, the failure of the board to break through entrenched corruption meant that it was not the solution to the problem. Nor did the church nomination of agency personnel provide a satisfactory answer by furnishing presumably honest men to deal with the Indians, for evils continued to crop up, and even Christian gentlemen in the office of commissioner of Indian affairs were forced from office because tainted by corrupt practices for which they may or may not have been personally responsible.

A special case that received much publicity showed the continuing problem: charges leveled against Red Cloud Agent J. J. Saville by Chief Red

9. *Report of the Board of Indian Commissioners*, 1871, p. 161; ibid., 1878, pp. 19–24. The latter gives specific cases.

10. George Hay Stuart, *The Life of George Hay Stuart: Written by Himself*, ed. Robert Ellis Thompson (Philadelphia: J. M. Stoddart, 1890), pp. 242–43.

Cloud and highly publicized by the noted Yale paleontologist, Othniel C. Marsh.[11] When Marsh was in Dakota hunting fossils, Red Cloud complained to him about the ill treatment he received and showed him samples of bad supplies furnished by the government. Marsh in turn took the complaints to the Board of Indian Commissioners and to the public at large. The board called for an investigation, and Secretary Delano, not wanting to be left out, cooperated with the president of the board in appointing a special committee to investigate the charges.[12] The whole affair was pretty much a fiasco. Red Cloud admitted that the samples he had shown Marsh were not typical of goods the Indians received. Marsh himself was less than completely helpful to the investigating committee, filing his complaints in the form of a pamphlet addressed to the president of the United States that he released to the press before the committee received it. He had laid the matter directly before the president, he said, because he had "no confidence whatever in the sincerity of the Secretary of the Interior or the Commissioner of Indian Affairs." Delano's response, also printed as a pamphlet, questioned Marsh's competence and judgment in the case and blamed the affair on attempts of the press to injure him.[13]

The committee determined that Red Cloud's samples were not representative of goods issued the Sioux, but it did find inferior supplies and agreed that the government and the Indians were being defrauded. The committee members recommended replacing the contractors for pork and flour and generally tightening the supply procedures. They thought, too, that Saville should be removed as agent, not because they found him guilty of fraud but because of lax administration that made fraud possible. Commissioner Edward P. Smith considered the committee's report a vindication of the Indian Office, however, and little came of the inquiry except the public airing of conditions in the Indian service that plainly called for remedy.[14]

The first significant moves came with the appointment of Carl Schurz as secretary of the interior. A reformer of long standing, Schurz was deter-

---

11. An excellent discussion of the case is in James C. Olson, *Red Cloud and the Sioux Problem* (Lincoln: University of Nebraska Press, 1965), pp. 179, 183–84, 189–98. The most important documents are in *Report of the Special Commission Appointed to Investigate the Affairs of the Red Cloud Indian Agency, July, 1875* (Washington: GPO, 1875). Marsh's side of the affair is recounted in Charles Schuchert and Clara Mae LaVene, *O. C. Marsh: Pioneer in Paleontology* (New Haven: Yale University Press, 1940), pp. 145–68.

12. Minutes of April 28 and 29, 1875, Minutes of the Board of Indian Commissioners, National Archives, Record Group 75.

13. O. C. Marsh, *A Statement of Affairs at Red Cloud Agency: Made to the President of the United States* (n.p., 1875); *Documents Relating to the Charges of Professor O. C. Marsh of Fraud and Mismanagement at the Red Cloud Agency* (n.p., 1875).

14. CIA Report, 1875, serial 1680, pp. 538–39.

mined to end the fraud and the conditions that made it possible. He noted in his first report, among other problems, "the temptations to fraud and peculation in furnishing and distributing supplies; [and] the careless and blundering management of agents, removed from immediate supervision." Schurz was a realist and knew that correction of the evils he saw would require time, patient labor, and "above all things, an honest and efficient Indian service."[15] The key, as always, was the character of the men who managed Indian affairs, and Schurz moved quickly, beginning at the top. After Commissioner J. Q. Smith, who had been carried over from the previous administration, resigned under pressure, Schurz turned to investigate the work of the chief clerk of the Indian Office, S. A. Galpin. A special committee of three, appointed by Schurz, not only judged specific charges against Galpin but reviewed broadly the whole operation of the Indian Office. Its report, dated December 31, 1877, found much carelessness and mismanagement to condemn all along the line, and Galpin was removed from office.[16]

But Schurz did not succeed completely. Even his carefully picked commissioner of Indian affairs, Ezra Hayt, proved a disappointment in the end, and the problem of finding proper men to conduct an absolutely honest and efficient service remained.

INSPECTORS AND SPECIAL AGENTS

One special remedy that was used to ease the problem was a corps of inspectors to keep tab on operations in the field and to give the central headquarters closer supervision over the activities of the agents and other personnel on the reservations. First put into effect in 1873, the provision for Indian inspectors rested on earlier recommendations. The Doolittle Committee's major practical suggestion for eliminating abuses had been a system of five inspection districts, each to be served by a three-man commission. Senator Doolittle's bill incorporating the inspection provisions passed the Senate in March 1866, but it never came to vote in the House.[17]

15. Report of the Secretary of the Interior, 1877, *House Executive Document* no. 1, part 5, 45–2, serial 1800, pp. x–xii.

16. *Report of the Board of Inquiry Convened by Authority of the Secretary of the Interior of June 7, 1877, to Investigate Certain Charges against S. A. Galpin, Chief Clerk of the Indian Bureau, and Concerning Irregularities in Said Bureau* (Washington: GPO, 1878). There is an account of the episode in Loring Benson Priest, *Uncle Sam's Stepchildren: The Reformation of United States Indian Policy, 1865–1887* (New Brunswick: Rutgers University Press, 1942), pp. 68–69.

17. *Senate Journal*, 39–1, serial 1236, pp. 235, 243, 246. See Doolittle's support of the measure and debate on it in *Congressional Globe*, 39th Congress, 1st session, pp. 1449–50, 1485–92.

The supervisory duties envisaged by Doolittle were then carried out in part by the Board of Indian Commissioners. Because the board's unofficial status led to conflict with the official bureaucracy, however, that group did not function well as the watchdog it was intended to be, except to some extent in its supervision of the purchase of Indian goods. An inspection mechanism within the Indian Office itself was needed, and the Board of Indian Commissioners, in fact, in its report of 1872 called for a "board of inspectors" of at least five persons to be appointed by the president from names recommended by the annual meetings of the various religious denominations.[18]

In January 1873, when the Indian appropriation bill reached the Senate, Senator William M. Stewart of Nevada offered an amendment as an added section of the bill. He proposed that the president detail an army officer to visit each agency every six months to examine the agency and its reservation and to report back to the president how its business was conducted, how the money was spent, how the Indians were being treated, and what progress they were making in civilization. The officer would be given authority to investigate all records and to examine agents and others under oath. When objections arose against such use of army officers and the conflict that was likely to occur between the two branches of government, Stewart proposed a substitute amendment by which the president would appoint "a person" to inspect the agencies every six months. To a suggestion that the Board of Indian Commissioners could fulfill the function, he replied: "The present Indian commission is composed of very nice men, very well-disposed men, men whom I have every reason to have the highest confidence in, so far as I know, but they are old men, they are not very active men; they have not seen all the reservations; they cannot give you this information, they cannot make this examination." After agreeing that the superintendencies as well as the agencies should be inspected and haggling over the number of inspectors and the salary to be paid them, the Senate on January 10 passed an amendment providing for no more than five inspectors, with annual salary of $3,000 plus traveling expenses. The inspectors would have power not only to inspect all records but to suspend superintendents, agents, and agency employees and appoint others in their places, subject to the president's approval.[19]

When the amendment reached the House of Representatives, the inspection scheme was combined with the question of whether the superintendencies should be continued. Added to the Senate amendment when it was reported to the House by the Committee on Appropriations was a clause abolishing all superintendencies as of June 30, 1873, and using the

18. *Report of the Board of Indian Commissioners,* 1872, p. 19.
19. *Congressional Globe,* 42d Congress, 3d session, pp. 436, 439–40, 480–81.

funds provided for their salaries to pay the inspectors. Some members pointed to the continuing need for superintendents in some parts of the country, but Representative Aaron A. Sargent of California, the chief advocate of the amendment, noted that the Board of Indian Commissioners in its 1872 report had recommended the discontinuation of the superintendencies; he thought it would be "unjust to this board, and rather a dangerous experiment, to adopt one part of their suggestions [inspectors] and reject the other." At any rate, he wanted to see if the country could not get along without "this expensive machinery of superintendents and superintendents clerks." The House concurred in the abolition of all superintendencies, of which there were eight at the time.[20]

This attack on the superintendencies as unnecessary was not a new thing. Congress in 1870 had authorized the president "to discontinue any one or more of the Indian superintendencies, and to require the Indian agents of such superintendencies to report directly to the commissioner of Indian affairs." In the following year it had charged the president to dispense with agents and superintendencies when feasible. The moves came from a desire for economy, ever present in Indian appropriations, but they were also due no doubt to changing conditions on the frontier. When diplomatic relations with the tribes were uppermost and treaty negotiations an important element in the handling of Indian affairs by the United States, the superintendents played a large role, for they often took part in the treaty making. With the developing reservation system and the emphasis on changing patterns of Indian life, the agent on the reservation assumed a new and more important role in directing the Indians toward civilization.[21]

In 1873 the measure that came out of the conference committee was a compromise. The appointment, pay, number, and duties of the inspectors were left untouched, for the House had concurred in this part of the Senate amendment. But the bill now directed that only four of the eight superintendencies be abolished. The president was to have authority to assign the four remaining superintendents over such agencies as he thought proper and to dispense with all of them at his discretion. In this form the measure became law on February 14, 1873.[22] The Indian service now had its board of inspectors.

20. Ibid., pp. 916–17. The recommendation of the Board of Indian Commissioners is in *Report of the Board of Indian Commissioners*, 1872, p. 19. Congress in 1873 authorized the following superintendencies: two east of the Rockies, one each for Oregon and California, and one each for the territories of Washington, New Mexico, Arizona, and Montana. 17 *United States Statutes* 438.

21. 16 *United States Statutes* 360–61, 545; Paul Stuart, *The Indian Office: Growth and Development of an American Institution, 1865–1900* (Ann Arbor: UMI Research Press, 1979), pp. 73–78.

22. *Congressional Globe*, 42d Congress, 3d session, p. 1079; 17 *United States Statutes* 463.

The Indian inspectors were hardly a panacea, but they provided an instrument that, with the right personnel and the right use, could facilitate reform and a tighter and more formal organization of the service. Inspections had of course been carried on before by special agents or commissioners appointed for particular one-time duties, but the inspectors authorized in 1873 were a new element between the agencies and the Washington office—men who, unlike the superintendents, viewed headquarters rather than the agents as the object of their first loyalty. Even though the number of inspectors was reduced to three in 1875 and the semi-annual inspection of each agency was no longer required, the new office hastened the demise of the remaining superintendencies, the last of which was closed in January 1878. Then in 1880 the number of inspectors was raised again to five. In addition, Congress in 1878 authorized two special agents and in 1882 doubled the number. These men were used to strengthen the inspection service.[23]

In 1873, when the inspectors were authorized, the system of church management of the agencies and superintendencies was in full force, and the first inspectors were chosen from men connected with the church-run agencies, with consequent interdenominational rivalry. Later inspectors were chosen from former agents and superintendents. The inspectors performed a great variety of tasks, although their primary function was to monitor the activities of the agents and make sure that laws and regulations were obeyed. They were used frequently to investigate specific complaints lodged against agents, often by whites in the neighborhood who charged discrimination against their economic interests. They aided in the removal of tribes (for example, the Ponca removal of 1877). They helped in problems resulting from the dissolution of the superintendencies, negotiated with tribes for railroad rights of way through the reservations, and made recommendations about transfers of personnel.[24]

At first the inspectors and the special agents both reported to the commissioner of Indian affairs, but in 1880 Schurz directed the inspectors to report directly to him. Because the legislation authorizing the Indian inspectors called for reports to be sent to the president, Schurz reasoned that in legal effect he acted for the president in the matter and should get the reports. Under his direction the work of the inspectors became more routinized, for he required them to report regularly on their activities. As in-

23. 18 *United States Statutes* 422–23; 20 *United States Statutes* 60; 21 *United States Statutes* 116; 22 *United States Statutes* 70. Stuart, *Indian Office*, chapters 6–9, discusses the work of the inspectors and the part they played in the formalization and institutionalization of the Indian Office.

24. Stuart, *Indian Office*, pp. 80–81, 87–96. Details on the inspection at three agencies, 1873–1906, are given on pp. 101–18.

structions to the inspectors became more detailed, their reports in turn became more patterned. In 1883 a formal set of instructions was issued.[25]

POLICIES AND PROGRAMS

As they struggled to control and improve the administration of Indian affairs, the commissioners, despite their diversity of background and short tenures, nevertheless had a uniform policy. All of them, in varying degrees, continued the promotion of Indian civilization that was the corollary of the reservation system. And in this they had the support of their superiors, the secretaries of the interior. Although in the period from the Civil War to 1880 no major legislative enactments effected the reforms advocated by humanitarians and their supporters in the government, the proposals that were to mark the last two decades of the nineteenth century began to assume a form that was generally agreed upon. By the end of Carl Schurz's administration in the Interior Department, the formulations were ready for the intensive campaign that followed to get Congress to enact them into law.

The policies were based on an increasingly clear realization that the expansion of the white population across the nation had forever doomed the Indians' traditional way of life. Ignatius Donnelly, then a young representative from Minnesota, predicted the outcome before the Civil War had ended. He saw white population closing in on the Indians from both the east and the west. "With the termination of our great war, now near its close," he said in the House on February 7, 1865, "a migration will spring up of which the world has as yet known no parallel; and in a few short years every tract capable of settlement and cultivation will pass into the occupancy of the white man. What is to become of the Indians as the races of the world thus draw together from the opposite shores of the continent?" Dennis Cooley in 1866 saw the white population "rapidly crowding westward upon the Indians, either in the search for farming lands or for the precious minerals; and the people who have held these lands are compelled to give way before the advancing tide." He saw a continued increase in the difficulties, for there was no way to avoid the collision. "It is the law of nature and of the progress of mankind," he said, "and its operation cannot be stayed."[26]

The movement of railroads westward and the climactic event of the completion of the Union Pacific transcontinental line in 1869 greatly

25. Ibid., pp. 82–83.
26. *Congressional Globe*, 38th Congress, 2d session, appendix, p. 61; CIA Report, 1866, serial 1284, p. 2.

speeded the process. "The completion of one of the great lines of railway to the Pacific coast has totally changed the conditions under which the civilized population of the country come in contact with the wild tribes," Secretary Cox noted in that year. "Instead of a slowly advancing tide of migration, making its gradual inroads upon the circumference of the great interior wilderness, the very center of the desert has been pierced. Every station upon the railway has become a nucleus for a civilized settlement, and a base from which lines of exploration for both mineral and agricultural wealth are pushed in every direction." The inevitability of the advance was taken for granted; the westward course of white population could not—and should not—be stopped or delayed by the Indians. Francis Walker lectured the humanitarian reformers in 1872 that they should exert themselves "not feebly and futilely to attempt to stay this tide, whose depth and strength can hardly be measured, but to snatch the remnants of the Indian race from destruction before it."[27]

The first step in saving the Indians from destruction had been the reservation system, which sought to remove the Indians from the path of the onrushing whites; by 1880 the pattern of reservations was set, although some of them would later be reduced again in size. But once that measure was accomplished, proposals for how to treat the Indians now confined to the reservations became the important elements of United States Indian policy. The Indians, having lost the independence and freedom that marked their aboriginal existence, now became in fact the wards and dependents of a paternal government, and the officials of the Department of the Interior and the Indian Office accepted that fact. They saw it as their responsibility to provide the means for the Indians to move from their traditional life to the white man's civilization—and to force this change upon the Indians for their own good. Commissioner Walker expressed the conclusion with his usual forcefulness:

> The Government should extend over them a rigid reformatory discipline, to save them from falling hopelessly into the condition of pauperism and petty crime. Merely to disarm the savages, and to surround them by forces which it is hopeless in them to resist, without exercising over them for a series of years a system of paternal control, requiring them to learn and practice the arts of industry at least until one generation has been fairly started on a course of self-improvement, is to make it pretty much a matter of certainty that by far the larger part of the now roving Indians will become simply vagabonds in the midst of civilization, forming little camps here and there over the

27. Report of the Secretary of the Interior, 1869, *House Executive Document* no. 1, 41–2, serial 1414, p. vii; CIA Report, 1872, serial 1560, p. 397.

face of the Western States, which will be festering sores on the communities near which they are located; the men resorting for a living to basket-making and hog-stealing; the women to fortune-telling and harlotry.[28]

When Carl Schurz left office, almost a decade later, he expressed the same concern and recommended strong government control. "Nothing is more indispensable," he said, "than the protecting and guiding care of the Government during the dangerous period of transition from savage to civilized life. . . . [The Indian] is overcome by a feeling of helplessness, and he naturally looks to the 'Great Father' to take him by the hand and guide him on. That guiding hand must necessarily be one of authority and power to command confidence and respect. It can be only that of the government which the Indian is accustomed to regard as a sort of omnipotence on earth. Everything depends upon the wisdom and justice of that guidance."[29]

A list of priorities in Indian policy emerged during the 1870s that the secretaries of the interior and the commissioners of Indian affairs, aided and abetted by reform sentiment (such as that expressed in the reports of the Board of Indian Commissioners), all espoused. They were set forth in excellent summary form by Schurz in 1879:

1. To set the Indians to work as agriculturists or herders, thus to break up their habits of savage life and to make them self-supporting.

2. To educate their youth of both sexes, so as to introduce to the growing generation civilized ideas, wants, and aspirations.

3. To allot parcels of land to Indians in severalty and to give them individual title to their farms in fee, inalienable for a certain period, thus to foster the pride of individual ownership of property instead of their former dependence upon the tribe, with its territory held in common.

4. When settlement in severalty with individual title is accomplished, to dispose, with their consent, of those lands on their reservations which are not settled and used by them, the proceeds to form a fund for their benefit, which will gradually relieve the government of the expenses at present provided for by annual appropriations.

5. When this is accomplished, to treat the Indians like other inhabitants of the United States, under the laws of the land.

To Schurz these elements of an Indian policy would solve the problems without injustice to the Indians or hindrance to the development of white

28. CIA Report, 1872, serial 1560, p. 399.
29. Carl Schurz, "Present Aspects of the Indian Problem," *North American Review* 133 (July 1881): 8–9.

The Peace Policy

settlement. The Indians would be raised to a high level of civilization because of the stimulus of individual ownership of property. The policy would not deprive them by force of what belonged to them but would induce them to part with, for a just compensation, lands they did not need and did not cultivate, which could then be opened to progress and improvement.[30]

The policies and programs carried out or recommended by the Indian Office and its supporters continued to rest upon a belief that the Indians were fully capable of adopting civilized ways. Although there were always voices raised against the competence of the Indians and ridicule made of attempts to raise the "savages" to the level of the whites, the dominant official views remained strong in the Christian humanitarian tradition, echoing in many ways such classic statements as those of Commissioner Taylor in 1868. This, of course, was to be expected from the commissioners who by experience and religious outlook were cast in the same mold. Among the most optimistic was Commissioner E. P. Smith, who in 1874 and 1875 was ready to declare large numbers of the Indians ready to be absorbed as citizens into American society. His successor, J. Q. Smith, though more aware of the long road ahead for many Indians, declared in 1876: "From the fact that for so long a period Indian civilization has been retarded, it must not be concluded that some inherent characteristic in the race disqualified it for civilized life. It may well be doubted whether this be true of any race of men. Surely it cannot be true of a race, any portion of which has made the actual progress realized by some of our Indians. They can and do learn to labor; they can and do learn to read. Many thousands to-day are engaged in civilized occupations." Carl Schurz, more hardheaded than the sentimental philanthropists with whom he sparred, held the same opinion. "That all the Indians on this northern continent have been savages and that many of them are savages now is true," he wrote in 1879; "but it is also true that many tribes have risen to a promising degree of civilization, and there is no reason to doubt that the rest, if wisely guided, will be found capable of following their example."[31]

Mundane policies of law and land allotment and self-support were not the only forces at work. Suffusing all was the powerful spirit of Christianity, and missionaries continued to be the primary agents of the government's program for Indian improvement. The assignment of agencies to Christian denominations gave the greatest momentum to the drive, but that was a result, not the cause, of the Christian philanthropic spirit. The

30. Report of the Secretary of the Interior, 1879, *House Executive Document* no. 1, part 5, 46–2, serial 1910, pp. 5–6.

31. CIA Report, 1874, serial 1639, pp. 313, 316; CIA Report, 1875, serial 1680, pp. 527–31; CIA Report, 1876, serial 1749, pp. 384–85; Report of the Secretary of the Interior, 1879, *House Executive Document* no. 1, part 5, 46–2, serial 1910, p. 4.

peace policy enlisted the kind of aid "for which the Government has no substitute," E. P. Smith said, "and without which all effort for civilization will drag heavily until it is abandoned." Then he put his finger on the peculiarly American manifestation of religious aid:

> No movement for changing the character and habits and prevailing condition of a people or a class can attain anything worthy the name of success without calling for the help which a volunteer benevolent or religious organization outside of the Government alone can give. The Sanitary and Christian Commissions of the war, Prison Associations, Children's Aid and other Relief Societies, and the multitude of benevolent organizations which the Government and the States call to their aid whenever any work of humanity or recovery of man is to be undertaken, bear abundant testimony to the prevailing opinion on this subject which has grown out of experience.[32]

The missionaries, whose aid was so generally praised, continued to play an especially important role in educating the Indians; one of the motives behind the allotment of agencies to religious denominations had been to encourage the educational and other work of the missionaries on the reservations by eliminating conflict between them and agents. It is difficult, however, to determine exactly the proportion of Indian school work done by church groups. The United States supplied funds to tribes for their own schools in accord with treaty specifications and used some funds designated for "civilization" for school support. In 1870 Congress for the first time appropriated money "for the support of industrial and other schools among the Indian tribes not otherwise provided for." The sum of $100,000 was provided, but the Indian Office that year expended only $37,597, and the money was reappropriated for later use. Money spent for schools rose only slowly until after 1880, when the sums advanced dramatically, reaching $2,277,557 in fiscal year 1893. Even though the government thus became firmly committed to maintaining a system of public schools for the Indians, it continued to rely for much Indian education on mission schools on a contract basis in which the church groups built the schoolhouses and supplied the teachers in return for an annual per capita payment for the students they enrolled. A considerable number of schools, in addition, were supported entirely by the churches.[33]

---

32. CIA Report, 1875, serial 1680, p. 524.

33. 16 *United States Statutes* 359; Stuart, *Indian Office*, pp. 119–34. A useful history and analysis of school development and expenditures is provided in the Report of the Indian School Superintendent (John H. Oberly) for 1885, CIA Report, 1885, serial 2379, pp. 75–127.

LAW AND ORDER

Much of the program of civilization, Christianization, and education, of course, was no more than a continuation and intensification of ideas long promoted by officials and others interested in Indian affairs. Newer was the emphasis on law for the Indians. It had been an assumption of United States Indian policy that the tribes were political entities within which law and order were maintained by Indian custom or law. But the traumatic changes brought by reservation life and the stepped-up attacks on Indian tribalism and Indian ways that were part of the reform movement brought with them a general disorganization and disintegration of Indian societies. "A serious detriment to the progress of the partially civilized Indians," the Board of Indian Commissioners declared in 1871, "is found in the fact that they are not brought under the domination of law, so far as regards crimes committed against each other." The board admitted that Indian tribes differed greatly among themselves and that all were not yet suited to white legal norms. "But when they have adopted civilized costume and civilized modes of subsistence," it said, "we owe it to them, and to ourselves, to teach them the majesty of civilized law, and to extend to them its protection against the lawless among themselves."[34]

A sharp blow at the traditional status of the Indian tribes was the legislation of 1871 declaring that thereafter no Indian tribe would be recognized as an independent nation with whom the United States could contract by treaty. Although agreements still were concluded that were no different from previous treaties except in mode of ratification, the formal end of treaty making and the conscious intention thereby to denigrate the power of the chiefs resulted in a loss of old systems of internal order without the substitution of anything in their place. Francis A. Walker clearly defined the problem:

> While the Act of 1871 strikes down at a blow the hereditary authority of the chiefs, no legislation has invested Indian agents with magisterial power, or provided for the assembling of the Indian *demos.* There is at this time no semblance of authority for the punishment of any crime which one Indian may commit against another, nor any mode of procedure, recognized by treaty or statute, for the regulation of matters between the government and the several tribes. So far as the law is concerned, complete anarchy exists in Indian affairs; and

34. *Report of the Board of Indian Commissioners,* 1871, pp. 7–8; see also ibid., 1873, p. 6. In this section I use material from Francis Paul Prucha, *American Indian Policy in Crisis: Christian Reformers and the Indian, 1865–1900* (Norman: University of Oklahoma Press, 1976), pp. 201–8, 329–31.

nothing but the singular homogeneity of Indian communities, and the almost unaccountable spontaneity and unanimity of public sentiment within them, has thus far prevented the attention of Congress and the country being called most painfully to the unpardonable negligence of the national legislature in failing to provide a substitute for the time-honored policy which was destroyed by the Act of 1871.[35]

Walker's successor, who inherited the problem, was no less concerned, and he recommended the application of United States courts to the Indian territories as a substitute for the former tribal authority. This became the common cry of reformers both in and out of the government. Even among white men, they asserted, civilization would not long exist without the guarantees of law. How, then, could there be any hope of civilizing the Indians without law? "That the benevolent efforts and purposes of the Government have proved so largely fruitless," the commissioner of Indian affairs declared in 1876, "is, in my judgment, due more to its failure to make these people amenable to our laws than to any other cause, or to all other causes combined." From all sides the refrain sounded. Bishop William Hare, the Episcopal missionary among the Sioux, wrote in 1877: "Wish well to the Indians as we may, and do for them what we will, the efforts of civil agents, teachers, and missionaries are like the struggles of drowning men weighted with lead, as long as by the absence of law Indian society is left without a base." Indians, too, were appealed to, and the commissioner of Indian affairs in 1878 said that Chief Joseph, the famous Nez Perce leader, believed that the greatest need of the Indians was a system of law by which controversies among Indians and between Indians and whites could be settled without appealing to physical force.[36]

A bill was introduced in Congress early in 1879 that authorized the president to prescribe police regulations for the Indian reservations and that provided for the laws of the respective states and territories relating to major crimes to be in force on the reservations. Both Schurz and Hayt strongly supported the measure. The latter declared: "A civilized community could not exist as such without law, and a semi-civilized and barbarous people are in a hopeless state of anarchy without its protection and sanctions. It is true the various tribes have regulations and customs of their own, which, however, are founded on superstition and ignorance of the usages of civilized communities, and generally tend to perpetuate feuds and keep alive animosities. To supply their place it is the bounden

---

35. Walker, *The Indian Question*, pp. 12–13.
36. CIA Report, 1873, serial 1601, pp. 372–73; CIA Report, 1875, serial 1680, pp. 517–18; CIA Report, 1876, serial 1749, pp. 387–88; CIA Report, 1878, serial 1850, p. 465. Bishop Hare is quoted in CIA Report, 1883, serial 2191, p. 7.

duty of the government to provide laws suited to the dependent condition of the Indians."[37] Congress could not be persuaded to enact the bill, but agitation kept the idea strong, and increasing pressure arose for law as a necessary means to bring about the reform and civilization among the Indians that humanitarians wanted. Under the paternal care of the United States, the Indians were to be introduced to white concepts of law.

A new agency of law that developed in the 1870s, which became a regular element on the reservations, was an Indian police force, quasi-military units under the command of the agents that emerged as substitutes for the authority of the chiefs or for military control of the reservations.[38] Some sort of police force was necessary in the best-ordered societies, it was argued, and to think that the Indian reservations, whose traditional tribal governments were weakened by the white reformers' attacks, could get along without law enforcers was absurd. It was all very well to condemn military management of Indian affairs, but if army troops were not on hand, the agent had to find some other way to back up his decisions.

The idea of a constabulary force of Indian policemen arose spontaneously on several reservations. Indians enrolled by the army as scouts had performed well, and it was not a difficult step to conceive of Indians as a temporary or even a permanent civilian corps. When Benjamin F. Lushbaugh became agent of the Pawnees in 1862, he was immediately annoyed by the frequent thefts, chiefly of horses, by young men of the tribe, and he organized a makeshift Indian police force to facilitate the recovery of property. In 1872–1873 a group of Navajo policemen, placed under a war chief, served well in preventing depredations and in expediting the return of stolen stock. Similar expedients for preserving order were used with success among the Klamaths, the Chippewas in Wisconsin, the Sioux, and the Blackfeet.[39]

The Apache police force established by John P. Clum, the extraordinary young agent at the San Carlos Reservation, was the best example. Clum had been nominated by the Dutch Reformed Church, which had been allotted the agency under Grant's peace policy and which, having no missionaries of its own willing to accept the hazards of the post, had turned to Rutgers College to find recruits. Clum had attended there briefly before

---

37. Report of the Secretary of the Interior, 1879, *House Executive Document* no. 1, part 5, 46–2, serial 1910, pp. 12–13; CIA Report, 1879, serial 1910, pp. 105–6.

38. An excellent, thorough treatment of Indian police and Indian judges is William T. Hagan, *Indian Police and Judges: Experiments in Acculturation and Control* (New Haven: Yale University Press, 1966).

39. Lushbaugh to Charles E. Mix, September 15, 1862, CIA Report, 1862, serial 1157, p. 266; Oakah L. Jones, Jr., "The Origins of the Navajo Indian Police, 1872–1873," *Arizona and the West* 8 (Autumn 1966): 225–38; Hagan, *Indian Police and Judges*, pp. 25–27, 39–40.

going west with the United States Weather Service, and former classmates recommended him for the position. He arrived at San Carlos on August 8, 1874, a cocky twenty-two year old "with instructions to assume *entire* control of the San Carlos agency." This meant forcing out the military and setting up his own enforcement agency. Two days after his arrival, Clum held a big talk with the Apaches and explained his plans. "I then told them that I intended to appoint some Indians as police-men," he later wrote; "that we would establish a supreme court for the trial of offenders; that I would preside as chief justice, and four or five Apache chiefs would serve as assistant justices; that Indians would be called as witnesses at the trials. Under this system, all Apache offenders would be arrested by Apache police, brought before an Apache court, with Apaches as witnesses, and, if convicted, sentenced by Apache judges, and finally delivered into the custody of Apache guards." The self-government plan worked, and Clum controlled the volatile Apaches without the aid of the army. The Indian Office and the Dutch Reformed Church supported him, and his Apache police were accepted as an integral part of the agency.[40]

The Board of Indian Commissioners raised the question of Indian police formally in its report for 1874. In a section entitled "Enforcement of Order," it noted that the power of the chiefs was limited and that outside intervention was resented. The result was that although the wild tribes had treaty obligations to maintain order, to educate their children, to apprehend and deliver offenders for punishment, and to labor for their own support, no machinery existed to enforce these stipulations and they had remained nugatory. The solution would be a "police or constabulary force" made up of the Indians themselves. Noting the successful attempts along this line at various reservations, the board concluded that there was abundant evidence to prove that a small, disciplined, and well-instructed police force of Indians would be a safe and effective means of preserving order and of assisting the tribe in enforcing its treaty obligations. And such a force in many cases, the board asserted, would obviate the necessity of a military post near the agency.[41]

In the following year the board moved ahead vigorously with its scheme. On August 1, 1875, it sent a circular letter to all the Indian agents as part of

40. Woodworth Clum, *Apache Agent: The Story of John P. Clum* (Boston: Houghton Mifflin Company, 1936), pp. 119–21, 132, 134–35. Clum's annual reports appear in the annual reports of the commissioner of Indian affairs, 1874–1877. Clum in later life wrote about his Apache police in "The San Carlos Apache Police," *New Mexico Historical Review* 4 (July 1929): 203–19; 5 (January 1930): 67–92. For a detailed, heavily documented account of Clum's career as agent, with emphasis on his struggle with the military, see Ralph Henrick Ogle, *Federal Control of the Western Apaches, 1848–1886* (Albuquerque: University of New Mexico Press, 1970).

41. *Report of the Board of Indian Commissioners*, 1874, p. 9.

its campaign against military control of the reservations. After requesting information about the existence of military forces in their vicinity and the effect of the troops on the Indians, the letter posed a specific question about Indian police: "Would the organization of an armed Indian police, under proper restrictions and discipline, for the enforcement of order, arrest of criminals, and the prevention of incursions of evil-disposed persons upon your reservation, prove safe or advisable; and to what extent would such an organization supersede the necessity of a military force?" A number of the agents saw no need for a police force because their charges were peaceful and well-ordered, and some believed that the Indian distaste for taking punitive action against other Indians would make such a police force useless, but the great majority replied favorably, some even enthusiastically. Agents who had already employed Indians as police of one sort or another pointed to the success of their efforts.[42]

It took some time for the work of the board to bear fruit. Commissioner Hayt picked up the recommendation in 1877 and urged the creation of a general system of Indian police. He noted the successes where such police had already been tried and the practice of using police in Canada. The police system, he said, would relieve the army from police duty on Indian reservations, would save lives and property, and would "materially aid in placing the entire Indian population of the country on the road to civilization." But Congress, where supporters of military control of the reservations were numerous and influential, held back. Finally, on May 27, 1878, a system of Indian police got congressional authorization. A section of the Indian appropriation act provided $30,000 to pay for 430 privates at $5 a month and fifty officers at $8 a month, "to be employed in maintaining order and prohibiting illegal traffic in liquor on the several Indian reservations." By the end of the year, the commissioner reported success at the thirty agencies where police forces had been organized, and in 1879 Congress doubled the number of policemen authorized. By 1880 there were police at forty agencies and a decade later at fifty-nine.[43]

The police were immediately useful to the agents as an extension of their authority. The tasks they performed were in many cases hardly police duties at all. An Indian policeman was the "reservation handyman." The police served as couriers and messengers, slaughtered cattle for the beef ration, kept accounts of births and deaths in the tribe, and took censuses for the agent; and they augmented the labor force of the agency by building roads, clearing out irrigation ditches, and doing other chores. In all this

42. Ibid., 1875, pp. 64–103.

43. CIA Report, 1877, serial 1800, pp. 398–99; CIA Report, 1878, serial 1850, pp. 471–72; CIA Report, 1880, serial 1959, pp. 88–89; CIA Report, 1890, serial 2841, pp. xc–xciv; 20 *United States Statutes* 86, 315.

they contributed substantially to the smooth operation of the agency. Routine labor, however, did not obscure the enforcement of order, which had been foremost on the minds of advocates of the police system. The Indian police were armed and often mounted, at the beck and call of the agent when disorder threatened or force was needed to see that rules and regulations on the reservation were properly observed. The police arrested or turned back intruders on the Indian lands and tore out the squatters' stakes, arrested horse thieves, escorted surveying parties, and served as scouts. They acted as guards at annuity payments, preserved order at ration issues, protected agency buildings and other property, and returned truant children to school. They searched for and returned lost or stolen goods, prevented depredations in timber, and brought whiskey sellers to trial. They arrested Indians for disorderly conduct, drunkenness, wife beating, and theft, and reported the comings and goings of strangers on the reservation.[44]

The reformers soon became aware, if they had not been from the start, that these duties and responsibilities of the Indian police were means to an end of greater worth than day-to-day good order on the reservations. The police were to become important chiefly for their moral influence. The police force on a reservation impressed the Indians with the supremacy of law; it discouraged the traditional practice of personal revenge; it imbued a sense of duty and personal responsibility, subjected the policemen themselves to strict discipline and self-control, and inspired them with a pride of good conduct; it taught respect for the personal and property rights of others; by strengthening the authority of the government agent against that of the chiefs, it prepared the Indians for the dissolution of their tribal relations and pushed them forward toward incorporation into American society. The Indian police taught by good example as well as by the enforcement of precepts. They were expected to have only one wife and to dress in the accepted white man's costume, with short hair and unpainted faces. The police force, Commissioner Hiram Price commented in 1881, was "a perpetual educator."

All in all, the Indian police worked remarkably well in fulfilling the reformers' designs. Four years after the program began, the commissioner of Indian affairs reported: "Tried as an experiment, it has proved a decided success. It has accomplished all that was claimed for it, and at many agencies has become an absolute necessity." Compared with white police forces throughout the country, he declared two years later, the Indian police could not be surpassed for faithfulness and the impartial performance of duty. And this was all the more remarkable considering that the police

44. Hagan, *Indian Police and Judges*, pp. 69–81. See also the annual reports of the commissioner of Indian affairs.

were asked to enforce against members of their own race laws made by
white officials, many of which went strongly against established practices
and customs, often of a religious nature.[45] The success rested to a large extent on the fact that the police forces often paralleled or replaced similar
institutions within the tribes themselves. The soldier societies that had
regulated much of tribal life had performed functions not unlike those assigned to the Indian police, and wittingly or unwittingly, agents drew their
policemen from the membership of such societies.[46]

There were, of course, some nay sayers. The strongest argument made
against the Indian police was that they gave too much power to the agent.
The chairman of the House Committee on Indian Affairs in 1880 argued
strongly against the continuation of the police on that basis. "This provision turns him [the Indian] over, bound hand and foot, to the agents," he
said. "These men had authority before almost without restriction, except
as they are restricted by the want of physical force. Now we give them
eight hundred men armed and equipped, and thus the fullest authority is
allowed with fearful power to execute not known laws, but the will of the
agent."[47] There was no doubt that an obedient police force in the hands of
an authoritarian or unscrupulous agent would be a dangerous thing. But
isolated examples of dangerous behavior did not outweigh the over-
whelmingly favorable impression made by the Indian police on white
observers.[48]

Part of the agitation for law for the Indians came, not from fear of disor-
ders within the Indian societies, which the Indian police might ease, but
from the difficulties of protecting Indians from crimes perpetrated upon
them by white aggressors. The instrument that was supposed to offer protection from such attacks was the Indian Trade and Intercourse Act of
1834, with its array of restrictions upon white contacts with Indians and
penalties for violating them. Like the officials in the 1850s, who lamented
the inapplicability of the old law to changed conditions, the secretaries
and commissioners of the 1860s and 1870s saw urgent need for revision.
Commissioner Cooley in 1866 began the refrain: "The intercourse laws,

45. CIA Report, 1882, serial 2100, pp. 35–36; CIA Report, 1884, serial 2287, p. 12.
See also CIA Report, 1890, serial 2841, pp. xci–xciv, for extracts of agents' reports prais-
ing the Indian police.

46. Clark Wissler, *Indian Cavalcade; or, Life on the Old-Time Indian Reservations*
(New York: Sheridan House, 1938), pp. 128–29; Hagan, *Indian Police and Judges*, p. 161.

47. *Congressional Record*, 10: 2487. Several other members of the House spoke
strongly in favor of the police, and the objection was not sustained. See the debate, ibid.,
pp. 2487–89.

48. George E. Hyde, *A Sioux Chronicle* (Norman: University of Oklahoma Press,
1956), generally supports the critics' position, but Hagan's *Indian Police and Judges* gives
a more sober and favorable evaluation of the police.

passed over thirty years since, and apparently sufficient at that time, before the tide of emigration had begun to set strongly towards the frontier, and while none but occasional hunters or trappers interfered with the occupancy of the country by the Indians, are insufficient now, when the white population west of the Mississippi begins to number its millions." A typical echo was that of Columbus Delano in 1874, who declared that the provisions of the act of 1834 were "entirely inadequate to meet the present requirements of the service" and that experience had shown that the law was no longer sufficient to protect the Indians.[49]

The problem was twofold. First, the Indians needed more effective protection against crimes committed against their persons and property by whites. What was called for was "a plain, comprehensive code, by which the superintendents and agents may dispense justice within their jurisdictions, and the infliction of appropriate penalties may be rendered certain, whether the offender be red or white." The longtime discrimination in favor of whites could not escape notice. "In too many cases, indeed almost universally," the commissioner wrote in 1866, "where a white offender against the rights or life of an Indian is brought into our courts through the efforts of the agent, he is sure of acquittal; but reverse the case, and the Indian almost surely suffers. It does seem practicable," he concluded, "to improve upon this condition of things." Secretary Delano, almost a decade later, pointed to the same problems.[50]

The second major concern was the inadequacy of the regulations for trade with the Indians. Indiscriminate granting of licenses to American citizens was a norm, and Congress in fact in 1866 had reinforced the principle by authorizing any loyal citizen to trade with the Indians. Such looseness aggravated the problems, for the Indian Office had authority neither to restrict the number of traders nor eliminate those judged unfit or unable to supply the Indians fairly and adequately.[51]

The result in both cases was severe irritation of the Indians, who sought revenge against the abuses and kept the frontier in turmoil. But more important, in the minds of the reformers, the situation left the Indians in an anomalous state in regard to law. The failure of Congress to act in providing a code of law for the Indians led Commissioner E. P. Smith in 1875 to

49. CIA Report, 1866, serial 1284, pp. 16–17; Report of the Secretary of the Interior, 1874, *House Executive Document* no. 1, part 5, 43–2, serial 1639, p. viii. See also CIA Report, 1867, serial 1326, part 2, p. 5; CIA Report, 1871, serial 1505, p. 422.

50. CIA Report, 1866, serial 1284, p. 17; Report of the Secretary of the Interior, 1874, *House Executive Document* no. 1, part 5, 43–2, serial 1639, p. viii. See the plea for better law for the Indians, both among themselves and in relation to whites, in CIA Report, 1874, serial 1639, pp. 324–25.

51. 14 *United States Statutes* 280; CIA Report, 1866, serial 1284, p. 17; CIA Report, 1877, serial 1800, pp. 404–5.

recommend the "divorcement of the United States and Indians as 'citizens of a domestic sovereignty within our borders,' and the transfer of the Indians and their property to the States where they reside." This could be done at once, he thought, in New York and for some of the Indians in Michigan, Wisconsin, and Minnesota; it could be done for others as soon as they were advanced enough in civilization to be treated as ordinary citizens.[52]

All the plans and the progress that came from them in implementing the peace policy fell short of the firm legislative enactments that were the ultimate goal of the reformers. Again and again the commissioners and the secretaries of the interior, supported and urged forward by church and other reform groups, had recommended legal support of land allotment, a system of courts, and increased educational facilities for Indians. To a large extent their exhortations were ineffective at the time, but they were not in vain. The ideas espoused in the 1860s and 1870s became the platform for a concentrated and successful drive in the next two decades that transformed the relations between the United States government and the Indians.

52. CIA Report, 1875, serial 1680, pp. 519–20. This was close to the policy of "termination" of the 1950s, although that term was not used.

Illustration
and Map Credits
Volume I

1. American Numismatic Society, New York City. 2. Charles Allen Munn Collection, Fordham University Library, Bronx, New York, Frick Art Reference Library print no. 21170. 3. New-York Historical Society, New York City, negative no. 1111. 4. National Archives, Washington, D.C. 5. New-York Historical Society, negative no. 6282 (painting by Edward Savage). 6. U.S. Signal Corps photograph no. 111–SC–90825 (from an engraving in Benson L. Lossing, *The Pictorial Field-Book of the War of 1812*) in the National Archives. 7–9. Independence National Historical Park Collection, Philadelphia. 10. Nebraska State Historical Society, Lincoln. 11. Library of Congress, Washington, D.C. 12. Architect of the Capitol, Washington, D.C. 13. In the collection of the Corcoran Gallery of Art, Washington, D.C., bequest of James C. McGuire. 14. National Archives. 15. State Historical Society of Wisconsin, Madison, negative no. WHI (x3) 35374 (from Marcius Willson, *American History*). 16. American Numismatic Society. 17. Chicago Historical Society, Chicago. 18. William L. Clements Library, University of Michigan, Ann Arbor. 19. Philbrook Art Center, Tulsa, Oklahoma. 20. National Anthropological Archives, Smithsonian Institution, Washington, D.C. (from a McKenney and Hall lithograph). 21. E. C. Tracy, *Memoir of the Life of Jeremiah Evarts, Esq.* (Boston: Crocker and Brewster, 1845), frontispiece (after a painting by Samuel F. B. Morse). 22. Kansas State Historical Society, Topeka. 23–24. National Portrait Gallery, Smithsonian Institution, Washington, D.C., on loan from the National Museum of American Art. 25. Illinois State Historical Library, Springfield. 26. California Historical Society, San Francisco; photograph by Edouart, San Francisco. 27. Hazard Stevens, *The Life of Isaac Ingalls Stevens* (Boston: Houghton Mifflin Company, 1900), frontispiece. 28. National Anthropological Archives,

Smithsonian Institution. 29. Library of
Congress (photograph by George Prince,
1898). 30. Smithsonian Institution. 31.
U.S. Signal Corps photograph no.
111–SC–87714 in the National Archives.
32. American Numismatic Society. 33.
Charles Lewis Slattery, *Felix Reville
Brunot*, frontispiece. 34–36. Library of
Congress. 37. U.S. Signal Corps photograph no. 111–SC–82311 (photograph by
Louis Heller, 1873) in the National Archives. 38. Library of Congress, Brady collection. 39. *Harper's Weekly*, January 25,
1879. 40. National Archives, photograph
no. 111–B–4990. 41. U.S. Signal Corps
photograph no. 111–SC–96773 (D. F.
Barry photograph, 1877) in the National
Archives.

MAP CREDITS

The maps in this volume were drawn by
the Cartographic Laboratory, University of
Nebraska–Lincoln. The following sources
were drawn upon for the maps. 1. Edgar
Bruce Wesley, *Guarding the Frontier: A
Study in Frontier Defense from 1814 to
1825* (Minneapolis: University of Minnesota Press, 1935), p. 39; Herman J.
Viola, *Thomas L. McKenney: Architect
of America's Early Indian Policy, 1816–*

1830 (Chicago: Swallow Press, 1974). 2.
*The American Heritage Pictorial Atlas of
United States History* (New York: Ameri-
can Heritage Publishing Company, 1966),
p. 148; Charles C. Royce, comp., *Indian
Land Cessions in the United States*, Eigh-
teenth Annual Report of the Bureau of
American Ethnology, 1896–1897, part 2
(Washington: Government Printing
Office, 1899), appropriate state plates. 3.
R. David Edmunds, *The Potawatomis:
Keepers of the Fire* (Norman: University
of Oklahoma Press, 1978), p. 245; Royce,
Indian Land Cessions. 4. *American Heri-
tage Pictorial Atlas of United States His-
tory*, p. 148; Royce, *Indian Land
Cessions*. 5. Arrell Morgan Gibson, *The
American Indian: Prehistory to the Pres-
ent* (Lexington, Massachusetts: D. C.
Heath and Company, 1980), p. 313; Royce,
Indian Land Cessions. 6. John W. Morris,
Charles R. Goins, and Edwin C. Mc-
Reynolds, *Historical Atlas of Oklahoma*,
2d ed. (Norman: University of Oklahoma
Press, 1976). 7. Gerald Thompson, *The
Army and the Navajo* (Tucson: Univer-
sity of Arizona Press, 1976), p. xii. 8. Fran-
cis Paul Prucha, *A Guide to the Military
Posts of the United States, 1789–1895*
(Madison: State Historical Society of
Wisconsin, 1964). 9. *Annual Report of the
Commissioner of Indian Affairs*, 1880.

The Great Father

Volume II

PART SIX

Americanizing the American Indians

The drive to acculturate and assimilate the American Indians culminated in the last two decades of the nineteenth century. The policies that statesmen and reformers had advocated through the previous decades now came to fruition. The military struggles were over except for isolated conflicts, and the programs for Americanizing the Indians were pushed with new energy and enthusiasm.

The method to accomplish this ultimate reform was no longer direct participation by laymen in Indian administration, for the early attempts of the Board of Indian Commissioners and the assignment of Indian agencies to missionary groups had proved unworkable. The movement turned now in another direction. By arousing and channeling public sentiment, humanitarians forced through Congress a program of reform that was considered the final answer to "the Indian problem." Uniting reformers in voluntary associations, flooding the nation with press reports and pamphlet propaganda, lobbying in Washington for specific measures, investigating the actual conditions of the Indians in the West, fighting for Indian rights in particular cases—these became the means of revolutionizing the relations of the Indians with the rest of the nation.

A concerted drive on the part of earnest men and women who unabashedly called themselves "the Friends of the Indians" made Congress listen at last. The reformers and their sympathetic friends in government had great confidence in the righteousness of their cause. Convinced of the superiority of the Christian civilization they enjoyed, they were determined to do away with Indianness and tribal relations and to turn the individual Indian into a patriotic American citizen, indistinguishable from his white brothers.

With great faith in the principles they espoused and unwilling to admit that earlier application of the same principles had not totally succeeded, the reformers drove steadily ahead. They got a general allotment in severalty law, which provided citizenship for the allotted Indians, and an expanded national school system for the Indians that would fit them for their new privileges and duties. Although the initial base for their programs was the reservation, the reformers expected soon to eliminate altogether the reservations and the communal life they symbolized and fostered. By proper regulations and administration, they hoped to remove all remnants of tribal customs and practices and welcome the transformed Indians into the great body of American society. "The logic of events," the commissioner of Indian affairs asserted in 1889, "demands the absorption of the Indians into our national life, not as Indians, but as American citizens."[1]

Here was a high point of paternalism, although the Great Father image had largely faded from the rhetoric. The reformers knew what was best for the wards of the government. Lacking all appreciation of the Indian cultures, they were intent on forcing upon the natives the qualities that they themselves embodied. It was an ethnocentrism of frightening intensity, and it set a pattern that was not easily eradicated.

1. CIA Report, 1889, serial 2725, p. 3.

CHAPTER 24

The New Christian Reformers

Reform Organizations.

Christian Humanitarianism.

Americanization.

Other Voices.

The reformers, in traditional American fashion, worked principally through voluntary associations or societies. Initiated by concerned individuals who often continued to energize the whole, the organizations united likeminded persons in a needed and noble work. By means of branches and auxiliaries they could boast a national membership and bring pressure to bear from all sections of the country. Eastern philanthropists and humanitarians, chiefly from Boston and Philadelphia, led the fight, but they elicited a sympathetic response across the land and brought a unity to the movement that was a primary basis for success.[1]

REFORM ORGANIZATIONS

New organizations devoted to Indian affairs seemed to spring up spontaneously and to attract enough membership and money to keep them viable. The first of these was the Boston Indian Citizenship Committee, which grew out of the furor created by the Ponca affair in the late 1870s. At

1. This chapter includes parts of Francis Paul Prucha, *American Indian Policy in Crisis: Christian Reformers and the Indian, 1865–1900* (Norman: University of Oklahoma Press, 1976), pp. 132–68. The material appears also in Francis Paul Prucha, "Indian Policy Reform and American Protestantism," in *People of the Plains and Mountains: Essays*

a public meeting of the merchants of Boston held on November 26, 1879, a committee of five prominent men was appointed to investigate the wrongs of the Ponca Indians and the general management of Indian affairs. The committee, in a report addressed "To the People of the United States," found in favor of the Poncas and against the government. In considering Indian affairs in general, it noted two evils, "absence of protection of law, and insecurity of titles to lands," and it took as its platform the fulfillment of treaties, recognition of the Indian as a person and as a fellow citizen, granting of Indian reservations to the tribes in fee simple (but inalienable for twenty-five years), and individual allotments of land to Indians who wanted them.[2] Although it spent much of its energy at first in a controversy with Secretary of the Interior Carl Schurz over the Ponca tragedy, the Boston Indian Citizenship Committee continued to keep interest alive in Indian welfare. Some of its members played a continuing role among the Indian reformers, emphasizing the need to secure for the Indians their political and civil rights.

At the same time that the Boston group began its work, a similar organization was established in Philadelphia, first as an Indian committee of the Women's Home Mission Society of the First Baptist Church. The work began in the spring of 1879 in an informal fashion; but under the amazing organizational ability of Amelia S. Quinton, the dominant force in the group, the eager women soon developed into a national body. Like the Boston businessmen, they had been aroused by injustices to the Indians and hoped to stir up the God-fearing people of the United States to demand reform in Indian affairs. In June 1881 the organization took the name the Indian Treaty-Keeping and Protective Association and in October 1883, the Women's National Indian Association.[3]

The work of the association was manifold. Its most cherished projects at the beginning were petitions sent to the president and to Congress, the first of which, with thirteen thousand signatures condemning the invasion of the Indian Territory by white settlers, was sent to Washington in February 1880. Two years later a mammoth petition, claiming to represent no

---

in the History of the West Dedicated to Everett Dick, ed. Ray Allen Billington (Westport, Connecticut: Greenwood Press, 1973), pp. 120–45. The sentiments of the reformers can be seen in detail in Francis Paul Prucha, ed., *Americanizing the American Indians: Writings by the "Friends of the Indian," 1880–1900* (Cambridge: Harvard University Press, 1973).

2. *The Indian Question: Report of the Committee Appointed by Hon. John D. Long, Governor of Massachusetts* (Boston: Frank Wood, 1880). The report included a large number of short extracts from government reports in support of its contentions.

3. See *Sketch and Plans of the Indian Treaty-Keeping and Protective Association, with Suggestions to Workers* (Philadelphia, 1881). The history of the origin of the association and its early years is given in Amelia S. Quinton, "Care of the Indian," in Annie Nathan Meyer, ed., *Woman's Work in America* (New York: Henry Holt and Company,

fewer than one hundred thousand persons and wrapped in white bunting tied with red, white, and blue ribbons, was delivered to President Arthur by a committee of the association. It was presented in the Senate on February 21, 1882, by Senator Henry L. Dawes of Massachusetts, who warmly supported the petitioners and their pleas. The petition itself and a memorial letter accompanying it, both of which were read to the Senate by Dawes, gave a dramatic picture of the thrust of the sentimental reform movement that the women's organization signally represented. The petition asked four things: the maintenance of all treaties "with scrupulous fidelity" until they were abrogated or modified with the free consent of the Indians involved; provision of common schools on the reservations "sufficient for the education of every child of every tribe" and of industrial schools as well; allotment of land in severalty (160 acres in fee simple, inalienable for twenty years) to all Indians who desired it; and full rights under the law for the Indians, making them amenable to the laws of the United States, granting full religious liberty, and encouraging them in industry and trade.[4]

Senators Preston B. Plumb of Kansas and Henry M. Teller of Colorado argued strongly against the petition and memorial. "I have noticed," Plumb remarked, ". . . that interest of a certain kind in the Indian is in the exact ratio of distance from him, and perhaps I might add in increased ratio to their knowledge of him or his actual need." And he complained that there were "barrels of tears, oceans of sympathy for the Indians, and a fragmentary and passing word only for the men who suffered at their hands." Teller insisted, as he had frequently before, that the Indians were eager for neither land in severalty nor the white man's education. Dawes's plea, he said, was "full of pathos and full of enthusiasm, but utterly lacking in common sense."[5] But such criticism did little to stay the flood of reform sentiment.

1891), pp. 373–91; Mary E. Dewey, *Historical Sketch of the Formation and Achievements of the Women's National Indian Association in the United States* (Philadelphia, 1900); *Annual Meeting and Report of the Women's National Indian Association* (Philadelphia, 1883), pp. 6–7; *Fourth Annual Report of the Women's National Indian Association* (Philadelphia, 1884), pp. 7–8. The constitution appears in *Fourth Annual Report* (1884), pp. 57–59. A careful scholarly study of the association is Helen M. Wanken, "'Woman's Sphere' and Indian Reform: The Women's National Indian Association, 1879–1901" (Ph.D. dissertation, Marquette University, 1981). The word "Women's" was included to distinguish the group from the Indian Rights Association, but in 1901 the organization's title reverted to simply the National Indian Association.

4. The petitions and memorial letters of the first three years are printed in footnotes in Quinton, "Care of the Indian." The 1882 petition, memorial, and remarks of Dawes are in *Congressional Record*, 13: 1326–27; extracts are given in *Council Fire* 5 (March 1882): 88–92.

5. *Congressional Record*, 13: 1327–29.

A second work of the Women's National Indian Association was the circulation of literature. The women distributed copies of their annual reports and thousands of copies of leaflets on Indian topics printed by the association, as well as the pamphlets printed by the Indian Rights Association. It made efforts also to gain wide circulation for books that agreed with its positions on the Indian question, and it furnished information on the Indian question to the press. The local branches secured the publication in both religious and secular papers of articles on Indian education, on national duty to the Indians, and on missionary work, together with extracts of pamphlets and books. Finally, the women presented their cause at public meetings, often with the cooperation of church groups. Mrs. Quinton herself in 1884 traveled more than ten thousand miles in promoting the work of the association and addressed more than one hundred meetings in the East and Middle West.[6]

The success of the petitions and the other work of the association depended on the active support of branches organized throughout the country. By 1886 there were eighty-three such branches, and contributions rose rapidly. Some of the branches, like those of Connecticut and Massachusetts, became important in their own right. In order to have a medium of communication between the national headquarters and the branches, the association in 1888 began to publish a monthly paper called *The Indian's Friend*, which recorded current legislation concerning Indians, made appeals for help in the association's work, and chronicled the efforts being made by other reform groups.[7]

In 1883 the Women's National Indian Association reduced its interest in propagandizing for Indian reform. "Providence has answered our prayers," Mrs. Quinton said, "by bringing the gentlemen's INDIAN RIGHTS ASSOCIATION into existence to pursue as their chief work, and with great advantages, this very object." The women were thus left free to devote most of their time "to uplifting Indian homes; to aiding the vastly needed work with Indian hearts, minds, and souls, while not intermitting the effort to secure to the race civil rights." The women's group cooperated with the new men's organization and other reform-minded groups, but it more and more devoted its energies to direct missionary activity. One of its projects was providing aid to young Indian couples in building homes, and the association established a special Indian Home Building Department.[8]

6. *Fourth Annual Report* (1884), pp. 14–15, 27–30.

7. Quinton, "Care of the Indian," pp. 385–86. The branches are discussed thoroughly in Wanken, "'Woman's Sphere' and Indian Reform."

8. *Annual Meeting and Report* (1883), pp. 10, 16–17. Mrs. Quinton regularly reported on the work of her organization at the meetings of the reformers; see, for example, *Lake Mohonk Conference Proceedings*, 1889, pp. 103–7, and *Report of the Board of Indian Commissioners*, 1891, p. 131.

The Indian Rights Association soon became the most important of the reform organizations. It was founded in December 1882 in Philadelphia, a direct outgrowth of a visit of two young Philadelphians, Henry S. Pancoast and Herbert Welsh, to the Great Sioux Reserve in Dakota during the previous summer.[9] "This visit," Welsh later recorded, "resulted in a revolution of many preconceived opinions and in fixing in our minds clearly and firmly two important truths:—1st. That the Indians were capable of civilization, and 2d. That it was largely due to the injustice or inefficiency of the government's dealings with him that the Indian had attained to civilization so imperfectly." Welsh and his companion were struck by the solid accomplishments of the missionaries whose work they inspected, which pointed to a humane solution to the Indian problem, but they were disturbed that so few of the general public were aware of what they themselves had witnessed. "The Indian must have just and faithful friends," Welsh decided, "who will plead his cause with the people, who will represent him in the East and at Washington, until his rights are accorded, and his days of tutelage are over."[10]

Back in Philadelphia, these young humanitarians determined to establish an organization to promote their views. In December, at a meeting in Welsh's home, the Indian Rights Association was founded, and it quickly became a dominant force in Indian affairs. Welsh, son of John Welsh, former minister to Great Britain, and nephew of the ardent Indian reformer William Welsh, became the secretary and for all practical purposes the guiding genius of the organization.

While not denying or denigrating the good accomplished in the past by missionaries, teachers, and government agents, the association turned its attention primarily to the question of vital legislation. "No man in these United States to-day," it asserted, "can be rightly termed civilized, nor can his position be considered a safe one, who is removed from both the protection and the punishment of law, who is denied a protected title to land and the right of holding it as an individual, or who is deprived of the blessings of a practical education." Since these conditions did not obtain for the Indians, the Indian Rights Association believed its program was necessary, and it claimed moral and financial support from the general public. In incisive statements, it set forth its aims for the Indians.

9. Accounts of the trip to Dakota and the subsequent founding of the Indian Rights Association are in Henry S. Pancoast, *Impressions of the Sioux Tribes in 1882; With Some First Principles in the Indian Question* (Philadelphia, 1883); Herbert Welsh, *Four Weeks among Some of the Sioux Tribes of Dakota and Nebraska, Together with a Brief Consideration of the Indian Problem* (Germantown, Pennsylvania, 1882); *Report of the Indian Rights Association*, 1883, p. 5; Herbert Welsh, *The Indian Question Past and Present* (Philadelphia, 1890), pp. 14–16; Herbert Welsh, "The Meaning of the Dakota Outbreak," *Scribner's Magazine* 9 (April 1891): 439.

10. Welsh, *Indian Question*, pp. 14–15.

I. Law, and to awaken the spirit of even-handed justice in the nation which will alone make law, when secured, fully operative.

II. Education. Signifying by this broad term the developing for their highest use physical, intellectual and moral powers.

III. A protected individual title to land. This is the entering-wedge by which tribal organization is to be rent asunder.[11]

The methods by which this was to be accomplished were just as clearly enunciated.[12] Branch associations were organized in principal cities; they kept in close contact with the central headquarters, receiving information on questions of concern to the association. Representatives were sent out to the Indian reservations in order to get complete, independent, and accurate information on which to base recommendations. Here lay much of the reason for the association's success, for it soon became evident to reasonable men that the Indian Rights Association, although often aggressively promoting its own point of view, had abundant facts behind its arguments. When it investigated an alleged evil or some unjust treatment of the Indians, it could not easily be dismissed as a group of unthinking sentimentalists who did not know what they were talking about. To place its information and its program before the public, the association embarked on an extensive publication program. It circulated in pamphlet form the reports of its own members' trips of investigation, and it reprinted and spread abroad newspaper articles, speeches, and other materials to further its program. Moreover, Welsh and his associates lectured frequently to interested groups, spelling out their ideas and eliciting support. In the first years of the organization, Welsh alone averaged more than forty talks a year, usually before church groups or local Indian reform associations.

Even more important was the direct and effective lobbying in Washington done by the Indian Rights Association's full-time representative in the capital, Charles C. Painter, and after Painter's death in 1895, Francis E. Leupp. Painter followed the progress of legislation on Indian matters,

11. *Report of the Indian Rights Association*, 1884, pp. 5–6. The Constitution of the Indian Rights Association included the following statements of purpose: "II. The object of the Association shall be to secure to the Indians of the United States the political and civil rights already guaranteed to them by treaty and statutes of the United States, and such as their civilization and circumstances may justify. . . . IV. For the purpose of carrying out its object, the Association shall endeavor in every proper way to influence public opinion and the legislation of Congress, and assist the executive officers of the Government in the enforcement of the laws passed for the protection and education of the Indians."

12. *Report of the Indian Rights Association*, 1884, pp. 7–8. A useful account of the association is Herbert Welsh, *A Brief Statement of the Objects, Achievements and Needs of the Indian Rights Association* (Philadelphia, 1887).

brought information to the attention of the members of the Indian commit-tees of Congress and other legislators, and pressed for measures deemed ben-eficial to the Indians while opposing those considered injurious. In his work he kept in close touch with Welsh in Philadelphia and as much as possible with branches of the association. To gain firsthand information to aid him in his work, Painter made frequent visits to the Indian country.[13]

The grandiose schemes for a massive uniting of the people across the land, however, were not matched by the actual numbers who actively joined the association. By 1892 only thirteen hundred members could be counted in all parts of the country, but the influence of Welsh and his friends was not measured in membership statistics. Welsh's own evalua-tion was accurate: "It is fair to claim that out of all proportion to its mem-bers or its expenditures has been its influence upon public sentiment and upon legislation and executive management. It has won general public re-spect and confidence by the general accuracy of its statements of fact, and by its impartial attitude, its freedom from partisan bias in judging men and measures within the range of Indian work."[14] The Indian Rights Associa-tion cooperated effectively with other Indian reform groups, and the pro-gram Welsh enunciated at the start of his career was largely enacted by 1900.

The work of the various reform groups came to a focus in a conference held each autumn at a resort hotel on Lake Mohonk, near New Paltz, New York. There men and women interested in Indian affairs met to discuss In-dian reform, to hear speakers on matters of concern, and to formulate reso-lutions that could be broadcast to the public and used to lobby for specific goals in Congress. The instigator of these Lake Mohonk Conferences of Friends of the Indian and a continuing presence behind them was a Quaker schoolteacher, Albert K. Smiley, who with his brother Alfred had pur-chased the Lake Mohonk property in 1869 and developed it into a summer resort that quickly gained popularity with a substantial religious-minded clientele. Smiley, who had been appointed a member of the Board of Indian Commissioners in 1879, found the meetings of the board in Washington too short to allow time for adequate consideration of Indian matters, so he determined to invite the members of the board and other interested indi-viduals to Lake Mohonk each fall. The first group assembled in October 1883. It was a small gathering, but as the idea took hold, the yearly con-ferences grew in size until they averaged in the late 1880s and early 1890s more than 150 persons. The format of the meetings was set, yet relaxed.

13. The work of Painter and Leupp can be followed in their contributions to the an-nual reports of the association.

14. *Report of the Indian Rights Association*, 1892, p. 4.

The mornings were devoted to formal sessions in the spacious parlors of the hotel. A president of the conference was designated (regularly a member of the Board of Indian Commissioners), a resolutions and platform committee chosen, the group welcomed by Smiley, and opening remarks made by the president as the conference got under way. Prepared papers on Indian matters by a variety of experts served as the focus for discussion. The afternoons were free for informal conversations, often on walks through the well-kept grounds of the resort, and the evenings were devoted again to formal sessions.[15]

The Lake Mohonk Conference had no official status other than as a loose extension of the Board of Indian Commissioners. Its work, instead, was the deliberate focusing of public opinion behind specific measures of Indian policy and the aggressive propagandizing of these measures in the press and in the halls of government. The aim, as Smiley expressed it, was "to unite the best minds interested in Indian affairs, so that all should act together and be in harmony, and so that the prominent persons connected with Indian affairs should act as one body and create a public sentiment in favor of the Indians." The group was in fact closely knit. Although it appeared on the surface that the net had been thrown wide to bring in the members in attendance, the large numbers were deceiving, for a small core of dedicated men gave direction to the movement. "The Lake Mohonk Conference is and has been a power," one of its active members asserted in 1889, "but why? It does not represent a solid constituency; it casts no vote; it exercises no political influence, in the ordinary sense of that term; nor does it exercise any ecclesiastical or church influence." The answer was clear; the conference represented "the conscience of the American people on the Indian question." History had taught that "when the conscience of the American people is aroused, it is the most potent factor in American politics, defeating and bringing to shame the cunningly devised schemes of politicians that disregard or condemn it."[16]

15. Smiley's accounts of the founding of the conference are in *Lake Mohonk Conference Proceedings*, 1885, p. 1, and 1894, p. 38. Histories of the conference are Larry E. Burgess, "The Lake Mohonk Conferences on the Indian, 1883–1916" (Ph.D. dissertation, Claremont Graduate School, 1972), and Larry E. Burgess, "'We'll Discuss It at Mohonk,'" *Quaker History* 40 (Spring 1971): 14–28. The indexes to the conference proceedings are reprinted in Larry E. Burgess, *The Lake Mohonk Conference of Friends of the Indian: Guide to the Annual Reports* (New York: Clearwater Publishing Company, 1975). For the story of the Lake Mohonk resort, see Larry E. Burgess, *Mohonk, Its People and Spirit: A History of One Hundred Years of Growth and Service* (New Paltz, New York: Mohonk Mountain House, 1980). There is material on the organization of the conferences and on their participants in the Smiley Family Papers, Quaker Collection, Haverford College Library.

16. *Lake Mohonk Conference Proceedings*, 1885, p. 1, and 1889, p. 13.

CHRISTIAN HUMANITARIANISM

The harmony that marked the Lake Mohonk Conferences was based on a common religious outlook. The Women's National Indian Association, which had been established under Baptist auspices, assumed a non-denominational stance, but it consciously drew on support from the evangelical churches. Its executive board in 1884 comprised members from eight Protestant denominations, and the support of Christian congregations throughout the country was essential for its reform crusade. In 1883, moreover, the organization specifically added missionary and school work to its efforts and took on many of the characteristics of a home missionary society. The new work was a direct endeavor to supply Christian training for Indians in areas where no one else was providing it and then, whenever possible, to turn over the work to the care of some regular missionary group. By 1892 the association had established twenty-five mission stations, which had been transferred to Methodist, Episcopal, Baptist, Presbyterian, or Moravian care.[17]

The Indian Rights Association, too, acknowledged the Christian motivation of its work. Herbert Welsh asserted that the Indian needed to be "taught to labor, to live in civilized ways, and to serve God." He remarked further that "the best Christian sentiment of the country is needed to redeem the Indian, to stimulate and guide the constantly changing functionaries of the government who are charged with the task of his civilization."[18]

The atmosphere of deep religiosity in which the reformers worked was most noticeable at the Lake Mohonk Conferences. The meetings were begun with an invocation, and the discussions were full of religious spirit and religious terminology. Part of this was due, no doubt, to the influence of the Quaker host; part, also, to the heavy clerical participation in the gatherings. Of the names listed in the membership roster, 1883–1900, more than a fourth were ministers, their wives, and representatives of religious groups, and a great many more were prominent lay leaders in their churches. The editors of the leading religious journals and papers, too, were regularly on hand. All had strong religious motivation for their work in Indian affairs. "It may be taken for granted," the Reverend Lyman Abbott observed at Lake Mohonk in 1885, "that we are Christian men and

17. The missionary work is described in the annual reports and in special pamphlets published by the association. See, for example, *Missionary Work of the Women's National Indian Association, and Letters of Missionaries* (Philadelphia, 1885); *Christian Civilization and Missionary Work of the Women's National Indian Association* (Philadelphia, 1887); *Sketches of Delightful Work* (Philadelphia, 1893); *Our Work—What! How! Why!* (Philadelphia, 1893).

18. Welsh, *Indian Question*, pp. 15, 18.

women; that we believe in justice, good-will, and charity, and the brother-hood of the human race." And the president of the conference, Merrill E. Gates, declared in 1891: "This is essentially a philanthropic and Christian reform. Whatever may be our views, our slight differences of view or differ-ences that may seem to us profound, we all gather here believing that, ever since God himself became incarnate, for a man to see God truly, he must learn to see something of God in his fellow-man, and to work for his fellow-men. We come in the spirit of service."[19]

The word *Christian* dropped unselfconsciously from the lips of the re-formers as they set about to do God's will, to guide the Indian "from the night of barbarism into the fair dawn of Christian civilization," as Herbert Welsh expressed it in 1886. The only hope for a solution to the Indian prob-lem, Gates declared at the end of nearly two decades of organized humani-tarian effort, would be to bring the Indians "under the sway of Christian thought and Christian life, and into touch with the people of this Chris-tian nation under the laws and institutions which govern the life of our States and Territories." As he welcomed the members of the Lake Mohonk Conference of 1900, he recalled the Christian foundation of their work for Indian reform. "Nothing less than decades of years of persistent effort," he said, "years of effort prompted by that love of one's fellow-men which has its perennial root in the love of Christ for us, can do the work which here we contemplate and discuss." He welcomed especially the devoted mis-sionaries who worked so diligently for the Indians; but he gave a clue to the pervasive Christianity of the age when he turned to welcome, too, rep-resentatives of the Indian Office, whom he described as "Christian men of high purpose, whose aim in the issuing of regulations and the administra-tion of Indian affairs is identical with the aims of the Christian workers in the field, and the Christian friends of the Indian who gather here."[20]

The decades at the end of the century in which Indian reform flourished were marked by an intensification of the desire on the part of zealous evan-gelicals to create a "righteous empire" in America, and the Indians were caught up in that thrust. The coincidence of an ultimate crisis in Indian affairs, brought about by the overwhelming pressure of expanding white civilization upon the Indians and their reservations, and the intensified re-ligious drive for a unified American society provided the momentum for the new program of Indian policy reform.[21]

19. *Lake Mohonk Conference Proceedings*, 1885, p. 50, and 1891, p. 11.
20. Ibid., 1886, p. 13, and 1900, pp. 13, 21.
21. For my understanding of evangelical Protestantism, I have learned much from Robert T. Handy, "The Protestant Quest for a Christian America," *Church History* 22 (March 1953): 8–20; Robert T. Handy, *A Christian America: Protestant Hopes and His-torical Realities* (New York: Oxford University Press, 1971); Martin E. Marty, *Righteous*

The distinguishing mark of American evangelicalism was its insistence on individual salvation: conversion and reformation of individuals was the means to correct evils or wrongs in society. The Indian reformers eventually realized the fundamental conflict between this principle and the communal life and customs of the Indians. Rather than approach the Indian problem in Indian terms, the reformers insisted adamantly on the individualization of the Indians and their acculturation as individuals freed from bondage to the tribe. "The philosophy of the present [Indian] policy," Senator Dawes said in January 1884, "is to treat him as an individual, and not as an insoluble substance that the civilization of this country has been unable, hitherto, to digest, but to take him as an individual, a human being, and treat him as you find him." Merrill Gates epitomizd the sentiments of the reformers as he summed up their work in 1900:

> If civilization, education and Christianity are to do their work, we must get at the individual. They must lay hold of men and women and children, one by one. The deadening sway of tribal custom must be interfered with. The sad uniformity of savage tribal life must be broken up! Individuality must be cultivated. Personality must be developed. And personality is strengthened only by the direction of one's own life through voluntary obedience to recognized moral law. At last, as a nation, we are coming to recognize the great truth that if we would do justice to the Indians, we must get at them, one by one, with American ideals, American schools, American laws, the privileges and the pressures of American rights and duties.[22]

The fight for individualization was carried on on many fronts by the evangelical reformers and sympathetic Indian Office officials. They intended to break up tribal ownership of land and substitute allotment of Indian lands in severalty. They wished to end tribal jurisdiction and to treat the Indians as individual citizens before the law. Their individualism, moreover, was tied closely to the Puritan work ethic. Hard work and thrift were virtues that seemed to be at the very basis of individual salvation. No transformation for the Indians that did not include self-support could be conceived in the reformers' minds. Annuities to the tribes and rations to subsist the Indians were imposing blocks that prevented realization of the

---

Empire: The Protestant Experience in America (New York: Dial Press, 1970); William G. McLoughlin, ed., *The American Evangelicals, 1800–1900: An Anthology* (New York: Harper and Row, 1968); and Sidney E. Mead, *The Lively Experiment: The Shaping of Christianity in America* (New York: Harper and Row, 1963).

22. *Report of the Board of Indian Commissioners*, 1883, p. 69; *Lake Mohonk Conference Proceedings*, 1900, p. 14.

ideal; until these were abolished and the Indians made to labor to support themselves and their families, there would be no solution to the Indian problem. Allotment of land in severalty to the Indians was insisted upon because the reformers believed that without the personal labor needed to maintain the private homestead the virtue of hard work could never be inculcated. It was common for the reformers to see in labor a fulfillment of an essential command of God, as Gates did in 1885, when he criticized past efforts to aid the Indians. "Above all else we have utterly neglected to teach them the value of honest labor," he said. "Nay, by rations dealt out whether needed or not, we have interfered to suspend the efficient teaching by which God leads men to love and honor labor. We have taken from them the compelling inspiration that grows out of His law, 'if a man will not work, neither shall he eat!'"[23]

Individual development and the stimulation of honest labor, in the evangelical Protestant worldview, were possible only in the perspective of the family. Glorification of hearth and home was an essential element in their program for Christian living, for the Christian purity and virtues that they extolled could take root and be nurtured to full maturity only within the Christian family. What the reformers saw of Indian life, therefore, seriously offended their sensibilities. Not understanding a culture and a family life that differed so markedly from their own experience, the humanitarians saw only heathen practices, which they felt it their duty to stamp out as quickly and as thoroughly as possible. Polygamy was a special abomination, and the whole tribal arrangement was thought to create and perpetuate un-Christian modes of life. Gates's lengthy attack upon tribalism in 1885 was premised fundamentally on the belief that it destroyed the family. "The family is God's unit of society," he declared. "On the integrity of the family depends that of the State. There is no civilization deserving of the name where the family is not the unit in civil government." But the tribal system, he believed, paralyzed both "the desire for property and the family life that ennobles that desire." As allegiance to the tribe and its chiefs grew less, its place would be taken "by the sanctities of family life and an allegiance to the laws which grow naturally out of the family."[24]

The goals envisaged for the Indians were deemed possible because the humanitarians believed in the unity of mankind. If the Indians were basically no different from other human beings—except for the conditioning that came from their environment—then there could be no real obstacle to their assimilation. "Let us forget once and forever the word 'Indian' and all that it has signified in the past," Charles C. Painter told the Lake Mohonk

23. *Report of the Board of Indian Commissioners,* 1885, p. 18.
24. Ibid., pp. 27–29.

Conference in 1889, "and remember only that we are dealing with so many children of a common Father." The doctrine of the brotherhood of man was a cardinal principle of the reformers, who wanted to erase all lines of distinction that separated the Indians from the rest of the nation. And in the process traditional Indian customs were to be simply pushed aside. In speaking of the proposal for severalty legislation, Philip C. Garrett, a regular participant at Lake Mohonk, said in 1886: "If an act of emancipation will buy them life, manhood, civilization, and Christianity, at the sacrifice of a few chieftain's feathers, a few worthless bits of parchment, the cohesion of the tribal relation, and the traditions of their race; then, in the name of all that is really worth having, let us shed the few tears necessary to embalm these relics of the past, and have done with them; and, with fraternal cordiality, let us welcome to the bosom of the nation this brother whom we have wronged long enough." Commissioner of Indian Affairs Thomas J. Morgan, speaking of Indian children, stressed first of all "their kinship with us." He observed that "they, too, are human and endowed with all the faculties of human nature, made in the image of God, bearing the likeness of their Creator, and having the same possibilities of growth and development that are possessed by any other class of children."[25]

The reformers accepted the traditional view that mankind had passed through distinct stages of society in the advance from savagery to civilization, and their goal, like that of so many before them, was to speed up the process by educational and other civilizing programs. They quietly ignored scientific studies that pointed to the slowness of change or the racial inferiority of the Indians, and they ridiculed those who challenged their convictions.[26]

AMERICANIZATION

What especially marked the last decades of the nineteenth century in the development of evangelical Protestantism and gave it its peculiar flavor was the subtle transformation that brought about an almost complete identification of Protestantism and Americanism, the culmination of a

---

25. *Lake Mohonk Conference Proceedings*, 1886, p. 11, and 1889, p. 88; Thomas J. Morgan, *A Plea for the Papoose: An Address at Albany, N.Y., by Gen. T. J. Morgan* (n.p., n.d.), pp. 2–3.

26. Lewis Henry Morgan, whose classic study *Ancient Society; or, Researches in the Lines of Human Progress from Savagery through Barbarism into Civilization* was published in 1877, died in 1881, just as the revitalization of Indian reform began to take effect. On scientific racism of the late nineteenth century, see John S. Haller, Jr., *Outcasts from Evolution: Scientific Attitudes of Racial Inferiority, 1859–1900* (Urbana: University of Illinois Press, 1971).

movement that had extended through the century. "So close was the bond, so deep the union," wrote the religious historian Martin Marty, "that a basic attack on American institutions would have meant an attack on Protestant Christianity itself. Positively, defense of America meant defense of the evangelical empire."[27] The amalgamation of Protestantism and Americanism was not simply an acceptance of evangelical religion by the officials of the state. It came increasingly to be a complacent defense of the social and economic status quo by the churches. Despite warnings of the necessity of separation of church and state, the churches gave a religious endorsement to the American way of life. The perceptive English observer Lord Bryce noted in 1885: "Christianity is in fact understood to be, though not the legally established religion, yet the national religion."[28]

As the nineteenth century drew to a close, two tendencies or forces intensified the union between Protestantism and Americanism. One was the weakening of traditional theological interest, so that the principles of Americanism became in large part the religious creed. The other was the growing threat to the dominance of the "righteous empire" by new forces in the United States, principally the influx of millions of European immigrants, many of whom did not fit the Anglo-Saxon Protestant pattern of America, as well as the growing industrialization and urbanization of the nation, which upset the foundations of the traditional rural Protestant outlook. Afraid that the unity of America was being weakened, the churches sought to strengthen union and conformity.

The Indians were engulfed in this flood of Americanism. Their Americanization, indeed, became the all-embracing goal of the reformers in the last two decades of the century. The reformers were convinced of the divine approbation of the spread of American culture; and the development of the West as an indication of that progress was part of the Protestant mission. There was no intention among the friends of the Indian to protect tribal rights that would obstruct the fruitful exploitation of the nation's domain. "Three hundred thousand people have no right to hold a continent and keep at bay a race able to people it and provide the happy homes of civilization," Lyman Abbott told his colleagues at Lake Mohonk. "We do owe the Indians sacred rights and obligations, but one of those duties is not the right to let them hold forever the land they did not occupy, and which they were not making fruitful for themselves or others." The Indian reservations should be abolished, letting the full blast of civilization rush in upon the Indians. "Christianity is not merely a thing of churches and school-houses," Abbott insisted. "The post-office is a Christianizing in-

27. Marty, *Righteous Empire*, p. 89.
28. Quoted in McLoughlin, *American Evangelicals*, p. 26. See also John Edwin Smylie, "National Ethos and the Church," *Theology Today* 20 (October 1963): 313–21.

stitution; the railroad, with all its corruptions, is a Christianizing power, and will do more to teach the people punctuality than schoolmaster or preacher can."[29]

The government alone could not provide the Christian influence that Americanization demanded, and the reformers continued to rely on the Protestant churches. When President Edward H. Magill of Swarthmore College addressed the Lake Mohonk gathering in 1887, he asserted: "For the realization of all our highest hopes for the Indian, for his education and training, for his introduction as an equal among a civilized people, and for his preparation for the high and responsible duties of American citizenship, we must look largely, if not chiefly, to the religious organizations of our country." The reformers, of course, agreed, and they insisted in 1895: "The government alone cannot solve the Indian problem. Our American civilization is founded upon Christianity. A pagan people cannot be fitted for citizenship without learning the principles and acquiring something of the spirit of a Christian people." As the government made progress in providing secular education, so the duty of the churches was increased "to furnish that contribution which nothing but unofficial, voluntary, and Christian service can furnish toward the emancipation and elevation of the Indian."[30]

The Christian reformers who promoted the Americanization of the Indians were not a small, peripheral group of men and women, who by clever machinations and unjustified propaganda foisted a program upon Congress and the Indian service, as they have sometimes been depicted.[31] Rather, they represented or reflected a powerful and predominant segment of Protestant church membership, and thereby of late nineteenth-century American society. When they spoke, they spoke for a large majority of the nation, expressing views that were widely held, consciously or unconsciously. They were the chief channel through which this Americanism came to bear upon the Indians.[32] It was the fate of the Indians that the solution of the "Indian problem," which had troubled the conscience of many Ameri-

29. *Lake Mohonk Conference Proceedings*, 1885, pp. 51–52.

30. Ibid., 1887, p. 60, and 1895, pp. 106–7.

31. This is the view expressed in George E. Hyde, *A Sioux Chronicle* (Norman: University of Oklahoma Press, 1956). See his chapter "The Brethren," pp. 145–63.

32. The religious men and women who met each year at Lake Mohonk to plot the course of Indian policy represented conservative lines of evangelicalism. They emphasized private elements in their tradition—emphasis upon the conversion and salvation of the individual. The growing social movements in American Protestantism that appeared in response to the problems of industrialization and urbanization were little represented. Of the leaders in humanitarian Indian reform in the 1880s and 1890s, only Lyman Abbott was a notable figure in the movement we label the Social Gospel. For a discussion of "private" Protestantism and "public" Protestantism, see Marty, *Righteous Empire*, p. 179.

cans throughout the nineteenth century, should have been formulated at the end of the century, when such a group was in command. The friends of the Indian set about with good intentions to stamp out Indianness altogether and to substitute for it a uniform Americanness, to destroy all remnants of corporate existence or tribalism and to replace them with an absolute rugged individualism that was foreign to the traditions and to the hearts of the Indian peoples.

OTHER VOICES

A singular voice in Indian reform was that of Helen Hunt Jackson, whose memory stimulated the reformers represented at Lake Mohonk. Born Helen Maria Fiske in Amherst, Massachusetts, in 1830, she married an army engineer, Edward B. Hunt, in 1852. When he died accidentally in 1863, she returned to New England and began a literary career. She wrote articles for *The Independent* and other journals, published travel pieces, and in 1870 brought out a book of poetry. While passing the winter of 1873–1874 in Colorado Springs she met a Quaker businessman, William Sharpless Jackson, whom she married in 1875. Making Colorado Springs her home, she continued writing, producing a series of novels and short stories.[33]

By chance, Mrs. Jackson was in Boston in the winter of 1879–1880, when the great furor over Ponca removal was at its height. In November 1879 she heard Chief Standing Bear and Bright Eyes lecture on the wrongs of the Indians. She had never been noticeably interested in Indians before, but she was suddenly fired by a tremendous indignation and threw herself headlong into the controversy raging over the Ponca affair. She attacked Secretary of the Interior Carl Schurz in a letter in the *New York Tribune*, December 15, 1879, and when his reply did not satisfy her, carried on direct correspondence with him, some of which was printed in the *Tribune* and in the *Boston Daily Advertiser*.[34]

To confirm her position that the government was to blame for the Indians' troubles, she undertook extensive research in the Astor Library in

33. A sympathetic appraisal of Helen Hunt Jackson by a close friend is Thomas Wentworth Higginson, *Contemporaries* (Boston: Houghton, Mifflin and Company, 1899), pp. 142–67. A full-scale biography is Ruth Odell, *Helen Hunt Jackson (H. H.)* (New York: D. Appleton-Century Company, 1939), which includes an exhaustive bibliography of Mrs. Jackson's writings.

34. This correspondence is printed in Helen Hunt Jackson, *A Century of Dishonor: A Sketch of the United States Government's Dealings with Some of the Indian Tribes* (New York: Harper and Brothers, 1881), pp. 359–66.

New York City; as she came across evidence of broken treaties or unjust treatment, she wrote up and published her findings. In a whirlwind of activity, she became a veritable one-person reform movement, circulating petitions and tracts, rebuking editors, army officers, clergymen, college presidents, and congressmen, and filling the press with stinging letters. The material she had gathered she incorporated into her famous volume *A Century of Dishonor: A Sketch of the United States Government's Dealings with Some of the Indian Tribes.* The book was published in January 1881 with a preface by Bishop Henry B. Whipple and an introduction by President Julius H. Seelye of Amherst College.

A Century of Dishonor was a strange book, a disorganized, cluttered compilation of fragments, which told the story of the government's relations with seven tribes. It was a polemic, not balanced history, and everywhere evidenced the haste with which it had been put together. Thrown into the appendix was a further miscellany of data—letters, extracts of reports, abridgments of treaties, and the like. The intention was to awaken the conscience of America to the flagrant wrongs that had been perpetrated upon the Indians. "The history of the United States Government's repeated violations of faith with the Indians," she wrote in the introductory pages of the book, ". . . convicts us, as a nation, not only of having outraged the principles of justice, which are the basis of international law; and of having laid ourselves open to the accusation of both cruelty and perfidy; but of having made ourselves liable to all punishments which follow upon such sins—to arbitrary punishment at the hands of any civilized nation who might see fit to call us to account, and to that more certain natural punishment which, sooner or later, as surely comes from evil-doing as harvest comes from sown seed." Once the people were aroused, she was convinced that they would demand that Congress right the wrongs. She also took care to see that the members of Congress got her message directly, sending a copy of the book to every one of them at her own expense. "What an opportunity for the Congress of 1880," she exclaimed, "to cover itself with a lustre of glory, as the first to cut short our nation's record of cruelties and perjuries! the first to attempt to redeem the name of the United States from the stain of a century of dishonor!"[35]

The book was a sentimental overdramatization of a complex problem, and it was of little help to the statesmen who had to wrestle with practical solutions to Indian questions. But there is no doubt that its author touched sympathetic chords among the reformers and much of the public.[36] Her

35. Ibid., pp. 29, 31.
36. A perceptive analysis of Jackson's work is Allan Nevins, "Helen Hunt Jackson: Sentimentalist vs. Realist," *American Scholar* 10 (Summer 1941): 269–85. There is a biting criticism of *A Century of Dishonor* in Theodore Roosevelt, *The Winning of the West*

writings brought her fame; and her later concern for the Mission Indians in California helped their cause. Her fictionalized treatment of the California Indian story in *Ramona*, published in 1884, enjoyed more popular success than *A Century of Dishonor*, although it never quite fulfilled its author's hope that it would be another *Uncle Tom's Cabin* in the drive for racial justice. But the strain of her crusade was too much, and she died in Colorado Springs in August 1885, concerned for the Indians to the very last.

With her recitation of wrongs, Helen Hunt Jackson looked to the past rather than to the future. Her death just as the great thrust in Indian reform was starting meant that, except for the case of the Mission Indians, she never became part of the positive movement for reform. Yet the title of her book, if not its substance, stuck in men's minds, and her name became irrevocably associated with nineteenth-century Indian reform.[37]

The humanitarian Indian reformers enjoyed a near unanimity. To be sure, they faced western sentiment expressed by men like Senators Plumb and Teller, who claimed that easterners were unacquainted with the Indians and offered impractical solutions to problems they did not really understand, but there was little counterreform activity. The notable exception was Dr. Thomas A. Bland, who began his reform career as the associate of Alfred B. Meacham in the 1870s. Meacham and Bland in the early pages of their publication *The Council Fire* did not depart materially from the programs that were so enthusiastically promoted by the new reform organizations. Even when Bland succeeded to full control of the journal on Meacham's death early in 1882, he did not appear to be in opposition to the main currents of Indian reform. The *Council Fire* reported favorably on the 1882 petition of the Women's National Indian Association and strongly sympathized with Dawes's support of the petition against the western senators. The editor welcomed the formation of the Indian Rights Association and other reform organizations and offered them the columns of the *Coun-*

(New York: G. P. Putnam's Sons, 1889), 1: 257–64: "The purpose of the book is excellent, but the spirit in which it is written cannot be called even technically honest. As a polemic, it is possible that it did not do harm (though the effect of even a polemic is marred by hysterical indifference to facts). As a history it would be beneath criticism, were it not that the high character of the author and her excellent literary work in other directions have given it a fictitious value and made it much quoted by the large class of amiable but maudlin fanatics concerning whom it may be said that the excellence of their intentions but indifferently atones for the invariable folly and ill effect of their actions. It is not too much to say that the book is thoroughly untrustworthy from cover to cover, and that not a single statement it contains should be accepted without independent proof; for even those that are not absolutely false are often as bad on account of so much of the truth having been suppressed."

37. Tributes of the reformers to Helen Hunt Jackson appear in *Lake Mohonk Conference Proceedings*, 1885, pp. 68–71.

cil Fire for communicating with each other and with the public. The allotment of land in severalty, a key proposal of the reformers, was agreed to in
principle, provided that Indian consent be obtained.[38]

But Bland soon parted company with the rest of the reformers. In November 1885 he organized the National Indian Defence Association and
gathered supporters in the East, who preferred to conserve Indian ways,
and among the chiefs and squawmen on the reservations, who held fast to
the old ways that benefited them. The National Indian Defence Association hoped to slow down if not stop the movement for land in severalty
and for citizenship. It argued that the immediate dissolution of tribal relations would be an impediment to the civilization of the Indians, that individual allotments would motivate the Indians to part with their holdings,
and that although education might help the next generation, it could not
solve the problems of the present one.[39] Bland and his friends actively promoted their views in Washington and in the national press and appeared to
have some influence in high places.

The Indian Rights Association fought strongly against that influence,
insisting upon the view of Indian policy espoused by the Lake Mohonk reformers. When President Grover Cleveland, in a meeting with Charles C.
Painter, asked whether the Indian Rights Association might not reach
an understanding with the Indian Defence Association, Painter answered
bluntly: "No Sir! Our views of the policy to be pursued are diametrically
opposite. . . . We are entirely opposed to the ideas of that Association. It
seems to me as if they are defending the Indian's right to be an Indian, and
would perpetuate the conditions which must force him to remain Indian."
In a long letter printed in the *Boston Herald* on December 27, 1886, and
then circulated in pamphlet form, Herbert Welsh made the same sort of
analysis of the "irreconcilable difference of opinion" that separated Dr.
Bland and his association from Senator Dawes and "other prominent defenders of Indian rights":

> Dr. Bland's efforts have been directed toward keeping the Indian as he
> is, his tribal relations untouched, his reservations intact; and in op-
> posing the sale of his unused lands, upon no matter how equitable
> conditions, for white settlement. . . . Senator Dawes and the Indian
> Rights Association, on the other hand, believe that such a theory is
> prejudicial to the best interests of the Indians, and even were it not so

38. *Council Fire* 5 (March 1882): 88–92; 6 (June 1883): 84; 6 (September 1883): 121–
22; 6 (October 1883): 137–38; 7 (January 1884): 7.

39. *Preamble, Platform, and Constitution of the National Indian Defence Association* (Philadelphia: Rufus H. Darby, 1885), reprinted in Prucha, *Americanizing the
American Indians*, pp. 141–45.

that it is wholly impracticable, that the settlement of the Indian question, in view of the uncontrollable pressure of white civilization upon the reservations, can only be reached through a careful, wise and equitable adjustment of the rights and needs of the white man and of the Indian; that under fair conditions the Indian should be persuaded to sell unused and unneeded land, upon which the white should be permitted to enter for *bona fide* settlement.[40]

Bland's attempts to defeat the severalty bill and his threat to challenge it in the courts were met by accusations that he was in the pay of the chiefs who opposed reforms.[41] Bland's views if not his methods, however, look better in the perspective of time than many of those of the united humanitarian reformers, who in the 1880s regarded criticism from the National Indian Defence Association as little more than the nipping of a dog at their heels. "Vituperation from that source," Senator Dawes declared in 1887, "is considered by all acquainted with it as a certificate of fidelity to public trust."[42]

40. Charles C. Painter to Herbert Welsh, January 22, 1887, in Indian Rights Association Papers, Welsh Collection, Historical Society of Pennsylvania; see also Painter to Welsh, January 8, 1886, and February 9, 1887, ibid; Herbert Welsh, *The Indian Problem: Secretary Welsh of the Indian Rights Association Reviews and Criticises Dr. Bland's Recent Statements—Dr. Sunderland a Self-Confessed Novice* (Philadelphia, 1886), p. 6.

41. See the flier of the Indian Rights Association, *Friendship That Asks for Pay: Pretended Friends of the Indians and Their Methods* (Philadelphia, 1887), reprinting an article from the *New York Tribune*, March 13, 1887; Frank Wood to Dawes, December 23, 1886, and T. H. Tibbles to Dawes, March 16, 1887, in Henry L. Dawes Papers, Library of Congress. A reasonable statement of Bland's opposition to the Dawes Severalty Act is "The New Indian Policy: Land in Severalty," *American* 14 (May 21, 1887): 73–74.

42. Dawes to John J. Janney, April 29, 1887, Dawes Papers, Letter Book, p. 139.

CHAPTER 25

The Reservations and Reform

Dismantling the Great Sioux Reserve.

Mission Indians of California. Promotion of

Civilization. Continuing Liquor Problems.

Opposition to Reservations.

When the new Christian reformers came on the scene about 1880, the reservation system was firmly established and had become the foundation of United States Indian policy. The reformers at first accepted the reservations and worked within the system, seeking to protect the land rights of the Indians, although they did not hesitate to promote the reduction of reservations in order to speed the Indians' acceptance of an individualized agricultural existence. They supported the reservations, too, as protected enclaves in which the programs of civilization and Americanization could move forward. Yet in the end the reservations became an abomination, for they symbolized the great separation between the Indians and the rest of American society, a separation that precluded the absolute Americanization that was the ultimate goal of the reform organizations and their friends in the government.[1]

DISMANTLING THE GREAT SIOUX RESERVE

Division of the Great Sioux Reserve was the most blatant example of reduction of a large reservation as a humanitarian measure in order to force

1. Some of the material in this chapter is taken directly from Francis Paul Prucha, *American Indian Policy in Crisis: Christian Reformers and the Indian, 1865–1900* (Norman: University of Oklahoma Press, 1976), pp. 169–226.

the Indians into an economic and social pattern acceptable to the whites. Driven by the fear that if the Indians did not agree to give up some of their holdings for fair compensation they were likely to lose them all without recompense, the reformers led the movement to cut down the reservation held by the Teton Sioux in Dakota.[2]

The Great Sioux Reserve, stretching from the Missouri River to the western boundary of Dakota, had been set off for the Indians by the Treaty of Fort Laramie in 1868. Although they were allowed to use the Powder River country as hunting grounds, the Sioux chiefs who signed the treaty agreed to settle on the new reserve, and the treaty was full of provisions for promoting civilization. With the Sioux boundaries clearly set, the government in article 12 of the treaty assured the Indians that no future cession of any part of the reservation would be valid until approved by at least three-fourths of the adult male Indians occupying or interested in it.[3]

It was not long before the discovery of gold in the Black Hills in the southwestern portion of the Sioux reserve upset the 1868 arrangements. Whites swarmed into the area, eager for gold, and the government found it difficult to live up to its pledge to guarantee the reservation for the Sioux. The familiar tactics of attempting to persuade the Indians to cede the coveted section soon began. A commission headed by Senator William B. Allison of Iowa was appointed on June 18, 1875, to treat with the Sioux for the relinquishing of the Black Hills, but its meetings with the Indians accomplished nothing, and its report ended with the recommendation that Congress should simply fix a fair price for the Black Hills and present the matter to the Indians "as a finality."[4]

After the defeat of Custer, while the army was still engaged against the hostiles, Congress decided on such an ultimatum. On August 15, 1876, it directed that the Indians were to receive no further subsistence unless they relinquished all claims to land outside the 1868 reserve and all of that reservation lying west of the 103d meridian (an area including the Black Hills).[5] The president appointed a commission to carry this word to the Sioux. The commission—headed by George W. Manypenny, former commissioner of Indian affairs, and including among others Newton Edmunds, onetime governor of Dakota Territory, and Bishop Henry B. Whipple, the

2. An excellent brief account, which emphasizes the effect on the Sioux, is Robert M. Utley, *The Last Days of the Sioux Nation* (New Haven: Yale University Press, 1963), pp. 40–59. A somewhat more detailed account is James C. Olson, *Red Cloud and the Sioux Problem* (Lincoln: University of Nebraska Press, 1965), pp. 286–319.

3. Kappler, pp. 998–1007.

4. "Report of the Commission Appointed to Treat with the Sioux Indians for the Relinquishment of the Black Hills," CIA Report, 1875, serial 1680, pp. 686–702.

5. 19 *United States Statutes* 192.

old reformer—met with the Indians at the Red Cloud Agency in early September. There Manypenny laid down the government's terms, and other commissioners lectured the Indians about the paths to civilization. Although it seems clear from the speeches of the Indians at the signing that they did not fully understand the import of the agreement, the chiefs marked their Xs and the scene was repeated at each of the agencies. "We finished our labors in the Indian country," the commissioners said, "with our hearts full of gratitude to God, who had guarded and protected us, and had directed our labors to a successful issue." They had won the cession of the Black Hills, but only by ignoring article 12 of the treaty of 1868. They had settled for the signatures of the chiefs and headmen only of each tribe, but this seemed not to trouble the good men on the commission, who concluded their report with a fine-sounding plea for good faith and justice.[6]

The commission's work was enthusiastically received by the Board of Indian Commissioners. Its report, the board said, "so truthfully reflects the firm convictions of the members of this board, that we would, if possible, emphasize those views by adopting them as our own."[7] This blindness of the commission and of the board to the disregard of the treaty stipulations calling for consent of the Indians is hard to understand. Yet so strong was their belief in the necessity of changing the Indians into counterparts of white farmers that they vividly saw past wrongs but did not notice the ones they themselves were perpetrating.

The land hunger of the whites was not sated by the large bite into the Sioux homelands made by the agreement of 1876. By the early 1880s, new pressures had built up along the borders of the reservation that were all but irresistible. The Chicago and Northwestern Railroad had reached Pierre, and the Chicago, Milwaukee, and St. Paul had built as far as Chamberlain, one hundred miles south on the Missouri. Here they were stopped in their drive to reach the Black Hills beyond. It seemed to Dakota promoters that civilization had come to a halt, blocked by the Great Sioux Reserve to the west. On August 7, 1882, at the instigation of Richard F. Pettigrew, Dakota delegate in Congress, a rider to the sundry civil appropriations bill provided for negotiations with the Sioux in order to modify existing treaties. To carry out this mandate Secretary of the Interior Henry M. Teller named a commission headed by Newton Edmunds, by now an experienced Indian negotiator, and comprising Peter Shannon, onetime chief justice of the Da-

---

6. The commission's report, dated December 18, 1876, is in *Senate Executive Document* no. 9, 44–2, serial 1718. The document also includes the journal of proceedings. The agreement, ratified by Congress on February 28, 1877, is in 19 *United States Statutes* 254–64.

7. *Report of the Board of Indian Commissioners*, 1876, p. 4.

kota territorial supreme court, and James H. Teller, of Cleveland, Ohio, his own brother. Samuel D. Hinman, a missionary who had often participated in councils with the Sioux, served as interpreter.[8]

The Edmunds commission presented to the Indians an agreement it had brought along already prepared. The document called for the cession of reservation lands between the White and Cheyenne rivers and for the lands north of the Cheyenne and west of the 102d meridian—altogether some eleven million acres, including a wide corridor from the Missouri River to the Black Hills. What was left was divided into five separate reservations, one for each of the agencies: Standing Rock, Cheyenne River, Lower Brulé, Rosebud, and Pine Ridge. In return, each head of a family was to be allowed to choose a 320-acre tract, plus 80 acres for each minor child. Those who made a selection of land would receive a cow and a team of oxen, and the government agreed to provide twenty-five thousand cows and one thousand bulls (all carrying the brand of the Indian Office and not to be sold or slaughtered without permission) as a foundation herd to be divided among the reservations according to population. By cajolery and threats the commission gathered the signatures of a number of chiefs and headmen and, disregarding the need for approval of three-fourths of the adult males, submitted the agreement as an accomplished fact. Secretary Teller sent it to the president to be forwarded to Congress for ratification with the remark that he considered it "favorable alike to the Indians and the Government."[9]

Outcries of protest arose immediately from the Indians, who claimed with good cause that they had been victimized, and from the Indian Rights Association and other humanitarian friends of the Indians, who pointed to the failure to obtain the necessary consent of the Sioux. Senator Dawes was able to block the measure, and the commission was sent back for more signatures. The second round, entrusted to Hinman, was little more successful than the first, and Congress refused to approve the agreement.

The reformers now entered the picture in full force; here was a cause in which they could fight for Indian rights and justice and at the same time promote the advance of civilization. The Indian Rights Association, successful in its drive to defeat the Edmunds agreement, determined to push the matter to the fullest. In May 1883 Herbert Welsh visited the Sioux at the Dakota agencies and produced a lengthy report that roundly condemned the terms of the Edmunds agreement and the methods of the commission. The Board of Indian Commissioners sent two of its members to visit the Sioux during the same summer to study "the conditions of the

8. 22 *United States Statutes* 328. Documents on the formation of the commission as well as its report are in *Senate Executive Document* no. 70, 48–1, serial 2165.

9. Teller to the president, February 1, 1883, *Senate Executive Document* no. 70, 48–1, serial 2165, p. 31. The agreements are printed ibid., pp. 34–41.

several Sioux tribes and their attitudes toward the proposed reduction of their reservation."[10] And a committee of missionaries, with Bishop William H. Hare as chairman, drew up its own statement, which scored the Edmunds commission because it did not offer appropriate compensation to the Indians, did not get the proper consent of the tribesmen, and did not make enough provision for taking land in severalty and the development of farming. All the reformers agreed, however, that the reserve should be reduced and divided. The missionaries reported:

> The undersigned advocate the division in any just way, of the Great Sioux Reservation into a number of separate reserves for the several tribes, and the cession, on equitable terms, of a portion of the present reservation to the United States for settlement by the whites. The reservation in its present shape and size is, in their opinion, a serious hindrance to the prosperity and welfare of the whites, and a great impediment to the civilization of the Indians. But, while holding this opinion, they think that the method of division provided for in the proposed agreement is not just, and that the consideration offered is not equitable.[11]

Welsh eagerly accepted this position, and his report reinforced the missionaries' statement; he was especially outspoken on the pressure that had been used to force the reluctant Indians to sign. The young Indian Rights Association for whom he spoke then forged ahead energetically to accomplish the end in view, and it was strongly seconded by the Lake Mohonk Conference, which met in October 1883. The first topic on the Lake Mohonk agenda was the Sioux agreement, and the conference reiterated in formal resolutions what Welsh and the others had concluded from their visits. The Board of Indian Commissioners at its January meeting with the representatives of the missionary boards adopted another resolution of the same tenor.[12]

Senator Dawes soon gave official support to the position of the reform groups. When the Senate refused to approve the Edmunds commission agreement, largely at Dawes's insistence, it appointed a select committee with Dawes as chairman to investigate the Sioux reservation situation. Dawes's committee visited all the Sioux agencies, interviewed Indians and agency personnel, and interrogated the Edmunds commission as well. Its

10. Herbert Welsh, *Report of a Visit to the Great Sioux Reserve, Dakota; Made during the Months of May and June, 1883, in Behalf of the Indian Rights Association* (Philadelphia, 1883); *Report of the Board of Indian Commissioners, 1883*, pp. 3, 33–38.

11. *Report of the Board of Indian Commissioners, 1883*, pp. 34–35.

12. *Report of the Indian Rights Association, 1883*, pp. 13–14; *Lake Mohonk Conference Proceedings, 1883*, pp. 4–8; *Report of the Board of Indian Commissioners, 1883*, pp. 68–69.

condemnation of the commission was, if anything, stronger than that of Welsh and the missionaries, with whose general line of argument it substantially agreed. But Dawes was no more in favor of the status quo of the Sioux in Dakota than were Welsh and his friends. He much favored cutting up the large reservation and opening part of it to white settlement if it could be done without violating treaty stipulations, and he hoped to convert what he considered the useless and unnecessary Indian lands into a permanent fund, the annual income of which could be devoted to "the civilization, education, and advancement in agriculture and other self-supporting pursuits" of the Sioux.[13]

Dawes submitted with the report of his select committee a bill that incorporated the changes he advocated. The main point was the establishment of a permanent fund for the Sioux. The fund was to total $1 million and be held in the Treasury of the United States to the credit of the Indians at 5 percent interest, one half of the income to be used for the promotion of "industrial and other suitable education" and the other half in whatever way the secretary of the interior would judge best for the advancement of the Indians "in civilization and self-support." All the land acquired by the bill was to be disposed of under existing homestead acts, but the settler would pay fifty cents an acre, in four equal annual payments. The money thus received would reimburse the government for the permanent fund, for the purchase of stock for the Indians to encourage them in herding, and for government expenses in administering the act. The bands were to receive a patent in fee for the reduced separate reservations, although the lands would be held in trust for twenty-five years. Beyond this, however, the president was authorized to issue allotments in severalty to Indians who seemed to him to be ready for them, and patents for such individual allotments were to override those granted to the tribes for lands held in common. The bill provided explicitly that the law would be null and void without the consent of three-fourths of the Indian men.[14]

The passage of this bill, known as Senator Dawes's Sioux Bill, became one of the primary objectives of the reform groups. The Indian Rights Association warmly supported the measure, and to promote it Welsh prepared an abstract of the bill together with arguments in favor of its passage, which he circulated widely as a means of stirring up public sentiment that would influence Congress. He pointed first to the benefits to the whites, for the cession would furnish a "magnificent highway" between "the civilization of Eastern and Western Dakota" and thus provide a "grand step forward in the march of prosperity" for the people of Dakota Territory. But

---

13. The Dawes committee report, dated March 7, 1884, is in *Senate Report* no. 283, 48–1, serial 2174.

14. Senate bill 1755, 48th Congress, 1st session.

second, in an argument "of equal weight," he noted that the bill would provide "ample justice for the Sioux Indians" and "swell the number of that class among them which is looking and striving toward civilization."[15] The Board of Indian Commissioners urged the prompt passage of the bill; and the Lake Mohonk Conference heartily approved it, proffered thanks to Senator Dawes, and commended the bill to all friends of the Indians.[16]

Dawes's Sioux bill passed easily in the Senate, but it had trouble in the House, where it was joined with the general land in severalty bill and a bill to provide relief for the Mission Indians as the essential package of legislation demanded by the humanitarians. Although the severalty bill finally passed early in 1887, the other two measures were put off again. The reformers continued their efforts, for they were convinced of the rightness of their cause. "The waves of an importunate civilization that cannot long be either staid or stopped, at the bidding of any man," Welsh wrote, "are breaking incessantly upon the border of the Great Reservation. It is the deep conviction of the Indian Rights Association that sound policy now demands the opening of a lawful channel for the advance of this mighty tide. Hesitation at the present critical time invites a possible catastrophe."[17]

The House at last bowed to the pressure. On April 30, 1888, Dawes's measure became law, and Secretary of the Interior William F. Vilas appointed a commission led by Richard Henry Pratt, head of the Carlisle Indian School, to submit the act to the various bands of Sioux to get their consent. There was to be no negotiation; the commissioners were to inform the Indians that Congress had drawn up the agreement with care and that the president after wise scrutiny had approved it and that it embodied "the desire and purpose of the Government of the United States for the advancement and civilization" of the Sioux. The commissioners, moreover, were to impress upon the Indians the fact that new conditions made the old reservation no longer viable and that if they did not accept the "generous and beneficent" arrangements now proposed by Congress, their future would be "problematical and uncertain."[18]

The Pratt commission made little headway against the intransigence of the Indians, who united in opposition to the new agreement. Having been severely burned before, the Sioux were now careful to stay far away from

15. *Report of the Indian Rights Association*, 1884, pp. 14–15; *Lake Mohonk Conference Proceedings*, 1884, pp. 17–19.

16. *Report of the Board of Indian Commissioners*, 1884, p. 11; *Lake Mohonk Conference Proceedings*, 1884, p. 16. Secretary Teller urged the passage of the measure in Report of the Secretary of the Interior, 1884, *House Executive Document* no. 1, part 5, 48–2, serial 2286, p. xiii.

17. Indian Rights Association leaflet, February 23, 1886.

18. 25 *United States Statutes* 94–104; instructions of Vilas to commissioners, July 9, 1888, in *Senate Executive Document* no. 17, 50–2, serial 2610, pp. 30–33.

the fire. Even when Little Wound, American Horse, and other tribal leaders were called to Washington for new talks, no progress was made. Although Vilas proposed to double the permanent fund, the Indians demanded still higher compensation, and the secretary sent them home. He judged their demands excessive and did not think that large sums would benefit them, for the interest would yield so much money for distribution "as to remove the incentive for their personal effort at subsistence and improvement."[19]

The Pratt commission's report, submitted on November 24, 1888, was full of the reformers' views. It excoriated the nonprogressive chiefs who controlled the bands in order to keep things as they were and thus prevent the elevation of the masses. "In brief," it said, "the defeat of this act was a victory for indolence, barbarism, and degradation as against the influence of the farm, the work-shop, the schools, and the Gospel."[20]

The supporters of the program were not yet ready to give up, for the urgency of the need had increased with the passage of the Omnibus Bill in February 1889 providing for the admission to statehood of North and South Dakota in November. On March 3, 1889, Congress authorized a new commission to negotiate for the reduction and division of the Sioux reservation. A separate act approved the same day set forth a new and decidedly more generous agreement, which the commission proposed to the Indians for their consent. The permanent fund was increased to $3 million; homesteaders were to pay $1.25 an acre for the first three years, $.75 for the next two, and $.50 thereafter, and the expenses of the program no longer would be deducted from the income. Allotments in severalty were not to be undertaken on any of the reservations until favored by a majority of adult males, and the size of the allotment was raised from 160 to 320 acres. Unrelated to the main issue, but helpful in getting assent to the agreement, was a provision to pay for ponies seized by the army during the war of 1876.[21]

The new commission was dominated by Major General George Crook, who used his long experience and his knowledge of Indian temperament and customs to succeed where previous commissions had failed. The commission put on feasts for the Indians, permitted tribal dances that had long been proscribed, and in general put the Sioux at ease, until little by little the Indians' will to resist was broken. But Crook also spoke bluntly to the Indians: "Last year when you refused to accept that bill, Congress came very near opening this reservation anyhow. It is certain that you will never get any better terms than are offered in this bill, and the chances are that

19. Commission's report, November 24, 1888, *Senate Executive Document* no. 17, 50–2, serial 2610; Report of the Secretary of the Interior, 1888, *House Executive Document* no. 1, part 5, 50–2, serial 2636, p. lxv.

20. *Senate Executive Document* no. 17, 50–2, serial 2610, pp. 13, 23, 29–30.

21. 25 *United States Statutes* 888–99, 1002.

MAP 10: The Sioux Reservations, 1890

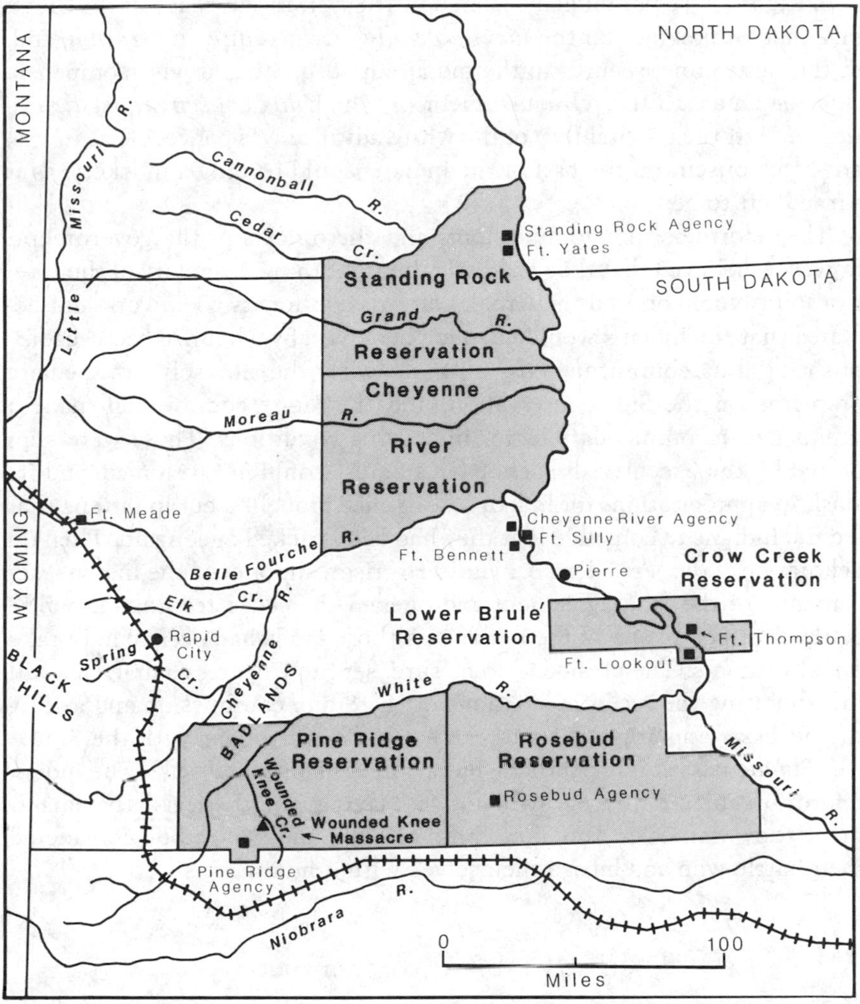

you will not get so good. And it strikes me that instead of complaining of the past, you had better provide for the future."[22]

In the end, out of 5,678 eligible to vote, 4,463 signified their approval.[23]

22. The report of the Sioux commission, dated December 24, 1889, with proceedings and other related material is in *Senate Executive Document* no. 51, 51–1, serial 2682; the quotation is on p. 172. There is an excellent account of the work of the commission in winning Sioux approval in Utley, *Last Days of the Sioux Nation*, pp. 50–54.

23. A table showing the number of eligible voters and the number who signed at each agency is given in *Senate Executive Document* no. 51, 51–1, serial 2682, p. 35. Crook wrote at Pine Ridge on July 9: "Lovely day. Tuned different Indians up. Got a good many

But the paradox of the reformers' position had become apparent. The Indian Rights Association had declared in 1885, in its advocacy of the Sioux bill, that "it provides for the *inevitable advance of white civilization*, and, at the same time, secures to the Indian an adequate and wise compensation for lands, to the relinquishment of which *his consent must be obtained*."[24] If the inevitability of the white advance was conceded, as it was, any free consent on the part of the Indians could be only a mockery, as it turned out to be.

The reformers, the commissions, and the officers of the government, however, believed that they had done the right thing. Secretary of the Interior John Noble praised the Crook commission for its good work and declared that the Indians would be much benefited by what had been accomplished.[25] But commitment to ultimate goals did not solve immediate problems on the Sioux reservation, and the Sioux commission made a number of recommendations for improving conditions. These were supported by the executive branch, but Congress could not be forced, and its slash in appropriations for Indian subsistence brought a cut in rations that led the Indians to conclude that they had been tricked once again. Then on February 9, 1890, President Benjamin Harrison announced the Indians' acceptance of the land agreement and opened the ceded territory to white settlement before any of the Indians on those lands had been able to take out allotments. The president, to be sure, sent to Congress a draft of a bill incorporating the recommendations of the Sioux commission and asking the necessary appropriations to carry out the agreement with the Sioux. The Senate passed it on April 26, but again the House refused.[26] The Indian reform organizations took little notice. Having won the legislative enactment they wanted in the Sioux bills of 1888 and 1889, they considered their battle won and busied themselves with other matters.

MISSION INDIANS OF CALIFORNIA

While the Indian Rights Association and other humanitarian reformers were carrying on their fight for the Sioux bill, they paid special attention

---

signatures by different young Indians who were made to see that they must think for themselves, and in this way it is breaking down the opposition of the old, unreconstructed chiefs." Martin F. Schmitt, ed., *General George Crook: His Autobiography* (Norman: University of Oklahoma Press, 1946), p. 286.

24. *Report of the Indian Rights Association*, 1885, p. 14, emphasis added.

25. Report of the Secretary of the Interior, 1889, *House Executive Document* no. 1, part 5, 51–1, serial 2724, p. xi.

26. The story is told in Utley, *Last Days of the Sioux Nation*, pp. 54–59.

also to the Mission Indians of California, "a singularly helpless race in a singularly anomalous position." Left unprotected by federal policy in California because of the failure to ratify treaties with them, these Indians and the loss of their lands became renewed concerns as reform sentiment grew after the Civil War. Although the Board of Indian Commissioners in 1871 had recommended that the Indians be given clear title to their lands, and the Indian Office, after a special agent had been sent to investigate in 1873, had recommended congressional action, nothing was done. In 1880 the commissioner of Indian affairs could report only that "the condition of the Mission Indians in California becomes, yearly, more deplorable."[27]

Then came the new burst of reforming energy and the stirring up of public sentiment to demand a righting of all Indian wrongs. The Mission Indians were not forgotten. In January 1883 Helen Hunt Jackson was appointed to investigate their condition and to make recommendations for correcting injustices. With the aid of Abbot Kinney, a Californian of sympathetic views, she submitted a report on July 13, 1883. Declaring that, with such long neglect and multiplication of wrongs, it was no longer possible to render the Indians a full measure of justice and that what was possible was only some measure of atonement, Jackson and Kinney made ten recommendations, which focused on confirmation of land titles to the Indians, appointment of lawyers to safeguard the Indians' rights, more schools, and agricultural and other assistance. The recommendations were incorporated into a bill by the Indian Office and submitted to Congress, where it passed the Senate but was not acted upon by the House.[28]

Jackson used material from her California investigations in her popular novel *Ramona*, which romanticized the Mission Indians and dramatized their plight. But the failure of Congress to act disheartened her, and she wrote to Senator Dawes in August 1884, "I am sick at heart, and discouraged, I see nothing more I can do, or write." She was considerably cheered, however, when the Indian Rights Association took up the cause. The association's Washington agent, Charles C. Painter, visited her shortly before her death and accepted for the Indian Rights Association a "most solemn obligation" to carry on where she left off, a trust the reform group

27. Helen Hunt Jackson and Abbot Kinney, *Report on the Condition and Needs of the Mission Indians of California* (Washington: GPO, 1883); *Report of the Board of Indian Commissioners*, 1871, pp. 9–10; CIA Report, 1873, serial 1601, pp. 397–409; CIA Report, 1875, serial 1680, pp. 511–14; CIA Report, 1880, serial 1959, pp. 99–101.

28. Jackson and Kinney, *Condition and Needs of the Mission Indians*, pp. 7–13. The report is summarized in CIA Report, 1883, serial 2191, pp. 36–37. It furnished the basis for the program of the reformers in regard to the Mission Indians. The proposed bill and Commissioner Hiram Price's support of it are in *Senate Executive Document* no. 49, 48–1, serial 2162, pp. 2–7.

earnestly fulfilled. Most of this responsibility came to rest upon Painter, whose first visit to the Mission Indians in 1885 left him with a conviction that their condition was deplorable but also that their title to the land could be vindicated in the courts. In 1886 Painter traveled to California again, this time not only as the agent of the Indian Rights Association, but having been delegated as well by a special committee on the Mission Indians appointed by the Lake Mohonk Conference in October 1886. His task was to investigate legal means of supporting the Indians' rights and to find legal counsel in California to undertake the work. "We are approaching the end of the period," Painter wrote, "when mere agitation can accomplish anything of great value." Even legislation in the Indians' favor was not enough; someone had to pay attention to particular cases of wrong and hardship as they arose and devote the time, labor, and money required in the defense of Indian rights. It was this work in which Painter and the Indian Rights Association intended to engage. In fact, the association paid the expenses of the special attorney appointed by the government to defend the Mission Indians when government funds were not forthcoming. In 1887 Painter went once again to California as agent of the Indian Rights Association and of the Lake Mohonk committee, to survey in detail the circumstances of the Indians and search out intelligent solutions.[29]

The reformers' pressure brought some action on the part of the Indian Office, which did what it could to remove intruders from lands on which the Indians lived. Then on January 31, 1888, the Supreme Court of California, in the case of *Byrne* v. *Alas et al.*, decided in favor of Indian rights to the land. Painter received the decision with great joy. "In this case," he said, "we turn down the last page of the history of our shame, and are about to enter upon a brighter and more creditable chapter, in which is to be recorded our atonement for these wrongs." The commissioner of Indian affairs declared the decision "the most valuable thing which has been definitely secured for these Indians since public attention has been turned to their sufferings and wrongs."[30]

29. Jackson to Dawes, August 27, 1884, Henry L. Dawes Papers, Box 26, Library of Congress; Charles C. Painter, *A Visit to the Mission Indians of Southern California and Other Western Tribes* (Philadelphia, 1886), pp. 12, 14–18; Indian Rights Association, *The Case of the Mission Indians in Southern California, and the Action of the Indian Rights Association in Supporting the Defense of Their Legal Rights* (Philadelphia, 1886), p. 4; Painter, *A Visit to the Mission Indians of California* (Philadelphia, 1887), pp. 4, 18; Painter, *The Condition of Affairs in Indian Territory and California* (Philadelphia, 1888), pp. 49–102. The special concern shown for the Mission Indians by a member of the Women's National Indian Association is discussed in Francis Paul Prucha, "A 'Friend of the Indian' in Milwaukee: Mrs. O. J. Hiles and the Wisconsin Indian Association," *Historical Messenger of the Milwaukee County Historical Society* 29 (Autumn 1973): 80–84.
30. Painter, *Condition of Affairs in Indian Territory and California*, p. 92; CIA

The judicial support of Indian titles in California did not put an end to pleas for congressional action, for although the Senate had passed bills for their relief in the Forty-eighth, Forty-ninth, and Fiftieth Congresses, the House still refused to act. The reformers kept up their demands, for as delay continued, the situation of the Indians deteriorated. Finally the House gave in. An act of January 12, 1891, provided that the secretary of the interior appoint three disinterested persons as commissioners to arrange a just and satisfactory settlement. The commissioners were to select reservations for the Indians to be held in trust by the government for twenty-five years. White settlers were to be removed and compensated for their improvements and allotments provided for individuals judged to be "so advanced in civilization as to be capable of owning and managing land in severalty." The act allowed each head of family not more than 640 acres of grazing land plus 20 acres of arable land, and smaller amounts were designated for single persons. The allotments would be granted in fee simple after a twenty-five-year trust period.[31]

The law fitted perfectly into the patterns of land tenure that the humanitarian reformers had decided upon for the Indians, emphasizing individual holdings in fee simple but with restrictions against alienation for a term of years. The Mission Indians were no more successful in attaining the great benefits envisaged than were the majority of American Indians, who soon lost most of the land that reformers had hoped to guarantee them forever. But with the passage of the law, the reformers rejoiced that they had accomplished their goal, and concern for the Mission Indians ceased to be a major element in Indian reform.

PROMOTION OF CIVILIZATION

The reservations segregated the Indians from the whites in order to prevent violent conflict, but the reformers initially gave them enthusiastic support also as hothouses in which the seedlings of civilization could get a protected start. Because the reservations were to serve this purpose, humanitarians had always had an interest in agency affairs, and the government accepted their help.

As the nineteenth century waned and the Indians were forced to accept reservations and were then squeezed ever more tightly together on reduced

---

Report, 1888, serial 2637, p. lxiv. Both Painter and the commissioner reprinted the decision in full, so important did they deem it.

31. 26 *United States Statutes* 712–14. For recommendations of the Mission Indian commission and some of its problems, see *House Executive Document* no. 96, 52–1, serial 2954.

holdings, the reservations and the agencies that governed them became of greater and greater critical importance. Because the great majority of the Indians with whom the reformers were concerned lived on reservations, these land areas were the places in which the Indian policies were applied. They were the means to transform the Indians into American ciizens, for the segregation and isolation they provided allowed the civilization process to proceed unhindered by outside forces. The reservations were a controlled society in which, the sooner the better, tribal ways would fall before the ways of the dominant white society.

The inhabitants of the reservation, however, were not a homogeneous group in their reaction to the purposes the government and the reformers had in mind. Most reservations, in fact, were split into two factions, designated by the reformers as "progressives" and "nonprogressives," or "conservatives." Herbert Welsh in 1891 described the divisions among the Sioux in typical terms:

> There are two great and sharply defined parties among the Sioux Indians to-day, either of which is the creation and representation of an idea. These ideas are antagonistic and irreconcilable.
>
> First. There is the old pagan and non-progressive party. Inspired by sentiments of hostility to the Government and to white civilization, it believes in what is Indian, and hates what belongs to the white man. It delights in the past, and its dream is that the past shall come back again—the illimitable prairie, with vast herds of the vanished buffalo, the deer, the antelope, all the excitement of the chase, and the still fiercer thrill of bloody struggles with rival savage men. Consider what has been the education of the men who form this party— eating Government rations paid them in lieu of ceded lands, idleness, visits to distant relatives and friends, constant feasts and dances, with oft-repeated recitals from the older men of their own deeds of valor and the achievements of their ancestors. . . .
>
> Second. A new, progressive, and what may properly be termed Christian party, whose life was begotten, nourished, and trained by missionary enterprise and devotion. . . . In these Christian Indians is to be found abundant food for a study of the germs and first awakenings of civilized life rich in variety and suggestion. They present all possible differences of age, condition, and of moral and mental attainments. . . . And yet in all this diversity to be found in the progressive party among the Sioux is clearly shown one controlling principle— an awakened moral purpose, newborn, or well-developed, the stirring of an enlightened conscience, and of a long-dormant intellect.[32]

32. Herbert Welsh, "The Meaning of the Dakota Outbreak," *Scribner's Magazine* 9 (April 1891): 43–45.

It was the reformers' mission to encourage the progressives and to stamp out the nonprogressives, to support men and measures that promoted the former and restricted or crushed the latter.

The key figure in the process was the Indian agent. The regulations for the Indian service promulgated by the Indian Office said bluntly: "The chief duty of an agent is to induce his Indians to labor in civilized pursuits. To attain this end every possible influence should be brought to bear, and in proportion as it is attained, other things being equal, an agent's administration is successful or unsuccessful."[33] If the agent was a man of strength and integrity who could control the conservative chiefs and who would aggressively foster the civilization programs, he won the commendation of the humanitarians and their support against attack.

The official personnel of the agency and others permitted by law to live on the reservation were considered instruments for carrying out the program of civilization. One such group was the licensed traders, who could be a force for evil if they exploited the Indians, supplied them with liquor, and promoted the interests of the nonprogressives, but who could also be a force for good. Commissioner of Indian Affairs Ezra Hayt in 1877 issued special regulations to develop a system of fair trading that would make the traders "most potent instruments in the civilizing process." In 1889 Commissioner Thomas J. Morgan instructed the special agents to pay close attention to the traders, to make sure they dealt with the Indians honestly, supplied them with useful goods only, provided good example by their own lives, and prevented loafing, gambling, and hurtful amusements on their premises. But Morgan soon realized that times were changing. He came to consider the system of the licensed trader "a relic of the old system of considering an Indian as a ward, a reservation as a corral, and a tradership as a golden opportunity for plunder and profit." He sought to encourage competition of trade on the reservations and to stimulate the Indians themselves to engage in the trade as one of the "civilized pursuits" that they were to adopt as a means of livelihood. And as towns developed near the reservations, the absolute dependence of the Indians upon the licensed reservation trader diminished and with it the importance of the traders in the scheme of reservation life.[34]

33. *Regulations of the Indian Department* (Washington, 1884), paragraph 486, p. 84. The same message was repeated when the *Regulations* were reissued in 1894, paragraph 563, p. 102. The section in the *Regulations* in which the paragraph appears is headed "Civilization" and contains directives on employment of Indians, on suppressing the liquor traffic, and on other civilizing duties.

34. CIA Report, 1877, serial 1800, pp. 404–5; CIA Report, 1889, serial 2725, p. 30; CIA Report, 1890, serial 2841, pp. lix–lx. Clark Wissler in *Indian Cavalcade; or, Life on the Old-Time Indian Reservations* (New York: Sheridan House, 1938), pp. 97–116, gives a sympathetic picture of the traders. For a detailed account of traders in the Southwest, see Frank McNitt, *The Indian Traders* (Norman: University of Oklahoma Press, 1962).

Other critical instruments of change were the agency physicians. The drive of the reformers and the government officials to replace the Indians' cultural patterns with their own civilization was often slowed by the medicine men, who worked effectively to preserve the old ways. If the belief in "sorcery and evil spirits" could be overcome, Commissioner Hiram Price remarked in 1884, "a long stride would be made in the work of civilization." No one had greater opportunity in this direction, he felt, than the agency doctor. Commissioner John D. C. Atkins, two years later, instructed the doctors not only to educate the Indians in the proper care of the sick but to use every effort to overcome the influence of the native medicine men, and he reported some success. He recommended, furthermore, the establishment of agency hospitals as an effective means of weakening the hold of ancient superstitions and traditions upon the Indians.[35]

The physicians faced a difficult task, for they worked in a situation that lacked adequate sanitary facilities. They were expected to care for the sick, to improve hygienic conditions on the reservations, and to instruct pupils in the schools on elementary principles of health; but as members of a complicated bureaucracy they were also plagued with monthly reports to be filled out on diseases treated and sanitary conditions observed and were expected to promote harmony on the reservation by prompt and cheerful obedience to the agent. The physician was told by Commissioner Morgan, however, that he would be compensated for his poor accommodations and low salary among the Indians by the realization of "the noble part he may perform in helping to lift this people out of their superstitious regard for the grotesque rites of the 'medicine men.'"[36] The high regard in which doctors were held on the reservations and the influence they had with the Indians came from their concern for their charges and their success in healing physical ills. Few, apparently, made it their business to mount a frontal attack upon the traditional Indian culture.

Preeminent supporters of the agent were the Indian police, instituted in the 1870s as a substitute for military control of the reservations but seen as a potent means, by law enforcement and good example, to foster civilization.[37] In the 1880s, the police were joined by a complementary institution, the courts of Indian offenses. The instigator of the courts was Secretary of the Interior Henry M. Teller, who in December 1882 called attention to "a great hindrance to the civilization of the Indians, viz, the continuance of the old heathenish dances, such as the sun-dance, scalp-dance, etc." Such practices, he insisted, led to a war spirit and demoralized the young. He

---

35. CIA Report, 1884, serial 2287, p. 28; CIA Report, 1886, serial 2467, pp. 116–17.
36. CIA Report, 1889, serial 2725, pp. 12–13.
37. See discussion of the Indian police above, pp. 600–604.

objected further to the practice of polygamy among the Indians, which could not be afforded when the Indians supported themselves by the chase but which now seemed to flourish when the government furnished rations. A third hindrance to the advancement of the Indians he found in the influence of the medicine men, who kept children from attending school and promoted heathenish customs. Nor could he abide the practice among the Indians of giving away or destroying the property of a man who died. "It will be extremely difficult to accomplish much towards the civilization of the Indians," Teller concluded, "while these adverse influences are allowed to exist."[38]

Following the secretary's orders, Commissioner Price on April 10, 1883, issued a directive to the agents for the establishment of courts. The judges were to be "intelligent, honest, and upright and of undoubted integrity," and could not practice polygamy. The courts were to meet twice a month and rule upon all questions presented to them for consideration by the agent. Specific jurisdiction was granted over the dances objected to by Teller, polygamous marriages, interference of the medicine men with the civilization program, thefts and destruction of property, intoxication and the liquor traffic, and misdemeanors. The civil jurisdiction of the courts was the same as that of justices of the peace in the state or territory where the courts were located. "There is no good reason," Price asserted, "why an Indian should be permitted to indulge in practices which are alike repugnant to common decency and morality; and the preservation of good order on the reservations demands that some active measure should be taken to discourage and, if possible, put a stop to the demoralizing influence of heathenish rites."[39]

A court comprised the first three officers in rank of the police force, if the agent approved, otherwise three other persons selected by the agent. The courts, like the police, were an extension of the agent's authority. Punishments were usually in the form of a fine, although imprisonment also could be ordered. All the decrees of the court were subject to the approval or disapproval of the agent, and appeal could be made to the commissioner of Indian affairs, but there was no intention that the courts should handle major crimes. Courts of Indian offenses were not established for the Five Civilized Tribes, Indians of New York, Osages, Pueblos, and Eastern Cherokees because these tribes had recognized tribal governments. On other

38. Teller to the commissioner of Indian affairs, December 2, 1882, Report of the Secretary of the Interior, 1883, *House Executive Document* no. 1, part 5, 48–1, serial 2190, pp. xi–xii.

39. CIA Report, 1883, serial 2191, p. 11. See "Rules for the Courts of Indian Offenses," April 10, 1883; a revision of these rules is in CIA Report, 1892, serial 3088, pp. 28–31.

reservations, they were set up as commissioners of Indian affairs saw need; at the height of the system, in about 1900, approximately two-thirds of the agencies had courts.[40]

The legal basis on which the courts of Indian offenses rested was extremely vague. Congress in 1888 authorized pay for the judges, but that was as close as the courts came to legislative formalization, despite continual requests from the Indian Office.[41] The specific offenses listed in the rules for the courts were geared to the promotion of civilizaton, and in 1892 the revised rules added as another provision "that if an Indian refuses or neglects to adopt the habits of industry, or to engage in civilized pursuits or employments, and habitually spends his time in idleness and loafing, he shall be deemed a vagrant and guilty of a misdemeanor."[42]

Everyone spoke favorably of the work of the courts. Teller was enthusiastic from the beginning, and Price after a year's experience with the system noted that the decisions of the judges had been quietly accepted and peaceably enforced and that at some agencies the courts had been instrumental in abolishing "many of the most barbarous and pernicious customs that have existed among the Indians from time immemorial." Within a few years he looked for the complete end to "polygamy and the heathenish customs of the sun dance, scalp dance, and war dance."[43] Reports from agents substantiated his opinion.

No tribal custom on the reservations was overlooked by the zealous reformers. One that particularly distressed them was the practice among the Sioux of killing the annuity beef cattle in ways reminiscent of the bygone buffalo hunts. The cattle were driven out of the corrals, pursued over the prairies, and killed in flight by the excited warriors. A member of the Indian Rights Association, who visited the Sioux reservations in the summer of 1886, was appalled by what he saw and even more by the apparent acceptance of the practice by whites as a sporting event. His disgust is evident in his description: "As we drive homeward, threading our way between the bloody groups around the flayed and dismembered beasts, many Indians are already beginning their feast. They are seated on the ground, eating the raw blood-hot liver. . . . The next day, at the great Government boarding school, the principal told us that his boys and girls had behaved

---

40. See the discussion of the courts in William T. Hagan, *Indian Police and Judges: Experiments in Acculturation and Control* (New Haven: Yale University Press, 1966).

41. 25 *United States Statutes* 233.

42. CIA Report, 1892, serial 3088, p. 30.

43. Report of the Secretary of the Interior, 1884, *House Executive Document* no. 1, part 5, 48–2, serial 2286, pp. ix–x; CIA Report, 1884, serial 2287, pp. 6–8; CIA Report, 1886, serial 2467, p. 103.

so well through the term that he meant to take them out in a body to see the next beef issue as a reward for their good conduct. It is a brutal and brutalizing spectacle."[44]

The beef issue was seized upon by Thomas J. Morgan with his usual forcefulness when he became commissioner of Indian affairs. It became his goal to end the "savage sport" and to substitute properly equipped slaughterhouses where the slaughter of the cattle and the handling of the beef could be done as painlessly and cleanly as possible. In July 1890 he issued a set of detailed directions on the killing and distribution of the beef. The slaughtering was to be done by competent men, with proper implements, and in a private place where cleanliness could be provided. Women and children were specifically forbidden to be present. Consumption of the blood and the intestines—a "savage and filthy custom"—was strictly prohibited because it served "to nourish brutal instincts" and was a source of disease. Morgan directed that men cut up the beefs and that the meat be distributed to the Indian men, not to the women, except in special exigencies. "In short," he declared, "I intend that this branch of the work, which at many agencies has been so conducted as to be a scandal on the service and a stimulus to the brutal instincts of the Indians, shall become an object lesson to them of the difference in this respect between the civilized man and the savage."[45] When he left office, he considered the reform almost entirely successful.

The Indian Office and its humanitarian supporters also waged an incessant war, which they never quite won, against intruders and other discordant elements on the reservations. The treaties and executive orders by which the reservations were established uniformly prohibited the entrance of whites who were not official agency personnel or licensed for some special purpose. Casual intruders were expelled by the agents and their police forces, and in serious cases, of which the infiltrations into the Indian Territory were most notorious, a call was made upon the troops of the United States army. Two groups, however, caused special trouble.

The first of these were squawmen, white men who had married Indian women and lived as members of the tribe. These men sometimes exploited the Indians by using without charge large portions of the reservation for grazing or agricultural purposes, but often they merely lived off the tribe with little work. Everywhere they were a discordant element, backed

---

44. J. B. Harrison, *The Latest Studies in Indian Reservations* (Philadelphia: Indian Rights Association, 1887), pp. 128–29. The Sioux commission headed by Richard Henry Pratt was equally dismayed; see *Senate Document* no. 17, 50–2, serial 2610, p. 19.

45. "Instructions to Agents in Regard to Manner of Issuing Beef," July 21, 1890, CIA Report, 1890, serial 2841, p. clxvi.

the chiefs in their resistance to change, and earned the enmity of the reformers.[46]

A second serious challenge to the isolation that the reservations were supposed to provide came from the intrusion of white cattlemen and their herds upon the Indian lands. The reservation of the Cheyennes and Arapahos in the Indian Territory was an especially attractive target, for the sparse population left vast acres of grassland lying vacant. In 1883 enterprising men entered into agreements with certain Indians within this reservation at minimal fees and began to exploit the lands; of 4,297,771 acres in the reservation, only 465,651 were left in Indian hands. Similar leases were made on other reservations.[47] Such actions were opposed by the reformers. The members of the Lake Mohonk Conference in 1883 considered the leasing of Indian lands for grazing as "inexpedient"; they wanted the Indians themselves to become herders on these lands and suggested that Congress appropriate money to buy herds to get the Indians started.[48]

The government, unfortunately, was caught without a policy. The Indian Office declined to approve the leases because it doubted its legal authority to do so, but it permitted the Indians to make them under the pretense that they were merely licenses granted by the Indians to the whites to enter the reservations. The average annual rental price, however, ran to about two cents an acre, which government officials considered altogether too low. The Senate during the Forty-eighth Congress directed two inquiries into the matter of the leasing, and when the attorney general was asked for a ruling, he decided in July 1885 that "no general power appears to be conferred by statute upon either the President or Secretary or any other officer of the Government to make, authorize, or approve leases of lands held by Indian tribes," and that "Indian tribes cannot lease their reservations without the authority of some law of the United States."[49]

46. See William T. Hagan, "Squaw Men on the Kiowa, Comanche, and Apache Reservation: Advance Agents of Civilization or Disturbers of the Peace?" in John G. Clark, ed., *The Frontier Challenge: Responses to the Trans-Mississippi West* (Lawrence: University Press of Kansas, 1971), pp. 171–202. Harry H. Anderson, "Fur Traders as Fathers: The Origins of the Mixed-Blooded Community among the Rosebud Sioux," *South Dakota History* 3 (Summer 1973): 233–70, emphasizes the importance of the mixed-bloods and their influence on tribal decisions.

47. An account of the leases is given in Report of the Secretary of the Interior, 1885, *House Executive Document* no. 1, part 5, 49–1, serial 2378, pp. 14–19. Full accounts of the Cheyenne-Arapaho leases are in Edward Everett Dale, "Ranching on the Cheyenne-Arapaho Reservation 1880–1885," *Chronicles of Oklahoma* 6 (March 1928): 35–59; and Donald J. Berthrong, "Cattlemen on the Cheyenne-Arapaho Reservation, 1883–1885," *Arizona and the West* 13 (Spring 1971): 5–32.

48. *Lake Mohonk Conference Proceedings*, 1883, p. 9.

49. Report of the Secretary of the Interior, 1885, serial 2378, p. 18. The Senate inquiries led to the publication of *Senate Executive Document* no. 54, 48–1, serial 2165, and

The leases of the Cheyennes and Arapahos, meanwhile, had caused great dissension among the Indians themselves. Powerful traditionalist groups within the reservation fought against the presence of the cattlemen and their herds, and the factionalism threatened to result in open conflict. President Cleveland issued a proclamation on July 23, 1885, declaring the leases null and void and calling for the removal of the whites and their cattle from the Indian lands. By the end of the year the cattlemen and their herds were gone.[50]

On the Kiowa, Comanche, and Apache reservation, lying south of the Cheyennes and Arapahos along the Texas border, the encroachment of cattlemen was less successfully resisted. Texas cattlemen moved across the Red River with large herds, and leases signed with influential chiefs gave a color of legality to their operations. The Indian Office, unsure of its ground, let the leases stand. The cattlemen here formed a powerful lobby supporting the Indians in opposition to the allotment of their lands in severalty and the opening of the surplus to white settlement, but their presence was in many ways harmful to the Indians. The money they poured into the pockets of the Indians corrupted the leaders, contributed to tribal factionalism, and did little to stimulate personal economic effort on the part of the tribesmen. Moreover, the isolation that the reservations were intended to provide was destroyed. At the reservations in the Pacific Northwest, too, cattlemen moved in unbidden to make use of the grasslands, and the efforts to remove them were continuous but largely ineffective.[51]

The problem of white cattlemen on the reservations was never satisfactorily faced because of the ambivalence of the government and the reformers toward the matter. Vast areas of the reservations were lying empty—a condition abhorrent to men imbued with the exploitative sentiment of the day. If the lands were not profitably used by the Indians, should they not be utilized by others who would pay for the use and provide funds for the benefit of the Indians? And could not the Indians learn by observing the profit-making enterprise of the whites in their midst? Would not such

Senate Executive Document no. 17, 48–2, serial 2261, both of which contain extensive documentation pertaining to the leases.

50. Berthrong, "Cattlemen on the Cheyenne-Arapaho Reservation," pp. 29–32.

51. William T. Hagan, "Kiowas, Comanches, and Cattlemen, 1867–1906: A Case Study of the Failure of the U.S. Reservation Policy," *Pacific Historical Review* 40 (August 1971): 333–55. See also Martha Buntin, "Beginning of the Leasing of the Surplus Grazing Lands on the Kiowa and Comanche Reservation," *Chronicles of Oklahoma* 10 (September 1932): 369–82; J. Orin Oliphant, "Encroachments of Cattlemen on Indian Reservations in the Pacific Northwest, 1870–1890," *Agricultural History* 24 (January 1950): 42–58. An excellent discussion of the problem of grazing leases on the Cherokee Outlet is in William W. Savage, Jr., *The Cherokee Strip Live Stock Association: Federal Regulation and the Cattleman's Last Frontier* (Columbia: University of Missouri Press, 1973).

benefits outweigh the evils of white infiltration? No final answers were forthcoming. The solution instead was to eliminate the questions by cutting down the holdings of the Indians as they were moved toward accepting land in severalty, and making the surplus lands directly accessible to the whites.

In one notable case the progress toward the civilization on the reservations was impeded by continued warfare, a last holdout of hostile Indians who rejected reservation life and the restrictions it entailed. The Apaches of the Southwest, led finally by the Chiricahua chief Geronimo, had been placed on reservations in Arizona and New Mexico, but they remained restless, and inefficient administration brought disorder rather than calm. The intermixture of Apache bands, moreover, increased the tensions. All the while, expanding white population in the region intensified the likelihood of Indian-white conflicts. As Indian bands left the reservations to renew their raiding, in Mexico as well as in the United States, new military campaigns were organized to subdue them and return them to the reservations. It was a long and weary conflict, for the guerilla warfare of the Indians was more than a match for the United States regulars. Not until September 1886 did Geronimo and the last of the hostile Apaches finally surrender. No chances could be taken that surrendered Indians would break loose again to terrify the countryside. This time the hostile Indians, and neutral Indians as well, were loaded into railroad cars and sent into exile in Florida.[52]

The forced removal of the Apaches from their homeland, although it undoubtedly ended the Apache dangers in Arizona and New Mexico, caused great concern among the reformers in the East, who took up the exiled Indians as one of their causes. Many Indians died in Florida; and the Indian warriors at first were separated from their families. The families were united in 1887 and moved to a more healthful location at Mount Vernon Barracks in Alabama. In 1894 they were moved once more, this time to Fort Sill, Oklahoma. There Geronimo died in 1909, having become a sort of celebrity. Some of the Apaches were transferred in 1913 to the Mescalero Reservation in New Mexico, but others remained at Fort Sill.[53]

52. There is an extensive literature on the Apache wars and the Geronimo campaign. A good account, with details of the operations, is Robert M. Utley, *Frontier Regulars: The United States Army and the Indian, 1866–1891* (New York: Macmillan Company, 1973), pp. 369–96. A brief popular survey is Odie B. Faulk, *The Geronimo Campaign* (New York: Oxford University Press, 1969). For a full biography, see Angie Debo, *Geronimo: The Man, His Time, His Place* (Norman: University of Oklahoma Press, 1976).

53. The postsurrender life of Geronimo is well told in Debo, *Geronimo*, pp. 299–444. For an example of humanitarian concern, see Herbert Welsh, *The Apache Prisoners at Fort Marion, St. Augustine, Florida* (Philadelphia: Indian Rights Association, 1887).

CONTINUING LIQUOR PROBLEMS

A strong argument for segregating the Indians had always been that a special curse of drunkenness afflicted Indians who were in contact with frontier whites. A vile breed of whiskey traders seemed to appear as if by magic wherever there were Indians with goods or money that could be exchanged for intoxicating liquor. Such vendors had been the bane of every frontier from the Atlantic coast to the Pacific, and increasingly stringent laws to prevent their nefarious business had never been quite effective. In the decades after the Civil War, the condemnation of the liquor traffic on or near the reservations was a strident echo of earlier charges, and the attempts to plug all the loopholes by legislation were intensified.

Commissioner Hiram Price fumed against the problems during his four years in office with a crescendo of complaint. He recommended a law prohibiting the manufacture or sale of liquor in any territory of the United States or, if that was impossible, within twenty miles of any Indian reservation. He was vehemently against allowing the introduction of whiskey by the army. "Fire should not be permitted near a powder-magazine," he said, "nor whiskey near an Indian reservation. Army whiskey is no better than other whiskey; it does not appear that its effects are any more desirable." He opposed, too, the exclusion of malt liquors from the prohibiting legislation. While he asked for and got an appropriation to aid in ferreting out and prosecuting persons who furnished the Indians with liquor, he considered this insufficient and called for the establishment of stiff minimum fines and imprisonment. "What must an Indian think of a Government claiming to be governed by the principles of Christianity," he asked, "and urging them to abandon their heathenish practices and adopt the white man's ways, which at the same time allows the meanest and vilest creatures in the persons of white men to demoralize and debauch their young men by furnishing them with that which brutalizes and destroys them?"[54]

Price's agitation was in vain, but the evangelical reformers, whose orga-

---

There is a series of articles on the Apache exiles by John Anthony Turcheneske, Jr., including, "Arizonans and the Apache Prisoners at Mount Vernon Barracks, Alabama: 'They Do Not Die Fast Enough!'" *Military History of Texas and the Southwest* 11 (1973): 197–226; "The United States Congress and the Release of the Apache Prisoners of War at Fort Sill," *Chronicles of Oklahoma* 54 (Summer 1976): 199–226; and "'It Is Right That They Should Set Us Free': The Role of the War and Interior Departments in the Release of the Apache Prisoners of War, 1909–1913," *Red River Valley Historical Review* 4 (Summer 1979): 4–32.

54. CIA Report, 1881, serial 2018, pp. 24–25; CIA Report, 1882, serial 2100, p. 12; CIA Report, 1883, serial 2191, pp. 2–4; CIA Report, 1884, serial 2287, p. 5.

nizations to aid the Indians came into full bloom during his administration of Indian affairs, carried on the crusade, for these men and women had a strong temperance bent. Amelia Quinton, for example, had been a temperance lecturer before she started work in Indian reform, and Clinton B. Fisk, an ardent Methodist who was president of the Board of Indian Commissioners from 1881 to 1890, ran for president in 1888 as the nominee of the Prohibition Party. Such leaders, backed by the ranks of Baptists, Methodists, and other evangelicals who staffed the reform organizations, made the liquor problems on the reservations one of their concerns. The Indian Office, too, continued to contribute its share of strong temperance men. Notable were Commissioner Morgan, an ordained Baptist minister, and his superintendent of Indian schools, Daniel Dorchester, a Methodist minister, who had written a number of temperance tracts and who served as president of the National League for the Suppression of the Liquor Traffic.

Morgan first of all hit at the problem through means that did not require legislative action and in accord with his views of educating the Indians to a high state of morality. He dismissed agency personnel who were themselves guilty of intemperance and refused to appoint anyone who would not pledge to abstain from drinking. He also used the Indian school system to "inculcate principles of temperance" and instituted instruction in the evil effects of alcohol and narcotics. But Morgan did not cease the campaign for stronger legislation, and he rejoiced that Congress in 1892 heeded his repetition of Price's demand that malt liquors as well as spirituous liquors be excluded from the Indian Territory and other Indian lands.[55]

The very civilization programs that the reformers promoted, however, weakened their temperance crusade. For the question soon arose whether the Indians who adopted the white man's ways could still be subject to special prohibitory legislation. One difficulty came from Indians who enlisted in the United States army. They bought liquor with their army pay and not only indulged to excess themselves but also supplied the Indians on nearby reservations, and it was questioned whether persons who sold liquor to these Indian soldiers could be indicted. The Indian Office in 1893 in answer declared its position to be that "the United States is not relieved from the responsibility assumed by it for the protection of Indians against influences calculated to degrade them morally and prevent them from advancing in the knowledge and customs of civilization by the mere fact of their having been enlisted in the armies of the Government."[56] The courts upheld this decision.

55. CIA Report, 1890, serial 2841, pp. liv, lvii; CIA Report, 1891, serial 2934, pp. 74–76; 27 *United States Statutes* 260–61.
    56. CIA Report, 1893, serial 3210, pp. 57–58.

A more serious challenge to prohibition on the reservations came with the allotment of lands in severalty to the Indians. Indians who had received allotments and thereby had become citizens of the United States were judged by some courts no longer to fall under the laws forbidding the sale of liquor to Indians. Such a judicial interpretation seemed to counteract any advantages coming from allotments with the danger of opening the reservations to whiskey sellers.[57] The solution would have to be new legislation, and in 1894 Representative George Meiklejohn of Nebraska introduced such a bill, which had the support of all the reforming elements. Although it passed slowly through the legislative process, it became law on January 30, 1897. The measure made it unlawful to sell or give to the Indians "any essence, extract, bitters, preparation, compound, composition, or any article whatsoever under any name, label, or brand, which produces intoxication"—thus hitting at the patent medicines and at the practice of providing pickles, fruits, and other foods with an alcoholic base for the Indian trade. Second, it changed the penalty for offenses from a maximum to a minimum imprisonment of not less than sixty days and a fine of not less than one hundred dollars for the first offense and not less than two hundred dollars for each subsequent offense. Finally, it defined the term *Indian* to include those who had received allotments as long as the allotment was held in trust by the government, any Indian under the charge of a superintendent or agent, and mixed-bloods over whom the government exercised guardianship.[58] The commissioner said the measure was "of unusual importance to the service," and the Indian Rights Association called it a piece of legislation "in which every friend of the red race will rejoice." Good results seemed to follow the law even though the problem of Indian drunkenness was by no means solved.[59]

OPPOSITION TO RESERVATIONS

The reformers were more successful in enacting programs for "elevating" the Indians than they were in providing for the basic human needs of the Indians in the process. The plains tribes, who got most of the attention,

57. The problem is discussed in CIA Report, 1894, serial 3306, pp. 60–64. The difficulties in enforcing the laws are illustrated in George Bird Grinnell, *The Enforcement of Liquor Laws a Necessary Protection to the Indians* (Philadelphia: Indian Rights Association, 1893).

58. *House Report* no. 1781, 53–3, serial 3346; *Senate Report* no. 1209, 54–1, serial 3461; 29 *United States Statutes* 506–7.

59. CIA Report, 1897, serial 3641, pp. 56–57; *Report of the Indian Rights Association*, 1897, p. 32. See also *Lake Mohonk Conference Proceedings*, 1897, p. 115.

had been self-sufficient in their hunting culture. With the buffalo gone, these Indians were supposed to become self-sustaining agriculturalists almost immediately. For a short period the government was willing to provide subsistence—either through annuity arrangements or as gratuities—and it publicly proclaimed that it was cheaper to feed the Indians than to fight them. The rations in many cases, however, had to continue indefinitely, for the conversion to agriculture came slowly if at all, and large numbers of the formerly energetic and aggressive warriors became enervated and dispirited recipients of the dole. In such an unanticipated circumstance, it was perhaps understandable that the rations supplied were insufficient and often poor in quality. Conditions of starvation and near starvation were prevalent, and the reformers and the Indian Office again and again had to make special appeals to stir Congress into making the necessary appropriations to prevent disaster. Cattle supplied for the purpose of starting a grazing economy among the Indians frequently disappeared to assuage hunger before they could begin to thrive. Other goods—clothing and farming implements, for example—were of bad quality and not plentiful enough to answer the Indians' needs.[60]

Such circumstances made the reservations appear to be mammoth poorhouses rather than nurseries of civilization, and they seriously undercut the positive efforts made to convert the Indians into American citizens. The reformers had looked with optimism to the reservations as halfway houses in which the native Americans could make a more or less speedy transition from their traditional ways to full acculturation. The change was to be made from the nomadic life of a buffalo hunter to the sedentary life of a small farmer, from communal patterns to fiercely individualistic ones, from native religious ceremonials to Christian practices, from Indian languages and oral traditions to spoken and written English. For most of the reservation Indians the changes were a shattering experience, demoralizing rather than uplifting. The self-reliance and self-support that underlay the hopes of reformers for the Indians were little in evidence.[61]

The realization that the Indians were not changing as the reformers had so confidently believed they would led to an outright condemnation of the reservations as an unmitigated evil to be destroyed. The strongest voice

60. See William T. Hagan, "The Reservation Policy: Too Little and Too Late," in Jane F. Smith and Robert M. Kvasnicka, eds., *Indian-White Relations: A Persistent Paradox* (Washington: Howard University Press, 1976), pp. 157–69.

61. For an excellent account of how the goals of the reformers fell short of accomplishment on the Kiowa and Comanche Reservation, see William T. Hagan, "Indian Policy after the Civil War: The Reservation Experience," *American Indian Policy: Indiana Historical Society Lectures, 1970–1971* (Indianapolis: Indiana Historical Society, 1971), pp. 20–36.

was that of Lyman Abbott, the vigorous proponent of so many reforms. Abbott admitted that his knowledge of the Indians was limited, that he had never visited an Indian reservation and had never known more than ten Indians, but his convictions about what was best for the Indians were absolute. The solution to the Indian problem, he believed, lay "in the annihilation of the reservation system root and branch." To make sure that his views had wide impact, Abbott published them in his paper *The Christian Union*.[62] But more than that, he hoped to have them adopted by the Lake Mohonk Conference. It soon became clear, however, that Abbott's views were too radical to suit the rest of the reformers, for he argued that treaties made with the Indians should be unilaterally abrogated by the United States if they stood in the way of abolishing the reservation system. Herbert Welsh took it upon himself to head off "the crude and radical views" of Abbott, speaking against them to his colleagues and writing to Dawes to enlist his support. At Lake Mohonk Dawes spoke eloquently against Abbott's position, insisting that the treaties with the Indians were inviolable and could not in justice be overthrown.[63]

Abbott was not easily put down and spoke his mind forcefully at the conference. "If we have made a bad contract," he said, "it is better broken than kept. . . . It is not right to do a wrong thing, and if you have agreed to do a wrong thing, that agreement does not make it right." He continued:

> I declare my conviction then that the reservation system is hopelessly wrong; that it cannot be amended or modified; that it can only be uprooted, root, trunk, branch, and leaf, and a new system put in its place. We evangelical ministers believe in immediate repentance. I hold to immediate repentance as a national duty. Cease to do evil, cease instantly, abruptly, immediately. I hold that the reservation barriers should be cast down and the land given to the Indians in severalty; that every Indian should be protected in his right to his home, and in his right to free intercourse and free trade, whether the rest of the tribe wish him so protected or not; that these are his individual, personal rights, which no tribe has the right to take from him, and no nation the right to sanction the robbery of.[64]

62. Lyman Abbott, *Reminiscences* (Boston: Houghton Mifflin Company, 1915), pp. 425–26; editorials in the *Christian Union* for July 16, 23, 30, and August 6, 13, 1885.

63. On Abbott's planning for the Lake Mohonk Conference and reaction thereto, see copy of "Proceedings of Informal Indian Meeting Held by Request of Dr. Lyman Abbott," sent to Dawes by Herbert Welsh, in Dawes Papers, Box 27. Welsh's concern over Abbott's views and his attempts to get support for opposition to Abbott at Lake Mohonk are shown in Welsh to Dawes, July 25, August 19 and 31, 1885, ibid. Dawes's remarks are in *Lake Mohonk Conference Proceedings*, 1885, p. 41.

64. *Lake Mohonk Conference Proceedings*, 1885, pp. 50–53.

Most of his listeners were not quite ready for immediate repentance, for they were strongly committed to maintaining the formal treaty rights of the Indians. Although Abbott served on the resolutions committee at the conference, he was unable to swing the gathering completely to his way of thinking. The platform adopted was a compromise. It agreed to the principle of allotting the lands of the reservations in severalty, and it urged that negotiations be undertaken to modify existing treaties and that "these negotiations should be pressed in every honorable way until the consent of the Indians be obtained." But it rejected the proposal to abrogate the treaties or to force severalty upon the Indians.[65]

There could be little doubt, however, that the powerful drive then under way for general allotment of land in severalty and for extending United States law over the Indians was intended ultimately to destroy the reservation system.

65. Ibid., p. 49.

CHAPTER 26

Severalty, Law, and Citizenship

The Drive for a General Allotment Law.

The Dawes Act. Leasing of Allotments.

Renaming the Indians. Law for the Indians.

Citizenship.

No panacea for the Indian problem was more persistently proposed than allotment of land to the Indians in severalty. It was an article of faith with the reformers that civilization was impossible without the incentive to work that came only from individual ownership of a piece of property. The upsurge of humanitarian concern for Indian reform in the post-Civil War era gave a new impetus to the severalty principle, which was almost universally accepted and aggressively promoted, until Congress finally passed a general allotment law. This is not surprising in the light of the long history of provision for allotments; what is surprising is the almost blind enthusiasm with which the policy was advocated despite considerable evidence from the previous half-century of experience that allotment had been a mixed blessing. Allotment of land in severalty, however, was part of the drive to individualize the Indian that became the obsession of the late nineteenth-century Christian reformers and their friends in government and did not stand by itself. The breakup of tribalism, a major goal of this Indian policy, had been moved forward by the abolition of the treaty system and would be carried on by a government educational system and by the extension of American law over the Indian communities. Yet for many years the dissolution of communal lands by allotment, together with the citizenship attached to private landowning, was the central issue.[1]

1. This chapter uses material from Francis Paul Prucha, *American Indian Policy in Crisis: Christian Reformers and the Indian, 1865–1900* (Norman: University of Oklahoma Press, 1976), pp. 227–64, 328–52.

THE DRIVE FOR A GENERAL ALLOTMENT LAW

The advocates of change wanted general legislation that would permit or require the allotment of lands in severalty for all the Indians on reservations, but they did not hesitate to support halfway measures that pointed in the proper direction. One such measure was provision for Indians to take out homesteads under the Homestead Law of 1862. "An extension to the Indians of the benefits of the homestead-laws," Secretary of the Interior Columbus Delano commented in 1874, ". . . will greatly facilitate the work of their civilization. It will rapidly break up tribal organizations and Indian communities; it will bring Indians into subjection to our laws, civil and criminal; it will induce them to abandon roving habits; and teach them the benefits of industry and individual ownership, and thus prove highly advantageous in promoting their prosperity." He recommended, further, that the homesteads patented by Indians should be inalienable except by permission of the president. In the next year, Congress provided that all the benefits of the Homestead Law should apply to the Indians without their losing any share in tribal funds. To protect the Indians, the lands were declared inalienable for five years after the issuance of the final patent.[2]

The Indian homestead legislation had little effect. It was enacted in a hurry as part of a deficiency appropriation bill on the last day of a session and as a result was never debated. The Senate included provisions for the Indians to cut their tribal ties and to become citizens of the United States. When the House refused to concur, the conference committee eliminated the citizenship clause and provided for the continuation of annuity payments and other tribal benefits to Indians taking advantage of the law. Then Congress in 1884 declared that Indians could take full advantage of the homestead laws without paying fees or commissions, and it appropriated $1,000 to aid them in making selections of land. Homesteads were to be held in trust for the Indians by the United States for a period of twenty-five years, at the end of which time they would be conveyed to the Indian or his heirs in fee simple.[3] Government officials, unfortunately, seemed to be unaware of the homesteading opportunities, and few Indians availed themselves of the chance for private land ownership thus furnished.

A pilot case on severalty occurred as a result of the outbreak among the

2. Report of the Secretary of the Interior, 1874, *House Executive Document* no. 1, part 5, 43–2, serial 1639, pp. v, vii; 18 *United States Statutes* 420; CIA Report, 1875, serial 1680, p. 517.

3. *Senate Journal*, 43–2, serial 1628, pp. 418, 423, 432; *Congressional Record*, 3: 2182, 2205; 23 *United States Statutes* 96.

Utes in Colorado in 1879. Secretary of the Interior Carl Schurz was alert to the violent opposition to the Utes from white Coloradans and the inflaming of the opposition by the Meeker murder, and he saw no solution to the explosive situation other than to settle the Utes on allotments and open remaining lands to the whites. An agreement signed in Washington by representatives of the Utes on March 6, 1880, which assigned the Indians to reservations in Utah and in southwestern Colorado, contained a provision for 160-acre allotments, plus additional land for grazing. Consent of three-fourths of the adult males was required before the agreement would take effect. The agreement, when it was sent to Congress for ratification, elicited heated debate, and the arguments for and against severalty were well aired. The debates on a general severalty law, which followed shortly, were in many respects only a repetition of this earlier debate.[4]

Senator Richard Coke of Texas, chairman of the Committee on Indian Affairs, reported the bill in the Senate and set forth clearly the position of the proponents of allotment:

> The policy of the bill is to break up this large reservation, to individualize the Indians upon allotments of land; to break up their tribal relations and pass them under the jurisdiction of the Constitution and laws of the United States and the laws of the States and Territories in which the lands are situated, to aid them with stock and with agricultural implements, and by building houses upon their allotments of land, to become self-supporting, to be cultivators of the soil; in a word, to place them on the highway to American citizenship, and to aid them in arriving at that conclusion as rapidly as can be done.
>
> The bill is in many respects a departure from the ancient and established policy of the Government with reference to the Indian tribes. The advance of settlements in the West has been so rapid that it has been found inexpedient and impolitic, as leading to collisions between the whites and the Indians, to continue the system of locking or attempting to lock up large tracts of land within their exclusive occupancy. The whites cannot be restrained from intrusion upon these large reservations. The Indians will not use them except for hunting purposes and the whites will not permit them to remain unused.
>
> The bill simply recognizes the logic of events, which shows that it is impossible to preserve peace between the Indians and the whites

4. The agreement is in *Senate Executive Document* no. 114, 46–2, serial 1885, and in 21 *United States Statutes* 200–202. Congressional debate is in *Congressional Record*, 10: 2027–30, 2058–67, 2152–64, 2189–2202, 2221–28, 2249–68, 2309–20, 4251–63, and appendix, pp. 100–105, 233–37, 274–76.

with these immense bodies of land attempted to be locked up as Indian reservations.[5]

Underlying all the arguments in favor of the bill was the sense of inevitability that Coke expressed. Secretary Schurz, in his strong support of the bill before the joint committees on Indian affairs, candidly admitted that the system of large reservations would "in the course of time, become utterly untenable," that as available lands became scarcer and more valuable it was "not unnatural that the withholding of large tracts from settlement and development so as to maintain a savage aristocracy in the enjoyment of their chivalrous pastimes, should be looked upon by many as a system incompatible with the progress of civilization and injurious to the material interests of the country." He saw the impossibility of the government's being able always to control the action of people in the West. So he urged the "new system." Its ultimate and necessary end, he said, was that "the Indians be gradually assimilated to and merged in the body of citizens."[6]

An attack on the Ute bill in Congress was led by Senator Henry Teller of Colorado. A New Yorker by birth who had moved to Colorado shortly before the Civil War, Teller had been elected senator when Colorado became a state in 1876. He could claim to have more firsthand contact with the Indian problem and a sounder understanding of Indian culture than most of those who wanted to reform Indian policy, and his views on severalty were decidedly negative. He denied that allotment was a means of civilizing the Indians, asserted that it would not work until the Indians were already civilized, and declared that individual ownership of parcels of land went against the customs and religious beliefs of the Indians. But Teller's cries to a large extent reflected his personal views and were colored by his personal animus toward Schurz, and the Ute bill was supported by Teller's partner in the Senate, Nathaniel Hill, and by Colorado's Representative James B. Belford.[7]

No doubt aided by the exigencies of the Colorado situation as well as by the support of strong advocates of a fundamental change in Indian policy, the bill passed easily in both House and Senate, and when divergent amendments of the two houses were straightened out in committee, it be-

5. *Congressional Record*, 10: 2059.

6. *House Report* no. 1401, 46–2, serial 1937, pp. 2–3. Support of Schurz's position is in *Report of the Board of Indian Commissioners*, 1879, pp. 11–12.

7. *Congressional Record*, 10: 2059–61, 2066–67, and appendix, pp. 233–36. A biography of Teller that pays considerable attention to his long concern for Indian affairs is Elmer Ellis, *Henry Moore Teller: Defender of the West* (Caldwell, Idaho: Caxton Printers, 1941).

came law on June 15, 1880. The act provided for a commission of five men to present the amended agreement to the Utes for their approval, to draw up a census of the tribe, and to arrange for the survey of the lands and for their allotment. The commission, with George W. Manypenny as chairman and the Indian reformer A. B. Meacham as one of its members, obtained the consent of the Indians and set about allotting the lands.[8]

Meanwhile, the drive for a general allotment law was stepped up. Early in 1879, Commissioner of Indian Affairs Ezra Hayt drew up a draft of such legislation, which he announced to the meeting of the Board of Indian Commissioners and the missionary societies on January 15. Then on January 24 he sent the bill to Schurz, with arguments similar to those used to support the Ute bill. Hayt pointed to the numerous treaties with allotment provisions as support of his proposal, but he criticized them for failure to protect the Indian allotments adequately from imprudent alienation, and his own proposal included a provision against alienation for a period of twenty-five years. The inefficiency of the old system of common title and of the treaties that granted land in severalty with a title in fee had been demonstrated, he thought, and he believed that his plan with delayed title would solve the problem. By such a measure, he was convinced that "the race can be led in a few years to a condition where they may be clothed with citizenship and left to their own resources to maintain themselves as citizens of the republic."[9]

Hayt's bill was sent to the House with strong approval by Schurz; it was introduced on January 31, 1879, and won the support of the House Committee on Indian Affairs. On February 6 a similar measure was introduced in the Senate, but neither bill progressed to a vote. In April, in the next session of Congress, general severalty bills were introduced in both houses, but to no avail. Renewed attempts were made in 1880. A revised bill in the House again got support of the Committee on Indian Affairs, although a strong

---

8. 21 *United States Statutes* 199–205; "Report of Ute Commission," *Senate Executive Document* no. 31, 46–3, serial 1943.

9. *Report of the Board of Indian Commissioners*, 1878, pp. 122, 129–33; Hayt to Schurz, January 24, 1879, *House Report* no. 165, 45–3, serial 1866, pp. 2–3; CIA Report, 1879, serial 1910, p. 70. A detailed account of the general allotment law, the motives behind it, and its effects is D. S. Otis, *The Dawes Act and the Allotment of Indian Lands*, ed. Francis Paul Prucha (Norman: University of Oklahoma Press, 1973), a monograph that appeared originally in published congressional hearings in 1934. A useful volume that contains a discussion of the Dawes Act as well as pertinent documents is Wilcomb E. Washburn, *The Assault on Indian Tribalism: The General Allotment Law (Dawes Act) of 1887* (Philadelphia: J. B. Lippincott Company, 1975). The reform movement culminating in the Dawes Act is studied in Loring Benson Priest, *Uncle Sam's Stepchildren: The Reformation of United States Indian Policy, 1865–1887* (New Brunswick: Rutgers University Press, 1942).

minority report was submitted, but the measure did not get as far as discussion on the floor. In the Senate, new bills were introduced in January
and again in May.[10]

The Senate bill introduced on May 19, 1880, by Senator Coke became
the center of attention for the advocates of the allotment policy, and it was
debated vigorously in the Senate over a period of several days in January
and February 1881. The bill provided that in cases where the president decided that reservations were fit for agricultural purposes, he could direct
the allotment of lands in severalty and negotiate with the tribes for sale
of the excess lands to the government. The allotment of the reservation
could be made only with the consent of two-thirds of the males of the tribe
over twenty-one years of age; and the allotments were to be inalienable for
twenty-five years. Once the allotments had been made, the laws of the
state or territory in which the Indians lived would govern the Indians. The
bill did not apply to the Five Civilized Tribes, who consistently opposed
the measure.[11]

The Coke bill had tremendous support from many sides, most impor-
tantly, perhaps, from Schurz, who again and again urged its passage. He insisted that the agricultural industry of the Indians would be greatly stimulated if the Indians could be sure of the title to their lands; he spoke of the
Coke bill as "the most essential step in the solution of the Indian problem." His statement of the advantages that would accrue summed up the
views of the reformers generally:

> It will inspire the Indians with a feeling of assurance as to the perma-
> nency of their ownership of the lands they occupy and cultivate; it
> will give them a clear and legal standing as landed proprietors in the
> courts of law; it will secure to them for the first time fixed homes
> under the protection of the same law under which white men own
> theirs; it will eventually open to settlement by white men the large
> tracts of land now belonging to the reservations, but not used by the
> Indians. It will thus put the relations between the Indians and their
> white neighbors in the Western country upon a new basis, by gradu-
> ally doing away with the system of large reservations, which has so
> frequently provoked those encroachments which in the past have led
> to so much cruel injustice and so many disastrous collisions. It will

10. Reports of congressional action are cited in Prucha, *American Indian Policy in
Crisis*, p. 242.
11. *Congressional Record*, 11: 778–88, 933–34, 994–1003, 1060–70. A summary of
the provisions is given by Senator Coke, ibid., 778–79. See also the abstract of the bill in
Lake Mohonk Conference Proceedings, 1884, pp. 7–13. The opposition of the Five Civilized Tribes can be seen in their memorial printed in *Congressional Record*, 11: 781.

also by the sale, with their consent, of reservation lands not used by the Indians, create for the benefit of the Indians a fund, which will gradually relieve the government of those expenditures which have now to be provided for by appropriations. It will be the most effective measure to place the Indians and white men upon an equal footing as to the protection and restraints of law common to both.[12]

In this he had the strong support of the commissioners of Indian affairs and of the Board of Indian Commissioners, which from the very first had included allotments in severalty as part of their basic Indian reform program. The Lake Mohonk Conference, too, in 1884, passed a formal resolution "earnestly and heartily" approving the Coke bill, which it characterized as "the best practicable measure yet brought before Congress for the preservation of the Indians from aggression, for the disintegration of the tribal organization, and for the ultimate breaking up of the reservation system." The Indian Rights Association looked upon the bill with favor because it seemed to provide solutions for the possible difficulties that long experience with allotments had suggested.[13]

There were, to be sure, a few voices who spoke out against allotment and who criticized the humanitarians' arguments. The minority report of the House Committee on Indian Affairs in 1880 attacked the measure as an experiment without practical basis, a "hobby of speculative philanthropists." An Indian could not be changed into a farmer, these congressmen argued, merely by giving him a quarter-section of land, for his whole tradition and culture predisposed him against the "scheme for his improvement, devised by those who judge him exclusively from *their* standpoint instead of from *his*." Nor was the measure logical, because it began by assuming that the Indian was a man like other men, then hedged his allotment around with such restrictions as would make sense only for a ward. Most basic of all, the report charged that the main purpose of the bill was not to help the Indians at all, but to get at the valuable Indian lands and open them up to white settlement.[14]

By far the strongest of the opponents of the severalty bill was Senator Teller, who repeated many of the arguments he had used in the Ute debate. He criticized the reformers' desire for a universal and uniform measure,

---

12. Report of the Secretary of the Interior, 1880, *House Executive Document* no. 1, part 5, 46–3, serial 1959, pp. 5–6.

13. CIA Report, 1881, serial 2018, pp. 17, 19, and CIA Report, 1882, serial 2100, pp. 34–35; *Report of the Board of Indian Commissioners*, 1880, p. 10, and 1881, pp. 7–8; *Lake Mohonk Conference Proceedings*, 1884, p. 7; *Report of the Indian Rights Association*, 1884, p. 15.

14. *House Report* no. 1576, 46–2, serial 1938, pp. 7–10.

which did not take into account the tremendous diversity among the Indian tribes, and he flatly denied the claims of the advocates of severalty that the Indians were clamoring for allotments in fee simple. In Teller's view, the friends of severalty had the whole matter turned around, mistaking the end for the means. Once the Indians were civilized and Christianized and knew the value of property and the value of a home, then give them an allotment of their own, he argued. But do not expect the allotment to civilize and Christianize and transform the Indians. The Senator was not afraid to advance his unpopular view. In a remarkably prescient declaration, he took his stand: "If I stand alone in the Senate, I want to put upon the record my prophecy in this matter, that when thirty or forty years shall have passed and these Indians shall have parted with their title, they will curse the hand that was raised professedly in their defense to secure this kind of legislation, and if all the people who are clamoring for it understood Indian character, and Indian laws, and Indian morals, and Indian religion, they would not be here clamoring for this at all."[15]

On April 17, 1882, Teller became secretary of the interior in President Chester A. Arthur's cabinet, but he was not able to stem the movement for a general allotment law. Commissioner of Indian Affairs Hiram Price strongly supported allotment, and hardly a session of Congress passed without the introduction of severalty measures in both houses. The Coke bill was passed again in the Senate on April 24, 1882, and on March 26, 1884. It was reported favorably by the House Committee on Indian Affairs in January 1885 but never reached the floor of the House for debate.[16]

THE DAWES ACT

When the severalty bill came before the Senate again on December 8, 1885, it was introduced by Senator Henry L. Dawes, now chairman of the Committee on Indian Affairs. His name stuck to the final act, although he had been relatively late in climbing on the allotment bandwagon, and Senator Coke was soon forgotten.[17] Dawes, perhaps because he despaired of any other answer, became one of the most active supporters of the individual-

15. *Congressional Record,* 11: 780–83, 934–35.
16. CIA Report, 1882, serial 2100, pp. 34–35; *Senate Journal,* 47–1, serial 1984, p. 622; *Senate Journal,* 48–1, serial 2161, p. 469; *Congressional Record,* 13: 3213; 15: 2240–42, 2277–80; *House Report* no. 2247, 48–2, serial 2328.
17. *Senate Journal,* 49–1, serial 2332, p. 49. Dawes himself declared that to Coke "more than to any other Senator is due the credit of this which I believe will be considered hereafter one of the wisest measures with reference to the Indian." *Congressional Record,* 17: 1559.

ization of the Indian through private property, answering questions in public meetings about the details of the proposal and ultimately pushing the measure through Congress.

The bill Dawes proposed in 1886 passed the Senate on February 25, in the first session of the Forty-ninth Congress, but the usual delay occurred in the House. The House Committee on Indian Affairs reported the bill favorably on April 20, but then matters stalled again. The Indian reformers, who were eager to get the enactment not only of the severalty bill but of Dawes's Sioux bill and the Mission Indian measure as well, were beside themselves; victory for their proposals seemed within grasp if only the bills could be brought to a vote. The House put the bills on the calendar for May 27 and 29, but then the Indian matters were shouldered aside as the House debated a proposal to tax the manufacture and sale of oleomargarine as a means of protecting dairy farmers from imitation products. The advocates redoubled their efforts in promoting the allotment measure, which finally, early in the second session of the Forty-ninth Congress, was debated on December 15, 1886, and passed the following day. The House, however, added amendments to the Senate bill, and when the Senate refused to approve the changes, a conference committee was appointed to iron out the difficulties. Both houses promptly agreed to the compromises. In the process the provision requiring tribal consent, which had been insisted upon in the House, was dropped altogether. President Grover Cleveland signed the bill on February 8, 1887, and the Dawes General Allotment Act became the law of the land.[18]

The law dealt primarily with ownership of the land. It authorized but did not require the president, in cases where Indian reservations had good agricultural and grazing land, to survey the reservations or selected parts of them and to allot the land to individual Indians. The amounts to be allotted reflected the strong tradition of a quarter-section homestead for the yeoman farmer. One-quarter of a section (160 acres) was to be allotted to each head of family, one-eighth of a section (80 acres) to each single person over eighteen years of age and to each orphan child under eighteen, and one-sixteenth of a section (40 acres) to other single persons under eighteen

---

18. The sources for the legislative history of the Dawes Act are given in Prucha, *American Indian Policy in Crisis*, pp. 250–52. The reformers' dismay over the inaction of the House can be seen in Charles C. Painter, *Oleomargarine versus the Indian* (Philadelphia: Indian Rights Association, 1886); debate on the oleomargarine tax, much of it frivolous in nature, can be followed in *Congressional Record*, 17: 5009–12, 5032–56, 5074–92. The Dawes Act is in 24 *United States Statutes* 388–91. A clear discussion of its provisions appears in James B. Thayer, "The Dawes Bill and the Indians," *Atlantic Monthly* 61 (March 1888): 315–22.

then living or born prior to the time when the president ordered allotment.[19] In cases where lands were suitable only for grazing, the allotments would be doubled, and if prior treaty provisions specified larger allotments, the treaty would govern. If anyone entitled to an allotment did not make the selection within four years after the president had directed allotment, the law authorized the secretary of the interior to order the agent of the tribe or a special agent to make such selection. Indians who did not live on reservations or whose tribe had no reservation could make their selection on any part of the public domain, surveyed or not surveyed, and receive an allotment under the same provisions. When the secretary of the interior approved the allotments, he would issue to each Indian a patent, which declared that the United States would hold the allotted lands in trust for twenty-five years for the Indian and for his sole benefit or that of his heirs. At the expiration of the trust period, the Indian would receive the land in fee simple. Any conveyance or contract touching the land during the trust period was null and void, and the president at his discretion could extend the period. Once an Indian had received his allotment, he would become a citizen of the United States.

After the lands had been allotted on a reservation, or sooner if the president thought it was in the best interests of the tribe, the secretary of the interior could negotiate with the tribe for the purchase of the remaining or surplus lands, the purchase to be ratified by Congress before becoming effective. If the lands so purchased were suitable for agricultural purposes, they were to be used only for actual homesteaders in 160-acre tracts. The money paid to the Indians for the surplus lands was to be held in the Treasury for the sole use of the tribes to whom the reservations belonged, and

19. These specifications were soon changed to equal allotments for all persons. Commissioner Thomas J. Morgan in his first annual report in 1889 pointed to the need to protect married women, who were excluded from the allotments by the Dawes Act; Indian women could be turned out of their homes by their husbands and then would be without any rights to land. The Board of Indian Commissioners in the same year listened to Alice Fletcher speak in favor of equal allotments to women and to her argument that equalization would benefit as well the young and able-bodied, who under the Dawes Act got only 40 acres while the old and infirm were given 160. The board urged Congress to equalize all the allotments. In March 1890, a bill drawn up by Commissioner Morgan providing 160 acres for every Indian, man, woman, and child, was introduced by Senator Dawes. As the bill proceeded through Congress, there was considerable debate about the size of the equalized allotments—whether they should be 160 acres or only 80 acres— but little disagreement apparently about the need for equalization. The Senate, originally voting for a uniform 160-acre allotment, in the end gave in to the wishes of the House and agreed to 80 acres, the provision that was finally written into the law. CIA Report, 1889, serial 2725, p. 17; *Report of the Board of Indian Commissioners*, 1889, pp. 8–9. The legislative history of the measure is given in Otis, *Dawes Act*, pp. 111–14; the final law is in 26 *United States Statutes* 794–95.

the funds were subject to appropriation by Congress for the education and civilization of the Indians concerned. Excluded from the provisions of the act were the Five Civilized Tribes, the Osages, Miamis, Peorias, and Sacs and Foxes in the Indian Territory, the Seneca Indians in New York, and the strip of Sioux lands in Nebraska.[20]

The Dawes Act, as one historian of the measure observed, was "an act of faith." It was an act pushed through Congress, not by western interests greedy for Indian lands, but by eastern humanitarians who deeply believed that communal landholding was an obstacle to the civilization they wanted the Indians to acquire and who were convinced that they had the history of human experience on their side.[21]

Beyond this basic philosophical position was the persistent fear that without individually owned parcels of land that could be defended in the courts, the Indians would soon lose everything, for there seemed to be no way for the government to protect the tribal reservations from the on-slaught of the whites. Carl Schurz had seen this when he advocated the Ute allotment law, and a pathetic echo came from Senator Dawes as he defended the Dawes Act at the Lake Mohonk Conference in 1887, for he knew that the Indian could not remain as he was in the face of white pres-sures. The government simply was unable to govern effectively. The for-eign observer M. I. Ostragorski wrote in 1902: "From one end of the scale to the other, the constituted authorities are unequal to their duty. . . . The spring of government is weakened or warped everywhere." The Indian re-formers did not speak of the "weakened spring of government," but they would have understood the metaphor. They were caught in the crisis of their times, and they sought to meet it with the remedies they had at hand.[22]

Because there was no roll call vote on the Dawes Act, it is impossible to determine a sectional breakdown of support and opposition to the mea-sure. The great delay in getting action in the House of Representatives shows, however, that there was no concerted popular pressure, either west-ern or eastern, for the bill. Only the persistent agitation of the Lake Mo-honk reformers finally brought the legislation to a successful conclusion.

---

20. The act also provided that religious organizations occupying lands subject to the provisions of the act could be confirmed in their possession, up to 160 acres, and it di-rected that Indians who had availed themselves of the provisions of the act were to be preferred in appointments as Indian police or as other employees of the Indian service.

21. Otis, *Dawes Act*, p. 56.

22. M. I. Ostrogorski, *Democracy and the Organization of Political Parties*, 2 vols. (London, 1902), 2: 550, quoted in Wallace D. Farnham, " 'The Weakened Spring of Gov-ernment': A Study in Nineteenth-Century American History," *American Historical Re-view* 68 (April 1963): 678. Farnham's article is a perceptive analysis of the ineffectiveness of government in post–Civil War America.

The eventual passage of the bill by the House, Dawes claimed, was due to Representative Samuel Jackson Randall's daughter, who, inspired by the discussions at Lake Mohonk, persuaded her father that the measure should be passed. "Public sentiment for the Indian has been manufactured *here*," Dawes told the gathering at Lake Mohonk. "Power to carry legislation in Congress has had its inspiration *here*. This Conference it was that insisted upon it that the House of Representatives should pass the allotment bill, which had been twice through the Senate."[23]

Whatever the forces that brought the passage of the Dawes Act, the victory caused great exultation among the reformers who had fought so persistently for the proposal. "In securing the passage of this law the Indian Rights Association achieved the greatest success in its history," the executive committee of the association declared, "and its enactment was the most important step forward ever taken by the national Government in its methods of dealing with the Indians." Clinton B. Fisk, chairman of the Board of Indian Commissioners, spoke of a "new epoch in Indian affairs" and called the act "the star of the East for the Indian tribes." Secretary of the Interior L. Q. C. Lamar described it as "the most important measure of legislation ever enacted in this country affecting our Indian affairs . . . [and] practically a general naturalization law for the American Indians." It was to his mind "the only escape open to these people from the dire alternative of impending extirpation."[24]

The Dawes Act was put into operation with a speed that frightened Dawes himself. When President Cleveland signed the bill, he remarked that he intended to apply it at first to one reservation only and then gradually extend its provisions to others. But when the Lake Mohonk Conference met seven months later, Dawes reported that the act had already been applied to half a dozen reservations. Such haste was disturbing to Dawes, who voiced a fear that the land grabbers would force allotment quickly so that they could get the surplus lands: "There is no danger but this will come most rapidly—too rapidly, I think,—the greed and hunger and thirst of the white man for the Indian's land is almost equal to his 'hunger and thirst for righteousness.'"[25]

23. *Lake Mohonk Conference Proceedings*, 1890, p. 84.

24. *Report of the Indian Rights Association*, 1887, p. 36; *Lake Mohonk Conference Proceedings*, 1887, p. 2; Fisk to Dawes, December 27, 1886, Dawes Papers, Box 27, Library of Congress; Report of the Secretary of the Interior, 1887, *House Executive Document* no. 1, part 5, 50–1, serial 2541, pp. 25–26. See also Charles C. Painter, *The Dawes Land in Severalty Bill and Indian Emancipation* (Philadelphia: Indian Rights Association, 1887).

25. *Lake Mohonk Conference Proceedings*, 1887, p. 67. Another warning came from James E. Rhoads of the Indian Rights Association, who stressed the need to make sure that the provisions of the Dawes Act were wisely carried out. See his pamphlet *Our Next Duty to the Indians* (Philadelphia: Indian Rights Association, 1887).

In general, however, the reformers were eager to see the panacea applied. Why should the remedy to the Indian problem be delayed any longer than was necessary, they asked; and the arguments that had been advanced for the passage of the act were now repeated as justification for its rapid application. The act, Merrill E. Gates told the Lake Mohonk Conference in 1900, was "a mighty pulverizing engine for breaking up the tribal mass." Year by year, in fact, the process of allotment was stepped up, and the surplus lands were rapidly transferred to the whites. The Indians held 155,632,312 acres in 1881; by 1890 they had 104,314,349, and by 1900 only 77,865,373, of which 5,409,530 had been allotted. So successful did the process seem that the reformers looked forward to the day when government supervision over the Indians would disappear entirely and the Indians would all be absorbed into American society.[26]

LEASING OF ALLOTMENTS

Dissatisfaction with the Dawes Act soon arose, when it was realized that the allotment of a homestead to an Indian did not automatically turn him into a practical farmer. The provisions of the act that prohibited the leasing or other such conveyance of the allotments—wisely intended to protect the Indian holdings for an extended period—actually seemed to work a hardship on many Indians. Women and children and Indians who were in some way disabled could not reap the benefits of the allotments because they were unable to farm them. Moreover, lands belonging to students who were away at school lay fallow or were used illegally by whites with no benefit to the Indians. If leasing were allowed for these needy persons, an income from the land could be provided for them. Other Indians, it turned out, did not have the work animals or agricultural implements indispensable for effective use of their allotments. If a portion of their land could be rented, the income could be used to provide the tools needed to farm the rest.[27]

26. *Lake Mohonk Conference Proceedings*, 1900, p. 16. President Theodore Roosevelt liked Gates's phrase and used it in his first annual message to Congress on December 3, 1901. The figures on allotment, compiled by the Land Division of the Indian Office, are cited in Otis, *Dawes Act*, p. 87. Chapter 7 of Otis's study gives a detailed analysis of the working out of allotment up to 1900 and evaluates its success and failure.

27. The best discussion of the leasing of allotments, on which I have relied, is Otis, *Dawes Act*, pp. 107–31. See also Everett Arthur Gilcreast, "Richard Henry Pratt and American Indian Policy, 1877–1906: A Study of the Assimilation Movement" (Ph.D. dissertation, Yale University, 1967), pp. 231–36; Laurence F. Schmeckebier, *The Office of Indian Affairs: Its History, Activities, and Organization* (Baltimore: Johns Hopkins Press, 1927), pp. 84, 177–79.

There was in addition the question of advancing the Indians toward full participation in American society by letting them assume the full responsibility for their own property. To hedge their ownership around with all kinds of restrictions in its use hardly was conducive to Indian growth in maturity, and the interspersing of white farmers among the Indians, it was argued, would furnish object lessons of great value in teaching the Indians how to farm.[28]

It is strange how readily the reformers accepted these arguments—the same men and women who had championed allotment in severalty as the way to move the Indians from idleness to hard work on their own land. Only a few voices were raised against the proposals to make leasing legal under set conditions. Among them was that of Senator Dawes, who saw in leasing the danger of a speedy collapse of the whole allotment system, for "the Indian would abandon his own work, his own land, and his own home, which we have talked about as the central pivot of our efforts in attempting to civilize the Indian."[29]

The opposition was too slight to stem the movement, however; and in fact the basic idea was accepted by the reformers, provided safeguards were set up to prevent indiscriminate leasing. By a law of February 28, 1891, Congress made leasing possible. It allowed Indians who "by reason of age or other disability" were personally unable to occupy and improve their allotments to lease their lands for set periods, subject to the approval of the secretary of the interior.[30] Although the Indian Office moved slowly at first in applying the leasing law, the program soon gained a momentum that swept away the restrictions the advocates had intended. The law provided that approval be given by the secretary of the interior to all requests for leasing, but by 1893 the matter of leasing had been placed in the hands of the Indian agents, who easily succumbed to pressure put upon them by whites who desired to farm the Indian lands. Moreover, the wording of the law was loosened in 1894 by adding "inability" to age and disability as a reason for leasing allotments and by extending the period of lease. The number of leases steadily climbed. In 1897, there was a temporary check to the leasing of allotments, with a drop in the number of leases, but the figure shot up again in subsequent years.[31]

---

28. *Lake Mohonk Conference Proceedings*, 1889, pp. 84–89; report of Robert H. Ashley, August 26, 1890, in CIA Report, 1890, serial 2841, p. 137.

29. *Lake Mohonk Conference Proceedings*, 1890, pp. 82–83.

30. 26 *United States Statutes* 795. See Otis, *Dawes Act*, pp. 111–14, for the legislative history of the bill. In 1893 the Indian Office defined "age" and "disability"; see "Rules and Regulations to be Observed in the Execution of Leases of Indian Allotments," CIA Report, 1893, serial 3210, pp. 476–77.

31. 30 *United States Statutes* 85. There were 948 leases in 1898, 1,185 in 1899, and 2,590 in 1900. Otis, *Dawes Act*, p. 121. A law of May 31, 1900, set the maximum period

The effects on the Indians could have been predicted. The Indians of the Omaha and Winnebago reservations in Nebraska, for example, who had been the great hope of the promoters of allotment, by the end of the decade were suffering the evil effects of leasing. By 1898, out of 140,000 acres allotted on the two reservations 112,000 had been leased. The low character of the whites who thus came to mingle with the Indians contributed further to their demoralization. One student of the Omahas concluded that these Indians—not good enough farmers to make a better or more reliable income than the rent from a white tenant and with no incentive to improve a standard of living that was alien to them—found in leasing a way out. Two-thirds of the men "ceased to make any further economic struggle."[32]

There is no doubt that the leasing policy ate deeply into the goals envisaged by reformers for the allotment policy, for many Indians came to look upon the land as a source of revenue from the labor of a tenant, not as a homestead to be worked personally by an independent small farmer. The leasing, furthermore, was a step toward complete alienation of the allotments by sale, a process that soon began to appear as a break in the dike of protection erected around the allotments by the reformers.[33]

RENAMING THE INDIANS

The allotment of Indian lands, which was intended to fit the Indians into Anglo-American systems of land tenure and inheritance, was complicated by the traditional system of Indian personal names. If the Indians were to be fully assimilated into American life, they would have to be renamed. To this end, Commissioner Thomas J. Morgan issued a circular to Indian agents and school superintendents on March 19, 1890. "When the Indians become citizens of the United States, under the allotment act," he said, "the inheritance of property will be governed by the laws of the respective States, and it will cause needless confusion and, doubtless, considerable

---

for leases at five years and restricted leasing to farming only. 31 *United States Statutes* 229.

32. Otis, *Dawes Act*, p. 130; Margaret Mead, *The Changing Culture of an Indian Tribe* (New York: Columbia University Press, 1932), p. 27. A variety of views on the effects of leasing can be found in the replies of agents to questions asked by the Board of Indian Commissioners in 1898. *Report of the Board of Indian Commissioners*, 1898, pp. 12–25. Leasing among the Santee Sioux is discussed in Roy W. Meyer, *History of the Santee Sioux: United States Indian Policy on Trial* (Lincoln: University of Nebraska Press, 1967), p. 196.

33. Otis, *Dawes Act*, pp. 149–50. By 1916 more than one-third of allotted agricultural lands were leased.

ultimate loss to the Indians if no attempt is made to have the different members of a family known by the same family name on the records and by general reputation. Among other customs of the white people it is becoming important that the Indians adopt that in regard to names." Morgan was not unmindful of Indian interests and directed that whenever possible the Indian name should be retained, and he condemned the translation of Indian names into English, which often resulted in "awkward and uncouth" names. Nor would he tolerate "the habit of adopting sobriquets given to Indians such as 'Tobacco,' 'Mogul,' 'Tom,' 'Pete,' etc., by which they become generally known." He did authorize, however, the substitution of English names for Indian ones too difficult for whites to pronounce and the introduction of Christian given names before the surnames. Indian names that were "unusually long and difficult" were to be shortened arbitrarily.[34]

Morgan's plan was endorsed by John Wesley Powell, director of the Bureau of Ethnology, who saw the advantages of the renaming for the inheritance of property and for accurate census taking among the tribes. Powell, in addition, stressed the value of the new system of naming in breaking up the tribal organization, which was "perpetuated and ever kept in mind by the Indian's own system of names." He wrote, "In selecting aboriginal names, I do not think it will be necessary to limit the choice to such names as Indians already bear. Excellent names may frequently be selected from the Indian's vocabulary of geographic terms, such as the names of rivers, lakes, mountains, etc., and where these are suitable and euphonic, I think they may be substituted for personal names which are less desirable."[35]

Despite the enthusiasm of Morgan and Powell, little renaming was accomplished in the 1890s, and Commissioner William A. Jones admitted in 1902 that Morgan's circular had become "practically a dead letter."[36] But soon the naming process took on new life under the prodding of the noted American literary figure Hamlin Garland, who took up the cause with great energy. Garland gained the interest of President Theodore Roosevelt and laid the matter before Secretary of the Interior Ethan Allen Hitchcock and Commissioner Jones. After listening to Garland and soliciting advice from George Bird Grinnell and others, Jones issued a new circular on De-

34. Morgan's circular is printed with his "Rules for Indian Schools," in the appendix to CIA Report, 1890, serial 2841, p. clx. An extended discussion of the renaming program is in Daniel F. Littlefield, Jr., and Lonnie E. Underhill, "Renaming the American Indian, 1890–1913," *American Studies* 12 (Fall 1971): 33–45.

35. J. W. Powell to T. J. Morgan, April 4, 1890, CIA Report, 1890, serial 2841, p. clxi.

36. W. A. Jones to Hamlin Garland, September 5, 1902, OIA LS, Miscellaneous Division, vol. 18.

cember 1, 1902, by which the 1890 circular was "amplified and reissued." The new directive followed closely the principles set forth by Garland, who continually urged the retention wherever possible of Indian names instead of a wholesale substitution of English ones.[37]

Considerable work was done on transforming Cheyenne and Arapaho names in the Indian Territory, and rolls with new names were sent to Garland for approval. Garland thought the names were an improvement, but he wrote: "I should like to know whether there are insuperable objections or whether the ones working on the rolls are not revising from the white man's point of view with the feeling that the names ought to be as nearly white as possible. My notion is to treat them as we would Polish or Russian names—*retain as much of the Cheyenne as we can easily pronounce* and above all secure the pleased co-operation of the red people themselves."[38]

Meanwhile, the renaming of the Sioux was delegated to the Sioux physician Charles A. Eastman, who, at Garland's insistence, was transferred from his position as agency physician at Crow Creek to work full time on the naming project. As an Indian himself, Eastman was able to get substantial cooperation from the Indians. He copied the allotment rolls, traveled to the agencies to learn family relationships, and by 1909 had revised the names of about twenty-five thousand Sioux.[39] Garland's plan for other tribes did not work as well, for Washington officials seem to have lost interest in the program. Regularization of Indian family names to fit the Anglo-American system came slowly over the years, as it might have done anyway without Garland's project.

While the renaming of the Indians undoubtedly eased some of the confusion surrounding allotment and the inheritance of allotted lands, it was a notable example of the insensitivity of white reformers to Indian cultural patterns. Like allotment of land in severalty, the program was a paternalis-

---

37. W. A. Jones to agents, allotting agents, school superintendents and teachers, December 1, 1902, OIA LS, Miscellaneous Division, vol. 18. The circular was based on Garland's letter to Jones, November 3, 1902, OIA LR, 1902–65943. There is an account of Garland's conversation with President Roosevelt and other officials in his autobiographical *Companions on the Trail* (New York: Macmillan Company, 1931), pp. 136–39. Garland's work is discussed in detail in Littlefield and Underhill, "Renaming the American Indian," pp. 37–42.

38. Garland to Jones, July 11, 1903, OIA LR, 1903–43254.

39. Garland's directing influence in the project can be seen in his frequent correspondence with the commissioner of Indian affairs; see, for example, letters of April 18 and December 7, 1903, OIA LR, 1903–27126 and 1903—83395. Seven volumes of rolls with the revised names that Eastman prepared for the Sioux are in Records of the Office of Indian Affairs, inventory entry no. 617, National Archives, Record Group 75. Eastman's work is described in Raymond Wilson, *Ohiyesa: Charles Eastman, Santee Sioux* (Urbana: University of Illinois Press, 1983), pp. 120–30.

tic attempt to transform the Indians quickly into American citizens and to erase as much as possible all remnants of Indian ways.

LAW FOR THE INDIANS

Paralleling the drive for allotment in severalty was strong agitation to make the Indians amenable to white law. The reformers attacked this problem with their usual gusto, and some of them offered a theoretical solution that had all the earmarks of a new panacea.

The historical starting point was clear enough. The Indian tribes were treated as "nations," and although John Marshall had characterized them as "domestic" and "dependent" in order to distinguish them from foreign states, the internal independence of the Indian group was assumed. The reformers after the Civil War, however, discovered weaknesses in this traditional arrangement, and various elements in their program eventually so changed the status of the Indians that the problem of law for the Indians acquired new and threatening dimensions. "A serious detriment to the progress of the partially civilized Indians," the Board of Indian Commissioners declared in 1871, "is found in the fact that they are not brought under the domination of law, so far as regards crimes committed against each other." The board admitted that Indian tribes differed greatly among themselves and that all were not yet suited to white legal norms. "But when they have adopted civilized costume and civilized modes of subsistence," it said, "we owe it to them, and to ourselves, to teach them the majesty of civilized law, and to extend to them its protection against the lawless among themselves."[40]

A sharp blow at the traditional status of the Indian groups was the legislation of 1871 declaring that no Indian tribe would be recognized as an independent nation with whom the United States might contract by treaty. Although agreements were still concluded that were no different from previous treaties except in mode of ratification, the formal end of treaty making and the conscious intention thereby to denigrate the power of the chiefs resulted in a loss of old systems of internal order without the substitution of new ones in their place. Reformers both in and out of government called for the application of United States courts to the Indian territories. Even among white men, they asserted, civilization would not long exist without the guarantees of law. How, then, could there be any hope of civilizing the Indians without law? "That the benevolent efforts and purposes of the Government have proved so largely fruitless," the commissioner of Indian affairs declared in 1876, "is, in my judgment, due more to

40. *Report of the Board of Indian Commissioners,* 1871, pp. 7–8.

its failure to make these people amenable to our laws than to any other cause, or to all other causes combined." From all sides the refrain sounded. Bishop William Hare, the Episcopal missionary among the Sioux, wrote in 1877: "Wish well to the Indians as we may, and do for them what we will, the efforts of civil agents, teachers, and missionaries are like the struggles of drowning men weighted with lead, as long as by the absence of law Indian society is left without a base."[41]

A bill was introduced in Congress in 1879 that authorized the president to prescribe police regulations for the Indian reservations and provided that the laws of the respective states and territories relating to major crimes should be in force on the reservations. Both Secretary Schurz and Commissioner Hayt strongly supported the measure, but Congress could not be persuaded to enact the bill. Agitation kept the idea strong, however, and increasing pressure arose for law as a necessary means to bring about the Indian reform and civilization the humanitarians wanted.[42]

By 1882 well-worked-out arguments, which increasingly shifted their emphasis as the reform movement that aimed to individualize the Indians gained momentum, began to appear with regularity. Although punishment for crimes committed by Indians on other Indians was not lost sight of, the dominant concern came to be the protection of the individual Indian in his personal and property rights. "That law is the solution of the Indian problem would seem to be a self-evident proposition," declared a writer in the *North American Review* in March 1882. Everything that was sought for the Indians—inducements to make them labor, educational facilities, and land in severalty—rested, he argued, upon adequate protection of law. To declare that the Indian is "a *person* before the law" was the first and all-important thing. "When his possessions are secure," the writer concluded, "his labor will be both profitable and attractive; when he feels himself a man, he will desire his own and his children's education; when he can be protected by law, the granting of land to him in severalty will be something more than a pretentious form."[43]

Similar sentiments were promoted by the Indian Rights Association, which established a standing committee on law under the chairmanship of one of the founders of the association, Henry S. Pancoast. Pancoast, a young lawyer of reforming temperament, returned home from his trip to the Sioux reservations in 1882 with strong convictions about what should

41. Francis A. Walker, *The Indian Question* (Boston: James R. Osgood and Company, 1874), pp. 12–13; CIA Report, 1873, serial 1601, pp. 372–73; CIA Report, 1876, serial 1749, pp. 387–88; Hare quoted in CIA Report, 1883, serial 2191, p. 7.

42. CIA Report, 1879, serial 1910, pp. 105–6; Report of the Secretary of the Interior, 1879, *House Executive Document* no. 1, part 5, 46–2, serial 1910, pp. 12–13.

43. William Justin Harsha, "Law for the Indians," *North American Review* 134 (March 1882): 272–92.

be done to solve the Indian problem. "Acknowledge that the Indian is a man," he said, "and as such give him that standing in our courts which is freely given as a right and a necessity to every other man." Because the Indians were neither citizens, nor aliens, nor foreign nations, they had no standing in court either individually or collectively and were therefore robbed and cheated with impunity. Their only resort was to demand their rights by force, and if they did so they were crushed by the military power of the United States. "If we want to make them like other people," Pancoast wrote, "we will never do it by studiously treating them differently from everybody else."[44]

While concern for general Indian rights and recognition of the individual Indian's manhood was thus pushed as an essential part of the program to introduce the Indian into the mainstream of American society as a man like other men, the question of a criminal code for the reservations came again to the forefront in the dramatic case of the Brulé Sioux Indian Crow Dog, who had been sentenced to death by the territorial court of Dakota for murdering Chief Spotted Tail. In the case of *ex parte Crow Dog*, decided on December 17, 1883, the United States Supreme Court ordered Crow Dog's immediate release because the United States had no jurisdiction over crimes committed by one Indian against another. Since Congress had provided no national jurisdiction over Indian crimes, even a murderer could not be punished, and the chief was permitted to return to his tribe.[45]

The decision caused great consternation, for such a state of lawlessness could not be tolerated in the republic. The Indian Rights Association drew up a bill to establish special courts of criminal jurisdiction on the reservations. But such a temporary expedient did not satisfy all the reformers, many of whom wanted no distinction whatever between the Indians and the whites in legal matters. The Board of Indian Commissioners objected that such a separate code of law for the Indians was not only expensive but would perpetuate the evil that had grown out of the treaty and reservation policies of keeping the Indians apart from the whites. "We believe," the board said, "that the laws which are good enough for all other kindreds and peoples and tribes and nations are good enough for Indians."[46]

---

44. Henry S. Pancoast, *Impressions of the Sioux Tribes in 1882; With Some First Principles in the Indian Question* (Philadelphia: Franklin Printing House, 1883), p. 22. See also Pancoast's pamphlet *The Indian before the Law* (Philadelphia: Indian Rights Association, 1884); an appendix to the pamphlet contains a questionnaire sent to Indian agents about a system of law for the Indians and their replies. The concern for law is shown in CIA Report, 1883, serial 2191, pp. 7–10, and *Report of the Board of Indian Commissioners*, 1884, pp. 6–7.

45. 109 *U.S. Reports* 556.

46. *Report of the Board of Indian Commissioners*, 1884, p. 6.

Finally, in a law of March 3, 1885, Congress extended federal criminal jurisdiction over the Indians for seven major crimes (murder, manslaughter, rape, assault with intent to kill, arson, burglary, and larceny). Restricted though it was, this legislation was revolutionary. For the first time the United States asserted its jurisdiction over strictly internal crimes of Indians against Indians, a major blow at the integrity of the Indian tribes and a fundamental readjustment in relations between the Indians and the United States government. When the Supreme Court in *United States* v. *Kagama* on May 10, 1886, upheld the right of Congress to take this step, the way was open for unlimited interference by the federal government in the affairs of the Indians. "It was laid down in this case, one of the landmarks of our Indian law," explained a leading legal expert of the day, "that the government of the United States has full power, under the Constitution, to govern the Indians as its own subjects, if it sees fit to do so, and to such partial or full extent as it sees fit; that nothing in the tribal relation or in any previous recognition of it by the United States cuts down this legislative power; that this is so not merely in the Territories, but on reservations within the States."[47]

For a while the efforts to bring further legal reforms, measures that would extend civil as well as criminal law over the Indians, were diverted by interest in the land in severalty bills that resulted in the Dawes Act. There was no doubt in the reformers' minds that the Dawes Act was a major step in the direction they aimed to go in making the Indians individually indistinguishable from other Americans. Senator Dawes and many others felt that this act answered all the needs of the Indians for legal protection and equality. Whenever Indians were judged by the president to be ready for the transition, they would get their homesteads, their citizenship, and their equality before the law and could merge with the general population. As the provisions of the Dawes Act were extended to tribe after tribe, the Indian problem would disappear without any resort to hasty or radical measures. But for men interested primarily in the Indians' legal status, the Dawes Act was too slow. Its legal provisions and opportunities for citizenship did not immediately embrace all the Indians, and in the long transition period until the act had taken effect everywhere, some further legislation, they felt, was absolutely necessary.

The man most eager for this to happen and most earnest and articulate in its promotion was a learned and highly respected professor in the Har-

---

47. 23 *United States Statutes* 385; 118 *U.S. Reports* 375; James Bradley Thayer, "A People without Law," *Atlantic Monthly* 68 (November 1891): 677. The *Kagama* case was hailed at the time as of equal importance with John Marshall's Cherokee cases. See Robert Weil, *The Legal Status of the Indians* (New York, 1888).

vard Law School, James Bradley Thayer. Thayer was well known for his
work in constitutional law and the rules of evidence, but he was also a
deeply religious man and one with an active social conscience, and in the
mid-1880s he turned his attention to the Indian question. He strongly supported the Dawes Act and wrote an intelligent article explaining the act to
the public. But Thayer considered the Dawes Act merely "one great step to
be followed by others." He declared: "We must not leave things alone for
one or two generations, to be worked out by the Severalty Law unaided." It
mattered little to him whether the Indians wanted to abandon their tribal
relations; the United States could simply ignore the tribes and deal directly
with the individuals. "There is little harm in men associating together,"
Thayer said, "whether in tribes of Shakers or Oneida communities, or Odd
Fellows, or Masons, or Germans, or colored men, or Indians, if they like;
but as we do not carry on a separate commerce with the tribe of Shakers
we had better stop doing it with the Indians."[48]

Thayer stressed the foolishness of maintaining a "gigantic, complicated,
costly, and, in a degree, needless body of laws and administration" to handle the Indians. There were fewer Indians in the whole United States than
there were people in Boston, Thayer pointed out, and the whole Indian
Office and its numerous personnel were set up to care for them outside of
the American judicial system. This, perhaps, would not have been so bad
had it provided a reasonable system of law and adminstration for the Indians. Instead it resulted in the exercise of arbitrary power over them,
which was repugnant to the American system of government.[49]

Men like Thayer and Pancoast made much of the arbitrary authority of
the Indian agents over the Indians on the reservations, speaking of the "irresponsible power" and "tyrannical power" of these men. "Here in the
midst of us," Pancoast wrote, "is an unauthorized power so despotic as to
be utterly irreconcilable with every principle of liberty we profess. The
agent is permitted to arrest and imprison Indians without trial. Here in
America, in the nineteenth century, does our Government deny these men
a right which Englishmen gained for themselves in the thirteenth."[50]

Thayer and his friends drew up a bill to accomplish what they had in
mind for the Indians. It provided that all Indians be given the full protec-

48. Thayer, "A People without Law," pp. 682, 686; Thayer, *Remarks Made at a Meeting in Cambridge, Mass., Called by the Women's Indian Association of That City, May
3, 1886* (n.p., n.d.). For Thayer's career, see *Dictionary of American Biography*, s.v. James
Bradley Thayer, by Samuel Williston; James Parker Hall, "James Bradley Thayer, 1831–
1902," in William Draper Lewis, ed., *Great American Lawyers*, 8 vols. (Philadelphia:
John C. Winston Company, 1907–1909), 8: 345–84.

49. Thayer, *Remarks Made before the Worcester Indian Association at Worcester,
Mass., February 13, 1887* (n.p., n.d.), pp. 4–5.

50. Pancoast, *Impressions of the Sioux Tribes*, p. 25; Pancoast, *The Indian before the
Law*, p. 15.

tion of the law and enabled them to sue and be sued in all courts and to make contracts and enter into trade or business. It provided, furthermore, for the immediate extension over every reservation of the civil and criminal laws of the state or territory in which it was located. To administer these laws, special commissioners' courts would be established, for until the Indians generally became taxpayers, the burden would be too heavy for the local courts to bear. Senator Dawes was prevailed upon to introduce the bill in Congress, although he himself did not favor it, and the passage of the "Thayer bill" became the object of an influential group of reformers and legal experts.[51]

As strong as the backers of the bill were, they were unable to force the legislation through Congress, primarily because of conflict within the ranks of the reformers themselves. The chief opponent of the measure was Dawes, who had qualms about the constitutionality of Thayer's proposal and who, more fundamentally, pinned his hopes for Indian salvation on the severalty measure he had sponsored. As the allotment went forward and the Indians became citizens and subject to state and territorial laws, there would be no need for Thayer's radical measure. He opposed its elaborate and expensive solution for a problem that to his mind would soon vanish. The charge made by the Thayer group that the Indians were "without law" exasperated Dawes, who pointed to the Dawes Act, the Major Crimes Act of 1885, and the courts of Indian offenses organized on many reservations.[52]

Without someone of Dawes's stature to manage the bill, it made no headway in Congress. Thayer lamented that "the whole Indian question gets little hold on public men, and is crowded aside by tariffs and silver and President-making and office-jobbing and pension-giving," and that too much attention was paid to patching up the existing Indian system instead of radically changing the status of the Indian before the law.[53]

CITIZENSHIP

Although the question of law for the Indians and Indian citizenship were intimately related, such strong advocates of a system of law as Pancoast

---

51. A summary of the bill is given in Austin Abbott, "Indians and the Law," *Harvard Law Review* 2 (November 1888): 177–78, and in *Report of the Indian Rights Association*, 1888, pp. 26–27. An account of the work that went into the framing of the bill was given by Thayer in *Lake Mohonk Conference Proceedings*, 1888, pp. 42–48. For examples of agitation for the bill, see Prucha, *American Indian Policy in Crisis*, pp. 338–41.

52. Dawes to the editors of the *Christian Union*, January 31, 1892, Dawes Papers, Box 29; *Lake Mohonk Conference Proceedings*, 1891, pp. 43–48. See also Dawes to J. W. Davis, June 5, 1892, Dawes Papers, in which he sets forth his position at length.

53. Thayer, "A People without Law," p. 686.

and Thayer were careful not to equate the two. Pancoast asserted that "the idea of declaring all Indians citizens at once, without warning or preparation, is crude and unpractical, devoutly as we may wish it were not so." He pointed to the duties of citizenship for which many Indians were not yet ready and declared that there had to be at least "an approximate fitness in the individual Indian for the duties of citizenship" before he could be made a citizen. But that did not preclude measures to make sure that all Indians, citizens or not, were protected by the law. Thayer, too, argued that the ballot and citizenship should not be granted immediately to all, as it had been to the former slaves.[54]

The question of citizenship for the Indians, nevertheless, could not be kept down. To make the Indians into acceptable American citizens was the great goal of the humanitarian reformers and of the Indian Office. There was little if any controversy about that. Yet the niceties of the precise legal formulation and how and when legal citizenship should be acquired by the red men were all matters of divided opinion. The immediate granting of citizenship, unlike most of the reforms proposed at the end of the nineteenth century for the Indians, was not universally accepted as a panacea. The anomalous legal status of the Indians was the major difficulty. As long as the Indians were members of tribes or nations, which treated with the United States as quasi-independent political units but which were also subject to the United States, they could not be considered American citizens.[55]

The status of the Indians came into question with the adoption of the Fourteenth Amendment to the Constitution in 1868. That Reconstruction measure provided in section 1: "All persons born or naturalized in the United States, and subject to the jurisdiction thereof, are citizens of the United States and of the State wherein they reside." Although the amendment was aimed at the recently emancipated slaves, the Indians did not escape attention when the amendment was being debated in Congress. Senator James R. Doolittle of Wisconsin, assuming that the amendment as worded would make citizens of the Indians as well as of the blacks, strongly opposed such a move, for he believed that the Indians were not yet prepared for citizenship. He thereupon proposed adding the words "excluding Indians not taxed" to the section. Other senators, although they agreed with Doolittle's views on Indian citizenship, held that the added phrase was unnecessary because the Indians with their tribal connections could

---

54. Pancoast, *The Indian before the Law*, p. 25; Thayer, "A People without Law," p. 683.

55. A clear formulation of the dependent status of the Indians was given by Attorney General Caleb Cushing in 1856. *Opinions of the Attorney General*, 7: 749–50. There is a brief survey of the citizenship question in Michael T. Smith, "The History of Indian Citizenship," *Great Plains Journal* 10 (Fall 1970): 25–35.

not be considered "subject to the jurisdiction" of the United States, and Doolittle's amendment was voted down thirty to ten.[56] That such a difference of opinion could obtain among senators, many of whom were well trained in law, indicates the confusion that existed about the precise status of the Indians under the Constitution.

Doolittle's view, in fact, continued to be expressed. In debate in the House on treaty making on April 6, 1869, Representative Benjamin F. Butler of Massachusetts asserted his belief that the Indians became citizens by virtue of the Fourteenth Amendment and argued that the United States could not make treaties with such groups. A year later the Senate, still in doubt, instructed its Committee on the Judiciary to report on the effect of the Fourteenth Amendment upon the Indian tribes, whether or not the amendment made the Indians citizens, and if so whether the treaties existing between the tribes and the United States were annulled. The report, submitted on December 14, 1870, presented a long historical exposition and then declared that the Indians did not become citizens because they were not subject to the jurisdiction of the United States in the sense meant by the amendment. Moreover, section 2 of the Fourteenth Amendment, which determined the apportionment of representatives in Congress, excluded "Indians not taxed" from the calculations. The committee's opinion became generally accepted so far as Indians holding tribal relations were concerned, and Congress, subsequent to the adoption of the Fourteenth Amendment, passed special laws granting citizenship to various tribes.[57]

What was still not clear, however, was the citizenship status of Indians who voluntarily severed their connections with their tribes and took up the ways of white society. Did they, by such an act, automatically receive citizenship? The Senate Judiciary Committee seemed to imply that they did, for it limited its restriction to tribes and to "individuals, members of such tribes, while they adhere to and form a part of the tribes to which they belong." This theory was current for more than a decade.[58]

In actual decisions of the Department of the Interior, however, the theory did not hold. The matter came up specifically in connection with making the Homestead Law available to Indians, since the law applied to citi-

56. *Congressional Globe*, 39th Congress, 1st session, pp. 2890–97.

57. Ibid., 41st Congress, 1st session, p. 560; *Senate Report* no. 268, 41–3, serial 1443; G. M. Lambertson, "Indian Citizenship," *American Law Review* 20 (March–April 1886): 184; Felix S. Cohen, *Handbook of Federal Indian Law* (Washington: GPO, 1942), p. 154. See also R. Alton Lee, "Indian Citizenship and the Fourteenth Amendment," *South Dakota History* 4 (Spring 1974): 198–221.

58. See *The Political Status of the American Indian* (n.p., n.d.), pp. 8–9; George F. Canfield, "The Legal Position of the Indian," *American Law Review* 15 (January 1881): 33.

zens of the United States. Secretary of the Interior Delano in 1874 saw no problem if an Indian tribe had been dissolved by treaty or by act of Congress (as had happened with certain Ottawa and Chippewa Indians by a treaty of July 31, 1855); the members of such a tribe, he declared, "become *ipso facto* citizens of the United States, and entitled to all the privileges and immunities belonging to other citizens." It was quite different, in his opinion, when an individual Indian withdrew from his tribe and adopted the habits and customs of civilized life. It was, he said, "inconsistent with sound law, as well as with public policy, to permit an individual Indian, by voluntarily withdrawing from his tribe, to become a citizen without some act of the Government recognizing his citizenship." Delano thought the time had arrived for some general law regulating Indian citizenship, but he had to be satisfied with legislation that extended homesteading privileges to Indians without reference to the larger matter of their citizenship.[59]

Not until November 3, 1884, was there a definite answer to questions about the status of an Indian who had withdrawn from his tribe and adopted the ways of white civilization. On that date the Supreme Court handed down its decision in the case of *Elk* v. *Wilkins*. John Elk, an Indian who had separated from his tribe, was refused permission to register to vote in a local election in Omaha, Nebraska, and when he later appeared at the polls he was again refused the right to vote. Elk met the residence and other requirements of the state of Nebraska and of the city of Omaha, but he was turned back because it was alleged that as an Indian he was not a citizen. The majority of the court held against the plaintiff, declaring that an Indian who was born a member of an Indian tribe, although he voluntarily separated himself from the tribe and took up residence among white citizens, was not thereby a citizen of the United States. Some specific act of Congress was necessary to naturalize him. "Indians born within the territorial limits of the United States, members of and owing allegiance to, one of the Indian tribes (an alien though dependent power)," the decision said, "although in a geographical sense born in the United States, are no more 'born in the United States and subject to the jurisdiction thereof,' within the meaning of the first section of the Fourteenth Amendment, than the children . . . born within the United States, of ambassadors or other public ministers of foreign nations."[60]

Granted the necessity, then, of some sort of congressional action to make Indians citizens, would such an enactment be wise and in the best interests of the Indians and of the United States? It was on this ques-

59. Report of the Secretary of the Interior, 1874, *House Executive Document* no. 1, part 5, 43–2, serial 1639, pp. v–vii, ix. The Chippewa treaty is in Kappler, p. 729.
60. 112 *U.S. Reports* 94, 102. Two justices dissented from the majority opinion.

tion that disagreement prevailed. Was citizenship a reward to be conferred when an Indian had demonstrated his desire and his competence to live among the whites, or was citizenship to be a means whereby the Indian would advance on the road to civilization? At first the reformers seemed to agree that preparation was necessary for citizenship and that Indians should not all suddenly be made citizens in a mass.[61] But by the end of 1884 a reversal had occurred on this point, and the Board of Indian Commissioners could assert: "The solution of the Indian problem is citizenship, and we believe that the time has come to declare by an act of Congress that every Indian born within the territorial limits of the United States is a citizen of the United States and subject to the jurisdiction thereof."[62]

The movement gained considerable momentum in the next two years. Merrill E. Gates of the Board of Indian Commissioners prepared a paper in 1885 entitled "Land and Law as Agents in Educating Indians." He asked, "For what ought we to hope as the future of the Indian? What should the Indian become?" And he replied, "To this there is one answer—and but one. He should become an intelligent citizen of the United States. There is no other 'manifest destiny' for any man or any body of men on our domain." Gates was no longer willing to wait until the Indians had proved their worth. "By the stupendous precedent of eight millions of freedmen made citizens in a day," he declared, "we have committed ourselves to the theory that the way to fit men for citizenship is to make them citizens." In the following year the Lake Mohonk Conference formally adopted Gates's view.[63]

There were more cautious voices, however. Dr. Thomas A. Bland of the Indian Defence Association described citizenship as "just such a policy as those who hang about the borders of Indian reservations, awaiting an opportunity to rob the Indians of their lands, would propose, if they dared." Less radical men than Bland did not want to push the Indians headlong into citizenship without guarding them from a precipitous descent into pauperdom. Secretary of the Interior Lamar, meeting in November 1885 with a committee from the Lake Mohonk Conference, answered a question about making the Pueblos citizens by declaring: "After swallowing four million black slaves and digesting that pretty well we need not strain at this. We could do that; but in my opinion it would be most sad service to

61. *Lake Mohonk Conference Proceedings*, 1883, p. 8, and 1884, p. 21. The repeated attempts to get citizenship legislation are discussed in Prucha, *American Indian Policy in Crisis*, pp. 347–49.

62. *Report of the Board of Indian Commissioners*, 1884, pp. 7–10.

63. Ibid., 1885, p. 17; *Lake Mohonk Conference Proceedings*, 1886, p. 46.

the Indian, and there would not be much of him left if that were done suddenly." But most important was Senator Dawes, the towering figure in Indian reform legislation. He persisted in his opinion that indiscriminate granting of citizenship to all Indians would be bad and held to the position that citizenship should be tied to taking land in severalty.[64]

The final provisions on citizenship in the Dawes Act were a compromise:

> And every Indian born within the territorial limits of the United States to whom allotments shall have been made under the provisions of this act, or under any law or treaty, and every Indian born within the territorial limits of the United States who has voluntarily taken up, within said limits, his residence separate and apart from any tribe of Indians therein, and has adopted the habits of civilized life, is hereby declared to be a citizen of the United States, and is entitled to all the rights, privileges, and immunities of such citizens, whether said Indian has been or not, by birth or otherwise, a member of any tribe of Indians within the territorial limits of the United States without in any manner impairing or otherwise affecting the right of any such Indian to tribal or other property.[65]

As a compromise, it did not fully satisfy either faction. Dawes complained about the House amendment to his bill that had provided citizenship for others than allottees under the severalty provisions of the bill. Advocates of immediate citizenship for all Indians were disappointed because tribal Indians on reservations were still excluded.[66]

The Indians frequently did not welcome federal citizenship, and the effects of citizenship in the end were meager, for the actual situation of the Indians was changed very little. Citizenship did not impair tribal law or affect tribal existence. It was not considered incompatible with federal powers of guardianship, nor was it inconsistent with restriction on the right to alienate property.[67] The great drive to make American citizens out of the Indians in the late 1880s and the 1890s through a system of national Indian schools was not a matter of legal citizenship but of cultural amalgamation of the Indians into the mass of white citizens, a much more comprehensive matter.

---

64. *Council Fire* 9: 29, quoted in Priest, *Uncle Sam's Stepchildren*, pp. 210–11; *Report of the Board of Indian Commissioners*, 1885, p. 116.

65. 24 *United States Statutes* 390.

66. The movement toward universal Indian citizenship continued. An act of August 9, 1888, provided that an Indian woman would become an American citizen by marrying a citizen. 25 *United States Statutes* 392. An act of May 3, 1901, declared all Indians in the Indian Territory citizens of the United States. 31 *United States Statutes* 1447.

67. See the discussion in Cohen, *Handbook of Federal Indian Law*, pp. 155–57.

Americanization & Wardship

42. Henry L. Dawes

The chief spokesman in Congress for Americanization of the Indians was Senator Dawes of Massachusetts. His sponsorship of a law to allot the tribal lands of the reservations to individual Indians (Dawes Act of 1887) made his name synonymous with Indian reform. He worked closely with the reform groups and was an example of a humane Christian gentleman promoting programs that were unsuited to the Indians and ultimately disastrous for them.

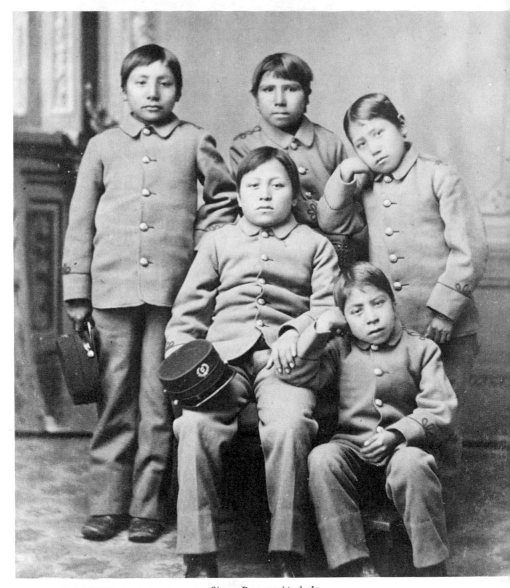

43. Sioux Boys at Carlisle

Pratt was an army officer who devoted much of his life to Indian education. He founded the Indian Industrial School at Carlisle, Pennsylvania, in 1879 and used it to promote his philosophy of absolute assimilation of the Indians through off-reservation boarding school education. The Sioux boys at Carlisle show the external transformation that Pratt insisted upon.

44. Richard Henry Pratt

45. Herbert Welsh

Two leaders in the movement to Americanize the Indians were Herbert Welsh, who founded the Indian Rights Association in Philadelphia in 1882, and Thomas J. Morgan, a professional educator who served as commissioner of Indian affairs, 1889–1893. Welsh and Morgan, together with other reformers interested in Indian affairs, met annually at the Lake Mohonk resort of Albert K. Smiley. There they formulated policies and programs to transform the Indians into counterparts of the white citizens of the nation.

46. Thomas Jefferson Morgan

47. Lake Mohonk Resort

48. Transformation of an Indian

Reformers delighted to witness the transformation of Indians from their native culture to white American ways. The change was often symbolized in before-and-after photographs, such as these formal portraits of Pat Tyhee, a Shoshoni.

The federal government's national school system for Indians called for numerous reservation boarding schools. This massive building located on the Pine Ridge Reservation in South Dakota contrasted sharply with the Indian camp in the foreground.

The resistance of Indians in the Indian Territory to white settlement in their lands was ultimately broken, and large areas not actually occupied by Indians were opened to homesteaders. The openings called out many prospective home seekers, who lined up along the borders waiting for a signal to open the "run." This scene was at the opening of the Cherokee Outlet in 1893.

49. Pine Ridge Indian Boarding School

50. Oklahoma Land Run

51. Estelle Reel

Estelle Reel served as United States superintendent of Indian schools, 1898–1910.
While state superintendent of schools in
Wyoming she had earned a reputation as
an effective educator, but her appointment to high federal office was influenced
by Republican politicians who sought
party gain by appointing a woman from
one of the states that had woman suffrage.

Commissioner of Indian Affairs Jones
(1897–1904) was a transition figure. In
large part he followed the principles of
the humanitarian reformers of the late
nineteenth century, but he also looked to
the future with a practical concern to
adapt education to Indian needs and to
supply programs of self-support for the
Indians.

Leupp, commissioner of Indian affairs
1905–1909, was well acquainted with Indian matters, and he had a self-confidence
in his understanding of Indian problems
that annoyed the oldtime reformers.
Leupp reflected the goal of administrative
efficiency that marked the Progressive
Era, and he was one of the first federal officials to recognize values in the Indians'
culture.

52. William A. Jones

53. Francis E. Leupp

The effect of Indian boarding school education can be seen in the Society of American Indians, an organization of educated Indians established in 1911 that sought assimilation into white society while at the same time retaining a pride in Indianness. This scene shows the society's banquet in Philadelphia in 1914.

54. Society of American Indians Banquet

55. Indian Industrial School, Genoa, Nebraska

The boarding schools for Indians sought the complete transformation of the Indians to white ways. These scenes from the school at Genoa, Nebraska, about 1910 show a girls' sewing class, the fourth grade classroom, and the school band.

Sells, as commissioner of Indian affairs (1913–1920), was obsessed with the idea of "freeing" competent Indians from federal protection and supervision and pushed the granting of competency certificates to Indians, who would then get fee patents for their lands. During his administration, competency commissions traveled to the reservations to seek out Indians judged to be able to handle their own affairs. At some reservations formal ceremonies were conducted—a symbolic shooting of a last arrow and the acceptance of a plow. This scene was at the Crow Creek Reservation in 1916.

56. Cato Sells

57. Competency Ceremony

CHAPTER 27

Education for Patriotic Citizenship

Promotion of Indian Schools. Carlisle Indian

Industrial School. Thomas Jefferson Morgan

and Indian Schools. Conflict over the Contract Schools.

Competition from the Wild West Shows.

Education of the Indians was the ultimate reform. The Lake Mohonk Conference resolved in 1884 that "education is essential to civilization." The reformers declared: "The Indian must have a knowledge of the English language, that he may associate with his white neighbors and transact business as they do. He must have practical industrial training to fit him to compete with others in the struggle for life. He must have a Christian education to enable him to perform the duties of the family, the State, and the Church." Despite the intense agitation for land in severalty and equality under the law for the Indians, there was fundamental agreement that neither homesteads nor legal citizenship would benefit the Indians if they were not properly educated to appreciate the responsibilities as well as the benefits of both.[1]

PROMOTION OF INDIAN SCHOOLS

Indian education, of course, was not new. From earliest colonial days there had been attempts—sporadic and ill-supported—to provide schools for In-

1. *Lake Mohonk Conference Proceedings*, 1884, p. 14. This chapter is in large part a revision and condensation of the material in Francis Paul Prucha, *American Indian Policy in Crisis: Christian Reformers and the Indian, 1865–1900* (Norman: University of Oklahoma Press, 1976), pp. 265–327.

dian children. Much of the effort came from Christian missionaries, for whom education and Christianization were almost interchangeable terms, but the United States government had recognized a responsibility to educate Indians, either by encouraging and supporting missionary endeavors or by providing schools on its own. From an early date education efforts were aimed toward the three goals enunciated by the Lake Mohonk reformers in the 1880s: English language, manual labor training, and knowledge of the Christian religion. Interest in Indian education increased as public education in the United States became a growing concern of the white citizenry.[2]

After the Civil War, when the nation faced the great mass of new Indians who had come within the immediate scope of American Indian policy and needed "civilizing," government officials continued the long tradition, but with a new urgency. The same principles and programs that had been promoted so ardently in the 1840s for the Shawnees, the Potawatomis, and the Cherokees were advocated with renewed vigor in the 1870s and 1880s for the Sioux, the Cheyennes, and the Comanches. Commissioner Dennis Cooley in 1866 made an extensive survey of the condition of the schools and endeavored to revive interest in the work of Indian education, which he characterized as "the only means of saving any considerable portion of the race from the life and death of heathen." Having recently become aware of the German kindergarten system, he sent books explaining it to several teachers and expressed great hopes that the system might attract the younger Indian children to the schools. Education had a central place in the peace policy of Grant's administration, for the church groups who assumed responsibility for the Indian agencies were expected to make education a primary concern. Commissioner Edward P. Smith argued in 1873 that "any plan for civilization which does not provide for training the young, even though at a largely increased expenditure, is short-sighted and expensive." He thought that with proper facilities half the Indian children then growing up in barbarism could be put into schools. The Board of Indian Commissioners in 1875 noted that in order to civilize the Indians and establish them in a permanent condition of self-support, "*education must be regarded as a fundamental and indispensable factor,*" and the board proposed a universal common school system by the federal govern-

2. There have been few general histories of Indian education. Evelyn C. Adams, *American Indian Education: Government Schools and Economic Progress* (New York: King's Crown Press, 1946), is a very brief survey. Unpublished Ph.D. dissertations include Martha Elizabeth Layman, "A History of Indian Education in the United States" (University of Minnesota, 1942), and Theodore Fischbacher, "A Study of the Role of the Federal Government in the Education of the American Indian" (Arizona State University, 1967).

ment for all its Indian wards just as the states provided public schools for their children.[3]

No one pushed more strenuously for Indian education than Carl Schurz. When he outlined his comprehensive Indian program in 1877, he gave extended space to education, and in subsequent years he repeated and refined his ideas. Secretary Henry Teller hammered incessantly on the same theme, and like many of his predecessors, he thought he had finally found the answer to the Indian problem. "The greatest agency for the civilization of the Indian," he wrote in 1884, "is the manual-labor school. Indeed, I do not think I shall be far out of the way if I say the only agency for that purpose is the manual-labor school. . . . The history of the few manual-labor schools established for the education of Indian children has demonstrated their great value, and that it is only necessary to multiply their number, so as to include all the Indian children of school age, to forever set at rest the question as to 'what shall be done with the Indians.'"[4]

Teller's plan reflected the primary concern in all Indian education schemes, to make the Indian self-supporting—not only as a means of advancing the individual's manhood but, quite practically, to end the enormous governmental outlays needed to maintain large numbers of Indians who had lost their old means of subsistence and had not taken up any new ones. To this end, training in agriculture or the common trades for the boys and in the domestic tasks of white households for the girls was considered indispensable. Despite the heavier costs of providing such schools—equipping them with stock, wagons, farming implements, and tools—they were proposed as the only economical policy in the long run. And the manual labor schools had to be boarding schools. Although day schools were provided on the reservations and were an important means of bringing the first lessons of civilization to the young, they were not satisfactory for accomplishing the complete transformation of the Indian children that the reformers had in mind. As Commissioner Ezra Hayt remarked in 1877, "the exposure of children who attend only day-schools to the demoralization and degradation of an Indian home neutralized the efforts of the schoolteacher, especially those efforts which are directed to advancement in morality and civilization." How could the Indian child become properly

3. CIA Report, 1866, serial 1284, pp. 20–21; CIA Report, 1873, serial 1601, p. 377; Report of the Secretary of the Interior, 1871, *House Executive Document* no. 1, part 5, 42–2, serial 1505, pp. 4–5; ibid., 1876, *House Executive Document* no. 1, part 5, 44–2, serial 1749, pp. iii–iv; *Report of the Board of Indian Commissioners*, 1875, pp. 8–9.

4. Report of the Secretary of the Interior, 1877, *House Executive Document* no. 1, part 5, 45–2, serial 1800, pp. xi–xii; ibid., 1884, *House Executive Document* no. 1, part 5, 48–2, serial 2286, p. vii.

acculturated, the reformers asked, if he were not removed from the Indian life and language of his home? What was needed was a substitute home, and this the boarding school provided.[5]

The cultural imperialism of the reformers was exhibited sharply in the demand that Indian languages be prohibited and only English allowed in the Indian schools. The principle was stated clearly by Carl Schurz: "If Indian children are to be civilized they must learn the language of civilization. They will become far more accessible to civilized ideas and ways of thinking when they are enabled to receive those ideas and ways of thinking through the most direct channel of expression." Schurz dismissed efforts to draw up Indian grammars and to instruct the Indians in their native languages as "certainly very interesting and meritorious philological work" but of little use to the Indians. The policy of teaching English in the government schools was praised by the Board of Indian Commissioners as "eminently wise," for if the Indians were to become useful American citizens, they had to know the common language of the country.[6]

The most radical promoter of English was J. D. C. Atkins, commissioner of Indian affairs from 1885 to 1888. Atkins rejoiced that there was not an Indian pupil whose tuition or maintenance in school was paid for by the United States government who was permitted to study any language but English—"the language of the greatest, most powerful, and enterprising nationalities beneath the sun." The superiority of English was a first principle with Atkins, and he was convinced that the Indians should acquire the language as rapidly as possible. He had no qualms about pushing the Indians' native tongues completely aside. English, he said, "which is good enough for a white man and a black man, ought to be good enough for the red man." To allow the Indian to continue with his native tongue was in fact a detriment to him. "The first step to be taken toward civilization, toward teaching the Indians the mischief and folly of continuing in their barbarous practices, is to teach them the English language."[7]

To make sure that his principles were carried out in practice, Atkins issued a series of regulations to the agents and to the representatives of missionary groups to insist that only English be used as a means of instruction in both government and church schools. The directives raised an im-

5. CIA Report, 1873, serial 1601, pp. 376–77; CIA Report, 1877, serial 1800, pp. 399–400; CIA Report, 1882, serial 2100, pp. 25–34; *Report of the Board of Indian Commissioners*, 1871, p. 11, and 1879, p. 14.

6. Report of the Secretary of the Interior, 1877, *House Executive Document* no. 1, part 5, 45–2, serial 1800, p. xii; *Report of the Board of Indian Commissioners*, 1888, pp. 10–11.

7. CIA Report, 1886, serial 2467, pp. 99–100; CIA Report, 1887, serial 2542, pp. 19–21.

mediate storm, largely from missionaries who interpreted them to mean a prohibition on all use of Indian vernacular by missionary teachers. They had been preaching the Gospel in Indian languages and cried that Atkins's order amounted to religious persecution, for the native tongue was the only way to bring Christian teachings to the adult Indians. The commissioner tried to soothe the ruffled feelings of the missionaries and made allowances for certain situations in which the vernacular would be permitted, but he was determined to allow few loopholes in his policy for the schools. "No text-books in the vernacular," he directed, "will be allowed in any school where children are placed under contract, or where the Government contributes to the support of the school; no oral instruction in the vernacular will be allowed at such schools. The entire curriculum must be in the English language."[8]

Atkins insisted that "in the schools established for the rising generation of Indians shall be taught the language of the Republic of which they are to become citizens." If the vernacular were allowed in the schools sponsored by the churches, the Indian students and their parents might be prejudiced against English and against the government schools where it was used exclusively. He stood firm, too, against the charge that his mandatory English struck a cruel blow at the sacred rights of the Indians. "Is it cruelty to the Indian," he asked, "to force him to give up his scalping-knife and tomahawk? Is it cruelty to force him to abandon the vicious and barbarous sun dance, where he lacerates his flesh, and dances and tortures himself even unto death? Is it cruelty to the Indians to force him to have his daughters educated and married under the laws of the land, instead of selling them at a tender age for a stipulated price into concubinage to gratify the brutal lusts of ignorance and barbarism?" He consoled himself in the face of criticism from the missionaries with the argument that he had been governed in his action solely by what he believed to be "the real interests of the Indians," and by the fact that he was supported in his stand by eminent educators and missionaries.[9]

Because the Indians did not respond enthusiastically to English education, whose purpose was to replace their traditional culture, compulsory education became a vital issue. Secretary of the Interior Columbus Delano thought it might be well to withhold annuities from those individuals who

8. Atkins's regulations, dated December 14, 1886, and February 2 and July 16, 1887, are printed in CIA Report, 1887, serial 2542, pp. 20–21. His exchange with the missionaries and other material on the subject are in *Correspondence on the Subject of Teaching the Vernacular in Indian Schools, 1887–'88* (Washington, 1888).

9. CIA Report, 1887, serial 2542, pp. 20–22; *Teaching the Vernacular in Indian Schools*, pp. 17, 20–21.

refused to use the educational facilities offered, and Schurz recommended compulsory education "as far as practicable." By 1884 some steps had been taken. Compulsory education had been tried at four agencies, at two by withholding rations and at two by withholding annuity payments, and the commissioner of Indian affairs noted that as soon as enough school buildings could be provided, all the Sioux could have a similar system of enforcement applied under the terms of their treaty. But no general regulation was enacted at once, despite repeated recommendations that only compulsory education would save the Indians for civilization.[10] There was a general feeling, no doubt, that civilizing and assimilating the Indians must rest on persuasion, not force. And the failure of the government to provide needed funds to care for the education of the entire population of Indian children made compulsion infeasible for a number of years.

Considerable progress was made in the system of Indian education in the quarter-century following the Civil War, even though the enthusiastic proclamations made periodically by officials in Washington have to be accepted with caution. Commissioner Hayt in 1878 provided statistical tables to show the "steady increase" in the number of Indian children attending school. "The results, after trial during the few years past, of the peace policy, imperfectly carried out as it has been," he asserted, "prove beyond a doubt that the eventual civilization of Indians may be reached through the education of their children; and further, that it can be brought about more speedily by that method than by any other." By 1884 Secretary Teller was able to report eighty-one boarding schools, seventy-six day schools, and six industrial or manual labor schools under government control, including new schools at Chilocco, Indian Territory, at Lawrence, Kansas, and at Genoa, Nebraska, plus the schools run by religious denominations.[11]

Secretary L. Q. C. Lamar in 1885, noting the progress in the schools, remarked, "The practicability of Indian education is no longer a question." Two years later he transmitted to the president data for the past decade of work. At the beginning of the decade, in 1878, there had been 137 Indian schools of all kinds provided by the government, with an average atten-

---

10. Report of the Secretary of the Interior, 1871, *House Executive Document* no. 1, part 5, 42–2, serial 1505, pp. 4–5; ibid., 1877, *House Executive Document* no. 1, part 5, 45–2, serial 1800, pp. xi–xii; CIA Report, 1884, serial 2287, p. 18. For recommendations on compulsory education, see Report of the Superintendent of Indian Schools in CIA Report, 1885, serial 2379, pp. 113–14, and Report of the Secretary of the Interior, 1887, *House Executive Document* no. 1, part 5, 50–1, serial 2541, pp. 29–30.

11. CIA Report, 1878, serial 1850, pp. 457–58; Report of the Secretary of the Interior, 1884, *House Executive Document* no. 1, part 5, 48–2, serial 2286, pp. iii–v. See also CIA Report, 1879, serial 1910, pp. 73–74, and CIA Report, 1880, serial 1959, pp. 85–88.

dance of about thirty-five hundred, maintained at a total cost of nearly $196,000. In 1887 there were 231 schools, with over ten thousand students, at a cost of almost $1,200,000. Lamar considered this "a gratifying improvement," which showed how interest in education was growing among the Indians.[12]

The figures surely indicated substantial growth, but even a cursory examination of them indicates that the surface had been little more than scratched. Ten thousand pupils out of an Indian population estimated at one-third of a million could hardly be considered satisfactory. The fact, of course, did not escape the proponents of Indian education, and the commissioners of Indian affairs kept pounding on the doors of Congress for additional funds needed to establish a reasonably inclusive system for the Indian children. Ely S. Parker in 1869 lamented that Congress had reduced the estimates for educational expenses that he had submitted, Edward P. Smith in 1873 argued that a "large expenditure for a few years in the proper direction will be more economical than a smaller expenditure perpetuated," Hiram Price in 1881 noted that the State of Rhode Island spent $600,000 annually for forty-nine thousand students, compared with the government's $215,000 for the same number of Indian children, Atkins in 1887 pointed out that the "cost of the schools is immeasurably less than that of the wars they supplant, to say nothing of the sacrifices of lives of both soldiers and Indians." Everyone, in fact, urged greater appropriations for Indian education.[13]

Since the appropriations, although they were increasing, were by no means equal to the task, the government continued to rely on missionary effort for many schools. By means of so-called "contract schools," the government gave financial aid on a per capita basis to religious groups that set up schools on the reservations. By 1883, these groups were conducting twenty-two boarding schools and sixteen day schools with government aid, in addition to those they conducted on their own. The aggregate monetary contribution to these schools came to $252,061, but this was considered to be only a part of the value contributed by the missionaries. "The influence of men and women whose lives are devoted to the uplifting of the degraded and ignorant cannot be measured by dollars and cents," Commissioner Price asserted. "Moreover, the very fact that he represents a

12. Report of the Secretary of the Interior, 1885, *House Executive Document* no. 1, part 5, 49–1, serial 2378, p. 29; ibid., 1887, *House Executive Document* no. 1, part 5, 50–1, serial 2541, p. 29. See also CIA Report, 1887, serial 2542, pp. 12–15, 757–91. For a table showing annual appropriations for Indian schools, 1877–1894, see CIA Report, 1893, serial 3210, p. 18.

13. CIA Report, 1869, serial 1414, p. 455; CIA Report, 1873, serial 1601, p. 377; CIA Report, 1881, serial 2018, pp. 25–30; CIA Report, 1887, serial 2542, p. 18.

great religious denomination, that a Christian community is his constituency, and that the funds which come into his hands have been consecrated by prayer and self-denial, gives to a man and his work a moral force and momentum which Government patronage does not impart." Price's successors, Atkins and John Oberly, continued the system, and the religious groups responded generously, putting more money into Indian school buildings than did the government. The increase in enrollment between 1887 and 1888, for example, was substantially greater in the contract schools than in the government schools because the contract schools had increased their accommodations more.[14] The Christian interest in Indian matters explicitly acknowledged by government officials made such an arrangement seem unexceptionable.

CARLISLE INDIAN INDUSTRIAL SCHOOL

A showpiece of Indian education, which some reformers considered a model of what could be done to transform the Indians, was the Indian school at Carlisle, Pennsylvania. It was the work of a remarkable young army officer named Richard Henry Pratt, whose appearance on the scene in the mid-1870s gave a new impetus and, in a sense, a new direction to Indian schooling.[15] Pratt, born in New York State in 1840, served in the Civil War as a cavalry officer and after the war reentered the army as a second lieutenant. He was assigned to the Tenth Cavalry, a black regiment,

14. CIA Report, 1883, serial 2191, p. 32; CIA Report, 1887, serial 2542, pp. 16–17; CIA Report, 1888, serial 2637, pp. xii–xv. For a detailed tabular account of religious educational work among the Indians in 1883, see CIA Report, 1883, serial 2191, pp. 298–303.

15. Pratt's career and the history of his educational work with the Indians can best be followed in his memoirs and related papers printed in *Battlefield and Classroom: Four Decades with the American Indian, 1876–1904,* ed. Robert M. Utley (New Haven: Yale University Press, 1964). Valuable also is Pratt's *The Indian Industrial School, Carlisle, Pennsylvania: Its Origin, Purpose, Progress and the Difficulties Surmounted* (Carlisle: Hamilton Library Association, 1908). Elaine Goodale Eastman, *Pratt: The Red Man's Moses* (Norman: University of Oklahoma Press, 1935), is an uncritical biography written by a person much involved in Indian reform. A great deal of detail can be found in Carmelita S. Ryan, "The Carlisle Indian Industrial School" (Ph.D. dissertation, Georgetown University, 1962); Everett Arthur Gilcreast, "Richard Henry Pratt and American Indian Policy, 1877–1906: A Study of the Assimilation Movement" (Ph.D. dissertation, Yale University, 1967); and Pearl Lee Walker-McNeil, "The Carlisle Indian School: A Study of Acculturation" (Ph.D. dissertation, American University, 1979). See also Robert L. Brunhouse, "The Founding of the Carlisle Indian School," *Pennsylvania History* 6 (April 1939): 72–85; Louis Morton, "How the Indians Came to Carlisle," ibid. 39 (January 1962): 53–73; and Thomas G. Tousey, *Military History of Carlisle and Carlisle Barracks* (Richmond, Virginia: Dietz Press, 1939), pp. 273–355.

and saw considerable action on the southern plains against hostile Indians in 1868–1869 and in the Red River War of 1874–1875. As commander of Indian scouts, he gained firsthand knowledge of the Indian's character and capabilities.

When the fighting ended, Pratt was detailed to take a group of seventy-two Indian prisoners to Fort Marion at St. Augustine, Florida. As he cared for the prisoners there, he began a program of education that was to make him a national figure. He got permission to release the Indians from close confinement, replaced their guards with some of the Indian prisoners themselves, instituted classes for them, and found useful work for them in the St. Augustine area. Determined to advance the Indians in their progress toward acceptance of white ways by treating them with dignity and providing opportunities for them to mix with whites, he had remarkable success. He interested white benefactors in his cause and persuaded his army superiors to assign him to the work of Indian education, where he could promote and expand the approach to Indian assimilation that he had begun so dramatically at Fort Marion. When the Indians' imprisonment came to an end, Pratt was assigned to Hampton Normal and Agricultural Institute in Virginia, and he took with him twenty-two of his Indian students, who were supported by private benefactors.

Hampton had already become well known for its educational work with freedmen under the direction of General Samuel C. Armstrong, who had commanded black troops during the Civil War and then served as an agent of the Freedmen's Bureau. Armstrong developed and promoted a plan of combining mental and manual training for the blacks, and he founded Hampton Institute for that purpose in 1868 with the support of the American Missionary Association and private benefactors. The strong similarity that reformers saw between the needs of the ex-slaves and those of the Indians in preparing for full participation in American society made it reasonable to provide room for Indians as well as blacks at Hampton. Pratt and his Indian charges arrived in April 1878, and soon Pratt was off to the West to recruit more Indians for his educational experiment. He returned with forty-three additional students for the Indian department at Hampton.[16]

16. On Hampton Institute, see Francis Greenwood Peabody, *Education for Life: The Story of Hampton Institute* (Garden City, New York: Doubleday, Page and Company, 1919); David Wallace Adams, "Education in Hues: Red and Black at Hampton Institute, 1878–1893," *South Atlantic Quarterly* 76 (Spring 1977): 159–76; Joseph Willard Tingey, "Indians and Blacks Together: An Experiment in Biracial Education at Hampton Institute, 1878–1923" (Ed.D. dissertation, Columbia University Teachers College, 1978). See also "Report of Lieut. R. H. Pratt, Special Agent to Collect Indian Youths to Be Educated at Hampton Institute, Va.," *House Executive Document* no. 1, part 5, 45–3, serial 1850, pp. 669–71.

Despite this promising beginning, Pratt chafed under the conditions at Hampton and feared that popular prejudices against the blacks would rub off on his Indians, whom he wished to see associate and mix fully with whites. He proposed, therefore, to set up an industrial training school solely for Indians, where he could carry out his educational principles unhampered. He importuned his superiors in the army and the officials of the Interior Department for a chance to prove the value of his program. He found in Secretary Schurz a sympathetic friend, and by a series of bureaucratic maneuvers he got permission to use the abandoned military barracks at Carlisle for his work. The federal government continued to support Indian students at Hampton until 1912, and for another decade a few Indians still attended, but attention soon became focused on Pratt's new venture at Carlisle.

Pratt went west in the summer of 1879 to recruit students for his school. At the Rosebud Agency, he persuaded Spotted Tail to send his children to Carlisle, and other Sioux there and at Pine Ridge followed the chief's example. Eighty-two children, who were in a sense hostages for the good behavior of their parents, made a dramatic entry into Carlisle on October 6, 1879, still wearing their tribal costumes, and the Carlisle Indian Industrial School began its influential history. The Sioux were soon joined by fifty-five students from tribes in the Indian Territory, and on November 1, 1879, the school was officially opened. Enrollment steadily increased as facilities grew and the fame of the school spread, until it reached about a thousand students.

Pratt's views on Indian matters were simple. He insisted upon complete integration of the Indians into white society, and his whole program was geared to that goal. Anything that tended to isolate or segregate the Indians was to him anathema. Reservations were an unmitigated evil and tribal status a preservation of outmoded ways and attitudes; he condemned what he called "this whole segregating and reservating process." He was only half jesting when he noted that there were about 260,000 Indians in the United States and twenty-seven hundred counties and suggested that the Indians be divided up and sprinkled, nine to a county, across the nation.[17] There were no twilight zones in Pratt's mind; his principle shone as a brilliant light, and he wavered not an inch from the path it marked out. He held as tenaciously to his views at the end of his long career as he had at the beginning, despite the setbacks he had received and the loss of friends who had broken with him.

Pratt firmly believed that human beings were products of their environ-

17. Eastman, *Pratt*, pp. 77, 221.

ment. "There is no resistless clog placed upon us by birth," he insisted. "We are not born with language, nor are we born with ideas of either civilization or savagery. Language, savagery and civilization are forced upon us entirely by our environment after birth." If the Indians were kept in tribal surroundings on the reservation, he said, the nation would "not lack material for Wild West shows which the gaping throngs of our great cities may scoff at and the crowned heads of Europe patronize, for centuries to come." He repeatedly pointed to the example of the blacks, who had learned the white man's language and his customs by associating with him, and to Europeans, who had immigrated in large numbers but were being rapidly integrated, while the Indians still remained Indians.[18]

Pratt was a man of tremendous drive, with an impatience to get things done that could not brook opposition or delay. "If I were asked to characterize in one word Captain Pratt's work for the Indian," one of his contemporaries said, "I should call it *uncompromising*. He does not hesitate—he stops at no half-way measures. His goal is American citizenship; and, while others are working gradually and tentatively *toward* that end, he works directly *for* it—flings himself *at* it with all the force and combativeness of his vigorous nature."[19] This singlemindedness carried with it a stubborn streak and an inability to admit mistakes. Those who disagreed with him he charged with stupidity or jealousy, and he easily imagined plots against him. But he was scrupulously honest and a deeply religious man.

The Carlisle Indian Industrial School was to be but the beginning, the prototype of a system of similar schools that would eventually provide all Indian youth with training for assimilation. Pratt wanted the results to be so convincing that other off-reservation schools would follow until the universal training he envisaged would obtain, and he used his considerable promotional skills to make sure that the story of Carlisle was widely known. He himself lectured widely, influential men and women were invited to visit the school, and he gave the Carlisle band full exposure at parades and other public gatherings. In this he was much helped by the discovery in the 1890s that the Indians at Carlisle could play great football, holding their own on the gridiron with the best of the Ivy League schools.[20]

18. Richard Henry Pratt, *How to Deal with the Indians: The Potency of Environment* (Carlisle: Carlisle Indian School, 1903), p. 3. An excellent statement of Pratt's views is given in his paper "The Advantages of Mingling Indians with Whites," read at the Nineteenth Annual Conference of Charities and Correction, Denver, 1892.

19. Elaine Goodale in *Captain Pratt and His Work for Indian Education* (Philadelphia: Indian Rights Association, 1886), p. 6.

20. Much information about Carlisle was spread through the school papers published there. The publications—variously called *School News, The Red Man, The Red Man and*

The athletic association with Harvard and Cornell and Pennsylvania was a grossly inaccurate indication of the academic level that Carlisle was able to achieve, for its level of instruction was basically that of a grammar school. Indian students came to Carlisle with little or no schooling, and some of them had to learn English after they arrived. Not until 1889, a decade after its opening, did Carlisle graduate its first class. Ultimately the course was extended to include the first two years of high school and some teacher training.

Pratt's success, however, did not depend entirely upon the academic competence and accomplishments of his students. Following Armstrong's lead, he insisted upon education for the hand and the heart as well as the head, and various manual labor or industrial pursuits formed a large part of the training. An essential part of the Carlisle program was the "outing system," a program of placing students during the summer and sometimes throughout the year with rural families in the vicinity of Carlisle, many of whom were Quakers and shared the traditional interest of their church in Indian welfare. The outing system exemplified Pratt's principle of associating Indian children closely with whites so that they could learn by example and observation the benefits of white family and economic life. It was a tightly controlled system, however, in which rigid rules were enforced.[21]

Pratt's prominence made him the focus of attacks by men who opposed the idea of trying to educate the Indians in the East and who objected strenuously to the expenditure of government funds for that purpose.[22] That there were good points in Pratt's educational philosophy, however, was recognized by most of the persons who sought to improve the condition of the Indians. The prominence of Carlisle in the public eye and the unmistakable achievements of many of the students were convincing proof to many former skeptics that Indians were indeed educable and could take their places in white society. Still, few of the reformers or the

---

Indian Helper, and *The Carlisle Arrow*—provided a vehicle for Pratt's views and were another proof of the capabilities of the students.

21. Pratt described the outing system in *Lake Mohonk Conference Proceedings,* 1891, pp. 60–65. See also George Bird Grinnell, "The Indians and the Outing System," *Outlook* 75 (September 12, 1903): 167–73. The outing system did not work so well at the other off-reservation training schools. The public-spirited Quaker farmers and Pratt with his unusual dynamic force were no doubt responsible for the success of the system at Carlisle.

22. A chief critic was Senator Preston B. Plumb of Kansas, who railed against Pratt, whom he considered a fraud and a swindler bent on self-aggrandizement. See the debate in the Senate over a special grant to Pratt, January 21, 1881, *Congressional Record,* 11: 817–21.

officials in the Indian Office wanted to go down Pratt's single track. After the initial years of enthusiastic support and rich praise, Pratt's doctrine ran into opposition, and alternative programs were projected that ultimately won the day. Pratt's position that the Indian problem would be solved only if every Indian student were enrolled in an off-reservation school, to move from there to public schools and thence into the mainstream of white society (with the consequent destruction of reservations and any other form of segregation), was pushed aside by a more varied and comprehensive system of Indian education, which emphasized reservation schools instead of those away from the reservations.

A problem that bothered Pratt's critics was the eventual status of the alumni of the eastern industrial training schools. Were they, in fact, absorbed into white society as Pratt hoped? Or did they return to the reservation, and if so, did their eastern off-reservation schooling fit them for the lives they actually led? The advocates of Hampton and Carlisle published careful reports to show that few graduates reverted to their old ways when they returned to their reservations.[23] But there were serious problems of adjustment, and the solution seemed to be to raise the general level of education on the reservations so that there would be less disparity between the returned students and those they had left behind. To attain this goal, emphasis would have to be placed on reservation schools. Planting a school on a reservation, it was argued, would bring the older members of the tribe within the school's sphere of influence. Off-reservation schools like Carlisle could then best serve as a capstone for a system of education beginning with day schools and boarding schools on the reservations, which would feed those youths best qualified for advanced studies to Carlisle and similar academies.[24]

As the movement for reservation schools grew, Pratt struck back at his opponents. He attacked the missionaries for fostering Indian ways and the Indian Rights Association because it openly supported day schools and other schools on the reservations. Ethnologists, too, were victims of his tirades, and he accused them of persuading the Indians to remain in their old ways and teaching them to be proud of their race. Pratt saved his strong-

---

23. Herbert Welsh, *Are the Eastern Industrial Training Schools for Indian Children a Failure?* (Philadelphia: Indian Rights Association, 1886); J. J. Gravatt, *The Record of Hampton's Returned Indian Pupils* (Philadelphia: Indian Rights Association, 1885); *Senate Executive Document* no. 31, 52–1, serial 2892. The last item is a long report, dated December 1891, on 639 returned students, with photographs of some of them at home on the reservations.

24. Pratt, however, charged that the reservation schools refused to send their best students on to Carlisle and generally allowed him "to have the rubbish." See the discussion in Gilcreast, "Pratt and American Indian Policy," pp. 305–6.

est denunciations, however, for the Office of Indian Affairs because of its educational policy and because it dealt with tribes and thought in terms of reservations. He accused the bureau of seeking only to perpetuate itself and referred to it as a "barnacle to be knocked off some time." His intemperate remarks and cantankerous attitude were too much for Washington officialdom. On June 15, 1904, Pratt was informed by the commissioner of Indian affairs that he had been dismissed from his post at Carlisle.[25] But he did not quietly fade away. Retired from the army with a rank of brigadier general, he continued to fight singlemindedly until his death in 1924 for the cause and principles he had espoused.

Pratt's goal was never attained, and the system on which he had placed his hope was rejected. His basic assumption that it was possible to eradicate completely the culture of the Indians and assimilate them as European immigrants were assimilated into American society was a questionable one and could not have been accomplished without great human cost. His importance lies not in promoting this impossible dream, but in his part in awakening public opinion to the capabilities of the Indians and in mobilizing forces to promote their education. "General Pratt," Herbert Welsh said, "was, in my opinion, the greatest moral force effecting the great change that has taken place in the minds of our citizens touching the Indians."[26]

THOMAS JEFFERSON MORGAN AND INDIAN SCHOOLS

The early efforts to create an Indian school system look anemic compared with the earnest drive for Indian education that came after the passage of the Dawes Act in 1887. The Lake Mohonk Conference of 1888, with a fearful sense of urgency, turned most of its attention to Indian education. The question, as formulated by one member of the conference, was "How can we make the individual red man a member of the white man's civilization?" The answer was obvious to him: "We have got to train him and fit him for it by the slow process of education." There was a lengthy discussion about how this might best be done, and the conference in the end called for a thorough system of government Indian schools, pledging its cooperation in efforts "to remove at once the National dishonor of supporting ignorant and barbaric people in the heart of a Christian civilization."[27]

25. Gilcreast, "Pratt and American Indian Policy," pp. 252–301, gives a long discussion of Pratt's quarrels with the humanitarians, Catholic and Protestant missionaries, his army superiors, and the Indian Office.
26. Quoted in Eastman, *Pratt*, p. 8.
27. *Lake Mohonk Conference Proceedings*, 1888, pp. 24, 94–95.

To forward this work the reformers soon had the powerful aid of Thomas Jefferson Morgan, commissioner of Indian affairs from 1889 to 1893 and the most significant national figure in Indian education in the nineteenth century. Not only was Morgan a professional educator, but he epitomized important intellectual trends of his age. His ardent and aggressive Americanism, his unquestioning belief in the public school system, his professional Protestantism (with its corollary of anti-Catholicism), and his deep humanitarianism brought together strands of American thought that had been slowly but steadily intertwining in the preceding decades. With him the United States government embarked upon a comprehensive system of Indian education that had enduring effects for the Indians and for the nation. Morgan was a symbol of the realization taking shape that education was the indispensable instrument that would make possible the final goal envisaged for the Indians.[28]

This goal was aptly expressed by the title of a book Morgan published two years after he left office, a sort of catechism for public school pupils that expounded the nationalistic fervor that nineteenth-century America reveled in. The book, a distillation of Morgan's philosophy developed during his years as soldier, clergyman, educator, and government administrator, was called *Patriotic Citizenship*. The title expressed Morgan's highest aspiration for the nation he loved. It could serve as well as the motto of his four-year term as commissioner of Indian affairs, for he energetically sought to usher the Indians, at last, into the great republican edifice as citizens indistinguishable from other Americans.[29]

Morgan, born in Franklin, Indiana, on August 17, 1839, served in the Civil War, first as a lieutenant under Benjamin Harrison in the Seventieth Indiana Volunteer Infantry and then as a commander of black troops. When the war ended, he entered Rochester Theological Seminary and in 1869 was ordained a Baptist minister. Alternating between ministerial work and public education—he served as head of state normal schools in Nebraska, New York, and Rhode Island—Morgan emerged as a national figure in the burgeoning public school movement. He gained attention in the educational world through his writings and public addresses. In addition, he was a regular participant in the annual meetings of the National Education Association and served as a vice president of that organization from 1887 to 1889. Although he maintained his interest in Baptist educa-

28. A convenient summary of Morgan's work as commissioner is Francis Paul Prucha, "Thomas Jefferson Morgan, 1889–93," in Robert M. Kvasnicka and Herman J. Viola, eds., *The Commissioners of Indian Affairs, 1824–1977* (Lincoln: University of Nebraska Press, 1979), pp. 193–203.
29. Thomas J. Morgan, *Patriotic Citizenship* (New York: American Book Company, 1895).

tional activities and served as corresponding secretary of the Providence branch of the Indian Rights Association, it was as a public educator that he prided himself and first sought public office.[30]

When his old Civil War commander, Benjamin Harrison, was elected to the presidency, Morgan hoped to be appointed United States commissioner of education, but he was offered instead the post of commissioner of Indian affairs, which he eagerly accepted. He came to the Indian Office with firm opinions on the value of education as an essential means for the promotion of American citizenship and on the necessity of a public school system. In his book *Studies in Pedagogy*, he extolled the virtues of the "free schools of America," which would create a universal Americanism. The goal of the teachers, he wrote, should be to bring about a common life among the various peoples who made up the nation. The children of Germans, Italians, and Africans, of Protestants, Catholics, and atheists, of anarchists, socialists, and communists entered the classroom representing divergent and often antagonistic groups. They should leave the schools "speaking the same language, eager in the same pursuits of knowledge, loving the same institutions, loyal to the same flag, proud of the same history, and acknowledging the one God the maker of us all."[31] In his new office, Morgan added the American Indians to this vision.

His first annual report as commissioner, submitted on October 1, 1889, presented his general position on Indian affairs—a position clearly in accord with the views advanced by the Board of Indian Commissioners, the Lake Mohonk Conference, and other associated Indian reform groups. He had entered into his office, he said, with "a few simple, well-defined, and strongly-cherished convictions." He asserted that the "anomalous position heretofore occupied by the Indians in this country can not much longer be maintained." The reservation system had to cease, and the "logic of events" demanded the absorption of the Indians into the national life, not as Indians but as American citizens. The relation of the Indians to the government must come to rest solely upon a recognition of their individuality, and in the end the Indians must conform to American civilization.[32] The day following the submission of this statement of his philosophy, Morgan appeared at the Lake Mohonk Conference to present in detail a proposal for an Indian educational system and to elicit support. His goal was clear:

30. For facts on Morgan's career, see *Dictionary of American Biography*, s.v. Morgan, Thomas Jefferson, by Conrad Henry Moehlman, and an autobiographical sketch attached to letter of Morgan to E. W. Halford, January 14, 1889, in OSI, Appointments Division, Commissioners of Indian Affairs, 1889.

31. Thomas J. Morgan, *Studies in Pedagogy* (Boston: Silver, Burdett and Company, 1889), pp. 327–28, 348–50.

32. CIA Report, 1889, serial 2725, pp. 3–4.

When we speak of the education of the Indians, we mean that comprehensive system of training and instruction which will convert them into American citizens, put within their reach the blessings which the rest of us enjoy, and enable them to compete successfully with the white man on his own ground and with his own methods. Education is to be the medium through which the rising generation of Indians are to be brought into fraternal and harmonious relationship with their white fellow-citizens, and with them enjoy the sweets of refined homes, the delight of social intercourse, the emoluments of commerce and trade, the advantages of travel, together with the pleasures that come from literature, science, and philosophy, and the solace and stimulus afforded by a true religion.[33]

Morgan pointed out that the education of the Indians was a responsibility of the national government that could not safely be shirked or delegated to any other party. And he insisted that the government of the United States, "now one of the richest on the face of the earth, with an overflowing treasury," could undertake the work without finding it a burden. To accomplish the work he set forth a series of stipulations. The schools should accommodate all the Indian children and be completely systematized. The common schools on the reservations, the agency boarding schools, and the great national industrial schools like Carlisle and Hampton should be properly related to form one whole. There should be a uniform course of study, similar methods of instruction, and standard textbooks, so that the Indian schools would conform to the public school system of the states. Although Morgan placed special stress on industrial training that would fit the Indian to earn an honest living, he asked for provision as well for "that general literary culture which the experience of the white race has shown to be the very essence of education." To this end command of the English language was necessary, and Morgan proposed that in schools supported wholly or in part by the government only English-speaking teachers be employed and that no language but English be allowed in the schools.

"The Indian youth," he said, "should be instructed in their rights, privileges, and duties as American citizens; should be taught to love the American flag; should be imbued with genuine patriotism, and made to feel that the United States, and not some paltry reservation, is their home." He urged those responsible for educating the Indians to waken in them "a

---

33. *Lake Mohonk Conference Proceedings,* 1889, pp. 16–17. The full address, "The Education of American Indians," is on pp. 16–34; it was also printed separately. The quotations in the paragraphs following are taken from this address.

sense of independence, self-reliance, and self-respect." He was worried that Indian youth, after studying at the off-reservation schools, would return to the reservations rather than put their former life of the tribe behind them. "Education should seek the disintegration of the tribes, and not their segregation. They should be educated, not as Indians, but as Americans. In short, public schools should do for them what they are so successfully doing for all the other races in this country,—assimilate them."

Coeducation was another part of Morgan's plan. It was the surest way, he thought, to lift Indian women out of their position of "servility and degradation" up to a plane where they would be treated with "the same gallantry and respect which is accorded to their more favored white sisters." For both girls and boys he proposed an extension of the outing system that had been developed at Carlisle. By this means the Indian children would acquire "habits of industry, a practical acquaintance with civilized life, a sense of independence, enthusiasm for home, and the practical ability to earn their own living." In this system he found a promise of their "complete emancipation."

With the enthusiastic support of the Lake Mohonk Conference, Morgan moved ahead boldly with his elaboration of a school system for the Indians. In a "Supplemental Report on Indian Education" of December 1, 1889, he explained in specific detail what he proposed for high schools, grammar schools, and primary schools, consciously modeling them on the public school system that he knew. His plans were pervaded by his overall philosophy of turning Indians as rapidly as possible into patriotic American citizens. His optimism was unbounded. If the government would provide the means to establish the schools called for in his supplemental report, it would be only a matter of time—"two or three years I think will suffice"—before all Indian youth of school age would be in school.[34]

Still another of Morgan's basic principles was patriotic training for the Indian pupils, for love of America was the keystone in his arch of American citizenship. As part of the students' training, he asserted, it was important that they understand the significance of national holidays and be encouraged to celebrate them. He sent instructions to the schools for appropriate celebrations of New Year's Day, Washington's Birthday, Decoration Day, the Fourth of July, Thanksgiving, Christmas, and Arbor Day, and he directed that a special holiday (to be called Franchise Day) be celebrated on February 8, the date on which the Dawes Act was signed. "The Indian heroes of the camp-fire need not be disparaged," he said, "but gradually and unobtrusively the heroes of American homes and history may be substi-

34. "Supplemental Report on Indian Education," December 1, 1889, in CIA Report, 1889, serial 2725, pp. 93–114; CIA Report, 1890, serial 2841, pp. vi–viii, xiv–xvii.

tuted as models and ideals." The students were to be taught that the highest privilege that could be conferred on them was American citizenship.[35]

Everything Morgan wrote manifested the philosophy of the reform groups he represented. These principles shine through in clearest fashion in a paper he read at Albany under the sentimental title *A Plea for the Papoose.* In a long fantasy in which he spoke for an Indian infant and set forth what the child was dreaming of for himself, Morgan displayed his strong adherence to the theory of the unity of humanity on which so much reform effort rested. The savagery and brutishness of the Indians, he noted, were due "rather to unfortunate circumstances, for which they are not always responsible, than to any inherent defect of nature." Granted this principle, the need for providing proper environment and training followed logically. "The pretty, innocent papoose has in itself the potency of a painted savage, prowling like a beast of prey," he continued, "or the possibility of a sweet and gentle womanhood or a noble and useful manhood." It was up to the nation to provide the education necessary to make the latter possibility come true.[36]

Morgan did not completely succeed, of course. His plan was based on a hierarchy of schools, beginning with primary schools on the reservation, proceeding through reservation boarding schools, and culminating in the off-reservation industrial schools. Unless a steady flow of students could be maintained from the lower to the higher schools, the system of producing American citizens would break down. The number of off-reservation schools, he pointed out to one agent who complained about students being taken away from his school, had increased from eight to twenty in a comparatively short time and had a capacity of five thousand, and they could not be run economically unless they had full enrollment. Children had to be brought there from the reservation schools and this had to be done "not once, twice or thrice during the year, but many times in order that all these schools may be filled." The reservation schools were to be considered "recruiting stations for the non-reservation schools."[37]

Morgan realized that persuasion alone would not succeed in making his theoretically wonderful system work. The depth of his conviction that it must succeed can be seen in his ultimate willingness to resort to force. The Indian Office, he told the secretary of the interior in 1892, "has argued with the Indians; has pleaded with them; has offered every inducement in

35. CIA Report, 1890, serial 2841, pp. xviii–xix, clxvii–clxix.

36. *A Plea for the Papoose: An Address at Albany, N.Y., by Gen. T. J. Morgan* (n.p., n.d.), pp. 2–4.

37. Morgan to C. W. Crouse, October 24, 1892, OIA LS, Education, vol. 44, pp. 128–30 (second pagination).

its power to cause them voluntarily to put their children into school; has, wherever it seemed wise, resorted to mild punishment by the withholding of rations or supplies, and, where necessary, has directed Agents to use their Indian police as truant officers in compelling attendance." There had been some encouraging results and a sizable increase in the number of pupils in school, and he refused to admit any error in principle. "After 25 years of experience in educational work, with exceptional opportunities for studying the question, I have no hesitation in saying that the present scheme of Government education for Indians has in it the 'promise and potency' of accomplishing for these people all that its most zealous friends have claimed for it."[38]

Morgan's educational system with its pattern of courses was attuned to the purposes the reformers had in mind. But the schools in actuality were less than perfect. Emphasis on manual training meant that the students progressed more slowly in the three Rs than did white students in state public schools, and the great spread of ages among students in the lower grades was a further challenge to the teachers, many of whom were not well trained for the difficult education task they faced. The physical condition of the buildings was often deficient, and the schools succeeded far less than the reformers assumed.

The advance of the government school system for the Indians, in fact, was resisted everywhere. Indian parents, not appreciating the value of the schools, and medicine men, who feared the enlightenment of the people, Morgan charged, threw themselves against the new movement. The commissioner might have interpreted such evidence as an indication that perhaps all was not right with his theory, but no such doubts crossed his mind. He remained convinced that the great work of making acceptable citizens through education must go on. "I would not needlessly nor lightly interfere with the rights of Indian parents," he wrote. "But I do not believe that Indians like the Bannacks and Shoshones at Fort Hall, the Southern Utes in Colorado, the Apaches, or the Navajoes of Arizona,—people who, for the most part, speak no English, live in squalor and degradation, make little progress from year to year, who are a perpetual source of expense to the Government and a constant menace to thousands of their white neighbors, a hindrance to civilization and a clog on our progress—have any right to forcibly keep their children out of school to grow up like themselves, a race of barbarians and semi-savages. We owe it to those children to prevent, forcibly if need be, so great and appalling a calamity from befalling them." He asked for a show of military force in order to convince the Indians that the government was in earnest in the matter and that the au-

---

38. Morgan to the secretary of the interior, November 30, 1892, copy in Henry L. Dawes Papers, Library of Congress.

thority of its agents was to be respected. Such a move Morgan believed "to be dictated by every honorable, patriotic, philanthropic, and humanitarian consideration."[39]

Morgan had expressed similar views publicly at the Lake Mohonk Conference in October 1892 and had won the support of the meeting. The platform adopted at the conference read in part: "In cases where parents, without good reason, refuse to educate their children, we believe that the government is justified, as a last resort, in using power to compel attendance. We do not think it desirable to rear another generation of savages."[40]

CONFLICT OVER THE CONTRACT SCHOOLS

Morgan's carefully conceived plan for a universal public school system of Indian education was challenged most seriously by the system of schools run by Catholic missionaries. The conflict was in large part an outgrowth of Catholic-Protestant antagonism that arose during the peace policy in the decade after the Civil War. Catholics were aggrieved by the assignment of so few agencies to them, and their determination to have a bigger role in Indian affairs gradually gained momentum under the direction of the Bureau of Catholic Indian Missions.[41]

The establishment of the Catholic Bureau in 1874 signaled—indeed, helped to stimulate—a new surge in Catholic activity. As Catholic population steadily increased in the United States, a vigorous and growing Church stepped up its mission work. Much of this, of course, was the work of religious orders and congregations of men and women, which, like the Catholic Church in the United States generally, were heavily staffed by foreign immigrants. Significant, too, was the continuing benefaction of Katharine Drexel, daughter of the wealthy Philadelphia financier Francis Drexel. She and her two sisters used large sums of their inheritance to build schools for Catholic Indian missions and to help staff them. And in 1891 Katharine Drexel founded a new congregation of nuns, the Sisters of the Blessed Sacrament, to work exclusively among Indians and blacks.[42]

39. Ibid.

40. *Lake Mohonk Conference Proceedings*, 1892, pp. 51–54, 121.

41. A detailed study of the Protestant-Catholic controversy, upon which this account draws, is Francis Paul Prucha, *The Churches and the Indian Schools, 1888–1912* (Lincoln: University of Nebraska Press, 1979); the book is based on the records of the Bureau of Catholic Indian Missions, Marquette University; the Indian Rights Association Papers, Historical Society of Pennsylvania; and the records of the Bureau of Indian Affairs, National Archives.

42. See Consuela Marie Duffy, *Katharine Drexel: A Biography* (Philadelphia: Peter Reilly Company, 1966), which is based on the extensive archives of the Sisters of the

The contract school system was especially attractive to Catholics, for the government funds, together with the Drexel gifts and the teaching staffs of priests and nuns, provided support for many schools. It was easy to expand under such circumstances, and expansion was seen as a necessary means to outmaneuver Protestant educational efforts. In May 1889 the president of the Catholic Bureau, Bishop Martin Marty, summarized the Catholic advance:

> The rapid growth of the Bureau almost surpasses belief. When the Bureau was first organized, in 1874, the Catholic Missions and Sisters had two boarding and five day schools, supported by the United States government at an expense of $8,000; there were, June 30, 1883, eighteen boarding schools, receiving a government allotment of $54,000. Our contracts with the Government during the year just closing aggregate $394,533, and we estimate that during the year about to commence the amount will be $431,933. Since the Council of Baltimore was held, five years ago, the Bureau has acquired property to the value of one million dollars. These results have not been accomplished without labor. We have fought every inch of the way. We must not let this work flag.[43]

The result of the aggressive Catholic action, coupled with declining Protestant interest, was a dominance of Catholics in Indian missions and the receipt by their schools of the overwhelming proportion of contract funds. In addition, an increasing number of Catholics appeared on the rolls of Indian service personnel during the Democratic administration of Grover Cleveland. Squeezed out, as they viewed it, under Grant's peace policy, the Catholics had come back in force.

This resurgence was not lost on the Protestant formulators of American Indian policy. In 1887 and 1888 Herbert Welsh of the Indian Rights Association began to spread the alarm, asserting that "very significant favoritism is being shown the Roman Catholic Church by the Indian Bureau." He warned of an aggressive "Romanist" influence in Indian matters that threatened the traditional Protestant hegemony.[44] A formal complaint of Welsh

---

Blessed Sacrament. A similar but undocumented work is Katherine Burton, *The Golden Door: The Life of Katharine Drexel* (New York: P. J. Kenedy and Sons, 1957).

43. Marty to James Cardinal Gibbons, May 31, 1889, printed flier, 86–K–10, Archives of the Archdiocese of Baltimore. See also *Statistics of Catholic Indian Education, July 1, 1886, to June 30, 1887; Issued by the Bureau of Catholic Indian Missions, Washington, D.C., March, 1887*, ibid., 82–P–4.

44. For examples of Welsh's activity, see his separate letters of October 14, 1887, to William Hayes Ward, Samuel Armstrong, and James E. Rhoads, Indian Rights Association Papers (reel 68). The *Independent* supported the Protestant position by occasional editorials. See 40 (February 9, 1888): 170; (October 25, 1888): 1371.

to Secretary of the Interior William F. Vilas was brushed aside by a disclaimer of any favoritism, and Commissioner of Indian Affairs John Oberly took pains to refute the charge that the Indian Office had discriminated in favor of Catholics. No organization with adequate facilities that had asked for contracts had ever been refused, he said; the Catholics had received more contracts simply because they had expended larger sums of money in the erection of school buildings and could accommodate more pupils under contract. In fiscal year 1887 the Catholics had spent $115,000 for Indian school buildings and furnishings, Oberly reported, and altogether had laid out about $1 million.[45]

When the Lake Mohonk Conference in 1888 began its serious promotion of a comprehensive government school system for Indians, it did so in the context of the mission school controversy, which played a large part in the discussion. The arguments were couched in general terms of secular versus religious responsibility for Indian education. But Lyman Abbott, the chief protagonist, noted as "an incidental evil of this anomalous condition of affairs" that in 1886, out of fifty religious schools supported in part by the government and in part by religious societies, thirty-eight with 2,068 pupils were under Catholic control and only twelve with 500 pupils were under Protestant control. Moderate voices argued that secular education alone was insufficient to work the transformation in the Indians that the reformers all wanted and that there was no likelihood that the government could at once step into the void that would be created if the religious schools were closed. So in the end the conference of 1888 compromised. It accepted the principle that Indian education should become totally the responsibility of the government, while urging the liberty of the Christian churches to continue their religious training of Indians and to supplement the work of the government with schools supported entirely by the missionary societies themselves. But it proposed that aid be continued to contract schools until the government was prepared to assume the entire work of secular education.[46] Catholic success, however, continued to irk the Protestants, who publicized widely the statistics for contract school funds in 1889: out of a total of $530,905, the Catholic schools received $347,672; the Presbyterians, with $41,825, ran a poor second.[47]

The election of Benjamin Harrison and the appointment of Morgan as commissioner of Indian affairs and of Daniel Dorchester, a Methodist minister, as superintendent of Indian schools brought great relief to the Protes-

45. Welsh to Vilas, July 9, 1888, and Vilas to Welsh, July 20, 1888, Indian Rights Association Papers (reels 69 and 3), published also in *Church at Home and Abroad* 4 (September 1888): 209; CIA Report, 1888, serial 2637, p. xv.

46. *Lake Mohonk Conference Proceedings*, 1888, pp. 11–16, 32–33, 36, 94–95, 102.

47. CIA Report, 1890, serial 2841, p. xvii.

tant reformers at Lake Mohonk, and they expected these men to reverse the dangerous trend toward Catholic dominance. They were not disappointed, for Morgan from the first made clear his unconditional opposition to the contract school concept, although he did not intend suddenly to kill the schools already in operation. To the Catholic missionaries, on the other hand, the appointment of Morgan and Dorchester spelled disaster. Both men had a record of public anti-Catholic statements, and Morgan's opposition to government support of mission schools and his dismissal of Catholics from the Indian service—for incompetence, insubordination, and intemperance, he claimed—led to a concerted effort on the part of Catholics to unseat him. Directed by the Reverend Joseph Stephan, who had become head of the Bureau of Catholic Indian Missions in 1884 after a stint as agent at Standing Rock, the initial maneuver was an attempt to prevent Senate confirmation of Morgan and Dorchester. It was an ardent campaign, waged by Stephan and his Catholic cohorts on one side and Welsh and his Protestant friends on the other, as each hoped to bring decisive influence to bear on the Senate.[48]

The confirmation of both men in early February 1890 did not end the controversy, and Morgan throughout his term, holding firm to his position in regard to contract schools, suffered almost incessant attacks from Stephan and other Catholic forces. In 1891 Morgan finally broke off all relations with the Catholic Bureau and dealt directly with the individual contract schools.[49] The issue did not die, for anti-Catholic forces still were articulate at Lake Mohonk, where the Reverend James M. King, spokesman for the National League for the Protection of American Institutions, periodically proclaimed his message. In 1892, referring to an "unscrupulous" attack by Father Stephan on the government schools "because they have the Protestant Bible and Gospel Hymns in them," King went on to make his point: "In this Columbian year it becomes us to remember that our civilization is not Latin, because God did not permit North America to be settled and controlled by that civilization. The Huguenot, the Hollander, and the Puritan created our civilization. Let us not put a premium by national grants on a rejected civilization in the education of a race who were here when Columbus came." Americanism and Protestantism thus coalesced. King concluded that "much Roman Catholic teaching among the Indians does not prepare them for intelligent and loyal citizenship. The solution of the Indian problem consists in educating them for citizenship, as we educate all other races."[50]

48. Prucha, *Churches and the Indian Schools*, pp. 10–17.
49. Ibid., pp. 18–24.
50. *Lake Mohonk Conference Proceedings*, 1892, pp. 63–64.

In the presidential election of 1892 Catholic promoters used the contract school question to attack Harrison and the Republicans, charging Morgan with anti-Catholic bigotry that rubbed off on the whole administration. It was a sorry spectacle.[51] Yet the defeat of the Republicans and the election of Grover Cleveland did not bring the support of their schools that the Catholics had hoped for. The new administration was no more sympathetic than Morgan had been, and Congress in the 1890s little by little whittled away the money appropriated for contract schools. When the Protestant churches, realizing the inconsistency of attacking support for Catholic mission schools while continuing to receive federal funds for their own, in 1892 withdrew from the contract school system, the issue became simply that of government schools (which were strongly Protestant in nature) versus the Catholic schools.[52]

Congressional opposition was sparked and supported by the strong nativistic and anti-Catholic movement of that decade, represented by the American Protective Association (APA). Despite the efforts of Stephan and churchmen like James Cardinal Gibbons and Archbishop Patrick J. Ryan of Philadelphia, Congress beginning in 1896 voted a 20-percent reduction year by year until in 1900 it declared "the final appropriation for sectarian schools." So ended the long partnership between the United States government and the Catholic Indian mission schools based on support of the schools by direct congressional appropriations. It had been a profitable relationship for the Catholic schools: Father Stephan totaled up the funds received from the federal government through fiscal year 1899, including estimates of the value of rations and clothing given to pupils, as $4,493,276.[53]

---

51. Harry J. Sievers, "The Catholic Indian School Issue and the Presidential Election of 1892," *Catholic Historical Review* 38 (July 1952): 129–55.

52. When Morgan left the Indian Office, he became corresponding secretary of the Baptist Home Mission Society and editor of *The Home Mission Monthly*, a platform for his anti-Catholicism, which seemed suddenly to burst forth when he left public office. He lectured and wrote against the Catholics and became a speaker at rallies of the American Protective Association. See, for example, his pamphlet, *Roman Catholics and Indian Education* (Boston: American Citizen Company, 1893), and his chapter in *Errors of the Roman Catholic Church and Its Insidious Influence in the United States and Other Countries* (St. Louis: J. H. Chambers and Company, 1895), pp. xxxii–xlix. Another example of strong anti-Catholic sentiment in regard to the Indian school question can be found in James M. King, *Facing the Twentieth Century: Our Country, Its Power and Peril* (New York: American Union League Society, 1899).

53. Prucha, *Churches and the Indian Schools*, pp. 26–40. Stephan's figures are in a memorandum dated August 1, 1898, records of the Bureau of Catholic Indian Missions, 1898, DC.

COMPETITION FROM THE WILD WEST SHOWS

The Indian schools, trying doggedly to convert the Indians from their old customs by a thoroughly American education, had sharp competition in the public eye from another institution, equally American in its enterprising spirit: the Wild West shows. In the last decades of the nineteenth century the exploitation of Indians by the promoters of these shows reached new heights. The best known of the showmen was William F. "Buffalo Bill" Cody, whose extravaganzas in the United States and Europe made him a celebrity—and a thorn in the side of the Indian reformers.[54]

As Cody enticed Indians to leave the reservations to work for him, it became clear to the humanitarians interested in Indian education that the Wild West shows were retrogressive, that for both the Indians who performed and the whites who were entertained the image presented of the Indians was the wrong one. Glorification of the savage past was hardly a way to lead the Indians down the paths of decorous white civilization. Nor was the life of the theatrical circuit a suitable introduction of reservation Indians to white manners and customs. By the end of the 1880s, therefore, considerable agitation arose to proscribe the employment of Indians in such enterprises. Commissioner of Indian Affairs Oberly set the tone in a statement of 1889:

> The effect of traveling all over the country among, and associated with, the class of people usually accompanying Shows, Circuses and Exhibitions, attended by all the immoral and unchristianizing surroundings incident to such a life, is not only most demoralizing to the present and future welfare of the Indian, but it creates a roaming and unsettled disposition and educates him in a manner entirely foreign and antagonistic to that which has been and now is the policy of the Government, as well as the aim of all good christian people who are doing so much for the welfare and benefit of the Indian.

Oberly argued that the moral, religious, and financial interests of the Indians would all be better served if they stayed on their reservations and made a home for themselves and their families, sent their children to school, and prepared themselves for the privileges and responsibilities of citizenship.[55]

---

54. The best account of Buffalo Bill's career is Don Russell, *The Lives and Legends of Buffalo Bill* (Norman: University of Oklahoma Press, 1960). See also Henry Blackman Sell and Victor Weybright, *Buffalo Bill and the Wild West* (New York: Oxford University Press, 1955), and Don Russell, *The Wild West: A History of the Wild West Shows* (Fort Worth: Amon Carter Museum of Western Art, 1970).

55. John H. Oberly to the secretary of the interior, March 20, 1889, copy in Dawes Papers.

When Oberly hesitated to act because he thought he lacked authority to restrict the Indians' participation, he was prodded by more ardent reformers. Senator Dawes ridiculed Oberly's reluctance. "Don't tell me," he wrote, "that the Government has no power to keep Indians on their reservations. They have for forty years hunted and chased with the whole force of the army, whenever they chose, Indians off their reservations without leave, and brought them back, sometimes in irons." The commissioner stuck to his guns and lectured Dawes on the right of a peaceful Indian to come and go as he wished.[56] This struck a very tender nerve in the reformers. They fought against government action in regard to Indians that they took to be oppressive or unjust, but they had no qualms about forcing upon the Indians measures that they considered to be for the Indians' own good.

Morgan, who succeeded Oberly, had no scruples about Indian freedom. On November 1, 1889, he sent an official circular to the Indian agents, calling for information about the effect of the shows, morally and physically, upon the Indians. The answers he received confirmed his opinion that the shows were diametrically opposed to the government's efforts to educate and civilize the Indians. "The influence of these shows is antagonistic to that of the schools," he wrote. "The schools elevate, the shows degrade. The schools teach industry and thrift, the shows encourage idleness and waste. The schools inculcate morality, the shows lead almost inevitably to vice. The schools encourage the Indians to abandon their paint, blankets, feathers, and savage customs, while the retention and exhibition of these is the chief attraction of the shows." The growth of public opinion supporting the possibility of civilizing the Indians, he noted, had led Congress to appropriate nearly $2 million that year for Indian education. But the impression left by the Wild West shows was that the Indians were incapable of civilization, and such an impression worked "directly and powerfully against the Government in its beneficent work." He continued to instruct the agents to use every legitimate means to prevent the Indians from joining the shows.[57]

Yet the legal authority was too questionable for the commissioner to overcome the perceived evil, and Cody was generally successful in getting Indians for his performances. The high point of his shows came in 1893, with the Columbian Exposition at Chicago. In April the Indian Office gave Cody permission to engage one hundred Indians for exhibition in Chicago. The terms of the agreement were intended to protect the Indians from the evils feared by the critics of Indian participation. The promoters agreed to

56. Oberly to Dawes, April 15, 1889, Dawes Papers.
57. Morgan to Herbert Welsh, June 13, 1891, OIA LS, Land, vol. 109, pp. 324–25 (second pagination); CIA Report, 1890, serial 2841, pp. lvii–lix; "Instructions to Indian Agents in Regard to Wild West Shows," October 1, 1890, ibid., pp. clxv–clxvi.

compensate the Indians fairly, to feed and clothe them properly, to pay travel and incidental expenses from the agencies to Chicago and back, to protect them from "all immoral influences and surroundings," to furnish medical care, and "to do everything that may be requisite for their health, comfort, and welfare." The showman was required to furnish a bond of $10,000 for faithful performance of the agreements signed with the various Indians.[58] The Wild West show was a tremendous success at Chicago. Cody, unable to gain a spot within the official limits of the exposition, leased a lot near the entrance to the fair, and to most of the visitors Buffalo Bill's Wild West and Rough Riders of the World seemed an integral part not to be missed.

The conspicuous and popular participation of the "wild" Indians with Buffalo Bill presented a striking contrast to Commissioner Morgan's attempts to use the exposition as propaganda for his Indian industrial school system. Morgan had begun to lay plans for an exhibition at Chicago as early as 1891. It was his desire, he said, "to set forth as graphically as practicable the progress made by Indians in the various lines of civilization, especially in industrial pursuits and in education." He wanted displays of products made by Indians, specimens of the work of school children, and Indians on hand pursuing various occupations. He hoped that Congress would make generous provision for representing at the exposition "the process of evolving United States citizens out of American savages."[59]

The commissioner's hopes for congressional generosity were ill-founded. Instead of a lavish, eye catching display to compete with the grand buildings that created the "White City," the Indian Office was forced to curtail its plans and to cut down expenses in every way in order to stay within the meager sums appropriated for its exhibit. The result was a two-story frame building, devoid of ornamentation and as inexpensively built as safety permitted. It had a school room, dining room, kitchen, dormitory, sitting rooms, and industrial rooms, and it was plainly furnished to accommodate thirty pupils and half a dozen employees. It was described by the secretary of the Board of Indian Commissioners as "a little mean-looking building in the midst of those grand and imposing structures."[60] Private enterprise had won out over government impecuniousness. Buffalo Bill's romantic and exciting version of the Indians in America was more than a

---

58. CIA Report, 1893, serial 3210, p. 59.

59. CIA Report, 1891, serial 2934, pp. 79–80. See also the remarks of Morgan in *Report of the Board of Indian Commissioners*, 1891, p. 153, and CIA Report, 1892, serial 3088, pp. 61–62.

60. CIA Report, 1893, serial 3210, pp. 20–21; *Lake Mohonk Conference Proceedings*, 1893, p. 134.

match for the Indian Office's meager display of the new Indians in school on their way to becoming exemplary American citizens.

Government Indian schools continued unabated, and so too for a time did the Wild West shows. But time was on the side of the Indian schools. The Wild West shows lost much of their dynamism when Buffalo Bill passed from the scene, and the dramatic charge of the Indian braves upon the Deadwood coach faded slowly from memory.[61]

61. Not all persons concerned with Indian welfare saw the Wild West shows as evil. Some argued that employment in the shows was an economic benefit and gave the Indians valuable lessons in self-support. For praise of the effect of employment by Cody on the Indians, see *Correspondence in Relation to the Employment of Indians with the Wild West Exhibition*, copy in Miscellaneous Documents Relating to Indian Affairs, vol. 35, pp. 32538–42, Interior Department Library. Continuing concern about the Wild West shows is indicated in CIA Report, 1900–1916.

CHAPTER 28

The Indian Service: Bureaucratization and Reform

Growth of the Indian Service. Civil Service

Reform. The Lesson of Wounded Knee.

Replacing the Political Agents.

The reform program of the late nineteenth century aimed to solve the Indian problem by helping the Indians disappear into white American society as independent landowners and United States citizens. When the process was complete there would be no more need for an Indian Office to manage the government's relations with the Indians, for there would be no more identifiable Indians. Little by little, many believed, the Indian service would wither away. What happened instead was that the Indian Office was formalized as an institution—and its bureaucracy grew tremendously. Thus while the Lake Mohonk reformers, intent on the substantive elements in their program for the Indians, pushed for allotment, law, and citizenship and persuaded the federal government to establish a government Indian school system, they did not lose sight of the need to improve the administration of Indian affairs.[1]

---

1. Amid the voluminous literature on the formulation of Indian policy there are few substantial works on administration and bureaucratic development. A welcome study is Paul Stuart, *The Indian Office: Growth and Development of an American Institution, 1865–1900* (Ann Arbor: UMI Research Press, 1979). Stuart uses such sociological constructs as formalization, boundary definition, organizational control, differentiation and specialization, and organizational goals to describe the institutionalization of the Indian Office.

TABLE 4: Employees in the Field Service

Year	Agents and Clerks	Education	Law and Order	Medical	Other	Total
1881	128 (6.1%)	238 (11.3%)	824 (39.2%)	60 (2.9%)	852 (40.5%)	2,102
1885	111 (5.9)	403 (21.3)	639 (33.8)	59 (3.1)	680 (35.9)	1,892
1889	117 (5.0)	708 (30.3)	795 (34.0)	65 (2.8)	654 (28.0)	2,339
1893	128 (4.1)	1,326 (42.5)	937 (30.0)	78 (2.5)	650 (20.8)	3,119
1897	141 (3.6)	1,936 (49.4)	954 (24.4)	86 (2.2)	800 (20.4)	3,917

SOURCE: Adapted from Paul Stuart, *The Indian Office: Growth and Development of an American Institution, 1865–1900* (Ann Arbor, Michigan: UMI Research Press, 1979), pp. 130–31, based on *Official Register of the United States, 1865–1897*.

GROWTH OF THE INDIAN SERVICE

As the Indians were individualized and as the federal government took increasing responsibility for them as individual citizens, the work and size of the Indian Office multiplied. Table 4 shows the dramatic growth.

With the increase in numbers came striking shifts in personnel occasioned by new programs. The institution of the Indian police forces at the agencies and the subsequent organization of courts of Indian offenses placed a considerable number of Indians on the agency payrolls, even though the remuneration allowed them was small. Much more significant was the concentration of agency employees in school work. In 1875 educational employees made up about 16.5 percent of the total personnel in the field; by 1895 they were nearly one-half of the work force, and they continued to dominate the rolls.[2]

Such growth depended, of course, upon the willingness of Congress to provide increased funds for the Indian service, and the annual augmentation was increasingly for education. Year after year the rise in expenditures for schools was greater than the increase in total costs (see Table 5).

Because of the steadily growing purchasing power of the dollar after 1875, the absolute figures conceal some of the growth. In constant dollars,

---

2. The allotment program, unlike the schools, did not greatly augment the personnel of the Indian service, and the allotting agents and surveyors appointed tended to be temporary. The number of such persons employed by the Indian Office was eight in 1889, twenty-five in 1891, fourteen in 1893, and fifteen in 1895 and 1897. Stuart, *Indian Office*, p. 122, and n. 13, p. 202.

TABLE 5: Selected Expenditures of the Indian Office

Fiscal Year	Total Expenditures	Schools: Amount/Percentage		Civilization: Amount/Percentage	
1873–1874	$4,676,222.90	$37,597.31	(.804%)	$1,796.12	(.038%)
1877–1878	3,969,749.25	127,649.41	(3.216)	17,101.75	(.431)
1881–1882	4,897,165.83	244,209.18	(4.987)	233,364.48	(4.765)
1885–1886	4,912,736.44	979,716.32	(19.942)	69,115.76	(1.407)
1889–1890	5,188,619.70	1,317,426.35	(25.391)	16,751.89	(.323)
1894–1895	6,364,494.25	1,962,415.80	(30.818)	84,373.57	(1.326)

SOURCE: Adapted from Paul Stuart, *The Indian Office: Growth and Development of an American Institution, 1865–1900* (Ann Arbor, Michigan: UMI Research Press, 1979), p. 125, based on annual statements of disbursement made from the appropriations for the Indian department.

while the total expenditures for the Indian service doubled between 1874–1875 and 1894–1895, school funds increased almost ten times.[3]

The increasing detail in the work of the Indian Office required systematization within the office itself, and the movement toward differentiation of function and the regularization of the work in the field that had begun in mid-century was continued and amplified. Circulars containing directions on administration were sent to the agents, school superintendents, and other agency personnel to govern their activities, sometimes in minute detail. In this Commissioner Thomas J. Morgan, with his obsession for systematization, was notable, as his circulars for celebrating national holidays and for the slaughtering of beef cattle bear witness. Beginning in 1897 the Education Division issued its own circulars, and there was a series of orders relating chiefly to the organization and procedures of the central office. From time to time cumulations of directives were published. In 1874 the Indian Office reissued its set of laws and regulations from 1850, with recent circulars through January 1874 added. In 1876 and 1877 appeared new compilations of instructions to superintendents and agents that dealt primarily with purchase of supplies and accounting for public funds—a perpetual and time-consuming concern of Indian service personnel.[4] When these instructions were reissued in 1880, they were greatly ex-

3. Stuart, *Indian Office*, p. 124.

4. *Office Copy of the Laws, Regulations, etc., of the Indian Bureau, 1850* (Washington: GPO, 1874); *Instructions to Superintendents and Indian Agents Relative to Purchasing Supplies, Accounting for Public Funds and Property, etc.* (Washington: GPO, 1876, 1877).

panded to include directions to the agents on "all matters relating to the proper administration of their duties." The new publication sharply reflected the increasing concern of the Indian Office for civilization and education as it instructed the agents in their responsibilities. The following extracts set the tone.

Sec. 231. The chief duty of an agent is to induce his Indians to labor in civilized pursuits. To attain this end every possible influence should be brought to bear, and in proportion as it is attained, other things being equal, an agent's administration is successful or unsuccessful.

Sec. 232. No Indian should be idle for want of an opportunity to labor or of instructions as to how to go to work, and, if farm work is not extensive enough to employ all idle hands, some other occupation should be introduced. No work must be given white men which can be done by Indians, and it is expected that hereafter no payments will be made to white laborers for cutting hay or wood, splitting rails, or gathering crops. Plowing and fencing should also be done by Indians.

Sec. 233. An agency farm should be used as a school where Indians shall be taught to labor, not by watching others, but by taking hold themselves. It is believed, however, that the best and most permanent results will be realized where the agency farm is *abandoned*, and all the time and effort of agency employes are expended in persuading Indians to cultivate small patches or farms of their own, and in directing and aiding such individual effort, even though the manner of farming be rude and the crops much smaller than a model agency farm would have produced. A well-ordered agency farm and "establishment" is far less creditable to an agent than a large number of comparatively unprofitably managed Indian farms, which will awaken in their Indian owners a sense of proprietorship, and will serve as beginnings in the direction of self-support.[5]

In addition the instructions noted the agent's duty in enforcing the prohibitions against liquor and his responsibility to provide and supervise English education and industrial training for his charges in the agency school. The publication directed the agent to allow the Indians to leave the reservation only with a permit (to be granted to worthy Indians as a reward for meritorious conduct) and to prohibit the custom of visiting between reser-

5. *Instructions to Indian Agents Relative to Purchasing Supplies, Accounting for Public Funds and Property, and All Matters Relating to the Proper Administration of Their Duties* (Washington: GPO, 1880), p. 71.

vations for the purpose of giving or receiving presents of ponies or other property.[6]

The 1880 instructions were repeated and amplified in 1884, 1894, and 1904, as centralization of control by the Indian Office grew.[7] There were in addition special compilations, of which the *Rules for Indian Schools*, in a series of editions beginning in 1890, were the most important. Most of these books of regulations contained appendixes comprising copies of the forms that were required for periodic reports to headquarters.[8]

The increased centralization of administration indicated by the directives increased the work of the office in Washington. The old divisions inaugurated in 1846—commonly known as the Land Division, Civilization Division, Finance Division, and Files and Records Division—still functioned, but there were additions and changes in title as work was shifted around. From 1873 to 1881 a Medical and Educational Division assumed some of the duties of the Civilization Division, and in 1884 the Civilization Division was changed to the Education Division. From 1885 to 1893 there was a separate Depredations Division to process the multitude of depredation claims, but in 1893 it merged with the Land Division. In 1889 a Miscellaneous Division was established, which dealt largely with the issuance of traders' licenses. The total staff in Washington increased from 70 in 1881 to 129 in 1901, and in addition there were inspectors and special agents, as well as allotting agents, who worked in the field but were responsible to headquarters.[9]

The handling of claims for depredations allegedly committed by Indians is one example of time-consuming work carried on in the Indian Office that had little direct bearing on normal Indian policy or administration. At the end of 1891 Commissioner Morgan reported 7,985 claims on file, with a total sum claimed of $25,589,006. He provided tables to show claims arising from depredations year by year from 1812 to 1890 and the tribes

6. Ibid., pp. 72–78.

7. *Regulations of the Indian Department, with an Appendix Containing the Forms Used* (Washington: GPO, 1884); *Regulations of the Indian Office, with an Appendix Containing the Forms Used* (Washington: GPO, 1894); *Regulations of the Indian Office, Effective April 1, 1904* (Washington: GPO, 1904).

8. Many of the rules and regulations were also printed in the annual reports of the commissioner of Indian affairs. Since there is no complete compilation of Indian Office circulars in the National Archives, it is difficult to trace the increase in their numbers from year to year.

9. Figures on staff are taken from the *Official Register of the United States, Containing a List of Officers and Employés in the Civil, Military, and Naval Service*, 1881 and 1901. An excellent discussion of the confusing shuffling of divisions within the Indian Office is in Edward E. Hill, *Records of the Bureau of Indian Affairs*, Preliminary Inventories no. 163 (Washington: National Archives, 1965), pp. 3–5.

against which the claims were lodged. He noted: "The 'care and custody' of these claims devolves upon this office a considerable amount of labor, of which no visible sign appears. Attorneys and claimants must obtain the data from these papers before they can prepare their petitions. The searching and verification of the records; the making of copies of lost papers or records; the large and miscellaneous correspondence involved; the transmittal, under the orders of the court, of the various papers with all the records pertaining thereto, necessitating as it does laborious search and careful scrutiny in order that errors may be guarded against; as well as other points too numerous to be specifically mentioned, make the work onerous and exacting."[10]

The management of the growing and varied activities, one senses, came to depend largely on the bureaucracy of clerks, for the commissioners of Indian affairs came and went with the changes in presidential administrations. Yet in the last two decades of the century the Indian Office was perhaps better served than usual in the commissioners appointed, for they did not let their political appointment becloud all the reform goals that dominated the period. Hiram Price, who was appointed in 1881 by his former congressional colleague President James A. Garfield, was the epitome of the "peace policy" official. Not only did he advocate the measures deemed vital to the transformation of the Indians, but he brought a moralistic sense to his office that rivaled that of Nathaniel Taylor a dozen years before. Price was an Iowa banker and railroad executive who had served in the House of Representatives 1863–1869 and 1877–1881, and he was also an ardent lay leader in the Methodist Church. He carried his religious principles and religious sentiments into the Indian Office, where he urged cooperation with religious societies and exhorted Indian service employees and the Indians as well to live Christian lives. Yet, despite some interest in Indian reform while he was in Congress, Price came to the Indian Office without any special competence for the job aside from his reputation for honesty, integrity, and good management—by no means negligible attributes, of course. He supported and encouraged the new reform organizations that came into national prominence during his term of office. Most symbolic of his administration, perhaps, was the attack on Indian customs embodied in the courts of Indian offenses.[11]

Price was followed by John DeWitt Clinton Atkins, a Tennessee Democrat who left the House of Representatives at the time of the Civil War and

10. CIA Report, 1891, serial 2934, pp. 113–19.

11. There is a useful survey of Price's administration in Floyd A. O'Neil, "Hiram Price, 1881–85," in Robert M. Kvasnicka and Herman J. Viola, eds., *The Commissioners of Indian Affairs, 1824–1977* (Lincoln: University of Nebraska Press, 1979), pp. 173–79.

served as a general in the Confederate army and as a member of the Confederate Congress. Returned to Congress after the war in 1873, he gained bipartisan support, and his appointment as commissioner in 1885 was well received. Atkins stood for all the right reform measures, and during his term of office significant changes in Indian policy occurred: improvements in Indian education, the beginning of a federal judicial system for the reservations, and the culmination of the severalty movement in the Dawes Act of 1887. But Atkins was a politician, and he lost the support of the reform groups by his patronage appointments in the Indian service. A special committee of the National Civil Service Reform League reported that up to November 16, 1886, of sixty-one Indian agents appointed by the previous administration, only eleven remained and that at many agencies not only the agents but nearly all of the employees had been changed. "The conclusion is irresistible," the report concluded, "that the Indian Bureau has been managed in the interest of a party, and not primarily in the interest of the public service, and, consequently, that the administration of Indian affairs has been thrown into an unhappy and confused condition." The chief villains were Atkins and his assistant commissioner, Alexander B. Upshaw, described by the Indian Rights Association as "Tennessee politicians of small range and the most thoroughgoing partisan principles, who . . . regarded the Indian reservations as a green pasture where their political herds might comfortably browse and fatten." The *Nation* exonerated Atkins as "much too simple-minded and good-natured for his place" and settled the blame on Upshaw. But it concluded that the Indian service had suffered as no other department had done from the change of administration in 1884. The Indian Rights Association continued to hound Atkins, until in 1888 its executive committee could report: "Messrs. Atkins and Upshaw were pursued in their predatory course by the incessant exposures and criticisms of the Indian Rights Association; these, passing through many channels of influence, finally produced tangible results. The Commissioner resigned his post, to follow less sharply contested ambitions; while the power of evil of the Assistant Commissioner rapidly diminished, if it did not wholly cease, and he also at last resigned."[12]

John H. Oberly, who was appointed to succeed Atkins in October 1888,

---

12. Extract, *Report of the Special Committee of the National Civil-Service Reform League upon the Present Condition of the Reform Movement* (Philadelphia: Indian Rights Association, 1887); *Report of the Indian Rights Association*, 1888, p. 32; "A Good Field for Reform," *Nation* 46 (March 15, 1888): 210–11. There is more criticism of Atkins and Upshaw in Herbert Welsh, "Indian Affairs under the Present Administration," *Civil-Service Reporter* 4 (August 1888): 90–92. A positive view of Atkins is given in Gregory C. Thompson, "John D. C. Atkins, 1885–88," in Kvasnicka and Viola, *Commissioners of Indian Affairs*, pp. 181–88.

was of a different breed. He was one of the few commisioners who was chosen for competence rather than for political considerations. A newspaperman from Illinois, Oberly had served effectively as superintendent of Indian education, and President Cleveland had named him to the civil service commission. He was just the kind of person the reformers wanted, but before he had completed a month of service as commissioner of Indian affairs, Cleveland was defeated at the polls and the Republican Benjamin Harrison elected to the presidency. Oberly did not have a chance to restore a disorganized and demoralized service to a state of efficiency.[13]

Thomas Jefferson Morgan, who followed Oberly, was without doubt one of the most important commissioners in the nation's history. His absolute and unwavering conviction that the Indians must all be completely Americanized made him a key figure in strengthening and completing the reforms that marked the closing decades of the century. Although, like most others, he was not an Indian expert, he was an education specialist, and he represented and in large measure directed the change that made Indian education the dominant activity of the Indian Office. His successor, Daniel M. Browning, who served as commissioner from 1893 to 1897, by contrast, left no mark on Indian policy or on the Indian Office. A faithful judge and party worker from Illinois, Browning had hoped to use the commissioner's office to reward his political friends, but he found few openings to fill, and in the daily work of the office he seems to have succumbed to the influence of the entrenched bureaucracy. His own assistant commissioner, Frank Armstrong, had a stronger voice than he.[14]

CIVIL SERVICE REFORM

The growth of personnel in the Indian service and the increasing importance of the agent in the civilization and education programs, to say nothing of the appearance of men like Atkins and Upshaw, highlighted a continuing problem of serious dimensions: the appointment of the Indian agents and other agency personnel under a political patronage system. The Indian reformers realized that their programs and policies for Indian betterment depended upon the quality of the men who administered them. Without honest and competent men in the Indian service—especially in

---

13. Floyd A. O'Neil, "John H. Oberly, 1888–89," in Kvasnicka and Viola, *Commissioners of Indian Affairs*, pp. 189–91.

14. Morgan's work is discussed above, pp. 700–707. For Browning, see William T. Hagan, "Daniel M. Browning, 1893–97," in Kvasnicka and Viola, *Commissioners of Indian Affairs*, pp. 205–9.

the office of agent—the best-laid plans would amount to little. Concomitant, therefore, with other proposals for reform was long-continuing agitation to improve the agents and their subordinates; and at times the drive to ensure adequate staffing of the agencies took on the characteristics of a major crusade.[15]

Although Carl Schurz's attack on corruption in the Indian service had brought a temporary calm, by the end of the 1880s a cry was again raised against the politicization of the Indian service and the degradation that followed in its wake. For the better part of a decade, a sustained drive to bring civil service reform to the Indian Office vied with education and a system of law for the Indians as the major concern of the Indian reformers.[16]

Several converging developments gave impetus to this movement for reform in Indian administration. For one thing, the changes in political parties in the executive branch of the government that occurred with four-year regularity between 1884 and 1896 brought the spoils system into new prominence. The Democrats, capturing the presidency for the first time since the Civil War with the election of Grover Cleveland in 1884, had a hunger for the fruits of victory that could not be denied, and the house that had been cleaned out by Schurz began again to show unmistakably the messy accumulations of partisan favors under Commissioner Atkins. A second factor was the Indian reform movement itself. In 1887, just as the worst evils of partisan appointments were beginning to be noticed, the humanitarians won a great victory with the Dawes Act. The allotment and citizenship provisions of that measure and the plans for a federal Indian school system marked the successful completion of the legislative program that the reformers had advocated. What remained to be achieved, then, was not new legislation but careful and competent carrying out of the laws already enacted. "It will thus be seen," declared one prominent reformer, "that legislation has largely done its part, and that *administration* of Indian affairs now claims the most serious attention."[17] The key to

---

15. In the decades after the Civil War, there was a continual plea on the part of Interior Department officials and the humanitarian reformers for an increase in the pay of Indian agents, for the $1,500 per year that agents received was insufficient to attract men of capacity and integrity. See, for example, Report of the Secretary of the Interior, 1867, *House Executive Document* no. 1, 40–2, serial 1326, p. 9; ibid., 1888, *House Executive Document* no. 1, part 5, 50–2, serial 2636, pp. xxix–xxx; CIA Report, 1873, serial 1601, pp. 377–78; *Lake Mohonk Conference Proceedings*, 1883, p. 12.

16. The following discussion on civil service reform uses materials from Francis Paul Prucha, *American Indian Policy in Crisis: Christian Reformers and the Indian, 1865–1900* (Norman: University of Oklahoma Press, 1976), pp. 353–72.

17. James E. Rhoads, *Our Next Duty to the Indians* (Philadelphia: Indian Rights Association, 1887), p. 5.

administration, of course, was the Indian agent and the men and women under him. Unless they were appointed on the basis of merit alone, they could hardly be depended upon to carry out the important work of the Dawes Act or the educational program that was coming to the fore. The third element was the national movement for civil service reform, which provided ready-made principles and rules to govern the Indian reformers in purifying the Indian service. The Pendleton Act of 1883 supplied the necessary structure for reform, and the humanitarian friends of the Indian soon began a campaign to have the whole Indian service classified under the reform legislation.[18]

The driving force behind the growing demand that civil service rules be applied to the Indian service was the Indian Rights Association and most particularly its secretary, Herbert Welsh, who made the reform his principal goal for more than a decade. Welsh, hoping to bring good business methods into Indian administration, said, "Civil-service reform is simply the putting into operation of a principle which is universally recognized in all business affairs excepting those of the government. . . . It is the selection of officials and employees on account of fitness, not on account of partisan politics, and their retention, so long as their work is well done."[19] The subject occupied much of the association's attention in 1886 and continued to be one of its primary activities. A long series of pamphlets and fliers began to appear from the press of the association, and its agent in Washington also brought to bear whatever pressure he could. At first it seemed that no headway was possible, but persistence in calling attention to the need and the support of other reforming groups began to tell. William F. Vilas, who became secretary of the interior in January 1888, was willing to listen to the pleas of the reformers, and his approval of Oberly as commissioner of Indian affairs met the high standards set by the Indian Rights Association.

When the change of presidents spelled Oberly's doom, Welsh determined to meet the danger by campaigning to retain him as commissioner under the new administration. If he could succeed in this, he would strike a blow at the spoils system, set a precedent for future times, and provide an opportunity for an upright commissioner to retain and to appoint qualified men in the service. Welsh was unable to break such a sturdy barrier, how-

---

18. A detailed monograph on civil service reform is Adelbert Bower Sageser, *The First Two Decades of the Pendleton Act: A Study of Civil Service Reform* (Lincoln: University of Nebraska Press, 1935). The progress of the reform can be traced in the annual *Report of the United States Civil Service Commission*. See also Ari Hoogenboom, "The Pendleton Act and the Civil Service," *American Historical Review* 64 (January 1959): 301–18.

19. *Lake Mohonk Conference Proceedings*, 1891, pp. 74–75.

ever, and he had to be satisfied with his second choice, Thomas J. Morgan, who saw pretty much eye to eye with the reformers and was determined in his own way to improve the quality and efficiency of the Indian service. Morgan's initial report gave Welsh and his friends considerable satisfaction, for the new commissioner declared, "The chief thing to be considered in the administration of this office is the character of the men and women employed to carry out the designs of the Government." He favored integrity, justice, patience, and good sense, and said that dishonesty, injustice, favoritism, and incompetency had no place in the Indian service.[20]

THE LESSON OF WOUNDED KNEE

The disastrous outbreak of the Sioux in 1890, shortly after Morgan had taken office, provided substantial fuel for the fires of the civil service reformers. The reservation life for the Sioux had brought degradation rather than the revitalization that its promoters envisaged. They had many grievances, and the reduction of their large reserve in 1889, instead of moving them more rapidly toward acculturation, had been a great disaster. "Despair came again," Chief Red Cloud said, and the Sioux were ready to grasp at any promise that could restore some of the hope and well-being of the old times.[21]

Then came news of a messiah. Far to the west in a remote corner of Nevada a Paiute shaman named Wovoka was preaching a wonderful message, compounded of Christian doctrines and Indian mysticism, which promised the Indians a new paradise if they would remain at peace, live honest and industrious lives, and perform a ghost dance that God had taught to the messiah.[22] The Sioux, like many other tribes, sent a delegation to Wovoka to investigate the new religion. The emissaries, returning to the reservation in March 1890, told remarkable tales of the messiah.

20. *The Question of Indian Commissioner Oberly's Retention* (Philadelphia: Indian Rights Association, 1889) contains statements by Welsh and Charles C. Painter in favor of retaining Oberly; see also *Report of the Indian Rights Association*, 1889, pp. 10–11. Morgan's position is given in CIA Report, 1889, serial 2725, p. 4.

21. The best work on the Sioux troubles is Robert M. Utley, *The Last Days of the Sioux Nation* (New Haven: Yale University Press, 1963).

22. The most thorough study of the ghost dance religion is James Mooney, *The Ghost-Dance Religion and the Sioux Outbreak of 1890*, Annual Report of the Bureau of Ethnology, 1892–1893, part 2 (Washington: GPO, 1896). A briefer, more popular exposition by the same author is "The Indian Ghost Dance," *Collections of the Nebraska State Historical Society* 16 (1911): 168–82. For a biography of the messiah, see Paul D. Bailey, *Wovoka: The Indian Messiah* (Los Angeles: Westernlore Press, 1957).

The Sioux, however, modified the nonviolent peace message of Wovoka and made it into one of antagonism toward the whites, who were held responsible for the present misery of the tribes. At first little disturbance was caused, and the Indian agents did not take the ghost dance religion seriously. Had the troubles of the Sioux not multiplied during the summer of 1890, it is possible that Wovoka's teachings and the ghost dance would have quietly faded away as they did in other tribes. But the specter of hunger still rode over the Dakota reservations, for rations were short and the promising crops of early summer were destroyed by the scorching heat of midsummer. Under such conditions other grievances assumed mountainous proportions. New boundary lines between reservations upset traditional tribal ties, and the taking of a census presaged in the minds of the Indians still another ration cut. The restlessness of the Indians led to movements of troops into uncomfortably close proximity to the reservations.[23]

The troubles and misery of the summer furnished an occasion for conservative chiefs to assert their leadership in opposition to government policies with a reasonable hope of gaining adherents. Sitting Bull at Standing Rock Agency, Hump and Big Foot at Cheyenne River, Red Cloud at Pine Ridge, and a group at Rosebud began to take courage that the old ways might yet be saved. The deep distress of the Sioux offered a favorable climate for their efforts, and when the most aggressive of the ghost dance apostles, Kicking Bear, returned in midsummer from a visit to the Arapahos and told of the regeneration of that tribe through Wovoka's religion, he gained important converts. Ghost dances multiplied among the Sioux, the dancers garbed in ghost shirts supposed to be invested with magic qualities that made the wearers invulnerable to bullets. Trances were common, with visions of earth regenerated and repeopled by the Indians. In alarm, as the movement spread, the Indian agents warned of its dangers and attempted with little success to suppress it with the agency police. Hump and Big Foot enthusiastically espoused the new religion at Cheyenne River Agency; and at Standing Rock, Sitting Bull became its apostle.

To meet this growing challenge to government authority, there were new and ineffectual agents, spawned by the spoils system. James McLaughlin at Standing Rock was a man of experience and ability, although he was faced with troubles enough in handling the shrewd Sitting Bull. At Cheyenne River a Republican without experience, Perain P. Palmer, was cast in the difficult role of dealing with Kicking Bear, Hump, and Big Foot.

---

23. An excellent, temperate account of the development of the Sioux crisis with a listing of twelve "causes of the trouble" appears in CIA Report, 1891, serial 2934, pp. 123–35.

But the greatest crisis of leadership came at Pine Ridge, where the powerful agent Valentine McGillycuddy had fallen victim to the system and been replaced in 1886 by the well-meaning but weak Democrat Hugh Gallagher. In October 1890 Gallagher in turn was dismissed to make room for the patronage appointment of a South Dakota Republican, Daniel F. Royer, whom the Indians in derision called Young-Man-Afraid-of-Indians. Royer soon lost all control of the situation as the dancers openly defied him. On November 15, he frantically telegraphed for troops: "Indians are dancing in the snow and are wild and crazy. . . . *We need protection and we need it now.*"[24] Two days later the order was given to send troops to Pine Ridge and Rosebud. The coming of the soldiers excited the ghost dancers and united them in armed defiance of the government. Although at other agencies the nearness of the troops seemed to bring a measure of quiet, the disaffected Pine Ridge and Rosebud Indians massed in the Bad Lands in the northwest corner of the Pine Ridge Reservation and threw themselves into a continuous frenzy of dancing. General Nelson A. Miles, commanding the Division of the Missouri, prepared to restore order on the Sioux reservations, depending on military control rather than on the agents, whom he in principle considered incapable of the task.

To end the troubles, government officials proposed to arrest the ghost dance leaders. High on the government's list was Sitting Bull at Standing Rock. Efforts of Indian police to arrest the chief, however, led to a shooting match between the chief's supporters and the police in which Sitting Bull was killed, along with seven of his Indians and six of the police.[25] At Cheyenne River, Hump unexpectedly gave up without trouble, but Big Foot, befriending refugees from Sitting Bull's followers, was treated as an outlaw, and with his people he fled south from the reservation.

Meanwhile the hostiles in the Bad Lands, pressed by troops to the north and west and suffering from cold and weariness, moved in toward the Pine Ridge Agency to surrender. When Big Foot approached the Bad Lands, they had already moved out, and Big Foot and his band were intercepted by troops of the Seventh Cavalry, who led the band to a spot on Wounded Knee Creek, northeast of the agency, where they were surrounded by more troops under Colonel James W. Forsyth, the regimental commander. On the following day, December 29, Forsyth prepared to disarm the Indians. The situation was tense, and when one of the Indians discharged a con-

24. Royer to R. V. Belt, November 15, 1890, quoted in Utley, *Last Days of the Sioux Nation*, p. 111.

25. McLaughlin's own account of his relations with Sitting Bull and the death of the chief is in *My Friend the Indian* (Boston: Houghton Mifflin Company, 1910). A detailed analysis of the affair is presented in Louis Pfaller, *James McLaughlin: The Man with an Indian Heart* (New York: Vantage Press, 1978), pp. 146–65.

cealed gun, the troops surrounding the camp interpreted it as an outbreak and opened fire on the encampment. Both sides fought in fury. Hotchkiss guns mounted on the overlooking hill raked the camp with murderous fire, catching many of the women and children. Fleeing Indians were shot down by the soldiers without discrimination of age or sex. A total of 146 Indians were buried on the battlefield, 84 men and boys, 44 women, and 18 children, many of them frozen in distraught postures by the blizzard that swept down upon the scene after the massacre. Seven more Indians of the 51 wounded died later; how many more were carried away by the Indians is not known. The whites lost 25 killed and 39 wounded.

The Indians from the Bad Lands who had come in to surrender became hostile again when the battle of Wounded Knee occurred. They attacked the agency and small troop detachments, but their efforts were half-hearted, and by January 16, 1891, they had been rounded up again and surrendered. When General Miles left Pine Ridge for Chicago at the end of January, he took with him twenty-five ghost dance leaders to be imprisoned at Fort Sheridan. It was the end of the Indian wars.

The reaction to Wounded Knee was polarized at two extremes in the press.[26] Some papers saw the battle as a victorious triumph of the soldiers over treacherous Indians. Others condemned the action as a brutal revenge for Custer's defeat (the soldiers were of the same regiment), in which women and children were wantonly butchered. Neither position was right, for neither side in the conflict had planned or foreseen the tragedy that occurred. Big Foot and his people sought peace, but they were afraid and suspicious, and when the shooting started they reacted violently. The soldiers fought back savagely against what they considered Indian treachery. "It is time that Wounded Knee be viewed for what it was," historian Robert Utley concludes, "—a regrettable, tragic accident of war that neither side intended, and that called forth behavior for which some individuals on both sides, in unemotional retrospect, may be judged culpable, but for which neither side as a whole may be properly condemned."[27]

The Sioux troubles that led to Wounded Knee in 1890 convinced the advocates of reform more than ever that they were right. Herbert Welsh and his friends declared that the troubles could have been prevented had not the spoils system operated to weaken the administrative control so necessary at Pine Ridge. The executive committee of the Indian Rights Association, issuing a statement in 1891 called *A Crisis in Indian Affairs*, discussed a number of causes of the Sioux outbreak—increased opposition of the nonprogressive Indians as the progressive party gained strength, ex-

26. Elmo Scott Watson, "The Last Indian War, 1890–91: A Study of Newspaper Jingoism," *Journalism Quarterly* 20 (September 1943): 205–19.

27. Utley, *Last Days of the Sioux Nation*, p. 230.

treme suffering among the Sioux because of food shortages, and the religious fanaticism of the messiah craze. But then the committee came to its point: "These causes linked together produced serious conditions, but in our opinion, the danger might have been averted had it not been for the last, most potent and determining cause, viz.:—the spoils system of appointments in the management of the Indian service, which supplied at the two most critical points in the Sioux country—Pine Ridge and Cheyenne River Agencies—a disastrously inadequate management and control." It lashed out at the principle of leaving appointments effectively in the hands of local politicians, for such "home rule" paid no attention to the merits of the appointees. The urgings of the Indian Rights Association through two administrations, it lamented, had been largely in vain, for the spoils system had "continued on its remorseless way." "Perhaps," the committee suggested, "it is one of those evils from which without shedding of blood there is no remission." Francis E. Leupp, the association's Washington agent, forcefully stated the same view: "There is no doubt—now that we can go back and study the Pine Ridge incident in the cold light of history—that all the upheaval, and riot, and bloodshed and suffering might have been spared if the first blunder had not been made in the removal of McGillicuddy—an act of political partisanship utterly hostile to the principles of Civil Service Reform."[28]

The humanitarians drew what comfort they could from the tragedy. Commissioner Morgan, speaking to the missionary boards in January 1891, noted that the Sioux troubles were confined to a small locality compared with the whole extent of the Indian country and that the number of hostile Indians was less than 3,000 compared with the total Indian population of 250,000. He urged his audience not to exaggerate the importance of the Sioux outbreak "in its relation to the great Indian question of the country," and he said with pride: "Do you know that the Government boarding school at Pine Ridge, at the seat of this trouble, has not been interrupted? It goes on to-day." Merrill Gates at Lake Mohonk looked upon the outbreak as a source "of especial encouragement," for it showed that the United States could now deal with small groups of Indians as individuals under law and not undertake a war against a whole Indian nation. "I think that the Dakota disaster shows," he said, "that we shall not need to have taught us again the lesson of the difference between savagery and civilization."[29]

28. *A Crisis in Indian Affairs* (Philadelphia: Indian Rights Association, 1891), p. 4; Francis E. Leupp, *Civil Service Reform Essential to a Successful Indian Administration* (Philadelphia: Indian Rights Association, 1895), p. 7. Welsh expressed his views in "The Meaning of the Dakota Outbreak," *Scribner's Magazine* 9 (April 1891): 439–52.

29. *Report of the Board of Indian Commissioners*, 1890, p. 166; *Lake Mohonk Conference Proceedings*, 1891, p. 8.

The prevention of a general Indian war was proof to the reformers that their policies of education and civilization had been a success. Secretary of the Interior John W. Noble spoke for them in his analysis of the outbreak as he pointed to the good behavior of the majority of the Indians. "They did not go upon the 'warpath' in the usual and aggressive way of Indians generally, and of the Sioux in particular," he noted. "The councils and efforts of much of the larger portion of the tribe were for peace, and they rendered good service in persuading their turbulent brethren to submit to the authority of the United States. They were held in check, undoubtedly, by the influences of civilization, which had been brought to bear upon a large number of them by the work of the schools, by the practical training in industry, and by the labors of the faithful missionaries and religious institutions established among them. Christianity, education, and industrial discipline, with an intelligent appreciation by many of the power of the United States restrained them more than arms."[30]

The policy of peaceful relations with the Indians had to fall back upon military force in the crisis, and General Miles made use of this opportunity to implement his views that the army should run the reservations. In a series of orders in January 1891 he assigned officers to duties at the Dakota agencies that brought divided authority and came close to negating civilian authority altogether. Commissioner Morgan fought back vigorously for the principle of civilian control. Before an open conflict between the two departments could materialize, however, an army reorganization in July 1891 removed Miles from authority over the Sioux, and although a military agent continued to run Pine Ridge, the other agencies returned to civilian management.[31]

Wounded Knee gave new impetus to the movement for civil service reform. The missionary boards, meeting in January 1891, passed resolutions in favor of the retention of agents with experience and "the extension of civil-service-reform regulations to the subordinate appointments in the Indian Department." The Board of Indian Commissioners itself formally petitioned the president to the same end. The pleas were not in vain, for on April 13, 1891, the president extended the civil service rules to cover all physicians, superintendents of schools, assistant superintendents, teachers, and matrons in the Indian service.[32]

---

30. Report of the Secretary of the Interior, 1891, *House Executive Document* no. 1, part 5, 52–1, serial 2933, pp. lvi–lvii.

31. On military control, see Utley, *Last Days of the Sioux Nation*, pp. 277–82.

32. *Report of the Board of Indian Commissioners*, 1890, pp. 4–5, 186; James D. Richardson, ed., *A Compilation of the Messages and Papers of the Presidents*, 10 vols. (Washington: GPO, 1896–1899), 9: 173; *Eighth Report of the United States Civil Service Commission, July 1, 1890, to June 30, 1891*, p. 72.

It was a substantial beginning, and the reformers rejoiced, but the success only whetted their appetite for more. Their goal was to bring the rest of the agency employees under the classified service and then, if possible, make sure that the agents, too, were freed from the political rotation that interrupted the smooth continuation of policy. If rules could not formally be extended, the reformers pleaded that at least the spirit of the law be followed. If the Indians were to be fitted for citizenship, the spoils system would have to be abandoned entirely, Welsh declared in 1892. "We may tolerate the spoils system with its false appointments and its wanton removals in our post-offices and custom houses," he said, "but in the Indian service, which concerns the welfare of a people, where the fortunes of human beings—even life and death!—hang in the balance, it is wholly intolerable!"[33]

For employees below the level of agent, the civil service reformers won their case. By direction of President Cleveland, the Department of the Interior on March 30, 1896, amended the classification of the Indian service to include all physicians, school superintendents, assistant superintendents, supervisors of schools, day school inspectors, school teachers, assistant teachers, industrial teachers, teachers of industries, disciplinarians, kindergarten teachers, matrons, assistant matrons, farmers, seamstresses, and nurses. All of these, without regard to salary level, were made subject to competitive examination for appointment. Another order of the same date included all clerks, assistant clerks, issue clerks, property clerks, and other clerical positions and storekeepers at Indian agencies and Indian schools. Furthermore, on May 6, 1896, the scope of the classified service was enlarged still more to include all officers and employees, of whatever designation, except persons employed merely as laborers or workmen and persons nominated for confirmation by the Senate. These regulations, however, did not apply to Indians themselves, who in increasing numbers were employed at the agencies, usually in positions of lower rank.[34]

A report on personnel in the field in the Indian service on June 30, 1896, showed how extensively the civil service rules were applied. There were 552 white persons in the classified service and 83 in the unclassified service. Of the latter, there were 38 agents, 5 inspectors, and 5 commissioners to the Five Civilized Tribes who held positions confirmed by the Senate;

33. *Lake Mohonk Conference Proceedings*, 1891, pp. 112–13; 1892, pp. 10, 121; 1893, pp. 141–42; *Report of the Board of Indian Commissioners*, 1891, p. 154; 1892, p. 9; 1894, p. 11; 1895, p. 9; *Report of the Indian Rights Association*, 1894, p. 12. For Welsh's views, see Herbert Welsh, *How to Bring the Indian to Citizenship, and Citizenship to the Indian* (Philadelphia: Indian Rights Association, 1892), pp. 13–14.

34. CIA Report, 1896, serial 3489, pp. 3–4.

17 military officers acting as agents, 3 physicians paid for occasional services, 3 transportation agents, and 12 employees at compensation below classification levels. In addition there were 1,434 whites and 705 Indians employed in the schools. "The recognition of the merit system in the Indian service is a long step forward," the commissioner of Indian affairs said, "and will undoubtedly elevate its standard, improve its morale, and promote its efficiency. The removal of all partisan influence from appointments will give added dignity to the positions and increase the zeal of those engaged in the work." The Indian Rights Association reported in 1896 that the year had "probably been the most encouraging and satisfactory" it had ever experienced.[35]

REPLACING THE POLITICAL AGENTS

This extension of the civil service system, however, still left the key men, the agents, under the spoils system. Until the political pressures that kept them there could be dissipated, other expedients were tried. One of these—remarkable as it may seem after the controversy that raged over the transfer issue in the 1870s—was the assignment of army officers as Indian agents. A law of July 13, 1892, provided that thereafter when any vacancies occurred, the president was to detail army officers to fill them, although he could appoint civilians if the good of the service would be better promoted thereby. The military men were to act under the orders and direction of the secretary of the interior in their duties as agents. Support for this measure came principally from the Indian Rights Association. Herbert Welsh, returning from a visit to the Sioux reservations in 1892, recommended the appointment of "judiciously selected Army Officers to serve as Agents *at many of the Agencies* whose present incumbents are unsatisfactory," and the reports of the association commended the measure. Francis E. Leupp stressed the continuity that the military appointments would ensure, even to the point that although the officers might change, the uniform remained the same. "In this one respect at least," he noted, "a

---

35. Ibid., pp. 4–5; *Report of the Indian Rights Association*, 1896, p. 3. The civil service reform efforts of the Indian Rights Association brought Welsh and his organization into sharp conflict with Richard Henry Pratt, head of the Carlisle Indian Industrial School. Pratt vigorously objected to the application of the civil service rules to Carlisle personnel and, more basically, objected to the emphasis put on civil service reform at the expense of educational efforts by the Indian Rights Association. The story is told in detail in Everett Arthur Gilcreast, "Richard Henry Pratt and American Indian Policy, 1877–1906: A Study of the Assimilation Movement" (Ph.D. dissertation, Yale University, 1967), pp. 284–99.

series of army officers are alike. In dealing with uniformed officers, the Indian does not have forced upon him in quite so pointed a way the fact that he has been passed from hand to hand."[36]

Other humanitarians, remembering no doubt the fearful cry they had made against military control of Indians, were less sure that the move was a wise one. Commissioner Morgan regarded the policy "with grave apprehension," and although he admitted that the idea of stopping the spoils system was a good one, he hoped it might be accomplished in some other way. He reemphasized the point that the work of an agent was civil, not military in nature and that an army officer's training did not fit him for it. The Board of Indian Commissioners, too, protested on the same grounds when the measure was before Congress, but they were willing to withhold judgment until the effects could be evaluated. President Cleveland moved ahead under the new legislation. By the end of 1893, twenty-seven out of fifty-seven agencies were under the charge of army officers.[37]

A more radical and ultimately more satisfactory expedient was to eliminate the position of agent altogether. Morgan made such a suggestion in his annual report of 1892, declaring that it was "entirely feasible and very desirable to modify the agency system and prepare the way for its complete abolition by placing the agency affairs, in certain cases, in the hands of school superintendents." He argued that on reservations where allotment had gone forward the work of the agent was greatly reduced, and he noted that the school superintendents were "generally men of high personal character and large business capacity." An act of March 3, 1893, authorized the commissioner, with the approval of the secretary of the interior, to assign the agent's duties to the superintendent at any agency where he felt the superintendent was qualified for the job. The agent's position at the Eastern Cherokee Agency in North Carolina, in fact, was abolished by the same law and the duties turned over to the school superintendent, but no other such assignments seem to have been made until after 1900.[38]

The millennium, clearly, had not yet arrived, and the advent of William McKinley's administration brought forebodings to the Indian reformers. The Indian Rights Association feared that a plan was afloat for getting rid of a number of the army officers who served as agents in order to make room for civilian appointees, who were more likely than the officers to

36. 27 *United States Statutes* 120–21; Herbert Welsh, *Civilization among the Sioux Indians: Report of a Visit to Some of the Sioux Reservations of South Dakota and Nebraska* (Philadelphia: Indian Rights Association, 1893), p. 58; *Report of the Indian Rights Association,* 1893, pp. 5–7; Leupp, *Civil Service Reform,* pp. 4–5.

37. CIA Report, 1892, serial 3088, pp. 10–12; CIA Report, 1893, serial 3210, p. 6; *Report of the Board of Indian Commissioners,* 1893, p. 11.

38. CIA Report, 1892, serial 3088, pp. 9–10; 27 *United States Statutes* 614; Sageser, *Pendleton Act,* p. 227.

serve local or personal interests at the cost of the Indians. And in fact the number of army officers in the service greatly declined.[39] The McKinley administration got low marks in general from the Indian Rights Association, which asserted in 1898 that the advances made in the two previous administrations had been negated and that affairs were worse than ever. After noting the positive accomplishments of Harrison and Cleveland, the association concluded: "So far in the present administration the credit sheet remains virtually blank."[40] In 1900 the annual report devoted extensive space to accounts of the appointment of bad agents under the spoils system. The singlemindedness of the association on this point is evident in its conclusion:

> It may seem to the casual reader that an undue amount of space is devoted to the abuse of power on the part of the appointing officer, but when it is considered that the Indian Agent is really the key to the proper solution of the Indian problem, the importance of securing good men for these positions and retaining them so long as they faithfully perform their duties will be apparent. As a matter of fact, a great part of the Association's work during the past eighteen years has been to counteract the disastrous results too often caused by placing unworthy, if not dishonest, men in charge of Indian agencies. Had the Government selected the proper kind of agents and other employees, it is safe to say that the Indian problem would have been solved by this time, and the Indian Rights Association would never have been organized.[41]

The Board of Indian Commissioners, too, continued its agitation for including the agents in the classified civil service and for a strict application of the existing laws to correct abuses on the reservations. At the end of the century it repeated its conviction, "never more deeply felt, that *Indian agents should be appointed solely for merit and fitness for the work*, and *should be retained in the service when they prove themselves to be efficient and helpful by their* character and moral influence, as well as by their experience." The evils that remained in the Indian service it attributed to "the partisan and political influences which still surround the appointment and removal of Indian agents."[42]

39. *Report of the Indian Rights Association*, 1897, pp. 12–14. The decline was steady; in 1898 there were only three out of a total of fifty-six agents. CIA Report, 1898, serial 3757, pp. 117–18.

40. *Report of the Indian Rights Association*, 1898, pp. 4–5; Sageser, *Pendleton Act*, p. 210.

41. *Report of the Indian Rights Association*, 1900, p. 18.

42. *Report of the Board of Indian Commissioners*, 1899, p. 22, and 1897, p. 12. See also *Lake Mohonk Conference Proceedings*, 1897, p. 115.

The advent of Theodore Roosevelt, soon after the turn of the century, brought the culmination of the movement. Roosevelt had been a civil service crusader and member of the civil service commission, and during his presidency the remaining agents were replaced by school superintendents. The president considered the matter significant enough to note in his final annual message to Congress on December 8, 1908. He spoke of the agency system as "gradually falling to pieces from natural or purely evolutionary causes" and as "decaying slowly in its later stages." Now was the time, he asserted, to bring about its final extinction "so that ground can be cleared for larger constructive work on behalf of the Indians, preparatory to their induction into the full measure of responsible citizenship." He noted that of eighteen agencies remaining on November 1, all but two (because of temporary legal problems) had been changed to superintendencies and their heads brought into the classified civil service.[43]

Like views about most panaceas, the reformers' insistence that the civil service would solve the problems of Indian administration was too simple. Bureaucratic personnel, securely protected by civil service rules, were not necessarily enlightened in their administration of Indian affairs, nor would perfection in administration alone have been able to solve the Indian problem. Once again the Indian reformers, seizing upon a remedy that was important in the general reform atmosphere of the day, mistakenly thought they had found the answer.

43. Fred L. Israel, ed., *The State of the Union Messages of the Presidents, 1790–1966*, 3 vols. (New York: Chelsea House, 1966), 3: 2323.

CHAPTER 29

Liquidating the Indian Territory

The Drive for Territorial Organization.

Invasion of the Indian Territory.

Defeat of the Five Civilized Tribes.

Oklahoma Statehood.

The dreams of the Indian reformers for the Americanization of all the Indians and the desire of western settlers for Indian lands that lay unused were long frustrated by the Indian Territory. Here were the Five Civilized Tribes—Cherokee, Creek, Choctaw, Chickasaw, and Seminole—who had advanced the farthest along the white man's road and who seemed most apt for final absorption into American society as individualized, land-owning citizens. Here too were rich acres only partially used by the Indians, which were coveted by white farmers as the surrounding states of Arkansas, Texas, and Kansas grew rapidly in population, and rich mineral resources that beckoned developers. The transformation seemed almost inevitable. Eliphalet Whittlesey, secretary of the Board of Indian Commissioners, was a prophet of impending change in 1882:

> A vague expectation of coming change seems to prevail to a considerable extent in all parts of the Territory. . . . One thing is clear: the new order of things must include the abandonment of communism and seclusion. Great progress and improvement cannot be expected without individual ownership of the soil. A permanent home, and a right to all the value that labor may give it, form the great incentive to effort and enterprise. The Indian needs that incentive as much as the white man. The citizens of the Indian Territory need it now to lift them to a higher plane of civilization. . . .

The Indian Territory cannot always remain in seclusion, impeding commerce from ocean to ocean. The rapid growth of the country will ere long demand that it fall into line and join the march of human progress.[1]

The situation in the Indian Territory was complex and confused. Indians, seeking economic well-being within their autonomous nations, private white corporations driven by the spirit of enterprise and profit, and the United States government, hoping both to protect the Indians and to encourage "progress," all contributed to the political and economic cauldron. Development of the region pitted corporations against the tribal governments, which in the long run were no match for the economic monsters. The Indian Territory stood across the lines of commerce, north and south and east and west, and agitation for railroad lines through the territory developed soon after the Civil War. The treaties of 1866 had authorized rights of way, and Congress in July 1866 made conditional grants to railroad companies. Ten or twenty alternate sections of land along the right of way would go to the railroads "whenever the Indian title shall be extinguished by treaty or otherwise" and the lands became part of the public domain. Hopes for profit intrigued the Indians as well as the whites, and tremendous pressures, only partially resisted, came to bear on the tribal governments and the federal government to promote the railroad interests. Then coal resources became the goal of corporate developers, and finally the new riches of oil and gas. And always there was the magnet of valuable lands for grazing cattle and ultimately for agricultural homesteaders.[2]

The drive to open the Indian Territory to these economic forces filled much of the period between the Civil War and the end of the century. As the invasion proceeded, the independence of the tribes declined in almost direct proportion. Although the Indians skillfully postponed the day of destruction, in the end the demand for progress and conformity won out. It is an instructive story of the force of the reforming spirit, which, blocked time and again in its efforts to eradicate this last great obstacle to the fulfillment of its promise, by the end of the century here too had triumphed.[3]

---

1. *Report of the Board of Indian Commissioners*, 1882, pp. 35–36.
2. A detailed, heavily documented account of the invasion of the Indian Territory by corporations is given by H. Craig Miner, *The Corporation and the Indian: Tribal Sovereignty and Industrial Civilization in Indian Territory, 1865–1907* (Columbia: University of Missouri Press, 1976). The conditional railroad grants are in 14 *United States Statutes* 238, 291, 294.
3. This chapter is taken in large part from Francis Paul Prucha, *American Indian Policy in Crisis: Christian Reformers and the Indian, 1865–1900* (Norman: University of Oklahoma Press, 1976), pp. 373–401. The most detailed and fully documented history of the changes in the Indian Territory is Roy Gittinger, *The Formation of the State of Oklahoma, 1803–1906* (Norman: University of Oklahoma Press, 1939).

THE DRIVE FOR TERRITORIAL ORGANIZATION

The ultimate goal was to bring the Indian Territory into the regular political structure of the United States, beginning with territorial status that would lead to statehood. There seemed no hope for full economic development until the region could be open to all citizens of the United States on an equal footing. That goal fitted perfectly with the program of Americanization espoused by the humanitarian reformers. As early as the end of the Civil War, the plans of the federal government for the Indian Territory, in addition to the emancipation of the slaves and the reduction of territory as a punishment for joining the Confederacy, included a determination to replace the independent tribal governments with a consolidated or confederated government that would be a regular territory of the United States. The persistent efforts to end tribal control and establish such a government were reflected in the numerous bills introduced into Congress for that purpose. One such measure was introduced on March 17, 1870, by Senator Benjamin F. Rice of Arkansas, for the organization of the "Territory of Ok-la-homa." The Committee on Territories, in favorably reporting the bill, argued that the Indians, or at least a large proportion of them, were fitted for citizenship and should be admitted to its rights and duties. "It is in consonance with the new policy of the government, born of the war and matured by the fifteenth amendment," the report said, "that no alien race shall exist upon our soil; all shall be citizens irrespective of race, color, or previous condition of servitude. It is part of the inexorable logic of the times that the Indian must adapt himself to the rights and duties of citizenship. He must wield the franchise and fulfill the obligations imposed thereby, otherwise he will gradually disappear as the waste soil becomes more and more absorbed by the increasing necessities of agriculture." At the heart of the matter was the conviction that there were too few Indians on too much land, that if the Indians could be forced to work 160-acre homesteads of their own, they would find their salvation and the rest of the land could be put into profitable production by whites.[4]

Aside from the purported advantages to the Indians from territorial government, American citizenship, and land in severalty, the advocates of territorial organization were deeply concerned about lawlessness in the Indian Territory. They saw ineffective governments, inadequate courts, and

4. *Senate Report* no. 131, 41–2, serial 1409, p. 4. The principal bills introduced between 1865 and 1879 to organize the Indian Territory or otherwise to extend federal jurisdiction over the area are listed in Gittinger, *Formation of the State of Oklahoma*, pp. 221–23. Examples of the argument about unused lands are in *Senate Report* no. 336, 41–3, serial 1443, and Report of the Secretary of the Interior, 1871, *House Executive Document* no. 1, part 5, 42–2, serial 1505, pp. 7–8.

no protection of the rights of whites and freedmen. Severely complicating the matter was the growing number of whites within the Five Civilized Tribes. Some of these had intermarried into the tribes or been adopted as tribal citizens and caused no special problem. A few others were simply intruders, who infiltrated into the territory unbidden and unwanted. The great majority, however, were farmers or other laborers who had been invited in by the Indians. Although the Five Civilized Tribes all prohibited the leasing of Indian lands, contracts or permits were given to whites to open up farms in return for a share of the crops. By such means ambitious Indians or mixed-bloods were able to establish large holdings not greatly different from antebellum plantations. Railroad and mineral development augmented still more the number of whites within the Indian nations. Because the tribal governments pertained to Indians alone, the demand arose for an adequate means to protect the personal and property rights of the whites. As the years passed and the white population continued to increase, the complaints multiplied, and the patience of the federal officials was severely strained. Commissioner of Indian Affairs John Q. Smith put the matter bluntly in 1876: "The anomalous form of government, if government it can be called, at present existing in the Indian Territory must soon be changed. . . . The idea that that Territory is to consist forever of a collection of little independent or semi-independent nationalities is preposterous."[5]

Congressional pressures did not subside. The Senate Committee on Territories, which sent members to the Indian Territory to interview inhabitants and collected extensive historial documentation, in 1878 confirmed the previous analysis of the situation. It found twenty thousand white and black citizens of the United States lawfully residing among the Five Civilized Tribes and almost without the protection of any law against violence and crime. The committee recommended that the Indian Territory should have a United States court with criminal and civil jurisdiction, that the Indians should become citizens of the United States, and that they should have representation in Congress similar to that of other territories. It asserted that the lands could be divided in severalty without confirming the railroad grants, but it did not press the matter of individual allotment.[6]

The agitation for changes in the Indian Territory in the 1870s bore no fruit. Bill after bill was introduced in Congress, but all failed. Although

5. CIA Report, 1876, serial 1749, p. 390. See also Report of the Secretary of the Interior, 1873, *House Executive Document* no. 1, part 5, 43–1, serial 1601, p. x; ibid., 1876, *House Executive Document* no. 1, part 5, 44–2, serial 1749, p. vii.

6. *Senate Miscellaneous Document* no. 77, 45–2, serial 1786; *Senate Report* no. 744, 45–3, serial 1839.

the arguments were repeated without end and the conditions complained about not only did not disappear but worsened, opponents of territorial organization were able to hold off the threat of radical change. Among these opponents the Indians themselves were foremost. The Five Civilized Tribes had astute and articulate spokesmen, who countered each congressional move toward territorial status with forceful memorials protesting the action. Many of the memorials were drawn up and presented by the national delegates maintained in Washington to look after tribal interests and to oppose changes in the political status or in the land tenure system. Other protests came from intertribal councils or from the principal chiefs of the various nations.[7]

The Indian delegates overlooked no opportunity to get support for their position. No sooner was the Board of Indian Commissioners organized in 1869, for example, than the Indians became regular attendants at the board's meetings and at the conferences of the board with the missionary societies each winter in Washington. At first the Board of Indian Commissioners was a useful ally, and it brought to bear pressure to uphold the Indians' treaty rights and protect their independence. But after 1874 the board moved firmly in the direction of the general reform sentiment that favored territorial organization and allotment of Indian lands. The delegates continued to importune the board for support, and they teamed up with Dr. Thomas Bland's National Indian Defence Association at the January meetings of the board to oppose severalty, but despite their eloquent statements, the Indians were unable to hold back the tide.[8]

The Indians' first defense was to rely upon the treaties that had guaranteed them self-government without white interference, and their statements and memorials skillfully marshaled the historical evidence in support of their stand. They argued that the establishment of a territorial government over them would "work our ruin and speedy extinction, by subjecting us to the absolute rule of a people foreign to us in blood, language, customs, traditions, and interest, who would speedily possess themselves of our homes, degrade us in our own estimation, and leave us prey to the politician and land speculator, thus destroying the unity of our race,

7. A convenient listing of these memorials, together with other pertinent documents, appears in Grant Foreman, *A History of Oklahoma* (Norman: University of Oklahoma Press, 1942), pp. 363–66. For an account of the activity of one of the tribal delegates, see W. David Baird, *Peter Pitchlynn: Chief of the Choctaws* (Norman: University of Oklahoma Press, 1972), pp. 181–212.

8. Statements of the Indian position and of board action appear in *Report of the Board of Indian Commissioners*. A full discussion of the subject is Francis Paul Prucha, "The Board of Indian Commissioners and the Delegates of the Five Tribes," *Chronicles of Oklahoma* 56 (Fall 1978): 247–64.

and producing national disintegration." They denied, moreover, the condition of lawlessness, which was the foundation for so much of the pro-territorial argument, and they lectured Congress that it should not be misled by "mischievous falsehoods." The thrust of the whole policy was well understood by the Indians. The "inexorable logic of the times" brought a sharp rejoinder from the Indian delegates: "Ah! this is the plea of 'manifest destiny' again." The argument signified that "the Indian must be compelled to abandon his present organized government, surrender what he has, and disappear before the white race."[9]

A basic fear of the Indians was that proposed changes would mean the ultimate loss of their lands. Especially disturbing were the conditional land grants. The Indians charged that territorial organization and the end of tribal independence would fulfill these conditions and that the land would then fall to the railroads. Most of the Indian protests adverted to the danger inherent in the railroad grants, and there was strong sympathy for the Indian position. Bills proposed for territorial organization at the end of the 1870s, in fact, added sections specifically repealing the earlier conditional grants.[10]

The Indians, of course, did not lack support. Cattlemen who benefited from leasing Indian lands fought for the maintenance of the status quo, and many persons agreed with the Indians' analysis of their treaty rights. A strong minority report from the House Committee on Territories was lodged against one of the proposed territory bills on the grounds that the bill would contravene treaty agreements and that the movement for territorial organization came from the railroads. "These soulless corporations," it said, "hover like greedy cormorants over this Territory, and incite Congress to remove all restraint, and allow them to swoop down and swallow over twenty-three million acres of land of this Territory, destroying alike the last hope of the Indian and the honor of the Government."[11] In 1879 the committee reported unfavorably on a bill to organize the Indian

9. Creek resolution of February 10, 1870, *Senate Miscellaneous Document* no. 76, 41–2, serial 1408, p. 3; protest of Creek and Cherokee delegates, March 3, 1873, *House Miscellaneous Document* no. 110, 42–3, serial 1573, p. 2; memorial of Cherokee, Creek, and Choctaw delegates, May 23, 1870, *Senate Miscellaneous Document* no. 143, 41–2, serial 1408, p. 11.

10. An example of a bill to repeal the conditional land grants is House Bill 1596, 45th Congress, 3d session.

11. Report of May 27, 1872, *House Report* no. 89, 42–2, serial 1543. The absurdity of the 23-million-acre figure is clear from the fact that the Dawes Commission found a total of only 19,525,976 acres among the Five Civilized Tribes. Elias C. Boudinot at the time pointed out the exaggeration, charging that the figure was at least 20 million acres off. Elias Cornelius Boudinot, *Oklahoma: Argument of Col. E. C. Boudinot before the Committee on Territories, January 29, 1878* (Alexandria, Virginia: G. H. Ramey and Son, 1878), pp. 27–28.

Territory and divide the land in severalty, arguing that the measure would conflict with treaty agreements, that there was no need to invalidate the treaties, and that past experience had shown that allotment of land in severalty and granting of citizenship to Indians had had uniformly bad results. The report, of course, was lauded by the Indian delegates.[12]

INVASION OF THE INDIAN TERRITORY

White agitation for changes in the Indian Territory intensified in the 1880s as new elements came to the fore. Westerners' desire for land, played upon by railroad interests, caused a decade of increasing pressure to open parts of the Territory to homesteaders, and federal officials supported by the humanitarian reformers found new arguments for dividing the Indians' land and absorbing the Indians as citizens of the United States.

The business interests were tireless advocates. Aided by Elias Cornelius Boudinot, of the prominent Ridge faction of the Cherokees, they fostered a group of professional promoters called "boomers," who by propaganda and direct action determined to force open the lands in the territory. Boudinot had wholeheartedly accepted the white vision of the future of the Five Civilized Tribes that called for citizenship and allotment of land. Now he claimed that fourteen million acres of land in the Indian Territory were in fact already in the public domain and subject to homestead entry. He paid special attention to the two million acres in the Oklahoma District, a central area that had been purchased from the Five Civilized Tribes but never assigned as reservations to the immigrating western Indians, but he also designated other lands in the Kiowa, Comanche, and Cheyenne-Arapaho reservations and in Greer County, the southwestern section in dispute with Texas. Boudinot made his assertions in an article in the Chicago *Times* for February 17, 1879, and he provided a map of Indian Territory with the "public lands" plainly marked. Such activities, together with a tremendous flood of boomer literature, led to organized Oklahoma colonies on the borders of the Indian Territory in Kansas and Texas that claimed the right to homestead in the territory and that, led by such organizers as C. C. Carpenter, David L. Payne, and William L. Couch, made forays into the territory and established incipient communities before they were driven out by federal troops.[13]

12. *House Report* no. 188, 45–3, serial 1867. The report supplied a long historical argument.

13. Elias Cornelius Boudinot, "The Indian Territory and Its Inhabitants," *Geographical Magazine* 1 (June 1874): 92–94; Boudinot, *Oklahoma*. Boudinot's assertions about free land were printed in *Senate Executive Document* no. 20, 46–1, serial 1869, pp.

The illegal invasions of the Indian Territory stirred new support for the Indians among humanitarians concerned with Indian rights, but the pressure was too great to withstand. Carl Schurz told the Indians in 1879 that "the difficulties of protecting the integrity of the Territory might in the course of time increase beyond control," and he urged them to meet the emergency by dividing their lands and obtaining individual titles in fee, which could be defended against attack.[14]

The vacant lands of the Oklahoma District were a powerful magnet for land-hungry westerners, and the reformers, too, could not abide continuing failure to make full use of the lands. When Commissioner J. D. C. Atkins proposed to move various Indian groups into the district in an attempt to end the agitation for white settlement of the region, Charles C. Painter of the Indian Rights Association replied vigorously. "The purpose to fill up Oklahoma [District] with settlers will never sleep, and ought never to sleep, until it is accomplished," he wrote. "Such an anomaly as is there presented can never be sanctioned and made permanent—that of an immense territory, valuable for its vast resources, and needed to meet the demand for homes by our increasing population, kept empty by the use of the army. It must, it will be opened in some way; it will be occupied and used by somebody."[15]

Little by little the government gave way. Congressional friends of the boomers regularly introduced bills for opening lands in the territory for homesteading, and in 1889 they succeeded. On March 2, 1889, Congress authorized homesteading in the Oklahoma District, and President Benjamin Harrison proclaimed the lands open to settlement at noon on April 22, 1889. Fifty thousand homeseekers lined the area waiting for the signal to advance, and when the blast of the bugle sounded, the first of the dramatic Oklahoma "runs" was under way. For a year the new inhabitants were forced to maintain their own communities, for Congress had failed to provide government for the region. Then on May 2, 1890, with the Oklahoma Organic Act, a formal territorial government was established for the Oklahoma District and for "No Man's Land" (the Oklahoma panhandle), which was joined to it. This was a far cry from the organization of the

---

7–10; a copy of the map is appended to the document. There is a good survey of boomer activity in Gittinger, *Formation of the State of Oklahoma*, chapters 7–10; see also Solon J. Buck, "The Settlement of Oklahoma," *Transactions of the Wisconsin Academy of Sciences, Arts, and Letters* 15 (1907): 325–80; Carl Coke Rister, *Land Hunger: David L. Payne and the Oklahoma Boomers* (Norman: University of Oklahoma Press, 1942).

14. Report of the Secretary of the Interior, 1879, *House Executive Document* no. 1, part 5, 46–2, serial 1910, p. 15.

15. Charles C. Painter, *The Proposed Removal of Indians to Oklahoma* (Philadelphia: Indian Rights Association, 1888), p. 3.

whole Indian Territory that had been advocated so strenuously; but white settlers had at last broken the barrier and begun their legal invasion of the once sacrosanct region.[16]

Meanwhile, the attack on the independent status of the Five Civilized Tribes went on. Commissioner Atkins was especially vehement. He asserted in 1885 that the idea of Indian nationality was fast melting away and that the tribal relations would sooner or later have to be broken up. When the Indians had taken their lands in severalty and become citizens, they would be prepared to dispose of their surplus lands to their own advantage and for the public good. Atkins hammered ceaselessly upon this theme, insisting that he did not want to do anything contrary to the treaties but only to convince the Five Civilized Tribes to adopt his views. But ultimately he admitted that the feelings of nationality among the Indians should not be the final arbiter. "These Indians," he declared in 1886, "have no right to obstruct civilization and commerce and set up an exclusive claim to self-government, establishing a government within a government, and then expect and claim that the United States shall protect them from all harm, while insisting that it shall not be the ultimate judge as to what is best to be done for them in a political point of view. I repeat, to maintain any such view is to acknowledge a foreign sovereignty, with the right of eminent domain, upon American soil—a thing utterly repugnant to the spirit and genius of our laws, and wholly unwarranted by the Constitution of the United States."[17]

Atkins made much of the recurring argument used by the proponents of forced change that the nations were controlled by aristocratic leaders who had built up huge land monopolies. He pointed to large holdings within the nations controlled by certain important men who had acquired land that belonged to all in common. "What a baronial estate!" he exclaimed about one such holding. "In theory the lands are held in common under the tribal relation, and are equally owned by each member of the tribe, but in point of fact they are simply held in the grasping hand of moneyed monopolists and powerful and influential leaders and politicians, who pay no rental to the other members of the tribe." Such a situation, the commissioner insisted, needed radical reformation. "Are these the sacred rights secured by treaty, which the United States are pledged to respect and defend?" he asked. "If so, the United States are pledged to uphold and maintain a stupendous land monopoly and aristocracy that finds no parallel in the

16. 25 *United States Statutes* 1005; 26 *United States Statutes* 81–100; proclamation of March 23, 1889, James D. Richardson, ed., *A Compilation of the Messages and Papers of the Presidents*, 10 vols. (Washington: GPO, 1896–1899), 9: 15–18.

17. CIA Report, 1885, serial 2379, p. 13; CIA Report, 1886, serial 2467, p. 87.

country except in two or three localities in the far West." He saw the need, he said, for "some potent influence or power to dispel this system and establish a new order of things"—some change that would raise up the downtrodden people to their proper level and bring down the mighty.[18]

DEFEAT OF THE FIVE CIVILIZED TRIBES

The humanitarian reformers who aimed to turn the Indians into landowning, civilized, Christian citizens of the United States wanted the Five Civilized Tribes to be the model for the rest of the Indian tribes. Not only would the incorporation of these Indians into the American system solve the problems that beset the Indian Territory, but it would provide encouragement for other Indians to follow suit. The reformers, however, were to be disappointed. Because of the insistent opposition of the Five Civilized Tribes to proposed land in severalty and citizenship legislation, Congress excluded them from the Dawes Act of 1887. Thus the very tribes that might have been the first to whom the Dawes Act could be applied and who had been a prime target of such proposals for two decades slipped out of the net.

Although the reformers lost this battle, they had not yet lost the war. The acquisition of lands for homesteading was accomplished by direct negotiation with the Cherokees for sale of the Cherokee Outlet and with other tribes residing west of the Five Civilized Tribes for cession of their surplus lands. This work was undertaken by the so-called Cherokee Commission, the result of legislation of March 2, 1889, which authorized the president to appoint three commissioners "to negotiate with the Cherokee Indians and with all other Indians owning or claiming lands lying west of the ninety-sixth degree of longitude in the Indian Territory for the cession to the United States of all their title, claim, or interest of every kind or character in and to such lands." Lands so obtained were to become part of the public domain.[19]

In July 1889 the president appointed the members of the commission: Lucius Fairchild, former governor of Wisconsin; John F. Hantranft, former governor of Pennsylvania; and Judge Alfred M. Wilson of Arkansas. The

---

18. CIA Report, 1886, serial 2467, pp. 82–84.

19. 25 *United States Statutes* 1005–6. The history of the Cherokee Commission is told in Berlin B. Chapman, "The Cherokee Commission, 1889–1893," *Indiana Magazine of History* 62 (June 1946): 177–90, and in a series of articles by Chapman in *Chronicles of Oklahoma* 15 (September 1937): 291–321; 16 (June 1938): 135–62; 17 (March 1939): 62–74; 19 (December 1941): 356–67; 26 (Winter 1948–1949): 449–58.

commissioners proceeded first to negotiate with the Cherokees for the Outlet. They offered $1.25 an acre, the price fixed by Congress, but the Cherokees, hoping to gain more from leasing to cattlemen, refused. After long and futile conferring, the negotiations were broken off at the end of December. Following the death of Hantranft in October 1889 and the resignation of Fairchild on January 1, 1890, the commission was reconstituted by the appointment of David H. Jerome, former governor of Michigan, and Warren G. Sayre of Indiana. The new commission (now frequently called the Jerome Commission) began its work in May 1890. Much opposition came from the Indians, but the persistence of the commissioners resulted finally in eleven agreements with plains Indians and Indians who had moved to the Indian Territory from the Old Northwest, by which the tribes gave up more than fifteen million acres. The common pattern provided for 160-acre allotments in severalty to each man, woman, and child on the tribal rolls. The remainder of the land was declared surplus and bought by the government for homesteading. As the areas were opened to white settlers, new counties were organized and incorporated into Oklahoma Territory. The Cherokee Outlet was the largest transfer of land. The Indians' reliance on grazing leases there was undercut by a presidential proclamation on February 17, 1890, that such leases were illegal and by an order that all livestock be removed by December 1890. When the Jerome Commission resumed negotiations in November 1890, therefore, the Cherokees were in a compliant mood, and an agreement was reached by which they sold more than six million acres of the Outlet for $8,595,736.12. On September 16, 1893, the Cherokee Outlet was opened to homesteaders, and the greatest of the Oklahoma land runs occurred as a hundred thousand persons rushed in to locate homes on the new land.[20]

A second line of attack on the problems of the Indian Territory was the extension of the federal judicial system over the region. Criminal cases in the territory involving white citizens of the United States had been handled by the United States District Court at Fort Smith, Arkansas, but the distance and expense involved in bringing cases before the court were so great that only important ones were brought in. There were no courts

---

20. Details on each of the agreements are given in Foreman, *History of Oklahoma*, pp. 244–53. An enlightening discussion of the conflicts that arose between Indians and whites on the Cheyenne-Arapaho Reservation after the Indians received allotments and the surplus lands were opened to settlement appears in Donald J. Berthrong, "White Neighbors Come among the Southern Cheyenne and Arapaho," *Kansas Quarterly* 3 (Fall 1971): 105–15. Berthrong speaks of the relations as "tragic" and concludes: "The first full contact of these tribesmen with whites delayed and perhaps even prevented them from attaining the goal of self-support demanded by Congress and the officials of the Bureau of Indian Affairs."

to take care of civil cases. Then in 1889 a United States court was established at Muskogee, with jurisdiction in civil cases affecting citizens of the United States if the amount involved was more than one hundred dollars, and the court was given criminal jurisdiction over cases in which the offense was not punishable by death or imprisonment at hard labor. But the more serious cases still had to go to Fort Smith or to the United States District Court at Paris, Texas, which had been designated for criminal cases arising in the Choctaw and Chickasaw nations. In the following year, nine United States commissioners for the Indian Territory were authorized and given powers of justices of the peace over United States citizens. The laws of Arkansas were made applicable if not in conflict with federal law. These provisions were a start in furnishing a judicial system for the whites who resided in the Indian nations.[21]

On March 1, 1895, Congress created two new United States courts for the Indian Territory and ended the jurisdiction of the courts in the neighboring states, and the system was gradually expanded. The dissolution of the Indian governments was thus rapidly advanced. In 1897 Congress provided that after January 1, 1898, all civil and criminal cases should be tried in the United States courts. The Curtis Act of June 28, 1898, abolished tribal laws and tribal courts and brought all persons in the Indian Territory, regardless of race, under United States authority. The act, entitled "an act for the protection of the people of the Indian Territory," was unilateral action by the United States that signaled the end of the tribal governments; it was practically an organic act for the establishment of the long-sought territorial government.[22]

Paralleling this dissolution of the tribal governments, and in fact a strong force in their destruction, was the work of the Commission to the Five Civilized Tribes (usually known as the Dawes Commission), which accomplished the allotment of land that had been the goal of the government and of the reformers for nearly three decades. By an act of March 3, 1893, Congress authorized the appointment of three commissioners to negotiate with the Five Civilized Tribes for the extinguishment of the national or tribal title to their lands and for consent to measures that would be "requisite and suitable to enable the ultimate creation of a State or States of the Union" out of the Indian Territory. The commissioners were directed to endeavor to procure first the allotment of the lands in severalty and then the cession of any surplus lands to the United States. It is significant that President Grover Cleveland chose Henry L. Dawes, who had retired from the Senate in 1893, to head the commission. Dawes's strong views as to the future of the Indians and the necessity of incorporation into

21. 25 *United States Statutes* 783–88; 26 *United States Statutes* 93–99.
22. 28 *United States Statutes* 693–98; 30 *United States Statutes* 83, 495–519.

white society through allotment of lands and citizenship made him a fit instrument to carry out the mandate of Congress. There is no doubt of his conviction that the goal was the proper one.[23]

After a preliminary meeting in Washington in December 1893, the Dawes Commission in January moved to the Indian Territory. It began at once a series of conferences with tribal leaders, to whom it submitted as the basis for discussion a series of proposals dealing with allotment, provisions for townsites and mineral lands, and the establishment of a territorial government. The Indians refused to negotiate, and the Dawes Commission could report little but frustration at the end of its first year's work.[24]

The reformers, who had long been agitated by conditions in the Indian Territory, soon had strong supporting evidence for their position. A Senate committee headed by Senator Henry M. Teller investigated the Indian Territory early in 1894 and submitted a report in May. This report, as well as the report of the Dawes Commission submitted in November 1894, emphasized the crisis resulting from the great influx of whites into the territory and from the monopolization of land by a few individuals. The whites were estimated to number 250,000 or more, and they had for the most part been invited in by the Indians themselves, despite provisions in the treaties that the lands were to be for the exclusive use of the Indians. The United States, Teller asserted, had made it possible for the Indians to maintain their tribal relations and Indian laws and customs. "And, if now," he continued, "the isolation and exclusiveness sought to be given to them by our solemn treaties is destroyed, and they are overrun by a population of strangers five times in number to their own, it is not the fault of the Government of the United States, but comes from their own acts in admitting whites to citizenship under their laws and by inviting white people to come within their jurisdiction, to become traders, farmers, and to follow professional pursuits." Most of these persons were not subject to the Indian law and lacked adequate protection of life and property.[25]

---

23. 27 *United States Statutes* 645–46. The history of the Dawes Commission is given in Loren N. Brown, "The Dawes Commission," *Chronicles of Oklahoma* 9 (March 1931): 71–105, and Loren N. Brown, "The Establishment of the Dawes Commission for Indian Territory," ibid. 18 (June 1940): 171–81. Official reports and related documents are in the *Annual Report of the Commission to the Five Civilized Tribes, 1894–1905* (issued under varying titles). See also *Index to the Annual Reports of the Commission to the Five Civilized Tribes for the Years 1894 to 1905, Inclusive* (Washington: GPO, 1906), and *Laws, Decisions, and Regulations Affecting the Work of the Commissioner to the Five Civilized Tribes, 1893 to 1906* (Washington: GPO, 1906).

24. *Annual Report of the Commission to the Five Civilized Tribes, 1894.*

25. Report of Select Committee on the Five Civilized Tribes, May 7, 1894, *Senate Report* no. 377, 53–2, serial 3183. The quotation is on p. 7. The same kinds of remarks occur in the *Annual Report, 1894,* p. 17.

It had been the theory, the reports noted, that when the government made over title to the lands to the Indian nations that the lands would be held in trust for *all* the Indians. Instead, Teller reported, a few enterprising citizens of the tribe, frequently Indian not by blood but by intermarriage, had become the practical owners of the largest and best part of the lands, even though the title still remained in the tribe. The monopoly was so great that in one tribe a hundred persons were reported to have appropriated fully one-half of the best land. The trust had been broken, nor would it ever be properly executed, Teller thought, if left to the Indians. The Dawes Commission faced the question of the duty of the government of the United States with reference to the trust. "These tribal governments," it asserted, "have wholly perverted their high trust, and it is the plain duty of the United States to enforce the trust it has so created and recover for its original uses the domain and all the gains derived from the perversion of the trust or discharge the trustee." Noted too were the inequities in the condition of the freedmen—despite the clear provisions of the 1866 treaties—and "corruption of the grossest kind, openly and unblushingly practiced" in all branches of the tribal governments.[26]

It was apparent to these official observers that the existing system could not continue. "It is not only non-American," Teller said, "but it is radically wrong, and a change is imperatively demanded in the interest of the Indian and whites alike, and such change cannot be much longer delayed. . . . There can be no modification of the system. It cannot be reformed. It must be abandoned and a better one substituted." There was only one solution: Congress had to act whether or not the Indians liked it. "The United States . . . granted to these tribes the power of self-government not to conflict with the Constitution," the Dawes Commission concluded its report. "They have demonstrated their incapacity to so govern themselves, and no higher duty can rest upon the Government that granted this authority than to revoke it when it has so lamentably failed."[27]

Despite its convictions, the Teller committee made no specific recommendations, preferring, it said, to await the outcome of the Dawes Commission's negotiations. The commission, for its part, continued to treat with the tribal governments. Its report at the end of 1895, however, indicated how hopeless it considered the work to be. It declared that the tribal governments were "wholly corrupt, irresponsible, and unworthy to be longer trusted" and that the promises of self-government made in the treaties were no longer binding under the changed conditions. "It is . . . the imperative duty of Congress," the commissioners declared, "to assume at

26. Report of Select Committee, pp. 11–12; *Annual Report,* 1894, pp. 17, 20.
27. Report of Select Committee, p. 12; *Annual Report,* 1894, p. 20.

once the political control of the Indian Territory." The reformers at Lake
Mohonk placed themselves firmly on the side of the commission. Their
platform for 1895 included this forthright statement:

> The nation possesses a supreme sovereignty over every foot of soil
> within its boundaries. Its legislative authority over its people it has
> neither right nor power to alienate. Its attempt to do so by Indian
> treaties in the past does not relieve it from the responsibility for the
> condition of government in the reservations and in the Indian Terri-
> tory; and, despite those treaties, it is under a sacred obligation to
> exercise its sovereignty extending over the three hundred thousand
> whites and fifty thousand so-called Indians in the Indian Territory
> the same restraints and protection of government which other parts
> of the country enjoy.[28]

Congress heeded the message. A law of June 10, 1896, directed the
Dawes Commission to make out rolls of Indian citizens in preparation for
allotment and stated: "It is hereby declared to be the duty of the United
States to establish a government in the Indian Territory which will rectify
the many inequalities and discriminations now existing in said Territory
and afford needful protection to the lives and property of all citizens and
residents thereof."[29] Under these new mandates, the commission moved
rapidly ahead toward the dissolution of the Five Civilized Tribes.

The Indian reformers followed the work of the Dawes Commission
with interest and at first with some concern, and Dawes regularly reported
to the Lake Mohonk Conference, in person or by letter, on the progress of
his work. Critics of the commission, however, had broadcast their complaints, charging that the commission aimed to violate the treaty rights of
the tribes. Such accusations could not go unnoticed, and the Indian Rights
Association, which considered itself the watchdog of Indian rights, decided
in 1896 to send a special agent of its own to investigate the conditions in
the Indian Territory and the work of the Dawes Commission. The man
chosen was Charles M. Meserve, president of Shaw College in Raleigh,
North Carolina, and former superintendent of Haskell Institute.[30]

Brushing aside the complaints he had heard—emanating, he said,
"largely, if not wholly, from paid attorneys, from Indian and white coal,
cattle, or timber monopolists, from Indian officials or other influential
people, all of whom are profiting from the present abnormal condition of

28. *Annual Report,* 1895, p. 78; *Lake Mohonk Conference Proceedings,* 1895, p. 106.
29. 29 *United States Statutes* 339–40.
30. Dawes's remarks in *Lake Mohonk Conference Proceedings,* 1895, 1896, 1897,
1898, 1900, and 1902; *Report of the Indian Rights Association,* 1896, p. 9.

affairs, and consequently are interested in the continuance of the *status quo*"—Meserve set about to seek the facts for himself. He spent the summer of 1896 in the Indian Territory, and his findings corroborated those of the Dawes Commission and the Teller committee. He saw crime, corruption, and monopoly; and everywhere he saw the overpowering presence of the whites.[31]

In October 1896 Meserve appeared at Lake Mohonk, where he repeated verbatim large sections of his printed report. He was followed on the platform by Dawes, who offered an apologia for the work of his commission, expressed his deep gratitude for Meserve's findings, and urged the members to continue their support. Dawes asked how it was that the Five Civilized Tribes enjoyed an autonomous political status within the territorial limits of the United States, and he then answered: "It grows out of the belief in a large portion of the people of the United States that somehow and in some way they have bound themselves to let it be so; the belief that the United States has abdicated authority over this people. If it is really and rightly so, it is to be respected and adhered to so long as public safety will permit *and no longer.*" But for his part, Dawes denied that the United States had ever abdicated authority over any of its territory and said that it in fact did not have the power to do so. The governmental arrangements of the Indians had been made by the United States, he insisted, "and if the government of the United States made it, it can unmake it." He emphasized the fact that the lands of the Indians in the Indian Territory were granted to them to be held in common, lands put in the hands of those nations "as *trustees for each and every one of the citizen Indians.*" Dawes wanted to return to that state of affairs, and he asserted that the commission "has asked for the violation of no treaty obligations. . . . They ask that these treaty stipulations may be enforced." If the Indian governments had failed as trustees and had misappropriated the trust by allowing monopolization of the land, they should be removed. Dawes understandably placed his primary reliance on the allotment of the lands in severalty and was less concerned about the details of territorial or state governmental arrangements, since he was convinced that once the Indians owned their land individually they would see to it that they got a proper government to protect it.[32]

Dawes got the support at Lake Mohonk that he was seeking, and in fact his listeners needed little persuading. The old reformer Bishop Henry Whipple, for one, asserted that the Indians had forfeited their old treaty

31. Charles F. Meserve, *The Dawes Commission and the Five Civilized Tribes of Indian Territory* (Philadelphia: Indian Rights Association, 1896).

32. *Lake Mohonk Conference Proceedings*, 1896, pp. 44–55.

rights by taking the side of the Confederacy during the Civil War and that after the war they had been received back into friendship under quite different conditions. "Familiar as I am with Indian wrongs," he concluded, "I have never had my heart more deeply stirred than in listening to Senator Dawes and to Mr. Meserve; and from my heart I can only say, God be praised for raising up such men to do his work." The desire to see the Indians as individual landowners and the belief that this was necessary for the advance of American civilization were so strong that they seemed to block out other considerations. Thomas J. Morgan, returning to Lake Mohonk in 1895, declared that the condition of things in Indian Territory was so anomalous that it was "irreconcilable with any philosophy of our national life," that the Indian governments had proved inadequate to meet the needs of the times, and that the Indian Territory was obstructing the "march of civilization." The time had come, Morgan said, when "the solution of the problem *must* be reached." It was a hard and perplexing situation, he admitted, but action had to be taken and the Indian Territory moved to territorial and then to state organization. In the final analysis the United States had to act, whether or not the Indians agreed.[33]

Support of the Meserve report by the Indian Rights Association placed that organization on Dawes's side. In an analysis of the question of the Five Civilized Tribes in 1896, the association spokesmen opted for a middle course between "a purely sentimental policy which considered the present situation of the five civilized tribes an autonomous one" and urged that the Indians be left alone, and a change overriding all rights of the Indians, forced by outside interests, not by friends of the Indians—between "landgrabbing and spoliation on the one side; a sentimentalism which takes no account of facts on the other." But ultimately the Indian Rights Association was "quite content to let the tribe go." It noted that all recent Indian legislation had contemplated the extinction of the tribes and that the great majority of Indian reformers were agreed on that policy. The association wanted to do all that could be done wisely "to save and guard the individual Indian."[34]

The tribes finally saw the futility of further resistance and gave in. On April 23, 1897, the Dawes Commission negotiated the Atoka Agreement with the Choctaws and Chickasaws, which determined the fundamental formula for allotment in those nations. An agreement was reached with the Seminoles in 1898, with the Creeks in 1901, and with the Cherokees finally in 1902. Meanwhile the Curtis Act authorized the Dawes Commis-

33. Ibid., p. 57; ibid., 1895, pp. 99–101.
34. *Report of the Indian Rights Association*, 1896, p. 12.

sion to proceed with the allotment of lands as soon as the tribal rolls were completed.[35]

The work of the Dawes Commission was exacting. The lands had to be surveyed, not only for extent but also for quality of land, since the agreements specified that allotments would be based on the value of the land, not simply on acreage. In addition the commission was responsible for determining the eligibility of allottees, a tremendous job, for more than 300,000 persons claimed membership in the Five Civilized Tribes. Beginning in 1898 and continuing until the rolls were closed in 1907, the commission entered 101,506 persons on the rolls. The size of the allotments varied from tribe to tribe. Choctaws and Chickasaws received 320 acres each, Cherokees 110 acres, Creeks 160 acres, and Seminoles 120 acres. Freedmen among the Cherokees, Creeks, and Seminoles shared equally with the Indians; those among the Chickasaws and Choctaws received 40-acre allotments. Some part of each allotment was designated a homestead and made inalienable for a period of years. Altogether 19,526,966 acres were surveyed in the Five Civilized Tribes, of which 15,794,400 were allotted to persons on the tribal rolls. The rest comprised land for townsites, schools, and other public purposes, and coal and mineral lands held for tribal benefit. There were few surplus lands within the Five Civilized Tribes to be opened to whites.[36]

These moves meant that members of the Five Civilized Tribes were to lose their tribal citizenship and become citizens of the United States. Congress in 1890, in fact, had provided that individuals could apply at the federal court at Muskogee for United States citizenship, and the allotment agreements drawn up by the Dawes Commission provided for a switch in citizenship. Finally, in 1901, Congress made every Indian in the Indian Territory a citizen of the United States.[37]

---

35. The Atoka Agreement was incorporated in the Curtis Act, in 30 *United States Statutes* 505–13. The other agreements appear as follows: Seminole, 30 *United States Statutes* 567–69; Creek, 31 *United States Statutes* 861–73; Cherokee, 32 *United States Statutes* 716–27. For a detailed listing of agreements with the tribes, see Gittinger, *Formation of the State of Oklahoma*, p. 194n.

36. Loren N. Brown, "The Appraisal of the Lands of the Choctaws and Chickasaws by the Dawes Commission," *Chronicles of Oklahoma* 22 (Summer 1944): 177–91. There is a tabulation of the final rolls, showing full-bloods, mixed-bloods, whites, and freedmen enrolled in each tribe in Angie Debo, *And Still the Waters Run: The Betrayal of the Five Civilized Tribes* (Princeton: Princeton University Press, 1940), p. 47. Figures on enrollment differ because some names were removed and the rolls were opened from time to time to admit new members. Figures on allotment are given in Arrell M. Gibson, *Oklahoma: A History of Five Centuries* (Norman: Harlow Publishing Corporation, 1965), pp. 325–26, and Gittinger, *Formation of the State of Oklahoma*, p. 230.

37. 26 *United States Statutes* 99. The Atoka Agreement, for example, provided that "the Choctaws and Chickasaws, when their tribal governments cease, shall become pos-

Thus ended the campaign to destroy the exclusiveness of the Indians in the Indian Territory. For more than three decades after the Civil War the Indian nations struggled to preserve their national existence, but the odds were too great. There was the continual tension between traditional tribal independence on one side and economic development on the other, for the two in practice seemed to be contradictory. As railroad or mining corporations gained power, tribal self-determination was weakened, and often even the moves of the federal government to protect the Indians' welfare were made in a paternalistic spirit independently of the tribal governments and thus were another wound to Indian sovereignty. More damaging, perhaps, was the factionalism that developed within the Indian tribes themselves over the question of economic exploitation of their resources. There were strong elements among the Indians—Elias Cornelius Boudinot is but a striking example—who on principle or for personal gain were on the side of the white corporations. These advocates of change were for the most part mixed-bloods, whereas the full-bloods in the more isolated country regions clung to the old ways. Events moved too rapidly for the federal government to develop a firm and consistent policy in regard to leasing and other elements of economic development; and the tribes, too, had to make decisions—often irrevocable—before they fully grasped the significance of their actions. Hesitation on the part of the government and informal permissions allowed business interests to get a vested interest in the Indian Territory, and then they influenced the circumstances under which formal policy decisions were made.[38]

The tribal governments were allowed to continue until their property was liquidated, and national councils were allowed to meet, but their acts were all subject to approval by the president of the United States. The Indian nations had succumbed to the pressures of the whites, who could brook no alien economic or political enclaves within their completely Americanized society.

OKLAHOMA STATEHOOD

Strong agitation for Oklahoma statehood developed at the end of the century, and the growing population in both Oklahoma Territory and the Indian Territory fully justified it; but delay came because of the question of

---

sessed of all the rights and privileges of citizens of the United States." 30 *United States Statutes* 513. Citizenship for all the Indians in the territory came fittingly enough as an amendment to the Dawes Act of 1887. 31 *United States Statutes* 1447.

38. See Miner, *Corporation and the Indian*, pp. 205–15, for a perceptive analysis of the conditions leading to the end of the national existence of the tribes.

what should be included in the new state or states. Some wanted the immediate admission of Oklahoma Territory, leaving the status of the Indian Territory undecided (but it could possibly join Oklahoma at a later date); others wanted the admission of Oklahoma Territory and the Indian Territory as separate states; still others wanted the admission of the two territories as a single state.[39]

The leaders of the Five Civilized Tribes made a valiant attempt to preserve their identity within the federal system by promoting separate statehood for the Indian Territory. On November 28, 1902, at Eufaula in the Creek Nation, officials of the Creeks, Cherokees, and Choctaws (supported by the Chickasaws as well) adopted a statement against union with Oklahoma Territory. The individual tribes also made separate protests.[40] But the movement seemed to have little effect at the time in convincing a majority of the citizens or the federal officials to accept the Indians' view.

In the summer of 1905 new agitation for a separate state developed, and strong arguments were presented. The Indian Territory had a population as large as that of Maine; its resources for economic development surpassed those of Oklahoma Territory, and it had numerous railroads and incorporated towns. Union with Oklahoma, moreover, would bring together two political entities with different histories and different current problems. The Indians pointed, too, to the Atoka Agreement of 1897, which spoke of the preparation of the lands of the Indian nations "for admission as a state of the Union." In July the heads of four of the five tribes issued a call for a constitutional convention to meet on August 21 at Muskogee. All the residents of the Indian Territory were invited to vote for delegates, and many whites cooperated with the Indians. The convention drew up a constitution for a proposed state of Sequoyah, and in an election on November 7 the document was ratified by a vote of fifty-six thousand to nine thousand (though not more than half of the qualified voters went to the polls).[41]

This seeming success was blocked in Congress. Although bills for admission of the separate state were introduced in both houses, no action was taken, and the whole movement died. President Theodore Roosevelt recommended joint statehood in his annual message on December 4, 1905, and Congress proceeded with its plans to unite the two territories. Under an enabling act passed on June 16, 1906, a constitutional convention was

---

39. The best discussion of the movement toward statehood is in Gittinger, *Formation of the State of Oklahoma*, pp. 236–58.

40. The Eufaula resolutions are printed in *Congressional Record*, 36: 567. For action by the various tribes, see *Senate Document* no. 143, 59–1, serial 4912.

41. *Senate Document* no. 143, 59–1, serial 4912. The memorial for the proposed state of Sequoyah is on pp. 1–27; the constitution on pp. 47–87.

held and a constitution drawn up, which was ratified by an overwhelming majority on September 17, 1907. A month later President Roosevelt issued a proclamation declaring that Oklahoma was a state of the Union.[42] According to a special census of 1907, the population of the new state stood at 1,414,177, slightly less than half of which was in the former Indian Territory. Of this total, there were 101,228 persons in the Five Civilized Tribes, including intermarried whites and the freedmen, and 15,603 other Indians.[43]

The Indians of Oklahoma were an anomaly in Indian-white relations. Many had long been acculturated to the white man's ways and took an active part in the formation of the new state and in its economic and political life. Yet they maintained an identity as Indians and for many years far surpassed the Indian population of other states. There are no Indian reservations in Oklahoma, however, and the reservation experience that was fundamental for most Indian groups in the twentieth century was not part of Oklahoma Indian history.[44]

42. Message of December 4, 1905, in Fred L. Israel, ed., *The State of the Union Messages of the Presidents, 1790–1966,* 3 vols. (New York: Chelsea House, 1966), 3: 2191; 34 *United States Statutes* 267 and 35 *United States Statutes* 2160.

43. Report of the Secretary of the Interior, 1907, *House Document* no. 5, 60–1, serial 5295, pp. 21, 49.

44. The fate of the Indians of the Five Civilized Tribes after the end of tribal autonomy is critically recounted in Debo, *And Still the Waters Run.*

PART SEVEN

The Nation's
Wards

The individualization and Americanization of the Indians that was the goal of the Christian reformers in the last two decades of the nineteenth century were worked out in practice in the first three decades of the twentieth. The theory embodied in the Dawes Act, with its allotment of land in severalty and its provisions for citizenship, and the establishment of a national school system for the Indians that had been the dream of Thomas Jefferson Morgan and his Lake Mohonk supporters were refined and implemented after 1900. The policy had been set; now the administration of the policy became the crucial matter. Perhaps because the period was devoid of striking policy changes, historians have neglected it, jumping for the most part from the Dawes Act of 1887 to its antithesis, the Indian Reorganization Act of 1934. Yet it was in the intervening years that the late-nineteenth-century policy was tested in the fire of experience. It was in these years that the Indian Office came face to face with the problems of dealing with the Indians, not as a relatively few tribal units, but as thousands upon thousands of individual wards of the federal government. Under these conditions the paternalism of the federal government, which was supposed to end when the individual Indians disappeared into the dominant American society, increased instead of diminished, until the bureaucracy of the Indian Service dominated every aspect of the Indians' lives.[1]

1. There are, unfortunately, no published general studies devoted to this crucial period. Frederick E. Hoxie, "Beyond Savagery: The Campaign to Assimilate the American

In its concern for the nation's wards, the federal government after 1900 moved in two directions. On the one hand, following to its logical conclusion the philosophy of assimilation, it sought rapidly—at times even recklessly—to end government supervision of individual Indians who were deemed competent to manage their own affairs. Most of the reservation lands that were suitable for allotment were granted in severalty, for allotment as a goal was strongly supported even after its destructive effects were visible. Then thousands of allottees were pushed into independence through the granting of fee simple patents or the removal of restrictions on their land and other property. For these Indians, the government no longer was to be the Great Father, for they were to stand on their own feet, not as children or wards who needed protection and guidance, but as independent adult citizens of the nation. When asked what happened to Indians who had received full control of their property, the commissioner of Indian affairs asserted in 1920 that he did not know, for he had no records on such individuals. "After an Indian receives a patent in fee to his land," he said, "he is no longer under our supervision or jurisdiction."[2] On the other hand, it became clear that many thousands of Indians were not prepared immediately—or within the near future—to compete on their own with their white neighbors. For these the federal government continued its guardianship, and its supervision became increasingly detailed, as provisions for health, for schools, and for management of Indian land and funds multiplied. The great problem was to decide just where the line should be drawn between "competent" and "incompetent" Indians. The Indian Office was caught between pressures from those who wanted all Indians freed at once and those who urged a continuing and more effective guardianship of the wards by the government.

Although the basic philosophy of assimilation continued to be the foundation of the government's relations with the Indians, there were important changes in outlook or in emphasis after 1900. Most noticeable was a change from the theoretical, religiously oriented dream of the Christian reformers of the late nineteenth century, with their faith that the individu-

---

Indians, 1880–1920" (Ph.D. dissertation, Brandeis University, 1977) treats aspects of the period in great detail but ends in 1920 and stresses a radical change in policy after 1900 that does not take account of significant evidence of continuity in policy. Some recent tribal histories carry the story through the period. See also Thomas M. Holm, "Indians and Progressives: From Vanishing Policy to the Indian New Deal" (Ph.D. dissertation, University of Oklahoma, 1978), and Kenneth O'Reilly, "Progressive Era and New Era American Indian Policy: The Gospel of Self-Support," *Journal of Historical Studies* 5 (Fall 1981): 35–56.

2. Cato Sells to John Barton Payne, December 3, 1920, OSI CCF 5–6, General, Patents.

alization and Christianization of the Indians would abruptly and dramatically transform them and result in a rapid disappearance of the "Indian
problem," to a pragmatic, practical approach, with the emphasis on efficiency and businesslike management that marked the Progressive Era. In
1893 the president of the Lake Mohonk Conference set the tone of much
of the earlier reform when he spoke of drawing the Indians out of their
old associations and immersing them "in the strong currents of Christian
life and Christian citizenship" and sending among them "the sanctifying
streams of Christian life and Christian work." In contrast, the new commissioner of Indian affairs in 1909 spoke in secular terms: "Whether in the
schoolroom or on the irrigation ditch, whether in leasing part of an allotment or in the issuance of a patent in fee or in the use of individual or
tribal funds, the one test to be brought to the business aspect of the case is,
Will doing this and way of doing it educate the child or the woman or the
man for citizenship?"[3] The key words in the new age were *self-support* and
self-reliance. The Indian must be turned into an efficient worker who
could care for himself and his family and no longer be dependent upon the
government. Even those who needed long-term protection and guardianship would eventually reach this ultimate state with improved education
and proper guidance.

The drive for practical programs that matched the actual conditions of
the Indians brought modifications in the theoretical positions of the old
reformers, but the basic conviction that the Indians were capable of incorporation into the body politic was never lost. The age was one of increasing awareness of race and racial distinctions, and some social scientists
preached a hierarchy of superior and inferior races; but the men who formulated federal Indian policy and programs did not accept such dogmas.
The inferiority that they saw and admitted, they considered to be not inherent but cultural, and they devoted tremendous energy to a melioration
of the circumstances that would improve the Indians.

So convinced were the Indian officials of the goal of ultimate incorporation and so diligently did they work to free the "competent" and to
improve the "incompetent" that they did not read the signals of failure
that flashed along the way. By the end of the 1920s, however, it was clear
to many observers that the individualization of the Indians—through
allotment and related programs—had not turned the Indians into self-
supporting, self-reliant farmers, that the programs of education and health
care administered by the federal government with increasing expense had
not kept pace with those services for the white population, and that those

3. *Lake Mohonk Conference Proceedings*, 1893, p. 12; CIA Report, 1909, serial 5747,
p. 4.

Indians who had been freed from government guardianship had not risen to prosperity but had fallen instead into poverty and degradation. The policy that had sought to promote individualism, self-support, independence, and hope for the Indians had instead increased government paternalism and Indian dependency and despair.

In the decade of the 1920s there was a continuation of the policies and programs of the preceding decades, a sort of culmination of the philosophy of individualism of the Dawes Act. But there was also the beginning of a dynamic reform movement that looked critically at the work and accomplishments of the Indian Office and, finding them wanting, proposed a reformulation of Indian policy that in the next decade revolutionized the United States government's relations with the Indians.

The six chapters of Part Seven first present an overview of the period, then treat in greater depth the development of Indian education, the growing concern for Indian health, the disposition and development of Indian lands, and the special problems connected with the Indians of Oklahoma and New York.

CHAPTER 30

The Indian Office:
The Indians' Guardian

Progressives in the Indian Office.

The Decline of the Christian Reformers.

Administrative Efficiency.

Liquor and Peyote.

The Indian Office in the Progressive Era was directed by men of ability and personal integrity, however much they may have been blinded to the deleterious effects their progressive programs had upon the Indian wards. It was in general a period of continuity and stability in Indian affairs. In the thirty-two years between the beginning of Commissioner William A. Jones's adminstration in 1897 and the resignation of Charles H. Burke in 1929, only five men held the office of commissioner of Indian affairs. Jones, who served until the end of 1904, held office longer than any of his predecessors. Francis E. Leupp, who succeeded him, served for four and a half years under Presidents Theodore Roosevelt and William Howard Taft, and Robert G. Valentine followed him for a little more than three years. The Democrat Cato Sells was in office for the full eight years of Woodrow Wilson's presidency, and Burke endured through eight years under Warren G. Harding and Calvin Coolidge. The assistant commissioner appointed by Sells, Edgar B. Meritt, also held that position during Burke's administration. These men took seriously their charge as guardians of the Indians, and although they were subject to considerable just criticism, they were free of fraud and corruption, misguided as their policies might seem to later generations.[1]

1. These five commissioners had exceptional longevity in office compared with the fourteen who held office for a comparable period of thirty-two years from 1865 to 1897.

PROGRESSIVES IN THE INDIAN OFFICE

William A. Jones, from Mineral Point, Wisconsin, had been a teacher and superintendent of schools and then a prominent banker and businessman. He was a staunch Republican who had served as mayor of Mineral Point and in the state assembly. It was his support of William McKinley in 1896, his place in the Wisconsin Republican Party, and his experience in business, not any contact with Indian affairs, that won him the appointment as commissioner in 1897. Coming into office while the Christian reform sentiment was strong, he reflected its principles in his handling of Indian affairs, but he also moved away from strict adherence to those theories when changed conditions or a better understanding of them demanded modifications. He was a transition figure, carrying on the Christian reform he inherited but bringing to the office, too, a keen interest in administrative efficiency to meet modern needs.[2]

One example of the older tradition that Jones exemplified was his notorious "short hair" order to agents and superintendents in late December 1901 and early January 1902, which matched the earlier strictures against Indian customs by Secretary of the Interior Henry M. Teller and Commissioner Hiram Price. Jones directed attention to "a few customs among the Indians which, it is believed, should be modified or discontinued." The first was the wearing of long hair by the men, which was "not in keeping with the advancement they are making, or will soon be expected to make, in civilization." If Indians who were employed by the Indian service or drawing rations refused to comply, they could be discharged and their supplies stopped. If they became obstreperous, "a short confinement in the guard-house at hard labor, with shorn locks, should furnish a cure." "Certainly all the younger men should wear short hair," Jones directed, "and it is believed that by tact, perseverance, firmness, and withdrawal of supplies the superintendent can induce *all* to comply with this order." He also directed action against painting of the face and against dances and Indian feasts, which were "simply subterfuges to cover degrading acts and to disguise immoral purposes." The superintendents and agents were directed, too, to encourage the wearing of citizen's dress instead of Indian costumes and blankets. The reaction in the press was immediate and widespread in criticism of the order, as though it would trigger a new Indian revolt. Jones himself saw in the press's reporting good-natured bantering rather than se-

---

In much of that earlier period graft was rampant; one commissioner was not confirmed by the Senate, and three others were removed from office or left under a cloud.

2. The only scholarly treatment of Jones is W. David Baird, "William A. Jones, 1897–1904," in Robert M. Kvasnicka and Herman J. Viola, eds., *The Commissioners of Indian Affairs, 1824–1977* (Lincoln: University of Nebraska Press, 1979), pp. 211–20.

rious criticism, and he affirmed the purpose of the order, calling attention to Teller's previous action and the courts of Indian offenses that had resulted. He thought it quite proper to enforce the order against employees of the Indian service and against returned students, who had been the recipients of "bounteous favors." Jones stated his philosophy candidly:

It is a familiar saying that error lies at two extremes and truth in the middle, and a striking illustration of the truth of this is found in the Indian question. At one extreme there is a cold brutality which recognizes the dead Indian as the only good Indian, and at the other a sickly sentimentalism that crowns the Indian with a halo and looks up to him as a persecuted saint. Between the two will be found the true friends of the Indian, who, looking upon him as he really is and recognizing his inevitable absorption by a stronger race, are endeavoring in a practical way to fit him under new conditions for the struggle of life. With these I desire to be numbered.[3]

Of more substance was Jones's strong promotion of all measures that would lead to Indian self-support, which became a kind of leitmotif of his administration. His annual report of 1900 began with a long section entitled "Obstacles to Self-Support," in which he lashed out at distribution of rations and annuities to the Indians and the practice of leasing allotments. To these, in the following year, he added the educational system, which coddled the Indians in boarding schools. "Whatever the condition of the Indian may be," he wrote, "he should be removed from a state of dependence to one of independence. And the only way to do this is to take away those things that encourage him to lead an idle life, and, after giving him a fair start, leave him to take care of himself." Jones in 1901 instructed the agents at the Sioux agencies and other ration agencies to cut from the ration rolls all able-bodied Indians who were self-supporting and those who could work but refused to do so. Above all else, the Indians must be taught *to work.*[4]

As Jones was preparing to leave office at the end of 1904, he summarized the accomplishments made in the seven years since he had taken office:

Reservations are being broken up. Inherited lands are being sold, and sturdy American citizens are buying them and settling among

---

3. Jones to the secretary of the interior, February 19, 1902, printed in CIA Report, 1902, serial 4458, pp. 13–16. The letter quotes the order and discusses the furor it caused. See also Jones's criticism of Indian dances in CIA Report, 1903, serial 4645, pp. 8–9.

4. CIA Report, 1900, serial 4101, pp. 5–13; CIA Report, 1901, serial 4290, pp. 1–6; CIA Report, 1902, serial 4458, pp. 1–13; CIA Report, 1903, serial 4645, p. 3; CIA Report, 1904, serial 4798, p. 28.

the Indians, and following the wake of all comes the public school, where in time the white and Indian will mingle. The indiscriminate issuance of rations has been discontinued. The old, infirm, and helpless receive this aid, and "old folks homes" are being established to care for those who can no longer care for themselves. At the old ration agencies work has been provided in lieu of the pauperizing allowance of subsistence. The able-bodied are thus compelled to work in order to meet the demands of existence. The teaching of the schools is being practically put into operation. Effort is constantly being made to "give the Indian a white man's chance." The logical results will be the extermination of the Indian as an Indian. Year by year there will be added to the body of the people a class of citizens who will do credit and honor to the generosity of a great nation.[5]

Jones could speak so optimistically because he saw the inferiority of the Indian not as an inherent quality but as a "husk of savagery and barbarism" to be taken away by "the gradual evolution of educational processes." He admired the Indian's love of freedom, his pride of ancestry, and his intense and fervent love of his children. "Such a race," he asserted, "is worthy of all the time, money, and labor expended on it by a generous Congress and people."[6]

Francis Ellington Leupp, who took office on January 1, 1905, carried on the policies and programs of his predecessor but managed to leave his own mark on the Indian Office. He came with a remarkably extensive background of interest in the Indians, a tremendous commitment to efficiency and economy, and a self-confidence that his detractors considered sheer arrogance. He was, moreover, a longtime personal friend of Theodore Roosevelt, with whom he worked directly on Indian affairs, largely bypassing the secretary of the interior. Leupp's credentials were excellent. Born in New York City in 1849, he had developed an early interest in Indians through visits to reservations in New York State. He earned a law degree at Columbia Law School in 1872 but soon turned to a career in journalism and in 1874 began a long connection with the *New York Evening Post*, serving many years as Washington correspondent for that paper. He became involved in the civil service reform movement, which led him into Indian affairs. When Charles C. Painter, Washington agent for the Indian Rights Association, died suddenly in 1895, Leupp was appointed to replace him, and in 1896 he became a member of the Board of Indian Commissioners. For a brief period he was deeply immersed in Indian affairs and controver-

5. CIA Report, 1904, serial 4798, p. 29.
6. Ibid., p. 30.

sies, but in 1897 he resigned from the Board of Indian Commissioners and in the following year gave up his Indian Rights Association position to return to journalism. Theodore Roosevelt picked him now and again to make special investigations dealing with the Indian reservations, however, and it was no surprise when he was chosen to replace Jones as commissioner.[7]

Leupp set the tone for his administration in a formal statement, "Outlines of an Indian Policy," which he published in *Outlook* in April 1905. In it he parted company with earlier reformers and asserted that the Indians had qualities and a heritage of art and music that should be preserved and cultivated, not eradicated. "The Indian is a natural warrior, a natural logician, a natural artist," he insisted. "We have room for all three in our highly organized social system. Let us not make the mistake, in the process of absorbing them, of washing out of them whatever is distinctly Indian. Our aboriginal brother brings, as his contribution to the common store of character, a great deal which is admirable, and which needs only to be developed along the right line. Our proper work with him is improvement, not transformation." Although thus recognizing the racial distinctiveness of the Indian, Leupp was impressed with the "strong family likeness between most of his traits and those of our own remote ancestors" and insisted that the Indian problem was "a human rather than a race question."[8]

But this general refusal to assume that the Indian was "simply a white man with a red skin" did not stop Leupp from energetically promoting programs to improve the Indians, and what he considered *improvement* differed little from *transformation*. Like Jones, he felt that the chief need was to turn the Indian into a self-reliant, independent worker, individualized both as to his land and his money, and "an active factor in the upbuilding of the community in which he is going to live." It was, Leupp declared, a "policy of shrinkage," for as Indian names were stricken from the tribal rolls, the number of dependents was reduced. "If we can thus gradually

7. Donald L. Parman, "Francis Ellington Leupp, 1905–1909," in Kvasnicka and Viola, *Commissioners of Indian Affairs*, pp. 221–32; Nicah Furman, "Seedtime for Indian Reform: An Evaluation of the Administration of Commissioner Francis Ellington Leupp," *Red River Valley Historical Review* 2 (Winter 1975): 495–517. Leupp left many writings about his role in Indian affairs. A summary statement of his administration is in Leupp to Secretary of the Interior James R. Garfield, February 20, 1909, OSI CCF 5–11, Administration, General, part 1. After Leupp left office he wrote a long apologia, which drew heavily on his annual reports and other writings: *The Indian and His Problem* (New York: Charles Scribner's Sons, 1910).

8. Leupp, "Outlines of an Indian Policy," *Outlook* 79 (April 15, 1905): 946–50; he repeated this statement at the beginning of his first annual report, CIA Report, 1905, serial 4959, pp. 1–12, from which the quotations here are taken. The views on race are in *The Indian and His Problem*, pp. 42–43; see also CIA Report, 1905, serial 4959, pp. 6–7.

watch our body of dependent Indians shrink, even by one member at a time," he thought, "We may congratulate ourselves that the final solution is indeed only a question of a few years."[9]

One program on which Leupp pinned his hopes was an Indian employment office. With a mixed-blood Peoria Indian from Oklahoma, Charles E. Daganett, in charge, this office sought to find jobs outside the reservation, inducing Indians who had no profitable work at home to "go out into the world to make a living as white men do" and to learn the importance of "regular and often prolonged hours of labor." Leupp also encouraged Indian employment in the sugar beet industry near western reservations.[10]

Leupp's forthright handling of Indian affairs according to his own positive views soon brought him into conflict with the Indian Rights Association, which still considered its independent concern for Indian rights a necessary influence on Indian policy and its voice one to be listened to. Leupp was irritated by what he thought was meddling in official matters, and he ended his career as commissioner in a storm of controversy with Herbert Welsh and the association. Although there was strong support for Leupp from men who were acknowledged experts in Indian affairs— George Bird Grinnell, Charles Lummis, Edward S. Curtis, and Warren K. Moorehead, for example—and who urged Taft to keep the able commissioner in office, Leupp used ill health as an excuse to resign, effective June 18, 1909, early in Taft's presidency.[11] He left office as he had begun with a public summation of his views (and this time of his accomplishments as well) in an article in *Outlook*, called in typical fashion "The Story of Four Strenuous Years."[12]

Leupp picked his own successor, Robert G. Valentine, who had taken office with him as his personal secretary and then moved into the position of assistant commissioner. A native of Massachusetts and a graduate of Harvard, Valentine had taught literature at Massachusetts Institute of Technology and worked for banks in New York City and for the Union Pacific Railroad in Omaha. He was only thirty-six years old when Taft appointed him commissioner of Indian affairs on June 19, 1909. Valentine was a solid Progressive, committed to economy and efficiency, who energetically continued the policies of his mentor. He gave high priority in his

9. CIA Report, 1905, serial 4959, p. 5.

10. CIA Report, 1906, serial 5118, pp. 6–16, offers a detailed account of employment projects for Indians. See also CIA Report, 1907, serial 5296, pp. 15–17; CIA Report, 1908, serial 5453, pp. 29–33.

11. See letters of Grinnell, Lummis, Curtis, Moorehead, and others to Taft and to R. A. Ballinger, January–March 1909, and Leupp's letter of resignation to Taft, June 8, 1909, OSI CCF, 22–33, Francis E. Leupp.

12. Leupp, "The Story of Four Strenuous Years," *Outlook* 92 (June 5, 1909): 328–31.

administration to the crucial problems of Indian health, promoted the industrial education program of the Indian Office, and developed its forestry program. In all he did he sought to advance the professional and businesslike performance of the Indian service, noting on one occasion "the only things I care for . . . [are] speed, economy and efficiency."[13] As might perhaps have been expected for a man so closely associated with Leupp, Valentine ran into criticism from the Indian Rights Association (over Pima water rights), and in 1912 he was investigated by a House committee on trumped-up charges.[14] He got ensnared, too, in church-state matters relating to Catholic missionaries teaching in government schools while wearing religious garb. Never a man of robust health, Valentine found the strain of administration and controversy too much to bear. On September 12, 1912, while the congressional investigation was still under way and the religious garb issue unsettled, he resigned in order to work for Roosevelt's Bull Moose Party. In an address to the Lake Mohonk Conference the following month, he gave an intimate glimpse into the commissioner's job and also into his own temperament:

> I found that I could give efficiently about three hours in the morning and three hours in the afternoon on the average to Indian affairs. The mental wear and tear, the struggle between all kinds of opposing forces, some good, some bad, were so great that even though I have prided myself on having that quality which it was said was necessary for a chief of the Iroquois Indians to possess in order to be chief of that tribe, namely . . . skin seven times the span of the hand in thickness—although I pride myself a little bit on having that quality, no man can stand up to the remorseless inconsequence of things below and of things above him and take all the attacks from right, left, behind, and before and not have it reduce his efficiency. So the result is, although twenty-four hours after I left the Indian office I began work with the rising of the sun and worked, with just time to eat, until one or two o'clock the next morning, I have not once in all that time, neither in each day nor in an accumulation of several days, been able to get as tired as I could in two hours in the Indian office.[15]

13. Valentine to E. P. Holcombe, February 20, 1911, quoted in Diane T. Putney, "Robert Grosvenor Valentine, 1909–12," in Kvasnicka and Viola, *Commissioners of Indian Affairs*, p. 237; Putney's biographical sketch on pp. 233–42 is a brief summary of his career.

14. The report of the investigation is in *House Report* no. 1279, 62–3, serial 6336. The report, which urged Valentine's dismissal, was issued after he had resigned, and nothing came of it; note also the minority report, which exonerated and supported Valentine.

15. *Lake Mohonk Conference Proceedings*, 1912, pp. 81–82.

Cato Sells, whom President Wilson appointed commissioner, had considerably more stamina than Valentine; but he carried on the tradition of Leupp and Valentine. Born in Iowa in 1859 and trained as a lawyer, he entered Democratic politics and became city attorney and mayor of La Porte, Iowa. From 1894 to 1899 he was United States district attorney and three times a delegate to the Democratic National Convention. In January 1907, however, Sells moved from Iowa to Cleburne, Texas, where he established a bank and trust company and continued his active Democratic politics. Sells backed Wilson and held the Texas delegates behind Wilson in the fight for nomination at the convention in 1912. He got the commissionership as a reward.[16]

Franklin K. Lane, a California lawyer and newspaperman, who became secretary of the interior in the new Democratic administration, played a fuller role in Indian policy than most of his predecessors. Lane endorsed the accepted philosophy that the Indians would advance to full citizenship through hard work leading to self-support. He chose Sells, who had no previous experience or knowledge of Indians, as a man who could with vigor and administrative ability carry out those policies. After a thorough investigation of the man's background, Lane presented him to Wilson. "Mr. Sells is not a great man," the secretary told the president, "but he will give whole-hearted devotion to the cause of the Indians. Being both a businessman and a lawyer, he will be able to protect them against the harpies, and being a man of a strong social sense, he will look carefully after their education and morals."[17]

Sells did not disappoint his superior. He combined a deep concern for Indians who needed the help of the government with a ruthless determination to rid the government of responsibility for those Indians whom he judged able to manage fully their own affairs. On taking office he estimated the land and other property of the Indians to be worth $900 million, and he declared: "The Government is the guardian of this vast Indian estate. How this property is to be conserved for the benefit of the Indians and how they shall be taught to make the best possible use thereof so that they may ultimately take their rightful place as self-supporting citizens of the Republic are the greatest problems confronting this bureau."[18] Yet his cooperation with Lane in speeding the release of "competent" Indians and his Declaration of Policy in 1917 were highwater marks in government policy that resulted in the loss of Indian economic resources, especially land. It was his

16. Lawrence C. Kelly, "Cato Sells, 1913–21," in Kvasnicka and Viola, *Commissioners of Indian Affairs*, pp. 243–50.

17. Lane to Wilson, May 22, 1913, OSI CCF 22–33, Presidential Appointments, Commissioner of Indian Affairs, Cato Sells.

18. CIA Report, 1913, serial 6634, pp. 3–4.

"fixed purpose to bring about the speedy individualizing of the Indians," he said early in his administration, and the Declaration of Policy moved to the next stage—the removal from guardianship of those individualized Indians who presumably could stand on their own.[19]

Sells's administration of Indian affairs was seriously interrupted by World War I, which called for new efforts in Indian agriculture, stock raising, and forestry to support the war effort, while at the same time it decimated Indian service personnel. The commissioner met the challenge with characteristic energy and enthusiasm, and he found in the wartime experiences of the Indians a great and positive advance toward the ultimate goal of American citizenship. The Indians increased food production, supported the relief work of the Red Cross, and contributed money to the war bond drives. More significantly, a large number of Indians entered military service: in 1918 Sells estimated that there were eight thousand in training or on active duty in some branch of the army and navy and that six thousand of them had enlisted, and he later spoke of ten thousand in the services. In addition, many Indians from the northern reservations had enlisted in Canadian military units before the United States declared war on Germany. Sells, however, refused to sanction separate Indian military units, which some persons proposed, as "not in harmony with our plans for developing the Indian's citizenship." The Indian, he said, should fight shoulder to shoulder with the white man in a common cause and go into the war "as the equal and comrade of every man who assails autocracy and ancient might, and to come home with a new light in his face and a clearer conception of the democracy in which he may participate and prosper."[20]

When Sells in 1919 looked back over the war experiences of the Indians, he included in his annual report a section called "War as a Civilizer," in which he wrote of the civilizing effect of the war, the irresistible march of democracy, and the effect of all this on the Indians. He said:

> The immediate benefit comes from the equal opportunity they had with white comrades for gaining knowledge, for maturing judgment, for developing courage through contact with events and conditions that trained and toughened character in the defense of a just cause and a great ideal. No education serves a man better than this in any circumstances. It puts into him the ability to "go over the top" anywhere. The great lesson mastered by American soldiers, as their achievements clearly show, was to get things done. They are not likely to forget how. No Hindenburg line across the field of civil

19. Ibid., p. 45.
20. CIA Report, 1918, serial 7498, pp. 3–18. See also *Senate Report* no. 222, 66–1, serial 7590.

progress can stand against such fellows. They are destined for to-morrow's leadership. The wondrously multiplied interests of trade, industry, education, and professions, statesmanship, await them. The same sort of splendid initiative and self-reliance should find expression in action wherever the Indian soldier returns to his people.[21]

This was a vision more than the reality, but the war did positively affect the drive for Indian citizenship. By an act of November 6, 1919, Congress provided that any Indian who received an honorable discharge from military service during World War I could, if he desired it, apply for citizenship and be granted it by a competent court without affecting rights to tribal property. Sells greeted the legislation enthusiastically as a "just and fitting tribute to the intelligence, patriotism, and courage of the young men of a virile and enduring race."[22]

THE DECLINE OF THE CHRISTIAN REFORMERS

Protestant Christian reformers had dominated the formulation of Indian policy in the late nineteenth century, operating effectively through the Board of Indian Commissioners and such voluntary organizations as the Indian Rights Association and the Lake Mohonk Conference. By 1900 these men and women could look down from a high plateau of success, for they had established their legislative programs. They looked upon themselves as the guardians of the Indians and the watchdogs and arbiters of national Indian policy. They saw themselves, not unrealistically, as the effective force in moving the Indians into an individualized, Americanized society (which meant to them a Protestant Christian nation). In the dozen or so years after the turn of the century their position of dominance was severely shaken, if not indeed shattered. To be sure, many of the principles for which they had fought had become accepted doctrine in Indian affairs, but the privileged place of their organizations and the strongly religious orientation of the programs had faded away.[23]

In the first place, the old reformers were no longer able to control the

21. CIA Report, 1919, serial 7706, p. 9.
22. 41 *United States Statutes* 350; *House Report* no. 140, 66–1, serial 7592; *Senate Report* no. 222, 66–1, serial 7590; CIA Report, 1920, serial 7820, pp. 10–11.
23. I draw here upon Francis Paul Prucha, "The Decline of the Christian Reformers," in *Indian Policy in the United States: Historical Essays* (Lincoln: University of Nebraska Press, 1981), pp. 252–62. See also John F. Berens, "Old Campaigners, New Realities: Indian Policy Reform in the Progressive Era, 1900–1912," *Mid-America* 59 (January 1977): 51–64.

legislative formulation of Indian policy. Their ineffectiveness could be seen in the Burke Act of 1906, which postponed citizenship for the Indians until the end of the trust period, thus reversing, or at least slowing down, the individualizing, Americanizing process of the Dawes Act. The act was severely criticized and strongly opposed by the reformers' groups, but to no avail.[24] A second law in which the reform groups failed to obtain their goals was the Lacey Act of 1907, which dealt with the allotment of money held in trust for the Indians in the United States Treasury. It was intended, in the minds of the reformers who initiated it, to break up the Indian trust funds (held in common by each tribe) exactly as the Dawes Act had broken up the reservation lands. Such a measure was considered a second necessary step on the Indians' road to civilization.[25] But when the act finally passed in Congress, it had been emasculated. Instead of being a directive that authorized the president to allot the trust funds when he considered a tribe ready, the law was merely permissive, and it required an Indian to apply for his allotment before any action could be taken. Spokesmen for the Indian Rights Association strongly objected. The association's Washington agent wrote that the tribal relation "defeats the effort for individual advancement and responsibility, a weakness too apparent in all systems of communal ownership of property." The revised bill, he said, would not remedy that evil, for it would affect only those Indians who applied for their pro rata share of the money, and precisely those who needed the law most would be least likely to take advantage of it. But Congress did not listen now as it had in the 1880s. The Lacey Act was, to the reformers, no more than a "makeshift substitute."[26] In basic legislation, then, the old Christian reformers lost the battle.

Second, the reformers lost their decisive influence with the commissioner of Indian affairs and the executive branch in general. The reform groups, with their investigative trips, their yearly conferences at Lake Mohonk, where they formulated programs and strategies, and their effective lobbying, had been a force to be reckoned with. They had spoken out fearlessly and had become accustomed to being listened to. They were con-

24. *Report of the Board of Indian Commissioners*, 1906, p. 8; *Report of the Indian Rights Association*, 1906, pp. 45–48. For further discussion of the Burke Act, see chapter 34.

25. See, for example, *Lake Mohonk Conference Proceedings*, 1900, pp. 18–20; 1901, pp. 5–8; *Report of the Board of Indian Commissioners*, 1902, p. 22.

26. S. M. Brosius to James S. Sherman, March 27, 1906, Indian Rights Association Papers, Historical Society of Pennsylvania (reel 18); *Report of the Indian Rights Association*, 1911, pp. 28–29. For further information on the Lacey Act and on its relation to Protestant-Catholic controversies, see Francis Paul Prucha, *The Churches and the Indian Schools, 1888–1912* (Lincoln: University of Nebraska Press, 1979), pp. 138–48.

vinced that they were the special guardians of Indian rights and could not be turned aside in their righteous campaigns. Then they ran into Commissioner Leupp. To their dismay, they learned that Leupp, despite the fact that he had once been one of their number, had a mind of his own and that he intended to run his office without their advice and in fact sometimes in sharp opposition to them.

One celebrated case concerned the Crow Agency in Montana, where the Indian Rights Association sought an investigation into alleged violations of Indian rights by the stockmen and the Indian agent. The Washington representative of the association was turned away when he went to Montana to investigate, and the secretary of the association was actually arrested by agency personnel when he appeared for the same purpose. The Indian Rights Association fought unsuccessfully to defeat Senate confirmation of a special inspector sent out to look into the charges. "I have been twenty-six years a student of Indian affairs," Herbert Welsh wrote to a friend, ". . . and it is my deliberate opinion that this Crow agency affair is the worst piece of business on the part of the government that has come within my knowledge. Heretofore our endeavors to correct wrongs in the Indian Service have on the whole been sympathetically received by the Indian Department and our cooperation accepted. Mr. Leupp, in my opinion, clearly intended to drive the Indian Rights Association from the field."[27]

The second case involved eight Navajo Indian outlaws, led by Bai-a-lil-le, who were arrested in 1907 and confined without specific charges and without trial. The Indian Rights Association insisted that the Indians be released; Leupp countered that he would do what he thought necessary to protect the peaceful Indians, "law or no law." Suit was brought to free the Indians, and the Supreme Court of Arizona Territory ordered their release on March 20, 1909. Although Leupp's opponents won their case in the end, the affair showed the strong opposition of views between the commissioner and the Indian Rights Association and Leupp's strong and independent action.[28]

27. *Report of the Indian Rights Association*, 1908, pp. 4–20; Herbert Welsh to Richard H. Dana, January 25, 1909, Indian Rights Association Papers (reel 78). A full account of the Crow Agency affair is Donald L. Parman, "A White Man's Fight: The Crow Scandal, 1906–1913," in Ronald Lora, ed., *The American West: Essays in Honor of W. Eugene Hollon* (Toledo, Ohio: University of Toledo, 1980), pp. 73–96.

28. A scholarly account is Donald L. Parman, "The 'Big Stick' in Indian Affairs: The Bai-a-lil-le Incident in 1909," *Arizona and the West* 20 (Winter 1978): 343–60. Details are in the report of an investigation of the affair in *Senate Document* no. 517, 60–1, serial 5269. See also Francis E. Leupp, "'Law or No Law' in Indian Administration," *Outlook* 91 (January 30, 1909): 261–63, and reply of Carl E. Grammer, ibid. (March 20, 1909): 629–30. President Roosevelt's strong support of Leupp in the case can be seen in *The Letters of Theodore Roosevelt*, ed. Elting E. Morison, 8 vols. (Cambridge: Harvard University Press, 1951–1954), 6: 1448–53.

The Indian Rights Association was delighted when Leupp resigned. "It is a cause of congratulations," the president of the association wrote, "that a commissioner whose egotism had made it impossible for him to catch other people's point of view, should give place to one of a more open mind and less assured infallibility."[29]

The Board of Indian Commissioners fared little better than the Indian Rights Association, and under Secretary of the Interior Ethan Allen Hitchcock it had to defend its authority, if not its very existence.[30] Although the board survived through the 1920s and was used from time to time by the Indian Office, its position as an independent force in Indian administration was not strong. Its pristine Protestantism, moreover, was eroded by the appointment of two Catholics to the board by Roosevelt in 1902. The Lake Mohonk Conference, with which the Board of Indian Commissioners was informally linked, also declined in its influence in Indian affairs. To begin with, after 1900 it broadened its activities to include the peoples in the territories acquired after the Spanish American War. It changed its name in fact to Friends of the Indian and Other Dependent Peoples. Then its founder and guiding light, Albert K. Smiley, grew old, moved to California, and died in 1912. The year 1916 marked the last in the regular series of historic Lake Mohonk Conferences.

The attempts of the reform organizations to use the courts to promote their ends were no more successful than their attempts to influence the legislative and executive branches. The Indian Rights Association undertook two cases that went to the Supreme Court, in which it supported Indian litigants against the federal government. In both instances the court ruled against the Indian Rights Association and its clients.

The first case, *Lone Wolf* v. *Hitchcock*, was a landmark decision that in significance went far beyond the question of reform influence. Under the provisions of article 12 of the Treaty of Medicine Lodge Creek of 1867, no part of the reservation set up for the Kiowas and Comanches could be ceded without the approval of three-fourths of the adult males. Nevertheless, the Jerome Commission on October 6, 1892, concluded an agreement with the Indians for the allotment of their lands and the disposition of the surplus to the United States to be opened to settlement, without obtaining the three-fourths approval. When Congress, by an act of June 6, 1900, accepted

29. Statement of Carl E. Grammer, published in the *North American* (Philadelphia), June 16, 1909. Leupp, however, had the last word in *The Indian and His Problem*, in which he lectured the philanthropists for their unrealistic positions. See chapter 15, "Philanthropy and Criticism," pp. 305–27.

30. There is material on the conflict with Hitchcock in the correspondence between Merrill E. Gates and Charles J. Bonaparte, June–November 1903, in Charles J. Bonaparte Papers, Library of Congress.

and confirmed the agreement, Lone Wolf, a prominent Kiowa, brought suit to enjoin the secretary of the interior, the commissioner of Indian affairs, and the commissioner of the general land office from implementing the act.[31] After the injunction was denied by the Supreme Court of the District of Columbia and the United States Court of Appeals for the District of Columbia, the Indian Rights Association gave its support. The case was appealed to the Supreme Court of the United States, which on January 5, 1903, rendered its decision against Lone Wolf. The court, in rejecting the arguments of the Indians' attorneys, asserted the plenary authority of Congress over Indian relations and its power to pass laws abrogating treaty stipulations.

> The contention in effect ignores the status of the contracting Indians in the relation of dependency they bore and continue to bear towards the government of the United States. To uphold the claim would be to adjudge that the indirect operation of the treaty was to materially limit and qualify the controlling authority of Congress in respect to the care and protection of the Indians. . . .
>
> Plenary authority over the tribal relations of the Indians has been exercised by Congress from the beginning, and the power has always been deemed a political one, not subject to be controlled by the judicial department of the government. . . .
>
> The power exists to abrogate the provisions of an Indian treaty, though presumably such power will be exercised only when circumstances arise which will not only justify the government in disregarding the stipulations of the treaty, but may demand, in the interest of the country and the Indians themselves, that it should do so.[32]

Leupp in commenting on the decision, noted that it "carried dismay to the hearts of many excellent persons whose benevolent interest in the Indians had led them to share the Indian views of unqualified ownership, and who could hardly reconcile themselves to the discovery that their long-cherished notion was a delusion." The result of the decision was that thereafter Congress proceeded with the opening of reservations without seeking preliminary agreements with the Indians, although Leupp tried to substitute for that by sending out a special agent to inform and counsel the Indians regarding proposed action.[33]

A second case was *Quick Bear* v. *Leupp*, in which the Indian Rights

31. 31 *United States Statutes* 676–79. The 1892 agreement is included in the act.

32. 187 *U.S. Reports* 553–68. The case is discussed in *Report of the Indian Rights Association*, 1903, pp. 20–24. The action of the Indian Rights Association in the case can be followed in Indian Rights Association Papers, 1901–1902.

33. Leupp, *The Indian and His Problem*, pp. 82–85.

Association, in the name of certain Rosebud Sioux Indians, sought an injunction against the use of Indian trust and treaty funds for support of Catholic Indian mission schools. This was the culmination of a renewed attack upon Catholic mission interests by Protestant forces and a resounding defeat for the hegemony that those forces had enjoyed in national Indian affairs. The conflict had its foundation in the congressional action of the 1890s eliminating direct support for sectarian schools. With such funds cut off, and unable to collect sufficient money from the Catholic faithful, the Bureau of Catholic Indian Missions began a bitter, but ultimately successful, battle to gain alternative support. In this battle it had the active legal and political aid of President Roosevelt's close friend Charles J. Bonaparte (who served as secretary of the navy and as attorney general, a position he held when the *Quick Bear* case came before the Supreme Court). The Catholic missionaries first won restoration of rations to Indian children attending mission schools, which Commissioner Jones had cut off in 1901. Then in 1904 they persuaded Roosevelt to approve the use of trust funds and treaty funds held in the Treasury for the Indians for new per capita contracts in support of their schools. The Indian Rights Association led the fight against the practice, even though the Indians by signing petitions signified that they approved such use of their funds, and argued that the earlier congressional prohibition against support of sectarian schools applied to these funds as well as to gratuitous appropriations by Congress. The Indian Rights Association, however, failed to convince Roosevelt and Leupp with their arguments. Congress, moreover, refused to pass the bills introduced to prohibit absolutely the use of tribal funds for the Catholic schools, and it did not provide for the mandatory segregation of the tribal funds in the names of the individual Indians, which would have eliminated the funds on which the Catholics drew. The Indian Rights Association then resorted to the courts.[34]

The United States Court of Appeals of the District of Columbia ruled against the Indian Rights Association on December 29, 1907. The court analyzed in considerable detail the nature and character of the two funds involved, recalling the provisions of the Sioux treaty of 1868, which provided for educational facilities for a set period of years (a provision extended in 1889), and the act of 1889, which provided a $3-million Sioux trust fund in return for the cession of parts of the Great Sioux Reserve. In creating these funds, the court argued, Congress had "made public money Indian money." In the one instance it paid a treaty debt, in the other a debt for lands. "The money," it said, "has changed owners; what had been money of the public in the Treasury of the United States is now money of

---

34. The history of the conflict is recounted in detail in Prucha, *Churches and the Indian Schools*, pp. 41–160.

the Indians in the Treasury." These funds were quite distinct from the gratuitous appropriations for Indian education, and the court spoke at length about the distinction between the two classes of money. To the contention that sectarian use of the Indians' money violated the First Amendment of the Constitution, the court gave a strong negative response. "It seems inconceivable," the decision read, "that Congress shall have intended to prohibit them from receiving religious education at their own cost, if they desire it; such an intent would be one to 'prohibit the free exercise of religion' amongst the Indians; and such would be the effect of the construction for which the complainants contend." The Supreme Court, to which the case was appealed, upheld the lower court's decision and repeated its arguments.[35]

The Catholic contract schools, thus saved by the *Quick Bear* decision, could not of course provide education for all Indian children of Catholic faith. Those who were forced to attend government schools, the Catholic missionaries charged, were subjected to undue Protestant influence in common religious services, Sunday school lessons, the work of the YMCA and YWCA, and even in singing from the popular Protestant hymnal, *Gospel Hymns*. The Bureau of Catholic Indian Missions campaigned to protect the religious rights of the Catholic pupils, and despite the cries of Protestant missionary groups, who had been willing to curtail their own Indian schools because the government schools served them so well, the Indian Office prescribed equal religious rights for the Catholic Indian students in government schools and eliminated many of the positive Protestant elements in the schools, including the *Gospel Hymns*.[36] One more Protestant-Catholic controversy arose over the wearing of religious garb by nuns who continued to teach in formerly Catholic Indian schools taken over by the government. When Valentine, on January 17, 1912, prohibited such garb, Catholic remonstrances forced the abrogation of his order by the secretary of the interior. In the end, President Taft decided that the nuns then employed could continue as they were, but that no new ones would be accepted.[37]

35. Ibid., pp. 149–60; *Reports of Cases Adjudged in the Court of Appeals of the District of Columbia* (New York: Lawyers Co-operative Publishing Company, 1908), 30: 151–64; 210 *U.S. Reports* 77–82. For essential documents in the case see *Transcript of Record, Supreme Court of the United States, October Term, 1907*, no. 569.

36. Prucha, *Churches and the Indian Schools*, pp. 161–88. The directives regarding religious instruction in the government Indian schools are in Education Circular no. 87, December 20, 1902, OIA, Circulars Issued by the Education Division; "General Regulations for Religious Worship and Instruction of Pupils in Government Indian Schools," March 12, 1910, reprinted in Prucha, *Churches and the Indian Schools*, pp. 213–16.

37. Prucha, *Churches and the Indian Schools*, pp. 189–205. See also William H. Ketcham, *Religious "Garb" and "Insignia" in Government Indian Schools* (Washington: Bureau of Catholic Indian Missions, 1912), which includes Valentine's Circular no. 601.

The Catholic victories in these matters were evidence of the breakdown of evangelical Protestant domination that came with the advent of large numbers of Catholics through the new immigration. The loss of Protestant influence came also from the increasing secularization of American society, an inchoative spirit that burst out full-blown in the 1920s. It could be seen in the importance attached to efficient administration on the part of Progressive government officials, which was a sort of secular force.

ADMINISTRATIVE EFFICIENCY

Since the goal in Indian affairs was to individualize the Indians and ultimately see them disappear as wards of the government, there was a good deal of talk about the dismantling of the Indian Office. The Board of Indian Commissioners in 1901 declared the object of the Indian Office to be to *"make all Indians self-supporting, self-respecting, and useful citizens of the United States,"* and it asserted that unlike other divisions of the government, *"the Indian Bureau should always aim at its own speedy discontinuance!"* "Its success," it said, "is to be shown not in self-perpetuation, but in self-destruction!" Within ten years, the board thought, the work of the office could be accomplished and whatever administration remained to be done could be turned over to the United States Treasury, the courts, and the public school system. The board was upset by the Burke Act because it threatened a prolonged perpetuation of special departmental control of Indian affairs.[38]

There was no argument from government officials, who believed, too, that they were directing a disappearing agency, although they frequently asked for more personnel and more money for salaries with the comment that such *temporary* increases were needed to speed the dissolution of the Indian Office. One step taken to complete the process was the closing out of agencies by transferring the agents' duties to bonded school superintendents, thus eliminating one level in the administrative structure. Leupp spoke of this action as "a final step in the disintegration of the old system" and one that allowed the business matters of the Indian to be "more expeditiously and intelligently acted upon than through the former roundabout mechanism." Another move made by Leupp in his drive to streamline the office was the promotion of cooperation between the Indian Office and other bureaus of the government. "The Office of Indian Affairs, when I assumed charge of it," he said in 1908, "not only performed the functions naturally to be expected of a benevolent guardian engaged in raising a race of human beings from barbarism to civilization, but maintained a little

38. *Report of the Board of Indian Commissioners,* 1901, pp. 4–5; 1906, pp. 8–9.

reclamation service, a little forestry branch, and several other minor organizations for work along lines commonly cared for, and presumptively better cared for, by special bureaus established by law for the benefit of the
American people at large." He pointed with pride to his negotiations for
turning Indian irrigation projects over to the Reclamation Service. "All my
work," he noted, "is guided by my general aim of preparing the whole Indian establishment for going out of business at no very distant date."[39]

Although these were sincere and noble aims, what actually occurred
was a tremendous growth in administrative work as a result of the individualizing of the Indians. Despite the shrinkage in the number of Indians
who remained wards of the government, the work of handling their health,
education, and property seemed to mount steadily, and the final dissolution that was supposed to come was indefinitely postponed. The paradox
was well expressed by Valentine when he made a survey of Indian administration over ten years (1902–1912):

> In 1906, 77,000 letters were received by the Indian Office, which
> to conduct its correspondence had 132 employees; in 1911, 209,000
> letters were received and there were 227 employees; in other words,
> the volume of correspondence had increased almost threefold,
> whereas the number of employees had not increased twofold. Even
> these figures do not nearly represent the added responsibilities of the
> office, for in the last 10 years the Indian Office affairs have taken on a
> magnitude, a breadth, and a detail which are significant of a real at-
> tempt to master the Indian problem by preparing the Indians to leave
> their status of wardship, at last to close their anomalous character as
> a people set apart and to join their white neighbors in the body of
> American citizenship.[40]

The flood of work continued. When Cato Sells left office, the proliferation of correspondence and of personnel to handle it strongly reinforced his
predecessor's concerns (see Table 6).

The commissioners of Indian affairs during the Progressive Era were
chosen in large part because of their business and administrative abilities,
and Leupp and Valentine especially considered themselves efficiency experts. It was only natural that they would attempt to reorganize the Indian
administration, and Leupp began with a vengeance in 1907 and 1908. He
redistributed the office work by reorganizing the divisions within the office and by creating in addition sections within the divisions, all intended,
as he said, "to put an end to all duplication of labor, to bring all closely

39. CIA Report, 1907, serial 5296, p. 9; CIA Report, 1908, serial 5453, pp. 4, 11.
40. CIA Report, 1912, serial 6409, p. 3. The survey of Indian affairs covers pp. 3–17.

TABLE 6: Work and Employees in the Office
of Indian Affairs

Year	Communications Received	Total Employees in Indian Office
1900	62,691	115
1905	98,322	149
1910	194,241	203
1915	298,240	260
1920	261,486	262

SOURCE: CIA Report, 1920, serial 7820, p. 63.

allied subjects under one head, and to provide a system of checks on the one hand and of automatic cooperation on the other, designed at once to guard against errors, lighten the present expenditure of energy, increase the capacity for output, and result progressively in substantial economies." By proper grouping of the divisions, he hoped to stimulate better leadership, and he expected to improve the quality of the clerical force. The filing system, too, was revamped. The old system of files of folded letters and cumbersome letter books was abolished and replaced by a system in which all the papers on a single case or a single subject were filed together under an elaborate decimal classification scheme.[41]

Valentine thoroughly approved, and he credited the changes with making possible the handling of business "with a directness and a dispatch which were unknown before." His own scheme to improve speed, economy, and efficiency was to centralize field supervision in an office in Denver, with a chief supervisor there to direct eight subdivisions of the field service, each with its own supervisor. His plan, however, was vetoed by the secretary of the interior before it could be given a fair trial.[42] Yet with all the innovations, Sells, when he took office nine months after Valentine's resignation, found the work of the bureau "very materially in arrears" and the Indian service "disorganized and discouraged," a condition he hoped to correct by placing the service "on a sound, economical, efficient business basis, working in harmony and with enthusiasm with a view of promoting the best interests of the Indians, who are wards of the Government." Sells worked hard, and his reorganization of the bureau

41. CIA Report, 1908, serial 5453, pp. 11–17; there is an organizational chart on p. 13.
42. CIA Report, 1912, serial 6409, pp. 12, 67–69; Putney, "Valentine," p. 237.

was called "the work of a genius" by the secretary of the Indian Rights Association.[43]

While the commissioners of Indian affairs were working to improve the efficiency of the Indian Office—against tremendous odds of rapidly increasing work—the Society of American Indians was vociferously calling for abolition of the organization altogether. The society, a group of educated Indians, had been organized in 1911 to promote race consciousness among Indians and at the same time to find ways to be both an Indian and a member of modern society, not wards of the nation set apart from their fellow citizens. Led by such Indians as Arthur Parker, a Seneca anthropologist, Charles E. Eastman, a Sioux physician and writer, and Carlos Montezuma, a Mojave-Apache physician, and counseled and encouraged by the white sociologist Fayette McKenzie, the society held annual conferences and published a *Quarterly Journal* (later named the *American Indian Magazine*). The society opposed the Indian Office and the governmental paternalism it represented, although there was great dissension within the ranks over the issue. The bureau, to these critics, despite its claims, failed to promote self-help, self-reliance, and initiative among Indians and in fact stifled such tendencies when they appeared. The leader in this attack, almost to the point of irrationality, was Montezuma, who demanded an immediate end to the bureau. In a printed speech, "Let My People Go," and in the journal he published, called *Wassaja*, he campaigned vigorously to get rid of the Indian Office.[44]

In the end this crusade of Montezuma and his supporters accomplished nothing, for Indians like Charles Daganett, who worked for the Indian Office, withdrew support, and others came to realize that the protective hand of the government was still needed by many Indians. The immediate abolition of the Indian Office was too simple a solution and was doomed to

43. CIA Report, 1913, serial 6634, p. 7; CIA Report, 1914, serial 6815, p. 6; M. K. Sniffen, *A Man and His Opportunity* (Philadelphia: Indian Rights Association, 1914), a very laudatory account of Sells after he had been in office for nine months.

44. The history of the Society of American Indians is told in Hazel W. Hertzberg, *The Search for an American Indian Identity: Modern Pan-Indian Movements* (Syracuse: Syracuse University Press, 1971), pp. 31–209. On Montezuma, see Peter Iverson, *Carlos Montezuma and the Changing World of American Indians* (Albuquerque: University of New Mexico Press, 1982). Useful shorter accounts are Neil M. Clark, "Dr. Montezuma, Apache: Warrior in Two Worlds," *Montana: The Magazine of Western History* 23 (Spring 1973): 56–65; Peter Iverson, "Carlos Montezuma," in R. David Edmunds, ed., *American Indian Leaders: Studies in Diversity* (Lincoln: University of Nebraska Press, 1980), pp. 206–20; Janet McDonnell, "Carlos Montezuma's Crusade against the Indian Bureau," *Journal of Arizona History* 22 (Winter 1981): 429–44. See also Montezuma's testimony on June 15–16, 1911, in *Hearings before the Committee on Expenditures in the Interior Department of the House of Representatives on House Resolution no. 103, to Investigate the Expenditures in the Interior Department* (1911), pp. 349–97.

fail. The Society of American Indians, committed to an impossible task and deeply divided, faded away in the 1920s. The Indian Office continued on its course, soon to be assailed by equally vocal and much more significant critics.[45]

LIQUOR AND PEYOTE

The major concerns of the Indian Office—education, health, and allotment and use of Indian resources—were paralleled by a continuing determination to prevent the deleterious effects of liquor among the Indians and by the undertaking of a new fight against another presumed evil, peyote.

All the past efforts to end intoxication among Indians had failed to achieve complete success, and recognition of the liquor problem was sharpened as the drive for self-support gained momentum in the first decades of the twentieth century. "The use of intoxicating liquors is a direct and incalculable injury to Indians in undermining health and in making them undependable as workmen," Commissioner Valentine declared in 1911; and all the commissioners of the period issued the same warning. "The use of intoxicating liquor is an insurmountable bar between the Indian and progress," Cato Sells said. "Education, health campaigns, appropriations to encourage industry, all fail so long as he uses intoxicants."[46]

Commissioner Jones began the new crusade to enforce liquor prohibitions by announcing in 1901: "Illicit traffic in liquor with the Indians should be utterly stamped out—not merely suppressed." He urged special appropriations to provide agents to obtain evidence against liquor traffickers, a plea picked up by his successors.[47] A serious obstacle to these efforts, however, came in the decision of the United States Supreme Court on April 10, 1905, in *Matter of Heff*, which struck down a conviction against a man who had sold liquor to an allotted Indian. The United States, the court said,

> is under no constitutional obligation to perpetually continue the relationship of guardian and ward. It may at any time abandon its guardianship and leave the ward to assume and be subject to all the privileges and burdens of one *sui juris*. . . . We are of the opinion that when the United States grants the privileges of citizenship to an In-

45. Hertzberg, *Search for an American Indian Identity*, p. 178.

46. CIA Report, 1911, serial 6223, p. 32; CIA Report, 1913, serial 6634, p. 12. See the discussion of liquor laws in Felix S. Cohen, *Handbook of Federal Indian Law* (Washington: GPO, 1942), pp. 352–57, and in the 1982 revision, pp. 305–8.

47. CIA Report, 1901, serial 4290, p. 51; CIA Report, 1902, serial 4458, pp. 52–53; CIA Report, 1903, serial 4645, pp. 34–36; CIA Report, 1905, serial 4959, pp. 20–27. The legal basis on which the commissioners worked was the law of January 30, 1897; see discussion above, p. 655.

dian, gives to him the benefit of and requires him to be subject to the laws, both civil and criminal, of the State, it places him outside the reach of police regulations on the part of Congress.[48]

But the Indian Office maintained that as long as the United States held the allotments in trust it could prevent the taking of liquor into allotted lands, and it persevered in the drive to crack down on the traffic. The Burke Act of May 8, 1906, met the challenge of the court's ruling by postponing citizenship for Indian allottees until the end of the twenty-five-year trust period. The Indian Office was materially aided, too, by the appropriation of the funds asked for by Jones and his successors, and Commissioner Leupp declared that his hopes for the suppression of the liquor traffic had been "realized beyond all expectation."[49] The annual fund, which was first set at $25,000 in 1906, was increased to $40,000 in 1908 and soon reached $150,000.[50] With this money the Indian Office hired a chief special officer, William E. Johnson (known as "Pussyfoot" Johnson in Oklahoma), who with deputies and various local officers began an effective campaign of arrests and convictions.[51]

Cato Sells was an especially strong preacher against the evils of liquor and was very active against the traffic. Not only did he strongly support the measure for suppressing it, but he also encouraged temperance movements among the Indians and used the schools to promote sobriety—with an essay contest in 1915 in the third, fourth, and fifth grades on "What Do I Know about Alcohol?" and in the higher grades on "Alcohol and My Future."[52] Sells, as was his wont, in 1916 reported considerable success:

> During the last three years a vigorous, continuous and effective assault has been made upon the liquor interests which have debauched the Indian race. Increased appropriations have enabled the Indian

48. 197 *U.S. Reports* 499, 509. The effect of the decision is discussed in CIA Report, 1905, serial 4959, pp. 24–27.

49. CIA Report, 1907, serial 5296, p. 26.

50. 34 *United States Statutes* 328; 35 *United States Statutes* 72; 39 *United States Statutes* 124.

51. Johnson's work is described and praised in CIA Report, 1907, serial 5296, pp. 26–33; CIA Report, 1908, serial 5453, pp. 34–40; CIA Report, 1909, serial 5747, pp. 12–13. There is a report by Johnson on his activities, dated August 15, 1910, in *Senate Document* no. 767, 61–3, serial 5943. The Board of Indian Commissioners declared in 1908, "The work of Special Officer Johnson and his associates commands the interest and commendation of all who care for the welfare of the Indians in that period of transition which is so heavily fraught with dangers to our Indian fellow-countrymen." *Report of the Board of Indian Commissioners*, 1908, p. 15.

52. CIA Report, 1913, serial 6634, pp. 14–15; CIA Report, 1914, serial 6815, pp. 43–47; CIA Report, 1915, serial 6992, pp. 8–12.

Office to place in the field a corps of detectives who have become a terror to the bootlegger and drinking man in the Indian country. . . .

While the strong arm of the law is being invoked to prevent the Indian from obtaining whisky and to punish the man who provides him with it, a moral awakening is being brought about through more peaceful means. My personal appeal to every employee in the Indian Service and to persons of prominence in local communities has made possible a most successful pledge-signing campaign among the Indians, in school and out of school, young and old, pledging themselves to abstain from the use of all kinds of intoxicants.[53]

The times, of course, were auspicious. In 1916 the Supreme Court in *United States* v. *Nice* expressly overruled the Heff decision, declaring that "citizenship is not incompatible with tribal existence or continued guardianship, and so may be conferred without completely emancipating the Indians or placing them beyond the reach of congressional regulations adopted for their protection." More significantly, the demand for national prohibition was gaining strength, and as states with Indian populations went "dry," the alcohol problem was lessened. Congress, too, helped the Indian Office with special legislation that made the mere possession of intoxicating liquor within the Indian country illegal.[54] Then, with the ratification of the Eighteenth Amendment on January 16, 1919, to take effect one year later, it became much more difficult for the Indians to obtain liquor. As a result, the special appropriations for suppressing the liquor traffic among the Indians were drastically cut. The Indian Office, nevertheless, kept alert, for the location of reservations in remote and secluded areas or near the Canadian and Mexican borders encouraged the introduction of illegal liquor. "The bootlegger is a cunning, resourceful, and treacherous offender," the commissioner of Indian affairs wrote in 1924, "and finds the Indian an easy prey."[55] So, unfortunately, there was still no end to the liquor problem.

Meanwhile, a new danger appeared in the form of peyote, a drug obtained from a cactus that was alleged to be a narcotic with serious harmful effects.[56] The use of peyote by Indians in the southern parts of the nation

53. CIA Report, 1916, serial 7160, p. 60.

54. 241 *U.S. Reports* 598; 40 *United States Statutes* 563; 41 *United States Statutes* 4. See accounts of progress in suppressing liquor among the Indians in CIA Report, 1917, serial 7358, pp. 21–25; CIA Report, 1918, serial 7498, pp. 69–78; CIA Report, 1919, serial 7706, pp. 31–32.

55. CIA Report, 1924, p. 21.

56. There is an extensive literature on peyote, much of it concerning the chemistry of the drug and the religious cult connected with peyote. A recent comprehensive study, which includes an extensive bibliography, is Edward F. Anderson, *Peyote: The Divine*

went back into the nineteenth century and beyond, but aside from some localized cases it had not attracted the attention of the Indian Office. By the end of the first decade of the twentieth century, however, a cry arose against the drug, and federal officials and the old-time reformers joined hands in an attempt to proscribe it. In 1909 Commissioner Valentine called attention to the problem, and in 1911 he came down heavily against peyote:

> The information now on hand concerning the physiological and sociological results of the use of this drug is such that the office will in every way practicable prevent the Indians from indulging in it further. . . .
>
> Even if the physiological effects of this drug were not serious, its use would have to be prohibited for the same sociological reasons as have led the Government strongly but tactfully to modify Indian dances. As is well known, exercises which the Indians consider of a religious nature are made the occasion of taking the drug. These meetings are held as often as twice a week and invariably last throughout the night. The time occupied in going to these meetings, the demoralizing effects of all-night seances, and consequent nervous languor and exhaustion, very considerably encroach upon the time that should normally be devoted to work. Furthermore, the effects of the drug in making the Indian contented with his present attainments seriously interfere with his progress by cutting off from him the possibility of healthful aspirations.[57]

The concern of the Indian Office was supported and no doubt to a large extent stimulated by the frenzy against peyote that developed among the humanitarian reformers. The Board of Indian Commissioners in 1912 voted formally to condemn all use of the drug, and the Lake Mohonk Conference in 1914 and 1915 urged its prohibition. The Indian Rights Association in 1916 entered a section on "The Ravages of Peyote" in its annual report, which described the harmful effects of peyote and ridiculed the Indians' claim that the religious use of the drug demanded protection under the Constitution.[58]

Cactus (Tucson: University of Arizona Press, 1980). Other valuable studies are Weston La Barre, *The Peyote Cult*, 4th ed. (New York: Archon Books, 1975); J. S. Slotkin, *The Peyote Religion: A Study in Indian-White Relations* (Glencoe, Illinois: Free Press, 1956); and Alice Marriott and Carol K. Rachlin, *Peyote* (New York: Thomas Y. Crowell Company, 1971).

57. CIA Report, 1909, serial 5747, pp. 15–16; CIA Report, 1911, serial 6223, p. 33. See also the concern voiced in subsequent annual reports.

58. *Report of the Board of Indian Commissioners*, 1912, p. 15, and 1914, p. 13; *Lake*

Repeated attempts were made beginning in 1914 to obtain legislation to prohibit the use of peyote, usually by adding it to the proscriptions of the 1897 law against liquor among Indians.[59] The most important of these was a bill (H.R. 2614) introduced at the request of the Indian Office by Representative Carl Hayden of Arizona on April 10, 1917, for it generated hearings on the measure that set forth in detail the arguments pro and con. The opponents of the drug marshaled impressive evidence from scientists (especially Dr. Harvey W. Wiley, who for twenty-nine years had been chief of the Bureau of Chemistry of the Department of Agriculture), from Indians who had witnessed harmful effects of peyote use, and from reformers and missionaries (men like S. M. Brosius of the Indian Rights Association, Richard Henry Pratt, former head of Carlisle Indian School, and the Reverend William H. Ketcham, director of the Bureau of Catholic Indian Missions), all of whom condemned the deleterious effects of the drug and urged absolute prohibition. But their remarks were matched by the testimony of others, who saw good, not evil, in peyote and who argued that its religious use should be protected. Chief among the proponents was the noted ethnologist James Mooney, of the Bureau of American Ethnology, who had long studied the use of the drug; he was joined by Indians who had used peyote and who described its beneficial and harmless effects.[60]

The condemnation of peyote in the hearings was strong, and the House Committee on Indian Affairs reported Hayden's bill favorably. "It is apparent," the committee said, ". . . that this dangerous drug should be absolutely prohibited. The proof is clear that the physicians, the chemists, the missionaries, and many of those who are endeavoring to uplift the Indian, are convinced of the harmful effects of peyote and desire to see its use discontinued." It rejected the testimony of the supporters of peyote as "to some extent interested" and threw out the religious argument in these strong words:

Mohonk Conference Proceedings, 1914, pp. 8, 62–76, and 1915, pp. 7, 75; Report of the Indian Rights Association, 1916, p. 37. See also Mrs. Delevan L. Pierson, "American Indian Peyote Worship," Missionary Review 38 (March 1915): 201–6; "The Case against 'Peyote,'" Outlook 113 (May 24, 1916): 162–63; "Peyote," ibid. 115 (April 11, 1917): 645–46.

59. There is a summary of these legislative attempts in Congressional Digest 1 (February 1922): 12; and a list of bills introduced, 1916–1937, in Slotkin, Peyote Religion, p. 54.

60. "Peyote," Hearings before a Subcommittee of the Committee on Indian Affairs of the House of Representatives, on H.R. 2614, 2 parts (1918). A summary of the hearings is given in Hertzberg, Search for an American Indian Identity, pp. 259–71. For Mooney's support of the use of peyote and the resultant opposition to him by the Indian Office, see L. G. Moses, "James Mooney and the Peyote Controversy," Chronicles of Oklahoma 56 (Summer 1978): 127–44.

The claim, stoutly maintained, that the all night orgies in a close tent polluted with foul air, should not be outlawed because of the religious character of the ceremonies should receive scant credit, although picturesque and eloquent Indian orators before this subcommittee pleaded persuasively for the "peyote religion," and insisted that it would be an unwarranted interference with their "constitutional" rights to curtail the "worship" of the peyote god. They cite scripture to prove the biblical justification of this alleged sacrament. In view of the fact that many reputable witnesses testify that many of these peyote feasts are attended with unrestrained libertinism, this particular claim, urged by Indian orators with great force, earnestness, and eloquence, might be met with the much quoted question: "What plea so tainted and corrupted, but being seasoned with a gracious voice obscures the show of evil; what damned error, but some sober brow will bless it and approve it with a text?"[61]

This was enough to frighten the peyotists, who organized formally as the Native American Church in order to fall clearly under the protective umbrella of the First Amendment.[62] But it was not effective enough to secure prohibitory legislation. Hayden's bill passed the House on October 3, 1919, but it failed in the Senate; nor were subsequent bills any more successful, although a new bill introduced by Hayden passed the House in May 1920.[63]

The reasons for the failure were clear enough. In the first place, evidence of the narcotic and addictive effects of peyote was not convincing, and counter-evidence cast doubts on the justice of prohibiting the drug. Even the reform-minded Committee of One Hundred in 1923 was still calling for "an immediate and definite study of the effects of peyote," despite the fact that the Indian Office remained adamant in its opposition to peyote.[64] Ironically, one of the arguments in favor of peyote was that it

---

61. *House Report* no. 560, 65–2, serial 7308, p. 26. The Indian Rights Association collected arguments against peyote in *Peyote—An Insidious Evil* (Philadelphia: Indian Rights Association, 1918).

62. Slotkin, *Peyote Religion*, pp. 57–67. An account of the Native American Church as a pan-Indian movement is in Hertzberg, *Search for an American Indian Identity*, pp. 239–84.

63. See House debate on Hayden's original bill in *Congressional Record*, 56: 11113–15.

64. "The Indian Problem: Resolutions of the Committee of One Hundred," *House Document* no. 149, 68–1, serial 8273, p. 3. The position of the Indian Office is presented in a pamphlet prepared by Robert E. L. Newberne, *Peyote: An Abridged Compilation from the Files of the Bureau of Indian Affairs* (Washington: GPO, 1922), and in Office of Indian Affairs Bulletin 21 (1923), *Peyote*.

curbed intoxication from liquor. Second, the ceremonial religious use of peyote made it difficult to proscribe use of the drug universally, especially after the organization and spread of the Native American Church. Thus, when there was an attempt in 1921 to add the suppression of peyote to the list of activities of the Indian Office for which general authorization for expenditures was provided, the Senate removed the phrase at the instigation of Senator Robert L. Owen of Oklahoma, who noted that Congress had never declared peyote to be a deleterious drug and insisted that the Indians of Oklahoma used peyote for religious ceremonies without any gross abuse.[65]

The changed atmosphere of the 1920s, with strong voices speaking out in favor of Indian customs and religious rites, doomed to failure the crusade for the national prohibition of peyote. At the end of the decade there had not yet been convincing demonstration that peyote was an evil.[66]

65. *Congressional Record*, 61: 6529. See the whole debate, ibid., pp. 4685–91, 6529–30.

66. The Meriam Report noted, "The habit-forming character of this drug has not been definitely determined." *The Problem of Indian Administration* (Baltimore: Johns Hopkins Press, 1928), p. 222. A survey of the literature on peyote made by Donald Collier in 1932 concluded: "Until more is known about the peyote cult, we have no right to suppress it." "Peyote: A General Study of the Plant, the Cult, and the Drug," printed in "Survey of Conditions of the Indians in the United States," *Hearings before a Subcommittee of the Committee on Indian Affairs, United States Senate, 70th Congress to 78th Congress* (1928–1943), part 34, pp. 18234–58.

CHAPTER 31

The 1920s:
The Guardian on Trial

Continuity and Development.

The Bureau under Siege.

Investigations and Reports.

The decade of the 1920s was a difficult period for the administration of Indian policy. The federal officials in charge of Indian programs were committed to the assimilationist policy they had inherited and were concerned about the progressive development of education and health care for those Indians who remained wards of the government and about the protection and utilization of Indian lands and other resources. The decade, thus, must be viewed first of all as a continuation and culmination of the Indian program begun in the late 1880s with the Dawes Act and the national Indian school system of Thomas J. Morgan. Yet it was a time, also, of widespread and bitter criticism of the Indian Office, its officials, and the program they promoted. The cry for reform was in the air and it grew in volume as the decade passed, but the period was not a period of reform, unless one equates the demands with the substance. There were no significant changes in policy, but rather defense of existing ways on the part of the Indian Office and its supporters. It was a time of unrest and questioning, however, in which the ground was prepared and the seeds planted in the public mind for the radical change that came in the 1930s.

CONTINUITY AND DEVELOPMENT

The direction of federal Indian policy fell to Charles H. Burke, who succeeded Cato Sells as commissioner of Indian affairs when the Democratic administration of Woodrow Wilson gave way to the Republican administration of Warren G. Harding in 1921. Burke was a man of long official contact with Indian affairs. Born in Batavia, New York, in 1861, he had moved to Dakota Territory as a young man, was admitted to the bar there, and established a real estate company in Pierre. After service in the South Dakota legislature he entered Congress, where he served in the House of Representatives from 1899 to 1907 and again from 1909 to 1915. He was a member of the Committee on Indian Affairs and was known for the Burke Act of 1906, which was a major amendment to the Dawes Act. Sixty years old when he became commissioner, Burke was no innovator and continued with some modifications the programs in education, health, and land ownership of his predecessors.[1] A statement he wrote in 1923 about his philosophy and his program could stand as a summary of the work of the Indian Office in the 1920s:

> Practically all our work for the civilization of the Indian has become educational: teaching the language he must of necessity adopt, the academic knowledge essential to ordinary business transactions, the common arts and crafts of the home and field, how to provide a settled dwelling and elevate its domestic quality, how to get well when he is sick and how to stay well, how to make the best use of his land and the water accessible to it, how to raise the right kind of livestock, how to work for a living, save money and start a bank account, how to want something he can call his own, a material possession with the happiness and comforts of family life and a pride in the prosperity of his children; teaching him to see the future as a new era and one inevitably different from his past, in which individual ambition, unaided by the show and trappings of ancient custom, must contend with the complexities and competition of a modern world. It is the policy of sympathy, patience, and humanity, which for thirty years has encountered no hostile Indian uprisings such as marked every previous decades for three centuries, that is preserving and reconstructing the Red Race.[2]

Burke served under two quite different secretaries of the interior. The first was Albert J. Fall, the New Mexico politician who had been one of the

---

1. Lawrence C. Kelly, "Charles Henry Burke, 1921–29," in Robert M. Kvasnicka and Herman J. Viola, eds., *The Commissioners of Indian Affairs, 1824–1977* (Lincoln: University of Nebraska Press, 1979), pp. 251–61. There is a very favorable contemporary view of Burke in Herbert Corey, "He Carries the White Man's Burden," *Collier's* 71 (May 12, 1923): 13.

2. Foreword to G. E. E. Lindquist, *The Red Man in the United States: An Intimate Study of the Social, Economic and Religious Life of the American Indian* (New York: George H. Doran Company, 1923), p. vi.

first senators from the state and who had been chosen for the cabinet by Harding in 1921. Although the commissioner supported departmental policy, he was embarrassed by Fall's greater concern for white economic interests than for Indian welfare, particularly in the matter of oil leases and land claims, and he was no doubt relieved when the secretary resigned in 1923. Fall's successor was Dr. Hubert Work, a physician from Colorado, who had been president of the American Medical Association and active in Republican Party affairs. He had served briefly in Harding's cabinet as postmaster general. Although Burke on occasion disagreed with the policies of the new secretary, the two men in general worked closely together on Indian affairs.[3]

It was Burke's lot to be the target of the growing dissatisfaction with the old approach to Indian affairs. During his long term the Indian Office was attacked from many sides, and the criticism came to be leveled at him personally and at his assistant commissioner, Edgar B. Meritt. One contributing factor to the uproar experienced by Burke was the inflation that followed World War I and the new administration's attempt to counter it with a policy of retrenchment. At a time when Indian health and education programs needed massive increases in funding if they were to accomplish their goals, the Indian Office was expected to economize instead, and Burke seemed willing to follow the new philosophy. When the newly established Bureau of the Budget called for reduced expenditures, Burke acquiesced and told his adminstrative officers in 1921: "The administration from the President down is solemnly committed to *rigid economy with increased efficiency*; and I expect and shall require every officer and employee of the Indian Service to cooperate with me in the early fulfillment of that policy."[4] The harmful effects of such a policy on Indian welfare haunted Burke through his whole term. Year by year the appropriations were too small to serve the needs of the Indian service. The secretary of the interior's report on Indian affairs in 1927, in fact, was headed by a seven-page section called "The Poverty of the Indian Service." It began with this summary statement:

> The Indian Service has not kept pace with the progress elsewhere along health, educational, industrial, and social lines. The appropriations for general purposes for the fiscal year 1923 were $10,316,221.30, and in the five fiscal years since they have been increased by about $2,338,463.70, principally for medical and health activities. But the

3. For a brief account of Work's career, see Eugene P. Trani, "Hubert Work and the Department of the Interior, 1923–28," *Pacific Northwest Quarterly* 61 (January 1970): 31–40.

4. Order no. 82, June 20, 1921, OIA Circulars (M1121, reel 3).

cumulative effect of many years of financial neglect has demanded even larger appropriations, if the Government may perform its full duty to the American Indian. Underrating the requirements of the Indian Service has continued so long that it has become a habit difficult to correct.[5]

Burke saw the culmination of the movement for Indian citizenship. Through the Dawes Act and the Burke Act, the blanket grants of citizenship to tribes such as the Five Civilized Tribes and the Osage Indians, and the provisions made for citizenship for veterans of World War I, a majority of the Indians—some estimates put the figure at two-thirds—had achieved citizenship.[6] But the patriotic fervor that persisted after the war seemed to call for a measure to complete the circle. It came in 1924. On January 29, Representative Homer P. Snyder of New York introduced a bill to authorize the secretary of the interior, at his discretion, to issue certificates of citizenship to any Indian born within the United States who was not yet a citizen, upon application by the Indian. The bill easily passed the House, but the Senate radically changed its nature by eliminating the discretionary authority of the secretary of the interior and declared flatly that the Indians were citizens by action of the law itself. The Committee on Indian Affairs, reporting the amended bill, had concluded "that as citizenship had been extended to the Five Civilized Tribes, and that as a large number of other Indians had become citizens under various acts of Congress, it was only just and fair that all Indians be declared citizens." The House without question accepted the change, and the bill became law on June 2.[7]

The effect of the citizenship act was nebulous. Like earlier Indian citizenship measures, it specified that the granting of citizenship would not "in any manner impair or otherwise affect the right of any Indian to tribal or other property." So the complete transition from tribal status to individualized citizenship that the Dawes Act reformers had had in mind when they talked about citizenship did not occur. The Indians were both citizens of the United States and persons with tribal relations. Nor did citizenship

5. CIA Report, 1927, p. 1.

6. A useful summary of citizenship provisions is Office of Indian Affairs Bulletin 20, 1922, "Indian Citizenship," printed in *House Report* no. 222, 68–1, serial 8227, pp. 2–3.

7. *Congressional Record*, 65: 1665, 2977, 4446, 6753, 8621–22, 9303–4; *House Report* no. 222, 68–1, serial 8227; *Senate Report* no. 441, 68–1, serial 8221; 43 *United States Statutes* 253. The Senate in changing the substance of the bill also changed its title correspondingly, but for some reason the change was not picked up, and the *United States Statutes* retains the original—no longer applicable—title referring to the issuance of certificates of citizenship by the secretary of the interior.

necessarily signify withdrawal from the protective guardianship of the United States government, as the Supreme Court declared in 1916 in *United States* v. *Nice.*[8] Burke, who called the citizenship law "a very important enactment of legislation," was at pains to point out that property rights would continue to be protected, that the Indians would not be "thrown en masse upon the mercies, or subject to the prey, of unscrupulous persons," and that the release of the trust or restrictions on Indian property would be determined upon the merit of individual cases.[9]

Enfranchisement as citizens was another matter. At one time *enfranchisement* was considered synonymous with *citizenship*, but that turned out not to be the case. The question had been raised explicitly in the House of Representatives when the act was passed. Did the act affect state laws concerning suffrage? Representative Snyder, the sponsor of the bill and speaking for the Committee on Indian Affairs, answered that it was "not the intention of the law to have any effect upon the suffrage qualifications of any State." Commissioner Burke urged the Indians to investigate the election laws of their states and to comply with the requirements necessary to entitle them to vote; but in fact Indians were prohibited from voting in a number of western states, and not until 1948 did Arizona and New Mexico extend the franchise to them.[10]

While the Indians were being pushed willy-nilly into citizenship, the Indian Office continued to be a honeycomb of offices and programs, all dedicated to the administration of affairs for Indian citizens who were still wards of the government. It was a bureaucracy of great size and complexity, which made a mockery of the earlier pronouncements that it was soon to go out of business. In the best of times, the supervision of such machinery would require high administrative ability, yet the maintenance and operation of the structure was always hindered by the lack of sufficient money to turn the organization into a first-class enterprise. The Indian Office, with its paternalistic control of numerous aspects of the Indians'

8. 241 *U.S. Reports* 591–601; the quotation is from p. 598. This decision explicitly overturned the decision in *Matter of Heff* (1905).

9. CIA Report, 1924, p. 20. On Indian citizenship, see *Felix S. Cohen's Handbook of Federal Indian Law*, 1982 ed. (Charlottesville, Virginia: Michie, Bobbs-Merrill, 1982), pp. 639–45.

10. *Congressional Record*, 65: 9303; CIA Report, 1924, p. 20. See N. D. Houghton, "The Legal Status of Indian Suffrage in the U.S.," *California Law Review* 19 (July 1931): 507–20, which discusses Arizona's refusal to allow Indians to vote because they were "persons under guardianship." See also the remarks on the reaction of New York Indians to the citizenship law in the report of Flora W. Seymour, in *Report of the Board of Indian Commissioners*, 1928, p. 36.

lives, became the object of growing criticism, not only for its policies but for its mode of operation.

Some sort of decentralization was strongly urged, especially by Hugh L. Scott and Warren K. Moorehead of the Board of Indian Commissioners, and in 1926 Burke instituted a considerable reorganization of the Indian service in that direction. Not only was the medical service reorganized with a chief medical supervisor and four medical districts, each with a district supervisor, but a general administrative change was made for the direction and supervision of all educational, agricultural, and industrial activities. A general superintendent of Indian affairs was appointed (H. B. Peairs, longtime superintendent of Haskell Institute and then chief supervisor of education), and the nation was divided into nine districts, each with a district superintendent to direct the activities within his area. Burke listed some of their duties as "assistance in the preparation of budgets, responsibility for the interpretation and execution of the policies of the commissioner, inspection of school and agency activities, supervision of school and agency organization and of classroom and vocational instruction, examination of the condition and needs of material plants and of personnel, conference with State and county officials, and conduct of special investigations when directed." The new system began with a conference in Washington in May 1926 of all the district superintendents, who discussed plans and procedures for the future and drew up a list of recommendations.[11]

A detailed picture of the structure and activities of the Office of Indian Affairs in 1926 was offered in a monograph prepared by Laurence F. Schmeckebier for a series on various bureaus of the federal government published by the Institute for Government Research. The series was based on the belief that "the first essential to efficient administration of any enterprise is full knowledge of its present make-up and operation." The Indian Office volume caught at a set moment in time the policies and programs of the federal government in its relations with the American Indians.[12] One of the goals of the institute in the monograph series was "to list and classify in all practicable detail the specific activities engaged in by the several services of the national government." The list for the Office of Indian Affairs provided an admirable summary of the multifarious operations of the bureau:

11. CIA Report, 1926, pp. 4–5. The Board of Indian Commissioners called the reorganization "the most advanced steps in the direction of increased efficiency and of a long-needed coordination of administrative functions that have been taken in many years." Report of the Board of Indian Commissioners, 1926, p. 1.

12. Laurence F. Schmeckebier, The Office of Indian Affairs: Its History, Activities, and Organization, Service Monographs of the United States Government, no. 48 (Baltimore: Johns Hopkins Press, 1927).

Classification of Activities

1. Making Allotments in Severalty
2. Issuance of Patents in Fee and Certificates of Competency
3. Supervision over Real Estate
   a. Determining heirs and approval of wills
   b. Distribution of property inter vivos
   c. Sale of land
   d. Leasing
   e. Granting rights of way and easements
   f. Administration of forest lands
4. Custody of Indian Money
   a. Tribal funds
   b. Individual money
5. Education of the Indian
6. Furnishing Medical Relief
7. Promoting Industrial Advancement
   a. Through construction and operation of irrigation, water supply, and drainage systems
   b. Through engineering works other than irrigation, water supply, and drainage
   c. Through advances of money
   d. Through promotion of agriculture and stock raising
   e. Through obtaining employment
8. Promotion of Home Economics
9. Support of Indians
10. Policing of Reservations
11. Suppression of Liquor Traffic
12. Control over Traders
13. Supervising Contracts with Attorneys.[13]

13. Ibid., pp. 393–94. There is discussion of these activities below in the chapters on education, health, and land. An act of November 2, 1921, known as the Snyder Act, provided a general and comprehensive authorization for appropriations and expenditures for administering Indian affairs, including the following purposes: "General support and civilization, including education. For relief of distress and conservation of health. For industrial assistance and advancement and general administration of Indian property. For extension, improvement, operation, and maintenance of existing Indian irrigation systems and for development of water supplies. For the enlargement, extension, improvement and repair of the buildings and grounds of existing plants and projects. For the employment of inspectors, supervisors, superintendents, clerks, field matrons, farmers, physicians, Indian police, Indian judges, and other employees. For the suppression of traffic in intoxicating liquors and deleterious drugs. For the purchase of horse-drawn and motor propelled passenger-carrying vehicles for official use. And for general and incidental expenses in connection with the administration of Indian affairs." 42 *United States Statutes* 208–9. There is a brief discussion of the act in *Cohen's Federal Indian Law*, 1982 ed., pp. 141–42.

THE BUREAU UNDER SIEGE

The Office of Indian Affairs, generally referred to as the "Indian Bureau" by its critics, came under heavy attack in the 1920s, and its work was carried on in an atmosphere of tension. New groups arose to challenge the very principles upon which federal policy was based and to demand reform. Burke and his supporters fought back, denying the legitimacy of the most extreme criticism but showing a willingness to listen and to compromise where they judged benefits would come to the Indians. It was a question of whose vision for the Indian future was the right one, and the issue was in doubt throughout the decade. Would the existing system be overturned, or would there be gradual change and reform from within?

The lines of the conflict were drawn over the question of land rights of the Pueblo Indians in New Mexico. These Indians, with territorial grants going back to Spanish times, had come within the limits of the United States with the Mexican Cession in 1848 by the Treaty of Guadalupe Hidalgo. The treaty specified that all Mexican citizens in the cession would enjoy the full rights and privileges of citizens of the United States. Because the Pueblos had been considered citizens by Mexico, the federal government treated them differently from other Indians, although some provisions were made for their welfare. Laws protecting Indian lands and prohibiting the encroachment of whites were not enforced against Anglo-Americans and Mexicans who settled on the Pueblo grants, for the territorial courts denied the applicability of the intercourse law of 1834 to the Pueblos, and that position was upheld by the United States Supreme Court in 1876 in *United States* v. *Joseph*. There was a change, however, when New Mexico became a state, and the lines between state authority and federal authority over the Indians became sharply drawn. The enabling act for the state of New Mexico specifically provided that "the terms 'Indian' and 'Indian country' shall include the Pueblo Indians of New Mexico and the lands now owned or occupied by them." This extension of federal control over the Pueblos was upheld by the Supreme Court in 1913 in *United States* v. *Sandoval*, which reversed the decision of the *Joseph* case.[14]

The *Sandoval* decision called into question the titles of non-Indians who had settled on lands claimed by the Pueblos, titles in many cases acquired in good faith. New Mexicans, of course, were deeply interested in

14. *United States* v. *Joseph, 94 U.S. Reports* 614–19; *United States* v. *Sandoval,* 231 *U.S. Reports* 28–49; 36 *United States Statutes* 558–60. For a discussion of the Pueblo land question, see Felix S. Cohen, *Handbook of Federal Indian Law* (Washington: GPO, 1942), pp. 383–93; Herbert O. Brayer, *Pueblo Indian Land Grants of the "Rio Abajo," New Mexico*, University of New Mexico Bulletin no. 334 (Albuquerque: University of New Mexico Press, 1938), pp. 7–31.

the matter, and Albert J. Fall, as senator from the state and then as secretary of the interior, represented their interests. In order to settle the controversy over the land claims, Holm O. Bursum, who had taken Fall's seat
in the Senate, introduced a bill on July 20, 1922, "to quiet title to lands
within Pueblo Indian land grants." At first sight the bill seemed to resolve
the problem, and it passed the Senate without much stir.[15] But more careful study showed that the Bursum bill strongly favored the non-Indian
claimants and placed the burden of proving title not on the claimants but
on the Pueblos.

The Pueblos were not without friends, and a tremendous protest arose
that changed the course of American Indian affairs. The leadership devolved upon John Collier, a one-time social worker in New York City, who
had been introduced to the Pueblos in 1920 by Mabel Dodge, a member of
the artists' colony at Taos. In 1922 Collier was employed as field representative for Stella M. Atwood's Indian Welfare Committee of the General
Federation of Women's Clubs. Collier found in the Pueblo communal and
ceremonial life an answer to the problems of human society, and he eagerly
joined with others (including Father Fridolin Schuster, a Franciscan missionary among the Pueblos, and Francis C. Wilson, a Santa Fe attorney
employed by the General Federation of Women's Clubs) in organizing opposition to the Bursum bill. They used the pages of *Survey*, a progressive journal staffed by reformers, and the liberal *Sunset*, edited by Walter
Woehlke, to take their case to the American people. Meanwhile Mrs. Atwood mobilized the two million members of the Federation to lobby against
the bill. A statement drawn up by Collier and Wilson entitled "Shall the
Pueblo Indians of New Mexico Be Destroyed?" was widely circulated and
sent to members of Congress.[16]

---

15. *Congressional Record*, 62: 12323–25. Secretary Fall, in commenting officially on
the bill, claimed that all parties were agreed on its provisions and that therefore it could
be called "an administration measure." Fall to Reed Smoot, July 31, 1922, printed in *Senate Report* no. 909, 67–2, serial 7951.

16. The best study of the protest movement is Lawrence C. Kelly, *The Assault on Assimilation: John Collier and the Origins of Indian Policy Reform* (Albuquerque: University of New Mexico Press, 1983). Another excellent study, upon which I have relied, is
Kenneth R. Philp, *John Collier's Crusade for Indian Reform, 1920–1954* (Tucson: University of Arizona Press, 1977), pp. 1–91. An older, brief account still of value is Randolph C. Downes, "A Crusade for Indian Reform, 1922–1934," *Mississippi Valley Historical Review* 32 (December 1945): 331–54. Downes gives a list of the muckraking articles
of Collier and his friends on pp. 335–39. An emphasis on the internal dynamics of the
reform movement, with an excellent treatment of the part played by the artists' and writers' colony at Taos, is given in Michael M. Dorcy, "Friends of the American Indian,
1922–1934: Patterns of Patronage and Philanthropy" (Ph.D. dissertation, University of
Pennsylvania, 1978). Collier reported on the Pueblo question in such articles as "Plundering the Pueblo Indians," *Sunset* 50 (January 1923): 21–25, 56; "The Pueblos' Last

When Burke supported the bill as an administration measure, the open conflict between Collier's forces and the Indian Office began. An All Pueblo Council (organized and run to a large extent by the Indians' white friends) denounced the bill in "An Appeal by the Pueblo Indians of New Mexico to the People of the United States," and Collier led delegates of Indians to Chicago, New York, and Washington to demonstrate against it. He was backed by the venerable Indian Rights Association and by the Eastern Association on Indian Affairs and the New Mexico Association on Indian Affairs, new white reform groups that had come into being in response to the Pueblo crisis. In May 1923 Collier organized the American Indian Defense Association, which soon became the chief vehicle for promoting his reforms. Collier served as its executive secretary from 1923 until 1933.[17]

Before congressional committees conducting hearings on the Pueblo bills and in a muckraking barrage, Collier and his friends pounded home their defense of the Indians' rights. The propaganda of the Collier camp was roundly condemned, of course, by supporters of the administration. The House Committee on Indian Affairs, reporting favorably on the Bursum bill, called the propaganda "insidious, untruthful, and malicious" and charged that some of it was "nothing more nor less than criminal libel." But official defense of the bill and condemnation of the propaganda techniques of its opponents could not save it. The question was about the nature of an alternative. A counter-proposal, the Jones-Leatherwood bill, was brought forward by the Collier forces. It would have established a commission of three persons to examine and rule on contested claims and provided funds for irrigation systems, but it made no progress.[18]

A new measure, reported by Senator Irvine L. Lenroot on February 24, 1923, continued the bitter controversy.[19] The bill provided for a land board

---

Stand," ibid. (February 1923): 19–22, 65–66; "No Trespassing," ibid. (May 1923): 14–15, 58–60; "The Pueblos' Land Problem," ibid. 51 (November 1923): 15, 101; "The Red Atlantis," *Survey* 49 (October 1922): 15–20, 63, 66; "The American Congo," ibid. 50 (August 1923): 467–76. Collier described the whole reform movement of the 1920s in *The Indians of the Americas* (New York: W. W. Norton and Company, 1947), pp. 246–60.

17. The fullest collection of materials on the American Indian Defense Association and on Collier's part in the reform movement in the 1920s is the John Collier Papers, Yale University, which I have used on microfilm.

18. There were extensive hearings on the bills to settle the Pueblo land question, at which both sides offered lengthy arguments. See "Pueblo Indian Lands," *Hearings before a Subcommittee of the Committee on Public Lands and Surveys, United States Senate, 67th Congress, 4th Session, on S. 3865 and S. 4223, Bills Relative to the Pueblo Indian Lands* (1923); "Pueblo Indian Land Titles," *Hearings before the Committee on Indian Affairs, House of Representatives, 67th Congress, 4th Session, on H.R. 13452 and H.R. 13674* (1923). Philp summarizes the hearings in *John Collier's Crusade*, pp. 42–45.

19. *Senate Report* no. 1175, 67–4, serial 8155, gives a detailed summary of the provisions.

appointed by the president to determine Pueblo land titles, and it eliminated some of the objectionable features of the Bursum bill. But it relied upon a statute of limitations that favored non-Indian claimants and made no provision to compensate Indians for land or water rights lost to white settlers. The Lenroot bill seriously divided the reform groups. Francis Wilson approved the measure as a compromise, and the New Mexico Association and the Eastern Association on Indian Affairs joined him, for they had developed some sympathy for the non-Indian settlers and were critical of Collier's dominating influence over the Pueblos. Collier, however, was adamant in his opposition to the Lenroot bill and fought strenuously to prevent its passage, and he tightened his control over the American Indian Defense Association by eliminating from its ranks those who disagreed with him.[20]

Finally, on June 7, 1924, a measure that seemed to satisfy both sides, the Pueblo Lands Act, became law. It established a Pueblo land board, which was to determine the boundaries of the Pueblo land grants and then fix the status of lands within those limits. To establish title, non-Indian claimants had to prove either continuous possession under color of title since January 6, 1902, or without color of title since March 16, 1889, supported by tax payments in both cases. The United States would compensate the Indians for land and water rights lost; and the value of improvements lost by unsuccessful non-Indian claimants was to be reported to Congress for compensation. To prevent further controversy, the act provided that no future transfer of Pueblo land would be valid unless approved beforehand by the secretary of the interior.[21] Under the law, the process of examining claims and evicting settlers proceeded slowly until by 1938 the Pueblo land question was generally settled.

Although defense of Pueblo land rights could engage the support of a broad range of Indian welfare organizations and the Indian Office as well, despite controversy over the precise method of protecting Indian rights in the face of counter-claims by non-Indians, a second challenge to the Indian Office by Collier and his supporters created a sharp split into two irreconcilable camps. This was the issue of Indian dances and other Indian customs. From the beginning of the decade the Indian Rights Association and missionaries among the Indians had complained to the Indian Office about Indian dances, which they argued were inconsistent with the Indians' progress. Commissioner Cato Sells, too, had been alert to problems that affected Indian advancement and in 1920 had asked for specific information from the superintendents. He wanted to know, among other things, the extent to which Indians indulged in the "old Indian dances" and the

20. Philp, *John Collier's Crusade*, pp. 47–49.
21. 43 *United States Statutes* 636–42; *Senate Report* no. 492, 68–1, serial 8221.

"extent such dances tend to retard the advancement of the Indians and what effect it has on their morals." The replies about the dances were assembled and laid before Burke when he took office. In general they reported few difficulties, although the superintendents expressed some concern about absence from work occasioned by the dances.[22]

On April 26, 1921, Burke issued a special circular to the superintendents on dances, in which he asserted: "The dance *per se* is not condemned. It is recognized as a manifestation of something inherent in human nature, widely evidenced by both sacred and profane history, and as a medium through which elevated minds may happily unite art, refinement, and healthful exercise." But he then called attention to dances that involved "acts of self-torture, immoral relations between the sexes, the sacrificial destruction of clothing or other useful articles, the reckless giving away of property, the use of injurious drugs or intoxicants, and frequent or prolonged periods of celebration which bring the Indians together from remote points to the neglect of their crops, livestock, and home interest." In such cases the regulations that prohibited ."Indian offenses" were to be enforced.[23]

Two years later, after attending a meeting of missionaries to the Sioux, Burke issued a supplement to his 1921 circular, urging the superintendents to "persistently encourage and emphasize the Indian's attention to those practical, useful, thrifty, and orderly activities that are indispensable to his well-being and underlie the preservation of his race in the midst of complex and highly competitive conditions." The superintendents, however, were to proceed with patience and charity and use tact, persuasion, and appeals to the Indians' good sense.[24] With the supplement Burke sent a "Message to All Indians," which the superintendents were directed to disseminate widely. In it he appealed to the Indians to stop the dances and celebrations that interfered with their making a living and to do so of their own free will. He told the Indians:

> I do not want to deprive you of decent amusement or occasional feast days, but you should not do evil or foolish things or take so much time for these occasions. No good comes from your "give-

22. *Report of the Indian Rights Association*, 1921, p. 11; minutes of October 2, 1920, OIA, Minutes of the Board of Indian Commissioners; Circular no. 1604, April 21, 1920, OIA Circulars (M1121, reel 12). Extracts of the superintendents' reports are in OIA CCF, General Service 063, 86448–1920. See also the discussion of the dance controversy in Philp, *John Collier's Crusade*, pp. 55–70.

23. Circular no. 1665, April 26, 1921, OIA Circulars (M1121, reel 12).

24. Supplement to Circular no. 1665, February 14, 1923, ibid. Reports from superintendents in answer to this directive are in OIA CCF, General Service 063, 10429–1922. This is a thick file in three parts and contains many letters attacking and supporting Burke's directives on Indian dances.

away" custom and dances and it should be stopped. It is not right to torture your bodies or handle poisonous snakes in your ceremonies. All such extreme things are wrong and should be put aside and forgotten. You do yourselves and your families great injustice when at dances you give away money or other property, perhaps clothing, a cow, a horse or a team and wagon, and then after an absence of several days go home to find everything going to waste and yourselves with less to work with than you had before.[25]

It was clear from the reports of the superintendents, the humanitarian criticism of the dances, and Burke's circulars and message to the Indians that the initial concern was about interruption in the work of earning a livelihood that were caused by the dances, not the isolated examples of behavior that was considered immoral. As the controversy over the dances developed, however, the focus of criticism came to be placed on alleged sexual excesses in the religious dances among the Indians of the Southwest (the Hopi snake dance was a favorite example). There was repeated talk about "the most depraved and immoral practices" and fear that young returned students were being drawn into the evil practices. The Indian Rights Association kept a file of testimony ("of an unprintable nature") about the immoral character of the dances, which it invited people to look at in its office.[26]

The commissioner's earnest efforts to strengthen Christian morality among the Indians won large support. The Indian Rights Association reported enthusiastically on Burke's directives, the Board of Indian Commissioners offered full support, and the Committee of One Hundred commended Burke for his stand.[27] The new secretary of the interior, Hubert Work, thoroughly agreed with Burke's position; in a letter to Tewa Indians at San Ildefonso Pueblo, who had complained about attacks on their cus-

25. "A Message to All Indians," February 24, 1923, copy in OIA CCF, General Service 063, 10429–1922, part 1.

26. *Report of the Indian Rights Association*, 1923, pp. 20–21, 26–27; *Indian Truth* 1 (April 1924): 3–4.

27. *Report of the Indian Rights Association*, 1923, pp. 20–21; *Report of the Board of Indian Commissioners*, 1923, pp. 6–7; "The Indian Problem: Resolutions of the Committee of One Hundred," *House Document* no. 149, 68–1, serial 8273. Herbert Welsh, the aging president of the Indian Rights Association, declared that Burke's stand had the support of all missionary groups because "these dances are incompatible in their very nature with the fundamental principles of Christian teaching." He said, "The time for their cessation has certainly come, unless these Indians are to be considered as archeological, or artistic, or literary pets, who are to have no concern with American taxation, with American education, with American farm or commercial life." Welsh to George Wharton Pepper, March 31, 1923, OIA CCF, General Service 063, 10429–1922, part 1.

toms, he firmly elaborated the department's stand. There was no intention to interfere with "any dance that has a religious significance, or those given for pleasure and entertainment, which are not degrading." But then he lectured the Indians on Christian morality.

There are certain practices, however, that are against the laws of nature, or moral laws, and all who wish to perpetuate the integrity of their race must refrain from them. The white man did not make these laws, although he has adopted some of them into his beliefs and customs, but they were ordained by that Supreme Being, who created all of us, and who has been worshipped by nearly all tribes and races in their own way since the beginning.

It is contrary to these moral laws to exaggerate the sex instinct of man, or become subservient to it, and the Indian, no more than the white man, cannot afford to contribute to his own spiritual and physical downfall by indulging in practices which appeal to lower animal emotions only.[28]

All this attack upon Indian culture, much of it aimed specifically at the Indians of the Southwest, infuriated John Collier. It was further proof to him of the bureau's disregard of Indian rights, and he mounted a campaign in support of religious liberty for the Indians. Whereas Burke saw immorality and degradation in the dances, Collier saw beauty and mystical experience. When Edith M. Dabb, of the Indian department of the YWCA, wrote to the *New York Times* in support of Burke and declared that "sentimentalists who dwell on the beauties of the quaint and primitive would do well to remember that primitive beauty is frequently found in close company with primitive cruelty and primitive ugliness," Collier replied with an eloquent defense of the Indians' religious rites. He accused the government of destroying Indian culture in its striving to Americanize and civilize the Indians. He insisted that "among these resources of civilization is an understanding, gained in our age, of the profound way in which personality, moral stability and culture are dependent on one another, and of the sacredness of primitive religion to the primitive, and the beauty and nobility of it to the eyes of the informed civilized man." Collier defended the dances in an article, "Persecuting the Pueblos," in *Sunset* magazine in July

28. Members of the Tawa Tribe to the secretary of the interior, January 16, 1924, and Hubert Work to Council of the Tawa Tribe, February 20, 1924, OIA CCF, General Service 063, 10429–1922, part 2. Work's letter is printed in his response to the resolutions of the Committee of One Hundred as a statement of the department's policy. Hubert Work, *Indian Policies: Comments on the Resolutions of the Advisory Council on Indian Affairs* (Washington: GPO, 1924), pp. 10–11. See also Hubert Work, "Our American Indians," *Saturday Evening Post* 196 (May 31, 1924): 27, 92–98.

1924, and most strongly of all in a pamphlet published by the American Indian Defense Association in the same month, called *The Indian and Religious Freedom*. The Eastern Association on Indian Affairs issued a special bulletin entitled "Concerning Indian Dances," in which it objected to the "slander of a noble and disappearing race" and printed letters from ethnologists and anthropologists refuting the charges of immorality made against the dances by such persons as Edith Dabb.[29]

The battle was spirited and enduring. Each attempt of the Indian Office to enforce its sanctions against the dances or to prevent the withdrawal of Indian children from school so they could be trained in the religious ceremonies brought new cries from defenders of the Indians' rights. The Indians themselves, however, were divided, and Protestant Indians passed resolutions condemning the domination of the Indian priests, who forced them to retain pagan customs. Such evidence led the Indian Rights Association to charge violation of individual religious liberty by "the oligarchy of caciques" who controlled the pueblos.[30]

Burke at length sought congressional support for his position. He drafted a bill, introduced in the House in January 1926 by Scott Leavitt of Montana, extending federal civil and criminal laws over Indians and granting United States district courts jurisdiction over these crimes and misdemeanors. For offenses not subject to federal law, the bill gave authority to the courts of Indian offenses, which could levy fines and impose jail sentences. The measure also prohibited marriages and divorces according to Indian custom and authorized fines and imprisonment for violations. The proposal met strong opposition. Collier testified at the hearings on the bill and vehemently criticized its sanctions against Indian customs of marriage and divorce. He condemned, too, the added authority given to the Indian courts and asserted that the bill would institute "a system of rule not differing in principle from that maintained by the Czar in Russia and by Leopold of Belgium in his management of his Congo victims." Although S. M.

---

29. *New York Times*, December 2 and 16, 1923; John Collier, "Persecuting the Pueblos," *Sunset* 53 (July 1924): 50, 92–93; *The Indian and Religious Freedom* (New York: American Indian Defense Association, 1924); Eastern Association on Indian Affairs, *Bulletin Number Three*. See also Collier, "Do Indians Have Rights of Conscience?" *Christian Century* 42 (March 12, 1925): 346–49.

30. Philp, *John Collier's Crusade*, pp. 59–65; *Indian Truth* 1 (April 1924): 3–4; (May 1924): 3. The Reverend William Hughes, director of the Bureau of Catholic Indian Missions, joined Protestant groups in objecting to Collier's position and supported the view that Christian Indians were being persecuted by pagan chiefs. See copy of his article in the *Sacramento Bee*, July 26, 1924, and the favorable reaction it received from Burke and from Herbert Welsh in papers of the Bureau of Catholic Indian Missions, New Mexico, Pueblo, 1924, Marquette University Library.

Brosius of the Indian Rights Association favored the bill's provision on marriage and divorce, he felt that strengthening the Indian courts would be "a step backward in Indian management." Assistant Commissioner Meritt replied to the criticisms and strongly supported the Leavitt bill as an aid to the bureau in prosecuting a long list of offenses, from assault with intent to commit rape, through robbery, mayhem, perjury, kidnapping, fraud, and embezzlement, to unlawful cohabitation, fornication, bigamy, incest, lewdness, and soliciting females for immoral purposes. Then he lashed out against the administration's critics, whom he called "paid propagandists making malicious, lying statements about the Indian Bureau," and he denied that the bureau was seeking more power.[31] The Leavitt bill did not pass; Collier's campaign had killed it, although the alternative legislation that he proposed was not enacted.

Pueblo lands and Indian religious liberty were by no means the only basis of attack upon Burke and the Indian Office, for all aspects of Indian administration came under the critical gaze of Collier and the American Indian Defense Association. The failures in the Indian schools, the deplorable state of Indian health, and the loss of Indian lands through allotment and fee patents furnished material for a constant chorus of complaint. The question of Indian rights to oil reserves in executive order reservations, the use of Indian funds on a reimbursable basis to construct improvements alleged to be of more use to whites than to Indians (the Lee's Ferry Bridge on the Navajo Reservation was an example), and the part played by Burke in handling the estate of a rich Oklahoma Indian, Jackson Barnett, furnished more rich grist for the critics' mill. In all of this Collier had the support in Congress of Representatives James A. Frear of Wisconsin, who aggressively pounced upon what he considered the wrongdoings of Commissioner Burke and Assistant Commissioner Meritt. Burke at length replied point by point to Frear's attack and accused him of being the mouthpiece of the American Indian Defense Association and thus of being seriously misinformed. Meritt for his part, in a speech on December 1, 1926, before the Oakland Forum in California, refuted Frear's criticism on

---

31. "Reservation Courts of Indian Offenses," *Hearings before the Committee on Indian Affairs, House of Representatives*, 69th Congress, 1st Session, on H.R. 7826 (1926). The hearings include a copy of the bill, pp. 1–2; Collier's testimony, pp. 18–29; Brosius's testimony, pp. 72–85; Meritt's testimony, pp. 85–111. Collier entered a prepared statement called "A Bill Authorizing Tyranny" and Meritt one called "The American Indian and Government Administration," in which he presented a survey of constructive government action for the Indians. The Leavitt bill was supported by the Board of Indian Commissioners. *Report of the Board of Indian Commissioners*, 1926, pp. 6–7; 1927, pp. 6–8.

fifteen points and then offered fifteen points of his own showing the constructive work of the Indian Office.[32]

Pervading all the controversy on particular issues was the charge that the Indian Office ignored the Indians themselves and their views and rode roughshod over their rights. The assimilationist policy was wrong, Collier charged, and must be replaced by one that respected the Indians as human beings with a dignity and culture of their own. In a forceful statement at the beginning of his crusade for Indian policy reform, he wrote:

> The policy of denying to the Indian a group existence, and at the same time of denying him personal option in matters of property, of parental authority, of amusement, and even of religion—this policy which is sanctioned by the belief that the Indian as a race must perish from the earth in order that, naked of memories, homeless, inferior and fugitive, some creatures with Amerindian blood in their veins may rush to the arms of Civilization: this policy, historically so natural but now so inhuman and un-American, is still the policy of that guardian before whose command all Indians must bow down.

Collier now called for an end to "monopolistic and autocratic control over person and property by a single bureau of the Federal Government" and for protection of Indian property rights, for respect of "elementary rights guaranteed to other Americans by the Constitution or long-established tradition," and for the use of cultural pride and "native social endowments and institutions" in the education of the Indians.[33]

INVESTIGATIONS AND REPORTS

It was inevitable that so much outspoken criticism would generate demands for a thorough study of the situation of the Indians and the work of

32. Examples of Frear's unscrupulous attacks are in *Congressional Record*, 67: 5032–51 (March 4, 1926); 68: 1066–78 (January 4, 1927); 68: 5707–20 (March 3, 1927). A reply by Burke was entered in the *Congressional Record* on April 23, 1926, by Representative William Williamson of South Dakota, 67: 8094–8109. Meritt's California speech is printed in the *Indian American* 27 (January 15, 1927): 13–28. When Representative Leavitt attempted to enter the speech in the *Congressional Record* on January 10, 1927, he was prevented from doing so by Frear, but he managed to read sections of it, which appear in *Congressional Record*, 68: 1401–4.

33. John Collier, "America's Treatment of Her Indians," *Current History* 18 (August 1923): 772, 779–81. See also the sharp distinction drawn between the traditional government policy and the new policy proposed by Collier in "The Red Indian Problem," *Public Health Nurse* 15 (November 1923): 557–58. Others of Collier's numerous writings carry the same theme.

the Indian Office. Investigation of Indian conditions, in fact, had long been an element in Indian administration. The special agents and Indian inspectors of the Interior Department and the Office of Indian Affairs were called upon again and again to examine particular problems, the Board of Indian Commissioners sent investigating committees to the reservations, and Congress and the Interior Department from time to time authorized special examinations of critical areas. The Indian Rights Association, too, continued its longtime role as watchdog. Yet those investigations and the reports they produced provided only a piecemeal approach to a critical appraisal of Indian policy and of Indian programs. John Collier and the American Indian Defense Association and other groups and individuals who joined with them in the 1920s demanded a more universal approach. Secretary Work slowly began to see the wisdom, if not the necessity, of a broad independent study from outside the normal course of government operations.

His first attempt, shortly after he took office and in response to the crusade of the Collier forces in the Pueblo lands question, was the establishment of an Advisory Council on Indian Affairs, more generally known as the Committee of One Hundred. In the spring of 1923 Work appointed about one hundred men and women to the committee "for the purpose of discussion and recommendation on the Government's Indian policy," and a meeting was called for December 12 and 13. The membership represented all the groups concerned with Indian affairs—Collier and his associates, members of the Indian Rights Association and the Board of Indian Commissioners, anthropologists and missionaries, political figures and educators, journalists and military men, and a sizable group of educated Indians.[34]

Although Work called the council "a landmark in the history of the Government's effort to handle the Indian question" and spoke of its importance in "unifying the thought of representative citizens, in arousing an informed public interest and discussion, and in presenting constructive measures for the benefit of the Indian," in fact the Committee of One Hundred accomplished little or nothing. Both the critics and the supporters of the Indian Office hoped to turn the conference to their own advantage, but the conservatives won out in the appointment of Arthur C. Parker, the Seneca ethnologist, as chairman, and the resolutions of the committee offered no radical recommendations. John Collier called it "the most representative conference on Indian affairs ever held" and spoke of the goodwill and spirit of mutuality exhibited, but he concluded: "Pre-conference poli-

---

34. Work tells of the establishment of the Committee of One Hundred and gives a list of persons invited to take part in *Indian Policies*, pp. iv–v.

tics and the absence of fundamental concepts held in common by the members defeated the results. Not one fundamental proposition (save in health matters where the conference merely echoed a previous official decision) was put across." The conference was clearly not the critical appraisal of Indian affairs that the reformers had called for.[35]

As the critics stepped up their attacks, Secretary Work took more constructive action. In the spring of 1926, at the instigation of the Board of Indian Commissioners, he began conversations with the Institute for Government Research, an independent organization that became the political division of the Brookings Institution, about a comprehensive survey of Indian affairs. On June 12, 1926, he formally requested W. F. Willoughby, the director of the institute, to undertake such a study "in a thoroughly impartial and scientific spirit with the object of making the result of its work a constructive contribution in this difficult field of government administration." With financial support from John D. Rockefeller, Jr., the work quickly got under way.[36]

The man chosen to direct the survey was Lewis Meriam, a permanent staff member of the Institute for Government Research, a Harvard graduate with two law degrees and long experience in technical study of government operations. He epitomized the concern of the institute with efficiency and expertise in government administration and was "a model of the modern scientific expert." To aid Meriam there was a staff of nine technical specialists in the fields of law, economic conditions, health, education, agriculture, family life, and the conditions of Indians in urban communities, and one "Indian adviser," the Winnebago Henry Roe Cloud, a Yale graduate and head of the American Indian Institute. It was a stellar group of eight men and two women, "persons highly qualified as specialists in their respective fields, scientific in their approach, not sensationalists, and free from preconceived views and opinions that would interfere with their impartiality and fairness in gathering and interpreting

35. The resolutions of the Committee of One Hundred are printed in *House Document* no. 149, 68–1, serial 8273. Work replied to each of the resolutions in *Indian Policies*. A mimeographed copy of the sketchy minutes kept by Matthew K. Sniffen, which contains a list of the sixty-six persons who actually attended, is in OIA, Board of Indian Commissioners, Reference Material, Committee of One Hundred; this file also contains Malcolm McDowell to members of the Board of Indian Commissioners, January 8, 1924, and other material on the conference. John Collier described the conference at considerable length in "The Red Slaves of Oklahoma," *Sunset* 52 (March 1924): 95–100.

36. There is a detailed account of the undertaking in Willoughby's letter of transmittal and in the foreword to *The Problem of Indian Administration* [Meriam Report] (Baltimore: Johns Hopkins Press, 1928), pp. vii–x, 56–85. For the part of the Board of Indian Commissioners, see minutes of January 26, 1926, OIA, Minutes of the Board of Indian Commissioners.

the facts."[37] In seven months of fieldwork the members of the staff visited ninety-five reservations, agencies, hospitals, and schools, as well as many communities of Indians who had moved from the reservations; they made a remarkably thorough investigation of all aspects of government work touching the Indians. The report was submitted to Secretary Work on February 21, 1928, and published by the Johns Hopkins Press under the title *The Problem of Indian Administration*.[38]

To understand the report's critical description of conditions among the Indians and in the Indian service, one must appreciate the approach outlined by Willoughby when he submitted it. The survey rejected the plan of comparing existing conditions with conditions that had existed at the time various activities undertaken for the Indians were begun—an approach that would have judged the progress made and evaluated the work of the employees on that basis, taking into consideration the limitations imposed by appropriations. Instead, the survey compared the activities of the Indian service with other agencies, public and private, engaged in comparable work for the general population or other special groups and thus compared "present conditions with the practical ideal." "The object of the Institute," Willoughby asserted, "was not to say whether the Indian Service has done well with the funds at its disposal but rather to look to the future and insofar as possible to indicate what remains to be done to adjust the Indians to the prevailing civilization so that they may maintain themselves in the presence of that civilization according at least to a minimum standard of health and decency." In other words, the object was not "to take sides for or against the Indian Office," but to point the way, through constructive criticism, toward improvement.[39]

37. Donald T. Critchlow, "Lewis Meriam, Expertise, and Indian Reform," *Historian* 43 (May 1981): 328–31; *Problem of Indian Administration*, pp. 57, 79–85. The technical experts were Ray A. Brown, assistant professor of law, University of Wisconsin (legal aspects of Indian problems); Henry Roe Cloud, president of the American Indian Institute, Wichita, Kansas (Indian adviser); Edward Everett Dale, professor of history, University of Oklahoma (economic conditions); Emma Duke (conditions of Indian migrants to urban communities); Herbert R. Edwards, medical field secretary of the National Tuberculosis Association (health); Fayette A. McKenzie, professor of sociology, Juniata College, Huntington, Pennsylvania (existing material relating to Indians); Mary Louise Mark, professor of sociology, Ohio State University (family life and activities of women); W. Carson Ryan, Jr., professor of education, Swarthmore College (education); William J. Spillman, agricultural economist, United States Department of Agriculture (agriculture).

38. There is a table showing the visits of the staff and an excellent description of the methods of the survey in the report, pp. 60–79. The "General Summary and Findings and Recommendations" and "Recommendations for Immediate Action" were published as a pamphlet, *The Problem of Indian Administration: Summary of Findings and Recommendations* (Washington: Institute for Government Research, 1928).

39. *Problem of Indian Administration*, pp. viii–ix.

The report, as was to be expected, found conditions far short of the "practical ideal." It reported deplorable conditions in health, education, and economic welfare and found incompetent and inefficient personnel. Almost nothing that it found met the progressive standards that governed the views of the survey team. The recommendations were in line with the findings and the outlook of the experts: generous appropriations to improve the administration of the Indian service in health care, education, and economic development and the institution of a Division of Planning and Development in the Indian Office that would consist of a group of experts not burdened with the details of routine administration and with time free for research and planning of Indian programs. The report admitted that for several years the necessary additional funds might double the present appropriations, but it spoke of this as "the economy of efficiency," for if the Indian service were brought to an acceptable level of efficiency, there could be a gradual reduction of expenses as more and more Indians became self-supporting and Indian services were turned over to state and local governments.[40]

The Meriam Report was not a radical innovative document seeking to overturn existing policy. "Meriam and his associates," a recent study of Meriam concludes, "were less interested in changing current governmental Indian policies than with ensuring that existing policies were implemented efficiently through a properly organized administration run by well-trained specialists." It was asking, in fact, what commissioners of Indian affairs had been asking since the beginning of the century: more money at once so that the process of preparing the Indian wards to enter American society as self-supporting, independent citizens could be efficiently speeded up and the Indian problem of the federal government dissolved. After the report was completed, Meriam spent the next four years seeking, unsuccessfully, to reform the Indian service by means of a reorganization that would make possible more efficient administration.[41]

40. Ibid., pp. 50–51.

41. Critchlow, "Lewis Meriam," p. 327; see pp. 335–44 for Meriam's work toward reform of the Indian Office. Warren K. Moorehead, a member of the Board of Indian Commissioners, severely criticized the Meriam Report for not explicitly noting the great many previous investigations and reports that had turned up similar material. "Research men in both History and Science," he said, "are careful to give credit to those who proceeded [sic] them, especially where similar recommendations or theories of the identical sort and covering the same field are presented." He declared, "It is true—although regrettable—that much old straw already threshed by others has been industriously put through the machine again." Warren King Moorehead, "An Analysis of The Problem of Indian Administration Published by the Institute for Government Research," a 23-page statement, copy in OIA, Board of Indian Commissioners, Reference Material, Indian Service.

The moderate tone and scientific impartiality of the Meriam Report almost guaranteed a favorable acceptance. Secretary Work and Commissioner Burke accepted the criticism with equanimity and set about to study the report in detail, and reform groups appreciated both the confirmation of their charges that all was not well and the recommendations for betterment. The Indian Rights Association called a meeting of interested persons at Atlantic City on December 14 and 15, 1928, to consider the report. The assembly unanimously approved the report and declared that it "constitutes the basis upon which to proceed constructively to secure the early reorganization of the Indian Service, and the adequate support of a modernized agency devoted to the human welfare of the American Indian."[42]

John Collier and the American Indian Defense Association received the Meriam Report favorably; Collier thought it had set the stage for a radical change in the government's Indian policy.[43] But these critics seemed to notice most the shortcomings that the survey discovered, and they used them as a whip with which to chastise the government for its mismanagement of Indian affairs. In an open letter addressed to the presidential candidates of 1928, the American Indian Defense Association, after calling attention to Helen Hunt Jackson's indictment in *A Century of Dishonor*, asserted

> that the record of the past is being rivalled at the present day through similar violation of obligations, through the misuse and misapplication of property held in guardianship, through an arbitrary and tyrannical denial of the fundamental safeguards to life, liberty and property which the Constitution guarantees to other citizens of the land:
> —and that the governmental Bureau to which we have entrusted our guardianship is, ignorantly or willfully, annihilating its 250,000 wards through starvation enforced by the waste and misapplication of their income, through the creation of centers for the spread of disease, and through the denial of health service that might serve, in some measure, to counteract the effects of its other activities.

42. The Board of Indian Commissioners issued a report on the Meriam Report on January 10, 1929, and a committee appointed by the secretary of the interior submitted a report on December 5, 1929; there are copies of these reports in Indian Rights Association Papers, Historical Society of Pennsylvania (reel 124, items 115 and 125). The work of the Atlantic City Conference is reported in *Report of the Indian Rights Association*, 1928, pp. 4, 14–17, and in Francis Fisher Kane, "East and West: The Atlantic City Conference on the American Indian," *Survey* 61 (January 15, 1929): 472–74. See also *The Atlantic City Conference* (Philadelphia: Indian Rights Association, 1928).

43. "Now It Can Be Told," *American Indian Life*, June 1928, pp. 1–14.

Appended to support these charges were a dozen pages of quotations from the Meriam Report.[44]

While the Meriam Report was in preparation, the secretary of the interior instituted a companion investigation. Because the Meriam survey team lacked specialists in the important and complex problems related to Indian irrigation projects, a separate study was undertaken. For this task Work appointed two irrigation experts—Porter J. Preston, an engineer from the Bureau of Reclamation, and Charles A. Engle, supervising engineer from the Office of Indian Affairs—to make a critical study of irrigation projects. Their report, submitted on June 8, 1928, was a severe indictment of the government's irrigation program on Indian reservations.[45]

The enemies of Burke's administration in the end were not satisfied with the moderate tone of the Meriam Report. Even before the survey team had turned in its findings, Collier aggressively supported a move in the Senate for a full-scale congressional investigation of the administration of Indian affairs. Senator William H. King of Utah on December 17, 1927, introduced a resolution to "make a general survey of the condition of the Indians and of the operation and effect of the laws which Congress has passed for the civilization and protection of Indian tribes; to investigate the relation of the Bureau of Indian Affairs to the persons and property of Indians and the effects of the acts, regulations, and administration of said bureau upon the health, improvement, and welfare of the Indians."[46]

In hearings on the resolution before the Senate Committee on Indian Affairs in January 1928, Burke insisted that the Meriam survey team had made an extensive study and that its forthcoming report would obviate any need for a Senate investigation, but Collier argued the necessity, and the Senate passed the resolution on February 2.[47] Thus began a series of hearings and investigations that ran from November 1928 to August 1943

44. *Our Indian Citizens, Their Crisis: A Letter Addressed to the Presidential Candidates and a Supporting Statement* (Washington: American Indian Defense Association, 1928). A particularly strong attack on the bureau by Collier was published just before the Meriam Report appeared. John Collier, "The Vanquished Indian," *Nation* 126 (January 11, 1928): 38–41.

45. Porter J. Preston and Charles A. Engle, "Report of Advisers on Irrigation on Indian Reservations," June 8, 1928, printed in "Survey of Conditions of the Indians in the United States," *Hearings before a Subcommittee of the Committee on Indian Affairs, United States Senate, 71st Congress, 2d Session* (1930), part 6, pp. 2210–2661. The substance of the report is treated below, p. 894.

46. *Congressional Record*, 69: 786.

47. "Survey of Conditions of the Indians in the United States," *Hearings before the Committee on Indian Affairs, United States Senate, 70th Congress, 1st Session, Pursuant to S. Res. 79* (1928). There is testimony of Frear, Collier, Meritt, Gertrude Bonnin, Clyde Kelly, and Burke, January 10 and 13, 1928.

and resulted in 23,069 printed pages of reports in forty-one parts.[48] Under the prodding of Collier and of Representative Frear, the tone of the subcommittee's questioning of Burke was hostile. Burke finally exploded, accusing Senator W. B. Pine, one of the committee members, of cooperating with Collier in an attempt "to hinder and obstruct the efforts of myself and other officials of the Indian Bureau to carry on its administration, and whose purpose is to overthrow the aims and policies of the Bureau for the advancement and protection of the Indians and their property."[49] When Burke testified in January 1929 he was nearly sixty-eight years old and at the end of his public career. On March 4, 1929, he submitted his resignation.

Agitation for reform in Indian affairs passed then to a new administration with new men in charge of Indian affairs, from whom, at first, much was expected.[50]

48. "Survey of Conditions of the Indians in the United States," *Hearings before a Subcommittee of the Committee on Indian Affairs, United States Senate, 70th Congress to 78th Congress* (1928–1943).

49. "Survey of Conditions," part 3, p. 1315. See also *Senate Report* no. 1490, 70–2, serial 8978.

50. Discussion of Indian affairs under the Hoover administration is below in chapter 36.

CHAPTER 32

Education
for Self-Support

The Indian School System.

Public Schools for Indians.

Courses of Study.

Success and Failure.

No means was more important than education in leading the Indians to-ward the goal of self-support. The ideal suffused all that was planned and proposed for Indian schools as the nation moved into the twentieth cen-tury. The superintendent of Indian schools, Estelle Reel, at the end of 1900 declared: "We are aiming at the unification of the Indian school system in all that tends to the formation of self-supporting, God-fearing Indian men and women." The emphasis in education continued to be heavily on prac-tical work. "A civilization without the elements of labor in it rests on a foundation of sand," Reel said. "Labor is the basis of all lasting civilization and the most potent influence for good in the world. Whenever any race, of its own volition, begins to labor its future is assured." The developing school system for the Indians was intended to make this possible and to fit Indian youth for the world into which they were to be absorbed.[1]

1. CIA Report, 1900, serial 4101, pp. 431–32. Despite the importance of education, there has been little scholarly writing about the Indian schools of the early twentieth century except for some studies of individual schools. There is a long chapter in Freder-ick E. Hoxie, "Beyond Savagery: The Campaign to Assimilate the American Indians, 1880–1920" (Ph.D. dissertation, Brandeis University, 1977), pp. 488–561, but I disagree with the author's thesis that the nature of Indian policy changed radically in the new century.

THE INDIAN SCHOOL SYSTEM

The aggressive promotion of Indian schools that began with Thomas J. Morgan in 1889 had accomplished much by the end of the century. Excluding the schools of the New York Indians (which were under state control) and the schools in the Indian Territory, Commissioner William A. Jones in 1900 reported impressive statistics. There were twenty-five off-reservation industrial schools with a total enrollment of 7,430. The largest (with over 1,000 pupils) was Carlisle, with Phoenix and Haskell (600–700 pupils) next in order. Eighteen of the schools had been established since 1890. There were eighty-one boarding schools on the reservations, which made the necessary modifications in the elaborate industrial training that the better-equipped off-reservation schools could offer but pursued the same policy; in addition they stood "as object lessons among the homes of the Indians" to present them with "ideals for emulation." These schools were smaller—rarely with a capacity as large as 200—and the total enrollment was 9,600. Next was a collection of government day schools with 30–40 pupils each, located in remote parts of the reservations and conducted by a single teacher and a housekeeper, if possible a man and wife team. These schools totaled 147 and enrolled about 5,000 pupils. There were also some 250 students in twenty-two public schools, the modest seeds of a program that would soon blossom forth with larger and larger proportions of the Indian students, and Jones counted thirty-two contract schools with an enrollment of 2,800 and twenty-two mission schools with 1,275 students.[2] The tremendous growth of the government's commitment can be seen in Tables 7 and 8.

Jones justified the increased expenditures by what had been accomplished in educating Indian children, and he noted that the figures compared favorably with the costs of similar white institutions. "The amount appropriated for the year may appear large," he admitted, "but it is insignificant compared with the value of the lands of these people which have been purchased or obtained from them by treaties. It is a small sum compared with the cost of the Indian wars of the United States and with what it would cost to hold them as semiprisoners upon reservations and feed them for an indefinite term of years. Humanity and economical considerations demand these appropriations, so that all the Indians may be educated to become self-supporting producers instead of idle consumers and mischief-makers."[3]

2. CIA Report, 1900, serial 4101, pp. 16–21. Average attendance figures were generally lower than enrollment figures.
3. CIA Report, 1900, serial 4101, p. 44.

TABLE 7: Number of Indian Schools and Average Attendance,
1877–1900

Selected Years	Boarding Schools		Day Schools		Total	
	Number	Average Attendance	Number	Average Attendance	Number	Average Attendance
1877	48	—	102	—	150	3,598
1881	68	—	106	—	174	4,976
1885	114	6,201	86	1,942	200	8,143
1889	136	9,146	103	2,406	239	11,552
1893	156	13,635	119	2,668	275	16,303
1897	145	15,026	143	3,650	288	18,676
1900	153	17,708	154	3,860	307	21,568

SOURCE: CIA Report, 1900, serial 4101, p. 23.

TABLE 8: Annual Appropriations for the Support
of Indian Schools, 1877–1901

Year	Appropriation	Year	Appropriation
1877	$20,000	1893	$2,315,612
1881	75,000	1897	2,517,265
1885	992,800	1901	3,080,367
1889	1,348,015		

SOURCE: CIA Report, 1900, serial 4101, p. 44.

Although Jones spoke with pride of the increase in the number of off-reservation boarding schools during the previous decade, in fact a strong movement against such schools had already begun—and Jones was one of the leaders. Those schools, of which the Carlisle Indian Industrial School was the first and prime example, had represented Richard Henry Pratt's strong insistence on "bringing the Indian to civilization and keeping him there," immersing the Indian children in white ways, both at school and in the "outing" system, far away from the traditional influences of camp life on the reservations. By means of such schools, which Pratt hoped would be multiplied until all Indians were cared for, the rising generation would be abruptly and completely inducted into white society, where Pratt expected them to remain. But hard reality quickly punctured the dream. In the first place, it was difficult to fill the schools with suitable pupils, as Carlisle itself experienced, and the pressures to "collect students" (as the saying went) in order to keep the off-reservation institutions at an efficient capacity led to abuses and tensions with the teachers and superintendents on the reservations, to say nothing of the Indian parents. In the second place, it was soon apparent that the graduates of such schools did not stay to take their places in white society but drifted back to their homes, and the problem of these "returned students" and their readjustment to reservation life attracted much attention. The interest and hope that had once been pinned on the off-reservation schools was diverted to the schools on the reservations. There schools could be better adapted to the actual life the students would live when they left school, and the educational center could widen its immediate influence to include parents and the whole Indian community.

Jones began his attack in 1901. Although he still spoke highly of the educational efforts of off-reservation schools, he began to voice some criticism. "Analysis of the data obtained by this office," he said, "indicates that the methods of education which have been pursued for the past generation have not produced the results anticipated."[4] To the three obstacles in the way of the Indian "toward independence and self-support"—rations, distribution of money to Indians, and general leasing of allotments—he now added the existing system of education. What bothered him was the contrast between the boarding schools and the ordinary life of the Indian. Transported from the poverty of his home to the affluence of the government school, where everything was provided for him and he lived in relative luxury without any special effort on his part, the Indian at the end of his school years returned to the squalid conditions of his home and was left to make his way against the ignorance and bigotry of his tribe.[5]

The next year Jones came out unequivocally for reservation schools:

> With conditions as they are, and which probably will remain for many years, the strength and foundation of Indian education must be

---

4. CIA Report, 1901, serial 4290, pp. 39–41. In Education Circular no. 55, October 10, 1901, sent to agents and superintendents, Jones had said: "It is believed essential to the ultimate civilization of the Indian that he should be gotten away from the reservations as much as possible. The work of the reservation day and boarding schools is not by any means minimized, but the transfer of pupils to non-reservation schools brings them into broader contact with civilization, and tends more to enlarge their aspirations, and cause them to seek citizenship earlier than otherwise." OIA, Circulars Issued by the Education Division, entry no. 718. But Jones soon sang a different tune.

5. CIA Report, 1901, serial 4290, p. 2.

the reservation boarding schools. They are located at the home of the parent, where he can from time to time see his child; while the child, on the other hand, during the evolutionary process it is undergoing, does not get out of touch with its home and people. For a generation or more the adult Indians are fixed to their present homes, and therefore the school is a nucleus for the best elements, while its employees are brought in contact with and still hold an influence over the boy and girl who have left its walls. The Government officials become more and more friends and advisers to their grown-up pupils. Thus the influence of the school expands in widening circles. The child thus educated does not get out of touch with its future environment, and while its talents may not have been as completely unfolded as at a nonreservation school, it is probably better fitted for association with those with whom it must make its home.

Jones concluded that the number of off-reservation schools could be materially reduced and the remainder, without increasing their capacity, could be refined and developed, and he said flatly, "More reservation boarding schools and less nonreservation institutions are required." He predicted that in another generation, as graduates of the reservation boarding schools learned to live by the sweat of their brow, the boarding schools, too, could be phased out and replaced by day schools.[6]

The shifting emphasis in the school system could be accomplished only gradually, but Jones struck immediately at the abuses that had arisen in collecting students on the reservation to fill the off-reservation schools. The competition for students was stiff, and elaborate pressures and promises were the stock-in-trade of the collecting agents, who accomplished their task, the commissioner said, "partly by cajolery and partly by threats; partly by bribery and partly by fraud; partly by persuasion and partly by force." On November 6, 1902, Jones assigned specific recruiting territory to each school, within which the collecting agents were to limit their activities. Only Carlisle and Haskell were permitted to attract students from throughout the United States.[7]

Jones continued to fight the off-reservation schools, whose number he found excessive, and he asserted as he left office that "the fallacious idea of 'bringing the Indian into civilization and keeping him there' was made too prominent." To him such schools were a waste of public money, for they brought an Indian to an eastern school to "educate him for years upon the

6. CIA Report, 1902, serial 4458, pp. 25–31.

7. CIA Report, 1901, serial 4290, p. 2; "Rules for the Collection of Pupils for Nonreservation Schools" (Education Circular no. 85), November 6, 1902, OIA, Circulars Issued by the Education Division, entry no. 718.

theory that his reservation home is a hell on earth, when inevitably he must and does return to his home." He concluded: "That the policy is wrong has been sufficiently demonstrated to justify its discontinuance. Home education of the average Indian, not out of his environment, but near his own people, will and does produce lasting results."[8]

When he left office, Jones could point to modest developments in his new policy. Although the number of off-reservation schools was the same as in 1900 and their enrollment had increased, the largest growth had been in the reservation boarding schools, which in 1904 numbered ninety with an enrollment of 11,514. The total attendance in all schools stood at 25,104 and appropriations at $3,880,740.[9]

The movement away from off-reservation schools was carried a step further by Francis E. Leupp. After two years of hinting at "a marked change in the Indian educational establishment, always in the direction of greater simplicity and a more logical fitness to the end for which it was designed," Leupp announced his plans. He intended to enlarge the system of day schools as opposed to any increase in boarding schools and to prefer reservation boarding schools to those off the reservation. It was a question, he said, of "whether we are to carry civilization to the Indian or carry the Indian to civilization, and the former seems to me infinitely the wiser plan." In 1906 Leupp had reported with pleasure an increase of day schools, for such schools "radiate knowledge of better habits of life and higher morality through the tepees, cabins, and camps to which the children return every night." He considered them "the greatest general civilizing agency of any through which we try to operate upon the rising generation." He saw the boarding schools as an anomaly, "simply educational almshouses" he called them, in which everything was provided for the Indians and nothing won by hard work. Although he realized that a sudden shift from boarding schools to day schools could not be made at once, he intended to give the movement a start, for aside from the educational superiority of day schools for the Indians he noted, too, that education of an Indian in such a school cost only one-fourth or one-fifth of the amount needed in a boarding school.[10]

---

8. CIA Report, 1904, serial 4798, pp. 32–33. Jones's report was dated October 17, 1904. Just four months earlier, on June 15, Pratt had been removed from his post as head of Carlisle. It was a new era.

9. CIA Report, 1904, serial 4798, pp. 39–49. In this report Jones surveyed the advances made in the seven years since he took office in 1897; he painted a very rosy picture of accomplishments and of Indian potential.

10. CIA Report, 1906, serial 5118, p. 44; CIA Report, 1907, serial 5296, pp. 17–26. See also Education Circular no. 161, July 1, 1907, OIA, Circulars Issued by the Education Division, entry no. 718.

Leupp, knowing that "the resistant force of error long persisted in is great," willingly answered the criticisms of his plan that arose. The old system, he insisted, had "passed the height of its usefulness, and henceforward must be tolerated only as a survival and allowed to disintegrate by degrees." He did not, however, intend to let the transition take place of itself. To rein in the off-reservation schools and prevent "future annoyance and squabbling over children," he tightened the regulations governing the collecting agents. Then he abrogated altogether the assigned recruiting areas that Jones had set up and directed that "no collecting agent shall canvass any territory in the interest of a non-reservation school." Indian parents who wanted to send their children away to such a school could designate the one they wanted, and the superintendents were to make the necessary arrangements following the parents' wishes. All that was allowed to the schools themselves was a certain amount of promotional literature and correspondence to point out the special merits of their institutions. Leupp sent a special directive to the reservation superintendents, directing their compliance. "No pressure must be brought to bear, by you or any other Government employee, to force any child into a nonreservation school, or to keep him from going to a school designated by the parents or guardian."[11]

Leupp could not get Congress to cut appropriations for well established off-reservation schools that had popular support—like Carlisle and Hampton—so he undertook to turn them into specialized institutions. Carlisle could give special emphasis to applied skills whose products found their largest market in the East; Haskell could concentrate on its business course, training Indians in stenography, typewriting, and bookkeeping to supply the market for Indian clerical labor in the Midwest; and Sherman Institute, in the heart of the orange-growing region of California, could find a large place in its curriculum for fruit culture.[12] Gradually the off-reservation schools that persisted came to be thought of as "advanced" schools (that is, of upper grades and eventually some high school courses) in which students who had completed the limited courses at day schools and reservation boarding schools might transfer to further their education. But in order to keep enrollment up, most off-reservation schools continued to offer primary and elementary education as well.

11. CIA Report, 1907, serial 5296, pp. 24–26; CIA Report, 1908, serial 5453, pp. 17–22; Education Circular no. 157, June 12, 1907, and Education Circulars nos. 216 and 217, June 2, 1908, OIA, Circulars Issued by the Education Division, entry no. 718.

12. CIA Report, 1908, serial 5453, pp. 21–22. Strong feelings against off-reservation schools continued in some circles; see O. H. Lipps to Cato Sells, June 7, 1918, OIA CCF, General Service 800, 59854.–1918.

Leupp had plans for everything he touched. He proposed changes in the reservation boarding schools and sought to improve the day schools. His fertile mind suggested a simpler construction of the schools, and he experimented in the warm, dry Southwest with buildings open to the air (called "bird cages"); for the still nomadic tribes he advocated "portable schools," which could follow the Indians from encampment to encampment.[13] When he left office, Leupp reported a modest but noticeable trend toward the educational changes he had promoted. There was one additional off-reservation school (authorized, he was careful to point out, before he became commissioner), but those schools showed a decrease of average attendance, whereas the day schools had grown from 138 when he took office to 167 (with an enrollment of 5,535).[14]

Indian education under Jones and Leupp was colored by the strong personality and views of Estelle Reel, who was appointed superintendent of Indian schools on June 20, 1898, to replace William N. Hailmann. Raised in Illinois, Reel had moved to Wyoming to teach in the public schools, and after a successful term as superintendent of schools for Laramie County, she had been elected state superintendent of schools. She was effective in that post and demonstrated not only her educational ability but her business capacity as well. Support for her appointment to the national post was strong—as an educator, to be sure, but also as a Republican and a woman from one of the four western states with woman suffrage. Wyoming's two senators, Francis E. Warren and Clarence D. Clark, pushed her candidacy as a means of drawing the woman suffrage states into the Republican fold, and an array of United States senators, Republican League clubs, women's organizations, national educational leaders, and prominent Protestant churchmen all added words of praise. Reel was described as physically strong and equal to any man for the job, yet withal very refined and womanly and the kind of person who would be like a mother to Indian children. She was remembered by one who met her for her "bright, cheery, breezy, western ways."[15]

Reel brought her professional educational interests to her office. She was a strong supporter of summer institutes for Indian school superinten-

13. CIA Report, 1908, serial 5453, pp. 23–25. The open air schools were tried at a Mission Indian school in California, but they were not widely adopted. See reports and photographs of the buildings in OIA CCF, General Service 806, 39393–1910.

14. CIA Report, 1908, serial 5453, pp. 41–42. See the statistics on attendance, number of schools, and appropriations for 1877–1908, pp. 53–54.

15. Francis E. Warren to Willis Van Devanter, October 27, 1897; Warren and C. D. Clark to the president, February 15, 1898; Joseph M. Craig to the president, February 1, 1898; Frank A. Hill to Estelle Reel, March 25, 1898, and numerous other letters of recommendation in OSI CCF 22–36, box 2179.

dents, teachers, and other employees, and in 1899 persuaded the National Educational Association (NEA) to institute a Department of Indian Education. The annual meetings of the NEA then provided an excellent forum for the discussion of topics of concern to Indian schools, both by the school personnel and by prominent outside educators. School personnel were urged to attend the institutes and the NEA meetings and were allowed academic leave at their regular salaries in order to attend.[16] Reel's reports of inspections of individual schools, her annual reports to the commissioner of Indian affairs, and the circulars she issued to school superintendents all show her insistence on practical industrial education for the Indians. In 1901 she drew up a new course of study that incorporated her educational philosophy for the Indians.[17]

With the change in presidential administrations in 1909, however, Reel's days were numbered. When rumors arose that she was to be replaced by a man, her many friends rallied to her support and deluged President William Howard Taft and Secretary of the Interior R. A. Ballinger with commendations and pleas for her retention. But Congress in its appropriations for fiscal year 1911 eliminated support for her position, and she left office on June 30, 1910. Ballinger asserted that her work had been "in large sense a duplication of the work of the Indian Office" and that in the best interests of the service the position should be discontinued.[18] Instead, Commissioner Robert G. Valentine, in what he termed "an improvement of signal importance" in the administration of the Indian school service, divided the country into six districts with a supervisor in charge of each, and a chief supervisor of schools was placed over them all.[19]

16. Minutes of the Board of Directors, National Educational Association, July 11, 1899, in National Educational Association, *Journal of Proceedings and Addresses*, 1899, pp. 35–36. The *Journal* from 1900 to 1908 carried a section on the Department of Indian Education, including transcripts and abstracts of the talks given. A list of the topics, 1900–1906, is given in the *Journal*, 1906, pp. 650–51. For a brief account of the NEA's involvement in Indian education, see Edgar B. Wesley, *NEA: The First Hundred Years: The Building of the Teaching Profession* (New York: Harper and Brothers, 1957), pp. 289–91.

17. Reel's annual reports as superintendent of Indian schools for the years 1898–1906 are printed in the annual reports of the commissioner of Indian affairs. A sampling of her reports on individual schools is in OIA, Special Series A, File 66415/07 (Correspondence of Estelle Reel). Her instructions on such matters as curriculum, employee reading circles, school gardens, attendance at institutes, and the making and arrangement of beds are found in OIA, Circulars Issued by the Superintendent of Indian Schools, 1899–1908, entry no. 719. The 1901 course of study is discussed below, pp. 827–29.

18. R. A. Ballinger to R. H. Pratt, February 10, 1910, and C. F. Hauke to the secretary of the interior, July 15, 1910, OSI CCF 22–36, box 2179. Letters in support of Reel's retention are in this file.

19. CIA Report, 1910, serial 5976, pp. 13–14. The top position, which was in a sense

PUBLIC SCHOOLS FOR INDIANS

The final goal in revamping the Indian school system was to disband the strictly Indian schools and let the Indians enroll in the public schools of the states. The germ of this idea had been planted in Commissioner Morgan's time: he saw as a final culmination of his elaborately systematized educational plan the movement of Indian children into the public school system he so cherished. At first Morgan advocated the mixing of children from many tribes in the industrial schools like Carlisle, but ultimately he envisaged the time when the mixing would take place in regular public schools. "Indeed," he had said, "it is reasonable to expect that at no distant day, when the Indians shall have all taken up their lands in severalty and have become American citizens, there will cease to be any necessity for Indian schools maintained by the government."[20] The time was more distant than Morgan had hoped, but little by little the balance began to swing toward public schools as white settlements multiplied in the West and the opened reservations stimulated the establishment of district schools in the neighborhoods of allotted Indians. The trickle of students in the public schools that Jones reported in 1900 eventually grew to a sizable flood.

In 1912 Commissioner Valentine noted that a larger number of Indian pupils were in public schools than ever before. It was, he said, the "final step" and the "way out" for Indian education. The advance in enrollment in public schools was so rapid that two years later almost as many Indian pupils were in these schools as in all the Indian schools under government control. Commissioner Cato Sells rejoiced in this development, which he himself studiously encouraged. He praised what he saw on the allotted reservations, where white settlers were moving in and organizing district public schools, which the Indian children, too, could attend. "This process of disintegration of the Indian reservations," Sells claimed, "is a splendid example of the elimination of the Indian as a distinct problem for the Federal or the State governments. The most distinctive element aiding in this growth is the public school. In the acquiring of a practical knowledge of conversational English and in the opportunities that are there afforded the Indians to learn and appreciate the 'better ways' of the white man the public schools are the trysting place in the winning of the race."[21]

a continuation of the office of superintendent of Indian schools, was first held by Hervey B. Peairs, who had been superintendent of the Haskell Indian School.

20. Thomas J. Morgan, "Education of American Indians," *Lake Mohonk Conference Proceedings,* 1889, p. 19.

21. CIA Report, 1912, serial 6409, p. 37; CIA Report, 1914, serial 6815, p. 9. In 1912 there were 17,011 Indians in public schools; in 1914 there were 27,755 in government schools, 25,180 in public schools, and 4,943 in mission and private schools. CIA Report, 1912, serial 6409, pp. 181–93; CIA Report, 1914, serial 6815, p. 136.

In his Declaration of Policy in 1917, Sells moved to eliminate from the government Indian schools all pupils whose parents could pay for their education and who had public school facilities at or near their homes. And in 1919, in what he called a radical departure on enrollment, he tightened the requirements for attendance at government-supported schools by forcefully instructing the superintendents to eliminate children of parents who had received patents in fee for their allotments and those who were "near-whites," except in particular cases of which the commissioner would be the final judge. If there were "at least average" public school facilities at hand, Indian students were not to be sent to off-reservation schools for vocational training, even if the government school might in fact be better. The question to be asked was "Does such Indian boy or girl have the same school privileges in the community in which he or she lives that other children enjoy?" As a result of this policy, Sells in 1920 listed government boarding schools that had been abolished in Oklahoma, Washington, Colorado, South Dakota, North Dakota, Wisconsin, Minnesota, and Kansas, as well as a number of day schools.[22]

The flow of Indian children into the public schools continued. In 1923 Commissioner Burke called it "unprecedented." Five years later there were 34,103 Indians in public schools, compared with 25,174 in government schools and 7,621 in mission and private schools. In areas where there were few public schools and where the Indians continued as wards of the government, however, the federal Indian schools were absolutely necessary, and Congress during the 1920s year by year appropriated more money for these schools, until in 1928 the total appropriation stood at $5,923,000. Both Sells and Burke were especially concerned about the large number of Indians in the Southwest, notably the Navajos, who lagged behind in school facilities and school enrollment. Burke saw "almost an emergency demand for additional school privileges to save non-English speaking children from reaching their majority unfitted for American citizenship." In 1928 there were still 11,419 eligible children not in school.[23]

The federal government paid tuition for the Indian children attending public schools because many Indians were not taxed, and the additional burden of instruction could not well be borne by the states. Congress in 1914 provided $20,000 for such tuition; in 1917 the sum was raised to $200,000, and in 1924 it reached $350,000. Yet the increases did not meet the demand, and many applications were refused for lack of funds. The appropriation of $375,000 for fiscal year 1929 was exhausted before the year

22. CIA Report, 1917, serial 7358, p. 4; circulars to superintendents, July 29, 1919, in CIA Report, 1919, serial 7706, pp. 18–21, and CIA Report, 1920, serial 7820, pp. 13–14.
23. CIA Report, 1920, serial 7820, p. 14; CIA Report, 1923, p. 1; CIA Report, 1928, pp. 2–3, 49.

ran out.[24] Where Indian children were entitled to public school education according to state constitutions, as in California and Oklahoma, the comptroller of the treasury ruled that it was illegal for the federal government to pay the tuition, and where Indian parents paid taxes the same principle held.[25]

The enthusiastic promotion of public schools for Indians and the favorable reports about snowballing enrollment, however, covered over some disturbing facts. "Enrollment" did not necessarily mean regular attendance, and as the numbers in district schools multiplied, so did a realization that the solution of the Indian school problem was not yet in sight. The Board of Indian Commissioners, for example, although in general an uncritical ally of the Indian Office in the period, sounded a warning early in the 1920s as reports of observation of the Indians in the public schools came in. Too often, the board found, the Indians enrolled in public schools were "practically non-attendants." The irregularity of attendance had several causes. Indian children were often ridiculed by their white classmates and would then refuse to return to class. The poverty of Indian families also affected attendance. In some areas whites opposed the admission of Indians. But the principal cause was that Indian pupils were simply not competent enough in English to mix in classes with white children their own age, and older Indian boys and girls were ashamed and uncomfortable sitting in classes with younger white children. The board in 1921 called the public schools "an end to be patiently pursued, but it cannot be wisely hastened." Two years later it flatly declared: "In our opinion the Indian Service schools, day, reservation, and nonreservation boarding, provide the best, the speediest, and the most satisfactory means for educating the Indian youth."[26] The movement toward public schools, which had looked so promising to government officials, continued, and increasing percentages of Indians were cared for by them, but the Indian school system put together after 1890 did not wither away. Government schools became a permanent fixture on the reservation landscape.[27]

24. 38 *United States Statutes* 584; 39 *United States Statutes* 970; 45 *United States Statutes* 215.

25. CIA Report, 1914, serial 6815, p. 8. See also E. B. Meritt to J. F. West, December 15, 1915, and Meritt to Gertrude Hartley, April 6, 1927, in OIA CCF, General Service 803, 130907–1915 and 18451–1927.

26. *Report of the Board of Indian Commissioners*, 1921, p. 12, and 1923, p. 4; "Some Memoranda Concerning American Indians," by Malcolm McDowell, secretary of the Board of Indian Commissioners, in "The Indian Problem: Resolutions of the Committee of One Hundred," *House Document* no. 149, 68–1, serial 8273, pp. 34–35.

27. In 1930 federal schools enrolled 39 percent of Indian school children, in 1970 only 26 percent. Margaret Szasz, *Education and the American Indian: The Road to Self-Determination, 1928–1973* (Albuquerque: University of New Mexico Press, 1974), p. 89.

The Indian schools were grammar schools, for Thomas J. Morgan's plan for a graded hierarchy of primary schools, grammar schools, and high schools was never fully realized. At the beginning of the twentieth century, in fact, the goal was explicitly more modest. Jones set the tone in 1900:

> The Indian school system aims to provide a training which will prepare the Indian boy or girl for the everyday life of the average American citizen. It does not contemplate, as some have supposed on a superficial examination, an elaborate preparation for a collegiate course through an extended high-school curriculum. The course of instruction in these schools is limited to that usually taught in the common schools of the country. . . . It is not considered the province of the Government to provide either its wards or citizens with what is known as "higher education."[28]

Character building and moral uplift were always in the minds of the educators, for education was equated with civilization. "With education," Superintendent Reel asserted in 1900, "will come morality, cleanliness, self-respect, industry, and, above all, a Christianized humanity, the foundation stone of the world's progress and well being." The only means to that end for the Indian children was industrial education aimed at self-support, as the superintendent explained:

> The overshadowing importance of industrial training in our work of Indian education becomes more clearly recognized as time passes. The theory of cramming the Indian child with mere book knowledge has been and for generations will be a failure, and that fact is being brought home every day to the workers in the cause of Indian regeneration. It is necessary for the child to read and write, since, in these days, no life can be intelligently lived without these rudiments. A practical knowledge of numbers as they relate to his daily work will be most helpful; but it is not wise to spend years over subjects for which he will have no use in later life and for which he has but little taste now, when the time could be more wisely employed in acquiring skill in the industrial arts, which will also train the judgment, will power, and all that combines to make up strength of character.
>
> The Indian must be brought to a point where he will feel the work

---

28. CIA Report, 1900, serial 4101, p. 14. See also Education Circular no. 43, September 19, 1900, OIA, Circulars Issued by the Education Division, entry no. 718.

spirit and become self-supporting, where he will have the ambition to support his family and not look to the Government for help. This point will be reached only through patient application and faithful work along industrial lines.[29]

The content of that "industrial" education was set forth in explicit terms in the new course of study drawn up by Reel and promulgated for the Indian schools with Jones's approval on August 10, 1901.[30] Under alphabetically arranged headings the directive specified what sort of training would be provided year by year for Indian boys and girls. There were academic branches of arithmetic, geography, history, music, nature study, physiology and hygiene, reading, spelling, and writing, but the greatest attention was paid to agriculture, baking, basketry, blacksmithing, caning, carpentry, cooking, dairying, engineering, gardening, harness making, housekeeping, laundering, painting, printing, sewing, shoemaking, tailoring, and upholstering. The severely practical intent of this education system was indicated in the directive that accompanied the course of study:

> In this course practical lessons in every branch are outlined. The child learns to speak the English language through doing the work that must be accomplished in any well-regulated home, and at the same time is being trained in habits of industry, cleanliness, and system. He learns to read by telling of his daily interests and work with the chalk on the blackboard. In dealing with barrels of fruit, bushels of wheat, yards of gingham, and quarts of milk, in keeping count of his poultry, and in measuring his garden he becomes familiar with numbers in such a practical way that he knows how to use them in daily life as well as on the blackboard in the schoolroom.[31]

The *Course of Study* received extravagant praise from Reel's supporters. Charles F. Lummis, who admitted an initial prejudice against her, exclaimed when he read the volume: "The work shows remarkably faithful and thorough labor, a genuine desire for light, and a practical common-sense which in comparison with Miss Reel's predecessors seems almost supernatural. . . . It is better to have invented such a book—though few will ever see it—than the 'best-selling novel' of the year." George Bird Grinnell praised the course for its practical adaptation to the Indians' life

29. CIA Report, 1900, serial 4101, pp. 425–26, 430–32.
30. *Course of Study for the Indian Schools of the United States, Industrial and Literary* (Washington: GPO, 1901). The volume was a hefty 276 pages; a brief summary of the course of study was printed in Reel's report for 1901, CIA Report, 1901, serial 4290, pp. 419–57.
31. CIA Report, 1901, serial 4290, p. 419.

and concluded, "I have seen the failure of many well meant but unintelligent efforts to legislate the Indian into civilization, but I am greatly encouraged by the efforts being made to treat him intelligently."[32] When Reel's retention in office came under attack in 1910, many prominent people rallied to her support and praised her efforts.

Of course, there were some nay-sayers. One was Thomas J. Morgan, who, in an address to the American Social Science Association in 1902 a few weeks before his death, condemned the course of study and the approach that posited only a rudimentary practical education for the Indians. "Now why should the national government offer to its wards so much less in the way of schooling than is offered by the States to the pupils in the public schools?" he asked. ". . . The Indian child has a right to demand of the government, which has assumed the responsibility of his training, that he shall not be hopelessly handicapped by such an inferior training as from the very beginning dooms him to failure in the struggle for existence and the competition for life's prizes."[33] General Pratt, too, was no friend of Reel, although he seems to have been irked more by her manner on her inspection visits to Carlisle than by the *Course of Study*. In fact, he charged that her new curriculum was "simply a compilation based on the Carlisle course of study."[34]

The *Course of Study* went into effect throughout the Indian school system in 1901, and in subsequent years Reel submitted glowing reports of progress under the new program. In the schools, one-half of the day was devoted to the academic classroom work, the other half to the industrial and domestic arts (much of which was simply performing the work necessary to keep the boarding schools operating economically). Not all the schools, of course, offered all the lines of work that Reel outlined. The large off-reservation schools might include most of them, but the smaller schools concentrated on skills most appropriate to their locality. Most of the "industrial training" at all the schools was agricultural in a broad sense, to enable the average Indian man, as Jones candidly expressed it in 1903, "to wring an existence from the too-frequently ungenerous soils the white man has allowed him to retain." It was accepted that "nature, environ-

32. Clipping of Lummis's editorial in *Out West*, June 1902, pp. 659–60, and Grinnell to Reel, April 14, 1902, OSI CCF 22–36, box 2179. There are other letters of support in this file.

33. Thomas J. Morgan, "Indian Education," *Journal of Social Science* 40 (December 1902): 165–76; quotation is from page 173. See also Frederick E. Hoxie, "Redefining Indian Education: Thomas J. Morgan's Program in Disarray," *Arizona and the West* 24 (Spring 1982): 5–18.

34. Pratt to R. A. Ballinger, February 8, 1910, OSI CCF 22–36, box 2179.

ment, and necessity will and should make at least nine-tenths of the Indian youth tillers of the soil and breeders of stock."[35]

Although the course of study was planned to transform Indian children into hardworking American citizens, there were occasional breaks in the absolute ethnocentrism of the program. Native arts in basketry and weaving were encouraged, and Jones showed a remarkable sensitivity for his times in recognizing the deep value that Indianness gave to the products. "There is an unknown value," he wrote, "in the basket of the Indian squaw who month after month in a primitive tepee weaves her soul, her religion, her woes, and her joys into every graceful curve and color of her handiwork." But it was Leupp who systematically hoped to save instead of crush what was characteristically Indian. He promoted a revival of Indian music and plastic arts in the schools as a means of encouraging the Indians' pride in their ancestry.[36]

As the years passed and initial enthusiasm for the 1901 course of study cooled, it was quietly shelved. In 1911 Commissioner Valentine reported: "[This course of study] has not been in general use for some time. In order that the Indian pupils may be prepared to enter the public schools the teachers have been directed to follow as closely as practicable the courses of study of their respective States, not however to the neglect of the present work of industrial training."[37]

A new course of study was adopted in 1916. That it was not a radical departure from the philosophy of Indian education which had dominated the earlier years of the century can be seen in Cato Sells's statement in 1915 as he planned the new course: "The aim of our Indian schools is not the perfect farmer or the perfect housewife, but the development of character and sufficient industrial efficiency to enable the returned boy or girl to derive happiness and comfort from a home created by individual efforts. This is attempted by thorough instruction in the agricultural, mechanical,

35. CIA Report, 1903, serial 4645, pp. 10–12.

36. Ibid., p. 11; CIA Report, 1905, serial 4959, pp. 12–13; CIA Report, 1906, serial 5118, pp. 65–67.

37. Valentine to Susan F. Nichols, August 24, 1911, OIA CCF, General Service 810, 52850–1911. This emphasis on conformity of the Indian school curriculum to that of the public schools, allowing for the extra industrial training, can be seen also in the *Manual for Indian Schools* (Washington: GPO, 1910), written by Valentine. It was carried over in the new *Rules for the Indian School Service* (Washington: GPO, 1913), section 78, pp. 12–13. Some insight into the nature of the training is furnished by a series of pamphlets issued by the Indian Office in 1911, including *Some Things That Girls Should Know How to Do and Hence Should Learn How to Do in School; Outline Lessons in Housekeeping, Including Cooking, Laundering, Dairying, and Nursing, for Use in Indian Schools;* and *Farm and Home Mechanics: Some Things That Every Boy Should Know How to Do and Hence Should Learn How to Do in School.*

and domestic arts, and an adequate balance of practical field and shop work." What distinguished it, however, was a conscious move toward what had come to be called "vocational training."[38]

The Indian Office reflected the current educational modes of the day, in which *vocational* education became a highly publicized development, giving a new name and new impetus to what had earlier been called *industrial* education. A strong drive for industrial education in the public schools of the nation had begun in 1906 with the publication of the *Report of the Massachusetts Commission on Industrial and Technical Education* (often referred to as the Douglas Commission Report, named after the governor of Massachusetts who appointed the commission) and the organization of the National Society for the Promotion of Industrial Education, which attempted to spread nationwide the concern and findings of the Douglas Commission. There was broad support for industrial education as a necessity in the increasingly technological world, and President Theodore Roosevelt in his message to Congress in 1907 joined the movement. "Our school system," he said, "is gravely defective in so far as it puts a premium upon mere literary training and tends therefore to train the boy away from the farm and the workshop. Nothing is more needed than the best type of industrial school, the school for mechanical industries in the city, the school for practically teaching agriculture in the country." A separate movement for vocational guidance in the schools merged with the movement for industrial education and lent its name to the whole development. In 1912 the National Education Association appointed a Committee on Vocational Education and Vocational Guidance; in 1914 Congress authorized a Commission on National Aid to Vocational Education, and in 1917 it passed the Vocational Education Act (Smith-Hughes Act), which provided federal aid for vocational training programs. Although the goal of this national public school movement was aimed at preparing youth for a technological society and looked toward problems that were different from those facing the Indian schools, the Indian Office could not help but be influenced by the agitation.[39]

Sells in fact noted in 1916: "For many years the general country has rec-

38. CIA Report, 1915, serial 6992, p. 8; *Tentative Course of Study for United States Indian Schools* (Washington: GPO, 1915).

39. The movement toward vocational training is traced in Grant Venn, *Man, Education, and Work: Postsecondary Vocational and Technical Education* (Washington: American Council on Education, 1964), pp. 38–66; Arthur G. Wirth, *Education in the Technological Society: The Vocational-Liberal Studies Controversy in the Early Twentieth Century* (Scranton, Pennsylvania: Intext Educational Publishers, 1972). Roosevelt's statement is in Fred L. Israel, ed., *The State of the Union Messages of the Presidents, 1790–1966*, 3 vols. (New York: Chelsea House, 1966), 3: 2262.

ognized a vital deficiency in its system of education. There has been a chasm, often impassable, between the completion of a course in school and the selection of a vocation in life. The Indian Service has recognized a similar deficiency, although partially overcome in its system. The new vocational course of study for Indian schools is believed to provide a safe and substantial passage from school life to success in real life." In the fall of 1915 the commissioner had called to Washington a group of experienced workers in Indian education. They collected samples of courses of study from around the country and picked what they thought best suited the condition of Indian children. The course they drew up was divided into three stages. The first comprised the first three grades and was labeled "primary"; the second covered the next three grades and was called "prevocational." These six grades paralleled the public school courses in academic work. The prevocational training aimed to provide industrial and domestic training centered around improving the rural home. In the final stage of four years, called "vocational," the vocational aim was dominant as the Indian students applied themselves to their likely callings—with the emphasis still clearly on agriculture and home making.[40]

Another goal of the new program was to restrict the various kinds of schools in the level of their instruction in order to eliminate "the scramble and competition for enrollment" that had resulted in each school accepting "any Indian pupils who could be secured irrespective of attainment or desirability or age." Early in 1916 Sells attempted to remedy the situation by prescribing the following arrangement of grades:

Day Schools	Grades 1–3
Reservation boarding schools	Grades 1–6
Off-reservation schools	Grades 4 and higher

The commissioner soon discovered, however, that this system would require a large transfer of older students out of the reservation schools and of younger students out of the off-reservation schools and that the latter could not survive financially if they lost their early grades, since Congress in 1905 had limited annual expenses for any pupil to $167. So on July 31, 1916, the Indian Office took away most of the restrictions it had set up earlier in the year.[41]

40. CIA Report, 1916, serial 7160, pp. 9–23.
41. An undated memorandum with attached copies of the following circulars: Circular no. 1069, January 13, 1916, and supplement of April 18, 1916, and Circular no. 1164, July 31, 1916, in OIA CCF, General Service 810, 25964–1917. The per capita limit was suspended for fiscal year 1918 and then raised to $200 and $250 for schools with fewer than one hundred pupils. 33 *United States Statutes* 1077; 39 *United States Statutes* 741; 40 *United States Statutes* 490.

The new course had been introduced tentatively on February 1, 1916, and with some modifications was installed in all the schools the following school year.[42] To further institutionalize the program—and to make sure that fieldworkers adhered to it—the Indian Office in 1917 prepared uniform examination questions, which the schools were directed to use at the end of the course in May. But that experiment lasted only a year, for diversity in school schedules and programs made a uniform exam at a set date difficult, and the costs were too heavy for the Indian Office to bear.[43]

Sells's course was soon modified to keep up with changing times. With the help of the Indian school supervisors, Commissioner Burke prepared a new course of study promulgated in 1922. It divided the vocational phase into two stages: junior vocational (corresponding to seventh and eighth grades) and senior vocational (which contemplated a four-year course above the eighth grade to correspond to a regular high school course). It added work on gas engines and auto mechanics, for example, to meet the new demands of the times, and it revised the time allotment in the primary grades to call for full days instead of only half-days devoted to academic work. But the fundamentals had not changed, as Chief Supervisor H. B. Peairs noted in the preface to the new course: "It emphasizes the study of home economics and agricultural subjects, because any attempt to change the Indian population of this country from a dependent to an independent people within a reasonable length of time must give special consideration to the improvement of the Indians' homes and to the development of their lands. The usual subjects of such school instruction are not neglected, but they are coordinated with subjects, which, if learned practically, lead directly to productive efficiency and self-support."[44]

In 1926 a further change was made in the program of the boarding schools to emphasize formal instruction. The old half-work, half-study regimen was replaced by one that called for one-half time for classroom instruction in academic subjects, one-fourth time for vocational instruction, and one-fourth time for school work details. The reduction in the noneducational routine labor was to be made possible by the introduction of such labor-saving equipment as dishwashers and laundry machines and by simplifica-

42. CIA Report, 1916, serial 7160, pp. 22–23. In his 1918 report Sells gave a number of sample daily lessons under the new course. CIA Report, 1918, serial 7498, pp. 22–26.

43. Circular no. 1330, July 18, 1917, and Circular no. 1384, December 28, 1917, OIA Circulars (M1121, reel 11). See also Sells to Oscar H. Lipps, July 18, 1918, OIA CCF, General Service 801, 57803–1918.

44. *Course of Study for United States Indian Schools* (Washington: GPO, 1922). Burke described the program in CIA Report, 1922, p. 5. There is an extended summary of the course of study in Laurence F. Schmeckebier, *The Office of Indian Affairs: Its History, Activities, and Organization* (Baltimore: Johns Hopkins Press, 1927), pp. 217–22.

tion in the construction of the children's clothing. Such an increase in classroom work, whether academic or vocational, put a new strain on the finances of the schools. Burke hoped to meet that problem by the adoption of a new pedagogical technique of the day advocated by the Bureau of Education: the "platoon system." The system was so called because the children were divided into two alternating groups or platoons. While one group pursued standard courses in the homeroom, the pupils of the other platoon were taught such subjects as music, civics, dramatics, physical education, and oral English in large groups in the school auditorium, obviating the immediate necessity of additional classroom space. Only an additional teacher for the auditorium classes and a special vocational teacher would be needed.[45] When Burke in the spring of the next year asked for reports on the new system, however, the reports were discouraging, for many schools had not been able to hire the additional two teachers needed to make the program work. In fact, the proposed salaries were so low that the Civil Service Commission did not schedule examinations because it considered it impossible to hire competent persons at that pay.[46]

All the courses of study, of course, depended upon having the children in the schools, and to accomplish that it was necessary to resort to compulsion. Thomas J. Morgan had been willing to resort to force and was supported by the Board of Indian Commissioners. Congress, too, gave some backing, for in 1893 it authorized the secretary of the interior to withhold rations or subsistence from Indians who did not send their children to school. But this authority was soon restricted to schooling on the reservations, for Congress in 1894 forbade "any Indian agent or other employee of the Government to induce, or seek to induce, by withholding rations or by other improper means, the parents or next of kin of any Indian to consent to the removal of any Indian child beyond the limits of any reservation."[47] Jones was unhappy with the restrictions and was insistent in the matter. The Indian child needed to be taken from his home to the boarding school,

45. CIA Report, 1926, pp. 708. Acting Commissioner E. B. Meritt outlined the changes in letters, dated June 18, 1926, to superintendents of the schools where the new system was to begin in September 1926. Copies in OIA CCF, General Service 810, 35244–1926. The new system was described and promoted in Charles L. Spain, "The Platoon School— Its Advantages," National Education Association of the United States, *Proceedings*, 1926, pp. 797–800, and in Charles L. Spain, *The Platoon School: A Study of the Adaptation of the Elementary School Organization to the Curriculum* (New York: Macmillan Company, 1924). Meritt urged the superintendents to study Spain's book.

46. CIA Report, 1927, pp. 4–5; Burke to school superintendents, March 15, 1927, and replies, OIA CCF, General Service 810, 35244–1926.

47. 26 *United States Statutes* 1014; 27 *United States Statutes* 143, 635; 28 *United States Statutes* 313, 906.

"where the moral influences of white civilization and culture may be thrown around it and love of the civilized home instilled in its heart, in the hope that it will bear fruit in future generations," and the older and conservative Indians could not be permitted to stand in the way. The commissioner wanted legislation that would "take from ignorant parents the privilege of continuing their children in a state of savagery and will bring the children into contact with the highest types of civilization," and he drafted a bill for consideration.[48] But Congress was slow to respond; persuasion, not compulsion, was the norm, and agents and superintendents were repeatedly urged to make sure that the schools were filled and that all the eligible children were in attendance. The increasing enrollment of the Indians in public schools was welcomed, among other reasons, because the children would be liable to state compulsory education laws.

At length, on February 14, 1920, Congress provided that "hereafter the Secretary of the Interior is authorized to make and enforce such rules and regulations as may be necessary to secure the enrollment and regular attendance of eligible Indian children who are wards of the Government in schools maintained for their benefit by the United States or in public schools." Cato Sells, a year later, promulgated appropriate regulations with elaborate procedures for hearings before special boards in cases where parents refused to send a child to school. If the board decided against the parents, the child was to be sent to the designated school, "with escort if necessary." The regulations ended with the admonition: "All existing school facilities for Indians, whether Government, public, or otherwise, must be utilized to the fullest extent." On June 14, 1921, Commissioner Burke formally amended the regulations to include the compulsory education laws and regulations of the state in which the Indians resided.[49]

Although the Indian schools may have kept pace with the times in the matter of industrial training, they fared badly in comparison with the white public school system in regard to level of instruction. At the end of four decades following Morgan's initial drive for an Indian school system in 1889, the government schools were almost universally still only primary and elementary schools. A high school course was added to one school in 1921, and three more appeared in 1925 and one each in 1926 and 1927, so that at the end of Burke's administration there were only six

---

48. CIA Report, 1900, serial 4101, pp. 32–36; CIA Report, 1901, serial 4290, pp. 15–17.

49. 41 *United States Statutes* 410–11; "Regulations Concerning Enrollment and Attendance of Indian Children in Schools, Pursuant to the Act of February 14, 1920," February 28, 1921, and Burke's amendment of June 14, 1921, in OIA CCF, General Service 802, 50122–1921.

schools maintained by the federal government where an Indian could receive a high school education, and in all of them the high school course was appended to elementary and junior high school programs. There was no Indian school that was strictly a high school. "The enrollment in the public high schools in the United States is approximately 1 to every 6 pupils of school age," Burke ruefully reported in 1928, "while among Indians it is only 1 to every 20. The aggregate number of Indians in institutions of higher learning or who are pursuing extension courses is negligible."[50]

SUCCESS AND FAILURE

Evaluation of the Indian school system in the first three decades of the twentieth century depends upon the viewpoint of the judge. The teachers and administrators in the Indian service and professional educators of the time considered the schools a primary tool in the improvement and transformation of the Indians—and that meant knowledge of English and of white American culture and the skills necessary to make one's way in the white-dominated world around them. And these teachers and administrators could point to considerable success. Commissioner Sells presented a very favorable picture at the end of World War I:

> The pressing demand of the war period for all kinds of efficient labor found a fully proportionate supply from the output of our Indian schools. A large force of young men entered the Government shipbuilding service with excellent results. Many young women entered hospital service, quite a number going abroad as trained nurses. Scores of others were accepted as stenographers and typists and fully evidenced their ability. Nothing has equaled the power of the school in producing the large percentage of Indians who today attend church, live in well arranged houses, are English-speaking citizens and voters, efficient artisans, successful in business, in the learned professions, in literature, and in legislative assemblies.
>
> Our Indian soldiers, probably seventy-five per cent of them, were the product of the schools where they were developed not only in the power to think and comprehend and classify facts, but acquired conceptions of civic rights and duties, patriotic ideals, and received through systematic athletics, physical discipline and vigor, all of which combined to make them dependable factors in warfare on land and sea. They entered this world-saving service largely as volunteers

50. CIA Report, 1928, p. 3.

and, with little exception, side by side with the white man. They fought with the courage of intelligence.[51]

Sells's point of view was shared by Malcolm McDowell, secretary of the Board of Indian Commissioners. In "Some Memoranda Concerning American Indians," published in 1924 with the resolutions of the Committee of One Hundred, McDowell asserted: "In the education of the Indian children the Indian Service has scored its highest mark. . . . After many years of discouragement, of apparently small results which caused much criticism against the Government's educational policy in and out of Congress, there now seems to be every indication that success in educating Indian children has been attained."[52]

Commissioner Burke, of course, agreed. In 1925 he pointed to the day and boarding school system and to the large numbers of Indians in the public schools, and he declared of the school program: "Its results are now unmistakable and the best argument for its continuance through some years to come. It has enabled the Indians to make greater progress than any other pagan race in a like period of which there is any written record. Of the 347,000 Indians in the United States, approximately two-thirds speak English and nearly 150,000 can read and write that language."[53]

The Society of American Indians, too, with its cadre of highly educated Indians, many of them products of the government's off-reservation schools, was witness to the successful working of the system. Education was a major topic at the conferences of the society and in its *Quarterly Journal*, and although there was considerable discussion of reform in Indian education, it was couched in much the same terms that the commissioners and educators in the Indian schools used.[54]

The favorable—at times even exuberant—reports about progress in Indian education that marked the early decades of the twentieth century, however, were strongly contradicted by two serious national studies that occurred at the end of the 1920s: the Meriam Report (1928) and the report of the National Advisory Committee on Education (1931). Their findings, as is usually the case with committees who are seeking improvement in

---

51. Sells to Joseph McGaheran, Jr., February 24, 1919, OIA CCF, General Service 800, 17276–1919. McGaheran, editor of the high school yearbook at La Porte, Iowa, where Sells once lived, had asked for an essay from Sells. The statement as a whole is an excellent summary of Sells's philosophy of Indian education.

52. "The Indian Problem: Resolutions of the Committee of One Hundred," pp. 29–30.

53. Burke article in *Yale Daily News*, March 19, 1925, copy in OIA CCF, General Service 800, 14662–1925.

54. See the discussion in Hazel W. Hertzberg, *The Search for an American Indian Identity: Modern Pan-Indian Movements* (Syracuse: Syracuse University Press, 1971), part 1.

the existing state of affairs, were detailed and very critical, and they must have come as a heavy blow to the men and women in the Indian school system. The reports help immeasurably in forming a balanced view of Indian education in the perspective of the times.

In its general findings and recommendations the Meriam Report was blunt: "The survey staff finds itself obliged to say frankly and unequivocally that the provisions for the care of the Indian children in boarding schools are grossly inadequate." The "outstanding deficiency" was the children's diet, but then came overcrowding in dormitories, below-standard medical service, too much labor on the part of the students (without much distinction between work to maintain the schools and vocational training), a teaching staff that could not meet "the standards set by reasonably progressive white communities," restrictive rather than "developmental" school discipline, and an obsolete industrial curriculum.[55]

The fundamental need, the report declared, was for a change in point of view. The Indian schools still operated on the theory that it was necessary to remove the Indian children from their home environment instead of adopting the "modern point of view in education and social work," which stressed education in the natural setting of home and family. The Indian educational system, it said, needed to be less concerned with a conventional school system and more with the understanding of human beings. "The methods of the average public school in the United States cannot safely be taken over bodily and applied to Indian education," the report noted, and it condemned the idea of a standard course of study and a system of uniform examinations. The minimum standards applied to education should be directed not toward courses and examinations, but to the qualifications of the personnel, and here the Indian school service fared badly. "After all is said that can be said about the skill and devotion of some employees," the report asserted, "the fact remains that the government of the United States regularly takes into the instructional staff of its Indian schools teachers whose credentials would not be accepted in good public school systems, and into the institutional side of these schools key employees—matrons and the like—who could not meet the standards set up by modern social agencies." The fault lay of course in lack of sufficient appropriations to pay adequate salaries. "From the point of view of education," it concluded, "the Indian service is almost literally a 'starved' service."[56]

---

55. *The Problem of Indian Administration* [Meriam Report] (Baltimore: Johns Hopkins Press, 1928), pp. 11–14.

56. Ibid., pp. 346–48. The Indian Office, of course, was aware of the financial needs. The report of 1927 began with a section labeled "The Poverty of the Indian Service." CIA Report, 1927, pp. 1–7.

What the Meriam survey staff looked for was an educational program of great breadth—not simply a traditional type of school—and a course of study that was suggestive rather than prescriptive, so that it could be adapted to different tribes and different individuals. The existing system it castigated as "a highly mechanical content of education handled in a mechanical way." The system of half-study, half-work that marked the Indian schools disturbed the survey team, for it found young children doing work beyond their strength, and it charged that "the labor of children as carried on in Indian boarding schools would . . . constitute a violation of child labor laws in most states." Children at least through age fourteen should be in school for education, not for "work." The vocational training, too, was criticized, as not clearly enough directed to the kind of work the students would do when they left school. It urged special attention to health education, to practical religious education, and to adult education.[57]

The Meriam Report supported the plans of the Indian Office regarding types of schools, but it found inadequacies in implementation. The off-reservation schools, it argued, should be deemphasized and reserved for pupils above the sixth grade and soon for ninth grade and above, and overcrowding in the schools should be eliminated. The reservation boarding schools, too, it hoped to see disappear, although it did not recommend a wholesale program of getting rid of them. The day schools were especially recommended as "the best opportunity available at present to furnish schooling to Indian children and at the same time build up a needed home and community education." In the end, it was the public schools, however, that appeared to be the solution. "Any policy for Indians based on the notion that they can or should be kept permanently isolated from other Americans is bound to fail," the report said; "mingling is inevitable, and Indian children brought up in public schools with white children have the advantage of early contacts with whites while still retaining their connection with their own Indian family and home." Yet it warned about pushing the principle too fast and condemned the idea of the government's washing its hands of the Indians and saving money by moving them into public schools before those schools were prepared to give them the special attention they might need.[58]

The Meriam Report recommended finally that the education staff of the Indian Office in Washington be only a small technical staff to furnish professional direction for the entire service and that the focus of responsibility be in the superintendents of the schools.[59]

57. *Problem of Indian Administration*, pp. 373–402.
58. Ibid., pp. 411–16.
59. Ibid., pp. 424–25.

The general tone and criticism of the Meriam Report was repeated in the report of the National Advisory Committee on Education. Organized by Secretary of the Interior Ray Lyman Wilbur at President Herbert Hoover's instigation in May 1929, the committee and its staff undertook extensive fieldwork and elicited the cooperation of numerous public and private organizations interested in education. The committee concluded that the government's educational policy for Indians was "a tragic failure." It considered the transfer of the ordinary American elementary school to the Indian reservations as a mistake; and it asserted: "What we normally call the school becomes a conveniently located Indian welfare center in and out of which all sort of practical educative functionaries operate. We mean social workers, public health nurses, teaching farmers and artisans, as well as teachers of the usual academic sort." Like the Meriam Report, the report of the National Advisory Committee condemned centralization in the school system, the inadequacy of the existing vocational training, and the failure to attract competent teachers and other staff.[60]

These critical surveys of Indian education were not revolutionary, and even in their emphasis on orientation of the educational system to meet the needs of Indian children rather than to match some conventional, traditional types of school system, they did not depart greatly from the ultimate goals and principles long enunciated by the educational leaders of the Indian service. The kernel of the criticism was that what had been attempted had not been well done, and again and again a finger was pointed at the incompetence of the teachers and other personnel who made up the Indian school service. The reports could be taken—as in fact they were—as a program for improvement in the education that the federal government would continue to provide for many Indian children.

The criticisms of the time did not touch what became a central point later in the twentieth century: the intent of the Indian schools to transfer Indian children from their own culture into white civilization. Despite some feeble attempts to include elements of Indian culture, like Leupp's promotion of Indian music and Indian art, the curriculum ignored the Indian heritage of the students and followed as closely as possible the curriculum in the public schools of the state in which each school was located. Though it might lament the sacrifice of traditional customs "as a picturesque factor in the national life," the Indian Office was convinced that the ancient laws and customs that did not coincide with national laws must inevitably give way. "However desirable, from an aesthetic point of view, it might be to maintain this quaint, old, semi-civilization in our midst," the

---

60. *Federal Relations to Education: Report of the National Advisory Committee on Education*, 2 vols. (Washington, 1931), 1: 47–53.

assistant commissioner of Indian affairs wrote in 1910 to a person who urged preservation of the arts and customs of the Pueblo Indians, "it is not altogether practicable. In its educational capacity, as a civilizing agent, the Office has a special duty to discharge toward the children of these Indians, who must be prepared for the future and to finally adjust themselves as citizens to our modern civilization."[61]

The textbooks and lessons in the Indian schools were geared to produce American citizens and were heavy with history and civics lessons that made little sense to the native pupils. A stark example is the series of examination questions in history administered to the children at the Albuquerque Indian School in 1911, of which these samples are typical:

Third grade
  Tell about the voyage of Columbus and why he wished to go.
  Who were the Pilgrims and where did they land?
  Tell what a good citizen is and what he does.
Fifth grade
  Why did England tax the colonies? Tell about the "Stamp Act."
  Who wrote the Declaration of Independence and when
    was it signed?
  Who was Robert Morris? Name the first three presidents of the
    United States.
Eighth grade
  Name the kinds of government and a country that has each kind.
  Explain the difference between the township government of New
    England and the county government of Virginia.[62]

There can be little doubt that failures in educating the Indians throughout the decades stemmed in part from the unwillingness of the educators to consider the Indians' cultural heritage and its persistence in spite of the efforts to eradicate it.

61. F. H. Abbott to Charles Francis Saunders, September 29, 1910, OIA CCF, General Service 810, 73672–1910.
62. These come from an interesting packet of documents dealing with examinations at the schools and with criticism of the questions and of the grading of the answers made by officials of the Indian Office. OIA, Office File of Hervey B. Peairs, entry no. 722.

CHAPTER 33

Concern for Indian Health

The Condition of Indian Health.

Initial Campaigns against Disease.

A Continuing but Insufficient Fight.

The Critics.

Education for self-support was inextricably intertwined with the health of the Indians. Here a strange paradox appeared. As more and more Indian children were enrolled in school, where they could be observed and examined, awareness of the prevalence of serious diseases was immeasurably sharpened. Even more troublesome was the realization that the very conditions of the schools under which the pupils lived aggravated, if indeed they did not cause, the shocking status of morbidity among the Indians. As the twentieth century advanced, the Indian Office devoted increasing attention to the problems of health, until that topic became one of the major areas of the federal government's paternalistic activity in regard to its Indian wards. It was unfortunately the case, however, that both the realization of the magnitude of the problem and the programs adopted to combat it came much too slowly. Despite two decades and more of effort on the part of the Indian Office and other segments of the federal government and the American public, the picture at the end of the 1920s was still a dismal one. It was a classic example of "too little and too late."[1]

1. An excellent account of Indian health policy and programs in the first three decades of the twentieth century is Diane T. Putney, "Fighting the Scourge: American Indian Morbidity and Federal Policy, 1897–1928" (Ph.D. dissertation, Marquette University, 1980). It has been, to some extent, a guide for my own research on Indian health policy in this period.

THE CONDITION OF INDIAN HEALTH

There had long been some attention paid to Indian health, and agency and school physicians were a common part of the reservation scene. A good many of them had regular appointments, but many others (local doctors) served only part-time as "contract physicians." Under the regulations issued by the Indian Office these physicians treated sickness, reported on health and sanitary conditions, and (if Commissioner Thomas J. Morgan had his way) served as civilizing agents to counter the influence of the Indian "medicine men."[2] There were isolated examples, too, of attention to specific diseases. Vaccination for smallpox had been promoted by the Indian Office for many years, and that dread disease had been largely eradicated by the end of the century. Tuberculosis among the Indians was another disease that caught the eye of medical men, and Washington Matthews, for one, published reports on its incidence and causes.[3] But the commissioners of Indian affairs, whose annual reports included sections on all sorts of topics of special concern, found no occasion to devote any space to health until 1904, when Jones reported the results of a survey of Indian health, and then 1908, when Leupp wrote a section on "Fighting the White Plague."[4]

Earlier, however, the urgency of Indian health conditions had been pressed upon the Indian Office, for deficiencies could no longer be overlooked or pushed aside. Although many persons were becoming increasingly aware of the high rates of morbidity and mortality among the Indians, it was easy to shrug one's shoulders and assume the inevitability of it all. But soon charges were leveled against the Indian Office for its negligence. The strongest critic, who fearlessly exposed the shocking conditions in Indian schools and on the reservations, was one of the Interior Department's Indian inspectors, William J. McConnell, who spent his four-year term from 1897 to 1901 as a stinging gadfly. McConnell was a man of

2. *Regulations for the Indian Department* (Washington: GPO, 1884), pp. 97–99. There was no indication of concern for "health problems" in this 1884 edition, but by 1894 certain "public health" activities were specified in directions to the doctors to heed the condition of buildings, sewerage, water supply, ventilation, and the like. The physicians were directed to "endeavor to improve sanitary and hygienic conditions generally, and instruct the Indians how to do so." *Regulations for the Indian Office* (Washington: GPO, 1894), pp. 89–92.

3. See, for example, Washington Matthews, "Consumption among the Indians," *Transactions of the American Climatological Association*, 1886, pp. 234–41; and "Further Contribution to the Study of Consumption among the Indians," ibid., 1888, pp. 136–55.

4. CIA Report, 1904, serial 4798, pp. 33–38; CIA Report, 1908, serial 5453, pp. 25–26. From that time on health was a regular topic in the reports and sometimes had the most prominent place.

strong character. Born in Michigan in 1839, he had moved to the West in 1860 and lived in Oregon and Idaho, and he was elected to the United States Senate when Idaho became a state in 1890. Although he stayed in the Senate only a few months, he subsequently served two terms as governor of Idaho and was a political force in his region. As he made his inspection rounds, he was astounded by the health conditions he found. He railed especially against the policy of filling the schools at all costs and pointed to the common acceptance of diseased children in order to keep the enrollment high, as the schools were repeatedly urged to do by the Indian Office. "The habit prevails at San Carlos," he wrote from Arizona in the summer of 1899, "as well as at most of these southern schools of taking in such pupils as can be obtained, some of whom are superficially examined and others not at all. Tuberculosis frequently develops, and apparently for no other reason than to maintain a full attendance, they are kept until the last stage is reached, when to prevent a death occurring at the school, they are carted home, to their tepe, where in some instances even a few days suffices to bring the end. In this manner the disease is diseminated among the pupils in the schools, and the few days they occupy the home tepe may be, and no doubt is, frequently the cause of other members of the family becoming affected."[5]

Everywhere McConnell found unconscionable overcrowding in the schools. The approved norms of cubic feet of air per pupil were ignored, ventilation of the classrooms and dormitories was faulty, and—worst of all—the diseased children were mixed with healthy ones in the dormitories. The inspector reported from the Blackfeet Agency in 1901: "30 girls being lodged in one dormitory with only 160 cubic feet of air to each child. I made an examination of this room and found that two at all times, and frequently three children are required to sleep in a single bed with only one pillow. . . . Among the children thus packed away are sandwiched in cases of both pulmonary and lymphatic tuberculosis sometimes sleeping in the same bed with those not yet affected. *No child sleeps alone.*"[6]

McConnell was not satisfied to describe conditions; he blasted the responsible officials in the Interior Department for what he found. He told

5. McConnell to the secretary of the interior, July 29, 1899, OIA, Official Letters of W. J. McConnell, U.S. Indian Inspector, entry 952. At the very time McConnell was writing, Jones was urging the agents "to put forth every effort at your command to fill each school, boarding and day, under your charge to the limit of its capacity during the first quarter of the new fiscal year. A thorough canvass of the reservations should be made at once, and every child located and assigned for whom you have quarters." Education Circular no. 31, August 5, 1899, OIA, Circulars Issued by the Education Department, entry 718. All education circulars cited below are in this file.

6. McConnell to the secretary of the interior, June 17, 1901, OSI, Indian Division, Inspection Reports, Blackfeet, 5119.

the secretary of the interior that of one group of fifteen boys sent to Carlisle from the Shoshone Agency "11 died there or returned home to die" and that out of two groups sent to boarding schools in Nebraska the mortality rate was nearly as great. "The word murder is a fearful word," he wrote, "but yet the transfer of pupils and subjecting them to such fearful mortality is little less"; he hoped God "would have mercy upon those responsible for such work." He told the secretary when he wrote from the Yakima Agency in 1899: "The United States declared war against Spain, our people being impelled to this course largely by the abuses imposed upon the Cubans by the Spaniards. Yet I venture to say that upon every one of our Indian Reservations in the Northwest there are conditions as bad or worse than any which were exposed in Cuba." It was not the rules of the Indian Office that he criticized, for he found them generally admirable, but, he said, "that they are not followed out is generally understood."[7]

A large part of the problem, which the inspector immediately pinpointed, was the sad state of the medical service of the Indian Office. Because of low pay, the personnel were often ill-trained, uninterested, and generally incompetent. The physicians had to get along without adequate equipment and medicines and with little chance to improve their knowledge either through professional associations or by reading the latest journals, and esprit de corps was almost entirely lacking. McConnell pointed to the vast difference in the medical corps of the army, where all that he missed among the Indian physicians he found in abundant measure.[8] To be sure, there had been some stirrings of professional interest on the part of the Indian service doctors. In 1898 Dr. Joseph R. Finney, of the Fort Berthold Agency, attempted to establish an Association of Physicians of the United States Indian Service, and in the same year, at the summer institute in Denver, Dr. Joseph G. Bulloch, of the Oneida Indian School in Wisconsin, began to organize a United States Indian Medical Service comparable to state medical societies. In Denver, Bulloch and other physicians pointed to the bad conditions existing at the schools and reservations. But the message was not heard by Commissioner William Jones, who discouraged the doctors' activities, and the enthusiasm that might have blossomed into a more effective medical service for the Indians died away.[9]

7. McConnell to the secretary of the interior, July 5, 1901, OSI, Appointments Division, Indian Inspectors, Wm. J. McConnell; McConnell to the secretary of the interior, February 10, 1899, OIA, Official Letters of W. J. McConnell.

8. Undated memorandum, "U.S. Indian Medical Service," OSI, Appointments Division, Indian Inspectors, Wm. J. McConnell.

9. Report of the Superintendent of Indian Schools, 1898, in CIA Report, 1898, serial 3757, pp. 340–41. The abortive attempt to form an association of Indian service physicians is described in Putney, "Fighting the Scourge," pp. 54–66.

Although McConnell was not reappointed in 1901, no doubt because he was too outspoken, and although Jones was slow to heed the warning signals and seemed satisfied to rely on the generally ineffective regulations and circulars sent to the agents and school superintendents directing their attention to measures to avoid contagion, the Indian Office at last began to move.[10] Jones was forced to adopt a new position because of the charge that the demand for increasing enrollment in the Indian schools led to overcrowding and to the admission of students with contagious diseases. As the school year began in the fall of 1903, the commissioner spoke to the agents and superintendents in forceful terms:

At the beginning of the present school year I wish to emphasize the necessity of your taking every precaution to place your school buildings in a thoroughly hygienic condition. While you are urged to fill your school to the limit of its capacity, it must be with sound and healthy children. There must, most positively, be *no overcrowding* in the dormitories to the detriment of the children sleeping in them. If you have an insufficient number of healthy children to fill up your school, do not place any more therein. A statement to this effect is to your credit and not your discredit. . . .

Indian children should be educated, but should not, however, be destroyed in the process. Health is the greatest consideration. Therefore, if you cannot accommodate your present enrollment, without lowering the vitality of the pupils, a decrease should be made. War should be made upon dust, filth, foul odors, and all disease breeding spots promptly attended to. Adequate ventilation and antiseptic methods should be adopted, especially in dormitories. Cuspidors should be provided, if not on hand. Individual towels furnished. In fact, the rules relating to the health of pupils strictly observed.[11]

Jones lamented that the high cost of building and the small appropriations made it impossible to construct new school plants "absolutely sani-

10. Jones's negative or noncommittal response to McConnell's reports can be seen in Jones to the secretary of the interior, January 28, 1898, and July 12, 1901, OIA LS, Education, vols. 92 and 142. For examples of regulations, see sections 53 and 68 in *Rules for the Indian School Service* (Washington: GPO, 1898). Estelle Reel's *Course of Study for the Indian Schools of the United States, Industrial and Literary* (Washington: GPO, 1901) contained a good number of suggestions on health and specific instructions about preventing the spread of tuberculosis.

11. Education Circular no. 102, September 21, 1903. See also Education Circular no. 85, November 6, 1902, which directed off-reservations schools that "only sound and healthy children shall be enrolled, each of whom must be accompanied with physician's certificate as required by Section 17, Indian School Rules, 1900."

tary from the latest hygienic and medical standpoint," and he urged elimination of overcrowding as the temporary expedient.[12]

In the summer of 1903 Jones took another step to move the Indian Office toward a sounder medical service: the first comprehensive survey of health conditions in the Indian schools and on the reservations. He directed the physicians to prepare a detailed report embodying statistical information on the present health record compared with previous years. The physicians were asked to include comparisons of the health of adult Indians with that of students returned from off-reservation schools and to indicate the standing of adult Indians, Indian students, and whites living in the same environment in regard to specific diseases. The reports were to note death rates, too, describe the conditions of the school buildings and their relation to disease, and include any facts that pertained to health or sanitation.[13]

The replies should have shocked the Indian Office out of any complacency. They showed that tuberculosis was more widespread among the Indians than among an equal number of whites—even though many Indians lived in healthful climates. The causes were clear: poor sanitation, lack of cleanliness, and specifically failure to destroy tubercular sputum; improper and poorly prepared food; overcrowding in dormitories; and lack of proper medical attention after infection. "Of these causes," a summary report of the responses noted, "failure to disinfect sputum is undoubtedly the most active. The Indian naturally lives in filthy surroundings. He coughs and expectorates without regard for the laws of health; the sputum dries rapidly, mixes with the dust and the germs it contains soon become widely disseminated." The report referred, too, to such general causes as use of alcohol, the change of children from camp life to confinement in school, and general weakening of the Indians by intermarriage, as well as Indian cultural patterns and the "ignorance and superstitions [which] often make it impossible to institute many of the procedures deemed advisable." The replies called attention to the prevalence of eye diseases but noted that, contrary to popular belief, venereal diseases were not widespread. "In summing up," the report concluded, "it may [be] said that the physical welfare of the Indian is and always must be the fundamental consideration in any scheme to educate or civilize him. It is impossible to develop his mental and moral capabilities without healthy material to work on and the government has no right to deny him ordinary health conditions." The report was shared with the agents and superintendents, and they received new directives for thorough examination of the pupils for tuberculosis,

---

12. Education Circular no. 102, September 21, 1903.
13. Education Circular no. 99, July 1, 1903.

provisiõn of cuspidors for the schools, cleanliness and proper ventilation to prevent spread of disease, and proper attention to eye diseases.[14] Yet such directives were only slowly and imperfectly implemented, and two years later it was necessary to repeat the health circulars of 1903 and 1904.[15]

INITIAL CAMPAIGNS AGAINST DISEASE

The business-as-usual approach to the problems of contagion that marked much of Jones's administration was eventually replaced by more intense action under Commissioner Francis E. Leupp. Leupp, however, was almost as slow as Jones had been to react effectively to the serious health problem of the Indians. His widely publicized "Outlines of an Indian Policy," issued in his first annual report and then published as an article in *Outlook*, contained no mention of health problems aside from the brief recommendation for a sanatorium in the Southwest to care for tubercular Indians.[16] Not until the end of his administration did he show an appreciation of the scope of the problem and begin to act as energetically as he did in other matters.

Tuberculosis was the first item on the agenda, for its fatal nature threatened to decimate the tribes. What sparked Leupp's interest was the Sixth International Congress on Tuberculosis, held in Washington in 1908. The Indian Office and the Smithsonian Institution cooperated in preparing material dealing with the Indians for the congress. Leupp appointed Elsie E. Newton, an Indian service supervisor, to prepare an exhibit, and the Smithsonian detailed the noted scholar Ales Hrdlicka to make a survey of tuberculosis on the Indian reservations. In the summer of 1908 Hrdlicka made an intensive study of selected Indian tribes across the nation: Menominee, Oglala Sioux, Quinaelt, Hupa, and Mojave. His report presented sobering statistics on tuberculosis among the Indians and concluded that "the morbidity and mortality from all forms of tuberculosis among the Indians today exceed by far those among the whites generally; and that their average exceeds even the very high rate among the American negroes." The causes he listed as "a frequent hereditary taint among the young," the great facility of infection arising from overcrowding at home and at school and the

14. "Brief of Replies to Education Circular no. 99," March 15, 1904, OIA, Records of the Education Division, Briefs of Inspection, vol. 1, pp. 432–40; Education Circular no. 106, March 23, 1904. The results of the survey were also reported in detail in CIA Report, 1904, serial 4798, pp. 33–38.

15. Education Circular no. 127, August 12, 1906.

16. CIA Report, 1905, serial 4959, pp. 1–15; Francis E. Leupp, "Outlines of an Indian Policy," *Outlook* 79 (April 15, 1905): 946–50.

common practice of spitting, the general poverty and undernourishment of the Indians, and infection from milk of tubercular cows. He called for a campaign to combat ignorance about the disease, special camps for isolating tubercular patients, improvement in houses and other home conditions, better nutrition, and repression of alcoholism. He also urged a better medical service.[17]

Leupp was caught up in the movement. He himself gave an address at the international congress, in which he admitted that tuberculosis was "the greatest single menace to the Indian race," and he pointed out the serious obstacles to improvement that lay in the communal life of the Indians, their conservatism and superstition, and the "conditions which afford fruitful soil for the spread of tuberculosis among a people who are exceedingly susceptible to it, to whom cleanliness means nothing, and to whose vocabulary sanitation and hygiene are unknown terms." But he could point, too, to some serious efforts. His "bird cage" schools were one example he cited, and the building of a sanatorium school at the Colville Reservation was another.[18] He had earlier ordered a special report on tuberculosis from the physicians and on special camps for affected students, and to strengthen the hand of the doctors he had designated them "health officers" with authority to inspect homes of Indians and employees and enforce correction of insanitary conditions. Then he directed the disinfection of band instruments at the Indian schools, to prevent contagion through common use; school books, too, were to be fumigated periodically. A special committee was appointed to draw up ways to combat the disease.[19]

One important action of Leupp was the appointment in 1908 of Dr. Joseph A. Murphy as medical supervisor for the Indian service. Murphy was an outstanding choice, for he was an expert in the treatment of tuberculosis and an intelligent and energetic medical leader. Until he resigned at the end of World War I, he gave forceful direction to the health campaigns of the Indian Office, although he operated against great odds. Murphy was an able promoter of the cause. He spoke to the assembly at Lake

17. Hrdlicka's investigation of tuberculosis for the international congress was reported in *Tuberculosis among Certain Indian Tribes of the United States,* Bureau of American Ethnology Bulletin no. 42 (Washington: GPO, 1909). His talk at the congress, "Contribution to the Knowledge of Tuberculosis in the Indian," is in *Transactions of the Sixth International Congress on Tuberculosis,* 6 vols. (Philadelphia: William F. Fell, 1908), 3: 480–93.

18. Francis E. Leupp, "Fighting the Scourge among the Indians," *Transactions of the Sixth International Congress on Tuberculosis,* 4, part 1: 428–35.

19. Education Circulars no. 209, April 25, 1908; no. 242, September 30, 1908; no. 246, October 27, 1908; no. 254, November 18, 1908; no. 266, December 29, 1908. A summary of Leupp's work is in CIA Report, 1908, serial 5453, pp. 25–26.

Mohonk in 1909 (on detail from the Indian Office); testified at congressional appropriation hearings; developed formal lectures on disease, which he gave at Indian schools; and at the end of 1909, at Commissioner Robert G. Valentine's instigation, prepared a *Manual on Tuberculosis: Its Cause, Prevention, and Treatment* for distribution to Indian service employees, Indian students, and adult Indians who could read.[20]

Following close upon tuberculosis as a malady of serious proportions was trachoma, which for undetermined reasons struck especially hard at the Indian schools and reservations. Jones's survey of health conditions in 1903 had noted that "eye diseases, as trachoma or granulated lids, and skin diseases are prevalent and are due to strumous or scrofulous tendencies coupled with uncleanliness and, in the case of diseases of the eye, with neglect of simple inflammations." The commissioner thereupon told agents and superintendents in 1904: "Eye diseases are to receive proper attention. . . . It must be borne in mind that many of these conditions are contagious, and precautions such as furnishing of individual towels, etc., should be taken to prevent their spread." Not until 1909, however, was any special concern given to the matter beyond the repeated injunctions against the common roller towels that were a feature of Indian schools. In that year the near disastrous dimensions of trachoma at the Phoenix Indian School came to light. Backed by a strong letter from Surgeon General Walter Wyman, who pointed to the loss of economic efficiency caused by the disease and the danger to white populations in contact with the Indians, Leupp was successful in persuading Congress to appropriate $12,000 "to investigate, treat, and prevent the spread of trachoma among the Indian population."[21]

20. *Lake Mohonk Conference Proceedings,* 1909, pp. 23–26; Joseph A. Murphy, *Manual on Tuberculosis: Its Cause, Prevention, and Treatment* (Washington: GPO, 1910). Material on Murphy's activities, including a copy of a 1911 lecture on tuberculosis and trachoma and his "Annual Report on Field Medical Work, Fiscal Year Ending June 30, 1911," are in OIA, Records of the Inspection Division, Special Agents File, J. A. Murphy. See also Joseph A. Murphy, "The Prevention of Tuberculosis in the Indian Schools," National Education Association, *Journal of Proceedings and Addresses,* 1909, pp. 919–24; Murphy, "Health Problems of the Indians," *Annals of the American Academy of Political and Social Science* 37 (March 1911): 347–53. Commissioner Valentine praised Murphy's work and outlined a ten-point plan of attack against disease in CIA Report, 1909, serial 5747, pp. 4–6. A candid statement of the seriousness of the health problems and of the attack being made on them is in "Memorandum of Health Conditions among the Indians," December 28, 1910, OIA CCF, General Service 732, 36688–1911. Further activities against tuberculosis are discussed in Putney, "Fighting the Scourge," pp. 110–19.

21. "Brief of Replies to Education Circular no. 99," March 15, 1904; Education Circular no. 106, March 23, 1904; 35 *United States Statutes* 642; "Trachoma in Certain Indian Schools," *Senate Report* no. 1025, 60–2, serial 5380, which printed the letter of Walter Wyman to Leupp, February 13, 1909.

The investigation of trachoma turned up new statistics of the heavy incidence of the disease, and the seriousness of the situation could not be denied. Congress began to make separate appropriations "to relieve distress among Indians and to provide for their care and for the prevention and treatment of tuberculosis, trachoma, smallpox, and other contagious and infectious diseases." The first appropriation, for fiscal year 1911, was $40,000, but the sums were rapidly increased as more information was received about the tragic prevalence of disease among the Indians.[22] Valentine viewed all these developments with considerable satisfaction. The medical work, which aimed to increase the vitality and physical wellbeing of the Indians, he said, was "being scientifically developed along lines which have already been successfully tried out by modern preventive medicine." He spoke of a three-pronged program: (1) an intensive attack upon tuberculosis and trachoma, (2) preventive work on a large scale through education and sanitary inspections, and (3) increased attention to the physical welfare of the schoolchildren.[23]

A great boost to the cause came from President William Howard Taft, who on August 10, 1912, sent a special message to Congress on Indian health. "In many parts of the Indian country," he told Congress, "infant mortality, tuberculosis, and disastrous diseases generally prevail to an extent exceeded only in some of the most insanitary of our white rural districts and in the worst slums of our large cities." The death rate from these causes among Indians, he pointed out, was thirty-five per thousand, compared with fifteen per thousand for the United States as a whole, and he cited striking statistics about the prevalence of disease. The home conditions of many of the Indians he called "almost beyond belief." "As guardians of the welfare of the Indians," he said, "it is our immediate duty to give to the race a fair chance for an unmaimed birth, healthy childhood, and a physically efficient maturity." He asked for an additional appropriation of $253,350 to step up the fight against disease and to augment and improve the Indian medical service.[24]

22. 36 *United States Statutes* 271. In 1912 the amount was $60,000, in 1913 it was $90,000, and then the figures jumped dramatically.

23. CIA Report, 1910, serial 5976, pp. 9–10; see also CIA Report, 1911, serial 6223, pp. 3–6. In April 1912 Valentine sent a special circular addressed to "every Indian and to every Indian Service employee," entitled "Our Task." It stressed two aims, "Health and Industry," and included among its directives: "3) Leave no stone unturned to get every family *sanitarily housed. Fresh air.* 4) Take immediate emergency measures to greatly *reduce infant mortality. Save the babies.* . . . 9) In every school rigidly segregate children with trachoma, tuberculosis, and any other infectious or contagious disease, and run the school in compartments, no matter at what loss to scholastic work." Circular no. 633, April 29, 1912, OIA Circulars, (M1121, reel 10). For a detailed analysis of trachoma and early methods of treatment, see Putney, "Fighting the Scourge," pp. 141–69.

24. Taft's message is printed as *Senate Document* no. 907, 62–2, serial 6179. The

Not trusting the statistics of the Indian Office, Congress authorized $10,000 to enable the United States Public Health Service "to make a thorough examination as to the prevalence of tuberculosis, trachoma, smallpox, and other contagious and infectious diseases among the Indians of the United States."[25] Under the direction of Assistant Surgeon General J. W. Kerr, who headed the Division of Scientific Research, the Public Health Service conducted a systematic study—examining morbidity and mortality records at the agencies, inspecting students at all types of schools, visiting sanatoriums, and making house-to-house inspections of Indian homes. By dividing the country into districts and detailing officers to them under careful guidelines, the survey was able to examine 39,231 Indians out of an estimated population of 322,715. The findings substantiated the earlier reports: 22.7 percent of the Indians examined had trachoma (29.86 percent of children in the boarding schools), and the incidence of tuberculosis ranged from a high of 32.6 percent among the Pyramid Lake Paiutes to a low of 2.33 percent among the Indians of Michigan. The prevalence of tuberculosis was "very greatly in excess of that among the white race" and "so serious as to require the prosecution of vigorous measures for its relief." Trachoma was more prevalent in the schools than on the reservations, and the survey concluded that the infection was frequently picked up at the boarding schools and then spread to the reservations when the students returned home. Other diseases, though present, gave less concern.[26]

The report noted, as usual, the highly unsanitary conditions on the reservations: overcrowded homes, uncleanliness, and poor food. It included an extract from the field survey of Dr. Paul Preble, who inspected the reservations in South Dakota, which gave "an excellent idea of conditions too frequently met with on Indian reservations and the opportunities for the transfer of infection which overcrowding affords":

> In one such house, a well-built, two-room framed building about six
> months old, eight individuals were found living and sleeping in one
> small room about 12 by 14 feet. Three of these people were between 8

---

breakdown of the $253,350 requested—for a tuberculosis hospital, extra medical inspectors, increased salaries for physicians and other health personnel, a pathological laboratory, new equipment, medical journals—was provided by the commissioner of Indian affairs, who also supplied a chart comparing pay in the Indian medical service with the much higher pay in the army, navy, and Public Health Service. *Senate Document* no. 920, 62–2, serial 6182. Taft's message and the Indian Office estimates are also in CIA Report, 1912, serial 6409, pp. 17–22.

25. 37 *United States Statutes* 519.

26. "Contagious and Infectious Diseases among the Indians," *Senate Document* no. 1038, 62–3, serial 6365.

months and 3 years of age. An apology for a bed occupied one side of the room and on it sat a young mother holding a 3-year-old girl suffering from advanced tuberculosis. In the center of this room was a worn-out cookstove, giving off great quantities of heat and foul odors. The air in the room was stifling. On the other side of the room, two women, about 30 years of age, were sitting on a number of extremely filthy rags and hides, both nearly blind as the result of acute trachoma. One was nursing an 8-month-old baby and, when an examination of their eyes was attempted, this mother wiped the discharges from her own eyes with her fingers and then attempted to assist in opening her baby's eyes for examination.[27]

The Public Health Service doctors found the schools generally overcrowded, with diseased children mingling among the others. Insufficient measures were taken to prevent the spread of disease through towels and by means of flies. The status of the physicians in the medical service was declared unsatisfactory from the standpoint of compensation, organization, and esprit de corps, and record keeping ("the foundation of public-health work") was indefinite and fragmentary. The general conclusion was inevitable: "It was found that the curative efforts of the physicians of the Office of Indian Affairs were largely nullified by the conditions under which work is attempted and by the indifference and ignorance of the primitive Indians. The important problem is not so much the medical treatment of the Indians for disease as the improvement of insanitary conditions causing such diseases."[28]

A CONTINUING BUT INSUFFICIENT FIGHT

In response to the president's plea and the disheartening facts presented by the Public Health Survey of 1912, Congress raised the annual appropriation for relieving distress and fighting disease to $200,000 for 1914, $300,000 for 1915 and 1916, and $350,000 for 1917. The sums were considerably below what was actually needed, but Commissioner Cato Sells enthusiastically continued the fight to protect and improve the condition of the Indians. He built new hospitals, appointed ophthalmologists to special districts of the Indian country, stressed educational measures to prevent disease, promoted lectures (illustrated with stereopticon slides and motion pictures) at

27. Ibid., pp. 62–63.
28. A summary of the findings is given ibid., pp. 73–80, and recommendations are on pp. 82–85.

the schools and on the reservations, and pushed the standard remedies of better sanitary conditions in Indian homes, better ventilation, and sufficient nourishing food. "The maintenance of good health," he declared in 1915, "is a prime requisite in the process of civilizing the Indian and placing him upon a self-supporting basis. Large sums of money and much scientific thought have been given to the improvement of sanitary conditions among these people. Results indicate that there has been wonderful improvement."[29] The improvement, however, fell much short of perfection, for the two chief diseases continued to be a great menace. A study on trachoma written by an Indian service physician and published by the Indian Office in 1915 declared that trachoma existed among the Indians in several states "to such an extent that if it were measles, whooping cough, scarlet fever, or smallpox its prevalence would be declared an epidemic and panic among the people of these districts would prevail."[30]

One of Sells's special concerns was the high infant mortality rate among the Indians. Building on one of Valentine's stated priorities, "save the babies," and the increasing awareness of infant mortality among reformers of the age, Sells promoted measures to increase the nourishment of Indian mothers, and he sent reading material on child care to the matrons, who could then instruct the mothers. He pushed exhibits on child care at Indian fairs, prepared and distributed pamphlets on child care (*Indian Mothers, Save Your Babies*), and—with little success—tried to persuade Indian mothers to have their babies delivered in hospitals instead of at home. He carried his concern to all Indian service employees in an emotional letter of January 10, 1916, in which he asked all to develop "a righteous passion to see that every Indian child has a fair chance to live," and he said, "If we have an Indian policy worthy of the name," he said, "its goal must be an enduring and sturdy race, true to the noblest of its original instincts and virtues and loyally sympathetic with our social and national life; a body of efficient citizens blending their unique poise and powers with the keen and sleepless vigor of the white man." The first step in his campaign, he said, was "to save the babies."[31]

Sells was pleased with the results, and in 1917 he announced: "The In-

29. CIA Report, 1913, serial 6634, pp. 20–21; CIA Report, 1914, serial 6815, pp. 14–17; CIA Report, 1915, serial 6992, pp. 12–14.

30. W. H. Harrison, *Trachoma: Its Cause, Prevention, and Treatment* (Washington: GPO, 1915), pp. 3–4.

31. Sells's letter of January 10, 1916, is printed in CIA Report, 1916, serial 7160, pp. 5–8. For directives on infant care, see the following circulars: no. 764, July 31, 1913; no. 865, May 20, 1914; no. 933, June 9, 1915; no. 1003, July 10, 1915, OIA Circulars (M1121, reels 10–11). For more information on the campaign against infant mortality, see Putney, "Fighting the Scourge," pp. 176–83.

dian is no longer a vanishing race." Birth rates were exceeding death rates, and there had been a significant drop in the number of deaths of infants under three years of age.[32]

Another of Sells's interests was the "Swat the Fly" campaign, for it was generally agreed that flies were responsible for the spread of disease, especially tuberculosis and trachoma. The commissioner directed superintendents to make reservation privies fly proof, and he distributed information on removing conditions that bred flies, on sanitary garbage cans, and on special fly traps.[33] He continued dental programs initiated by Commissioner Valentine, concerned himself with physically and mentally handicapped Indian children, and fought alcoholism as a contributing condition to poor health.[34]

It is impossible to judge what might have been the results of the steadily increasing appropriations for Indian health and the strenuous campaigns directed by Sells if they had continued unabated. The fight, unfortunately, was obstructed, cut back, and in some cases halted by World War I and the postwar inflation and government retrenchment. The wartime demands for personnel made a shambles of the Indian medical service. Nearly 40 percent of the positions for regular physicians were vacant in 1918, and similar cuts had been made among the nurses, as figures supplied by the Indian Office to the House Committee on Indian Affairs showed (see Table 9).

The contract physicians who made up almost half the medical service in 1918 rendered little more than emergency service. Thus, to meet the serious health needs of the Indians that had been repeatedly identified, the essential medical personnel were greatly cut instead of increased. Related supporting services of teachers and matrons, too, were reduced, as men and women went into military service or took better-paying jobs outside the Indian service. At the end of the war, the strength of the medical service remained considerably below the authorized strength, and the turnover rate was high. Wartime shortages of materials and rising prices further undercut the effectiveness of health care.[35]

---

32. CIA Report, 1917, serial 7358, p. 19. The idea was in the air. See "The Indian Is No Longer a Vanishing Race," a talk at Lake Mohonk in 1916 by Dr. Lawrence W. White. *Lake Mohonk Conference Proceedings*, 1916, pp. 59–65. Sells printed the talk as an appendix to the Indian Office pamphlet *Tuberculosis among Indians* (Washington: Acme Printing Company, 1917).

33. See, for example, Circular no. 707, November 9, 1912, and supplement of January 6, 1914; Circular no. 1263, February 15, 1917, OIA Circulars (M1121, reels 10–11).

34. These programs are described in Putney, "Fighting the Scourge," pp. 170–76.

35. Sells noted the problems in 1918, but he insisted that the positive work was going ahead nevertheless. CIA Report, 1918, serial 7498, pp. 34–36. He gave a more serious description of the decimation of the service in CIA Report, 1919, serial 7706, pp. 25–26,

TABLE 9: Indian Medical Service Personnel

	Regular Physicians	Contract Physicians	Nurses
Authorized for 1917	128	69	99
In service January 1, 1917	116	70	91
In service August 31, 1917	108	60	90
In service November 1, 1918	79	60	55

SOURCE: "Indians of the United States," *Hearings before the Committee on Indian Affairs, House of Representatives, on Conditions of Various Tribes of Indians* (1919), p. 285.

Added to this already dismal picture was the devastating influenza epidemic of 1918–1919, which struck some Indian reservations with even more terrifying force than it did the army units and the general public. Nurses and physicians were hired from Public Health Service funds during the height of the emergency at the end of 1918, but no means seemed effective in controlling the disease. Indian Office statistics showed that between October 1, 1918, and March 31, 1919, out of a total Indian population of 304,854, there were 73,651 cases of influenza and 6,270 deaths. Thus more than 2 percent of the Indians died from the epidemic, with the mortality especially high in Colorado, Utah, and New Mexico. The death rate for Indians far exceeded that of the white population in the same period.[36]

The Indian medical service never did get back to "normal," because of the postwar drive for economy and retrenchment, which Commissioner Charles H. Burke did not effectively oppose. In the face of continuing needs for Indian health, which he recognized and with which he sympathized, Burke nevertheless seemed comfortable in adhering to the retrenchment moves of the Republican administration.[37]

The attacks on the Indian Office by the rising tide of reformers in the 1920s, however, shocked the administration into new efforts. Secretary of

---

but he did not lose heart. See his exhortatory letter on health to all Indian service employees, June 18, 1919, in CIA Report, 1919, serial 7706, pp. 29—31.

36. "Influenza among American Indians," *Public Health Reports* 34 (May 9, 1919): 1008–9. These figures do not include the second, less serious wave of the epidemic in 1919. Extensive reports on influenza, reservation by reservation, are in OIA CCF, General Service 731, 732.

37. A critical account of Burke's policy of economy and retrenchment is in Putney, "Fighting the Scourge," pp. 211–18.

the Interior Hubert Work, who replaced Albert Fall in 1923, was himself trained as a physician and had been president of the American Medical Association; he responded to criticisms of Indian health policy by requesting an additional $100,000 from Congress in 1924, for which he gained the support of the Committee of One Hundred. From the increased appropriation that Congress voted for fiscal year 1925 ($500,000 for "the relief and care of destitute Indians not otherwise provided for, and for the prevention and treatment of tuberculosis, trachoma, smallpox, and other contagious and infectious diseases"), $65,000 was devoted to a campaign against trachoma in the Southwest, principally among the Navajos. A serious program was inaugurated, although it was handicapped by bickering among the directors and by sincere disagreement over the best methods for curing the disease.[38]

A crucial decision made by the Indian Office was to support radical surgery on the eyelids, which was promoted by Dr. L. Webster Fox, an ophthalmologist at the University of Pennsylvania Medical School. At special clinics he taught the Indian service trachoma specialists the Fox techniques, and they in turn instructed the regular physicians. This appeared to be the solution to the troubling problem, and the Indian Office accepted it uncritically, directing its resources to the surgery for "curing" the disease, to the neglect of preventive measures. The Board of Indian Commissioners applauded the work. "The unquestionable success of the intensive effort," it reported in 1925, "through a well-organized campaign to fight trachoma, warrants the strong hope that in a comparatively few years our Indian people will be clear eyed and reservations will be rid of the disease

38. The Committee of One Hundred's resolution on health and sanitation said in part: "We recognize the national responsibility to combat such evils as tuberculosis, pyorrhea, and trachoma, and we favor the use of whatever means will quickly and effectively meet the situation represented by them. We urge earnestly upon Congress the appropriation of the sum of $100,000 asked by the Bureau of Indian Affairs for this purpose." In "The Indian Problem: Resolutions of the Committee of One Hundred," *House Document* no. 149, 68–1, serial 8273, p. 2. The appropriation is in 43 *United States Statutes* 408. Putney, "Fighting the Scourge," pp. 227–50, describes the Southwest trachoma campaign in detail.

The widespread interest in the trachoma problem can be seen in the numerous publications dealing with the matter. See, for example, John McMullen, *Trachoma: Its Nature and Prevention* (Washington: GPO, 1923), a publication of the Public Health Service; "The Trachoma Problem among the Indians," *Medical Searchlight* 1 (April 1925): 17–21; Lewis H. Carris, *Trachoma among the Indians: What Uncle Sam Should Do about It*, Eastern Association of Indian Affairs, Bulletin no. 7 (1925), written by the managing director of the National Committee for the Prevention of Blindness; and *Trachoma among the Indians*, Eastern Association on Indian Affairs, Bulletin no. 10 (1925), which contains abstracts of speeches given at a joint meeting of the Association and the National Committee for the Prevention of Blindness, December 2, 1925. Copies of these materials are in OIA, Board of Indian Commissioners, Reference Material, Health.

which has made blind men and women common objects in Indian communities."[39] In the end, however, better judgment ruled against Fox's measures. Not only had the technique been universally prescribed whether it was indicated or not, but it was often performed by unskilled persons, and the needed postoperative treatment was neglected. The whole trachoma campaign was seriously discredited.[40]

The concentration on curing diseases among the Indians—of which the Southwest trachoma campaign was a fine example—was open to serious criticism, for in the long run preventive measures promised the only effective control of disease. That would have entailed an emphasis on public health measures, which the Indian Office seemed unable or unwilling to undertake. The ineffectiveness of the Indian medical service in this matter was strikingly revealed by a report prepared in the early 1920s by the American Red Cross. At the request of Commissioner Burke, the Red Cross commissioned Florence Patterson, a Red Cross public health nurse with extensive experience in America and Europe during and after World War I, to study Indian health. Beginning in October 1922, Patterson spent nine months in the field, visiting thirteen superintendencies and examining some forty thousand Indians. This was the most thorough investigation since the Public Health Service study of a decade earlier. What Patterson reported was not of much consolation to the Indian Office, for she still found rampant disease. Worse still, she reported extremely spotty and ineffective record keeping and an indifference, if not outright hostility, toward preventive medicine, which was the foundation of a public health approach. At the boarding schools she scored the diets, carelessness in regard to contagion, harsh institutional routine with its heavy work schedule, and renewed overcrowding (with a resultant increase in the incidence of tuberculosis) that resulted from Burke's campaign to fill the schools to capacity. Patterson was especially critical of the field matrons, so essential in promoting hygiene on the reservations, and she insisted that they should be replaced by trained public health nurses.[41]

39. *Report of the Board of Indian Commissioners*, 1925, pp. 14–15.

40. Putney, "Fighting the Scourge," pp. 233–44. The Indian Office had also been assisted by a special advisory committee on trachoma appointed by the American Medical Association. See material on this committee in OIA CCF, General Service 732, 78136–1924 and 40506–1925.

41. Patterson's report, "A Study of the Need for Public-Health Nursing on Indian Reservations," was not made public until 1928, when it was included in "Survey of Conditions of the Indians in the United States," *Hearings before a Subcommittee of the Committee on Indian Affairs, United States Senate*, 43 vols. (1928–1943), 3: 955–1005. The Indian Office's directives for increasing enrollment in 1921 are in Circular no. 1705, August 12, 1921, OIA Circulars (M1121, reel 12); see also Circular no. 2254, August 11, 1926, ibid. (M1121, reel 13).

Although Burke had suggested that such a report could be used as lever-
age upon Congress for increased appropriations, he in fact suppressed the
report when he received it in June 1924. He asked the Red Cross not to
make the report public and buried his copy in the files, for he feared that
John Collier and others of his critics might seize the evidence it presented
and make capital of it in their fight against the Indian Office. The Indian
service's medical supervisor, Dr. Robert E. L. Newberne, prepared an analysis of Patterson's report, which lamely refuted the charges, supported the
field matrons, and suggested that Patterson was promoting the self-interests
of the Public Health Service Nursing Association. The chief positive result
of Patterson's work was the appointment of a Red Cross public health
nurse, Elinor D. Gregg, as supervisor of nurses and field matrons; but the
effectiveness of her work was hindered by conservative physicians and superintendents, who did not appreciate the innovations that a public health
approach entailed.[42]

Yet, despite such criticism as that in Florence Patterson's report, there
were advances in the medical service in the 1920s. The Classification Act
of 1923, with its extension to field positions in 1924, redefined positions in
the civil service system and upgraded salaries for the Indian service, including those of physicians; Burke remarked that "unquestionably the increase
in salaries under reclassification has had much to do with a marked improvement in the personnel of the service." The pay of the doctors still did
not equal that of other government physicians, but the move was in the
right direction.[43] And, although Burke in his concern for the economy
eliminated positions in the Indian service as a whole, the appropriations
and numbers for the medical service slowly increased (see Table 10).

A large share of the increased appropriations that came from time to
time went into hospitals, which were classified as sanatoriums, primarily
for the treatment of tuberculosis (there were eleven in 1925), general and
agency hospitals, and school hospitals for treatment of children in the
boarding schools. In addition, the government had built an insane asylum
for Indians at Canton, South Dakota, which admitted its first patients in
1903 and gradually expanded its capacity; in 1915 the asylum had about
fifty patients, in 1925 one hundred. Although the inadequacy of these institutions for the total Indian population and the poor equipment and lim-

42. Robert E. L. Newberne, "A Review of Miss Patterson's Report Entitled 'A Study of
the Need for Public-Health Nursing on Indian Reservations,'" in "Survey of Conditions
of the Indians in the United States," 3: 1005–17. A thorough account of Patterson's report and the reaction of the Indian Office is in Putney, "Fighting the Scourge," pp. 255–
90. Elinor D. Gregg, The Indians and the Nurse (Norman: University of Oklahoma Press,
1965), a book of reminiscences, gives insight into the work of nurses on the reservations.
43. 42 United States Statutes 1488–99; 43 United States Statutes 704–5.

TABLE 10: Indian Medical Service, 1911–1926

Year	General Appropriation	Hospitals	Capacity (beds)	Physicians[a]	Nurses	Hospital Employees	Field Matrons
1911	$40,000	50	1,268	—	—	—	—
1914	200,000	51	1,432	—	—	—	—
1917	350,000	81	2,273	—	—	—	—
1920	375,000	85	2,190	160	98	158	78
1923	370,000	77	—	177	106	154	63
1926	700,000	91	2,750	194	132	229	27

SOURCE: Data from Laurence F. Schmeckebier, *The Office of Indian Affairs: Its History, Activities and Organization* (Baltimore: Johns Hopkins Press, 1927), p. 232.
[a] One-fourth to one-third of the physicians reported were contracted.

ited staff that marked most of them were frequent targets of critics of the Indian medical service, the system was a considerable advance over the few hospitals that had existed at the beginning of the century.[44]

In 1924 the Indian Office designed a new health education program for the Indian schools, which Burke called "the most important educational event of the year." Implementation of the course of study, however, was left pretty much to the local authorities.[45]

THE CRITICS

The Indian Office worked within an atmosphere of growing criticism from John Collier and the American Indian Defense Association and other individuals outside the government who lamented the state of Indian health.

44. Extensive data on the hospitals is provided in Laurence F. Schmeckebier, *The Office of Indian Affairs: Its History, Activities, and Organization* (Baltimore: Johns Hopkins Press, 1927), pp. 234–66. The annual reports of the commissioner of Indian affairs frequently commented on hospital development and on the insane asylum. For pictures and floor plans of the hospitals, see Arthur E. Middleton, "Supplementing the Medicine Man," *Modern Hospital* 19 (July 1922): 41–43; (August 1922): 139–42.
45. CIA Report, 1925, p. 8; Office of Indian Affairs, Office of the Chief Supervisor of Education, *A Program of Health Education for Indian Schools* (Lawrence, Kansas: Haskell Printing Department, 1924). The program was prepared with the cooperation of the American Child Health Association and was based on a report of the Joint Committee on Health Problems in Education of the National Education Association and the American Medical Association.

The ineffectiveness of the health programs for Indians that was revealed in the surveys and the continuing high morbidity statistics led critics to recommend transfer of the responsibility for Indian health to the Public Health Service, which was directed by the surgeon general within the Treasury Department. The idea was broached as early as 1919, when the House Committee on Indian Affairs investigated the reorganization of the Indian service. Because the Public Health Service was highly respected, whereas the Indian medical service seemed unable to accomplish effectively what was needed in Indian health care, such a transfer won many supporters. The Indian Office, however, strongly opposed such a move, which it called "a proposition so extraordinary and so radically at variance with administrative procedures." The main argument was that medical problems could not be separated from "the educational, social, and industrial problems that concern a race that is in the critical transformation period of evolution from one social plane to another." And if the Public Health Service would have to care for Indian health under existing appropriations, it could do no better than the Indian Office; but "if additional appropriations were made for the United States Indian Medical Service, it would be an easy matter to place it upon a Public Health Service efficiency basis." Dr. Rupert Blue, the surgeon general, also opposed transfer, for he claimed that he was already overwhelmed with caring for disabled veterans. He absolved the Indian Office from blame for the high prevalence of disease among the Indians, which he attributed largely to their "aboriginal characteristics."[46] The idea did not die, and transfer was promoted by Collier and the American Indian Defense Association and a variety of other concerned persons. But even when the House Committee on Indian Affairs reported favorably on the plan, Congress took no action.[47]

What happened was a half-measure but one of considerable importance. When Dr. Newberne, the chief medical supervisor of the Indian service, died in early 1926, Secretary Work asked the Public Health Service to assign one of its officers to act in that position. In March 1926 Dr. Marshall C. Guthrie assumed the post. At the same time, the Indian reserva-

46. "Indians of the United States," *Hearings before the Committee on Indian Affairs, House of Representatives, on the Condition of Various Tribes of Indians* (1919), pp. 285–89, 436–37.

47. "Reorganizing the Indian Service," *House Report* no. 1189, 66–3, serial 7776, p. 3. Examples of support for transfer are G. E. E. Lindquist, *The Red Man in the United States: An Intimate Study of the Social, Economic and Religious Life of the American Indian* (New York: George H. Doran Company, 1923), p. 391; letters to the editor of the *Journal of the American Medical Association* by Frederick L. Hoffman, 75 (August 14, 1920): 493–94, and 81 (September 8, 1923): 848–49; by L. Webster Fox, 81 (November 3, 1923): 1544–45.

tions were divided into four geographical districts, each with a district medical officer whose duties were to keep tab on the medical services within his district, coordinate the activities of the Indian physicians, and promote friendly relations with state and local health agencies.[48]

A strong criticism of the Indian medical service continued to be the sad status of the records kept on diseases and deaths, a charge that was well to the point. The confusion as to mortality rates and the incidence of diseases was shocking and embarrassing to the Indian Office and made difficult if not impossible any efficient drive against the health problems.[49] One persistent critic, who spoke with authority on the subject, was Frederick L. Hoffman, a statistician of the Prudential Insurance Company, who attempted to stir up action among the members of the American Medical Association. He called the Indian medical situation "as deplorable as it is disgraceful," and spoke of "the most regrettable apathy on the part of the nation which has assumed responsibility for the medical needs of the Indian population."[50] Another general, and more violent, critic was Dr. Haven Emerson, a professor of Public Health Administration at Columbia University, who was a close associate of Collier and president of the American Indian Defense Association. He called the Indian medical service "the most disgraceful apology for scientific or humane medical care under the federal or state government" and used the health and sanitary conditions among the Indians as a whip against the Indian Office.[51]

Naturally enough, the commissioner of Indian affairs and the secretary of the interior were defensive in the face of attacks on their Indian health policies and programs, and they prepared statements that pointed to the

48. CIA Report, 1926, pp. 1–2; Circular no. 2230, June 5, 1926, OIA Circulars (M1121, reel 13).

49. Putney, "Fighting the Scourge," pp. 298–302.

50. *Journal of the American Medical Association* 75 (August 14, 1920): 493–94; 81 (September 8, 1923): 848–49. In a talk before the Eastern Association on Indian Affairs on February 5, 1925, however, Hoffman, while still voicing strong criticism about the Indian medical service and urging its transfer to the Public Health Service, softened his views of the Indian Office. He offered his "profound appreciation of what the Office of Indian Affairs has done or aimed at doing in its 100 years of Indian Administration" and spoke of "the obvious sincerity of the various Indian Commissioners during recent years, who, in season and out, have tried to improve conditions of Indian life." Frederick L. Hoffman, *Medical Problems of Our Indian Population*, Eastern Association on Indian Affairs, Bulletin no. 6 (1925).

51. Haven Emerson, "Morbidity of the American Indians," *Science* 63 (February 26, 1926): 229–31; *Journal of the American Medical Association* 88 (February 5, 1927): 424. See also Bulletin no. 8 of the American Indian Defense Association, entitled *Our Near East*, the criticisms of which were repeated in an editorial, "The Fate of Our Indians," *Medical World* 42 (November 1924): 355–57.

advances made, while admitting that serious problems still remained. Their ultimate refuge was the insufficiency of the appropriations made by Congress for Indian health.[52]

If the commissioner of Indian affairs and the secretary of the interior were well pleased because they had accomplished so much for Indian health, the Meriam survey staff was appalled that they had accomplished so little. "Taken as a whole," the Meriam Report stated, "practically every activity undertaken by the national government for the promotion of the health of the Indians is below a reasonable standard of efficiency." The cause it saw was lack of sufficient money to set salaries high enough to hire really competent people and to provide facilities for health care that met even minimum standards from a scientific standpoint. More telling was the criticism that "lack of vision and real understanding have precluded the establishment in the Indian service of a real program of preventive medicine," and the report ridiculed the attempts to prevent trachoma as consisting "mainly in providing separate towels in boarding schools, displaying posters in Indian communities, and in a small amount of rather ineffective segregating of cases in schools." The position of the Meriam staff was that an effective public health program—with public health nurses in place of matrons and physicians who were "public health men" —would have to be substituted for the existing system, which was largely relief of the sick, not the prevention and eradication of disease.[53]

The recommendations were in line with these positions: strengthening the personnel in number and qualifications, inauguration of an adequate public health program (including complete medical records, public health nurses, home demonstration agents, and social workers to reach the Indians in their homes, regular clinics for early diagnosis and treatment of disease, and adequate hospitals and sanatoriums), and revising the whole regime of the boarding schools "to make them institutions for developing health" (with better food, less overcrowding, thorough periodic physical examinations, reduction of the labor required of the children, and greater effort to prevent contagion).[54]

52. See Hubert Work's letter in *Journal of the American Medical Association* 81 (October 20, 1923): 1382, in reply to Hoffman; Work to William Barton Brader, December 10, 1924, OIA CCF, General Service 732, 83084–1924, in which he supplies a long answer to the article in the *Medical World* of November 1924; Charles H. Burke to Walter W. Woehlke, November 10, 1928, ibid., 53800–1928, in which Burke refutes charges made in an article in *Sunset*; and letter of M. C. Guthrie, *Journal of the American Medical Association* 88 (April 9, 1927): 1198–99, which challenges Haven Emerson's letter.

53. *The Problem of Indian Administration* [Meriam Report] (Baltimore: Johns Hopkins Press, 1928). Health received more attention than any other subject; it is treated briefly on pp. 3–4 and 9–11 and at great length on pp. 189–345.

54. Ibid., p. 195.

In trachoma work, the Indian Office was properly criticized for its whole-sale acceptance of Dr. Fox's radical surgery without follow-up examina-tions to see if it was in truth effective. The report also suggested the possi-bility that trachoma was a deficiency disease, not one caused by the spread of infection, and it criticized the Indian Office for not acting upon the like-lihood. (Here, of course, the report was on the wrong track, and in fact no cure for trachoma was found until it was treated in 1937 with sulpha drugs.) The organization of the medical service, also, received critical at-tention, especially because of the subordination of the physicians to the superintendents and the failure to maintain adequate records. It noted, however, that the new organization under Dr. Guthrie had inaugurated "a marked change for the better."[55] The Meriam Report furnished a stimulus and a guide for bettering the care of Indian health, but health conditions improved very slowly and never kept pace with the advances made by the general society of the United States.

55. Ibid., pp. 208–16, 244–74.

CHAPTER 34

The Indians' Land

Continuing Allotment. Modifications

of the Dawes Act. Competency and Fee Patents.

Land Policy in the 1920s. Forestry and

Irrigation. Appraisal of the Allotment Policy.

The key to Indian self-support was the ability to make a living from the land. The Dawes Act of 1887 was the fruit of the philosophy that individual pieces of property—homesteads—would not only protect the Indians' title to the land but would be the paramount means of turning them into hardworking farmers. Then, when the Indians had become self-supporting citizens under the working of the allotment law, they would disappear into American society, and the government could gradually go out of the Indian business. Although allotment began almost at once after the Dawes Act was passed, the great period of allotment was the first decade of the twentieth century, as the machinery shifted into high gear and as the pressure from white farmers for the opening of the reservations grew. But allotment was only the first step in the program for the Indians. The final step was the issuing of patents in fee to the allottees so that they would at last have full control of their property and could use it or dispose of it as they pleased. Until allotment was ended in 1934, managing individual allotments, granting fee patents, and leasing and selling Indian lands were a principal work of the federal government. Instead of withering away according to the blueprint, the Indian Office vastly increased its involvement; it became a sort of real estate agent, handling a multitude of land transactions for individual Indians. And in the end, the results were not at all what the advocates of allotment intended. Nothing seemed to work right. Many Indians turned into petty landlords, who leased their lands and eked out a pitiful existence on the rents, and many others, once they had gained full title to the land, sold it. In the first third of the twentieth century, the Indians' estate was dissipated.[1]

CONTINUING ALLOTMENT

Allotment continued to be the goal of the Indian Office and the reform groups after the turn of the century. Commissioner Robert Valentine expressed the spirit of the times in 1910: "The essential feature of the Government's great educational program for the Indians is the abolition of the old tribal relations and the treatment of every Indian as an individual. The basis of this individualization is the breaking up of tribal lands into allotments to the individuals of the tribe. This step is fundamental to the present Indian policy of the Government. Until their lands are allotted, the Government is merely marking time in dealing with any group of Indians."[2] Year by year the number of allotted acres was totaled up as a sign of progress. In 1900 there were 55,996 allotments, covering 6,736,504 acres; by 1910 these figures had swelled to 190,401 allotments covering 31,093,647 acres. In 1911 Valentine reported that roughly two-thirds of the Indians had been allotted. After that the process slowed down, for most of the land in reservations that were amenable to allotment had been allotted, and what was left was in areas, especially in the Southwest, where division of the lands was not immediately feasible. By 1920 the number of allotments on reservations had advanced to only 217,572 and the acres allotted to 35,897,069.[3] These allotments were made fundamentally under the provisions of the Dawes Act, but Congress passed many particular laws providing for specific reservations. These special acts (or sections in the annual Indian appropriation laws) came in response to pressure to open

---

1. There is no thorough modern study of Indian land policy and problems in this period. A compilation of data is found in J. P. Kinney, *A Continent Lost—A Civilization Won: Indian Land Tenure in America* (Baltimore: Johns Hopkins Press, 1937), pp .214–343. For legal aspects, see Felix S. Cohen, *Handbook of Federal Indian Law* (Washington: GPO, 1942), and its 1982 revision. A helpful introduction to the literature is Imre Sutton, *Indian Land Tenure: Bibliographical Essays and a Guide to the Literature* (New York: Clearwater Publishing Company, 1975). Part of the period is covered in Janet McDonnell, "The Disintegration of the Indian Estate: Indian Land Policy, 1913–1929" (Ph.D. dissertation, Marquette University, 1980).

2. CIA Report, 1910, serial 5976, p. 28.

3. CIA Report, 1900, serial 4101, p. 600; CIA Report, 1910, serial 5976, p. 67; CIA Report, 1911, serial 6223, pp. 22–23; CIA Report, 1920, serial 7820, p. 82.

the Indians' land to settlement but also because conditions on the various reservations necessitated special provisions for division of the land and disposition of the surplus.[4]

A special problem concerned allotments on the public domain. Section 4 of the Dawes Act had authorized such allotments for Indians who did not reside on a reservation or for whose tribe no reservation had been set aside, but these limitations were generally overlooked. Through the years a number of Indians took advantage of the provisions; by 1920, 8,776 allotments had been made on the public domain, covering 1,261,586 acres.[5] Questions arose, however, about reservation Indians who wanted to augment their holdings and about the wives of Indians whose husbands had public domain allotments. Could they move onto the public domain, and under what conditions of settlement? The General Land Office, which officially issued the patents to allottees, tended to equate such settlement with regular homesteading procedures and thus to require a set period of residence on the land. This Commissioner Cato Sells steadfastly opposed, for he realized that the nomadic habits of many of the Indians—and it was the Navajos and other Indians of the Southwest to whom public domain allotments most appealed—made it infeasible to require formal continuous occupation.[6] In the end Sells won out. The new *Regulations Governing Indian Allotments on the Public Domain*, issued on April 15, 1918, required only that the Indian "assert a claim to the land based upon the reasonable use or occupation thereof consistent with his mode of life and the character of the land and climate," although the issuance of the trust patent was to be suspended for two years in order to test the good faith of the allottee. Wives who qualified for allotments were provided for in regulations issued in 1921.[7] The situation in the Southwest, however, was greatly complicated by conflicts in New Mexico and Arizona, where the move of the Navajos to expand their holdings by means of public domain allotments

4. Kinney, *A Continent Lost*, p. 245n, gives a list of such acts passed 1900–1910. An excellent case study of local pressures for special legislation to open a reservation is Burton M. Smith, "The Politics of Allotment: The Flathead Indian Reservation as a Test Case," *Pacific Northwest Quarterly*, 70 (July 1979): 131–40.

5. CIA Report, 1920, serial 7820, p. 82.

6. This controversy can be traced in the correspondence in OSI CCF 506, General, Allotments, Public Domain; for examples see Sells to the secretary of the interior, November 12, 1913; Clay Tallman to Alexander T. Vogelsang, November 30, 1917; and Sells to Vogelsang, January 14, 1918.

7. *Regulations Governing Indian Allotments on the Public Domain under Section 4 of the Act of February 8, 1887 (24 Stat., 388), As Amended by the Act of February 28, 1891 (26 Stat., 794), and As Further Amended by the Act of June 25, 1910 (36 Stat., 855)* (Washington: GPO, 1918), pp. 5–6; CIA Report, 1921, pp. 22–23.

was opposed by white land interests, who wanted to prevent any such expansion.[8]

The allotment of mineral lands, as opposed to agricultural lands, raised other difficult problems. The purpose of the Dawes Act had been to turn the Indians into farmers or stockmen, and it specified only agricultural and grazing lands. When it became evident that some reservation land was rich in coal or oil or other minerals, controversies arose about whether individual Indians should be allowed to take such lands as allotments (with the concomitant problem of then opening the remaining mineral lands as "surplus"), or whether the government should act to protect the mineral wealth for the tribe as a whole. The questions were settled chiefly in the laws dealing with particular reservations, which were generally in favor of allotting the mineral lands to the Indians.[9]

The allotment of Indian reservation lands was accompanied by the disposal of the "surplus" land to white settlers. The Dawes Act had specified negotiation with the Indians for the sale of lands remaining after the allotments had been made—"such portions of its reservation not allotted as such tribe shall, from time to time, consent to sell, on such terms and conditions as shall be considered just and equitable between the United States and such tribe of Indians"—and agreements had been made with the tribes and approved by Congress. After the Supreme Court in *Lone Wolf* v. *Hitchcock* in 1903 declared that Congress had power to dispose of Indian lands without Indian consent, the process was speeded up.

The opening of a part of the Rosebud Reservation in South Dakota in 1904 set the pattern. In order to avoid appropriations for buying Indian lands, Congress proposed that instead of the outright purchase of surplus lands to add to the public domain, the actual settlers on those lands should be required to pay the Indians directly. The House Committee on Indian Affairs, chaired by Charles H. Burke of South Dakota, in favorably reporting the new measure admitted that it broke with the past in its method of paying for Indian lands, and it justified acting without Indian consent. The arguments of advantages to the Indians were an echo of those used to promote the Dawes Act twenty years earlier:

> The passage of this bill will open for settlement 416,000 acres of land, which will be settled upon, cultivated, and improved, and

8. This complex story is told in Lawrence C. Kelly, *The Navajo Indians and Federal Indian Policy, 1900–1935* (Tucson: University of Arizona Press, 1968), pp. 18–36. On public domain allotments and the problems involved, see McDonnell, "Disintegration of the Indian Estate," pp. 24–40.

9. McDonnell, "Disintegration of the Indian Estate," pp. 19–24. The question of mineral leases is treated in *Felix S. Cohen's Handbook of Federal Indian Law*, 1982 ed. (Charlottesville, Virginia: Michie, Bobbs-Merrill, 1982), pp. 531–38.

turned into actual homes. This will enhance very materially the value of the 452 Indian allotments which are within the area proposed to be ceded, and give them the benefit of learning how to farm and raise stock from actual observation, and will tend to make them more self-supporting, and be a great improvement upon their present condition, many of them being dependent upon the bounty of the Government, and the sooner the Indian reservations are broken up and the Indians required to take their allotments and their surplus lands opened to settlement, the better it will be for the advancement and higher civilization of the Indian.[10]

The committee relied upon the Lone Wolf decision (which it reprinted in its report) in asserting the power of Congress to act without consulting the Indians, and it quoted at length testimony before the committee given by Commissioner of Indian Affairs William A. Jones:

> If you depend upon the consent of the Indians as to the disposition of the land where they have the fee to the land, you will have difficulty in getting it, and I think the decision in the Lone Wolf case, that Congress can do as it sees fit with the property of the Indians will enable you to dispose of that land without the consent of the Indians. If you wait for their consent in these matters, it will be fifty years before you can do away with the reservations. . . .
>
> I know I am running counter to the traditions of the office of my superiors in this, but hereafter, when asked to make any report on these bills, I shall report in favor of Congress taking the property of the Indians without their consent.
>
> MR. BURKE. Would you make that statement general or would you except reservations where there may be in existence treaty relations that provide directly to the contrary? For instance, do you know there is in existence among the Sioux—I think in the treaty of 1868—a provision that the Indians will not be deprived of their lands without the consent of three-fourths, and that provision was reenacted, I think, in the treaty of 1889.
>
> COMMISSIONER JONES. I will go to the extreme. I do not think I would ask the consent of the Indians in that case. Supposing you were the guardian or ward [sic] of a child 8 or 10 years of age, would you ask the consent of the child as to the investment of its fund? No; you would not, and I do not think it is a good business principle in this case.[11]

---

10. *House Report* no. 443, 58–2, serial 4578, p. 3.

11. Ibid., pp. 4–5. In a letter to the secretary of the interior, January 9, 1904, Jones wrote: "As a general proposition the Office has to say that after careful and mature con-

Both the committee and the commissioner, in accepting the authority to act without Indian consent, asserted the responsibility of the government to act in good faith in the Indians' best interests.[12] These statements, however, did not satisfy the watchdogs of Indian rights, and there was soon harsh criticism of the proposed Rosebud bill from the Indian Rights Association and other Indian advocates. The association, having lost its attempt to prevent the Lone Wolf decision, accepted the principle of plenary legislative power over Indian affairs and turned its attention to the fairness of the proposed legislation. The three dollars an acre that the Rosebud bill proposed was condemned as completely inadequate. Marshaling evidence from the Indians and from others about the substantially greater value of the lands in question, the Indian Rights Association petitioned Congress to set at least five dollars an acre as the price (a compromise, it said, that the Indians were willing to accept). Although it broadcast its plea through newspaper articles and a special pamphlet, the association was unable to prevent the passage of the measure and could not persuade the president to veto it, and the bill became law on April 23, 1904.[13] Congress, with the continued support of Commissioner Jones, similarly revised an earlier agreement with the Crow Indians and provided for opening their lands in the pattern of the Rosebud legislation, and other measures followed suit.[14]

---

sideration it is of the opinion that the time has come when Congress and the Indian Department are warranted in administering the tribal interests of the Indians in the United States, including the matter of disposing of such of their lands as they do not need and do not use, without consulting the Indians affected in reference thereto." Ibid., p. 8.

12. Ibid., pp. 5, 8.

13. "Memorial of the Indian Rights Association on Behalf of the Rosebud Indians," February 15, 1904, Senate Document no. 158, 58–2, serial 4590; Another "Century of Dishonor"? (Philadelphia: Indian Rights Association, 1904); 33 United States Statutes 254–58. See also George Kennan, "Indian Lands and Fair Play," Outlook 76 (February 27, 1904): 498–501, which the Indian Rights Association reprinted in its pamphlet.

14. House Report no. 890, 58–2, serial 4579; 33 United States Statutes 352–62. There is discussion of these land openings in Frederick E. Hoxie, "Beyond Savagery: The Campaign to Assimilate the American Indians, 1890–1920" (Ph.D. dissertation, Brandeis University, 1977), pp. 381–92.

Another invasion of Indian lands occurred in the increased granting of rights of way through Indian reservations and allotted lands still held in trust to railroads and other means of communication. Many Indian treaties from early times had provided for rights of way for roads through Indian lands, and particular legislation had authorized railroad construction. At the end of the nineteenth and beginning of the twentieth century the need for separate pieces of legislation was obviated by laws that gave general authorization, under the direction of the secretary of the interior. An act of March 2, 1899, granted rights of way for the construction of railroads and telegraph and telephone lines to any railroad company organized under federal or state laws. 30 United States Statutes 990–92. An act of March 3, 1901, authorized easements for telephone and telegraph lines, and an act of February 15, 1901, authorized power plants and power lines for the generation

Although allotment of Indian lands moved forward rapidly, until the great bulk of allottable land had been divided into small individual parcels and the tribal landed estate destroyed, much communal property still existed in the form of trust funds of the various tribes in the Treasury of the United States. In 1900 these funds amounted to $34,317,955.[15] If allotment of land was necessary for the civilization of the Indians and their disappearance into the dominant American society, so too was it necessary to divide the tribal moneys among the individual Indians. A drive for "segregation" of these funds—at least dividing them into separate accounts for the individual Indians entitled to them, if not actually paying them out to the Indians—gained momentum in the twentieth century. Theodore Roosevelt in his first State of the Union Message on December 3, 1901, after praising the Dawes Act, said, "We should now break up the tribal funds, doing for them what allotment does for the tribal lands." The president was merely echoing what had already become a firm principle of the Board of Indian Commissioners, the Indian Rights Association, and the Lake Mohonk Conference. Merrill Gates, secretary of the board and frequent president of the Lake Mohonk meetings, was a principal spokesman for the policy. He talked in 1901 of the "intensively conservative force of vested funds in maintaining an established order of things" and in the following year presented all the arguments in an address at Lake Mohonk entitled "The Next Great Step to Break Up Tribal Funds into Individual Holdings." The conference included in its recommendations of that year the segregation of tribal funds into individual holdings "for the good of the Indian and for his protection from the machinations of designing white men."[16]

The Board of Indian Commissioners did not let the matter rest. It argued in 1901 that "the expectation of annuities and of a share of undivided tribal funds keeps Indians out of civilized life and prevents them from engaging in self-supporting labor. In general, it tends to pauperize and degrade them." It was all part of "the new method" of Indian policy, the

---

and distribution of electrical power. 31 *United States Statutes* 790–91, 1083–84. On March 11, 1904, grants of right of way for pipes for the conveyance of oil and gas were authorized. 33 *United States Statutes* 65. The annual reports of the commissioner of Indian affairs give details on the laws and on the extensive activity under them.

15. CIA Report, 1900, serial 4101, pp. 587–88. The story of the drive to individualize the trust funds is told in Francis Paul Prucha, *The Churches and the Indian Schools, 1888–1912* (Lincoln: University of Nebraska Press, 1979), pp. 138–48; I have drawn upon that account here.

16. Fred L. Israel, ed., *The State of the Union Messages of the Presidents, 1790–1966,* 3 vols. (New York: Chelsea House, 1966), 2: 2047; *Lake Mohonk Conference Proceedings,* 1900, pp. 18–20; 1901, pp. 5–8; 1902, pp. 9, 118–19.

breaking up of tribal reservation life and the training of the Indians in the duties of American citizenship.[17] The Indian Rights Association, too, gave strong support. Its Washington agent said in 1902: "Public opinion is gradually being aroused to the anomalous condition of the Indian tribes regarding the perpetual tribal relation—the transmitting from parent to child an interest in the communal property that of itself might continue forever. Such a system renders futile the best efforts to create a sense of individuality, and to arouse a feeling of responsibility among the members of the tribe, which is absolutely essential to advancement." The Indian Office agreed. Commissioner Jones called the trust funds "a constant menace to the welfare of the Indian," and Francis E. Leupp in his "Outlines of an Indian Policy" hoped for a division of the tribal funds similar to the division of communal lands under the Dawes Act. In 1906 Leupp explained his stand at some length. "The positive moral damage inflicted upon the character of an undeveloped or only partly developed people by having with them always the assurance of a fund in the Treasury from which they are to receive such and such benefits," he said, "is as serious as that suffered by a young white man whose career is blighted by the knowledge that he is heir to a fortune. Until we can eliminate this disturbing factor from the problem of Indian civilization our progress toward its solution is bound to be limping rather than strong."[18]

The movement to divide the trust funds ran into trouble. Not only was the issue complicated by the fight over use of the tribal funds by Catholic missionaries for their Indian schools, but there was congressional opposition based on doubts about the Indians' capabilities to use such funds wisely. A bill was introduced by Representative John F. Lacey of Iowa on January 5, 1905, which would have been a counterpart of the Dawes Act by authorizing the president to order the distribution and payment of their tribal funds to the tribal members. But before the bill reached the floor of the House, its contents were replaced by a proposal made by Representative Burke, which emasculated the original measure by directing that the segregation of funds would apply only to those Indians who personally requested it. In that form the bill became law as the Lacey Act on March 2, 1907. The absolute faith of the Indian Rights Association and similar humanitarian reformers in the immediate civilizing power of a division of tribal property—be it land or money—was not held by Congress, for the

---

17. *Report of the Board of Indian Commissioners*, 1901, p. 7. See also the reports of 1899, pp. 17–19; 1900, pp. 9–10; 1902, p. 22; 1903, pp. 11–12; 1904, pp. 5–10.

18. *Report of the Indian Rights Association*, 1902, p. 25; CIA Report, 1900, serial 4101, pp. 11–12; CIA Report, 1905, serial 4959, p. 4; CIA Report, 1906, serial 5118, p. 24.

experience of allotment of land under the Dawes Act indicated that not all Indians were ready for sudden immersion into the white man's economic world.[19]

Promoters of full division of the trust funds were much upset by the outcome, and the Board of Indian Commissioners continued its recommendations. In 1911 Secretary of the Interior Richard A. Ballinger sent Congress a draft of a bill to amend the Lacey Act by broadening the classes of Indians to whom the secretary of the interior could pay pro rata shares of the trust funds; but Congress took no action despite the favorable report of the House Committee on Indian Affairs.[20] Not until 1918 did Congress act. In a law of May 25 it authorized the secretary of the interior to segregate tribal funds in the United States Treasury and to deposit the funds in the Indians' names in banks selected by him. But since the law specified that none of this could take place until final rolls of the tribes had been prepared, no immediate action was possible. In the following year, however, Congress provided for the drawing up of such final rolls whenever the secretary of the interior judged it would be "for the best interest of the Indians." Calling the segregation "one of the most significant indications of the progress of the Indians, and their consequent release from Government control," Sells began the work. The practice was to pay the shares directly to competent Indians to use as they saw fit and to place the shares of non-competent and minor Indians to the credit of their accounts, subject to the regulations covering individual Indian money.[21]

MODIFICATIONS OF THE DAWES ACT

The Dawes Act was intended to give the Indians a protected title to individual parcels of land, for the allotments were to be held in trust by the

19. The Lacey Act is in 34 *United States Statutes* 1121–22. For support of the original proposal, see *House Report* no. 4547, 58–3, serial 4762, which appended a letter of Leupp giving unqualified approval, the correspondence of Secretary of the Interior Hitchcock, and a letter of support from President Roosevelt. Opposition to the substitute measure and Burke's support of it are in Charles C. Binney to Burke, April 4, 1906, and Burke to Binney, April 7, 1906, Indian Rights Association Papers, Historical Society of Pennsylvania (reels 77 and 18).

20. *Report of the Board of Indian Commissioners*, 1907, p. 17; 1908, pp. 8ff, 21; 1909, p. 19; *House Report* no. 925, 62–2, serial 6132; *House Report* no. 422, 63–2, serial 6559.

21. 40 *United States Statutes* 591; 41 *United States Statutes* 9; CIA Report, 1920, serial 7820, p. 50; CIA Report, 1921, p. 26. A table showing tribal funds distributed 1920–1924 is in Laurence F. Schmeckebier, *The Office of Indian Affairs: Its History, Activities, and Organization* (Baltimore: Johns Hopkins Press, 1927), p. 194. Detailed instructions for use of money belonging to individual Indians are in R. G. Valentine to Walter L. Fisher, May 21, 1912, OSI CCF 5–6, General, Competent Indians, and *Regulations Concerning the Handling of Individual Indian Money* (Washington: GPO, 1913).

United States government for twenty-five years. During that time the land would be completely inalienable. When, at the end of the period, the Indians received fee simple patents to the land and could do with it as they pleased, it was judged that they would have become competent to deal with the pressures that surrounded them. How quickly the act proved unworkable can be seen in the breakdown of the inalienability of the land in the provisions for leasing that were enacted by Congress in 1891. And soon new modifications were made in the original act. The center of gravity throughout the first decade of the century, Felix S. Cohen noted in surveying legislation on Indian affairs, was "almost entirely in the problem of how Indian lands or interests therein may be transferred from Indian tribe to individual Indian or from individual Indian to individual white man."[22]

A serious problem with the allotment machinery arose with the death of Indians who held trust patents to allotments. Under the Dawes Act the heirs were to be determined according to the laws of the state or territory in which the land was located, and because most Indians died intestate, the interests in these allotments were divided equally among the heirs. Many of the heirs already held allotments in their own names, which they were not farming themselves, and they lacked the incentive or capital needed to utilize the inherited lands. Moreover, in many cases the lands could not be divided in any useful way, and the leasing of small parcels was often impracticable. The solution seemed to be to sell the inherited lands and divide the proceeds among the Indians. In 1902 Congress authorized such sale, with the approval of the secretary of the interior.[23]

In 1910 Congress provided for the making of wills by Indians, but this did not solve the heirship problem, which became increasingly serious as allotments were divided and subdivided on the death of heirs.[24] The fractionalization of the land made a mockery of the concern to turn the Indians into landowning farmers by means of individual allotments, for generation by generation the division of inherited land broke down a single allotment into a multitude of tiny pieces that were economically unmanageable. In thirty-seven years following the death of one Chippewa Indian allottee, for example, the Indian Office probated the estate five times. There were then thirty-nine living heirs, among whom the original eighty-acre allotment was distributed as follows:

22. Cohen, *Federal Indian Law*, p. 80. On leasing provisions of the 1890s, see discussion in chapter 26.

23. 32 *United States Statutes* 275. Further provisions were made in the Burke Act of 1906 and in the omnibus bill of 1910. 34 *United States Statutes* 183; 36 *United States Statutes* 855–56. The laws were augmented by regulations issued by the Indian Office and by circulars sent to the superintendents.

24. 36 *United States Statutes* 856.

3 heirs had an interest of 8.88 acres each
4 heirs had an interest of 4.44 acres each
3 heirs had an interest of 2.96 acres each
6 heirs had an interest of 1.48 acres each
6 heirs had an interest of 1.12 acres each
10 heirs had an interest of .98 acre each
1 heir had an interest of .80 acre
4 heirs had an interest of .22 acre each
2 heirs had an interest of .11 acre each[25]

And this was not an unusual case. As more deaths occurred among the heirs, further subdivisions of the interest in the land reached ludicrous figures.[26]

On the other hand, a single Indian might be heir to a number of allotments, with an interest in each so small as to be infinitesimal. There was no way he could gather these pieces together into a usable parcel, so leasing or sale were the only alternatives, and outright sale often seemed the better choice because leasing income was received in very small amounts.

Meanwhile the Indian Office had to handle the multifarious transactions necessitated by the sale and leasing of Indian lands, and a tremendous backlog of cases developed; by 1913 there were 40,000 cases awaiting determination, with land worth $60 million involved. The costs of such administration put a strain on the Indian Office funds, which was relieved somewhat when Congress authorized a fifteen-dollar fee for handling each estate.[27]

25. *Indian Land Tenure, Economic Status, and Population Trends*, Supplementary Report of the Land Planning Committee to the National Resources Board, part 10 (Washington: GPO, 1935), p. 17.

26. What could happen to inherited allotments is dramatically shown in the case of Santee Sioux in the late 1930s. "The extreme case was that of the allotment of Akipa (Joseph Renville), who had died in 1891 and whose land was now owned by more than 150 heirs. Probating the estate cost $2,400 and required more than 250 typewritten pages. If the land were sold at its appraised value, Arie Redearth's share would have been 1.6 cents. Rentals would have had to accumulate to $250 before she would be entitled to one cent in income; and since checks were not normally issued for less than a dollar, it was estimated that 1,600 years would have to elapse before sufficient funds would accumulate so that a check might be issued, assuming that the current rate of rentals continued. [Superintendent] Smith reported in 1937 that unless something was done shortly, the agency would have to buy a larger adding machine to use in making the divisions of equities on rentals coming in; his clerk was then using 56,582,064,000 as a common denominator." Roy W. Meyer, *History of the Santee Sioux: United States Indian Policy on Trial* (Lincoln: University of Nebraska Press, 1967), p. 332.

27. CIA Report, 1913, serial 6634, p. 4; 38 *United States Statutes* 80, 586. The fee was initially set at $15, but few fees were collected because the land involved was often not worth that much. In 1917 Congress dropped the fee for estates worth less than $250

A major change in allotment policy came with the Burke Act of May 8, 1906.[28] It was the result of growing dissatisfaction with the trust and citizenship provisions of the law. The original legislation provided that with the acceptance of an allotment (even though it was to be held in trust for twenty-five years) the Indian became a citizen. The paradoxical situation of granting citizenship to a person who at the same time was declared incompetent to manage his property was not unnoticed, but the change in the law came from more practical considerations. Commissioner Leupp, early in 1906, noted the pressing need for new legislation:

> Experience has demonstrated that citizenship has been a disadvantage to many Indians. They are not fitted for its duties or able to take advantage of its benefits. Many causes operate to their detriment. Some communities are too indifferent and others are financially unable to enforce the local laws where Indians are involved. The result is that the newly enfranchised people are free from any restraining influence. Degraded by unprincipled whites, who cater to their weaknesses, no protection is given them, because the United States courts have no jurisdiction and the local authorities do not enforce State laws.[29]

The particular event that brought the issue to the fore was the Supreme Court's decision *Matter of Heff* in 1905, which declared that an Indian who was a citizen was no longer a ward of the nation and was not subject to the liquor restriction laws.[30] To solve that problem, the Burke Act declared that Indians allotted land in the future would not become citizens until the end of the trust period and receipt of a fee patent to their land. To remove any doubt about the Indians in trust status, the law provided that they should be "subject to the exclusive jurisdiction of the United States" until they received their fee simple patents. The act also authorized the president to extend the trust status of Indians beyond the twenty-five-year period if conditions warranted.

But if some Indians were not yet ready for citizenship, others were competent to manage their own land; for them a twenty-five-year trust period seemed unnecessary and unwise. The Burke Act, therefore, authorized the secretary of the interior to issue a fee patent to any Indian deemed "competent and capable of managing his or her affairs" before the end of the trust

---

and later established a sliding scale. 39 *United States Statutes* 127; 41 *United States Statutes* 413; 42 *United States Statutes* 1185.

28. 34 *United States Statutes* 182–83.

29. Leupp to the secretary of the interior, February 8, 1906, *House Report* no. 1558, 59–1, serial 4906.

30. 197 *U.S. Reports* 488–509. See also *House Report* no. 1558, 59–1, serial 4906, and *Senate Report* no. 1998, 59–1, serial 4904.

period. In supporting the bill, Leupp called this provision "perhaps the most important in the bill . . . a long step in the right direction." He argued, "If such allottees are given full control of their property they will be absorbed into the community in which they reside and bear their share of its burdens, while at the same time the number of 'wards of the Government' will be gradually reduced." Leupp lauded the Burke Act in his report of 1906 and gave examples of what he meant by a competent Indian: "I would make industry the primary test and use this as a lever to force Indians to earn their bread by labor."[31]

The Board of Indian Commissioners, however, still strongly imbued with the Dawes Act mentality, objected vigorously to postponing citizenship. Although it admitted the evils of unrestricted access to liquor, the board considered "this prolonged period of exclusion from the duties and rights of citizenship . . . too heavy a price for the Indian to pay for protection by the Indian Bureau." The Burke Act took away the presumption in favor of citizenship, the board complained, and threw the presumption *against* it, placing on the individual Indian the burden of proving his competence in order to become a citizen before the trust period expired.[32]

The real difficulty with the law, however, was that it opened the door to early alienation of allotments. Although it was the intention of the legislators that great care should be taken by the secretary of the interior in determining competency, in practice the safeguards were often neglected. Leupp noted in 1907 that 881 applications had been received and a total of 753 of them approved, and he believed the effects to be "most beneficial"; but two years later he began to have second thoughts. On many reservations where land speculators were active, Indian allottees had been importuned to apply for patents in fee, and "in many instances the Indians were defrauded out of a large portion of the value of their lands." More stringent regulations were promulgated; the number of applicants fell from 1,787 in 1908 to 1,116 in 1909, and the number of refusals increased from 68 to 836.[33] Yet a beginning had been made in a serious reduction of the Indian estate by premature issue of patents in fee and the removal of restrictions on alienation. No doubt some Indians kept their allotments and profited from them, but for most the patent in fee was soon followed by sale of the land. Then in 1907 Congress took still another step in the alienation of Indian lands. It authorized the sale of restricted lands of noncompetent Indians under rules to be prescribed by the secretary of the interior, with the

31. Leupp to the secretary of the interior, February 8, 1906, *House Report* no. 1558, 59–1, serial 4906; CIA Report, 1906, serial 5118, pp. 27–30.

32. *Report of the Board of Indian Commissioners*, 1906, pp. 8–9, 18.

33. CIA Report, 1907, serial 5296, pp. 63–64; CIA Report, 1909, serial 5747, p. 65.

proceeds used to benefit the seller. The provision was necessary for certain special cases, but it let down the clear safeguard intended by the sponsors of the Dawes Act and became an effective instrument in the dissipation of Indian landholdings.[34]

The leasing of Indian lands, probating of estates, determination of heirs, adjustment in the size of allotments, declaration of competency, and issuance of patents, to say nothing of the management of forestry operations and irrigation projects, required new legislation, a flood of regulations and circulars, and the multiplication of official correspondence, as the Indian Office had to deal more and more with individual cases. In order to refine and clarify procedures in many of these activities, Congress on June 25, 1910, passed an act "to provide for determining the heirs of deceased Indians, for the disposition and sale of allotments of deceased Indians, for the leasing of allotments, and for other purposes." It was an "omnibus bill," gathering together a variety of measures, many of which had been introduced as separate bills.[35]

The law of 1910 also indicated a realization that allotment could not apply uniformly to all Indian communities—a realization that was long in coming. As irrigation projects were promoted, it became clear that the across-the-board allotment of 80 acres of farming land or 160 acres of grazing land was not suitable in many regions. Leupp in 1906 had noted that nearly all the reservations still to be allotted contained little or no agricultural land that could be cultivated without irrigation, and he urged legislation that would be "very flexible, permitting the authorities who have it in charge to take into account the altitude, character of the soil, climate, productive possibilities and proximity to market, as well as the habits of the tribe." For individual tribes, this sort of discretion was authorized from time to time. The original allotments of the Jicarilla Apaches, for example,

---

34. 34 *United States Statutes* 1018. In January 1908, Leupp defined what was meant by "noncompetent" Indians: "That general class of Indians, who, through mental or physical infirmities incident to accident, disease, or old age, are unable to avail themselves of the benefits arising from the development of their allotments, and whose best interests require that their lands be converted into money, so that funds may be available for medical attendance, and for their support." Circular no. 181, January 9, 1908, OIA Circulars (M1121, reel 9). In order to eliminate uncertainty of title in the conveyance of Indian lands, Congress, at the request of Secretary of the Interior James R. Garfield, provided that the secretary of the interior issue a patent directly to the purchaser, rather than have the land pass by patent to the Indian and then by deed from the Indian to the purchaser. 35 *United States Statutes* 444. See also *Senate Document* no. 61, 60–1, serial 5267; *House Report* no. 1187, 60–1, serial 5225.

35. 36 *United States Statutes* 855–63. See the long explanatory statement, presented section by section, sent to Congress by Leupp, March 3, 1908, in *Senate Document* no. 395, 60–1, serial 5265.

were canceled, in part because 80-acre allotments to each person were wholly unsuited to the region, and new allotments were authorized not to exceed 10 acres of agricultural land or 640 acres of other land. Similarly, the secretary of the interior received authority to allot the lands of the Hopi Indians "in such quantities as may be for their best interests."[36] Secretary of the Interior James R. Garfield urged Congress in 1908 to make such particular provisions general. "I do not believe that any one Indian should be given 80 acres of irrigated land," he said, "much less each Indian—man, woman, or child—who may be alive when the allotments are being made. Indeed there are many cases where 5 acres would be more than an Indian would make good use of, and some where it would be advisable to give even a less area. On the other hand, 160 acres of grazing land is in many places wholly insufficient to sustain an Indian who may elect to engage in raising stock." Garfield wanted general discretionary power to allot no more than 40 irrigable or 640 grazing acres. Congress in the omnibus bill met only part of the request, by authorizing allotments of irrigable land "in such areas [quantities] as may be for their best interest not to exceed, however, forty acres to any one Indian." The rest of an Indian's entitlement to allotted land was to be filled from nonirrigable land.[37]

The omnibus bill also authorized the issuance of patents for village lots to Indians in the state of Washington whose livelihood came from the sea and for whom agricultural plots made no sense. Secretary of the Interior Richard A. Ballinger had realized this and noted that "any attempts to force agriculture on such Indians as a regular vocation would undoubtedly spoil a lot of good watermen in order to make a few poor farmers."[38] The patents, however, restricted alienation of the lots to other members of the tribe.

How far the government by 1910 had departed from the philosophy of the Dawes Act, which insisted on the individual ownership and use of a plot of farmland (under firm protection from alienation for a set period of years), can be seen in the regulations issued in 1910 to implement the omnibus bill. At the head of the document stood this significant statement:

> Any Indian of 21 years or over who holds an allotment of land under a trust patent can—
> (1) Procure a patent in fee under the act of May 8, 1906 (34 Stat., 182), provided it is shown that he is competent to care for his welfare.

36. CIA Report, 1906, serial 5118, pp. 80–81; C. F. Larabee to Hans Aspaas, May 23, 1907, OIA, Instructions to Allotting Agents; 34 United States Statutes 1021, 1413.

37. Garfield to the speaker of the House, February 19, 1908, House Document no. 705, 60–1, serial 5377; 36 United States Statutes 859–60.

38. Ballinger to the speaker of the House, February 9, 1910, quoted in House Report no. 1135, 61–2, serial 5593, p. 4.

Reform & Reaction

58. John Collier

The most important commissioner of Indian affairs in the twentieth century was John Collier. In the 1920s he had been a violent critic of Indian Bureau policies; then as commissioner (1933–1945) he promoted a new approach to Indian affairs, one in which Indian culture was respected and Indians were encouraged to direct their own destinies. He irrevocably changed the Indians' status.

59. Hubert Work

60. Charles H. Burke

The 1920s were a period of agitation for reform of Indian policy, most of it aimed against Secretary of the Interior Work and Commissioner of Indian Affairs Burke. Collier and his followers attacked these officials for adhering to the old assimilationist policies instead of encouraging Indian rights and Indian cultures. Rhoads, a Quaker banker who succeeded Burke as commissioner in 1929, began reforms but did not move quickly enough to satisfy Collier.

A special Indian division of the Civilian Conservation Corps began the relief and rehabilitation of Indian communities that was an initial goal of the Indian New Deal. Unlike the regular CCC, which had camps only for men, the Indian CCC allowed family camps, like this one at the Flathead Indian Agency in Montana. The Indians in the CCC did a great variety of work, including stabilizing the ruins at Pecos Mission in New Mexico.

61. Charles J. Rhoads

62. Indian CCC, Family Camp

63. Indian CCC, Stabilization of Ruins

64. WPA Project, Shoshoni Women

65. Woody Crumbo, Potawatomi Artist

The Indian Bureau made use of New Deal relief agencies to bring economic assistance to Indians and to Indian communities. One WPA project was the tanning of elk hides at the Shoshoni Indian Agency in 1936. Another was the employment of Indian artists to paint murals in government buildings. Shown here is the Potawatomi Woody Crumbo and one of his murals in the Department of the Interior building.

Indian education was a primary activity of the Bureau of Indian Affairs. Ryan, who was director of Indian education from 1930 to 1935, was a strong proponent of day schools on the reservations, which could serve as community centers as well as academic institutions. One such school, built in 1937–1938, was that at Rocky Boys Reservation, Montana.

66. W. Carson Ryan, Jr.

67. Indian Day School, Rocky Boys Reservation

68. Indian Soldiers, World War II

World War II had a revolutionary impact on Indian communities, for large numbers of men and women left the reservations for military service or for jobs in war industries. This immersion in white society created a new outlook for many Indians. Here four Indian airmen—Winnebago, Sioux, Pawnee, and Ute—stage a mock war dance at Sheppard Field, Texas, and a Rosebud Sioux army nurse adjusts her hospital equipment.

69. Indian Nurse, World War II

70. Students at Intermountain School

A special Navajo education project initiated in 1946 provided an accelerated program for adolescents whose education had been neglected. The project made use of off-reservation boarding schools where space was available. A sudden expansion occurred in 1950 with the opening of the Intermountain School in Brigham City, Utah, in the abandoned Bushnell General Hospital.

Beatty, director of education in the Bureau of Indian Affairs 1936–1952, was a national figure in progressive education. He applied great zeal and energy in providing an educational program that was adapted to the Indians and that allowed individual children to develop according to each one's own interests and abilities.

71. Willard Walcott Beatty

72. Dillon S. Myer

73. Glenn L. Emmons

A strong move on the part of Congress and the executive branch to terminate federal responsibility for Indian tribes was a reaction to the policies of the Collier era. Three men who promoted the policy were Commissioners of Indian Affairs Myer and Emmons and Senator Watkins of Utah. The program had barely begun, however, before strong Indian opposition to being cut off from federal protection and support halted the termination policy, although the threat of termination continued to frighten Indian groups.

74. Arthur V. Watkins

(2) Devise his land by will under the act of June 25, 1910 (36 Stat., 855), provided the land is not located in Oklahoma.

(3) Sell his land under the act of March 1, 1907 (34 Stat., 1015–1018).[39]

COMPETENCY AND FEE PATENTS

The radical switch from emphasis on protection of the Indian allotments toward provisions for alienation of the Indian landholdings reached its height in the period 1913–1920, under the leadership of Secretary of the Interior Franklin K. Lane and Commissioner Cato Sells, with whom the issuance of fee patents to competent Indians became a high priority. There was a double motivation for such a position.

In the first place, both Lane and Sells were obsessed with the idea that land and other natural resources should be fully utilized. Efficient use became more important than protection and conservation. Lane, in his first year as secretary, advocated a policy that went beyond ending monopolies (a goal of the conservation movement) to embrace a concept of developing the land and its riches in the most beneficial way.[40] The secretary and his commissioner applied this principle to Indian lands, which they were committed to making as productive as possible. "The Indian's rich agricultural lands, his vast acres of grass land, his great forests should be so utilized as to become a powerful instrument for his civilization," Sells told the superintendents in 1914. "I hold it to be an economic and social crime, in this age and under modern conditions, to permit thousands of acres of fertile land belonging to the Indians and capable of great industrial development to lie in unproductive idleness. . . . Former widespread negligency and mismanagement in the cultivation of the soil, the breeding of stock, and the handling of grazing land is no excuse for the continuance of such conditions, and they will not be permitted to exist on an Indian reservation during my administration." So the Indian Office promoted programs for Indian work and self-support. One instrument pushed by Sells was the agricultural fair, at which Indians could display the products of their farms. He wanted the fairs to be conducted in such a way as "to open to the Indians the vision of the industrial achievements to which they should

39. *Rules and Regulations Relating to the Issuance of Patents in Fee and Certificates of Competency and the Sale of Allotted and Inherited Indian Lands, Except Those Belonging to the Five Civilized Tribes* (Washington: GPO, 1910), p. 5.

40. Report of the Secretary of the Interior, 1913, *House Document* no. 1069, 63–2, serial 6633, pp. 3–5. For a discussion of Lane's philosophy, see McDonnell, "Disintegration of the Indian Estate," pp. 4–12. The brief biography by Keith W. Olson, *Biography of a Progressive: Franklin K. Lane, 1864–1921* (Westport, Connecticut: Greenwood Press, 1979), has very little on Indian affairs.

aspire." Additional farmers were employed to teach the Indians farming methods, and stock-raising programs were instituted. Sells, in the usual commissioner's pattern, reported considerable success. "It cannot be expected that all Indians shall advance from plainsmen to intensive farmers in one generation," he remarked in 1916, "but that they are now making tremendous progress is apparent through the entire country." And stock raising, because the Indians were natural herdsmen, was even more successful.[41]

Despite these promising developments, many Indians still did not utilize their lands effectively, and such inefficiency disturbed the Indian Office, which was insistent that the land be used. To this end, leasing was encouraged and approved. The sale of allotted land continued, too, and Sells encouraged superintendents to make sure that the Indians got a fair price for their lands.[42]

If efficient utilization of the land was one guiding principle of policy in the Wilson administration, a second—perhaps the dominant one—was to free "competent" Indians from wardship status and set them and their land loose from federal supervision. Here was a zenith in the drive that began in the late nineteenth century to let the Indians take their places, on their own, in American society. Lane and Sells pursued this termination principle with a vengeance. By eliminating Indians who did not need government care from the responsibility of the Indian Office, attention could then be concentrated on those wards who still needed help. Secretary Lane promoted the idea forcefully and publicized his views widely. "I am of the opinion that it would be better, far better, to sever all ties between the Indians and the government," he wrote in the *National Geographic* early in 1915, "give every man his own and let him go, rather than keep alive in the Indian the belief that he is to remain a ward of the Government. . . . Our goal is the free Indian. The orphan-asylum idea must be killed in the mind of the Indian and the white man. The Indian should know that he is upon the road to enjoy or suffer full capacity. He is to have his opportunity as a 'forward-looking man.'"[43]

With such backing, Sells proceeded enthusiastically, despite reports

41. Circular no. 892, August 10, 1914, OIA Circulars (M1121, reel 10); CIA Report, 1914, serial 6815, pp. 26–28; CIA Report, 1916, serial 7160, p. 29.

42. McDonnell, "Disintegration of the Indian Estate," pp. 83–91. Circular no. 969, April 6, 1916, OIA Circulars (M1121, reel 10), gave directions and prescribed forms for leasing allotments; on land sales see Circular no. 1095, March 11, 1916, ibid. (M1121, reel 11).

43. Franklin K. Lane, "From the Warpath to the Plow," *National Geographic* 27 (January 1915): 80. This article was adapted from Lane's annual report of 1914, in *House Document* no. 1475, 63–3, serial 6814, pp. 3–12.

from superintendents (whom he had directed to make a special study of the qualifications of the Indians) that the Indians did not fare well when released from government supervision. The instrument to be used was the declaration of competency and the issuance of fee simple patents, authorized by the Burke Act of 1906. But the task of determining competent Indians was a job of frightening magnitude if the decision had to be made carefully one by one. The first move to speed up the granting of the patents was the establishment of a "competency commission." In 1915 Lane appointed James McLaughlin, an Indian inspector of high reputation, and Frank A. Thackery, the highly regarded superintendent of the Pima Reservation, as a commission or board to move from reservation to reservation and, in conjunction with the local superintendent, determine the "qualifications of each Indian who may apply for a severance of tribal relations, or who, in its judgment, has arrived at the degree of business competency that he should assume the duties of citizenship."[44] The following year the original commission was split into two, and then a third one was created. Effectiveness was at once demonstrated. During fiscal year 1916, on the recommendation of the commission, 576 fee patents were issued. These were added to the 949 approved through other channels for a total of 1,525 fee patents for the year, covering about 220,490 acres.[45]

The competency commissions also delivered the patents that were issued to the Indians, and in 1916 an elaborate ceremony was devised to portray the change that the patented Indian was to experience. Before large gatherings on the reservations the Indian emerged from a tepee, shot a bow and arrow as a final act of his Indian status, then received symbols of his new status—a plow, a purse, and an American flag. A badge of citizenship was pinned on his breast. The ceremonies were festive occasions and appeared to be appreciated by the Indians, but when Secretary Lane arrived at the Yankton Reservation for the first ceremony, he found that many of the patentees had already agreed to sell their land, and he removed twenty-five Indians from the list of those who were to receive patents that day.[46]

---

44. CIA Report, 1915, serial 6992, p. 25. See the correspondence on the competency commissions, including reports of the commissioners to the secretary of the interior, in OSI CCF 5–6, General, Competent Indians. The work of the commissions is discussed in McDonnell, "Disintegration of the Indian Estate," pp. 100–143, and in Janet McDonnell, "Competency Commissions and Indian Land Policy, 1913–1920," *South Dakota History* 11 (Winter 1980): 21–34. McLaughlin's role is treated in Louis L. Pfaller, *James McLaughlin: The Man with an Indian Heart* (New York: Vantage Press, 1978), pp. 325–45.

45. CIA Report, 1916, serial 7160, p. 49.

46. The ceremonies are described in McDonnell, "Disintegration of the Indian Estate," pp. 120–23, and in Pfaller, *McLaughlin*, pp. 333–38. There is a copy of the "Ritual on Admission of Indians to Full American Citizenship" and other material on the

The competency commissions did not solve all the problems. Even the experienced men appointed to the positions found it difficult to reach all the Indians on a reservation and determine personally who was and who was not competent. Often the time allowed for each Indian was too short to make the necessary inquiry, and some of the commissioners' work was carelessly done. Nor were they able to persuade all those judged competent to agree to accept the fee patents, and the Indian Office resorted finally to forcing the patents upon unwilling Indians, for the goal had been to smoke out just such persons. These activities brought the usual chorus of criticism. Opponents of the process pointed out that the patentees sold their lands, wasted the sale money, and ended up worse off than before, but supporters of the program, although they admitted some evils in it, were convinced that fee patents and citizenship were the only road along which Indians could advance. Even Indians who lost their land gained valuable experience and learned a lesson in responsibility.[47]

Despite the abuses, Sells was pleased with the program of freeing the Indians from wardship, and he was determined not to let the momentum be lost. He was pressured, besides, by persons in and out of Congress who felt that the Indian Office was moving too slowly to free the Indians. Accordingly, on April 17, 1917, Sells issued a "Declaration of Policy in the Administration of Indian Affairs." He pointed to the successful activities under way in regard to health, vocational training, suppression of the liquor traffic, and protection of Indian property, and said that he was ready to take "the next step." He declared:

> The time has come for discontinuing guardianship of all competent Indians and giving even closer attention to the incompetent that they may more speedily achieve competency.
>
> Broadly speaking, a policy of greater liberalism will henceforth prevail in Indian administration to the end that every Indian, as soon as he has been determined to be as competent to transact his own business as the average white man, shall be given full control of his property and have all his lands and moneys turned over to him, after which he will no longer be a ward of the Government.[48]

The guidelines issued in the new policy set blood quantum as a norm. Patents in fee, as a general rule, would be issued to Indians who had less

---

ceremonies, including photographs, in OSI CCF 5–6, General, Competent Indians. Lane reported one ceremony in Lane to H. B. Brougham, May 20, 1916, *The Letters of Franklin K. Lane, Personal and Political*, ed. Anne Wintermute Lane and Louise Herrick Wall (Boston: Houghton Mifflin Company, 1922), pp. 208–10. See also Myrle Wright, "A Ritual for Citizenship," *National Magazine* 45 (December 1916): 331–33.

47. McDonnell, "Disintegration of the Indian Estate," pp. 124–43.

48. CIA Report, 1917, serial 7358, p. 3.

than one-half Indian blood, as well as to those with more than half Indian blood if they were found to be competent. Moreover, Indians over twenty-one years of age who had received diplomas from government Indian schools, if they demonstrated competence, would be so declared. In addition, the sale of inherited Indian lands and the sale of lands of incompetent Indians who were old and feeble and needed the proceeds for support would be done under a "liberal ruling." The use of individual Indian moneys, too, would be unrestricted for competent Indians, and pro rata shares of tribal moneys would be set aside for them "as speedily as possible." One safeguard against creating a new group of completely landless Indians was a provision for holding in restricted status a small homestead of forty acres for persons with more than one-half Indian blood.[49]

Sells presented his policy with a tone of exultation: "This is a new and far-reaching declaration of policy. It means the dawn of a new era in Indian administration. It means that the competent Indian will no longer be treated as half ward and half citizen. It means reduced appropriations by the Government and more self-respect and independence for the Indian. It means the ultimate absorption of the Indian race into the body politic of the Nation. It means in short, the beginning of the end of the Indian problem."

The Declaration of Policy was received very favorably. The Indian Rights Association voiced its approval, and the Board of Indian Commissioners, too, endorsed the policy, which it said was "in line with policies which the Board of Indian Commissioners has advocated, consistently and continuously, for more than a quarter of a century.[50] Sells proceeded quickly. He asked the superintendents to submit lists of Indians on their reservations who were less than half Indian and to indicate reasons for those judged noncompetent. When the lists arrived, the commissioner sent them to the secretary of the interior for approval, and then the secretary directed the issuance of patents. The blood quantum was taken as a norm (unless there were exceptional circumstances), and the "white Indians" were turned loose.

Although it was evident almost immediately that on some reservations a very high percentage of the patentees quickly sold or mortgaged their land and wasted the proceeds, Sells was not deterred. He and many of the superintendents who saw the evils firsthand argued that sooner or later the Indians would have to face the world without government protection, and

49. The final section of the Declaration of Policy concerned the elimination of ineligible pupils from government Indian schools.

50. *Report of the Indian Rights Association,* 1917, p. 38: *Report of the Board of Indian Commissioners,* 1917, p. 14. See McDonnell, "Disintegration of the Indian Estate," pp. 147–49, for other indications of support.

that although some would fail, many would rise to meet the challenge. They would realize, at last, that work was necessary if they were to be saved. In fact, in 1919, Sells liberalized his policy one step further, by including Indians who had just one-half Indian blood.[51]

The policy of hastening the patenting of Indian allottees took place during the war years, in which the need for foodstuffs demanded full use of the agricultural resources of the Indian reservations. The national food campaign was strongly supported by the Indian Office, which sought to arouse the Indians' interest in more production and to increase the amount of Indian land under cultivation, whether by the Indians themselves or by white lessees, thus accelerating the process of assimilating the Indians into the nation's economic life. "There yet remain thousands of acres of uncultivated agricultural land on the different reservations," Sells told the superintendents, "with many able-bodied Indians not making their best effort toward self-support, many of whom should no doubt be farming. . . . Every uncultivated acre of tillable land is an opportunity and a challenge which we must not neglect."[52] Many Indians enthusiastically took part in the campaign, and the high prices caused by wartime demand stirred the interest of whites in using or acquiring Indian lands. The Indian Office eagerly promoted the leasing of unused Indian lands, both for agricultural production and for mineral resources, and approved the sale of land if that move would expedite its productive use. In 1917 Lane reported a 25- to 50-percent increase in cultivated acreage of Indian lands and predicted the addition of forty thousand to fifty thousand acres cultivated under leases for the next year.[53]

At the end of the war, however, Sells refused to go along with some members of Congress and other citizens who complained that the Indian Office was dragging its feet in releasing Indians from government supervision. He was especially concerned about the Indians on the Navajo, Hualapai, Hopi, and Apache reservations, whose property could not wisely be allotted for many years to come, and the many other full-bloods or near full-bloods who were not qualified to enter into competition in the economic world of the whites. "To abandon these at this point in their progress where elementary acquirements are shaping into self-reliance and a comprehension of practical methods," he warned, "would be to leave them a prey to every kind of unscrupulous trickery that masks itself in the con-

51. CIA Report, 1919, serial 7706, p. 4.

52. Circular no. 1268, March 2, 1917, and Circular no. 1399, March 4, 1918, OIA Circulars (M1121, reel 11).

53. Report of the Secretary of the Interior, 1917, *House Document* no. 915, 65–2, serial 7357, p. 16. McDonnell, "Disintegration of the Indian Estate," pp. 171–202, discusses the effects of World War I on Indian land policy. See also David L. Wood, "American Indian Farmland and the Great War," *Agricultural History* 55 (July 1981): 249–65.

ventions of civilization." Sells stood firmly at the line he had drawn and refused to be moved by the agitation around him for terminating federal supervision of all the Indians. He condemned "misrepresentations to the public by speakers and writers of superficial knowledge or excessive zeal" and the "selfish adventurers" who were looking only for personal gain. "Few things have been more obstructive to Indian welfare," he said, "than the professional agitator who claims the abolishment of government supervision as the salvation of the Indian."[54]

Before Sells left office a critical reaction had set in against his "liberal" policy, for its disastrous effects in loss of Indian lands were becoming evident to many. The Board of Indian Commissioners, which three years earlier had hailed the Declaration of Policy, now spoke with a cautious voice, lest unprotected incompetent Indians be handed over to exploiters. The Indian Rights Association, too, had become critical of Sells and his program.[55] A sharp change in policy came when Secretary Lane resigned in early 1920 and President Wilson appointed John Barton Payne to replace him. Payne saw no need to rush the Indians into full citizenship status. "It may take the Indians a very long, long time to become really competent," he told Sells; "but we should be patient and not permit ourselves to be hurried. . . . for a long time yet the Indians must continue the wards of the nation, and the nation must take care of them." The new secretary ended the policy of blanket issuance of patents and returned to the policy of examining each case for competency on its merits; he rejected many of the applications forwarded by the competency commissions and then abolished the commissions altogether, turning the work of judging competence back to the superintendents. Unfortunately, the reversal came after many Indians had already lost their property.[56]

54. CIA Report, 1919, serial 7706, pp. 3–4; Sells to Mrs. F. W. Haman, March 21, 1920, printed in CIA Report, 1920, serial 7820, pp. 7–10.

55. *Report of the Board of Indian Commissioners,* 1920, p. 8; *Report of the Indian Rights Association,* 1920, pp. 4–5. In 1921 the board conducted a survey of superintendents to determine the present condition of the Indians who had received fee patents. Out of the eighty-seven replies, seventy-one superintendents (81.5 percent) stated that the majority of the Indians had disposed of their property shortly after receiving their patents, and only ten (11.5 percent) thought the majority of the fee patented Indians were successful. *Report of the Board of Indian Commissioners,* 1921, p. 9.

56. [Payne] to Sells, November 16, 1920, OSI CCF 5–6, General, Patents. For the change in policy see the terse notification to the superintendents in Circular no. 1649, November 23, 1920, OIA Circulars (M1121, reel 12). Sells, in answer to a query from Payne, asserted that he had no records to show what happened to patented Indians, but he admitted, "I do know, in a general way, that a large percentage of the Indians to whom patents in fee have been issued soon dispose of their lands, frequently for an inadequate consideration, and that in many cases the Indians are left homeless." Sells to Payne, December 3, 1920, OSI CCF 5–6, General, Patents.

LAND POLICY IN THE 1920S

Charles H. Burke, who replaced Sells in 1921, did not forsake the philosophy that allotment and assimilation were the proper goals of the government in dealing with the Indians, and in his eight-year term as commissioner of Indian affairs he continued the general policies that had been established in earlier decades. He moved much more cautiously, however, than Lane and Sells, both because he saw the evils resulting from the attempt to free the government of responsibility for Indian property and because of the whirlwind of criticism and demands for reform in Indian affairs that stirred around him in the 1920s. The reform movement spawned by the controversy over the Bursum bill in 1922 (a fundamental matter of protecting Pueblo rights to their lands) was intensely critical of allotment and related policies of lease, sale, and patenting. John Collier and his friends pointed to the loss of lands under fee patenting—"to thrust a fee simple ownership on the Indians was to give away the public domain and to ruin the Indians"—and they were critical of the bureaucratic control that the Indian Office exerted over the lives and property of the Indians. "Reservation Indians are slaves," Collier cried, "and their enslavement is not benevolent. There are few instances of modern slavery wherein the destruction of life and social values has equaled the current record of our Indian slavery." For Collier, the basic wrong lay in the allotment policy, which had dominated Indian life for thirty or forty years, much to the detriment of the Indians. "Indian poverty," he charged, "is chiefly poverty of allot[t]ed Indians. Indian idleness is idleness of allot[t]ed Indians. Indian disinheritance, moving ahead faster each year, is almost exclusively a disinheritance of allot[t]ed Indians. And the government's Indian bureaucracy spends millions a year in the supervision, admittedly without hopeful issue, of allotment matters."[57]

Within such an atmosphere the Indian Office under Burke faced a number of particular problems. One early issue concerned allotment of the Mission Indians in California. Burke insisted that this would be the best thing for the Indians, but Collier and his associates damned the measure as a scheme to defraud the Indians of what little they had left. Another involved the allotment of timber lands, a question as controversial as that concerning mineral lands; and the questions of public domain allotments and the exchange of allotments further troubled the Indian Office.[58]

Burke also faced the decline in economic well-being that struck the In-

57. John Collier, "Our Indian Policy," *Sunset* 50 (March 1923): 13–14; Collier, "Are We Making Red Slaves?" *Survey* 57 (January 1, 1927); 454–55; Collier, "Indians, Inc.," *Survey Graphic*, February 1930, pp. 519–22, 547–49.

58. McDonnell, "Disintegration of the Indian Estate," pp. 207–34.

dians in the immediate postwar years. The sale of land and the dispersal of stock during the war made it difficult for the Indians to prosper, and the Indian Office sought to encourage new development. On the Blackfeet Reservation a Five Year Program was launched in 1921; it showed that success was possible under a concentrated drive for economic development, and the program spread to other reservations. By 1927 Five Year Programs had been established at fifty-five reservations, and increases in farming and stock raising were reported. Yet the progress was not universal, and the Indian reservations remained depressed areas.[59]

As in previous decades, there was a great deal of pressure for leasing Indian lands. Burke acknowledged the long-held government policy of giving each Indian "a tract of land that he could call his own and from the cultivation of which he might gain a livelihood, and at the same time acquire the arts of civilization." He directed the superintendents to encourage the Indians "to go upon their allotments and establish homes and work their lands, either themselves or by hired help, rather than to depend upon the small rents received." But if an Indian could not or would not make productive use of his land, Burke permitted leasing, even though he knew it subverted the intention of the allotment policy of turning the Indians into hardworking citizens. A new controversy arose, however, over the leasing of oil and mineral lands on Indian reservations established not by treaty or by act of Congress but by executive order. The question was whether the Indians had full title to such reservations or whether the reservations were in fact still part of the public domain. In the latter case the General Leasing Act of February 25, 1920, which controlled leasing on the public domain, would have to be followed. The act placed leasing under the General Land Office, not the Indian Office, and divided the proceeds between reclamation projects, the state, and the United States Treasury, and thus cut the Indians out of any return from the leasing. Secretary Albert Fall decided, in fact, that the General Leasing Act did apply and issued some leases, and a cry was immediately raised by Burke and by the Indian Rights Association.[60]

There was a long fight in Congress over the precise nature of Indian rights in executive order reservations, and Commissioner Burke was willing to compromise if he could get a law that recognized Indian title even though it would authorize division of the returns between the Indians and the states. A bill introduced by Representative Carl Hayden of Arizona in

59. CIA Report, 1922, p. 11; CIA Report, 1923, pp. 11–12; CIA Report, 1924, p. 12; CIA Report, 1927, p. 16. The economic development is discussed in McDonnell, "Disintegration of the Indian Estate," pp. 238–50.

60. *Regulations Governing the Execution of Leases of Indian Allotted and Tribal Lands for Farming, Grazing, and Business Purposes* (Washington: GPO, 1924); these regulations were approved July 20, 1923. Burke repeated much the same directive in Circular no. 2209, April 19, 1926, OIA Circulars (M1121, reel 13).

February 1926 provided that the Indian Oil Leasing Act of 1924, which applied to treaty reservations and allowed 37.5 percent of the rentals and royalties to go to the state for roads on Indian reservations and for public schools attended by Indians, would also apply to executive order reservation leases. Thus the Indian Office, not the General Land Office, would be in control, and the Indians would receive a relatively large return. When Burke supported the bill as a responsible compromise, he was attacked by the American Indian Defense Association. The Hayden bill as amended was vetoed by President Calvin Coolidge on July 2, 1926, but in 1927 a new Indian Oil Leasing Act was approved. It vindicated the rights of the Indians to executive order reservations and their right to proceeds from leases; states would tax oil and mineral production directly. Boundaries of executive order reservations, according to another section of the act, could no longer be changed except by act of Congress. It was an important victory for the Indians.[61]

In regard to issuing fee patents to Indians, Burke took a cautious stand. He objected to any automatic determination of competency—such as blood quantum or amount of schooling—and was determined to protect noncompetent Indians. Yet he was unable to devise any policy that would ensure that the patented Indian did not dispose of his property, and the land loss continued. Burke was critical of the free and easy policy of Lane and Sells, and he attempted to undo some of the damage that had resulted under the "liberal policy" by promoting cancellation of patents issued to Indians who had not applied for them or against their will. In 1927 Congress authorized cancellation of such patents in cases where the land had not been encumbered or sold.[62] Such attempts to save Indian lands and Indian rights, however, were piecemeal solutions. The demand for a complete rejection of allotment and its corollaries did not die.

FORESTRY AND IRRIGATION

Two economic developments closely related to the land and its use were the management of Indian forests and the building of irrigation projects on the reservations. Although concern for these matters began in the late nineteenth century, it was only in the twentieth that they became con-

61. 44 *United States Statutes* 1347–48. The complicated story is told in Kelly, *Navajo Indians*, pp. 76–103.

62. CIA Report, 1921, pp. 23–24; CIA Report, 1927, p. 12; 44 *United States Statutes* 1247. Burke in 1928 directed the superintendents to send him detailed information about all Indians who had received fee patents prior to 1921 without having made application for them, in order to determine those upon whom patents had been forced. Circular no. 2464, June 18, 1928, OIA Circulars (M1121, reel 13).

suming interests and heavy administrative duties of the Indian Office. In both there was a fundamental question of safeguarding Indian interests while promoting utilization and development of the nation's natural resources.

Because many tribal lands were covered in part by forests, the question of Indian rights to the timber arose early. Most Indian tribes were accorded only a right of occupancy in their reservations while the fee remained in the United States, and it was a common opinion that Indian rights did not extend to the timber except where the timber was cut off arable lands in the process of making them available for cultivation.[63] From time to time Congress passed special acts authorizing disposition of the timber on Indian lands, but there was no general legislation until February 16, 1889, when Congress permitted the sale of dead and down timber only, under presidential regulations. Then gradually the principle developed that the establishment of a reservation for use and occupancy of the Indians conveyed to the Indians a title in the timber that was comparable to their title in the land and that the disposition of the timber was subject to congressional legislation. The omnibus act of 1910 expressly recognized the theory and provided that the forests could contribute to the support and advancement of the Indians through the sale of timber. Section 7 read: "That the mature living and dead and down timber on unallotted lands of any Indian reservation may be sold under regulations to be prescribed by the Secretary of the Interior, and the proceeds from such sales shall be used for the benefit of the Indians of the reservation in such manner as he may direct." Section 8 provided that timber on trust allotments could be sold by the allottee for his benefit, under Interior Department regulations. The extensive supervision of the Department of the Interior over the cutting and sale of timber was comparable to that over lands; the underlying purpose of the regulations, even though it often was not realized, was to protect the forests against covetous whites and to save resources for later generations.[64]

The question of cutting and sale of timber was only one side of the government's concern, for the conservation movement of the early twentieth century also had an impact. One result was the attempt to withdraw forested Indian lands from the reservations and add them to national forests as a conservation measure. Although it was recognized that reservations

---

63. *United States* v. *Cook*, 19 Wallace 591 (1873). In 1888 the attorney general confirmed this view. Opinion of A. H. Garland, November 20, 1888, *Official Opinions of the Attorneys-General of the United States*, 19: 194–96. For a discussion of rights to timber, see Cohen, *Federal Indian Law*, pp. 313–16, and the 1982 revision, pp. 538–42, 624–26, 734–35; Kinney, *A Continent Lost*, pp. 253–78.

64. 25 *United States Statutes* 673; 36 *United States Statutes* 857. There is a table of data on acres of timber land and the value of the timber in 1912, 1916, 1920, and 1925 in Schmeckebier, *Office of Indian Affairs*, p. 189.

set up by treaty or by act of Congress could not be thus altered by act of the president, executive order reservations were treated differently. Two days before the end of his term, Theodore Roosevelt in a series of executive orders transferred approximately 2.5 million acres of forest land from executive order reservations to contiguous or nearby national forests—by far the greater part of salable timber on reservations in New Mexico, Arizona, and California. But on February 17, 1912, after adverse opinions from the attorney general, Taft restored the forested lands of the eight reservations to their former status as Indian reservation lands.[65]

A second and less controversial move was the establishment of administrative structures to survey and protect the Indian forests, to prevent what the Board of Indian Commissioners in 1908 called the "wholesale slaughter of forests" on Indian reservations.[66] First there was an abortive attempt to enlist the aid of the Forestry Service of the Department of Agriculture, which between January 1908 and July 1909 supervised forest operations while the Indian office paid the bills. The arrangement did not work, for the Forest Service was interested primarily in the practice of scientific forestry on the reservations, and the Indian Office looked to the welfare and advancement of the Indians who owned the forests. And there were problems arising from one service doing the work and another keeping the responsibility and control of funds. Beginning with the Indian appropriation act of 1910, Congress authorized $100,000 annually to enable the Indian Service "to make investigations on Indian reservations and take measures for the purpose of preserving living and growing timber, and removing dead timber, standing or fallen; to advise the Indians as to the proper care of forests, and to conduct such timber operations and sales of timber as may be deemed advisable and provided for by law." The funds made it possible to organize a separate unit, first the Forestry Section in 1910 and then in 1926 a full Forestry Division. A chief supervisor of forests was in charge, and special forestry officers were assigned to some reservations, but regular superintendents also played a part in directing forestry activities. The work of appraising timber stands, providing means to prevent and fight forest fires and to protect the forests from severe insect damage, and cutting and selling timber continued year by year.[67]

65. Kinney, *A Continent Lost*, pp. 276–77; Kappler, vol. 3, pp. 636–53, 670–72, 674, 677, 684–85.

66. The board noted: "For the last forty years pressure from those who are interested in the manufacture and sale of lumber has been intense, to secure opportunities to clear off trees from Indian reservations." *Report of the Board of Indian Commissioners*, 1908, p. 24.

67. Schmeckebier, *Office of Indian Affairs*, pp. 186–88; 35 *United States Statutes* 783. A detailed history of the Indian forestry service, written by a man who was intimately involved, is J. P. Kinney, *Indian Forest and Range: A History of the Administration and Conservation of the Redman's Heritage* (Washington: Forestry Enterprises,

During World War I the forest resources, like the land, were turned toward war uses. More timber was sold, and the government mill on the Menominee Reservation, for example, produced lumber needed by the war effort. At the end of the war the market notably declined, but it revived somewhat during that decade. In 1926 Burke noted the end of ten years of large-scale lumbering activity, especially on the reservations in the western states. Between 1916 and 1926, on lands under the direct administration of the Indian Office, income derived from timber had totaled approximately $16 million. As he asked Congress for increased appropriations to protect and manage the Indian forests, Burke called attention to the value that had been derived from the sale of timber in promoting educational, health, and industrial work among the Indians.[68]

Of greater investment but ultimately of less benefit to the Indians were the irrigation projects initiated by the government on Indian reservations. Much of the land of the reservations was arid or semi-arid and could support the Indian communities only if intensive agriculture under irrigation were undertaken. The government's interest in irrigation of Indian lands began shortly after the Civil War, when Congress in 1867 appropriated $50,000 for relocating the Colorado River Indians of Arizona, "including the expense of constructing a canal for irrigating said reservation." Year by year funds were provided for this and other particular projects, and in 1884 Congress began the practice of appropriating in addition a general irrigation fund to be spent at the discretion of the secretary of the interior. The sum in 1884 was $50,000, and in 1892 a similar appropriation of $40,000 was made for irrigation projects. From that time on there was an annual appropriation; before 1902 the amounts were small, but then they shot up, with $100,000 in 1902 and a high of $335,000 in fiscal years 1914, 1915, and 1916. After 1919, however, the fund was specified for particular projects. These "general" funds continued to be small in relation to the total moneys provided for particular projects, of which the most important were on the Blackfeet, Colorado River, Crow, Flathead, Fort Belknap, Fort Hall, Fort Peck, San Carlos, Uintah, Wind River, and Yakima reservations (see Table 11).[69]

The projects at first were under control of the agents or superintendents. A primary interest in irrigation from the viewpoint of the Indian Office was, as Commissioner Leupp noted in 1906, "affording employment for

---

1950). Each annual report of the commissioner of Indian affairs has a special section devoted to forestry; the progress and increasing realization of the value of the forests for Indian economic well-being can be followed in them.

68. CIA Report, 1918, serial 7498, pp. 62–63; CIA Report, 1921, p. 29; CIA Report, 1926, p. 21; CIA Report, 1927, p. 21.

69. 14 *United States Statutes* 514–15; 23 *United States Statutes* 94; 27 *United States Statutes* 137; 38 *United States Statutes* 78. Cohen, *Federal Indian Law*, pp. 250–52, gives data on the particular projects.

TABLE 11: Appropriations for Irrigation, 1907–1928

	Fiscal Year				
	1907	1910	1917	1924	1928
General appropriations for irrigation	$155,000	$200,000	$244,700	$197,450	$150,000
Appropriations for specific projects	515,000	865,000	1,713,000	2,211,300	1,517,125
Total	670,000	1,065,000	1,957,700	2,408,750	1,667,127

SOURCE: Data from Laurence F. Schmeckebier, *The Office of Indian Affairs: Its History, Activities and Organization* (Baltimore: Johns Hopkins Press, 1927), p. 239.

the Indians on which their daily bread should depend, and thus undermining the racial prejudice against common manual labor."[70] But the haphazard approach of the early years was gradually replaced, as the nation as a whole took up interest in reclamation of the arid lands in the West and as irrigation became increasingly essential on both allotted and unallotted Indian lands. National demands for efficient utilization of the land and Indian needs for economic subsistence resulted in a continually more regulated approach.

In 1899 provision had been made for two superintendents of irrigation, and the number was gradually increased to seven. Then, beginning in 1907, some of the major projects (Blackfeet, Fort Peck, Flathead, and Yuma) were transferred to the Bureau of Reclamation, which took charge of constructing the irrigation systems. A closer control over irrigation projects was instituted in 1910 by limiting to $35,000 projects undertaken without express authorization by Congress and by the necessity of estimating ultimate costs before new projects could begin. The omnibus bill of 1910 allowed the secretary of the interior to reserve from allotment or sale valuable power or reservoir sites and to cancel and exchange trust patents already issued for such sites.[71]

As the costs of irrigation projects increased, they came to be charged against the Indian tribes themselves in the form of reimbursable funds. Such reimbursement was frequently provided for in acts authorizing specific projects, but until 1914 the general appropriations for irrigation were considered gratuities. On August 1, 1914, however, Congress provided that

70. CIA Report, 1906, serial 5118, p. 82. In 1911 Valentine noted the sizable amounts paid out of irrigation appropriations for Indian labor. CIA Report, 1911, serial 6223, p. 14.

71. Schmeckebier, *Office of Indian Affairs*, pp. 240–41; CIA Report, 1907, serial 5296, pp. 50–51; 36 *United States Statutes* 270, 858. In 1924 the Indian Office took back the operation of the irrigation projects that had been in the hands of the Reclamation Service. 43 *United States Statutes* 402.

both the earlier grants and future grants should be charged against Indian funds if they were available and furthermore that the costs should be borne, not by the tribe as a whole, but by the individual Indians who benefited from the water. It was next to impossible to enforce the law, and little attempt was made to do so until Congress in 1920 directed the secretary of the interior to enforce at least partial reimbursement. But nearly all money collected under the laws of 1914 and 1920 was paid by white landowners on Indian reservation projects. The Meriam Report of 1928 urged the canceling of reimbursable debts if the money had been originally given as a gratuity, and in 1932 Congress canceled all outstanding debts due on construction of irrigation projects.[72]

The primary concern of the federal irrigation program administrators seemed to be the construction of reservoirs and ditches and their maintenance. A more important matter, the protection of the water rights of Indians so that there would be a continuing adequate supply of water for the projects, was slighted. Some attention was paid to water rights, to be sure, in the Dawes Act, which declared that in cases where water for irrigation was necessary to render the lands within any Indian reservation suitable for agricultural purposes, the secretary of the interior was to secure "a just and equal distribution" of water among the Indians. But, except for special cases like that of the Pimas, there was no special problem for a considerable number of years.[73] In 1908 the Supreme Court, in the landmark case *Winters* v. *United States*, decreed that where land was reserved by treaty to an Indian tribe, there was an implied reservation of water necessary for the irrigation of their lands, and the Indian Office tended to rely on this decision, without taking other action to protect the water rights of the Indians.[74]

---

72. 38 *United States Statutes* 583; 41 *United States Statutes* 409; 47 *United States Statutes* 564–65; *The Problem of Indian Administration* [Meriam Report] (Baltimore: Johns Hopkins Press, 1928), p. 510. The Preston–Engle Report on irrigation projects also strongly criticized the system of reimbursable funds.

73. 24 *United States Statutes* 390. On the Pimas, see CIA Report, 1904, serial 4798, pp. 7–21. The Pima case was taken up by the reform groups. See *Report of the Board of Indian Commissioners*, 1904, pp. 15–16; 1905, p. 9; 1906, pp. 13–14; Stella M. Atwood, "The S.O.S. of the Pimas: They Must Have Water for Their Crops to Avoid Starvation and Beggary," *Sunset Magazine* 50 (April 1923): 24. The Pima water case is treated historically in Alfonso Ortiz, "The Gila River Piman Water Problem: An Ethnohistorical Account," in Albert H. Schroeder, ed., *The Changing Ways of Southwestern Indians: A Historic Perspective* (Glorieta, New Mexico: Rio Grande Press, 1973), pp. 245–57.

74. 207 *U.S. Reports* 564. See Cohen, *Federal Indian Law*, pp. 220–21, 316–19, and the 1982 revision, pp. 575–604, for a discussion of water rights. The *Winters* decision and later applications are treated in two articles by Norris Hundley, Jr.: "The Dark and Bloody Ground of Indian Water Rights: Confusion Elevated to Principle," *Western Historical Quarterly* 9 (October 1978): 455–82, and "The 'Winters' Decision and Indian Water Rights: A Mystery Reexamined," ibid. 13 (January 1982): 17–42.

The overriding question in the end, however, was whether and to what extent the irrigation projects in fact benefited the Indians. Were the Indians actually using the lands for successful irrigated agriculture? The answer was no. It became increasingly clear through the 1920s that irrigation projects were authorized for Indian reservations, not with the primary intent of aiding Indian advance toward self-sufficiency, but to develop the arid West for the benefit of white interests. And, in fact, the whites were the ones who profited from the irrigation. The conclusion was inescapable from the special report on Indian irrigation projects submitted in June 1928 by Porter J. Preston and Charles A. Engle.[75] The statistics submitted in the report pretty much tell the story. As of June 30, 1927, government projects had prepared 692,057 acres for irrigation on reservations, at a total expenditure since the first appropriation in 1867 of $35,967,925.72. Of these acres, 70 percent were owned by the Indians and 30 percent by whites. Only 52 percent of the total acreage susceptible of irrigation, however, was actually being irrigated, and of this 32 percent was farmed by Indians and the rest by whites, either as owners (37 percent) or lessees (31 percent). On the large projects studied especially by Preston and Engle (which accounted for 91 percent of the acreage), the Indians irrigated only 23 percent.[76]

Preston and Engle placed the blame chiefly on the allotment system, which gave the Indians more land than they could beneficially use. With 40-acre allotments of irrigable land to each individual—"the speechless babe and the gray-haired man are given allotments the same as the ablebodied head of a family"—an average family would have about 200 acres, whereas it could efficiently irrigate no more than 40 or 50. The result was the leasing of land to whites, while the Indians lived in indolence and dissipation, or the outright sale of the land. In the end much land was not used at all, yet the costs of construction and maintenance were geared to full utilization. The report criticized the system of reimbursable charges, the failure to keep accurate records, and the lack of attention to protecting the water rights of the Indians. There were seventy-five recommendations for correcting the faults the investigation had uncovered, including the abandonment of unprofitable projects and the transfer of others to the Reclamation Service.[77]

75. Porter J. Preston and Charles A. Engle, "Report of Advisors on Irrigation on Indian Reservations," June 8, 1928, printed in "Survey of Conditions of the Indians in the United States," *Hearings before a Subcommittee of the Committee on Indian Affairs, United States Senate, 71st Congress, 2d Session* (1930), part 6, pp. 2210–2661.
76. Ibid., p. 2217.
77. Ibid., pp. 2211–2300. The remainder of the report, pp. 2300–2661, deals with specific irrigation projects.

APPRAISAL OF THE ALLOTMENT POLICY

The allotment policy, begun and carried out by federal officials imbued with the philosophy of individualizing the Indians, failed miserably. The paternalistic concern to transform the Indians into independent farmers and stockmen did not take sufficiently into consideration the nature of traditional Indian ways or the geographical conditions of the area in which the allotted Indians were supposed to work out their destiny.

Allotment did not perform its primary function: to turn the Indians generally into agriculturalists. Many Indians had farmed successfully under their communal land patterns, with individuals and families using designated sections of tribal land for their cultivation, and as allotment began it was hoped that more and more Indians would become self-sufficient through the land. Yet in fact, under allotment, the amount of Indian farming declined rather than grew. In the first decade of allotment, the 1890s, there were already clear indications that the expectations of the advocates of the policy were not being fulfilled.[78] In the twentieth century, after the burgeoning of allotment between 1900 and 1910, the situation was no more encouraging. In the ten states in which the great majority of Indian allotments were made, excluding Oklahoma, the total area farmed by Indians in 1910 was estimated at 2,131,477 acres. In the next decade Indian farming declined in all the states except Montana, with a total of 1,836,191 acres in 1920, and in the 1920s the decline was universal, with a total of 1,519,368 acres farmed by Indians in 1930. Moreover, the position of Indians in relation to white farmers deteriorated. In 1910 the value of land and buildings on an Indian farm was 44 percent of that on the average white farm; in 1930 it was only 31 percent. A similar decline occurred in the relative value of machinery and implements on Indian and white farms. "Allotment in severalty, judged either as a program to advance the welfare of American Indians or to promote economic development among reservation Indians," a careful economic study has concluded, "was a disaster. Rather than encourage Indian farming, it led to a significant decline in Indian farming."[79]

A primary cause of this decline, of course, was the loss of Indian lands in the allotment period. When John Collier testified before a congressional committee in 1934 on legislation to reverse allotment, he declared that

78. D. S. Otis, *The Dawes Act and the Allotment of Indian Lands*, ed. Francis Paul Prucha (Norman: University of Oklahoma Press, 1973), pp. 138–41. The final chapter in this book, pp. 124–53, is an appraisal of allotment to 1900.

79. Leonard A. Carlson, *Indians, Bureaucrats, and Land: The Dawes Act and the Decline of Indian Farming* (Westport, Connecticut: Greenwood Press, 1981), pp. 146–55, 174.

"two thirds of the Indians in two thirds of the Indian country for many years have been drifting toward complete impoverishment." He asserted that Indian lands had been cut from 138 million acres in 1887 to 48 million in 1934, and that of the residual lands nearly one-half were desert or semi-desert. About one hundred thousand Indians, he said, were "totally land-less as a result of allotment."[80]

Of the 118 allotted reservations (with three-fourths of the Indian population), 44 had been opened to homestead entry under public land laws after the surplus lands had been ceded to the federal government. At least 38 million acres of Indian land were lost in this way. By a similar practice, surplus lands on the reservations were thrown open to settlement, and the homesteaders remunerated the Indians for the land settled. Some 22 million acres were disposed of in this way. Another 23 million acres were alienated by Indians who had received fee patents to their allotments. Under the provisions of 1902 for sale of inherited land and of 1907 for the sale of land of noncompetent Indians, 3,730,265 acres of land passed out of Indian hands. Of the 52,142,935 acres still owned by Indians in 1934, 21.9 percent (11,369,974 acres) was in original allotments, 12 percent (6,252,726 acres) was in heirship allotments, and .5 percent (232,899 acres) was held in reserve for schools and agencies. The rest, 65.6 percent (34,287,336 acres), was still tribal land. Most of the tribal land (84 percent) was in unallotted reservations in Arizona, New Mexico, Utah, Wyoming, Oregon, and Montana. The allotted acreage was chiefly in Montana, South Dakota, Oklahoma, New Mexico, and North Dakota, where 82 percent of all allotted land was located.[81]

Thus the grand dream of Henry Dawes and his friends and followers came to naught. However one looks at allotment, it was disappointing and damaging.[82] A principal goal of Collier and the reform movement he inaugurated was to correct the evils that had come with the individualizing of Indian economic activity, the subdivision of the lands into economically unsound parcels, and the loss of so much of the Indian landed estate.

80. "Readjustment of Indian Affairs," *Hearings before the Committee on Indian Affairs, House of Representatives, on H.R. 7902, 73d Congress, 2d Session* (1934), pp. 15, 17. A careful study made in 1934 showed better than 52 million acres still in Indian hands, but Collier's point was still valid. *Indian Land Tenure, Economic Status, and Population Trends,* p. 6.

81. Ibid., pp. 6–7, 27.

82. A number of studies describe the working out of allotment and its failure. See, for example, David M. Holford, "The Subversion of the Indian Land Allotment System, 1887–1934," *Indian Historian* 8 (Spring 1975): 11–21; Ross R. Cotroneo and Jack Dozier, "A Time of Disintegration: The Coeur d'Alene and the Dawes Act," *Western Historical Quarterly* 5 (October 1974): 405–19; Allen G. Harper, "Salvaging the Wreckage of Indian Land Allotment," in Oliver La Farge, ed., *The Changing Indian* (Norman: University of Oklahoma Press, 1942), pp. 84–109.

CHAPTER 35

Indians of Oklahoma and New York

Final Dissolution of the Five Civilized Tribes.

Removal of Restrictions. The Scandal of the Probate

Courts. Indian Schools in Oklahoma.

The Indians of New York State.

The Five Civilized Tribes had unique relations with the federal government. The Dawes Act and many other measures that embodied federal Indian policy specifically exempted the Five Tribes—and sometimes all the Indians of Oklahoma. Yet until the census of 1950 Oklahoma was the most populous Indian state (it was overtaken in that year by Arizona), and in the first decades of the twentieth century Oklahoma Indians comprised about one-third of the Indian population in the United States. The Cherokees, Creeks, Choctaws, Chickasaws, and Seminoles clearly did not fit the general pattern of Indian existence that determined much of federal policy. Although many aspects of federal activity among Indians applied to Oklahoma Indians as well as to other tribes, peculiar circumstances dictated special relations with the United States government in the matter of political status, control of land and other resources, and education. Similarly, the Indians in New York state fell somewhat outside the general course of Indian affairs.[1]

1. An extended account of the Five Civilized Tribes in the early twentieth century, which includes many individual cases, is Angie Debo, *And Still the Waters Run: The Betrayal of the Five Civilized Tribes* (Princeton: Princeton University Press, 1940). The complexities of the legal relationships are outlined in Felix S. Cohen, *Handbook of Federal Indian Law* (Washington: GPO, 1942), chapter 23, "Special Laws Relating to Oklahoma," pp. 425–55, and the 1982 revision, pp. 770–97.

FINAL DISSOLUTION OF THE FIVE CIVILIZED TRIBES

The Dawes Commission, appointed in 1893 to work for the allotment of Indian lands and the dissolution of tribal governments, the Curtis Act of 1898, which gave legislative sanction to the commission's work, and the agreements made by the commission with the separate tribes were the foundation upon which the new political relations with the Five Civilized Tribes rested. But the transformation from tribal governments to an aggregate of individualized American citizens did not happen instantaneously. It was a long and complicated process, and it engaged much of the time and energy of the Indian Office.[2]

In March 1901, by an amendment to the Dawes Act, Congress conferred United States citizenship on all the Indians in the Indian Territory. Skeletal tribal administrations were still maintained as a necessary means to expedite the disposition of tribal property, but the act "to provide for the final disposition of the affairs of the Five Civilized Tribes in the Indian Territory" of April 26, 1906, indicated what puppet regimes the continuing tribal governments were. If any tribal executive refused or neglected to perform his duties, he could be removed from office by the president of the United States, who could fill any vacancy arising from removal, disability, or death of the incumbent. Moreover, if an executive officer, after receiving notice that any document was ready for his signature, failed to appear within thirty days to sign it, the secretary of the interior could approve the measure instead. The tribal revenues were to be collected by an officer appointed by the secretary, and although the law authorized the existing tribal governments to continue "in full force and effect for all purposes authorized by law," the legislature could not be in session for more than thirty days in any one year, and no act was valid until approved by the president.[3]

Gradually, as their work was accomplished, the tribal governments became mere shadows. Cato Sells noted at the end of 1914 that the tribal form of government of the Cherokees was "practically abolished." The tribal officers tendered their resignations as of June 30, 1914, and all were accepted except that of the governor, whose temporary continuance in office was "required to assist in the disposal of the few remaining details incident to the complete dissolution of the tribal government." Similarly, the Choctaw, Chickasaw, and Seminole tribes had lost their legislative and

2. The work of the Dawes Commission has been discussed in chapter 29. Extended sections in the annual reports of the commissioner of Indian affairs deal with implementation of the Curtis Act and the agreements.

3. 31 *United States Statutes* 1447; 34 *United States Statutes* 137–48.

judicial functions and retained only a small corps of officers to transact necessary business. Among the Creeks a limited force was kept until the work of equalizing allotments could be accomplished.[4]

There was no regret in Washington about the end of the once-flourishing Indian governments. Secretary of the Interior Franklin K. Lane expressed the general attitude:

> On the 1st of last July the Cherokee Nation ceased to exist. This act was the culmination of a treaty promise made over 80 years ago, extended by statute, and at last placed within administrative discretion. The word of the white man has been made good. These native and aspiring people have been lifted as American citizens into full fellowship with their civilized conquerors. The Cherokee Nation, with its senate and house, governor and officers, laws, property, and authority exists no longer. Surely there is something fine in this slight bit of history. It takes hold upon the imagination and the memory, arouses dreams of the day when the Indian shall be wholly blended into our life, and at the same time draws the mind backward over the stumbling story of our relationship with him.[5]

The American citizenship of the Indians and the dissolution of their tribal governments, however, did not end the federal government's business with them. Citizenship, in fact, had little effect upon the paternalistic directing of the individual Indians from Washington. This was one of the paradoxes that continued to mark Indian affairs, and it was noted at the time. A select committee of the Senate, sent to investigate conditions in the Indian Territory in connection with the act of 1906, reported much embarrassment arising out of the discrepancy between citizenship and continuing wardship. It cited the law conferring citizenship in 1901 and remarked: "Yet notwithstanding this express legislative naturalization, Congress in its subsequent legislation, and the Department of the Interior, acting under such legislation, has apparently ignored entirely this established citizenship, and in nearly every instance has treated the questions arising within the Five Civilized Tribes as though no such act had ever been passed and as though the Indians were still in the broadest sense wards of the Government." Even statehood for Oklahoma in 1907 did not materially affect this condition, for in the enabling act Congress had set the provision that the constitution of a new state could not be construed

---

4. CIA Report, 1914, serial 6815, pp. 50–51; CIA Report, 1916, serial 7160, pp. 55–56.

5. Report of the Secretary of the Interior, 1914, *House Document* no. 1475, 63–3, serial 6814, p. 3.

"to limit or impair the rights of person or property pertaining to the Indians of said Territories (so long as such rights shall remain unextinguished) or to limit or affect the authority of the Government of the United States to make any law or regulation respecting such Indians, their lands, property, or other rights by treaties, agreement, law, or otherwise, which it would have been competent to make if this Act had never been passed."[6]

To attend to the multifarious duties regarding the Five Civilized Tribes, the United States at first had three governmental units: the Commission to the Five Civilized Tribes (Dawes Commission), an Indian inspector for Indian Territory authorized by the Curtis Act, and the superintendent of the Union Agency at Muskogee. Changes in this structure soon occurred. The Dawes Commission was discontinued on July 1, 1905. In its place the secretary of the interior conferred its duties on a commissioner to the Five Civilized Tribes, who after June 30, 1907, also performed the duties of the inspector.[7] Thus after 1907 the affairs of the Five Civilized Tribes were administered by the commissioner and the superintendent of the Union Agency. In 1914, however, these two offices were discontinued by Congress and replaced by a superintendent for the Five Civilized Tribes, to be appointed by the president with the advice and consent of the Senate.[8] This return to a political appointee for a sensitive position in the Indian service was strongly criticized by the reform groups, for whom civil service appointment was a basic principle.

REMOVAL OF RESTRICTIONS

When the rolls were closed, 101,506 persons had been enrolled in the Five Civilized Tribes, including 2,582 whites married into the tribes and 23,405 freedmen. Out of the 19,525,966 acres of land embraced within these five nations, 15,794,351.48 were allotted to the enrolled members.[9] Of the surplus about 150,000 acres were set aside for townsites and other public

---

6. "Report of the Select Committee to Investigate Matters Connected with Affairs in the Indian Territory," January 16, 1907, *Senate Report* no. 5013, 59–2, serial 5062, p. ii; 34 *United States Statutes* 267–68.

7. The first commissioner to the Five Civilized Tribes was Tams Bixby, who had replaced Dawes as chairman of the commission; then came J. George Wright, who had been inspector for the Indian Territory.

8. 38 *United States Statutes* 598.

9. Debo, *And Still the Waters Run*, p. 47, gives a table of enrollment by tribe. Figures on enrollment differ because some names were removed and the rolls were opened from time to time to admit new members. A table of allotted acreage by tribe appears ibid., p. 51.

uses. The act of 1906 authorized the sale of the remainder under the direction of the secretary of the interior, and Commissioner Sells reported in 1914 that 2,178,174 acres had been sold at public auction for the sum of $12,189,193. In addition, 1,274,024 acres of Choctaw and Chickasaw timberlands had been offered for sale, of which 306,286 acres had been sold for $1,460,244.85, leaving about a million and a half acres of timberlands and segregated coal and asphalt lands still to be marketed.[10]

What concerned the federal government and the people of Oklahoma most, however, were the individual allotments of the enrolled tribal members. Unlike allotments made under the Dawes Act, in which the allottees received trust patents from the United States for a period of twenty-five years and full title when a fee patent was issued at the end of the trust period, the patents for allotments under the agreements made with the tribes by the Dawes Commission were granted by the tribes, but with exemptions from taxation and specific restrictions against alienation, which varied from agreement to agreement. In general, a set portion—usually forty acres—of the allotment was designated a homestead and made inalienable for twenty-one years; the rest was called "surplus lands." By the act of 1906 the allotments of full-bloods were restricted against alienation for a period of twenty-five years, that is, until 1931. Additional provisions in the tribal agreements and in the 1906 legislation dealt with the complicated details of wills, inheritance, and leasing.[11]

The handling of the allotment process provided extensive opportunity for graft, and S. M. Brosius, the Washington agent of the Indian Rights Association, brought charges against the Dawes Commission and the federal officials in the Indian Territory for speculating in Indian lands. In the fall of 1903 the Department of the Interior sent Charles J. Bonaparte, a member of the Board of Indian Commissioners, to investigate the charges, and the Justice Department sent three examiners to look into the activities of the courts and court employees. The investigators did indeed turn up

10. CIA Report, 1914, serial 6815, p. 50. Only the surface of the mineral lands was to be sold.

11. Debo, *And Still the Waters Run*, p. 90, gives a brief summary of alienation restrictions; Cohen, *Federal Indian Law*, pp. 434–42, provides data on alienation and taxation of the allotted lands of the Five Tribes. A number of legal treatises on Indian land laws were published at the time as guides to the complexities of the situation. See S. T. Bledsoe, *Indian Land Laws: Being a Treatise on the Law of Acquiring Title to, and the Alienation of, Allotted Indian Land* (Kansas City: Pipes-Reed Book Company, 1909); J. E. Bennett, *The Law of Titles to Indian Lands* (Oklahoma City: Harlow Publishing Company, 1917); Lawrence Mills, *The Lands of the Five Civilized Tribes: A Treatise upon the Law Applicable to the Lands of the Five Civilized Tribes in Oklahoma* (St. Louis: F. H. Thomas Law Book Company, 1919); and Lawrence Mills, *Oklahoma Land Laws* (St. Louis: Thomas Law Book Company, 1924).

questionable dealings, although it was difficult to pinpoint wrongdoing, and the Interior Department forbade its employees to lease or purchase Indian land for speculation. Congress in the Indian appropriation act of April 21, 1904, prohibited the payment of any money appropriated for the Indian Territory to any federal official until he had taken an oath that he had "no financial interest with any person or corporation dealing with Indian lands in the Indian Territory."[12]

To the whites, who comprised the great majority of the Oklahoma population, the restricted, nontaxable lands in the hands of the Indians appeared as an obstacle to economic development, and pressures soon mounted for a removal of restrictions. An example was the gathering of citizens at Muskogee in January 1904, which sent a delegate to Washington with a memorial praying Congress to remove restrictions on the alienation of certain categories of land. "Under the present plan relating to sales and leases," the memorial read, "the development of Indian Territory is grievously retarded," and it pointed to the very large number of Indian citizens who felt that the restrictions were "a humiliating reflection upon their intelligence and rob them of what they regard as substantial benefits." The memorialists recognized that full-bloods and others who did not speak English needed to be protected. But they insisted that "25 percent or more" of allottees who had no Indian blood and those with only a little, as well as the Indians who were responsible and competent, should be allowed freely to dispose of their surplus lands.[13]

These eager citizens did not have long to wait. Congress in 1904 removed restrictions from all lands allotted to whites and to black freedmen, except for the homesteads and the lands of minors, and authorized the secretary of the interior to remove restrictions on lands of other Indians, with the same exceptions. This was but the beginning, as Indian blood quantum came to be the basis for dividing restricted from nonrestricted Indians. The law of May 27, 1908, "an act for the removal of restrictions from part of the lands of allottees of the Five Civilized Tribes," opened the gates wide. First, it removed all restrictions (including those on homesteads and the lands of minors) from the allotments of intermarried whites, freedmen, and mixed-blood Indians with less than half Indian blood. Second, all the lands, except homesteads, of mixed-blood Indians with half or more but less than three-fourths Indian blood, were freed of restrictions. This meant that restrictions applied only to homesteads of mixed-blood Indians having

12. 33 *United States Statutes* 205. Bonaparte's investigation is reported in *Senate Document* no. 189, 58–2, serial 4591; that of the Justice Department in *House Document* no. 528, 58–2, serial 4675.

13. "Removal of Restrictions upon the Sale of Surplus Allotments," *Senate Document* no. 169, 58–2, serial 4590, pp. 2–7. Attached to the memorial were numerous petitions and other documents of the same tenor.

half or more than half Indian blood (including minors) and to all allotted lands of full-bloods and mixed-bloods of three-fourth or more Indian blood (including minors). But the secretary of the interior was empowered to remove even these restrictions. Moreover, all restricted land other than homesteads could be leased by adult allottees and by guardians of minors or incompetent adults for a period not to exceed five years, and the secretary of the interior could approve other leases.[14] By 1914, when the tribal governments ended, out of the total enrolled population of 101,209 members and freedmen of the Five Civilized Tribes, only 36,967 were in the restricted class. Then, under the "liberal" policy of Commissioner Cato Sells, by an order of August 6, 1919, restrictions were unconditionally removed from all allottees of one-half Indian blood, and the number of restricted Indians fell to 21,213, holding 2,683,819 acres.[15]

THE SCANDAL OF THE PROBATE COURTS

The act of 1908 that removed the restrictions from the land of large numbers of Indians went a step further. It subjected minors in the Five Civilized Tribes to the jurisdiction of the probate courts of Oklahoma. This removed them from the protection of the federal government and left to the secretary of the interior only the innocuous authority to appoint local agents within Oklahoma to investigate the actions of guardians appointed for minor allottees. It turned out to be throwing these defenseless children to the wolves. Grafters of all sorts exploited the situation, and a class of "professional guardians" arose whose sole occupation was caring for the estates of Indian minors and of adult Indians declared incompetent.[16]

The evils of the situation came to light in a report of an investigation made by M. L. Mott, the attorney for the Creek Nation, in 1912. Mott compared the costs of administering the estates of Indian minors by the "professional guardians" with costs under competent relatives or businessmen and with the costs of administering the estates of white minors, and he found scandalously high costs charged against the estates of the Indians, as well as poor record keeping of the transactions.[17] Commissioner Sells, on taking office, noted the serious problem:

14. 33 *United States Statutes* 204; 35 *United States Statutes* 312–13.

15. CIA Report, 1914, serial 6815, pp. 51–52; CIA Report, 1920, serial 7820, p. 38.

16. 35 *United States Statutes* 313–14. Much has been written about the exploitation. A strongly condemnatory account is in Debo, *And Still the Waters Run*. There is a critical but moderately toned account in *The Problem of Indian Administration* [Meriam Report] (Baltimore: Johns Hopkins Press, 1928), pp. 798–804.

17. Mott's report of November 21, 1912, is printed in a pamphlet he published in 1925 on the probate scandals, *A National Blunder: The Act of May 27, 1908, Placing in the*

It is apparent that many guardians were appointed without regard to their fitness and insolvent bondsmen accepted. It is not uncommon for lands of minor Indian children to be sold on appraisements influenced by perspective [*sic*] purchasers and for inadequate prices. Excessive compensation was many times allowed guardians and unconscionably large fees paid to attorneys. Under these conditions the property of Indian children was frequently so ravished that when final reports were called for they were not forthcoming, and estates were often found to have been dissipated and their bondsmen financially irresponsible. Altogether it developed a condition demanding speedy and radical reform.[18]

In an attempt to correct the abuses, Sells arranged conferences with the county judges, prosecuting attorneys, and district judges in eastern Oklahoma. A set of probate procedures was adopted by the county judges, approved by the State County Judges Association, and then officially adopted and promulgated by the Supreme Court of Oklahoma. In addition, a number of special probate attorneys were appointed by the secretary of the interior to be watchdogs in probate matters, under the authority of the Indian appropriation act of June 30, 1913. In 1914 a specific sum of eighty-five thousand dollars was provided for these attorneys. Sells reported immediate improvement in prosecution of wrongdoers, recovery of estates, removal of dishonest and incompetent guardians, and appointment of responsible bondsmen, and in "the moral influence which has resulted, operating powerfully to prevent a repetition of wrongdoing and to insure better conditions in the future."[19]

In actual fact, the situation was not as favorable as Sells reported, and it rapidly deteriorated. The rules of 1914 were opposed by local courts, and on April 4, 1919, the Oklahoma legislature abrogated all rules adopted by the Supreme Court and required each local court to promulgate its own rules. Moreover, the federal appropriations for the probate attorneys after 1920 were steadily reduced so that the number declined from the twenty originally appointed to nine.[20]

Probate Courts of Oklahoma Indian Jurisdiction (Washington, 1925), pp. 64–75. It was supported and quoted by Representative Charles H. Burke in the House on December 13, 1912, *Congressional Record*, 49: 596–602.

18. CIA Report, 1914, serial 6815, p. 53. See also CIA Report, 1913, serial 6634, p. 8.

19. 38 *United States Statutes* 95, 598; CIA Report, 1914, serial 6815, pp. 53–54. The "Rules of Procedure in Probate Matters Adopted by the Justices of the Supreme Court of Oklahoma" are printed ibid., pp. 54–57. In 1920 Sells was still commenting favorably on the correction of abuses in probate matters in the Five Civilized Tribes. See CIA Report, 1920, serial 7820, pp. 39–40.

20. Laurence F. Schmeckebier, *The Office of Indian Affairs: Its History, Activities,*

In the early 1920s, conditions in Oklahoma occasioned a new and dramatic exposé. An official report came at the end of 1923 from S. E. Wallen, superintendent of the Five Civilized Tribes at Muskogee, who had been instructed by Commissioner Charles H. Burke to investigate the probate activities. Wallen's report read very much like that of Mott a decade earlier. He cited case after case and concluded: "that there are many cases in which bad management and great waste of the estates have been the rule; that there are extravagant and unwarranted allowances for maintenance and personal expenses for the wards; that guardians' and attorneys' fees are excessive, and in many cases unconscionable; and that the costs of administration through the Probate Courts of Oklahoma constitute an unfair tax upon the estates. That in many cases the concern of the guardian is in the handling of the funds and property, and not in regard to the best interest and welfare of the Indian ward." Wallen saw no solution except to take the matter of Indian lands out of local courts and to confer upon the secretary of the interior exclusive jurisdiction in all matters pertaining to restricted Indians.[21]

More startling was the muckraking pamphlet published by the Indian Rights Association early in 1924 under the inflammatory title *Oklahoma's Poor Rich Indians: An Orgy of Graft and Exploitation of the Five Civilized Tribes—Legalized Robbery.* The Indian Rights Association had decided to make "a thorough study of this amazing Oklahoma Probate situation," and it gained the cooperation of the Indian Welfare Committee of the General Federation of Women's Clubs and the American Indian Defense Association. For about five weeks in November and December 1923, Matthew K. Sniffen of the Indian Rights Association, Gertrude Bonnin of the General Federation of Women's Clubs, and Charles H. Fabens of the American Indian Defense Association carried on an investigation in Oklahoma. The pamphlet named above, which was their report, began with a series of bold, dramatic charges—that the estates of members of the Five Civilized Tribes were "shamelessly and openly robbed in a scientific and ruthless manner"; that the efforts of the secretary of the interior to correct abuses had failed; that "excessive and unnecessary administrative costs, unconscionable fees and commissions" were allowed to professional guardians and attorneys; that "Indian guardianships are the plums to be distributed to the faithful friends of the judges as a reward for their support at the polls"; and that, when oil was found on an Indian's property, "it is usually considered prima facie evidence that he is incompetent, and in the ap-

and Organization (Baltimore: Johns Hopkins Press, 1927), pp. 174–75. The Meriam Report, p. 799, commented on the ineffectiveness of the probate attorneys.

21. S. E. Wallen to Burke, December 31, 1923, printed in Mott, *A National Blunder*, pp. 16–44. Wallen's conclusions are on pp. 42–44.

pointment of a guardian for him his wishes in the matter are rarely considered." The bulk of the pamphlet was filled with a "bill of particulars" giving lurid details of the graft and corruption. Sniffen and his associates called the law of 1908 that passed jurisdiction to the Oklahoma courts The Crime of 1908 and declared that there was no hope of any reform in the existing system. They called for legislation that would return to the Department of the Interior "as a complete control of all Indian property and Indian minors and incompetents as constitutional limits will permit."[22]

The Oklahoma delegation in Congress could not let such a condemnation of their state go unanswered, and a special subcommittee of the House of Representatives issued a report on February 19, 1925. It accused the Indian Rights Association of sensationalism, spoke of "ill-founded publicity," and declared that the wholesale charges against judges, attorneys, and businessmen of Oklahoma were not substantiated. Yet the report also noted the loss of lands by restricted Indians and spoke of "reprehensible and indefensible practices" by "unconscionable attorneys and persons who make it a profession to obtain appointments as guardians." Such acknowledgment of evils in the system was an invitation for a rebuttal, which Sniffen soon furnished in another Indian Rights Association pamphlet, *"Out of Thine Own Mouth": An Analysis of the House Subcommittee Report Denying and Confirming the Looting of Oklahoma's "Poor Rich Indians."* He declared the report a "whitewash" and thanked the subcommittee for "proving a condition of affairs which it declared did not exist."[23]

The agitation continued at a somewhat subdued level. A bill was introduced in Congress in 1924 to give the secretary of the interior exclusive jurisdiction and control of restricted funds and lands of the Five Civilized Tribes, but it got nowhere in either house. In 1926 the Board of Indian Commissioners made a long report on Oklahoma matters, in which it repeated the established litany of evils in the work of the probate courts and called again for return to the federal government of the protective authority over Indian estates that had been taken away by the act of 1908.[24]

22. Gertrude Bonnin, Charles H. Fabens, and Matthew K. Sniffen, *Oklahoma's Poor Rich Indians: An Orgy of Graft and Exploitation of the Five Civilized Tribes—Legalized Robbery* (Philadelphia: Indian Rights Association, 1924), pp. 3, 5–8, 39.

23. "Indian Affairs in Oklahoma," *House Report* no. 1527, 68–2, serial 8392; Matthew K. Sniffen, *"Out of Thine Own Mouth": An Analysis of the House Subcommittee Report Denying and Confirming the Looting of Oklahoma's "Poor Rich Indians"* (Philadelphia: Indian Rights Association, 1925).

24. *Congressional Record*, 65: 1774, 2333. There is a summary of the special report in *Report of the Board of Indian Commissioners*, 1926, pp. 9–21; the records of the investigation are in OIA, Records of the Board of Indian Commissioners, Records Concerning Investigation of Administration of Affairs of the Five Civilized Tribes in Oklahoma. See also *Report of the Indian Rights Association*, 1924, pp. 6–12; 1925, p. 6.

All the publicity, which took its place amid the growing general criticisms of the handling of Indian affairs, brought no specific action, but it alerted the nation to the scandals and bolstered the resolve of responsible citizens of Oklahoma to end the evils in their state. The Meriam Report in 1928 called the turning over of probate matters to the state courts "a deviation from the usual mode of dealing with the government's wards" that re-sulted in "a flagrant example of the white man's brutal and unscrupulous domination over a weaker race." Yet it noted that the investigations and reports had brought about an improvement in conditions. And in 1928, as the date drew near for removing all restrictions under the 1906 act, Con-gress, pushed by the recommendation of the Meriam Report and the con-tinuing agitation of the Board of Indian Commissioners, extended the re-strictions on the allotments of Indians of one-half Indian blood or more for another twenty-five years. By then there were only about twelve thousand restricted Indians in the Five Civilized Tribes, with allotted lands aggregat-ing approximately 1,727,702 acres.[25]

The whole affair highlighted the paradox of combining citizenship with wardship. There was a strong feeling that the Indians should be allowed to exercise responsibility for their own property as one of the rights and privi-leges of citizenship, and the Indians of the Five Civilized Tribes—with a long history of acculturation to the white man's ways—were thought to be particularly good cases in which to push for freedom from federal guardian-ship and paternalistic control of all their affairs. But in practice the Indians proved unable to protect their own interests. The only answer was to con-tinue the protection of the United States government. This was the prof-fered solution of the critics of the Oklahoma probate situation, and the Meriam Report noted that "the Indians of the Five Tribes are still the easy victims of the greedy and unscrupulous" and that the federal government owed "a duty to preserve to the Indians their patrimony."[26]

The Osage Indians presented another special case. They had been re-moved from Kansas in the early 1870s to a tract immediately west of the Cherokee Nation in the Outlet. Largely destitute at the time of their re-moval, they were located by chance on lands of tremendous riches in oil and gas resources, and they became probably the richest class of people in the world. In 1906 Congress provided for the allotment of the Osage lands. Each of the approximately twenty-two hundred Indians was entitled to make three selections of 160 acres each, one of which would be a home-stead and inalienable for the life of the allottee. The other sections were "surplus lands," inalienable for twenty-five years unless a certificate of

25. Meriam Report, pp. 798, 801; CIA Report, 1928, p. 29; 45 *United States Statutes* 495.
26. Meriam Report, pp. 800–801.

competency was issued to the owner by the secretary of the interior—
although in 1909 the secretary was authorized, on application, to sell surplus lands. All subsurface mineral rights were reserved to the tribe for
twenty-five years, at which time they were to pass to the individual owners. The returns on the leases of oil and gas lands became immense, and
they were divided per capita and deposited to the credit of the individual
Indians. The interest on these funds was paid quarterly to the individuals
and to the parents of minor children. The segregated funds were restricted,
but when an Indian received a certificate of competency, he acquired access to his money.[27]

Unfortunately, most Osages did not make good use of their riches. The
chairman of the Board of Indian Commissioners, George Vaux, Jr., reported
what he had seen in 1920:

> Their wealth literally has been thrust upon them, unwittingly on
> their part. They are almost, if not quite, dazed by it. I have been over
> many of their household accounts—bills for family expenses run up
> with local merchants. Many of the totals are appalling. For example,
> in a family of two, an average for months of over $400 per month for
> meats alone; while four or five pairs of blankets a month are being
> purchased by the same couple. Other expenditures are in proportion.
> These people do not know what they are doing; they have never been
> trained, nor have they the opportunity to learn what it all means.
>
> That the money is being largely squandered is evident. Of course,
> a great deal of it goes into automobiles; many Osages have several,
> and they are all high-priced cars. One rarely sees an Osage in a Ford.
> Apart from this expenditure, however, not any very valuable personal
> property appears to be acquired.[28]

Some of these conditions were remedied in 1921, when Congress provided that full payments could be made only to competent Indians. For
noncompetent adults a maximum payment of one thousand dollars quarterly was authorized; for minors the quarterly payment was limited to five
hundred dollars for maintenance and education. The same law granted
citizenship to all members of the Osage tribe and removed all restrictions
on homesteads and surplus lands of adults of less than one-half Indian
blood. It also extended tribal rights to oil and other minerals until 1946. In
1925 additional safeguards were provided by reasserting control of the secretary of the interior or the superintendent of the Osage Agency over many

---

27. 34 *United States Statutes* 539–45; 35 *United States Statutes* 778; Cohen, *Federal Indian Law*, pp. 446–55, and 1982 revision, pp. 788–97.
28. *Report of the Board of Indian Commissioners*, 1920, p. 116.

actions of the legal guardians of Osages. The secretary was also authorized to revoke certificates of competency granted to Indians of more than one-half Indian blood who were guilty of "squandering or misusing" funds.[29]

INDIAN SCHOOLS IN OKLAHOMA

Although most of the special federal concern for affairs of the Five Civilized Tribes was related to land and other property of the individual Indians, the government also had a special relation to the schools. Each of the Five Tribes had maintained its own school system, but the Curtis Act and the agreements with the tribes that worked toward the dissolution of the tribal governments also heralded an end to tribal schools. The secretary of the interior assumed that he was invested with management of the schools, and in 1899 he appointed a superintendent of schools for the Indian Territory (John D. Benedict of Illinois) and a school supervisor for each of the tribes except the Seminoles. Because it seemed impossible for the Indian Office to take over full management of the schools all at once, "Regulations Concerning Education in the Indian Territory" were formulated to govern federal supervision as a temporary expedient. Commissioner Jones's report on the character of the Indian schools at the time of the change was extremely critical. He found incompetent administrators and teachers, deplorable financial management, dilapidated buildings, and an inadequate curriculum, especially in regard to English language training and agricultural or other industrial education. He noted Benedict's work and spoke highly of his zeal and tact in "rescuing the education matters of these Indians from their present chaotic condition." Adhering to his general principles of Indian education, Jones criticized the tribes for spending money "on large academies, seminaries, and colleges, where the ornamental curriculum of a white fashionable boarding school was given to the favored few, leaving the full bloods and poorer classes of mixed bloods to depend upon poorly equipped, miserable little schools, usually erected by subscriptions or donations." Year by year, he reported improvements under his regulations, although a system of day schools developed only slowly. The schools continued, however, to operate under a dual system of tribal and federal control, and there was considerable resentment on the part of the tribal school officials.[30]

By 1904 Jones was beginning to seek an end to the dual supervision of

29. 41 *United States Statutes* 1249–50; 43 *United States Statutes* 1008–11.
30. CIA Report, 1899, serial 3915, pp. 86–92; CIA Report, 1900, serial 4101, pp. 105–7; Debo, *And Still the Waters Run*, pp. 66–69.

the schools. In that year Congress appropriated one hundred thousand dollars for the "maintenance, strengthening, and enlarging of the tribal schools of the Cherokee, Creek, Choctaw, Chickasaw, and Seminole nations, and making provision for the attendance of children of non-citizens therein, and the establishment of new schools under the control of the tribal school boards and the Department of the Interior." The commissioner issued new rules and regulations for the application of the fund that strengthened the hand of the superintendent of schools in the appointment of teachers, setting of salaries, and general management of the schools. These rules were amended the following year, moving still closer to full federal control as the date for ending the tribal governments approached. Congress continued and increased the appropriations in subsequent years, using the funds not only for Indian education but also to provide educational facilities for whites and blacks, who as noncitizens of the tribes were excluded from Indian tribal schools.[31]

The act of April 26, 1906, placed the school system of the Five Civilized Tribes completely in the hands of the federal government. Section 10 of the law read: "The Secretary of the Interior is hereby authorized and directed to assume control and direction of the schools in the Choctaw, Chickasaw, Cherokee, Creek, and Seminole tribes, with the lands and all school property pertaining thereto . . . , retaining tribal educational officers, subject to dismissal by the Secretary of the Interior, and the present system so far as practicable, until such time as a public school system shall have been established under Territorial or State government." The schools were to be supported by tribal moneys in the Treasury of the United States up to the amount spent in the year ending June 30, 1905, supplemented by the congressional appropriations for tribal schools.[32]

Commissioner Francis E. Leupp remarked that the principal change to begin with was in the manner of paying expenses, for the superintendent of schools, the supervisors, and the tribal school officials all continued in office. At the beginning of July 1906, the secretary of the interior promulgated regulations for the conduct of the schools. "An effort was made," Leupp said, "to apply the same general rules as far as possible to all the nations in order that a uniform system might be established prior to their schools being placed under State supervision."[33]

---

31. 33 *United States Statutes* 215; CIA Report, 1904, serial 4798, pp. 89–92; CIA Report, 1905, serial 4959, pp. 108–16; Debo, *And Still the Waters Run*, pp. 70–72.

32. 34 *United States Statutes* 140.

33. CIA Report, 1906, serial 5118, p. 129; *Regulations for Tribal Indian Schools among the Five Civilized Tribes* (Washington: GPO, 1906). The regulations directed that "the supervisor of schools in each nation shall act jointly with the tribal school authorities thereof in supervising the work of the schools of such nation," but it was clear from the regulations that all authority rested in the federal officials.

In the fall of 1909 the Indian boarding schools in eastern Oklahoma were inspected by Inspector E. B. Linnen and other Indian Office agents. Their report was very critical, for they found the schools filthy, dilapidated, and lacking proper sanitation, medical care, and vocational training. The blame was placed on Superintendent Benedict, and as a result of the investigation, the school administration was reorganized. The positions of the superintendent of Indian schools and the tribal supervisors were abolished, and the regular Indian service personnel took over, with the supervisor at Muskogee directing the work. The most seriously rundown boarding schools were closed and the others repaired, and rural Indians were encouraged to attend public schools instead of Indian day schools. The congressional appropriations were used to pay tuition of Indian children in these schools.[34]

But conditions remained far from ideal, and the Meriam Report singled out the state in its discussion of Indians in public schools. "In Oklahoma," it noted, "where by far the largest numbers of Indian children live, it was clear in some localities that the right to attend public school meant little to full-blood Indians; they were attending irregularly or not at all." The rate of federal tuition was fixed to cover the loss to the state or local community resulting from nontaxation of Indian lands, and the area of the Five Civilized Tribes received the lowest rate. "Some of the poorest public school facilities for Indian children," the report declared, "are in those parts of Oklahoma where only ten cents per day per child is paid—quite insufficient to induce the school authorities to put forth any effort to get and keep Indian children in school." There is no reason to believe that the strictures against Indian education made by the Meriam Report in regard to medical care, sanitation, diet, and curriculum did not apply to Oklahoma as well as to the rest of the nation, for nine of the ten members of the survey team visited the Five Civilized Tribes and the Osages, a high proportion compared with the average number visiting the various jurisdictions as a whole.[35]

THE INDIANS OF NEW YORK STATE

The Indians of New York State, numbering about fifty-four hundred in 1900, were another instance of peculiar circumstances. There were two small communities on Long Island of Shinnecock and Poosepatuck Indians, which were under state control and did not concern the United

34. Debo, *And Still the Waters Run*, pp. 73–74, 276–78; CIA Report, 1910, serial 5976, pp. 223–30; CIA Report, 1911, serial 6223, pp. 459–68.
35. Meriam Report, pp. 416–17. See the table showing staff visits, pp. 64–65.

States government. The remainder were members of the Iroquois nations of Senecas, Mohawks, Onondagas, Cayugas, Oneidas, and Tuscaroras, who lived on reserves scattered across the state.[36] The largest group and the one that attracted most attention was the Seneca Nation on the Allegany and Cattaraugus reserves in western New York. The unique situation of these Indians arose in part from the question of federal, state, and tribal jurisdiction over their affairs, for the United States government had paid little attention to New York, and the state government had assumed considerable authority, building and maintaining schools and highways on the reservations and exercising some control over law and order and property rights.[37] The Indians were acculturated to white ways, and although the lands of the reserves were tribally owned, individual Indians had rights to designated parcels of land, which they cultivated and improved.

The status of Seneca land titles was seriously complicated by the confused question of the claims of the Ogden Land Company. Massachusetts, which claimed a preemptive right to lands in western New York on the basis of a royal grant, disposed of these rights in the late eighteenth century. They came to rest finally, after a number of transactions, in David A. Ogden, who had purchased the interest in Seneca lands in 1810. The rights of the Ogden Land Company, made up of heirs of Ogden and his partners, were variously interpreted to mean that the land belonged to the Seneca Nation, subject to the right of preemption of the land company, or that it belonged to the Ogden Land Company, under the grant from the crown to Massachusetts but subject to the perpetual right of occupancy by the Indians. Whatever the precise legal status of the claim, it was generally held to be an existing right, and it meant that Seneca lands could not be conveyed to anyone but the Ogden Land Company.[38]

The Senecas, like the Five Civilized tribes, had been specifically exempted from the operation of the Dawes Act, and they were determined to maintain their tribal ownership and tribal identity. The federal government and the reformers who supported and influenced government Indian policy, on the other hand, were equally determined that the reservations be

---

36. There is a table of population figures in CIA Report, 1900, serial 4101, p. 646. A brief history of the status of New York Indians is given in Cohen, *Federal Indian Law*, chapter 22, "New York Indians," pp. 416–24. Many of the reports and articles cited below also contain general historical information.

37. The New York code of laws had a special chapter called "The Indian Law."

38. Every investigation of Indian affairs in New York State had to take into account the Ogden claims, and the various reports examined the matter in great detail. See the reports cited below in notes 40–41; there is a useful brief account in Laurence M. Hauptman, "Senecas and Subdividers: Resistance to Allotment of Indian Lands in New York, 1875–1906," *Prologue* 9 (Summer 1977): 105–16.

allotted and the Indians made citizens and absorbed into the general population. New York, too, was eager for this to happen, and the whites who leased lands of the Senecas wanted to obtain full title.[39] Through much of the later nineteenth century, various commissions and individuals investigated the condition of the Senecas and the status of the Ogden claims, and attempts were repeatedly made to get federal or state legislation that would allot the Indians' lands. In 1888 the New York Assembly appointed a special committee, chaired by J. S. Whipple, to investigate the state's Indian problem. The long report submitted on February 1, 1889, traced the history of the conflicting claims and recommended a compulsory school attendance law, extinguishment of the Ogden land claims, allotment of the reservations in severalty, and the repeal of special state laws relating to Indians. "These Indian people have been kept as 'wards' or children long enough," the report concluded. "They should now be educated to be men, not Indians. . . . [When] the Indians of the State are absorbed into the great mass of the American people, then, and not before, will the 'Indian problem' be solved."[40]

In 1891 Philip C. Garrett, a member of the Board of Indian Commissioners, toured the New York reservations and submitted to the board a report that duplicated the recommendations of the Whipple committee. Garrett asserted that "the recognition of independent nationalities in the midst of our American nationality is absurd and untenable," and he expressed his view that "the New York Indians are entirely capable of civilization, as much so as the population around them, more so than the negroes." Four years later, in a detailed report to the secretary of the interior, Commissioner Daniel M. Browning reasserted the same principles. Then, when Congress asked for further negotiation on the Ogden claims, the secretary sent Philip Garrett on another mission to New York, all without avail.[41] The next move came from Theodore Roosevelt, governor

39. The problems of leasing are illustrated in the case of Salamanca, a white-inhabited city on the Allegany Reserve, in which ninety-nine-year leases, approved by the federal government, will lapse in 1991. See Thomas E. Hogan, "City in a Quandary: Salamanca and the Allegany Leases," *New York History* 55 (January 1974): 79–101.

40. *Report of Special Committee to Investigate the Indian Problem of the State of New York, Appointed by the Assembly in 1888*, Report no. 51 (Albany: Troy Press Company, 1889), p. 79.

41. "Report on New York Indians," Philip C. Garrett to Merrill E. Gates, June 9, 1891, in *Report of the Board of Indian Commissioners*, 1891, pp. 18–25; D. M. Browning to the secretary of the interior, January 19, 1895, *Senate Executive Document* no. 52, 53–3, serial 3275; Garrett to the secretary of the interior, December 4, 1896, and Garrett to D. M. Browning, December 10, 1896, in *House Document* no. 309, 54–2, serial 3534; CIA Report, 1897, serial 3641, pp. 88–90.

of New York, who was pushed by Garrett and likeminded reformers to take state action. Roosevelt appointed a commission headed by Garrett to investigate. The commission submitted its report on December 30, 1900, the day before Roosevelt's term ended, and no action was taken on it.[42] Meanwhile, as all the investigations and reports were being made by reform-minded committees, whites interested in the Indians' lands continued to push, still unsuccessfully, for some sort of allotment legislation.

The strongest agitation for allotment of the New York reservations came shortly after the turn of the century, in the form of a bill (H.R. 12270) introduced in Congress in 1902 by Representative Edward B. Vreeland of New York, a man who had important economic interests in Seneca land and oil. The Christian reform organizations closed ranks behind Vreeland's bill. The Board of Indian Commissioners persistently promoted severalty for the New York Indians, and the Lake Mohonk Conference in October 1902 devoted a whole session to the subject, beginning with an address by Vreeland and continuing with long discussion by both supporters and opponents of the measure. The conference formally endorsed allotment in severalty and the Vreeland bill specifically, and in the following year reaffirmed its support. Commissioner Jones, too, was heartily in favor. His only objection to the bill was a provision that required submission of the measure to the Indians for ratification, which he wanted stricken out. "If the enforcement of the bill, should it become law, depends upon the consent of the tribe," he said, "it will be a long time before any change is seen."[43]

Vreeland's bill passed the House of Representatives on December 15, 1902, and a similar measure (H.R. 7262) introduced in December 1903 was approved by the House on April 20, 1904, but neither bill was reported out of the Committee on Indian Affairs in the Senate. The reason lay in the able opposition provided by the Indians and their friends and in the specter of the Ogden Land Company claims. Although the Indians themselves were divided over the issue of allotment, the Seneca opposition to the measure was led by shrewd politicians like William C. Hoag and Andrew John, Jr., and by strong spokesmen from the white citizenry—especially Wil-

---

42. The report is printed in *Report of the Board of Indian Commissioners*, 1900, pp. 20–22. See also Laurence M. Hauptman, "Governor Theodore Roosevelt and the Indians of New York State," *Proceedings of the American Philosophical Society* 119 (February 21, 1975): 1–7.

43. *Report of the Board of Indian Commissioners*, 1901, pp. 9–12; 1902, pp. 16–17; 1903, pp. 17–18; *Lake Mohonk Conference Proceedings*, 1902, pp. 9, 57–101; 1903, pp. 112, 120–21; CIA Report, 1903, serial 4645, pp. 96–97; CIA Report, 1904, serial 4798, pp. 119–20. The original Vreeland bill is printed in *Lake Mohonk Conference Proceedings*, 1902, pp. 101–5.

liam D. Walker, Episcopal bishop of western New York, former Representative John Van Voorhis, and Senator Matthew Quay of Pennsylvania—who effectively stymied the thrust of the pro-allotment forces. Ogden claims were always in the background. Until they could be extinguished, it seemed impossible to proceed with allotment, and the land company refused to consider the buying out of its claims for any reasonable amount.[44]

The Vreeland bills were the greatest threat to Seneca tribal existence, and with their defeat the likelihood of allotment passed, but the New York Indians continued to be a matter of concern. It is understandable that the administration of Lane and Sells would object to the continuation of acculturated Indians like the Senecas as wards. Sells noted in 1914 the failure of the earlier measures and began new agitation to place the New York Indians "on a basis of citizenship equal to other residents of the State—a place which they should have occupied long ago." On September 10 a new allotment bill for New York Indians was introduced in the House by John R. Clancy of New York, which authorized the attorney general to institute suits to test the extent and validity of the Ogden claims and provided for appointment of a commission to appraise the Indian lands and divide and allot them in severalty. The Indian Office sent an employee, John R. T. Reeves, to investigate the Indian situation in New York once more, and as Assistant Commissioner Edgar Meritt told him, "to get to the bottom of it." Reeves's report, submitted on December 26, 1914, presented an able historical survey of the Indians' rights and Ogden claims, but neither his report nor statements from the attorney general and the secretary of the interior were enough to push the bill through Congress.[45]

From time to time there were flutters of new interest in the status of the New York Indians. The Lake Mohonk Conference appointed a special committee on the matter in 1909, which urged once more extinguishing the Ogden claims and allotment of lands; but soon attempts to allot the reservations disappeared, and attention focused instead on the critical problems of jurisdiction—federal, state, and tribal—on the reservations and the de-

---

44. *Congressional Record*, 36: 335–39, 365; 38: 147, 3475, 4253–55, 5199–5207; *House Report* no. 1793, 58–2, serial 4581. There is an excellent treatment of the Vreeland measure and opposition to it in Hauptman, "Senecas and Subdividers." For able statements on both sides of the question, see *Hearing before the Committee on Indian Affairs, House of Representatives, on H.R. 7262, to Provide for the Allotment of Lands in Severalty to the Indians in the State of New York, and for Other Purposes* (1904).

45. CIA Report, 1914, serial 6815, pp. 57–58. *House Document* no. 1590, 63–3, serial 6889, contains a copy of the bill, letters of Assistant Attorney General Ernest Knoedel to John H. Stephens, chairman of the Committee on Indian Affairs, September 28, 1914, and Franklin K. Lane to Stephens, January 22, 1915, and the Reeves report of December 26, 1914.

plorable conditions that were said to arise from the confusion. Commissioner Sells adverted to the matter in 1919, and the Indian Rights Association in 1919 and 1920 asserted: "Chaos reigns by reason of the fact that sovereignty has not been definitely determined."[46] Yet no fundamental action was taken by the United States government or by the state of New York, and development came only in individual cases of property or other rights adjudicated by the courts.[47]

46. *Lake Mohonk Conference Proceedings,* 1909, pp. 188–89; 1910, p. 32; 1911, pp. 10, 89; 1912, pp. 73–74; 1913, pp. 189–92; 1916, pp. 7, 56; CIA Report, 1919, serial 7706, pp. 57–58; *Report of the Indian Rights Association,* 1920, pp. 23–25; 1921, pp. 43–44; 1924, pp. 29–30. An innocuous report made to the Board of Indian Commissioners in 1920 by one of its members, Samuel A. Eliot, repeated the old song of allotment. *Report of the Board of Indian Commissioners,* 1920, pp. 95–100.

47. The following articles in legal journals discuss the jurisdictional problems of the New York Indians: Cuthbert W. Pound, "Nationals without a Nation: The New York State Tribal Indians," *Columbia Law Review* 22 (February 1922): 97–102; Gerald Gunther, "Governmental Power and the New York Indian Lands—A Reassessment of a Persistent Problem of Federal-State Relations," *Buffalo Law Review* 8 (Fall 1958): 1–26; Henry S. Manley, "Indian Reservation Ownership in New York," *New York State Bar Bulletin* 32 (April 1960): 134–38; James W. Clute, "The New York Indians' Right to Self-Determination," *Buffalo Law Review* 22 (Spring 1973): 985–1019. See also *Felix S. Cohen's Handbook of Federal Indian Law,* 1982 ed. (Charlottesville, Virginia: Michie, Bobbs-Merrill, 1982), pp. 372–73.

PART EIGHT

The Indian
New Deal

The decade of the 1930s was a watershed in American Indian policy; the agitation for reform that had been building up through the previous decade now turned into substantial, and to some degree, revolutionary action. There was hope at first that the Hoover administration would mark the beginning of the new age, that with Charles Burke and Edgar Meritt gone from the Indian Office and with the Meriam Report as a blueprint, the evils of the past would be remedied. But the new officials failed to fulfill the reformers' hopes. Not until the Democratic victory that brought Franklin Delano Roosevelt into the White House was there a real turnabout in policy and a new philosophy about Indian-white relations to guide the policy makers.

The New Deal of Roosevelt brought with it a set of circumstances that made Indian policy changes possible, for the Great Depression had nearly destroyed long-held convictions about the illimitable progress of industrial America. The relief activities of the New Deal immediately benefited the depressed Indian reservations; the concern for corporate action ("socialism" in the minds of critics) overcame the rampant individualism of American society and made Indian communal life and desires seem less out of place; the problems of urbanization made a back-to-the-land movement a reality, and Indian devotion to the land appeared to be wise and reasonable. At a time when innovation and experimentation were in the air, it was possible to think of modifying if not reversing government Indian policies that had been sacrosanct. Congress, caught up in the excitement of the New Deal, accepted too a "new deal" for Indians.[1]

John Collier, the gadfly and critic who was appointed commissioner of Indian affairs by Roosevelt, was now in a position to effect his reforms. A large part of his program, though not all, he sold to Congress, and much that Congress refused to accept he managed to achieve by administrative means. The Christian missionaries, who so long had influenced official thinking and action in regard to the Indians, were pushed aside—not without some complaints—and social scientists became the cutting edge of Indian reform.

Collier, with all his enthusiasm and deep conviction about the rightness of his course, soon met serious criticism and opposition. The world war, too, disrupted the plans that he had seen developing early in his tenure of office. In 1945, after the longest term of office of any commissioner of Indian affairs, he resigned, and the forces opposing him gained dominance once again. But Collier had left an indelible mark. On his retirement, the *New Republic* entered a brief editorial note:

> The peculiarities of a little man named John Collier have often been the subject of conversation in Washington. He was credited with being a dreamer, a thing which always arouses the suspicions of Congress; he smoked a corncob pipe, worked in an old green sweater, wore his hair long and unbrushed and, according to the gossips, sometimes carried a pet frog in his pocket. The most peculiar thing about John Collier, however, was that he had a deep and abiding interest in the welfare of the Indians of this country, and the intelligence and courage to fight in their behalf. . . .

1. There are numerous works on the Indian New Deal, for it was one of the significant developments in the history of Indian affairs. The best general work, upon which I have relied to a considerable extent, is Kenneth R. Philp, *John Collier's Crusade for Indian Reform, 1920–1954* (Tucson: University of Arizona Press, 1977). Other critical works are Graham D. Taylor, *The New Deal and American Indian Tribalism: The Administration of the Indian Reorganization Act, 1934–45* (Lincoln: University of Nebraska Press, 1980); Lawrence C. Kelly, "John Collier and the Indian New Deal: An Assessment," in Jane F. Smith and Robert M. Kvasnicka, eds., *Indian-White Relations: A Persistent Paradox* (Washington: Howard University Press, 1976), pp. 227–41; Lawrence C. Kelly, "The Indian Reorganization Act: The Dream and the Reality," *Pacific Historical Review* 44 (August 1975): 291–312. Collier's own view is expressed in John Collier, *The Indians of the Americas* (New York: W. W. Norton and Company, 1947), chapter 14, "The Indian New Deal," pp. 261–87. Studies of the Indian New Deal as it affected particular tribes are Donald L. Parman, *The Navajos and the New Deal* (New Haven: Yale University Press, 1976), and Laurence M. Hauptman, *The Iroquois and the New Deal* (Syracuse: Syracuse University Press, 1981).

He leaves behind him a consistent record of progress, a record achieved in spite of frequent opposition from Congress. . . . As a result of his effort, the condition of the Indian is better today than ever before under our government, and his future is brighter.[2]

However one sees the final outcome in details, the general truth was that Collier's Indian New Deal did set in motion forces that could never be stamped out. Appreciation of Indian culture, respect for Indian rights, renewal of Indian tribal communities—in a word, Indian self-determination —in spite of Indian hesitation and external setbacks, became the road to the future.

2. "People in the Limelight—Collier and Brophy," *New Republic* 112 (March 5, 1945): 319.

CHAPTER 36

Transition: The Hoover Years

New Officials.

Progress and Reform.

Failures.

Attacks and Rebuttals.

The presidency of Herbert Hoover was a transition period in the administration of Indian affairs. The attacks on the Office of Indian Affairs as it had been run by Hubert Work, Charles H. Burke, and Edgar B. Meritt had been too severe to be ignored, and the Meriam Report and the report of Preston and Engle, although generally moderate in their critical tone, left no doubt that immediate and far-reaching changes were needed. The men appointed by Hoover to handle the government's relations with the American Indians were sincerely committed to correcting the evils that existed, and at the end of their four-year term they could point to significant accomplishments. Yet they accepted the traditional view of their predecessors that the goal of government Indian policies and programs was the assimilation of the individual Indians into the nation's citizenry and the ultimate dissolution of the federal Indian service. In the end, although they pointed the way to a new future, they failed to revolutionize Indian affairs, and much of what they did accomplish was done too slowly and too cautiously for radical critics like John Collier and the American Indian Defense Association.[1]

---

1. A valuable account of the Hoover period that emphasizes Collier's role is Kenneth R. Philp, *John Collier's Crusade for Indian Reform, 1920–1954* (Tucson: University of Arizona Press, 1977), pp. 92–112. See also Randolph C. Downes, "A Crusade for Indian Reform, 1922–1934," *Mississippi Valley Historical Review* 32 (December 1945): 334–51.

NEW OFFICIALS

President Hoover, himself known for humanitarian work during World War I, chose for his secretary of the interior a likeminded man, who had assisted him with war relief, Ray Lyman Wilbur. Wilbur, born in Iowa in 1875, had moved to California as a youth. There he attended Stanford University, completed medical school, and from 1910 to 1916 served as dean of the medical school at Stanford. He became president of Stanford in 1916 and won national respect as an educator and some political exposure as a prominent Republican who campaigned for Hoover in 1928. Although reluctant to leave his university position for the political problems in Washington, Wilbur was persuaded by Hoover to accept the secretaryship.[2]

Wilbur had more than a passing interest in Indian affairs, for he had been in contact with the Indian Rights Association since 1913 and had aided the Indian Defense Association of Central and Northern California. He had been named as a member of the Committee of One Hundred (although he did not attend the conference), and he advised Secretary Work on matters of Indian health and education. He took office with a firm conviction that he had expressed in 1924: "The government as soon as possible should get out of the position of guardian for a portion of its citizens. Indians must as speedily as possible depend upon themselves if they are ever to amount to anything except dying remnants."[3] In his annual reports to the president he reiterated this position. "The fundamental aim of the Indian Service," he wrote in 1929, "will be to make the Indian a self-supporting and self-respecting citizen as rapidly as it can be brought about. He will be considered a potential citizen, instead of a ward of the Government. . . . The new policy can be characterized briefly as meaning a new deal for the young Indian and a square deal for the old Indian. It will have as its objective the placing of the Indian and his property upon a normal basis and the elimination of the Indian Bureau within a period of 25 years."[4] Wilbur admitted that until the states could be depended upon to protect the Indians' property, the responsibility of the federal government

---

2. Wilbur's life can be traced in *The Memoirs of Ray Lyman Wilbur, 1875–1949*, ed. Edgar Eugene Robinson and Paul Carroll Edwards (Stanford, California: Stanford University Press, 1960); chapter 27, "Wards of the Nation," pp. 479–92, deals with Indian affairs.

3. Wilbur to Hubert Work, December 15, 1924, quoted in *Memoirs*, p. 482.

4. *Annual Report of the Secretary of the Interior*, 1929, pp. 13–14. Elaine Goodale Eastman, who weathered the vicissitudes of Indian reform for half a century, noted that Wilbur was proposing nothing new. "There were hopeful souls in 1885 who gave the bureau a bare thirty years to live! The self-same knotty questions of day versus boarding schools, of possible moral harm in the performance of native ceremonies and 'pagan' dances, the methods of safeguarding the Indian's lawful property interests, while at the same time the door of civilized opportunity is thrown wide open to the young—these,

would have to continue, but he saw no good reason to maintain separate educational and health programs for Indians. He insistently promoted a division between the *person* and the *property* of the Indians.[5]

More than most secretaries of the interior, Wilbur considered it his duty and prerogative to explain to the general public the government's Indian policy and to answer the critics of that policy. In June 1929 he placed an article in the *Saturday Evening Post* entitled "Uncle Sam Has a New Indian Policy," in which he advocated making the Indians self-sustaining and free of government wardship and urged land allotment and other measures that would hasten contact of the Indians with whites and thus their eventual assimilation. Two years later he published an optimistic article in the Sunday supplements of the nation's major newspapers. He called it "A New Day for the Indian" and spoke with high praise of the accomplishments of the Indian Office, which carried "the promise that the bureau will try to work itself out of existence within a generation by educating the Indians to become a free, independent, self-supporting people." It was to be the beginning of a "new era for the Indians."[6]

To run the Indian Office, Hoover turned to two highly respected Quakers. As commissioner of Indian affairs he selected Charles J. Rhoads, a prominent Philadelphia banker who had succeeded Herbert Welsh as president of the Indian Rights Association. Rhoads initially turned down the invitation and recommended instead J. Henry Scattergood, treasurer of Haverford and Bryn Mawr colleges and another long-term member of the Indian Rights Association. Scattergood hesitated, and in the end the two men accepted what amounted to a joint commissionership—Rhoads as commissioner and Scattergood as assistant commissioner but in fact a coordinated team. The work of the Indian Office was carried on not by a "commissioner," but by two "commissioners," and the two officials signed the reports of the Indian Office jointly. An indication of their outlook came in a letter from Rhoads to the president on behalf of the Indian Rights Association before he had been invited to take office. "We feel," he said, "that there is an imperative need for a prompt and thorough reorganization of the Indian Service that will put it on a modern basis equal to the welfare work conducted by the Government in other Departments."[7]

---

and others of like nature, were debated even more ardently than now, some forty or fifty years ago." Eastman, "Our New-Old Indian Policy," *Christian Century* 46 (November 27, 1929): 1491.

5. See *Annual Report of the Secretary of the Interior*, 1931, pp. 9–10.

6. Ray Lyman Wilbur, as told to William Atherton DuPuy, "Uncle Sam Has a New Indian Policy," *Saturday Evening Post* 201 (June 8, 1929): 5, 136–37; Ray Lyman Wilbur, "A New Day for the Indian," *New York Herald Tribune Magazine*, May 24, 1931, pp. 1–2, 12.

7. Rhoads to Hoover, March 12, 1929, OSI CCF 22–33, Presidential Appointments,

Universal enthusiasm greeted the appointments. Even John Collier spoke of "the coming of day" and noted that "each of these new men is a revolutionary type from the standpoint of the Indian Bureau old-guard." With the clean sweep in Interior Department and Indian Office leadership and with the Senate investigations continuing, Collier declared: "Every condition favorable to a large reorganization of Indian affairs now exists," and he asked, "Has the 'century of dishonor' neared its end?" Collier and the American Indian Defense Association expected to have a substantial part in the new regime. The officers of the association in December 1929, in fact, drew up an agenda of reform measures that they thought the Indian Office would accept, and they hoped to be the effective right hand of the administration in researching the topics, drawing up bills and briefs, and lobbying for the measures in Congress. Their list comprised the following items:

1. The California Indian Plan for sharing responsibility for Indian affairs with the states.
2. An arts and crafts marketing corporation.
3. Amendment of the allotment laws.
4. Revision of methods of handling tribal estates.
5. Cancellation of reimbursable debts owed by the Indians.
6. A special Indian claims commission.
7. Protection of Indian rights, tribal life, and culture.
8. Demobilization of Indian boarding schools.
9. Amendment of the Pueblo Lands Act, enlargement of the Navajo reservation, and distribution of responsibility for the New York Indians between the federal and state governments.
10. Protection of Indian water power sites.
11. Continuation of the Senate Indian investigation.[8]

Commissioner of Indian Affairs, Charles J. Rhoads. This file contains documents concerning Rhoads's appointment. *Indian Truth*, May 1929, was devoted entirely to the appointment of the two men and provided biographical sketches. It quoted a columnist from the *Philadelphia Inquirer* who described Rhoads in these terms: "A very quiet man is he. Were all the tin in the world converted into horns, Mr. Rhoads would never blow one of them. But doesn't he get things done? Ask any Philadelphia banker. He's a student, a thinker, a worker, much of an idealist, and yet extremely practical." An excellent brief survey of Rhoads's commissionership is Lawrence C. Kelly, "Charles James Rhoads, 1929–33," in Robert M. Kvasnicka and Herman J. Viola, eds., *The Commissioners of Indian Affairs, 1824–1977* (Lincoln: University of Nebraska Press, 1979), pp. 263–71.

8. Mimeographed bulletin of the American Indian Defense Association, "The Immediate Tasks of the American Indian Defense Association, Inc.," December 10, 1929, John Collier Papers, Yale University (reel 9, no. 283). Similar attention to the commissioners came from a resurrected Lake Mohonk Conference, which met on October 16–18, 1929, after a lapse of thirteen years. Its platform expressed a need for increased funding and

The new administration moved quickly to set a positive tone. Acting upon the emergency recommendations of the Meriam Report, President Hoover requested additional funds to supply adequate food and clothing for pupils in the Indian schools, both through deficiency appropriations for the remainder of fiscal year 1930 and through a $3.1-million augmentation in the budget for 1931. Meanwhile Rhoads, with Wilbur's formal approval, sent four letters to the committees on Indian affairs in Congress, outlining legislation that would significantly reform the administration of Indian affairs.[9]

The first letter pointed to the heavy burden placed on the Indians by the obligation to pay reimbursable loans on irrigation projects and to the serious problems with the allotment laws, by which inherited lands were sold and the Indian landed estate inevitably lost. "I have become convinced," Rhoads said, "that the difficulties and problems here stated are very close to the heart of the Indian situation and of the perplexities which beset the Indian Office. Constructive thinking is needed, and I make bold to suggest that the allotment act in its entirety, along with the system of reimbursable loans in its entirety, need legislative reconsideration." He even suggested the possibility of having the allotted lands revert to the tribes. The second letter hit upon the problem of the tribally held resources, the "indivisible tribal estates of the Indians." Rhoads noted the mineral and oil deposits, power sites, timber stands, grazing lands, and unallotted agricultural lands of the southwestern Indians. Under existing law, he said, "the Government through the Interior Department, is charged with the direct and highly paternalistic administration of these properties, and unless existing law be changed it may well be that the Government 100 years from now will find itself still charged with this responsibility and still maintaining the paternalistic administration." In order to preserve these resources, they needed to be treated as "estates not capable of subdivision," and Rhoads urged consideration of incorporation of the tribes in a way that would enable them, instead of the government, to manage the estates. A third proposal concerned tribal claims. Rhoads noted the vexa-

---

outlined proposals for education, health and family life, industrial development, missionary activities, law and order, and land claims. *Report of the Thirty-Fifth Lake Mohonk Conference on the Indian*, 1929, pp. 7–12.

9. "Annual Budget Message to Congress, Fiscal Year 1931," December 4, 1929, *Public Papers of the Presidents of the United States: Herbert Hoover, 1929* (Washington: GPO, 1974), pp. 441–42. Rhoads's letters were each dated December 11, 1929, and approved by Wilbur on December 18; they are printed in *Congressional Record*, 72: 1051–53. John Collier claimed that he had prepared the statements in consultation with Matthew K. Sniffen of the Indian Rights Association and Lewis Meriam. Collier, *From Every Zenith: A Memoir and Some Essays on Life and Thought* (Denver: Sage Books, 1963), p. 152.

tious existing situation under which tribes had to get special authorization to bring their claims to the Court of Claims, as well as the numerous claims that were not amenable even to that solution. He recommended a special Indian claims commission, independent of the Interior Department, that "should hear all causes, those that are human and moral as well as those that are legal and equitable; and its findings, submitted to Congress, could be the basis of settlement of a gratuitous kind which Congress might authorize." He noted, too, that unless something like this were done, the claims might well run on for another century. "There can be no liquidation of the Government's guardianship over Indians," he declared, "until this inheritance to treaties and alleged broken treaties and governmental laches of the past is absorbed. . . . Hence, any plan contemplating the gradual diminution and the ultimate and final termination of Indian tutelage must concern itself with this aspect of the situation." Rhoads's final letter dealt with Indian irrigation projects; he described the problems of financing them and the influx of white lessees or owners. He suggested transferring the projects to the Bureau of Reclamation.[10]

The proposals offered a farsighted and statesmanlike approach to problems of long standing and placed before Congress significant suggestions for study and for legislation. Collier called them "epoch making announcements concerning Indian law" and "the most adequate statement, official or unofficial, ever made, dealing with those phases of the Indian problem which are more baffling and more insistent than any others."[11]

PROGRESS AND REFORM

On many fronts, the new administrators of Indian affairs made important progress. The request for added appropriations to provide adequate food and clothing for Indian students was a case in point. Hoover's budget requests at first met a formidable roadblock in Representative Louis C. Cramton of Michigan, chairman of the subcommittee on appropriations that handled the Interior Department budget. Cramton showed no sympathy for the Indians' plight and cut back the proposals, shifting funds away from food and clothing to labor-saving machinery to reduce the work required of the children. But the Senate restored the funds, and in the final compromise Congress authorized enough money to bring the average daily food ration from 20 cents per student, which it had been in 1929, to 37.8 cents, and the annual clothing allowance from $22 to $40. Thus the board-

10. *Congressional Record,* 72: 1051–53.
11. *American Indian Life,* January 1930. The letters are summarized in this issue.

ing schools at long last were able to meet acceptable standards, and the undernourishment or starvation of the Indian children that the Meriam Report had described and the reformers had cried out against was corrected. The near doubling of the allowances was a significant step forward, although the commissioners stirred up considerable criticism because they had been willing to acquiesce in Cramton's initial cuts.[12]

Congress in time accepted Rhoads's recommendations in regard to the reimbursable debts that were weighing so heavily upon the Indians and stifling their economic development. Although a measure introduced in the Seventy-first Congress by Congressman Scott Leavitt on March 18, 1930, was killed by Cramton's objections, the bill fared better when it was reintroduced on March 28, 1932. It authorized the secretary of the interior to adjust or forgive the debts. The House Committee on Indian Affairs urged its passage "as a matter of simple justice" and noted that its purpose was not "to wipe out any just or proper debts," but to enable the secretary "to do justice in connection with ill-founded or unjust obligations." The Senate concurred, but it amended the bill to *direct* the secretary to act, not merely to authorize action, and to require approval by Congress of the secretary's actions. By a compromise, the final act, approved on July 1, 1932, let the secretary make the decision but postponed the effective date for sixty days. During this time Congress, if it chose, could approve or disapprove his action.[13]

The Rhoads-Scattergood administration made perhaps its most significant advance in the field of Indian education, for it made a determined effort to change the Indian school system into one that would suit the background and needs of the Indians. The goals, as well as the practical limitations in attaining them, were clearly set forth by the commissioners in 1931:

> The purpose of education for any indigenous peoples at the present day is to help these peoples, both as groups and as individuals, to adjust themselves to modern life, protecting and preserving as much of their own ways of living as possible, and capitalizing their economic and cultural resources for their own benefit and their contribution to modern civilization.
>
> Accordingly, if the Indian Service were starting afresh on the task of Indian education, with what is now known of the processes of

12. CIA Report, 1930, p. 2. The role of Cramton is discussed critically in Ruby A. Black, "A New Deal for the Red Man," *Nation* 130 (April 2, 1930): 388–90.

13. *Congressional Record*, 72: 5562, 6980–81; 75: 6981, 8142–44, 12316, 13829–30; *House Report* no. 951, 72–1, serial 9492; *Senate Report* no. 752, 72–1, serial 9488; *House Report* no. 1725, 72–1, serial 9493; 47 *United States Statutes* 564.

change and adjustment through schools and other agencies, it would undoubtedly begin with the Indian people in their own environment or in some comparable environment in which they could develop their own resources. It would employ other methods than some of those that have been employed—it would not use to any extent the reservation, "rations," or distant boarding schools for young children. But we are not starting afresh and we cannot; one kind of philosophy and one kind of a system have been established a long time. The basic Indian Service educational problem, therefore, is to work over from a more or less conventional institutional conception of education to one that is local and individual. It means abandoning boarding schools wherever possible, eliminating small children from the larger boarding schools, setting up day schools or making arrangements with local public schools to receive these children, providing the necessary family follow-up for such children, and directing the boarding schools into specialized purposes, at least partially vocational; in the meantime all these boarding schools (those that should be abandoned soon as well as those that have a degree of permanence) should be made as effective educationally as it is possible to make them, utilizing Indian arts and crafts and Indian culture generally wherever these exist or can be revived, and developing throughout the service at all levels a staff of workers who understand the new point of view.[14]

This philosophy of education reflected the influence of the man appointed director of Indian education on August 19, 1930, W. Carson Ryan, Jr. Ryan, professor of education at Swarthmore College and an ardent proponent of progressive education, had been the education specialist on the Meriam survey team, and in his deliberate manner he began slowly to implement changes that had been called for in the Meriam Report. Ryan sought a true community school system, directed toward the needs of the whole reservation population. These needs were essentially rural, and he adapted the curriculum to them. The uniform course of study that had been one of the pillars of the Indian school system, in its attempt to turn the Indians into white citizens, was discarded by Ryan. Courses that did not fit the Indian children's background and experience were gradually eliminated, and special courses adapted to Indian culture were introduced, with appropriate concern for the great diversity in these cultures from region to region. To aid in reaching these goals, decentralization of the school service was encouraged. No longer was everything to depend on the central Indian Office in Washington. A corollary of this decentralization was the

14. CIA Report, 1931, pp. 4–5.

move toward state control of Indian education. More and more Indian children were enrolled in public schools, and the number of contracts with boards of education increased. Practical vocational training adapted to the localities in which the schools were situated was another abiding concern of Ryan's, and though progress was slow, he was able in 1932 to secure a position in the Indian Office for a director of vocational guidance.[15]

A major obstacle to a program of local community schools was the federal boarding school system. "We make no secret of the fact that we hope to eliminate gradually practically all the Government boarding schools," Ryan wrote in 1931, ". . . but we do not intend to do this until a real study is made of each school and the necessary guarantee of follow-up of the children is obtained."[16] Between 1928 and 1933 a dozen boarding schools were closed, but the increase in school population meant that in fact the number of children in boarding schools increased. During the depression years it was difficult to build the new day schools that were needed, and in any case local interests fought strongly to prevent the closing of boarding schools, which were often an important economic activity in the locality.

The schools improved markedly in management, and they became less like prisons or reform schools. The strict discipline and sometimes cruel punishments prevalent earlier had been a large part of the reformers' arsenal for attacking the Indian Office. Commissioner Burke, in fact, on January 10, 1929, had responded to the criticism by prohibiting corporal punishment and "other means of discipline of a degrading character." But Rhoads, on assuming office, studied the effect of the directive and concluded that discipline had eroded under it, and on March 20, 1930, he issued a new directive on "student control." He urged that the students be trained in self-discipline and that there be parent-child relationships between the superintendent and the pupils, and he directed that a "quiet room" where offending students could "think things over in comfort and self-respect" be substituted for the jails maintained at some schools. But if such measures failed, he authorized "emergency measures." Although the commissioner intended that there be careful supervision and moderate use of authority, he was attacked at once for reinstituting harsh disciplinary measures.[17] Ryan's approach eased the whole situation, making use of "advisers" in the schools rather than "disciplinarians." At the same time, the

---

15. Margaret Szasz, *Education and the American Indian: The Road to Self-Determination, 1928–1953* (Albuquerque: University of New Mexico Press, 1974), pp. 16–36.

16. W. Carson Ryan, Jr., "Federal-State Cooperation in Education," *School and Society* 34 (September 26, 1931): 422.

17. Circular no. 2526, January 10, 1929 (Burke), and Circular no. 2666, March 20, 1930 (Rhoads), OIA Circulars (M1121, reel 14).

heavy labor that had made boarding school life drudgery for many students was reduced, and care was taken to see that the youngest students were not subjected to boarding school routine. Finally, sincere efforts were made to improve standards for teachers and other Indian school personnel. A degree was required for principals of the government schools, and salary increases enabled higher standards to be set for newly hired persons, even though the "old guard" long impeded the development of the new point of view in Indian education that Ryan fostered.

The educational program was a bright spot in the Rhoads-Scattergood administration, and it received wide acclaim. Lewis Meriam, in an article called "Indian Education Moves Ahead," congratulated Rhoads and Scattergood for "substantial progress in the field of Indian education" and declared: "Even vigorous critics of the new Indian administration would, I believe, endorse that statement. Insofar as criticism has been directed against the commissioners' work in education it has related to details and delay." [18]

Ryan himself was a realist and did not expect to accomplish the impossible. He divided the Indians into two groups, the mixed-blood, largely acculturated Indians and the Indians of the Southwest, who still retained many of their traditional ways. For the first he encouraged rapid commingling with the rest of the population and attendance at public schools; for them he had little hope of preserving aboriginal culture. "The most one dares to hope," he wrote in 1932, "is that occasionally an observant teacher may rescue some of the forgotten elements. In other respects, however, we can do much; we can at least help the Indian to stand on his own feet and learn to get along with his neighbors." It was with the second group, he thought, that opportunity lay. "Our task here," he said, "is to help the Indians to capitalize to the full their contribution and to educate the rest of the United States to an intelligent rather than a merely sentimental appreciation of the value of this contribution." [19] This was a philosophy well in accord with John Collier's views, and in fact, when Collier became commissioner of Indian affairs in 1933, Ryan stayed on as director of Indian education for another two and a half years.

The programs for Indian health urged by the Meriam Report were advanced by Rhoads and Scattergood, although no great breakthroughs occurred. Appropriations for public health purposes increased, and all the

18. Lewis Meriam, "Indian Education Moves Ahead," *Survey* 66 (June 1, 1931): 253–57, 293. Collier praised Ryan and his direction of the Indian schools in *American Indian Life*, January 1931.

19. W. Carson Ryan, Jr., and Rose K. Brant, "Indian Education Today," *Progressive Education* 9 (February 1932): 82–83.

indicators (number of public health nurses, salaries for health service personnel, examinations for trachoma, hospital facilities, hospitalization for victims of tuberculosis, and live births in hospitals) showed marked improvement.[20]

Another positive contribution of Rhoads and Scattergood was a reorganization of the Indian Office—a move that had been urged for many years, one of the key points in the critics' demands for change, and a strong recommendation of the Meriam Report. On March 9, 1931, an extensive reorganization was directed, which placed "directors of high technical and professional ability" in charge of five field divisions: health, education, agricultural extension and industry, forestry, and irrigation. A great volume of correspondence was now handled directly by the division heads, freeing the commissioners of that burden. The first three divisions were grouped together under an assistant to the commissioner in charge of human relations; the other two were placed under an assistant to the commissioner in charge of property. This was intended to decentralize the office's operations and make the Washington office more responsive to needs in the field. But more than that, it represented the division in functions that Secretary Wilbur so strongly emphasized—that between the Indian as a person and his property. In point of fact, however, the reorganization did not solve the problem of longtime employees whose competence was questionable, whose outlook was not in accord with the reforms that were initiated, and whose foot-dragging could negate the best of plans. Nor did it provide for a planning and development division, which was central to the Meriam Report's recommendations.[21]

FAILURES

The Rhoads-Scattergood administration did not bring the total reform that early expectations had indicated. Although notable progress was made in

---

20. Downes, "Crusade for Indian Reform," p. 348; Charles J. Rhoads and J. Henry Scattergood, "Indian Administration since July 1, 1929," pp. 51–56, copy in Indian Rights Association Papers, Historical Society of Pennsylvania (reel 124, no. 131).

21. The reorganization is reported in CIA Report, 1931, pp. 3–4, and described for the field service in Circular no. 2758, April 6, 1931, OIA Circulars, (M1121, reel 14). Meriam called the reorganization "a step equaled only by the appointment of Carson Ryan as Director of Education." Quoted in *New Opportunities for Indians* (Philadelphia, 1931), p. 14; this pamphlet is a laudatory appraisal of Indian administration prepared by the Indian Rights Association and published by the Philadelphia Yearly Meeting of Friends. Meriam's part in the reform is treated in Donald T. Critchlow, "Lewis Meriam, Expertise, and Indian Reform," *Historian* 43 (May 1981): 339–42.

education, in reorganizing the Indian Office, and in lifting the burden of reimbursable debts, not all of the early proposals made to Congress by Rhoads were implemented.[22] One of the failures was the matter of irrigation. Although Rhoads had clearly delineated the problem in December 1929 and had suggested as a remedy the transfer of Indian irrigation projects to the Reclamation Bureau, Congress refused to take that action, and the commissioners and the secretary of the interior were willing to let things ride without a determined fight.

Similarly, no significant action was taken to establish federal-state cooperation in Indian affairs, which had been an objective of Wilbur in phasing out federal domination of Indian lives. Rhoads supported a measure introduced by Representative Philip D. Swing and Senator Hiram W. Johnson of California that would have stimulated state responsibility in the areas of health, education, and relief for the indigent by contracting with the states for these functions and turning over federal institutions to the states. It was, the commissioner said, an experimental move before more radical legislation could be planned, and it would not affect the citizenship or property rights of the Indians. The measure was stopped by Cramton in the House. When it was reintroduced in the next Congress, Rhoads repeated his support. The Senate Committee on Indian Affairs again favorably reported the bill. The committee called it a move toward "the development of the Indian to the point where he can take his place as a normal contributing citizen of the community. It contemplates the administration of problems having to do with his well-being on a basis that is the same as and a part of that of the normal community." But the action came so late in the session that the Swing-Johnson bill, although it reached the floor of the House, was ultimately lost.[23]

A signal failure, especially from the standpoint of the Collier forces, was the inability or unwillingness of Rhoads and Scattergood to gain legislation to promote Indian arts and crafts. Appreciation of Indian artistic work had slowly increased from the beginning of the century, and white artists and literary figures became enamored of Indian art; government officials, too, began to see the wisdom of preserving aspects of the Indians' cultural heritage. There soon developed a double-headed campaign to preserve and stimulate arts and crafts. One element continued to be a strong interest in the arts as an expression of Indian culture, a truly American artistic ex-

22. There is an excellent discussion of the relations of Rhoads and of Collier with Congress in John Leiper Freeman, Jr., "The New Deal for Indians: A Study in Bureau-Committee Relations in American Government" (Ph.D. dissertation, Princeton University, 1952), pp. 49–102.

23. Memorandum of Rhoads, February 27, 1930, *Senate Report* no. 449, 71–2, serial 9185; *Senate Report* no. 271, 72–1, serial 9487; *House Report* no. 1100, 72–1, serial 9492; Philp, *John Collier's Crusade*, p. 102.

pression that would not only encourage Indians' pride in their heritage but also greatly enrich the nation as a whole. A second element was the realization that markets could be developed for Indian products that would mean a strengthening of the economic well-being of the Indian communities.[24]

An early and vigorous proponent of the movement was the novelist Mary Austin, who from her home in Sante Fe continually prodded the federal officials. In 1919, for example, she wrote to Secretary of the Interior Franklin Lane, urging government attention to "the great treasures of Indian art which, after all, were developed out of living on American soil." She outlined a program:

What we have to do in America is
> For the Government itself to become aware of native art
> To spread the appreciation of native art in its schools and press
> To take steps to preserve the sources of native art
> To correlate these American movements
> To establish routes over which native art may travel from the producer to the consumer.[25]

Although little came from Austin's efforts at the time, she continued her interest and had considerable influence on the later development of Indian arts and crafts.

Through the 1920s interest in Indian arts widened, and their preservation became one of the staples of the reform agitation of the Eastern Association on Indian Affairs, the New Mexico Association on Indian Affairs, and Collier's American Indian Defense Association. The Committee of One Hundred in 1924 spoke favorably of incorporating into the life of the nation "the genius of the Indians in music, literature, and the decorative arts," and Secretary Work responded with the remark that the Indian service "encourages native arts and crafts, blanket weaving, basketry, pottery, and many other forms for both cultural and commercial benefit." But no substantial efforts were made during the 1920s to promote arts and crafts actively. The Meriam Report recommended both a program to secure marketable handcrafted products and the organization of a market. It urged as well attention to the quality of the products and some means to guarantee genuineness.[26]

---

24. The movement in support of Indian arts and crafts is traced in Robert Fay Schrader, *The Indian Arts and Crafts Board: An Aspect of New Deal Indian Policy* (Albuquerque: University of New Mexico Press, 1983).

25. Mary Austin to Franklin K. Lane, January 16, 1919, OSI CCF 5–3, Indian Office, Indian Art, General.

26. John Collier, "Announcement of Purpose of the American Indian Defense Association, Inc.," May 21, 1923, Collier Papers (reel 9, no. 277); "The Indian Problem: Resolutions of the Committee of One Hundred," *House Document* no. 149, 68–1, serial 8273,

Roy O. West, who replaced Work as secretary of the interior on July 20, 1928, shortly after the Meriam Report was submitted, took a special interest in the matter. He published figures on income from arts and crafts in his report of 1928 and suggested that the government might "recognize these products in some official manner and thereby render a real service to those Indians now engaged in such crafts and to those who might be encouraged to interest themselves in them." He supported a proposal to adopt a trademark design to guarantee the genuineness of Indian products, and a trademark was in fact designed, but the Patent Office refused to approve it.[27]

The advent of the Hoover administration raised high hopes among promoters of Indian arts and crafts, and John Collier began a campaign for a comprehensive marketing plan. Under his prodding a scheme was drawn up by James Young, a wealthy advertising executive and member of the board of directors of the American Indian Defense Association, and submitted to Rhoads on September 1, 1929. Although Rhoads showed no great eagerness to push the plan, he finally called Young to Washington to prepare necessary legislation. Collier considered legislation for an Indian arts and crafts marketing corporation one of the immediate tasks of the American Indian Defense Association.[28]

On February 10, 1930, a bill was introduced by Lynn Frazier in the Senate and by Scott Leavitt in the House to promote the production and sale of Indian products and to create a board and a marketing corporation to carry on the work. The proposal immediately became mired in controversy, in large part because of opposition from white friends of the Indians in the Southwest, who thought their advice had been bypassed in the formulation of the bill and who, like Mary Austin, believed that no legislation was really necessary. Their organization (the Indian Arts Fund at Santa Fe), they thought, could accomplish the same ends. Representative Cramton, of course, objected to the costs of the proposal, and the Bureau of the Budget objected to the government-controlled corporation that was part of the measure. Collier and his friends fought on to provide acceptable modifications, but Wilbur, Rhoads, and Scattergood did nothing to push the measure or to amend it to satisfy the critics. When Rhoads in December 1930 refused to report the Frazier-Leavitt bill favorably to either the Senate or the House committee, the measure died. Such inaction became for Collier just one more indication of the incompetence of the administration.[29]

---

p. 5; *The Problem of Indian Administration* (Baltimore: Johns Hopkins Press, 1928), pp. 645–52.

27. *Annual Report of the Secretary of the Interior*, 1928, pp. 20–21; Schrader, *Indian Arts and Crafts Board*, pp. 23–24.

28. Ibid., pp. 25–30.

29. Ibid., pp. 30–43.

ATTACKS AND REBUTTALS

John Collier had greeted Rhoads and Scattergood with great enthusiasm. Along with Lewis Meriam and others, he had been allowed to have a hand in formulating the plans and programs of the new commissioners. In January 1930 Collier declared that the new men were accomplishing their tasks "with success visibly increasing as each month goes by."[30] Then, less than six months later, he was back in his old role as an aggressive and vocal critic of Indian Office administration. The new day that he had discerned in 1929 had turned out to be a "false dawn." He claimed now that the old guard in Congress and in the Indian service were "devouring the new commissioners." The proof was a list of failures to act vigorously in immediately implementing the program that had earlier looked so promising. Rhoads and Scattergood had buckled too easily in the face of Cramton's opposition to new programs and policy changes. There was no reorganization of irrigation projects, no revision of allotment legislation, and no court of claims; there were no tribal incorporations, and there was a return to corporal punishment in the Indian schools.[31] Collier pointed to Rhoads's testimony before the Senate investigating committee as "a true picture of the bankruptcy of legislative ideas or purpose in the Indian Bureau," for when Rhoads had met with the committee on January 21, 1930, to consider the reimbursable features of irrigation projects, he had displayed a less than vigorous approach. "I am coming here," he told the Senators, "more to learn than to tell you how it should be done. I am altogether new to this, and I am very much bewildered by the complexity of the whole question of reimbursable debts." The self-effacing ways of the Quaker humanitarian did not meet the demands of the fiery activist.[32]

Collier's attack on Rhoads was backed up by a letter sent to Secretary Wilbur by Haven Emerson in the name of the American Indian Defense Association on May 6, 1930. Emerson asserted that Rhoads and Scattergood had been in office for ten months but that their accomplishment had been practically nothing. "They have not rectified the extreme abuses in the treatment of the Indians," Emerson charged, "nor have they put into effect a single constructive plan." Because the Indian Office had failed to put up any real right for necessary reforms, it was in a worse situation than under Burke and Meritt. Wilbur responded to the attack in a gentlemanly

---

30. *American Indian Life*, January 1930, p. 27.

31. *American Indian Life*, July 1930. Collier describes his disillusionment in *From Every Zenith*, chapter 12, "False Dawn," pp. 148–66.

32. *American Indian Life*, July 1930, p. 8; "Survey of Conditions of the Indians in the United States," *Hearings before a Subcommittee of the Committee on Indian Affairs, United States Senate*, 70th Congress to 78th Congress (1928–1943), part 6, p. 2197.

fashion, pointing out that the commissioners worked under serious handicaps, for they had had no part in the construction of the current budget, had to deal with civil service employees whom they had not appointed, and were obliged to operate under legislation that was not under their control, and he praised them for success in getting additional funds appropriated in the new budget. But he also charged that the American Indian Defense Association was taking up the valuable time of the department with petty matters and was turning the legislators against the Indian Office. "I hope," Wilbur told Emerson, "there can be more sober acceptance of legitimate responsibility on the part of the officials of your organization rather than a continuation of widespread intemperate and illy digested emotional attacks."[33]

Wilbur's reply did nothing to ease the situation, and throughout the rest of his administration the secretary and his Indian commissioners were subjected to a continuing barrage of criticism emanating from the Collier forces and their friends in Congress. Two special cases of dereliction that figured prominently in the attack were the retention in office of Herbert J. Hagerman, a member of the Pueblo Lands Board and special attorney for the Navajos, whom Collier accused of sacrificing the Indians' interests, and the licensing of a valuable power site on the Flathead Reservation to the Montana Power Company, which he charged was paying too little for the license.[34] A key person in the attack on the Indian Office was Senator William H. King of Utah. On March 9, 1932, he presented to the Senate a long bill of charges against the Indian administrators, dated February 26, 1932, signed "in the name of all Indians" by delegates of a number of Indian tribes, and countersigned by Collier, Emerson, Mrs. Atwood, and other white reformers. The tone of the statement was set by one of the opening paragraphs: "When Secretary Wilbur and Commissioners Rhoads and Scattergood took office in 1929 we were led to feel a wonderful hope. They announced great programs and made great promises. We assert that they have forsaken their programs. They have broken their promises. They have set up new evils of far-reaching kinds—evils which their predecessors did not sponsor." The statement specified the broken promises in re-

---

33. Emerson to Wilbur, May 6, 1930, and Wilbur to Emerson, May 7, 1930, printed in *American Indian Life*, July 1930, pp. 20–23. Emerson answered Wilbur in a letter of May 9, 1930; and the board of directors of the American Indian Defense Association on May 27, 1930, sent him a long list of existing evils. Ibid., pp. 23–25.

34. Collier made a lot of the Hagerman affair and asserted in his memoirs: "Our major break with the Rhoades-Scattergood administration came at last with Rhoades' support, with a zeal approaching fanaticism, of the acts of Herbert J. Hagerman." *From Every Zenith*, p. 153. There is extended discussion of the Hagerman affair in Philp, *John Collier's Crusade*, pp. 103–12. On the Flathead controversy, see Collier, "The Flathead Water Power Lease," *New Republic* 64 (August 20, 1930): 20–21.

gard to loss of Indian lands, diversion of Indian moneys, reimbursable debts, continuation of the boarding school system, and ignoring of "an appalling condition of Indian distress and starvation." In addition, it focused on the retention of Hagerman. "The forcing of H. J. Hagerman upon the Indians as their representative holding their power of attorney, in the face of the record now made," the statement read, "is not only a material injury, it is an insult flaunted in the face of all Indians."[35]

Wilbur quickly replied to the statement, and he showed none of the hesitancy that frequently marked Rhoads. He placed the whole responsibility for the statement King read, which "purported to come from the Indians," at Collier's door. It was a biting personal attack:

> Mr. Collier is a fanatical Indian enthusiast with good intentions, but so charged with personal bias and the desire to get a victim every so often, that he does much more harm than good. His statements can not be depended upon to be either fair, factual or complete. He presents facts the way the curved mirrors make the people look who attend the chamber of horrors of the side show. . . . Constant badgering of faithful and devoted men who are working hard in the national service is pretty poor business. When a man reaches a point where he conducts an inquisition because those in responsibility will not follow his irresponsible directions, it is about time for his own organization to carry out its purpose under new leadership.[36]

The next day, in a long and detailed memorandum prepared by the Indian Office, Wilbur answered the specific charges presented by King, and he called the statement "a series of distorted misrepresentations almost approaching blackmail." He called attention to the intricate and difficult problems involved in the administration of Indian affairs. "It is easy to complain and to blame either Congress or the Indian Office, as the case may be," he said, "for every hardship or difficulty, real or imaginary, confronting two or three hundred thousand people." Then, even though he considered the charges "vague, unfair, and misleading," he presented detailed answers to them—showing "an entirely different state of affairs than that indicated by the statement to Congress." It was a reasoned statement of what the Indian Office was doing, and it placed considerable blame upon Congress for not enacting measures proposed, but it did nothing to ease the tension between the administration and Collier.[37]

---

35. *Congressional Record*, 75: 5547–49.

36. Department of the Interior, Memorandum for the Press, March 9, 1932, OSI CCF 1–127, Administrative General, Publicity, Press Notices.

37. Memorandum for the Press, March 10, 1932, printed in *Congressional Record*, 75: 5677–81. Wilbur with some satisfaction reported in his memoirs, written in 1948 after Collier's long tenure as commissioner of Indian affairs had ended: "There is some

Collier returned to the charge with a brief answer to Wilbur's personal attack and then a critical appraisal of the Indian Office's record in the October 1932 issue of the *Nation*, in which he once more described the great hopes entertained when Wilbur, Rhoads, and Scattergood had taken office in 1929, only to have them become "the apologist and protector of the inherited 'system.'" "The 'system' of 1929," he declared, "is the 'system' of today." And he flayed away again at Cramton, the retention of Hagerman, and the Flathead power case.[38]

After the presidential election had determined the fate of Wilbur and the commissioners, Senator King returned with one final blast. In a speech delivered in the Senate on February 8, 1933, prepared in large part by Collier, King repeated at great length all the old charges. It was clearly too late, of course, for the men of the Hoover administration to satisfy the critics. But King's statement, as Senator Frazier noted, was "an impressive challenge to the new administration. . . . The success or failure of the new administration in its Indian work will determine the future of many tribes for all time to come."[39]

For their part, Rhoads and Scattergood drew up a formal statement, dated March 3, 1933, which was a sort of apologia for their work, a detailed account of what had been accomplished by means of legislation and administrative reform since they had taken office on July 1, 1929. It was a long and positive list, and the commissioners called special attention to the increase in appropriations from $12,925,626.36 for regular expenses of the Indian Office in fiscal year 1929 to $17,984,945.67 for fiscal year 1934, an increase of well over $5 million. The commissioners noted, too, the effects on the Indians of the depression, which had curtailed their income and created tremendous demands for relief.[40] Their conclusion was in line with the evidence presented and with the basic philosophy that had guided their administration:

---

advantage in living long enough to see what happens to certain kinds of people as the calendar keeps working away in its deadly and persistent manner. I admit I have watched with some interest Mr. Collier's rather allergic reactions to doses of his own medicine, when his turn came to get complaints and attacks and to be 'investigated.'" *Memoirs*, p. 491.

38. *Congressional Record*, 75: 5681–82; John Collier, "The Indian Bureau's Record," *Nation* 135 (October 5, 1932): 303–5.

39. *Congressional Record*, 76: 3602–22. The speech, with introductory remarks by Senator Frazier, was printed as *Senate Document*, no. 214, 72–2, serial 9665, a document of 76 pages.

40. Rhoads and Scattergood, "Indian Administration since July 1, 1929," pp. 9, 30–33. An account of how the depression affected the Indians in Oklahoma is B. T. Quinten, "Oklahoma Tribes, the Great Depression, and the Indian Bureau," *Mid-America* 49 (January 1967): 29–43.

Progress has been made during the present administration, both in continuing sound established policies and in introducing new ones. Practically all lines of endeavor have shown marked improvement. . . . Notwithstanding the adverse conditions that have prevailed, it is believed real progress has been made in advancing the day when the Indian will be a self-sustaining American citizen, with full responsibility for himself, no longer viewed as a ward of the Government, but as a citizen absorbed in the economic and social life of the Nation.[41]

The two evaluations of Indian administration from 1929 to 1933—those of Senator King and of the two commissioners—were like ships passing in the night. The one noted the failures to correct all the evils; the other reported the constructive improvements in Indian affairs. The one expressed the outsider's impatience with a bureaucracy that moved slowly and incompletely; the other represented the bureaucrat's concern for continuity and the practical limitations imposed upon innovative changes. Much of what the Meriam Report had recommended was accomplished or initiated under Rhoads and Scattergood. Their work was a substantial move in the direction of the reform Collier demanded, even though their philosophy of reform was traditional, not revolutionary. Yet despite the advances in education, health care, and other benefits to the Indians, there had been failure to change things very much on two fundamental points—allotment with its consequences and tribal incorporation—and there had been no success in getting an Indian claims commission, an arts and crafts board, or a law promoting state cooperation. Rhoads and Scattergood tried hard with good intentions, but they belonged to the old school. When it was time for the Roosevelt administration to choose its commissioner of Indian affairs, the noted anthropologist Franz Boas wrote to the president to argue against the reappointment of the two men, which many people urged. "In my opinion," he said, "one fundamental error in their attitude was the same as the one made by Carl Schurz when he was the Secretary of the Interior, namely to assume that by administrative measures the Indian can be changed immediately into a White citizen. I believe they fail to understand the impossibility of overcoming the deep influence that the old ways of Indian life still exert upon the Indian community. Whoever is in charge of the Bureau of Indian Affairs ought to understand this fact."[42]

It would be up to Collier to see what he could do when he was placed in the position of responsibility that had been held by Rhoads and Scattergood.

41. Rhoads and Scattergood, "Indian Administration since July 1, 1929," p. 61.
42. Franz Boas to Franklin D. Roosevelt, March 17, 1933, OSI CCF 22–33, Rhoads.

CHAPTER 37

The New Reform

John Collier, Commissioner. Conservation and Relief.

New Deal Measures. John Collier's Reform Proposal.

The Wheeler-Howard (Indian Reorganization) Act.

Indian Organization.

The election of Franklin Delano Roosevelt in November 1932 presaged a change in Indian administration. The Indian Rights Association and many individuals urged that Rhoads and Scattergood be retained as heads of the Indian Bureau, but the two really had no chance of reappointment. It was time for a "new deal" for the Indians; the crucial question was who would direct it.

JOHN COLLIER, COMMISSIONER

John Collier, even before the election, had named himself—together with Lewis Meriam and Nathan Margold, a protégé of Felix Frankfurter who had acted as legal counsel for minority groups—as the most acceptable candidates for the commissionership. There were other candidates as well. Harold L. Ickes wanted the job, but he soon turned his eye toward the position of assistant secretary, or even secretary, of the interior. A strong candidate, because pushed by Senator Joseph T. Robinson of Arkansas as a favorite son, was Edgar B. Meritt, who of course was absolutely unacceptable to the Collier forces. Collier campaigned aggressively for the post, lining up support of the American Indian Defense Association, the All Pueblo Council, and numerous friends around the nation. Meriam withdrew his candidacy, and Margold seemed better suited for the office of solicitor in the Depart-

ment of the Interior (a position he in fact received). When Ickes, to his considerable surprise, was offered the secretaryship, he backed Collier for
commissioner. Only Senator Robinson and Meritt seemed to stand in the
way, and in the confrontation between Robinson and Ickes in Roosevelt's
office the president stood behind the secretary. In reply to a critic of the
appointment, Ickes wrote of Collier:

> I do believe . . . that no one exceeds him in knowledge of Indian mat-
> ters or his sympathy with the point of view of the Indians them-
> selves. I want some one in that office who is the advocate of the
> Indians. The whites can take care of themselves, but the Indians need
> some one to protect them from exploitation. I want a man who will
> respect their customs and have a sympathetic point of view with ref-
> erence to their culture. I want the Indians to be helped to help them-
> selves. John Collier, with whatever faults of temperament he may
> have, has to a higher degree than any one available for that office, the
> point of view towards the Indians that I want in the Commissioner of
> Indian Affairs.[1]

Collier took office as commissioner of Indian affairs on April 21, 1933.
It was now his chance to bring about the revolutionary change that he had
long demanded. He began with great bursts of energy and created an enthusiasm and excitement among his staff matching that generated by President Roosevelt for the New Deal as a whole. "Even after twenty-four years,"
William Zimmerman, Jr., Collier's assistant commissioner, wrote in 1957,
"it is easy to relive the first months of the new administration. There were
endless meetings, inside and outside of working hours. . . . There was zest
and fun in those meetings, but also always a sense of urgency, of fighting
time, of doing things now, before it should be too late; but there was always a feeling of accomplishment."[2] Collier assembled an eager and capable staff, including the lawyer, Felix S. Cohen, who joined Margold in the
solicitor's office.

Collier depended, too, on the expert support of anthropologists, to whom
he offered a part in determining the policies and programs of his administration. On November 20, 1933, he addressed a circular letter, with an
attached questionnaire, to a number of anthropologists, asking for infor-

1. Ickes to Francis C. Wilson, April 18, 1933, quoted in Lawrence C. Kelly, "Choosing
the New Deal Indian Commissioner: Ickes vs. Collier," *New Mexico Historical Review*
49 (October 1974): 284. This article traces in full detail the intricate political maneuvering that went into the commissioner's appointment.

2. William Zimmerman, Jr., "The Role of the Bureau of Indian Affairs since 1933,"
Annals of the American Academy of Political and Social Science 311 (May 1957): 31.

mation about tribal structures and activities. "In particular," he said, "we are anxious to build upon the potentialities of cooperative economic activity that exist today within the social organization of various Indian tribes and communities, with a view to enlarging the tribal ownership of land in lieu of the present system of individual allotments." The replies were mixed; some respondents were enthusiastic, others openly skeptical, and throughout there was an expression of doubt about how much tribal organization was left or could be put to Collier's uses.[3] But the commissioner seemed not to hear any warning and went ahead with his plans. He continued to call upon the anthropologists and polled them again in April 1934 for their reactions to his draft of a bill for land reform and Indian self-government. Then in December 1934, at the meeting of the American Association for the Advancement of Science in Pittsburgh, Collier and members of his staff met with a select group of anthropologists to discuss the Indian bureau's plans and enlist support.[4]

Collier brought anthropologists into his staff to assist in planning and carrying out his reorganization programs. He established an applied anthropology staff from 1935 to 1938, and anthropologists were employed in a planning group called Technical Cooperation—Bureau of Indian Affairs (TC–BIA), which was set up to coordinate the work of the bureau with the Soil Conservation Service. Its goal was to see that conservation projects would strengthen the traditional social and economic institutions of the tribes and foster Indian values. Considerable use was made of anthropologists, too, in the Indian education division, where they conducted surveys and studies of Indian patterns on which educational programs might be based. If the cutting edge of Indian reform had earlier been the Christian missionaries of the Dawes Act era, now it was to be the social scientists.[5]

3. Circular letter, Collier to anthropologists, November 20, 1933, OIA Circulars (M1121, reel 6). The replies to the letter are in OIA, Records concerning the Wheeler-Howard Act, part 10–A, box 8; they are summarized in Graham D. Taylor, "Anthropologists, Reformers, and the Indian New Deal," Prologue 7 (Fall 1975): 156–57.

4. Collier to anthropologists, April 3, 1934, and replies to the circular letter, OIA, Records concerning the Wheeler-Howard Act, part 10–B, box 8; "Anthropologists and the Federal Indian Program," Science 81 (February 15, 1935): 170–71; W. Carson Ryan, Jr., "Anthropologists and the Indian Program," Indians at Work 2 (January 15, 1935): 35–40. Ryan included a list of persons at Pittsburgh and the memorandum sent to the anthropologists before the meeting.

5. General studies of the anthropologists' work are Lawrence C. Kelly, "Anthropology and Anthropologists in the Indian New Deal," Journal of the History of the Behavioral Sciences 16 (January 1980): 6–24, which is heavily documented and especially good on the personalities involved; Taylor, "Anthropologists, Reformers, and the Indian New Deal"; and David L. Marden, "Anthropologists and Federal Indian Policy prior to 1940," Indian Historian 5 (Winter 1972): 19–26. See also Felix S. Cohen, "Anthropology and the Problem of Indian Administration," Southwest Social Science Quarterly 18 (September

The anthropologists, however, found difficulties in their relations with Collier, and their contributions to the Indian New Deal fell far short of what Collier had at first expected. Their viewpoints and modes of action differed in fundamental ways from Collier's and still more from those of many old-time Indian service employees. The commissioner and his close advisers were interested in problem solving, not theoretical research, and they tended to be critical of the scientists' careful studies, which might not be suitable for application to immediate problems. More fundamentally, Collier operated on the assumption that tribal groups existed that, with Indian Bureau encouragement, could take over the government and economic organization of the tribes. The anthropologists were to identify such traditional groups and help to organize programs that would not undermine old tribal patterns. But the anthropologists, who often discovered that such traditional tribal bases for modern organization were weak or lacking entirely, were not allowed to question Collier's basic premise. Collier, too, insisted on working with *tribes*, whereas the anthropologists often found that the Indian unit was a band or a village, not the tribe.[6] Moreover, Indian service personnel obstructed much of the program. "A good deal of what Mr. Collier and his associates planned in a sophisticated way in Washington," an astute report on anthropologists and the New Deal asserted, "was not put into effect because insufficient attention was paid to the habitual ways of thinking and reacting of the groups in the field. It was not that Indian Service field representatives were irresponsible, or insincere, or unintelligent, by and large. It was simply that their own subculture screened both the instructions they got from Washington and their appraisal of the local situation." Collier, it was suggested, should have turned the anthropologists not only toward the Indian tribes but toward that "other tribe," the United States Indian Service.[7]

1937): 171–80, and Edward A. Kennard and Gordon Macgregor, "Applied Anthropology in Government: United States," in A. L. Kroeber, ed., *Anthropology Today: An Encyclopedic Inventory* (Chicago: University of Chicago Press, 1953), pp. 832–35. A series of studies, partly supported by the Indian Bureau, resulted in books on the Navajos by Clyde Kluckhohn and Dorothea Leighton, on the Pine Ridge Sioux by Gordon Macgregor, on the Hopis by Laura Thompson and Alice Joseph, on the Papagos by Rosamond Spicer, and on Indian administration research by Laura Thompson.

6. Taylor, "Anthropologists, Reformers, and the Indian New Deal," pp. 160–62; Marden, "Anthropologists and Federal Indian Policy," pp. 24–25. Some of the conflict can be seen in Scudder Mekeel, "An Appraisal of the Indian Reorganization Act," *American Anthropologist* 46 (April–June 1944): 209–17, and Collier, "Collier Replies to Mekeel," ibid. (July–September 1944): 422–26.

7. Clyde Kluckhohn and Robert Hackenberg, "Social Science Principles and the Indian Reorganization Act," in William H. Kelly, ed., *Indian Affairs and the Indian Reorganization Act: The Twenty Year Record* (Tucson: University of Arizona, 1954), p. 31.

The ultimate fact was that Collier had already made up his mind about what needed to be done. He often seemed not to hear warnings or alternative suggestions, and conversely, his own program was not always understood by those who worked with him. During the 1920s Collier had been primarily a critic. He had insistently pointed out evils in the administration of Indian affairs and had been less concerned to advance his own vision of what the future of the Indians should be. He attracted followers inside and outside of Congress who agreed with his attack on existing wrongs but who never pressed him for and never understood his basic social philosophy. Since his days in New York City, when he had worked for the People's Institute (an organization that provided evening lectures and forums for the city's immigrant masses), he had sought to develop communities where cooperation would replace individual competition and where aesthetic values would be more important than material ones. He thought he had found such a utopia among the Pueblo Indians whom he visited in the early 1920s, and he hoped that he could promote among all the Indian tribes some sort of a Red Atlantis. This would mean a restoration of Indian culture, a return to Indian political autonomy, and communal ownership of land and resources instead of the individualism of allotment.[8]

As Collier looked back upon his commissionership, he spoke about seven basic principles that had guided his administration of Indian affairs. They were his philosophy of reform:

1. "Indian societies must and can be discovered in their continuing existence, or regenerated, or set into being *de novo* and made use of."

2. "The Indian societies, whether ancient, regenerated or created anew, must be given status, responsibility and power."

3. "The land, held, used and cherished in the way the particular Indian group desires, is fundamental in any lifesaving program."

4. "Each and all of the freedoms should be extended to Indians, and in the most convincing and dramatic manner possible." Collier asked for "proclamation and enforcement of cultural liberty, religious liberty, and unimpeded relationships of the generations."

5. Positive means must be used to ensure freedom: credit, education (of a broad and technical sort), and grants of responsibility.

6. "The experience of responsible democracy, is, of all experience, the most therapeutic, the most disciplinary, the most dynamogenic and the most productive of efficiency. In this one affirmation, we, the workers who knew so well the diversity of the Indian situation and its recalcitrancy to-

---

8. A useful analysis that places Collier in the context of Progressive thought is Stephen J. Kunitz, "The Social Philosophy of John Collier," *Ethnohistory* 18 (Summer 1971): 213–29.

ward monistic programs, were prepared to be unreserved, absolute, even at the risk of blunders and of turmoil."

7. "The seventh principle I would call the first and the last: That research and then more research is essential to the program, that in the ethnic field research can be made a tool of action essential to all the other tools, indeed, that it ought to be the master tool."[9]

This was the humane vision that guided Collier. Yet, despite the high-sounding rhetoric of Indian self-determination, it was a paternalistic program for the Indians, who were expected to accept it willy-nilly.

CONSERVATION AND RELIEF

Collier began with a dramatic attack upon the depression conditions that engulfed the Indian reservations. Following a suggestion that had been made in the Indian Office before he had become commissioner, he worked for a separate Indian Civilian Conservation Corps (originally entitled Emergency Conservation Work). He was strongly supported by Secretary Ickes, who argued in a memorandum to Robert Fechner, director of the CCC, that special Indian conditions demanded a separate program, so that the Indians themselves could do the conservation work needed on the reservations and not be subjected to the army-type camps that marked the regular program. Near the end of April 1933, President Roosevelt approved an Indian CCC following Ickes's suggestions, and Congress appropriated $5,875,000 for the first six months of the program. The Office of Indian Affairs assumed responsibility for the supervision of the projects, for medical examinations of enrollees, and for camp discipline and administration. The Indian CCC operated on its own rules. Married or unmarried men seventeen years of age or over were enrolled, and there was great flexibility in the nature of the camps. Besides the usual boarding camps for single men, the Indian program established camps for married men with families and in some cases operated the programs by transporting the enrollees each day from their own homes. Most of the projects dealt with soil erosion control, forestation, and range development, but dozens of other projects were instituted. Collier's goal was not the improvement of the public domain, toward which the parent organization was directed, but the conservation of reservation land and the training of Indians to make good use of it. In ad-

9. These principles were set forth in Collier, "United States Indian Administration as a Laboratory of Ethnic Relations," *Social Research* 12 (September 1945): 274–75. The article is repeated substantially in John Collier, *The Indians of the Americas* (New York: W. W. Norton and Company, 1947), pp. 261–63, from which I have taken my quotations.

dition, especially after 1938, an enrollee program of training in practical industrial skills was a prominent part of the Indian program, and about 50,000 individuals took part in it. Collier established a new office in the bureau to administer the CCC program, headed at first by Jay B. Nash and then by Daniel Murphy, and six district offices were set up to coordinate the reservation projects. World War II seriously interrupted the program, for many enrollees left to join the army or to enter the war industries. Then on July 2, 1942, Congress abruptly ended the whole CCC program.[10]

Collier had had high hopes for the program. "No previous undertaking in the Indian Service," he wrote after it had begun, "has so largely been the Indians' own undertaking, as the emergency conservation work." And in 1939, when the program was in full stride, he wrote with pride but quite accurately: "Indian CCC, now six years old, is bone of the bone and flesh of the flesh of the Indian's new achievement. There is no part of Indian country, there are few functions of Indian life, where it has not made an indispensable contribution. Truly, Indian CCC has been a creative force. 'Sociogenic,' to use a highbrow word. Other factors have been no less essential, but none has operated more universally than CCC." When the CCC was abolished, he could still exult over its accomplishments: "Along with tribal self-government, it has wrought itself into the personalities of tens of thousands of Indians! How it has held high a beacon for all of the 30,000,000 Indians of our Western world!"[11]

The impact of the Indian CCC can be seen in its statistics: 85,349 en-

10. Donald L. Parman, "The Indian and the Civilian Conservation Corps," *Pacific Historical Review* 40 (February 1971): 39–57; Parman, "The Indian Civilian Conservation Corps" (Ph.D. dissertation, University of Oklahoma, 1967); Calvin W. Gower, "The CCC Indian Division: Aid for Depressed Americans, 1933–1942," *Minnesota History* 43 (Spring 1972): 3–13. The records of the Indian CCC have been segregated in the National Archives as OIA, Records of the Civilian Conservation Corps—Indian Division. Of special value is "Final Report of Indian Emergency Conservation Work and Civilian Conservation Corps—Indian Division, 1933–1942," September 11, 1943, file 32114–44–344, General Service, box 10; the Narrative and Pictorial Reports, 1937–1942, are full of snapshots of CCC projects and camp activities. See also reports in the commissioner's annual reports, for example, CIA Report, 1933, pp. 69–70; CIA Report, 1934, pp. 102–5; CIA Report, 1935, pp. 144–47.

The Indian Office began publishing *Indians at Work*, with the subtitle "An Emergency Conservation News Sheet for Ourselves," in August 1933, as a newsletter for the Indian CCC. The publication was soon broadened to include general news of Indian service activities, and its subtitle was changed on January 1, 1934, to "A News Sheet for Indians and the Indian Service." Although it continued to carry much conservation news, it became an excellent source on the day-to-day operations of the Indian New Deal until it ceased publication in the summer of 1945.

11. *Indians at Work*, first issue undated, p. 1; 6 (April 1939): 2; 9 (May–June 1942): inside back cover.

rollees, nearly all of them Indians, seventy-one jurisdictions (reservations, schools, and the like) in twenty-three states, and $72 million expended. The relief of economic suffering was immediate, and the conservation and other constructive work on the reservations was extensive. Equally important was the effect of the camp life and its training programs on the Indians, who made use of the experience and skills obtained there as they went into military service or entered the general work force. But the long-term results did not meet Collier's expectations of rehabilitating the reservations and training the Indians to make better use of their resources as farmers, foresters, and ranchers. "Ironically," the historian of the Indian Civilian Conservation Corps concluded, "a conservation program designed to improve Indian land probably had its greatest impact in permitting former enrollees to take up careers in industrial centers."[12]

Other federal relief programs were made available to the Indians. Secretary of Agriculture Henry A. Wallace and his assistant Rexford Tugwell were deeply concerned about Indian matters and through the Agricultural Adjustment Administration allocated $800,000 for the purchase of stock to establish herds on a number of reservations. The Soil Erosion Service benefited the Indians, and at Collier's insistence the Federal Emergency Relief Administration extended its programs to Indians. Oklahoma Indians, for example, were paid to build roads and bridges, and FERA funds purchased sheep and goats from the Navajos and distributed the meat to Indians on the northern plains. Indians were paid from federal funds, as well, under the Civil Works Administration, which employed more than 4,000 Indians in the winter of 1934 to repair buildings, build roads, dig wells, and perform office work. The CWA also hired Indians to paint murals in government buildings and to make rugs and pottery for Indian Service facilities. The Public Works Administration established in June 1933 improved the reservations with day schools, hospitals, roads, irrigation projects, and sewerage systems. And other funds under the National Industrial Recovery Act set up five subsistence homesteads for Indians. When Congress passed the Emergency Relief Appropriations Act in 1935, the Indians participated in both the Works Progress Administration and the National Youth Administration. Moreover, Indians used the Resettlement Administration's program of crop loans, drought relief, and subsistence grants.[13]

---

12. Parman, "The Indian and the Civilian Conservation Corps," p. 56. The "Final Report" gives statistics on enrollees, money spent, and projects completed.

13. Kenneth R. Philp, *John Collier's Crusade for Indian Reform, 1920–1954* (Tucson: University of Arizona Press, 1977), pp. 122–26. *Indians at Work* contains news of many of the relief activities.

There is no doubt that these measures helped to lift the pall of despair that had spread over many reservations. Of course there were mistakes made in the hurriedly put together programs, many of which provided short-term relief without striking deeply at the long-term problem of Indian poverty, but both Ickes and Collier were justifiably proud of their record in conservation and relief. Ickes wrote to Roosevelt in December 1935 that he had been "a real White Father to the Indians and they appreciated it deeply." He told the president that his administration would "go down in history as the most humane and far seeing with respect to the Indians that this country ever had."[14]

NEW DEAL MEASURES

The first legislative enactments of the Indian New Deal came quickly, for the way had been prepared for them in the previous administration. On May 31, 1933, the Pueblo Relief Act was approved. This was a measure for which reformers had fought for many years, and it corrected inadequacies in compensation allowed by the Pueblo Lands Board by appropriating $761,954.88 for the Pueblos and $232,086.80 for the white settlers who had been evicted. The Indian funds were to be used for purchase of lands, water rights, and other economic benefits, but the Pueblos had a veto on how the money was spent. The law also provided a fifty-year renewable permit to Taos Pueblo for economic and religious use of government lands surrounding their sacred Blue Lake.[15]

The drive to share responsibility with the states for Indian programs, which had been stopped when Congress failed to pass the Swing-Johnson bills in 1930 and 1932, was now successful. The Johnson-O'Malley Act of April 16, 1934, authorized the secretary of the interior to sign contracts with states for "the education, medical attention, agricultural assistance, and social welfare, including relief of distress, of Indians," and to expend under the contracts moneys appropriated by Congress for such purposes. States could make use of the existing federal buildings. The impact of the law, however, was not as great as Collier hoped, especially in regard to schools, for the Indian Bureau could not control its funds if the states insisted on independence, states were reluctant to establish special Indian programs, and conflicts between federal and state adminstrators soon appeared.[16]

14. Ickes to Roosevelt, December 19, 1935, quoted in Philp, *John Collier's Crusade*, p. 126.

15. CIA Report, 1933, p. 101; 48 *United States Statutes* 108–11.

16. 48 *United States Statutes* 596; *Senate Report* no. 511, 73–2, serial 9769; *House*

Other early legislation extended the Navajo reservation, a project that had long been afoot to eliminate the checkerboard nature of part of the tribal domain. Early in 1934 administrative bills were introduced to establish new boundaries and eliminate private landholdings within them. Secretary Ickes pushed the bills as the only means by which proper range management and control of soil erosion could be carried on. Funds, reimbursable by the Navajo tribe, of $482,136 for New Mexico and $481,897 for Arizona were to be provided. The Arizona bill, which resulted in the addition of about one million acres to the reservation, became law on June 14, 1934, but the New Mexico bill after passing the Senate failed in the House.[17]

It was not necessary to wait for congressional action on many aspects of reform, for executive action by the president, the secretary of the interior, or the commissioner of Indian affairs could suffice. One such move abolished the Board of Indian Commissioners, which in the 1920s and early 1930s had sided with Burke and then Rhoads and Scattergood against the radical reformers' attacks.[18] The board was a conservative body, composed mostly of Republicans, who clung fast to the assimilationist views that Collier wanted to overturn. Attacks on the board had begun early in 1932, when there were attempts, ultimately unsuccessful, made in the Senate Appropriations Committee to eliminate the board's budget, a move that some board members believed originated with Collier. Although well aware of its precarious existence, the board in its report of 1932 restated its assimilationist philosophy: "The Board refuses to believe that an Indian is incapable of living the life of a normal American citizen and the department is assured of the support of this board in every endeavor to hasten the time when the Indian can be justly expected to forego the special privileges which set him apart from other citizens. . . . Self-support and self-reliance must be not only the ultimate goal but also the touchstone by which we test all plans and policies."[19]

Report no. 864, 73–2, serial 9775. John Collier argued for the measure in a letter of February 26, 1934, printed in both reports. The working of the Johnson-O'Malley Act in the area of education is discussed in Margaret Szasz, *Education and the American Indian: The Road to Self-Determination, 1928–1973* (Albuquerque: University of New Mexico Press, 1974), pp. 91–105.

17. 48 *United States Statutes* 960–62; *Senate Report* no. 1074, 73–2, serial 9770; *House Report* no. 1602, 73–2, serial 9776. Ickes's letter of May 5, 1934, in support of the measure, is printed in both reports. For a discussion of the matter in the larger context of Navajo reservation extension, see Lawrence C. Kelly, *The Navajo Indians and Federal Indian Policy, 1900–1935* (Tucson: University of Arizona Press, 1968), pp. 127–30.

18. I have relied here on an unpublished seminar paper by Harold E. Stine, Jr., "The 'Fifth Wheel' of American Indian Reform: The U.S. Board of Indian Commissioners, 1920–1933," Marquette University, 1979.

19. *Report of the Board of Indian Commissioners,* 1932, p. 16.

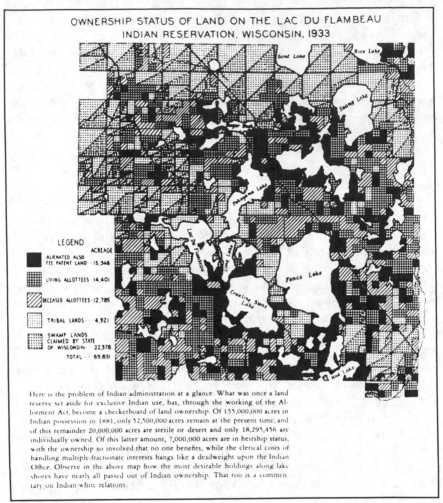

OWNERSHIP STATUS OF LAND ON THE LAC DU FLAMBEAU
INDIAN RESERVATION, WISCONSIN, 1933

LEGEND

		ACREAGE
ALIENATED ALSO FEE PATENT LAND	15,346
LIVING ALLOTTEES	14,401
DECEASED ALLOTTEES	12,785
TRIBAL LANDS	4,921
SWAMP LANDS CLAIMED BY STATE OF WISCONSIN	22,378
TOTAL	69,831

Here is the problem of Indian administration at a glance. What was once a land reserve set aside for exclusive Indian use, has, through the working of the Allotment Act, become a checkerboard of land ownership. Of 155,000,000 acres in Indian possession in 1881, only 52,500,000 acres remain at the present time; and of this remainder 20,000,000 acres are sterile or desert and only 18,295,456 are individually owned. Of this latter amount, 7,000,000 acres are in heirship status, with the ownership so involved that no one benefits, while the clerical costs of handling multiple-fractionate interests hangs like a deadweight upon the Indian Office. Observe in the above map how the most desirable holdings along lake shores have nearly all passed out of Indian ownership. That too is a commentary on Indian-white relations.

Some board members fought diligently for the appointment of Meritt rather than Collier as commissioner, and when Collier won, the board realized its days were numbered. Collier addressed its last meeting, on May 10–11, 1933, about his proposed reforms. Fifteen days later, on May 25, 1933, President Roosevelt signed an executive order abolishing the Board of Indian Commissioners. The president justified the move on the basis of economy and the elimination of overlapping and duplication of effort, but the action was in fact a symbol of the changing of the guard in the management of Indian affairs.[20]

20. Minutes of the Board of Indian Commissioners, May 10–11, 1933, OIA, Records of the Board of Indian Commissioners; Executive Order no. 6145, "Abolition of Board of Indian Commissioners and Transfer of the Records, Property, and Personnel of Said Board to the Secretary of the Interior," printed in *House Document* no. 57, 73–1, serial 9751.

Collier also began his attack on the land allotment system. In his first annual report he declared:

It is only recently that we have come fully to realize the magnitude of the disaster which the allotment law of 1887 has wrought upon the Indians. . . .

It is clear that the allotment system has not changed the Indians into responsible, self-supporting citizens. Neither has it fitted them to enter into urban industrial pursuits. It has merely deprived vast numbers of them of their land, turned them into paupers, and imposed an ever-growing relief problem on the Government. As a starting point for a rational policy, we can categorically say that the immediate problem is not that of absorbing the Indians into the white population, but first of all lifting them out of material and spiritual dependency and hopelessness. It is equally clear that the place to begin this process is on the land; for if the Indian cannot pursue the relatively simple and primitive arts of agriculture, grazing, and forestry, there seems little prospect that he can be fitted for the more exacting technology of urban society. Even if he could be at once so fitted, the industrial depression has taught us that we already have far too many industrial workers.[21]

Collier sought to reorient Indian land policy by reversing the allotment system, and he began with partial steps that were within his administrative competence. On August 12, 1933, he directed the superintendents to stop the sale of trust or restricted Indian land, allotted or inherited, and ordered them not to submit certificates of competency, patents in fee, or requests for removal of restrictions on Indian property, except "in individual cases of great distress or other emergency."[22]

Much more controversial were Collier's executive reforms dealing with religion and with missionary work on the reservations. By Circular no. 2970, January 3, 1934, entitled "Indian Religious Freedom and Indian Culture," he demanded "the fullest constitutional liberty, in all matters affecting religion, conscience, and culture" for all Indians and that the employees in the Indian Service show an "affirmative, appreciative attitude toward Indian cultural values." He directed unequivocally: "No interference with Indian religious life or ceremonial expression will hereafter be tolerated. The cultural liberty of Indians is in all respects to be considered equal to that of any non-Indian group." Moreover, Indian arts and crafts were to be "prized, nourished and honored." A second directive, issued on January 15, 1934, dealt with religious services at government schools and replaced the

21. CIA Report, 1933, pp. 108–9.
22. Order no. 420, John Collier to all Indian superintendents, August 12, 1933, CIA Report, 1933, p. 100.

existing regulations, which were largely a restatement of the directives worked out by Leupp and promulgated by Valentine in 1910. The new "Regulations for Religious Worship and Instruction" prohibited compulsory attendance at services, although religious denominations could make use of school facilities if the children's attendance was by their own choice or that of their parents. At the day schools, religious instruction was permitted for one hour a week, with the written permission of the parents. What made the regulations distinctive, however, was that they applied to representatives of native religions as well as to Christian missionaries.[23]

Religion was a sensitive subject. Many of the missionaries who had long used the schools as the focus of their Christianizing efforts looked upon Collier's moves to protect religious freedom for the Indians as a direct attack upon them, and there were cries of atheism and anti-religion. If Collier had his way, they feared, the Indians would all return to paganism. Criticism of Collier was widespread in Protestant circles; many Indians, too, having firmly accepted Christianity, were offended by Collier's actions. The old Christian reformer Elaine Goodale Eastman deplored the acceptance of Indian ceremonials and religious expressions. Many of them had reached complete degradation, she asserted, and she feared that "some such pseudo-native institution as the 'Peyote church' or a new 'Messiah craze' invented by self-seeking fakirs, may serve to drug the Indian masses into forgetfulness of the fact that the present Indian policy tends not to be the promised full enfranchisement, but rather to a perpetual twilight of insincere praise and actual inferiority." A year later, Flora Warren Seymour, once a member of the Board of Indian Commissioners, made a similar attack on what she called federal favor for fetishism. "Under the high-sounding slogans of 'toleration' and 'religious liberty,'" she charged, "missionaries of all denominations working among the American Indians are meeting with such obstructions to their work as have not been encountered for more than a century past." The missionaries, she said, were committed to the belief "that there is a higher way of life than that beset by shamanism and savage fears."[24]

Collier held his ground and refused to give up the principles of religious

---

23. Circular no. 2970, "Indian Religious Freedom and Indian Culture," January 3, 1934, OIA Circulars (M1121, reel 14); "Regulations for Religious Worship and Instruction, Amendment no. 2," January 15, 1934, copy in OIA CCF 110, General Service, 10637–1934.

24. Elaine Goodale Eastman, "Does Uncle Sam Foster Paganism," *Christian Century* 51 (August 8, 1934): 1016–18; Flora Warren Seymour, "Federal Favor for Fetishism: The American Government and the American Indian," *Missionary Review of the World* 58 (September 1935): 397–400. See also the material in OIA, Office File of Commissioner John Collier, folders marked Religious Freedom and Propaganda, Adverse, box 14.

liberty for the Indians that he had fought for since the early 1920s. He forthrightly answered Mrs. Eastman by pointing out the profound character of Indian religions like that of the Pueblos, and he declared that his administration would "continue to try to admit Indians to the most important of all the human birthrights—affirmative liberty of conscience." In a widely circulated statement dated February 19, 1936, and addressed to Ben Dwight, editor of the Stroud, Oklahoma, *Tushkahomman*, Collier formally replied to the missionary critics. He flatly denied that he was an infidel or an atheist or that he was hostile to missionary effort. But he did insist that Indians be granted "the fullest constitutional liberty, in all matters affecting religion, conscience and culture." Religious liberty, he said, does not extend only to Christians.[25] But the issue would not die; Collier's radical rightwing opponents continued to hammer on the theme of irreligion and atheism, and the Wheeler-Howard bill was criticized for promoting a return to tribalism.

In addition to fighting for the Indians' rights of conscience, Collier intended to relieve the Indians of numerous restrictions that had built up on the reservations through the decades. Many of these had been reasonable answers to specific needs when they were introduced, but they made little sense in the 1930s, at a time when the policy was to treat Indians as other citizens. At the instigation of the commissioner, Congress in May 1934 abolished twelve sections in the *United States Code* that, among other things, authorized military activities on the reservations, required passports of foreigners entering the Indian country, prohibited seditious messages to Indians, and gave the commissioner power to remove persons from the reservations whom he considered detrimental to the welfare of the Indians.[26]

Then changes were made in the administrative powers by which the reservation Indians had been subjected to what Felix Cohen called "perhaps the greatest concentration of administrative absolutism in our governmental structure." The Indian Bureau, represented by the superintendent, he noted, combined "the functions of an employer, landlord, policeman, judge, physician, banker, teacher, relief administrator, and employment agency." An important mechanism for much of the superintendent's exercise of authority was the court of Indian offenses, which had been instituted in 1882

25. Collier, "A Reply to Mrs. Eastman," *Christian Century* 51 (August 8, 1934): 1018–20; "The Policy of the Office of Indian Affairs on Religious Liberty among Indians," February 19, 1936, copy attached to Circular no. 2970, January 3, 1934, OIA Circulars (M1121, reel 14).

26. 48 *United States Statutes* 787, repealing *United States Code*, title 25, sections 171–73, 186, 219–26. See also Felix S. Cohen, *Handbook of Federal Indian Law* (Washington: GPO, 1942), pp. 174–75.

as a means of eliminating cultural practices that were offensive to the white officials. The rules governing the courts and the offenses had been written into the *Regulations of the Indian Department* of 1884 and were repeated substantially intact in subsequent editions of the regulations. In regulations issued by the secretary of the interior on November 27, 1935, these old rules were revoked and new ones substituted.[27] Collier described the change:

> Indian Service Officers are prohibited from controlling, obstructing, or interfering with the functions of the Indian courts. The appointment and removal of Indian judges on those reservations where courts of Indian offenses are now maintained is made subject to confirmation by the Indians of the reservation. Indian defendants will hereafter have the benefit of formal charges, the power to summon witnesses, the privilege of bail, and the right of trial by jury. . . .
>
> The revision of law and order regulations is one step in the program of the present administration to eliminate obsolete regulations and bureaucratic procedures governing the conduct of Indians, and to endow the Indian tribes themselves with increased responsibility and freedom in local self-government.[28]

JOHN COLLIER'S REFORM PROPOSAL

Collier's great goal was legislation to reverse the allotment policy, which had not only had deleterious effects upon the Indian communities but symbolized the assimilationist philosophy with which he was at odds. To promote his goal Collier called a conference on January 7, 1934, at the Cosmos Club in Washington, D.C., to discuss the issue and outline a program. He invited persons from the American Indian Defense Association, the Indian Rights Association, the National Association on Indian Affairs (formerly the Eastern Association on Indian Affairs), the American Civil Liberties Union, the National Council of American Indians, and the General Federation of Women's Clubs, with the hope of uniting diverse groups behind legislation to replace the Dawes Act. Lewis Meriam chaired the meeting. With its eye on the criticisms made by the Meriam Report, the conference recommended repeal of the allotment laws, consolidation of trust lands under tribal ownership, change in inheritance laws, organiza-

---

27. Cohen, *Federal Indian Law*, p. 175; "Law and Order Regulations," November 27, 1935, copy in *Miscellaneous Regulations*, vol. 3, Department of Interior Library.
28. CIA Report, 1936, p. 166.

tion of the Indian communities, and transfer of power from the federal government to Indian tribes.[29]

Next Collier began a campaign to prepare the Indians for his new program. On January 20, 1934, he addressed a circular letter entitled "Indian Self-Government" to superintendents, tribal councils, and individual Indians, in which he directed superintendents to meet with tribal councils, where they existed, or to call special meetings of tribal leaders to present to them the government's plans and get their reactions. This was an attempt on the part of the commissioner to get some input from the Indians, but the lengthy circular, with its detailed guidelines of what the discussions should include, showed heavy-handed direction from the top. The superintendents were to point out the evils of the allotment system and suggest the establishment of Indian self-government. "As a possible solution for the evils of the heirship and like problems caused by the allotment system," Collier wrote, "it is suggested that the underlying principle of the modern corporation be applied to Indian communities. In brief, it is suggested that instead of retaining their interest in particular pieces of land the Indians transfer control over their lands to an incorporated Indian Community and receive in exchange a proportionate interest in the entire landholdings of the community. Such a system would permit the establishment of proper economic timber units, grazing units and farm tracts as well as home and garden areas." Rights would terminate at death, and the only inheritance would be the improvements made on a piece of property assigned for use. The goal was to have the self-governing Indian community control its funds, its employees, and in general all internal affairs. Collier hoped that "ultimately the Indian Bureau may serve the Indians in an advisory capacity, on a purely voluntary basis, as for instance, the Department of Agriculture serves the American farmer." The commissioner directed that reports in response to the circular be forwarded to the Indian Office no later than February 15, 1934.[30]

Despite the short time allowed, the superintendents faithfully complied. They presented the circular to tribal groups and sent to Collier very candid reports. In many cases, the Indian groups themselves responded. To Collier, who was so intent on returning to the Indians the communal life and autonomy they had once enjoyed, the negative tone of most of the replies must have been disconcerting. Some groups, like the Eastern Chero-

29. "Washington Conference," *Indian Truth* 11 (January 1934): 3–4; Vera Connolly, "The End of a Long, Long Trail," *Good Housekeeping* 98 (April 1934): 250.

30. "Indian Self-Government," circular letter of John Collier to superintendents, tribal councils, and individual Indians, January 20, 1934, copy in OIA, Records concerning the Wheeler-Howard Act, part 8, box 7.

kees, replied that they were already operating under procedures much like Collier's scheme, but from other areas criticism of the circular's suggestions was strong. The superintendent of the Sacramento Agency, O. H. Lipps, saw great difficulty in organizing any kind of Indian community action or self-government among the California Indians. "These Indians," he said, "were never united like many other tribes and their whole history has been one of inter-tribal warfare and family feuds engendered by suspicion and petty jealousies. . . . If they ever possessed a common tribal culture and strong, virile civic institutions they have long since lost them." The superintendent of the Rosebud Sioux Agency, W. O. Roberts, reported unusual excitement and all shades of opinion caused by the circular. He thought he might be able to put the program across, but he warned, "It would be a fatal error to treat the Sioux Indian in the same manner and to think of him as the same type of person as the southwestern Indians." The greatest difficulty, he believed, lay in the jealousy and hatred that existed between full-bloods and mixed-bloods. From neighboring Pine Ridge Agency, Superintendent James H. McGregor reported the same kind of division. Similarly, in what was a common attitude, the Pawnee superintendent, P. W. Danielson, reported that the reason his Indians rejected the proposal was "the fact that those now owning lands were of the opinion that they should not be penalized for having kept their property intact, and as a result do not desire to pool their interests in a community holding and let others who have dissipated their funds and property, share and share alike with them."[31]

Indian petitions and reports from tribal business committees voiced these and other objections. The Nez Perces said, "We object most strenuously to taking away of our independence to control our own affairs and transact our own business. We want our children's future to be preserved and our people kept in safe ground. We do not want them to be turned back forty years to take up the old communal life which never made for progress. After forty years of advancement we object to going back to the status of the Navajoes and Pueblos which you mention in your letter." Others, like the Indians at the Colville Agency, asserted that they had no members who were well educated enough to take responsibility for tribal affairs. The resolutions passed at meetings of the Cheyenne River Agency asserted the impossibility of perfecting a community organization and insisted that pooling interests would be too great a sacrifice for a majority of the tribe. They added:

31. O. H. Lipps to Collier, February 1, 1934; W. O. Roberts to Collier, January 31, 1934; James H. McGregor to Collier, February 2, 1934; P. W. Danielson to Collier, February 15, 1934—all in OIA, Records concerning the Wheeler-Howard Act, part 2–A, box 2. There are other reports in this file.

We submit: That our people have lived for too many years with our white neighbors; that we have become accustomed to the white man's law; that our children have been and are being taught to obey the white man's law; that there is no longer any tribal government by chiefs and we have no desire to be segregated as an Indian organization from the State and Civil government with whom we have affiliated, and with whom we have an equal opportunity at the polls and in their courts. Some of our members serve on election boards and take part in the community activities of the Civil Government.[32]

THE WHEELER-HOWARD (INDIAN REORGANIZATION) ACT

One might wonder, for all his talk about Indians taking part in measures that affected them, whether Collier really intended to make use of the replies to his circular or whether the circular was merely a first step in his campaign to prepare the Indians for what he had in mind for them. At any rate, even before the deadline set for submission of the reports, he had drawn up a detailed legislative measure. The bill, which was the work in large part of Nathan Margold and his assistants, Felix Cohen and Charles Fahy, was introduced on February 12, 1934, by Representative Edgar Howard of Nebraska and on February 13 by Senator Burton K. Wheeler of Montana. It was a forty-eight-page document as a printed bill and bore the long but indicative title "A bill to grant to Indians living under Federal tutelage the freedom to organize for the purposes of local self-government and economic enterprise; to provide for the necessary training of Indians in administrative and economic affairs; to conserve and develop Indian lands; and to promote the more effective administration of justice in matters affecting Indian tribes and communities by establishing a Federal Court of Indian Affairs." The bill, which was significantly modified before it became law, embodied Collier's key proposals for revolutionizing Indian policy.[33]

The original Wheeler-Howard bill had four sections. Title I, "Indian Self-Government," granted Indians the right to organize for local self-government and for economic activities. To those who wanted to take part, the secretary of the interior would grant a charter indicating their

---

32. Tribal Business Committee of Nez Perce Indians to Collier, February 8, 1934; petition of 94 members of Colville Agency, included in Harvey K. Meyer to Collier, February 14, 1934; resolutions of meetings at Cheyenne River Agency, February 15, 1934—all in OIA, Records concerning the Wheeler-Howard Act, part 1–A, box 1.

33. *Congressional Record*, 78: 2437, 2440; H.R. 7902 and S. 2755, 73d Congress, 2d session.

rights and responsibilities; then the secretary would give to the new corporation powers of government and control of funds that federal law invested in him. Congress would create a revolving credit fund to aid in the economic development of the Indian communities. Title II, "Special Education for Indians," directed the promotion of the study of Indian civilization, including arts, crafts, and traditions, and support of this policy by special appropriations. Title III, "Indian Lands," abolished the allotment system, restored existing "surplus" lands to the tribe, and appropriated two million dollars a year for the purchase of new lands. The most controversial parts authorized the secretary of the interior to transfer individual land interests to the tribe "if, in his opinion, such transfer is necessary for the proper consolidation of Indian lands," and directed that at the death of an allottee the restricted lands would pass not to his heirs but to the chartered community or tribe. Finally, Title IV, "Court of Indian Affairs," created a special court of Indian affairs, to be conducted according to Indian traditions, which would serve as a court of original jurisdiction for cases involving the Indian communities or their members. In short, the Indians would be granted control of their own affairs, allotment would end and lands would be consolidated and augmented, and federal administration of the self-governing tribes would cease.[34]

Brief hearings on the bill were held by the Senate and House committees on Indian affairs in February 1934. From the first there was strong opposition to any policy of segregation or communal ownership of property.[35] Because of this congressional hostility, and mindful of the criticism evoked by his circular on "Indian Self-Government," Collier moved dramatically to lessen or eliminate the Indians' misunderstandings about the bill and to gain their support when Congress took up the bills again. He announced a series of Indian congresses to be held across the country, to be attended by tribal councils and business committees, superintendents and other reser-

34. Collier prepared an elaborate twenty-six-page analysis of the bill, "The Purpose and Operation of the Wheeler-Howard Indian Rights Bill (S. 2755; H.R. 7902)," February 19, 1934. It was a "memorandum of explanation" sent to the Senate and House committees on Indian affairs, but it was used also to educate the Indians and others about the measure. There is a copy in OIA, Records concerning the Wheeler-Howard Act, part 8, box 7, and it is printed in the House and Senate hearings on the bill. For a brief analysis of the bill, see Philp, *John Collier's Crusade*, pp. 141–43.

35. "Readjustment of Indian Affairs," *Hearings before the Committee on Indian Affairs, House of Representatives, 73d Congress, 2d Session, on H.R. 7902* (1934); "To Grant to Indians Living under Federal Tutelage the Freedom to Organize for Purposes of Local Self-Government and Economic Enterprise," *Hearings before the Committee on Indian Affairs, United States Senate, 73d Congress, 2d Session, on S. 2755 and S. 3645* (1934).

vation employees, and the commissioner, the assistant commissioner, and other staff members from the Washington office, at which the Wheeler-Howard bill could be openly and thoroughly discussed and misconceptions dispelled. To prepare for the meetings he sent to the reservations copies of the detailed analysis of the bill that he had prepared for the congressional committees. In all, ten Indian congresses were held in March and April 1934, at Rapid City, South Dakota (March 2–5), Chemawa, Oregon (March 8–9), Fort Defiance, Arizona (March 12–13), Santo Domingo, New Mexico (March 15), Phoenix, Arizona (March 15–16), Riverside, California (March 17–18), Anadarko, Oklahoma (March 20), Muskogee, Oklahoma (March 22–23), Miami, Oklahoma (March 24), and Hayward, Wisconsin (April 23–24).[36]

Collier attended most of the congresses himself, but when he was unable to do so (as in the case of those at Chemawa, Phoenix, and Riverside), the assistant commissioner or other staff officers explained the bill to the assembled Indians. Large numbers of the Indians supported Collier, but at all the meetings objections were raised and at some open hostility broke out. There were fears about allotments held by individuals who wanted to keep them and about the proposals for self-government, and there was frequent suspicion about any changes in Indian policy. Indians voiced objections to a revival of tribal segregation, which would mean regression from the progress they had made. And rumors that the measure was communistic or socialistic were circulated, especially among the Oklahoma Indians.[37] All in all, though, Collier returned to Washington confident that the congresses had been successful and that the great majority of the Indians were behind his reforms. The opposition, he declared, almost without exception had been "fomented and fanned by the crass, unadulterated self-interest of whites and Indian persons who are afraid, often without reason, that under the proposed act they will lose advantages they now possess." He asserted: "On nearly all reservations the Indians had been told that the Wheeler-Howard bill was a scheme to confiscate the land of Indians who still retained their holdings, under the guise of providing land for homeless Indians; that it was a communistic scheme to expropriate Indian lands as was done in Russia. Again and again this fantastic allegation popped up, the frequency and universality of its appearance indicating a common

---

36. Circular letter, Collier to superintendents, tribal councils, business committees, and individual Indians, March 6, 1934, copy in OIA, Records concerning the Wheeler-Howard Act, part 8, box 7. The minutes of the various congresses are in the same file, parts 1–A and 2–A, boxes 1 and 2, and in John Collier Papers, Yale University (reel 30).

37. The congresses are summarized in Philp, *John Collier's Crusade*, pp. 146–54. See also the minutes of the congresses cited in note 36.

source and a deliberate attempt to sow these poison statements through-out the Indian country."[38]

But Collier met with more than the opposition of fanatics. The unity he had hoped to build among the Indian reform organizations at the Cosmos Club meeting, he discovered when he returned to Washington, had fallen apart. Although the National Association of Indian Affairs, led by Oliver La Farge, and the American Indian Defense Association, directed by Allan Harper, supported Collier's measure, the Indian Rights Association broke away. In an article called, "Stop, Look—and Consider," in the March 1934 issue of *Indian Truth*, Matthew K. Sniffen issued a stern warning against the bill. "It proposes revolutionary departures in Indian policy," he said. "It perpetuates segregation under the guise of self-government. It jeopardizes individual Indian property rights, and shifts the incentive which the au-thors of the Allotment Act had in mind for individual ownership of prop-erty leading toward citizenship. The policy is a reversal of the past." A sec-ond issue of the magazine spelled out in more detail the objections of the Indian Rights Association to the Wheeler-Howard bill. It printed a state-ment adopted by the board of directors of the association at a special meet-ing on May 14, 1934, which criticized the bill title by title. "Whether we wish it to be so or not, whether we encourage or discourage it," the state-ment read, "the amalgamation of the Indian with the white race in the United States is in process."[39]

If this was not bad enough, Collier's program met obstruction from some Indian service employees, who, perhaps naturally enough, were wed-ded to old ways and who looked upon the innovations with suspicion if not outright hostility. Because the effectiveness of new programs depended so largely on the loyalty and enthusiasm of the fieldworkers, Secretary Ickes took strong action to scotch any obstructionism. In a letter of April 30, 1934, addressed to all employees, he condemned "subtle, misleading prop-aganda against the new Indian program emanating from a minority of em-ployees within the Indian service," which propaganda he characterized as "disloyal and pernicious." He threatened dismissal to "all of those engaged in this scheme to defeat our program."[40]

Collier faced up to the criticism and the recommendations made at the Indian congresses, and he prepared more than thirty amendments to the

38. "Statement of John Collier, Commissioner of Indian Affairs," undated, in OIA, Records concerning the Wheeler-Howard Act, part 2–B, box 3.

39. "Stop, Look—and Consider," *Indian Truth* 11 (March 1934): 1–3; "The Collier Bill," ibid. (May 1934): 1–8.

40. Harold L. Ickes to all employees of the Indian service, April 30, 1934, copy in OIA, Records concerning the Wheeler-Howard Act, part 7, box 7; it is printed in "Readjust-ment of Indian Affairs," pp. 233–34.

bill. These looked to protection of individual allotments, which could not be transferred to communal control without consent, continued division of allotments among heirs if the land so divided could be used effectively, preservation of individual title to mineral resources, protection of Indian claims, and allowance for tribes to exclude themselves from the provisions of the bill by tribal referendum.[41] Collier in the original bill had intended not only to end allotment but, as much as possible, to undo its evil effects by returning individually owned parcels of land to tribal ownership and also to prohibit the further inheritance of lands by providing that at the death of an Indian his land interests would revert to the tribe. This was more than many Indians and most of the old-line reformers could stomach, and in the amendments Collier wisely retreated to what he thought he could get enacted.

Yet even with his willingness to amend the bill to meet objections, Collier faced strong opposition in Congress, when during April and May hearings were renewed in both the Senate and the House. Senator Wheeler, one of the original sponsors of the bill, now turned against its key provisions and condemned the anti-assimilationist results it would bring. Instead of setting up self-governing Indian communities, Wheeler believed, the government should help the tribes to adopt the white man's ways and laws. He questioned the expense of setting up tribal governments and asserted that Congress would never appropriate money and then turn it over to the tribes to administer. Elmer Thomas, senator from Oklahoma, vigorously seconded Wheeler's objections. In the House hearings, too, a similar pattern developed. Although Collier pointed out that the votes taken by the tribes at the congresses and afterward showed fifty-four tribes (with a population of 141,881) in support of the bill and only twelve tribes (with 15,106 Indians) against it, a good many committee members were not impressed.[42]

Collier sought President Roosevelt's aid against the congressional opposition. Ickes and Secretary of Agriculture Wallace interceded with the president, who promised to give the legislation high priority. In letters to the chairmen of the Indian committees in Congress, April 28, 1934, Roosevelt called for an end to allotment and for the extension of self-government and political liberty to the Indians. The Wheeler-Howard bill, he said, would establish "a new standard of dealing between the Federal Govern-

41. The amendments were announced in Department of the Interior, Memorandum for the Press, April 15, 1934, OSI CCF 1–127, Press Notices. There is a summary of the amendments in *Indians at Work* 1 (April 15, 1934): 20–22, and the amendments themselves are printed in "Readjustment of Indian Affairs," pp. 195–99.
42. Philp, *John Collier's Crusade*, pp. 156–57. See the hearings cited in note 35.

ment and its wards" and was "a measure of justice that is long overdue."
Collier also took his plea to the public. In a radio address over the National
Broadcasting Company on May 7, 1934, he told the American people that
"the Indian wards of our Government, supported by President Roosevelt,
are pleading before Congress for a chance to live." And he pinned the responsibility on all citizens to support "this supreme effort of the Indians
and their friends to win for them freedom, to win for them the right to
continue to exist."[43]

Under pressure from many sides, the House committee redrafted the
entire bill along the lines of Collier's amendments and reported it back to
the House. Even this weakened version was further amended by the Senate—including exclusion of the Indians of Oklahoma from the law's provisions.[44] The heavily amended bill, a considerably shorter measure than the
original Wheeler-Howard bill, became law on June 18, 1934. Collier got
only half his cake, but it was far better than none and was in fact a substantial piece of legislation that ranked in importance with the laws of 1834
and the Dawes Act of 1887. And he was jubilant. "One becomes a little
breathless," he exclaimed, "when one realizes that the Allotment Law—
the agony and ruin of the Indians—has been repealed." He noted that any
one of the parts of the law alone would have been an important change in
government policy.[45]

The first sections dealt with land: further allotment was prohibited,
existing trust periods and restriction on alienation for Indian land were
indefinitely extended, remaining surplus lands could be restored to tribal
ownership by the secretary of the interior, individual allotments could
be voluntarily transferred to tribal ownership, and the secretary was
authorized to acquire additional lands for reservations (with an annual
appropriation not to exceed $2 million). Collier rejoiced in these provi-
sions, although they fell short of directing the consolidation of Indian
lands checkerboarded with white holdings by the allotment process. "The
allotment system with its train of evil consequences," he said, "was definitely abandoned as the backbone of the national Indian policy." And he
spoke of "economic rehabilitation," noting that "the policy of common
ownership of land enunciated in section 1 . . . is reaffirmed and implemented throughout the body of the statute."[46]

43. Roosevelt to Burton K. Wheeler, April 28, 1934, printed in *Senate Report* no.
1080, 73–2, serial 9770, pp. 3–4; transcript of address in Department of the Interior,
Memorandum for the Press, May 8, 1934, OSI CCF 1–127, Press Notices.
44. *Congressional Record*, 78: 11122–39, 11724–44, 12161–65; *Senate Report* no.
1080, 73–2, serial 9770; *House Report* no. 1804, 73–2, serial 9776. The Senate introduced a new amended bill (S. 3645), which was passed by the House also in lieu of H.R.
7902.
45. 48 *United States Statutes* 984–88; *Indians at Work* 1 (July 1, 1934): 1–2.
46. CIA Report, 1934, pp. 79–80.

The law granted any Indian tribe the right to organize for its common welfare and to adopt appropriate constitution and bylaws, to be ratified by a majority vote of adult members of the tribe. Such an organized tribe would have powers to employ legal counsel, to prevent the sale or other disposition of tribal assets, and to negotiate with federal, state, and local governments. Moreover, the secretary of the interior could issue a charter of incorporation to the tribe, so that it could manage its own property. The act authorized an appropriation of $250,000 a year to defray the expenses of organizing the tribes and chartering the corporations. A revolving fund of $10 million was provided, from which the secretary of the interior could make loans to the corporations to promote economic development. The law in addition authorized the preferential appointment of qualified Indians to positions in the Indian service without regard to civil service laws, and it provided an annual appropriation of $250,000 for loans to Indian students in vocational and trade schools. Collier saw these measures as "spiritual rehabilitation." They would help to destroy the Indians' inferiority complex brought about by fifty years of individualization and arbitrary supervision of their affairs, by which "the Indians have been robbed of initiative, their spirit has been broken, their health undermined, and their native pride ground into the dust."[47]

The law directed that the secretary of the interior make rules and regulations to operate Indian forests on the principle of sustained yield management, to restrict the number of livestock grazed on Indian ranges, and to prevent soil erosion and other deterioration of the ranges. It protected Indian claims or suits against the United States and declared that no expenditures under the act could be considered offsets against claims. The Indians of Oklahoma were excluded from the provisions of the act, and finally, the act directed that it would not apply to any reservation where a majority of the adult Indians, voting in a special election called by the secretary of the interior within a year after the approval of the act, voted to exclude themselves from its application. There was no provision at all for a special court of Indian affairs.

INDIAN ORGANIZATION

The Indian Office set out at once to put the act into operation. The first step was the referendums on the reservations by which the tribes voted to accept the act or to exclude themselves from its provisions. Collier realized that an educational campaign would be necessary on all the reservations, so that the Indians could appreciate the advantages that would come

47. Ibid., p. 82.

to them from the new legislation. This was not an easy job. Congress adjourned before it had appropriated the money authorized to organize the tribes, and Collier had to appeal to the men in the field for extra duty both in preparing the Indians and in helping him select first those reservations that were best informed and most favorably inclined toward the act.[48] Meetings were held with local superintendents, booklets of questions and answers about the act were prepared, and all possible steps were taken to make sure that the Indians would vote affirmatively. Many Indians were confused and still had in mind the provisions of the original bill, which had been discussed with them at length in the Indian congresses of March and April. Collier prepared a sixteen-page statement, in which he outlined the essential changes and described the final provisions. But the information was accompanied by a clear threat of what the results would be if a tribe voted to reject the measure.

> If they do this, they remain exactly as before the passage and approval of the Act. The tribe that rejects the Act does not have the trust period automatically extended; the tribe does not share in the land-purchase fund; its members cannot receive the new educational loans; they cannot receive exemption from the general civil service law; they cannot participate in the ten-million-dollar credit fund; they cannot incorporate under the terms of the Act; the Government can continue to do as it pleases with their tribal assets; they cannot share in the tribal-organization fund.

Collier insisted that rejecting the act would not mean rejection of the Indians by the federal government, and he asserted that there could be no discrimination against a tribe that voted against the act, but he added: "It will merely drift to the rear of the great advance open to the Indian race. It will stand still and will probably continue to lose its lands while those who accept the Act, its benefits and responsibilities can preserve and increase their lands and will move forward."[49]

The referendums moved forward in the fall of 1934, and Collier tallied up the results of each one, noting the tribes and the number of Indians they represented on each side. It was, by and large, a favorable vote. Within the two-year period from 1934 to 1936, in which votes were eventually allowed, 181 tribes (with a population of 129,750) accepted the law and 77

---

48. Collier to M. L. Burns, undated, OIA, Records of the Indian Organization Division, Correspondence with Officials, box 1.

49. Collier, "Facts about the New Indian Reorganization Act: An Explanation and Interpretation of the Wheeler-Howard Bill as Modified, Amended and Passed by Congress," undated, copy in OIA, Records concerning the Wheeler-Howard Act, part 8, box 7.

tribes (86,365 Indians) voted to reject it. Fourteen more groups came under the act because they did not hold elections to exclude themselves from its operation.[50] Yet Collier was not satisfied to accept without complaint the democratic vote that turned out to be less than unanimous approval of his program. The delay in getting the appropriations slowed his campaign to prepare the Indians, and he complained that the area leaders and superintendents had not been able to educate the Indians effectively. Then there was the work of opponents of the measure, who sent lawyers and other agents to the reservations to stress the controversial aspects of the original bill even though those sections had been eliminated in the final act. "At certain places," Collier charged, "there was a deliberate campaign to mislead the Indians as to the content of the actual legislation." He regretted having had no means to counteract such misinformation, and he was sorry that there was no provision by which those tribes who had voted against the act could be given a second opportunity to accept it.[51]

The heaviest blow was the rejection of the act by the Navajos, the largest of the Indian tribes, who made up about half of the Indians who voted against its application. Under the leadership of J. C. Morgan, there was continuing opposition to Collier and his whole program among large numbers of Navajos.[52] An especially sore point was the stock reduction program that Collier had instituted in an attempt to prevent the destruction of the Navajo range by overgrazing and resulting soil erosion. Collier was adamant on the need for reducing the number of sheep on the ranges, but his move appeared to many Indians to strike at their economic basis and well-being. Opponents of Collier were able to tie together stock reduction and the Indian Reorganization Act, and Collier complained: "The Navajo vote was largely controlled by the untrue statement, spread by word of mouth in the Navajo language, that upon the acceptance of the Act, immediately the sheep and goats of the tribe would be taken away." In his disappointment, Collier petulantly told the Navajos the mistake they had made. "Stock reduction, past or future, and the Indian Reorganization Act," declared, "have had and will have nothing to do with each other." He pointed out, item by item, the money that the Navajos would not get because they

50. Theodore H. Haas, *Ten Years of Tribal Government under I.R.A.*, Tribal Relations Pamphlets no. 1 (Chicago: United States Indian Service, 1947), p. 3. Table A, pp. 13–29, in this pamphlet provides a list of tribes and the action they took on the Indian Reorganization Act.

51. "Why the Indian Reorganization Act Was Rejected by a Number of Tribes," *Indians at Work* 2 (July 1, 1935): 44–45.

52. Donald L. Parman, *The Navajos and the New Deal* (New Haven: Yale University Press, 1976); Parman, "J. C. Morgan, Navajo Apostle of Assimilation," *Prologue* 4 (Summer 1972): 83–98.

had not approved the act. He noted the difficulties already facing the tribe and concluded: "Through rejecting the Reorganization Act, the tribe has made its task indefinitely [sic] harder, and has added grievously, even critically, to the handicaps under which it and its old and young people must labor."[53]

Collier moved ahead with the Navajo stock reduction program, setting up land management districts with the designated maximum carrying capacity for livestock. If cooperation between the Navajo tribal council and the federal agencies (the Indian Bureau and the Soil Conservation Service) did not bring the necessary results, the commissioner of Indian affairs was "to take such action as he may deem necessary to bring about such reduction or to establish such management plan in order to protect the interests of the Navajo people."[54]

The necessity of obtaining an absolute majority of the tribal adults, not simply a majority of those voting, in order for a tribe to exclude itself from the act brought a challenge from those who opposed the Collier program, for it meant that Indians who did not turn out to vote were in fact counted as voting for the act. Collier favored this interpretation because he did not believe that the Indians should be given an opportunity to escape the general application of the law. But he did not like the provision for the same absolute majority of all tribal adults in the voting to accept constitutions and charters, for it made the work of reorganization difficult. The result, after long hearings before a hostile subcommittee of the House Committee on Indian Affairs, chaired by Abe Murdock of Utah, was a compromise: a simple majority of those voting (provided at least 30 percent of eligible voters participated) would be sufficient both to reject the act and to approve constitutions and charters.[55]

The vote to accept the Indian Reorganization Act, however the majority was determined, by itself did no more than identify the tribes to which the

53. *Indians at Work* 2 (July 1, 1935): 45; "A Message to the Navajo People through the Superintendent from Commissioner Collier," June 21, 1935, copy in OIA, Office File of Commissioner Collier, Navajo Documents, box 8.

54. "Regulations Affecting the Carrying Capacity and Management of the Navajo Range," November 6, 1935, OIA, Office File of Collier, Navajo Documents, box 8. Parman, *Navajos and the New Deal*, treats the stock reduction program at great length. There is an enlightening discussion of stock reduction among the Navajos in Richard White, *The Roots of Dependency: Subsistence, Environment, and Social Change among the Choctaws, Pawnees, and Navajos* (Lincoln: University of Nebraska Press, 1983), chapters 10–13.

55. 49 *United States Statutes* 379; *Senate Report* no. 564, 74–1, serial 9879; *House Report* no. 865, 74–1, serial 9887; "Indian Conditions and Affairs," *Hearings before the Subcommittee on General Bills of the Committee on Indian Affairs, House of Representatives, 74th Congress, 1st Session, on H.R. 7781 and Other Matters* (1935).

legislation would be applied. The next step was to organize the tribes, for their economic development as well as their self-government depended upon the drawing up of constitutions, bylaws, and corporate charters. In March 1935 Collier sent a circular to those tribes that had expressed an interest in tribal organization under the new law and an outline for a tribal constitution and bylaws that indicated the points to be included. It was clear, however, that many tribes had not the slightest idea of what was involved in the process, and to direct this basic work Collier set up an Indian Organization Division within the bureau. Field representatives, field agents, and men on special detail were appointed to work with the superintendents and the Indian tribal leaders in drafting and preparing the documents, and a "systematic educational campaign" was initiated to inform the Indians and to prepare them to vote intelligently on the acceptance of the documents.[56] Collier impressed upon the fieldworkers the significance of what was being done.

> We are establishing a new kind of relationship between the Indians and government service: the relation of active, responsible and authoritative partnership. All these many new enterprises first and last are meant to bring the Indians into group self-help and into wisely used power. The flood of detail of the new enterprises and of the established enterprises must not be permitted to smother this first, last and supreme duty: partnership with the Indians here and now; and above all, partnership in the making of the plans which will fix the future mold of Indian service and largely of Indian life.[57]

Collier was enthusiastic about tribal organization and what enduring effects it would have on the Indians. The experience alone had great benefits, he thought, and his optimism blinded him to fundamental problems in the whole business. He wrote to Secretary Ickes in November 1935 from the Cheyenne River Agency about how encouraged he was by his visit to the Sioux. "Two things are clear," he said. "One of them is that the Sioux Indians are getting a fundamental political and economic education through the process of working out their constitutions. It genuinely is a mass participation, and I doubt whether any white community in our lifetime has struggled with political questions as fundamental as those which the In-

---

56. Circular letter, Collier to superintendents, tribal councils, and individual Indians, March 6, 1935, OIA, Records concerning the Wheeler-Howard Act, box 8; "Outline of Tribal Constitution and Bylaws," ibid., part 8, box 7; "To Members of Tribal Councils, Indians, Reservation Superintendents, Employees, and Others Interested in Indian Reorganization," *Indians at Work* 2 (July 1, 1935): 6–9.

57. *Indians at Work* 2 (June 1, 1935): 1–2.

dians are now meeting, and they are bringing a real wisdom to bear. My other good impression is that the Superintendents and Service employees at large are genuinely and even intensely working in the direction of the new program."[58]

The work was slow and difficult; but within ten years, ninety-three tribes, bands, and Indian communities had adopted constitutions and by-laws and seventy-three were granted charters. This was far from total acceptance of Collier's dream, but a new period in Indian relations with the government had begun, and the tribal councils became the basis for later developments in tribal autonomy.[59]

58. Collier to Ickes, November 23, 1935, OSI, Office File of Harold Ickes, Miscellaneous, part 1, box 5.

59. Haas, *Ten Years of Tribal Government*, p. 3; tables B, C, and D, pp. 21–34, give data as of October 1946 on tribes operating under constitutions approved in accordance with the Indian Reorganization Act, the Oklahoma Indian Welfare Act, and the Alaska Reorganization Act; tribes and bands which approved the IRA but operated under constitutions approved prior to that act; and other groups, not under the IRA, which operated under constitutions. For comparable listings, circa 1970, see Theodore W. Taylor, *The States and Their Indian Citizens* (Washington: Bureau of Indian Affairs, 1972), appendix K, "Federally Recognized Tribes," pp. 233–45. A compilation of the documents is George E. Fay, comp., *Charters, Constitutions, and By-Laws of the Indian Tribes of North America*, Occasional Publications in Anthropology, Ethnology Series, 19 vols. (Greeley, Colorado: University of Northern Colorado, Museum of Anthropology, 1967–). Many of the documents appear in microfiche in *Pamphlets in American History*, Indian series (Sanford, North Carolina: Microfilming Corporation of America).

CHAPTER 38

Rounding Out
the New Deal

Extending the Indian Reorganization Act.

Indian Arts and Crafts. Continuing

Educational Reform. Health Programs.

Economic Development.

The Bureaucracy.

The Indian Reorganization Act, even though it was a weakened version of what John Collier had originally proposed, was the heart of New Deal Indian reform. The principles on which it was based—appreciation for Indian culture, concern for Indian self-determination and self-government, and a movement toward tribal economic activity—suffused all of what the Collier administration attempted and what it accomplished.

EXTENDING THE INDIAN REORGANIZATION ACT

To Collier's dismay, large groups of Indians lay outside the full benefits of the Indian Reorganization Act. Although the act did not apply to any territories, colonies, or insular possessions of the United States, the Territory of Alaska was specifically included under the sections that provided various funds for Indian benefit, preferential hiring of Indians, and adoption of constitutions and bylaws. By oversight, however, section 17, which authorized the incorporation of tribes, was omitted from the list of sections applicable to Alaska Natives, and without incorporation the credit facilities of the act were not available to them. A remedy was provided on May 1, 1936, by the Alaska Reorganization Act, which extended the rest of the Indian Reorganization Act to Alaska, excepting only four sections that related to tribal lands and reservations and were largely inapplicable to the territory. Moreover, acknowledging the unique characteristics of Alaskan native life, Congress in the new law authorized adoption of constitutions and bylaws, incorporation, and credit loans for "groups of Indians in Alaska not heretofore recognized as bands or tribes but having a common bond of occupation, or association, or residence within a well-defined neighborhood, community or rural district." Collier saw in the law a remedy for the problems of the Alaska Natives, "who in the past have seen their land rights almost universally disregarded, their fishing rights increasingly invaded, and their economic situation grow each year more desperate." There was little debate over the measure, since it was basically an amendment to the earlier law that corrected an unintentional omission.[1]

There were special complications, however, in organizing the Alaska Natives. Their villages were widely separated and transportation between them was difficult and expensive, and as Collier noted, unlike tribes in the United States, they did not "fall into well-defined tribal groups occupying definite geographical areas and having a tradition of tribal organization and background of governmental recognition." He noted too that the status of land ownership was ambiguous and would often have to be clarified before organization could begin.[2] Yet by February 1941 thirty-eight native groups in Alaska had adopted constitutions and received charters, and by the end of the New Deal period forty-nine were so established. The Alaska Reorganization Act also authorized the secretary of the interior to designate reservations for the Alaska Natives, with the approval of the residents by secret ballot. Six small reservations were thus created, but in other instances local opposition frustrated the attempts to secure the natives' property rights by this means.[3]

To bring the Indians of Oklahoma under the Indian New Deal umbrella was a much more difficult problem than caring for the Alaska Natives, and Collier walked a rocky road in his relations with them. The Oklahoma Indians had not supported Collier for commissioner in 1933, and Senator

1. 49 *United States Statutes* 1250–51; CIA Report, 1936, p. 163; *Senate Report* nos. 1748 and 1908, 74–2, serial 9988; *House Report* no. 2244, 74–2, serial 9992. There is useful discussion of the measure in Felix S. Cohen, *Handbook of Federal Indian Law* (Washington: GPO, 1942), pp. 413–15; and in John Leiper Freeman, Jr., "The New Deal for Indians: A Study in Bureau-Committee Relations in American Government" (Ph.D. dissertation, Princeton University, 1952), pp. 302–5.

2. CIA Report, 1937, pp. 200–201.

3. Lists of groups adopting constitutions and charters are given in Cohen, *Federal Indian Law*, p. 414, and Theodore H. Haas, *Ten Years of Tribal Government under I.R.A.* (Chicago: United States Indian Service, 1947), pp. 29–30. The reservations established are noted in CIA Report, 1944, p. 239.

Elmer Thomas and other members of the Oklahoma delegation in Congress (especially W. W. Hastings, a Cherokee member of the House) were among Collier's strong opponents. When the new commissioner toured the Indian regions in March 1934 to explain the Wheeler-Howard bill, he faced strong opposition at the three congresses held in Oklahoma, for many allotted Indians did not want to return to a condition of tribal ownership and segregation from the white community. Most support of Collier's plans came from the tribes in western Oklahoma, for the Five Civilized Tribes in the eastern part of the state seemed too deeply integrated into white society to be concerned about tribal reorganization. It is likely, however, that Collier generated enough support so that the Oklahoma Indians as a whole would not have fought the amended bill that finally became law in June 1934; but Senator Thomas, without consulting the Indians of his state, managed to exclude them from the basic sections of the final act. He later justified his action in this way: "The Wheeler-Howard bill was evidently prepared having in view the large Indian reservations located in the western and southwestern States. The Oklahoma Indians having made progress beyond the reservation plan, it was thought best not to encourage a return to reservation life."[4]

Collier considered the Oklahoma tribes "penalized" and deeply regretted that they did not come under the law. "Through this exclusion," he pointed out, "the Oklahoma Indians lose the benefits of Section 2, which automatically extends the protective trust period on all restricted land; no new reservations can be established in Oklahoma; Oklahoma tribes can not organize under the new act, nor can they form tribal corporations. Because they are denied the incorporation privilege, they cannot receive loans from the revolving credit fund, which loans can be made only to tribal corporations." Yet Collier did not give up, and he hoped that Congress would enact legislation to bring the benefits of his reorganization policy to the Oklahoma Indians. In July and August he wrote a series of explanatory articles in an Oklahoma newspaper, and many of the Indians began to see the advantages that the Indian Reorganization Act would have for them. Then in October Senator Thomas and Collier toured Oklahoma and held a series of conferences with the Indians to get their views and to propose the New Deal programs. The meetings were often a debate between Collier, who extolled the advantages of the Indian Reorganization Act, and Thomas, who criticized the law, but they also brought forward a variety of Indian opinions, and in the end it was clear that existing legislation was not satisfactory for Oklahoma. Some law was needed to allow for land ac-

4. *Senate Report* no. 1232, 74–1, serial 9989, p. 6.

quisition and credit, for tribal incorporation, and for better safeguards to protect the Indians from white encroachment.[5]

Early in 1935 Collier, with Senator Thomas and Representative Will Rogers, the Oklahomans who now chaired the Senate and House committees on Indian affairs, drew up a bill to fit the Oklahoma tribes. It made a division between Indians of one-half Indian blood or more, whose property would be held in trust, and those of less Indian blood, for whom restrictions would be rapidly removed. To decide the competency of this latter group, special competency commissions would be established. The first class of Indians was placed under federal guardianship in regard to wills, determination of heirship, and administration of property. Voluntary organization of the tribes was permitted, corporate bodies could draw on the credit funds of the Wheeler-Howard Act, and the secretary of the interior could acquire restricted lands to form new reservations. The bill also promised adequate health services and educational facilities for the Oklahoma Indians. Secretary Ickes expressed his "wholehearted accord" with the measure because he believed it endeavored "to remove certain inequalities arising from historical causes, which at present bar the assumption by the Federal Government of generous responsibilities for the welfare of all the Indians of all Oklahoma."[6]

The history of the Thomas-Rogers bill was a reenactment on a smaller scale of the bitter fight over the original Wheeler-Howard bill. Both Indians and whites attacked the bill in the committee hearings, and in the face of the objections Thomas drafted a new measure, which was passed by the Senate on August 16, 1935. Congress adjourned before the House could consider the bill, and in the interval before the new session opened renewed attacks were made by radical opponents of Collier, who charged that the goal of the bill was to establish communism in the United States, and by lobbyists for special interests in Oklahoma. Finally the Senate version was amended by the House, and in this considerably modified and weakened version, the Oklahoma Indian Welfare Act became law on June 26, 1936.[7]

---

5. CIA Report, 1934, p. 83. For discussion of the Oklahoma Indian Welfare Act, see Peter M. Wright, "John Collier and the Oklahoma Indian Welfare Act of 1936," *Chronicles of Oklahoma* 50 (Autumn 1972): 347–71; Angie Debo, *And Still the Waters Run* (Princeton: Princeton University Press, 1940), pp. 370–73. A summary of the conferences with the Oklahoma Indians is given in Kenneth R. Philp, *John Collier's Crusade for Indian Reform, 1920–1954* (Tucson: University of Arizona Press, 1977), pp. 177–79.

6. Ickes to Elmer Thomas, February 23, 1935, printed in "To Promote the General Welfare of the Indians of Oklahoma," *Hearings before the Committee on Indian Affairs, United States Senate, 74th Congress, 1st Session, on S. 2047* (1935), p. 8. The original bill is printed ibid., pp. 1–8.

7. "To Promote the General Welfare of the Indians of Oklahoma," *Hearings before*

The law had none of the protective measures of the original bill; it made no provision for continuing restrictions on Indian property and left heirship and probate matters in the hands of the state courts. But it did enable the Oklahoma Indians (except the Osages, who were excluded from the act) to participate in self-government, corporate organization, credit, and land purchase provisions similar to those of the Indian Reorganization Act. Moreover, any ten or more Indians residing "in convenient proximity to each other" could be granted a charter as a local cooperative association and draw upon a special loan fund of $2 million. A considerable number of Oklahoma tribes took advantage of the act to adopt constitutions and charters. These differed in some respects, however, from those of Indians in other states, for the constitutions were restricted to such elements as tribal membership and tribal organization, whereas substantive powers of government were set forth in the charters. None of the documents provided for the broad police and judicial powers that were part of many other tribal constitutions.[8]

INDIAN ARTS AND CRAFTS

A distinct legislative victory for Collier's Indian New Deal was the passage of the Indian Arts and Crafts Act of 1935. The promotion of a marketing scheme for Indian products had long been one of Collier's goals, and the defeat of the Frazier-Leavitt bill of 1930 was only a temporary setback. When the new administration began, immediate steps were taken to combat the deleterious effects of the depressed economic condition on the production and sale of handcrafted articles. With a view toward educating the public about Indian art and stimulating sales, small exhibits of Indian work were set up at the Chicago World's Fair in 1933 and at Atlanta, Georgia, and an exhibit room and sales office for Indian arts and crafts were opened in the Interior Department. Within the Public Works of Art Project of the Civil Works Administration, Indian artists were employed to paint murals and to make rugs, pottery, and other artwork for new Indian schools, hospitals, and community centers that were constructed under the program of the Public Works Administration. Collier's daughter-in-law, Nina

---

the Committee on Indian Affairs, United States Senate, 74th Congress, 1st Session, on *S. 2047* (1935); ibid., 74th Congress, 2d Session (1936); "To Promote the General Welfare of the Indians of Oklahoma," *Hearings before the Committee on Indian Affairs, House of Representatives, 74th Congress, 1st Session, on H.R. 6234* (1935); ibid., 74th Congress, 2d Session, on *S. 2047* (1936); *Senate Report* no. 1232, 74–1, serial 9880; *House Report* no. 2408, 74–2, serial 9993; 49 *United States Statutes* 1967–68. The legislative history of the measure is discussed in Wright, "John Collier and the Oklahoma Indian Welfare Act," pp. 368–70, and Freeman, "The New Deal for Indians," pp. 278–301.

8. Haas, *Ten Years of Tribal Government*, p. 28; Cohen, *Federal Indian Law*, p. 455.

Collier, drew up extensive plans for an Indian art project that would employ Indian artists who were out of work, and she promoted a display of Indian art at Macy's in New York City. Meanwhile, Secretary Ickes, in an attempt to safeguard Indian craftsmen from competition from machine-made imitations, ordered the national parks to sell nothing but authentic Indian craftwork (despite the fact that there were no standards to determine what was genuine and what imitation).[9]

Such halfway measures did not satisfy Collier, who stressed the need to develop Indian crafts as part of a successful economic policy for the Indians, which would be the underpinning of cultural preservation. The depression made this need all the more urgent. He turned again to James Young, who was persuaded to head a Committee on Indian Arts and Crafts, which was "to study and make recommendations concerning the whole problem of Indian arts and crafts, in their relation to the economic and cultural welfare of the American Indian." The committee, after meeting in March and August 1934, submitted a report in September.[10]

The report was a balanced evaluation of the arts and crafts situation and was alert to both cultural and economic aspects, but it asserted that "in the economic one lies the real heart of the problem." It found that the products were no longer made primarily for the Indians' own use but were created for a market that would bring to the Indians a cash income to supplement the subsistence obtained from the land. The problem posed by the report was fundamental: "How can the economic welfare of the Indians be advanced by the Government, in cooperation with the Indians through arts and crafts, without loss to the vitality of Indian art, and without danger to the integrity of Indian life?" Could increased and more effective production and a change of products to those that might be more marketable be accomplished without radically changing the essential Indian character of the products? The committee asserted that the "key to a materially wider market and materially increased income for the Indian arts and crafts lies . . . in an improved production—through improved production processes,

---

9. Robert F. Schrader, *The Indian Arts and Crafts Board: An Aspect of New Deal Indian Policy* (Albuquerque: University of New Mexico Press, 1983), pp. 77–89. *Indians at Work* followed the developments in arts and crafts; see, for example, 1 (April 1, 1934): 37–38; (June 1, 1934): 4–10; (July 1, 1934): 29–30; 2 (February 1, 1935): 31–32; (February 15, 1935): 39–40.

10. Department of the Interior, Memorandum for the Press, January 11, 1934, OSI CCF 5–3, Indian Office, Indian Art; "Report of the Committee on Indian Arts and Crafts," September 1934, Records of the Indian Arts and Crafts Board, box 4, National Archives, Record Group 435, also printed in *Senate Report* no. 900, 74–1, serial 9879, pp. 5–12. Schrader, *Indian Arts and Crafts Board*, pp. 90–104, discusses the committee and its report.

through better products, and through better adaptation of products to American usage." But it cautioned that any action taken should meet three criteria: it should not be detrimental to Indian life, it should not change the essential handcrafted character of the product, and it should not lower the artistic standards. To bring all this about, the committee recommended the formation of a government agency to undertake market research, provide technical assistance, coordinate the activities of private and government agencies concerned, supply management personnel, create government marks of genuineness, and establish standards of quality. But the committee did not want the agency itself to become a trader in Indian goods.

On March 6, 1935, a bill was introduced in the House and on March 8 one in the Senate "to promote the development of Indian arts and crafts and to create a board to assist therein." The measure varied little from the recommendations of the Young committee, and despite vigorous opposition from traders and from members of the House who feared an increase in bureaucracy, the bill became law on August 27, 1935. The law created an Indian Arts and Crafts Board of five members appointed by the secretary of the interior. In order to promote Indian arts and crafts and expand the market for the products, the board was empowered to undertake market research and technical research, to correlate the activities of various interested agencies, both private and public, to assist the management of specific projects, to create government trademarks of genuineness and standards of quality, and to employ a general manager and other personnel. Finally, it provided fines and imprisonment for persons selling counterfeit goods.[11]

It was no easy matter to get suitable members for the board, and Collier himself finally assumed the position of chairman. Congress, moreover, was reluctant to appropriate adequate funds to enable the board to begin its work. Not until René d'Harnoncourt was appointed assistant to Louis C. West (the first general manager) on September 11, 1936, and then general manager himself on June 15, 1937, did the work of the board really get under way. D'Harnoncourt, born in Vienna, Austria, in 1901, had gained experience with native arts in Mexico. He proved to be an extremely able promoter of the arts and an effective manager of the Arts and Crafts Board. He chose talented staff members and soon caught the enthusiastic atten-

11. The Senate bill (S. 2203) introduced by Senator Thomas was accepted by the House in lieu of its own bill (H.R. 6468), introduced by Representative Will Rogers. *Congressional Record,* 79: 3066, 3180, 9402, 11961–62, 14030; 49 *United States Statutes* 891–93. See also *Senate Report* no. 900, 74–1, serial 9879, and *House Report* no. 973, 74–1, serial 9887.

tion of the public with remarkable displays of Indian art at the San Francisco Golden Gate International Exposition of 1939 and at the Museum of Modern Art in New York City in 1941. Meanwhile, the board worked to establish standards for Navajo weaving, silver and turquoise jewelry, and other products, to survey Indian arts and crafts production and possibilities, and to organize production and marketing units among various groups of Indians, from a wool spinning project among the Choctaws to wood carving among the Alaska Natives and leather glove making among the Coeur d'Alenes.[12]

As Collier encountered increasing opposition in Congress to his Indian program, resistance to appropriations for the Arts and Crafts Board hindered development of its work and at times threatened its very existence. There was strong objection, notably, to d'Harnoncourt and his foreign birth (he spoke almost flawless English, but with a German accent) and to his high salary. Year by year Collier had to fight in the hearings on appropriation bills to maintain the essential work of the board. Then the war, which brought a large exodus from reservations, cut seriously into handicraft production, even though demand was heightened by the cutting off of foreign products and the purchases by United States servicemen in Indian areas. The move of the Indian Office to Chicago further disrupted the board's work. In January 1944 d'Harnoncourt resigned as general manager, although he replaced Collier as unsalaried chairman of the board.[13]

The Indian Arts and Crafts Board was a notable example of Collier's New Deal policy. It stressed economic advance for the tribes and a recognition and preservation of their artistic heritage—both with strong government encouragement and management. Congressional opposition to the board was in large part opposition to Collier and d'Harnoncourt and did not reflect a fundamental attack on the principles behind the board's work. Indian arts and crafts obtained a solid and continuing acceptance by government officials and, more important, by the general public, in considerable measure because of the work of the board. After World War II, with the departure of Collier and d'Harnoncourt, the work of the board expanded, as did congressional support.

---

12. Schrader, *Indian Arts and Crafts Board*, pp. 105–241. A year-by-year account of the board's activities and the views of d'Harnoncourt are given in "Indian Department Appropriation Bill for 1943," *Hearings before a Subcommittee of the Committee on Appropriations, United States Senate, 77th Congress, 2d Session, on H.R. 6845* (1942), pp. 695–99, 706–10. See also René d'Harnoncourt, "Indian Arts and Crafts and Their Place in the Modern World," in Oliver La Farge, ed., *The Changing Indian* (Norman: University of Oklahoma Press, 1942), pp. 144–57.

13. Schrader, *Indian Arts and Crafts Board*, pp. 242–98.

CONTINUING EDUCATIONAL REFORM

Education was basic to Collier's Indian New Deal, even though the Wheeler-Howard Act did not directly touch Indian education, except for its support of special vocational training for Indians. There was, however, no dramatic change in educational policy or programs when Collier entered office, for the administration of Rhoads and Scattergood had already started on the road that Collier would follow. From his appointment by Rhoads in 1930 until his resignation in 1935, W. Carson Ryan worked toward continuity in the field of education. The principles of progressive education that he followed were carried on—although perhaps in more intensive form— by his successor. How well Ryan fitted in with Collier's overall philosophy of Indian administration can be seen in an address he gave in late 1935.

> Behind the present program of Indian administration in the United States, and particularly Indian education, there is an assumption that is new with us and I believe is still relatively infrequent in the administration of native affairs generally—namely, that native life itself has values that urgently need to be maintained. The customary assumption of white superiority is abandoned in the new program, so far as it is humanly possible to do it. It is assumed that in all efforts carried on by the Government or other outside interests in behalf of Indians the purpose is to be helpful while interfering as little as possible with existing modes of life. Indian ways of doing things are considered to be right except as they are found, by the experience of members of the tribe or others unselfishly interested in their welfare, to be positively detrimental to the Indians or harmful to the rights of others. . . .
>
> Nothing in this program is intended, of course, to prevent Indians from utilizing as much of modern methods as they care to adopt. . . . in a word . . . to help Indians to see that they need not—and should not—surrender all that they have in order to be "modern"; but that they have rather, an unusual opportunity to combine such advantages as there are in modern civilization with the special advantages of their own culture.[14]

Although education was a major element in Collier's Indian policy, there were no legislative enactments by which one can mark change or development. The work of the schools depended upon administrative direction from the Office of Indian Affairs. It was, of course, greatly affected by

14. *Indians at Work* 3 (October 15, 1935): 36.

the quality of the persons in the field who implemented official policy and by the appropriations of Congress for education. The latter was a particularly serious limitation, for the depression years brought severe cuts in the Indian Office budget. From a total appropriation for fiscal year 1933 of $22,140,000, of which $9,771,000 was for education, the funds fell to $19,156,064 in 1935, of which $7,900,000 was for the schools.[15] Fortunately, in this crucial period of New Deal activity, Collier was able to draw on other funds to develop educational programs. The CCC–Indian Division was an important educational activity, and under the PWA numerous school buildings were constructed, fulfilling a longtime need.

The most important force in the New Deal education program was Willard W. Beatty, who replaced Ryan early in 1936. Whereas Ryan had been a cautious man, planning carefully before acting, Beatty was a dynamic and forceful personality. Born in 1891 and raised in Berkeley, California, by 1936 Beatty had become a national leader in progressive education. By establishing model progressive schools in Winnetka, Illinois, and Bronxville, New York, he was in the forefront of the movement, and from 1933 to 1937 he was president of the Progressive Education Association. When he took office, *Time* remarked: "The titular leader of U.S. Progressive Education settled himself in the Bureau of Indian Affairs in Washington last week and prepared to dispense the blessings of his faith to 81,000 young Amerindians. . . . His appointment as Director of Indian Education indicated a new attempt to develop some sort of education to which Indians will respond."[16] It was a huge undertaking, of course, but Beatty went to work with tremendous zeal and energy.

He continued the progressive education ideas of Ryan—a program of cross-cultural education in which the curriculum and methods were to be adapted to the Indians and their environment and in which the children could develop according to their individual interests and abilities. In this he had the assistance and encouragement of the anthropologists whom Collier recruited for his staff. The anthropologists seemed to work better with the Education Division than they did with the bureau's administrators in general, for despite some tensions and disagreements the scientists were an important force in the educational development of the period.[17]

The major policies that concerned Indian educational leaders were less

15. CIA Report, 1938, p. 263.

16. *Time* 27 (February 10, 1936): 36. For Beatty and his work, see Margaret Szasz, *Education and the American Indian: The Road to Self-Determination, 1928–1973* (Albuquerque: University of New Mexico Press, 1974), pp. 37–122. A brief summary of education policy and activities is Margaret Szasz, "Thirty Years Too Soon: Indian Education under the Indian New Deal," *Integrated Education* 13 (July–August 1975): 3–9.

17. An excellent statement is H. Scudder Mekeel, "An Anthropologist's Observations on Indian Education," *Progressive Education* 13 (March 1936): 151–59.

innovations than they were a new emphasis on policies introduced earlier, and Collier noted three major tasks in education: "(a) improving existing schools; (b) reducing and eliminating Indian boarding schools and transferring Indian children back to their own homes; (c) developing day schools that will work with adults as well as children and become real centers for Indian community life."[18]

The boarding schools, the symbol of the old ways with their separation of the Indian children from home and community and their emphasis on training for the white man's world, were attacked by Collier as they had been by Jones and Leupp and all their successors. The commissioner pointed out that between 1928 and 1933 twelve boarding schools had been closed, whereas in his first year in office ten had been either closed or turned into community schools. The 22,000 children in attendance at the boarding schools at the end of the 1932 school year had been reduced to 17,500 for 1933–1934; and for the new year, Congress appropriated funds for only 13,000. "This decrease of 9,000 in 2 years," Collier declared, "means that the decline of the boarding school as the dominant factor in the education of Indian children is at last an accomplished fact." But the downward trend leveled off, and in 1941 there were still forty-nine boarding schools and about 14,500 Indians attending them.[19]

The correlative of abolishing boarding schools was the establishment of community day schools, and here there was substantial progress. Between 1933 and 1941 the number of day schools rose from 132 to 226, and in 1941 the enrollment was 15,789.[20] A great increase in the number of day schools came with construction under PWA, and Ryan, Beatty, and Collier all put heavy emphasis on this element in Indian education. "The foundation stone . . . of the new educational policy," Beatty declared when he took office, "has been the establishment of community day schools in which we have undertaken to educate the Indian child in the home community, wherein he remains an active member of his family group. The community day school has undertaken to be something more than the usual American public school. It recognized that in introducing new ideas and new experiences to its pupils in order to adapt them more successfully to their necessary contacts with white society and white economic practices it is necessary for the adults of the community to understand and sympathize with the experiences to which the young people are being exposed."[21] Collier, for his part, when the new PWA schools were being built,

18. CIA Report, 1933, pp. 68, 72; CIA Report, 1934, p. 84.
19. CIA Report, 1934, p. 84; CIA Report, 1941, pp. 514–16.
20. CIA Report, 1941, p. 415.
21. Willard W. Beatty, "Planning Indian Education in Terms of Pupil and Community Needs," *Indians at Work* 4 (September 1, 1936): 5–7. Beatty described the community

set forth the clear rationale behind their function in his directions to the architects:

    1. The schools are to be community schools of the activity type, for the use of all members of the community, adults as well as children, and the buildings should be adapted to local needs rather than conform to any conventional school plans. The simplest possible construction should be used, with local materials and Indian labor, not only for the usual reasons inherent in the Public Works program, but as part of the Indian participation in school and community work.

    2. Even the smallest schools are to have a varied program. They are to be "one-teacher" rather than one-room schools—that is, there should be, in addition to the main "classroom," space for workshop, library, school lunch, washing (frequently for community washing and laundering as well as for children's use), and other needs that will develop for both pupils and community.

    3. In schools larger than one-teacher schools there should be abundant space for shopwork, crafts, science, agriculture, music, home economics, library, play and assembly facilities, and such other school and community activities as are indicated in the detailed set-up for each school. A general community meeting place is to be assumed regardless of the size of the school.[22]

Changes occurred in the regimen of the boarding schools that remained. They became less like military institutions, for the restrictions on the lives of the students were relaxed, and Collier and Ickes insisted that "corporal punishment, and stupid, humiliating punishments of boys and girls" would not be tolerated.[23] Yet much of the student labor that had caught the critical eye of reformers in previous times continued, often out of necessity during the depression years and as a patriotic duty during World War II. The industrial training of the schools was shifted in some degree from urban to rural job training, for the latter provided a link between the schools and the life at home that the student would be expected to live after finishing school, and it was realized that urban centers during the depression were not likely to furnish jobs for Indian workers. Serious attempts were made, too, to include instruction in Indian arts and crafts and other aspects of Indian culture. Bilingual education made little headway, however, for it

---

day schools in "Uncle Sam Develops a New Kind of Rural School," *Elementary School Journal* 41 (November 1940): 185–94.

    22. Printed in CIA Report, 1934, p. 86.

    23. Ickes to superintendents, principals, and teachers in the Indian service, August 16, 1934, and Collier to all field supervisors of education, August 22, 1934, printed in *Indians at Work* 2 (September 1, 1934): 5–6.

faced the almost insurmountable obstacles of lack of trained instructors and of bilingual books, to say nothing of the traditional disdain for Indian languages within the Indian service. Beatty made some beginning steps with Sioux, Navajo, and Pueblo texts, and he initiated training courses for bilingual teachers, but these promising beginnings had to be curtailed when the war came. And there was no real success—as perhaps none was possible in so short a period—in providing an integrated cross-cultural education for Indian children in the boarding schools. The day schools, tied as they were to home and community, worked better, but here too there was generally far less than total success.[24]

Both Ryan and Beatty realized that the key to the kind of education they sought for the Indians was teachers and other school personnel, and they promoted in-service training for these persons. Beatty was especially zealous in the matter, and he reinvigorated the old idea of summer institutes, with intensive sessions to make the teachers aware of Indian cultures, to train them in the special methods needed to teach Indian children, and to indoctrinate them as well in the principles and ideals of progressive education. In order to carry on this educative work throughout the year, he began in 1936 a bimonthly bulletin for Indian service teachers called *Indian Education*, which he filled with his own views and with professional articles on theories of education and practical advice on particular problems.[25]

While the Indian Office worked to fulfill its objectives in the federal boarding schools and day schools, it continued to promote the enrollment of Indian children in the state public schools. Federal-state cooperation had been a major concern of Ryan, and Beatty moved in the same direction. The Johnson-O'Malley Act of 1934 laid the legislative groundwork for contracts between the federal government and the states for the education of Indians, and before World War II contracts were signed with four states: California (1934), Washington (1935), Minnesota (1937), and Arizona (1938). These states presented a wide variety of conditions, but in all of them to some extent there were fundamental problems. The states had

---

24. Szasz, *Education and the American Indian*, pp. 64–75. A report on Indian schools made for the Advisory Committee on Education in 1938 reported: "The objective is no longer merely personal improvement or intellectual discipline; it is distinctly social in purpose. Inspired by this objective, the schools for Indians have taken on renewed life and significance both for the Indians and for the leaders directing their activities. The day schools appear to be functioning as community centers of education and social regeneration to a degree never before realized in Indian administration." Lloyd E. Blauch, *Educational Service for Indians* (Washington: GPO, 1939), p. 131.

25. Szasz, *Education and the American Indian*, pp. 81–88. A representative selection of articles from the newsletter was reprinted in Willard W. Beatty and associates, *Education for Action: Selected Articles from Indian Education, 1936–43* (Washington: Education Division, United States Indian Service, 1944).

educational bureaucracies of their own, which clashed from time to time
with the educators of the Indian Office. The federal administrators felt that
they knew the Indians and the type of schooling they should get, whereas
the state systems were intent on maintaining their autonomy. Moreover,
Beatty and his staff, as they moved toward special education for the Indians, began to have doubts about how well the public schools could supply the curriculum that was deemed essential for Indian students and
whether the attitudes toward Indians were conducive to good learning.
The bureau had little means to correct the faults detected in the public
school systems, and it came to regard its own schools as superior. Although Beatty admitted that he probably had transferred more children
from federal schools to the public schools than had any other official, he
questioned the wisdom of pushing the policy too far. "I am convinced," he
wrote, "that there is nothing in the administration and curriculum of the
average rural public school that is better for children than what is offered
by a Federal school." And he claimed that teachers in the Indian service
were better trained than those in many small rural public schools and that
they were more carefully supervised. Many Indian parents, too, preferred
the government schools, because they supplied lunches and clothing for
the children. Thus, like other New Deal policies, the move to pass educative responsibility to the states was in many respects unsatisfactory and
unsuccessful. The Education Division could not implement its progressive
ideas in the public schools, where ill-trained teachers and unsympathetic
attitudes toward the Indians were the rule.[26]

In 1938, when the educational policies of the Collier administration
were in place, the enrollment figures in the various types of schools were
as shown in Table 12.

A special educational task of the Office of Indian Affairs was the administration of schools in the Territory of Alaska. From 1884 to 1931 those
schools had been the responsibility of the United States Office of Education but on March 16, 1931, they were transferred to the Indian Office. The
Alaska schools were community schools in a full sense, for the teachers
were social workers, medical aides, economic advisers, and recreational directors. In 1938 there were ninety-eight government day schools in Alaska
with an enrollment of 4,417 pupils. Nearly three-fourths of these were
one-teacher schools. There was trend, however, toward enrollment of native children in the territorial schools, and by 1938 about one-third of the
students in these schools were natives.[27]

26. Szasz, *Education and the American Indian*, pp. 89–105; Willard W. Beatty,
"Twenty Years of Indian Education," in David A. Baerreis, ed., *The Indian in Modern
America* (Madison: State Historical Society of Wisconsin, 1956), pp. 45–46.
27. Blauch, *Educational Service for Indians*, pp. 107–28. See also Lloyd E. Blauch,

TABLE 12: Schools, Teachers, and Indian Pupils, 1938

Type of School	Number of Schools	Number of Teachers	Number of Pupils
Federal government			
Nonreservation boarding	18	253	5,412
Reservation boarding	27	298	4,769
Community day	211	479	13,797
Sanatoriums	6	8	433
Total	262	1,038	24,411
Mission, private, and state			
Boarding			4,936
Day			2,039
Total			6,975
Public and special			
Public			33,645
Special			135
			33,780
Total pupils			65,166

SOURCE: Lloyd E. Blauch, *Educational Service for Indians* (Washington: GPO, 1939), p. 49.

The war exerted a powerful influence on Indian education. The war budget dramatically cut back the appropriations for the Indian service; many of the teachers and other school employees left the Indian schools for military service or more lucrative war jobs; and thousands of Indians left school to fight or to work in industry. The war, in fact, was a great dividing line. It brought many Indians into close contact with white society for the first time and impressed upon them the need of education, which they demanded for themselves and for their children at the end of the war. And, as employment opportunities shifted during the war and postwar years, Indian schools, still under Beatty's direction, changed their emphasis from cross-cultural education and vocational training to suit the Indians' rural community needs to training young Indians for urban society and assimilation into the mainstream.[28]

Public Education in the Territories and Outlying Possessions (Washington: GPO, 1939), pp. 18–52; Katherine M. Cook, *Public Education in Alaska*, Bulletin 1936, no. 2 (Washington: Department of the Interior, Office of Education, 1936).

28. Szasz, *Education and the American Indian*, pp. 106–11; CIA Report, 1941, p. 412; CIA Report, 1944, pp. 246–47; CIA Report, 1945, pp. 245–46.

HEALTH PROGRAMS

Another serious concern of the Indian New Deal was Indian health. As a critic of health conditions on Indian reservations during the 1920s and early 1930s, Collier had dramatized the tragic state of Indian health and charged the Indian Office with serious neglect. But as commissioner he found that it was not easy to find the funds needed for the reforms he had so facilely demanded before. After two years in office he praised the health service for its quality but admitted that it was "quantitatively, very much insufficient." The Indian mortality rate was 50 pecent higher than that of whites, Indian morbidity rates were extremely high in various categories, and the tuberculosis rate was still seven times that of the general population. "There is no question," Collier told a House committee on April 2, 1935, "but what our medical appropriation for the Indian Service is tragically inadequate. The limitations of our medical service are limitations of appropriations in the main."[29] The commissioner was able to find some help, however, outside the regular appropriations for his bureau, and he used PWA funds to begin construction of eleven new hospitals and to improve facilities at ten others. Then when Congress increased the appropriations for fiscal year 1936 by more than half a million dollars, he could report some progress in hiring more physicians and nurses and in improving hospital facilities.[30]

Year by year Collier combined reports of progress—more general use of hospitals, more births in hospitals, a decrease in death rate and increase in birth rate, new health surveys—with a cry that much more needed to be done. Tuberculosis rates remained far above the national average, and in 1942 the director of Indian health services declared that "tuberculosis is still the great Indian-killer." Advances were made, nevertheless, in studying the incidence of the disease. Numerous surveys were made on the reservations and in Alaska, and help was received from the Henry Phipps Institute of Philadelphia for X-ray studies of the Indians. Dental facilities remained woefully short, and sanitation needed much improvement.[31]

The one important breakthrough came in the treatment of trachoma, which, with tuberculosis, had been the great scourge of the Indian schools and reservations. Cooperative research work carried on by Indian medical service physicians and Columbia University staff determined in 1936 that

29. "Indian Conditions and Affairs," *Hearings before the Subcommittee on General Bills of the Committee on Indian Affairs, House of Representatives, 74th Congress, 1st Session, on H.R. 7781 and Other Matters* (1935), pp. 743–44.

30. CIA Report, 1934, pp. 93–94; CIA Report, 1936, pp. 174–75. There is a brief discussion on health matters in Philp, *John Collier's Crusade*, pp. 129–31.

31. J. G. Townsend, "Indian Health—Past, Present, and Future," in La Farge, *The Changing Indian*, pp. 28–41; CIA Report, 1936, p. 176; CIA Report, 1938, pp. 238–39.

trachoma was caused by a virus, and in 1938 a report was made to the meeting of the American Medical Association on the findings and on successful treatment of the disease with sulfanilamide. The Indian service introduced sulfanilamide treatment generally in 1939, and trachoma incidence among the Indians dropped from 30 percent to 5 percent in 1943.[32]

Indian health activities were stimulated also by the Johnson-O'Malley Act. In the first year cooperative agreements were made with North Carolina for care of the Eastern Cherokees and with Florida to begin health services for the Seminoles, and in subsequent years agreements were worked out with other states. When the Social Security Act was passed in 1935, additional health services were provided for the Indians, for the act was applicable to them.[33]

Collier was pleased with the advances that had been made, especially with the breaking down of cultural barriers that for years had kept the Indians from fully using modern medical facilities and the white physicians from an appreciation of Indian medical practices. In 1941 he noted a growing demand by Indians for hospitals and clinics. At the same time he saw an increased appreciation on the part of physicians for the role of the Indian medicine men. "Not only are they discovering values in the Indians' medicinal herbs, massages, sweat baths, cathartics, and cauterizations," he wrote, "but they are sensing a strong psychotherapeutic value in the songs, prayers, and ceremonies of the Indians."[34]

World War II had a deleterious effect on the Indian medical service, for it created a critical shortage of personnel. On January 1, 1944, there were 73 vacancies for full-time physicians, 27 for part-time physicians, and 188 for nurses. Employment of local persons on a temporary basis was sometimes possible, but no more than essential emergency services could be provided. After the war health conditions remained far from ideal, with scandalously high morbidity and mortality rates.[35]

ECONOMIC DEVELOPMENT

Collier's plans for self-government and community development rested on a foundation of economic well-being for the Indians. Although the Indian Civilian Conservation Corps and other emergency relief projects elimi-

---

32. CIA Report, 1938, p. 239; CIA Report, 1940, p. 383; CIA Report, 1943, p. 281; "Trachoma Eradication," *Science* 90 (December 15, 1939): supplement, 10.

33. CIA Report, 1934, p. 93; CIA Report, 1938, pp. 237–38, 240; Cohen, *Federal Indian Law*, p. 245.

34. CIA Report, 1941, pp. 433–44.

35. CIA Report, 1944, p. 249. Two biting criticisms of Indian health services by knowledgeable medical men were Arthur S. Foard, "The Health of the American Indians,"

nated much of the critical unemployment and debilitation that came with the depression, the Indian service was continuously concerned with the long-term economic development of the Indian reservations. At the end of the New Deal period these reservations comprised some fifty-six million acres of land, of which about seven million acres were agricultural, more than sixteen million acres were forests, and about 32 million acres were open grazing land. Because much of the Indian land was in arid or semi-arid regions, agriculture to a large extent depended upon irrigation. Thus, the administration of irrigation, forestry, and grazing formed a substantial part of Indian service activity. Collier and his associates realized that viable Indian communities depended upon the success of these operations. "It is pleasant to talk of spiritual development, moral awakening, and educational growth," Collier wrote in 1938, "but unless the Indian has enough to eat and enough to take care of the normal, decent clothing and shelter needs of himself and his family, he has little heart or spirit, or even strength, to give to other things."[36]

Collier turned quickly to irrigation problems, moving first to cancel unjust and uncollectable reimbursable debts. Secretary Ickes made use of the Leavitt Act of 1932, which authorized the adjustment or elimination of reimbursable debts, to cancel more than $2 million of debt during the first year of the New Deal. Thus began a process that by 1936 had cancelled over $12 million of debt, much of it for irrigation projects. Then Collier directed the Irrigation Division to locate and develop supplies of water that would actually be used by the Indians themselves in the cultivation of their lands. After that came new construction on irrigation projects under the CCC and under the Public Works Administration, which in 1934 allotted about $8 million for irrigation work on Indian reservations. The projects on the reservations varied greatly in size, from those of a few acres for subsistence gardens to projects of tens of thousands of acres, and consisted of small diversion dams and ditches with small pumps to large dams and extensive distribution systems, and Collier noted that the use of irrigated lands by the Indians increased greatly.[37]

The forestry activities of the Indian Service were directed toward the

American Journal of Public Health 39 (November 1949): 1403–6; Haven Emerson, "Indian Health—Victim of Neglect," *Survey* 87 (May 1951): 219–21.

36. CIA Report, 1938, p. 227; CIA Report, 1945, p. 235. The annual reports of the commissioner of Indian affairs devote long sections to irrigation, forestry, grazing, and other economic topics, but historians of the Indian New Deal have paid little attention to them, concentrating instead on the more dramatic anti-allotment and self-government elements of Collier's program.

37. Philp, *John Collier's Crusade*, p. 127; CIA Report, 1933, p. 90; CIA Report, 1939, p. 32.

preservation of the forests through scientific management and their utilization for maximum economic and social benefit to the Indians. To this
end new general forest regulations were issued on April 23, 1936, which
had as a preamble a strong policy statement. The first goal was to preserve
the Indian forests "in a perpetually productive state by providing effective
protection, preventing clear cutting of large contiguous areas, and making
adequate provision for new forest growth when the mature timber is removed." The forestry business, moreover, was to be conducted in a manner that would promote self-sustaining Indian communities, and the forests were to be managed to regulate runoff and minimize erosion. Thus,
while promoting scientific sustained-yield management of the forests,
Collier did not neglect broader interests. Unlike forests in the public domain, which could be governed strictly by technical considerations, the
Indian forests, Collier insisted, required a more flexible management,
which would "take cognizance of the general Indian problem and be coordinated with the whole Indian Service program of social and economic betterment."[38]

When Collier took office the economic returns from timber on the reservations were very small, for the depression had practically stopped timber sales. But a gradual upswing followed, and when the United States
geared for war in 1941 the business boomed. During fiscal year 1941, approximately six hundred million feet of timber valued at $1,835,000 was
cut from Indian reservations, and Indian lumber went into the building of
army cantonments and many defense industrial uses, including airplane
construction.[39]

Proper range management, to control grazing on the Indian reservations
with the corollary objective of soil conservation by controlling erosion,
was a major work of the Indian New Deal. The work was complicated by
the checkerboard pattern of many allotted reservations that made range
control difficult if not impossible. By a special leasing system the Indian
Office had some success in organizing solid units for range control, and on
December 28, 1935, it issued new grazing regulations, with these objectives:

> 1. The preservation through proper grazing practice of the forest,
> the forage, the land, and the water resources on Indian reservations,
> and the building up of these resources where they have deteriorated.

38. CIA Report, 1934, p. 106; CIA Report, 1936, pp. 198–99; CIA Report, 1939, p. 38;
"General Forest Regulations," April 23, 1936 (approved by the secretary of the interior,
May 18, 1936).
39. CIA Report, 1933, p. 87; CIA Report, 1941, p. 428. A great deal of information
about forestry development and timber sales is contained in J. P. Kinney, *Indian Forest
and Range: A History of the Administration and Conservation of the Redman's Heritage* (Washington: Forestry Enterprises, 1950), pp. 280–335.

2. The utilization of these resources to give the Indians an opportunity to earn a living through grazing their own livestock.

3. The granting of grazing privileges on surplus range lands not
needed by Indians under such safeguards as will yield the highest return consistent with undiminished future use.

4. The protection of the interests of the Indians from the encroachment of unduly aggressive and antisocial individuals.[40]

The Indian CCC was instrumental in initiating much soil conservation
work, and the Indian service cooperated closely with the Soil Conservation
Service of the Department of Agriculture. The closest cooperation was
in the Navajo and Pueblo areas, where administrative unification was
achieved. The results, Collier said in 1936, were "so startling and convincing" that additional agreements were undertaken.[41]

One ubiquitous activity on the reservations was road construction,
which began in earnest with the Indian CCC and a $4 million allotment
from Public Works Administration funds in August 1933. The PWA grant
like the CCC work fulfilled two immediate ends, the employment of destitute Indians and the provision of badly needed roads on the reservations.
The funds continued to come—$2 million in June 1934 under the Emer-
gency Appropriation Act and then sizable annual appropriations. The building of roads and their year-round upkeep were especially essential if the
day school program of the Indian Office was to work, for transportation of
the children by school buses was a necessary part of the plan. Similarly, the
road system made possible increased medical service to isolated parts of
the reservations. The roads, in fact, aided all manner of reservation activity, and Collier was careful to see that they were built for practical purposes of the Indians and not to satisfy tourist interests in Indians and Indian culture. The war cut road work to basic maintenance, but as it drew
to a close plans were immediately set in motion for postwar construction
to continue the development of reservation road systems.[42]

THE BUREAUCRACY

To administer the many facets of the Indian service, to plan for new activities, and to coordinate the work of the bureau with other government

40. CIA Report, 1934, pp. 106–7; CIA Report, 1936, p. 198; "General Grazing Regulations," December 28, 1935.

41. CIA Report, 1935, p. 143; CIA Report, 1936, pp. 187–88. The Navajo story is told
in detail in Donald L. Parman, *The Navajos and the New Deal* (New Haven: Yale University Press, 1976).

42. CIA Report, 1936, p. 201; CIA Report, 1937, p. 223; CIA Report, 1944, p. 246.

agencies required a numerous staff and complicated organization. The fading away of the bureau—which Collier, like his many predecessors, confidently predicted—had not yet begun. The organization chart of the Office of Indian Affairs in 1940 (Table 13) shows the variety of the administrative duties.

The Washington office was divided into seventeen divisions or sections, each with a director. The commissioner of Indian affairs and the assistant commissioner were aided by three field representatives (who were in charge of contacts with Indian tribes, new projects and management problems, and cooperation with other agencies) and four assistants to the commissioner with specialized duties. The legal division and the probate division were under the jurisdiction of the solicitor of the Interior Department. In 1939 this Washington staff included 356 persons. In 1941, because of the growing business of the office, the divisions were grouped under five branches: Administration, Planning and Development, Community Services, Indian Resources, and Engineering, adding a new level to the top bureaucracy.[43]

Directly responsible to the Office of Indian Affairs in 1940 were eighty-nine field organizations, comprising sixty-four superintendents of jurisdictions, nine district offices, ten schools, and six sanatoriums. Collier wanted a system of decentralization in which the superintendents and the Indians and employees with whom they worked would handle local problems. To carry out this intent he issued on July 14, 1934, a "Statement of New Indian Service Policies," which he asserted would mark the beginning of a new era in administration. It was a fine scheme, which he hoped would result in

(1) The Washington Office recognizing its lack of information so that it should take action on field matters only after consultation and in cooperation with reservation administrators.

(2) Superintendents cooperatively (a) with Indian leaders participating at each step, (b) with their staffs, and (c) with the advice of specialists from the Washington Office developing local programs which meet recognized needs.

(3) The Indians, through Indian organization, carrying their share of community responsibility so that local problems may be taken care of locally and the Washington Office relieved of decisions which it is ill prepared to make.

(4) A better knowledge by all employees and by Indians of policies, of appropriations, of expenditures, and of governmental restric-

---

43. CIA Report, 1941, pp. 440–41; *Statistical Supplement to the Annual Report of the Commissioner of Indian Affairs*, 1939, table VII.

TABLE 13: Organization of the Office of Indian Affairs, 1940

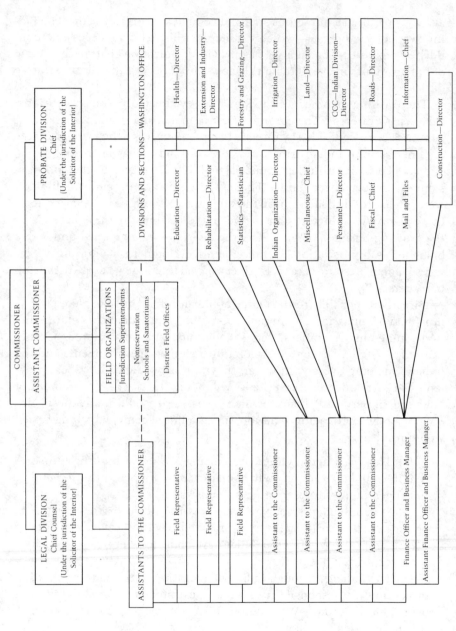

Source: Felix S. Cohen, *Handbook of Federal Indian Law* (Washington: GPO, 1942) p. 20.

tions, all of which is essential to a complete understanding of what can be planned and put into operation locally without reference to the Washington Office.[44]

Then, in 1937, in order to regularize the relations of the various divisions in the Washington office with the jurisdictions in the field, Collier divided the United States into ten geographical districts, each with one or more headquarters, through which all the business between the division heads and the field operations would be channeled. When the order was issued, he took the occasion to restate his principle that the superintendents were the responsible officers and that they reported directly to him; supervisory employees in the districts representing the various divisions were advisers and consultants only, who exercised no administrative authority over the employees in any jurisdiction.[45]

The work of the field units was governed in large part by specific regulations on a wide variety of topics. Between 1938 and 1943, in addition to special regulations, codified regulations were issued on the following topics:

Alaska
Attorneys and agents
Civilian Conservation Corps, Indian Division
Credit to Indians
Education of Indians
Enrollment and reallotment of Indians
Forestry
Grazing
Heirs and wills
Hospital and medical care of Indians
Irrigation projects
Law and order
Leases and permits on restricted Indian lands
Leases and sale of minerals, restricted Indian lands
Moneys, tribal and individual
Patents in fee, competency certificates, sale and
    reinvestment of proceeds

---

44. Cohen, *Federal Indian Law,* p. 30; "Statement of New Indian Service Policies," Circular 3011, July 14, 1934, OIA Circulars (M1121, reel 15); *Statistical Supplement,* 1939, table VII.

45. Order no. 481, "Field District Plan," June 21, 1937, OIA Circulars (M1121, reel 4). Although this direct chain of command no doubt had advantages, it was disliked by the medical service physicians, who objected to having nonmedical superintendents with superior authority. See Foard, "Health of the American Indians."

Records (Oklahoma tribes)
Relief of Indians
Rights of way
Roads and highways
Trading with Indians
Wilderness and roadless areas
Wildlife [46]

The Indian Reorganization Act authorized preferential hiring of Indians in the Indian service, and the effects of the legislation were soon evident. Whereas in 1933 there were only a few hundred permanent Indian employees, by June 30, 1940, the number had risen to 4,682. Of these, 8 were superintendents, 251 held professional positions, 935 were clerical workers, and approximately 3,475 were in other skilled jobs. In addition, a large number of Indians were employed temporarily in construction work on the reservations, so that Indians in regular and temporary positions represented over half the entire Indian Service personnel. [47]

The work of the Indian Office under the New Deal was notably different from that in previous decades in the amount of cooperation established between it and other federal agencies; this brought a degree of decentralization that had never before existed. Where in the past there had been cooperation, it had been only between the bureau and the other agencies. Now some of these units—Soil Conservation Service, Farm Security Administration, Social Security Board, National Youth Administration, Public Works Administration, and Works Progress Administration—had direct contact with the Indians. Moreover, the Indian service received help from the General Land Office and the Federal Power Commission and continued to work with the Department of Agriculture and the Public Health Service. Thus, the monopoly over Indian affairs once held by the Indian Office was broken. From another viewpoint, the Indian Office had available a great range of skills and expert knowledge that it could never have acquired as an isolated bureau. And, of course, the movement to transfer responsibilities to the newly formed tribal governments and corporations, and to state governments in certain areas, further decentralized the government's management of Indian affairs. [48]

46. *Cumulative Supplement to the Code of Federal Regulations of the United States, 1938–1943* (Washington: GPO, 1944), pp. 5745–48.

47. CIA Report, 1940, pp. 389—90. See also *Statistical Supplements*.

48. Cohen, *Federal Indian Law*, p. 32; Joseph C. McCaskill, "The Cessation of Monopolistic Control of Indians by the Indian Office," *Indians of the United States: Contributions of the Delegation of the United States, First Inter-American Conference on Indian Life, Patzcuaro, Mexico, April 1940*, 2 vols. (Washington: Office of Indian Affairs, 1940), 2: 69–76.

CHAPTER 39

The End of the
Indian New Deal

John Collier's Travail. Congressional Attacks.

The Indians and World War II.

The Legacy of the Indian New Deal.

The Indian New Deal, like Roosevelt's New Deal in general, had a limited life. After a period of enthusiasm and success in getting reform measures enacted, John Collier ran into increasing opposition. After 1937 he managed only a holding operation against antagonistic groups, to whom Congress gave a receptive ear. Then World War II turned the nation's attention away from such domestic concerns as the American Indians, and in 1945 Collier, overwhelmed by frustration, resigned. With his departure, the Indian New Deal came to an end; yet its legacy was of tremendous importance. Relations between the government and the Indians could never again return to the situation in the pre-Collier days.[1]

JOHN COLLIER'S TRAVAIL

The opposition to the original Wheeler-Howard bill that Collier had met from Indians, reform groups, and Congress forced him to curtail much of

1. Discussion of the opposition to Collier and critical evaluations of his work are found in Kenneth R. Philp, *John Collier's Crusade for Indian Reform, 1920–1954* (Tucson: University of Arizona Press, 1977), pp. 187–213, 237–44; John Leiper Freeman, Jr., "The New Deal for Indians: A Study of Bureau-Committee Relations in American Government" (Ph.D. dissertation, Princeton University, 1952), pp. 274–514; Graham D.

his reform plan, yet in many ways he marched bravely ahead as though nothing had happened. The goals of reasserting Indian cultural patterns, Indian self-determination, and Indian self-government, deliberately cut back by Congress in the Indian Reorganization Act, remained the guiding principles of Collier's activity, which he promoted through administrative means when legislative ones failed. He thus left himself open to continuing charges that he sought a revival of tribalism, segregation of the Indians from white society, and a slowing down if not an absolute halt in the drive for assimilation. Collier was an aggressive publicist and propagandist for his own policies and programs, and he drew strong counteraction in return. In the first four years he succeeded to a large extent in overcoming opposition, and he got his program enacted, at least in amended form. But in 1935 and 1936 a case against the Collier administration slowly built up. Those who lost out in the battle over the Wheeler-Howard Act regrouped their forces and renewed the fight. Moreover, many local interests were affected as the new policies were put into operation, especially as land acquisition was pushed, and these interests joined the growing opposition. From 1937 to 1945 Collier was a man besieged.

The tactics of the opposition were twofold. In the first place, critics painted the Indian New Deal as an extremist movement for which Collier was responsible; they asserted that the Indian Reorganization Act aimed to promote Indian culture, traditions, and religion and that ultimately it was a communistic scheme, imposing a dictatorial regime upon the Indians. A second attack focused on Collier's administration of the bureau, with charges that he was an empire builder who sought, despite all his talk about Indian self-determination, to perpetuate federal guardianship of the Indians and thus the bureaucracy of the Indian Office. The attack came more and more to be leveled at Collier the man as well as at the abstract policies, and Collier furnished grist for the mill by acting as though his original plans were all in effect.[2]

One vocal group that kept Collier in trouble was the missionaries, who would not drop the issue of his stand on freedom of religion for the Indians. When the strong statement on promotion of Indian culture was eliminated from the Indian Reorganization Act, criticism of Collier was temporarily moderated, but it soon flared up again.[3] In addition there was opposition from strong elements in the Indian Rights Association. Jacob C. Morgan, Collier's Navajo critic, received considerable support from the association,

Taylor, *The New Deal and American Indian Tribalism: The Administration of the Indian Reorganization Act, 1934–45* (Lincoln: University of Nebraska Press, 1980).

2. Freeman, "The New Deal for Indians," pp. 315–19.

3. Ibid., pp. 323–25.

which took up his views against the stock reduction program and the reorganization of the tribal council. Then on August 27, 1938, the association addressed a long open letter to President Roosevelt, in which it charged mismanagement of Navajo Indian affairs by the Indian Office. Secretary Ickes at first counseled ignoring the attack, but it was too serious to pass by, and Roosevelt sent a strong reply. He noted that the letter to him had been released to the press before it reached his office; and he declared that the letter, "in its indefiniteness of reference, in the anonymity of most of its charges, and in the extravagance of some of them," failed to convince him. The Indian Office then prepared a point-by-point rebuttal.[4]

Collier remained worried about the Indian Rights Association letter, and he charged that "active control of the Association had passed into the hands of a very small and unrepresentative minority of workers who were either completely misinformed themselves or were deliberately and for their own ends, misleading the large body of responsible but inactive supporters of the Association's work." He considered the letter to the president a pulling together of allegations made by Jacob C. Morgan, G. E. E. Lindquist, and others, and he feared that these allegations would continue in the context of the association's letter, which would give them a certain prestige. Finally, to resolve the difficulty, he enlisted the aid of the Phelps-Stokes Fund to make an independent investigation of the Navajo situation. The study, conducted early in 1939 with the blessings of the Indian Rights Association as well as the Indian Bureau, in general vindicated Collier but not without some barbed critical comments about his methods. "The present administration, as demonstrated on the Navajo Reservation," the report concluded, "is vigorously idealistic, impatient of the experimentation required to test methods to be used, and, though sincerely devoted to human welfare, determined to push through the programs without adequate regard for the natural apathy or ignorance of the group to be helped. Under the temptation and almost the compulsion of large funds easily available, the danger of drastic reforms can hardly be exaggerated." Yet it declared

---

4. The Indian Rights Association criticized Collier and his programs, especially that among the Navajos, repeatedly in *Indian Truth* in 1936–1938; see, for example, 13 (May 1936): 2–3; 14 (March 1937): 1–4; 15 (January 1938): 1–4; 15 (April 1938): 1–3. The association, however, did not support repeal of the Indian Reorganization Act; see *Indian Truth* 14 (April 1937): 1–5. The reaction to the Indian Rights Association letter to the president is recorded in Harold L. Ickes, Memorandum for Commissioner Collier, August 31, 1938, and "Memorandum on Letter to the President from the Indian Rights Association of Philadelphia," September 9, 1938, in OSI, Office File of Harold L. Ickes, Miscellaneous File on the Indian Office, part 2, box 5; Franklin D. Roosevelt to Jonathan M. Steere, president of the Indian Rights Association, September 8, 1938, copy in OIA, Office File of Commissioner John Collier, Indian Rights Association, box 6.

that "trends in the right direction are being discovered and developed," and it refuted particular charges made against Collier's Navajo program.[5]

More insistent and more aggressive in its attack on Collier and all his works was the American Indian Federation, a small but vocal Indian group led by an Oklahoma Creek named Joseph Bruner and his dynamic lieutenant, Alice Lee Jemison, a Seneca activist. Organized in 1934, the group had attracted a variety of dissidents who objected to Collier's program and had gained a hearing with the Indian Rights Association and, more important, with congressional committees, who listened to its testimony at great length. The platform of the federation was clear: free the Indians immediately from their status of wardship under the guardianship of the Indian Office, turn over to the states the services for Indians, remove Collier from office because he did not represent the Indian people and was an atheist and Communist, and repeal the Indian Reorganization Act, which had been drawn up by the Communist-dominated American Civil Liberties Union and which turned the Indians away from American citizenship.[6]

In December 1934 the federation circulated a memorial to the president and to Congress that was written in the inflammatory language typical of the organization: "We charge that Commissioner Collier has, and is, with deliberate intent, and contrary to the desires of the American people, who desire justice due to the American Indian, seeking to frustrate the opportunity of the Indian to enter American life as a citizen, and, instead is perpetuating an in[i]quitous, un-American Bureau, and forcing a subdued, Bureau-controlled (a subject) people into a segregated serfdom, continued

5. The Navajo Indian Problem: An Inquiry Sponsored by the Phelps-Stokes Fund (New York: Phelps-Stokes Fund, 1939). The Indian Office prepared a 22-page analysis of the report. See Office of Indian Affairs Press Release, undated, in OIA, Office File of Collier, Indian Rights Association, box 6; there are other materials on the controversy in the same file.

6. Freeman, "The New Deal for Indians," pp. 325–33 and passim. The anti-Collier testimony of the American Indian Federation is printed at great length in "Indian Conditions and Affairs," Hearings before the Subcommittee on General Bills of the Committee on Indian Affairs, House of Representatives, 74th Congress, 1st Session, on H.R. 7781 and Other Matters (1935); "Wheeler-Howard Act—Exempt Certain Indians," Hearings before the Committee on Indian Affairs, House of Representatives, 76th Congress, 3d Session, on S. 2103 (1940); and "Survey of Conditions of the Indians in the United States," Hearings before a Subcommittee of the Committee on Indian Affairs, United States Senate, 76th Congress, Pursuant to S. Res. 79 (70th Cong.) and Subsequent Continuing Resolutions, part 37 (1940). Laurence M. Hauptman, "Alice Jemison: Seneca Political Activist, 1901–1964," Indian Historian 12 (Summer 1979): 15–22, 60–62, presents Mrs. Jemison's career is a very favorable light in an attempt to balance the criticism she received from Collier and Ickes; this material is repeated in Laurence M. Hauptman, The Iroquois and the New Deal (Syracuse: Syracuse University Press, 1981), pp. 34–55.

to be ruled by the dictatorship of a Government Bureau, which has held the American Indian in chains since 1871."[7]

A year and a half later, in another letter to Roosevelt, the federation charged that the Indian Office was dominated and controlled by "the Christ-mocking, Communist-aiding, subversive and seditious American Civil Liberties Union." It pushed strongly for the repeal of the Indian Reorganization Act, which it claimed was "opposed by intelligent Indian leaders all over the United States" and had been passed only because of Collier's propaganda tactics and silencing of Indian opposition by threats of economic sanctions. Collier dismissed the federation as a very small group of Indians who spoke for nobody but themselves and who attracted all sorts of right-wing radicals and drew support from American Nazi sympathizers like the Silvershirts of William Dudley Pelley and the German-American Bund. Unfortunately for Collier, however, the federation's charges were given repeated and to some extent sympathetic hearing by the congressional committees on Indian affairs.[8]

CONGRESSIONAL ATTACKS

The debate between Collier and his opponents began in the subcommittee of the House Committee on Indian Affairs chaired by Representative Abe Murdock of Utah, in February, March, and April 1935, over the bill to amend the election process under the Indian Reorganization Act. Then it moved in 1936 to the Senate Investigating Subcommittee, where the same arguments were displayed and the American Indian Federation began a concerted movement to gain the sympathy of the subcommittee. At first the attacks on Collier did little more than stir up misgivings about his competence as commissioner, but as time passed his program was seriously endangered. The appropriations authorized for land purchase and for organization were never fully provided, and in 1937 Collier suffered the first major blow to his proposals when the House refused to pass the In-

7. "A Memorial of American Indians to Honorable Franklin D. Roosevelt, the President, and to the Congress of the United States," December 21, 1934, signed by Joseph Bruner, copy in OIA, Office File of Collier, American Indian Federation, box 1; it is printed also in "Indian Conditions and Affairs," pp. 20–21.

8. Joseph Bruner to Roosevelt, June 19, 1936, and "Bulletin of American Indian Federation," March 26, 1937, in OIA, Office File of Collier, American Indian Federation, box 1. There is a good deal of material in Collier's Office File under such headings as Bruner *et al.*, German-American Bund, O. K. Chandler, Alice Lee Jemison, and Silvershirts of America.

dian Claims Commission bill that had been passed by the Senate and favorably reported by the House Committee on Indian Affairs.[9]

Soon there were attempts to undo what Collier had achieved, by repeal of the Indian Reorganization Act or by elimination of large blocks of Indians from its provisions. A number of bills were introduced early in 1937 to repeal the act for specific groups of Indians, and on March 1, 1937, Senators Wheeler and Frazier introduced a measure for the outright repeal of the entire law. Collier immediately challenged the move. In a statement released to the Associated Press on March 3 he refuted the senators' complaints against the Indian Reorganization Act, and in another prepared statement he declared: "Were the Wheeler-Frazier bill to become law it would bring the beginning of a long Indian night, perhaps the last." He was sure that such a disastrous step would not be taken, and he believed that the onslaught would remind the Indians that their cause was "a battlefield, now as long ago; an enduring labor, and a battleground." Behind the repeal drive he saw two groups of people. One was the special economic interests who profited from Indian lands and Indian timber. "Did anyone expect that the interests adversely concerned with so huge a property stake," Collier asked, "would yield instantly and supinely and would *not* strike back?" The second group comprised those who wanted to protect the Indians' property but who disliked the Indian Reorganization Act because of its reinforcement of Indian self-determination. To them Collier refused to bend. "The right of the Indians to group self-determination, to the pursuit of *their own vision of the good*," he insisted, "is so fundamental that it cannot be surrendered; nor can it be segregated and walled-off from the material part; the Indians must assert this right even if it loses them some friends."[10]

The bill never came out of committee, but it was an indication of Senator Wheeler's disaffection with Collier and his program. Senator Elmer Thomas, who succeeded Wheeler as chairman of the Senate Committee on Indian Affairs, was generally in opposition, too, and the two were joined by Senator Dennis Chavez of New Mexico, who seemed to have a special dis-

---

9. Freeman, "The New Deal for Indians," pp. 333–52; "Indian Conditions and Affairs"; "Survey of Conditions of the Indians in the United States," part 37. For discussion on the Indian Claims Commission bill, see chapter 40.

10. "Statement by Commissioner John Collier, of the Office of Indian Affairs to the Associated Press, on the Attempted Destruction of the Indian Reorganization Act by Senate Bill 1736," March 3, 1937; Collier, "Six Efforts in Congress to Destroy the Indian Reorganization Act," March 4, 1937; Collier, "Senator Wheeler and the Indian Reorganization Act," March 19, 1937—all in OIA, Records concerning the Wheeler-Howard Act, part 8, box 7. See also "More Trouble for the Indians," *New Republic* 90 (March 31, 1937): 226.

like for the commissioner. Behind these senators stood the special assistant to the Senate Investigating Subcommittee, Albert A. Grorud, a friend of Wheeler's from Montana, who had a personal grudge against the bureau and was an undying opponent of Collier. Grorud did much of the work of the committee, and its reports may have reflected his views more than those of the senators.[11]

Collier suffered severely at the hands of the Senate Committee on Indian Affairs, which prepared two devastating reports, based to a large extent on the ideas of the American Indian Federation. The first of these came in connection with a bill introduced on April 7, 1939, renewing the proposal to repeal the Indian Reorganization Act. The committee's report of August 2, 1939, charged that the Indian Office had spent large sums in promoting the Indian Reorganization Act and discriminated against Indians who opposed it, that individual rights and private property of Indians were being destroyed and the Indians forced back into a communal status, that primitive tribalism was being promoted, that the Indian Reorganization Act actually resulted in increased power for federal administrators and continued wardship status instead of moving the Indians toward full citizenship, and that Collier by administrative measures was putting into operation elements of the original Wheeler-Howard Act that had been explicitly eliminated by Congress. The committee, however, rewrote the bill so that it did not call for outright repeal of the Indian Reorganization Act but provided for the exemption of more than seventy tribes from its provisions. In this modified form it passed the Senate on February 19, 1940.[12]

The House Committee on Indian Affairs, which held its own extensive hearing on the bill in June 1940, acted in a more balanced way and gave Collier ample opportunity to strike back. This he did, pointing especially to the Nazi connections of the American Indian Federation and accusing it of being a "fifth column" movement. "It cannot be said," he concluded, "that the 'fifth column' drive has been wholly in vain. It has not reached the Indians, but it has reached the office of the Senate's Indian Committee, and as a matter of parliamentary fact it has encircled and captured the unwatchful committee as a whole." The House committee submitted its own amended bill, which had Collier's approval. The House version struck out the entire contents of the bill passed by the Senate; it substituted a provision to allow new tribal elections for exclusion from the operation of the Indian Reorganization Act when one-third of the adult Indians petitioned for such an election and provisions, as well, for rescinding action on con-

11. Freeman, "The New Deal for Indians," pp. 423–34.
12. *Congressional Record*, 84: 3945, 10739; 86: 469–72, 1587; *Senate Report* no. 1047, 76–1, serial 10295.

stitutions and charters. In this form it passed the House in August 1940, but the fundamental difference between the two versions made it impossible for the conference committee to come up with a compromise acceptable to both houses, and the measure died.[13]

A second Senate report came from the investigating subcommittee, which on June 11, 1943, issued *Senate Report* no. 310. The earlier debates, especially in the House hearings of 1940, had to a large extent dissipated the charges of atheism and communism and discredited the radicals who had made them, but fundamental criticisms of Collier and his program remained, and they were the substance of the Senate report. They touched the basic question of whether the Indian New Deal was moving the Indians toward real self-sufficiency, which would mean the end of federal guardianship and absorption into the mass of the nation's citizenry, or whether the bureau was instead building up and perpetuating itself, continuing its guardianship as the Indians returned to tribalism and their old ways. Collier believed that the only way the Indians could adjust to the dominant white society was through group processes, not individual ones, and that adaptation should come from free choice on the part of the Indians working within their own traditions and not be imposed from without. The Senate committee reflected quite an opposite viewpoint, and its condemnation of the Indian Bureau was complete:

> The Bureau has been concerned with building up a system instead of service; attempting to build self-perpetuating institutions; making material improvements for the Indian Service at the expense of Indian life; furnishing physical relief that was not needed nearly so much as economic and civic encouragement; breaking down assisting agencies; segregating the Indian from the general citizenry; condemning the Indian to perpetual wardship; making the Indian the guinea pig for experimentation; grouping the Indians for convenience of supervision for which they are presumed to exist; tieing him to the land in perpetuity; forcing a conventional type of education on him; attempting to compel all Indians to engage in agriculture and stock raising under the supervision of an extension department which is an end in itself.
>
> Since the Indian Bureau has been built up by adventitious accretions, it may be reduced to a minimum by the orderly elimination of such accretions.

In a series of thirty-three recommendations the committee proposed elimination of bureau staff, cutting of funds, transfer of nearly all bureau

---

13. *Congressional Record*, 86: 10787, 12848, 13060, 13323; "Wheeler-Howard Act—Exempt Certain Indians"; *House Report* no. 2876, 76–3, serial 10444.

services to other agencies or their complete elimination, the end of federal trusteeship over individual Indian lands and the end of any kind of wardship, the closing out of individual Indian money accounts, and the per capita distribution of all trust funds. To have carried out these recommendations would nearly have abolished the Office of Indian Affairs altogether.[14]

A corollary to *Senate Report* no. 310 came from a special House investigating committee directed by Representative Karl E. Mundt of South Dakota. Although it made no radical and sweeping proposals such as those of the Senate committee, the Mundt committee, after extensive hearings from March 1943 to December 1944, offered a critical appraisal of the Indian Bureau's operations. The goal espoused by the committee for the Indian—"to take his place in the white man's community on the white man's level and with the white man's opportunity and security status"—it found to be slowed down by inadequate economic and educational opportunities, inadequate guidance for adult Indians, and lack of proper laws and regulations regarding claims, heirship lands, and the freeing of competent Indians for full citizenship. Although the committee recognized that the American Indians as a group were not yet ready to be turned loose from federal guardianship and that it would be unwise to remove restrictions on Indian lands by blanket legislation, it made some specific recommendations. It suggested elections for tribes that wanted to withdraw from the Indian Reorganization Act, extension of credit facilities to all tribes (whether under the act or not), liquidation of fractionalized heirship lands by negotiation with the heirs, and economies in bureau administration through further decentralization. The tone of the report was distinctly assimilationist. In terms reminiscent of Thomas Jefferson Morgan in the 1890s, it said:

> The goal of Indian education should be to make the Indian child a better American rather than to equip him simply to be a better In-

14. "Survey of Conditions among the Indians of the United States: Analysis of the Statement of the Commissioner of Indian Affairs in Justification of Appropriations for 1944, and the Liquidation of the Indian Bureau," *Senate Report* no. 310, 78–1, serial 10756, described as a "Partial Report Pursuant to S. Res. 17 Extending S. Res. 79, 70th Congress." A statement of Collier's principles appeared in *Indians at Work* 9 (April 1942): 1–3. One of Collier's New Deal assistants, D'Arcy McNickle, thirty years later denied that Collier had been anti-assimilationist and asserted that he had had a correct sense of assimilation—"the idea of people of different cultures coming together and adapting to each other, without coercion on either side. . . . He [Collier] was saying that Indians are people, as good as any other people. They love their own values, and they should be allowed to work out their own destinies without being beaten down by superior power. That really is what the argument was all about." D'Arcy McNickle, "Commentary," in Jane F. Smith and Robert M. Kvasnicka, eds., *Indian-White Relations: A Persistent Paradox* (Washington: Howard University Press, 1976), p. 255.

dian. The goal of our whole Indian program should be, in the opinion of your committee, to develop better Indian Americans rather than to perpetuate and develop better American Indians. The present Indian education program tends to operate too much in the direction of perpetuating the Indian as a special-status individual rather than preparing him for independent citizenship.

The Mundt report was hardly an endorsement of Collier's administration, but it stopped far short of the radical proposal of the Senate that the bureau be destroyed.[15]

Collier's fight with Congress did not occur in a vacuum, for Roosevelt's New Deal itself underwent a similar estrangement from Congress, and Collier's adherence to administration measures cost him support from members of Congress who increasingly opposed Roosevelt. A special blow to Collier's status with Congress was his staunch endorsement of the president's court-packing plan of 1937, which Senator Wheeler bitterly attacked. Collier's active support of Roosevelt on the court issue in *Indians at Work* in March 1937 aggravated the Wheeler-Collier tension. Again, the strong isolationist bloc in Congress, of which Wheeler was a leader, tended to sympathize with some of the very groups who attacked Collier, and Collier's belief that United States Indian affairs had relevance for other native peoples around the world raised isolationist hackles.[16]

The conflict over Collier's policies that erupted in Congress, of course, was carried on, too, outside congressional committee rooms. Collier continued his effective promotional efforts, and he received support from old friends. Both the National Association on Indian Affairs and the American Indian Defense Association stood behind his programs, and when in 1937 these two organizations merged to form the American Association on Indian Affairs (with Oliver La Farge as president and Haven Emerson as vice president), the new group became a focus for Collier support. Strong support came, as well, from the American Civil Liberties Union, which in 1938 promoted the publication of a very favorable statement on the Indian

---

15. "Investigate Indian Affairs," *Hearings before the Committee on Indian Affairs, House of Representatives, 78th Congress, 1st Session, on H. Res. 166, a Bill to Authorize and Direct and Conduct an Investigation to Determine Whether the Changed Status of the Indian Requires a Revision of the Laws and Regulations Affecting the American Indian* (1943–1945); House Report no. 2091, 78–2, serial 10848. The committee also recommended an Official Indian Advisory Council, with at least two Indian members, to replace the Board of Indian Commissioners. Collier had appeared before the committee and pointed out areas in Indian affairs that needed investigation. See *Indians at Work* 10 (Spring 1943): 1–2.

16. Freeman, "The New Deal for Indians," pp. 419–42. Collier supported the court plan in *Indians at Work* 4 (March 1, 1937): 1–9.

New Deal called *The New Day for the Indians*. The booklet had been suggested by Roger Baldwin, head of the ACLU, and financed by him, but it was put together with the cooperation of the Indian Office and was edited by Jay B. Nash, Oliver La Farge, and W. Carson Ryan, all active Collier supporters. Although it quoted opponents like Joseph Bruner, the pamphlet was a justification of Collier's work and urged continued public support. It was signed by a large number of sponsors—Indians, anthropologists, and members of reform groups—who thus endorsed "the principle of the Reorganization Act of 1934." Collier himself called the booklet the "most objective and comprehensive appraisal of the present administration of Indian affairs thus far consummated," and he circulated and publicized the pamphlet widely.[17] Meanwhile, favorable publicity for Collier's work came in articles in such national magazines as *Collier's, Nation,* and *New Republic*. In the September 1942 issue of *Atlantic Monthly*, Collier himself eloquently stated his case. He wrote, in part:

> In 1933, when President Franklin D. Roosevelt took office, Indian policy was changed in fashions radical and exhaustive. The change, in principle, was from maximal to minimal authority; from denial of Indian cultural values to their emphasis; from expectation of Indian doom to expectation of Indian triumph; from one-pattern policy to a policy of multiple options; but first and last from denial to intense encouragement of group self-determination and self-government. Self-determination under the impact of difficulties and challenges crowding fast. Self-determination even where failure might be very damaging. Above all, self-determination oriented toward regenerating the land and toward using it beneficially. In a word, restoration to the Indian of his two inseparable heritages wherein he had been great—democracy and land, one and indivisible.[18]

Collier's combat with the House and Senate committees on Indian affairs was disturbing, for it resulted from attacks upon his character and

17. Jay B. Nash, Oliver La Farge, and W. Carson Ryan, *The New Day for the Indians: A Survey of the Working of the Indian Reorganization Act of 1934* (New York: Academy Press, 1938); John Collier, Memorandum for the Secretary, December 22, 1938, OIA, Office File of Collier, New Day for the Indians, box 11.

18. John Collier, "Indians Come Alive," *Atlantic Monthly* 170 (September 1942): 78. Articles favorable to Collier were Owen P. White, "Lo, the Poor Indian," *Collier's* 99 (February 6, 1937): 16–17, 40; Elizabeth Shepley Sergeant, "A New Deal for the Indians," *New Republic* 95 (June 15, 1938): 151–54. The other side, of course, was presented to the public as well. See Flora Warren Seymour, "Thunder over the Southwest," *Saturday Evening Post* 211 (April 1, 1939): 23, 71–76; Oswald Garrison Villard, "Wardship and the Indian," *Christian Century* 61 (March 29, 1944): 397–98.

upon the vision he had for the Indians' future; but the attacks were for the
most part driven back. The Indian Reorganization Act was not repealed,
and there were no fundamental revisions of New Deal policy. But the key
to the government's programs was the appropriations made for them by
Congress, and here Collier encountered great setbacks.

Collier had begun his administration with no lack of funds, for although
regular appropriations for the Indian service were curtailed in the depression years, emergency funding was plentiful. The appropriations for fiscal
year 1933, with which Collier began, were about $23 million; for fiscal year
1934, counting emergency appropriations, he had about $52 million to work
with, and he continued to enjoy considerable financial support. But as the
tension between Collier and Congress heightened in Collier's last three
years in office, the appropriations plummeted. And these reductions came
at a time when appropriations for other nonwar activities were increasing.
The bureau's reduction in funding in 1943 of about 25 percent was matched
by a 4-percent increase in total nonwar funds, and when in 1944 the bureau
was cut by 4 percent, total nonwar appropriations increased by 13.5 percent over the previous year. In 1945 the Indian service received a slight
increase of about 2 percent, whereas nonwar appropriations as a whole increased by more than 63 percent. So Collier suffered not only in absolute
loss of dollars but also heavily in comparison with other agencies. If the
reduced purchasing power of the dollar is taken into account, his status
was even worse. Much of the difficulty, of course, lay in the decrease of
emergency funding; from 1934 to 1942 the Indian Office had received an
average of $12 million a year in such money, but in 1943–1945 the yearly
average was only about $466,000. The lack of emergency funding applied
to other agencies as well, but they seemed to have received increased regular appropriations to take up the slack. Especially hard hit were the Indian
programs of land purchase, credit, and construction on the reservations.
The appropriations for health and education, perhaps because they struck
a more responsive chord in Congress or were requested with more dramatic appeals, did not suffer, although they were never as high as the need
dictated.[19]

Although it was the Bureau of the Budget that reduced the funds sought
from Congress for the Indian Office, the antagonism of the powerful chairman of the House Appropriations Subcommittee on Interior Department
Appropriations, Jed Johnson of Oklahoma, was nonetheless a great obsta-

19. Freeman, "The New Deal for Indians," pp. 438–51. The figures are based on Freeman's study for the Hoover Commission; see *Report of the Committee on Indian Affairs
to the Commission on Organization of the Executive Branch of the Government*, October 1948, pp. 51, 204–9.

cle for Collier. Johnson was an arch foe of the commissioner and the bureau, and he seemed to take special delight in Collier's discomfiture. It was finally Johnson's subcommittee that triggered Collier's resignation, for Johnson indicated that the appropriations for the bureau would be severely cut for 1946 unless there was a new commissioner. Collier sent a letter of resignation to President Roosevelt on January 19, 1945, in time for a successor to appear at the appropriations hearings for the new year. In it he said that he wanted to be free to devote more time to his concern for native peoples outside the United States, but he noted also the special hardship that came with the move of the Indian Bureau to Chicago and the "unfortunate trend" in appropriations for Indian services.[20]

THE INDIANS AND WORLD WAR II

World War II was an event of great importance in the lives of the American Indians and in the history of the Indian service. In the first place, the direct participation of Indians in the war and in wartime activities far exceeded what might have been expected. In spite of the long history of conflict between whites and Indians and of the Indians' dissatisfaction with the treatment they had often received at the hand of the federal government, the Indian response to the war was almost uniformly positive. "Strange as it may seem," Collier remarked in 1942, "the Indians have responded earnestly and even enthusiastically to the challenge of the war. From the remotest parts of isolated reservations has come evidence of Indian concern over the war."[21]

Even before Pearl Harbor, many Indians became involved in the war effort. Because all Indians were citizens of the United States, they were subject to Selective Service. They registered for the draft without any serious resistance, although some thought the draft impinged upon their

20. Freeman, "The New Deal for Indians," pp. 456–62. See also Lawrence C. Kelly, "The Indian Reorganization Act: The Dream and the Reality," *Pacific Historical Review* 44 (August 1975): 306–9. Collier's letter of resignation and Roosevelt's reply are printed in *Indians at Work* 12 (January–February 1945): 2–5.

21. CIA Report, 1942, p. 238. There was a surge of enthusiastic articles about Indian participation in the war; see John Collier, "The Indian in a Wartime Nation," *Annals of the American Academy of Political and Social Science* 223 (September 1942): 29–35; Elizabeth S. Sergeant, "The Indian Goes to War," *New Republic* 107 (November 30, 1942): 708–9; Richard L. Neuberger, "The American Indian Enlists," *Asia and the Americas* 42 (November 1942): 628–31. A survey of the subject is Tom Holm, "Fighting a White Man's War: The Extent and Legacy of American Indian Participation in World War II," *Journal of Ethnic Studies* 9 (Summer 1981): 69–81. The issues of *Indians at Work* for 1942–1945 are full of information and illustrations on Indians in the war.

rights as "sovereign" nations.[22] Large numbers of Indians volunteered for military service, and others were inducted through National Guard units. Still others entered Canadian military units. When the country formally entered the war, Indian participation greatly expanded. By mid-1943 there were 18,000 Indians in military service. As of April 1, 1944, there were 21,756 Indians, exclusive of officers, in the fighting forces. The great majority (19,284) were in the Army, but there were 1,555 in the Navy, 574 in the Marine Corps, 127 in the Coast Guard, and 216 in the WAC and WAVES. These men and women served in all the battle zones of the world, and the number who received battlefield citations was impressive.[23]

It was common at the time to comment on the Indians' aptitude for war and the special contributions they made to the fighting. Secretary Ickes was typical; he wrote in January 1944: "The inherited talents of the Indian make him uniquely valuable. He has endurance, rhythm, a feeling for timing, co-ordination, sense perception, an uncanny ability to get over any sort of terrain at night, and, better than all else, an enthusiasm for fighting. He takes a rough job and makes a game of it. Rigors of combat hold no terrors for him; severe discipline and hard duties do not deter him." A special contribution was made by the Navajo "code talkers," who passed voice messages in their native tongue, which the enemy was unable to decode. But Collier credited the Indians' enthusiastic support for the war to something deeper than "their traditional love of fighting," asserting that they had a clear understanding of the issues involved in the war. He wrote in September 1942:

It may not be too great a stretch of the imagination to suggest that the Indians have identified the struggle of democracies the world over with their own struggle of the last century. It may be that they see in a victory of the democracies a guarantee that they too shall be permitted to live their own lives. Perhaps their experiences of the last ten years, in which there has been a rebirth of spirit, a reviving of the smoldering fire of local democracy, and a step toward economic rehabilitation, have helped them to see the possibilities in a world of the Four Freedoms.[24]

22. The Indians of the Six Nations solved the problem by a symbolic declaration of war against the Axis Powers. These tribes in 1917 had separately declared war on Germany, but they never ratified the peace treaty. Collier, "The Indian in a Wartime Nation," p. 34. See also "Six Nations Declare War on Axis," *Indians at Work* 9 (May–June 1942): 17–18.

23. CIA Report, 1943, p. 290; CIA Report, 1944, p. 235. By the spring of 1945 there were 24,521 Indians, exclusive of officers, in the armed forces. CIA Report, 1945, p. 249.

24. Collier, "The Indian in a Wartime Nation," p. 30; Harold L. Ickes, "Indians Have a Name for Hitler," *Collier's* 113 (January 15, 1944): 58. There is a discussion of the war-

Military service was only part of the Indians' role, for thousands worked in war industries, where they made use of skills acquired in the vocational training of the boarding schools or in the Indian Civilian Conservation Corps. The Indian Office in 1945 reported that more than 40,000 Indians had left the reservations for war work. Meanwhile those at home devoted their energies toward aiding the war effort. Collier noted that there was a "continual recasting of the functions of the [Indian] Service," and that much of its time and effort was devoted to problems that arose directly from the war. "Essential war activities must go on," he said in 1942, "such as food production, mining of strategic minerals, protection and utilization of forests, power production and protection, and cooperation with the War Department in securing gunnery and bombing ranges and airports."[25]

The war thus brought a substantial change in the operations of the Indian Office. The great drive that Collier had conducted for the rejuvenation of Indian culture and for Indian self-government was halted, as Congress cut appropriations for nonwar activities and as the great exodus of field employees to the armed services and to war industries occurred. The bureau's coordinator of field services at Minneapolis wrote with alarm in October 1942 that the program of organizing the tribes as well as the credit and land programs would be "seriously endangered" by the war because local Indian groups were losing members, and that several tribal councils in his area were already "on the verge of collapse because of the absence of officers or lack of acting quorums." Educational and medical services were curtailed by the shortage of personnel. Collier asserted in 1942 that personnel administration had suffered "the worst year, perhaps of all times." A final blow was the move of the Indian Office from Washington to Chicago in the summer of 1942 to make room in the capital for more essential war activities. Exiled from the center of government, the bureau found it difficult to keep up its coordinated efforts with other agencies of the federal government, on which services to the Indians increasingly had come to depend.[26]

One remarkable activity of the Indian service in wartime concerned the

---

rior tradition among the Indians in Holm, "Fighting a White Man's War," pp. 74–75. For anecdotes about the code talkers, see Doris A. Paul, *The Navajo Code Talkers* (Philadelphia: Dorrance and Company, 1973).

25. CIA.Report, 1942, pp. 233, 240–41, 256; CIA Report, 1944, p. 237; CIA Report, 1945, p. 233.

26. M. L. Burns to commissioner of Indian affairs, October 2, 1942, and Burns to William Zimmerman, Jr., November 6, 1942, OIA, Indian Organization Division, Correspondence with Officials, box 1; CIA Report, 1942, pp. 455–56; "Removal of Indian Office to Chicago Is Accomplished," *Indians at Work* 10 (July–August–September 1942): 17.

forced relocation of Japanese from their West Coast homes for the duration of the war. When the federal government, deciding in March 1942 to evacuate the Japanese from sensitive areas and settle them in isolated detention camps, established an independent War Relocation Authority to administer this difficult project, John Collier immediately urged that the Department of the Interior be given the responsibility of caring for the evacuees. "The Interior Department," he told Secretary Ickes, "is better equipped than any other Agency of the Federal Government to provide for the Japanese aliens the type of treatment and care which will make them more acceptable as members of American populations and is better equipped to provide the rehabilitation of this group subsequent to the war and its reintegration into the stream of American life." He called attention to the suitable areas for relocation in grazing lands, national parks, and Indian reservations under the jurisdiction of the department and to "the Indian Service's long experience in handling a minority group."[27]

Collier and the Indian service were given the responsibility for the largest Japanese relocation camp, the Poston Center, set up on the Colorado River Indian Reservation in southwestern Arizona. Here some 20,000 Japanese were interned, creating tremendous activity on the quiescent reservation as barracks arose to house the newcomers and as the Japanese began to build irrigation works and to improve the land for cultivation. Collier, who loved to have his hand in this sort of social experimentation, intended to turn the relocation center into a model of community living, and he negotiated with the Rochsdale Institute for assistance in establishing cooperatives in the camp. He was much interested, too, in the permanent improvement that the Japanese might create on the reservation, which would accrue to the Indians' advantage at the termination of the war.[28] As the relocation program developed, however, Collier became disillusioned with the War Relocation Authority, which turned from a program of economic develop-

27. Collier, Memorandum for the Secretary, March 4, 1942, OIA, Office File of Collier, Internment of Japanese on Indian Lands, part 1, box 17. Two general accounts of the Japanese internment are Edward H. Spicer and others, *Impounded People: Japanese-Americans in the Relocation Centers* (Tucson: University of Arizona Press, 1969), and Dillon S. Myer, *Uprooted Americans: The Japanese Americans and the War Relocation Authority during World War II* (Tucson: University of Arizona Press, 1971). Spicer had been community analyst at the Poston Center, and Myer headed the War Relocation Authority and later became commissioner of Indian affairs.

28. "Memorandum of Understanding between the Director of the War Relocation Authority and the Secretary of the Interior," April 14, 1942, OIA, Office File of Collier, Internment of Japanese on Indian Lands, part 1, box 17; Collier, "The Indian in a Wartime Nation," p. 31. Other Japanese were located on the Gila River Reservation, but that center was run by the War Relocation Authority, not by the Indian Office.

ment at the centers to one of mere subsistence. He continued to urge that the Department of the Interior take over the whole operation in order "to achieve the salvaging and rehabilitation of the evacuated population," and in fact the War Relocation Authority was transferred to the Interior Department in February 1944. By that time, however, the responsibility for running the Poston Center had been taken away from the Indian service.[29]

The impact of the wartime experience on the Indians was immeasurable, for the war suddenly threw thousands of reservation Indians into the midst of white society and greatly accelerated the movement toward assimilation. The orderly adjustment of "the ancient social forms and archaic cultures of primitive Indian groups to the demands being made upon them by modern society," which was Collier's goal, was upset by the rapidity of change brought about by the war. An anthropologist who interviewed Navajo and Pueblo veterans in the summer of 1946 asserted that the war had "exerted a great impact on the cultures of these peoples, perhaps the greatest since the arrival of the Spaniards four hundred years ago." A large part of the impact was the freedom of association and action that the Indians enjoyed in the military service, which contrasted with the regulations and discrimination they encountered when they returned home. And the higher standard of living that war incomes had brought meant that a return to old reservation ways would not satisfy many of the veterans and war industry workers. Collier, because he resigned before the war ended, did not have responsibility for the crucial problems of readjustment. This was perhaps fortunate for him, for the effect of the war on Indian policy augmented the movement toward assimilation that had been so prominent a part of the congressional attack on him and his policies in 1943–1945.[30]

THE LEGACY OF THE INDIAN NEW DEAL

John Collier was an effective publicist, and he wanted everyone to believe—as no doubt he himself believed—that the Indian New Deal had been a resounding success. A harder look will reveal that Collier's dream fell short of realization. The Indian Reorganization Act, which was the key

29. Collier, Memorandum for Secretary Ickes, undated, OIA, Office File of Collier, file no. 1–188, part 1, box 17; "Memorandum of Understanding," January 1944, ibid., Miscellaneous WRA Publications, box 17.

30. Collier, "The Indian in a Wartime Nation," p. 32; John Adair, "The Navajo and Pueblo Veteran: A Force for Cultural Change," *American Indian* 4, no. 1 (1947): 5–11. See also John Adair and Evon Vogt, "Navajo and Zuni Veterans: A Study of Contrasting Modes of Culture Change," *American Anthropologist* 51 (October–December 1949): 547–61.

to his policy and programs, was not only in its very inception a truncated version of what Collier had in mind for the regeneration of Indian communities, but the implementation of the act was flawed. Collier's vision of a return to communal life and government was not accepted by all the Indians; for many of them the transition to an individualized life intermingled in white society had progressed too far for them to turn back. Moreover, even the Indians who voted to accept the act's provisions did not all adopt constitutions, and even fewer organized economically under corporate charters. The goal of reestablishing the old land base was not met because of the refusal of Congress to sanction the compulsory return of allotments or heirship lands to communal ownership and its failure to appropriate the large funds envisaged for the purchase of additional lands. Although there were sincere moves made by Collier, Ryan, and Beatty to reorder the Indian schools to make them more responsive to Indian needs and Indian culture, there were no attempts to give Indian communities a fundamental role in managing their schools.[31]

The most telling failures came in the organization of the Indian groups. Collier in a sense imposed upon the Indians a *tribal* government and a *tribal* economy, when traditional Indian ways called rather for organization on a smaller basis of bands or villages. And the paraphernalia of electoral districts, tribal councils, and majority vote all fitted better an Anglo-Saxon conception of democratic government than the systems that many Indians were accustomed to. It became clear as the Organization Division of the Indian Bureau went about its work that most Indian communities were ill-prepared to draw up the needed instruments of government; and, although Collier insisted with technical correctness that no two of the constitutions were the same, the pattern of most of them was supplied by his office. Collier's administration was caught in a dilemma. Its overriding concern for sound economic development of the Indian reservations demanded a total reservation and tribal approach, whereas the community development so much talked about called for less universal conformity. Thus factionalization of the tribes, a phenomenon long antedating white interference in Indian matters, was seriously aggravated by the very measures that Collier intended should solidify the tribal communities. The charge was made again and again, with some justification, that Collier was as paternalistic as any of his predecessors—perhaps even more so—and

---

31. See assessments in Kelly, "The Indian Reorganization Act: The Dream and the Reality"; Lawrence C. Kelly, "John Collier and the Indian New Deal: An Assessment," in Smith and Kvasnicka, *Indian-White Relations*, pp. 227–41; William H. Kelly, ed., *Indian Affairs and the Indian Reorganization Act: The Twenty Year Record* (Tucson: University of Arizona, 1954).

that the Indian Bureau had a tighter hold on Indian affairs and interfered more in them than ever before. And paradoxically, much of the reform that Collier intended was obstructed or negated by old-time employees who could not be shaken out of their past views on government policies toward the Indians.[32]

Yet Collier's positive mark on Indian affairs was indelible. If nothing else, the allotment of land was stopped, reversing a key element in previous Indian policy. The conservation and rehabilitation of the land and other resources on the reservations were greatly forwarded by the soil erosion control programs, the sustained-yield forestry policy, and roads and irrigation projects that flourished in the early years of the New Deal. The credit facilities of the Indian Reorganization Act had positive results, although they were short of what Collier wanted, and the preferential hiring of Indians aided Indian employment and changed the composition of the Indian service.

The assimilationist movement that Collier had fought so vigorously in the 1920s and again in the last years of his tenure as commissioner and which appeared to triumph when he left office could never return to its status in the Dawes Act era. The acceptance and encouragement of Indian culture that Collier had promoted left a mark, not only in the white mind, but most especially among the Indians, in reviving a pride in their heritage and an interest in preserving and, if need be, rediscovering their culture. The upsurge of Indian self-determination that occurred in the 1970s would have been inconceivable without the developments of John Collier's administration.

The tribal councils, whatever their faults, were a fact of life. They furnished a focus for tribal dealings with the federal government and added an element to reservation life and development that was a giant step beyond the autocratic agents or superintendents with their unlimited authority, who had been targets of criticism from the late nineteenth century on. Although traditionalists among some of the tribes would come to ridicule the tribal governments established under the Indian Reorganization Act as puppets of the Bureau of Indian Affairs and deny that they truly represented the Indians, the councils and their elected tribal chairmen became a continuing and powerful force in Indian affairs. The emphasis of the Indian New Deal on tribal government made possible the perpetuation of the concept of tribal sovereignty that at a later date would play a dominant role in relations between the Indians and white society.

The Indian New Deal also, in indirect ways, stimulated pan-Indian de-

---

32. There is a perceptive analysis of why the Indian Reorganization Act did not fully succeed in Taylor, *The New Deal and American Indian Tribalism.*

velopments. The congresses that Collier held to promote the Wheeler-Howard bill had pan-Indian overtones, and Joseph Bruner's American Indian Federation, despite its bizarre character, brought together disparate Indian individuals to combat Collier's programs. The renewed role of tribal governments created a group of Indian leaders who frequently realized their common interests in dealing with the United States government, and in 1944 a group of Indians, including many tribal leaders, organized the National Congress of American Indians. Similar in many respects to the then defunct Society of American Indians, the NCAI set forth its purposes in the preamble to its constitution: "to enlighten the public, preserve Indian cultural values, seek an equitable adjustment of tribal affairs, and secure and preserve their rights under treaties." The organization became important in promoting Indian interests on the national level.[33]

It is obvious now that the great dream Collier had for regenerated Indian communities and acceptance of Indian culture as a positive contribution to American life never became a total reality. He had to compromise and fight off attacks. He was so firm in his convictions of what was right for the Indians that he sometimes imposed conformity or manipulated the Indians to behave in ways that he thought best. He fell far short of reforming the nation on the model of Indian communities. Yet, in balance, John Collier was the most important figure in the history of American Indian policy. Just as the nation could never turn back from the reforms of Roosevelt's New Deal, so Indian affairs, in subtle if not in overt ways, exist in a situation that is the legacy of Collier and the Indian New Deal.

33. Hazel W. Hertzberg, *The Search for an American Indian Identity: Modern Pan-Indian Movements* (Syracuse: Syracuse University Press, 1971), pp. 289–91; N. B. Johnson, "The National Congress of American Indians," *American Indian* 3 (Summer 1946): 1–4; Johnson, "The National Congress of American Indians," *Chronicles of Oklahoma* 30 (Summer 1952): 140–48.

PART NINE

Termination

The assimilation of Indians as individuals into the mainstream of American society, promoted so strenuously by congressional and other opponents of John Collier, had long been a dominant principle in United States Indian policy. Collier's crusade to reverse that position and stress instead group self-determination and the preservation and restoration of Indian culture was looked upon by many as an aberration. After Collier left office in 1945 and his strong supporter Harold Ickes resigned as secretary of the interior in 1946, the executive branch of the government joined the Congress in a massive drive to assimilate the Indians once and for all and thus to end the responsibility of the federal government for Indian affairs.[1]

1. The policy of termination has been studied in considerable depth. An early and widely cited study, which concentrates on the termination of the Menominee Indians is Gary Orfield, "A Study of the Termination Policy," printed in *The Education of American Indians*, vol. 4: *The Organizational Question*, Committee Print of the Subcommittee on Indian Education of the Committee on Labor and Public Welfare, United States Senate, 91st Congress, 1st Session (Washington: GPO, 1970), pp. 673–816; the study was originally issued in 1965 by the National Congress of American Indians. Three recent studies treat the termination period: Larry W. Burt, *Tribalism in Crisis: Federal Indian Policy, 1953–1961* (Albuquerque: University of New Mexico Press, 1982); Larry J. Hasse, "Termination and Assimilation: Federal Indian Policy, 1943 to 1961" (Ph.D. dissertation, Washington State University, 1974); Donald Lee Fixico, "Termination and Relocation: Federal Indian Policy in the 1950s" (Ph.D. dissertation, University of Oklahoma, 1980). See also Charles F. Wilkinson and Eric R. Biggs, "The Evolution of the Termination

The rhetoric of the new age was varied. There was talk of *freeing* or *emancipating* the Indians from a status that bound them by special laws and regulations and placing them instead on an absolutely equal footing with white citizens. The other side of the coin was *withdrawal* or *termination* of federal responsibility and federal programs for Indian groups and Indian individuals. At one time the Bureau of Indian Affairs preferred the word *readjustment*, in an attempt to avoid words that had developed emotional overtones. But overall, it was *termination* that best described the movement, and the word came to be used not only of the government's responsibilities toward the Indians but of the Indians themselves. It became common, thus, to speak of terminated Indians and tribes.

The action of the federal government looking toward termination fell into four general categories: (1) repealing laws that set the Indians apart from other citizens and thereby ending certain restrictions that were deemed discriminatory; (2) ending services provided by the Bureau of Indian Affairs for Indians by transferring responsibility for those services to other agencies of the federal government, to state and local governments, to private agencies, or to Indian tribes; (3) freeing individual Indians from federal supervision and guardianship and removing them from restrictions and disabilities applicable only to Indians; (4) terminating federal responsibility for the affairs of specified tribes.[2] Thus some actions were national in scope, affecting all Indians or all tribes but in a partial manner or touching individual Indians who fell into certain categories. Other actions were aimed at geographical areas (selected states). Finally came the total termination of individual tribes, which severed their connections with the federal government completely and ended for them all federal programs provided specifically for Indians.

Although termination came to be thought of as a single principle that lined up promoters against opponents, in fact there were many ambiguities. The repeal of discriminatory legislation was sought by Indians and their friends and was, in fact, a continuation of action inaugurated by Collier. Transfer of some services for Indians—education, health, and welfare—to other federal agencies or to the states had been an important ingredient of the Indian New Deal, as the Johnson-O'Malley Act of 1934

Policy," *American Indian Law Review* 5, no. 1 (1977): 139–84; S. Lyman Tyler, *A History of Indian Policy* (Washington: Bureau of Indian Affairs, 1973), pp. 151–88; "Termination (1943–1961)" and "Terminated Tribes" in *Felix S. Cohen's Handbook of Federal Indian Law*, 1982 ed. (Charlottesville, Virginia: Michie, Bobbs-Merrill, 1982), pp. 152–80, 811–81.

2. These categories were used by the House Committee on Interior and Insular Affairs in 1953 as a context for specific legislative proposals. See, for example, *House Report* no. 841, 83–1, serial 11666, and *House Report* no. 870, 83–1, serial 11667.

demonstrated. The concept of a special claims commission to handle Indian claims against the government, which was a part of Collier's program that he had failed to accomplish, became tied in with terminationist philosophy. *Freedom* and *emancipation* resonated with both Collier's policies of self-determination and the insistence of Indian New Deal critics like the American Indian Federation that the Indian Bureau be abolished. Thus there came together in the termination policy of the 1950s a good many threads of history, not only from the assimilationist era of the nineteenth and early twentieth centuries but from the reform movement of the 1920s and 1930s as well.

Although there was a kind of inner dynamism within the movement that came from a firmly held philosophical position that the Indians must be integrated into white society and not be allowed or encouraged to remain a segregated segment within the nation, the termination era coincided with and was strengthened by the political and economic conditions of the decade. Postwar economy moves called for reduction of government spending. The period was a time of economic growth, and the tying up of Indian lands and other resources in tribal enclaves went against the prevailing mood. The Cold War between the United States and Russia placed particular value on national unity and conformity, and special groups, especially if they emphasized communal values, were considered out of line. Urban-industrial development, speeded by the war, caught the Indians, too, and as growing population pushed beyond the capabilities of the reservations to support it, a movement to urban centers, with consequent assimilationist pressures, coincided with the termination actions of the government.

As with most phases of United States Indian policy, termination had strong supporters and strong critics. The two streams of opinion and attitude toward the Indians that had existed during all of the nation's history—assimilation or separateness—continued to flow strongly, and each brought its own evaluation of the policy. Senator Arthur V. Watkins of Utah, the most ardent promoter of termination, considered the "freeing of the Indian from wardship status" not a subject for academic debate but "an ideal or universal truth, to which all men subscribe, and concerning which they differ only in their opinion as to how the ideal may be attained and in what degree and during what period of time." He saw the Indian Reorganization Act simply as an unfortunate delay in "the major and continuing Congressional movement toward full freedom," and he worked for "the full realization of [Indian] national citizenship with all other Americans." In 1957, at the height of the termination movement, he wrote: "Following in the footsteps of the Emancipation Proclamation of ninety-four years ago, I see the following words emblazoned in letters of fire above the heads of the Indians—*THESE PEOPLE SHALL BE FREE!"* On the other hand, Oliver La Farge, president of the Association on American Indian Affairs, the organization that most consistently fought to preserve federal responsibility for Indian welfare, saw termination as the latest attempt at "disintegration" of the Indians, at "de-Indianizing Indians, dissolving their communities, or destroying their cultural heritage." He condemned the "hasty impatience" in applying termination to tribes who did not want it.[3]

As some tribes were actually terminated and it became clear that their well-being greatly declined with loss of federal status, the cry against termination came to drown out once more the advocates of "freedom." When the stark reality of absolute cessation of federal responsibility for protection of Indian property and of federal services for Indians confronted the tribes and the nation, the full evil of terminating tribes that were not able to stand by themselves in the competitive technological world of the whites became apparent. The movement slowed and finally was reversed before irreparable damage had spread across the nation.

3. Watkins's and La Farge's positions were printed side by side: Oliver La Farge, "Termination of Federal Supervision: Disintegration and the American Indians," *Annals of the American Academy of Political and Social Science* 311 (May 1957): 41–46; Arthur V. Watkins, "Termination of Federal Supervision: The Removal of Restrictions over Indian Property and Person," ibid., pp. 47–55.

The Postwar Years

The years after Collier's departure from office were a period of transition to the new policy of federal withdrawal from Indian affairs. They were a time, too, of some confusion, for management of the Indian Bureau was in the hands of administrators whose actions contrasted sharply with the strong, purposeful leadership that Collier had provided. Vacillating between Collier's vision of Indian self-determination and the new principles of termination, the first two commissioners, William A. Brophy and John R. Nichols, left little mark on Indian affairs. Only when Dillon S. Myer became commissioner in 1950 did firm direction again appear, and by the end of his tenure in 1953 the bureau had been fully committed to termination.

THE INDIAN CLAIMS COMMISSION

The matter of Indian claims against the United States, however, still remained to be settled. Many tribes had grievances growing out of treaties or other contracts with the federal government, some of which were of long standing, and there was no expeditious way of coming to an equitable settlement. The claims were a continuing irritant to satisfactory relations between the Indians and the government, and the drawn-out process of dealing with them was a heavy burden upon Congress, the Indian Bureau, and the Justice Department. Reformers looked upon the elimination of just claims as something owed to the Indians, and those who envisaged the termination of federal guardianship knew that the ties could not be broken as long as the claims were not quieted with absolute finality. The Court of Claims, established in 1855 to permit suits against the federal government, had been prohibited in 1863 from considering claims "growing out of or dependent on any treaty stipulation entered into with foreign nations or with the Indian tribes." To bring an Indian claim before the court, therefore, required a special act of Congress; although some claims were handled by the court, beginning with a Choctaw case in 1881, the process was slow and uncertain. By 1946 nearly two hundred Indian claims had been filed with the Court of Claims, but only twenty-nine received awards; most of the rest were dismissed on technicalities.[1]

It was clear that more adequate machinery was necessary. The Meriam Report in 1928 had remarked: "The benevolent desire of the United States Government to educate and civilize the Indian cannot be realized with a tribe which has any considerable unsatisfied bona fide claim against the government. The expectation of large awards making all members of the tribe wealthy, the disturbing influence of outside agitators seeking personal emoluments, and the conviction in the Indian mind that justice is being denied, renders extremely difficult any cooperation between the government and its Indian wards. Besides these practical considerations, the simple canons of justice and morality demand that no Indian tribe should be denied an opportunity to present for adjustment before an appropriate tribunal the rights which the tribe claims under recognized principles of law and government." The report noted the inability of existing procedures to rectify the situation and recommended a special staff of experts to investigate tribal claims and draw up proper jurisdictional bills for Congress in order to expedite the work of the Court of Claims. Commissioner Charles J. Rhoads's proposed program of reform in 1929 included a recommendation for a "special Indian claims commission," to hear not only legal cases but also causes that were "human and moral," which might be settled in some gratuitous way by Congress. But the bill introduced by Representative Scott Leavitt on January 6, 1930, to create a United States Court of Indian Claims came to naught, largely because of the potential costs involved.[2]

1. Harvey D. Rosenthal, "Their Day in Court: A History of the Indian Claims Commission" (Ph.D. dissertation, Kent State University, 1976), pp. 7–60; Glen A. Wilkinson, "Indian Tribal Claims before the Court of Claims," *Georgetown Law Journal* 55 (December 1966): 511–28. See also E. B. Smith, ed., *Indian Tribal Claims Decided in the Court of Claims of the United States; Briefed and Compiled to June 30, 1947*, 2 vols. (Arlington, Virginia: University Publications of America, 1976).

2. *The Problem of Indian Administration* (Baltimore: Johns Hopkins Press, 1928), pp. 805–11; C. J. Rhoads to Lynn J. Frazier, December 11, 1929, in *Congressional Rec-*

John Collier, as commissioner of Indian affairs, considered Indian claims a matter of high priority, and he and Secretary Ickes decided upon a *commission* rather than a *court*, for the former, it was believed, could solve the problems better than adversary proceedings inherent in a judicial format. Numerous bills for creating such an Indian claims commission were introduced between 1935 and 1945, but none was able to overcome the strong opposition of members of Congress, some of whom looked upon the measure as a raid upon the Treasury intended to benefit not the Indians but their lawyers. Then in early 1945 new bills were introduced on which long hearings were held over a four-month period.[3] From these deliberations and testimony came a final bill, introduced by Representative Henry Jackson of Washington on October 25, 1945, embodying the ideas contained in the earlier measures. The House Committee on Indian Affairs, which Jackson chaired, submitted a long report and a strong favorable recommendation.[4] The bill easily passed the House and, with some minor alterations, the Senate. It became law on August 13, 1946. On signing the act, President Truman spoke with high optimism: "I hope that this bill will mark the beginning of a new era for our Indian citizens. They have valiantly served on every battlefront. They have proved by their loyalty the wisdom of a national policy built upon fair dealing. With the final settlement of all outstanding claims which this measure insures, Indians can take their place without special handicaps or special advantages in the economic life of our nation and share fully in its progress."[5]

The law provided for a commission of three persons (enlarged to five in 1967), with appropriate staff, to hear claims against the United States on behalf of "any Indian tribe, band, or other identifiable group of Indians re-

ord, 72: 1052–53; *Congressional Record*, 72: 1139. Note that a claims commission was one of the nine points in the agenda of the American Indian Defense Association, December 1929. See discussion above, p. 924.

3. There is extensive debate for and against a commission in connection with the bill of 1937 (S. 1902) in *Congressional Record*, 81: 6058–59, 6236–67. The hearings are in "Creation of Indian Claims Commission," *Hearings before the Committee on Indian Affairs, House of Representatives, 79th Congress, 1st Session, on H.R. 1198 and H.R. 1341* (1945). The legislative history of the various bills is given in Rosenthal, "Their Day in Court," pp. 71–124. See also the discussion of the defeat of the claims commission bills in John Leiper Freeman, Jr., "The New Deal for Indians: A Study in Bureau–Committee Relations in American Government" (Ph.D. dissertation, Princeton University, 1952), pp. 308–15. Freeman notes (p. 315) that the defeat of the measure in 1937, after passing the Senate and being favorably reported by the House committee, was "the first major legislative setback of the Collier administration. It stands somewhat as a symbol of the end of the offense and the beginning of a serious defensive struggle for survival by Collier, the Bureau, and the New Deal program for Indians."

4. *House Report* no. 1466, 79–1, serial 10936.

5. 60 *United States Statutes* 1049–56; *Public Papers of the Presidents of the United States: Harry S. Truman, 1946* (Washington: GPO, 1962), p. 414.

siding within the territorial limits of the United States or Alaska." The claims could be presented by any member of the group as its representative, but if a federally recognized tribal organization existed, it would have the exclusive right to represent the group. The commission was to notify the tribes of the act, and it could receive petitions for a period of five years from the date of the act. The classes of claims were broadly defined in five categories:

(1) claims in law or equity under the Constitution, laws, treaties of the United States, and Executive orders of the President;

(2) all other claims in law or equity, including those sounding in tort, with respect to which the claimant would have been entitled to sue in a court of the United States if the United States was subject to suit;

(3) claims which would result if the treaties, contracts, and agreements between the claimant and the United States were revised on the grounds of fraud, duress, unconscionable consideration, mutual or unilateral mistake, whether of law or fact, or any other ground cognizable by a court of equity;

(4) claims arising from the taking by the United States, whether as the result of treaty of cession or otherwise, of lands owned or occupied by the claimant without the payment for such lands of compensation agreed to by the claimant; and

(5) claims based upon fair and honorable dealings that are not recognized by any existing rule of law or equity.[6]

No statute of limitations or laches would have effect, but the United States could use all other defenses, and in the determination of relief deductions were to be made for payments made on the claims and other offsets, including "all money or property given to or funds expended gratuitously for the benefit of the claimant." Indians were to be represented by attorneys of their own selection, whose fees were to be fixed by the commission; the attorney general would represent the United States. Appeal to the Court of Claims was allowed. When the commission submitted its report at the end of a case, Congress would appropriate the sums necessary to make the awards. The payment of the claims would discharge the United States fully of all claims in the matter, and the law barred any further claims arising out of the matter involved. The life of the commission extended for ten years from the date of its first meeting. The law provided for the establishment of an Investigation Division, to investigate all the claims and determine the facts relating to them, but this section of the law was never implemented.

6. 60 *United States Statutes* 1050. The paragraph designations are not in the original.

Although the filing of claims proceeded slowly at first, by the end of the five-year petition period the commission was overwhelmed. Nearly all of the 176 tribes or bands who were notified of the act filed one or more claims on old grievances; in the end there were 370 petitions, which were broken down into 617 dockets. The great majority of cases were land cases, which involved three stages: determining the claimant's title to the land (either *Indian title* based on continuous, exclusive occupation or *recognized title* based on some treaty or law), determining the value of the land and the amount of liability of the United States, and then determining gratuitous offsets to be subtracted from the government's liability. A second class of cases comprised accounting cases concerned with fiduciary culpability on the part of the federal government in the management of Indian funds. The intention in establishing a claims *commission* rather than a claims *court* had been to make the deliberations more informal and to escape strict adversary proceedings. Unfortunately, with hired attorneys on the Indian side and lawyers from the Department of Justice defending the United States, a legal adversary proceeding quickly developed, and the fact that the commission looked to the Court of Claims for procedures and precedents further strengthened that situation. The result was serious delay, and Congress had to extend the life of the commission in 1956, 1961, 1967, 1972, and 1976, until the commission finally went out of existence on September 30, 1978, with unfinished cases transferred to the Court of Claims.[7]

7. An alphabetical list of cases and an index by docket number are given in *United States Indian Claims Commission, August 13, 1946–September 30, 1978: Final Report* (Washington: GPO, 1979), pp. 23–123. The *Final Report* contains a large map, "Indian Land Areas Judicially Established." The decisions themselves have been published by the Native American Rights Fund, Boulder, Colorado, and Clearwater Publishing Company, New York. See Norman A. Ross, ed., *Index to the Decisions of the Indian Claims Commission* (New York: Clearwater Publishing Company, 1973).

The *Final Report*, pp. 1–21, includes a "Historical Survey," by Harvey D. Rosenthal, based on his detailed dissertation, "Their Day in Court." The issues in land claims and the literature about them are discussed in Imre Sutton, *Indian Land Tenure: Bibliographical Essays and a Guide to the Literature* (New York: Clearwater Publishing Company, 1975), pp. 91–114. Other useful studies of the Indian Claims Commission and its work are Nancy Oestreich Lurie, "The Indian Claims Commission Act," *Annals of the American Academy of Political and Social Science* 311 (May 1957): 56–70; and Thomas Le Duc, "The Work of the Indian Claims Commission under the Act of 1946," *Pacific Historical Review* 26 (February 1957): 1–16. *Ethnohistory* 2 (Fall 1955) was devoted to articles on the commission. The gratuitous offsets are treated in John R. White, "Barmecide Revisited: The Gratuitous Offset in Indian Claims Cases," *Ethnohistory* 25 (Spring 1978): 179–92. Examples of studies dealing with specific tribes are Herbert T. Hoover, "Yankton Sioux Tribal Claims against the United States, 1917–1975," *Western Historical Quarterly* 7 (April 1976): 125–42, and Robert C. Carriker, "The Kalispel Tribe and the Indian Claims Commission Experience," ibid. 9 (January 1978): 19–31.

The work of the Indian Claims Commission was a mixture of positive results and substantial failure. The Indians had their day in court, and the very establishment of the commission indicated a strong willingness on the part of the United States to admit injustice toward the Indians in the past and to make amends. The total awards of more than $818 million meant a sizable injection of money into the Indian tribal economies, even though the lasting effects of the sum were not great, for many tribes insisted on per capita payments instead of investing the funds in tribal enterprises. The presentation of the cases before the commission greatly heightened the legal consciousness of the Indian communities, many of which became accustomed to hire legal counsel for their affairs. Moreover, the heavy reliance on expert witnesses, which was necessary in determining the land cases, resulted in a new awareness of documentary sources on the Indians' past and established cooperation between anthropologists and historians that resulted in an extensive and continuing interest in ethnohistory.[8]

But on a more fundamental level the Indian Claims Commission did not fulfill its purpose, for it did not bring the finality in the settlement of all claims that its framers had wanted. In some ways Indian grievances seemed to be heightened instead of diffused as the commission went about its work. The legalistic approach that developed, with rigorous appraisals of what the Indian lands were worth at the time of cession, and the concern of the United States attorneys to ferret out all gratuitous offsets, for example, often caused bitterness; and in the end the awards were smaller than the Indians had expected. Then, as the commission's work stretched out into the 1950s, it coincided with the congressional drive to terminate federal responsibility for the Indians, and in 1960 Arthur V. Watkins became chief commissioner. The Senate committee noted when considering extension of the commission in 1961: "It cannot be stressed too strongly that the Claims Commission Act was passed by Congress to give the Indians their day in court to present their claims of every kind, shape, and variety. Until all these claims are heard and settled, we may expect the In-

8. The written testimony of the expert witnesses has been published in the American Indian Ethnohistory Series (New York: Garland Publishing, 1974). A listing of the published studies is given in Francis Paul Prucha, *A Bibliographical Guide to the History of Indian-White Relations in the United States* (Chicago: University of Chicago Press, 1977), pp. 86–96. The testimony is available also on microfiche from the Clearwater Publishing Company; see Norman A. Ross, ed., *Index to the Expert Testimony before the Indian Claims Commission: The Written Reports* (New York: Clearwater Publishing Company, 1973). The cooperation of anthropologists and historians on Indian Claims Commission work led to the organization of the American Society for Ethnohistory and the establishment of the journal *Ethnohistory*.

dians to resist any effort to terminate Federal supervision and control over them."[9] The settlement of claims thus appeared to be, not a bold stroke to correct all past injustices, but simply a necessary preliminary step toward termination. Finally, the only remedy following the commission's decisions was monetary settlement, whereas more and more Indians insisted that they did not want money but the return of their lands. Indian agitation in the 1960s and 1970s—both from federally recognized tribes that had used the commission's machinery and from others, chiefly eastern tribes, that had been excluded—and the increasing number of legal cases drawn up by Indians seeking to right old wrongs made a mockery of the promise that the Indian Claims Commission would settle grievances once and for all.[10]

POSTWAR READJUSTMENT

On March 6, 1945, William A. Brophy assumed office as commissioner of Indian affairs. A New Mexican lawyer who had acted as attorney for the Pueblos, Brophy was Collier's choice as his successor. He broadly sympathized with the Indian New Deal and had the support of the Association on American Indian Affairs and a wide range of members of Congress. Yet he made it clear to the Senate when his nomination was under consideration that he was not a crusader in the Collier mold and that his responsibility was to implement the policy that Congress made. He was a middle-of-the-roader who hoped to get along with the terminationists in Congress without completely giving in to them. By accepting termination as a long-term goal, he hoped to hold back any precipitate action that could harm the Indians before they were fully prepared to give up their special status. And the problems of postwar readjustment demanded solution before termination could be seriously considered. Brophy sharply perceived the economic problems that faced the returning Indian veterans and war industry workers and realized that reservation resources alone could not provide for

9. *Senate Report* no. 208, 87–1, serial 12322, pp. 2–3.
10. The Conclusion in Rosenthal, "Their Day in Court," pp. 303–23, is very critical and speaks of the commission's "generally dismal record," but the historical survey by Rosenthal in the commission's *Final Report* emphasizes the positive aspects of its work. A critical appraisal of the commission appears in Nancy Oestreich Lurie, "The Indian Claims Commission," *Annals of the American Academy of Political and Social Science* 436 (March 1978): 97–110. She notes (p. 108) "the lack of meaningful Indian involvement in the cases" and that "no one really listened very carefully to the Indians." See also the criticisms in Sandra C. Danforth, "Repaying Historical Debts: The Indian Claims Commission," *North Dakota Law Review* 49 (Winter 1973): 359–403.

them. "So long as thousands of Indians exist below the subsistence level on poverty-stricken reservations," he wrote shortly after taking office, "so long as employment opportunities are scarce, Federal expenditures for program services to Indians cannot be appreciably decreased."[11]

Some segments of the public, however, were unwilling to proceed slowly. One indication of the popular mood was an article by O. K. Armstrong in the *Reader's Digest* for August 1945, called "Set the American Indians Free!" This highly charged piece sought to stir up public support, and it was full of the old clichés: that Indians needed to be "emancipated" from special restrictions and limitations, that the Indian Reorganization Act had forced a "collectivist system upon the Indians, with bigger doses of paternalism and regimentation," that lands were added to Indian reservations even though the Indians were not utilizing the lands they already had, and that the costs of the Indian service were increasing despite the fact that the most advanced Indians were those with the least connection with the Bureau of Indian Affairs. Strong answers were published in the *American Indian*, the journal of the Association on American Indian Affairs. Dr. Haven Emerson, president of the association, said of the article: "Had it appeared in some local journal, [it] should merely have been deplored as an ill-informed rehash of old fallacies and sentimentalities concerning our Indians. With the authority of the *Reader's Digest* behind it, however, the article becomes a potential danger to the very freedom which it demands. No one can be free unless he is independent." Emerson charged that if Armstrong's principles were followed, all hopes that the Indians would become independent would be destroyed. But the refutations in the association's journal reached few of Armstrong's readers.[12]

The cry for "freedom" was full-throated, and it was echoed in congressional chambers. Brophy's term was full of warnings, as bills were introduced that would have removed restrictions on Indian lands, subjected the Indian property to freedom from limitations, or in some other way thrown the Indians upon their own resources, ready or not. One proposal

---

11. "Nomination of William A. Brophy to Be Commissioner of Indian Affairs," *Hearings before the Committee on Indian Affairs, United States Senate, 79th Congress, 1st Session* (1945); CIA Report, 1945, p. 233. On Brophy, see S. Lyman Tyler, "William A. Brophy, 1945–48," in Robert M. Kvasnicka and Herman J. Viola, eds., *The Commissioners of Indian Affairs, 1824–1977* (Lincoln: University of Nebraska Press, 1979), pp. 283–87, and Larry J. Hasse, "Termination and Assimilation: Federal Indian Policy, 1943 to 1961" (Ph.D. dissertation, Washington State University, 1974), pp. 66–80.

12. O. K. Armstrong, "Set the American Indian Free!" *Reader's Digest* 47 (August 1945): 47–52; Haven Emerson, "Freedom or Exploitation! Is Mr. O. K. Armstrong's Recent Solution of the American Indian Problem Sound?" *American Indian* 2 (Fall 1945): 3–7; Randolph C. Downes, "The American Indians Can Be Free," ibid., pp. 8–11.

was to remove all restrictions on the property of Indian veterans, either by a blanket law or by enabling any such person to apply for the removal. A House bill (H.R. 1113) of the Eightieth Congress, for example, read: "Upon application by any Indian who shall have served honorably in the armed forces of the United States in time of war . . . [the secretary of the interior is directed] to remove all restrictions upon the lands, interest in lands, funds, or other property of such Indians, and, if such lands or interests in lands are held by the United States in trust for such Indians, to issue an unrestricted patent in fee therefor." Another proposal broadened the basis for "emancipation" to include Indians who were high school graduates, those who met the requirements for naturalization of aliens, those recommended by their superintendent, and those who had resided and provided self-support off the reservation for five years.[13] The Interior Department, however, did not favor such moves. D'Arcy McNickle, testifying before the Senate committee, foresaw a "wave of applicants for fee patents from the veterans of the various wars and a rapid transfer of Indian lands to non-Indian ownership." He feared the breaking up of established grazing units and forest management units and a "disastrous effect" upon the department's efforts to consolidate Indian landholdings.[14]

Commissioner Brophy spoke firmly for the protection of Indian property rights, and he appreciated the Indians' unalterable opposition to the disposal of tribal property and the placing of Indian lands on the tax rolls. He insisted that the Indians were not seeking special privileges but that they sought only to retain rights and guarantees granted long ago by the United States. "To remove trust status from their lands and remaining property," he said, "would be to destroy the last important guarantee remaining to them. It must be remembered that the guarantees were not wrung from a reluctant government but were freely given as part of a bargain by which the United States obtained the right to enter and dispose of lands which previously were in Indian ownership." Brophy fought strongly against damaging cuts in appropriations. He admitted that Congress, with

13. "Emancipation of Indians," *Hearings before the Subcommittee on Indian Affairs of the Committee on Public Lands, House of Representatives, 80th Congress, 1st Session, on H.R. 2958, H.R. 2165, and H.R. 1113* (1947). See also "Removal of Restrictions on Indian Property and for the Emancipation of Indians," *Hearings before the Committee on Indian Affairs, House of Representatives, 79th Congress, 2d Session, on H.R. 3680, H.R. 3681, and H.R. 3710* (1946); "Removal of Restrictions on Property of Indians Who Served in the Armed Forces," *Hearing before the Committee on Indian Affairs, United States Senate, 79th Congress, 2d Session, on S. 1093 and S. 1194* (1946).

14. "Removal of Restrictions on Property of Indians Who Served in the Armed Forces," pp. 2–3. See also Oscar L. Chapman to Richard J. Welsh, May 2, 1947, in *House Report* no. 691, 80–1, serial 11121.

its plenary power, could withhold all appropriations for Indian administration and remove trustee responsibilities, but he charged: "Entirely apart from the injustice which such precipitate action would inflict on these first Americans, whose property rights do not derive from any benevolence of the United States, it would prove economically disastrous to reduce the resources available to the Indians." He concluded: "Granted, perhaps, that the rate of progress has been slow, it nevertheless follows that we get ahead no faster if we reduce our present effort. A hungry and sick Indian is not brought nearer to the day when he may have food and good health if we allow his meager resources to be further diminished or wasted."[15]

Brophy did not last out the fight. His health was poor, and he frequently left matters in the hands of William Zimmerman, Jr., the assistant commissioner of Indian affairs, while he took sick leave. Finally, on June 3, 1948, he resigned.

Zimmerman, as acting commissioner, played an important role in the move toward termination. On February 8, 1947, he testified at hearings before the Senate Committee on Civil Service, which had asked for a statement of how the personnel and expenses of the Bureau of Indian Affairs could be reduced. Zimmerman's reply was couched in terms of decreasing the number of Indians to whom the expensive services of the bureau were provided, and he offered three lists of tribes. The first group, he said, could be denied federal services immediately; the second could function with minimal federal supervision within ten years; the third would need more than ten years to prepare for withdrawal of bureau support. The categories had been determined according to four criteria: (1) degree of acculturation of the tribe (admixture of white blood, percentage of illiteracy, business ability, acceptance of white institutions, and acceptance of the Indian by whites); (2) economic condition of the tribe (availability of resources and assets to enable a tribe or individuals to make a reasonably decent living); (3) willingness of a tribe and its members to dispense with federal aid; and (4) willingness and ability of the state in which a tribe lived to assume the responsibilities dropped by the federal government. In addition to the lists and criteria, Zimmerman presented three specimen bills, for the Klamath, Osage, and Menominee tribes, groups that he thought would be suitable for beginning the withdrawal process.[16]

15. William A. Brophy, Memorandum for the Secretary, July 8, 1946, OSI CCF 1937–1953, 5–11, Administration General, part 15; CIA Report, 1947, pp. 348–49.

16. "Officers and Employees of the Federal Government," *Hearings before the Committee on Civil Service, United States Senate, 80th Congress, 1st Session, on S. Res. 41* (1947), pp. 544–47; the lists of tribes are reprinted in S. Lyman Tyler, *A History of Indian Policy* (Washington: Bureau of Indian Affairs, 1973), pp. 163–64. See also CIA Report, 1947, pp. 348–49.

It was not Zimmerman's aim to prepare a blueprint for termination, but his "plan" soon became a jumping-off point for the terminationists. Senator Watkins said that the assistant commissioner's testimony "vividly recalled Congressional attention to the fact that specific groups of Indians were then regarded as prepared for on-the-spot freedom from their wardship status" and that it "served as an effective stimulus toward renewed consideration of an end of wardship." The plan was frequently cited in support of congressional withdrawal proposals, even though Zimmerman later insisted that his testimony before the committee had been "repeatedly misquoted and misinterpreted" and that the bills he had submitted differed greatly from the termination bills that were finally passed for the Klamaths and the Menominees.[17]

Whatever Zimmerman's later disclaimers, the Interior Department and the Bureau of Indian Affairs came to preach a moderate form of terminationism. One of the assistant commissioners of Indians affairs, John H. Provinse, worked out a "policy statement" for the department in March 1947, which began: "The policy of the Department of the Interior in the discharge of its responsibility for the administration of Indian affairs in the United States and Alaska, is one of liquidation of the Bureau of Indian Affairs as rapidly as is consistent with recognized American principles of fair dealing and the fulfillment of national trust obligations assumed or imposed over a period of many decades." The statement repeated Zimmerman's plan.[18] Provinse presented the policy publicly at the National Conference of Social Work on April 15. He discussed the various services provided for the Indians by the federal government, then summarized the bureau's policy under five heads: (1) the Zimmerman plan; (2) legislation to enable individual Indians to renounce tribal or federal status; (3) assumption of services for the Indians by other federal or state agencies or by Indian corporations; (4) maintenance of the federal government's trusteeship responsibilities for Indian resources "until such time as it can be assured that release of the lands will not result in the wholesale dispossession of Indians from their lands that occurred in the decades from 1890 to 1920"; and (5) encouragement of the Indians "to understand the full im-

17. Arthur V. Watkins, "Termination of Federal Supervision: The Removal of Restrictions over Indian Property and Persons," *Annals of the American Academy of Political and Social Science* 311 (May 1957): 49; William Zimmerman, Jr., "The Role of the Bureau of Indian Affairs since 1933," ibid., pp. 36—37.

18. "Policy Statement," March 25, 1947, in OIA, Office File of Assistant Commissioner John H. Provinse, Policy Statement. Felix Cohen, in a letter to Provinse of April 3, 1947, criticized the statement for "trying to force good things down [the Indians'] throats."

plications of their citizenship" and to stimulate a "constructive interest" on the part of non-Indians.[19]

The Brophy administration, through Acting Commissioner Zimmerman, also took definite steps toward planning for the withdrawal it espoused. In April 1948 Zimmerman prepared a memorandum for the assistant secretary of the interior on comprehensive long-range plans and programs, along the lines of the plan that had been drawn up for the Navajo Tribe. He considered the formulation of such plans "one of the most essential tasks now facing the Indian service" and wanted to assign it a high priority even at the expense of other activities, and he selected tribes for which to begin the planning. About the Klamath Indians and the Indians in California and in Minnesota he spoke bluntly. They "are considered to be sufficiently assimilated, educated, and possessed of sufficient resources," he wrote, "to warrant the withdrawal of the Indian Service in the near future. The long-range programs for these tribes would thus be, in effect, liquidation programs." In early May the memorandum was sent to regional directors and to the pertinent agency superintendents, with a schedule for the submission of reports, and at the end of the month a supplementary directive stated explicitly what was wanted:

> What is desired is the assembly in concise form of existing factual data as to the social and economic status of each group or tribe and, after a careful analysis and evaluation of the data, the projection of a comprehensive long-range program. The objective of the program should be the eventual discharge of the Federal government's obligation, legal, moral or otherwise, and the discontinuance of Federal supervision and control at the earliest date compatible with the government's trusteeship responsibility. This may mean the early termination of all Federal supervision for some groups, whereas for others it seems obvious that certain Federal activities including the development of resources, must be continued for many years.[20]

A major statement that reinforced the policy of assimilation was the report of the Commission on Organization of the Executive Branch of the

---

19. John H. Provinse, "The Withdrawal of Federal Supervision of the American Indian," a paper presented at the National Conference of Social Work, San Francisco, California, April 15, 1947, copies in OIA, Office File of Provinse, San Francisco. This paper was sent to all regional offices and all reservations as an aid to discussion of programs planned for eventual federal withdrawal. Circular no. 3675, May 28, 1948, OIA Circulars (M1121, reel 17).

20. Memorandum, William Zimmerman, Jr., to Assistant Secretary William E. Warne, April 30, 1948; Circular no. 3672, May 5, 1948; Circular no. 3675, May 28, 1948—all in OIA Circulars (M1121, reel 17).

Government (the Hoover Commission). The commission's special task force on Indian affairs asserted in its report that "assimilation must be the dominant goal of public policy," that in fact there was no other choice. "The basis for historic Indian culture has been swept away," it said. "Traditional tribal organization was smashed a generation ago. Americans of Indian descent who are still thought of as 'Indian' are a handful of people, not three-tenths of one percent of the total population. Assimilation cannot be prevented. The only questions are: What kind of assimilation, and how fast?"[21] The full commission picked up and endorsed the task force's position as "the keystone of the organization and of the activities of the Federal Government in the field of Indian affairs." It recommended complete integration of the Indians into the mass of the population as taxpaying citizens, and until that could occur it wanted the social programs for Indians to be transferred to the state governments, thus diminishing the activities of the Bureau of Indian Affairs. Tribal governments, it thought, should be regarded as a stage in the transition from federal tutelage to full participation in state and local government. There was strong dissent from the vice chairman of the commission, Dean Acheson, and from two other commission members, James Forrestal and James H. Rowe, Jr., who declared that the Indian task force and the commission had exceeded their authority and their competence in making a recommendation on substantive Indian policy. But in the widely disseminated general report of the commission the dissent was omitted, and the assimilationist position was given a decided boost. The Hoover Commission also recommended that the Bureau of Indian Affairs, while it continued to exist, be transferred from the Department of the Interior to a new department of social services, but nothing came of this proposal.[22]

The Hoover Commission report was published in 1949 during the administration of Commissioner John R. Nichols, who had been a member of the commission's Indian task force and had succeeded Brophy in March 1949. Nichols was a university administrator who at the time of his ap-

---

21. *Report of the Committee on Indian Affairs to the Commission on Organization of the Executive Branch of the Government,* October 1948 (mimeographed), pp. 54–55. The members of the task force were George A. Graham, chairman, Charles J. Rhoads, John R. Nichols, and Gilbert Darlington. See also John Leiper Freeman, Jr., "A Program for Indian Affairs: Summary of the Report of the Hoover Commission Task Force on Indian Affairs," *American Indian* 7 (Spring 1954): 48–62.

22. *Social Security and Education—Indian Affairs: A Report to the Congress by the Commission on Organization of the Executive Branch of the Government,* March 1949 (Washington: GPO, 1949); *The Hoover Commission Report on the Organization of the Executive Branch of the Government* (New York: McGraw-Hill Book Company, 1949), pp. 461–73.

pointment was president of the New Mexico College of Agriculture and Mechanical Arts at Las Cruces. He was commissioner for only eleven months and made no dramatic changes, yet he reinforced the bureau's endorsement of assimilation. Although he admitted that the federal government still needed to protect the Indians' property and provide services that were not otherwise available, he took as his goal for the Indians a statement of Thomas Jefferson: "The ultimate point of rest and happiness for them is to let our settlements and theirs meet and blend together, to intermix, and become one people."[23]

THE APPROACH OF TERMINATION

If Commissioner Nichols was an uncertain force whose term was too short for him to give strong leadership, the same cannot be said of his successor, Dillon S. Myer, who became commissioner of Indian affairs on May 5, 1950. Myer had been an agronomist and an administrator in the Department of Agriculture, and from 1942 to 1946 he served as director of the War Relocation Authority, handling the Japanese evacuees from the West Coast. After a short stint as head of the Federal Housing Administration, he became coordinator of the Institute of Inter-American Affairs. He was an efficient administrator, but he knew little of Indian affairs and seemed to his critics to be insensitive to Indian views and needs, and he surrounded himself with old friends from the War Relocation Authority, who replaced the holdovers from Collier's regime. His administration became a center of growing controversy as he pushed vigorously for termination and as criticism mounted against him. At the end of Myer's first year, Harold Ickes publicly called him "a Hitler and Mussolini rolled into one."[24]

Although there were no laws terminating Indian tribes during Myer's term, the movement in the direction of withdrawal of federal responsibility for Indians was pronounced. The commissioner's long-range objectives, as he stated them in 1951, were "(1) a standard of living for Indians comparable with that enjoyed by other segments of the population, and (2) the

23. CIA Report, 1949, p. 366; William J. Dennehy, "John Ralph Nichols, 1949–50," in Kvasnicka and Viola, *Commissioners of Indian Affairs*, pp. 289–92.

24. Harold L. Ickes, "'Justice' in a Deep Freeze," *New Republic* 124 (May 1951): 17. At this time Ickes wrote a weekly column for the *New Republic* in which he again and again castigated Myer's administration; see "Go East, Young Indian!" 125 (September 3, 1951): 17; and "The Indian Loses Again" 125 (September 24, 1951): 16. There is an excellent discussion of Myer's administration in Hasse, "Termination and Assimilation," pp. 108–64; a briefer sketch is Patricia K. Ourada, "Dillon Seymour Myer, 1950–53," in Kvasnicka and Viola, *Commissioners of Indian Affairs*, pp. 293–99.

step-by-step transfer of Bureau functions to the Indians themselves or to appropriate agencies of local, State, or Federal Government." In the next year he noted the "greatly increased emphasis" on the second of these objectives and called attention to the introduction of bills in Congress to withdraw bureau activities in California and part of Oregon, the acceleration of transferring educational responsibility to the public school systems, the transfer of health functions to the states, negotiations for transfer of jurisdictional responsibility on reservations to the states, an all-time high in the leasing of lands for oil and gas production, and the encouragement of Indians to seek loans from local agencies instead of from the bureau.[25] To make clear his stand to the Indians, Myer circulated among the tribes the following offer:

> 1. If any Indian tribe is convinced the Bureau of Indian Affairs is a handicap to its advancement, I am willing to recommend to the Secretary of the Interior that legislative authority be obtained from the Congress to terminate the Bureau's trusteeship responsibility with respect to that tribe.
> 2. If any Indian tribe desires modification of the existing trusteeship in order that some part or parts thereof be lifted (such as the control of tribal funds, the leasing of tribal land, as examples), and if the leaders of the tribe will sit down with Bureau officials to discuss the details of such a program of partial termination of trusteeship, we will be glad to assign staff members to work with the group with a view to developing appropriate legislative proposals.
> 3. If there are tribes desiring to assume themselves some of the responsibilities the Bureau now carries with respect to the furnishing of services, without termination of the trusteeship relationship, we are prepared to work with such tribes in the development of an appropriate agreement providing for the necessary safeguards to the tribe and its members.
> The statement constitutes, in effect, a standing offer by the Bureau to work constructively with any tribe which wishes to assume either full control or a greater degree of control over its own affairs.[26]

An important part of the planning for ultimate termination of the Indian tribes was to survey conditions existing on the various reservations. Whether Zimmerman's criteria or others were to be used, detailed information geared to answer questions about the readiness of tribes to be set

---

25. CIA Report, 1952, pp. 389–92. See list of bills "prepared or revised during the year by the Bureau's legal staff," ibid., p. 419.
26. CIA Report, 1952, pp. 393–94.

free was necessary, and study and planning that was hesitantly begun in Brophy's administration blossomed into a full-blown activity. It was stimulated by a joint resolution introduced by Representative Reva Beck Bosone of Utah on June 21, 1950, which called for the study of all the Indian groups "to determine their qualifications to manage their own affairs without supervision and control by the Federal Government." The resolution directed the secretary of the interior to report at the beginning of the first session of the Eighty-second Congress the Indian groups that could be relieved of all supervision and at the beginning of the second session the programs undertaken and the proposed legislation for terminating such supervision for the remaining tribes as soon as practicable. The resolution was strongly supported by the Interior Department and by Commissioner Myer, and it passed the House on July 27. Although favorably reported by the Senate Committee on Interior and Insular Affairs, the resolution finally failed on the floor of the Senate. There Senator Watkins, on December 15, spoke vigorously against it on the ground that a new study was not needed and would only delay action; and he objected to spending bureau appropriations for the study when funds were so badly needed for regular activities.[27]

Watkins's action only postponed Mrs. Bosone's proposal, for the House then proceeded on its own. On July 1, 1952, it directed the Committee on Interior and Insular Affairs or a subcommittee "to conduct a full and complete investigation and study of the activities and operations of the Bureau of Indian Affairs." The specific intention was to gather information about the readiness of the tribes for termination. Because no funds were provided for the investigation, the subcommittee charged with the study turned to the Bureau of Indian Affairs for its information, asking the commissioner to supply a complete report on the following points: (1) the manner in which the Bureau of Indian Affairs had performed its function of studying the various tribes, bands, and groups of Indians to determine their qualifications for managing their own affairs without further supervision by the federal government; (2) the manner in which the Bureau of Indian Affairs had fulfilled its obligations of trust as the agency of the federal government charged with the guardianship of Indian property; (3) the adequacy of law and regulations to assure the faithful performance of trust in the exchange, lease, or sale of surface or subsurface interests in or title to real property or the disposition of personal property of Indian wards; (4) the names of tribes, bands, or groups of Indians now qualified for full management of

27. *House Report* no. 2723, 81–2, serial 11383, which prints Assistant Secretary Dale E. Doty to J. Hardin Peterson, July 21, 1950; CIA Report, 1950, pp. 342–43; *Senate Report* no. 2488, 81–2, serial 11372; *Congressional Record*, 96: 16604.

their own affairs; (5) the legislative proposals designed to promote the earliest practicable termination of all federal supervision and control over Indians; (6) the functions carried on by the Bureau of Indian Affairs that could be discontinued or transferred to other agencies of the federal government or to the states; (7) the names of states where further operation of the Bureau of Indian Affairs should be discontinued; (8) recommended legislation for removal of legal disability of Indians by reason of guardianship by the federal government; and (9) findings concerning transactions involving the exchange, lease, or sale of lands or interests in lands belonging to Indian wards, with specific findings as to such transactions in the state of Oregon.[28]

Dillon Myer responded promptly and enthusiastically. On August 5 he sent a detailed questionnaire to bureau officials in the field, requesting the information. In a cover letter accompanying the questionnaire he stated unequivocally his policy on withdrawal:

> During the past fiscal year the Bureau has devoted a great deal of effort to the development of withdrawal concepts and policy. Bureau personnel have been encouraged to give increasing emphasis to withdrawal objectives in their work with Indian groups and individuals in program development and effectuation. At the central office, we have established a Division of Program, whose primary responsibilities are to render guidance and assistance to Bureau personnel engaged in withdrawal programming at area and agency levels and to formulate Bureau withdrawal programs in cooperation with other central-office staff at national levels. We have reached the stage where it has become desirable to crystallize certain Bureau withdrawal policies, establish methods basic to the development of withdrawal programing, and fix responsibilities for proceeding with the task.

In urging careful attention to the questionnaire, Myer warned that future appropriations by Congress for the Indian Bureau would "be limited largely to financing items which will facilitate withdrawal." He insisted that the programming for withdrawal be a cooperative effort with Indian leaders, but in the end he declared that the bureau must proceed even if Indian cooperation was lacking.[29]

The Bureau of Indian Affairs reported the results of the survey on December 3, 1952, with lengthy answers to the specific questions asked by the subcommittee and thirteen tables of data pertaining to the prepared-

---

28. *House Report* no. 2503, 83–2, serial 11582, pp. 2–3.

29. Memorandum, D. S. Myer to all bureau officials, August 5, 1952, printed in *House Report* no. 2503, pp. 3–4.

ness of Indian groups to dispense with services provided by the bureau. Myer noted problems of treaty claims, surplus population, heirship lands, the need for corporations to manage Indian resources, and subsidization of states that took over Indian services, and he declared that it was "extremely difficult to make a flat statement on which tribes . . . are now qualified for full management of their own affairs." In the following year, however, the bureau submitted a list of tribes, marked "yes" or "no" according to readiness for immediate withdrawal of federal supervision and support.[30]

Myer's forthright promotion of federal withdrawal drew violent criticism from Indians and from whites sympathetic to the Indian New Deal. John Collier, who saw his hard-won gains for Indian self-determination being rapidly dissipated, wrote an open letter to president-elect Dwight D. Eisenhower in January 1953 calling for the ousting of Myer. An even stronger attack came from Collier's legal friend Felix Cohen, who in a long article in the *Yale Law Journal* condemned the erosion of Indian rights that he alleged had occurred in Myer's administration.[31]

Fundamental differences existed between Myer and his critics. The Association on American Indian Affairs, which through Oliver La Farge and Felix Cohen was in the forefront of the attack on the new policies, sought a way out of the dilemma of freedom or protection by drawing a sharp distinction between wardship and trusteeship. Cohen argued that wardship, which he called an "archaic concept," had poisoned the thinking of officials, legislators, the general public, and even the Indians themselves. He defined *wardship* as restriction on personal freedom of action; he found only a few remnants of it, and they were about to be swept away. But in the public mind, he argued, the concept was still strong. "Through constant repetition of that phrase by the persons having greatest influence in shaping public opinion," he wrote, "the idea of wardship under a 'Great White Father' became firmly fixed in the popular imagination. The paternalistic attitude of Indian Bureau administrators during recent years has unfortunately served to buttress that illusion. But it remains an illusion,

---

30. *House Report* no. 2503; *House Report* no. 2680, 83–2, serial 11747, pp. 3–4. The committee submitting *House Report* no. 2680 was very critical of the Indians and the reformers who opposed termination, who it claimed misconstrued the government's program.

31. John Collier, "Letter to General Eisenhower," *Nation* 176 (January 10, 1953): 29–30; Felix S. Cohen, "The Erosion of Indian Rights, 1950–1953; A Case Study in Bureaucracy," *Yale Law Journal* 62 (February 1953): 348–90. The Bureau of Indian Affairs, under Myer's supervision, prepared a long and detailed rebuttal of Cohen's study: "Indian Bureau Comments on an Article by Felix S. Cohen, 'Erosion of Indian Rights, 1950–1953: A Case Study in Bureaucracy,'" copies in Interior Department Library.

unsupported by legal authority." It was this erroneous idea of wardship that lent such strong support for the "emancipation" bills. Trusteeship, on the other hand, in Cohen's analysis, did not touch the person of the Indian or his personal freedom as a citizen, but was a necessary means of protecting Indian property. It set up a trustee-beneficiary relation in which the trustee was the servant of the trust beneficiary. Cohen and other critics of termination were adamant in demanding the continual protection of Indian property by the trusteeship provision—which the termination bills almost universally sought to end.[32]

The separation between a person and his property—a disjunction that Ray Lyman Wilbur had advanced when he was secretary of the interior— was not as sharp a distinction when applied to the Indian situation as Cohen asserted. Myer was closer to the mark, to judge from the history of Indian-white relations, when he asserted, "You cannot have trusteeship without paternalism and practically all the paternalism which you find in the Indian Bureau program stems directly from our trusteeship responsibilities." In his view, therefore, the only way to end the paternalism of wardship or guardianship was to eliminate the trusteeship.[33] Thus was the issue joined.

One of Myer's most controversial actions concerned the appointment of attorneys by the Indian tribes. He found the statutory guidelines for hiring attorneys insufficient to prevent abuses, and he scrutinized and in some cases refused to approve pending contracts for tribal lawyers. Then he proposed a new policy, which established penalties for soliciting contracts, set a maximum of three years for general counsel contracts, and recommended that tribes seek local or nearby counsel. When he announced the stricter rules in a memorandum of November 9, 1950, which he sent to bureau officials and to tribal leaders, a tremendous outcry arose. Indian groups and white Indian reform groups charged that the commissioner was imposing his will on the tribes. Myer retreated a little and proposed changes

---

32. Felix S. Cohen, "Indian Wardship: The Twilight of a Myth," *American Indian* 6 (Summer 1953): 8–14. See also Oliver La Farge, "The New Administration: Indian Affairs in the Balance," ibid., pp. 3–7; and Oliver La Farge to Secretary of the Interior Douglas McKay, May 1, 1953, OSI CCF 1937–1953, 5–11, Administration General, part 18.

33. The quotation comes from a forthright statement on Indian policy by Myer given at the Western Governors' Conference in Phoenix, Arizona, December 7, 1952. The talk is printed in Dillon S. Myer, "Indian Administration: Problems and Goals," *Social Service Review* 27 (June 1953): 193–200. For other statements of Myer's policy, see Myer, "The Program of the Bureau of Indian Affairs," *Journal of Negro Education* 20 (Summer 1951): 346–53 (reprinted as a pamphlet by the Bureau of Indian Affairs); and Frank T. Wilson, "Interview with Dillon S. Myer, Commissioner of Indian Affairs," *Journal of Religious Thought* 7 (Spring–Summer 1950): 93–100.

in the memorandum to modify it "by softening most of the mandatory words ('shall' and 'must') and by placing more emphasis on flexibility in the application of some of the policies." But the revised regulations, printed in the *Federal Register* for August 11, 1951, did not calm the storm. The Association on American Indian Affairs continued its agitation, lawyer groups remonstrated, and a special committee of the American Bar Association added its sharp criticisms. Finally, on January 3 and 4, 1952, hearings were held by Secretary of the Interior Oscar Chapman in which arguments were presented against the proposed changes. In the end the critics won, for the department fell back to the procedures in use before Myer assumed office.[34]

BUREAU REORGANIZATION

The movement toward termination was accompanied by a reorganization of the Bureau of Indian Affairs. Effective July 1, 1947, the field installations within the continental United States were reorganized in order to increase administrative effectiveness. Five geographical districts were established, each including Indian service facilities within a group of states. The headquarters were at Minneapolis, Billings, Portland, Phoenix, and Oklahoma City. Thus there was established a hierarchical level between the commissioner and the local offices. But some saving was also instituted, as more than forty "at large" offices or stations were eliminated and their duties taken over by the district offices. Further simplification came in budgetary procedures, through consolidating the titles under which funds were requested from 116 to 29. "This amounted to a complete revision of budget structure," Brophy noted, "and has made for such efficiency that any inter-

---

34. The basic documents on the issue of tribal attorneys, including among other items statements of Secretary Chapman; Myer's memorandum of November 9, 1950; the opinion of Solicitor Mastin G. White, June 22, 1951; recommendations of the Association of American Indian Affairs (presented by Felix S. Cohen); memorandum on Indians' right to counsel of law firms and individual lawyers, September 7, 1951; report of a special committee of the American Bar Association; "Regulations Governing Negotiation and Execution of Attorney Contracts with Indian Tribes," May 2, 1938; and transcript of the hearings on the proposed regulations are in OSI CCF 1937–1953, 5–6, Attorneys and Agents, boxes 3517–19. The quotation is from D. S. Myer to the secretary of the interior, March 28, 1951, ibid., box 3519. See also Charles L. Black, Jr., "Counsel of Their Own Choosing," *American Indian* 6 (Fall 1951): 3–17; Clayton R. Koppes, "Oscar L. Chapman: A Liberal at the Interior Department, 1933–1953" (Ph.D. dissertation, University of Kansas, 1974), pp. 224–55. Support for Myer came in *Senate Report* no. 8, 83–1, serial 11659.

ested person, looking at the 29 permanent titles, can tell how much the administrative expense is, and how much each one of the major activities such as education, health, forestry, etc., cost in 1 year."[35]

Accompanying these structural changes was a new emphasis on decentralization through delegation of powers. A law of August 8, 1946, "to facilitate and simplify the administration of Indian affairs" authorized the secretary of the interior, in individual cases arising under general regulations, to delegate any powers he had to the commissioner of Indian affairs, and the commissioner, similarly, to delegate them to subordinate officials.[36] Accordingly, the secretary gave the commissioner final authority to act in certain matters pertaining to health and welfare, education, land and minerals, irrigation, forestry, grazing, and fiscal affairs, and the commissioner authorized field officers to make final decisions in the same cases. Brophy's purpose was clearly stated: "I am more convinced than ever that we must get closer to the people if our programs are to yield the greatest benefit to the Indians and the country. We must constantly strive to have greater participation by the Indians in the initiation, formulation, and execution of our policy work. There should be a real sharing of ideas about goals and how to reach them and their (the Indians') views as well as those of the entire staff of the Service should be weighed and considered."[37]

Brophy's attempt to decentralize the bureau's organization with the five district offices did not work effectively. The dominance of the old system of functional lines from Washington headquarters to the field jurisdictions and the set ways among the rank and file could not be replaced without more decisive leadership than Brophy was able to provide, and the whole concept of decentralization was inadequately worked out. Specific operating instructions were lacking, and the agency superintendents, resenting the new layer of authority, preferred to deal directly with Washington and often did so. Congress, moreover, in its appropriations for 1949 authorized funds for only the Portland and Billings district offices.[38]

35. CIA Report, 1946, p. 352.

36. 60 *United States Statutes* 939; *House Report* no. 1164, 79–1, serial 10935; *Senate Report* no. 1318, 79–1, serial 11015.

37. Department of the Interior, Order no. 2252, September 9, 1946, OSI CCF 1937–1953, 1–12, Administration General, Instructions and Orders, Interior, part 65; Memorandum, J. A. Krug, to the commissioner of Indian affairs, September 9, 1946, and Order no. 537, September 16, 1946, OIA Circulars (M1121, reel 4); CIA Report, 1947, pp. 349–50.

38. *Report of the Committee on Indian Affairs to the Commission on Organization of the Executive Branch of the Government*, pp. 42–43; 62 *United States Statutes* 1116. There is full discussion of the organization of regional offices in Theodore W. Taylor, "The Regional Organization of the Bureau of Indian Affairs" (Ph.D. dissertation, Harvard University, 1959); see especially pp. 186–90.

Yet the increasing work of the Washington office of the bureau called for another attempt at decentralization, which came in the fall of 1949. On September 3 Secretary J. A. Krug issued an order that set up three administrative units in headquarters—resources, community services, and administration—and established eleven area offices, at the following cities:

Juneau, Alaska	Albuquerque, New Mexico
Phoenix, Arizona	Anadarko, Oklahoma
Window Rock, Arizona	Muskogee, Oklahoma
Sacramento, California	Portland, Oregon
Minneapolis, Minnesota	Aberdeen, South Dakota
Billings, Montana	

Under the area offices were the agencies, boarding schools, hospitals and sanatoriums, and irrigation projects. In addition to the area offices, there were ten detached field offices: Seminole Agency, Haskell Institute, Choctaw Agency, Carson Indian Agency, Western Shoshone Agency, New York Agency, Cherokee Agency, Chilocco School, Osage Agency, and Intermountain School (see Table 14). Commissioner Nichols noted of the new organization: "I now have only six key employees reporting to me in the Washington Office as compared with twenty-four, on the day I took office. In the field service today only the eleven area directors and 10 superintendents of detached field offices report directly to me—as compared with nearly 100, previously."[39]

The new organization, if it was to work more effectively than the five district offices, needed firm administrative direction, and that was provided by Dillon Myer. By effectively reducing the division directors in Washington to staff officers, he concentrated administrative decision in his own hands, and by giving substantial authority to the area directors, who would play a key role in termination activities, he strengthened the move toward withdrawal. Officials below the area level lost many of their responsibilities. The changes not only tightened the machinery of the bureau, with centralized power in the hands of the commissioner, but they eliminated to a large extent residual Collier influence among the division heads and among the field superintendents. Myer insisted that a major purpose of the reorganization was to decentralize the administration of Indian

39. Department of the Interior, Order no. 2535, September 13, 1949, OSI CCF 1937–1953, 1–12, Instructions and Orders, Interior; Order no. 549, September 14, 1949, and supplements of October 21, November 8, 1949, October 6, 1950, OIA Circulars (M1121, reel 4); address of John R. Nichols to Oklahoma-Kansas Superintendents' Association, November 17, 1949, OSI CCF 1937–1953, 5–11, Administration General, part 16. See also United States Department of the Interior, *Official Organization Handbook for Use in 1949–1950.*

TABLE 14: Organization Chart of the Bureau of Indian Affairs, 1950

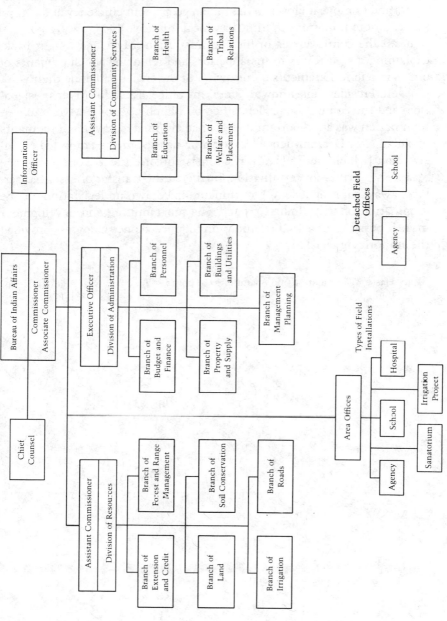

SOURCE: CIA Report, 1950, p. 344.

affairs and to move it closer to the Indian people; but efficiency and control seemed more important to him than local initiative.[40]

In all the controversies of his administration, Myer had fought back, explaining his positions to his superiors and rebutting the statements of critics in public statements of his own. But the critics had done their work too well. President Eisenhower, on taking office, asked for Myer's resignation, and the commissioner left office on March 20, 1953. Myer's role in termination was an important one. He had eliminated any major remnants of Indian New Deal influence by reorganizing the bureau, compiled extensive data (which were not always consistent or correct) concerning the readiness of tribes for termination, furthered the transfer of essential services away from the federal government, and drawn up legislation for the termination of some Indian groups. His programming and development made it possible for actual termination to proceed once Congress provided the authorizing legislation.[41]

40. Hasse, "Termination and Assimilation," pp. 126–29.
41. Ibid., p. 163.

CHAPTER 41

Termination
in Action

Legislative Action.

Termination Laws.

Reversal of Policy.

The eight years of President Dwight D. Eisenhower's administration were the high point of termination. Building on the policy that had evolved under Truman and on the planning and programming of Commissioner Dillon Myer, Congress in 1953 formally endorsed the policy of termination and in succeeding years enacted laws to withdraw federal supervision from a number of small Indian groups and from two major tribes, the Menominee Indians of Wisconsin and the Klamath Indians of Oregon.

LEGISLATIVE ACTION

The new commissioner of Indian affairs, chosen by Eisenhower after considerable consultation and delay, was Glenn L. Emmons. Emmons, a banker from Gallup, New Mexico, who had the support of the Navajos, was a mild-mannered man. He was concerned about traditional Indian interests, but he was committed enough to withdrawal of federal supervision that he cooperated with congressional and departmental moves toward termination. When Senator Watkins quizzed him at his nomination hearing, Emmons, although he noted that for some tribes it would take longer than for others, firmly asserted: "I think we should see that the Government trusteeship is liquidated just as rapidly as possible." He was careful to con-

vince Watkins, too, that he did not belong to any of the Indian rights organizations. Emmons consistently supported termination measures of Congress and drew up bills for the termination of specific tribes, although he
urged consultation with the Indians concerned and strongly promoted the
educational, health, and economic development of the tribes to enable
them to stand on their own after termination.[1]

Final commitment to termination, however, came before Emmons actually assumed office on August 10, 1953. The Department of the Interior
confirmed the policy in a conference on February 27, 1953, held by Assistant Secretary Orme Lewis with Senator Watkins and Representative
William H. Harrison of Wyoming. Lewis accepted Watkins's views and
outlined a policy of termination under which federal responsibility would
be withdrawn. In March this "basic departmental policy" was sent to all
bureau officials, and in June a circular announcing the policy was sent to
all area offices and agencies.[2]

The effective drive for termination came from within Congress, but it
was the work of a few men, for Indian affairs were not a major interest
of the legislators. The standing committees on Indian affairs, which had
played such an important role in the past, were eliminated by the Legislative Reorganization Act of 1946, and Indian matters were referred to the
Committee on Public Lands (later called the Committee on Interior and

1. "Nomination of Glenn L. Emmons," *Hearings before the Committee on Interior
and Insular Affairs, United States Senate, 83d Congress, 1st Session, on the Nomination
of Glenn L. Emmons to Be Commissioner of the Bureau of Indian Affairs* (1953), pp. 4–6,
18–27. Details of the political maneuvering in the selection of Emmons are given in
Larry W. Burt, *Tribalism in Crisis: Federal Indian Policy, 1953–1961* (Albuquerque: University of New Mexico Press, 1982), pp. 9–18; the book provides a full account of Emmons's administration. A shorter sketch is Patricia K. Ourada, "Glenn L. Emmons,
1953–61," in Robert M. Kvasnicka and Herman J. Viola, eds., *The Commissioners of Indian Affairs, 1824–1977* (Lincoln: University of Nebraska Press, 1979), pp. 301–10.
Debra R. Boender, "Termination and the Administration of Glenn L. Emmons as Commissioner of Indian Affairs, 1953–1961," *New Mexico Historical Review* 54 (October
1979): 287–304, argues, not quite convincingly, that "Emmons never fully understood
Congressional policies of termination" and that he was too fully occupied with tribal
development programs to be aware of the seriousness with which Congress was pursuing
termination. See also Larry J. Hasse, "Termination and Assimilation: Federal Indian Policy, 1943 to 1961" (Ph.D. dissertation, Washington State University, 1974), and Donald
Lee Fixico, "Termination and Relocation: Federal Indian Policy in the 1950s" (Ph.D. dissertation, University of Oklahoma, 1980).

2. Hasse, "Termination and Assimilation," pp. 177–78. Lewis's letter to Watkins,
March 13, 1953, and the memorandum to bureau officials, March 25, 1953, are printed in
S. Lyman Tyler, *Indian Affairs: A Work Paper on Termination, with an Attempt to Show
Its Antecedents* (Provo, Utah: Institute of American Indian Studies, Brigham Young Uni-
versity, 1964), pp. 70–72.

Insular Affairs) in the House and in the Senate. These committees were dominated by westerners, and the subcommittees on Indian affairs pretty much had their way; what they proposed was accepted by the full committees and by the houses without much question or debate. And the subcommittees were chaired and dominated by ardent terminationists: Senator Watkins and Representative E. Y. Berry of South Dakota. It was Watkins who directed the termination impulse, but he had important support from Representatives Berry, Harrison, Wesley A. D'Ewart of Montana, and A. L. Miller of Nebraska, who introduced much of the legislation Watkins wanted.[3]

The congressional leaders and their friends in the Department of the Interior were for the most part political conservatives who distrusted government control and direction of human lives and who exalted individualism and the rights of private property over group interests. The evidence they gathered about the Indian tribes was selected and interpreted from their conservative point of view, and many Americans shared their positions. The Indian policy they promoted was based on fundamental assumptions growing out of their philosophical views and cannot be understood simply as another white land-grabbing scheme. The assumptions have been well formulated by Gary Orfield, as follows:

1. That the more advanced Indian groups had achieved basic social progress, and that they now lived at a level comparable to a great many non-Indians.

2. That no important "cultural" differences existed between advanced Indian groups and other population segments, and that the Indians would respond to economic opportunity in the same manner as had other groups.

3. That many of the most important service functions for these tribes had already been transferred to the State government, and thus full transfer would not be difficult.

4. That a large number of the Indian people were in favor of an end to Federal trusteeship.

5. That the bureaucracy of the BIA was stifling the development of individual initiative and the economic development of tribal resources by trusteeship.

6. That Indian tribes largely self-sufficient under Federal supervision could easily meet the expenses of governing themselves under State law.

7. That the Indian communities were unified and had democratic

3. 60 *United States Statutes* 819, 828; Hasse, "Termination and Assimilation," pp. 168–73.

institutions by which they were capable of making basic decisions for their own future.[4]

The reconstruction of Indian communities that was attempted through the termination policy was a response to this interpretation of the facts. The assumptions were rejected by more liberal-minded politicians, but the full realization of their falsity and inadequacy as a basis for federal policy came only as the termination laws went into effect.

Congress committed itself to rapid termination of the Indian tribes by House Concurrent Resolution no. 108, adopted on August 1, 1953. The measure declared that "it is the policy of Congress, as rapidly as possible, to make the Indians within the territorial limits of the United States subject to the same laws and entitled to the same privileges and responsibilities as are applicable to other citizens of the United States, to end their status as wards of the United States and to grant them all of the rights and prerogatives pertaining to American citizenship." It was the sense of Congress, it then declared, that specific Indians and Indian groups "should be freed from Federal supervision and control and from all disabilities and limitations specially applicable to Indians" at the earliest possible time: that is, Indians within the states of California, Florida, New York, and Texas; the Flathead, Klamath, Menominee, and Potawatomi tribes, and the Chippewa Indians of the Turtle Mountain Reservation. All offices of the Bureau of Indian Affairs serving the affected states and tribes should be abolished. The resolution directed the secretary of the interior to report to Congress no later than January 1, 1954, with recommendations for legislation to carry out the purposes of the resolution.[5] Although President Eisenhower had made a strong point in his campaign about consultation with Indian tribes, this fundamental policy determination was made without any attempt to involve the Indians.

While awaiting specific legislative proposals for termination, Congress moved ahead with another significant withdrawal measure, approved on August 15, 1953, which came to be known simply as Public Law 280. It provided that for all the Indian country within the states of California, Minnesota, Nebraska, Oregon, and Wisconsin (except for the Red Lake Reservation in Minnesota, the Warm Springs Reservation in Oregon, and the Menominee Reservation in Wisconsin) jurisdiction over criminal offenses and civil causes would rest with the states; the criminal laws of the state would have the same force on Indian reservations that they had else-

---

4. Gary Orfield, "A Study of the Termination Policy," printed in *The Education of American Indians*, vol. 4: *The Organizational Question*, Committee Print of the Subcommittee on Indian Education of the Committee on Labor and Public Welfare, United States Senate, 91st Congress, 1st Session (Washington: GPO, 1970), p. 782.

5. 67 *United States Statutes* B132; *House Report* no. 841, 83–1, serial 11666.

where in the state. The law grew out of the confusing situation of jurisdiction in the Indian country, and the Bureau of Indian Affairs for a number of years, after consulting with Indian tribes and with state officials, had proposed particular pieces of legislation that were now consolidated in Public Law 280. The House committee reporting the bill commented: "As a practical matter, the enforcement of law and order among the Indians in the Indian country has been left largely to the Indian groups themselves. In many States, tribes are not adequately organized to perform that function; consequently, there has been created a hiatus in law-enforcement authority that could best be remedied by conferring criminal jurisdiction on States indicating an ability and willingness to accept such responsibility. Similarly, the Indians of several States have reached a stage of acculturation and development that makes desirable extension of State civil jurisdiction to the Indian country within their borders."[6]

Besides specifying the five states in the act, the legislation in section 7 provided that any other state could similarly assume jurisdiction over Indian reservations by its own legislative action. This section caused great concern to Indian groups, for it raised the pertinent question of consent by Indian tribes to such state assumption of jurisdiction, and agitation by Indians against this provision of the bill was noted by Eisenhower when he received the bill. The president, however, signed the legislation because its basic purpose, he said, represented "still another step in granting complete political equality to all Indians in our nation." Yet he expressed "grave doubts" about section 7 because it did not provide for full consultation with the Indians or for approval by the federal government before states assumed jurisdiction. He urged Congress to amend the law at its next session.[7]

The Senate in the first session of the Eighty-fourth Congress introduced an amendment that went further than the "consultation" asked for by Eisenhower and provided for "consent." The Senate Committee on Interior and Insular Affairs reported favorably on the bill, for it saw justice in the Indian request not to be deprived of tribal control over civil and criminal cases on the reservations, and it noted that the "consent theory is not an innovation in the field of Indian legislation," pointing to the Indian Reorganization Act and other laws. The Interior Department, however, opposed the idea of Indian consent, and Senator Watkins issued a strongly worded minority report against the measure. As citizens, he said, the Indians must be bound by laws just as the general citizenry, which had no

6. 67 *United States Statutes* 588–90; *House Report* no. 848, 83–1, serial 11666, p. 6.
7. *Public Papers of the Presidents of the United States: Dwight D. Eisenhower, 1953* (Washington: Office of the Federal Register, National Archives and Records Service, n.d.), p. 564–66.

power to veto measures it disliked. "The concept that the Indian people exist within the United States as independent nations," he added, "has been rejected."[8] Watkins's views were seconded by Secretary of the Interior Douglas McKay in an exchange with Oliver La Farge, president of the Association on American Indian Affairs. "What you are proposing—and let us be quite clear about this," he told La Farge, "—is that, over and above . . . the normal rights of citizens, the Indians should also have a special veto power over legislation which might affect them. No other element in our population (aside from the President himself) now has such a power and none ever has had in the history of our country." In the end, the Senate rejected the bill; not until the Civil Rights Act of 1968 was Indian consent required for the assumption of jurisdiction by states.[9]

Two other measures were approved on August 15, 1953, that were part of the drive to repeal legislation setting Indians apart from other citizens. One of these ended at last the long history of prohibition against the sale of liquor to Indians off the reservations and legalized the introduction of alcoholic beverages into the Indian country by the tribes on a local option basis. The Indians, especially since World War II, had agitated against the laws as discriminatory, and Congress and the Department of the Interior backed the new measure. "Termination of the subjection of Indians to Federal laws applicable only to Indians certainly appears to be desirable," the House committee noted in reporting the bill.[10] The second law repealed discriminatory laws of long standing that forbade the sale of firearms or ammunition to Indians, prohibited Indians from selling or trading guns or traps, farming implements, cooking utensils, and clothing, and restricted the sale of livestock by Indians.[11]

TERMINATION LAWS

In response to House Concurrent Resolution no. 108 the Bureau of Indian Affairs drafted terminal legislation for a number of tribes. As Emmons out-

---

8. *Senate Report* no. 357, 84–1, serial 11816, p. 3. A letter of Assistant Secretary Fred G. Aandahl to James E. Murray, April 27, 1955, is printed in the report, pp. 3–8. "We believe," it said, "that a consent requirement is contrary to the best interests of the Indians, and is unsound as a matter of Federal policy."

9. Douglas McKay to Oliver La Farge, November 30, 1955, quoted in S. Lyman Tyler, *A History of Indian Policy* (Washington: Bureau of Indian Affairs, 1973), p. 184; *Congressional Record*, 101: 11332, 11800, 12227; 82 *United States Statutes* 78–79.

10. 67 *United States Statutes* 586–87; *House Report* no. 775, 83–1, serial 11666; *Senate Report* no. 722, 83–1, serial 11661. The favorable report on the bill from the Department of the Interior is printed in the two reports. See also CIA Report, 1954, p. 244.

11. 67 *United States Statutes* 590; *House Report* no. 268, 83–1, serial 11664; *Senate Report* no. 793, 83–1, serial 11661.

lined the procedure, there were three steps: "(1) a preliminary draft of a proposed bill, covering each of the designated Indian groups, was developed solely for discussion purposes by area directors, superintendents, and central office staff; (2) representatives of area and agency offices arranged for meetings with Indian people, officials of State and local governments, and other interested persons to discuss with them the preliminary draft and invite an expression of their views and suggestions; and (3) proposed bills and basic information relating to the Indian groups were prepared and submitted to Congress through departmental channels." The proposed bills had common features, which included provisions for drawing up a final tribal roll, for dividing tribal property rights among the enrolled members, and for transfer to individual Indians of their trust property. Tribes could choose to manage tribal property themselves or place it in the hands of a private trustee. If they did not exercise an option within a specified time, the secretary of the interior could select a trustee for liquidation purposes. The bills specified a time, from two to five years, within which final termination was to be accomplished.[12]

Some twenty bills were introduced in the second session of the Eighty-third Congress beginning early in 1954 that pertained to the Indians named in the resolution as well as to other groups. Joint hearings before the Indian subcommittees of the House and Senate were held between February and April 1954 to consider the bills.[13] Some of the groups proposed for termination, like the Turtle Mountain Chippewas and the Seminoles of Florida, were clearly not prepared to give up federal supervision; but for others, despite opposition from Indian groups and warnings that precipitous termination would be deleterious, laws were enacted. The great rush to legislate termination came in 1954. The Menominees and Klamaths led the list, followed shortly by a group of small tribes in western Oregon, the Alabama-Coushatta Indians of Texas, and the Ute and Paiute Indians of Utah. Then the movement slowed, as the Democratic victories in the 1956 election changed the membership of congressional committees and as opposition mounted and deep problems in the process came to be realized. Later legislation was sporadic and touched relatively small groups without cohesive tribal organization or large land holdings (see Table 15).

The passage of an act by itself did not effect termination, since it was necessary to develop a detailed termination plan for each tribe. For the

12. CIA Report, 1954, pp. 231–32.

13. "Termination of Federal Supervision over Certain Tribes of Indians," *Joint Hearings before the Subcommittees of the Committees on Interior and Insular Affairs, Congress of the United States, 83d Congress, 2d Session . . . Providing for Legislation Pursuant to H. Con. Res. 108, 83d Congress, 1st Session* (1954). There were twelve parts to the published hearings; they are conveniently listed in Tyler, *Indian Policy*, pp. 172–73.

Indian Group	State	Population	Acres	Date of Act	Effective Date
Menominee	Wisconsin	3,270	233,881	June 17, 1954	1961
Klamath	Oregon	2,133	862,662	Aug. 13, 1954	1961
Western Oregon (61 tribes and bands)	Oregon	2,081	3,158	Aug. 13, 1954	1956
Alabama-Coushatta	Texas	450	3,200	Aug. 23, 1954	1955
Mixed-blood Ute	Utah	490	211,430	Aug. 27, 1954	1961
Southern Paiute	Utah	232	42,839	Sept. 1, 1954	1957
Wyandotte	Oklahoma	1,157	94	Aug. 1, 1956	1959
Peoria	Oklahoma	640	0	Aug. 2, 1956	1959
Ottawa	Oklahoma	630	0	Aug. 3, 1956	1959
California Rancherias	California	1,107	4,315	Aug. 18, 1958	1961–70
Catawba	South Carolina	631	3,388	Sept. 21, 1959	1962
Ponca	Nebraska	442	834	Sept. 5, 1962	1966
		13,263	1,365,801		

SOURCE: Data from Theodore W. Taylor, *The States and Their Indian Citizens* (Washington: Bureau of Indian Affairs, 1972), p. 180; Charles F. Wilkinson and Eric R. Biggs, "Evolution of the Termination Policy," *American Indian Law Review* 5, no. 1 (1977): 151.

smaller tribes this could be done relatively expeditiously; for the larger ones it meant complicated negotiations in regard to the trust status of lands, the determination of tribal members to receive per capita payments, and the assumption of services by the states, with the result that actual termination did not take effect until long after the passage of the act and at a time when the impulse for termination had been greatly weakened.

For terminated tribes and individuals the special status of federal supervision and federal programs that had long marked relations of the Indian groups with the United States government came to an abrupt end. The following common elements resulted from the termination laws and termination plans: (1) Land ownership patterns were changed. In some cases the land was simply appraised and sold, with the proceeds divided on a per capita basis; in others, corporations were established to manage what had previously been tribal land held in trust by the federal government. (2) The federal trust relationship was ended, and the federal government no longer protected Indian property and was no longer responsible for the management of land and other resources. (3) State legislative and judicial authority was imposed, replacing the authority of Congress or tribal councils. Civil and criminal cases went to state courts, and the buffer against discrimination that had been provided by federal and tribal law disappeared. Moreover, the special tax exemption that Indians had enjoyed on reservations was ended. (4) Special programs provided by the federal government specifically for Indian tribes and for individual Indians were discontinued. Numerous programs that provided education, health, and welfare assistance to Indians were not easily replaced by local, state, or tribal agencies. The loss of such special aid was one of the most severely felt of termination effects. (5) In practice, most aspects of tribal sovereignty were ended for terminated tribes because the land base over which sovereignty could be exercised was destroyed. Although "inherent sovereignty" of Indian groups may not have been touched by the termination laws, tribal sovereignty, which became a great rallying cry in the 1960s and 1970s, was struck a heavy blow in the terminated tribes. The loss of identity as Indians was a severe psychological loss.[14]

The Menominee Tribe was the most noted case of termination.[15] The tribe, on its small reservation established in northeastern Wisconsin in 1854, had long been considered a prime target for withdrawal of federal supervision. Its members were literate in English and appeared to be acculturated to white ways, and its forestry and lumber mill operations provided employment for a large proportion of the tribe. As an Indian tribe under federal trusteeship and exempt from taxation and federal and state regulations and licensing, the Menominees presented a picture of moderate prosperity. They were thus on all the lists of tribes to be terminated immediately. The actuality of termination, however, showed the disparity be-

---

14. These points are adapted from a list in Charles F. Wilkinson and Eric R. Biggs, "The Evolution of the Termination Policy," *American Indian Law Review* 5, no. 1 (1977): 152–54.

15. A detailed and judicious study is Nicholas C. Peroff, *Menominee Drums: Tribal Termination and Restoration, 1954–1974* (Norman: University of Oklahoma Press, 1982). Gary Orfield, "A Study of the Termination Policy," deals primarily with the Menominee case. Detailed and sympathetic accounts are presented by Stephen J. Herzberg in "The Menominee Indians: From Treaty to Termination," *Wisconsin Magazine of History* 60 (Summer 1977): 267–329, and "The Menominee Indians: Termination to Restoration," part 1, *American Indian Law Review* 6, no. 1 (1978): 143–86. An excellent analysis of the internal conditions in the tribe is David W. Ames and Burton R. Fisher, "The Menominee Termination Crisis: Barriers in the Way of a Rapid Cultural Transition," *Human Organization* 18 (Fall 1959): 101–11. There is a brief account in Patricia K. Ourada, *The Menominee Indians: A History* (Norman: University of Oklahoma Press, 1979), pp. 190–213. See also Burt, *Tribalism in Crisis*; Hasse, "Termination and Assimilation"; and Fixico, "Termination and Relocation."

tween the appearances of readiness and the harsh reality of continued dependency and demonstrated the coercive nature of measures taken to gain the acquiescence of the tribe to termination.

Menominee termination was tied to distribution of the award made to the tribe under cases in which the tribe had sued the United States for mismanagement of its forest resources and won an $8.5-million judgment. The success of the Indians in their suit was taken to be a further sign of their readiness to go their own way, and when the Menominees sought legislation to allow them to distribute part of the $8.5 million in per capita payments, the government delayed until plans for the ultimate future of the tribe could be worked out. A bill for a $1,500 per capita payment introduced by Representative Melvin Laird of Wisconsin and passed by the House was held up by Senator Watkins, who used the occasion to promote termination legislation for the Menominees. Watkins visited the reservation in Wisconsin and warned the Indians that they were likely to be terminated by Congress whether they wanted to be or not, and that unless they agreed the per capita payment would not be authorized. His hard line convinced the tribal council that termination was inevitable, and it passed a resolution in favor of termination by a vote of 169 to 5. Although the Menominees later argued that the resolution did not represent the mind of the tribe as a whole and was not a commitment to immediate termination, Watkins and other terminationists considered it binding.

Back in Washington, Watkins's Senate subcommittee amended one of the per capita payment bills to make it an immediate termination measure. The House managers of the conference committee agreed to the substantial change in the original bill because they considered it a response to House Concurrent Resolution no. 108, but when the conference report came to the floor of the House on August 1, 1953, there was long debate. The discussion was full of statements accepting the propriety of the measure. Representative John W. Byrnes of Wisconsin declared that there was no objection to termination of federal supervision. "There is no resistance whatever on our part or on the part of the tribe," he asserted; "in fact, we think it is indeed a step in the right direction, and that step should be taken at the earliest possible opportunity." His colleague Laird agreed: "I believe the Menominee Indian Tribe is ready for complete emancipation as set forth in the resolution of the tribe." But there was strong objection to the procedure by which the simple per capita payment bill had been transformed into an all-out termination bill and to the shortness of time it permitted for the transition to independence, and the House rejected the conference report.[16]

16. *House Report* no. 1034, 83–1, serial 11667; *Congressional Record*, 99: 10930–42 (quotations at pp. 10931–32).

Under the influence of Commissioner Emmons, who visited the Menominees in September 1953 and told the council that termination was inevitable and that they would be wise to plan for it, and of Representative Laird, who backed Emmons's position, the tribal council drafted a substitute termination measure that allowed five years for planning and preparation before termination would take effect. The council approved the measure on January 7, 1954, by a vote of 101 to 0, and the bill was promptly introduced in Congress by Laird. The three days of hearings on the bill before the joint committee in March were dominated by Senator Watkins; no effective opposition to the substance of the measure was presented either by the tribe, by officials of the state of Wisconsin, or by other witnesses. "We are not opposing the withdrawal program," the chairman of the Menominee Advisory Council, Antoine Waupochick, testified. "All we ask is sufficient time to accomplish our end of the bargain. Time is essential; withdrawal must be orderly, or we will face liquidation, for there are many in our tribe who do not know the white man's way of living." The president of the Indian Rights Association, Jonathan Steere, told the subcommittee that the Menominees were "probably better prepared for termination of Federal supervision than most Indian groups in the country."[17]

The Menominee termination bill was passed without dissent by both houses of Congress, with the effective date of termination set at December 31, 1958. President Eisenhower, signing the bill on June 17, 1954, said: "The Menominees have already demonstrated that they are able to manage their assets without supervision and take their place on an equal footing with other citizens of Wisconsin and the Nation. I extend my warmest commendations to the members of the Tribe for the impressive progress they have achieved and for the cooperation they have given the Congress in the development of this legislation. In a real sense, they have opened up a new era in Indian affairs—an era of growing self reliance which is the logical culmination and fulfillment of more than a hundred years of activity by the Federal Government among the Indian people." In August 1954 the per capita payment of $1,500 authorized by the law was made to members of the tribe.[18]

In preparation for federal withdrawal, the Menominees were directed by the law to draw up a termination plan, which was to be submitted to the secretary of the interior by December 31, 1957. It soon became clear, however, that the tribe did not have the resources or time to accomplish the

17. The Menominee hearings of March 10–12, 1954, are in "Termination of Federal Supervision over Certain Tribes of Indians," part 6, pp. 579–772. The quotations are at pp. 664, 741.

18. 68 *United States Statutes* 250–52; *Public Papers of the Presidents of the United States: Dwight D. Eisenhower, 1954,* p. 582; Ourada, *Menominee Indians,* p. 195.

necessary planning. The state of Wisconsin created a Menominee Indian Study Committee to assist, and the tribe petitioned Congress for more time and for financial support of the planning activities. On July 14, 1956, the original act was amended to reimburse the tribe from federal funds for expenditures in the planning process. This provision was changed on July 2, 1958, to provide for only 50-percent reimbursement after that date, a compromise accepted by the tribe in order to gain an extension of time— to February 1, 1959, for the submission of the termination plan and to December 31, 1960, for actual termination. The planning still did not proceed expeditiously, and the tribal council begged for a ten-year extension, but without avail. Finally, on October 31, 1959, the Menominee tribe and the Department of the Interior agreed upon a plan. A business corporation would hold title to and manage the tribe's property, and, according to an earlier tribal referendum, the reservation would be established as a separate county in Wisconsin, rather than be joined to an existing county or counties. There was one more attempt to gain a long delay in termination, but Congress granted only a four-month extension; on April 30, 1961, the property of the tribe held in trust by the federal government was transferred to a tribal corporation, Menominee Enterprises, Inc., and the individual Menominees were no longer entitled to any services provided for Indians and were subject to the laws of the state of Wisconsin.[19]

Menominee County, the least populated and poorest of Wisconsin's seventy-two counties, was in trouble from the start. Its experience made a mockery of the goals of termination. The Menominee Indians were not prepared to accept a place in the white man's competitive world. Their cultural values differed markedly from those of their white neighbors, however much of a superficial resemblance there might be in dress, language, and education. The apparently healthy economy of the reservation depended upon props which were pulled out with federal withdrawal, and the tribal government, dominated by a small group, was not accepted by the whole tribe as a representative decision-making body. The factional opposition to the council and then to the tribal corporation obstructed effective development. No sooner was termination accomplished than agitation grew for overturning it and restoring the Menominees to reservation status.[20]

19. 70 *United States Statutes* 544; 72 *United States Statutes* 290; 74 *United States Statutes* 867; *House Report* no. 2235, 84–2, serial 11899; *Senate Report* no. 2412, 84–2, serial 11889. The Menominee termination plan was extremely complex and covered about thirty pages of small type in 26 *Federal Register* 3727–55 (April 29, 1961). See the discussion in Herzberg, "Menominee Indians: From Treaty to Termination," pp. 324–26.

20. Menominee unpreparedness—social, economic, and especially governmental—is analyzed in Ames and Fisher, "Menominee Termination Crisis"; and Herzberg, "Meno-

The Klamath Indians' experience was similar to that of the Menominees. A tribe of some two thousand members living on a reservation in southern Oregon that was rich in timber resources, the Klamaths were pegged for quick termination. The Interior Department, in sending a draft of a bill for termination of the tribe to Congress in January 1954, declared: "It is our belief that the Klamath Tribe and the individual members thereof have in general attained sufficient skill and ability to manage their own affairs without special Federal assistance." It pointed to intermarriage with non-Indians, education in public schools, integration into the economic and social life of the area, and a standard of living that compared favorably with that of their white neighbors. In fact, for a good many years the Klamaths themselves had discussed plans—called "final settlement" proposals—whereby members who chose to do so could elect to receive pro rata shares of the tribal assets. They had considered, too, proposals for setting up a tribal corporation to manage property. The tribe was sharply factionalized, however, and the division became aggravated when the federal movement toward termination began. One group, led by Boyd Jackson, sought to hold the traditional homelands together; the other, vigorously led by Wade Crawford and his wife Ida, urged immediate liquidation of the tribal estate and distribution of the proceeds in per capita payments. But even the anti-termination party was badgered by government officials into the conviction that a move was inevitable. In February 1954 the tribal council conditionally accepted the termination bill that had been proposed.[21]

The Klamath termination act passed on August 13, 1954, directed the secretary of the interior to select and contract with qualified "management specialists" to prepare for termination with the following steps: (1) appraise the tribal property; (2) provide for an election by which tribal members could elect either to withdraw from the tribe and receive pro rata shares of the tribal assets converted into money or to remain in the tribe under a tribal management plan; (3) determine the portion of tribal property that would have to be sold in order to provide money for the withdrawing members and then distribute the proceeds; and (4) draw up a plan

---

minee Indians: From Treaty to Termination," pp. 307–10, 314–16, and "Menominee Indians: Termination to Restoration," pp. 170–86. For discussion of restoration to tribal status, see chapter 44.

21. The Interior Department view is expressed in Orme Lewis to Richard M. Nixon, January 4, 1954, in *Senate Report* no. 1631, 83–2, serial 11730, pp. 7–8. An excellent discussion of the Klamath situation is Theodore Stern, *The Klamath Tribe: A People and Their Reservation* (Seattle: University of Washington Press, 1965), pp. 249–55. See also Susan Hood, "Termination of the Klamath Tribe in Oregon," *Ethnohistory* 19 (Fall 1972): 379–92; and the discussion in Burt, *Tribalism in Crisis*, Hasse, "Termination and Assimilation, and Fixico, "Termination and Relocation."

for the management of remaining tribal property through a trustee or a corporation.[22]

The law did not satisfy either of the tribal factions, for the four years it allowed for preparation was too long a delay for the Crawfords and far short of the fifteen years that Jackson wanted as a transition period. The work of planning, however, fell not to the Indians but to the management specialists, especially to Thomas B. Watters, a local insurance and real estate man, who worked diligently for the Indians' interests. Watters soon discovered that the Klamaths were far from ready for federal withdrawal, and a study produced by the Stanford Research Institute reinforced that conclusion. Many of the Indians did not understand the full import of termination and were unprepared for the social and economic shock that it would bring. Yet the government was caught in a test of its policy, and a repeal of the law would look like a reversal of the whole termination policy.

Then the conservation of the Klamath forests became a major concern. The Interior Department acknowledged that the indiscriminate sale of the Klamath forests would result in accelerated cutting and cause "serious injury to the economy of the entire Klamath Basin"; but the original law of 1954 emphasized private property rights and omitted requirements for continued sustained-yield management of the forests.[23] The evils that would result both to the conservation of the forests and to the local economy by the dumping of massive amounts of timber on the market were not lost upon the people of Oregon. Agitation soon began for amendment of the law and in some circles for its outright repeal.[24] In August 1957 Congress passed an amendment that extended the termination date to August 13, 1960, so that the forest problems could be worked out, and other amendments were proposed to protect the forests. One of these, introduced by Senator Richard L. Neuberger of Oregon, provided for purchase of the forests by the federal government, but the elimination of private purchases was not acceptable. Finally, in 1958, a compromise measure was worked out that authorized either private or public purchase. How far the official position had changed can be seen in the strong arguments made for the bill by the new secretary of the interior, Fred A. Seaton:

22. 68 *United States Statutes* 719; the full law is on pp. 718–23. See also *House Report* no. 2483, 83–2, serial 11743, and *Senate Report* no. 1631, 83–2, serial 11730. Hearings on the Klamath termination bill are in "Termination of Federal Supervision over Certain Tribes of Indians," part 4, pp. 195–349, and part 4–A, pp. 1–112.

23. Lewis to Nixon, January 4, 1954, in *Senate Report* no. 1631.

24. The conservation issue was treated in detail in a series of articles in *American Forests* in 1957 and 1958. See, for example: Anthony Netbory, "Uproar on Klamath Reservation," 63 (January 1957): 20–21, 61–62; William Dean, "Klamath Hearings in Oregon," 63 (November 1957): 12, 65–67; and Richard L. Neuberger, "Solving the Stubborn Klamath Dilemma," 64 (April 1958): 20–22, 40–42.

The manner in which the Klamath Indian Forest is managed in the future will have a vital impact on the life and economy of the entire Klamath River Basin. If it is kept intact and managed according to sustained yield principles, the forest will remain a perpetually productive source of ponderosa pine and other commercial species. Such management will also assure continuation of its important function as a watershed. The large numbers of migratory waterfowl for which it now provides nesting and feeding grounds will be protected, as will the deer and other species of wild animals that now find sanctuary within its boundaries. Further development of the forest's recreational potential will also be made possible.[25]

The amendment of August 23, 1958, guaranteeing that the Klamath forests would be sold as sustained-yield units and at fair market prices, was an important conservation measure. It offered the forest for private purchase under sustained-yield requirements, and it provided for purchase by the federal government for a national forest of units not privately bought. It also authorized the purchase by the secretary of the interior of the marshlands for a natural wildlife refuge, and it extended the date of final termination an additional year, to August 13, 1961. Ninety million dollars was authorized for the purchases.[26]

In a tribal election of 1958 to determine which Indians chose withdrawal from tribal relations, 1,659 tribal members voted to withdraw, whereas only 474 (either by voting to remain or not voting at all) became part of the nonwithdrawing group. Thus, about 77 per cent of the Klamaths elected to receive a per capita payment (amounting to about $43,700) for their share of the tribal property, and most of the nearly one million acres of the reservation had to be sold in order to provide the money. The property of the remaining members, including about 145,000 acres of forest lands, was committed to the United States National Bank of Portland as trustee for these Indians. Little of the land sold went to private companies. One sustained-yield unit of 92,000 acres was sold to the Crown Zellerbach

25. Information on the Klamath amendments can be found in *House Report* no. 379, 85–1, serial 11985; *Senate Report* no. 1518, 85–2, serial 12062; *House Report* no. 2278, 85–2, serial 12075; "Klamath Indian Tribe—Termination of Federal Supervision," *Hearings before the Committee on Interior and Insular Affairs and Its Subcommittee on Indian Affairs, United States Senate, 84th Congress, 2d Session* (1957); "Amendments to the Klamath Termination Act of 1954," *Hearings before the Subcommittee on Indian Affairs of the Committee on Interior and Insular Affairs, United States Senate, 85th Congress, 2d Session, on S. 2047 and S. 3051*, parts 1 and 2 (1957–1958). The letter of Fred A. Seaton to Richard M. Nixon, January 13, 1958, is in *Senate Report* no. 1518. The amendment of August 14, 1957, is in 71 *United States Statutes* 347–48. See also discussion in Hasse, "Termination and Assimilation," pp. 281–87.

26. 72 *United States Statutes* 816–19.

Corporation, and tribal members bought other units, but the federal government purchased the bulk of the land for use as national forest or wildlife refuge.[27]

The Klamath Indian Reservation was gone and the Klamath Tribe effectively destroyed. The sequel showed again the problems that termination brought to a tribe. Many of the Indians who withdrew were incompetent to manage their own assets, and arrangements were made with local banks to act as trustees, thus in effect transferring the trusteeship responsibilities from the federal government to private agencies. Others lost their money, and poverty and social disorganization resulted. When terminated Oregon Indians were interviewed in 1976, the great majority declared that they had neither understood nor participated in the process by which the tribal lands were lost and federal services ended. The positive effects envisaged by Senator Watkins and other terminationists did not materialize.[28]

REVERSAL OF POLICY

The absolute termination of Indian tribes, which was so eagerly promoted in the Eighty-third Congress and which seemed to have become the settled policy of the United States, slowly ground to a halt. From the very beginning, the complete withdrawal of federal responsibility for the tribes had met opposition from Indian groups and Indian welfare organizations. As termination moved into full gear and the Menominee and Klamath developments became well known, the outcry against termination became too loud to ignore. The National Congress of American Indians led the fight for the Indians, and tribal and individual Indian protests flowed into Congress. The Association on American Indian Affairs, in its role as watchdog for Indian rights, pointed to the dangers of federal withdrawal. "What is not understood," one writer in the *American Indian* declared, ". . . is that the withdrawal of Federal responsibility opens the door for the kind of unscrupulous exploitation of Indian persons and properties which has so often characterized our relations in the past." And the Indian Rights Association warned against too rapid and coercive termination, filling issues of *Indian Truth* with material critical of federal policy.[29]

27. There is discussion of these matters in Hasse, "Termination and Assimilation," pp. 287–94.

28. Stern, *Klamath Tribe*, pp. 253–55; "Oregon Termination: A Study of the Process and Effects of the Federal Government's Policy of Termination on the Lives of Oregon Indians," in American Indian Policy Review Commission, Task Force Ten, *Report on Terminated and Nonfederally Recognized Indians* (Washington: GPO, 1976), pp. 17–70.

29. Solon T. Kimball, "The New Crisis in Indian Affairs," *American Indian* 7 (Spring

John Collier, too, entered the fray. In May 1954 he pointed to the threat of a new "century of dishonor." He wrote in the *Nation* in October:

> Beginning with Dillon S. Myer as Indian Commissioner in 1950, the ruling purpose, harshly intensified by the present Administration, has been to atomize and suffocate the group life of the tribes— that group life which is their vitality, maturation, and hope—and to prevent the continuance and adaptation of those Indian civilizations which have produced great human beings through hundreds of generations. The present Administration's central method is to destroy the Indian Reorganization Act and the life structure which the Indians have built within its authority. The technique is not to use an omnibus bill but a host of special bills—effective in scattering the opposition—designed to destroy the Reorganization Act and its results tribe by tribe and region by region. A looted Indian estate will be the most apparent result, as it was in the case of the allotment acts of sixty and fifty years ago. A less apparent result will be a looted Indian soul and looted national honor, a United States shamed before the forty million Indians of the hemisphere.

Journals of opinion were full of criticism of the talk of "liberating" the Indians.[30]

Such sentiments were matched by new voices in Congress after 1956, as liberals began to speak out against the termination policy. Foremost among these was Representative Lee Metcalf of Montana. Although he had not resisted the passage of House Concurrent Resolution no. 108, when he saw how it had become the basis for immediate termination of federal services to the tribes, he objected. Metcalf was joined by Senators James E. Murray and Mike Mansfield of Montana, Frank E. Church of Idaho, Richard L. Neuberger of Oregon, and Joseph C. O'Mahoney of Wyoming in challenging the rapid drive for termination. These men proposed massive economic development for the reservations as an alternative to termination. Senate Concurrent Resolution no. 3, introduced by Murray on Janu-

---

1954): 21. See also, for example, the following articles in *Indian Truth*: "Indian Land Holdings Threatened," 32 (April–July 1955): 1; "Congress Can Help Indians," 33 (Winter 1956–1957): 1; "A New Policy Statement by Congress Needed," 36 (May–July 1959): 1.

    30. John Collier, "Back to Dishonor?" *Christian Century* 71 (May 12, 1954): 578–80; Collier, "Indian Takeaway: Betrayal of a Trust," *Nation* 179 (October 2, 1954): 290–91; Collier, "The Unfinished Indian Wars," ibid. 184 (May 25, 1957): 458–59. Other critical articles include Dorothy Bohn, "'Liberating' the Indian: Euphemism for a Land Grab," *Nation* 178 (February 20, 1954): 150–51; Harold E. Fey, "Our National Indian Policy," *Christian Century* 72 (March 30, 1955): 395–97; "Are the Indians to Lose All Their Land?" ibid. (July 20, 1955): 835–36; Edith R. Mirrielees, "The Cloud of Mistrust," *Atlantic Monthly* 199 (February 1957): 55–59.

ary 7, 1957, declared that the purpose of the Bureau of Indian Affairs should be "to assist American Indian communities to reach the level of well-being enjoyed by other communities in the United States" and that the program should be offered to the Indians "without exacting termination of Federal protection of Indian property or of any other Indian rights as its price."[31] States and localities in which the Indians lived, moreover, began to have second thoughts about the wisdom of termination and the benefits it might bring to them.

The Department of the Interior, too, pulled back. Seaton, who was appointed secretary of the interior in June 1956 to replace McKay, was a moderate on the issue of termination. He symbolized the new direction in a speech at Flagstaff, Arizona, on September 18, 1958, in which he declared that House Concurrent Resolution no. 108 stated "an objective, not an immediate goal." He added: "To be specific, my own position is this: no Indian tribe or group should end its relationship with the Federal Government unless such tribe or group has clearly demonstrated—first, that it understands the plan under which such a program would go forward, and second, that the tribe or group affected concurs in and supports the plan proposed." It was unthinkable, Seaton insisted, that a termination plan should be forced upon any Indian tribe, and he declared that it would be "incredible, even criminal" to send any tribe out into the mainstream of American life until it was properly educated to shoulder the new responsibilities.[32]

Although it was at first confused by the change of direction, the Bureau of Indian Affairs accepted the new mandate, and Emmons declared that Seaton's speech was "one of the most important developments of the year in Federal administration of Indian affairs . . . , clarifying the Department's position on the centrally important question of terminating Federal trust responsibilities for Indian tribal groups." And he noted the favorable response that the secretary's remarks had brought from Indians.[33]

In reality, the coercive termination policy of Senator Watkins and his supporters, with its total withdrawal of federal support, had a short life. The Indians in the terminated groups numbered 13,263 out of an estimated tribal Indian population of 400,000, or not much more than 3 percent of federally recognized Indians. The 1,365,801 acres of trust land

31. Lee Metcalf, "The Need for Revision of Federal Policy in Indian Affairs," *Indian Truth* 35 (January–March 1958): 1–8; *Congressional Record*, 103: 278. On congressional changes, see Hasse, "Termination and Assimilation," pp. 264–71.

32. Seaton's Flagstaff speech is printed in *Congressional Record*, 105: 3105.

33. CIA Report, 1959, p. 231. The softening position of the Bureau of Indian Affairs is discussed in Burt, *Tribalism in Crisis*, pp. 107–23.

withdrawn amounted to about 3 percent of the approximately 43,000,000 acres held in trust in 1953.[34]

The psychological effects on all Indians, however, were enormous, for fear of termination filled the air. Opposition to the policy became a rallying point for Indian groups, and it unified Indian voices in a new and remarkable way. "Termination" became a hated word, and all government proposals on Indian matters were scrutinized with a new alertness, lest they be secret steps toward federal withdrawal. The Indian agitation of the 1960s and 1970s was, among other things, a response to the policies of the 1950s.

34. Wilkinson and Biggs, "Evolution of the Termination Policy," p. 151. There is a table on Indian groups freed from federal supervision as of June 30, 1964, in *Information on Removal of Restrictions on American Indians*, Committee Print no. 38, House Committee on Interior and Insular Affairs, 88th Congress, 2d session (Washington: GPO, 1964).

CHAPTER 42

Programs for
Indians

Education for Cultural Change.

Transfer of Indian Health Services.

Economic Development.

Relocation.

The absolute withdrawal of federal responsibility that was the fate of the Menominees, Klamaths, and other tribes falling under Watkins's program, however, was not the whole story of the termination era, for Indian development—in education, health, and economic resources—was an abiding goal. Programs in these areas were part of a continuing story that antedated termination and extended far beyond it, and they were promoted by groups interested in Indian welfare whether they favored federal withdrawal or opposed it. Yet these programs also had strong tinges of terminationist philosophy, for by enabling Indians and Indian groups to stand more firmly on their own feet and by transferring activities away from the Bureau of Indian Affairs, the programs looked toward the elimination of the traditional federal responsibility for Indians.

EDUCATION FOR CULTURAL CHANGE

At the end of Collier's administration in 1945, Willard W. Beatty stayed on as director of Indian education, thus providing a continuity of educational philosophy and programming. But Beatty also faced changes that World

War II had brought, as well as the hostile attitude of Congress toward the Collier outlook.[1]

The havoc that the war had brought to the Indian schools did not automatically disappear at war's end. The decimation in school personnel caused by war service and war industry jobs affected all the schools, and the lack of funds for construction and maintenance meant that the physical plant was in poor shape. The community day schools, which had been the central pillar in Collier's program, were especially hard hit, for they could not operate when buses broke down and were not replaced or when the reservation roads fell into disrepair. In some places, notably on the Navajo reservation, day schools were in fact turned into makeshift boarding schools, as crude dormitories were thrown together for the pupils by the Indians themselves. The war, too, had cut school enrollment. In 1945–1946 there were 22,770 pupils in school, down from 25,839 in 1941–1942.[2]

The war also brought a changed philosophy. Returning veterans of the armed forces and workers from war jobs carried back to the reservations a new respect and desire for education. The value of education in military service and in industry was not lost on the Indians, who demanded attention to their needs. More important, the ideal of educating to preserve Indian community patterns, which had been so strongly promoted under the New Deal, gave way now to an emphasis on preparation to succeed in the white man's world. Beatty changed with the times. In compiling a selection of articles from the newsletter *Indian Education* in 1944, he had written, "The schools of the Indian Service are primarily rural, and their most important job is to prepare young Indians to earn a successful living through the use of their own resources." When he edited a new compilation of articles in 1951, he took a different position:

> The new title to this second volume of reprints, *Education for Cultural Change*, serves to identify a phase of the basic purposes in Indian education, which has gained increasing endorsement from the Indian people. Over the last 15 years the adherence to traditional patterns and resistance to change that was characteristic of many adult Indians has given way to a recognition that the richest future for Indians in the United States lies in mastery of the material culture of the dominant race. Without sacrificing racial pride or identification with their Indian past, Indian parents and pupils are determined to

1. Beatty's work from 1945 to 1952 is treated in Margaret Szasz, *Education and the American Indian: The Road to Self-Determination, 1928–1973* (Albuquerque: University of New Mexico Press, 1974), pp. 106–22.

2. CIA Report, 1946, p. 357. For the problem of the buses and the roads, see Willard W. Beatty, "History of Navajo Education," *America Indigena* 21 (January 1961): 15.

gain from education a mastery of the English language and of the manual and intellectual skills of their white brethren.[3]

The federal Indian day school concept suffered heavily. The Mundt committee report in 1944 had set the tone when it contrasted the handicaps suffered by pupils in day schools with the "opportunities afforded Indian children in off-the-reservation boarding schools where they can acquire an education in healthful and cultural surroundings." The report declared; "If real progress is to be made in training the Indian children to accept and appreciate the white man's way of life, the children of elementary school age who live in violently substandard homes on reservations should be encouraged to attend off-the-reservation boarding schools where they can formulate habits of life equipping them for independent citizenship when they reach maturity."[4] The Bureau of the Budget, moreover, looked askance at authorizing new construction for reservation schools when the off-reservation schools were not filled to capacity. The movement away from boarding schools toward community day schools, therefore, was stopped, and a new appreciation of the boarding schools arose, both for acculturation of the young Indians and for vocational training to fit those who were approaching adulthood for jobs off the reservation. In 1946 the commissioner of Indian affairs reported an increase in boarding school attendance, both on and off the reservations, over the previous year, while day school attendance remained stationary. By 1952 there were 16,865 enrollments in federal day schools and 19,549 in boarding schools; in 1960 the comparable figures were 16,025 and 21,352.[5]

The most serious educational problem by far was that of the Navajos. Their schools had been neglected by the federal government, and many of the Indians had long resisted white schools. Then, at the end of the war, the severity of the situation suddenly was realized. The Navajos began to demand the educational facilities promised them in the treaty of 1868, and the government became aware at last of the results of its negligence. There were almost 20,000 Navajo children between the ages of six and eighteen, Commissioner William Brophy reported in 1945, and school facilities for fewer than 60 percent of them. "During the war period," he noted, "the

3. Willard W. Beatty and associates, *Education for Action: Selected Articles from Indian Education, 1936–43* (Washington: Education Division, United States Indian Service, 1944), p. 7; Beatty and associates, *Education for Cultural Change: Selected Articles from Indian Education, 1944–51* (Washington: Bureau of Indian Affairs, 1953), pp. 10–11.

4. *House Report* no. 2091, 78–2, serial 10848, p. 9.

5. CIA Report, 1946, p. 357; *Statistics Concerning Indian Education* (Washington: Branch of Education, Bureau of Indian Affairs), issues for 1952 and 1960.

lack of road maintenance and the limitations on tires, gasoline, and school bus replacements have interfered seriously with the maintenance of the day schools. As a result the largest enrollment ever recorded has crowded into the boarding schools of the area, and it has been necessary to turn away hundreds of children whose parents wished them to have the advantages of education."[6]

The inexcusable school conditions on the Navajo reservation were eloquently described in a study commissioned by the Indian Bureau in 1946. Written by George L. Sanchez, a rural education specialist at the University of Texas, the report described in detail the "makeshift schools" and condemned unmercifully what Sanchez called the "day school fallacy":

> The modern day school, everywhere else in the nation, presupposes a fundamental condition: the children must be within walking distance of the school or accessible to a school bus which can transport them back and forth comfortably, regularly, with safety, and without undue loss of time from either home life, school work, or rest and recreation. It is also dependent upon a cultural scheme wherein it is assumed that the home is in a position to further educational aims or that, at the very least, it will not negate the work of the school. For the vast majority of Navajo children, these conditions do not exist, and both the Navajo Service educators and the Navajo people themselves know that the day school, as known elsewhere, cannot function here.[7]

The Bureau of Indian Affairs forthrightly attacked the Navajo problem. To meet the needs of Navajo adolescents, who had had little or no schooling and who would soon approach adulthood thus handicapped, it established the Special Navajo Education Program. This innovative program had three aims: to develop sound skills and habits that would fit the youth to live effectively in a non-Indian culture, to teach basic English language skills and arithmetic skills necessary for earning a living in a non-Indian world, and to teach vocational skills that would enable the young Indians to make a living and support a family after graduation. Because of the advanced age of the students admitted to the program (twelve to eighteen), the educational program was limited to five years. Instruction was in both Navajo and English, but it all took place in off-reservation boarding schools, where space was available.[8]

6. CIA Report, 1945, pp. 245–46.

7. George I. Sanchez, *"The People": A Study of the Navajos* (Washington: United States Indian Service, 1948), p. 33. See also Beatty, "History of Navajo Education."

8. L. Madison Coombs, *Doorway toward the Light: The Story of the Special Navajo Education Program* (Washington: Bureau of Indian Affairs, 1962), is a full and enthusiastic

The program began at Sherman Institute, Riverside, California, in the fall of 1946 with 290 students enrolled for the first year. In 1947 the program was expanded to Chilocco Indian School in Oklahoma, the Phoenix Indian School in Arizona, and the Carson Indian School in Nevada; the following year the Albuquerque Indian School, the Chemawa Indian School in Oregon, and the Cheyenne-Arapaho School in Oklahoma were added. As these boarding schools opened their doors to the young Navajo men and women, the participants grew in number; in the spring of 1949 there were 1,650 enrolled. A sudden expansion in the program's capacity came when the government opened Intermountain School at Bushnell General Hospital, Brigham City, Utah, which had been declared surplus by the United States army. The school opened in January 1950 with 542 students; the next year it had 1,374 and in 1951–1952, 2214 (at which figure, roughly, the enrollment stabilized).[9]

The Special Navajo Education Program had considerable success in meeting its goals. From 1951, when the first group graduated, through 1959, 3,362 pupils were graduated, and many others attended for varying lengths of time. A large number of the graduates found jobs away from the reservation.[10] Thus the program—which ultimately trained some Papagos and Apaches as well as Navajos—was a significant arm of the concurrent Indian relocation program of the government, which sought to find employment or Indians off the reservations. It met less criticism than other relocation efforts, for the Indians' training was off-reservation, and the final year of school provided on-the-job training, which frequently turned into permanent employment after graduation. Thus those Indians in the program were already acquainted both with the geographical area and the nature of the work and were not moved into a completely strange world.[11]

The special program for adolescents did not solve the fundamental problem that numerous Navajo children still were not receiving formal educa-

---

report of the program. A promotional pamphlet is *Education for Cultural Adjustment: A Special Five-Year Program for Adolescent Indians* (Washington: Bureau of Indian Affairs, 1956). For the course of studies, see *Minimum Essential Goals: Special Five Year Adolescent Navajo Program, First, Second, and Third Years*, 2d ed. (Washington: Branch of Education, Bureau of Indian Affairs, 1952), and *Goals of the Special Five Year Navajo Program: Years Four and Five*, 2d ed. (Washington: Branch of Education, Bureau of Indian Affairs, 1953).

9. Coombs, *Doorway toward the Light;* see the table on p. 168.

10. Ibid., p. 133; see the table of graduates 1951–1959, p. 173. There is an account of the program in CIA Report, 1951, pp. 360–63.

11. James E. Officer, *Indians in School: A Study of the Development of Educational Facilities for Arizona Indians* (Tucson: Bureau of Ethnic Research, University of Arizona, 1956), p. 117.

tion. As late as 1953 nearly half of the school-age population of 27,016 were not enrolled in school. In the fall of 1954, therefore, a massive emergency program was undertaken, and within two years enough space in schools was made for an additional 13,000 Navajos. This was accomplished by expanding boarding school facilities on the reservation, crowding children into existing schools both on and off the reservation, and developing public schools at some locations on the reservation. Two special programs helped. The first was bordertown schools. Public schools on the periphery of the reservation were expanded, and boarding dormitories for the Indian students were provided at them. Thus the students would have the advantages that had been seen to come from mingling with white students in public schools, yet they would be provided for in a boarding school situation. Second, trailer schools were set up wherever concentrations of population would support a school on a day basis. Thus, through a crash program, the substantial backlog of unschooled Navajo children was partially corrected.[12]

The Navajo educational advances were directed in large part by Hildegard Thompson, who served as director of Navajo education. In 1952, when Beatty resigned because of a loss of authority under Commissioner Dillon S. Myer, Thompson succeeded him as director of education for the bureau. She called the emergency Navajo program an "unbelievable achievement which far outstripped any previous efforts to solve the out-of-school Navajo problem," and she credited the success to the full support and cooperation of the Indian people. Thompson was a persistent administrator, willing to compromise for small gains under circumstances that had led her stronger predecessor to leave office. She worked for improvement in basic academic and social skills and little by little advanced the number in school and the educational level of the Indian students, without any dramatic innovations.[13]

The move toward enrollment of Indian children in the regular public

12. Hildegard Thompson, "Education among American Indians: Institutional Aspects," *Annals of the American Academy of Political and Social Science* 311 (May 1957): 102. For a special report on the bordertown schools, see *Report to the Senate Appropriations Committee on the Navajo Bordertown Dormitory Program by the Commissioner of Indian Affairs* (Washington: Bureau of Indian Affairs, 1965).

13. Thompson's work is evaluated in Szasz, *Education and the American Indian*, pp. 123–40. Thompson described the educational work in the early years of her administration in "Education among American Indians"; the quotation is from p. 102. For her fundamental objectives, see the guides she issued: *Minimum Essential Goals for Indian Schools*, 3 vols. (Washington: Bureau of Indian Affairs, 1953), and Thompson and others, *Education for Cross-Cultural Enrichment: Selected Articles from Indian Education, 1952–64* (Washington: Branch of Education, Bureau of Indian Affairs, 1964).

TABLE 16: School Enrollments, Students 6–18 Years of Age,
United States and Alaska

	1952	1956	1960
Public schools	52,960	71,956	84,650
Federal schools			
Day	16,865	16,804	16,025
Boarding	19,549	22,872	21,353
Total	[36,414]	[39,676]	[37,377]
Mission and other	10,067	11,223	11,289
Total	99,441	122,855	133,316
Not in school		10,311	8,881

SOURCE: *Statistics Concerning Indian Education* (Washington: Branch of
Education, Bureau of Indian Affairs), issues for 1952, 1956, 1960.

schools of the state, which had begun early in the century, did not slacken.
It was in fact an important part of the new drive to get the government out
of the Indian business as quickly as possible, for education was a heavy
part of the government's Indian responsibilities (see Table 16). By 1956
there were no federal Indian schools in Michigan, Washington, Minnesota,
Idaho, Nebraska, or Wyoming, states in which the government had once
been involved. To provide for the transferred students, the Bureau of Indian
Affairs continued to make contracts with the states under the Johnson-
O'Malley Act of 1934. In 1956, for example, contracts that provided financial assistance for about 39,600 of the Indian children in public schools
were made with states and with local school districts in nineteen states
and the Territory of Alaska. Indians who lived in areas where their tax-
exempt status caused no hardship, however, received their education in
the public schools without federal aid; in 1956, excluding Alaska, about 45
percent of the Indian public school children were in this category. Federal
assistance was available to public schools also under laws passed in 1950
authorizing funds for construction and operation of schools in areas where
there was special impact from students who lived on federal property, for
"federal property" was defined to include trust or restricted land of individual Indians or Indian tribes.[14]

14. CIA Report, 1956, pp. 209–10; CIA Report, 1959, pp. 233–34; Thompson,
"Education among American Indians," p. 100. For the legislation on funds for school
construction and operation, see 64 *United States Statutes* 967–78, 1100–1109; 72
United States Statutes 559–61. As this increased aid was available, contracts under the
Johnson-O'Malley Act were reduced.

The transfer of a large part of the Indian educational program to the states (58.6 percent attended public schools in 1956) resulted in a considerable differentiation between Indian students in the public schools and those who were in federal schools. This difference became clear, in part, as a result of studies commissioned by the Bureau of Indian Affairs to investigate the academic achievement of Indian boys and girls. In general the studies found that the highest achievement came from Indian children in the public schools, then in federal boarding schools, and finally in federal day schools.[15] In justifying the poorer performance in the Indian Bureau schools, the bureau pointed to the different types of students in the different schools. Those in the public schools were largely mixed-bloods, whereas the reservation boarding schools and especially the day schools were heavy with full-bloods. In 1956, 83 percent of the students in the federal schools were full-blooded Indians and only 3 percent were less than half-blood. There was close correlation between achievement on the standard tests and the degree of Indian blood, which in turn reflected the acculturation of Indian homes to the English language and white ways.[16] A considerable number of students in the boarding schools were from broken homes or came from undesirable social and economic conditions at home.

A special concern was education for adult Indians. In 1955 a program was initiated on five reservations—Papago, Fort Hall, Turtle Mountain, Seminole, and Rosebud Sioux—for adult education. Its aims, Thompson said, were "to orient Indians and their children to a time-conscious, acquisitive, and competitive world and at the same time to give them sufficient command of English to function in an English-speaking society." By 1958 the program had been expanded to serve seventy-nine Indian communities or native villages in the United States and Alaska.[17] But strictly vocational aims, too, were part of the movement for adult education. In 1956 Congress appropriated funds for special vocational training for Indians eighteen to thirty-five years of age living on or near reservations. Programs

15. Shailer Peterson, *How Well Are Indian Children Educated?* (Washington: United States Indian Service, 1948); Kenneth E. Anderson, E. Gordon Collister, and Carl E. Ladd, *The Educational Achievement of Indian Children: A Re-examination of the Question, How Well Are Indian Children Educated?* (Washington: Bureau of Indian Affairs, 1953); L. Madison Coombs and others, *The Indian Child Goes to School: A Study of Interracial Difference* (Washington: Bureau of Indian Affairs, 1958).

16. CIA Report, 1956, p. 210; Thompson, "Education among American Indians," p. 103. See also the introduction by Willard W. Beatty in Homer H. Howard, *In Step with the States: A Comparison of State and Indian Service Educational Objectives and Methods* (Washington: Education Division, United States Indian Service, 1949).

17. CIA Report, 1956, p. 211; CIA Report, 1958, p. 203; Thompson, "Education among American Indians," p. 103.

were to provide "vocational counseling or guidance, institutional training
in a recognized vocation or trade, apprenticeship, and on the job training,
for periods that do not exceed twenty-four months, transportation to the
place of training and subsistence during the course of training." The purposes, according to the Interior Department, in promoting the measure
were to stimulate industries to locate near the reservations, where trained
manpower would be available, and to prepare and orient participating Indians for the relocation program. In fiscal year 1958 there were 376 Indians
enrolled in regularly accredited vocational schools, and the training was
provided in all ten of the bureau's areas and in eight of the cities where
relocation offices were located. Another 168 Indians were in on-the-job
training in plants near the reservations.[18]

High school education, which had barely begun for Indians in the 1920s,
had by the 1950s become a recognized part of the formal school system,
especially in the public schools and in off-reservation boarding schools.
Whereas in 1924 only one federal Indian school offered twelve grades of
instruction, in 1934 there were a dozen, and ten years later there were
thirty-seven high schools. By 1956 there were 5,406 Indians in government
high schools. The schools of the federal government, however, continued
to carry a heavy load of primary and elementary school pupils (in 1956
over half of the children in federal schools were in the first four grades), for
the older children were more likely to respond favorably to public schools.
Increasing attention now came to be paid, also, to higher education for Indians. Congress in 1957 appropriated seventy thousand dollars for grants to
Indians in college, tribal funds were set aside, and there were special grants
available from colleges and universities and from private organizations.[19]

TRANSFER OF INDIAN HEALTH SERVICES

Health problems, like educational ones, were enduring among the Indians.
The reduction of critical personnel in the Indian health services that came
during World War II aggravated an already serious situation, and the government in the postwar years struggled to improve conditions. Year by year
there was some progress as the morbidity and mortality rates dropped

18. Wesley A. D'Ewart to Clair Engle, May 18, 1956, in *House Report* no. 2532, 84–2,
serial 11900, pp. 2–4; *Senate Report* no. 2664, 84–2, serial 11890; 70 *United States
Statutes* 986; CIA Report, 1958, pp. 203, 222–23.

19. *Statistics Concerning Indian Education,* 1956; Thompson, "Education among
American Indians," p. 103. The bureau produced booklets describing sources of aid for
Indian college students; see, for example, Amanda H. Finley, *Higher Education Aids for
Indian Young People* (Washington: Bureau of Indian Affairs, 1956).

slightly and as more and more Indians made use of medical facilities. Yet these causes of optimism—eagerly reported by government officials— could not conceal radically deficient health care for the Indians. It was frequently declared that health conditions among the Indians were comparable to those among the general population half a century earlier. The great medical advances that had cut diseases and lengthened life expectancy for the white population still had not reached the Indians. The statistics were staggering: in 1953 among the Indian population the death rate from measles was twenty times that of the non-Indian population, from tuberculosis nine times, and from pneumonia and influenza four times. There were three times as many infant deaths and twice as many accidental deaths. Tuberculosis, despite the periodic attacks upon the disease, was still the most frequent cause of illness.[20]

The Navajos received special attention, for they were the largest tribe and in many ways the most in need. A survey conducted in September 1947 under the sponsorship of the American Medical Association found general undernourishment and vitamin deficiency, especially among schoolchildren, a wide prevalence of tuberculosis, a high death rate among infants and children, and a woeful lack of preventive measures to control communicable diseases.[21]

The reasons were easy enough to enumerate. The health conditions, as a report of the bureau's Branch of Health declared, occurred within a "framework of an essentially rural, isolated, culturally different and economically depressed population." The great distance many Indians had to travel to get general health services, the isolation of the facilities, which made adequate staffing very difficult, the cultural differences that increased the difficulty in communication and in explaining procedures for prevention and

20. CIA Report, 1954, p. 235. There were numerous reports about the bad state of Indian health. See, for example, Fred T. Foard, "The Health of the American Indians," *American Journal of Public Health* 39 (November 1949): 1403–6; Haven Emerson, "Indian Health—Victim of Neglect," *Survey* 87 (May 1951): 219–21; Raymond C. McKay, "Indian Health Needs and Services," *American Indian* 6 (Summer 1951): 29–32. See also *Current Facts about Indian Health* (Washington: Branch of Health, Bureau of Indian Affairs, 1953).

21. "Health Survey of Navajos," 1947, a 32-page mimeographed report, including the findings of the survey by Ozro T. Woods; *The Navajo Health Program* (Window Rock, Arizona: Window Rock Area Office, Bureau of Indian Affairs, 1951). See also Lewis J. Moorman, "Health of the Navajo-Hopi Indians: General Report of the American Medical Association Team," *Journal of the American Medical Association* 139 (February 5, 1949): 370–76. A very sympathetic account of the Navajo approach to health is John Adair, Kurt Deuschle, and Walsh McDermott, "Patterns of Health and Disease among the Navajos," *Annals of the American Academy of Political and Social Science* 311 (May 1957): 80–94.

treatment, and the "often intransigent attitudes of non-Indians toward Indian customs and practices" all contributed to the problem. Unsanitary housing and environment, unsafe and inadequate water supplies, and poor diet were widespread, and public health preventive medicine in many places was almost nonexistent. The absence of accurate statistics on the population base and on the incidence of disease and death made even an evaluation of the problem next to impossible. Corrective measures all required money, yet appropriations for medical services for the Indians seemed to do little more than keep up with inflation and allowed for no radical improvement in personnel or services.[22]

The only solution to the impasse seemed to be to transfer responsibility for Indian health out of the Bureau of Indian Affairs in the Department of the Interior to the Public Health Service in the Department of Health, Education, and Welfare. Such action would be in line with a developing movement. The supervision of Indian health activities by personnel from the Public Health Service, which had begun in 1926, had brought some improvement in efficiency and in recruitment of doctors and nurses. As much as possible the Bureau of Indian Affairs was committed in its withdrawal objectives not to operate any health facility where regular health care was available, and the Johnson-O'Malley Act authorized contracts with states, local governments, and private organizations for Indian medical services. A law of April 3, 1952, furthermore, authorized the secretary of the interior to transfer Indian hospitals and other health facilities to states, local governments, or appropriate private organizations for operation, provided that the health needs of the Indians would continue to have priority in those units.[23]

Action came finally in 1954. A bill for transfer to the Public Health Service had been introduced in January 1953, and hearings brought out arguments both for and against the measure. Proponents argued that transfer would ease the staffing problems of the Indian health program because the Public Health Service as an established career service could offer better salaries and other professional advantages. Second, the Public Health Service would assume direct medical supervision of the program, eliminating the continual conflicts that arose when agency superintendents and other lay officials exercised control over administrative matters related to health.

---

22. *Indian Health: A Problem and a Challenge* (Washington: Branch of Health, Bureau of Indian Affairs, 1955). Commissioner Myer gives an account of conditions contributing to the Indian health problem in CIA Report, 1950, p. 343. For a discussion of the problem of accurate statistics, see H. DeLien and J. Nixon Hadley, "How to Recognize an Indian Health Problem," *Human Organization* 11 (Fall 1952): 29–33.

23. 66 *United States Statutes* 35–36.

Indian Self-Determination

75. President Richard Nixon and the Return of Blue Lake

On December 15, 1970, President Nixon signed a bill to return the sacred Blue Lake to the Taos Pueblo Indians. It was an act of great symbolic value for Indian self-determination, for it marked the restoration of significant Indian lands and a recognition of Indian religious rights, and it began a decade of change. Looking on are Paul Bernal (left), interpreter, and Juan de Jesus Romero, religious leader.

76. Stewart L. Udall and W. W. Keeler

Secretary of the Interior Udall, who
served in the Kennedy and Johnson administrations, had firm views about promoting Indian self-determination and
reservation development. Early in his tenure he appointed a Task Force on Indian
Affairs to investigate Indian needs and a
Task Force on Alaska Native Affairs to
study the special problems in Alaska. The
chairman of both task forces was W. W.
Keeler, principal chief of the Cherokee
Nation and a high-ranking executive of
the Phillips Petroleum Company.

77. Philleo Nash

78. Robert L. Bennett

Nash, an anthropologist who had served
as lieutenant governor of Wisconsin, was
commissioner of Indian affairs 1961–1966.
He had been a member of Udall's Task
Force on Indian Affairs and promoted
policies of Indian participation in programs for their economic development.
The last non-Indian to serve as commissioner, Nash was replaced in 1966 by Robert L. Bennett, an Oneida Indian from
Wisconsin, who had worked his way
up through the BIA bureaucracy.

79. Navajo Community Action Program

Many of the programs authorized by the Economic Opportunity Act of 1964 were extended to Indian groups, which used them to provide community development. Of special note was the Community Action Program, in which Indian participation in planning and management was extensive. Under the Home Improvement Program of the Community Action Program, Navajo Indians were instructed in building new homes to replace their hogans.

A report of 1969 entitled "Indian Education: A National Tragedy—A National Challenge" stimulated Congress to pass new legislation to improve the condition of Indian schools. The report came from the Special Subcommittee on Indian Education, chaired first by Robert F. Kennedy and then by his brother Edward M. Kennedy.

Commissioner of Indian Affairs Bruce and Secretary of the Interior Hickel were the initial appointments to those offices by President Nixon. Bruce, of Mohawk-Sioux heritage, worked hard to reorganize the BIA to give Indians a greater voice in its deliberations, but he met opposition from old-line bureaucrats.

80. Senator Robert F. Kennedy and Indian Students

81. Louis R. Bruce and Walter J. Hickel

82. Indian Seizure of BIA Headquarters

In November 1972 militant Indians, led
by members of the American Indian
Movement, seized the BIA headquarters
building in Washington, D.C. Although
the embittered and frustrated Indians
thoroughly wrecked the interior of the
building, they finally were persuaded to
end the occupation and leave peacefully.

The seizure of the village of Wounded Knee by Indian activists on February 27, 1973, was intended to bring national attention to the plight of the Indians as well as to dramatize intratribal divisions among the Pine Ridge Sioux. Although the confrontation between the Indians and federal officers was deadly serious, the Indians capitalized on the affair as a "media event," and there was a good deal of dramatic posturing, as this photograph shows.

Ada Deer led the successful agitation of Menominee Indians against the termination of federal responsibility for their tribe. After Congress restored tribal status to the Menominees in December 1973, Deer was head of the Menominee Restoration Committee until she resigned in 1976. Milwaukee Journal Photo.

83. Wounded Knee, 1973

84. Ada Deer, Menominee Leader

85. Forrest Gerard

One goal of the Nixon administration was to establish an assistant secretary of the interior for Indian affairs in place of the commissioner of Indian affairs, thus upgrading the federal officer directly responsible for Indian policy. The move was finally accomplished by President Carter in 1977, when he appointed Forrest Gerard, a member of the Blackfeet Tribe, to the newly created position.

Claims of the Passamaquoddy and Penobscot Indians of Maine to much of the territory of the state, on the grounds that treaties of cession made with the state of Massachusetts had been invalid, threatened economic chaos in Maine. A settlement was finally negotiated, which was approved and funded by Congress in 1980. President Carter signed the bill on October 10.

86. President Jimmy Carter Signing the Maine Indian Claims Settlement Act

Moreover, the Public Health Service would offer tremendous professional and technical resources, especially in regard to public health measures, which would set the Indian health program within a larger medical context. Elimination of overlapping activities was another goal, and there was hope that the Public Health Service would obtain needed appropriations more successfully than had the Bureau of Indian Affairs. There was support for transfer from such groups as the Hoover Commission's task force on public welfare, the American Medical Association, the National Tuberculosis Association, and the Association on American Indian Affairs.[24]

Countering these forceful arguments was the fear that Indian health care was so closely tied to other activities that to separate it would cause confusion in the complex administration of affairs on the reservations. The bureau, it was noted, had worked long with the Indians and knew their special conditions and problems, a sympathetic understanding that the Public Health Service could hardly hope to match. In 1953, when the House considered the bill, the Department of the Interior opposed the transfer. "The various service programs for Indians are so closely related," Assistant Secretary Orme Lewis wrote, "that it is deemed inadvisable to separate the administration of the health services from the administration of other services to Indians. The education, welfare, law and order, and health functions of the Bureau are particularly interrelated." A year later, however, the department had changed its mind and argued that the Public Health Service could attain the health objectives of the Indians more quickly than could the Bureau of Indian Affairs. It admitted that there would be administrative problems but considered none of them insoluble. The Department of Health, Education, and Welfare, which would have to assume the transferred health responsibilities, nevertheless held firm in opposition to the change. The department feared administrative confusion with the fragmenting of responsibilities toward the Indians, and it declared: "The transfer of responsibility in itself would not constitute the solution to the health problems of the Indians. These problems are difficult and deep-seated, involving the geographic location, economic status, cultural and educational levels and lack of social and political integration of this special segment of the Nation's population."[25]

24. "Transfer of Indian Hospitals and Health Facilities to Public Health Service," *Hearings before a Subcommittee of the Commitee on Interior and Insular Affairs, United States Senate, 83d Congress, 2d Session, on H.R. 303* (1954).

25. Orme Lewis to A. L. Miller, May 5, 1953, in *House Report* no. 870, 83–1, serial 11667, pp. 10–11; Lewis to Hugh Butler, May 27, 1954, and Oveta Culp Hobby to Butler, May 28, 1954, in "Transfer of Indian Hospitals," pp. 2–5, 10–12. Discussion of the arguments for and against transfer are in *Health Services for Amerian Indians* (Washington: Public Health Service, 1957), pp. 95–96, and Ruth M. Raup, *The Indian Health Program*

What strongly motivated the congressional committees in their favorable consideration of the transfer bill was their commitment to termination and the withdrawal of special services to Indians. The House committee spoke bluntly:

> Transfer of the Indian Health Service is part of the pattern of legislation deemed necessary by the committee to effectuate the eventual termination of all Federal responsibility for providing Indian services.
>
> For a number of years, the Public Health Service has been assisting the Bureau of Indian Affairs in the planning and administration of health services to Indians; in addition policy has called for turning over this responsibility to State or local agencies wherever feasible— all aiming at erasing the line of distinction between services for Indians and the non-Indian population. For many years, State health agencies and numerous national health groups have emphasized the desirability of the transfer anticipated by this legislation.
>
> Your committee feels that the transfer of the health program is only an initial step, that Indian Bureau operations in the field of education and in the field of welfare should be transferred to other agencies serving these needs for non-Indians as soon as practicable programs can be worked out.[26]

In Senate debate on transfer, Senator Edward J. Thye of Minnesota succinctly summed up the objectives of the measure: "First, it will improve the health service for the Indian people. Second, it will coordinate the public health program. Third, it will further the long-range objective of the integration of the Indian people into the common life of the United States."[27]

The transfer bill was approved on August 5, 1954. All functions and responsibilities of the Bureau of Indian Affairs and the Department of the Interior relating to "the maintenance and operation of hospital and health facilities for Indians, and the conservation of the health of Indians" were given to the surgeon general of the United States Public Health Service, effective July 1, 1955, with provisions to protect the interest of particular tribes in hospitals serving them. The law specifically authorized the continuation of the policy of transferring Indian facilities to state or other agencies. The transfer, Commissioner Glenn Emmons noted, was "un-

---

from 1800–1955 (Washington: Division of Public Health Methods, Public Health Service, 1959), pp. 23–26.

26. *House Report* no. 870, 83–1, serial 11667, p. 14. See also *Senate Report* no. 1530, 83–2, serial 11729, p. 2.

27. *Congressional Record*, 100: 8959.

questionably the biggest reduction of program responsibilities in the history of the Bureau." The move affected thirty-six hundred employees and property valued at $40 million. There were 970 buildings in thirteen states and the Territory of Alaska, including 56 hospitals, 21 health centers, and 13 boarding school infirmaries, plus numerous field clinics.[28]

The transfer triggered a detailed new survey of Indian health care. In considering increased appropriations for Indian health under the new auspices, the House Committee on Appropriations noted: "Health services for Indians have been provided by the Federal Government for over a hundred years; but in spite of this fact the American Indian is still the victim of an appalling amount of sickness. The health facilities are either nonexistent in some areas, or, for the most part, obsolescent and in need of repair; personnel housing is lacking or inadequate; and workloads have been such as to test the patience and endurance of professional staff. This all points to a gross lack of resources equal to the present load of sickness and accumulated neglect." The committee asked the surgeon general for "a careful comprehensive evaluation of the Indian health problem," including a statement on what would be required to bring Indian health up to an acceptable level and how long it would take. In addition, it wanted a review of the social and economic resources available for Indian health purposes.[29]

The surgeon general, with the aid of staff from the Public Health Service, the Bureau of Indian Affairs, and other government agencies, plus studies on social and economic resources contracted for with scholars at five universities, submitted the required reports. The final report, *Health Services for American Indians*, dated February 11, 1957, was a comprehensive and forthright analysis of the Indian health situation. It outlined a program to meet the major health needs of the Indians that in substance asked for more of everything. But the report also put its finger on more basic problems beyond the scope of the Public Health Service's responsibilities: "To achieve good health, Indians need more than measures aimed directly at disease prevention and control. They need better general education, vocational training, housing, food, roads, and means of transportation. They need more understanding and acceptance by the rest of the population, particularly their own non-Indian neighbors. They also need adequate economic opportunities."[30]

28. 68 *United States Statutes* 674–75; CIA Report, 1955, p. 231.

29. *House Report* no. 228, 84–1, serial 11822, pp. 12–13. A preliminary report was requested by October 1955 and a final report by October 1956.

30. *Health Services for American Indians*, p. 3. The reports to the House committee were drawn upon for *Plan for Medical Facilities Needed for Indian Health Services*, prepared by the Division of Indian Health, Public Health Service, in 1958 or 1959.

With the transfer came an increase in appropriations, which permitted hiring more staff and extending services, and statistics on the Indians continued to show both increasing use of medical facilities and a slow decline in morbidity and mortality. The Public Health Service announced in 1957: "The gains of the past two or three years may be small in relation to the ultimate objective of this program, but they are clear indications that the goals in Indian health in time will be achieved." Yet there was no sudden solution to the social and economic basis upon which ultimately the good health of the Indian population rested.[31]

ECONOMIC DEVELOPMENT

That the education, health, and general welfare of the Indians depended upon economic development was well understood, and continuing efforts were made to shore up the economic basis of Indian existence. The goal, as in the past, was to make the Indians self-supporting at a level of well-being comparable to that of the non-Indian population. But now there was a new urgency, for successful withdrawal of federal responsibility for the Indians was premised upon conditions under which they could stand on their own like other citizens without special federal aid.

The problems were many and serious. The war had obstructed development of the reservations, and some of the gains made in earlier decades were lost as irrigation projects and roads, for example, were allowed to deteriorate. Increasing Indian population aggravated the problem because it made the disparity between the number of Indians on a reservation and the economic resources available for their support greater than ever before. Yet Indian expectations, especially among those who had been relatively prosperous during the war, had risen.[32]

The first response of the federal government was program planning. Indian Commissioners Brophy, Nichols, and Myer, sometimes stimulated by congressional inquiries, all undertook investigations upon which detailed programs could be devised, reservation by reservation. Thus, for example,

31. *Facts about Indian Health* (Washington: Public Health Service, 1957), pp. 4–5, 8. For accounts of progress see James Raymond Shaw, "Meeting the Challenge of Indian Health," *American Indian* 7 (Winter 1956): 3–12, and Arthur S. Flemming, "Indian Health," *Public Health Reports* 74 (June 1959): 521–22. The Public Health Service issued periodic reports under the following titles: *Indian Health Highlights* and *Indian Health Trends and Services*.

32. The Bureau of Indian Affairs in 1952 estimated that 31,301 families could be supported on the reservations and that there were 20,534 "excess" families. *House Report* no. 2503, 82–2, serial 11582, p. 110. A good picture of the Indian economic situation in the mid-1950s is presented in William H. Kelly, "The Economic Basis of Indian Life," *Annals of the American Academy of Political and Social Science* 311 (May 1957): 71–79.

Nichols in August 1949 set forth the objectives of the reservation programs that were being drawn up: "The establishment of the members of various tribes or groups of Indians on an economic level comparable to other citizens of the area; their integration into the social, economic and political life of the Nation; and the termination, at the appropriate future time, of Federal supervision and control special to Indians. The programs should outline plans for attaining these objectives at the earliest practicable date, and should contain cost estimates and time schedules based upon the best information available."[33]

The key, of course, was not planning but persuading Congress to appropriate the large funds necessary to make the program a reality. The one case where this was successfully done was the long-range rehabilitation program for the Navajos and the Hopis. The needs of these Indians were widely known. Reports on the Navajo situation were drawn up in the Indian Bureau in 1947, with an outline of a tentative reservation program; but the first action came as a response to emergency needs in December 1947, after a severe summer drought and winter storms combined with other economic problems to create a crisis. President Truman on December 2, 1947, made public a statement of Secretary of the Interior Julius A. Krug about the serious situation, and Congress responded with an emergency measure, signed by the president on December 19, that authorized $2 million for the relief of the two tribes. A section in the law directed the secretary of the interior to submit his recommendations for a long-range program dealing with the problems of these Indians.[34]

In March 1948 Krug presented his recommendations for a ten-year $90-million program, and a bill for the rehabilitation of the tribes was introduced. The secretary testified before the joint hearings of the Indian subcommittees in April on the desperate conditions facing the tribes, yet Congress did not act on the measure.[35] The next year Krug submitted the bill

33. Circular no. 3704, August 15, 1949, OIA Circulars (M1121, reel 17).

34. "Summary of Conditions and Outline of Tentative Reservation Program, Navajo Indian Reservation—Arizona—New Mexico—Utah," January 1947, and "Report on the Navajo Indian Situation," July 30, 1947, in OIA, Records of Assistant Commissioner William Zimmerman, Memoranda 1944–50, Walthen Report; Statement by the President Making Public a Report on the Needs of the Navajo Indians, December 2, 1947, *Public Papers of the Presidents of the United States: Harry S. Truman, 1947* (Washington: GPO, 1963), pp. 503–4; J. A. Krug, "Report to the President on Conditions of the Navajo Indians," December 2, 1947, copy in William Brophy Desk Files, 67A–721, WNRC; 61 *United States Statutes* 940.

35. J. A. Krug, *The Navajo: A Long-Range Program for Navajo Rehabilitation* (Washington: Department of the Interior, 1948); "Rehabilitation of Navajo and Hopi Indians," *Hearings before a Subcommittee of the Committee on Interior and Insular Affairs, United States Senate, 80th Congress, 2d Session, on S. 2363* (1948). Krug's testimony is on pp. 44–50 of these hearings.

again, with a new plea for the Navajos and the Hopis, and this time the bill passed quickly through Congress.[36]

On October 17, 1949, President Truman vetoed the bill. The president agreed with its rehabilitation sections, but Congress had attached a section providing for the extension of state civil and criminal jurisdiction over the reservations, and Truman, acting on the opposition of the tribal councils, sent Congress a blistering attack on that section of the bill. He found the legal provisions unclear and ambiguous and declared, furthermore, that such action was in conflict with "one of the fundamental principles of Indian law accepted by our Nation, namely, the principle of respect for tribal self-determination in matters of local government." Truman did not doubt that in the long run all Indian groups would be merged into the general body of population, but he refused to force legal integration upon the Navajos and Hopis when they were not prepared for it and did not want it. "It would be unjust and unwise," he said, "to compel them to abide by State laws written to fill other needs than theirs."[37]

The president indicated in his veto message that he would gladly approve a bill without the offending provisions, and Congress quickly enacted such a measure, which Truman signed on April 19, 1950. The law described its goals as follows: "to further the purposes of existing treaties with the Navajo Indians, to provide facilities, employment, and services essential in combating hunger, disease, poverty, and demoralization among the members of the Navajo and Hopi Tribes, to make available the resources of their reservations for use in promoting a self-supporting economy and self-reliant communities, and to lay a stable foundation on which these Indians can engage in diversified economic activities and ultimately attain standards of living comparable to those enjoyed by other citizens." Appropriations totaling $88,570,000 were authorized, with specific sums set for such projects as soil and water conservation, irrigation projects, development of industrial and business enterprises, off-reservation employment, relocation of Navajos and Hopis on the Colorado River Reservation, roads and communication systems, hospital and school construction, housing, and surveys of natural resources. The law established a revolving loan fund and provided preferential employment of Indians on the projects, with on-the-job training that would qualify them for more skilled employ-

---

36. "Rehabilitation of Navajo and Hopi Indians," *Hearings before a Subcommittee of the Committee on Interior and Insular Affairs, United States Senate, 81st Congress, 1st Session, on S. 1407* (1949); *Senate Report* no. 550, 81–1, serial 11293; *House Report* no. 963, 81–1, serial 11299.

37. *Public Papers of the Presidents of the United States: Harry S. Truman, 1949* (Washington: GPO, 1964), pp. 514–17.

ment. The program was to be completed, so far as practicable, within ten years.[38]

In order to facilitate the fullest possible participation by the Navajo Tribe in the program, the law authorized adoption of a tribal constitution, but the instrument drawn up was not approved by the tribe. The business was carried on under the tribal council and auxiliary bodies. Yet even without the new constitutional organization, the massive, wide-ranging rehabilitation program had an enormous effect upon the Navajos and the Hopis. The money supported school construction, health facilities, road building, and a variety of economic enterprises. The decade of the 1950s for the Navajos was one of remarkable progress in both economic and political development.[39]

A similar long-range program was planned for the Papago Indians, whose needs matched those of the Navajos and Hopis. A bill authorizing $23 million for rehabilitation purposes was introduced, but it made no progress despite support of the Department of the Interior and Indian welfare groups.[40]

Aside from such special rehabilitation programs aimed at particular tribes, the Bureau of Indian Affairs made a good deal of development of the reservations, and reports show positive activity year by year. Thus Commissioner Emmons reported in 1956: "On the economic side the progress was at least equally impressive [as in education]. Development of reservation resources was pressed forward through continued extension of Indian irrigation projects, further expansion of soil and moisture conservation work, and other similar activities. Sales of Indian timber were sharply stepped up in the calendar year 1955 and produced about a third more income to the Indian owners than in the preceding year. Combined Indian income from oil, gas, and other minerals reached an all-time high of more than $41 million." As he held conferences with the tribes between June and December 1956, Emmons talked much about the need for active In-

38. *Senate Report* no. 1202, 81–1, serial 11294; *House Report* no. 1474, 81–2, serial 11379; 64 *United States Statutes* 44–47.

39. Robert W. Young, *A Political History of the Navajo Tribe* (Tsaile, Arizona: Navajo Community College Press, 1978), pp. 140–51; Peter Iverson, *The Navajo Nation* (Westport, Connecticut: Greenwood Press, 1981), pp. 56–82. Much information about the progress achieved during the ten-year period of the long-range act is provided in Robert W. Young, *The Navajo Yearbook, 1951–1961: A Decade of Progress*, Report no. 8 (Window Rock, Arizona: Navajo Agency, 1961). See CIA Reports, 1951–1960, for yearly accounts of the program.

40. "Rehabilitation of the Papago Tribe of Indians, Arizona," *Hearing before a Subcommittee of the Committee on Interior and Insular Affairs, United States Senate, 82d Congress, 1st Session, on S. 107* (1952).

dian participation in developing the reservations—which, he told one group, was "the best assurance against too sudden termination."[41]

One of Commissioner Emmons's pet schemes was industrial development in the vicinity of reservations as a solution to the economic problems of the Indians. Beginning in 1956, he persuaded some companies to open plants near reservations, and he issued encouraging reports of success, but in reality the effect upon the total problem was negligible.[42]

At the end of the 1950s, Congress took up new interest in Indian economic development, to some extent as a substitute for termination. On January 7 Senator James E. Murray of Montana submitted Senate Concurrent Resolution no. 3, which proposed a Point 4 Program for Indians such as the United States had applied successfully to underdeveloped areas of the world. On January 23 Senator William Langer of North Dakota and twenty other senators sponsored a bill (S. 809) calling for $200 million in loans and grants for tribal enterprises or businesses of individual Indians and for non-Indian industries that located near reservations. Senator Langer set forth the needs of the Indians at great length, but the Interior Department held firm to its ongoing policies. Undersecretary Hatfield Chilson criticized Senate Bill no. 809 as ineffective and asserted that what it proposed was already being accomplished, and he objected to Senate Concurrent Resolution no. 3 because Point 4 Programs were more limited than the wide range of assistance already provided for Indians. He also spoke strongly against the provision in the resolution that said termination should not be the price demanded for economic aid. Such a reversal of House Concurrent Resolution no. 108, he said, would be undesirable. "An indefinite continuation of the Federal trust for all Indian tribes," he explained, "is undesirable because it is a paternalistic system that discourages initiative and tends to make the individual dependent upon the Government. If the Government is to perform its responsibilities toward the Indian people properly, Congress must make the ultimate decision about when the termination of the Federal trust will be in the best interests of the Indians." Glenn Emmons, too, testified that "House Concurrent Resolution 108 was a very, very wholesome resolution." "I think on the whole," he said, "the Indians of the country will someday reach the age of 21. It is probably high time that the Indians begin to plan toward that eventuality."[43]

41. CIA Report, 1956, p. 199; conference with Ponca tribal delegates, December 4, 1956, in Commissioner Emmons's Conferences with Tribes, 68A–2045, box 368, WNRC.

42. CIA Report, 1957, pp. 245–47; CIA Report, 1958, p. 221; Larry W. Burt, *Tribalism in Crisis: Federal Indian Policy, 1953–1961* (Albuquerque: University of New Mexico Press, 1982), pp. 85–88.

43. *Congressional Record*, 103: 278, 881–83; "Federal Indian Policy," *Hearings before the Subcommittee on Indian Affairs of the Committee on Interior and Insular Affairs, United States Senate, 85th Congress, 1st Session, on S. 809, S. Con. Res. 3, and S. 331* (1957), pp. 240–43, 261.

Langer's bill and Murray's resolution had insufficient support to meet the determined criticism of the Interior Department, and in the following year a new attack on the depressed economic condition of the Indians was made within the framework of a general "area redevelopment bill" introduced by Senator Paul H. Douglas of Illinois and a large number of other senators on April 23, 1958. The legislation was aimed at industrial and rural areas throughout the United States that had consistently high levels of unemployment or underemployment by providing funds for stimulating industrial location in the depressed areas or by special vocational training. Indian areas were to be included in the operation of the law. The bill passed Congress in the summer, but it received a pocket veto from President Eisenhower. The next year a new measure of the same import passed Congress, only to be vetoed again by the president.[44] Meanwhile, a new set of bills called Operation Bootstrap for the American Indian was introduced in the House in the summer of 1959. Hearings were held in May and June 1960, but the measure died.[45]

The Eisenhower administration thus ended without the massive attack against poverty on Indian reservations that was so obviously needed. It would come in the next decade.

RELOCATION

In the decade of the 1950s the federal government promoted an active policy of "relocating" Indians, that is, moving them from overcrowded reservations to urban areas, where employment possibilities might be better. Relocation was a corollary of termination. It was directly related to the

44. *Congressional Record*, 104: 7031–38; *Senate Report* no. 1494, 85–2, serial 12062; Memorandum of Disapproval of the Area Redevelopment Bill, September 6, 1958, *Public Papers of the Presidents of the United States: Dwight D. Eisenhower, 1958* (Washington: Office of the Federal Register, National Archives and Records Service, 1959), pp. 690–91; "Area Redevelopment Act," *Hearings before a Subcommittee of the Committee on Banking and Currency, United States Senate, 86th Congress, 1st Session, on S. 268, S. 722, and S. 1064* (1959); Veto of the Area Redevelopment Bill, May 13, 1960, *Public Papers of the Presidents: Eisenhower, 1960–61,* pp. 417–20.

45. "Operation Bootstrap for the American Indian," *Hearings before the Subcommittee on Indian Affairs of the Committee on Interior and Insular Affairs, House of Representatives, 86th Congress, 2d Session, on H.R. 7701, H.R. 8033, and H.R. 8590* (1960). Congress also tried to promote Indian economic welfare under measures proposed to combat juvenile delinquency. "Juvenile Delinquency (Indians)," *Hearings before the Subcommittee to Investigate Juvenile Delinquency of the Committee on the Judiciary, United States Senate, 83d Congress, 2d Session, Pursuant to S. Res. 89* (1954); a second set of hearings was conducted in the 84th Congress, 1st session, pursuant to S. Res. 62. See also *Senate Report* no. 1483, 84–2, serial 11886.

movement for better general education, more vocational training, adult education, and economic development plans, and it was another avenue for federal withdrawal from the Indian business. The rationale for the relocation or "placement" program was clearly set forth by Commissioner Myer at the beginning of the policy:

> On most Indian reservations the land resources are insufficient either in quantity or quality to support the present population. Population is increasing much faster than the national rate, industrial development is negligible, and a large portion of the inhabitants face the alternative of remaining wholly or partially unemployed or of leaving home to seek employment. In a study of 16 reservation areas where the problem is considered most serious, it is estimated that resources available within the reservation can support only 46 percent of the reservation population even at a minimum standard of subsistence. To attain a fully adequate standard of living comparable to that of the national average, it is probable that more than half of all Indians would have to seek their livelihood off reservation.
>
> The objectives of the Bureau placement program are to make known to Indians the opportunities existing for permanent off-reservation work and living, to assist those who are interested in improving their lot to plan for and successfully carry out their movement to places of greater opportunity, to ensure their acceptance in employment, and to facilitate their social adjustment in communities to which they may go.[46]

Beginning with placement programs for the Navajos and Hopis in 1948 and skeletal operations in the Aberdeen, Billings, Minneapolis, Muskogee, and Portland areas in 1950, the Bureau of Indian Affairs provided staffs to facilitate off-reservation employment. The placement personnel worked with Indians and Indian organizations to stimulate interest in seeking employment, to educate Indians for adjustment to the new life, and to assist them in using established employment agencies. On the other side, it assisted employer groups and employment agencies to recruit Indian workers. In fiscal year 1951, the staff aided in more than 20,000 placements,

---

46. CIA Report, 1951, p. 375. The relocation program in the 1950s and 1960s is discussed in detail in Elaine M. Neils, *Reservation to City: Indian Migration and Federal Relocation*, Research Paper no. 131 (Chicago: Department of Geography, University of Chicago, 1971). See also Joan Ablon, "American Indian Relocation: Problems of Dependency and Management in the City," *Phylon* 26 (Winter 1965): 362–71, and Donald Lee Fixico, "Termination and Relocation: Federal Indian Policy in the 1950s" (Ph.D. dissertation, University of Oklahoma, 1980), pp. 213–42.

two-thirds of which were for Navajos and Hopis. Of the placements, however, 90 percent were for seasonal employment only, with no more than
a small beginning of permanent employment in army installations and
other work near the reservations.[47]

Year by year the program expanded, and the bureau shifted away from
the placement activities for finding temporary jobs—work that it left to
local employment agencies—to permanent relocation programs. In January 1952 the bureau initiated financial assistance to aid the resettling Indians. Bureau relocation offices opened in the major cities in which the Indians sought employment, and in 1954 the former Branch of Placement
and Relocation was changed simply to the Branch of Relocation. In 1954
the bureau assisted 2,163 Indians, including 1,649 in over four hundred
family groups and 514 unattached men and women. Three hundred more
left the reservations without assistance to join relatives or friends already
in the cities. Of the 2,163, the bureau provided financial support, as well as
general assistance in relocating, to 1,637. Fifty-four percent of the Indians
aided came from the northern areas of Aberdeen, Billings, and Minneapolis, and the rest from Anadarko, Gallup, Muskogee, and Phoenix. The Indians moved to twenty different states. In the three succeeding years the
number of Indians aided under the bureau's relocation program increased
significantly, but then, as the economic recession of 1957–1958 hit the nation, the operation fell off dramatically (see Table 17).[48]

The number of relocation field offices grew or declined according to employment opportunities for the Indians. The first offices were in Chicago and
Los Angeles; in 1956 there were also offices in Denver and San Francisco; in
1957 San Jose and St. Louis were added; and in 1958 the number had expanded to twelve by the addition of Joliet, Waukegan, Oakland, Cincinnati,
Cleveland, and Dallas. Then a decline set in as the number of jobs in some
cities decreased. By 1960 only eight cities remained, four of them in California (Los Angeles, San Francisco, Oakland, and San Jose) and four others
across the country (Chicago, Cleveland, Denver, and Dallas). In some cities
where the federal government did not maintain a relocation field office, the
Bureau of Indian Affairs assisted in establishing local committees or groups
comprised of welfare agencies, church organizations, or individuals to assist
Indians seeking employment in those places.[49]

Considering the total Indian population in cities by 1960, roughly
166,000, the number of reservation Indians who took part in the govern-

47. CIA Report, 1951, pp. 375–76.

48. CIA Report, 1952, p. 403; CIA Report, 1954, pp. 242–43.

49. CIA Report, 1953, p. 40. The opening and closing of relocation offices is reported
year by year in CIA Reports.

TABLE 17: Relocation Program, 1953–1960

	1953	1954	1955	1956	1957	1958	1959	1960	Total
Total relocated	2,600	2,163	3,461	5,316	6,964	5,728	3,560	3,674	33,466
Number in family groups	–	1,649	2,656	4,211	5,384	4,331	–	–	
(Number of units)	–	(400)	(708)	(1,051)	(1,302)	(976)	–	–	
Unattached men and women	–	415	805	1,105	1,580	1,366	1,655[a]	1,798[a]	
Number given financial aid	1,300	1,637	2,415	4,402	6,543	–	–	–	

SOURCE: CIA Reports, 1953–1960
[a]Includes family heads.

ment's relocation program was comparatively small. There had been a flow of Indians to cities for a long time, and the Meriam Report in 1928 devoted a long chapter to these "migrated Indians."[50] World War II increased the numbers. Basic economic forces were at work, which the bureau's program merely augmented, and Indians established urban pockets in such cities as New York and Boston, where there was no government relocation activity at all. The decade of the 1950s brought increased consciousness of the fact that there were Indians in cities as well as on reservations.

As the work of relocation proceeded, the Bureau of Indian Affairs soon realized that finding employment for the Indians in the cities was only part of the problem and not the most difficult. The major concern was adjustment of the Indians to their new environment: securing housing, acquiring information about community facilities, and gaining acceptance from the urban communities into which they moved. In 1953 the bureau estimated that one-third of the Indians relocated returned to the reservations—persons who "found the adjustment to new working and living conditions more difficult than anticipated."[51]

To aid the Indians in their adjustment the relocation personnel were caught in a network of personal relations with the Indians that covered multiple aspects of the Indians' lives:

. . . a network encompassing decisions regarding city, neighborhood, building, and apartment of residence, type of eyeglass frames, choice of companions, purchase of food, housewares, and furniture, psychi-

50. *The Problem of Indian Administration* (Baltimore: Johns Hopkins Press, 1928), pp. 667–742.
51. CIA Report, 1953, pp. 40–41.

atric counselling, school tardiness and absenteeism, week-end travel, attendance at funerals, drinking habits, visits to the doctor, use of free time, church membership, home ownership, sexual relationships, lifetime career, social problems, family planning, clothing, personal style of living. Financial relationships entwined in this network cover costs of transportation over hundreds of miles, shipment of effects, personal appearance needs, rent and subsistence, health services, tuition, tools, emergencies. Federal employees caught up in this network function as furniture movers, realtors, property inspectors, chauffeurs, babysitting agents, tour guides and travel agents, public relations men, advertisers for doctors and drug stores, welcoming committees, agents of sobriety, morality and industry, friendly home visitors, employment, school, and community living counsellors, psychologists, family planners, confidants, and arbiters of personal destiny.[52]

The problems that Indians faced in the new urban environment, with resultant unemployment, slum living, and alcoholism for many of them, led to cries of criticism and outrage against the government's relocation program, even though the program touched only a minority of Indians who migrated to cities. An article in the *Atlantic Monthly* in March 1956 spoke recklessly of the "vast army of displaced persons which has been created by the government's policy of accelerating the 'integration' of the Indian" and described Indians "being turned loose upon the asphalt jungles of metropolitan centers in one of the most extraordinary forced migrations in history." A companion article in *Harper's* charged that the program was being used deliberately as a "cover for recently accelerated legislation to separate the Indians from their lands and resources, an old and dishonorable game," and argued, rightly enough, that relocation would not solve the "real Indian problems" of poverty, ill-health, poor education, and economic stagnation, which were merely transferred to the urban areas.[53] Although these were exaggerated, muckraking articles, there is no doubt that the federal government only slowly realized the magnitude of the problem, since it saw its obligations as limited largely to Indians residing on trust or restricted lands. As the Indians moved out of the reservations, they presum-

---

52. Neils, *Reservation to City*, pp. 55–56, based on the author's personal observation of the operations of the Chicago Field Employment Assistance Office.

53. Ruth Mulvey Harmer, "Uprooting the Indians," *Atlantic Monthly* 197 (March 1956): 54–57; Dorothy Van de Mark, "The Raid on the Reservations," *Harper's* 212 (March 1956): 48–53. There is still a tendency to blame all the urban woes of Indians upon the bureau's relocation program. See, for example, "Historical Review," in American Indian Policy Review Commission, Task Force Eight, *Final Report: Report on Urban and Rural Non-Reservation Indians* (Washington: GPO, 1976), pp. 23–43.

ably would disappear into the general population and no longer be of concern to the federal government. But the Indians did not so quickly adjust to their new homes. They kept their Indian identity and their place on tribal rolls, and many used the cities as only a temporary residence, still thinking of the reservation as their true home. There was a good deal of passing back and forth between reservation and city.

Sober appraisals uncovered a good many deficiencies in the program. A study sponsored by the Association on American Indian Affairs in 1956, although it noted improvements as the program had developed, criticized the government's promotion of relocation as a solution to the Indian problem, its intention that the movement to the city be permanent, its failure to prepare the Indians adequately for the migration, and its misleading promotional material, which, while calling the program "voluntary," pressured the Indians into relocating. It recommended development of economic alternatives to relocation for reservation Indians. A highly selective study of the program (seen largely through the eyes of relocation agents in Los Angeles and Chicago) made by a special subcommittee of the House of Representatives in 1957 presented a favorable report on employment and on living conditions. But the committee noted the considerable numbers who did not succeed in the cities, and it listened to recommendations from urban welfare groups that echoed some of the complaints of the Association on American Indian Affairs. When the General Accounting Office evaluated the program in 1958, it asserted that the Bureau of Indian Affairs had not put sufficient emphasis on successful relocations. "We noted," the report said, "that Indians were relocated to an area not offering adequate opportunities to relocatees, Indians were inadequately prepared for relocation, and minimum standards for selecting relocatees had not been prescribed by the Bureau."[54]

The Indian Bureau paid attention to the criticism, cutting back on the number of relocatees it aided in order to provide greater service over a longer period. Yet, like termination, the relocation program did not work as its promoters had hoped. The new administration that took office in 1961 would have to find new and better solutions.[55]

54. La Verne Madigan, *The American Indian Relocation Program* (New York: Association on American Indian Affairs, 1956); *Indian Relocation and Development Programs,* Report of a Special Subcommittee on Indian Affairs of the Committee on Interior and Insular Affairs, House of Representatives, 85th Congress, 1st session, Pursuant to H. Res. 94, October 1957, Committee Print no. 14 (Washington: GPO, 1958), pp. 1–20; *Administration of Withdrawal Activities by Bureau of Indian Affairs, Department of the Interior, March 1958: Report to the Congress of the United States by the Comptroller General of the United States,* August 1958, p. 20.

55. CIA Report, 1959, p. 250. For an account of the increased operations of the Relocation Program, renamed Employment Assistance Program, see Neils, *Reservation to City.* See also discussion of Indians in urban areas in chapter 47.

PART TEN

Indian
Self-Determination

Termination, for all the turmoil and fear it caused in Indian communities, was a temporary departure from the movement toward Indian self-determination that began with John Collier's principles and programs in the 1930s. The strongly assimilationist doctrine preached by the terminationists, often in the deceptively attractive rhetoric of "freedom," was not acceptable in a society that had begun to appreciate, however dimly, the values of pluralism. The two decades of the 1960s and 1970s were a period of public interest in Indian affairs and of governmental activity that rivaled in significance the era of Indian removal, the humanitarian reform movement of the late nineteenth century, and the agitation for change that Collier and his followers had sparked in the 1920s. To a large extent, the new Indian drive for recognition reflected the earlier agitation of American blacks, and Indians adopted techniques of protest from the black minority. The guilt felt by white Americans for past injustices to the Indians was a powerful stimulus to widespread support of Indian claims, both in Congress and among the general public.

The official policy of the administrations of John F. Kennedy and his successors was couched in terms of Indian participation in the formulation of Indian policy and overt rejection of involuntary termination of Indian tribes. There were ups and downs, to be sure; Indian activism and exaggerated demands triggered an occasional backlash that slowed or temporarily reversed the major trend, but by 1980 the impact of Indian communities upon their own future was greater than it had been since the days before the military subjugation of the tribes and their forced location on reservations throughout the West. Respect for Indian religious and civil rights, recognition of land claims and water rights, expanded programs for education and health care (increasingly under Indian control), and new life for the old concept of tribal sovereignty—all indicated a change in Indian relations of truly remarkable extent that should not be obscured by the loud cries about existing wrongs and demands for new programs and services that continued to issue from Indian groups and their advocates. The concept of the Indians as a disappearing race soon to be absorbed into white society and the concomitant view that ultimately the Bureau of Indian Affairs would be unnecessary no longer had validity.

All the high appointive offices concerned with Indians in the Department of the Interior and the Bureau of Indian Affairs were in the hands of Indian bureaucrats, and new Indian preference policies in hiring and promotion meant that 78 percent of all the bureau employees were Indians and Alaska Natives by 1980. Many programs once administered exclusively by agencies of the federal government, moreover, were turned over to Indian tribes or organizations. Pan-Indian activity flourished, and court decisions upheld many of the Indians' contentions about their rights. Yet the Indians, moving toward the self-determination indicated by these conditions and events, still faced pervasive federal paternalism, growing out of the continuing trust relationship between them and the government. It was a seemingly inescapable paradox.

CHAPTER 43

Turnabout in
the 1960s

The New Trail. The War against Poverty.

New Emphasis on Indian Self-Determination.

The State of Indian Education.

The Civil Rights Act of 1968.

The decade of the 1960s brought a new orientation to United States Indian policy. As the Kennedy administration replaced that of Eisenhower, the policy of termination, although it was not formally rejected by Congress and still caused great fear among the Indians, was shelved. The drive for economic betterment for the Indians received top priority, and the idea that plans and progress for Indians must be the work of the Indians themselves gained new strength.

THE NEW TRAIL

John F. Kennedy, campaigning for the presidency in 1960 promised the Indians "a sharp break with the policies of the Republican Party," and he specifically declared: "There would be no change in treaty or contractual relationships without the consent of the tribes concerned. No steps would be taken by the Federal Government to impair the cultural heritage of any group. There would be protection of the Indian land base, credit assistance, and encouragement of tribal planning for economic development." When he won the election, Kennedy appointed Stewart L. Udall, representative from Arizona, to be secretary of the interior, and Udall intended to carry out the administration's promises. He had a deep interest in Indian affairs and even considered briefly being his own commissioner of Indian affairs. He talked in terms of "maximum development," not termination.[1]

The decade opened with three notable examples of the new mood and outlook. The first was the publication in January 1961 of the summary report of the Commission on the Rights, Liberties, and Responsibilities of the American Indian. This private study group, established by the Fund for the Republic in 1957, made an independent study of Indian conditions. Its chairman was O. Meredith Wilson, president of the University of Minnesota, and its members were W. W. Keeler, principal chief of the Cherokee Nation and a high-ranking executive of the Phillips Petroleum Company, the Harvard historian Arthur Meier Schlesinger, Sr., Karl N. Llewellyn, professor of jurisprudence at the University of Chicago, and Charles A. Sprague, editor of the *Oregon Statesman*. The work of the commission was directed first by William A. Brophy, former commissioner of Indian affairs, and then by his wife, Sophie D. Aberle, who at one time had been superintendent of the United Pueblo Agency. A group of special studies was initiated by the commission to aid in its conclusions and recommendations.[2]

The 1961 report was a strongly worded statement that programs for Indians should not be imposed from above but that they should always be based on the initiative and intelligent cooperation of the Indians themselves. It condemned the termination policy and legislation of the 1950s and declared: "For the government to act out of a sense of frustration and of haste to rid itself of the vexing questions involved in administering Indian affairs is bound to ensure failure." If ultimate termination was to come, the commission asserted, it would have to be based on long preparation and the collaboration of the Indians. The report spoke of the "bounden duty" of the United States to assist the Indians in progressing "from their present poverty to a decent standard of living," and it made specific recommendations in regard to tribal government, education programs, and health care.

1. John F. Kennedy to Oliver La Farge, October 28, 1960, in *Senate Report* no. 944, part 1, 87–1, serial 12331, pp. 800–803; Stewart L. Udall to employees of the Bureau of Indian Affairs, September 26, 1961, Bureau of Indian Affairs news release, September 26, 1961; Stewart L. Udall, "The State of the Indian Nation—An Introduction," *Arizona Law Review* 10 (Winter 1968): 554.

2. *A Program for Indian Citizens: A Summary Report* (Albuquerque: Commission on the Rights, Liberties, and Responsibilities of the American Indian, 1961). The final report of the commission was published as William A. Brophy and Sophie D. Aberle, *The Indian, America's Unfinished Business: Report of the Commission on the Rights, Liberties, and Responsibilities of the American Indian* (Norman: University of Oklahoma Press, 1966). After the death of Karl Llewellyn in 1962, he was replaced on the commission by his wife, Soia Mentschikoff.

A second event—and a more remarkable one—was the American Indian Chicago Conference, held at the University of Chicago in June 1961. Originating with the anthropologist Sol Tax and endorsed by the National Congress of American Indians, the conference brought together more than 450 Indian delegates from ninety tribes for a week of discussion about problems and proposals. Although largely directed by Tax and his assistants, the meeting resulted in the formal Declaration of Indian Purpose, a forceful statement of Indian concerns. It called for abandonment of the "so-called termination policy of the last administration by revoking House Concurrent Resolution 108 of the 83rd Congress," for broad educational progress to remove the disabilities that prevented Indians from making use of their own resources, and for a reorganization of the Bureau of Indian Affairs with a view toward more local control. It urged economic assistance to the tribes and their members, with full Indian participation in development programs. It addressed, as well, specific problems of health, welfare, housing, education, and law and jurisdiction. "What we ask of America," the declaration concluded, "is not charity, nor paternalism, even when benevolent. We ask only that the nature of our situation be recognized and made the basis of policy and action. In short, the Indians ask for assistance, technical and financial, for the time needed, however long that may be, to regain in the America of the space age some measure of the adjustment they enjoyed as the original possessors of their native land."[3]

The American Indian Chicago Conference not only brought Indians of diverse tribes together for a joint statement of purpose—no mean accomplishment—but it also generated public interest, for it was widely publicized. On August 15, 1962, in a climaxing ceremony at the White House, a specially bound copy of the Declaration of Indian Purpose was presented to President Kennedy, who called it "a very useful reminder that there is still a good deal of unfinished business."[4]

The third report, and the most significant because it became the basis for official policy, was the report of the Task Force on Indian Affairs. Secretary Udall, shortly after his appointment, had established the task force to study Indian affairs and make recommendations to the new administration. The group, consisting of W. W. Keeler (chairman), Philleo Nash, James E. Officer, and William Zimmerman, Jr., submitted its report of

3. *Declaration of Indian Purpose* (Chicago: American Indian Chicago Conference, 1961), pp. 5–20. An excellent account of the conference, written by one of its coordinators, is Nancy Oestreich Lurie, "The Voice of the American Indian: Report on the American Indian Chicago Conference," *Current Anthropology* 2 (December 1961): 478–500.

4. *Public Papers of the Presidents of the United States: John F. Kennedy, 1962* (Washington: GPO, 1963), p. 619.

seventy-seven pages to Udall on July 10, 1961. Members of the group con-
ducted hearings on Indian reservations, met with tribal delegations in
Washington, conferred with Bureau of Indian Affairs personnel from the
Washington office as well as area directors and superintendents, met with
anthropologists, used questionnaires prepared by the National Congress of
American Indians, and attended the American Indian Chicago Conference.
From all of the opinions and information it gathered, the task force prepared a landmark report with suggestions for programs of development—of
people and of resources. "What we are attempting to do for those in the
underdeveloped areas of the world," it said, "we can and must also do for
the Indians here at home. Furthermore, to insure the success of our endeavor, we must solicit the collaboration of those whom we hope to benefit—the Indians themselves. To do otherwise is contrary to the American
concept of democracy."[5]

The task force rejected the current objectives of government Indian policy, which included termination. "The experience of the past few years," it
noted, "demonstrates that placing greater emphasis on termination than
on development impairs Indian morale and produces a hostile or apathetic
response which greatly limits the effectiveness of the Federal Indian program." The new objectives for the Bureau of Indian Affairs, as formulated
by the task force, were three: maximum Indian economic self-sufficiency,
full participation of Indians in American life, and equal citizenship privileges and responsibilities for Indians. The task force emphasized strongly
that the aid of the Indian communities was crucial for the achievement of
these objectives, and it declared: "The Indians can retain their tribal identities and much of their culture while working toward a greater adjustment and, for the further enrichment of our society, it is in our best interests to encourage them to do so."[6]

The report made specific recommendations in regard to industrial development, vocational training and placement, loan funds, protection of
the rights of off-reservation Indians, land problems, and educational facilities, and it concluded with a repetition of its theme: "The proper role
of the Federal government is to help Indians find their way along a new
trail—one which leads to equal citizenship, maximum self-sufficiency,
and full participation in American life."[7]

Secretary Udall endorsed the report and as an earnest of his intentions
to follow it he appointed one of its members, Philleo Nash, to be commis-

5. *Report to the Secretary of the Interior by the Task Force on Indian Affairs*, July 10,
1961, p. 4. A summary of the report is in CIA Report, 1961, pp. 277–79.
6. *Task Force Report*, pp. 5–8.
7. Ibid., p. 77.

sioner of Indian affairs. Nash, nominated after considerable delay on August 1, 1961, and sworn in on September 26, was an anthropologist by training who had had political experience as lieutenant governor of Wisconsin and business experience as an officer in his family's cranberry company. He was deeply concerned about Indian welfare and Indian rights, and he won the respect of Indian groups and substantially lessened their fear and antagonism toward federal activity. Nash accepted the "new trail" figure and considered the task force's objectives and recommendations a roadmap for his administration.[8]

THE WAR AGAINST POVERTY

Commissioner Nash stressed above all the drive for economic development and self-sufficiency, and he began at once to promote industrial development on or near the reservations, working with tribal leaders, civic organizations, and industrial groups. He pushed increasingly a proposal to build recreational facilities that would attract tourist business to the reser-

8. Margaret Connell Szasz, "Philleo Nash, 1961–66," in Robert M. Kvasnicka and Herman J. Viola, eds., *The Commissioners of Indian Affairs, 1824–1977* (Lincoln: University of Nebraska Press, 1979), pp. 311–13. Examples of Nash's policy statements are his address to the annual convention of the National Congress of American Indians, September 21, 1961, and his talk before the annual meeting of the Association on American Indian Affairs, May 7, 1962, attached to Department of the Interior, news releases, September 21, 1961, and May 8, 1962. There are other statements in the Desk Files of Philleo Nash, 69A–1697, WNRC. James E. Officer, an anthropologist from the University of Arizona and another member of the Task Force on Indian Affairs, was appointed associate commissioner of Indian affairs on September 26, 1961.

Running counter to the new concern for Indian development was the building of Kinzua Dam for flood control on the Allegheny River. The dam, which was completed in 1964, flooded the reservation of the Seneca Indians, and the Indians and their friends loudly protested this violation of a treaty of 1794 that had guaranteed their lands. The Indians lost their suit for an injunction against the dam, but Congress in 1964 provided compensation for the direct and indirect damages and funded a rehabilitation program for the Indians. Examples of protest against the dam are "The Shame Is Ours," *Social Education* 26 (May 1962): 233, 268, and Walter Taylor, "The Treaty We Broke," *Nation* 193 (September 2, 1961): 120–21. For the reparations, see *Senate Report* no. 969, 88–2, serial 12612–2, and 78 *United States Statutes* 738–43. There is a general discussion of the controversy in Levinus K. Painter, "The Seneca Nation and the Kinzua Dam," *Niagara Frontier* 17 (Summer 1970): 30–35, and in Alvin M. Josephy, Jr., *Now That the Buffalo's Gone: A Study of Today's American Indians* (New York: Alfred A. Knopf, 1982), chapter 4. A similar story about the flooding of Indian lands along the Missouri River as part of a flood control project is told in Michael L. Lawson, *Dammed Indians: The Pick-Sloan Plan and the Missouri River Sioux, 1944–1980* (Norman: University of Oklahoma Press, 1982).

vations. He established in the Bureau of Indian Affairs a new Division of Economic Development to bring the resource functions of the bureau (agricultural assistance, forestry, real estate appraisal, real property management, and road construction and maintenance) into closer relation with the industrial development work and the revolving credit program. In addition, he created a new position of economic adviser to the commissioner. At a meeting of agency superintendents at Denver in October 1961 to consider steps for putting into effect the major recommendations of the task force report, economic development and related topics had a prominent place.[9]

The programs and plans of the Bureau of Indian Affairs were soon augmented by national poverty programs that included the Indians within their scope. The first of these was the Area Redevelopment Administration, set up when President Kennedy on May 1, 1961, signed the Area Redevelopment Act, which Congress had reintroduced after Eisenhower's two vetoes. The law provided for the designation of "redevelopment areas" in places where there was substantial and persistent unemployment and where there were high numbers and percentages of low-income families, and loans and grants were authorized for economic development. Indian reservations were explicitly mentioned as coming under the law.[10] Fifty-one areas encompassing fifty-six reservations and four native areas in Alaska were designated "reservation development areas" under the act. Much of the money granted was used to support feasibility studies by private consulting firms for the economic development of the areas. When the Economic Development Administration succeeded the Area Development Administration in 1965, it continued loans and grants for work on Indian reservations. Emphasis was placed on construction of sewer, water, and communications facilities, without which industrial growth would be seriously obstructed.[11]

Perhaps the most significant augmentation to the bureau's economic programs was the general attack on poverty in the United States that was initiated by President Kennedy and enthusiastically carried forward by President Lyndon B. Johnson. Johnson, in a special message to Congress on

9. CIA Report, 1961, pp. 196–99; CIA Report, 1962, pp. 8, 9–10; CIA Report, 1965, p. 10.

10. 75 *United States Statutes* 47–53; Alan L. Sorkin, *American Indians and Federal Aid* (Washington: Brookings Institution, 1971), pp. 91–92. A full study of the Area Redevelopment Administration is Sar A. Levitan, *Federal Aid to Depressed Areas: An Evaluation of the Area Redevelopment Administration* (Baltimore: Johns Hopkins Press, 1964).

11. CIA Report, 1962, pp. 8–11; Sorkin, *American Indians and Federal Aid*, pp. 91–93, and table A–11, p. 200.

poverty, March 16, 1964, noted the great progress the United States had made, but he said: "We still have a long way to go. The distance which remains is the measure of the great unfinished work of our society. To finish that work I have called for a national war on poverty. Our objective: total victory." The president submitted with his message a detailed draft of legislation to accomplish the goal.[12]

There was much support for the president's program, and Congress immediately considered the proposed legislation with hearings and reports.[13] Special attention was paid to Indian property in an American Indian Capital Conference on Poverty, held under church auspices in Washington, D.C., in May 1964. The conference brought together many Indian leaders, and its recommendations called attention to Indian demands that they have an active part in the programs designed to alleviate poverty. Both Nash and Udall addressed the meeting; the secretary of the interior saw in the conference a "new determination to help our Indian people help themselves to achieve the very highest that they can achieve."[14]

The Economic Opportunity Act was approved on August 20, 1964, pretty much in the shape of the bill that Johnson had submitted. In it Congress declared that the policy of the United States was "to eliminate the paradox of poverty in the midst of plenty in this Nation by opening to everyone the opportunity for education and training, the opportunity to work, and the opportunity to live in decency and dignity." The law was a sort of catch-all of programs proposed earlier, but it had unifying themes in its concentration on youth and on education and training. It stressed local initiative by encouraging or requiring the poor themselves to take an active part in planning and carrying out the programs of the war. Under six titles the act provided for youth programs, community action programs, rural assistance, small loans, work experience, and VISTA (Volunteers in Service to America).[15]

12. *Public Papers of the Presidents of the United States: Lyndon B. Johnson, 1963–64,* 2 vols. (Washington: GPO, 1965), 1: 375–80; *House Document* no. 243, 88–2, serial 12631–1.

13. "Economic Opportunity Act of 1964," *Hearings before the Subcommittee on the War on Poverty Program of the Committee on Education and Labor, House of Representatives, 88th Congress, 2d Session, on H.R. 10440* (1964); "Economic Opportunity Act of 1964," *Hearings before the Select Committee on Poverty of the Committee on Labor and Public Welfare, United States Senate, 88th Congress, 2d Session, on S. 2642* (1964); *House Report* no. 1458, 88–2, serial 12619–2; *Senate Report* no. 1218, 88–2, serial 12616–3. For department support of the measure see Stewart L. Udall to Lister Hill, June 22, 1964, and other material in Desk Files of Philleo Nash, 69A–1697, Poverty, box 7.

14. Desk Files of Philleo Nash, 69A–1697, American Indian Capital Conference on Poverty, box 8.

15. 78 *United States Statutes* 508–34. For detailed analyses and evaluations of the

The Economic Opportunity Act opened up numerous new avenues of aid for depressed Americans, and Indians were quick to take advantage of them. When Sargent Shriver, who had been instrumental in drawing up the program, testified at the Senate hearings on June 23, 1964, he said: "We expect broad participation by Indians and tribal communities all across the nation. In every program there must be strong Indian involvement for consent and development. . . . Every aspect of this bill can be brought to focus on Indian poverty."[16] Shriver was not mistaken, for the tribal governments were an efficient mechanism for community action programs, and the tribal councils frequently designated themselves as community action agency boards. By June 30, 1968, there were sixty-three community action agencies serving 129 reservations, which had a total population of 312,000. They developed a wide variety of programs to combat poverty and created a large number of jobs to administer the programs. Funds came to the Neighborhood Youth Corps, which discouraged high school dropouts by providing constructive work projects, and to Operation Head Start, both in federal schools and in public school districts with heavy Indian populations. Job Corps centers (serving non-Indians as well as Indians) were set up on or near ten reservations, and VISTA workers were sent to many reservations. In addition, the Office of Economic Opportunity supported a consortium of universities to provide technical staff for the development of Indian community action programs.[17]

In 1968 the total Office of Economic Opportunity funding for Indian community action programs was more than $22 million. Of this sum, Head Start received the most and home improvement the next largest amount. This was about two-thirds of the total funds that flowed to Indian reservations under the Economic Opportunity Act. Altogether, however, the funding from the Office of Economic Opportunity was a very small part of total federal spending for Indians. In 1968 it amounted to about $35 million out of a total Indian budget of $448,393,000 (of which Bureau of

Economic Opportunity Act, see Sar A. Levitan, *The Great Society's Poor Law: A New Approach to Poverty* (Baltimore: Johns Hopkins Press, 1969), and Joseph A. Kershaw, with the assistance of Paul N. Courant, *Government against Poverty* (Washington: Brookings Institution, 1970).

16. "Economic Opportunity Act of 1964," *Senate Hearings*, 88th Congress, 2d session, pp. 137–38. See also "Prepared Statement by Association on American Indian Affairs, Inc.," ibid., pp. 299–302.

17. Indian participation in the programs of the Office of Economic Opportunity is described in CIA Report, 1965, pp. 20–22; Sorkin, *American Indians and Federal Aid*, pp. 165–69; Levitan, *The Great Society's Poor Law*, pp. 263–70. A handbook for tribal leaders was Henry W. Hough, *Development of Indian Resources* (Denver: World Press, 1967).

Indian Affairs funds represented $249,719,000 and Indian Health Service $103,552,000).[18]

More important than the amount of funds was the boost that the Office of Economic Opportunity programs gave to the Indian management of Indian programs. Grants were made directly to Indian groups, who used the money for programs they chose and developed themselves. All this was not done without criticism, of course. The community action programs had staffing problems, and there was talk of nepotism and favoritism in the distribution of jobs. The benefits of the programs went chiefly to the young, and they did not meet the needs of adults. The number of jobs provided overall was far short of the number needed.[19]

Commissioner Nash remained optimistic as the Bureau of Indian Affairs continued its firm commitment to the war on poverty, for broadening educational opportunities, from pre-schoolers to adult citizens, helped Indians take advantage of the economic developments. Yet the Office of Economic Opportunity programs and the traditional programs of the bureau were insufficient to lift the Indians out of their depressed condition. Nash realized this, and after noting much progress in 1965 he candidly admitted: "The gains made so far have not yet wiped out all Indian unemployment, nor raised the average level of Indian income above the poverty line, nor eliminated the substandard housing, nor brought equal educational opportunity to isolated communities. Poverty has haunted the reservations for too long to be banished so quickly."[20]

Nash worked effectively with bureau personnel and with the Indians, but he got along less well with Secretary Udall and with Congress. His work for long-term goals and his realization that there could be no dramatic changes in the Indians' situation did not satisfy Udall, who hoped for more radical reforms. Although Nash was largely responsible for re-establishing a sense of trust among the Indian people—without which no program for reservation development could work—he was eased out of office in March 1966.[21]

NEW EMPHASIS ON INDIAN SELF-DETERMINATION

The new commissioner was Robert L. Bennett, an Oneida Indian from Wisconsin and the first Indian to hold the office since Ely S. Parker nearly a

18. Levitan, *The Great Society's Poor Law*, pp. 267–69; CIA Report, 1968, p. 15.

19. Sorkin, *American Indians and Federal Aid*, pp. 168–69.

20. CIA Report, 1965, p. 2.

21. Szasz, "Philleo Nash," p. 320; D'Arcy McNickle, "The Indian Tests the Mainstream," *Nation* 203 (September 26, 1966): 275–79.

century before. Bennett, who had entered the Indian service in 1933, had worked his way up through the bureaucracy, and at the time of his appointment he was area director of the Juneau Area Office. His philosophy was that the tribes must set their own goals and priorities and that the Bureau of Indian Affairs should help them in their endeavors. "One of our first jobs," he said in his first year in office, "is to demonstrate to tribal leaders that we mean business—that their suggestions, plans, and proposals are urgently needed." He foresaw an increase in tribal responsibility, with the bureau acting simply as a coordinating and advisory agency. And he spoke confidently of a new era in federal-Indian relations, "an era in which the expressed wishes and hope of all Indians will be fulfilled through their own active participation in the making of policy and law."[22]

Bennett, like many past commissioners, was faced with the task of satisfying specific congressional concerns. When the Senate Committee on Interior and Insular Affairs reported on Bennett's nomination, it took the unusual step of submitting a written report, in which it elaborated on "the numerous subjects discussed at the hearing which reflect the committee's dissatisfaction with the pace of progress in elevating the American Indian to a level of parity with other citizens of the country." It noted that despite the increased budgets and steadily growing number of employees in the Bureau of Indian Affairs, "poverty and squalor continue to plague many reservations." Shocked by that situation, the committee declared: "That Indians remain at the bottom of the economic ladder, have the highest rate of unemployment, live in the poorest housing, and suffer chronic poverty, is a clear indictment of past programs and policies pursued by the Bureau." Specific problems mentioned involved Indian claims, heirship, education, unemployment, off-reservation Indians, and Alaska. The committee requested of Bennett a written report of the steps he had taken to begin meeting these problems, to be submitted ninety days after his confirmation.[23]

Bennett used the report he submitted on July 11, 1966, as a sort of prospectus for his administration of Indian affairs. Like other policy statements, however, it was long on fine-sounding but vague goals and short on specifics about how the goals would be achieved. Bennett agreed with the conclusions of the Senate committee, he said, and he intended "to meet the challenges of the unresolved Indian problems outlined in the Committee report." "Paternalism and its stifling effects brought about by the myr-

22. Richard N. Ellis, "Robert L. Bennett, 1966–69," in Kvasnicka and Viola, *Commissioners of Indian Affairs*, pp. 325–31; CIA Report, 1966, pp. 3–5; CIA Report, 1967, p. 4; Robert L. Bennett, "New Era for the American Indian," *Natural History* 76 (February 1967): 6–11.

23. "Nomination of Robert La Follette Bennett to be Commissioner of Indian Affairs," *Senate Executive Report* no. 1, 89th Congress, 2d session, April 8, 1966.

iad of laws and their administration affecting Indian people," he declared, "should be eliminated. Paternalism creates attitudes of dependency which restrains the social and economic advancement of Indian people. As I see it, the Congress and the Bureau must bring about a real, genuine, partnership with Indian leadership. There is no question in my mind that Indian leadership must be brought aboard to the fullest extent possible."[24]

Bennett continued the development programs of his predecessors, but he faced a continuing fear on the part of the Indians that any federal activity might lead to termination. There were grounds for the fear. The Senate report on Bennett's nomination contained a strongly terminationist statement, for it noted both the slowing of the termination drive and also that no legislation had been proposed by the bureau to end federal supervision of all the tribes designated as ready for termination in 1953. "If those tribes were prepared to go their own way more than a decade ago," the report said, "the committee can only conclude that the Bureau is more interested in perpetuating its hold on Indians and their property than in bringing them into the mainstream of American life." Bennett's reply to the Senate committee was considerably less than a forthright statement against the termination policy. "In my talks to Indian people," the commissioner said, "I find that the Indian leadership accepts the fact that at some time the Congress will change their special relationship with the Federal Government. Until the Congress reaches that decision, hopefully with their consent, it is their wish that the Congress meet its responsibilities to them, the same as its national commitment to others, of maximum social and economic development."[25]

The policy of turning over management of their own affairs to Indian groups—an obvious corollary of the emphasis on Indian leadership and participation—seemed to carry a threat of termination by undermining the trust relationship. One example of the apprehension felt by the Indians was their reaction to the administration's proposed Indian Resources Development Act of 1967. Secretary Udall called the measure "the most important legislation proposed for American Indians since the Wheeler-Howard Act of 1934," and he testified strongly in its favor before the congressional committees. The bill was clearly intended to increase Indian self-sufficiency. It provided five hundred million dollars for a loan guarantee and insurance fund, the issuance of federal charters to Indian tribes and groups to form corporations, and authority to issue tax-exempt bonds and to mortgage trust property. The bill would have expanded the supply of

24. Report submitted by Robert L. Bennett to Henry M. Jackson, July 11, 1966, copy in Desk Files of Robert L. Bennett, 70A–2935, box 150, WNRC. This file has considerable material on Bennett's administration.

25. *Senate Executive Report*, no. 1, p. 4; Bennett's report of July 11, 1966, p. 6.

funds available for industrial and other economic development. Indian objections to the bill, however, were strong. The Indians disliked the fact that approval was needed from the secretary of the interior for loans over sixty thousand dollars and objected to the provision for mortgaging tribal land. But mostly they feared that the bill would lead to termination. Udall, to be sure, gave them some grounds for apprehension. In the House hearings he said: "I think this type of legislation, which would encourage initiative, would encourage decisionmaking, would move us down the road toward the right kind of ultimate independence is what the Indian people want." But when asked whether "ultimate independence" meant doing away with reservations, he replied, "I think this is undoubtedly the ultimate end result; yes."[26] The bill did not come out of committee.

Another attempt to plan new directions in Indian policy was the formation of a Presidential Task Force on the American Indian in 1966. The chairman was Walsh McDermott of the Cornell University School of Medicine's Department of Public Health, and the members represented universities, industry, the law, and the Bureau of Indian Affairs. The report of the task force disavowed termination as a policy and concentrated on recommendations for economic and educational development, with a goal of sixty thousand new jobs on the reservations by 1977. It insisted, too, on full participation of the Indians in the programs developed for their benefit. But a major recommendation was the transfer of all Indian Bureau functions to the Department of Health, Education, and Welfare—a proposal that the Indians strongly condemned, for it brought new visions of termination of the special federal responsibilities toward Indians. The report, despite its substantial proposals, was quietly filed away.[27]

That the Indians were intended to be part of America's "Great Society," however, was made clear by President Johnson on March 6, 1968, in his

26. Department of the Interior news release, May 16, 1967; "Indian Resources Development Act of 1967," *Hearings before the Subcommittee on Indian Affairs of the Committee on Interior and Insular Affairs, House of Representatives, 90th Congress, 1st Session, on H.R. 10560* (1967), p. 48; Sorkin, *American Indians and Federal Aid*, pp. 97–99; Alvin M. Josephy, Jr., "The American Indian and the Bureau of Indian Affairs—1969," printed in "Indian Education, 1969," *Hearings before the Subcommittee on Indian Education of the Committee on Labor and Public Welfare, United States Senate, 91st Congress, 1st Session, on Policy, Organization, Administration, and New Legislation concerning the American Indians* (1969), pp. 1437–38. Secretary Udall blamed the failure of the measure on tactical errors in not explaining the bill effectively to Indian leaders and on bad timing. Udall, "The State of the Indian Nation," pp. 555–56.

27. The substance of the task force's report was published in Herbert E. Striner, *Toward a Fundamental Program for the Training, Employment and Economic Equality of the American Indian* (Washington: W. E. Upjohn Institute for Employment Research, 1968). There is a summary of the report in Josephy, "American Indian and the Bureau of Indian Affairs," pp. 1438–40.

"Special Message to Congress on the Problems of the American Indian: 'The Forgotten American.'" He proposed "a new goal for our Indian programs: a goal that ends the old debate about 'termination' of Indian programs and stresses self-determination; a goal that erases old attitudes of paternalism and promotes partnership self-help." To move toward the goals of better living, freer choice, and a full share in economic opportunity and social justice, he asked Congress to appropriate in 1969 five hundred million dollars for programs targeted for Indians, an increase of 10 percent over 1968. Although he noted the responsibility of the nation toward the Indians, Johnson emphasized Indian leadership and initiative in solving Indian problems, and he listed specific proposals in regard to education, health and medical care, jobs and economic development, community services, civil rights, off-reservation Indians, and Alaska Native claims. To coordinate efforts for Indians, he created a National Council on Indian Opportunity, chaired by the vice president of the United States and comprising the heads of the Departments of Interior, Agriculture, Commerce, Labor, Health, Education and Welfare, and Housing and Urban Development and the director of the Office of Economic Opportunity. In addition, the council had six Indian leaders.[28]

Bennett was greatly encouraged by the president's message, yet he was unable to overcome the Indians' fear of termination. In commenting on basic problems in Indian affairs in April 1969, he wrote:

> Positive attempts to bring about the development of the Indian people—to equip them with the tools necessary to that development—to imbue in them a sense and desire for independence and self-determination, meet with outright suspicion by the Indians which then must be laboriously overcome.
>
> It is this underlying problem with which we must cope in developing a program for Indian progress toward equality with other citizens. H. Con. Res. 108 of the 83rd Congress is still relied upon by the Senate Committee as the official Congressional Indian policy and it is anathema to the Indian people. Official policy statements expressing general opposition to the concept of precipitous termination have encouraged the Indians to some degree but have not erased the fear created by the Senate Committee in its continued reliance on the premise that H. Con. Res. 108 is the official Indian policy.[29]

28. *Public Papers of the Presidents of the United States: Lyndon B. Johnson, 1968–69* (Washington: GPO, 1970), pp. 335–44; CIA Report, 1968, p. 4; Executive Order 11399, "Establishing the National Council on Indian Opportunity," March 6, 1968, 33 *Federal Register* 4245 (March 7, 1967).

29. Memorandum on legislative activity and problems, Robert L. Bennett to the undersecretary of the interior, April 25, 1969, in Desk Files of Robert L. Bennett, 70A–2935, Legislation, box 150.

The termination resolution was only one of the legislative problems Bennett saw. He listed long-term leasing of Indian lands in order to attract industry to the reservations, conveyance of federal lands to Indians, the heirship lands, Alaska Native land rights, the controversy over Taos Pueblo's Blue Lake, and the donation of submarginal lands to the Indians as "basic problems" affecting the bureau's relations with Congress. "Most of the problems," he noted, "are of longstanding duration with little prospect of immediate solution."[30]

THE STATE OF INDIAN EDUCATION

Educational development was always linked with economic development as an essential goal of federal Indian policy, and in fact economic self-sufficiency depended upon educational improvements. Until the level of education among the Indians was raised to that of non-Indian citizens, it was unlikely that the economic level could meet the goals set in the pronouncements of the president, the secretary of the interior, and the commissioner of Indian affairs. And special vocational and adult education programs were in fact a constant part of the programs for economic development. "To a greater extent than many people realize," Philleo Nash asserted in 1962, "the Bureau of Indian Affairs is today, and has been for many years, basically an education agency. Funds spent for the operation of its extensive school system both on and off reservations together with construction appropriations used for building or rehabilitating various types of school-connected facilities account, in total, for more than 60 percent of the Bureau's budget. Involvement of Bureau personnel is in a similar ratio. And even some of the Bureau's more technical programs, such as forestry and agricultural assistance, are largely educational in nature."[31]

The trends of earlier decades in Indian education carried into the 1960s. The absolute number of Indian chidren in all types of schools increased substantially, and the percentage in public schools continued to grow (see Table 18). There were notable advances in high school enrollment and in the number of Indian youth in college.

There was, in addition, special progress made possible by new programs and new legislation. Beginning in 1960 remedial programs were estab-

---

30. Ibid. There is a valuable collection of essays on Indian economic development in *Toward Economic Development for Native American Communities: A Compendium of Papers Submitted to the Subcommittee on Economy in Government of the Joint Economic Committee, Congress of the United States*, Joint Committee Print, 91st Congress, 1st session, 2 vols. (Washington: GPO, 1969).

31. CIA Report, 1962, p. 27.

TABLE 18: Indian Children in School,
1961 and 1971

	1961	1971
Total in school	120,838	203,683
Ages 6–18[a]		
Public schools	64,987	103,885
Federal schools	38,876	48,761
Mission and other schools	8,883	10,528
Under 6 and over 18[b]	8,092	13,509
Number not enrolled	9,691	9,907

SOURCE: *Statistics Concerning Indian Education* (Washington: Branch of Education, Bureau of Indian Affairs), issues for 1961, 1971.
[a] For 1971, ages 5–18
[b] For 1971, over 18

lished during the summer, and year by year more students (although only a fraction of those in need of such additional study) were attracted to the programs. A special American Institute for Indian Art was opened in Santa Fe in 1962. Amendments to the Elementary and Secondary Education Act of 1965, passed in 1966 and 1968, provided special funds for Indian education that were effectively used for remedial programs, recreational activities, and field trips. In February 1968 Congress increased the annual authorization for adult Indian vocational training from fifteen to twenty-five million dollars. Interest in cross-cultural education was revived, and as a result of a study about bilingual education by the Center for Applied Linguistics, renewed emphasis was put on teaching English as a second language to Indian children. Stimulated perhaps by the success of the Head Start programs, the bureau in 1967 opened its own kindergartens.[32]

Moreover, the increasing concern about Indians' participation in the education of their children began to bear some small fruit. In 1967 a National Indian Education Advisory Committee, which included fifteen

32. These developments are noted year by year in CIA Reports. See also the discussion in Margaret Szasz, *Education and the American Indian: The Road to Self-Determination, 1928–1973* (Albuquerque: University of New Mexico Press, 1974), pp. 141–68, 181–87; Sorkin, *American Indians and Federal Aid*, pp. 28–30, and tables A–3 and A–4, p. 195. On bilingual education, see Sirarpi Ohannessian, *The Study of the Problems of Teaching English to American Indians: Report and Recommendations* (Washington: Center for Applied Linguistics, 1967); Robert L. Bennett to Walter F. Mondale, May 27, 1969, in "Indian Education, 1969," pp. 1508–12.

tribal leaders, was appointed by the commissioner of Indian affairs. Bennett set its objectives: "First, to stimulate keener interest among Indians in such basic issues as financing and operating programs for both children and adults; and second, to close the present gap between what Indian people feel they need and what others think they need." Indian educators themselves organized a National Indian Education Association, which held its first meeting in November 1969. The small beginning of Indian membership on school boards and in parent-teacher associations was given a boost by President Johnson's special message, in which he said, "To help make the Indian school a vital part of the Indian community, I am directing the Secretary of the Interior to establish Indian school boards for Federal Indian schools. School board members—selected by the communities—will receive whatever training is necessary to enable them to carry out their responsibilities." By May 1969, in accordance with this directive, 174 of the bureau's 222 schools (mostly in Alaska and on the Navajo reservation) had selected such boards. The boards, however, were advisory only and did not control the schools.[33]

Of special significance as a sign of the new direction was the establishment in 1966 of the Rough Rock Demonstration School on the Navajo Reservation, run on contract by the Indians. Rough Rock was a widely-noted experiment in Indian community control of education, and it was highly praised; but its abundant funding by the Bureau of Indian Affairs and the Office of Economic Opportunity (nearly twice the amount per pupil as at a regular boarding school) made it difficult to duplicate. Attempts to apply traditional educational norms and standards to this nontraditional school created unusual pressures. But other such schools, which made contracts with the bureau to become locally-run community enterprises, soon appeared. A similar move was the establishment in 1968, with the blessing of the bureau, of the Navajo Community College, the first college to be controlled and directed by Indians.[34]

---

33. Bureau of Indian Affairs news release, January 16, 1967; CIA Report, 1962, p. 32; *Public Papers of the Presidents: Johnson, 1968–69*, p. 338; Robert L. Bennett to Walter F. Mondale, May 27, 1969, in "Indian Education, 1969," pp. 1500–1501.

34. Szasz, *Education and the American Indian*, pp. 169–80. There is abundant literature on the Rough Rock Demonstration School; see, for example, Broderick H. Johnson, *Navaho Education at Rough Rock* (Rough Rock, Arizona: Rough Rock Demonstration School, 1968); Paul Conklin, "Good Day at Rough Rock: They're Giving Education Back to the Indians," *American Education* 3 (February 1967): 4–9; Robert A. Roessel, Jr., "An Overview of the Rough Rock Demonstration School," *Journal of American Indian Education* 7 (May 1968): 2–14. Robert Roessel was the first director at Rough Rock, and the success of the school was due in large part to his enthusiasm and energy. He was succeeded in July 1969 by Dillon Platero, a Navajo.

But all these gains, substantial as they were, could not disguise the essential failure of federal Indian education, and public criticism abounded. One proposal for correcting the evils was to transfer the Indian schools from the Bureau of Indian Affairs to the Office of Education in the Department of Health, Education, and Welfare. A joint committee of the two departments, however, in May 1967, recommended against the transfer. "Because education is inextricably linked to the other human service functions," the report said, "and because transfer of the education function would result in further fragmentation of the total spectrum of services now afforded American Indians by the Federal Government, the Departments recommend that the Bureau of Indian Affairs should retain the education function at this time, working in close cooperation with the Office of Education to develop a high quality program of Indian education. This recommendation also reflects prevailing Indian opinion." The committee, however, made fifteen recommendations for improving Indian education.[35]

The weaknesses in Indian education were described in abundant detail in a series of studies in the second half of the decade. An independent study sponsored by the Brookings Institution declared flatly: "The record of accomplishments in the field of Indian education is unsatisfactory." It noted slow progress in enrolling Indians in public schools, inadequate remedial programs, a heavy dropout rate (only one-half of all reservation Indians finished high school), outmoded and poorly-equipped vocational training in the federal schools, a serious shortage of adult education, a lack of trained psychologists, social workers, and guidance counselors, and an abnormally heavy turnover of the teaching staff. The description sounded too much like the findings of the Brookings study of forty years earlier, the Meriam Report, to give much consolation to those responsible for Indian education.[36]

More shocking—because more dramatically presented and more widely publicized—was the report of the Senate Special Subcommittee on Indian Education, November 3, 1969. Under a directive from the Senate, the subcommittee, first under the chairmanship of Robert F. Kennedy and, after his death, of Edward M. Kennedy, spent two years examining all aspects of Indian education: federal schools, state and local schools, and the mission schools. Its 4,077 pages of hearings and five volumes of committee prints,

35. "Interdepartmental Report on Organizational Location for Quality Education of American Indians," printed in *The Education of American Indians*, vol. 4: *The Organization Question*, Committee Print, 91st Congress, 1st session, prepared for the Subcommittee on Indian Education of the Committee on Labor and Public Welfare, United States Senate (Washington: GPO, 1969), pp. 569, 575–77.

36. Sorkin, *American Indians and Federal Aid*, pp. 21–50, 178–81.

distilled in its report, was a massive indictment. "We have concluded," the committee said, "that our national policies for educating American Indians are a failure of major proportions. They have not offered Indian children—either in years past or today—an educational opportunity anywhere near equal to that offered the great bulk of American children." It compared statistics for Indian schools and Indian students with those for non-Indians, and it was struck with "the low quality of virtually every aspect of the schooling available to Indian children. The school buildings themselves; the course materials and books; the attitude of teachers and administrative personnel; the accessibility of school buildings—all these are of shocking quality." The committee insisted on increased participation and control by Indians of their education, and it set forth at length a series of sixty recommendations to correct the evils.[37]

Such critiques and indictments pointed up the deficiencies in the education programs for Indian children, but it was easier to note the shortages than to correct them and more dramatic to point to continuing evils than to evaluate progress. Commissioner Bennett criticized the extremely harsh tone of some of the testimony before the Senate subcommittee, and a rebuttal to the report was written by L. Madison Coombs (director of educational research, Bureau of Indian Affairs). Coombs not only questioned some of the report's statistics but complained of its "unbelievably negative" judgment. He was afraid that instead of pointing to a solution of the problems, the Senate subcommittee had weakened the credibility of the bureau's educational work and thus its effectiveness in working with the Indians toward educational goals.[38]

37. "Indian Education: A National Tragedy—A National Challenge," *Senate Report no. 91–501, 91–1,* serial 12836–1; "Indian Education," *Hearings before the Special Subcommittee on Indian Education of the Committee on Labor and Public Welfare, United States Senate, 90th Congress, 1st and 2d Sessions, on the Study of the Education of Indian Children* (1969); "Indian Education, 1969," *Hearings before the Subcommittee on Indian Education of the Committee on Labor and Public Welfare, United States Senate, 91st Congress, 1st Session, on Policy, Organization, Administration, and New Legislation concerning the American Indians* (1969). The five volumes of committee prints included Brewton Berry, *The Education of American Indians: A Survey of the Literature,* a compilation of statutes, field investigations and reports, a compendium of federal boarding school evaluations, and a set of documents on the organization question. A number of critical articles also appeared; see, for example, Daniel Henninger and Nancy Esposito, "Regimented Non-Education: Indian Schools," *New Republic* 160 (February 15, 1969): 18–21; George D. Fischer and Walter F. Mondale, "Indian Education—A National Disgrace," *Today's Education* 59 (March 1970): 24–27.

38. Robert L. Bennett, "Commentary on the Testimony before the Senate Subcommittee on Indian Education," May 21, 1969, printed in "Indian Education, 1969," part 2, appendix, pp. 1479–89; L. Madison Coombs, "The Indian Student Is *Not* Low Man on the Totem Pole," *Journal of American Indian Education* 9 (May 1970): 1–9.

A more balanced view of the problems of Indian education was presented in the report of another major study sponsored by the federal government, this time by the Office of Education of the Department of Health, Education, and Welfare. For two years, 1968–1970, the National Study of American Indian Education, under the direction of Robert J. Havighurst of the University of Chicago and with a large staff working out of five university centers, investigated all aspects of Indian education. Although the study admitted the unsatisfactory conditions in Indian schools and Indian programs, it sought to understand the causes of the conditions—Indian social and cultural factors, as well as weaknesses in the schools—and to suggest feasible programs for improvement. "While criticism of schools has called public attention to important concerns," the directors of the study declared, "attacking the schools as a primary cause of educational failure oversimplifies the issues and, more important, directs attention from the basic economic and political problems of ethnic minorities." Like all those interested in Indian education in the late 1960s, the men and women involved in the National Study strongly emphasized the need to incorporate Indian planning and Indian decisions into the educational programs, and their concern for Indian participation was reflected in the number of Indians on the advisory committee and among the field workers.[39]

The work of the Education Division of the Bureau of Indian Affairs was thus, in large part, overshadowed by these nonbureau studies and reports, and the bureau did not provide the leadership that might have been expected. Hildegard Thompson continued her low-key approach until her resignation in 1965, and then the division was subjected to a rapid turnover of directors. In July 1966 Carl Marburger, who had worked with disadvantaged children under the Office of Education, was appointed to succeed Thompson. He resigned within a year because the area directors blocked his direct line of authority to the educational personnel in the field. His successor, Charles N. Zellers, trained in business administration rather than education, stayed only until 1969. The forces affecting Indian educa-

39. Estelle Fuchs and Robert J. Havighurst, *To Live on This Earth: American Indian Education* (Garden City, New York: Doubleday and Company, 1972), p. 300. This book, written by the director and one of the associate directors of the National Study of American Indian Education, draws heavily on that study. There is an "Overview of the National Study of American Indian Education" in appendix I, pp. 327–44. See also Herbert A. Aurbach, Estelle Fuchs, and Gordon Macgregor, *The Status of American Indian Education*, An Interim Report of the National Study of American Indian Education (University Park, Pennsylvania: Pennsylvania State University, 1970); Robert J. Havighurst, *The Education of Indian Children and Youth: Summary Report and Recommendations*, National Study of American Indian Education, Final Report, series 4, no. 6 (Minneapolis: Training Center for Community Programs, University of Minnesota, 1970).

tion came increasingly from outside the Bureau of Indian Affairs—from other agencies like the Office of Economic Opportunity, from public reports made by independent organizations, from Congress, and most of all from an awakened Indian leadership. But all these together could not suddenly change the scope or nature of Indian education.[40]

THE CIVIL RIGHTS ACT OF 1968

A significant but controversial move toward a guarantee of Indian rights came at the end of the 1960s in special Indian titles of the Civil Rights Act (P.L. 90–284) signed on April 11, 1968. The existence of tribal governments and tribal courts had raised the question of the rights of individual Indians with respect to these governments. Were the constitutional rights of Indian citizens fully protected? The issue arose sharply in a court case of November 17, 1959. In *Native American Church* v. *Navajo Tribal Council*, the United States Court of Appeals, Tenth Circuit, rejected an appeal from the Native American Church, which had brought suit on the basis of freedom of religion when the Navajo tribal government made it an offense to use peyote. The court argued that neither the First Amendment nor the Fourteenth Amendment applied to Indian tribal governments and that no law of Congress made them applicable. "It follows," the court ruled, "that neither under the Constitution or the laws of Congress, do the Federal courts have jurisdiction of tribal laws or regulations, even though they may have an impact to some extent on forms of religious worship."[41] At the same time there was increasing awareness of discrimination against Indians and of numerous violations of their civil rights.

Concern for the constitutional rights of the Indians became almost a crusade with Senator Sam J. Ervin, Jr., of North Carolina. In a time of growing agitation for protection of the rights of blacks, Ervin made it his business to look after "the first Americans, whose rights have been ignored by everyone."[42] Beginning in late August 1961, the Senate Subcommittee on Constitutional Rights, which Ervin chaired, began a series of hearings on Indian rights in order to bring to light the Indians' needs. Out of these hearings came a number of bills introduced by Ervin in 1965, which sought to correct the evils by subjecting tribal governments to the same limitations

40. Szasz, *Education and the American Indian*, pp. 141–55. A useful article, written by a member of the Senate Subcommittee on Indian Education, is Paul J. Fannin, "Indian Education: A Test for Democracy," *Arizona Law Review* 10 (Winter 1968): 661–73.
41. 272 *Federal Reporter, Second Series*, 131–35.
42. *Senate Report* no. 721, 90–1, serial 12750–4, p. 30.

and restraints as those imposed on the federal government by the Constitution and by providing measures to strengthen legal procedures. "The aim of these bills," Ervin explained, "is to provide the Indians living on reservations with a more adequate system of justice by insuring that the constitutional rights which apply to all citizens by the United States will also be made effectively available to Indians."[43]

It took a long time for Ervin to get Congress to accept his package. A consolidated bill was passed by the Senate on December 7, 1967, but the House took no action on it, and there was trouble getting agreement that the Indian measures should be included in general civil rights legislation. Substantively, the first of Ervin's proposals was the one most severely criticized. As he introduced it, it read simply: "That any Indian tribe in exercising its powers of local self-government shall be subject to the same limitations and restraints as those which are imposed on the Government of the United States by the United States Constitution." It soon became clear from the testimony of Indian leaders and federal officials that this was too sweeping a limitation. Indian tribal governments differed from the federal government; application of the full Bill of Rights to them did not make sense and would upset traditional governing practices. Especially crucial was the prohibition against the "establishment of religion," which would have obstructed the quasi-theocracies that ran some Indian communities. In the end the blanket extension of the Bill of Rights to tribal governments was replaced by a selective and specific list of individual rights that were to be protected.[44]

Ervin's proposals as amended were included as Titles II–VI in the Civil Rights Act of 1968. Title II listed ten limitations on the powers of Indian tribal governments, guaranteeing the freedoms of the Constitution that

43. "Constitutional Rights of the American Indian," *Hearings before the Subcommittee on Constitutional Rights of the Committee on the Judiciary, United States Senate, 87th Congress, 1st Session* [and 87th Congress, 2d session, and 88th Congress, 1st session], 4 parts (1962–1964); "Constitutional Rights of the American Indian," *Hearings before the Subcommittee on Constitutional Rights of the Committee on the Judiciary, United States Senate, 89th Congress, 1st Session, on S. 961–968 and S. J. Res. 40* (1965). In the latter hearings, pp. 1–5, Ervin provided a brief explanation of each bill; the bills are printed on pp. 5–14. There is a detailed discussion of Ervin's role in Donald L. Burnett, Jr., "An Historical Analysis of the 1968 'Indian Civil Rights' Act, *Harvard Journal of Legislation* 9 (May 1972): 557–626.

44. "Constitutional Rights of the American Indian," *Senate Hearings on S. 961–968 and S. J. Res. 40;* see, for example, the testimony of Frank J. Barry, solicitor of the Department of the Interior, pp. 17–19. See also *Senate Reports* nos. 721 and 841, 90–1, serials 12750–4 and 12750–5. There is a useful discussion in *Felix S. Cohen's Handbook of Federal Indian Law,* 1982 ed. (Charlottesville, Virginia: Michie, Bobbs-Merrill, 1982), pp. 666–70.

were judged to fit the Indian case, and it specifically authorized the writ of habeas corpus in federal courts for persons detained by order of an Indian tribe. Title III directed the secretary of the interior to draw up a model code for the administration of justice by courts of Indian offenses on the reservations. Title IV repealed section 7 of Public Law 280; it provided for tribal approval of the extension of state jurisdiction and authorized the retrocession of jurisdiction already assumed by a state. Title V added "assault resulting in serious bodily injury" to the offenses on reservations subject to federal jurisdiction. Title VI required the automatic approval of tribal contracts for legal counsel if the secretary of the interior did not act within ninety days. The final Indian title to the act directed the secretary of the interior to publish updated versions of Charles J. Kappler's *Indian Affairs: Laws and Treaties* and Felix S. Cohen's *Handbook of Federal Indian Law* and to prepare and publish a compilation of the official opinions of the solicitor of the Department of the Interior relating to Indian affairs.[45]

The Indian Civil Rights Act had a mixed reception. It was clearly Senator Ervin's intention to bring the Indian tribal governments within the constitutional framework of the United States, and it was precisely on this point that the act was criticized by Indian groups and their non-Indian advocates. Indians favored the amendment to Public Law 280 and the strengthening of their right to employ counsel, but they were concerned about the application of United States legal forms to their tribal governments and what this might do to self-government and tribal sovereignty. Most outspoken were the Pueblos of New Mexico, who objected strongly before the law was passed. Domingo Montoya, chairman of the All-Pueblo Council of New Mexico, testified that "the legislation would bar the effective administration of the tribal government," that the tribal governments could neither financially afford the required procedures nor provide the mechanics on the sophisticated level that would be necessary to meet legal standards. After the law had been enacted the Pueblos persuaded the New Mexico senators to introduce legislation to exclude them from the law, and other amendments were proposed to make sure that the law did not infringe on property rights or tribal self-government; but none of the proposals were enacted by Congress.[46]

---

45. 82 *United States Statutes* 73–92. It took a long time to implement the provision for updated legal compilations, but they eventually appeared, as follows: *Kappler's Indian Affairs: Laws and Treaties*, vols. 6, 7 (Washington: Department of the Interior, 1979), which carried the compilation through 1970; *Opinions of the Solicitor of the Department of the Interior Relating to Indian Affairs, 1917–1974*, 2 vols. (Washington: Department of the Interior, 1979); *Cohen's Federal Indian Law*, 1982 ed.

46. "Constitutional Rights of the American Indian," *Senate Hearings on S. 961–968 and S. J. Res. 40*, pp. 190–92; "Amendments to the Indian Bill of Rights," *Hearings*

Judicial interpretations of the Indian Civil Rights Act created tension between the congressional intent to protect the rights of individual Indians and the policy of encouraging tribal self-government. Cases were accepted by federal courts to enforce the Indian bill of rights in such matters as tribal membership, tribal elections, and selection of tribal officers, and the decisions were seen by critics of the act as intrusions upon the sovereignty of the tribes. Later cases, however, showed an inclination on the part of the courts to use tribal customs and traditions in interpreting the act.[47] Finally, in *Santa Clara Pueblo* v. *Martinez*, the Supreme Court on May 15, 1978, upheld the tribal objections. The suit arose when a plaintiff sued the pueblo in federal court because of a tribal ordinance that only children of tribal fathers could be members of the tribe, charging that this was sexual discrimination and that it violated the Civil Rights Act. The Supreme Court reversed a lower court decision that favored Martinez and declared that suits against a tribe under the Civil Rights Act were barred by the tribe's sovereign immunity to suit. The court noted that the act had two distinct purposes: to protect individual tribal members from violation of their civil rights by the tribe, but also to promote "the well-established federal policy" of encouraging self-government. "Creation of a federal cause of action for the enforcement of rights [in the act] . . . plainly would be at odds with the congressional goal of protecting tribal self govern-

---

before the Subcommittee on Constitutional Rights of the Committee on the Judiciary, United States Senate, 91st Congress, 1st Session, on Title II of the Civil Rights Act of 1968 (1970); *Senate Report* no. 91–294, 91–1, serial 12834–2. Exemplifying the criticism of the Indian Civil Rights Act is Wilcomb E. Washburn, *Red Man's Land/White Man's Law: A Study of the Past and Present Status of the American Indian* (New York: Charles Scribner's Sons, 1971), pp. 173–93. Washburn says: "[The act seeks to prescribe] that the legal culture evolving in Anglo-Saxon law shall be applied to the legal culture of the Indian communities whether or not they retain a distinct point of view after hundreds of years of similar assaults on their legal, moral, social, economic, political, and military culture. Though the recent assault is couched in terms of altruism on the part of the whites, and though considerable native support—particularly by acculturated individuals—is evident, it is cultural assault nevertheless, and one in the tradition of virtually every white policy imposed on the Indian. It is the tradition that somehow the Indian should conform, aspire or submit to the dominant white culture of the United States." On the other hand, Arthur Lazarus, Jr., "Title II of the 1968 Civil Rights Act: An Indian Bill of Rights," *North Dakota Law Review* 45 (Spring 1969): 337–52, argues: "The legislative history of Title II makes clear that Congress viewed extension of the Bill of Rights to Indian reservations as a tool for strengthening tribal institutions and organizations, not as a weapon for their destruction." For an account of Indian reaction to the law, see Ernest L. Schusky, "American Indians and the 1968 Civil Rights Act," *America Indigena* 29 (April 1969): 369–76.

47. Judy D. Lynch, "Indian Sovereignty and Judicial Interpretations of the Indian Civil Rights Act," *Washington University Law Quarterly*, Summer 1979, pp. 897–918.

ment," the court ruled. "Not only would it undermine the authority of tribal forums . . . but it would also impose serious financial burdens on already 'financially disadvantaged' tribes."[48] As in other instances, the ultimate interpretation of the legislation supported tribal autonomy.

48. *Santa Clara Pueblo* v. *Martinez*, 436 *U.S. Reports* 49–83; John T. Hardin, "Santa Clara Pueblo v. Martinez: Tribal Sovereignty and the Indian Civil Rights Act of 1968," *Arkansas Law Review* 33 (Summer 1979): 399–421. An argument that the court's decision "has all but destroyed any possible federal court protection of Indian political rights" is made in Dennis R. Holmes, *South Dakota Law Review* 24 (Spring 1979): 419–46.

CHAPTER 44

Signs of the
New Day

Nixon's Indian Policy. The New Indians

and Red Power. Turnover and Turmoil in the BIA.

Religious Freedom. Alaska Native Claims.

Menominee Restoration.

The movement for self-determination was continued with new force in the 1970s. The presidential administration of Richard M. Nixon carried it forward with considerable success. In many ways the years under Nixon and Gerald Ford produced more constructive legislation relating to Indians than any other period in the nation's history. This legislation included such notable achievements as the return of Blue Lake to the Pueblo Indians, the settlement of Alaska Native claims, and the restoration of the Menominee Tribe to federal status. At the same time, Indian voices and Indian actions, with new vigor, called for a righting of past wrongs and for increased Indian participation in the policy formulations of the federal government.

NIXON'S INDIAN POLICY

The principles of Nixon's Indian policy were clearly set forth in a campaign statement of September 27, 1968, in which Nixon asserted: "Termination of tribal recognition will not be a policy objective and in no case will it be imposed without Indian consent. . . . The right of self-determination of the Indian people will be respected and their participation in planning their own destiny will actively be encouraged." He spoke, too, of encouragement of economic development and listed as high priority items the training of Indians for employment on and off the reservation and the improvement of health services to the Indian people.[1]

At the twenty-fifth anniversary meeting of the National Congress of American Indians held in Albuquerque in October 1969, the concern of the Nixon administration was hammered home to somewhat skeptical Indians. Vice President Spiro Agnew was unequivocal: "The Administration *opposes* termination. This Administration *favors* the continuation of the trust relationship and the protection of Indian lands and Indian resources." His stand was reiterated by Secretary of the Interior Walter J. Hickel, former governor of Alaska, who received with good humor the Indian protests that greeted him in Albuquerque. Hickel was followed by the new commissioner of Indian affairs, Louis R. Bruce, who announced: "As Commissioner I want to get Indians fully involved in the decisions affecting their lives; then to get the Bureau of Indian Affairs to be totally responsive to Indian needs; and to develop a climate of understanding throughout the United States which will permit the full development of Indian people and their communities without threat of termination."[2]

A special message on Indian affairs sent to Congress by President Nixon on July 8, 1970, strongly stated the anti-termination policy of his administration and called for a series of measures to give substance to his pronouncements.[3] In a phrase that became the slogan of his Indian policy, Nixon called for self-determination without termination. "It is long past time," he said, "that the Indian policies of the Federal government began to build upon the capacities and insights of the Indian people. Both as a matter of justice and as a matter of enlightened social policy, we must begin to act on the basis of what the Indians themselves have long been telling us. The time has come to break decisively with the past and to create the conditions for a new era in which the Indian future is determined by Indian acts and Indian decisions." He spoke of the "immense moral and legal

1. Statement of Richard Nixon, September 27, 1968, printed in *Indian Record*, January 1969, pp. 1–2.

2. Address by Vice President Agnew, October 8, 1969; remarks of Walter J. Hickel, October 8, 1969; address of Louis B. Bruce, October 9, 1969, in Office of the Secretary of the Interior, news releases of those dates. Bruce repeated his stand strongly at a meeting of western Oklahoma Indian leaders in Oklahoma City, October 24, 1969, and at the convention of the National Congress of American Indians, October 20, 1972, in Office of the Secretary of the Interior, news releases of those dates. For an account of Indian reaction to Hickel's appearance at Albuquerque, see Vine Deloria, Jr., "The War between the Redskins and the Feds," *New York Times Magazine*, December 7, 1969, pp. 47, 82–88.

3. *Public Papers of the Presidents of the United States: Richard Nixon, 1970* (Washington: GPO, 1971), pp. 564–76.

force" of the agreements made between the tribes and the government through the decades and insisted that because the special relationship between the Indians and the United States rested on these solemn obligations it could not be terminated unilaterally. He noted, too, the harmful results of termination where it had been put into effect and the blighting effect on tribal progress caused by the fear of termination.

Nixon challenged as well the running of programs for Indians by non-Indians, which created an excessive Indian dependence upon the federal government. So he rejected two extremes, federal termination on the one hand and federal paternalism on the other. He concluded: "This, then, must be the goal of any new national policy toward the Indian people: to strengthen the Indian's sense of autonomy without threatening his sense of community. We must assure the Indian that he can assume control of his own life without being separated involuntarily from the tribal group. And we must make it clear that Indians can become independent of Federal control without being cut off from Federal concern and Federal support."

The proposals to Congress embodied in the message became the program for his administration. Nixon asked for nine things:

1. A "new Concurrent Resolution which would expressly renounce, repudiate and repeal the termination policy" of House Concurrent Resolution 108, a resolution that would "explicitly affirm the integrity and right to continued existence of all Indian tribes and Alaska native governments, recognizing that cultural pluralism is a source of national strength."

2. Legislation that would "empower a tribe or group of tribes or any other Indian community to take over control or operation of Federally-funded and administered programs" whenever the Indian group voted to do so. Technical assistance to help the Indians operate the programs successfully would still be provided by the federal government.

3. Restoration to Taos Pueblo of Blue Lake and the sacred Indian lands surrounding it.

4. The right of Indians to control their own Indian schools and authorization to channel Johnson-O'Malley funds to Indian tribes and communities.

5. Economic development legislation, which would provide financing, incentives, and coordinated planning for economic development of the reservations.

6. Allocation of additional funds for improving Indian health and for training Indians for health careers.

7. Help for urban Indians by aiding them to participate in social services and government programs for the poor and disadvantaged.

8. Creation of an Indian Trust Counsel Authority, an agency indepen-

dent of the Departments of the Interior and Justice, which would assure legal representation for the Indians' natural resource rights and eliminate existing conflicts of interest.

9. Creation of the position of assistant secretary for Indian and territorial affairs and "elevation of Indian affairs to their proper role within the Department of the Interior."

Secretary Hickel shortly sent to Congress a package of seven bills to implement the president's program, including proposals for financing economic development, for establishing the position of assistant secretary of the interior, for contracting with Indian tribes for Johnson-O'Malley funds and health care, and for the assumption of control and operation of other federal Indian programs by the Indians themselves. In addition, there was a bill to establish the Indian Trust Counsel Authority, for which Hickel argued: "The Indians of our country have for years felt that the Federal government, because of the inherent conflict of interest that the President discussed in his message, has not given their rights adequate legal protection. We believe that this bill will restore the confidence of the American Indians in the ability of our government to give their natural resource rights legal protection to which they are entitled. This will make it clear to the American Indian that the United States is meeting the legal obligation it has as trustee to advance the interest of the beneficiaries of the trust without reservation and to the highest degree of its ability and skill."[4] The National Council on Indian Opportunity held hearings with Indian groups in the states of Alaska, Arizona, Florida, Minnesota, Nevada, Oklahoma, South Dakota, and Washington on the president's message and his legislative package. These hearings were directed by Nixon "in order to establish a continuing dialogue between the Executive branch of government and the Indian population of our country."[5]

Congress did not act quickly on the proposed legislation, and when no action was taken in the Ninety-second Congress, the Interior Department resubmitted the bills on March 16, 1973. "If these bills were enacted into law by the 93rd Congress," the assistant to the secretary for Indians affairs told the annual meeting of the Association on American Indian Affairs, "it

4. Letters of Hickel to the speaker of the House, July 21, 1970, and to the president of the Senate, July 29, 1970. Copies of these letters, bound together as "President Nixon's Indian Legislative Program," are in Records of Presidential Committees, Commissions, and Boards, Records of the National Council on Indian Opportunity, 1968–74, Publications, box 116, National Archives, Record Group 220.

5. *Public Papers of the Presidents: Nixon, 1970*, p. 575; *Transcript of Regional Hearings on President's Indian Message, July 8, 1970, and on Attendant Legislative Package*, 4 vols. (Washington: National Council on Indian Opportunity, 1970), copy in Records of the National Council on Indian Opportunity, Publications, box 116.

would be the most positive step taken on behalf of Indians in decades."[6]
Large parts of the program were eventually enacted, but not in the complete package that Nixon wanted.

THE NEW INDIANS AND RED POWER

The Nixon administration's Indian policy initiatives were conceived and carried out in an atmosphere of high tension and widespread publicity of wrongs done to the Indians and of Indian demands. Many Indians were no longer willing to accept their lot passively, and their growing activism ultimately broke out in violent confrontations.[7]

The movement had developed through the 1960s. The successful pan-Indian experience at the American Indian Chicago Conference in 1961 evidenced a new articulation by Indians of their concerns. In the succeeding years the National Congress of American Indians became an outspoken advocate of Indian rights, and the National Indian Youth Council, established in 1960, augmented the increasingly clear calls for Indian self-determination with an element of militancy. These "new Indians," who demanded attention to their needs, forced the public and the federal government to face an Indian challenge that many thought had disappeared in the nineteenth century. By the end of the decade Red Power, imitating the Black Power movement of protest and political pressure, was a force to be reckoned with in government relations with the Indians.[8]

The number of collective actions by Indians multiplied rapidly during

6. Statement of John C. Whitaker, March 16, 1973, and remarks of Marvin L. Franklin, May 7, 1973, in Office of the Secretary of the Interior, news releases of those dates. For initial action, which ultimately was unsuccessful, on two of Nixon's proposals, see "Establishing within the Department of the Interior an Additional Assistant Secretary of the Interior for Indian Affairs," *House Report* no. 93–374, 93–1, serial 13020–4; and "Creation of the Indian Trust Counsel Authority," *Hearings before the Subcommittee on Indian Affairs, House of Representatives, 93d Congress, 1st Session, on H.R. 6106, H.R. 6374, and H.R. 6494* (1973).

7. There is voluminous literature dealing with Indian activism in the 1960s and 1970s, much of it advocacy. The notes below indicate useful and significant items.

8. The Indian activism of the 1960s is given general coverage in Stan Steiner, *The New Indians* (New York: Harper and Row, 1968); Alvin M. Josephy, Jr., ed., *Red Power: The American Indians' Fight for Freedom* (New York: American Heritage Press, 1971); Robert C. Day, "The Emergence of Activism as a Social Movement," in Howard M. Bahr, Bruce A. Chadwick, and Robert C. Day, eds., *Native Americans Today: Sociological Perspectives* (New York: Harper and Row, 1972), pp. 506–32. An example of the new articulate Indian voices is the writing of Vine Deloria, Jr.; see especially his *Custer Died for Your Sins: An Indian Manifesto* (New York: Macmillan Company, 1969), and *We Talk, You Listen: New Tribes, New Turf* (New York: Macmillan Company, 1970).

the 1970s, in both obstructive tactics (such as delaying or halting dam construction, hindering beach or island use, seizing or obstructing use of government facilities, and nonviolent picketing, sit-ins, marches, and boy-
cotts) and in positive group action (public relations projects, conferences
on Indian matters, and legal proceedings to reassert rights to land and
other resources).[9] The decade came to rival earlier periods of national attention to Indian matters, such as the removal controversy of the 1830s,
Indian wars after the Civil War, and the agitation for reform in the 1920s.
The Indians attracted substantial support for their positions from white
liberals and religious groups.

A number of events that received widespread publicity indicated the
militancy of the Indians and the charged atmosphere in which federal relations with them were conducted. One was the series of "fish-ins" in the
state of Washington, beginning in 1964. Dissatisfied with the interpretation of treaties with tribes that limited their fishing rights, groups of Indians including members of the National Indian Youth Council determined to continue fishing in opposition to the laws. Support of this action
by the motion-picture actor Marlon Brando brought much public attention, and the agitation spread.[10]

More important in its pan-Indian aspects was the Indian seizure of Alcatraz Island in San Francisco Bay. After an earlier abortive attempt to take
the island, which had been abandoned by the United States as a federal
penitentiary, a group of Indians from many tribes, most of whom were
students in the area, occupied the island on November 20, 1969. They
declared that they were taking the island in the name of the Indians,
facetiously offered to buy it for twenty-four dollars worth of beads, and announced plans to turn the barren rock into a site for a Center for Native
American Studies, an American Indian Spiritual Center, an Indian Center
of Ecology, a Great Indian Training School, and an American Indian Museum. The dramatic takeover captured the attention of the news media;
there was much sympathetic support of the Indians on Alcatraz; and the
federal government took no strong moves to dislodge them, although wa-

9. There is a year-by-year tabulation and account of Indian actions as reported by the
New York Times in Day, "Emergence of Activism," pp. 514–30.

10. A sympathetic account appears in Alvin M. Josephy, Jr., *Now That the Buffalo's
Gone: A Study of Today's American Indians* (New York: Alfred A. Knopf, 1982), chapter
6. A detailed account of the controversy is in *Uncommon Controversy: Fishing Rights of
the Muckleshoot, Puyallup, and Nisqually Indians* (Seattle: University of Washington
Press, 1970), a report prepared for the American Friends Service Committee. See also "Indian Fishing Rights," *Hearings before the Subcommittee on Indian Affairs of the Committee on Interior and Insular Affairs, United States Senate, 88th Congress, 2d Session,
on S. J. Res. 170 and S. J. Res. 171* (1964).

ter and electricity were cut off. The occupation served as a symbol of Indian unity, and the leaders, using the designation Indians of All Tribes, issued a call for national Indian support. The Indian population on the island averaged about one hundred, representing some fifty tribes. More than twelve thousand supporters, both Indians and non-Indians, visited the island, and large contributions of supplies and money flowed in.[11]

The federal government moved cautiously, but it did not admit the Indian claims to Alcatraz. It deemed the Indian plans for a university and cultural center "unreasonable and unrealistic, primarily because the island does not lend itself to any high-density proposal." It offered instead to make Alcatraz a national park with an Indian theme, an Indian name, and Indian employment preference in hiring the necessary park personnel. The Indians flatly rejected the government's proposals and held firm to their original demands. They did not have the means to carry out their own plans for the island, however, and dissension on the island and steadily worsening material conditions there finally led to its abandonment. The few who remained were removed by federal marshals on June 11, 1971.[12] The occupation of Alcatraz, however, triggered other Indian demonstrations for land: at Fort Lawton in Washington, Ellis Island in New York, and Mount Rushmore in South Dakota.

The occupation of Alcatraz was a symbolic gesture, on the periphery of government activity and concern. Not so the Trail of Broken Treaties with its attendant occupation and destruction of the headquarters building of the Bureau of Indian Affairs in Washington, D.C., that soon followed. In the fall of 1972 a caravan of Indians converged on the capital to make known their grievances and demand a righting of wrongs. The affair was dominated by members of the American Indian Movement (AIM), which had been organized in Minneapolis in 1968 to protect Indians there from

11. A small, handsome book that presents the Indian viewpoint on the occupation of Alcatraz is Peter Blue Cloud, ed., *Alcatraz Is Not an Island* (Berkeley, California: Wingbow Press, 1972); it reprints essential documents pertaining to the affair, including "Proclamation to the Great White Father and All His People," pp. 40–42, which states the goals and demands of the Indians. Other valuable accounts of the occupation are Richard Oakes, "Alcatraz Is Not an Island," *Ramparts* 11 (December 1972): 35–41, by the leader of the occupation group; John A. Coleman, "Lords of the Rock," *America* 122 (May 2, 1970): 465–67; Steve Talbot, "Free Alcatraz: The Culture of Native American Liberation," *Journal of Ethnic Studies* 6 (Fall 1978): 83–96.

12. The government's proposal for Alcatraz and the Indians' rejection of it are printed in Blue Cloud, *Alcatraz Is Not an Island*, pp. 65–68. See also letters of Robert Robertson, executive director of the National Council on Indian Opportunity, June 26, 1970, in Records of the National Council on Indian Opportunity, Alcatraz, box 4. The pathetic condition of the few Indians left on Alcatraz at the end of the occupation is described in "Anomie at Alcatraz," *Time* 97 (April 12, 1971): 21.

harassment and which soon became the cutting edge of Indian militancy. Under the direction of such men as Russell Means (an Oglala Sioux) and Dennis Banks (a Chippewa), AIM organized groups of Indians from various parts of the nation, who gathered adherents as they moved toward Washington. The plan for a peaceful demonstration and for serious negotiations with federal officials went awry as adequate facilities for meetings and for housing were not forthcoming and as high federal officials refused to negotiate with the Indian leaders. On November 2 the Indians occupied the Bureau of Indian Affairs building and, when forceful ejection was feared, barricaded the building. In a fit of anger and frustration, they utterly destroyed the interior of the building and its contents. An attack of riot police upon the barricaded Indians would without doubt have resulted in much bloodshed, since many Indians were resolved to die rather than give in. But no attack was ordered, for the government was determined to avoid violence, and the occupants, getting a face-saving indication that their complaints would be investigated, withdrew. Office of Economic Opportunity funds totaling sixty-six thousand dollars were channeled to the Indians through the National Congress of American Indians as travel expenses to get them home. The departing Indians took with them files of records, which they mistakenly thought could be used to prove government fraud and corruption in dealing with the Indians.[13]

13. A detailed account of the affair by an Indian participant of moderate views is in Robert Burnette and John Koster, *The Road to Wounded Knee* (New York: Bantam Books, 1974), pp. 195–219. A more extreme Indian position is given in *Trail of Broken Treaties: B.I.A., I'm Not Your Indian Anymore* (Mohawk Nation, Rooseveltown, New York: Akwesasne Notes, n.d.). Vine Deloria, Jr., gives a brief account in *Behind the Trail of Broken Treaties: An Indian Declaration of Independence* (New York: Delacorte Press, 1974), pp. 43–62. An account by a reporter for the *Washington Post* is Eugene I. Meyer, "Bury My Heart on the Potomac: Indians at the B.I.A.," *Ramparts* 11 (January 1973): 10–12. A House of Representatives investigation, which includes testimony from the government officials involved in the event, is "Seizure of Bureau of Indian Affairs Headquarters," *Hearings before the Subcommittee on Indian Affairs of the Committee on Interior and Insular Affairs, House of Representatives, 92d Congress, 2d Session* (1972). There is considerable material in Records of the National Council on Indian Opportunity, Caravans, box 16.

The American Indian Movement is hard to evaluate, for its supporters see it as a forceful advocate of Indian rights and its critics as a group of militants seeking to overturn the established order by revolutionary means. There is considerable information about AIM in "Revolutionary Activities within the United States: The American Indian Movement," *Hearing before the Subcommittee to Investigate the Administration of the Internal Security Act and Other Internal Security Laws of the Committee on the Judiciary, United States Senate, 94th Congress, 2d Session* (1976), which reported the testimony of Douglas Durham, a white who infiltrated AIM as an operative for the Federal Bureau of Investigation. See also the report on the hearing issued by the same committee. A sympathetic account of AIM is Peter Matthiesen, *In the Spirit of Crazy Horse* (New York: Viking Press, 1983).

The leaders of the Trail of Broken Treaties had brought to the government a list of twenty demands. These called for the renewal of a treaty relationship between the tribes and the federal government and a review of treaty violations, for a 110-million-acre Indian land base by July 4, 1976, for repeal of state laws enacted under Public Law 280, for tribal jurisdiction over non-Indians on Indian reservations, for repeal of termination laws, for the replacement of the Bureau of Indian Affairs by an Office of Federal Indian Relations and Community Reconstruction within the executive offices of the president, and for specific items of economic and cultural development. But in the dramatic confrontation at the Bureau of Indian Affairs these formal proposals were pushed into the background. When the government at length responded to the twenty points, it almost totally rejected them, much to the resentment of the militant Indians.[14]

The next militant action engineered by AIM was the seizure of the hamlet of Wounded Knee on the Pine Ridge Reservation in South Dakota on February 27, 1973. The site was consciously chosen as a symbol because of the disastrous confrontation there of Sioux and the Seventh Cavalry in 1890 and because Dee Brown's best-selling *Bury My Heart at Wounded Knee* had made Wounded Knee a household word.[15] The occupation of Wounded Knee in 1973 was intended as a new national event to call attention to the Indians' continuing woes, but it had an added dimension that Alcatraz and the Trail of Broken Treaties lacked—an intratribal conflict at Pine Ridge. The elected tribal chairman, Richard Wilson, was condemned by AIM leader Russell Means and his followers as a puppet of the Bureau of Indian Affairs who did not truly represent the Indian tribal members and who ruled the reservation with the help of a "goon squad."[16]

Federal marshals and agents of the Federal Bureau of Investigation

14. The twenty points and the response to them are printed in "Seizure of Bureau of Indian Affairs Headquarters," pp. 162–79.

15. Dee Brown, *Bury My Heart at Wounded Knee: An Indian History of the American West* (New York: Holt, Rinehart and Winston, 1971). The book, which was at the top of best-seller lists for months, presented a strongly pro-Indian account of the Indian wars and other Indian-related events of the nineteenth century. Only the final, very brief chapter dealt with Wounded Knee, 1890.

16. There are accounts in Burnette and Koster, *Road to Wounded Knee*, pp. 220–54; and Deloria, *Behind the Trail of Broken Treaties*, pp. 62–83. A detailed pro-Indian account is Bill Zimmerman, *Airlift to Wounded Knee* (Chicago: Swallow Press, 1976). A brief historical account, which sees the event in the perspective of the Sioux warrior tradition, is Clyde D. Dollar, "The Second Tragedy at Wounded Knee: A 1970s Confrontation and Its Historical Roots," *American West* 10 (September 1973): 4–11, 58–61. Testimony, especially on the intratribal conflict at Pine Ridge, is in "Occupation of Wounded Knee," *Hearings before the Subcommittee on Indian Affairs of the Committee on Interior and Insular Affairs, United States Senate, 93d Congress, 1st Session, on the Causes and Aftermath of the Wounded Knee Takeover* (1974).

quickly sealed off the occupied village, and a stand-off developed that won national and, indeed, worldwide news coverage. The AIM leaders were astute propagandists who fed the media their views and staged events that the television cameramen eagerly reported. For more than seventy days the impasse continued. The well-armed Indians were determined to hold out, and the government agents sought to end the occupation without a bloodbath. At length, through negotiations conducted in part with the aid of the National Council of Churches, the Indians withdrew on May 8, 1973.[17]

The militant actions at Alcatraz, the Bureau of Indian Affairs, and Wounded Knee were effective in spotlighting the grievances of the Indians. The violence was condemned by many Indians, who declared that the activists were largely young urban Indians who did not have deep roots in the reservations, and by many whites, among whom a mild backlash developed. The denouement of all three events showed that violent confrontation would not force the federal government to accept Indian demands and thus was ultimately ineffective and to some degree counterproductive. Yet the reality of the miserable conditions of many Indians and the deep desire of Indians to have a larger say in their own destiny were driven home to American society. The move for self-determination continued in the administration and in Congress with a new urgency because of the outbreaks.

TURNOVER AND TURMOIL IN THE BIA

The agitation exhibited in the public confrontations was paralleled by turmoil within the Bureau of Indian Affairs. President Nixon's search for a suitable Republican Indian to head the bureau ended with the nomination on August 7, 1969, of Louis R. Bruce, a Mohawk–Oglala Sioux. Bruce was not experienced in the bureau, nor was he prominent in the national Indian community of the day, but he had been one of the founders of the National Congress of American Indians and had played a part in other Indian-related activities. A man of reason and good sense, committed to the cause of Indian self-determination, he had the misfortune to hold office during a volatile and controversial period of Indian affairs. He surrounded himself with young activist Indians, a "new team," who sought to work around the bureaucratic inertia of the old administrative setup.[18]

17. The importance of the media in the events was noted and criticized in "Trap at Wounded Knee," *Time* 101 (March 26, 1973): 67; Desmond Smith, "Wounded Knee: The Media Coup d'Etat," *Nation* 216 (June 25, 1973): 806–9; Terri Schultz, "Bamboozle Me Not at Wounded Knee," *Harper's Magazine* 246 (June 1973): 46–48, 53–56.
18. A brief, sympathetic sketch of Bruce is Joseph H. Cash, "Louis Rook Bruce, 1969–73," in Robert M. Kvasnicka and Herman J. Viola, eds. *The Commissioners of Indian Affairs, 1824–1977* (Lincoln: University of Nebraska Press, 1979), pp. 333–40. Bruce dis-

When Bruce took office, the bureau was run by the commissioner, a deputy commission, and six assistant commissioners for community services, economic development, education, administration, engineering, and program coordination. The organization soon underwent realignment, which Secretary Hickel said would "help make the Bureau more responsive to the needs of the Indian people and . . . provide the necessary flexibility in developing and carrying out programs to meet those requirements." The deputy commissioner and the six assistant commissioners were eliminated and replaced by an associate commissioner for education and programs (overseeing staff directors for education programs, community services, and economic development) and an associate commissioner for support services (overseeing directors of management services and operating services). At the end of the year Hickel proposed sweeping changes as well in the field organization, to abolish the sixty-three agency superintendent positions and replace them with "field administrators" with increased authority, intended "to achieve the objections of President Nixon in placing the Indian people in closer contact with decision-makers and in broadening their opportunities to guide and improve their own affairs." The area directors were to keep their advisory capacity and retain technical and general service functions.[19] Thus began a decade of shuffling and reshuffling of the administration of national Indian affairs, an unfortunate situation in a time of great agitation and rapid change.

The Hickel-Bruce administration, which was geared to an increased voice of Indians in the high-level management of Indian affairs, was soon cut short. In November 1970 Hickel resigned, to be replaced by Rogers C. B. Morton at the end of January 1971. Morton was less flexible and innovative than Hickel, and he moved to tighten the administration of the bureau. On July 23 he appointed John O. Crow to the reactivated position of deputy commissioner. Crow, a part-Cherokee who had had long experience in the bureau (he had served as acting commissioner of Indian affairs between Nash and Bennett), with Morton's backing, opposed Bruce and his young advisers. In December Morton abolished the associate commissioner positions and made the major program offices (now thirteen in number) the district responsibility of the commissioner and the deputy commissioner.[20]

cussed his policies and programs in "The Bureau of Indian Affairs, 1972," in Jane F. Smith and Robert M. Kvasnicka, eds., *Indian-White Relations: A Persistent Paradox* (Washington: Howard University Press, 1976), pp. 242–50.

19. *Indian Record*, January 1969, p. 4; Office of the Secretary of the Interior, news releases of January 9 and November 25, 1970.

20. Office of the Secretary of the Interior, news release, December 8, 1971. The bitter struggle between opposing forces in the Bureau of Indian Affairs is described in Steve Nickeson, "The Structure of the Bureau of Indian Affairs," *Law and Contemporary*

The struggle for power within the bureau reflected the growing agitation among Indians outside. The seizure and destruction of the offices of the bureau in November 1972 brought complete disruption to the organization. Bruce, Crow, and Assistant Secretary Harrison Loesch resigned; management was placed in the hands of Richard S. Bodman, assistant secretary of the interior for management and budget; and the offices of the bureau were scattered.[21] On February 7, 1973, Morton appointed Marvin L. Franklin, a member of the Iowa Indian Tribe and an executive of the Phillips Petroleum Company, to a new position of assistant to the secretary for Indian affairs. Franklin assumed direct responsibility for all Indian programs and reported directly to the secretary. In May a new reorganization of the bureau was announced, "in order to implement the President's directive, reduce non-essential Central Office support staff and increase the effectiveness of the delivery system of services to Indians." The bureau was to be headed by a commissioner, who would report directly to the secretary of the interior, and a deputy commissioner. There were now six major offices: Indian education programs, tribal resource development, trust responsibilities, Indian services, public affairs, and administration. Until the commissioner and deputy could be chosen, the administration of Indian affairs remained in Franklin's hands.[22] One thing was clear from the rearrangements, whatever confusion might have resulted from the changes: the direction of Indian affairs, once in the hands of a commissioner who reported to the assistant secretary of the interior for public land management, had now achieved a direct line to the secretary.

It took some time to find an Indian to serve as commissioner. Finally, on October 30, 1973, Nixon nominated Morris Thompson, an Athabascan Indian from Alaska who was then serving as director of the Juneau Area Office. When Thompson was sworn in on December 3, he was, at thirty-four, the youngest person to hold the office. Morton arranged that the new commissioner, on a comparable level of responsibility and authority with the assistant secretaries of the Interior Department, would report directly to him. When Thompson resigned three years later to return to Alaska as vice president of the Alcan Pipeline Company, he was replaced on December 7, 1976, as a "recess appointment" by Ben Reifel, a former longtime employee of the bureau and South Dakota representative and a member of

---

Problems 40 (Winter 1976): 61–76. See also Peter Collier, "Wounded Knee: The New Indian War," *Ramparts* 11 (June 1973): 25–29, 56–59.

21. Office of the Secretary of the Interior, news release, December 8, 1972; Bureau of Indian Affairs, news release, December 8, 1972.

22. Office of the Secretary of the Interior, news releases, February 7 and May 15, 1973.

the Sioux Tribe, who served only until President Jimmy Carter asked for his resignation on January 28, 1977.[23]

The Carter administration accomplished by administrative action what Nixon had hoped but failed to achieve by legislation: elevation of the head of Indian affairs to the assistant secretary level. After six months of Indian consultation, speculation, and rumor, the White House on July 12, 1977, announced the nomination of Forrest J. Gerard for the new position. A member of the Blackfeet Tribe, Gerard from 1971 to 1976 had headed the professional staff of the Senate Subcommittee on Indian Affairs and had worked previously for the Indian Health Service as a tribal relations officer and for the Bureau of Indian Affairs as legislative liaison officer. He was formally installed on October 13, 1977.[24]

In December 1977, Carter's secretary of the interior, Cecil D. Andrus, appointed an eleven-member task force to develop recommendations for reorganizing the Bureau of Indian Affairs. After numerous meetings to elicit Indian input, the task force submitted its report on March 31, 1978. The report proposed that the top administration of Indian affairs be in the hands of the assistant secretary for Indian affairs and three deputies and that the area offices should be reviewed to determine the future role of each.[25] Forrest Gerard modified the recommendations according to his own judgment. He rejected the proposed assistant and three deputies and re-instituted the commissioner of Indian affairs—who, with a deputy commissioner, would direct the day to day activities of the Bureau of Indian Affairs, leaving the assistant secretary, also with a deputy, to emphasize policy, planning, and evaluation. The area offices were continued as intermediate levels of authority, pending studies to be made of each area. Until a new commissioner could be located, Martin E. Seneca, Jr., was appointed to run the bureau as acting deputy commissioner. A year later, on Septem-

23. Office of the Secretary of the Interior, news releases, October 30 and November 28, 1973; Bureau of Indian Affairs, news releases, December 4, 1973, and December 8, 1976. For brief biographies, see Michael T. Smith, "Morris Thompson, 1973–76," and "Benjamin Reifel, 1976–77," in Kvasnicka and Viola, *Commissioners of Indian Affairs*, pp. 341–48.

24. *Indian Record*, July–August 1977, p. 1, and October 1977, p. 4; Bureau of Indian Affairs, news release, October 14, 1977. The position of assistant secretary was formalized in 42 *Federal Register* 53682 (October 3, 1977).

25. 43 *Federal Register* 16284–304 (April 17, 1978). Note that the American Indian Policy Review Commission also had a task force working on the organization of the Bureau of Indian Affairs. See American Indian Policy Review Commission, Task Force Three, *Report on Federal Administration and Structure of Indian Affairs* (Washington: GPO, 1976), and American Indian Policy Review Commission, *Bureau of Indian Affairs Management Study* (Washington: GPO, 1976). These recommendations seem to have had little effect.

ber 28, 1979, President Carter nominated William E. Hallett, a Red Lake Chippewa, to be commissioner, and Hallett, thirty-seven years of age, was ceremoniously installed on December 14. A day earlier Forrest Gerard announced his resignation, effective January 19, 1980; on June 18, 1980, a member of the Mandan-Hidatsa Tribe, Thomas E. Fredericks, was nominated to succeed him.[26]

The commitment of the federal government to Indian self-determination of their own affairs hindered the effective management of Indian matters, for the wide consultation with Indian groups that was believed essential in selecting Indians for high office greatly slowed down the appointment process, and Indians of competence were passed over in the attempt to find someone not strongly opposed by any group. And those Indians who were finally appointed did not receive unanimous Indian support. The increasing number and authority of persons of Indian descent in the Indian service, moreover, heightened conflicts between new and old bureaucrats and between Indian and non-Indian employees of the bureau.

A sign of the increasing Indian influence in the Bureau of Indian Affairs was the amplification of the policy of preference for Indians in hiring personnel for the bureau. Section 12 of the Indian Reorganization Act of 1934 had established the policy: "The Secretary of the Interior is directed to establish standards of health, age, character, experience, knowledge, and ability for Indians who may be appointed, without regard to civil-service laws, to the various positions maintained, now or hereafter, by the Indian Office, in the administration of functions or services affecting any Indian tribe. Such qualified Indians shall hereafter have the preference to appointment to vacancies in any such positions."[27]

Despite the general nature of this authority, in practice Indian preference had been applied only to initial hiring or to reductions in force. In June 1972 Commissioner Bruce with the approval of Secretary Morton extended the policy to cover all vacancies, whether of original appointment, reinstatement, or promotion.[28] This action immediately elicited a response from non-Indian employees. A group of them working for the bureau in Albuquerque initiated a class action suit in the United States District

26. Bureau of Indian Affairs, news release, September 21, 1978; Office of the Secretary of the Interior, news releases, December 6 and 13, 1979, June 18, 1980. The rapid turnover of high-ranking personnel created uncertainty in the running of the bureau, yet lower-echelon people, sometimes almost unaware of the changes at the top, continued to administer the day-to-day operations.

27. 48 *United States Statutes* 986.

28. Bureau of Indian Affairs Personnel Management Letter no. 72–12, June 26, 1972, quoted in *Morton* v. *Mancari*, 417 *U.S. Reports* 538n; Office of the Secretary of the Interior, news release, June 23, 1972.

Court for the District of New Mexico, claiming that the Indian preference law had been repealed by the Equal Employment Opportunity Act of 1972 and that the preference measure deprived them of property rights without due process of law in violation of the Fifth Amendment. The judges of the district court held that Indian preference had indeed been implicitly repealed by the 1972 act, which prohibited racial discrimination in most federal employment, and they enjoined federal officials from implementing any Indian employment preference policy in the Bureau of Indian Affairs. Upon appeal, the Supreme Court of the United States on June 17, 1974, in *Morton* v. *Mancari*, reversed this decision, supported the preference policy, and recognized the special legal status of Indians.[29]

The court noted in this case the longstanding preference for Indians in Bureau of Indian Affairs employment and in employment by Indian tribes and by private industries on or near reservations and declared that it would be anomalous to conclude that Congress in the Equal Employment Opportunities Act had intended implicitly to end that practice. Moreover, shortly after the 1972 act Congress had enacted new Indian preference laws. The Supreme Court also considered the charge of violation of the Fifth Amendment, which it similarly rejected, basing its argument on "the unique legal status of Indian tribes under federal law and upon the plenary power of Congress, based on a history of treaties and the assumption of a 'guardian-ward' status, to legislate on behalf of federally recognized Indian tribes." The 1934 preference legislation, the court said, was a reaction to the "overly paternalistic approach of prior years," which had been exploitative and destructive of Indian interests. It thus threw out the charge that the preference was racial discrimination. The court concluded:

> Indeed, it is not even a "racial" preference. Rather, it is an employment criterion reasonably designed to further the cause of Indian self-government and to make the BIA more responsive to the needs of its constituent groups. It is directed to participation by the governed in the governing agency. . . . Congress has sought only to enable the BIA to draw more heavily from among the constituent groups in staffing its projects, all of which, either directly or indirectly, affect the lives of tribal Indians. The preference, as applied, is granted to Indians not as a discrete racial group, but, rather, as members of quasi-sovereign tribal entities whose lives and activities are governed by the BIA in a unique fashion.[30]

29. *Morton* v. *Mancari*, 417 *U.S. Reports* 535–55; Brian Douglas Baird, "*Morton* v. *Mancari*: New Vitality for the Indian Preference Statutes," *Tulsa Law Journal* 10, no. 3 (1975): 454–62.

30. *Morton* v. *Mancari*, 417 *U.S. Reports* 551–54.

The principle was thus firmly established, and the number of Indians employed by the Bureau of Indian Affairs steadily increased. Indian employment preference, however, was restricted generally to members of federally recognized tribes. New regulations issued on January 17, 1978, spelled out the eligibility in detail, including other Indians of one-half or more Indian blood and Eskimos and other aboriginal people of Alaska.[31] The political appointees to the positions of assistant secretary of the interior for Indian affairs, the assistant secretary's deputies, and the commissioner of Indian affairs, of course, were all Indians, and 78 percent of the bureau's employees were Indians and Alaska Natives by 1980. Furthermore, preference for Indians extended beyond employment in the Bureau of Indian Affairs. In health services, educational training, and the construction of Indian facilities, for example, legislation provided for Indian preference.[32] Although Indian criticism of federal programs continued, it was no longer possible to argue that white bureaucrats were solely responsible for Indian woes.

RELIGIOUS FREEDOM

A key element in the Indians' advance toward self-determination and cultural freedom in the United States was freedom of religious belief and practice. From the beginning of white contact, the zeal of Christian missionaries and government officials to Christianize and civilize the Indians had meant the denigration of aboriginal religions and an attempt to stamp them out, replacing them with European Christianity. Not until the 1920s, when John Collier began his crusade for reform, were there outspoken voices in support of full religious freedom for the American Indians. As American society became more tolerant of pluralism in religion and other aspects of culture, Indian religions were no longer directly attacked.

31. 43 *Federal Register* 2393–94 (January 17, 1978), codified as 25 *Code of Federal Regulations* 259. For a criticism of limitations on eligibility, see Karl A. Funke, "Educational Assistance and Employment Preference: Who Is an Indian?" *American Indian Law Review* 4, no. 1 (1976): 1–45. Commissioner of Indian Affairs William Hallett criticized the preferential employment practice because the Indians thus employed in the Bureau of Indian Affairs did not accumulate seniority rights that could be transferred to employment in other federal agencies. Interview with Hallett in "The New Commissioner Gets Down to Business," *American Indian Journal* 6 (March 1980): 20–21.

32. As of September 30, 1980, there were 13,602 Indians and Alaska Natives out of a total work force of 17,438. Bureau of Indian Affairs, "Workforce Profile by Pay Systems, Bureau Total Employment." See Kevin N. Anderson, "Indian Employment Preference: Legal Foundations and Limitations," *Tulsa Law Journal* 15 (Summer 1980): 736–38, and legislation cited there. Anderson's article pays special attention to tribal employment preference.

There were still areas of conflict, however, for certain federal and state laws and actions indirectly hindered the free exercise of religion for many Indians. One problem was that of free access to sites considered sacred by the tribes and used for religious ceremonies, some of which had passed from Indian ownership or control and been set aside as national parks or other federal reserves. Traditional burying grounds, too, had sometimes become inaccessible to the Indians. A second source of friction was the restriction on the use of certain substances that were an essential part of Indian rites, such as peyote (restricted as a hallucinogen) or eagle feathers (protected under endangered species laws). A third area of concern was occasional interference with actual ceremonies by overzealous officials or the merely curious, against which legal protection seemed necessary.[33]

One dramatic move to right these wrongs came in December 1970, when the sacred Blue Lake and surrounding lands of the Taos Pueblo were returned to the Indians. These lands had been taken from the Indians in 1906 when President Theodore Roosevelt added them to what is now Carson National Forest, thus restricting their use exclusively by Indians. After years of Indian struggle to regain the lands and persistent rejection of the idea of a monetary compensation for their loss, Congress authorized the return of forty-eight thousand acres.[34] In signing the bill on December 15, 1970, President Nixon called attention to the fact that the bill did not represent a gift to the Indians by the United States, but rather the return to them in justice of what was rightfully theirs. "This bill," he said, "also involves respect for religion. Those of us who know something about the background of the first Americans realize that long before any organized religion came to the United States, for 700 years the Taos Pueblo Indians worshiped in this place. We restore this place of worship to them for all the years to come."[35]

A direct and broad statement of policy in regard to Indian religious freedom came in Senate Joint Resolution 102 (P.L. 95–341) on August 11,

33. These points in support of new legislation were made in *Senate Report* no. 95–709, 95–2, serial 13197–1, pp. 3–4.

34. 84 *United States Statutes* 1437–39; "Taos Indians—Blue Lake Amendments," *Hearings before the Subcommittee on Indian Affairs of the Committee on Interior and Insular Affairs, United States Senate, 91st Congress, 2d Session, on S. 750 and H.R. 471* (1970); *Senate Report* no. 91–1345, 91–2, serial 12881–6. Useful articles about the Blue Lake affair are Dabney Otis Collins, "Battle for Blue Lake: The Taos Indians Finally Regain Their Sacred Land," *American West* 8 (September 1971): 32–37; John J. Bodine, "Blue Lake: A Struggle for Indian Rights," *American Indian Law Review* 1 (Winter 1973): 23–32; Bodine, "Taos Blue Lake Controversy," *Journal of Ethnic Studies* 6 (Spring 1978): 42–48. There is information on the Blue Lake issue in Records of the National Council on Indian Opportunity, Taos—Blue Lake, box 83.

35. *Public Papers of the Presidents: Nixon, 1970*, pp. 1131–32.

1978. After noting the American principle of freedom of religion and the infringement of that principle in regard to Indians, Congress resolved: "That henceforth it shall be the policy of the United States to protect and preserve for American Indians their inherent right of freedom to believe, express, and exercise the traditional religions of the American Indian, Eskimo, Aleut, and Native Hawaiian, including but not limited to access to sites, use and possession of sacred objects, and the freedom to worship through ceremonials and traditional rites." The resolution directed evaluation by the various federal departments and agencies of their policies and procedures in this regard and appropriate changes needed to protect religious rights and practices.[36]

Indian religious rights were further recognized in the Archaeological Resources Protection Act of 1979 (P.L. 96–95), which became law on October 31, 1979. The purpose of the act was to prevent the destruction of important archaeological sites, and it required special permits for persons studying or excavating them. If such a permit might result in harm to any religious or cultural site, the Indian tribe concerned was to be notified before a permit was issued. The ultimate disposition of archaeological resources excavated or removed from Indian lands was subject to the consent of the Indians or tribe.[37]

ALASKA NATIVE CLAIMS

Another signal event in the recognition of the rights of Indians and other native peoples was the settlement of Alaska Native claims in 1971. Alaska Natives—Indians, Eskimos, and Aleuts—offered unique problems, for they had never been fully encompassed in the federal policies and programs developed for the American Indians. Alaska for decades seemed remote and out of the way; no treaties were made with the natives there, few reservations were established for them, and only small appropriations were made for their benefit. Not until the mid-twentieth century did striking changes occur that demanded attention to the claims of the aboriginal peoples of Alaska.[38]

36. 92 *United States Statutes* 469–70.

37. 92 *United States Statutes* 721–28; *Senate Report* no. 96–179, 96–1, serial 13240; *House Report* no. 96–311, 96–1, serial 13297. Proposed regulations to implement the act were published in 46 *Federal Register* 5566–76 (January 19, 1981).

38. The best general account of claims of the Alaska Natives is Robert D. Arnold, *Alaska Native Land Claims* (Anchorage: Alaska Native Foundation, 1976). Other useful general accounts appear in Claus-M. Naske and Herman E. Slotnik, *Alaska: A History of the 49th State* (Grand Rapids, Michigan: William B. Eerdmans Publishing Company, 1979), pp. 195–232, and Mary Clay Berry, *The Alaska Pipeline: The Politics of Oil and Native Land Claims* (Bloomington: Indiana University Press, 1975).

When Russia ceded Alaska to the United States in 1867, the treaty declared that "the uncivilized tribes will be subject to such laws and regulations as the United States may, from time to time, adopt in regard to the aboriginal tribes of that country," but it did not touch aboriginal rights to the land and its resources. The Organic Act of 1884, which established a civil government for Alaska, did not recognize aboriginal ownership but merely continued the status quo; the law provided that "the Indians or other persons in said district shall not be disturbed in the possession of any lands actually in their use or occupation or now claimed by them but the terms under which such persons may acquire title to such lands is reserved for future legislation by Congress."[39]

From time to time the federal government passed legislation in regard to Indian lands, but the action was sporadic and never all-encompassing. In 1891, for example, Congress established the Metlakatla Indian Community (Annette Island Reserve) for a group of Indians who had migrated to Alaska from British Columbia, and after 1891 some small reserves were established by executive order. The Alaska Allotment Act of May 17, 1906, extended to Alaska the provisions of the Dawes Act, allowing allotments of 160 acres to individual Indians that would give clear title to their homesites; but quarter-section allotments made little sense in the subsistence economy carried on by most Alaska Natives.[40]

The social and political organization of the Alaska Natives was generally that of villages with traditional self-governing councils, although some communities organized municipal governments under the Territory of Alaska. The Indian Reorganization Act of 1934 and its extension in the Alaska Reorganization Act of 1936 made possible more formal tribal organization, provided for the incorporation of communities, and authorized the secretary of the interior to set aside reservations. Informal regional councils and broader voluntary organizations like the Alaska Native Brotherhood (organized in 1912) and in more recent years the influential Alaska Federation of Natives (organized in 1966) increased the effectiveness of the villages in voicing their concerns.

The crisis for the Alaska Natives came with the rush for exploitation of Alaska's tremendously rich natural resources. The arrival of white com-

---

39. Treaty with Russia, March 30, 1867, 15 *United States Statutes* 542; act of May 17, 1884, 23 *United States Statutes* 26. In *Tee-Hit Ton Indians* v. *United States*, February 7, 1955, the Supreme Court ruled that the tribe was not due compensation for sale of timber by the federal government because the government had never recognized the Indians' right to unrestricted possession, occupancy, or use of the land. 348 *U.S. Reports* 272–91.

40. 26 *United States Statutes* 1101; 34 *United States Statutes* 197. The Native Townsite Act of May 25, 1926, allowed the conveyance of public lands to individuals as townsites. 44 *United States Statutes* 629–30.

mercial fishermen in the second half of the nineteenth century and gold rushes in the late nineteenth and early twentieth centuries were harbingers of what was to come. By mid-twentieth century the white Alaska economy—long dependent upon United States military activities—was based on the natural resources of the territory. Exploration and development of oil, gas, and other mineral riches and the post–World War II population influx brought an insistent demand for statehood for the territory.

Statehood, which became a reality on January 3, 1959, was an ultimate challenge to the Alaska Natives, who formed about one-fifth of the new state's population in 1960. They continued to live in villages and settlements widely scattered throughout the state. But threats to their lands and to their traditional hunting and gathering economy now took on serious proportions. In the enabling act Congress, while asserting absolute jurisdiction and control over lands held by the natives, authorized the state to select 102.5 million acres from the "vacant, unappropriated, and unreserved" public domain, another 400,000 acres from national forests, and 400,000 acres from other public lands for disposition by the state. It was the intent of Congress to have the new state "achieve full equality with existing states not only in a technical, juridical sense, but in practical economic terms as well. . . . by making the new State master in fact of most of the natural resouces within its boundaries." By 1968 the state had selected 19.6 million acres, of which more than 6 million had been patented. To meet this threatening development the natives resorted to filing protests against the state land selections, and these protests ultimately covered much of the land in the state.[41]

Meanwhile the federal government had not been unmindful of the critical nature of the land claims problem in Alaska. Secretary of the Interior Stewart L. Udall, in addition to his general task force on Indian affairs, named a three-man Task Force on Alaska Native Affairs in May 1962. Its report, submitted on December 28, 1962, emphasized the need to resolve the land claims, but its recommendations for action were opposed by the Alaska Natives because there was no provision for compensation for lost lands or for mineral rights.[42] There was no dearth of other suggestions

41. 72 *United States Statutes* 339–40 (statehood act); 73 *United States Statutes* C16 (proclamation); *House Report* no. 624, 85–1, serial 11986, p. 2. The protests are reported in *Senate Report* no. 92–405, 92–1, serial 12929–4, pp. 96–98.

42. The Alaska Task Force was composed of William W. Keeler, chairman, Hugh J. Wade, and James E. Officer. There is a copy of the report in Desk Files of Philleo Nash, 69A–1697, box 2, WNRC. The Association on American Indian Affairs sharply criticized the task force report when it was released on March 5, 1963. See the association's press release of March 9, copy in Desk Files of Robert Bennett, 70A–2935, Alaska Task Force, box 48, WNRC.

about how to resolve the claims, whether by state or federal action or by judicial or legislative means. In the end, congressional legislation was decided upon.

By 1968 the lines of various proposals had been quite clearly drawn, separate bills embodying them introduced in Congress, and extensive hearings held both in Washington and in Alaska. One of the proposals was based on the report and recommendations made by the Federal Field Committee for Development Planning in Alaska, a study group created by executive order in 1964 to develop "coordinated plans for Federal programs which contribute to the economic and resources development in Alaska." At Senator Henry Jackson's request the committee compiled extensive data on Alaskan conditions—published as *Alaska Natives and the Land,* which became a sort of source book for the Senate committee—and outlined a proposal that was incorporated into a bill introduced by Jackson. An alternate bill was drawn up by the Department of the Interior and yet a third one by the Alaska Federation of Natives, which represented the views of the Alaska Natives. The bills differed on the amount of land to be withdrawn for native use and the surface and mineral rights to be acquired, on the amount and kind of compensation to be awarded, and on the machinery for resolution of conflicts and adjudicative decisions. The state of Alaska did not offer a separate bill, but it had its own position on a number of the points proposed.[43]

The conflicting interests on numerous points made it seem unlikely that a compromise agreeable to all could ever be reached, but there were increasing pressures for a settlement. The secretary of the interior had frozen the public lands in Alaska until Congress could settle the native claims, and the continuing freeze seriously hindered the economic development of the state. Then discovery of immense oil reserves on the North Slope and the proposal of a pipeline to transport the oil added new urgency for a quick settlement. The situation played into the hands of the Alaska

---

43. Executive Order no. 11182, October 2, 1964, 29 *Federal Register* 13629–32; *Alaska Natives and the Land* (Anchorage: Federal Field Committee for Development Planning in Alaska, 1968). A comparative analysis of the three bills, prepared by Esther Wunnicke, is in "Alaska Native Land Claims," *Hearings before the Committee on Interior and Insular Affairs, United States Senate, 91st Congress, 1st Session, on S. 1830,* 3 parts (1969), pp. 597–622. See also "Alaska Native Land Claims," *Hearings before the Subcommittee on Indian Affairs of the Committee on Interior and Insular Affairs, House of Representatives, 91st Congress, 1st Session, on H.R. 13142, H.R. 10193, and H.R. 14212,* 2 parts (1969–1970). There were also House and Senate hearings in 1968 and in 1971. The Alaska Federation of Natives' "Position with Respect to the Native Land Claim Issue," June 20, 1969, is printed, among other places, in "Alaska Native Land Claims," *House Hearings,* p. 49.

Federation of Natives, which had won the support of influential groups as well as the legal assistance of former Supreme Court Justice Arthur Goldberg and former Attorney General Ramsey Clark. Now the oil companies realized that the Alaska Natives would have to be satisfied before there was any chance for the pipeline. After intense lobbying and numerous compromise suggestions, the House and Senate in December 1971 finally agreed on a measure that became law on December 18 as the Alaska Native Claims Settlement Act. Though a complex compromise, it was by and large a victory for the Alaska Natives.[44] "After more than four hundred years," an Indian scholar wrote after passage of the act, "a native people and a colonizing power had come to terms. What had been expressed as a piety by Spanish humanists, then elevated into law in British North America, had met the harsh test of the market. The Natives of Alaska had asserted their rights as original owners of the soil—rights which priests, statesmen, and jurists had recognized, and frontier society had largely ignored—and their claim had been honored."[45]

The law granted the Alaska Natives legal title to 40 million acres, and in return all native claims in Alaska were extinguished. Existing reserves (except for Annette Island Reserve) were revoked, and the Alaska Allotment Act was repealed. Compensation of $462 million was provided, plus another $500 million in revenues from mineral rights to be paid over a number of years. The law required the secretary of the interior to divide Alaska into twelve geographic regions, for each of which a regional corporation was established. All Alaska Natives would be shareholders in one of these corporations or in a thirteenth corporation for nonresident natives. In addition, native village corporations would be formed to hold the lands distributed under the act and to administer other benefits. The law itself listed more than two hundred such villages, and the secretary of the interior was empowered to add or delete villages from the list. The village corporations dealt only with surface rights; title to subsurface mineral rights was held by the regional corporations, which distributed funds to villages and at-large stockholders according to a complex formula. The Joint Federal-State Land Use Planning Commission was created to make recommendations on the disposal of the Alaska lands.

The regional corporations were organized quickly and began to invest their funds in a wide variety of economic enterprises, but the transfer of

44. 85 *United States Statutes* 688–716; *Senate Report* no. 91–925, 91–2, serial 12881–3; *Senate Report* no. 92–405, 92–1, serial 12929–4; *House Report* no. 92–523, 92–1, serial 12932–4.

45. D'Arcy McNickle, *Native American Tribalism: Indian Survivals and Renewals* (New York: Oxford University Press, 1973), pp. 158–59.

land to native title moved very slowly. By the spring of 1977 only 3.5 million of the 40 million acres due the native corporations had been transferred. The slowness in conveyance of the lands and the general compromise nature of the act led to continuing complaints. Representative Lloyd Meeds, chairing the House Subcommittee on Indian Affairs, severely criticized the Department of the Interior in its implementation of the act. "Time allotted to the Natives in the act to enroll their members; organize their corporations; assess and select their land entitlements; and plan for the future of their people," he said, "has been eaten up in interminable conflict with Departmental politicians and bureaucrats."[46] The American Indian Policy Review Commission's special task force on Alaska Native issues, moreover, declared in its report of July 1976 that the Department of the Interior had "not performed at sufficiently high levels of effectiveness" in implementing the settlement act. It pointed to the "comparatively insignificant portion" of the land that had been conveyed and complained that the department, "rather than acting as advocate for Native needs, which it should pursuant to its continued legal-moral obligation to dependent native communities, . . . had consistently taken positions adverse, particularly with respect to easement, to Native interests." The agitation brought some results, for Congress provided amendments in an omnibus act of January 2, 1976, which clarified some of the original law's ambiguities; but uncertainties and problems remained.[47]

One problem concerned the conservation of wilderness areas in Alaska. Persons interested in preserving wildlife refuges and other such reserves worried that improper native claims under the settlement act might affect adversely the lands within the National Wildlife Refuge System, and in any case, it would be difficult to set aside wilderness areas until the natives had chosen their 40 million acres. Extensive hearings were held in the latter half of the decade, and Congress finally enacted the Alaska National

46. "Alaska Native Claims Settlement Act Amendments," *Hearings before the Subcommittee on Indian Affairs of the Committee on Interior and Insular Affairs, House of Representatives, 94th Congress, 1st Session, on H.R. 6644* (1975), pp. 11–12. See also "Amendments to Alaska Native Claims Settlement Act," *Hearings before the Committee on Interior and Insular Affairs, United States Senate, 94th Congress, 1st Session, on S. 131, S. 685, S. 1469, and S. 1501,* 4 parts (1975).

47. American Indian Policy Review Commission, *Special Joint Task Force Report on Alaskan Native Issues* (Washington: GPO, 1976), p. 25. The commission's *Final Report* deals with Alaska issues on pp. 489–503. For the amendments of 1976, see 89 *United States Statutes* 1145–503. There is discussion of ambiguities and problems in the legislation in Arthur Lazarus, Jr., and W. Richard West, Jr., "The Alaska Native Claims Settlement Act: A Flawed Victory," *Law and Contemporary Problems* 40 (Winter 1976): 132–65; "Alaska Native Claims Settlement Act: Long-Term Prospects," *American Indian Journal* 3 (May 1977): 10–17.

Map 12: Alaska: The Regional Corporations

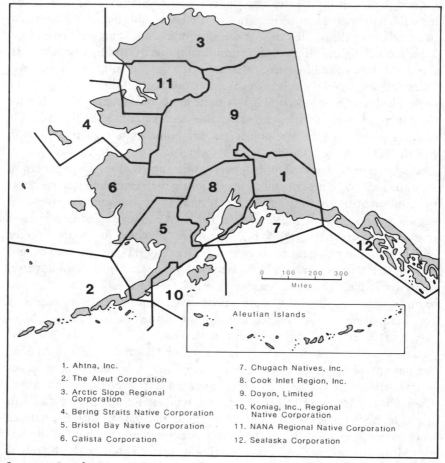

1. Ahtna, Inc.
2. The Aleut Corporation
3. Arctic Slope Regional Corporation
4. Bering Straits Native Corporation
5. Bristol Bay Native Corporation
6. Calista Corporation
7. Chugach Natives, Inc.
8. Cook Inlet Region, Inc.
9. Doyon, Limited
10. Koniag, Inc., Regional Native Corporation
11. NANA Regional Native Corporation
12. Sealaska Corporation

Interest Lands Conservation Act (P.L. 96–487), which became law on December 2, 1980.[48]

The Alaska Native Claims Settlement Act of 1971 provided a revolutionary solution to a problem of long standing, but the ultimate effects were not agreed upon. Some thought that the act freed the Alaska Natives and through grants of land and money gave them a basis for political power. The native community could now take its rightful place in Alaskan society. Others argued that in exchange for money and land the natives gave up their own lifestyle and traditional mode of living. They feared that hunters and gatherers would be transformed into corporation members interested in the development of resources and dividend payments, and that

48. 94 *United States Statutes* 2371–551. See also *House Report* no. 96–97, 96–1, serial 13290, and *Senate Report* no. 96–413, 96–1, serial 13247.

the political tribe as a dominant force in native life would be replaced by the economic corporation.[49]

MENOMINEE RESTORATION

Because deeds speak louder than words, the restoration of the terminated Menominee Indians to federal status as a tribe was one of the most significant actions of the Nixon administration. The move, supported by state and federal officials as well as by a majority of the Menominees, showed that in the new era of self-determination and Indian rights it was possible for an Indian community with determined leaders to reverse congressional action and policy.[50]

The disastrous results of termination for the Menominees were the springboard from which the drive for restoration took off. All the economic and social indicators pointed to intolerable conditions. Representative Harold Froehlich of Wisconsin, when he introduced a restoration bill, commented: "Whatever its motivation and objective, this Termination Act has proved in the ensuing years to be a misconceived and tragic experiment. It was an involuntary experiment that has produced cultural shock and severe economic hardship for the Menominee people. It has led to disorientation, disunity, and despair in the tribe. And it has written a sad and regrettable chapter in American social history."[51] The sawmill operation that had employed most of the tribe before termination had to modernize to make its operations pay under the new dispensation, and many Indians lost their jobs. Federal support of schools and hospital was withdrawn, and the tax base of the new county was too small to cover the costs. Menominee Enterprises, Inc. (MEI), the trust that had taken over the tribal assets, was hard-pressed financially. When MEI decided on the necessity of selling tribal land to white developers, it created hostility among the rank and file

49. Naske and Slotnik, *Alaska*, p. 232; Monroe E. Price, "A Moment in History: The Alaska Native Claims Settlement Act," *UCLA–Alaska Law Review* 8 (Spring 1979): 89–101.

50. The best account of the Menominee restoration movement, which presents a balanced account of the various factions of the tribe, is Nicholas C. Peroff, *Menominee Drums: Tribal Termination and Restoration, 1954–1974* (Norman: University of Oklahoma Press, 1982). Another useful study, written from the standpoint of the restoration advocates, is Deborah Shames, ed., *Freedom with Reservation: The Menominee Struggle to Save Their Land and People* (Madison, Wisconsin: National Committee to Save the Menominee People and Forests, 1972). A briefer account is in Patricia K. Ourada, *The Menominee Indians: A History* (Norman: University of Oklahoma Press, 1979), pp. 190–223.

51. *Congressional Record*, 119: 14052.

of the tribe, who were already disturbed because of the tight control over economic and political affairs that MEI held. Termination was supposed to save the federal government money, but instead both federal and state governments were forced to pump in funds to prevent complete collapse of the Menominees. Menominee County was the poorest of Wisconsin's seventy-two counties, with little hope of recovery.[52]

The Menominee governing group that ran MEI, however, did not despair. It hoped by prudent development to ride out the storm, and there were many Indians who survived and prospered and who were convinced that termination could be made to work. But this group was soon vigorously attacked by a new faction that called itself Determination of Rights and Unity for Menominee Stockholders (DRUMS). Under astute leadership furnished by Ada Deer and Jim White, DRUMS organized groups in Chicago and Milwaukee and then in Menominee County to oust the Indians who controlled MEI and eventually—as their ultimate goal—to bring about a reversal of termination and restore the Menominee tribe and its assets to federal responsibility. The new political force, through skillfully using protest tactics against MEI and the governing elite, enlisting wide public support, and stirring up the Menominees themselves to a new determination to preserve their old ways, managed to get its members elected to controlling offices in MEI. Then it put on a lobbying drive to get Congress to pass a restoration bill.[53]

In the political climate, supportive of minority rights, of the late 1960s and early 1970s, the drive under Ada Deer moved forward effectively and successfully. With support from Indian groups across the nation, who rightly saw the symbolic significance of restoration as a final rejection of the termination policy, and with endorsement from state officials and the Department of the Interior, the Menominees won congressional approval of their demands to be reinstated as a federally recognized tribe eligible for the federal services and benefits provided Indians. A bill was introduced by Wisconsin's senators and Representative Froehlich on May 2, 1973. Hearings were held in Menominee County as well as in Washington, and massive support for restoration was exhibited. Prominent among those testifying in favor of the measure was Ada Deer, who summarized once more the persuasive arguments of the Menominees:

> We believe that termination has produced three major long-range effects on the Menominee people, each one a disaster in itself.

52. For details on the troubles brought by termination, see Peroff, *Menominee Drums*, pp. 128–90; Shames, *Freedom with Reservation*, pp. 7–66; and the congressional hearings on restoration cited in note 54 below.
53. Peroff, *Menominee Drums*, pp. 175–224; Shames, *Freedom with Reservation*, pp. 67–107.

First, termination has transferred Menominee County into a "pocket of poverty" kept from total ruin only by massive transfusions of special Federal and State aid, welfare payments, and OEO spending.

Second, termination has forced our community to sell its assets. Consequently, both tribal and individual assets were lost at an incredible rate.

Third, the mechanics of the termination plan has denied the Menominee people a democracy.[54]

The House passed the measure 404 to 3 on October 16, and the Senate added its approval on December 7. President Nixon signed the bill on December 22. "The signing of H.R. 10717," he said, "represents an important turning point in the history of the American Indian people. By restoring the Menominee Indian Tribe to Federal trust status, the United States has at last made a clear reversal of a policy which was wrong, the policy of forcibly terminating Indian tribal status." The law (P.L. 93–197) repealed the termination act of June 17, 1954, and returned the Menominee Tribe to full federal status. It provided for the election of a Menominee Restoration Committee, which was authorized to implement the act and to govern the tribe until a constitution could be drawn up and a new government established. A new tribal roll would add members who were born since the roll was closed in 1954.[55]

Restoration was in the hands of its friends, and Ada Deer was chosen to head the Menominee Restoration Committee. Reversing termination was not a simple matter, however, for it meant disentangling public from private assets and sorting out jurisdictional responsibilities as the county became a reservation again. Finally, on April 22, 1975, Secretary of the Interior Morton and Ada Deer signed a deed conveying Menominee tribal land back to trust status. Unfortunately, internal tribal dissension marred the new order, and Deer and her associates in governing the tribe were soon subjected to criticisms similar to those they had made against the old MEI. A group of activists who called themselves the Menominee Warrior Society, in order to publicize their grievances, on New Year's Day 1975 seized

---

54. "Menominee Restoration Act," *Hearings before the Subcommittee on Indian Affairs of the Committee on Interior and Insular Affairs, House of Representatives, 93d Congress, 1st Session, on H.R. 7421* (1973), testimony of Ada Deer, May 25, 1973, p. 33; "Menominee Restoration Act," *Hearings before the Subcommittee on Indian Affairs of the Committee on Interior and Insular Affairs, United States Senate, 93d Congress, 1st Session, on S. 1687* (1973); *House Report* no. 93–572, 93–1, serial 13020–5; *Senate Report* no. 93–604, 93–1, serial 13017–8.

55. *Public Papers of the Presidents: Nixon, 1973,* p. 1023; 87 *United States Statutes* 770–73.

the Alexian Brothers novitiate at Gresham, Wisconsin. Their thirty-four day occupancy of the building under siege became a media event that rivaled the occupation of Wounded Knee. The Menominee People's Committee, dissidents who supported the Warrior Society, called for the immediate resignation of Deer and her friends, claiming that tribal disunity was a result of the "dictatorial, sarcastic, and arrogant attitudes" of the group.[56] Although the novitiate was evacuated and some of those who seized it were brought to trial, the turmoil among the Menominees did not cease. It led to considerable physical violence on the reservation, and it seriously obstructed the necessary formation of the new tribal government. Not until November 12, 1976, did the tribe vote approval of a constitution, and then by a relatively close vote of 468 to 426. When that was accomplished, Ada Deer resigned, saying it was time for new leadership to accept responsibility. "Perhaps she is right," the *Milwaukee Journal* editorialized, "for her work inevitably created controversy that must be overcome if the Menominees' new self-rule relationship with the federal government is to succeed."[57]

The restoration of the Menominee Tribe was possible because those Indians had maintained a cohesive community with their own government (beset by troubles as it was) and had preserved much of their tribal land base. A similar reversal of termination was not feasible for the Klamath Indians, but some smaller groups that had been terminated in the 1950s were restored to federal status. These were the Confederated Tribes of Siletz Indians in Oregon, the Wyandotte, Peoria, and Ottawa tribes of Oklahoma, and certain bands of Paiute Indians in Utah.[58]

The restoration actions effectively destroyed the termination policy, although Congress still did not formally reject House Concurrent Resolution no. 108 of 1953, which remained an irritating symbol of the hated program.

56. *Milwaukee Sentinel*, January 22, 1975. The story of the Warrior Society's actions was fully reported in the *Milwaukee Sentinel* and the *Milwaukee Journal*, as well as in national news media. A detailed account of the seizure of the novitiate and the negotiations for its evacuation by the Indians is in John P. Adams, "Why the Alexians Gave the Abbey to the Indians," *Christian Century* 92 (March 5, 1975): 223–28.

57. *Milwaukee Journal*, November 13 and December 10, 1976.

58. 91 *United States Statutes* 1415–19 (Siletz); 92 *United States Statutes* 246–47 (Oklahoma tribes); 94 *United States Statutes* 317–22 (Paiute). See also "The Siletz Restoration Bill: Background Information," *American Indian Journal* 1 (November 1976): 11–13.

CHAPTER 45

Advances in Indian Rights and Responsibilities

Indian Education. Indian Health.

Indian Child Welfare Act.

Indian Self-Determination Act.

American Indian Policy Review Commission.

Although the return of Blue Lake, the settlement of Alaska land claims, and the reversal of Menominee termination were important links in the new chain of Indian self-determination, they affected only particular tribes or regions. The federal government in the decade of the 1970s moved forward as well in areas that affected all Indians. The government was determined to broaden Indian participation in programs that touched their lives and thus to lessen the paternalism that everyone admitted had had a deleterious effect upon the Indian communities.

INDIAN EDUCATION

The drive for Indian self-determination was nowhere more pronounced than in education. The responsibility of the federal government to provide educational programs was recognized and increasingly supported by congressional appropriations, but there was a new insistence on the part of both the executive branch and Congress that the programs meet the special educational and cultural needs of the Indians and that direction and control of the schools be placed in Indian hands in order to assure these goals.[1]

1. There is a succinct account of education policies and programs in *Felix S. Cohen's Handbook of Federal Indian Law*, 1982 ed. (Charlottesville, Virginia: Michie, Bobbs-

The report on Indian education by the Senate Special Subcommittee on Indian Education in 1969, with its harsh criticism of the existing state of affairs, struck a responsive chord in Congress. An educational amendments bill introduced in the Ninety-second Congress in 1971 (S. 659) contained a special title relating to Indian education that the Senate committee considered "a vital first step" in responding to the recommendations of the 1969 report. The measure was the subject of extensive hearings and reports and was treated for a while as an entirely separate bill (S. 2482).[2]

As the Educational Amendments Act of 1972 (P.L. 92–318) finally emerged on June 23, 1972, it included Title IV, the Indian Education Act, which embodied the amended provisions of the original bills and provided striking advances and changes in the Indian educational scene. It directed input from Indian communities on the use of funds under the Federally Impacted Areas Act (P.L. 81–874), authorized grants for special programs to improve elementary and secondary education for Indians in both public schools and federal Indian schools, and provided aid for adult education.[3]

A dramatic departure from previous education programs was the establishment of an Office of Indian Education in the Department of Health, Education, and Welfare to administer the provisions of the act. The law also created a National Advisory Council on Indian Education, composed of fifteen Indians or Alaska Natives appointed by the president, to advise the commissioner of education, review applications for grants, evaluate programs and projects, and provide technical assistance to local educational agencies or to Indian agencies and organizations. The purpose of the new council was set forth by the Senate committee: "One of the primary findings of the Senate Special Subcommittee on Indian Education and the Education Subcommittee hearings was evidence of an overriding paternalism in Federal policy, resulting in programs and administration which crushed Indian culture and values. The Committee intends that the National Council, having a majority of Indian members, shall have sufficient

---

Merrill, 1982), pp. 192–95, 678–96. A description of recent education programs is given in American Indian Policy Review Commission, Task Force Five, *Report on Indian Education* (Washington: GPO, 1976). A useful article that deals with Indian education legislation is Daniel M. Rosenfelt, "Toward a More Coherent Policy for Funding Indian Education," *Law and Contemporary Problems* 40 (Winter 1976): 190–223.

2. "Indian Education Act of 1971," *Hearing before the Committee on Interior and Insular Affairs, United States Senate, 92d Congress, 1st Session, on S. 2482* (1971); "Indian Education Act of 1971," *Hearings before the General Subcommittee on Education of the Committee on Education and Labor, House of Representatives, 92d Congress, 2d Session, on H.R. 8937 and S. 2482* (1972); *Senate Report* no. 92–346, 92–1, serial 12931–2; *Senate Report* no. 92–384, 92–1, serial 12924–4.

3. 86 *United States Statutes* 334–45.

policy voice in the Office of Education to reverse this paternalism. . . . Indian programs should thus be fashioned to meet Indian needs and preserve Indian culture, language, and traditional values."[4]

Thus was established a dual system of federal aid to Indian education. The Bureau of Indian Affairs in the Department of the Interior continued to run its Indian schools, but now there were added as well the programs administered by the Office of Indian Education in the Department of Health, Education, and Welfare. In fiscal year 1980, appropriations for Indian education under the Department of the Interior amounted to $270 million; those under the Department of Education (established in 1979), to $214 million.[5] An important distinction between the two systems was the definition of those to be aided. The Bureau of Indian Affairs, by and large, provided schools for reservation Indians, with some off-reservation boarding schools for special needs, and it retained responsibility for the use of Johnson-O'Malley Act funds for Indian programs in the public schools. This limitation to Indians falling under the responsibility of the Bureau of Indian Affairs was too narrow for the senators who sponsored the Indian Education Act of 1972, and the law was worded to apply not only to federally recognized tribes but broadly to *all* Indians and Alaska Natives. The reasons were these:

> The broad definition is used in order to insure that State-recognized tribes and off-reservation Indians are included in the definitions . . . ; the exclusion of terminated Indians from this definition would not appear warranted. These native Americans do not become non-Indians by an Act of Congress; their formal relationship with the United States is simply changed by termination legislation. The In-

4. *Senate Report* no. 92–346, p. 102. The National Advisory Council on Indian Education sent annual reports to Congress beginning in 1974. The new council replaced the Special Indian Education Subcommittee of the National Council on Indian Opportunity, which had agreed in 1972 to serve as a special advisory board for the Office of Education. *NCIO News* 2 (June 1972): 8; memorandum from the secretary of health, education, and welfare to C. D. Ward, July 12, 1973, Records of the National Council on Indian Opportunity, National Advisory Council on Indian Education, box 59, National Archives, Record Group 220. See also *Between Two Milestones: The First Report to the President of the United States by the Special Education Subcommittee of the National Council on Indian Opportunity*, November 30, 1972, reprinted also in *First Annual Report to the Congress of the United States from the National Advisory Council on Indian Education*, May 1974, pp. 317–424.

5. "Fact Sheet, Government-Wide Funding for Indian Programs, 1980–1982," in "Department of the Interior and Related Agencies Appropriations for 1982," *Hearings before a Subcommittee of the Committee on Appropriations, House of Representatives, 97th Congress, 1st Session, Subcommittee on the Department of the Interior and Related Agencies* (1981), part 9, p. 1279.

dian Education Act provides special programs for Indians because of the special, remedial education needs of Indian children, not necessarily because of any trust responsibility towards, or treaty obligation to, these Indians. Non-terminated Indians in rural and urban areas across the country, just as Indians living on Federal trust lands, have special educational needs and problems of the nature described in the final report of the Special Subcommittee on Indian Education. The needs and problems of terminated Indians are no different in kind from these other groups; in fact, they may be more acute.[6]

The divided jurisdiction over Indian education almost came to an end in 1979, when the Department of Education was established as a separate cabinet-level agency, for the original House bill provided for transfer of the education programs of the Bureau of Indian Affairs to the new department. That proposal was vigorously opposed by Indians and Indian organizations, who (whatever their continuing cries about the bureaucratic evils of the Bureau of Indian Affairs) were convinced that the old bureau best understood their needs. Representative Dale E. Kildee of Michigan, after leading the successful attack on the transfer, remarked: "With one voice the Indians and native American tribes and nations across the breadth of the country opposed this effort to transfer the Bureau's Indian education responsibilities to the new Department of Education. . . . I have served in some capacity as a legislator for over 15 years, and I have never really seen such a massive grassroots lobbying effort." Commissioner of Indian Affairs William Hallett argued that removing Indian education from the Bureau of Indian Affairs would create an opportunity to lessen or discontinue treaty obligations to the tribes. Nevertheless, Indian leaders were disappointed when the secretary of education, under reorganization authority granted by Congress, did not continue the Office of Indian Education as a separate entity but placed it under the assistant secretary for elementary and secondary education.[7]

The Indian education programs that remained the responsibility of the

---

6. *Senate Report* no. 92–384, pp. 5–6. The definitions are set forth in section 453 of the law, 86 *United States Statutes* 345.

7. "Oversight Hearings on the Implementation of Indian Education Amendments," *Hearings before the Subcommittee on Elementary, Secondary, and Vocational Education of the Committee on Education and Labor, House of Representatives, 96th Congress, 1st Session* (1980), p. 168; foreword by Michael P. Doss, *Education for Indian Survival as a People, a Goal for the 1980's: The Seventh Annual Report [of the National Advisory Council on Indian Education] to the Congress of the United States,* June 1980, pp. v–vi; interview with William Hallett, "The New Commissioner Gets Down to Business," *American Indian Journal* 6 (March 1980): 20.

Bureau of Indian Affairs continued to change in the direction of greater attention to specific Indian needs and increasing control by the Indians of
their children's education. The policy was clearly stated when Morris
Thompson became commissioner:

> The Bureau of Indian Affairs proposes to be as responsible to In-
> dian requests for change as it can be and to make possible increasing
> acceptance of responsibility for the direction of their children's edu-
> cation by Indian people. The objectives are:
>
> (1) Provide for a legitimate Indian voice in all education programs
> operated by the BIA.
>
> (2) Help Indian communities provide for each student a program
> of high quality which will prepare the individual to make informed
> choices through his life including those instances where the schools
> are not operated by BIA.[8]

One instance of the new agitation for an effective Indian voice in education was the growing concern about the dichotomy in the use of Johnson-
O'Malley funds for basic support of the operating needs of the school districts, on the one hand, and for programs to meet the special needs of
Indian children, on the other. Bureau of Indian Affairs regulations of 1957
allowed the school districts to use Johnson-O'Malley funds for basic support "to accommodate unmet financial needs of school districts related to
the presence of large blocks of non-taxable Indian-owned property in the
district and relatively large numbers of Indian children which create situations which local funds are inadequate to meet." Although Congress in
1958 allowed public school districts to receive funds under both the Federally Impacted Areas Act and the Johnson-O'Malley Act, with the intention
that the former would be used for basic support in lieu of taxes and the
latter for special Indian programs, no clear regulations existed. School districts were generally allowed to spend Johnson-O'Malley funds as they saw
fit, to the neglect of the special educational needs of the Indians.[9]

Acting on the requests and recommendations of Indian groups, the Bureau of Indian Affairs on August 16, 1974, issued a new set of regulations
governing the use of Johnson-O'Malley funds. The regulations specified
that the funds were to be used for supplementary programs, defined as
those programs "designed to meet the special needs of Indian students that
may result from socio-economic conditions of the parents, or from cultural
or language difference, or other factors." And it severely restricted the use

---

8. *CHOICE: Indian Communities Have Options in Control of Education*, an undated and unpaginated pamphlet issued by the Bureau of Indian Affairs about 1974.

9. 22 *Federal Register* 10533 (December 24, 1957); 72 *United States Statutes* 559.

of the funds for operational support of the schools. More important, the
new regulations directed that the Indians concerned should, through Indian education committees, "participate in the planning, development,
evaluation, and monitoring of all programs." The Indian committees had
authority to approve or reject programs and thus in effect to control use
of the funds under contract. This was a dramatic move toward self-
determination. Indian tribes themselves, furthermore, received Johnson-
O'Malley contracts.[10]

The concern for Indian rights in education extended beyond parental
control of schools and their programs to the fundamental rights of the children in the schools. On September 4, 1974, the Bureau of Indian Affairs
published regulations governing student rights and due process procedures
for schools operated by the Bureau of Indian Affairs or under contract with
the bureau. These regulations, like all such documents, depended in large
part upon their implementation by local school personnel, but they were
evidence of the distance educational policies had come since the days
nearly half a century earlier when John Collier was railing against dictatorial and repressive control in the bureau's schools. The regulations listed
essential rights, some with a specificity that echoed the times, including:

> The right to freedom of religion and culture.
> The right to freedom of speech and expression, including symbolic
> expression, such as display of buttons, posters, choice of dress, and
> length of hair, so long as the symbolic expression does not unrea-
> sonably and in fact disrupt the educational process or endanger the
> health and safety of the student or others.
> The right to freedom from discrimination.[11]

The drive for greater control by the Indians of the education of their
children was given legislative sanction by Title II of the Indian Self-
Determination and Education Assistance Act of 1975. The law amended
the Johnson-O'Malley Act to require Indian parent advisory committees in
districts where the school boards had less than a majority of Indian members, with authority to develop new Johnson-O'Malley programs and to ap-

10. 39 *Federal Register* 30114−16. These regulations were codified in 25 *Code of Fed-
eral Regulations* 33, which was replaced in 1975 by parts 271−77; see especially part 273.
See also "Administration of the Johnson-O'Malley Act," *Hearing before the Committee
on Interior and Insular Affairs, United States Senate, 93d Congress, 2d Session, on
Rules and Regulations for the Administration of the Johnson-O'Malley Act* (1975). The
Navajo Tribe in 1976, for example, received a contract for $7.3 million for Johnson-
O'Malley programs serving the reservation; the tribe subcontracted with local schools
and school districts. Bureau of Indian Affairs, news release, August 24, 1976.
11. 39 *Federal Register* 32741−42, codified in 25 *Code of Federal Regulations* 35.3.

prove or disapprove existing contracts; and it directed the secretary of the interior to review education plans for contracting agencies to make sure that the special needs of Indian students were adequately cared for. Funds were authorized for the construction of schools for Indians residing on trust lands and for reimbursement of local schools for educating out-of-state Indian children boarding in federal dormitories.[12]

These progressive changes did not end congressional concern for Indian education. The House Committee on Education and Labor at the beginning of the Ninety-fifth Congress appointed a special Advisory Study Group on Indian Education, which in conjunction with the Subcommittee on Elementary, Secondary, and Vocational Education held hearings and conducted on-site visits. The study group pinpointed continuing problems: lack of adequate Indian involvement in the programs of both public and federal schools; need for increased funds for basic education programs for Indian children; lack of adequate funding for special Indian programs; and need for a better coordinated educational system within the Bureau of Indian Affairs. The group asserted that bureaucratic inertia thwarted possible administrative changes and that many bureau employees were still reluctant to solicit and encourage Indian input. "The Bureau employees, Indian and non-Indian alike," the subcommittee charged, "still support the outmoded concept of 'doing things for the Indians.' Congress must take immediate steps to see that this misguided policy, already repudiated by the Indian Self-Determination and Education Assistance Act of 1975, is changed forthwith." Especially criticized were the lack of standards for either education programs or boarding facilities, control over education programs by noneducators, lack of accountability on the part of bureau employees, and a dearth of information on school construction needs.[13]

To correct the defects, Congress inserted in the Education Amendments Act of 1978 (P.L. 95–561) a special section on Indian education (Title XI). The law made more specific the Indian input required for entitlements to federal assistance under the Federally Impacted Areas Act, provided for equitable distribution of school operational funds, and directed the establishment of priorities for school construction projects. It directed the secretary of the interior, in cooperation with Indian tribes and organizations, to develop standards for basic education in Bureau of Indian Affairs and

12. 88 *United States Statutes* 2213–17.
13. There were five sets of oversight hearings of the House Subcommittee on Elementary, Secondary, and Vocational Education in the 95th Congress, 1st session, running from February to October 1977. See also "Indian Basic Education Act," *Hearings before the Subcommittee on Elementary, Secondary, and Vocational Education of the Committee on Education and Labor, House of Representatives, 95th Congress, 2d Session, on H.R. 9810* (1978); *House Report* no. 95–1137, 95–2, serial 13204–4, pp. 112–13.

contract schools and for dormitory situations. In addition, there were amendments to the Indian Education Act of 1972, which increased the scope of assistance for special education needs of Indians, extended eligibility for funding to schools run by Indians under contract with the Bureau of Indian Affairs, and added programs for "gifted" Indian children and for preschool children. Regional centers were authorized to provide Indians with information on available grants and technical assistance in preparing grant proposals.[14]

A major innovation was the restructuring of the Bureau of Indian Affairs educational administration required by the legislation. Educational programs were still the ultimate responsibility of the secretary of the interior, but the programs were placed in the hands of the director of the bureau's Office of Indian Education Programs, who would formulate, monitor, and evaluate education policies and programs and would deal directly with educators in the field, bypassing the commissioner of Indian affairs, area directors, and agency superintendents. In December 1978 Earl J. Barlow, a Blackfoot Indian with extensive experience in Indian education in Montana, was appointed to the newly augmented position. The law also gave substantial authority to local Bureau of Indian Affairs school boards by allowing them to control daily program decisions, budget, and personnel. The Senate subcommittee saw this as a middle course between total control by the bureau and tribal contracting for a school under the Self-Determination Act of 1975. Another significant change was the removal of education personnel actions (teacher hiring and the like) from the civil service processes, with the hope of eliminating the "cumbersome process of recruitment" under the civil service system. The bureau issued elaborate regulations to govern this transfer and to protect the job security of the school personnel.[15]

The act of 1978 directed: "It shall be the policy of the Bureau, in carrying out the functions of the Bureau, to facilitate Indian control of Indian affairs in all matters relating to education," and it directed the secretary of the interior to develop and publish a "set of education policies, procedures, and practices for education-related action of the Bureau." These regulations were published in the *Federal Register* on October 9, 1979. The "mission statement," with which the regulations began, declared:

> The mission of the Bureau of Indian Affairs, Office of Indian Education Programs, is to provide quality education opportunities from

14. 92 *United States Statutes* 2313–33.
15. Ibid., 2319–26; 44 *Federal Register* 58095–104, codified in 25 *Code of Federal Regulations* 31; *House Report* no. 95–1137, pp. 119–20.

early childhood through life in accordance with the Tribes' needs for cultural and economic well-being in keeping with the wide diversity of Indian Tribes and Alaska Native villages as distinct cultural and governmental entities. The Bureau shall manifest consideration of the whole person, taking into account the spiritual, mental, physical and cultural aspects of the person within family and Tribal or Alaska Native village contexts.[16]

The regulations provided, among other things, specific policies for Indian participation in policy making, student rights, respect for family and religious freedom, multilingual education, choice of schools, recruitment of Indian educators, a community school concept, and alternative and innovative programs.[17]

Self-determination in the running of Indian community colleges was another element of the new educational policies. The model was the Navajo Community College, which had been founded in 1969 and supported largely by grants from the Office of Economic Opportunity. The college at first used space in the Many Farms High School building but soon needed its own quarters. In the Navajo Community College Act of December 15, 1971, Congress appropriated $5.5 million to aid in the construction and operation of the institution (augmenting other funds from the Department of Housing and Urban Development, the Economic Development Administration, industry and foundations, and the tribe itself). The college, with about one third of its students in an academic course and two-thirds in vocational training, enrolled Navajos of all ages. It was intended to supplement other college opportunities and aimed specifically at those Indians who were unwilling to leave home to enroll in colleges or were unable to adjust to new environments.[18]

Support of the successful Navajo institution was used as an argument for further aid to Indian community colleges, and in 1978 Congress passed the Tribally Controlled Community College Act, which provided (through grants of $4,000 per year for each full-time student) "for the operation and improvement of tribally controlled community colleges to insure continued and expanded educational opportunities for Indian students." The eligibility requirements dictated that a college must be governed by an Indian board and have a philosophy and plan of operation directed to meet the needs of Indians. The secretary of the interior was directed to provide

16. 44 *Federal Register* 58099, codified in 25 *Code of Federal Regulations* 31a.3.
17. 44 *Federal Register* 58099–101; 25 *Code of Federal Regulations* 31a.4.
18. 85 *United States Statutes* 646; *Senate Report* no. 92–548, 92–1, serial 12929–6; *House Report* no. 92–636, 92–1, serial 12932–5.

feasibility studies, aid in drawing up grant applications and budgets, and technical assistance in operating the schools.[19]

Amid all the innovations and legislative changes, the fundamental work of educating Indian children progressed, with notable increases in the number of students reached. In fiscal year 1979, Indian students numbering 221,271 received government funds for their schooling through the Bureau of Indian Affairs. The bureau itself ran 174 schools (68 boarding and 106 day) with an enrollment of 41,598 and maintained fifteen dormitories at public schools to care for 1,973 children (19.7 percent of known students). In addition, 33 schools (13 boarding and 20 day) with 6,412 students were run on contract by Indian groups (2.9 percent). Of the students in these categories of schools, 72.8 percent were full-bloods and only 6.9 percent had less than half Indian blood. In the public schools with funding under the Johnson-O'Malley Act there were 171,290 Indian children (77.7 percent).[20]

The bare statistics, of course, do not disclose the quality of the education, and there was always dissatisfaction on the part of Indians and other critics of government Indian education. A study of early childhood education mandated by Congress and carried out under contract with the Bureau of Indian Affairs reported in 1976 that the educational programs serving Indians were "inadequate in their responsiveness to the culture and life experiences of the children and families they serve; in staff training and development; in the number of Native Americans in professional positions; in health, psychological and social services; and in programs for handicapped children or for children who show unusual promise."[21]

That the programs were less than perfect was acknowledged by all, and it was to meet such deficiencies that Congress repeatedly provided new

19. 92 *United States Statutes* 1325–31; 44 *Federal Register* 67040–48, codified in 25 *Code of Federal Regulations* 32b. The Navajo Community College was excluded from the general operation of the act but got special support in Title II, the Navajo Community College Assistance Act of 1978. For arguments and legislative history, see "Indian Education," *Hearing before the Subcommittee on Postsecondary Education of the Committee on Education and Labor, House of Representatives, 95th Congress, 1st Session, on H.R. 9158, to Provide for Grants to Tribally Controlled Community Colleges* (1977); *Senate Report* no. 95–502, 95–1, serial 13168–11; *House Report* no. 95–1558, 95–2, serial 13201–12.

20. *Statistics concerning Indian Education*, 1979, pp. 1, 35. These figures do not include Indian children attending public or private schools that did not receive government funds. For an official and favorable description of the federal education programs, see *Indian Education: Steps to Progress in the 70's* (Washington: Office of Education Programs, Bureau of Indian Affairs, 1973).

21. *House Report* no. 93–1293, 93–2, serial 13061–8, p. 8; *Young Native Americans and Their Families: Educational Needs Assessment and Recommendations* (Washington: Office of Indian Education Programs, Bureau of Indian Affairs, 1976), p. iv.

legislation in attempts to bring Indian education up to acceptable standards. All measures leading to increased community control of the Indian schools, however, have been limited by the inescapable fact that the financial support of the schools comes from outside sources. Yet the heavy federal funding for Indian education through Bureau of Indian Affairs schools, support of special programs in public schools, and special scholarship programs for Indians undoubtedly will continue, whatever the commitment to Indian autonomy and self-determination.[22]

INDIAN HEALTH

The status of Indian health and of health services for Indians continued to exhibit the dichotomy that had been manifested ever since the beginning of active concern for Indian health early in the twentieth century. On the one hand, there was remarkable progress from year to year in the eradication of diseases among the Indians and substantial growth in health facilities and their use by the Indians. But on the other hand, there was the disquieting lag of Indian health behind that of the total population of the United States.[23]

The statistics on progress were indeed impressive, as reported by the Indian Health Service (see Table 19). Dr. Emery A. Johnson, director of the Indian Health Service, credited the improvements to increased availability and accessibility of health services, advances in the home environment (better housing, safe water supplies, proper sewage disposal), and increased emphasis on health education. "The investments made in providing health care for Indian people," he said, "are now showing sound dividends."[24]

The encouraging state of Indian health that Johnson reported was due in large part to the increases in appropriations that came after the health programs had been transferred to the Public Health Service in 1955. Funds appropriated for Indian health in 1955 were about $25 million; they had risen to about $72 million in 1965. Appropriations for the Indian Health Service

22. Daniel M. Rosenfelt, "Indian Schools and Community Control," *Stanford Law Review* 25 (April 1973): 550. For essays on aspects of Indian education written by Indian authors, see Thomas Thompson, ed., *The Schooling of Native Americans* (Washington: American Association of Colleges for Teacher Education, in collaboration with the Teacher Corps, United States Office of Education, 1978).

23. For an account of health developments between 1955 and 1967, see Alan L. Sorkin, *American Indians and Federal Aid* (Washington: Brookings Institution, 1971), pp. 51–65. A good guide to recent public documents on Indian health is *Cohen's Handbook of Federal Indian Law*, 1982 ed., pp. 698–701.

24. "Department of the Interior and Related Agencies Appropriations for 1982," part 9, pp. 1–4.

TABLE 19: Health Program Accomplishments

Health Improvements (calendar years 1954–1956 to 1976–1978)	Percentage decrease
Death rates	
Infant	74
Under 28 days	65
28 days to 11 months	75
Maternal	90
Influenza and pneumonia	67
Certain diseases of early infancy	75
Tuberculosis, all forms	91
Gastroenteritis, etc.	90
Congenital malformations	46
Incidence rates	
New active tuberculosis cases	78
Trachoma	96

Increased use of services (fiscal years 1955 to 1980)	Percentage Increase
Hospital admissions	122
Outpatient visits	792
Dental services	918

SOURCE: "Department of the Interior and Related Agencies Appropriations for 1982," *Hearings before a Subcommittee of the Committee on Appropriations, House of Representatives, 97th Congress, 1st Session, Subcommittee on the Department of the Interior and Related Agencies* (1981), part 9, p. 22.

in 1980 were a massive $547 million, with another $36 million for nutritional improvement from the Department of Agriculture.[25] In the 1970s, moreover, two pieces of legislation made a dramatic impact—the Indian Self-Determination and Education Assistance Act of 1975 and the Indian Health Care Improvement Act of 1976. The first of these did for health services what it did for education and other federal Indian programs: it enabled and encouraged Indian tribes to take over and run the programs themselves.[26] By 1980 a small but significant move had been made in this direction, and the rate of transfer was rapidly accelerating. Important health services formerly provided solely by the Indian Health Service were now provided by tribal organizations through contracts. Fully functioning health programs were operated by the Seneca Nation in New York, the Menomi-

25. Figures for 1955 and 1965 from Sorkin, *American Indians and Federal Aid*, p. 52; figures for 1980 from "Fact Sheet: Government-Wide Funding for Indian Programs," March 20, 1981, in "Department of the Interior and Related Agencies Appropriations for 1982," part 9, p. 1279.
26. 88 *United States Statutes* 2206–8.

nee Tribe in Wisconsin, and two Alaska Native corporations. The Creek Nation in Oklahoma, the Navajo Health Foundation in Arizona, and the two Alaska corporations operated their own hospitals. In addition, tribes ran 252 health clinics and stations. About 10 percent of the tribes delivered all their own health services, and many others ran smaller or single elements of health programs. Almost 90 percent of eligible tribes were responsible for some part of their own health services.[27]

The Indian Health Care Improvement Act (P.L. 94–437) of September 30, 1976, came as a result of strong agitation to lessen or remove the gap between Indian health conditions and those of the total population. Extensive congressional hearings in 1975 and 1976 placed in sharp focus, once again, what was described as the deplorable status of Indian health.[28] "The sad facts are," a House committee reported in the spring of 1976, "that the majority of Indians still live in an environment characterized by inadequate and understaffed health facilities; improper or nonexistent waste disposal and water supply systems; and continuing dangers of deadly or disabling diseases. These circumstances, in combination, cause Indians and Alaska Natives to suffer a health status far below that of the general population and plague Indian communities and Native villages with health concerns other American communities have forgotten as long as 25 years ago." Congress found inadequate and outdated facilities, a shortage of medical personnel, insufficient health services and lack of full access to those that existed, a shortage of housing for staff at isolated hospitals and health stations, and a severe lack of safe water and sanitary waste disposal systems. There was no doubt that Congress recognized the seriousness of the situation. As the House committee asserted:

The most basic human right must be the right to enjoy decent health. Certainly, any effort to fulfill Federal responsibilities to the

27. Statement of Emery A. Johnson, March 2, 1981, "Department of the Interior and Related Agencies Appropriations for 1982," part 9, p. 2. As of October 1, 1980, the Indian Health Service ran 49 hospitals, the tribes 4; the Indian Health Service ran 202 health centers and stations, the tribes 252. Ibid., p. 24.

28. "Indian Health Care Improvement Act," *Hearings before the Subcommittee on Indian Affairs of the Committee on Interior and Insular Affairs, House of Representatives, 94th Congress, 1st Session, on H.R. 2525 and Related Bills* (1975); "Indian Health Care Improvement Act," *Hearings before the Subcommittee on Health and the Environment of the Committee on Interstate and Foreign Commerce, House of Representatives, 94th Congress, 2d Session, on H.R. 2525* (1976). The task force on Indian health of the American Indian Policy Review Commission also studied the problems and made recommendations, but the task force was dissatisfied with its own work; see American Indian Policy Review Commission, Task Force Six, *Report on Indian Health* (Washington: GPO, 1976).

Indian people must begin with the provision of health services. In fact, heath services must be the cornerstone upon which rest all other Federal programs for the benefit of Indians. Without a proper health status, the Indian people will be unable to fully avail themselves of the many economic, educational, and social programs already directed to them or which this Congress and future Congresses will provide them.

The goal was "to raise the status of health care for American Indians and Alaska Natives, over a seven-year period, to a level equal to that enjoyed by other American citizens."[29]

The new law sought to attain this goal by a program of incremental funding rather than through a "crash" program. As originally drafted, it called for appropriations of $1.6 billion over the seven-year period, but that sum was too much for an administration worried about inflation, and in the end the law authorized specific appropriations of about $475 million for various programs in fiscal years 1978, 1979, and 1980 and called for new legislation to authorize appropriations for 1981–1984. The law established grants, scholarship programs, and continuing education allowances to aid in recruiting Indians and other persons for the Indian Health Service, authorized funds to eliminate backlogs in health care services and for the construction and renovation of hospitals and health centers, and lifted the prohibition against Medicare and Medicaid reimbursement for services performed by the Indian Health Service. Of particular significance was the provision for the establishment of urban health centers to care for the large urban Indian population. In addition, the law directed a feasibility study on a school of medicine to train Indians.[30]

The Indian Health Service in 1980 drew up a national plan for Indian health care service, based on 216 tribal and 34 urban health plans. A health service priority system was developed, with five levels of deficiencies, so that the tribes and urban groups most in need could receive special funding.[31]

The Indian Health Care Improvement Act did not usher in the millennium, to be sure, for many health problems facing Indian communities were not amenable to dramatic sudden solutions. And as old ones were eliminated, new ones appeared. "The scourges of yesterday such as tu-

29. *House Report* no. 94–1026 (4 parts), 94–2, serial 13134–4, quotations from part 1, pp. 13, 15; *Senate Report* no. 94–133, 94–1, serial 13096–3.

30. 90 *United States Statutes* 1400–1414. Regulations to implement the act were published in 42 *Federal Register* 59643–52 (November 18, 1977).

31. Statement of Emery A. Johnson, March 2, 1981, "Department of the Interior and Related Agencies Appropriations for 1982," part 9, p. 3.

berculosis and gastroenteritis," the Indian Health Service noted in 1980, "have been replaced by other more challenging problems, ones which require new ideas and new approaches. The Indians' health priorities of today—accidents, alcoholism, diabetes, mental health, suicides and homicides—stem not from organic causes, but from changes in their traditional lifestyles and values, and from deprivation."[32] Nor did the bureaucratic operation of the Indian Health Service escape continuing criticism.[33]

INDIAN CHILD WELFARE ACT

Nothing touched Indian self-determination more deeply than the problem of child custody and maintenance of Indian family life. White governmental concern for child welfare, however, had seriously eroded family rights. Indian children were taken from homes judged unsuitable or harmful to them by Bureau of Indian Affairs or state social workers and placed in foster or adoptive homes, usually non-Indian. What began as a sincere effort to protect the best interest of the child, as it was viewed by social workers, eventually was perceived more accurately as a force destructive of Indian families and Indian children. The involuntary separation of children from their parents that had marked the old boarding school experience was being continued now by child custody proceedings.

The Bureau of Indian Affairs became actively involved in the adoption of Indian children by non-Indian parents in 1958 with the establishment of an Indian Adoption Project, in which the bureau worked with the Child Welfare League of America. In 1961 the bureau provided funds to care for more than 2,300 dependent and neglected children from unstable or broken homes; and foster home placements began to grow, with bureau social workers referring homeless children to qualified adoptive agencies se-

32. *Indian Health Program, 1955–1980,* a pamphlet published by the Indian Health Service, 1980. See also the sections "Special Health Concerns," and "Manpower Needs," in *The Indian Health Program* (Washington: Indian Health Service, 1978), pp. 9–16, and Everett R. Rhoades, "Barriers to Health Care: The Unique Problems Facing American Indians," *Civil Rights Digest* 10 (Fall 1977): 25–31.

33. An especially sensitive point was the alleged involuntary sterilization of Indian women, which elicited public outcry from the Indians and Indian rights advocates. See Janet Karsten Larson, "'And Then There Were None': Is Federal Policy Endangering the American Indian 'Species'?" *Christian Century* 94 (January 26, 1977): 61–63; Mark Miller, Judith Miller, and Chris Szechenyi, "Native American Peoples on the Trail of Tears Once More," *America* 139 (December 9, 1978): 422–25; and a series of articles by Brint Dillingham in *American Indian Journal* in 1977. Continuing dissatisfaction with the delivery of Indian health care was expressed in two oversight hearings on Indian health before the Senate Select Committee on Indian Affairs, August 2, 1979, and January 4, 1980.

lected by the Child Welfare League.[34] The insensitivity of the bureau to Indian cultural needs can be seen in its news release of March 14, 1966,
which began: "One little, two little, three little Indians—and 206 more—
are brightening the homes and lives of 172 American families, mostly non-
Indians, who have taken the Indian waifs as their own." The bureau reported 209 children adopted during the previous seven years through the
Indian Adoption Project and a steadily growing rate of adoption. The children came from eleven states, with the majority from South Dakota (64)
and Arizona (52). "Almost all the placements," the report noted, "have
been in the east and midwest, with 49 in New York alone."[35]

By the end of the decade, as state welfare agencies moved into action,
the separation of Indian children from their families grew at an alarming
rate. The Association on American Indian Affairs, which made a special
survey of the problem in 1969 and monitored the condition of Indian families through an *Indian Family Defense* newsletter, soon brought the matter to public attention. In April 1974 the Senate Subcommittee on Indian
Affairs held hearings on "problems that American Indian families face in
raising their children and how these problems are affected by federal action
or inaction." Senator James Abourezk of South Dakota opened the hearings with a forceful statement:

> It appears that for decades Indian parents and their children have
> been at the mercy of arbitrary or abusive action of local, State, Fed-
> eral and private agency officials. Unwarranted removal of children
> from their homes is common in Indian communities. . . .
> Because of poverty and discrimination Indian families face many
> difficulties, but there is no reason or justification for believing that
> these problems make Indian parents unfit to raise their children; nor
> is there reason to believe that the Indian community itself cannot,
> within its own confines, deal with problems of child neglect when
> they do arise. Up to now, however, public and private welfare agen-
> cies seem to have operated on the premise that most Indian children
> would really be better off growing up non-Indian. The result of such
> policies has been unchecked, abusive child-removal practices, the
> lack of viable, practical rehabilitation and prevention programs for
> Indian families facing severe problems, and a practice of ignoring the
> all-important demands of Indian tribes to have a say in how their
> children and families are dealt with. Officials would seemingly rather
> place Indian children in non-Indian settings where their Indian cul-

34. CIA Report, 1961, p. 292.
35. Bureau of Indian Affairs, news release, March 14, 1966. See an update on the figures (sixty-seven more adoptions) in a news release of April 18, 1967.

ture, their Indian traditions and, in general, their entire Indian way of life is smothered.[36]

The key witness at the hearings was William Byler, executive director of the Association on American Indian Affairs, who supplied data from the association's surveys that became a staple in the arguments for reform. He asserted that "approximately 25–35 percent of all Indian children are separated from their families and placed in foster homes, adoptive homes, or institutions [including boarding schools]." In Minnesota, he reported, one child in eight under eighteen years of age was living in an adoptive home, and in 1971–1972 nearly one in four under one year of age was adopted. The disparity between rates of adoption for Indians and for non-Indians he found "shocking." In Minnesota the per capita rate was five times greater than for non-Indian children, in Montana thirteen times greater, in South Dakota sixteen times, and in Washington nineteen times. In sixteen states surveyed in 1969, about 85 percent of Indian children in foster care were in non-Indian homes. And in most of the cases Indian children had been removed from their natural families without due process of law.[37] The seriousness of the situation was confirmed by a new study done by the association for the American Indian Policy Review Commission in 1976. The study, in fact, disclosed that proportionate rates of foster care for Indians compared with non-Indians had increased, and so too had the percentage placed in non-Indian homes. The conclusions were based on a detailed investigation of nineteen states with high Indian populations.[38]

To meet the evils, legislation was introduced in both the House and the Senate in the Ninety-fifth Congress, and a new hearing was held by the Senate Select Committee on Indian Affairs on August 4, 1977, that emphasized once more the dire need for corrective action on the part of the federal government. "It is clear," the House committee reported, ". . . that the Indian child welfare crisis is of massive proportions and that Indian fam-

---

36. "Indian Child Welfare Program," *Hearings before the Subcommittee on Indian Affairs of the Committee on Interior and Insular Affairs, United States Senate, 93d Congress, 2d Session* (1975), pp. 1–2.

37. Ibid., pp. 3–8, 14–32. Byler's formal statement is reprinted in Steven Unger, ed., *The Destruction of American Indian Families* (New York: Association on American Indian Affairs, 1977), pp. 1–11; the book contains a number of essays describing the magnitude of the problem.

38. American Indian Policy Review Committee, Task Force Four, *Report on Federal, State, and Tribal Jurisdiction* (Washington: GPO, 1976), pp. 78–88, 177–242; American Indian Policy Review Commission, *Final Report* (Washington: GPO, 1977), pp. 35, 422–23. See also Gaylene J. McCartney, "The American Indian Child-Welfare Crisis: Cultural Genocide or First Amendment Preservation," *Columbia Human Rights Law Review* 7 (Fall–Winter 1975–1976): 529–51.

ilies face vastly greater risks of involuntary separation than are typical of our society as a whole."[39]

The result was the Indian Child Welfare Act of 1978 (P.L. 95–608), which became law on November 8, 1978. As had become congressional practice, the substantive sections of the law were preceded by a statement of findings and of policy. Congress asserted that "there is no measure that is more vital to the continued existence and integrity of Indian tribes than their children and that the United States has a direct interest, as trustee, in protecting Indian children." And it declared that the policy of the nation was "to protect the best interests of Indian children and to promote the stability of and security of Indian tribes and families." To do this it provided for the jurisdiction of Indian tribes in child custody proceedings and the right of the tribe or Indian parents to intervene in state court proceedings, and it set forth criteria for the placement of children removed from their parents or guardians. Preference in adoption was to be given to the child's extended family, other members of the child's tribe, or other Indian families. Protection was provided to make sure that the child was placed in an Indian cultural setting.[40]

The act, furthermore, authorized the secretary of the interior to make grants to Indian tribes and organizations for the establishment of child and family service programs on or near reservations and for the preparation and implementation of child welfare codes. The objective of these programs, the law said, was "to prevent the breaking up of Indian families and, in particular, to insure that the permanent removal of an Indian child from the custody of his parent or Indian custodian shall be a last resort." In order to strike at the problem of children absent from their families in federal boarding schools, Congress directed the secretary of the interior to prepare a study on the feasibility of providing Indian children with schools located near their homes. Detailed guidelines for the implementation of the act were published in the *Federal Register* on July 21, 1979. "In administering

39. "Indian Child Welfare Act of 1977," *Hearing before the United States Senate Select Committee on Indian Affairs, 95th Congress, 1st Session, on S. 1214, to Establish Standards for the Placement of Indian Children in Foster or Adoptive Homes, to Prevent the Breakup of Indian Families, and for Other Purposes* (1977); House Report no. 95–1386, 95–2, serial 13201–10, p. 9. See also *Senate Report* no. 95–597, 95–1, serial 13168–11. The Mormon Church had a particularly active Indian child placement center and feared that the bill would interfere with it. See the extensive Mormon testimony in the hearing.

40. 92 *United States Statutes* 3069–73. A useful general article on the act and its background is Manuel P. Guerrero, "Indian Child Welfare Act of 1978: A Response to the Threat to Indian Culture Caused by Foster and Adoptive Placements of Indian Children," *American Indian Law Review* 7, no. 1 (1979): 51–77.

the grant authority for Indian Child and Family Programs," the regulations read, "it shall be Bureau policy to emphasize the design and funding of programs to promote the stability of Indian families."[41]

Reaction to the child custody proceedings provision of the act was strongly positive. A Navajo spokesman said that there had been "many heartwarming success stories about the reunification of Navajo families," and Steven Unger, the new executive director of the Association on American Indian Affairs, reported that the tribes were "creatively and dynamically developing programs to halt and reverse the removal of children and to assure that they are well cared for within the tribal community" and that state courts and agencies were working with the tribes to see that the purposes of the act were fulfilled. The main complaints about the act and its implementation came in regard to the funding of the grant programs.[42]

Like other legislation, however, the Indian Child Welfare Act emitted mixed signals on the issue of self-determination. Although the law clearly aimed at preserving Indian culture through stable Indian families and established tribal jurisdiction over Indian child custody cases, it on the other hand justified federal intervention in the matter on the grounds that "Congress has plenary power over Indian affairs." The grants for tribal child and family service programs were firmly in the hands of the Bureau of Indian Affairs, and the funds came from federal, not Indian, sources.

INDIAN SELF-DETERMINATION ACT

Although nearly every act or set of regulations in the 1970s was touched by the philosophy of self-determination, of particular significance was Title I of the Indian Self-Determination and Education Assistance Act (P.L. 93–638) of January 4, 1975. This was the culmination of President Nixon's intention that the tribes should be able to escape the domination of the Bureau of Indian Affairs and take upon themselves the responsibility for programs and services provided by the federal government. "We have con-

---

41. 92 *United States Statutes* 3075–78; 44 *Federal Register* 45096–108, codified in 25 *Code of Federal Regulations* 23. Proposed new rules were printed in 45 *Federal Register* 81781–85.

42. Letter of Frank E. Paul, vice chairman of the Navajo Tribal Council, to Senate Select Committee on Indian Affairs, June 27, 1980, and statement of Steven Unger in "Oversight of the Indian Child Welfare Act," *Hearing before the Select Committee on Indian Affairs, United States Senate, 96th Congress, 2d Session* (1980), pp. 45, 118. This oversight hearing contains information on Indian dissatisfaction with the funding of the programs. A harsh criticism of the act is Russel Lawrence Barsh, "The Indian Child Welfare Act of 1978: A Critical Analysis," *Hastings Law Journal* 31 (July 1980): 1287–1336.

cluded," Nixon said in his special message on Indian affairs in 1970, "that Indians will get better programs and that public monies will be more effectively expended if the people who are most affected by these programs are responsible for operating them." To this end, the administration submitted a proposal, as part of its legislative package, to authorize transfer of programs run by the Bureau of Indian Affairs and the Indian Health Service to the Indian tribes themselves. One instance of the administration's proposal was S. 1573, introduced on April 19, 1971. The measure provided for the transfer to Indian tribes, at their request, of federal programs and services, with the federal government furnishing the funds and technical assistance. It was known as a "takeover" bill, by which the Indians would assume full responsibility. An alternative and less radical bill (S. 3157), introduced by Senator Henry Jackson on February 9, 1972, provided for limited contracting for progrms to be operated by the Indians. The two bills were the subject of hearings in May 1972.[43]

The Department of the Interior and the Department of Health, Education, and Welfare urged passage of the administration bill in preference to Senator Jackson's proposal, which they believed would fall short of what the Indians needed and wanted. Assistant Secretary of the Interior Harrison Loesch clearly distinguished the two measures: "S. 3157 is a contracting bill, designed to enable Indians to enter into contracts for the administration of Federal programs or portions thereof. S. 1573 is a bill for assumption of control of such programs by Indians. Under S. 3157 Indians would merely by parties to a contract to be negotiated between themselves and the appropriate Secretary: the terms of this contract would determine the amount of Indian involvement in a given program. Under S. 1573 Indians would obtain full control of any program for their benefit upon their request. Only this approach squarely meets the Administration goal of Indian self-determination." Loesch noted too the different manners in which program changes would be initiated. Jackson's bill gave the department secretaries authority to make decisions about which programs would be contracted for; the administration bill directed the secretaries to transfer programs to any Indian group that requested it.[44]

43. *Public Papers of the Presidents of the United States: Richard Nixon, 1970* (Washington: GPO, 1971), p. 576; *Congressional Record*, 117: 10671, 10692–93; "Indian Self-Determination," *Hearing before the Subcommittee on Indian Affairs of the Committee on Interior and Insular Affairs, United States Senate, 92d Congress, 2d Session, on S. 3157, a Bill on the "Indian Self-Determination Act of 1972," S. 1573, S. 1574, and S. 2238, Similar Measures* (1972).

44. Loesch to Jackson, April 21, 1972, and oral testimony, "Indian Self-Determination," pp. 11, 47–52. The position of the Department of Health, Education, and Welfare is given in the testimony of Assistant Secretary Laurence E. Lynn, Jr., pp. 58–67, and in Secretary Elliot L. Richardson to Jackson, May 22, 1972, p. 14.

Despite their criticism of bureau domination and their cries for self-determination, on this crucial measure the Indians backed away. When William Youpee, president of the National Tribal Chairmen's Association, was asked if there was any Indian consensus on the bills, he replied: "The only thing I would like to say, Mr. Chairman, is on the takeover bill [S. 1573], I think that perhaps this bill here, S. 3157 would probably be more receptive to the Indian people. Because I think the takeover bill is— most of the reservations kind of feel this would maybe eventually lead to termination. But in this, S. 3157, where they can contract any part of it and, more or less, are guaranteed additional funding." A similar position was taken by Franklin Ducheneaux, a spokesman for the National Congress of American Indians:

> S. 1573 and S. 1574 are companion bills providing for assumption of control by Indian tribes over BIA and IHS programs. While this approach may be the wave of the future, the bills are very complex and complicated and have not received substantial support from the Indian people. . . .
>
> This [S. 3157] is a fairly straight-forward bill. It authorizes the Secretary of Interior and HEW to contract with Indian tribes for the services the BIA and IHS carry out on Indian reservations. We favor enactment of the bill.[45]

Jackson's bill passed the Senate in August 1972 but received no action in the House in the Ninety-second Congress. It was introduced again in the next Congress as S. 1017. The administration still preferred its own assumption proposal but was willing now to support the contracting measure with some amendments as an "interim measure." New hearings indicated continued Indian support for the bill, and strong arguments were advanced for the measure. It would, at the very least, provide clear statutory authority to contract for services with the Indians tribes instead of relying on favorable interpretations of earlier scattered legislation.[46] After favor-

---

45. "Indian Self-Determination," p. 69.

46. *Senate Report* no. 92–1001, 92–2, serial 12971–5; "Indian Self-Determination and Education Program," *Hearings before the Subcommittee on Indian Affairs of the Committee on Interior and Insular Affairs, United States Senate, 93d Congress, 1st Session, on S. 1017 and Related Bills* (1973). There is a discussion of the legislative history of the bills in *Senate Report* no. 93–682, 93–2, serial 13057–1, pp. 18–19. Prior to the new law, authority for contracting with the Indians relied on a combination of four basic acts: the so-called "Buy Indian" Act of 1910 (36 *United States Statutes* 861), which waived competitive bidding on contracts with Indian tribes; the Johnson-O'Malley Act of 1934 (48 *United States Statutes* 596) for contracts for educational services; the Snyder Act of 1921 (42 *United States Statutes* 208); and an 1834 law (4 *United States Statutes* 737), which authorized tribal supervision over federal employees.

able action in both houses, the bill became law (P.L. 93–638) on January 4, 1975. Commissioner of Indian Affairs Morris Thompson said it "marked the beginning of a new era in Federal-Indian relations."[47]

The twofold policy of the government was asserted in the preamble to the law: the United States recognized its obligation to respect "the strong expression of the Indian people for self-determination by assuring maximum Indian participation in the direction of educational as well as other Federal services to Indian communities so as to render such services more responsive to the needs and desires of those communities"; and Congress declared its commitment to "the maintenance of the Federal Government's unique and continuing relationship with and responsibility to the Indian people" through a self-determination policy that would provide an orderly transition from federal domination to effective Indian participation in planning and administering programs.

The tension between the two points, however, was not eliminated by the law. The Bureau of Indian Affairs saw the law and the regulations issued to implement it as furnishing tribes with four new or improved tools for self-development and self-determination: (1) grants to tribal governing bodies to strengthen tribal governments and to help them prepare for planning, contracting for, and monitoring federal programs; (2) contracting for all or parts of specific federal programs and the redesigning of programs to conform better to tribal needs; (3) planning to redesign or restructure bureau programs without actually assuming administrative responsibility for them; and (4) the tribal use of federal personnel in carrying out programs.[48] Yet the secretaries of the federal departments still made basic decisions about which contracts to approve, and Indians charged that use of this ultimate authority negated the effects intended by Congress in the legislation. The law and the regulations stipulated that the burden of proof in declining a contract rested with the Bureau of Indian Affairs, that unless substantial evidence for a declination existed the bureau would enter into the proposed contract. But these assertions did not satisfy Indian spokesmen, who soon were aggressively asserting that Title I of the Indian Self-Determination Act was a disappointment, if not actually a fraud.

47. *Senate Report* no. 93–682, 93–2, serial 13057–1; *Senate Report* no. 93–762, 93–2, serial 13057–2; *House Report* no. 93–1600, 93–2, serial 13061–11; 88 *United States Statutes* 2203–17; Bureau of Indian Affairs, news release, November 26, 1975. Title II of the law, called the Indian Education Assistance Act, was in reality a separate piece of legislation; it is discussed above under Indian education.

48. *Handbook for Decision Makers on Title I of the Indian Self-Determination and Education Assistance Act* (Washington: Bureau of Indian Affairs, 1976). The regulations for implementing the act are in 40 *Federal Register* 51282–345 (November 4, 1975), codified in 25 *Code of Federal Regulations* 271.

At oversight hearings held by the Senate Select Committee on Indian Affairs in June 1977 Indian complaints were loud and clear. Tribal leaders spoke of massive resistance to contracting by employees of the Bureau of Indian Affairs—the "backlash of a paternalistic organization"—and insufficient technical assistance from the bureau. They objected to tying the contract process into the preexisting operation of the bureau with its line item budget, instead of allowing the tribes to shape their own programs, and to the increased burden of paper work. The law, the president of the National Tribal Chairmen's Association said, was "an extraordinary example of the institutional power and capacity of some Federal Bureaucracies to preserve and protect themselves against the will of the people they serve." Thus, representatives of the same organizations that had rejected legislation to allow tribes to assume full responsibility for programs and instead opted for a contracting scheme now were singing a different tune. On the other hand, there was also the fear so often expressed that contracting for programs was simply "concealed termination," or that it would lead to state jurisdiction over the reservations.[49]

The bureau's answer to the charges rested firmly on the contractural relationship between the tribe and the government, which by its very nature imposed some limitations on the contractor, and on the ultimate responsibility of the federal officials. "The act does not relieve the Bureau of program responsibility," noted Raymond Butler, acting deputy commissioner of Indian affairs. "Tribal assumption of program operations under contract is another, a different, method for carrying out the Bureau's program responsibility."[50]

Because of tribal testimony about the frustration of the intent of the act through faulty implementation, Senator Abourezk on January 31, 1978, introduced a bill to amend the law, primarily by permitting a tribe to develop a comprehensive tribal plan to be implemented by a single consolidated grant, thus simplifying the excessive paperwork and allowing for flexi-

49. "Indian Self-Determination and Education Assistance Act Implementation," *Hearings before the United States Senate Select Committee on Indian Affairs, 95th Congress, 1st Session, on Implementation of Public Law 93–638* (1977); see the statements and testimony of Albert W. Trimble, president of the Oglala Sioux Tribe, pp. 296–98; Mel Tonasket, president of the National Congress of American Indians, pp. 265–67; Joseph B. De La Cruz, president of the National Tribal Chairmen's Association, pp. 260–63; and Little Wound School Board, Kyle, South Dakota, pp. 250–53. A very critical appraisal of the act is Russel Lawrence Barsh and Ronald L. Trosper, "Title I of the Indian Self-Determination and Education Assistance Act of 1975," *American Indian Law Review* 3, no. 2 (1975): 361–95.

50. "Indian Self-Determination and Education Assistance Act Implementation," pp. 19–20.

bility in local policy determinations. There was Indian support for the amendment, but the Interior Department and the Indian Health Service opposed the measure as unnecessary because, they asserted, block grants could be made under existing authority. The bill passed the Senate in September, but it died in the House.[51]

Despite the strong rhetoric of Indian leaders about the failure of the act to provide genuine self-determination, in fact a large number of contracts were concluded under its provisions. In fiscal year 1980, 370 tribes contracted for the operation of $200 million worth of programs under the Indian Self-Determination Act, and $22.3 million was paid to the tribes to cover their overhead in the contracts. By the next year 480 grants had been made to tribal governments under the act to improve their capacity to operate federal programs under contract and in general to increase their effectiveness in serving tribal members.[52]

AMERICAN INDIAN POLICY REVIEW COMMISSION

The outbreaks of restless and frustrated Indians at the Bureau of Indian Affairs in 1972 and at Wounded Knee in early 1973 were clear evidence to many people that something needed to be done to meliorate the conditions in federal Indian relations that had led to such violence. One proposed solution came from Senator Abourezk, the leading congressional advocate of Indian rights. Abourezk on July 16, 1973, introduced a joint resolution to establish an American Indian Policy Review Commission. In defending the proposal, he criticized the existing legal relationship with the Indian people as "a complex mess" and declared: "No rational, uniform policy seems to be growing out of it. But every day, in some sort of headless, directionless way, it is shaping, or misshaping the lives of Indian people. Trying to make sense out of our Indian policy, that is, trying to come up with some coherent, rational, clear definition of it, is presently impossible. Our policy is labyrynthian. It is like a catacomb. It is layer upon layer of patchwork. Trying to sort it out makes playing three-dimensional chess look like child's play."[53]

51. "Amend the Indian Self-Determination and Education Assistance Act," *Hearings before the United States Senate Select Committee on Indian Affairs, 95th Congress, 2d Session, on S. 2460* (1978); *Senate Report* no. 95–1200, 95–2, serial 13197–12.
52. "United States Department of the Interior Budget Justifications, FY 1982: Bureau of Indian Affairs," printed in *Hearings before a Subcommittee of the Committee on Appropriations, House of Representatives, 97th Congress, 1st Session, Subcommittee on the Department of the Interior and Related Agencies* (1981), part 2, pp. 256–59.
53. *Congressional Record*, 119: 24030, 24464.

Abourezk's proposed solution was the appointment of a congressional commission with members from both houses and from the Indian community to undertake an exhaustive review of the historical and legal elements in federal-Indian relations and to recommend legislation. The presuppositions behind the resolution were evident in the senator's listing of purposes: "First, to affirm the unique and longstanding relationship between the Indian people and the U.S. Government, and to recognize that this unique relationship forms the basis to undertake fundamental reform in Indian policies. . . . Second, to admit openly that the Federal trust responsibility for the Indian people has not been fulfilled, and to admit further that by that failure Indian people have been denied full opportunity."[54]

Abourezk's resolution had a long preamble full of *whereas*'s castigating the federal government for its failures in regard to the Indians. The resolution proposed a commission with an executive director, a general counsel, and advisory groups to study and analyze treaties, statutes, and other documents in order to determine precisely what the unique relationship was, to revise the policies, practices, and structure of federal agencies dealing with Indians, to examine the current and future needs of the Indians, to seek ways to strengthen tribal governments, and to recommend modifications of policies in line with the purposes of the study.[55] What Abourezk and his supporters had in mind was a new Meriam Report that would provide a "systematic exploration of the contributing causes to the chaotic state of Indian affairs" with a "longer range objective of corrective action." The commission's report, it was hoped, would furnish a blueprint for future Indian policy. The Interior Department refused to take a stand on the resolution, declaring that the matter was entirely a congressional one that Congress should decide for itself. Senate hearings, however, showed strong support for the proposal from Indians and non-Indian advocates, and the Senate passed the resolution on December 5, 1973.[56]

The strong statements and the pro-Indian tone of the Senate resolution caused consternation among conservative congressmen and threatened a backlash that could destroy the positive features of the proposal, and the House of Representatives, under the leadership of Representative Lloyd Meeds of Washington, considerably moderated the resolution. It cut out

54. Ibid., p. 24464.

55. The original resolution is printed in *Congressional Record*, 119: 39587–89.

56. "Establishment of the American Indian Policy Review Commission," *Hearings before the Subcommittee on Indian Affairs of the Committee on Interior and Insular Affairs, United States Senate, 93d Congress, 1st Session, on S. J. Res. 133* (1973); *Senate Report* no. 93–594, 93–1, serial 13017–8. The Interior Department position is expressed in letters of Assistant Secretary John Kyl to Henry M. Jackson, July 19, 1973, and August 14, 1973, printed in *Senate Report* no. 93–594, pp. 4–5.

Abourezk's long preamble and substituted an innocuous statement calling attention to the shifts and changes in policy and the need for a general review of the conduct of Indian affairs to update the Meriam Report.[57]

The resolution as it became law (P.L. 93–580), January 2, 1975, established a commission of eleven members—three senators, three representatives, and five Indians (three from federally recognized tribes, one urban Indian, and one from nonrecognized groups). The commission was charged to analyze official documents to determine "the attributes of the unique relationship," review policies and practices, collect data on Indian needs, and in general accomplish what Abourezk had originally had in mind. The commission was directed, furthermore, to appoint investigative task forces to consider specific problems. Each task force was composed of three members, a majority of whom were to be Indians, and support staff for the task forces was authorized. The law provided $2.5 million for the work of the commission and extended the life of the body to June 30, 1977.[58]

In the end there were eleven task forces, and thirty-one of the thirty-three members were Indians. They worked in the following areas: (1) trust responsibilities and the federal-Indian relationship; (2) tribal government; (3) federal administration and the structure of Indian affairs; (4) federal, state, and tribal jurisdiction; (5) Indian education; (6) Indian health; (7) reservation and resource development and protection; (8) urban and rural nonreservation Indians; (9) Indian law consolidation, revision, and codification; (10) terminated and nonrecognized Indians; and (11) alcohol and drug abuse. In addition, two special task force reports were prepared on Alaska Native issues and on the management of the Bureau of Indian Affairs.[59]

The American Indian Policy Review Commission held out great promise; an expert, historically accurate, and balanced analysis of Indian status and of the legal responsibilities of the federal government would have been of tremendous value in understanding past policies and planning future development. Unfortunately, little of this was realized, and the commission must be judged a failure.

57. "Establishment of the American Indian Policy Review Commission," *Hearing before the Subcommittee on Indian Affairs of the Committee on Interior and Insular Affairs, House of Representatives, 93d Congress, 2d Session, on H. J. Res. 881, S. J. Res. 133* (1974); *House Report* no. 93–1420, 93–2, serial 13061–9.

58. 88 *United States Statutes* 1910–14. See also Kirke Kickingbird, "The American Indian Policy Review Commission: A Prospect for Future Change in Federal Indian Policy," *American Indian Law Review* 3, no. 2 (1975): 243–53.

59. The individual task force reports were published in 1976 and 1977 by the Government Printing Office. For the commission's findings and recommendations, see American Indian Policy Review Commission, *Final Report* (Washington: GPO, 1977).

The trouble began at the very start, with controversy over the appointment of the Indian members of the commission. Abourezk was chosen chairman of the commission and Meeds vice chairman, and they and the other congressional members selected the five Indian members: John Borbridge, Tlingit-Haida, Ada Deer, Menominee, and Jack Whitecrow, Quapaw-Seneca-Cayuga, representing federally recognized tribes; Louis R. Bruce, Mohawk-Sioux, representing urban Indians; and Adolph Dial, Lumbee, representing nonrecognized groups. These Indians were able and knowledgeable persons, but their appointment was violently criticized by other Indians as not being properly representative, and the National Congress of American Indians sought an injunction, unsuccessfully, to prevent the commission's operation on that ground. There was political maneuvering in the appointment of Ernest Stevens, an Oneida from Wisconsin, as executive director and in the appointment of the task force members.[60]

The commission in its *Final Report*, submitted to Congress on May 17, 1977, set forth its "policy for the future" in the following summary recommendations:

Foundations of Federal Indian Law

1. That Indian tribes are sovereign political bodies, having the power to determine their own membership and power to enact laws and enforce them within the boundaries of their reservations, and

2. That the relationship which exists between the tribes and the United States is premised on a special trust that must govern the conduct of the stronger toward the weaker.

The Trust Responsibility

1. The trust responsibility to American Indians extends from the protection and enhancement of Indian trust resources and tribal self-government to the provision of economic and social programs necessary to raise the standard of living and social well being of the Indian people to a level comparable to the non-Indian society.

2. The trust responsibility extends through the tribe to the Indian member, whether on or off the reservation.

3. The trust responsibility applies to all United States agencies and instrumentalities, not just those charged specifically with administration of Indian affairs.

---

60. For criticisms of the commission's formation, see Mark Thompson, "Nurturing the Forked Tree: Conception and Formation of the American Indian Policy Review Commission," and Donald A. Grinde, Jr., "Politics and the American Indian Policy Review Commission," in *New Directions in Federal Indian Policy: A Review of the American Indian Policy Review Commission* (Los Angeles: Amerian Indian Studies Center, University of California, Los Angeles, 1979), pp. 5–28.

Federal Administration

1. The executive branch should propose a plan for a consolidated Indian Department or independent agency. Indian programs should be transferred to this new consolidated agency where appropriate.

2. Bureaucratic processes must be revised to develop an Indian budget system operating from a "zero" base, consistent with long-range Indian priorities and needs. Those budget requests by the tribes should be submitted without interference to Congress.

3. Federal laws providing for delivery of domestic assistance to State and local governments must be revised to include Indian tribes as eligible recipients.

4. To the maximum extent possible, appropriations should be delivered directly to Indian tribes and organizations through grants and contracts; the first obligation being to trust requirements.

Economic Self-Sufficiency

1. The first order of business of future Indian policy must be the development of a viable economic base for the Indian communities.

2. Adequate credit systems must be established for Indian economic development projects; funds must be established to provide for land acquisition and consolidation; and policies must be adopted which will favor Indian control over leases of their own natural resources.

3. Technical assistance must be available to tribes both in the planning and management stages of operations.

4. Every effort must be made to encourage and aid tribes in the development of economic projects relevant to their natural resource base.

Restoration and Recognition

1. Tribes which were terminated must be restored to their formal political status and Congress must establish a legal process for restoration.

2. Tribes which have been overlooked, forgotten, or ignored must be recognized as possessing their full rights as tribes.

Urban Indians

1. Federal Indian programs should address the needs of off-reservation Indians.

2. Programs directed to the needs of urban Indians should encourage and utilize urban Indian service centers.[61]

61. *Final Report*, pp. 4–9.

Under thirteen chapters the report then listed and explained 206 specific recommendations for Congress to consider.

The *Final Report* and the reports of the eleven task forces on which it was based indicate why the work of the commission had so little effect. Instead of the balanced historical and legal report called for, the commission submitted a report based on the controversial positions of inherent full political sovereignty of the tribes and broad trust responsibilities of the federal government. The vice chairman of the commission submitted a vigorous dissent from the commission's report on these two points, claiming that the report was "one-sided advocacy" encompassing only a tribal view of the future of American Indian law and policy. Though Meeds's own position may have been as one-sided as the one he condemned, his minority report considerably weakened the impact of the commission's work.[62]

Even without the vice chairman's dissent, however, the report of the commission was unlikely to become a widely accepted general plan for future Indian policy. In the first place, it was caught in the theoretical dilemma that plagued the whole movement for self-determination. Although the report was premised on the concept of full political sovereignty of the tribes, most of the 206 recommendations of the commission were proposals for the federal government to appropriate funds for Indian programs or in some other way to deliver services to the "sovereign" tribes. There was, moreover, such a barrage of demands for funds or other congressional and administrative action that it was difficult to know where to begin. In the second place, the task forces' work and their reports were by and large not of high quality. These reports in many cases were an accumulation of raw data, often not expertly gathered, and were short on convincing analysis and interpretation. They showed neither the historical nor legal understanding that the purposes of the commission demanded. Compared with the well-organized information and tightly argued conclusions provided by the technical experts who made up the Meriam survey team in the 1920s, the material published by the American Indian Policy Review Commission was unsatisfactory. Part of the failure was due, no doubt, to the limited resources and limited time with which the task forces worked (the final reports were hastily put together), but the lack of highly competent personnel was also a factor.

The commission and the task forces did, of course, provide some useful material, and their findings and recommendations influenced action by

---

62. "Separate Dissenting Views of Congressman Lloyd Meeds, D-Wash., Vice Chairman of the American Indian Policy Review Commission," *Final Report*, pp. 571–612. A rebuttal to the dissent was supplied by Senator Abourezk and printed on pp. 615–17.

MAP 13: Indian Lands and Communities (Bureau of Indian Affairs Map, 1971)

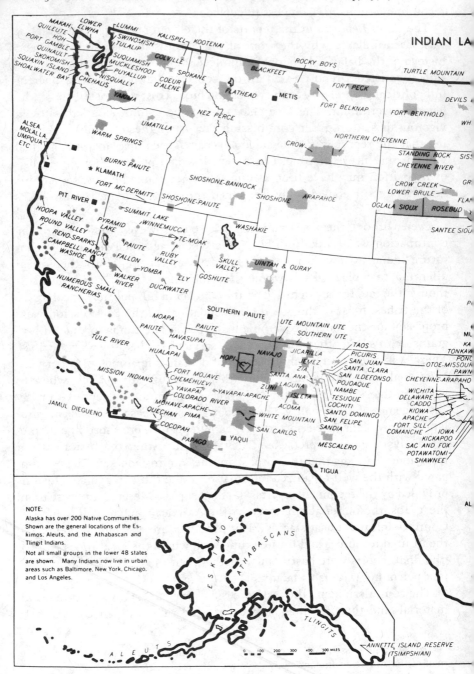

INDIAN LA

MAKAH, LOWER ELWHA, QUILEUTE, HOH, PORT GAMBLE, QUINAULT, SKOKOMISH, SQUAXIN ISLAND, SHOALWATER BAY, LUMMI, SWINOMISH, TULALIP, SUQUAMISH, MUCKLESHOOT, PUYALLUP, NISQUALLY, CHEHALIS, COLVILLE, KALISPEL, KOOTENAI, SPOKANE, COEUR D'ALENE, YAKIMA

BLACKFEET, ROCKY BOYS, FLATHEAD, METIS, FORT PECK, FORT BELKNAP, TURTLE MOUNTAIN, DEVILS, FORT BERTHOLD, WH

ALSEA MOLALLA UMPQUA ETC, WARM SPRINGS, UMATILLA, NEZ PERCE

BURNS PAIUTE, KLAMATH, FORT McDERMITT

CROW, NORTHERN CHEYENNE

STANDING ROCK, SIS, CHEYENNE RIVER, CROW CREEK, GR, LOWER BRULE, FLA, OGLALA SIOUX, ROSEBUD

SHOSHONE-BANNOCK, SHOSHONE-PAIUTE, SHOSHONE, ARAPAHOE

PIT RIVER, HOOPA VALLEY, ROUND VALLEY, RENO-SPARKS, CAMPBELL RANCH, WASHOE

SUMMIT LAKE, PYRAMID LAKE, WINNEMUCCA, PAIUTE, FALLON, RUBY VALLEY, TE-MOAK, WASHAKIE

SANTEE SIOU

NUMEROUS SMALL RANCHERIAS

WALKER RIVER, YOMBA, ELY, DUCKWATER, GOSHUTE, SKULL VALLEY, UINTAH & OURAY

SOUTHERN PAIUTE

TULE RIVER, MOAPA, PAIUTE, PAIUTE, HAVASUPAI, HUALAPAI

UTE MOUNTAIN UTE, SOUTHERN UTE

MISSION INDIANS, FORT MOJAVE, CHEMEHUEVI, YAVAPAI, COLORADO RIVER, YAVAPAI-APACHE

TAOS, PICURIS, SAN JUAN, SANTA CLARA, SAN ILDEFONSO, POJOAQUE, NAMBE, TESUQUE, COCHITI, SANTO DOMINGO, SAN FELIPE, SANDIA

JICARILLA, JEMEZ, ZIA, SANTA ANA, ZUNI, LAGUNA, ISLETA, ACOMA

CHEYENNE-ARAPAHO, WICHITA, DELAWARE, CADDO, KIOWA, APACHE, FORT SILL, COMANCHE, IOWA, KICKAPOO, SAC AND FOX, POTAWATOMI, SHAWNEE

MU, KA, TONKAWA, PONC, OTOE-MISSOURI, PAWN

JAMUL DIEGUENO, MOHAVE-APACHE, QUECHAN, PIMA, COCOPAH, PAPAGO, YAQUI, SAN CARLOS, WHITE MOUNTAIN, MESCALERO

TIGUA

AL

NOTE:

Alaska has over 200 Native Communities. Shown are the general locations of the Eskimos, Aleuts, and the Athabascan and Tlingit Indians.

Not all small groups in the lower 48 states are shown. Many Indians now live in urban areas such as Baltimore, New York, Chicago, and Los Angeles.

ESKIMOS, ATHABASCANS, TLINGITS, ALEUTS

0 100 200 300 400 500 MILES

ANNETTE ISLAND RESERVE (TSIMPSHIAN)

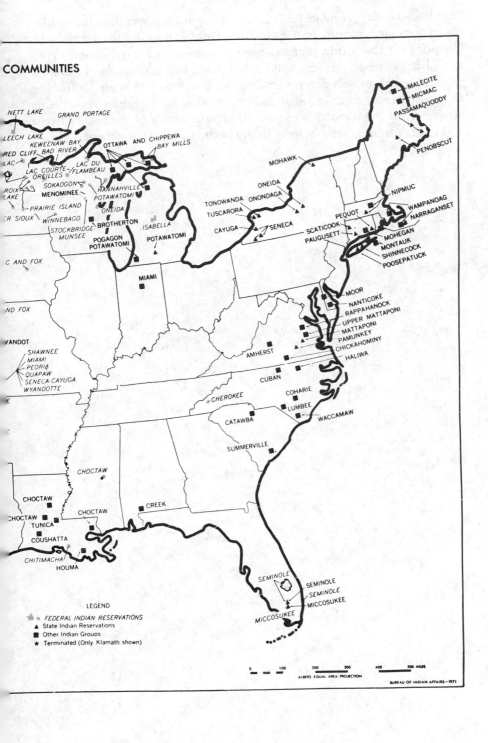

COMMUNITIES

MALECITE
MICMAC
PASSAMAQUODDY
PENOBSCOT

NETT LAKE   GRAND PORTAGE
LEECH LAKE
KEWEENAW BAY
RED CLIFF BAD RIVER
LAC
LAC COURTE   LAC DU
OREILLES   FLAMBEAU
ROIX   SOKAOGON
LAKE   MENOMINEE   HANNAHVILLE
POTAWATOMI
PRAIRIE ISLAND   ONEIDA
R SIOUX   WINNEBAGO
STOCKBRIDGE BROTHERTON
MUNSEE   ISABELLA
POGAGON   POTAWATOMI
POTAWATOMI

OTTAWA AND CHIPPEWA
BAY MILLS

MOHAWK
ONEIDA
TONOWANDA ONONDAGA
TUSCARORA
CAYUGA   SENECA

NIPMUC

WAMPANOAG
PEQUOT   NARRAGANSET
SCATICOOK
PAUGUSETT   MOHEGAN
MONTAUK
SHINNECOCK
POOSEPATUCK

C AND FOX

ND FOX

MIAMI

YANDOT
SHAWNEE
MIAMI
PEORIA
QUAPAW
SENECA-CAYUGA
WYANDOTTE

MOOR
NANTICOKE
RAPPAHANOCK
UPPER MATTAPONI
MATTAPONI
PAMUNKEY
CHICKAHOMINY
HALIWA

AMHERST

CUBAN

COHARIE
LUMBEE
WACCAMAW

CHEROKEE
CATAWBA

SUMMERVILLE

CHOCTAW

CHOCTAW
CHOCTAW   CHOCTAW   CREEK
TUNICA
COUSHATTA
CHITIMACHA
HOUMA

SEMINOLE   SEMINOLE
SEMINOLE
MICCOSUKEE
MICCOSUKEE

LEGEND
- FEDERAL INDIAN RESERVATIONS
- ▲ State Indian Reservations
- ■ Other Indian Groups
- ★ Terminated (Only Klamath shown)

0   100   200   300   400   500 MILES
ALBERS EQUAL AREA PROJECTION

BUREAU OF INDIAN AFFAIRS—1971

the executive departments and the Congress on a number of aspects of Indian policy and administration. But the *Final Report* did not furnish the blueprint for the future that had been hoped for. Piecemeal changes continued to be made, and these did move the Indian communities toward a greater degree of self-determination and protection of their rights, but there was no overarching plan and no solution to the inherent problems arising from the tension between self-determination of the Indian tribes and the continuing trust responsibility of the federal government.

CHAPTER 46

Legal and Judicial Maneuvering

Land Claims and Conflicts. Water Rights.

Fishing and Hunting Rights.

Inherent Sovereignty and Tribal Jurisdiction.

The 1970s were a decade of violent Indian protest, but they were also—and in the long run perhaps more significantly—a period in which Indians resorted to the courts to protect their rights and to demand a righting of old wrongs. With increasing skill and considerable success, Indians and their lawyers made use of the American legal system to gain recognition of their claims and remedies for their grievances.

Many of the suits brought by Indians to recover land or to vindicate other rights were encouraged and supported by the Native American Rights Fund (NARF), a national legal defense organization founded in 1971. With headquarters in Boulder, Colorado, and a permanent office in Washington, D.C., NARF assembled a group of young lawyers expert in Indian law, two-thirds of them Indian, and used its funds to pursue cases and projects that would have national impact. Its priorities were preservation of tribal existence, protection of tribal land and other natural resources, promotion of basic human rights for Indians, holding government accountable for proper enforcement of laws governing Indian affairs, and development of Indian law. Its report for 1981 listed ninety-four activities, from agitation for Indian water rights, support of land claims, and promotion of federal acknowledgment for nonrecognized tribes to continuing development of a national Indian law library at Boulder. The organization proved the value of working expertly within the system of American law to protect Indian rights of all sorts, and much of the Indians' success in vindicating claims was due to its work and support. NARF was not without critics among the Indians, of course, in part because it eschewed tactics of violent confrontation and in part because it was so largely dependent upon money from the federal government.[1]

LAND CLAIMS AND CONFLICTS

As Indians became more active in asserting claims, a new area of agitation opened up that soon gained the attention of the public press and the federal government. This was the claims of Indian groups in the eastern United States for land parcels that they alleged had been taken away from them illegally by eastern states. The most important of the claims were made by the Passamaquoddy Tribe and the Penobscot Nation in Maine, who demanded the return of about half the lands of the state. The Narragansetts in Rhode Island, remnants of Wampanoag Indians at Mashpee on Cape Cod, and other nonrecognized groups made similar claims.[2] The claims were based on the Indian Trade and Intercourse Act of 1790, which in section 4 declared: "That no sale of lands made by any Indians, or any nation or tribe of Indians within the United States, shall be valid to any person or persons, or to any state, whether having the right of pre-emption to such lands or not, unless the same shall be made and duly executed at some public treaty, held under the authority of the United States."[3]

The argument appeared first in the suits brought by the Passamaquoddy and Penobscot Indians under the tutelage of a young lawyer, Thomas Tureen, who became the leading advocate of the Indians' claims. When the

---

1. *Native American Rights Fund 1981 Report.* In fiscal year 1980, when $2,183,824 was the total revenue, Government sources supplied 68 percent, private foundations 21 percent, individuals and corporations 8 percent, and other sources 3 percent. NARF's law library holdings are reported in *National Indian Law Library Catalogue: An Index to Indian Legal Materials and Resources* (Boulder, Colorado: Native American Rights Fund, 1982). For Indian criticism of NARF, see "N.A.R.F.'s Ethics Questioned," *Akwesasne Notes*, Early Spring 1980, pp. 7, 31; *Wassaja*, January–February 1983, p. 3.

2. Tim Vollmann, "A Survey of Eastern Indian Land Claims, 1970–1979," *Maine Law Review* 31, no. 1 (1979): 5–16. Vollmann also discusses the case of *Oneida Indian Nation* v. *County of Oneida*, pp. 6–8.

3. 1 *United States Statutes* 138. It should be noted that the lawyers and judges who considered the claims consistently and erroneously referred to the law as the Nonintercourse Act, perhaps because of some vague remembrance from their school days of the Nonintercourse Act of Thomas Jefferson's administration. The 1790 law and its successors regulated trade and intercourse between whites and Indians; they did not interdict it.

secretary of the interior, on the ground that the tribes did not fall under the government's trust responsibility, refused to undertake the Indians' suit for recovery of lands lost under agreements made after the 1790 law, the Indians sued in the federal district court in Maine. In the case of *Passamaquoddy Tribe* v. *Morton*, Judge Edward T. Gignoux held that even though the tribe had never been federally recognized, the Trade and Intercourse Act was applicable to it and that the law established a trust relationship between the United States and the tribe. That decision was affirmed by the United States Court of Appeals, First Circuit, on December 23, 1975. Under these rulings the United States government was obliged to bring suit against Maine on behalf of the Indians.[4]

Gignoux's decision came as a bolt of lightning out of the blue, for the state's dealings with Indians outside the scope of federal Indian policy had been of long standing, without objection or interference from Washington, and it was a shock to discover the strong possibility that the agreements by which Maine (then part of Massachusetts) had cleared large areas of the land of Indian title were invalid. The courts' decisions cast a cloud over land titles in much of Maine; the Indians, private landowners, and the state of Maine geared up for a long period of complex litigation.[5]

An extended court battle (during which time land titles would be in doubt) would have brought tremendous economic hardship to Maine, and it was soon evident that a negotiated settlement, with the federal government picking up the bill, was the only solution. In a special report prepared at President Jimmy Carter's request by Judge William B. Gunter, a pattern was provided for a settlement, and Gunter's work was followed up by a three-man team appointed by the president to continue work toward a negotiated settlement.[6]

After long and difficult negotiations, a settlement was announced in March 1980. The agreement was approved by the Passamaquoddy Tribe,

4. 388 *Federal Supplement* 649–69 (January 20, 1975); 528 *Federal Reporter, Second Series* 370–81. An argument for federal authority over the Maine Indians is made in Francis J. O'Toole and Thomas N. Tureen, "State Power and the Passamaquoddy Tribe: 'A Gross National Hypocrisy?'" *Maine Law Review* 23, no. 1 (1971): 1–39. For a detailed account of the case, based largely on interviews with Thomas Tureen, see Paul Brodeur, "Annals of Law: Restitution," *New Yorker*, October 11, 1982, pp. 76–155.

5. The position of Maine is set forth by two members of the attorney general's office, John M. R. Paterson and David Roseman, in "A Reexamination of *Passamaquoddy* v. *Morton*," *Maine Law Review* 31, no. 1 (1979): 115–52. The article is based on research by Ronald Banks.

6. Recommendation to President Carter from William B. Gunter, July 15, 1977, and proposed Joint Memorandum of Understanding drawn up by Eliot R. Cutler, Leo M. Krulitz, and A. Stevens Clay, both printed in *Senate Report* no. 96–957, 96–2, serial 13330, pp. 55–61.

the Penobscot Nation, and the Houlton Band of Maliseet Indians (a small group that had also advanced claims), and it was adopted by the Maine legislature and signed by the governor on April 2, 1980. On June 13 the proposal was introduced into Congress by Maine's two senators, and hearings were held to gather the views of all interested parties. There was strong pressure on Congress to approve, even though the cost to the United States was considerably higher than the administration had previously supported.[7]

On October 10 the Maine Indian Claims Settlement Act of 1980 (P.L. 96–420) became law. It ratified all transfers of land and other natural resources by the Indians and thus extinguished all their claims to the land. In return Congress established a Maine Indian Claims Settlement Fund of $27 million, to be held in trust by the secretary of the interior for the tribes and the income used for their benefit. Another $54.5 million created a Maine Indian Claims Land Acquisition Fund ($26.8 million each for the Passamaquoddies and the Penobscots and $900,000 for the Houlton Band), from which 300,000 acres of land would be purchased for the Indians of the state. The tribes were recognized by the federal government and able to draw on the full federal services provided for Indian groups. They were, however, to be under the civil and criminal jurisdiction of the state.[8]

Before the Maine case had reached this successful conclusion, the claims of the Narragansett Indians in Rhode Island has been settled. The tribe claimed aboriginal title to 3,200 acres of land within the town of Charlestown and asserted that the alienation of those lands between 1790 and 1880 was null and void because of the provisions of the Trade and Intercourse Acts. The lawsuits clouded the title of most of the land in the town, and after lengthy negotiations the parties to the lawsuits, together with Governor J. Joseph Garrahy of Rhode Island and the Charlestown Town Council, signed a settlement agreement out of court, which Congress was asked to approve. The Rhode Island Indian Claims Settlement Act of September 30, 1978 (P.L. 95–395) confirmed the agreement. The state transferred to a state-chartered and Indian-controlled corporation about 900 acres of state land, and Congress appropriated $3.5 million to purchase another 900 acres for the Indians. In return all tribal land claims within Rhode Island were extinguished.[9]

7. "Proposed Settlement of Maine Indian Land Claims," *Hearings before the Select Committee on Indian Affairs, United States Senate, 96th Congress, 2d Session, on S. 2829,* 2 vols. (1980); "Settlement of Indian Land Claims in the State of Maine," *Hearing before the Committee on Interior and Insular Affairs, House of Representatives, 96th Congress, 2d Session, on H.R. 7919* (1980); *Senate Report* no. 96–957, 96–2, serial 13330; *House Report* no. 96–1353, 96–2, serial 13377.

8. 94 *United States Statutes* 1785–97.

9. "Rhode Island Indian Claims Settlement Act," *Joint Hearing before the United States Senate Select Committee on Indian Affairs and the U.S. House of Representatives*

The Mashpee case was similar, but it had quite a different outcome. These Indians, living in a small community on Cape Cod, brought suit as the "Mashpee Tribe" in the federal court in August 1976 and asked the court to declare that they were the legal owners of much of the land in the town of Mashpee because the provisions of the 1790 law had not been followed in alienating the land. This claim, like that of the Maine and Rhode Island Indians, immediately threw the town into economic turmoil because of the uncertainty of land titles. After a long trial on the question of the tribal status of the Mashpees, the jury found that although the Indians had been a federal Indian tribe in 1834 and 1842, they had ceased to be so by 1869, at which time their lands were sold to individual white purchasers, and that they were not a tribe when they brought suit in 1976. The district court approved the jury's decisions and dismissed the case in March 1978, and this action was upheld by the United States Court of Appeals, First Circuit, in February 1979. The United States Supreme Court declined to review the actions of the lower courts, thus ending the case unfavorably for the Indians.[10]

A case of quite a different sort arose from a festering land dispute between the Navajos and the Hopis. The dispute was of long standing, and the problem became critical in the 1970s. Congressional attempts to solve it by partition and relocation led to new cries of federal heartlessness.[11]

The Hopis, a sedentary people relying on farming and grazing for a livelihood, had inhabited their mesa-top villages for centuries. The Navajos were later arrivals—a semi-nomadic people for whom grazing was a pri-

---

Committee on Interior and Insular Affairs, Subcommittee on Indian Affairs and Public Lands, 95th Congress, 2d Session, on S. 3153 and H.R. 12860 (1978); Senate Report no. 95–972, 95–2, serial 13197–7; House Report no. 95–1453, 95–2, serial 13201–10; 92 *United States Statutes* 813–18. The necessary Rhode Island legislation to implement the act was signed on May 10, 1979.

10. *Mashpee Tribe* v. *Town of Mashpee*, 447 *Federal Supplement* 940–50; *Mashpee Tribe* v. *New Seabury Corp.*, 592 *Federal Reporter, Second Series* 575–95. The question of tribal existence is discussed in James D. St. Clair and William F. Lee, "Defense of Non-intercourse Act Claims: The Requirement of Tribal Existence," *Maine Law Review* 31, no. 1 (1979): 91–113. Useful accounts of the Mashpee Indians and their case are Francis G. Hutchins, *Mashpee: The Story of Cape Cod's Indian Town* (West Franklin, New Hampshire: Amarta Press, 1979), and Paul Brodeur, "The Mashpees," *New Yorker*, November 6, 1978, pp. 62–150.

11. Two useful analyses of the case are Kevin Tehan, "Of Indians, Land, and the Federal Government: The Navajo–Hopi Land Dispute," *Arizona State Law Journal*, 1976, pp. 173–212, and James M. Goodman and Gary L. Thompson, "The Hopi–Navaho Land Dispute," *American Indian Law Review* 3, no. 2 (1975): 397–417. A more detailed account, described as a combination of "history and investigative reporting," which describes the persons involved and the political maneuvering, is Jerry Kammer, *The Second Long Walk: The Navajo–Hopi Land Dispute* (Albuquerque: University of New Mexico Press, 1980).

mary occupation—and they gradually spread from their center in north-western New Mexico. After their return from forced exile at the Bosque Redondo in 1868, they expanded their reservation to keep pace with increasing population, ultimately surrounding the Hopis. To meet the growing Hopi complaints about Navajo encroachment, President Chester A. Arthur on December 16, 1882, by executive order set aside a reservation of nearly 2.5 million acres for the Hopis. The order was hastily drawn and imprecisely worded; it set the land aside "for the use and occupancy of the Moqui [Hopi], and such other Indians as the Secretary of the Interior may see fit to settle thereon." At the time there were an estimated three hundred Navajos living in the area.[12] The Hopis actually lived in a contracted area and did not use the full 1882 reservation, although their religious traditions required the use of shrines throughout the region; and the aggressive Navajos, still growing, moved onto it with their flocks and herds. By 1960 there were perhaps eighty-five hundred Navajos occupying land within the 1882 reservation boundaries. The acquiescence of the federal government in this encroachment was taken to be an application of the secretary of the interior's authority to settle other tribes there.

A related controversy developed around the Hopi village of Moencopi, located outside the 1882 reservation to the west of the main Hopi settlements. When Congress in 1934 defined the Navajo Reservation (which had grown piecemeal over the years), it specified that the lands were set aside for the Navajos and "such other Indians as are already settled thereon." Thus the Hopis got an undetermined interest in lands within the 1934 Navajo reservation, but the two tribes were unable to reach an agreement as to the precise interests held by the Hopis at Moencopi.[13]

Attempts to settle the question about the 1882 reservation by negotiation failed, and in 1958 a court settlement of conflicting interests was sought. By a law of July 22, 1958 (P.L. 85–547), Congress converted the tenancy by sufferance (which the Indians had under the executive order of 1882) to a vested interest with the government holding the lands in trust, and it authorized adjudication of the two tribes' claims by a three-member United States District Court in the District of Arizona—thus treating the issue primarily as a legal one, not one calling for a broader legislative resolution of the dispute. The court rendered its decision in the case of *Healing*

12. Executive order, December 16, 1882, printed in Kappler, vol. 1, p. 805. The area reserved was a rectangle approximately seventy miles from north to south and fifty-seven miles from east to west.

13. 48 *United States Statutes* 960–62. The act specifically declared that "nothing herein contained shall affect the existing status of the Moqui (Hopi) Indian Reservation created by Executive order of December 16, 1882." For a discussion of the Moencopi dispute, see Tehan, "Of Indians, Land, and the Federal Government," pp. 183–84, 198–203.

v. *Jones* on September 28, 1962. It held that the Hopis had an exclusive interest in that part of the reservation defined in 1943 as Land Management District Six (some 631,000 acres in the area they had traditionally inhabited) and that both tribes had a joint, undivided, and equal interest in the remaining 1.8 million acres. The court, however, asserted that the act of 1958 did not authorize it actually to partition the land held jointly.[14]

The *Healing* decision did not resolve the conflict. The Navajos' suggestion that they buy out Hopi interests in the areas of Navajo settlement was rejected by the Hopis, and new negotiations between the tribes were unsuccessful. When the Hopi Tribe sought court action to enable it to utilize the joint-use land and to remove Navajo stock from Hopi lands, the Court of Appeals for the Ninth Circuit directed the district court to determine appropriate relief. The district court in October 1972 ordered a program of stock reduction by the Navajos, restoration of overgrazed lands, and a limitation on Navajo construction within the joint-use area. When the Navajo Tribe failed to comply with the order, it was held in contempt of court.[15] The tension between the two tribes increased to such an extent that the *New York Times* in May 1974 could report the issue in a feature article with the headline "Rival Tribes Threaten War over Million Acres."[16]

Congress sought to end the impasse with new legislation, but it was not easy to decide what that legislation should contain. The House and Senate were faced with the genuine conflicting interests of the two tribes, a variety of proposals to solve the difficulties equitably, and a considerable amount of political agitation and maneuvering, so that it was difficult to find a solution that would be generally accepted. Three proposals were considered. The Hopis wanted a clear partition that would affirm their rights, which had been acknowledged in *Healing* v. *Jones*. The Navajos wanted to stay where they were in the disputed area and to buy out the Hopi interest in those lands. A third proposal urged still further negotiation and mediation. Extended hearings on the proposals brought forth

---

14. *Healing* v. *Jones*, 210 *Federal Supplement* 125–92, which includes a lengthy historical discussion of the dispute. There is an analysis of the decision in Tehan, "Of Indians, Land, and the Federal Government," pp. 189–94. The Navajo position is presented by two lawyers from the law firm representing the Navajos in Richard Schifter and W. Richard West, Jr., "Healing v. Jones: Mandate for Another Trail of Tears?" *North Dakota Law Review* 51 (Fall 1974): 73–106.

15. The post-*Healing* court action is traced in *Hamilton* v. *MacDonald*, 503 *Federal Reporter, Second Series* 1138–51. The various cases and court orders are printed in "Relocation of Certain Hopi and Navajo Indians," *Hearing before the United States Senate Select Committee on Indian Affairs, 95th Congress, 2d Session, on S. 1714* (1978), pp. 775–918.

16. *New York Times*, May 10, 1974, p. 39.

sharp disagreement. The Navajo chairman, Peter MacDonald, stressed the human suffering and disaster that would occur with forced removal and relocation of the Navajos and their livestock, repeating a common Navajo charge that partition and relocation would mean another Long Walk for his tribe comparable to the tragic episode of the 1860s, which was still vividly remembered by the Indians. Abbott Sekaquaptewa, chairman of the Hopi Tribe, on the other hand, spoke eloquently about the Hopis' long history of suffering under the aggressive encroachment of the Navajos and belittled the cries of hardship connected with relocation. "The Navajo Tribe has yet to explain," he said, "why great psychological harm will be done if they move off Hopi lands, and similar harm is not done to them when they up-root their homes and families and move in on Hopi territories."[17]

Congress sided with the Hopis, as did the Department of the Interior. The department at first opposed a legislative solution, hoping that an answer to the dispute could still be found through negotiation and court action, but it eventually despaired of such a solution and supported partition and relocation. "We recognize that a major relocation of people in this way is a grave human problem," Commissioner of Indian Affairs Morris Thompson asserted on June 24, 1974. "We earnestly hope that if [the relocation bill] is enacted, the affected peoples will move willingly and we are recommending a system of cash incentives to encourage early and voluntary relocation. However, we realize that some affected persons may resist relocation and that in some cases it may not be possible to carry out the court's partition on a voluntary basis."[18]

An act of December 22, 1974 (P.L. 93–531), provided for Navajo and Hopi negotiating teams under a federal mediator to settle the conflict, but if no agreement were reached within six months, it directed the district court to partition the joint-use area. To carry out the necessary relocations, it established a three-member Navajo and Hopi Relocation Commission and authorized the appropriation of funds to provide incentives for volun-

---

17. "Partition of Navajo and Hopi 1882 Reservation," *Hearings before the Sub-committee on Indian Affairs of the Committee on Interior and Insular Affairs, House of Representatives, 93d Congress, 1st Session, on H.R. 5647, H.R. 7679, and H.R. 7716 (Navajo-Hopi Dispute)* (1974); "Navajo-Hopi Land Dispute," *Hearing before the Committee on Interior and Insular Affairs, United States Senate, 93d Congress, 2d Session, on H.R. 10337, S. 2424, S. 3230, and S. 3724* (1974). See Sekaquaptewas's testimony and prepared statement on pp. 25–30 of the House hearings and MacDonald's on pp. 256–61 of the Senate hearings.

18. Statement of Morris Thompson, June 24, 1974, in "Navajo-Hopi Land Dispute," *Senate Hearings*, pp. 243–46. The political positions in the congressional action are treated in Kammer, *Second Long Walk*, pp. 91–137. See also *House Report* no. 93–909, 93–2, serial 13061–2, and *Senate Report* no. 93–1177, 93–2, serial 13057–8.

tary moving and to pay the costs of relocation. The secretary of the interior was authorized to sell the Navajos 250,000 acres of Bureau of Land Management lands on which to resettle the families forced to relocate. The final court decree on partition came in April 1979; it accepted the detailed partition plan worked out by the mediator. The Relocation Commission was required to submit a final relocation plan within two years. Five years were then allowed to complete the relocation.[19]

As removal approached, the Navajos dug in their heels to stay, and they sought amendment or repeal of the 1974 act. This time Congress was more sympathetic to them and, over the cries of the Hopis that their rights established by the court decision and affirmed in P.L. 93–531 were being washed away, provided for life estates to allow certain Navajos to stay on the land. It also authorized the acquisition of additional lands for the Navajos. This act of July 8, 1980, however, did not reverse the basic policy of partition and relocation.[20] As the Relocation Commission carried out its work, the anguished cries of the Navajos continued, and the final settlement of the long and bitter conflict remained in doubt.[21]

WATER RIGHTS

The 1970s brought a tremendous concern for the rights of Indians to water on their reservations. As population increased in the arid West, pressure on the limited water resources mounted, and the Indians were threatened by loss of water necessary for their existence. Fifty-five percent of all the In-

19. 88 *United States Statutes* 1712–23. The 1974 act also authorized court action regarding conflicting claims relating to areas within the Navajo reservation defined in 1934, that is, the Moencopi area. The mediator's report is printed in "Relocating Certain Hopi and Navajo Indians," pp. 919–1037. The regulations on procedures for the Relocation Commission are in 25 *Code of Federal Regulations* 700. There are copies of the commission's report, manual of procedure, and other related documents in "Relocation of Certain Hopi and Navajo Indians," pp. 161–774.

20. 94 *United States Statutes* 929–36. For the continuing disagreements between the Hopis and the Navajos and the congressional reasoning, see "Relocation of Certain Hopi and Navajo Indians," *Senate Hearing on S. 1714;* "Relocation of Certain Hopi and Navajo Indians," *Hearing before the Select Committee on Indian Affairs, United States Senate, 96th Congress, 1st Session on S. 751 and S. 1077* (1979); *Senate Report* no. 96–373, 96–1, serial 13245; *House Report* no. 96–544, 96–1, serial 13302.

21. The Navajos charged that the Hopis were unduly influenced by power companies interested in coal deposits in the disputed area, a charge that is difficult to substantiate. Certainly the basic dispute of the Hopis with the Navajos antedated serious energy development activities. See the discussion in Kammer, *Second Long Walk,* pp. 85–90, 133–37.

dian lands and 75 percent of the Indian reservation population lay within the zone of less than twenty inches of annual rainfall (the amount generally considered necessary for successful agriculture), and as Indians sought to improve their condition through economic development, the use of water for irrigation and for other uses became of supreme importance. The activism of the Indians in the 1970s was strongly reflected in strident demands that Indian water rights be protected. "There is no issue so critical to Indian affairs today," one Indian spokesman asserted in 1972, "as the issue of water rights and resources. It cannot be too often emphasized, or too strongly insisted, that this is *the* most important problem confronting us . . . a problem concerning our very survival."[22]

The determination of what rights the Indians had to water was a matter of judicial interpretation—which was complex and controverted and not yet clearly decided. The debate revolved around three fundamental questions: what priority do Indian reservations have to the limited water resources in relation to the rights of non-Indians, what quantum or volume of water are the Indians entitled to, and to what uses of water do the Indians' rights extend (to agricultural uses only or to other uses as well)? Initial formulations of answers to questions of the status of Indian water rights were worked out through the decades of the twentieth century. It was agreed that Indian water rights exist independent of state water management laws, for these rights arise under federal law, and that they come into being at the date of creation of the reservation (or in some cases from time immemorial, if the reservation was on lands owned aboriginally by the tribe). No actual diversion of water and application of it to beneficial uses is necessary to create the water rights of the Indians, nor do the priority principles of appropriation apply to their rights.

22. Rupert Costo, "Indian Water Rights: A Survival Issue," *Indian Historian* 5 (Fall 1972): 4. Indian water rights are discussed with heavy documentation in *Felix S. Cohen's Handbook of Federal Indian Law,* 1982 ed. (Charlottesville, Virginia: Michie, Bobbs-Merrill, 1982), pp. 575–604, and in Norris Hundley, Jr., "The Dark and Bloody Ground of Indian Water Rights: Confusion Elevated to Principle," *Western Historical Quarterly* 9 (October 1978): 455–82. One of the most persistent voices raised in defense of Indian water rights was that of William H. Veeder; see, for example, his "Federal Encroachment on Indian Water Rights and the Impairment of Reservation Development," in *Toward Economic Development for Native American Communities: A Compendium of Papers Submitted to the Subcommittee on Economy in Government of the Joint Economic Committee, Congress of the United States,* Joint Committee Print, 91st Congress, 1st session, 2 vols. (Washington: GPO, 1969), 2: 460–518; "Water Rights: Life or Death for the American Indian," *Indian Historian* 5 (Summer 1972): 4–21. See also *Water Rights: A Fact Book,* 1978, published by the Bureau of Indian Affairs, and Rennard Strickland, "American Indian Water Law Symposium," *Tulsa Law Journal* 15 (Summer 1980): 699–719.

The fundamental principles rest on the case of *Winters* v. *United States*, which the Supreme Court decided on January 6, 1908. The case involved the water rights of the Fort Belknap Indian Reservation, which had been established along the Milk River in Montana by agreement with the Indians in 1888. When white setlers diverted water from the reservation, the United States got an injunction against them, and the settlers appealed that action. The Supreme Court came down firmly on the side of the Indians and established the doctrine of "reserved rights" for the Indians that were different from all other rights to water. It declared that by the establishment of the Fort Belknap Reservation the Indians were entitled to a sufficient amount of water from the Milk River for irrigation purposes and that the water of the river could not be diverted by settlers on the public lands in a way that would prejudice the Indians' rights. It did not matter if the non-Indians had begun to use the water first (prior appropriation) or if the Indians in fact used any of the water at all. The water necessary for the purposes for which the reservation had been created had been reserved for Indian use. It was not immediately clear who reserved the water, the Indians or the federal government, how much was reserved, or for what purposes, but the *Winters* decision became the starting point for all future discussion of Indian water rights.[23]

Winters pertained to a reservation established by Congress in an agreement with the tribe (similar to the old treaty procedures). On June 3, 1963, in *Arizona* v. *California*, the Supreme Court confirmed the *Winters* doctrine and applied it to all reservations whether established by treaty, agreement, congressional act, or executive order. The court declared that the United States in establishing reservations reserved sufficient quantities of water for both present and future needs.[24] In *Cappaert* v. *United States*, June 7, 1976, the court included rights to groundwater as well as surface water in "the implied-reservation-of-water-rights doctrine." It has been argued, also, that the *Winters* doctrine applies not only to agricultural uses, but to any reasonable uses for developing the reservations, even though those uses might not have been foreseen at the time.[25]

Indians have seriously complained that the United States government, as trustee for Indian resources, failed to fulfill its responsibility to protect their water rights. Indians did not make full use of their water rights, and

23. 207 *U.S. Reports* 564–78. The literature on the *Winters* case is extensive. A useful discussion is Norris Hundley, Jr., "The 'Winters' Decision and Indian Water Rights: A Mystery Reexamined," *Western Historical Quarterly* 13 (January 1982): 17–42.

24. 373 *U.S. Reports* 546–602.

25. 426 *U.S. Reports* 128–47. This case did not concern Indian reservations but other federal reserved land. The development of the *Winters* doctrine is discussed in detail in *Cohen's Federal Indian Law*, 1982 ed., pp. 578–96.

as non-Indian users drew more and more heavily on the water resources, the government was caught in a conflict of interest between protecting Indian rights and concern for the economic development of the West. The National Water Commission, established by Congress in 1968, reported bluntly in 1973:

> With the encouragement, or at least the cooperation, of the Secretary of the Interior—the very office entrusted with protection of all Indian rights—many large irrigation projects were constructed on streams that flowed through or bordered Indian Reservations. . . . With few exceptions the projects were planned and built by the Federal Government without any attempt to define, let alone protect, prior rights that Indian tribes might have had in the waters used for the projects. . . . In the history of the United States Government's treatment of Indian tribes, its failure to protect Indian water rights for use on the Reservations it set aside for them is one of the sorrier chapters.[26]

Striking cases illustrate the Indians' concern and anger on this issue. One is the diversion of waters from Pyramid Lake in Nevada, in which waters from the Truckee River that supplied the lake were diverted to the Carson River watershed as part of the Newlands Reclamation Project. The Paiute Indians, who depended upon fishing in the lake for their livelihood, found the lake practically destroyed. Another is the serious diminution of underflow and groundwater of the Santa Cruz River in southern Arizona upon which the Papago Indian Tribe depended for irrigated agriculture. Upstream use of water by non-Indians drastically reduced the groundwater levels and hampered farming efforts of the Papagos. A third is the controversial Central Arizona Project, which is being constructed to divert waters from the Colorado River to central and southern Arizona and which seriously affects five Indian communities—the Ak Chin, Fort McDowell, Gila River, Papago, and Salt River Pima-Maricopa reservations.[27]

---

26. *Water Policies for the Future: Final Report to the President and to the Congress of the United States by the National Water Commission* (Washington: GPO, 1973), pp. 474–75.

27. For the Pyramid Lake issue, see Alvin M. Josephy, Jr., *Now That the Buffalo's Gone: A Study of Today's American Indians* (New York: Alfred A. Knopf, 1982), chapter 5, and Veeder, "Federal Encroachment on Indian Water Rights," pp. 497–512. The conflicting views of Indians and non-Indians about the Central Arizona Project are set forth at length in "Indian Water Rights of the Five Central Tribes of Arizona," *Hearings before the Committee on Interior and Insular Affairs, United States Senate, 94th Congress, 1st Session* (1976); and "Water for Five Central Arizona Indian Tribes for Farming Operations," *Hearings before the U.S. Senate Select Committee on Indian Affairs on S. 905* (1977). The secretary of the interior's allotment of water from the Central Arizona Project to the five reservations is in 41 *Federal Register* 45883–89 (October 18, 1976).

President Carter treated the problem of Indian water rights in the special federal water policy message that he sent to Congress on June 6, 1978, in which he urged prompt and expeditious inventory and quantification of federal reserved water rights, including those of the Indian reservations. Until that quantification was determined, he noted, the states would be unable effectively to allocate state water resources, and he emphasized negotiation rather than litigation whenever necessary.[28] But the issues at stake are so momentous that no easy solution is possible. Since the demand for water, from both Indians and non-Indians, seems bound to increase and the amount of water is strictly limited, the problem of Indian water rights and government protection of them will be a continuing one.

FISHING AND HUNTING RIGHTS

A similar issue of rights to natural resources concerned fishing and hunting off the reservations. Treaties signed with Indian tribes in the nineteenth century in some cases preserved for the Indians their traditional fishing and hunting rights in lands ceded to the federal government. For many years these clauses in the treaties were ignored or forgotten, since there was little conflict between Indians and whites over the resources. But in the mid-twentieth century, as the resources became depleted, these latent rights assumed new importance. Indian groups, in seeking to promote their economic well-being, demanded full recognition of their rights, but it was not clear what the extent of these rights was and how far the Indians were subject to state regulatory authority. Considerable litigation resulted, which by and large tended to vindicate the Indians' rights.[29]

Much of the litigation concerned fishing rights embodied in the treaties negotiated with the tribes of the Pacific Northwest in 1854 and 1855 by Isaac I. Stevens, the governor of Washington Territory. Those treaties reserved to the Indians "the right of taking fish, at all usual and accustomed grounds and stations . . . in common with all citizens of the Territory."[30] In

28. "Federal Water Policy," *Public Papers of the Presidents of the United States: Jimmy Carter, 1978* (Washington: GPO, 1979), pp. 1044–51.

29. There is a detailed discussion of these rights in *Cohen's Federal Indian Law*, 1982 ed., pp. 441–70; the book contains extensive citation of references. Note that the question of gathering rights was also at issue.

30. See, for example, the Treaty of Medicine Creek with the Nisqually, Puyallup, and other tribes, December 26, 1854, in Kappler, p. 662. The problem of fishing rights in Washington is studied in *Uncommon Controversy: Fishing Rights of the Muckleshoot, Puyallup, and Nisqually Indians*, a Report Prepared for the American Friends Service Committee (Seattle: University of Washington Press, 1970). A full account of these fish-

a series of cases over the years fundamental principles were established in regard to the Indians' rights. In *United States* v. *Winans*, decided on May 15, 1905, the Supreme Court declared that the Indians could not be barred from their usual sites and that they had easements over both public and private lands to get to those fishing places. Three cases involving Puyallup Indian rights in 1968, 1973, and 1977 further refined and augmented the rights the Indians could exercise. The Indians, however, were not accorded exclusive fishing rights and had to share them with non-Indians.[31]

A vital question was whether the Indians were entitled to a definite amount or percentage of the catch. In *United States* v. *State of Washington*, a case filed in the Federal District Court for the Western District of Washington in 1970, a group of Indian tribes sought a determination of their rights to a fair share of the catch. In 1974, after three and a half years of study, Judge George Boldt rendered his decision in an extensive opinion that thoroughly analyzed the treaties, the migratory patterns of the fish, Indian fishing patterns, and the history of state regulation. The analysis showed how Indian rights had been reduced over the years by state regulation and non-Indian encroachment, and Boldt set forth a series of principles to govern Indian fishing. He noted that the treaties reserved fishing rights for Indians that were distinct from those of other citizens, that off-reservation fishing rights extended to all places that a tribe had customarily fished, and that the state could regulate Indian fishing only to the extent needed to conserve the fish resources. The most controversial part of the decision was Boldt's determination that the right to "fish in common with the citizens of the Territory" meant not just the right of access to fishing sites but a fair share of the fish: up to 50 percent of the harvestable number of fish, exclusive of catches used for subsistence or for ceremonial

---

ing rights is given in *Indian Tribes: A Continuing Quest for Survival*, a Report of the United States Commission on Civil Rights, June 1981, pp. 61–100. The Commission on Civil Rights in 1977 and 1978 held extensive hearings in Seattle, which set forth the problems and proposed solutions. See *Hearing before the United States Commission on Civil Rights: American Indian Issues in the State of Washington*, October 19–20, 1977, vols. 1 and 2, and *Hearing before the United States Commission on Civil Rights: American Indian Fishing Rights in the State of Washington*, August 25, 1978, vols. 3 and 4.

31. *United States* v. *Winans*, 198 *U.S. Reports* 371–84; *Puyallup Tribe* v. *Department of Game of Washington* (*Puyallup I*), 391 *U.S. Reports* 392–403; *Department of Game of Washington* v. *Puyallup Tribe* (*Puyallup II*), 414 *U.S. Reports* 44–50; *Puyallup Tribe* v. *Department of Game of Washington* (*Puyallup III*), 433 *U.S. Reports* 165–85. Other significant cases were *Tulee* v. *Washington*, 315 *U.S. Reports* 681 (1942), which declared that the state could not regulate off-reservation Indian fishing, and *Menominee Tribe of Indians* v. *United States*, 391 *U.S. Reports* 404 (1968), which declared that the Menominee Indians did not lose treaty fishing and hunting rights because of termination.

purposes.[32] The appeals court confirmed the district court decision, and the Supreme Court refused to accept the case for review.[33]

Non-Indian reaction to the Boldt decision was violent, and much of the public outburst was aimed against Judge Boldt personally. Non-Indian fishermen declared that the decision constituted racial discrimination against them, and they openly violated the ruling by fishing illegally. A serious backlash against augmented Indian rights threatened to halt, if not reverse, recent Indian gains.[34] The federal answer, at the instigation of the Washington congressional delegation, was the appointment by the president in April 1977 of a Federal Task Force on Washington State Fisheries to work for an effective management system for fisheries in the Northwest. A regional team of the task force produced a settlement plan for Washington salmon and steelhead fisheries in 1978.[35]

New litigation also arose, for the state of Washington refused to enforce the Boldt decision. The federal district court itself took over that function, and its action was upheld by the appeals court. At length the United States Supreme Court agreed to hear the dispute, and on July 2, 1979, it issued its opinion on the case. It reviewed the Boldt decision and upheld it almost completely. The tribes did lose, however, by the court's inclusion in the 50 percent figure the fish caught for subsistence and ceremonial uses and those caught on the reservations—all of which had been excluded by Boldt's original decision.[36]

Another case involved Chippewa Indian fishing in Lake Michigan in violation of regulations promulgated by the state of Michigan. In *United States* v. *State of Michigan*, Judge Noel P. Fox, of the United States District Court for the Western District of Michigan, denied the power of Michigan to regulate Indian fishing based on aboriginal use and on a treaty of 1836

---

32. *United States* v. *State of Washington*, 384 *Federal Supplement* 312–423. I rely here on the summary in *Indian Tribes: A Continuing Quest for Survival*, pp. 70–71.

33. 520 *Federal Reporter, Second Series* 676; 423 *U.S. Reports* 1086.

34. For a statement of non-Indian views, see George Reiger, "Bury My Heart at the Western District Court," *Field and Stream* 80 (June 1975): 38, 102–4. An extreme reaction to the Boldt decision was the organization in 1976, by representatives from ten western states, of the Interstate Congress for Equal Rights and Responsibilities. See its material in *Hearing before the United States Commission on Civil Rights*, vol. 2, pp. 597–616. There is copious evidence of reaction to the decision, ibid., vols. 3 and 4.

35. The document is printed in *Hearing before the United States Commission on Civil Rights*, vol. 4, pp. 27–403. For a discussion of the matter, see *Indian Tribes: A Continuing Quest for Survival*, pp. 75–91.

36. *Washington* v. *Washington State Commercial Passenger Fishing Vessel Association*, 443 *U.S. Reports* 658–708. See the discussion in *Indian Tribes: A Continuing Quest for Survival*, pp. 91–98.

that reserved "the right of hunting in the lands ceded, with the other usual privileges of occupancy, until the land is required for settlement."[37]

New cases arose continually, and Indian tribes needed to stay alert to their rights and to resort to the courts for protection of them.[38]

INHERENT SOVEREIGNTY AND TRIBAL JURISDICTION

All elements of Indian self-determination were tied to the issue of tribal sovereignty, and the 1970s were a culmination of the gradual reawakening of tribal identity and autonomy. The nineteenth- and early twentieth-century attempts to divest Indians of their tribal relations and let them disappear as individual citizens into the body of the nation did not succeed. Contrary to the confident expectations of humanitarian reformers and federal officials, tribalism survived, and it became the basis for much of the legal maneuvering in the second half of the twentieth century. The tribal governments established under the Indian Reorganization Act of 1934 and other similar Indian bodies governed the reservations, and little by little federal courts recognized and protected this tribal authority.[39] It became an accepted position—a position clearly set forth by Felix S. Cohen in New Deal days—that Indian tribes had a retained inherent sovereignty, that they enjoyed the attributes of sovereignty that had not been taken away or given up. Cohen wrote in his *Handbook of Federal Indian Law*:

> Perhaps the most basic principle of all Indian law, supported by a host of decisions . . . is the principle that *those powers which are lawfully vested in an Indian tribe are not, in general, delegated powers granted by express acts of Congress, but rather inherent powers of a limited sovereignty which has never been extinguished.* Each Indian tribe begins its relationship with the Federal Government as a sovereign power, recognized as such in treaty and legislation. The powers of sovereignty have been limited from time to time by special treaties and laws designed to take from the Indian tribes control of

37. *United States* v. *State of Michigan*, 471 *Federal Supplement* 192–281. See also the action of the United States Court of Appeals, Sixth Circuit, which refused to reverse the decision. 623 *Federal Reporter, Second Series* 488 and 653 *Federal Reporter, Second Series* 277–80. The treaty in question is in Kappler, pp. 450–57.

38. See *Native American Rights Fund 1981 Annual Report*, pp. 27–42, for current actions involving Indian rights to resources.

39. The persistence of tribalism is the subject of William T. Hagan, "Tribalism Rejuvenated: The Native American since the Era of Termination," *Western Historical Quarterly* 12 (January 1981): 5–16.

matters which, in the judgment of Congress, these tribes could no longer be safely permitted to handle. The statutes of Congress, then, must be examined to determine the limitations of tribal sovereignty rather than to determine its sources or its positive content. What is not expressly limited remains within the domain of tribal sovereignty.[40]

This doctrine of inherent sovereign powers was accepted by the United States Supreme Court, notably in *United States* v. *Wheeler*, decided on March 22, 1978.[41] The question at issue was whether the double jeopardy clause of the Fifth Amendment barred prosecution of a Navajo Indian in a federal court when he had previously been convicted in a tribal court of a lesser included offense arising out of the same incident. The court declared that there was no double jeopardy because the tribal court and the federal court were arms of separate sovereigns. After quoting Cohen, the court said:

> Before the coming of the Europeans, the tribes were self-governing sovereign political communities. . . . Like all sovereign bodies, they then had inherent power to prescribe laws for their members and to punish infractions of those laws.
>
> Indian tribes are, of course, no longer possessed of the full attributes of sovereignty. . . . Their incorporation within the territory of the United States, and their acceptance of its protection, necessarily divested them of some aspects of the sovereignty which they had previously exercised. By specific treaty provision they yielded up other sovereign powers; by statutes, in the exercise of its plenary control, Congress has removed still others.
>
> But our cases recognize that the Indian tribes have not given up their full sovereignty. . . . The sovereignty that the Indian tribes retain is of a unique and limited character. It exists only at the suf-

40. Felix S. Cohen, *Handbook of Federal Indian Law* (Washington: GPO, 1942), p. 122. There are innumerable studies on the legal status of the tribes within the American nation, and the questions of sovereignty and jurisdiction are too complex to be treated fully here. For brief surveys of the topic, see Arthur Lazarus, Jr., "Tribal Sovereignty under United States Law," in William R. Swagerty, ed., *Indian Sovereignty: Proceedings of the Second Annual Conference on Problems concerning American Indians Today* (Chicago: Newberry Library, 1979), pp. 28–46; and John Niemisto, "The Legal Powers of Indian Tribal Governments," *Wisconsin Academy Review* 28 (March 1982): 7–11. The full complexity of the legal issues can be seen in the detailed discussion in *Cohen's Federal Indian Law*, 1982 ed., pp. 207–385; the volume contains separate chapters on federal, tribal, and state authority in Indian affairs and on jurisdiction. A useful workbook is Kirke Kickingbird and others, *Indian Sovereignty* (Washington: Institute for the Development of Indian Law, 1977).

41. 435 *U.S. Reports* 313–32.

ferance of Congress and is subject to complete defeasance. But until Congress acts, the tribes retain their existing sovereign powers. . . .

In sum, the power to punish offenses against tribal law committed by Tribe members, which was part of the Navajos' primeval sovereignty, has never been taken away from them either explicitly or implicitly, and is attributable in no way to any delegation to them of federal authority. It follows that when the Navajo Tribe exercises this power, it does so as part of its retained sovereignty and not as an arm of the Federal Government.[42]

And the court indicated that it favored leaving the inherent power intact. "Tribal courts," it said, "are important mechanisms for protecting significant tribal interests. Federal pre-emption of a tribe's jurisdiction to punish its members for infractions of tribal law would detract substantially from tribal self-government, just as federal pre-emption of state criminal jurisdiction would trench upon important state interests."[43]

In a variety of cases the courts have recognized that Indian tribes enjoy sovereign immunity from suit and are not subject to adverse possession, laches, or statutes of limitation. Tribes can exercise the right of eminent domain, tax, and create corporations. They can set up their own form of government, determine their own members, administer justice for tribal members, and regulate domestic relations and members' use of property. They can establish hunting and fishing regulations for their own members within their reservations and can zone and regulate land use. They can do a great many things that independent political entities do, insofar as federal law has not preempted their authority.[44]

It is true, as the courts have long held, that Indian tribes are subject to the legislative power of the United States, and the courts have spoken of the plenary power of Congress over Indian affairs.[45] The power of the United States government is not in question but rather whether Congress has in given cases exercised that power or intended to restrict tribal sovereignty. In some instances tribes are governed by general congressional legislation, in other cases not.

The question of state jurisdiction over Indian reservations has been cru-

---

42. Ibid., pp. 322–23, 328.

43. Ibid., p. 332.

44. The sovereign powers of Indian tribes are discussed in Lazarus, "Tribal Sovereignty"; Kickingbird and others, *Indian Sovereignty*, pp. 7–13; and *Cohen's Federal Indian Law*, 1982 ed., pp. 246–57.

45. See, for example, *United States* v. *Kagama*, 118 *U.S. Reports* 375 (1886); and *Lone Wolf* v. *Hitchcock*, 187 *U.S. Reports* 553 (1903). Federal authority over Indians is discussed in *Cohen's Federal Indian Law*, 1982 ed., pp. 207–28.

cial, for states have been irked by restrictions on enforcing their laws and regulations over areas within their boundaries. The courts have said that where federal law has preempted jurisdiction the states do not have authority, but the conflict between state and tribal jurisdiction is far from resolved. An especially disputed point is the extent of tribal authority over nontrust lands located within the original boundaries of the reservations.

The stickiest issue has been tribal jurisdiction over non-Indians on reservations. On March 6, 1978, the Supreme Court in the case of *Oliphant* v. *Suquamish Indian Tribe* reversed a district court decision and decided against tribal jurisdiction over non-Indians. Mark Oliphant, a non-Indian residing on the Port Madison Reservation in the state of Washington, had been arrested by tribal authorities during the Suquamish annual Chief Seattle Days celebration and charged with assaulting a tribal officer and resisting arrest. He claimed that he was not subject to tribal authority, and the Supreme Court upheld his claim. After a consideration of historical cases involving tribal jurisdiction, the court declared: "They have little relevance to the principles which lead us to conclude that Indian tribes do not have inherent jurisdiction to try and to punish non-Indians."[46]

Oliphant was taken by Indians as a damaging blow to their sovereign revival, a step backward in the progress made in recent years, and it emphasized the fragile nature of tribal sovereignty and the ultimate power of the federal government in determining the extent and limitations of that sovereignty.[47] The court, in fact, on March 24, 1981, restated the *Oliphant* doctrine in *Montana* v. *United States*, which concerned the right of the Crow Indian Tribe to regulate hunting and fishing of nonmembers on fee title lands held by non-Indians within the reservation. After noting inherent tribal power over tribal domestic concerns, the court said: "But exercise of tribal power beyond what is necessary to protect tribal self-government or to control internal relations is inconsistent with the dependent

---

46. *Oliphant* v. *Suquamish Indian Tribe*, 435 *U.S. Reports* 191–212. The proportion of non-Indians to Indians on the reservation was noted by the court. Sixty-three percent of the land on the reservation was owned in fee simple by non-Indians, and there were nearly three thousand non-Indians living on the reservation, compared with approximately fifty Indians. Ibid., p. 193n.

47. For strong criticism of the decision, see Russel Lawrence Barsh and James Youngblood Henderson, "The Betrayal: *Oliphant* v. *Suquamish Indian Tribe* and the Hunting of the Snark," *Minnesota Law Review* 63 (April 1978): 609–40; Jeff Larson, "Oliphant v. Suquamish Indian Tribe: A Jurisdictional Quagmire," *South Dakota Law Review* 24 (Winter 1979): 217–42; and Curtis G. Berkey, "Indian Law—Indian Tribes Have No Inherent Authority to Exercise Criminal Jurisdiction over Non-Indians Violating Tribal Criminal Laws within Reservation Boundaries . . . ," *Catholic University Law Review* 28 (1979): 663–87.

status of the tribes, and so cannot survive without express congressional delegation." It repeated bluntly "the general proposition that the inherent sovereign powers of an Indian tribe do not extend to the activities of non-members of the tribe."[48]

By the end of the eighth decade of the century the courts were thus moving toward a clearer definition of tribal sovereignty. Retained inherent power was affirmed as it applied to tribal members; its application in given cases to nonmembers was denied. New cases will no doubt further determine tribal jurisdiction, for it remains a problem of vital importance to Indian self-determination.

48. *Montana* v. *United States*, 450 *U.S. Reports* 544–81; quotations at pp. 564–65.

CHAPTER 47

The American Indians
in 1980

Urban Indians and Nonrecognized Tribes. Federal Programs

for Indians. Building an Economic Base.

Trust Responsibility: The Great Father Redivivus.

America's Unfinished Business.

The century from 1880 to 1980, which began with a strong sentiment that the Indians were the "vanishing Americans," ended with a resurgence of Indian visibility. Indian population steadily increased after 1900; the census of 1900 counted 237,196 Indians and that of 1980 counted 1,361,869. Recent census figures have reflected both an increased willingness of many persons to identify themselves as Indians and natural increases.[1] What at one time seemed an inexorable drive for complete assimilation has been slowed if not turned around, and new policies of self-determination have brought new hope to Indian communities. Indian protests and Indian legal actions have alerted the government and the general public to the continuing importance of Indians in American life.

URBAN INDIANS AND NONRECOGNIZED TRIBES

By 1980 it could no longer be said that the Indians as a whole were a reservation people. The urbanization of American Indians, which had become a

---

1. Indian population figures are given in the Appendix. Details for 1970 were compiled in *1970 Census of Population: Subject Report, American Indians*, and similar information will be available for 1980. Special efforts, in fact, were made in 1980 to gather information on Indians, and a fifteen-page "Supplementary Questionnaire for American Indians" was administered on reservations and historic areas of Oklahoma.

TABLE 20: Urban Indians, 1970 and 1980

SMSA[a]	1980[b]	1970	SMSA[a]	1980[b]	1970
Los Angeles	48,158	24,509	Anaheim–Santa Ana–Garden Grove	12,942	3,920
Tulsa	38,498	15,519			
Oklahoma City	24,752	13,033	Detroit	12,483	5,683
Phoenix	22,900	11,159	Dallas–Ft. Worth	11,225	6,632
Albuquerque	20,788	5,839	Sacramento	11,164	3,559
San Francisco	18,139	12,011	Chicago	10,709	8,996
			Fort Smith	9,297	3,812
San Bernardino–Riverside–Ontario	17,265	6,378	Denver–Boulder	9,117	4,348
Seattle–Everett	16,578	9,496	Anchorage	8,901	880
Minneapolis–St. Paul	15,959	9,852	Portland, Oregon	8,826	4,011
Tucson	14,927	8,837	San Jose	8,506	4,048
San Diego	14,616	5,880	Buffalo	7,113	5,775
New York	13,842	3,920	Yakima	6,656	416
			Milwaukee	6,534	4,075

SOURCE: *1980 Census of Population: Supplementary Reports, Standard Metropolitan Statistical Areas and Standard Consolidated Statistical Areas, 1980*, table 1; *1970 Census of Population*, vol. 1: *Characteristics of the Population*, part 1, section 1, table 67.
[a] These are the 25 Standard Metropolitan Statistical Areas with heaviest Indian population in 1980, with comparable 1970 figures.
[b] Includes Eskimo and Aleut.

major element in Indian life since World War II, did not slacken in the 1960s and 1970s. In the 1960 census, 27.9 percent of Indians enumerated lived in urban areas; in 1970 the percentage had climbed to 44.5 and in 1980 to 49. Some American cities, to which large numbers of Indians from disparate tribes migrated, became centers of Indian population that outdistanced reservations (see Table 20).[2] Many of these urban Indians main-

2. There is no general history of the Indian urban experience. The best recent study is Alan L. Sorkin, *The Urban American Indian* (Lexington, Massachusetts: D. C. Heath and Company, 1978). A collection of useful essays by anthropologists is Jack O. Waddell and O. Michael Watson, eds., *The American Indian in Urban Society* (Boston: Little, Brown and Company, 1971). For a listing and analysis of studies dealing with urban Indians, see Russell Thornton, Gary D. Sandefur, and Harold G. Grasmick, *The Urbanization of American Indians: A Critical Bibliography* (Bloomington: Indiana University Press, 1982).

tained tribal connections with the reservations, but second and third generations of Indians in cities often had no reservation experience at all. These city dwellers, however, for the most part steadfastly maintained their identity as Indians.

Although the movement to cities was a difficult uprooting for many Indians—a break from family and reservation patterns and removal from Bureau of Indian Affairs programs—the Indians in urban areas by most indicators fared better than their reservation counterparts. Studies for the 1960s and 1970s showed higher income, improved occupational status, a considerably higher level of education, lower rates of unemployment, and superior (but still inadequate) housing compared to rural Indians.[3]

The cultural, social, and economic changes that Indians were forced to make in the cities, nevertheless, were critical. Thrown into the white world in a more drastic way than on reservations, Indians faced conflicts between traditional behavioral patterns and urban ways. Extended families and tribal ties were diminished in the cities, and identification with one's occupation became an important element in social change. The changes—some of them in rapid and dramatic form—contributed to highly visible social pathology among urban Indians, especially alcoholism, crime, and mental illness. At the same time, the new situations stimulated a sense of social awareness and led to pan-Indian activities. In many cities "Indian centers" were established to provide social, cultural, and recreational activities for Indians residing there, to assist the Indians in developing job opportunities, and to attack the special problems (such as health and education needs) affecting urban Indians.[4]

The Bureau of Indian Affairs, which traditionally had been the contact between the federal government and the Indians, generally was unconcerned with nonreservation Indians. When asked by the Task Force on Urban and Rural Non-Reservation Indians of the American Indian Review Commission to respond to a questionnaire, Morris Thompson, commissioner of Indian affairs, declined because he said the questions did not apply to Bureau of Indian Affairs programs. He wrote:

3. Sorkin, *Urban American Indian*, summarizes studies through the mid-1970s. See also Sar A. Levitan and William B. Johnston, *Indian Giving: Federal Programs for Native Americans* (Baltimore: Johns Hopkins University Press, 1975), pp. 2–5; and Sol Tax, "The Impact of Urbanization on American Indians," *Annals of the American Academy of Political and Social Science* 436 (March 1978): 121–36.

4. Thornton and others, *Urbanization of American Indians*, pp. 32–53. Sorkin, *Urban American Indian*, has separate chapters on Indian health and alcoholism, housing and social services, urban Indian education, and urban institutions. For a state-by-state directory of urban Indian centers and other organizations, see American Indian Policy Review Commission, Task Force Eight, *Report on Urban and Rural Non-Reservation Indians* (Washington: GPO, 1976), pp. 97–133.

The basic reason for the BIA's providing services to Indians stems from the fact that the United States has a trust responsibility for Indian lands. We serve those Indian individuals who live on Indian reservations, trust, or restricted land. We also serve Indians who live so close to these areas that they can be considered socially, culturally, and economically affiliated with the tribe on that reservation or area held in trust. Hence the rule that we serve Indian individuals "on or near" Indian reservations. For all practical intents and purposes these individuals can be considered reservation Indians. They must be enrolled with the reservation and they are so near the reservation that they are dependent upon the facilities provided by BIA for their major community services.

Although Thompson admitted exceptions for the Indians of Oklahoma and Alaska growing out of special historical circumstances, in response to the question "If you have no specific programs for urban and rural non-reservation Indians, do you anticipate developing and/or extending services to these communities and individuals?" he answered, "No." Even the annual appropriations for funding urban Indian centers were turned over by the bureau to the Office of Native American Programs in the Department of Health, Education, and Welfare.[5] Federal relations with urban Indians, then, came from other departments and agencies than the Bureau of Indian Affairs, in programs developed specifically to meet Indian needs and in those applicable to Indians along with other citizens. There was overlapping and competition among programs, however, and many Indians preferred to work with specially Indian-related programs.[6] The accusation was made that urban Indians had become "victims of a Federal policy which denies services, if not thereby their very existence" to the urban Indian poor.[7] Demands reechoed for specific programs to meet the needs of the Indians in the cities.

Comparable problems, though of considerably lesser extent, faced Indian groups that were not formally recognized by the United States government and thus were not eligible for federal protection and for many federal

5. Morris Thompson to Al Elgin, August 2, 1976, printed in Task Force Eight, *Report on Urban and Rural Non-Reservation Indians*, pp. 143–44.

6. Task Force Eight reported: "The present state of federal funding for urban Indians can be compared with a jungle. Federal funding in most urban areas now goes to a host of fractionalized and competing urban organizations. The delivery of funds and services is not related to the objective needs of Indian individuals but is determined rather by political pressures and by the ability of individual factions to defeat their opponents through superior grantsmanship. Federal efforts to correct the situation seem to result only in the proliferation of more competing urban Indian organizations." *Report on Urban and Rural Non-Reservation Indians*, p. 11.

7. Ibid., p. 2.

services. These groups petitioned for recognition, and although some h. been considered on a case-by-case basis over the years, events of the 1970s made some regularization of the process necessary. Following Judge Boldt's decision in 1974 that "recognized" tribes were entitled to one-half of the commercial fish catch in the state of Washington, a number of Indian groups in that state petitioned for federal recognition. In 1975 the case of *Passamaquoddy* v. *Morton* held that the federal government had a trust responsibility for previously unrecognized groups. Recognition was seen by some Indians as an absolute right. Thus the American Indian Policy Review Commission asserted in its final report: "There is no legal basis for withholding general services from Indians, with the sole exception of specific termination acts. There is no legitimate foundation for denying Indian identification to any tribe or community. The BIA has no authority to refuse services to any member of the Indian population." The report spoke of "murky precedents and quirky administration."[8] But leaders of already recognized tribes were wary of widespread recognition of other groups, lest their own services and benefits be diluted by the addition of large numbers of newly recognized Indians.

Some government action was needed to set up criteria and procedures that would satisfy all parties. A move was made for congressional action by introduction of a bill in the Senate on December 15, 1977, and another in the House on May 11, 1978, to establish administrative procedures and guidelines for the secretary of the interior in acknowledging Indian tribes, but the goal was accomplished instead by administrative action. Proposed regulations drawn up by the Bureau of Indian Affairs were published on June 16, 1977, followed by consultation with tribes and other interested parties that was unprecedented in scope. There were, according to a bureau tabulation, "400 meetings, discussions, and conversations about Federal acknowledgment with other Federal agencies, State government officials, tribal representatives, petitioners, congressional staff members, and legal representatives of petitioning groups; 60 written comments on the initial proposed regulations of June 16, 1977; a national conference on Federal acknowledgment attended by approximately 350 representatives of Indian tribes and organizations; and 34 comments on the revised proposed regulations, published on June 1, 1978."[9]

8. American Indian Policy Review Commission, *Final Report* (Washington: GPO, 1977), pp. 461–62. See the whole chapter on nonrecognized tribes, which includes recommendations of the commission, pp. 457–84. See also American Indian Policy Review Commission, Task Force Ten, *Report on Terminated and Nonfederally Recognized Indians* (Washington: GPO, 1976), pp. 1651–1711.

9. 43 *Federal Register* 39361. A description of the conference called by the National Congress of American Indians in Nashville in the spring of 1978 and the resolutions adopted there appear in *American Indian Journal* 4 (May 1978): 2–4. For a discussion of

The final regulations were published on September 5, 1978.[10] In order ,or a petitioner to be recognized by the secretary of the interior as an Indian tribe having government-to-government relations with the United States and thus eligible for the protection, services, and benefits and subject to the responsibilities and obligations of such tribes, the regulations provided criteria to be applied to groups that were "ethnically and culturally identifiable," that could establish "a substantially continuous tribal existence," and that had "functioned as autonomous entities throughout history until the present." The seven criteria—all of them mandatory—were the following: (1) identification from historical times until the present on a continuous basis as "American Indian" or "aboriginal"; (2) habitation by a substantial portion of the group of a specific area or living in a community viewed as American Indian and distinct from other populations in the area, with members who were descendants of an Indian tribe which historically inhabited a specific area; (3) maintenance of tribal political influence over its members as an autonomous entity throughout history up to the present; (4) a governing document or statement describing membership criteria and governmental procedures; (5) a current list of members who could establish descendancy from a historical tribe or tribes; (6) membership composed principally of persons who were not members of any other Indian tribe; (7) not having been a subject of congressional legislation that expressly terminated or forbade federal relationship.[11]

The Bureau of Indian Affairs established a Federal Acknowledgment Branch, with a staff that included a historian, a genealogist, an anthropologist, and a sociologist, to check the evidence supplied by the petitioners and to do independent research on the status of each petitioning group. It promised to be a long process, for the branch estimated the number of unrecognized groups as 251, living in thirty-eight states, of which 150 might submit petitions.[12]

---

the issues and a harsh criticism of federal policy and action in the past, see Terry Anderson, "Federal Recognition: The Vicious Myth," ibid., pp. 7–19.

10. 43 *Federal Register* 39361–64, codified as 25 *Code of Federal Regulations* 54. Detailed guidelines for preparing a petition were issued by the Bureau of Indian Affairs in December 1978. A list of federally recognized tribes, directed by the regulations, appeared in 44 *Federal Register* 7235–37 (February 6, 1979). The list for 1980 is printed in the Appendix.

11. 25 *Code of Federal Regulations* 54.7.

12. Estimates are as of July 1981, furnished to the author by the Federal Acknowledgment Branch. Reports of action taken on petitions are published in the *Federal Register*. See, for example, the acknowledgment of the Grand Traverse Band of Ottawa and Chippewa Indians as an Indian tribe in 45 *Federal Register* 19321–22 (March 25, 1980), and the rejection of the petition of the Lower Muskogee Creek Tribe—East of the Mississippi, Inc., in 46 *Federal Register* 11718 (February 10, 1981).

FEDERAL PROGRAMS FOR INDIANS

In 1980 urban Indians and reservation Indians—and in some cases Indians, too, from terminated or nonrecognized tribes—benefited from a tremendous array of federal programs. The ultimate, although sometimes unexpressed, goal of the federal spending was to assist the Indians to become self-supporting. Yet Indian communities and individual Indians continued to need outside help to bring them up to the economic and social levels of other American citizens, and the federal government assumed most of the responsibility. Programs for education, health, and social services; for construction of schools, hospitals, and roads; for irrigation systems and resources development—all were provided from federal funds. Year by year the amounts had increased, as more needs were recognized and as Indian demands for goods and services became stronger and better articulated. Like other poverty-stricken groups in the nation, Indians drew upon general programs designed for all citizens, but their special relation with the United States government resulted in a continuation and proliferation of "Indian programs" that pertained to the recipients because of their special status as Indian people or Indian organizations.[13]

The chief supplier of these programs, of course, was the Bureau of Indian Affairs in the Department of the Interior. The bureau's budget for 1980 totaled more than a billion dollars (see Table 21), of which education costs made up the largest share. Yet the Bureau of Indian Affairs, although still considered by the Indians and by the public as the principal federal agency concerned with Indian matters, no longer controlled even a majority of the funds appropriated by Congress for the Indians. The Indian Health Service, in the Department of Health and Human Services, spent more each year for health care than the Bureau of Indian Affairs spent on education; and even in education, the bureau shared responsibility with the Department of Education. Because the bureau restricted its programs largely to Indians on or near reservations, to federally recognized tribes, and to trust obligations relating to land and other assets, Indians were forced to look to other agencies for social services, housing, employment assistance, and programs for economic development (see Table 22). The Department of the Interior, however, still administered the sizable Indian

---

13. The fullest compilation of federal programs for Indians is Richard S. Jones, *Federal Programs of Assistance to American Indians: A Report Prepared for the Senate Select Committee on Indian Affairs*, Committee Print, 97th Congress, 1st session, (Washington: GPO, 1981). See also *Felix S. Cohen's Handbook of Federal Indian Law*, 1982 ed. (Charlottesville, Virginia: Michie, Bobbs-Merrill, 1982), chapter 13, "Government Services to Indians," pp. 673–738; and Alan L. Sorkin, *American Indians and Federal Aid* (Washington: Brookings Institution, 1971).

TABLE 21: Bureau of Indian Affairs Budget, Fiscal Year 1980
(In Thousands of Dollars)

Education		271,762
School operations	(187,031)	
Johnson–O'Malley educational assistance	(29,388)	
Continuing education	(55,343)	
Indian Services		202,190
Tribal government services	(22,460)	
Social services	(87,401)	
Law enforcement	(27,709)	
Housing	(19,416)	
Self-determination services	(45,204)	
Economic Development and Employment Programs		78,253
Business enterprise development	(8,713)	
Employment development	(51,737)	
Road maintenance	(17,803)	
Natural Resources Development		74,622
Forestry and agriculture	(61,832)	
Minerals, mining, irrigation, and power	(12,790)	
Trust Responsibilities		51,047
Indian rights protection	(25,940)	
Real estate and financial trust services	(25,107)	
General Management and Facilities Operations		131,021
Management and administration	(49,434)	
Program support services	(4,074)	
Facilities management	(77,513)	
Construction		93,291
Irrigation systems	(43,449)	
Building and utilities	(44,725)	
Land acquisition	(5,117)	
Road Construction		66,479
Alaska Native Claims		30,000
Eastern Indians Land Claims		8,000
Total		1,006,665

SOURCE: Bureau of Indian Affairs, news release, January 30, 1980.
NOTE: Includes actual appropriations, pay-cost adjustments, and pending supplemental requests.

TABLE 22: Government-Wide Funding for Indian Programs, 1980
(In Millions of Dollars)

	Budget Authority	Actual Outlay		Budget Authority	Actual Outlay
Education	484	438	Management and		
Interior	(270)	(247)	Facilities	131	121
Education	(214)	(191)	Interior	(131)	(121)
Health Service/Nutrition	583	558	Construction	251	274
HHS	(547)	(525)	Interior	(160)	(189)
USDA	(36)	(33)	HHS	(74)	(73)
Housing	867	141	Education	(17)	(12)
Interior	(19)	(17)	Other Interior Funds	153	142
HUD	(848)	(124)			
Social Services	121	106	Revenue Sharing	10	10
Interior	(87)	(78)	Total Federal Funds	3,063	2,220
HHS	(34)	(28)	Interior Trust Funds	969	794
Employment	250	237	Total	4,032	3,014
Interior	(52)	(45)			
Labor	(198)	(192)	Recapitulation		
Economic Development	88	91	Interior	1,043	972
Interior	(26)	(31)	Education	231	203
Commerce	(26)	(24)	HHS	655	626
HUD	(36)	(36)	USDA	36	33
Natural Resources	74	66	HUD	884	160
Interior	(74)	(66)	Labor	198	192
			Commerce	26	24
Trust Activities	51	36	Revenue Sharing	10	10
Interior	(51)	(36)	Total	3,063	2,220

SOURCE: "Department of the Interior and Related Agencies Appropriations for 1982," *Hearings before a Subcommittee of the Committee on Appropriations, House of Representatives, 97th Congress, 1st Session, Subcommittee on the Department of the Interior and Related Agencies* (1981), part 9, pp. 1279–80.

trust funds that were held in the Treasury of the United States and that were appropriated for the Indians' benefit from year to year.[14]

14. See the two-page table prepared by the Office of Management and Budget regarding federal budgets for programs identified as serving Indians because of their status as Indians in "Department of the Interior and Related Agencies Appropriations for 1982," *Hearings before a Subcommittee of the Committee on Appropriations, House of Representatives, 97th Congress, 1st Session, Subcommittee on the Department of the Interior and Related Agencies* (1981), part 9, pp. 1279–80.

ı amazing array of federal programs gave assistance to American In-
ns in 1980. If to those designed exclusively to benefit Indian tribes and
ndividuals are added programs that specifically included Indians as eligible beneficiaries and those that were of special interest to Indians (without
specially naming them), the total is almost overwhelming. There were
many roads by which to approach the federal government for assistance.
Twelve of the executive departments—Agriculture, Commerce, Defense,
Education, Energy, Health and Human Services, Housing and Urban Development, Interior, Justice, Labor, Transportation, and Treasury—had
something to offer Indians. In addition, eight independent agencies were
concerned with Indian programs or Indian rights: the Commission on
Civil Rights, Environmental Protection Agency, Equal Employment Opportunity Commission, National Endowment for the Arts, National Science Foundation, Office of Personnel Management, Small Business Administration, and Smithsonian Institution.[15]

This proliferation caused confusion and competition and considerable
overlapping. It was impossible for all departments and agencies—even
with the establishment of special "Indian desks"—to show the understanding and sympathy for Indian needs that the Bureau of Indian Affairs
had developed over the decades. The negative results were pointed out by
the American Indian Policy Review Commission in 1977:

> Because of the layers of Federal, State and local employees charged
> with administering Indian programs, decisionmaking powers are
> often denied Indian people. One result of this bureaucratic entangle-
> ment is that Indian people do not know which agency to approach
> when they need assistance.
>
> Because of the complexity of many Indian programs, there is a se-
> rious lack of coordination within and between Federal agencies. As a
> result, Indian people often fail to realize many of the benefits in-
> tended for them.[16]

There was recurring agitation for a new centralization of Indian administration at the federal level, a reversal of the sporadic but long-lived condemnation of concentrated authority in the hands of the Bureau of Indian
Affairs. Thus the American Indian Policy Review Commission recommended that the special status of the Indians be "recognized and institu-
tionalized in the form of a separate Indian Department or independent
agency," under which all Indian programs would fall; other Indian groups
supported similar proposals.[17]

15. Jones, *Federal Programs of Assistance to American Indians.*
16. American Indian Policy Review Commission, *Final Report*, p. 248.
17. Ibid., pp. 284–88.

BUILDING AN ECONOMIC BASE

The most serious problem underlying the search for self-determination continued to be economic. Commissioner of Indian Affairs William E. Hallett described the situation candidly in 1980:

> During the past decade and a half, federal monies have gone to Indian communities in unprecedented amounts. Those dollars bought better education, health care, housing, public employment and roads. In some ways, at least, they resulted in a noticeable improvement in the quality of reservation life.
>
> What those dollars did not buy was substantive economic development. And if this trend continues, tribes may become overwhelmingly dependent upon direct and indirect government subsidies. That would be a tragedy for both the Indian people and the nation.
>
> Without a comprehensive economic development plan as one of our foremost priorities, the goals of self-determination and self-sufficiency will eventually topple back onto the heap of good intentions.[18]

In a series of oversight hearings in 1979, the House Committee on Interior and Insular Affairs gathered new testimony on the economic status of the reservations that it hoped would serve as the basis for "comprehensive reform legislation." But it uncovered in large part simply a duplication of reports on economic insufficiencies that had regularly appeared since 1960. There was no shortage of federal programs. In a statement submitted to the committee, Forrest J. Gerard, assistant secretary of the interior for Indian affairs, described activities under eleven headings: employment assistance, Indian Action Program, enterprise development, credit and financing, road maintenance, road construction, natural resources development, forestry and fire suppression, water resources, wildlife and parks, and minerals and mining. Yet his conclusion sounded like an echo from past decades. "Reservations," he noted, "lack some or all of the attributes necessary to support the economic enterprise functions. Reservations have no tax base, often are bleak and barren, remote from labor pools, raw materials, and markets; transportation and power may be minimal or non-existent."[19] The need was clear; the programs to meet it all seemed ineffective.

18. *BIA Profile: The Bureau of Indian Affairs and American Indians* (Washington: GPO, 1981), p. 6.

19. "Indian Economic Development Programs," *Oversight Hearings before the Committee on Interior and Insular Affairs, House of Representatives, 96th Congress, 1st*

One significant development was the formation in 1975 of the Council of Energy Resource Tribes (CERT), a consortium of tribes, originally twenty-two but later expanded, that had important mineral resources. Under the initial leadership of Peter MacDonald, Navajo tribal chairman, CERT sought to promote the development of Indian resources on terms favorable to the tribes. Supported by government funds and with an office in Washington, D.C., the council spoke out for Indian economic development needs. It worked for the renegotiation of old leases to bring a higher return to the Indians, and its members hoped, on the model of the Organization of Petroleum Exporting Countries (OPEC), to be able to use the rich natural resources of the reservations (oil, coal, uranium) as a bargaining tool for bettering Indian conditions. It also provided encouragement and technical assistance to tribal groups. But CERT was not the full answer, for it represented only the resource-rich tribes, a minority of the total number, and reduction in demand and lower prices for mineral resources dampened the original high hopes. The criticism of CERT voiced by Indians who feared that it was too closely tied to corporations and to the government also weakened its effectiveness.[20]

TRUST RESPONSIBILITY: THE GREAT FATHER REDIVIVUS

The heavy federal support of services for Indians was justified in the minds of many Indians by a new concept in federal-Indian relations that came to the fore in the 1970s: trust responsibility. If the concept was not entirely new, it was given greatly expanded meaning, and it was called "one of the most important" concepts governing relations between the United States government and the Indians and "one of the primary cornerstones of Indian law."[21] But the precise extent of the trust responsibility was far from clear.

Session (1979). Gerard's statement is on pp. 115–26. The hearings are an excellent survey of conditions, with testimony and statements from government officials, Indian spokesmen, and other interested parties.

20. There is discussion of CERT in "An 'OPEC' Right in America's Own Back Yard," *U.S. News and World Report* 81 (August 2, 1976): 29–30; "U.S. Indians Demand a Better Energy Deal," *Business Week*, December 19, 1977, p. 53; "Fuel Powwow," *Time* 114 (August 20, 1979): 17; Geoffrey O'Gara, "Canny CERT Gets Respect, Money Problems," *Wassaja/Indian Historian* 13 (June 1980): 24–28.

21. American Indian Policy Review Commission, *Final Report*, pp. 5, 125; *Cohen's Federal Indian Law*, 1982 ed., p. 221. Note that the use of the term and its expanded meaning are of recent vintage. Felix S. Cohen in his monumental analysis of Indian legal matters, *Handbook of Federal Indian Law* (Washington: GPO, 1942), did not use the term; and Wilcomb E. Washburn, in *Red Man's Land/White Man's Law: A Study of the*

There was agreement that the United States government acted trustee for Indian land and other property—both what was owned by t. tribes and what belonged to individual Indians. The obligations in this re gard were reasonably well defined. Much of the work of the Bureau of In- dian Affairs in the twentieth century focused on trust duties—for the al- lotted lands held in trust under the provision of the Dawes Act, for tribal and individual funds held in the Treasury of the United States, and for other Indian properties. The Department of the Interior and the Bureau of Indian Affairs argued that the obligations, in fact, were limited to those of trustees of property and only for tribes that were federally recognized. This position was represented in a statement prepared in 1973 by the solicitor of the Interior Department:

> The phrase "trust responsibility of the Secretary" is not only gen- erally misunderstood and misapplied, but also undefined in any trea- tise or statute. It has an emotional meaning when used by Indians and their advocates but it also has a legal meaning. It is generally used in two broad contexts: in connection with Indian lands and gov- ernmental social programs, but only with respect to the lands and re- lated property is the phrase appropriately applied.
>
> . . . Certain Indian lands, mineral resources, and water rights, put in Indian ownership by treaty or statute, and income derived there- from are held in trust by the United States for the benefit of the In- dian owner, whether it be a tribe or an individual. This "trust" rela- tionship between the Secretary and the Indian owner is similar to that between a bank which has been named trustee under a trust agreement and the beneficiaries of the trust. A distinguishing feature of the Secretary's responsibilty, however, is the manner in which he exercises it. That is, his decisions are made not unilaterally but in conjunction with the Indian beneficiaries. The responsibilities of the Secretary in this connection as well defined in the common law and can generally be said to impose a high degree of care upon the Secre- tary in the handling of these trust properties.[22]

Indians and their advocates were dissatisfied with this restrictive legal interpretation and insisted that trust responsibility had a much wider ap-

---

Past and Present Status of the American Indian (New York: Charles Scribner's Sons, 1971), was unaware of it. For treatments of trust responsibility, see American Indian Pol- icy Review Commission, *Final Report*, pp. 5–6, 11–13, 121–34; American Indian Policy Review Commission, Task Force One, *Report on Trust Responsibilities and the Federal- Indian Relationship, Including Treaty Review* (Washington: GPO, 1976); Gilbert L. Hall, *The Federal-Indian Trust Relationship* (Washington: Institute for the Development of Indian Law, 1979).

22. Quoted in Task Force One, *Report on Trust Responsibilities*, p. 48.

...ation. The National Tribal Chairmen's Association in February 1974, ... example, saw a threefold obligation of the federal government: not only ...he protection of tribal assets and the management of Indian funds and natural resources, but a duty to "protect . . . [the] sovereignty of Indian Tribes, so there is no further erosion of tribal sovereignty and to support tribes in their efforts to enhance tribal sovereignty" and to provide community and social services to Indian people. A more recent statement from the same association was brief and pointed:

> The federal government gained a territory in perpetuity over which to govern through treaties and other agreements with Indian nations, with promises to: 1) protect the Indians in their reserved territory and other private property, and 2) provide a variety of health, education and social services to Indian people, in perpetuity.
>
> The federal government historically has not lived up to its trust responsibility to fulfill these promises, and it is this reason that the Indian people today suffer from the poorest social and economic conditions of any population in the United States.[23]

Indians asserted that the federal government in fulfilling its trust responsibilities must provide Indians with education, health care, and other social services sufficient at least to bring them up to the level of the general population; that the responsibility extended to all Indians, not only to those of federally recognized tribes; and that the responsibility affected all agencies of the federal government, not only the Department of the Interior.[24]

The diversity of interpretation of trust responsibility between the federal government and the Indians was only one cause of the murkiness that surrounded the concept, for Indian spokesmen themselves were hesitant to offer a detailed definition of trust responsibility. The American Indian Policy Review Commission, a major force in promoting the broad application of the concept, declared in 1977: "The argument against a precise definition of the trust obligations with an enumeration of specific rights and obligations is that the Federal trust responsibility is a continually evolving concept." The commission wanted instead a general congressional statement of policy, which "would not place undue restrictions on the

---

23. Ibid., p. 47; response of National Tribal Chairmen's Association to President Ronald Reagan's policy statement, printed in *Indian Truth*, April 1983, p. 6. A useful analysis of trust responsibility, including its broad ramifications, is Reid Peyton Chambers, "Judicial Enforcement of the Federal Trust Responsibility to Indians," *Stanford Law Review* 27 (May 1975): 1213–48.

24. American Indian Policy Review Commission, *Final Report*, pp. 6, 129–38.

development of this doctrine but still would constitute an explicit recog-
tion of the scope of the obligation by Congress."[25]

A fundamental problem surrounding the whole question of federal responsibilities to Indians was that of Indian self-determination versus federal paternalism. In earlier decades attempts to solve the problem of paternalism had rested on a distinction between the *person* and the *property* of
the Indians. Thus Secretary of the Interior Ray Lyman Wilbur in 1931
wrote: "For a hundred years the wheels of Federal administration have
worn a deeper and deeper rut of dependence. We can probably make a distinction between the Indian's health and education and his property. Until
the States develop proper protective laws for the Indians' property, Federal
responsibility is inevitable, but there is no good reason for maintaining
separate schools and health programs for Indian boys and girls when the
State already provides them." And in his reorganization of the Indian Bureau, the administration of activities relating to the Indian's person and to
his property was divided.[26] At the time of the termination controversy in
the 1950s, Felix S. Cohen, in condemning the cry to end paternalism that
was behind much of the termination effort, fell back on the same sort of
distinction. Trusteeship was a necessary means of protecting Indian property, Cohen argued, and he distinguished it from wardship, which touched
the personal action of the Indians and which he called outmoded.[27]

In the decade of the 1970s, Indians, by rejecting the limitation of trusteeship to property and by expanding the concept of trust responsibility to
nearly all aspects of Indian existence, reopened the Pandora's box of federal
paternalism. Even the trust responsibilities regarding land and other assets
brought a large element of paternalism. Commissioner Dillon Myer's assertion in 1953 that "you cannot have trusteeship without paternalism"

25. Ibid., p. 132. Representative Lloyd Meeds of Washington, vice chairman of the
commission, issued a strongly dissenting view, declaring: "Because the United States has
assumed the role of trustee with respect to some tribal assets, the Commission would
also have us believe that the United States is under a permanent legal obligation to do all
things helpful to the protection and enhancement of Indian lands, resources, tribal self-
government, culture, prosperity, and material well-being. In addition, the Commission
charges that the entitlements under its new found obligation of the United States run to
all Indians wherever they may be located, however assimilated, and whether or not they
retain any ties with Indian culture or tribal self-government. In short, in seeking to find
some nonexistent legal basis for the creation of a special status for Indians, the Commission has created a new doctrine, unknown to the law. This would convert tribal political
aspirations into legal doctrine without the necessity of going through our democratic political processes." Ibid., p. 602.

26. *Report of the Secretary of the Interior*, 1931, pp. 9–10.

27. Felix S. Cohen, "Indian Wardship: The Twilight of a Myth," *American Indian* 6
(Summer 1953): 8–14.

reechoed by Interior Department officials twenty years later: "The exercise of a trust is paternalism. Indian leaders, government officials and the general public should understand that the Indian demands that the government continue its trust responsibility for Indian assets inescapably involves paternalism. The government has to approve proposed uses or disposition of the assets under its trust responsibility. To do otherwise is to violate the trust. If the Indians want to do otherwise—that is, have complete freedom for use of their assets—they should request legislation terminating the trust responsibility."[28]

When the trust responsibility is extended to include "health, education and social services to Indian people, in perpetuity," paternalism becomes almost unlimited in scope and in duration, for the federal government becomes the supplier of the Indians' essential needs. Some Indians have noted that in the old days before the coming of the white man, the buffalo provided all that the Indians needed: food, shelter, clothing. Then the white man took away the buffalo and gave the Indians the government instead—the new buffalo.[29] The figure of the government as the "new buffalo" is to the point. But a better figure is the historical one of the Great Father. Dependence on the federal government for schooling, health care, legal services, technical aid in tribal government, and economic development means the Great Father redivivus in pervasive form.[30]

AMERICA'S UNFINISHED BUSINESS

Relations between the federal government and the American Indians were an ever-developing continuum, but in the second half of the twentieth century changes have come at an especially rapid rate. The decade of the 1970s with its numerous laws and programs looking toward Indian self-determination (in education, religion, land and resource use, and tribal jurisdiction) was a remarkably busy time. The developments were the cumulative results of actions with roots far in the past, but they will un-

28. Dillon S. Myer, "Indian Administration: Problems and Goals," *Social Service Review* 27 (June 1953): 200; statement of Marvin Franklin, William Rogers, and Theodore Taylor, May 4, 1973, printed in Task Force One, *Report on Trust Responsibilities*, p. 49.

29. The "new buffalo" figure is reported in D'Arcy McNickle, "Commentary," in Jane F. Smith and Robert M. Kvasnicka, eds., *Indian-White Relations: A Persistent Paradox* (Washington: Howard University Press, 1976), pp. 251–52, and in William T. Hagan, "Tribalism Rejuvenated: The Native American since the Era of Termination," *Western Historical Quarterly* 12 (January 1981): 11.

30. See Russel L. Barsh, "U.S. v. Mitchell Decision Narrows Trust Responsibility," *American Indian Journal* 6 (August 1980): 2–14, especially pp. 13–14.

doubtedly be seen by later historians as a prelude to future—and per
radical—change in Indian-white relations.

Persistent themes from the previous two hundred years were still ev.
dent in 1980, and questions to be faced were often merely new manifestations of old problems still not solved. The dependency of the Indian
communities, heightened in times of economic stress, continued the paternalism of the federal government. Despite all the talk about cultural,
economic, and political autonomy, many Indian individuals and Indian
groups looked toward the federal government, even though no longer per-
sonified as the Great Father, for daily support and for relief from special
distress. The continuing tendency of many Indians to see the federal government as the cause of all their problems was an acknowledgment of the
dominant influence of the government in their lives and a reinforcement
of paternalism. Indian attempts to extend the idea of trust responsibility beyond trusteeship for Indian property to include a responsibility for
the general welfare of the Indians emphasized the paternalistic aspects of
government relations with the Indians at the very time that cries of self-
determination filled the air.

As the nation and the Indian tribes look toward the twenty-first century, certain problems seem sure to remain prominent. First is the continuing need for sound economic development—including coal, oil, and
other mineral resources as well as land—so that the Indian communities
asserting self-determination can indeed reach some degree of self-sufficiency. But the search for economic progress will also heighten tensions
within Indian groups between those who want to exploit the sources of
wealth for the sake of economic betterment and those who insist that the
environment, Mother Earth, should not be violated by strip mining or
other extractive operations.

A second continuing issue of major concern is the question of inherent
sovereignty of Indian tribes within their reservations and the increasing
assertion of such sovereignty. How is criminal and civil jurisdiction to be
divided between tribes, states, and the federal government, and especially,
what jurisdiction does a tribe have over non-Indians within the reservation
boundaries? Can viable and effective tribal governments be maintained to
carry on the government-to-government relations with the United States
that have become the announced goal of both Indian groups and the federal
government? Tribal factionalism and a division between supporters of federally recognized tribal governments (many of which stem from the Indian
Reorganization Act of 1934) and "traditional" Indian elders and spiritual leaders undercut effective modern government. Government-to-
government relations presume strong and well-supported tribal government structures that not only can deal with the federal government as

ependent political entities but can also manage and operate the pro-
ams for the Indian communities that have been the work and responsibility of the United States government.[31] Practically, however, "government-to-government" has been understood to apply simply to Indian
groups acknowledged by the Bureau of Indian Affairs as recipients of federal services provided by the bureau. In 1980 there were 278 such tribal
entities, ranging from the large Navajo tribe (with a greater population
than a good many member nations of the United Nations) to an array of
very small bands, colonies, and communities scattered through California
and Nevada, some with a population of less than a dozen people (see
Appendix C).

A third matter of concern is the federal government's responsibility for
that half of the Indian population no longer living under tribal governments on reservations. How much responsibility does the federal government have toward urban Indians, and in what way can that responsibility
be met? If the Bureau of Indian Affairs limits its concern to federally recognized tribes and emphasizes its trusteeship for land and related assets, can
other agencies of the United States government adequately care for continuing needs of the numerous Indians outside the reservations?

Paternalism seems abiding (although few Indians or government officials want to admit it), but the Great Father cannot act as arbitrarily as he
once did. Unilateral action of the federal government, common in the past,
is difficult if not impossible in an age of increasingly sophisticated Indian
initiatives. Tribal governments, with their astute lawyers and other specialists, skillfully draw upon the resources of the federal government and
adapt them more and more to their own ends.

The history of government relations with the Indians over two centuries
points with considerable clarity to the long-standing pressures for assimilation of the Indians into the mainstream of white American society. Only
the future will show whether the heavy dependence of the Indians upon
federal funds and federal management skills can be effectively lessened and
whether the destiny of the Indians as prosperous groups with separate
identities within a pluralistic society can be attained.

31. Statements of the government-to-government philosophy are in *BIA Profile*, p. 3,
and Indian policy statement of President Reagan, January 24, 1983, *Weekly Compilation
of Presidential Documents* 19 (January 31, 1983): 98–102. An example of criticism of
existing tribal governmental organization is the statement of William A. Means, director
of the International Indian Treaty Council, in *Indian Truth*, April 1983, p. 7. Means
says: "Unfortunately, these tribal governments do not represent the majority of the Indian population. Rather, they are administrative authorities imposed by the government
and managed by the Bureau of Indian Affairs." For a sharp exchange of views on this subject, see the statements of Wilcomb E. Washburn and Joseph De La Cruz in the *New York
Times* (op ed page), July 20 and August 2, 1978, on the occasion of an Indian protest called
the Longest Walk.

Appendixes
Bibliographical Essay
Index

Appendix A

President	Secretary of War	Commissioner
George Washington April 30, 1789	Henry Knox September 12, 1789 Timothy Pickering January 2, 1795 James McHenry February 6, 1796	
John Adams March 4, 1797	James McHenry (continued) Samuel Dexter June 12, 1800	
Thomas Jefferson March 4, 1801	Henry Dearborn March 5, 1801	
James Madison March 4, 1809	William Eustis April 8, 1809 John Armstrong February 5, 1813	

resident	Secretary of War	Commissioner
	James Monroe October 1, 1814 William Crawford August 8, 1815	
James Monroe March 4, 1817	John C. Calhoun December 10, 1817	Thomas L. McKenney[1] March 11, 1824
John Quincy Adams March 4, 1825	James Barbour March 7, 1825 Peter B. Porter June 21, 1828	Thomas L. McKenney (continued)
Andrew Jackson March 4, 1829	John H. Eaton March 9, 1829 Lewis Cass August 8, 1831	Thomas L. McKenney (continued) Samuel S. Hamilton[1] September 30, 1830 Elbert Herring[1] August 1831 July 10, 1832[2] Carey H. Harris July 4, 1836
Martin Van Buren March 4, 1837	Joel R. Poinsett March 14, 1837	Carey H. Harris (continued) T. Hartley Crawford October 22, 1838
William Henry Harrison March 4, 1841	John Bell March 5, 1841	T. Hartley Crawford (continued)
John Tyler April 6, 1841	John Bell (continued) John C. Spencer October 12, 1841 James M. Porter March 8, 1843 William Wilkins February 20, 1844	T. Hartley Crawford (continued)
James K. Polk March 4, 1845	William L. Marcy March 8, 1845	T. Hartley Crawford (continued) William Medill October 28, 1845

President	Secretary of the Interior	Commissioner
Zachary Taylor March 4, 1849	Thomas Ewing March 8, 1849	William Medill (continued) Orlando Brown June 30, 1849 Luke Lea July 1, 1850
Millard Fillmore July 10, 1850	Thomas Ewing (continued) Alexander H. H. Stuart September 16, 1850	Luke Lea (continued)
Franklin Pierce March 4, 1853	Robert McClelland March 7, 1853	George W. Manypenny March 24, 1853
James Buchanan March 4, 1857	Jacob Thompson March 10, 1857	George W. Manypenny (continued) James W. Denver April 17, 1857 Charles E. Mix June 14, 1858 James W. Denver November 8, 1858 Alfred B. Greenwood May 4, 1859
Abraham Lincoln March 4, 1861	Caleb Smith March 5, 1861 John P. Usher January 1, 1863	William P. Dole March 13, 1861
Andrew Johnson April 15, 1865	John P. Usher (continued) James Harlan May 15, 1865 Orville H. Browning September 1, 1866	William P. Dole (continued) Dennis N. Cooley July 10, 1865 Lewis V. Bogy[3] November 1, 1866 Nathaniel G. Taylor March 29, 1867
Ulysses S. Grant March 4, 1869	Jacob D. Cox March 9, 1869 Columbus Delano November 1, 1870	Nathaniel G. Taylor (continued) Ely S. Parker April 21, 1869

President	Secretary of the Interior	Commissioner
	Zachariah Chandler October 19, 1875	Francis A. Walker November 21, 1871 Edward P. Smith March 20, 1873 John Q. Smith December 11, 1875
Rutherford B. Hayes March 4, 1877	Carl Schurz March 12, 1877	John Q. Smith (continued) Ezra A. Hayt September 20, 1877 Roland E. Trowbridge March 15, 1880
James A. Garfield March 4, 1881	Samuel J. Kirkwood March 8, 1881	Hiram Price May 6, 1881
Chester A. Arthur September 20, 1881	Samuel J. Kirkwood (continued) Henry M. Teller April 17, 1882	Hiram Price (continued)
Grover Cleveland March 4, 1885	Lucius Q. C. Lamar March 6, 1885 William F. Vilas January 16, 1888	Hiram Price (continued) John D. C. Atkins March 21, 1885 John H. Oberly October 10, 1888
Benjamin Harrison March 4, 1889	John W. Noble March 7, 1889	John H. Oberly (continued) Thomas J. Morgan June 30, 1889
Grover Cleveland March 4, 1893	Hoke Smith March 6, 1893 David R. Francis September 4, 1896	Daniel M. Browning April 18, 1893
William McKinley March 4, 1897	Cornelius N. Bliss March 5, 1897 Ethan A. Hitchcock February 20, 1899	Daniel M. Browning (continued) William A. Jones May 3, 1897

President	Secretary of the Interior	Commissioner
Theodore Roosevelt September 14, 1901	Ethan A. Hitchcock (continued) James R. Garfield March 4, 1907	William A. Jones (continued) Francis E. Leupp January 1, 1905
William H. Taft March 4, 1909	Richard A. Ballinger March 5, 1909 Walter Lowrie Fisher March 7, 1911	Francis E. Leupp (continued) Robert G. Valentine June 19, 1909
Woodrow Wilson March 4, 1913	Franklin Knight Lane March 5, 1913 John Barton Payne March 13, 1920	Cato Sells June 2, 1913
Warren G. Harding March 4, 1921	Albert B. Fall March 5, 1921 Hubert Work March 5, 1923	Cato Sells (continued) Charles H. Burke May 7, 1921
Calvin Coolidge August 3, 1923	Hubert Work (continued) Roy O. West January 21, 1929	Charles H. Burke (continued)
Herbert C. Hoover March 4, 1929	Ray L. Wilbur March 5, 1929	Charles J. Rhoads April 18, 1929
Franklin Delano Roosevelt March 4, 1933	Harold L. Ickes March 4, 1933	Charles J. Rhoads (continued) John Collier April 21, 1933 William A. Brophy March 6, 1945
Harry S. Truman April 12, 1945	Harold L. Ickes (continued) Julius A. Krug March 18, 1946 Oscar L. Chapman January 19, 1950	William A. Brophy (continued) John R. Nichols April 13, 1949 Dillon S. Myer May 5, 1950
Dwight D. Eisenhower January 20, 1953	Douglas McKay January 21, 1953	Glenn L. Emmons August 10, 1953

President	Secretary of the Interior	Commissioner
	Frederick A. Seaton June 8, 1956	
John F. Kennedy January 20, 1961	Stewart L. Udall January 20, 1961	Philleo Nash September 26, 1961
Lyndon B. Johnson November 22, 1963	Stewart L. Udall (continued)	Philleo Nash (continued) Robert L. Bennett April 27, 1966
Richard M. Nixon January 20, 1969	Walter J. Hickel January 24, 1969 Rogers C. B. Morton January 29, 1971	Robert L. Bennett (continued) Louis R. Bruce August 8, 1969 Morris Thompson December 3, 1973
Gerald R. Ford August 9, 1974	Rogers C. B. Morton (continued) Stanley K. Hathaway June 11, 1975 Thomas S. Kleppe October 9, 1975	Morris Thompson (continued) Benjamin Reifel December 7, 1976
Jimmy Carter January 20, 1977	Cecil D. Andrus January 23, 1977 Forrest J. Gerard[4] October 13, 1977	William E. Hallett December 14, 1979

NOTE on dates of office: *Secretaries:* date entered upon duties if different from date of appointment. See *Biographical Directory of the American Congress* and Eugene P. Trani, *The Secretaries of the Department of the Interior* (Washington: National Anthropological Archives, 1975). *Commissioners:* date entered upon duties as indicated in the essays in Robert M. Kvasnicka and Herman J. Viola, eds., *The Commissioners of Indian Affairs, 1824–1977* (Lincoln: University of Nebraska Press, 1979); if no precise date is given, date of appointment used is that shown in Edward E. Hill, *Preliminary Inventory of the Records of the Bureau of Indian Affairs* (Washington: National Archives, 1965).
[1] Head of Bureau of Indian Affairs
[2] Appointed Commissioner of Indian Affairs
[3] Not confirmed by the Senate
[4] Assistant Secretary of the Interior for Indian Affairs

Appendix B

Indian Population

1900	237,196	1930	343,352	1960	532,591
1910	276,927	1940	345,252	1970	792,730
1920	244,437	1950	357,499	1980	1,361,869

	1970	1980		1970	1980
Alabama	2,443	7,483	Iowa	2,992	5,367
Alaska	16,276	21,849	Kansas	8,672	15,254
Arizona	95,812	152,610	Kentucky	1,531	3,518
Arkansas	2,014	9,346	Louisiana	5,294	11,950
California	91,018	198,095	Maine	2,195	4,057
Colorado	8,836	17,726	Maryland	4,239	7,823
Connecticut	2,222	4,431	Massachusetts	4,475	7,483
Delaware	656	1,309	Michigan	16,854	39,702
District of			Minnesota	23,128	34,841
Columbia	956	996	Mississippi	4,113	6,131
Florida	6,677	18,981	Missouri	5,405	12,127
Georgia	2,347	7,444	Montana	27,130	37,153
Hawaii	1,126	2,664	Nebraska	6,624	9,147
Idaho	6,687	10,418	Nevada	7,933	13,201
Illinois	11,413	15,833	New Hampshire	361	1,297
Indiana	3,887	7,681	New Jersey	4,706	8,176

	1970	1980		1970	1980
New Mexico	72,788	104,634	Vermont	229	968
New York	28,355	38,117	Virginia	4,853	9,093
North Carolina	44,406	64,519	Washington	33,386	58,159
North Dakota	14,369	20,119	West Virginia	751	1,555
Ohio	6,654	11,986	Wisconsin	19,924	29,318
Oklahoma	98,468	169,297	Wyoming	4,980	7,088
Oregon	13,510	26,587	Total Indians	792,730	1,361,869
Pennsylvania	5,533	9,173			
Rhode Island	1,390	2,872	Eskimos	28,186[1]	42,149
South Carolina	2,241	5,666	Aleuts	6,352[1]	14,177
South Dakota	32,365	45,081	Total	827,268	1,418,195
Tennessee	2,276	5,012			
Texas	17,957	39,374			
Utah	11,273	19,158			

SOURCES: *1970 Census of Population*, vol. 1: *Characteristics of the Population*, part 1, section 1, tables 48 and 60; *1980 Census of Population, Supplementary Reports: Race of the Population by States, 1980*, table 1.

[1] Alaska only

Appendix C

Indian Tribal Entities That Have

a Government-to-Government Relationship

with the United States, 1980

Absentee-Shawnee Tribe of Indians of Oklahoma

Agua Caliente Band of Cahuilla Indians of the Agua Caliente Indian Reservation, Palm Springs, California

Ak Chin Indian Community of Papago Indians of the Caricopa, Ak Chin Reservation, Arizona

Alabama-Quassarie Tribal Town of the Creek Nation of Indians of Oklahoma

Alturas Indian Rancheria of Pit River Indians of California

Apache Tribe of Oklahoma

Arapahoe Tribe of the Wind River Reservation, Wyoming

Assiniboine and Sioux Tribes of the Fort Peck Indian Reservation, Montana

Augustine Band of Cahuilla Mission Indians of the Augustine Reservation, California

Bad River Band of the Lake Superior Tribe of Chippewa Indians of the Bad River Reservation, Wisconsin

Barona Capitan Grande Band of Diegueno Mission Indians of the Barona Reservation, California

Bay Mills Indian Community of the Sault Ste. Marie Band of Chippewa Indians, Bay Mills Reservation, Michigan

Berry Creek Rancheria of Maidu Indians of California

Big Bend Rancheria of Pit River Indians of California

Big Lagoon Rancheria of Smith River Indians of California

Big Pine Band of Owens Valley Paiute Shoshone Indians of the Big Pine Reservation, California

Blackfeet Tribe of the Blackfeet Indian Reservation of Montana

Bridgeport Indian Colony of California

Burns Paiute Indian Colony, Oregon

Cabazon Band of Cahuilla Mission Indians of the Cabazon Reservation, California

Cachil DeHe Band of Wintun Indians of the Calusa Indian Community of the Colusa Rancheria, California

Caddo Indian Tribe of Oklahoma

Cahto Indian Tribe of the Laytonville Rancheria, California

Cahuilla Band of Mission Indians of the Cahuilla Reservation, California

Campo Band of Diegueno Mission Indians of the Campo Indian Reservation, California

Capitan Grande Band of Diegueno Mission Indians of the Capitan Grande Reservation, California

Cayuga Nation of New York

Cedarville Rancheria of Northern Paiute Indians of California

Chemehuevi Indian Tribe of the Chemehuevi Reservation, California

Cher-Ae Heights Indian Community of the Trinidad Rancheria of California

Cherokee Nation of Oklahoma

Cheyenne-Arapaho Tribes of Oklahoma

Cheyenne River Sioux Tribe of the Cheyenne River Reservation, South Dakota

Chickasaw Nation of Oklahoma

Chippewa-Cree Indians of the Rocky Boy's Reservation, Montana

Chitimacha Tribe of Louisiana

Choctaw Nation of Oklahoma

Citizen Band of Potawatomi Indians of Oklahoma

Coast Indian Community of Yurok Indians of the Resighini Rancheria, California

Cocopah Tribe of Arizona

Coeur D'Alene Tribe of the Coeur D'Alene Reservation, Idaho

Cold Springs Rancheria of Mono Indians of California

Colorado River Indian Tribes of the Colorado River Indian Reservation, Arizona and California

Comanche Indian Tribe of Oklahoma

Confederated Salish and Kootenai Tribes of the Flathead Reservation, Montana

Confederated Tribes of the Chehalis Reservation, Washington

Confederated Tribes of the Colville Reservation, Washington

Confederated Tribes of the Goshute Reservation, Nevada and Utah

Confederated Tribes of the Siletz Reservation, Oregon

Confederated Tribes of the Umatilla Reservation, Oregon

Confederated Tribes of the Warm Springs Reservation of Oregon

Confederated Tribes and Bands of the Yakima Indian Nation of the Yakima Reservation, Washington

Cortina Indian Rancheria of Wintun Indians of California

Coushatta Tribe of Louisiana

Covelo Indian Community of the Round Valley Reservation, California

Coyote Valley Band of Pomo Indians of California

Creek Nation of Oklahoma

Crow Creek Sioux Tribe of the Crow Creek Reservation, South Dakota

Crow Tribe of Montana

Cuyapaipe Band of Diegueno Mission Indians of the Cuyapiape Reservation, California

Delaware Tribe of Western Oklahoma

Devils Lake Sioux Tribe of the Devils Lake Sioux Reservation, North Dakota

Dry Creek Rancheria of Pomo Indians of California

Duckwater Shoshone Tribe of the Duckwater Reservation, Nevada

Eastern Band of Cherokee Indians of North Carolina

Eastern Shawnee Tribe of Oklahoma

Elem Indian Colony of Pomo Indians of the Sulphur Bank Rancheria, California

Ely Indian Colony of Nevada

Enterprise Rancheria of Maidu Indians of California

Flandreau Santee Sioux Tribe of South Dakota

Forest County Potawatomi Community of Wisconsin Potawatomie Indians, Wisconsin

Fort Belknap Indian Community of the Fort Belknap Reservation of Montana

Fort Bidwell Indian Community of Paiute Indians of the Fort Bidwell Reservation, California

Fort Independence Indian Community of Paiute Indians of the Fort Independence Reservation, California

Fort McDermitt Paiute and Shoshone Tribes of the Fort McDermitt Indian Reservation, Nevada

Fort McDowell Mohave-Apache Indian Community, Fort McDowell Band of Mohave Apache Indians of the Fort McDowell Indian Reservation, Arizona

Fort Mojave Indian Tribe of Arizona

Fort Sill Apache Tribe of Oklahoma

Gila River Pima-Maricopa Indian Community of the Gila River Indian Reservation of Arizona

Grindstone Indian Rancheria of Wintun-Wailaki Indians of California

Hannahville Indian Community of Wisconsin Potawatomie Indians of Michigan

Havasupai Tribe of the Havasupai Reservation, Arizona

Hoh Indian Tribe of the Hoh Indian Reservation, Washington

Hoopa Valley Tribe of the Hoopa Valley Reservation, California

Hopi Tribe of Arizona

Hopland Band of Pomo Indians of the Hopland Rancheria, California

Hualapai Tribe of the Hualapai Indian Reservation, Arizona

Inaja and Cosmit Reservation of Dieguena Indians, California

Iowa Tribe of Indians of the Iowa Reservation in Nebraska and Kansas

Iowa Tribe of Oklahoma

Jackson Rancheria of Me-Wuk Indians of California

Jicarilla Apache Tribe of the Jicarilla Apache Indian Reservation, New Mexico

Kaibab Band of Paiute Indians of the Kaibab Indian Reservation, Arizona

Kalispel Indian Community of the Kalispel Reservation, Washington

Karok Tribe of California

Kashia Band of Pomo Indians of the Stewarts Point Rancheria, California

Kaw Indian Tribe of Oklahoma

Keweenaw Bay Indian Community of L'Anse, Lac Vieux Desert, and Ontonagon Bands of Chippewa Indians of the L'Anse Reservation, Michigan

Kialegee Tribal Town of the Creek Indian Nation of Oklahoma

Kickapoo Tribe of Indians of the Kickapoo Reservation in Kansas

Kickapoo Tribe of Oklahoma

Kiowa Indian Tribe of Oklahoma

Kootenai Tribe of Idaho

Lac Courte Oreilles Band of Lake Superior Chippewa Indians of the Lac Courte Oreilles Reservation of Wisconsin

Lac du Flambeau Band of Lake Superior Chippewa Indians of the Lac du Flambeau Reservation of Wisconsin

La Jolla Band of Luiseno Mission Indians of the La Jolla Reservation, California

La Posta Band of Diegueno Mission Indians of the La Posta Indian Reservation, California

Las Vegas Tribe of Paiute Indians of the Las Vegas Indian Colony, Nevada

Lookout Rancheria of Pit River Indians, California

Los Coyotes Band of Cahuilla Mission Indians of the Los Coyotes Reservation, California

Lovelock Paiute Tribe of the Lovelock Indian Colony, Nevada

Lower Brule Sioux Tribe of the Lower Brule Reservation, South Dakota

Lower Elwha Tribal Community of the Lower Elwha Reservation, Washington

Lower Sioux Indian Community of the Minnesota Mdewakanton Sioux Indians of the Lower Sioux Reservation in Minnesota

Lummi Tribe of the Lummi Reservation, Washington

Makah Indian Tribe of the Makah Indian Reservation, Washington

Manchester Band of Pomo Indians of the Manchester–Point Arena Rancheria, California

Manzanita Band of Diegueno Mission Indians of the Manzanita Reservation, California

Menominee Indian Tribe of Wisconsin, Menominee Indian Reservation, Wisconsin

Mesa Grande Band of Diegueno Mission Indians of the Mesa Grande Reservation, California

Mescalero Apache Tribe of the Mescalero Reservation, New Mexico

Miami Tribe of Oklahoma

Miccosukee Tribe of Indians of Florida

Middletown Rancheria of Pomo Indians of California

Minnesota Chippewa Tribe, Minnesota (six component reservations: Boise Forte Band [Nett Lake], Fond du Lac Band, Grand Portage Band, Leech Lake Band, Mille Lac Band, White Earth Band)

Mississippi Band of Choctaw Indians, Mississippi

Moapa Band of Paiute Indians of the Moapa River Indian Reservation, Nevada

Modoc Tribe of Oklahoma

Montgomery Creek Rancheria of Pit River Indians of California

Morongo Band of Cahuilla Mission Indians of the Morongo Reservation, California

Muckleshoot Indian Tribe of the Muckleshoot Reservation, Washington

Navajo Tribe of Arizona, New Mexico and Utah

Nez Perce Tribe of Idaho, Nez Perce Reservation, Idaho

Nisqually Indian Community of the Nisqually Reservation, Washington

Nooksack Indian Tribe of Washington

Northern Cheyenne Tribe of the Northern Cheyenne Indian Reservation, Montana

Northwestern Band of Shoshone Indians of Utah (Washakie)

Oglala Sioux Tribe of the Pine Ridge Reservation, South Dakota

Omaha Tribe of Nebraska

Oneida Nation of New York

Oneida Tribe of Indians of Wisconsin, Oneida Reservation, Wisconsin

Onondaga Nation of New York

Osage Tribe of Oklahoma

Otoe-Missouri Tribe of Oklahoma

Ottawa Tribe of Oklahoma

Paiute-Shoshone Indians of the Bishop Community of the Bishop Colony, California

Paiute-Shoshone Indians of the Lone Pine Community of the Lone Pine Reservation, California

Paiute-Shoshone Tribe of the Fallon Reservation and Colony, Nevada

Pala Band of Luiseno Mission Indians of the Pala Reservation, California

Papago Tribe of the Sells, Gila Bend, and San Xavier Reservations, Arizona

Pascua Yaqui Tribe of Arizona

Passamaquoddy Tribe of Maine

Pauma Band of Luiseno Mission Indians of the Pauma and Yuima Reservation, California

Pawnee Indian Tribe of Oklahoma

Pechanga Band of Luiseno Mission Indians of the Pechango Reservation, California

Penobscot Tribe of Maine

Peoria Tribe of Oklahoma

Pit River Indian Tribe of the X-L Ranch Reservation, California

Ponca Tribe of Indians of Oklahoma

Port Gamble Indian Community, Port Gamble Band of Clallam Indians, Port Gamble Reservation, Washington

Prairie Band of Potawatomi Indians of Kansas

Prairie Island Indian Community of Minnesota Mdewakanton Sioux Indians of the Prairie Island Reservation, Minnesota

Pueblo of Acoma, New Mexico

Pueblo of Cochiti, New Mexico

Pueblo of Isleta, New Mexico

Pueblo of Jemez, New Mexico

Pueblo of Laguna, New Mexico

Pueblo of Nambe, New Mexico

Pueblo of Picuris, New Mexico

Pueblo of Pojoaque, New Mexico

Pueblo of Sandia, New Mexico

Pueblo of San Felipe, New Mexico

Pueblo of San Ildefonso, New Mexico

Pueblo of San Juan, New Mexico

Pueblo of Santa Ana, New Mexico

Pueblo of Santa Clara, New Mexico

Pueblo of Santo Domingo, New Mexico

Pueblo of Taos, New Mexico

Pueblo of Tesuque, New Mexico

Pueblo of Zia, New Mexico

Puyallup Tribe of the Puyallup Reservation, Washington

Pyramid Lake Paiute Tribe of the Pyramid Lake Reservation, Nevada

Quapaw Tribe of Oklahoma

Quechan Tribe of the Fort Yuma Indian Reservation, California

Quileute Tribe of the Quileute Reservation, Washington

Quinault Tribe of the Quinault Reservation, Washington

Ramona Reservation of California

Red Cliff Band of Lake Superior Chippewa Indians of Wisconsin, Red Cliff Reservation, Wisconsin

Red Lake Band of Chippewa Indians of the Red Lake Reservation, Minnesota

Reno–Sparks Indian Colony, Nevada

Rincon Band of Luiseno Mission Indians of the Rincon Reservation, California

Roaring Creek Rancheria of Pit River Indians of California

Robinson Rancheria of Pomo Indians of California

Rosebud Sioux Tribe of the Rosebud Indian Reservation, South Dakota

Rumsey Indian Rancheria of Wintun Indians of California

Sac and Fox Tribe of Indians of Oklahoma

Sac and Fox Tribe of the Mississippi in Iowa

Sac and Fox Tribe of Missouri of the Sac and Fox Reservation in Kansas and Nebraska

Saginaw Chippewa Indian Tribe of Michigan, Isabella Reservation, Michigan

St. Croix Chippewa Indians of Wisconsin, St. Croix Reservation, Wisconsin

St. Regis Band of Mohawk Indians of New York

Salt River Pima-Maricopa Indian Community of the Salt River Reservation, Arizona

San Carlos Apache Tribe of the San Carlos Reservation of Arizona

San Manual Band of Serrano Mission Indians of the San Manual Reservation, California

San Pasqual Band of Diegueno Mission Indians of the San Pasqual Reservation, California

Santa Rosa Band of Cahuilla Mission Indians of the Santa Rosa Reservation, California

Santa Rosa Indian Community of the Santa Rosa Rancheria of California

Santa Ynez Band of Chumash Mission Indians of the Santa Ynez Reservation, California

Santa Ysabel Band of Diegueno Mission Indians of the Santa Ysabel Reservation, California

Santee Sioux Tribe of the Santee Reservation of Nebraska

Sauk-Suiattle Indian Tribe of Washington

Sault Ste. Marie Tribe of Chippewa Indians of Michigan

Seminole Nation of Oklahoma

Seminole Tribe of Florida, Dania, Big Cypress, and Brighton Reservations, Florida

Seneca-Cayuga Tribe of Oklahoma

Seneca Nation of New York

Shakopee Mdewakanton Sioux Community of Minnesota (Prior Lake)

Sheep Ranch Rancheria of Me-Wuk Indians of California

Sherwood Valley Rancheria of Pomo Indians of California

Shingle Springs Band of Miwok Indians, Shingle Springs Rancheria (Verona Tract), California

Shoalwater Bay Tribe of the Shoalwater Bay Indian Reservation, Washington

Shoshone-Bannock Tribes of the Fort Hall Reservation of Idaho

Shoshone-Pauite Tribes of the Duck Valley Reservation, Nevada

Shoshone Tribe of the Wind River Reservation, Wyoming

Sisseton-Wahpeton Sioux Tribe of the Lake Traverse Reservation, South Dakota

Skokomish Indian Tribe of the Skokomish Reservation, Washington

Skull Valley Band of Goshute Indians of Utah

Soboba Band of Luiseno Mission Indians of the Soboba Reservation, California

Sokoagon Chippewa Community of the Mole Lake Band of Chippewa Indians, Wisconsin

Southern Ute Indian Tribe of the Southern Ute Reservation, Colorado

Spokane Tribe of the Spokane Reservation, Washington

Squaxin Island Tribe of the Squaxin Island Reservation, Washington

Standing Rock Sioux Tribe of the Standing Rock Reservation, North and South Dakota

Stillaguamish Tribe of Washington

Stockbridge-Munsee Community of Mohican Indians of Wisconsin

Summit Lake Paiute Tribe of the Summit Lake Reservation, Nevada

Suquamish Indian Tribe of the Port Madison Reservation, Washington

Susanville Indian Rancheria of Paiute, Maidu, Pit River, and Washoe Indians of California

Swinomish Indians of the Swinomish Reservation, Washington

Sycuan Band of Diegueno Mission Indians of the Sycuan Reservation, California

Table Bluff Rancheria of California

Table Mountain Rancheria of Yokut Indians of California

Te-Moak Bands of Western Shoshone Indians of the Battle Mountain, Elko, and South Fork Colonies of Nevada

Thlopthlocco Tribal Town of the Creek Indian Nation of Oklahoma

Three Affiliated Tribes of the Fort Berthold Reservation, North Dakota

Tonawanda Band of Seneca Indians of New York

Tonkawa Tribe of Indians of Oklahoma

Tonto Apache Tribe of Arizona

Torres-Martinez Band of Cahuilla Mission Indians of the Torres-Martinez Reservation, California

Tulalip Tribes of the Tulalip Reservation, Washington

Tule River Indian Tribe of the Tule River Indian Reservation, California

Tuolumne Band of the Me-Wuk Indians of the Tuolumne Rancheria of California

Turtle Mountain Band of Chippewa Indians, Turtle Mountain Indian Reservation, North Dakota

Tuscarora Nation of New York

Twenty-Nine Palms Band of Luiseno Mission Indians of the Twenty-Nine Palms Reservation, California

United Keetoowah Band of Cherokee Indians, Oklahoma

Upper Lake Band of Pomo Indians of Upper Lake Rancheria of California

Upper Sioux Indian Community of the Upper Sioux Reservation, Minnesota

Upper Skagit Indian Tribe of Washington

Ute Indian Tribe of the Uintah and Ouray Reservation, Utah

Ute Mountain Tribe of the Ute Mountain Reservation, Colorado, New Mexico, and Utah

Utu Utu Gwaiti Paiute Tribe of the Benton Paiute Reservation, California

Viejas Baron Long Capitan Grande Band of Diegueno Mission Indians of the Viejas Reservation, California

Walker River Paiute Tribe of the Walker River Reservation, Nevada

Washoe Tribe of Nevada and California (Carson Colony, Dresslerville, and Washoe Ranches)

White Mountain Apache Tribe of the Fort Apache Indian Reservation, Arizona

Wichita Indian Tribe of Oklahoma

Winnebago Tribe of the Winnebago Reservation of Nebraska

Winnemucca Indian Colony of Nevada

Wisconsin Winnebago Indian Tribe of Wisconsin

Wyandotte Tribe of Oklahoma

Yankton Sioux Tribe of South Dakota

Yavapai-Apache Indian Community of the Camp Verde Reservation, Arizona

Yavapai-Prescott Tribe of the Yavapai Reservation, Arizona

Yerington Paiute Tribe of the Yerington Colony and Campbell Ranch

Yorok Tribe of the Hoopa Valley Reservation, California

Zuni Tribe of the Zuni Reservation, New Mexico

Source: 45 *Federal Register* 27828-30 (April 24, 1980). Spelling follows that in the *Federal Register*.

Appendix D

Nomenclature of the
Bureau of Indian Affairs

The Bureau of Indian Affairs is the federal administrative unit that historically has had the primary responsibility for managing the United States government's relations with the American Indians. Unfortunately for those who like consistency, the terminology used to designate the organization has been inconsistent and confused.

On March 11, 1824, when Secretary of War John C. Calhoun set up an office within the War Department to handle Indian affairs, he called it the Bureau of Indian Affairs.[1] But the first incumbent, Thomas L. McKenney, and his successors did not use that term. Instead they headed their correspondence and reports Indian Office or Office of Indian Affairs. This practice continued through the nineteenth century and well into the twentieth. All the commissioners of Indian affairs until 1947, in fact, headed their annual reports Office of Indian Affairs.

There were, nevertheless, a good many departures from this usage. During the controversy about transferring Indian affairs from the Department of the Interior to the War Department that filled the decade after the Civil War, for example, it was common to speak of the Indian Bureau or the Bureau of Indian Affairs. During Carl Schurz's tenure as secretary of the interior (1877–1881), Thomas Nast, the noted cartoonist for *Harper's Weekly*,

1. *House Document* no. 146, 19–1, serial 138, p. 6.

liked to play on the word *bureau*—Indian Bureau and bureau as a chest of drawers—and drew Schurz as a carpenter repairing the *bureau* or pulling out the drawers to look for fraud in the *bureau*.[2] Until 1909, congressional appropriations for Indian affairs were designated for the Indian Department, but from 1910 on the designation was Bureau of Indian Affairs. The Snyder Act of 1921, which provided general authorization for appropriations for Indian affairs, moreover, spoke of the Bureau of Indian Affairs; and the *United States Code*, when it was initiated in 1925, designated chapter 1 of Title 25 as Indians, Bureau of Indian Affairs.[3] During the decade of the 1920s, when John Collier and his friends mounted a strong attack on the management of Indian affairs, their criticism was usually aimed at the "Bureau." So serious was this attack that Secretary of the Interior Ray Lyman Wilbur in 1929 directed that the term Bureau be avoided because of its unhappy connotations and that the term Indian Service be used instead.[4] Little, however, seems to have changed in the usage of the office.

Thus while the term Office of Indian Affairs was generally used on official documents and publications, the practice was not uniform within the government, and Bureau kept creeping in, no doubt because it was a generic term for administrative levels below the cabinet departments. Both Office and Bureau were used to designate the headquarters in Washington, D.C. When the extended field operations were included with the central headquarters, the terms Indian Department and later Indian Service were often used. The inconsistency shows clearly in Felix S. Cohen's authoritative *Handbook of Federal Indian Law*, published in 1942. His chapter entitled "The Office of Indian Affairs" has three sections, devoted to the development of the Indian Service, its policies, and its administration. But he also speaks in the text about the activities and practices of the Bureau of Indian Affairs. The varied usage can be seen also in the official description of the agency printed in the *Federal Register*, September 11, 1946, in response to the Administrative Procedure Act of 1946. The heading is Office

---

2. See report of Commissioner of Indian Affairs Nathaniel G. Taylor, November 23, 1868, in CIA Report, 1868, serial 1366, p. 467, and Nast's cartoons in *Harper's Weekly*, January 26, 1878, and January 25, 1879.

3. 35 *United States Statutes* 781; 36 *United States Statutes* 269; 42 *United States Statutes* 208; *The Code of the Laws of the United States of America of a General and Permanent Character in Force December 7, 1925*, Title 25: Indians, chapter 1 (printed as 44 *United States Statutes* part 1).

4. Department of the Interior, Order no. 342, April 4, 1929, OSI CCF 1–12, part 33. See also Memorandum for the Secretary: In re "Bureau of Indian Affairs," April 3, 1929, ibid.

of Indian Affairs, but the body of the statement uses Bureau of Indian Affairs.[5]

Finally, in 1947 Bureau of Indian Affairs was officially adopted as the name of the organization. On June 6 of that year the Senate Committee on Expenditures in the Executive Departments issued a report that, in order to eliminate the "startling heterogeneity" in the naming of administrative agencies, recommended a set nomenclature for all government departments, in descending order: department, bureau, division, branch, section, and unit. In this scheme, a bureau would be the principal component of an executive department.[6] Secretary of the Interior Julius A. Krug thereupon directed all his subordinates to conform to the new usage. Vernon D. Northrop, director of the Division of Budget and Administrative Management for the Department of the Interior, who was charged by Krug with carrying out the directive, wrote to the Office of Indian Affairs on September 17, 1947, remarking on the new nomenclature he had received from it: "Although there is no specific mention in your communication, we assume that henceforth your organization will be the 'Bureau of Indian Affairs,' and that 'Office of' and 'Service' will be avoided in all cases."[7] From that time on, although it took a while for everyone to conform, the title has been Bureau of Indian Affairs, for which the abbreviation BIA has become almost universal. The reports of the commissioner of Indian affairs beginning in 1947 used the title as a heading. The National Archives and Records Service has adopted the new terminology, and the records in Record Group 75 are uniformly designated Records of the Bureau of Indian Affairs, even though most of the historical documents themselves do not use that nomenclature.[8]

5. Felix S. Cohen, *Handbook of Federal Indian Law* (Washington: GPO, 1942), pp. 9–32; 11 *Federal Register* 177A–219.

6. *Senate Report* no. 243, 80–1, serial 11115; George D. Aiken to Julius A. Krug, June 12, 1947, OSI CCF 1–81, General, part 1.

7. Julius A. Krug to all bureaus and offices, June 21, 1947, OSI CCF 1–81, General, part 17; Vernon D. Northrop to Guy C. Williams, September 17, 1947, ibid.

8. Edward E. Hill, *Records of the Bureau of Indian Affairs*, Preliminary Inventories Number 163, 2 vols. (Washington: National Archives, 1965); Edward E. Hill, *Guide to the Records in the National Archives of the United States Relating to American Indians* (Washington: National Archives and Records Service, 1981).

Bibliographical
Essay

This is a selective bibliography for the two centuries of United States Indian policy covered in this study. Readers interested in a more detailed list of sources are directed to two bibliographies compiled by the author: *A Bibliographical Guide to the History of Indian-White Relations in the United States* (Chicago: University of Chicago Press, 1977), and *Indian-White Relations in the United States: A Bibliography of Works Published 1975–1980* (Lincoln: University of Nebraska Press, 1982). In addition, the footnotes herein contain references to primary documents and secondary works on which this study is based. Most of the monographs and dissertations cited in the footnotes have references to materials on their specific topics. This bibliographical essay discusses general sources and then cites some essential and useful works dealing with topics treated in the prologue and in each of the ten parts of the present volumes. It can serve as a guide for further investigation.

GENERAL SOURCES

The fundamental documents for reconstructing the history of United States Indian policy are the official archival records of the various departments and agencies of the federal government preserved in the National

Archives. An excellent guide to these Indian-related records is Edward E. Hill, *Guide to Records in the National Archives of the United States Relating to American Indians* (Washington: National Archives and Records Service, 1981). Of primary importance are the Records of the Bureau of Indian Affairs (Record Group 75); these are expertly described in Edward E. Hill, *Records of the Bureau of Indian Affairs*, Preliminary Inventories no. 163, 2 vols. (Washington: National Archives, 1965). Next in importance are the Records of the Office of the Secretary of the Interior (Record Group 48) and the Records of the Office of the Secretary of War (Record Group 107). Many of the pertinent collections of records dealing with Indians have been published on microfilm; see *The American Indian: Select Catalog of National Archives Microfilm Publications* (Washington: National Archives and Records Service, 1972); *Catalog of National Archives Microfilm Publications* (Washington: National Archives and Records Service, 1974); and "Supplementary List of National Archives Microfilm Publications, 1974–80," *Prologue* 13 (Spring 1981): 60–72. An excellent brief treatment of Indian-related records in the National Archives is Robert M. Kvasnicka, "Major Research Sources," in Robert M. Kvasnicka and Herman J. Viola, eds., *The Commissioners of Indian Affairs, 1824–1977* (Lincoln: University of Nebraska Press, 1979), pp. 349–56. Records of regional or local agencies are in the Federal Records Centers. There are papers of various government officials in the presidential libraries of Franklin D. Roosevelt, Truman, Eisenhower, Johnson, Kennedy, and Ford.

The papers of persons and organizations concerned with the formulation or implementation of United States Indian policy offer considerable material that supplements official archival and published sources. There is, unfortunately, no comprehensive guide to such collections of manuscript materials, and both general and specific manuscript guides must be relied upon. Examples of valuable manuscript collections in the Library of Congress are presidential papers and the papers of such men as Henry L. Dawes, Harold L. Ickes, Hugh S. Scott, and Charles Jerome Bonaparte. Among other collections of personal papers worthy of special note are the John Collier Papers, Yale University, and the Henry B. Whipple Papers, Minnesota Historical Society. Papers of Indian reform organizations and missionary groups interested in Indians offer special insight into Indian affairs. Among such collections are the papers of the Indian Rights Association, Historical Society of Pennsylvania; papers of the Association on American Indian Affairs, Princeton University; archives of the Bureau of Catholic Indian Missions, Marquette University; papers of the American Board of Commissioners for Foreign Missions, Harvard University; and the Indian Collection of the Presbyterian Historical Society. Many of these collections are available on microfilm.

Published documents of all three branches of the federal government provide a vast array of material on Indian affairs. Proceedings of the Senate and the House of Representatives—journals as well as debates—are essential for tracing the course of Indian policy as it was embodied in legislation. Reports and other documents ordered printed by Congress are in the serial set of congressional documents and include the long annual reports sent to Congress by the executive departments and many special reports called for by the House or Senate. This vast storehouse of information can be searched best through the *CIS US Serial Set Index*, 36 vols. (Washington: Congressional Information Service, 1975–1978), which covers the period 1789–1969; later years are covered in annual and cumulative indexes. Another useful index is Steven L. Johnson, *Guide to American Indian Documents in the Congressional Serial Set, 1817–1899* (New York: Clearwater Publishing Company, 1977). Transcripts of hearings before congressional committees are another rich source. Some early hearings appear in the serial set; but for most of the twentieth century, the hearings form a separate set of publications. Laws covering Indians are included in *United States Statutes at Large* and in later codifications. Treaties and laws on Indian affairs are conveniently available in Charles J. Kappler, comp., *Indian Affairs: Laws and Treaties*, 5 vols. (Washington: Government Printing Office, 1904–1941). Two additional volumes, entitled *Kappler's Indian Affairs: Laws and Treaties* (Washington: Department of the Interior, n.d.), extend the compilation through 1970.

Publications of the executive branch are of particular value because most Indian policy originated there. Of prime importance are the annual reports of the commissioner of Indian affairs. These began in 1824 (with the heads of the Indian Office who antedated the official commissionership) and continued in a variety of forms. Until 1920 they were printed in the serial set as part of the reports of the secretary of war or (after 1849) the secretary of the interior, and in some years they also appeared in separate departmental editions. Until 1906 the reports of superintendents and agents were included, and these subordinate reports are an extensive source of information. After 1920 the commissioners' reports were issued separately, but from 1933 to 1963 they appear only as part of the annual reports of the secretary of the interior. Beginning in 1964 the reports, in very brief form, were issued as *A Progress Report from the Commissioner of Indian Affairs*. A convenient listing of the annual reports in the serial set is given in Kvasnicka and Viola, *Commissioners of Indian Affairs*, pp. 357–64. The annual reports of the secretary of war and the secretary of the interior also contain valuable material. There are a great many printed regulations on Indian affairs issued by the secretary of the interior or the commissioner of Indian affairs from time to time, which supplement congressional enactments. There is no single compilation of them, and they are often difficult to locate. There are extensive collections in the library of the superintendent of documents (now National Archives Record Group 287, Publications of the U.S. Government) and in the library of the Department of the Interior (which includes the old Bureau of Indian Affairs library). More recent ones appear in the *Code of Federal Regulations*, Title 25: Indians. James D. Richardson's *Compilation of the Messages and Papers of the Presidents* provides basic documents, and *The Public Papers of the Presidents of the United States* offers material for recent presidents, although in general the presidents have not taken an active personal role in Indian affairs. The annual reports of the United States Board of Indian Commissioners (1869–1932) are a good place to trace movements in Indian affairs.

The decisions of the United States Supreme Court and sometimes of lower courts are essential for understanding the development of Indian policy. An indispensable guide to these decisions, as well as to legislation, is Felix S. Cohen, *Handbook of Federal Indian Law* (Washington: Government Printing Office, 1942). An updating of this classic work is *Felix S. Cohen's Handbook of Federal Indian Law*, 1982 ed. (Charlottesville, Virginia: Michie, Bobbs-Merrill, 1982).

A number of scholarly secondary works give general surveys of Indian affairs in the United States. Among the most useful, in alphabetical order, are Angie Debo, *A History of the Indians of the United States* (Norman: University of Oklahoma Press, 1970); Brian W. Dippie, *The Vanishing American: White Attitudes and U.S. Indian Policy* (Middletown, Connecticut: Wesleyan University Press, 1982); Arrell Morgan Gibson, *The American Indian: Prehistory to the Present* (Lexington, Massachusetts: D. C. Heath and Company, 1980); William T. Hagan, *American Indians*, rev. ed. (Chicago: University of Chicago Press, 1979); D'Arcy McNickle, *Native American Tribalism: Indian Survivals and Renewals* (New York: Oxford University Press, 1973); Edward H. Spicer, *A Short History of the Indians of the United States* (New York: Van Nostrand-Reinhold Company, 1969); and Wilcomb E. Washburn, *The Indian in America* (New York: Harper and Row, 1975). Other secondary studies on Indian-white relations are listed extensively in the two bibliographies cited at the beginning of this bibliographical note.

PROLOGUE: THE COLONIAL EXPERIENCE

A number of modern historical studies supply the colonial background necessary for understanding United States Indian policy. A perceptive analysis of these writings is James Axtell, "The Ethnohistory of Early

America: A Review Essay," *William and Mary Quarterly*, 3d series 35 (January 1978): 110–44. Douglas Edward Leach, *The Northern Colonial Frontier, 1607–1763* (New York: Rinehart and Winston, 1966), and W. Stitt Robinson, *The Southern Colonial Frontier, 1607–1763* (Albuquerque: University of New Mexico Press, 1979), present general accounts that include Indian relations. Of value are Gary B. Nash, *Red, White, and Black: The Peoples of Early America* (Englewood Cliffs, New Jersey: Prentice-Hall, 1974); a collection of essays by Wilbur R. Jacobs, *Dispossessing the American Indian: Indians and Whites on the Colonial Frontier* (New York: Charles Scribner's Sons, 1972); and a collection of essays by James Axtell, *The European and the Indian: Essays in the Ethnohistory of Colonial North America* (New York: Oxford University Press, 1981).

Sharply contrasting views of Puritan relations with the Indians are presented in Alden T. Vaughan, *New England Frontier: Puritans and Indians, 1620–1675*, rev. ed. (New York: W. W. Norton and Company, 1979), and Francis Jennings, *The Invasion of America: Indians, Colonialism and the Cant of Conquest* (Chapel Hill: University of North Carolina Press, 1975). Other regions are treated in Allen W. Trelease, *Indian Affairs in Colonial New York: The Seventeenth Century* (Ithaca: Cornell University Press, 1960), and chapter 2, "The Indian as Image and Factor in Southern Colonial Life," of Richard Beale Davis, *Intellectual Life in the Colonial South, 1585–1763*, 3 vols. (Knoxville: University of Tennessee Press, 1978), 1: 103–256. The images of the Indians developed by Englishmen are studied in Bernard W. Sheehan, *Savagism and Civility: Indians and Englishmen in Colonial Virginia* (Cambridge: Cambridge University Press, 1980); Karen Ordahl Kupperman, *Settling with the Indians: The Meeting of English and Indian Culture in America, 1580–1640* (Totowa, New Jersey: Rowman and Littlefield, 1980); and Robert F. Berkhofer, Jr., *The White Man's Indian: Images of the American Indian from Columbus to the Present* (New York: Alfred A. Knopf, 1978). For colonial military relations with the Indians, see Douglas Edward Leach, *Arms for Empire: A Military History of the British Colonies in North America, 1607–1763* (New York: Macmillan Company, 1973). Imperial Indian policy in the eighteenth century can be followed in Milton W. Hamilton, *Sir William Johnson: Colonial American, 1715–1763* (Port Washington, New York: Kennikat Press, 1976); John R. Alden, *John Stuart and the Southern Colonial Frontier: A Study of Indian Relations, War, Trade, and Land Problems in the Southern Wilderness, 1754–1775* (Ann Arbor: University of Michigan Press, 1944); and Helen Louise Shaw, *British Administration of the Southern Indians, 1756–1783* (Lancaster, Pennsylvania: Lancaster Press, 1931).

PART ONE: FORMATIVE YEARS

Indian affairs in the early national period are treated in Francis Paul Prucha, *American Indian Policy in the Formative Years: The Indian Trade
and Intercourse Acts, 1790–1834* (Cambridge: Harvard University Press,
1962). Another survey is George Dewey Harmon, *Sixty Years of Indian Affairs, Political, Economic, and Diplomatic, 1789–1850* (Chapel Hill: University of North Carolina Press, 1941). Excellent treatments of particular
parts of the period are Walter H. Mohr, *Federal Indian Relations, 1774–
1788* (Philadelphia: University of Pennsylvania Press, 1933); Randolph C.
Downes, *Council Fires on the Upper Ohio: A Narrative of Indian Affairs
in the Upper Ohio Valley until 1795* (Pittsburgh: University of Pittsburgh
Press, 1940); and Reginald Horsman, *Expansion and American Indian Policy, 1783–1812* (East Lansing: Michigan State University Press, 1967).
Both Downes and Horsman have also written valuable articles dealing
with Indian affairs in the early period. Essential for understanding Indian
affairs during the Revolutionary War are Barbara Graymont, *The Iroquois
in the American Revolution* (Syracuse: Syracuse University Press, 1972),
and James H. O'Donnell III, *Southern Indians in the American Revolution*
(Knoxville: University of Tennessee Press, 1973). Military aspects of Indian involvement can be traced also in such standard histories of the Revolutionary War as those of Don Higginbotham and Christopher Ward.

Military relations with the Indians in the post–Revolutionary War pe-
riod are discussed in Francis Paul Prucha, *The Sword of the Republic: The
United States Army on the Frontier, 1783–1846* (New York: Macmillan
Company, 1969); James Ripley Jacobs, *The Beginning of the U.S. Army,
1783–1812* (Princeton: Princeton University Press, 1947); and Richard H.
Kohn, *Eagle and Sword: The Federalists and the Creation of the Military
Establishment in America, 1783–1802* (New York: Free Press, 1975). Im-
portant documents are printed in Richard C. Knopf, ed., *Anthony Wayne, a
Name in Arms: The Wayne-Knox-Pickering-McHenry Correspondence*
(Pittsburgh: University of Pittsburgh Press, 1960). See also biographies of
such men as Henry Knox, Anthony Wayne, and James Wilkinson.

Documents on the key explorations of the Indian country are set forth
in Reuben Gold Thwaites, ed., *Original Journals of the Lewis and Clark
Expedition, 1804–1806,* 8 vols. (New York: Dodd, Mead and Company,
1904–1905), and in printed editions of more recently discovered documents edited by Milo Quaife and Ernest S. Osgood; Donald Jackson, ed.,
*Letters of the Lewis and Clark Expedition, with Related Documents,
1783–1854,* 2d ed., 2 vols. (Urbana: University of Illinois Press, 1978); and
Donald Jackson, ed., *The Journals of Zebulon Montgomery Pike with Letters and Related Documents,* 2 vols. (Norman: University of Oklahoma

Press, 1966). See also W. Eugene Hollon's biography of Pike and studies of Lewis and Clark by John Bakeless and by Richard Dillon.

The standard histories of the War of 1812 all cover Indian activities; see Harry L. Coles, *The War of 1812* (Chicago: University of Chicago Press, 1965); Alec R. Gilpin, *The War of 1812 in the Old Northwest* (East Lansing: Michigan State University Press, 1958); Reginald Horsman, *The War of 1812* (New York: Alfred A. Knopf, 1969); and John K. Mahon, *The War of 1812* (Gainesville: University of Florida Press, 1972). Aspects of the war in the south are thoroughly treated in Frank L. Owsley, Jr., *Struggle for the Gulf Borderlands: The Creek War and the Battle of New Orleans, 1812–1815* (Gainesville: University Presses of Florida, 1981).

Comprehensive studies of the government trading houses (factories) are Ora Brooks Peake, *A History of the United States Indian Factory System, 1795–1822* (Denver: Sage Books, 1954), and Aloysius Plaisance, "The United States Government Factory System, 1796–1822 (Ph.D. dissertation, Saint Louis University, 1954). For shorter accounts, see Royal B. Way, "The United States Factory System for Treating with the Indians, 1796–1822," *Mississippi Valley Historical Review* 6 (September 1919): 220–35, and Edgar B. Wesley, "The Government Factory System among the Indians, 1795–1822," *Journal of Economic and Business History* 4 (May 1932): 487–511. There are also a number of brief studies of individual factories. The work of the second superintendent of Indian trade, Thomas L. McKenney, is well delineated in Herman J. Viola, *Thomas L. McKenney: Architect of America's Early Indian Policy, 1816–1830* (Chicago: Swallow Press, 1974).

White men's perceptions of the Indians, which lay at the basis of Indian policy, are studied in Robert F. Berkhofer, Jr., *The White Man's Indian: Images of the American Indian from Columbus to the Present* (New York: Alfred A. Knopf, 1978), and Roy Harvey Pearce, *The Savages of America: A Study of the Indians and the Idea of Civilization* (Baltimore: Johns Hopkins Press, 1953). Jeffersonian views are treated thoroughly in Bernard W. Sheehan, *Seeds of Extinction: Jeffersonian Philanthropy and the American Indians* (Chapel Hill: University of North Carolina Press, 1973). Humanitarian views are discussed in Viola, *McKenney*, and in Jerome O. Steffen, *William Clark: Jeffersonian Man on the Frontier* (Norman: University of Oklahoma Press, 1977). For missionary efforts, see Robert F. Berkhofer, Jr., *Salvation and the Savage: An Analysis of Protestant Missions and American Indian Response, 1787–1862* (Lexington: University of Kentucky Press, 1965).

The development of the Indian Office is traced in Prucha, *American Indian Policy in the Formative Years*, and Viola, *McKenney*. For the work of early agents, see Edgar B. Wesley, *Guarding the Frontier: A Study of Fron-*

tier Defense from 1815 to 1825 (Minneapolis: University of Minnesota Press, 1935), and Ruth A. Gallaher, "The Indian Agent in the United States before 1850," *Iowa Journal of History and Politics* 14 (January 1916): 3–55. There are also studies of Benjamin Hawkins, Lawrence Taliaferro, William Clark, and Lewis Cass. Scholarly biographical sketches of early commissioners of Indian affairs appear in Robert M. Kvasnicka and Herman J. Viola, eds., *The Commissioners of Indian Affairs, 1824–1977* (Lincoln: University of Nebraska Press, 1979). The use of Indian peace medals in Indian diplomacy is treated in Francis Paul Prucha, *Indian Peace Medals in American History* (Madison: State Historical Society of Wisconsin, 1971); Indian delegations are described in Herman J. Viola, *Diplomats in Buckskins: A History of Indian Delegations in Washington City* (Washington: Smithsonian Institution Press, 1981).

PART TWO: INDIAN REMOVAL

The controversy of Indian removal has generated a great deal of historical study, much of it very critical of the removal policy associated with Andrew Jackson's presidency. An old but still valuable work that sets the tone for much writing on removal is Annie H. Abel, "The History of Events Resulting in Indian Consolidation West of the Mississippi," *Annual Report of the American Historical Association for the Year 1906*, 1: 233–450. Popular accounts in the same vein are Dale Van Every, *Disinherited: The Lost Birthright of the American Indian* (New York: Morrow, 1966), and Samuel Carter III, *Cherokee Sunset, a Nation Betrayed: A Narrative of Travail and Triumph, Persecution and Exile* (Garden City, New York: Doubleday and Company, 1976). An attempt to explain Jackson's policy in psychohistorical terms is Michael Paul Rogin, *Fathers and Children: Andrew Jackson and the Subjugation of the American Indian* (New York: Alfred A. Knopf, 1975). A detailed scholarly and generally balanced account is Ronald N. Satz, *American Indian Policy in the Jacksonian Era* (Lincoln: University of Nebraska Press, 1975). Studies that are more favorable toward the government policy are Francis Paul Prucha, "Andrew Jackson's Indian Policy: A Reassessment," *Journal of American History* 56 (December 1969): 527–39, and the pertinent sections in Francis Paul Prucha, *American Indian Policy in the Formative Years: The Indian Trade and Intercourse Acts, 1790–1834* (Cambridge: Harvard University Press, 1962). Grant Foreman, *Indian Removal: The Emigration of the Five Civilized Tribes of Indians* (Norman: University of Oklahoma Press, 1932), emphasizes the actual migration and the hardships encountered.

The Cherokees have received special attention because the agitation about removal centered on them. Wilson Lumpkin, *The Removal of the Cherokee Indians from Georgia*, 2 vols. (Wormsloe, Georgia, 1907; New York: Dodd, Mead and Company, 1907), is by a Georgia politician deeply involved in removal. The story of the Cherokee leader opposed to removal is Gary E. Moulton, *John Ross, Cherokee Chief* (Athens: University of Georgia Press, 1978). A sympathetic presentation of the other Cherokee party, which signed a removal treaty in 1835, is Thurman Wilkins, *Cherokee Tragedy: The Story of the Ridge Family and the Decimation of a People* (New York: Macmillan Company, 1970). The writings of the leader of the public, religiously-oriented opposition to Cherokee removal are reprinted in *Cherokee Removal: The "William Penn" Essays and Other Writings*, by Jeremiah Evarts, ed. Francis Paul Prucha (Knoxville: University of Tennessee Press, 1981). The role of black slavery in the Cherokee Nation is described in Theda Perdue, *Slavery and the Evolution of Cherokee Society, 1540–1866* (Knoxville: University of Tennessee Press, 1979), and in R. Halliburton, Jr., *Red over Black: Black Slavery among the Cherokee Indians* (Westport, Connecticut: Greenwood Press, 1977). The removal of other tribes has been less thoroughly covered, but see Arthur H. DeRosier, Jr., *The Removal of the Choctaw Indians* (Knoxville: University of Tennessee Press, 1970), and Arrell M. Gibson, *The Chickasaws* (Norman: University of Oklahoma Press, 1971). Histories of the other tribes also provide information on removal.

The famous Supreme Court cases dealing with Cherokee removal are skillfully analyzed in Joseph C. Burke, "The Cherokee Cases: A Study in Law, Politics, and Morality," *Stanford Law Review* 21 (February 1969): 500–531; William F. Swindler, "Politics as Law: The Cherokee Cases," *American Indian Law Review* 3, no. 1 (1975): 7–20; and Edwin A. Miles, "After John Marshall's Decision: *Worcester* v. *Georgia* and the Nullification Crisis," *Journal of Southern History* 39 (November 1973): 519–44.

The removal of the northern Indians was a piecemeal affair, and the historiography reflects that fact. A general book that treats the subject in part is Grant Foreman, *The Last Trek of the Indians* (Chicago: University of Chicago Press, 1946). Otherwise information must be gathered from histories of the tribes involved, such as Edmund J. Danziger, Jr., on the Chippewas, James A. Clifton and R. David Edmunds on the Potawatomis, Bert Anson on the Miamis, and Patricia K. Ourada on the Menominees, and from articles on specific migrations. The important part played by white traders in these movements is discussed in James L. Clayton, "The Impact of Traders' Claims on the American Fur Trade," in David M. Ellis, ed., *The Frontier in American Development: Essays in Honor of Paul Wallace Gates* (Ithaca: Cornell University Press, 1969), pp. 299–322; Lucile M. Kane, "The Sioux Treaties and the Traders," *Minnesota History* 32 (June

1951): 65–80; and Robert A. Trennert, *Indian Traders on the Middle Border: The House of Ewing, 1827–54* (Lincoln: University of Nebraska Press, 1981).

The two wars that resulted from the attempt to remove the Indians west of the Mississippi have been thoroughly studied. For the Black Hawk War, see Frank E. Stevens, *The Black Hawk War; Including a Review of Black Hawk's Life* (Chicago: Frank E. Stevens, 1903), and Cecil Eby, *"That Disgraceful Affair": The Black Hawk War* (New York: W. W. Norton and Company, 1973). Other accounts of value are William T. Hagan, *The Sac and Fox Indians* (Norman: University of Oklahoma Press, 1958), and Reuben Gold Thwaites, "The Story of the Black Hawk War," *Collections of the State Historical Society of Wisconsin* 12 (1892): 217–65. An excellent ethnohistorical account of the background of the war is Anthony F. C. Wallace, *Prelude to Disaster: The Course of Indian-White Relations which Led to the Black Hawk War of 1832* (Springfield: Illinois State Historical Library, 1970). The Wallace work is also printed as the introduction to the collection of documents edited by Ellen M. Whitney, *The Black Hawk War*, 3 vols. (Springfield: Illinois State Historical Library, 1970–1975). Black Hawk's own account is presented in Donald Jackson, ed., *Black Hawk (Ma-Ka-Tai-Me-She-Kia-Kiak): An Autobiography* (Urbana: University of Illinois Press, 1955).

The Florida War (Second Seminole War) is covered in detail in John K. Mahon, *History of the Second Seminole War, 1835–1842* (Gainesville: University of Florida Press, 1967). See also the contemporary account by John T. Sprague, *The Origin, Progress, and Conclusion of the Florida War* (New York: D. Appleton and Company, 1848), and Virginia Bergman Peters, *The Florida Wars* (Hamden, Connecticut: Archon Books, 1979). The importance of black slaves in the war is discussed in a series of articles by Kenneth W. Porter.

The history of the tribes in the West after removal can be followed in histories of the separate tribes and in Grant Foreman, *The Five Civilized Tribes* (Norman: University of Oklahoma Press, 1934). See also Brad Agnew, *Fort Gibson: Terminal on the Trail of Tears* (Norman: University of Oklahoma Press, 1980), and Francis Paul Prucha, "American Indian Policy in the 1840s: Visions of Reform," in John G. Clark, ed., *The Frontier Challenge: Responses to the Trans-Mississippi West* (Lawrence: University Press of Kansas, 1971), pp. 81–110. The missionaries' work is examined in Robert F. Berkhofer, Jr., *Salvation and the Savage: An Analysis of Protestant Missions and American Indian Response, 1787–1862* (Lexington: University of Kentucky Press, 1965). Military affairs are covered in Francis Paul Prucha, *The Sword of the Republic: The United States Army on the Frontier, 1783–1846* (New York: Macmillan Company, 1969).

The development of the Indian Office is traced in part in Prucha, *American Indian Policy in the Formative Years*. See also the biographical sketches in Robert M. Kvasnicka and Herman J. Viola, eds., *The Commissioners of Indian Affairs, 1824–1977* (Lincoln: University of Nebraska Press, 1979). There are useful sketches of the various field agencies in Edward E. Hill, *The Office of Indian Affairs, 1824–1880: Historical Sketches* (New York: Clearwater Publishing Company, 1974). Plans for an Indian state in the West are discussed in Annie H. Abel, "Proposals for an Indian State, 1778–1878," *Annual Report of the American Historical Association for the Year 1907*, 1: 87–104; and George A. Schultz, *An Indian Canaan: Isaac McCoy and the Vision of an Indian State* (Norman: University of Oklahoma Press, 1972).

PART THREE: AMERICAN EXPANSION AND THE RESERVATION SYSTEM

The development of Indian policy to meet American expansion in the Trans-Mississippi West in the 1840s and 1850s can be traced in James C. Malin, *Indian Policy and Westward Expansion* (Lawrence: University of Kansas, 1921); Alban W. Hoopes, *Indian Affairs and Their Administration, with Special Reference to the Far West, 1849–1860* (Philadelphia: University of Pennsylvania Press, 1932); and Robert A. Trennert, Jr., *Alternative to Extinction: Federal Indian Policy and the Beginnings of the Reservation System, 1846–51* (Philadelphia: Temple University Press, 1975). Military aspects of the expansion and contact with new western Indians are treated best in Robert M. Utley, *Frontiersmen in Blue: The United States Army and the Indian, 1848–1865* (New York: Macmillan Company, 1967). See also Averam B. Bender, *The March of Empire: Frontier Defense in the Southwest, 1848–1860* (Lawrence: University of Kansas Press, 1952).

There are particular studies dealing with the various geographical areas into which federal Indian policy was extended. For Texas, two articles are valuable: Lena Clara Koch, "The Federal Indian Policy in Texas, 1845–1860," *Southwestern Historical Quarterly* 28 (January 1925): 223–34; (April 1925): 259–86; 29 (July 1925): 19–25; (October 1925): 98–127; and George Dewey Harmon, "The United States Indian Policy in Texas, 1845–1860," *Mississippi Valley Historical Review* 17 (December 1930): 377–403. A series of articles by Kenneth F. Neighbours describes the work of the chief Indian agent in Texas, Robert S. Neighbors.

New Mexico Indian affairs are treated in Frank D. Reeve, "The Government and the Navaho, 1846–1858," *New Mexico Historical Review* 14 (January 1939): 82–114, and in L. R. Bailey, *The Long Walk: A History of the Navajo Wars, 1846–68* (Los Angeles: Westernlore Press, 1964). The papers of James S. Calhoun are in Annie Heloise Abel, ed., *The Official Correspondence of James S. Calhoun while Indian Agent at Santa Fe and Superintendent of Indian Affairs in New Mexico* (Washington: Government Printing Office, 1915). See also Ralph Hedrick Ogle, *Federal Control of the Western Apaches, 1848–1886* (Albuquerque: University of New Mexico Press, 1970), and Frank McNitt, *Navajo Wars: Military Campaigns, Slave Raids, and Reprisals* (Albuquerque: University of New Mexico Press, 1972).

Mormon relations with the Indians in Utah can be followed in Juanita Brooks, "Indian Relations on the Mormon Frontier," *Utah Historical Quarterly* 12 (January–April 1944): 1–48; Gustive O. Larson, "Brigham Young and the Indians," in Robert G. Ferris, ed., *The American West: An Appraisal* (Santa Fe: Museum of New Mexico Press, 1963), pp. 176–87; and Dale L. Morgan, "The Administration of Indian Affairs in Utah, 1851–1858," *Pacific Historical Review* 17 (November 1948): 383–409. A critical study of one tragic episode is Juanita Brooks, *The Mountain Meadows Massacre* (Norman: University of Oklahoma Press, 1962).

For California, see William H. Ellison, "The Federal Indian Policy in California, 1846–1860," *Mississippi Valley Historical Review* 9 (June 1922): 37–67. On the treaties made with the California bands, a critical analysis is Harry Kelsey, "The California Indian Treaty Myth," *Southern California Quarterly* 55 (Fall 1973): 225–35. For the work of the most important federal agent in California, see Gerald Thompson, *Edward F. Beale and the American West* (Albuquerque: University of New Mexico Press, 1983), and Richard W. Crouter and Andrew F. Rolle, "Edward Fitzgerald Beale and the Indian Peace Commissioners in California, 1851–1854," *Historical Society of Southern California Quarterly* 42 (June 1960): 107–32.

In the Pacific Northwest, Indian affairs were related first of all to the arrival of missionaries. Studies of Jason Lee, a Methodist missionary, are Cornelius J. Brosnan, *Jason Lee: Prophet of the New Oregon* (New York: Macmillan Company, 1932), and Robert J. Loewenberg, *Equality on the Oregon Frontier: Jason Lee and the Methodist Mission, 1834–43* (Seattle: University of Washington Press, 1976). Clifford M. Drury's *Marcus and Narcissa Whitman and the Opening of Old Oregon*, 2 vols. (Glendale, California: Arthur H. Clark Company, 1973), his *Henry Harmon Spalding: Pioneer of Old Oregon* (Caldwell, Idaho: Caxton Printers, 1936), and his *Elkanah and Mary Walker: Pioneers among the Spokanes* (Caldwell, Idaho: Caxton Printers, 1940), tell the full story of other Protestant missionaries. Catholic involvement in the Pacific Northwest is studied in Robert Ignatius Burns, *The Jesuits and the Indian Wars of the Northwest* (New Haven: Yale University Press, 1966). United States Indian policy is discussed in two articles by C. F. Coan: "The First Stage of the Federal Indian Policy in the Pacific Northwest, 1849–1852," *Oregon Historical Society Quarterly* 22 (March 1921): 46–65, and "The Adoption of the Reservation Policy in the Pacific Northwest, 1853–1855," ibid. 23 (March 1922): 3–27. A scholarly biography of the governor of Washington Territory and principal treaty maker with the Northwest Indians is Kent D. Richards, *Isaac I. Stevens: Young Man in a Hurry* (Provo: Brigham Young University Press, 1979). Considerable information on federal relations with the Indians can be obtained in such tribal histories as those of Alvin M. Josephy, Jr., on the Nez Perces, John C. Ewers on the Blackfeet, and Robert H. Ruby and John A. Brown on the Cayuse and the Spokane Indians.

The history of the Indian Office during the period is given in the sketches of the commissioners in Robert M. Kvasnicka and Herman J. Viola, eds., *The Commissioners of Indian Affairs, 1824–1977* (Lincoln: University of Nebraska Press, 1979). The creation of the Department of the Interior is discussed in Henry Barrett Learned, "The Establishing of the Secretaryship of the Interior," *American Historical Review* 16 (July 1911): 751–73.

PART FOUR: THE CIVIL WAR YEARS

General accounts dealing with the period of Lincoln's administration are David A. Nichols, *Lincoln and the Indians: Civil War Policy and Politics* (Columbia: University of Missouri Press, 1978), and Edmund J. Danziger, Jr., *Indians and Bureaucrats: Administering the Reservation Policy during the Civil War* (Urbana: University of Illinois Press, 1974). For the work of Lincoln's commissioner of Indian affairs, see Harry Kelsey, "William P. Dole and Mr. Lincoln's Indian Policy," *Journal of the West* 10 (July 1971): 484–92, and Donovan L. Hofsommer, "William Palmer Dole, Commissioner of Indian Affairs, 1861–1865," *Lincoln Herald* 75 (Fall 1973): 97–114.

The role of the southern Indians in the Civil War and their relations with both the Union and the Confederacy are exhaustively treated, with long extracts from documents, in three volumes by Annie H. Abel, collectively entitled *The Slaveholding Indians* (Cleveland: Arthur H. Clark Company), vol. 1: *The American Indian as Slaveholder and Secessionist: An Omitted Chapter in the Diplomatic History of the Southern Confederacy* (1915); vol. 2: *The American Indian as Participant in the Civil War* (1919); vol. 3: *The American Indian under Reconstruction* (1925). Abel also has a brief account, "The Indians in the Civil War," in *American Historical Review* 15 (January 1910): 281–96. See also Ohland Morton, "Confederate Government Relations with the Five Civilized Tribes," *Chronicles of Oklahoma* 31 (Summer 1953): 189–204; (August 1953): 299–322; and two articles by Kenny A. Franks: "An Analysis of the Confederate Treaties with the Five Civilized Tribes," ibid. 50 (Winter 1972–1973): 458–73, and "The Implementation of the Confederate Treaties with the Five Civilized Tribes," ibid. 51 (Spring 1973): 21–33. Military activities are described in Lary C. Rampp and Donald L. Rampp, *The Civil War in the Indian Territory* (Austin: Presidial Press, 1975). Biographies of the two opposing Cherokee leaders in the war period are Gary E. Moulton, *John Ross, Cherokee Chief* (Athens: University of Georgia Press, 1978), and Kenny A. Franks, *Stand Watie and the Agony of the Cherokee Nation* (Memphis: Memphis State University Press, 1979).

The history of the Sioux uprising in Minnesota is presented with many illustrations in Kenneth Carley, *The Sioux Uprising of 1862* (St. Paul: Minnesota Historical Society, 1961). An older work still of much value is William Watts Folwell, *A History of Minnesota*, 4 vols. (St. Paul: Minnesota Historical Society, 1921–1930), 2: 109–301. A popular account is C. M. Oehler, *The Great Sioux Uprising* (New York: Oxford University Press, 1959). The historical setting of the event is provided in Roy W. Meyer, *History of the Santee Sioux: United States Indian Policy on Trial* (Lincoln: University of Nebraska Press, 1967). Military aspects of the conflict are covered in Louis H. Roddis, *The Indian Wars of Minnesota* (Cedar Rapids, Iowa: Torch Press, 1956), and Robert Huhn Jones, *The Civil War in the Northwest: Nebraska, Wisconsin, Iowa, Minnesota, and the Dakotas* (Norman: University of Oklahoma Press, 1960). See also William E. Lass, "The Removal from Minnesota of the Sioux and Winnebago Indians," *Minnesota History* 38 (December 1963): 353–64.

The government's dealings with the southwestern Indians in the Civil War years concerned largely the pacification of the Navajos. Biographies of the army officers responsible for these events are Max L. Heyman, Jr., *Prudent Soldier: A Biography of Major General E. R. S. Canby, 1817–1873* (Glendale, California: Arthur H. Clark Company, 1959); Aurora Hunt, *Major General James Henry Carleton, 1814–1873: Western Frontier Dragoon* (Glendale, California: Arthur H. Clark Company, 1958); and Edwin L. Sabin, *Kit Carson Days, 1809–1869*, rev. ed., 2 vols. (New York: Press of the Pioneers, 1935). Relations with the Navajos leading to the exile of the Indians at the Bosque Redondo in eastern New Mexico are the subject of Lawrence C. Kelly, *Navajo Roundup: Selected Correspondence of Kit Carson's Expedition against the Navajo, 1863–1865* (Boulder, Colorado: Pruett Publishing Company, 1970), and Clifford E. Trafzer, *The Kit Carson Campaign: The Last Great Navajo War* (Norman: University of Oklahoma Press, 1982). The story of the Bosque Redondo is told in Gerald Thompson, *The Army and the Navajo: The Bosque Redondo Reservation Experiment, 1863–1868* (Tucson: University of Arizona Press, 1976), and Lynn R. Bailey, *Bosque Redondo: An American Concentration Camp* (Pasadena: Socio-Technical Books, 1970). For an interpretation of the treaty that ended the Navajo exile, see John L. Kessell, "General Sherman and the Navajo Treaty of 1868: A Basic and Expedient Misunderstanding," *Western Historical Quarterly* 12 (July 1981): 251–72.

The literature on Sand Creek is extensive. A survey of the event is Stan Hoig, *The Sand Creek Massacre* (Norman: University of Oklahoma Press, 1961). For a discussion of the historical controversies about the massacre, see Michael A. Sievers, "Sands of Sand Creek Historiography," *Colorado Magazine* 49 (Spring 1972): 116–42.

PART FIVE: THE PEACE POLICY

In the years after the Civil War there was a remarkable upsurge of reform sentiment in regard to the Indians. Four general works that describe the events of these decades, in order of their publication, are Loring Benson Priest, *Uncle Sam's Stepchildren: The Reformation of United States Indian Policy, 1865–1887* (New Brunswick: Rutgers University Press, 1942); Henry E. Fritz, *The Movement for Indian Assimilation, 1860–1890* (Philadelphia: University of Pennsylvania Press, 1963); Robert Winston Mardock, *The Reformers and the American Indian* (Columbia: University of Missouri Press, 1971); and Francis Paul Prucha, *American Indian Policy in Crisis: Christian Reformers and the Indian, 1865–1900* (Norman: University of Oklahoma Press, 1976).

The peace policy of Grant's administration has been well covered. The best general account, which concerns the participation of the Protestant churches, is Robert H. Keller, Jr., *American Protestantism and United States Indian Policy, 1869–82* (Lincoln: University of Nebraska Press, 1983). The Catholic activity is described in Peter J. Rahill, *The Catholic Indian Missions and Grant's Peace Policy, 1870–1884* (Washington: Catholic University of America Press, 1953). See also Robert L. Whitner, "The Methodist Episcopal Church and Grant's Peace Policy: A Study of the Methodist Agencies, 1870–1882" (Ph.D. dissertation, University of Minnesota, 1959), and Clyde A. Milner II, *With Good Intentions: Quaker Work among the Pawnees, Otos, and Omahas in the 1870s* (Lincoln: University of Nebraska Press, 1982). Biographies of two men influential in the beginning of the peace policy are William H. Armstrong, *Warrior in Two Camps: Ely S. Parker, Union General and Seneca Chief* (Syracuse: Syracuse University Press, 1978), and Charles Lewis Slattery, *Felix Reville Brunot, 1820–1898: A Civilian in the War for the Union, President of the First Board of Indian Commissioners* (New York: Longmans, Green and Company, 1901).

The years of the peace policy were also years of Indian wars, which have been the subject of innumerable scholarly and popular books. The best general account is Robert M. Utley, *Frontier Regulars: The United States Army and the Indians, 1866–1891* (New York: Macmillan Company, 1973). A popular account is Ralph K. Andrist, *The Long Death: The Last Days of the Plains Indians* (New York: Macmillan Company, 1964). More specific studies are William H. Leckie, *The Military Conquest of the Southern Plains* (Norman: University of Oklahoma Press, 1963); Keith A. Murray, *The Modocs and Their War* (Norman: University of Oklahoma Press, 1959); Dan L. Thrapp, *The Conquest of Apacheria* (Norman: University of Oklahoma Press, 1967); Merrill D. Beal, *"I Will Fight No More Forever": Chief Joseph and the Nez Perce War* (Seattle: University of Washington Press, 1963); and Robert Emmitt, *The Last War Trail: The Utes and the Settlement of Colorado* (Norman: University of Oklahoma Press, 1954). The most celebrated of the military encounters, Custer's defeat at the Little Bighorn, is the subject of a tremendous literature. A reasonable account is Edgar I. Stewart, *Custer's Luck* (Norman: University of Oklahoma Press, 1955). Much information is provided in biographies of military men, such as those of Robert G. Athearn on William T. Sherman, Carl Coke Rister on Philip Sheridan, Martin F. Schmitt on George Crook, Richard N. Ellis on John Pope, John A. Carpenter on Oliver O. Howard, and Virginia Weisel Johnson on Nelson A. Miles. An Indian view on Indian-white warfare is presented in Peter J. Powell, *People of the Sacred Mountain: A History of the Northern Cheyenne Chiefs and Warrior Societies, 1830–1879, with an Epilogue, 1969–1974*, 2 vols. (New York: Harper and Row, 1981).

Studies of special value dealing with specific tribes are James C. Olson, *Red Cloud and the Sioux Problem* (Lincoln: University of Nebraska Press, 1965); Alvin M. Josephy, Jr., *The Nez Perce Indians and the Opening of the Northwest* (New Haven: Yale University Press, 1965); and Donald J. Berthrong, *The Southern Cheyennes* (Norman: University of Oklahoma Press, 1963).

Administration of Indian affairs can be followed in the biographical sketches in Robert M. Kvasnicka and Herman J. Viola, eds., *The Commissioners of Indian Affairs, 1824–1977* (Lincoln: University of Nebraska Press, 1979). A perceptive view of Indian policy by one of the commissioners is Francis A. Walker, *The Indian Question* (Boston: James R. Osgood and Company, 1874). One successful innovation in running reservations, the Indian police, is studied in William T. Hagan, *Indian Police and Judges: Experiments in Acculturation and Control* (New Haven: Yale University Press, 1966).

PART SIX: AMERICANIZING THE AMERICAN INDIANS

The drive after 1880 to individualize and Americanize the Indians through allotment of land, education, and citizenship is treated in Francis Paul Prucha, *American Indian Policy in Crisis: Christian Reformers and the In-*

dian, 1865–1900 (Norman: University of Oklahoma Press, 1976). There is an extensive collection of the writings of the men and women who directed the movement in Francis Paul Prucha, ed., *Americanizing the American Indians: Writings by the "Friends of the Indian," 1880–1900* (Cambridge: Harvard University Press, 1973). The work of the reform organizations devoted to Indian affairs can be followed best in their annual reports and other publications, but see Helen M. Wanken, "'Woman's Sphere' and Indian Reform: The Women's National Indian Association, 1879–1901" (Ph.D. dissertation, Marquette University, 1981), and Larry E. Burgess, "'We'll Discuss It at Mohonk,'" *Quaker History* 40 (Spring 1971): 14–28. One reformer who has received some attention is Helen Hunt Jackson; see Ruth Odell, *Helen Hunt Jackson (H.H.)* (New York: D. Appleton-Century Company, 1939), and Allan Nevins, "Helen Hunt Jackson, Sentimentalist vs. Realist," *American Scholar* 10 (Summer 1941): 269–85.

Critical accounts of the reservations in the late nineteenth century include Robert M. Utley, *The Last Days of the Sioux Nation* (New Haven: Yale University Press, 1963); William T. Hagan, *United States–Comanche Relations: The Reservation Years* (New Haven: Yale University Press, 1976); and Donald J. Berthrong, *The Cheyenne and Arapaho Ordeal: Reservation and Agency Life in the Indian Territory, 1875–1907* (Norman: University of Oklahoma Press, 1976).

The primary means of detribalizing the Indians was the allotment of the reservation lands to individual Indians, which received legislative approval in the Dawes Act of 1887. Loring Benson Priest, in *Uncle Sam's Stepchildren: The Reformation of United States Indian Policy, 1865–1887* (New Brunswick: Rutgers University Press, 1942), sees the Dawes Act as the successful culmination of the post–Civil War reform movement. A thorough and more critical account of the measure is D. S. Otis, *The Dawes Act and the Allotment of Indian Lands*, ed. Francis Paul Prucha (Norman: University of Oklahoma Press, 1973). A briefer treatment, with appended documents, is Wilcomb E. Washburn, *The Assault on Indian Tribalism: The General Allotment Law (Dawes Act) of 1887* (Philadelphia: J. B. Lippincott Company, 1975). The question of citizenship for Indians, which was closely related to allotment, is discussed in Michael T. Smith, "The History of Indian Citizenship," *Great Plains Journal* 10 (Fall 1970): 25–35, and R. Alton Lee, "Indian Citizenship and the Fourteenth Amendment," *South Dakota History* 4 (Spring 1974): 198–221.

Although the most significant reform measures had to do with education, there are no detailed histories of Indian education. For information on the leading proponent of complete assimilation through education, Richard Henry Pratt, see Elaine Goodale Eastman, *Pratt: The Red Man's Moses* (Norman: University of Oklahoma Press, 1935), and a collection of

Pratt's writings edited by Robert M. Utley, *Battlefield and Classroom: Four Decades with the American Indian, 1876–1904* (New Haven: Yale University Press, 1964). A perceptive interpretation of Pratt and the movement he symbolized is Everett Arthur Gilcreast, "Richard Henry Pratt and American Indian Policy, 1877–1906: A Study of the Assimilation Movement" (Ph.D. dissertation, Yale University, 1967). The key figure in Indian education and the foremost promoter of a national Indian school system was Commissioner of Indian Affairs Thomas J. Morgan, but there is no study of him aside from the sketch in Robert M. Kvasnicka and Herman J. Viola, eds., *The Commissioners of Indian Affairs, 1824–1977* (Lincoln: University of Nebraska Press, 1979). A story of the controversy between Protestant and Catholic groups over government support of Indian mission schools is told in detail in Francis Paul Prucha, *The Churches and the Indian Schools, 1888–1912* (Lincoln: University of Nebraska Press, 1979).

The development of the bureaucracy to administer the new aspects of Indian policy is analyzed in a sociological study: Paul Stuart, *The Indian Office: Growth and Development of an American Institution, 1865–1900* (Ann Arbor: UMI Research Press, 1979).

The particular conditions of Indian affairs in the area that became the state of Oklahoma are described in Roy Gittinger, *The Formation of the State of Oklahoma, 1803–1906* (Norman: University of Oklahoma Press, 1939). A careful study of the invasion of the Indian Territory by corporations is H. Craig Miner, *The Corporation and the Indian: Tribal Sovereignty and Industrial Civilization in Indian Territory, 1865–1907* (Columbia: University of Missouri Press, 1976). The invasion by white settlers is recounted in Carl Coke Rister, *Land Hunger: David L. Payne and the Oklahoma Boomers* (Norman: University of Oklahoma Press, 1942). For the work of the Cherokee Commission, see Berlin B. Chapman, "The Cherokee Commission, 1889–1893," *Indiana Magazine of History* 62 (June 1946): 177–90, and a series of articles by the same author in *Chronicles of Oklahoma*. The history of the Dawes Commission is provided in two articles by Loren H. Brown: "The Dawes Commission," *Chronicles of Oklahoma* 9 (March 1931): 71–105, and "The Establishment of the Dawes Commission for Indian Territory," ibid. 18 (June 1940): 171–81. What happened to the Five Civilized Tribes as their tribal governments were destroyed by federal action is critically examined in Angie Debo, *And Still the Waters Run: The Betrayal of the Five Civilized Tribes* (Princeton: Princeton University Press, 1940).

PART SEVEN: THE NATION'S WARDS

The three decades after 1900, a period in which the Americanization programs were carried out, are singularly devoid of serious historical studies.

There are no published general works devoted to this crucial period. A detailed study that ends in 1920 and stresses a radical change in policy after 1900 is Frederick E. Hoxie, "Beyond Savagery: The Campaign to Assimilate the American Indians, 1880–1920" (Ph.D. dissertation, Brandeis University, 1977). Brief articles that deal with the period are John Berens, "'Old Campaigners, New Realities': Indian Policy Reform in the Progressive Era, 1900–1912," *Mid-America* 59 (January 1977): 51–64, and Kenneth O'Reilly, "Progressive Era and New Era American Indian Policy: The Gospel of Self-Support," *Journal of Historical Studies* 5 (Fall 1981): 35–56. Tribal histories that are especially useful for the twentieth century are Lawrence C. Kelly, *The Navajo Indians and Federal Indian Policy, 1900–1935* (Tucson: University of Arizona Press, 1968); and two books by Roy W. Meyer: *History of the Santee Sioux: United States Indian Policy on Trial* (Lincoln: University of Nebraska Press, 1967), and *The Village Indians of the Upper Missouri: The Mandans, Hidatsas, and Arikaras* (Lincoln: University of Nebraska Press, 1977).

The commissioners of the early twentieth century are treated in Robert M. Kvasnicka and Herman J. Viola, eds., *The Commissioners of Indian Affairs, 1824–1977* (Lincoln: University of Nebraska Press, 1979). For Francis E. Leupp, see also Nicah Furman, "Seedtime for Indian Reform: An Evaluation of the Administration of Commissioner Francis Ellington Leupp," *Red River Valley Historical Review* 2 (Winter 1975): 495–517, and Leupp's own book, *The Indian and His Problem* (New York: Charles Scribner's Sons, 1910). The work of the Society of American Indians is discussed in Hazel W. Hertzberg, *The Search for an American Indian Identity: Modern Pan-Indian Movements* (Syracuse: Syracuse University Press, 1971). A study of one of the leaders of that movement is Peter Iverson, *Carlos Montezuma and the Changing World of the American Indians* (Albuquerque: University of New Mexico Press, 1982).

The 1920s have been studied primarily for the incipient reform movement associated with John Collier, rather than as a continuation of the policies and programs of the preceding decades. The most thorough study of Collier in that period is Lawrence C. Kelly, *The Assault on Assimilation: John Collier and the Origins of Indian Policy Reform* (Albuquerque: University of New Mexico Press, 1983). An earlier study of Collier that is also of great value is Kenneth R. Philp, *John Collier's Crusade for Indian Reform, 1920–1954* (Tucson: University of Arizona Press, 1977). A pioneer article still of use is Randolph C. Downes, "A Crusade for Indian Reform, 1922–1934," *Mississippi Valley Historical Review* 32 (December 1945): 331–54. The work of the Office of Indian Affairs in the mid-1920s is set forth in detail, along with historical material, in Laurence F. Schmeckebier, *The Office of Indian Affairs: Its History, Activities, and Organization* (Baltimore: Johns Hopkins Press, 1927). A classic report on Indian affairs is

Lewis Meriam and others, *The Problem of Indian Administration* (Baltimore: Johns Hopkins Press, 1928).

Education was the increasingly dominant work of the Indian Office, yet there is no general history of Indian education for the early twentieth century. The very end of the period is covered in Margaret Szasz, *Education and the American Indian: The Road to Self-Determination, 1928–1973* (Albuquerque: University of New Mexico Press, 1974), and the climax of the controversy over Indian mission schools is treated in Francis Paul Prucha, *The Churches and the Indian Schools, 1888–1912* (Lincoln: University of Nebraska Press, 1979). Although after 1900 Indian health care became a significant concern of the federal government, the only scholarly study on the subject is Diane T. Putney, "Fighting the Scourge: American Indian Morbidity and Federal Policy, 1897–1928" (Ph.D. dissertation, Marquette University, 1980).

A detailed study on land policy, allotment, and fee patenting is Janet McDonnell, "The Disintegration of the Indian Estate: Indian Land Policy, 1913–1929" (Ph.D. dissertation, Marquette University, 1980). For a compilation of data on the subject, see J. P. Kinney, *A Continent Lost—A Civilization Won: Indian Land Tenure in America* (Baltimore: Johns Hopkins Press, 1937). A useful guide to writings is Imre Sutton, *Indian Land Tenure: Bibliographical Essays and a Guide to the Literature* (New York: Clearwater Publishing Company, 1975). Critical studies on the allotment program are Leonard A. Carlson, *Indians, Bureaucrats, and Land: The Dawes Act and the Decline of Indian Farming* (Westport, Connecticut: Greenwood Press, 1981); David M. Holford, "The Subversion of the Indian Land Allotment System, 1887–1934," *Indian Historian* 8 (Spring 1975): 11–21; Ross R. Cotroneo and Jack Dozier, "A Time of Disintegration: The Coeur d'Alene and the Dawes Act," *Western Historical Quarterly* 5 (October 1974): 405–19; and Allan G. Harper, "Salvaging the Wreckage of Indian Land Allotment," in Oliver La Farge, ed., *The Changing Indian* (Norman: University of Oklahoma Press, 1942), pp. 84–102. For the work of the competency commissions, see Janet McDonnell, "Competency Commissions and Indian Land Policy, 1913–1920," *South Dakota History* 11 (Winter 1980): 21–34.

The special Indian conditions in Oklahoma can be seen in the critical book by Angie Debo *And Still the Waters Run: The Betrayal of the Five Civilized Tribes* (Princeton: Princeton University Press, 1940). The pressures on the New York Indians are discussed in Laurence M. Hauptman, "Senecas and Subdividers: Resistance to Allotment of Indian Lands in New York, 1875–1906," *Prologue* 9 (Summer 1977): 105–16, and James W. Clute, "The New York Indians' Right to Self-Determination," *Buffalo Law Review* 22 (Spring 1973): 985–1019. See also Thomas E. Hogan, "City in a

Quandary: Salamanca and the Allegany Leases," *New York History* 55 (January 1974): 79–101.

PART EIGHT: THE INDIAN NEW DEAL

The reform in Indian policy that began in the Hoover administration and blossomed forth under Collier's commissionership from 1933 to 1945 is well treated in Kenneth R. Philp, *John Collier's Crusade for Indian Reform, 1920–1954* (Tucson: University of Arizona Press, 1977), and in two evaluative articles of Lawrence C. Kelly: "John Collier and the Indian New Deal: An Assessment," in Jane F. Smith and Robert M. Kvasnicka, eds., *Indian-White Relations: A Persistent Paradox* (Washington: Howard University Press, 1976), pp. 227–41, and "The Indian Reorganization Act: The Dream and the Reality," *Pacific Historical Review* 44 (August 1975): 291–312. A perceptive work that analyzes the working of the new tribal organizations is Graham D. Taylor, *The New Deal and American Indian Tribalism: The Administration of the Indian Reorganization Act, 1934–45* (Lincoln: University of Nebraska Press, 1980). A valuable early study is John Leiper Freeman, Jr., "The New Deal for Indians: A Study in Bureau–Committee Relations in American Government" (Ph.D. dissertation, Princeton University, 1952). Much can be learned also from studies of particular tribes; see Donald L. Parman, *The Navajos and the New Deal* (New Haven: Yale University Press, 1976), and Laurence M. Hauptman, *The Iroquois and the New Deal* (Syracuse: Syracuse University Press, 1981). Collier's own account can be found in his books *The Indians of the Americas* (New York: W. W. Norton and Company, 1947) and *From Every Zenith: A Memoir and Some Essays on Life and Thought* (Denver: Sage Books, 1963).

The work of anthropologists in the Indian New Deal is treated in Graham D. Taylor, "Anthropologists, Reformers, and the Indian New Deal," *Prologue* 7 (Fall 1975): 151–62; David L. Marden, "Anthropologists and Federal Indian Policy prior to 1940," *Indian Historian* 5 (Winter 1972): 19–26, and Lawrence C. Kelly, "Anthropology and Anthropologists in the Indian New Deal," *Journal of the History of the Behavioral Sciences* 16 (January 1980): 6–24. Other studies on particular topics are Lawrence C. Kelly, "Choosing the New Deal Indian Commissioner: Ickes vs. Collier," *New Mexico Historical Review* 49 (October 1974): 269–88; Stephen J. Kunitz, "The Social Philosophy of John Collier," *Ethnohistory* 18 (Summer 1971): 213–29; and Peter M. Wright, "John Collier and the Oklahoma Indian Welfare Act of 1936," *Chronicles of Oklahoma* 50 (Autumn 1972): 347–71.

The early relief measures of the Indian Civilian Conservation Corps are described in Donald L. Parman, "The Indian and the Civilian Conservation Corps," *Pacific Historical Review* 40 (February 1971): 39–57, and Calvin W. Gower, "The CCC Indian Division: Aid for Depressed Americans, 1933–1942," *Minnesota History* 43 (Spring 1972): 3–13. For the creation and work of the Indian Arts and Crafts Board, see Robert Fay Schrader, *The Indian Arts and Crafts Board: An Aspect of New Deal Indian Policy* (Albuquerque: University of New Mexico Press, 1983).

Education measures are well described in Margaret Szasz, *Education and the American Indian: The Road to Self-Determination, 1928–1973* (Albuquerque: University of New Mexico Press, 1974), and in a briefer treatment by the same author, "Thirty Years Too Soon: Indian Education under the Indian New Deal," *Integrated Education* 13 (July–August 1975): 3–9.

Although World War II had tremendous influence on Indian life, it has received little specific attention. A brief survey is Tom Holm, "Fighting a White Man's War: The Extent and Legacy of American Indian Participation in World War II," *Journal of Ethnic Studies* 9 (Summer 1981): 69–81.

PART NINE: TERMINATION

The termination of federal responsibility for Indians, a short-lived reaction against Collier's new emphasis on tribalism and Indian culture, has been thoroughly studied. An early investigation, which emphasizes the Menominee Indian case, is Gary Orfield, "A Study of the Termination Policy," printed in *The Education of American Indians*, vol. 4: *The Organizational Question*, Committee Print of the Subcommittee on Indian Education of the Committee on Labor and Public Welfare, United States Senate, 91st Congress, 1st session (Washington: Government Printing Office, 1970), pp. 673–816. More recent studies are Larry W. Burt, *Tribalism in Crisis: Federal Indian Policy, 1953–1961* (Albuquerque: University of New Mexico Press, 1982); Larry J. Hasse, "Termination and Assimilation: Federal Indian Policy, 1943 to 1961" (Ph.D. dissertation, Washington State University, 1974); and Donald Lee Fixico, "Termination and Relocation: Federal Indian Policy in the 1950s" (Ph.D. dissertation, University of Oklahoma, 1980). Shorter treatments of value are Charles F. Wilkinson and Eric R. Biggs, "The Evolution of the Termination Policy," *American Indian Law Review* 5, no. 1 (1977): 139–84; and the pertinent sections in S. Lyman Tyler, *A History of Indian Policy* (Washington: Bureau of Indian Affairs, 1973). For two opposing views on termination, see Oliver La Farge, "Termination of Federal Supervision: Disintegration and the American Indians," *Annals of the American Academy of Political and Social Science* 311 (May 1957): 41–46, and Arthur V. Watkins, "Termination of Federal

Supervision: The Removal of Restrictions over Indian Property and Person," ibid., pp. 47–55.

Application of the termination policy to two major tribes—Menominee and Klamath—has been carefully studied. For the Menominees, see Nicholas C. Peroff, *Menominee Drums: Tribal Termination and Restoration, 1954–1974* (Norman: University of Oklahoma Press, 1982); Stephen J. Herzberg, "The Menominee Indians: From Treaty to Termination," *Wisconsin Magazine of History* 60 (Summer 1977): 267–329; and David W. Ames and Burton R. Fisher, "The Menominee Termination Crisis: Barriers in the Way of a Rapid Cultural Transition," *Human Organization* 18 (Fall 1959): 101–11. For the Klamaths, see Theodore Stern, *The Klamath Tribe: A People and Their Reservation* (Seattle: University of Washington Press, 1965), and Susan Hood, "Termination of the Klamath Tribe in Oregon," *Ethnohistory* 19 (Fall 1972): 379–92.

Associated with termination was the federal government's encouragement of migration from reservations to urban areas. Useful studies are Elaine M. Neils, *Reservation to City: Indian Migration and Federal Relocation* (Chicago: Department of Geography, University of Chicago, 1971), and Joan Ablon, "American Indian Relocation: Problems of Dependency and Management in the City," *Phylon* 26 (Winter 1965): 362–71.

The work of the Indian Claims Commission is ably summarized in the *Final Report* of the commission (1979). A detailed and critical study is Harvey D. Rosenthal, "Their Day in Court: A History of the Indian Claims Commission" (Ph.D. dissertation, Kent State University, 1976). Among a good many articles on the commission, see especially Nancy Oestreich Lurie, "The Indian Claims Commission Act," *Annals of the American Academy of Political and Social Science* 311 (May 1957): 56–70, and Thomas Le Duc, "The Work of the Indian Claims Commission under the Act of 1946," *Pacific Historical Review* 26 (February 1957): 1–16. Two articles dealing with the application of the act to particular tribes are Herbert T. Hoover, "Yankton Sioux Tribal Claims against the United States, 1917–1975," *Western Historical Quarterly* 7 (April 1976): 125–42, and Robert C. Carriker, "The Kalispel Tribe and the Indian Claims Commission Experience," ibid. 9 (January 1978): 19–31. Criticism of the commission's work is found in Sandra C. Danforth, "Repaying Historical Debts: The Indian Claims Commission," *North Dakota Law Review* 49 (Winter 1973): 359–403, and Nancy Oestreich Lurie, "The Indian Claims Commission," *Annals of the American Academy of Political and Social Science* 436 (March 1978): 97–110.

Programs for Indian education, health, and economic development continued in the era of termination. Educational developments are discussed in Margaret Szasz, *Education and the American Indian: The Road to Self-Determination, 1928–1973* (Albuquerque: University of New Mexico

Press, 1974), and Hildegard Thompson, "Education among American Indians: Institutional Aspects," *Annals of the American Academy of Political and Social Science* 311 (May 1957): 95–104. A sympathetic account of the special program for the Navajos is L. Madison Coombs, *Doorway toward the Light: The Story of the Special Navajo Education Program* (Washington: Bureau of Indian Affairs, 1962). A general survey of health care for Indians is Ruth M. Raup, *The Indian Health Program from 1800–1955* (Washington: Division of Public Health Methods, Public Health Service, 1959). See also *Health Services for the American Indian* (Washington: Public Health Service, 1957). Indian economic conditions are surveyed in William H. Kelly, "The Economic Basis of Indian Life," *Annals of the American Academy of Political and Social Science* 311 (May 1957): 71–79.

The organization and administration of the Bureau of Indian Affairs is covered in Robert M. Kvasnicka and Herman J. Viola, eds., *The Commissioners of Indian Affairs, 1824–1977* (Lincoln: University of Nebraska Press, 1979). For the organization of regional offices, see Theodore W. Taylor, "The Regional Organization of the Bureau of Indian Affairs" (Ph.D. dissertation, Harvard University, 1959).

PART TEN: INDIAN SELF-DETERMINATION

The multifarious laws and programs of the 1960s and 1970s looking toward Indian self-determination are too recent to have received adequate scholarly treatment, and much of the writing has a tone of advocacy for one side or the other of controverted questions. A good brief introduction, however, is Donald L. Parman, "American Indians and the Bicentennial," *New Mexico Historical Review* 51 (July 1976): 233–49.

The new Indian voices, forcefully articulating their rights, are the subject of Stan Steiner, *The New Indians* (New York: Harper and Row, 1968), and Alvin M. Josephy, Jr., ed., *Red Power: The American Indians' Fight for Freedom* (New York: American Heritage Press, 1971). The writings of Vine Deloria, Jr., exemplify the new spirit; see, for example, *Custer Died for Your Sins: An Indian Manifesto* (New York: Macmillan Company, 1969); *We Talk, You Listen: New Tribes, New Turf* (New York: Macmillan Company, 1970); and *Behind the Trail of Broken Treaties: An Indian Declaration of Independence* (New York: Delacorte Press, 1974).

An indication of the reform sentiment of the period is found in reports of private organizations and governmental agencies. The Commission on the Rights, Liberties, and Responsibilities of the American Indian issued *A Program for Indian Citizens: A Summary Report* (Albuquerque: The Commission, 1961); its final report appeared as William A. Brophy and Sophie

D. Aberle, *The Indian, America's Unfinished Business: Report of the Commission on the Rights, Liberties, and Responsibilities of the American Indian* (Norman: University of Oklahoma Press, 1966). See also the *Declaration of the Indian Purpose* (Chicago: American Indian Chicago Conference, 1961); and Herbert E. Striner, *Toward a Fundamental Program for the Training, Employment and Economic Equality of the American Indian* (Washington: W. E. Upjohn Institute for Employment Research, 1968).

A valuable study on Indian economic progress is Alan L. Sorkin, *American Indians and Federal Aid* (Washington: Brookings Institute, 1971). Sar A. Levitan, *The Great Society's Poor Law: A New Approach to Poverty* (Baltimore: Johns Hopkins Press, 1969), discusses the Economic Opportunity Act, which greatly benefited Indian communities. See also the essays in Sam Stanley, ed., *American Indian Economic Development* (The Hague: Mouton Publishers, 1978).

Greater participation by Indians in the education of their children was a constant drive in the period, much of the action stemming from the devastating report of the Senate Special Subcommittee on Indian Education entitled *Indian Education: A National Tragedy—A National Challenge* (*Senate Report* no. 91–501, 91st Congress, 1st session, serial 12836–1). Another report, growing out of a study sponsored by the Office of Education, is Estelle Fuchs and Robert J. Havighurst, *To Live on This Earth: American Indian Education* (Garden City, New York: Doubleday and Company, 1972). The funding of Indian education is treated in Daniel M. Rosenfelt, "Toward a More Coherent Policy for Funding Indian Education," *Law and Contemporary Problems* 40 (Winter 1976): 190–223. Indian health care is described in *The Indian Health Program* (Washington: Indian Health Service, 1980), and in Everett R. Rhoades, "Barriers to Health Care: The Unique Problems Facing American Indians," *Civil Rights Digest* 10 (Fall 1977): 25–31.

For the critical—and heavily symbolic—events of the return of Blue Lake to Taos Pueblo and the restoration of the Menominee Indians to federal status, see Dabney Otis Collins, "Battle for Blue Lake: The Taos Indians Finally Regain Their Sacred Land," *American West* 8 (September 1971): 32–37; John J. Bodine, "Blue Lake: A Struggle for Indian Rights," *American Indian Law Review* 1 (Winter 1973): 23–32; and Nicholas C. Peroff, *Menominee Drums: Tribal Termination and Restoration, 1954–1974* (Norman: University of Oklahoma Press, 1982).

The settlement of the Alaska Native land claims is covered in Robert D. Arnold, *Alaska Native Land Claims* (Anchorage: Alaska Native Foundation, 1976), and Mary Clay Berry, *The Alaska Pipeline: The Politics of Oil and Native Land Claims* (Bloomington: Indiana University Press, 1975). See also Arthur Lazarus, Jr., and W. Richard West, Jr., "The Alaska Native

Claims Settlement Act: A Flawed Victory," *Law and Contemporary Problems* 40 (Winter 1976): 132–65, and Monroe E. Price, "A Moment in History: The Alaska Native Claims Settlement Act," *UCLA–Alaska Law Review* 8 (Spring 1979): 89–101.

The land claims of eastern Indians on the basis of the Indian Trade and Intercourse Act of 1790 are discussed in Tim Vollman, "A Survey of Eastern Indian Land Claims, 1970–1979," *Maine Law Review* 31, no. 1 (1979): 5–16. Two descriptive articles by Paul Brodeur on the Passamaquoddy and Penobscot case in Maine and the Mashpee case in Massachusetts are "Annals of Law: Restitution," *New Yorker*, October 11, 1982, pp. 76–155, and "The Mashpees," ibid., November 6, 1978, pp. 62–150. The issues in the land dispute between the Navajos and Hopis are discussed in Kevin Tehan, "Of Indians, Land, and the Federal Government: The Navajo-Hopi Land Dispute," *Arizona State Law Journal*, 1976, pp. 173–212, and Jerry Kammer, *The Second Long Walk: The Navajo-Hopi Land Dispute* (Albuquerque: University of New Mexico Press, 1980).

The concern for Indian rights is reflected in a growing literature, much of it of a legal nature. The background of the Indian titles of the Civil Rights Act of 1968 is given in Donald L. Burnett, Jr., "An Historical Analysis of the 1968 'Indian Civil Rights' Act," *Harvard Journal of Legislation* 9 (May 1972): 557–626. A favorable evaluation of the law is presented in Arthur Lazarus, Jr., "Title II of the 1968 Civil Rights Act: An Indian Bill of Rights," *North Dakota Law Review* 45 (Spring 1969): 337–52. Water rights are discussed in two excellent articles by Norris Hundley, Jr., "The Dark and Bloody Ground in Indian Water Rights: Confusion Elevated to Principle," *Western Historical Quarterly* 9 (October 1978): 455–82, and "The 'Winters' Decision and Indian Water Rights: A Mystery Reexamined," ibid. 13 (January 1982): 17–42. William H. Veeder has been a strong advocate of Indian water rights; see, for example, his "Water Rights: Life or Death for the American Indian," *Indian Historian* 5 (Summer 1972): 4–21.

Fishing rights are the subject of a report prepared for the American Friends Service Committee, *Uncommon Controversy: Fishing Rights of the Muckleshoot, Puyallup, and Nisqually Indians* (Seattle: University of Washington Press, 1970), and there is a detailed account of the controversy in the 1981 report of the United States Commission on Civil Rights, *Indian Tribes: A Continuing Quest for Survival*. The fight for Indian family rights culminating in the Indian Child Welfare Act of 1978 is traced in Manuel P. Guerrero, "Indian Child Welfare Act of 1978: A Response to the Threat to Indian Culture Caused by Foster and Adoptive Placements of Indian Children," *American Indian Law Review* 7, no. 1 (1979): 51–77. A harsh criticism of the act is Russel Lawrence Barsh, "The Indian Child Welfare Act of 1978: A Critical Analysis," *Hastings Law Journal* 31 (July

1980): 1287–1336. See also Steven Unger, ed., *The Destruction of American Indian Families* (New York: Association on American Indian Affairs, 1977). The important Indian Self-Determination Act of 1975 has received little attention in scholarly articles. A critical view is expressed in Russel Lawrence Barsh and Ronald L. Trosper, "Title I of the Indian Self-Determination and Education Assistance Act of 1975," *American Indian Law Review* 3, no. 2 (1975): 361–95.

The quest for Indian rights reopened the question of the sovereignty of tribes. Two brief surveys of this complex and controversial topic are Arthur Lazarus, Jr., "Tribal Sovereignty under United States Law," in William R. Swagerty, ed., *Indian Sovereignty: Proceedings of the Second Annual Conference on Problems concerning American Indians Today* (Chicago: Newberry Library, 1979), pp. 28–46, and John Niemisto, "The Legal Powers of Indian Tribal Governments," *Wisconsin Academy Review* 28 (March 1982): 7–11. The American Indian Policy Review Commission's *Final Report* (Washington: Government Printing Office, 1977) presents strong assertions of sovereignty with paradoxical strong insistence on the broad trust responsibilities of the United States government. For criticism of the commission and its work, see *New Directions in Federal Indian Policy: A Review of the American Indian Policy Review Commission* (Los Angeles: American Indian Studies Center, University of California, Los Angeles, 1979).

Urban Indians are slowly getting more attention. The best recent study is Alan L. Sorkin, *The Urban American Indian* (Lexington, Massachusetts: D. C. Heath and Company, 1978). Essays by anthropologists are collected in Jack O. Waddell and O. Michael Watson, eds., *The American Indian in Urban Society* (Boston: Little, Brown and Company, 1971). A useful introduction to urban Indian problems and literature is Russell Thornton, Gary D. Sandefur, and Harold G. Grasmick, *The Urbanization of American Indians: A Critical Bibliography* (Bloomington: Indiana University Press, 1982).

The turmoil that struck the Bureau of Indian Affairs in the early 1970s is well described in Steve Nickeson, "The Structure of the Bureau of Indian Affairs," *Law and Contemporary Problems* 40 (Winter 1976): 61–76. Brief biographies of the commissioners of the period are in Robert M. Kvasnicka and Herman J. Viola, eds., *The Commissioners of Indian Affairs, 1824–1977* (Lincoln: University of Nebraska Press, 1979).

Illustration
and Map Credits
Volume II

ILLUSTRATION CREDITS

42. Library of Congress, Washington, D.C., Brady Collection. 43. National Archives, Washington, D.C., Bureau of Indian Affairs photograph no. 75–IP–1–13. 44. National Archives, U.S. Signal Corps photograph no. 111–SC–85686. 45. Historical Society of Pennsylvania, Philadelphia. 46. James M. King, *Facing the Twentieth Century: Our Country, Its Power and Peril* (New York: American Union League Society, 1899), opposite p. 261. 47. A. Keith Smiley, Mohonk Mountain House, New Paltz, New York. 48. Idaho Historical Society, Boise. 49. Library of Congress, Grabill photograph. 50. Archives/Manuscripts Division, Oklahoma Historical Society, photograph no. 572. 51. Wyoming State Archives, Museums and Historical Department, Cheyenne. 52. State Historical Society of Wisconsin, photograph no. WHi (x3) 25819. 53. *Indian Craftsman*, April 1909. 54. National Archives, photograph no. 75–M–3. 55. National Archives, photograph nos., top to bottom, 75–GS–20, 75–GS–9, 75–GS–1 (photographs by Louis R. Bostwick). 56. *Report of the Indian Rights Association*, 1913, frontispiece. 57. National Archives, Records of the Office of the Secretary of the Interior (RG 48), Central Classified File 5–6, General, Competent Indians. 58. National Archives, photograph no. 268–PU–40BB–1–NS–5944. 59. Library of Congress, Underwood and Underwood portrait. 60. Library of Congress, Underwood and Underwood portrait. 61. Library of Congress, Herbert E. French Collection. 62. National Archives, photograph no. 75–RAFB–30B. 63. National Archives, photograph no. 35–G, 2134. 64. National Archives, photograph no. 75–RAS–67. 65. National Archives, photograph no. 75–N–WO–24. 66. Library of Congress, Underwood and Underwood photograph. 67. National Archives, photograph no. 75–RA–2–19B. 68. National

Archives, photograph no. 75–N–MISC–115. 69. National Archives, photograph no. 75–N–WO–51. 70. National Archives, photograph no. 75–N–MISC–42–52–53. 71. Margaret Szasz, *Education and the American Indian: The Road to Self-Determination, 1928–1973* (Albuquerque: University of New Mexico Press, 1974), courtesy of Walcott H. Beatty, San Francisco. 72. National Anthropological Archives, Smithsonian Institution. 73. National Archives, photograph no. 75–N–WO–E–6. 74. Library of Congress. 75. United Press International photo. 76. National Archives, photograph no. 75–CL–26–1. 77. National Anthropological Archives, Smithsonian Institution. 78. National Archives, photograph no. 75–CL–28–1. 79. National Archives, Records of Agencies for Economic Opportunity and Legal Services (RG 381), Community Action Program—Navajo, photograph by Paul Conklin. 80. National Archives, photograph no. 75–CL–22–1.

81. National Archives, photograph no. 75–CL–18–1. 82. United Press International photo. 83. United Press International photo. 84. *Milwaukee Journal* photo. 85. National Archives, photograph no. 75–IR–29–1. 86. *BIA Profile: The Bureau of Indian Affairs and American Indians* (Washington: GPO, 1981), p. 66.

MAP CREDITS

The maps for this volume were drawn by the Cartographic Laboratory, University of Nebraska–Lincoln. The following sources were drawn upon for the maps. 10. Ralph K. Andrist, *The Long Death: The Last Days of the Plains Indian* (New York: Macmillan Company, 1964), p. 339. 11. *Indians at Work: Reorganization Number* (1936). 12. Robert D. Arnold, *Alaska Native Land Claims* (Anchorage: Alaska Native Foundation, 1976), p. 166, inside back cover. 13. Bureau of Indian Affairs.

Index

About the Author

A foremost authority on American Indian policy, Francis Paul Prucha is a professor of history at Marquette University. He has also taught at Harvard University and the University of Oklahoma and from 1983 to 1985 was Thomas Gasson Professor at Boston College. He served as president of the Western History Association in 1982–83. His publications include a dozen and a half books dealing with the history of American Indian policy.